ELEMENTS OF
LITERATUR

THIRD COURSE

The Elements of Literature Program

ELEMENTS OF LITERATURE: First Course

ELEMENTS OF LITERATURE: Second Course

ELEMENTS OF LITERATURE: Third Course

ELEMENTS OF LITERATURE: Fourth Course

ELEMENTS OF LITERATURE: Fifth Course
Literature of the United States

ELEMENTS OF LITERATURE: Sixth Course
Literature of Britain

An Annotated Teacher's Edition and a variety of other ancillaries are available for each of the above titles.

The Authors

Robert Anderson is a playwright, novelist, screenwriter, and teacher. His plays include *Tea and Sympathy; Silent Night, Lonely Night; You Know I Can't Hear You When the Water's Running;* and *I Never Sang for My Father.* His screenplays include *The Nun's Story* and *The Sand Pebbles.* Mr. Anderson has taught at the Writer's Workshop at the University of Iowa, the American Theatre Wing Professional Training Program, and the Salzburg Seminar in American Studies. He is a Past President of the Dramatists' Guild, Vice-President of the Authors' League of America, and a member of the Theatre Hall of Fame. He makes his home in Connecticut and New York.

John Malcolm Brinnin, author of six volumes of poetry which have received many prizes and awards, is a member of the American Academy and Institute of Arts and Letters. He is also a critic of poetry and a biographer of poets and was for a number of years Director of New York's famous Poetry Center. His teaching career, begun at Vassar College, included long terms at the University of Connecticut and Boston University, where he succeeded Robert Lowell as professor of creative writing and contemporary letters. Mr. Brinnin has also written *Dylan Thomas in America: An Intimate Journal* and *Sextet: T. S. Eliot & Truman Capote & Others.* He divides his time between Duxbury, Massachusetts, and Key West, Florida.

John Leggett is a novelist, a biographer, and a teacher who went to the Writer's Workshop at the University of Iowa in the spring of 1969, expecting to put in a single semester. In 1970 he assumed temporary charge of the program and was its Director for the next seventeen years. Mr. Leggett's novels include *Wilder Stone, The Gloucester Branch, Who Took the Gold Away, Gulliver House,* and *Making Believe.* He is also the author of the highly acclaimed biography *Ross and Tom: Two American Tragedies.* His short fiction, articles, and reviews have appeared in *Harper's, Esquire, Mademoiselle, The Ladies Home Journal,* and the *Los Angeles Times.* A native New Yorker, Mr. Leggett now lives in San Francisco. He is currently at work on a biography of William Saroyan.

Janet Burroway is a novelist and teacher who has also written children's books and a textbook on writing fiction. She has taught at the University of Sussex, England; the University of Illinois; and the Writer's Workshop at the University of Iowa. She is currently FSU Foundation Professor of English at Florida State University in Tallahassee. Her novels include *Descend Again, The Dancer from the Dance, Eyes, The Buzzards* (nominated for the Pulitzer Prize), *Raw Silk* (nominated for the National Book Award), and *Opening Nights.*

Sandra Cisneros is a teacher and a novelist, an essayist, a poet, and a short-story writer. A graduate of the Writer's Workshop at the University of Iowa, she has written two books of fiction, *The House on Mango Street,* which won the Before Columbus American Book Award, and *Woman Hollering Creek.* Her collections of poems include *Bad Boys* and *My Wicked Wicked Ways.* She makes her home in Texas.

David Adams Leeming is a Professor of English at the University of Connecticut and the author of several books on mythology, including *Mythology: The Voyage of the Hero; Flights: Readings in Magic, Mysticism, Fantasy, and Myth;* and *The World of Myth.* For several years he taught English at the Robert College in Istanbul, Turkey. He also served as secretary-assistant to the writer James Baldwin in New York and Istanbul. Dr. Leeming lives in Stonington, Connecticut.

ELEMENTS OF
LITERATURE

THIRD COURSE

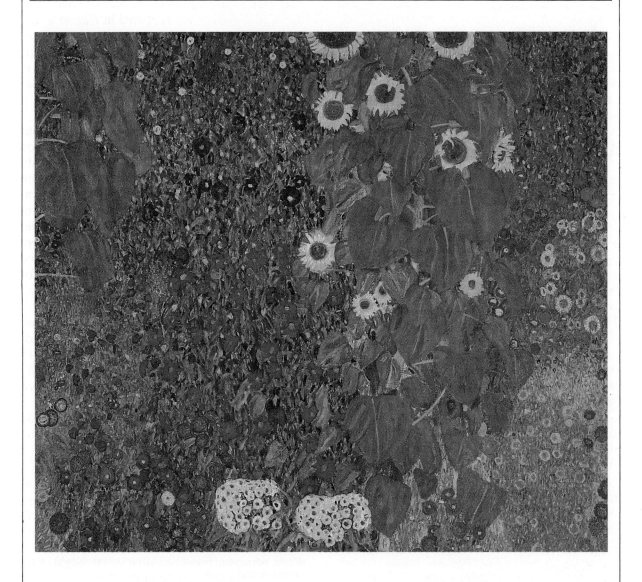

Holt, Rinehart and Winston, Inc.

Harcourt Brace Jovanovich, Inc.

Austin • Orlando • San Diego • Chicago • Dallas • Toronto

Candy Carter wrote the Exercises in Critical Thinking and Writing. Ms. Carter has served on the editorial committee of the NCTE and has been an editor of the California English Magazine. She has edited books and journal articles for the NCTE. She teaches English at McQueen High School in Reno, Nevada.

Nancy E. Wiseman Seminoff has served as Consultant in Reading and Questioning Strategies for the program. Dr. Seminoff is Dean, School of Education at the William Patterson College of New Jersey. She has served as a reading consultant at the secondary level and as a classroom teacher.

ISBN 0-03-074196-3

1 2 3 4 5 6 7 8 9 10 041 95 94 93 92 91

Acknowledgments

Grateful acknowledgment is made to the teachers who reviewed materials for the 1989 edition of ELEMENTS OF LITERATURE, in manuscript or in classroom tests.

Reviewers

Peggy Anatol
Warren High School
Downey, California

Larry Anders
Caroline County Schools
Denton, Maryland

Bernice Causey
Mobile County Public Schools
Mobile, Alabama

Anne Kelley
Milford Public Schools
Milford, Connecticut

Karen Libby
Hamilton Junior High School
Denver, Colorado

Carl Moyler
Dayton City Schools
Dayton, Ohio

Ruby Lee Norris
Moody Middle School
Richmond, Virginia

Delores Obermiller
Corpus Christi Independent School District
Corpus Christi, Texas

Gloria Pipkin
Mowat Junior High School
Lynn Haven, Florida

Sylvia Skarstad
Portland Public Schools
Portland, Oregon

Susan Stevens
South High School
Youngstown, Ohio

Gerry Tylavsky
Spratley Junior High School
Hampton, Virginia

Joe Wilson
Corpus Christi Independent School District
Corpus Christi, Texas

Classroom Testing

Peggy Ehlen
Maine East High School
Parkridge, Illinois

Marge Murphy
Riverdell Junior High School
River Edge, New Jersey

Doreatha Orr
Robert E. Lee Junior High School
Orlando, Florida

Emily Rich
Vines High School
Plano, Texas

Jim Sayers
Liberty Junior High School
Orlando, Florida

Cynthia Schaulis
Maine West High School
Des Plaines, Illinois

Grateful acknowledgment is also made to the teachers who evaluated materials for the 1993 edition of ELEMENTS OF LITERATURE and who recommended new selections:

Kansas City School District, Kansas City, Missouri:

Dr. Ula Manzo
Coordinator of Language Arts K–12

Ann Crockett
Metro Tech High School

Michael Lyons
Southwest High School

Patricia Lyons
Southwest High School

Elizabeth M. Smith
Van Horn High School

Linda Watkins
East High School

Killeen Independent School District, Killeen, Texas:

Phyllis Wheeler
Secondary Language Arts Consultant

Paula Brock
Killeen High School

Roberta Brooks
Ellison High School

Susie DeVault
Killeen High School

Glen Martin
Killeen High School

Bunnie Montgomery
Killeen High School

Mark Noblitt
Killeen High School

Debbie Prude
Ellison High School

Debbie Siegman
Killeen High School

Barbara Teer
Ellison High School

Veda Kay Waheed
Ellison High School

Washoe County School District, Reno, Nevada:

Joanne Walen
English/Language Arts Program Coordinator K–12

Rita Hambleton
Hug High School

Phil Harriman
Sparks High School

Olivia Martin
Reno High School

Mel Shields
McQueen High School

Beverly Wooster
Reed High School

CONTENTS

UNIT ONE: THE ELEMENTS OF A SHORT STORY

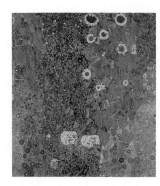

UNIT TWO: THE ELEMENTS OF POETRY

UNIT THREE: THE ELEMENTS OF NONFICTION

THE ELEMENTS OF A SHORT STORY

Interior with a Violin Case, Nice (winter 1918–1919) by Henri Matisse. Oil on canvas 28¾″ × 23⅝″.

UNIT ONE   **John Leggett**

THE ART OF STORYTELLING

An introduction by **John Leggett**

> *Neanderthal man listened to stories, if one may judge by the shape of his skull. The primitive audience was an audience of shockheads, gaping around the campfire, fatigued with contending against the mammoth or woolly rhinoceros, and only kept awake by suspense. What would happen next? The novelist droned on, and as soon as the audience guessed what happened next, they either fell asleep or killed him.*
>
> —E. M. Forster

> "A good storyteller is born with something special— with the kind of mind that sees and says things in an imaginative, original way. But a good storyteller also has learned certain skills."

Storytelling is an art, just as playing the guitar or drawing a portrait is, and we admire it when it is done well. When a story is told well, we are often astonished by how simple it seems. In fact, we often think we could write a story like it ourselves, equally well. Only when we actually try to write our own stories do we discover how even the simplest story can be told wrong. Our own story might bore us or confuse us or even pain us, just as sour notes from the guitar would spoil the song.

Even when we hear a story told well and then go home and try to repeat it, we often fail to reproduce the effect the story had on us. We thought the story was funny; why don't *we* get a laugh when we retell it? Thus, we tend to think of storytelling as a gift, a talent the storyteller is born with.

There is some truth in that, too. A good storyteller is born with something special—with the kind of mind that sees and says things in an imaginative, original way. But a good storyteller also has learned certain skills. In fact, student writers examine good fiction in order to learn these skills. They learn first to recognize the elements of a good story and then to use those elements in their own writing.

In this unit, you will look at the elements of fiction, just as a student writer would. You will see that understanding these elements not only makes better storytellers—it also makes more responsive readers of us all.

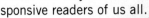

Pueblo storytelling dolls.

Plot is the element to start with, for it is story itself. **Plot** is a series of related events, each event connected to the next, like links in a chain. Each event in a plot "hooks" our curiosity and pulls us forward to the next event, in order to satisfy that curiosity.

> The King, preparing to lead the parade, looked on the royal hat rack for his crown and found it missing.

Right away, we wonder what has happened. Has the crown been stolen, or did the King misplace it?

> He asked the Queen if she had taken it.

Why? the reader wonders. Had he reason to suspect her? Would she have taken it away to be cleaned and polished? Or out of mischief?

> The Queen denied any knowledge of the crown's whereabouts. But after a moment's reflection, she reminded the King of the Prince's weakness for gambling. Now she recalled that while strolling about the palace grounds, she had seen the Prince riding off toward the village with a large box.

If our curiosity is aroused by these events, we await successive ones with mounting **suspense.** We want to know: "What happens next?" Has a theft taken place? Who is the thief—the Prince or the Queen or a new character yet to be introduced? This buildup of suspense is how a plot works. A series of related events plants the hook of curiosity in us, making us keep reading to find out: "What happens next?"

Plot: The "Hook" of Curiosity

> "**E**ach event in a plot 'hooks' our curiosity and pulls us forward to the next event . . ."

Sioux storyteller Lame Deer and some of his audience.

Conflict: The Fuel of Narrative

The degree to which we care about what happens next in a story depends largely on the amount of conflict that develops. A **conflict** is a struggle. This struggle might take place between two characters or it might take place inside a character's mind or it might take place between a character and something nonhuman—a typhoon or a shark or gas in the mine pit.

When the conflict takes place between a character and another person or between a character and something nonhuman, it is an **external conflict.** When the conflict takes place inside a character's mind, it is an **internal conflict.** Conflict is the fuel of narrative. The greater the conflict, the more we care about the outcome.

Imagine a situation in which Dorothy finds herself locked in a room without the key. Ho-hum? All right, suppose that in half an hour she is due to sing in a concert, one that might lead to a music scholarship. Are you getting more interested? Then suppose she has been deliberately locked in the room, and that the person who did this is her Great-Uncle Godfrey, who, far from playing a prank, is opposed to her musical career on the grounds that it will interfere with her care of him, and of the family's alligator farm.

Like sticks fueling a fire, these particulars feed Dorothy's desire to escape from the room and to overcome the forces holding her back. These details build an external conflict between Dorothy and her great-uncle. They also build an internal conflict in Dorothy's own heart, for we can presume that her desire to leave the alligators and get on with her singing is in conflict with her desire to be obedient to Great-Uncle Godfrey.

> " **T**he greater the conflict, the more we care about the outcome."

Father's Day by
Petra Mathers (1986).
Watercolor.

Courtesy of the artist.

The "Bare Bones" of a Plot

Stories, like houses and human beings, need a structure or framework to hold them together. Plots are usually built on four major parts, which we might think of as their "bare bones." The first part of a plot can be called the **basic situation.** This is the opening of the story, where the characters and their conflict are usually introduced. (Writers have many names for this part of the story. Some call it **exposition.** We might even think of it as a "doormat"— indicating that it is both the entry to the story and its "grounding." It tells us what is going on.)

> If we take the Cinderella story as an example, the basic situation shows us Cinderella, a beautiful and good heroine, in a conflict with her evil stepmother and two nasty stepsisters.

The second part of a plot is the **complication.** This is the part of the story in which the main character takes some action to resolve the conflict and meets with problems or complications: danger, hostility, indecision, fear.

> Cinderella wants to go to the ball. Her stepmother says "No," but a Fairy Godmother promises to get her to the ball if she obeys one rule: "Be home by midnight." Cinderella goes to the ball, the Prince falls in love with her at first sight, she flees at midnight, and she loses one of her glass slippers.

The third part of a story is the **climax.** This is the key scene of the story—that tense or exciting or terrifying moment when our emotional involvement is greatest because we realize what the outcome of the conflict is going to be.

> The Prince makes a house-to-house search for the foot that fits the slipper and finds that foot on Cinderella.

The final part of the story is the **resolution** (sometimes this is called the **denouement** (dā·n$\overline{oo}$·män'), a French word for "unraveling the knot"). The resolution occurs at the very end of the story (perhaps in only a paragraph), when all the struggles are over and we know what is going to happen to the people in the story. The resolution "closes" the story.

> Cinderella marries the Prince and they live happily ever after. If you are reading the original Grimm story, you'll also find ravens pecking out the eyes of the evil stepmother.

These four bare bones support a series of events that are intended to hook our curiosity—to keep us reading to find out what happens next. If one of these bare bones is weak, the story falls apart. We are not hooked by the characters and their struggle, and we might say that we just couldn't finish the story.

Now let's look at the way a professional writer uses his power to hook our curiosity and lead us through another series of related events.

"Now here comes the kicker."

Drawing by Modell.
© 1982 The New Yorker Magazine, Inc.

> "If one
> of these bare bones
> is weak,
> the story falls apart."

POISON

Roald Dahl

Here is Roald Dahl's suspenseful tale about a pair of Englishmen who share a house in colonial India. As Dahl describes this series of events and you begin to share in his characters' terror, be aware of how he is hooking into your own fears— fears that you bring to the story. As he builds up your suspense, ask yourself this: Could you stop reading and put this story aside, without ever knowing how it ends?

It must have been around midnight when I drove home, and as I approached the gates of the bungalow I switched off the headlamps of the car so the beam wouldn't swing in through the window of the side bedroom and wake Harry Pope. But I needn't have bothered. Coming up the drive I noticed his light was still on, so he was awake anyway—unless perhaps he'd dropped off while reading.

I parked the car and went up the five steps to the balcony, counting each step carefully in the dark so I wouldn't take an extra one which wasn't there when I got to the top. I crossed the balcony, pushed through the screen doors into the house itself, and switched on the light in the hall. I went across to the door of Harry's room, opened it quietly, and looked in.

He was lying on the bed and I could see he was awake. But he didn't move. He didn't even turn his head toward me, but I heard him say, "Timber, Timber, come here."

He spoke slowly, whispering each word carefully, separately, and I pushed the door right open and started to go quickly across the room.

"Stop. Wait a moment, Timber." I could hardly hear what he was saying. He seemed to be straining enormously to get the words out.

"What's the matter, Harry?"

"Sshhh!" he whispered. "Sshhh! For God's sake, don't make a noise. Take your shoes off before you come nearer. *Please* do as I say, Timber."

The way he was speaking reminded me of George Barling after he got shot in the stomach, when he stood leaning against a crate containing a spare airplane engine, holding both hands on his stomach and saying things about the German pilot in just the same hoarse, straining half whisper Harry was using now.

"Quickly, Timber, but take your shoes off first."

I couldn't understand about taking off the shoes but I figured that if he was as ill as he sounded I'd better humor him, so I bent down and removed the shoes and left them in the middle of the floor. Then I went over to his bed.

"Don't touch the bed! For God's sake, don't touch the bed!" He was still speaking like he'd been shot in the stomach, and I could see him lying there on his back with a single sheet covering three quarters of his body. He was wearing a pair of pajamas with blue, brown, and white stripes, and he was sweating terribly. It was a hot night and I was sweating a little myself, but not like Harry. His whole face was wet, and the pillow around his head was sodden with moisture. It looked like a bad go of malaria to me.

"What is it, Harry?"

"A krait,"[1] he said.

---

1. **krait** (krīt): a type of poisonous snake found in parts of Asia.

"A *krait!* Oh, my God! Where'd it bite you? How long ago?"

"Shut up," he whispered.

"Listen, Harry," I said, and I leaned forward and touched his shoulder. "We've got to be quick. Come on now, quickly, tell me where it bit you." He was lying there very still and tense as though he were holding on to himself hard because of sharp pain.

"I haven't been bitten," he whispered. "Not yet. It's on my stomach. Lying there asleep."

I took a quick pace backward; I couldn't help it, and I stared at his stomach or rather at the sheet that covered it. The sheet was rumpled in several places and it was impossible to tell if there was anything underneath.

"You don't really mean there's a krait lying on your stomach now?"

"I swear it."

"How did it get there?" I shouldn't have asked the question because it was easy to see he wasn't fooling. I should have told him to keep quiet.

"I was reading," Harry said, and he spoke very slowly, taking each word in turn and speaking it carefully so as not to move the muscles of his stomach. "Lying on my back reading and I felt something on my chest, behind the book. Sort of tickling. Then out of the corner of my eye saw this little krait sliding over my pajamas. Small, about ten inches. Knew I mustn't move. Couldn't have anyway. Lay there watching it. Thought it would go over top of the sheet." Harry paused and was silent for a few moments. His eyes looked down along his body toward the place where the sheet covered his stomach, and I could see he was watching to make sure his whispering wasn't disturbing the thing that lay there.

"There was a fold in the sheet," he said, speaking more slowly than ever now and so softly I had to lean close to hear him. "See it, it's still there. It went under that. I could feel it through my pajamas, moving on my stomach. Then it stopped moving and now it's lying there in the warmth. Probably asleep. I've been waiting for you." He raised his eyes and looked at me.

"How long ago?"

"Hours," he whispered. "Hours and bloody hours and hours. I can't keep still much longer. I've been wanting to cough."

There was not much doubt about the truth of Harry's story. As a matter of fact it wasn't a surprising thing for a krait to do. They hang around people's houses, and they go for the warm places. The surprising thing was that Harry hadn't been bitten. The bite is quite deadly except sometimes

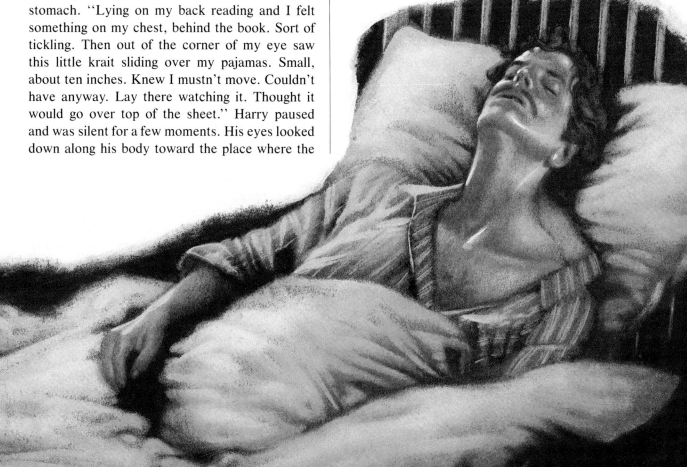

when you catch it at once, and they kill a fair number of people each year in Bengal, mostly in the villages.

"All right, Harry," I said, and now I was whispering too. "Don't move and don't talk anymore unless you have to. You know it won't bite unless it's frightened. We'll fix it in no time."

I went softly out of the room in my stocking feet and fetched a small sharp knife from the kitchen. I put it in my trouser pocket, ready to use instantly in case something went wrong while we were still thinking out a plan. If Harry coughed or moved or did something to frighten the krait and got bitten, I was going to be ready to cut the bitten place and try to suck the venom out. I came back to the bedroom and Harry was still lying there very quiet and sweating all over his face. His eyes followed me as I moved across the room to his bed, and I could see he was wondering what I'd been up to. I stood beside him, trying to think of the best thing to do.

"Harry," I said, and now when I spoke I put my mouth almost on his ear so I wouldn't have to raise my voice above the softest whisper, "I think the best thing to do is for me to draw the sheet back very, very gently. Then we could have a look first. I think I could do that without disturbing it."

"Don't be a fool." There was no expression in his voice. He spoke each word too slowly, too carefully, and too softly for that. The expression was in the eyes and around the corners of the mouth.

"Why not?"

"The light would frighten him. It's dark under there now."

"Then how about whipping the sheet back quick and brushing it off before it has time to strike?"

"Why don't you get a doctor?" Harry said. The way he looked at me told me I should have thought of that myself in the first place.

"A doctor. Of course. That's it. I'll get Ganderbai."

I tiptoed out to the hall, looked up Ganderbai's number in the book, lifted the phone, and told the operator to hurry.

"Doctor Ganderbai," I said. "This is Timber Woods."

"Hello, Mr. Woods. You not in bed yet?"

"Look, could you come round at once? And bring serum—for a krait bite."

"Who's been bitten?" The question came so sharply it was like a small explosion in my ear.

"No one. No one yet. But Harry Pope's in bed, and he's got one lying on his stomach—asleep under the sheet on his stomach."

For about three seconds there was silence on the line. Then speaking slowly, not like an explosion now but slowly, precisely, Ganderbai said, "Tell him to keep quite still. He is not to move or to talk. Do you understand?"

"Of course."

"I'll come at once!" He rang off and I went back to the bedroom. Harry's eyes watched me as I walked across to his bed.

"Ganderbai's coming. He said for you to lie still."

"What does he think I'm doing!"

"Look, Harry, he said no talking. Absolutely no talking. Either of us."

"Why don't you shut up then?" When he said this, one side of his mouth started twitching with rapid little downward movements that continued for a while after he finished speaking. I took out my handkerchief and very gently I wiped the sweat off his face and neck, and I could feel the slight twitching of the muscle—the one he used for smiling—as my fingers passed over it with the handkerchief.

I slipped out to the kitchen, got some ice from the icebox, rolled it up in a napkin, and began to crush it small. That business of the mouth, I didn't like that. Or the way he talked, either. I carried the ice pack back to the bedroom and laid it across Harry's forehead.

"Keep you cool."

He screwed up his eyes and drew breath sharply through his teeth. "Take it away," he whispered. "Make me cough." His smiling-muscle began to twitch again.

The beam of a headlamp shone through the window as Ganderbai's car swung around to the front of the bungalow. I went out to meet him, holding the ice pack with both hands.

"How is it?" Ganderbai asked, but he didn't stop to talk; he walked on past me across the balcony and through the screen doors into the hall. "Where is he? Which room?"

He put his bag down on a chair in the hall and followed me into Harry's room. He was wearing soft-soled bedroom slippers and he walked across the floor noiselessly, delicately, like a careful cat. Harry watched him out of the sides of his eyes. When Ganderbai reached the bed he looked down at Harry and smiled, confident and reassuring, nodding his head to tell Harry it was a simple matter and he was not to worry but just to leave it to Doctor Ganderbai. Then he turned and went back to the hall and I followed him.

"First thing is to try to get some serum into him," he said, and he opened his bag and started to make preparations. "Intravenously. But I must do it neatly. Don't want to make him flinch."

We went into the kitchen and he sterilized a needle. He had a hypodermic syringe in one hand and a small bottle in the other, and he stuck the needle through the rubber top of the bottle and began drawing a pale yellow liquid up into the syringe by pulling out the plunger. Then he handed the syringe to me.

"Hold that till I ask for it."

He picked up the bag and together we returned to the room. Harry's eyes were bright now and wide open. Ganderbai bent over Harry and very cautiously, like a man handling sixteenth-century lace, he rolled up the pajama sleeve to the elbow without moving the arm. I noticed he stood well away from the bed.

He whispered, "I'm going to give you an injection. Serum. Just a prick but try not to move. Don't tighten your stomach muscles. Let them go limp."

Harry looked at the syringe.

Ganderbai took a piece of red rubber tubing from his bag and slid one end under and up and around Harry's bicep; then he tied the tubing tight with a knot. He sponged a small area of the bare forearm with alcohol, handed the swab to me, and took the syringe from my hand. He held it up to the light, squinting at the calibrations, squirting out some of the yellow fluid. I stood still beside him, watching. Harry was watching too and sweating all over his face so it shone like it was smeared thick with face cream melting on his skin

and running down onto the pillow.

I could see the blue vein on the inside of Harry's forearm, swollen now because of the tourniquet, and then I saw the needle above the vein, Ganderbai holding the syringe almost flat against the arm, sliding the needle in sideways through the skin into the blue vein, sliding it slowly but so firmly it went in smooth as into cheese. Harry looked at the ceiling and closed his eyes and opened them again but he didn't move.

When it was finished Ganderbai leaned forward, putting his mouth close to Harry's ear. "Now you'll be all right even if you *are* bitten. But don't move. Please don't move. I'll be back in a moment."

He picked up his bag and went out to the hall and I followed.

"Is he safe now?" I asked.

"No."

"How safe is he?"

The little Indian doctor stood there in the hall rubbing his lower lip.

"It must give some protection, mustn't it?" I asked.

He turned away and walked to the screen doors that led onto the veranda. I thought he was going through them, but he stopped this side of the doors and stood looking out into the night.

"Isn't the serum very good?" I asked.

"Unfortunately not," he answered without turning round. "It might save him. It might not. I am trying to think of something else to do."

"Shall we draw the sheet back quick and brush it off before it has time to strike?"

"Never! We are not entitled to take a risk." He spoke sharply and his voice was pitched a little higher than usual.

"We can't very well leave him lying there," I said. "He's getting nervous."

"Please! Please!" he said, turning round, holding both hands up in the air. "Not so fast, please. This is not a matter to rush into baldheaded." He wiped his forehead with his handkerchief and stood there, frowning, nibbling his lip.

"You see," he said at last. "There is a way to do this. You know what we must do—we must administer an anesthetic to the creature where it lies."

It was a splendid idea.

"It is not safe," he continued, "because a snake is coldblooded and anesthetic does not work so well or so quick with such animals, but it is better than any other thing to do. We could use ether . . . chloroform . . ." He was speaking slowly and trying to think the thing out while he talked.

"Which shall we use?"

"Chloroform," he said suddenly. "Ordinary chloroform. That is best. Now quick!" He took my arm and pulled me toward the balcony. "Drive to my house! By the time you get there I will have waked up my boy on the telephone and he will show you my poisons cupboard. Here is the key of the cupboard. Take a bottle of chloroform. It has an orange label and the name is printed on it. I'll stay here in case anything happens. Be quick now, hurry! No, no, you don't need your shoes!"

I drove fast and in about fifteen minutes I was back with the bottle of chloroform. Ganderbai came out of Harry's room and met me in the hall. "You got it?" he said. "Good, good. I've just been telling him what we are going to do. But now we must hurry. It is not easy for him in there like that all this time. I am afraid he might move."

He went back to the bedroom and I followed, carrying the bottle carefully with both hands. Harry was lying on the bed in precisely the same position as before with the sweat pouring down his cheeks. His face was white and wet. He turned his eyes toward me, and I smiled at him and nodded confidently. He continued to look at me. I raised my thumb, giving him the okay signal. He closed his eyes. Ganderbai was squatted down by the bed, and on the floor beside him was the hollow rubber tube that he had previously used as a tourniquet, and he'd got a small paper funnel fitted into one end of the tube.

He began to pull a little piece of the sheet out from under the mattress. He was working directly in line with Harry's stomach, about eighteen inches from it, and I watched his fingers as they tugged gently at the edge of the sheet. He worked so slowly it was almost impossible to discern any movement either in his fingers or in the sheet that was being pulled.

Finally he succeeded in making an opening un-

der the sheet and he took the rubber tube and inserted one end of it in the opening so that it would slide under the sheet along the mattress toward Harry's body. I do not know how long it took him to slide that tube in a few inches. It may have been twenty minutes, it may have been forty. I never once saw the tube move. I knew it was going in because the visible part of it grew gradually shorter, but I doubted that the krait could have felt even the faintest vibration. Ganderbai himself was sweating now, large pearls of sweat standing out all over his forehead and along his upper lip. But his hands were steady, and I noticed that his eyes were watching, not the tube in his hands, but the area of crumpled sheet above Harry's stomach.

Without looking up, he held out a hand to me for the chloroform. I twisted out the ground-glass stopper and put the bottle right into his hand, not letting go till I was sure he had a good hold on it. Then he jerked his head for me to come closer, and he whispered, "Tell him I'm going to soak the mattress and that it will be very cold under his body. He must be ready for that and he must not move. Tell him now."

I bent over Harry and passed on the message.

"Why doesn't he get on with it?" Harry said.

"He's going to now, Harry. But it'll feel very cold, so be ready for it."

"Oh, get on!" For the first time he raised his voice, and Ganderbai glanced up sharply, watched him for a few seconds, then went back to his business.

Ganderbai poured a few drops of chloroform into the paper funnel and waited while it ran down the tube. Then he poured some more. Then he waited again, and the heavy, sickening smell of chloroform spread out over the room, bringing with it faint unpleasant memories of white-coated nurses and white surgeons standing in a white room around a long white table. Ganderbai was pouring steadily now, and I could see the heavy vapor of the chloroform swirling slowly like smoke above the paper funnel. He paused, held the bottle up to the light, poured one more funnelful, and handed the bottle back to me. Slowly he drew out the rubber tube from under the sheet; then he stood up.

The strain of inserting the tube and pouring the chloroform must have been great, and I recollect that when Ganderbai turned and whispered to me, his voice was small and tired. "We'll give it fifteen minutes. Just to be safe."

I leaned over to tell Harry. "We're going to give it fifteen minutes, just to be safe. But it's probably done for already."

"Then why don't you look and see!" Again he spoke loudly and Ganderbai sprang round, his small brown face suddenly very angry. He had almost pure black eyes and he stared at Harry and Harry's smiling-muscle started to twitch. I took my handkerchief and wiped his wet face, trying to stroke his forehead a little for comfort as I did so.

Then we stood and waited beside the bed, Ganderbai watching Harry's face all the time in a curious intense manner. The little Indian was concentrating all his willpower on keeping Harry quiet. He never once took his eyes from the patient and although he made no sound, he seemed somehow to be shouting at him all the time, saying: Now listen, you've got to listen, you're not going to go spoiling this now, d'you hear me; and Harry lay there twitching his mouth, sweating, closing his eyes, opening them, looking at me, at the sheet, at the ceiling, at me again, but never at Ganderbai. Yet somehow Ganderbai was holding him. The smell of chloroform was oppressive and it made me feel sick, but I couldn't leave the room now. I had the feeling someone was blowing up a huge balloon and I could see it was going to burst, but I couldn't look away.

At length Ganderbai turned and nodded and I knew he was ready to proceed. "You go over to the other side of the bed," he said. "We will each take one side of the sheet and draw it back together, but very slowly please, and very quietly."

"Keep still now, Harry," I said, and I went around to the other side of the bed and took hold of the sheet. Ganderbai stood opposite me, and together we began to draw back the sheet, lifting it up clear of Harry's body, taking it back very slowly, both of us standing well away but at the same time bending forward, trying to peer underneath it. The smell of chloroform was awful. I remember trying to hold my breath, and when I

couldn't do that any longer, I tried to breathe shallow so the stuff wouldn't get into my lungs.

The whole of Harry's chest was visible now, or rather the striped pajama top which covered it, and then I saw the white cord of his pajama trousers, neatly tied in a bow. A little farther and I saw a button, a mother-of-pearl button, and that was something I had never had on my pajamas, a fly button, let alone a mother-of-pearl one. This Harry, I thought, he is very refined. It is odd how one sometimes has frivolous thoughts at exciting moments, and I distinctly remember thinking about Harry being very refined when I saw that button.

Apart from the button there was nothing on his stomach.

We pulled the sheet back faster then, and when we had uncovered his legs and feet we let the sheet drop over the end of the bed onto the floor.

"Don't move," Ganderbai said, "don't move, Mr. Pope"; and he began to peer around along the side of Harry's body and under his legs.

"We must be careful," he said. "It may be anywhere. It could be up the leg of his pajamas."

When Ganderbai said this, Harry quickly raised his head from the pillow and looked down at his legs. It was the first time he had moved. Then suddenly he jumped up, stood on his bed, and shook his legs one after the other violently in the air. At that moment we both thought he had been bitten, and Ganderbai was already reaching down into his bag for a scalpel and a tourniquet when Harry ceased his caperings and stood still and looked at the mattress he was standing on and shouted, "It's not there!"

Ganderbai straightened up and for a moment he too looked at the mattress; then he looked up at Harry. Harry was all right. He hadn't been bitten and now he wasn't going to get bitten and he wasn't going to be killed and everything was fine. But that didn't seem to make anyone feel any better.

"Mr. Pope, you are of course *quite* sure you saw it in the first place?" There was a note of sarcasm in Ganderbai's voice that he would never have employed in ordinary circumstances. "You don't think you might possibly have been dreaming, do you, Mr. Pope?" The way Ganderbai was looking at Harry, I realized that the sarcasm was not seriously intended. He was only easing up a bit after the strain.

Harry stood on his bed in his striped pajamas, glaring at Ganderbai, and the color began to spread out over his cheeks.

"Are you telling me I'm a liar?" he shouted.

Ganderbai remained absolutely still, watching Harry. Harry took a pace forward on the bed and there was a shining look in his eyes.

"Why, you dirty little sewer rat!"

"Shut up, Harry!" I said.

"You dirty black——"

"Harry!" I called. "Shut up, Harry!" It was terrible, the things he was saying.

Ganderbai went out of the room as though nei-ther of us was there, and I followed him and put my arm around his shoulder as he walked across the hall and out onto the balcony.

"Don't you listen to Harry," I said. "This thing's made him so he doesn't know what he's saying."

We went down the steps from the balcony to the drive and across the drive in the darkness to where his old Morris car was parked. He opened the door and got in.

"You did a wonderful job," I said. "Thank you so very much for coming."

"All he needs is a good holiday," he said quietly, without looking at me; then he started the engine and drove off.

Responding to the Story

Analyzing the Story

Identifying Facts

1. What a strong line and a firm hook Roald Dahl has made for his plot here! Once we take it, our need to know what happens next pulls us straight to the last line. What clues tell us at once that something is wrong with Harry?
2. At what point do we learn precisely what the **conflict** is in the story? Why is this conflict so difficult to resolve?
3. See how the writer has his characters try to **resolve** their conflict by a succession of possible solutions. First, Timber gets a knife. What is it for? What plan does Dr. Ganderbai finally put into action?
4. As the plot unfolds, what details make us aware of Harry's fear? (His hoarse whisper is one thing.)
5. What is the outcome of the snake search?

Interpreting Meanings

6. What is the source of the terrifying **suspense** in this story—that is, what big question does the writer plant in your mind to keep you turning the pages?

7. Is it possible that there really was a krait under the sheet, or do you think Harry imagined it? What evidence can you find in the story to support both interpretations?
8. The major struggle in the story is an **external conflict,** which takes place between the three characters and the supposed snake. But **internal conflicts** are also at work. What feelings are the characters trying to control? By the story's end, what surprising external conflict between two of the characters has come out in the open?
9. How would you explain Harry's response to the generous native doctor? Now that you have finished the story, think again about Timber's earlier observation that Harry was "very refined." Explain how this comment is both true and false.
10. We might suspect that the title of the story refers to more than the venom of the krait. What other kinds of poison is the story about?

A Creative Response

1. **Making Up a Dialogue.** What do Timber and Harry

say to each other after Dr. Ganderbai drives off? The story doesn't tell us, but you might imagine a final scene. Suppose Timber turns to Harry. What does Timber say? How does Harry respond? Does he regret his harsh words to the doctor, or does he try to justify them? Does he convince Timber that there *was* a snake under the sheet? Write a dialogue that might end the story.

2. **Imagining a Character's Thoughts.** The final scene might also take place with Dr. Ganderbai in his car as he heads for home. What is he thinking? Will he come to the aid of Harry ever again? Does he understand Harry? What does he think *really* happened—does he believe there was a krait under the sheet? Write a paragraph telling what the doctor is thinking. Write as if you are Dr. Ganderbai, using the first-person pronoun, "I."

A Critical Response

3. **Explaining a Response.** What did you think of the surprise ending of this story? Do you like such surprise endings, or do you feel cheated by them? If you feel you were cheated by the ending of this story, what scene were you cheated of? Write a brief paragraph explaining how you felt about the story's ending.

4. **Summarizing a Plot.** For an exercise on summarizing the plot of this story, see page 57.

Analyzing Language and Vocabulary

Context Clues

The first sentence of this story mentions a *bungalow*, a word that might not be familiar to you. Most readers would be able to guess that a bungalow must be a kind of dwelling, probably a house. They would figure this out from various clues in the **context**—that is, the words and phrases that surround the word. One clue is that Timber has just said that he drove "home." Another is that the "bungalow" has gates leading to it. Another is that the "bungalow" has bedrooms and a balcony and screen doors. If you were really curious about exactly what kind of house a bungalow is, you would check the dictionary. There you would find that *bungalow*, in fact, comes from a Hindu word and that it specifically refers to a low, one-storied house in India, usually one with a wide, sweeping porch.

Find the context clues that will help you make an educated guess at the meaning of each italicized word. Check all the meanings in a dictionary.

1. "His whole face was wet, and the pillow around his head was *sodden* with moisture." What clues tell you that *sodden* probably means "soaked"?
2. "He . . . took the syringe from my hand. He held it up to the light, squinting at the *calibrations,* squirting out some of the yellow fluid." Why is the doctor "squinting" at the calibrations? Why does he squirt out some of the yellow fluid? What do you guess the "calibrations" must be?
3. "He turned away and walked to the screen doors that led onto the *veranda*." What do you picture the character doing? Given the clues in the passage, is a veranda most likely a table, a porch, a window, or a garage?
4. "Harry . . . jumped up, stood on his bed, and shook his legs one after the other violently in the air. At that moment we both thought he had been bitten, and Ganderbai was already reaching down into his bag for a scalpel and a tourniquet when Harry ceased his *caperings* and stood still. . . ." What clues tell you that *caperings* must be some kind of jumps and leaps?

Reading About the Writer

Roald Dahl (1916–1990) is an English writer known for his marvelous short stories and for his children's books (including *Charlie and the Chocolate Factory* and *James and the Giant Peach*). He is also known for his own dramatic life.

Dahl was a fighter pilot with Britain's Royal Air Force during World War II. He suffered serious injuries when his Hurricane fighter plane was shot down over North Africa. Eventually he left flying and went to work for the British Embassy in Washington, D.C. There he was interviewed about his flying experiences for a magazine article. Frustrated that the interview was interfering with his lunch, he volunteered to go home and scribble down some notes instead. In fact, what Dahl did was to sit down and write a perfect short story. *The Saturday Evening Post* published it at once.

Like "Poison," Dahl's other short stories almost always place ordinary characters in believable but bizarre situations. Many of his stories have surprise endings—some of them are shockers. Several of his stories have been made into TV movies.

THE MOST DANGEROUS GAME

Richard Connell

No story has had more popularity in school books than this story of a chase and of the dark, inhuman practices uncovered by a hunter named Rainsford, when he . . . but you read on to find out for yourself what happens to Rainsford. As you read, enjoy the story's heart-stopping suspense. Then think about the commentary following the story, and be ready for arguments.

But before you meet Rainsford as he speeds through the inky tropical night on his yacht, write down three things that you think the title might mean.

O ff there to the right—somewhere—is a large island," said Whitney. "It's rather a mystery——"

"What island is it?" Rainsford asked.

"The old charts call it 'Ship-Trap Island,'" Whitney replied. "A suggestive name, isn't it? Sailors have a curious dread of the place. I don't know why. Some superstition——"

"Can't see it," remarked Rainsford, trying to peer through the dank tropical night that was palpable as it pressed its thick warm blackness in upon the yacht.

"You've good eyes," said Whitney, with a laugh, "and I've seen you pick off a moose moving in the brown fall bush at four hundred yards, but even you can't see four miles or so through a moonless Caribbean night."

"Nor four yards," admitted Rainsford. "Ugh! It's like moist black velvet."

"It will be light in Rio," promised Whitney. "We should make it in a few days. I hope the jaguar guns have come from Purdey's.[1] We should have some good hunting up the Amazon. Great sport, hunting."

"The best sport in the world," agreed Rainsford.

"For the hunter," amended Whitney. "Not for the jaguar."

"Don't talk rot, Whitney," said Rainsford. "You're a big-game hunter, not a philosopher. Who cares how a jaguar feels?"

"Perhaps the jaguar does," observed Whitney.

"Bah! They've no understanding."

"Even so, I rather think they understand one thing—fear. The fear of pain and the fear of death."

"Nonsense," laughed Rainsford. "This hot weather is making you soft, Whitney. Be a realist. The world is made up of two classes—the hunters and the huntees. Luckily, you and I are the hunters. Do you think we've passed that island yet?"

"I can't tell in the dark. I hope so."

"Why?" asked Rainsford.

"The place has a reputation—a bad one."

"Cannibals?" suggested Rainsford.

"Hardly. Even cannibals wouldn't live in such a God-forsaken place. But it's gotten into sailor lore, somehow. Didn't you notice that the crew's nerves seemed a bit jumpy today?"

"They were a bit strange, now you mention it. Even Captain Nielsen——"

---

1. **Purdey's:** British manufacturer of hunting equipment.

"Yes, even that tough-minded old Swede, who'd go up to the devil himself and ask him for a light. Those fishy blue eyes held a look I never saw there before. All I could get out of him was: 'This place has an evil name among seafaring men, sir.' Then he said to me, very gravely: 'Don't you feel anything?'—as if the air about us was actually poisonous. Now, you mustn't laugh when I tell you this—I did feel something like a sudden chill.

"There was no breeze. The sea was as flat as a plate-glass window. We were drawing near the island then. What I felt was a—a mental chill; a sort of sudden dread."

"Pure imagination," said Rainsford. "One superstitious sailor can taint the whole ship's company with his fear."

"Maybe. But sometimes I think sailors have an extra sense that tells them when they are in danger. Sometimes I think evil is a tangible thing—with wave lengths, just as sound and light have. An evil place can, so to speak, broadcast vibrations of evil. Anyhow, I'm glad we're getting out of this zone. Well, I think I'll turn in now, Rainsford."

"I'm not sleepy," said Rainsford. "I'm going to smoke another pipe on the afterdeck."

Icarus by Julio Larraz (1987). Oil.

"Good night, then, Rainsford. See you at breakfast."

"Right. Good night, Whitney."

There was no sound in the night as Rainsford sat there, but the muffled throb of the engine that drove the yacht swiftly through the darkness, and the swish and ripple of the wash of the propeller.

Rainsford, reclining in a steamer chair, indolently puffed on his favorite brier.[2] The sensuous drowsiness of the night was on him. "It's so dark," he thought, "that I could sleep without closing my eyes; the night would be my eyelids——"

An abrupt sound startled him. Off to the right he heard it, and his ears, expert in such matters, could not be mistaken. Again he heard the sound, and again. Somewhere, off in the blackness, someone had fired a gun three times.

Rainsford sprang up and moved quickly to the rail, mystified. He strained his eyes in the direction from which the reports had come, but it was like trying to see through a blanket. He leaped upon the rail and balanced himself there, to get greater elevation; his pipe, striking a rope, was knocked from his mouth. He lunged for it; a short, hoarse cry came from his lips as he realized he had reached too far and had lost his balance. The cry was pinched off short as the blood-warm waters of the Caribbean Sea closed over his head.

He struggled up to the surface and tried to cry out, but the wash from the speeding yacht slapped him in the face and the salt water in his open mouth made him gag and strangle. Desperately he struck out with strong strokes after the receding lights of the yacht, but he stopped before he had swum fifty feet. A certain coolheadedness had come to him; it was not the first time he had been in a tight place. There was a chance that his cries could be heard by someone aboard the yacht, but that chance was slender and grew more slender as the yacht raced on. He wrestled himself out of his clothes and shouted with all his power. The lights of the yacht became faint and ever-vanishing fireflies; then they were blotted out entirely by the night.

Rainsford remembered the shots. They had come from the right, and doggedly he swam in that direction, swimming with slow, deliberate strokes, conserving his strength. For a seemingly endless time he fought the sea. He began to count his strokes; he could do possibly a hundred more and then——

Rainsford heard a sound. It came out of the darkness, a high screaming sound, the sound of an animal in an extremity of anguish and terror.

He did not recognize the animal that made the sound; he did not try to; with fresh vitality he swam toward the sound. He heard it again; then it was cut short by another noise, crisp, staccato.

"Pistol shot," muttered Rainsford, swimming on.

Ten minutes of determined effort brought another sound to his ears—the most welcome he had ever heard—the muttering and growling of the sea breaking on a rocky shore. He was almost on the rocks before he saw them; on a night less calm he would have been shattered against them. With his remaining strength he dragged himself from the swirling waters. Jagged crags appeared to jut into the opaqueness. He forced himself upward, hand over hand. Gasping, his hands raw, he reached a flat place at the top. Dense jungle came down to the very edge of the cliffs. What perils that tangle of trees and underbrush might hold for him did not concern Rainsford just then. All he knew was that he was safe from his enemy, the sea, and that utter weariness was on him. He flung himself down at the jungle edge and tumbled headlong into the deepest sleep of his life.

When he opened his eyes he knew from the position of the sun that it was late in the afternoon. Sleep had given him new vigor; a sharp hunger was picking at him. He looked about him, almost cheerfully.

"Where there are pistol shots, there are men. Where there are men, there is food," he thought. But what kind of men, he wondered, in so forbidding a place? An unbroken front of snarled and ragged jungle fringed the shore.

He saw no sign of a trail through the closely knit web of weeds and trees; it was easier to go

---

2. **brier** (brī′ər): a pipe made from the root of the brier plant.

along the shore, and Rainsford floundered along by the water. Not far from where he had landed, he stopped.

Some wounded thing, by the evidence a large animal, had thrashed about in the underbrush; the jungle weeds were crushed down and the moss was lacerated; one patch of weeds was stained crimson. A small, glittering object not far away caught Rainsford's eye and he picked it up. It was an empty cartridge.

"A twenty-two," he remarked. "That's odd. It must have been a fairly large animal too. The hunter had his nerve with him to tackle it with a light gun. It's clear that the brute put up a fight. I suppose the first three shots I heard was when the hunter flushed his quarry[3] and wounded it. The last shot was when he trailed it here and finished it."

He examined the ground closely and found what he had hoped to find—the print of hunting

---

3. **flushed his quarry:** drove his prey out of its cover.

boots. They pointed along the cliff in the direction he had been going. Eagerly he hurried along, now slipping on a rotten log or a loose stone, but making headway; night was beginning to settle down on the island.

Bleak darkness was blacking out the sea and jungle when Rainsford sighted the lights. He came upon them as he turned a crook in the coastline, and his first thought was that he had come upon a village, for there were many lights. But as he forged along he saw to his great astonishment that all the lights were in one enormous building—a lofty structure with pointed towers plunging upward into the gloom. His eyes made out the shadowy outlines of a palatial château; it was set on a high bluff, and on three sides of it cliffs dived down to where the sea licked greedy lips in the shadows.

"Mirage," thought Rainsford. But it was no mirage, he found, when he opened the tall spiked iron gate. The stone steps were real enough; the massive door with a leering gargoyle for a knocker was real enough; yet about it all hung an air of unreality.

He lifted the knocker, and it creaked up stiffly, as if it had never before been used. He let it fall, and it startled him with its booming loudness. He thought he heard steps within; the door remained closed. Again Rainsford lifted the heavy knocker and let it fall. The door opened then, opened as suddenly as if it were on a spring, and Rainsford stood blinking in the river of glaring gold light that poured out. The first thing Rainsford's eyes discerned was the largest man Rainsford had ever seen—a gigantic creature, solidly made and black-bearded to the waist. In his hand the man held a long-barreled revolver, and he was pointing it straight at Rainsford's heart.

Out of the snarl of beard two small eyes regarded Rainsford.

"Don't be alarmed," said Rainsford, with a smile which he hoped was disarming. "I'm no robber. I fell off a yacht. My name is Sanger Rainsford of New York City."

The menacing look in the eyes did not change. The revolver pointed as rigidly as if the giant were a statue. He gave no sign that he understood Rainsford's words, or that he had even heard them. He was dressed in uniform, a black uniform trimmed with gray astrakhan.[4]

"I'm Sanger Rainsford of New York," Rainsford began again. "I fell off a yacht. I am hungry."

The man's only answer was to raise with his thumb the hammer of his revolver. Then Rainsford saw the man's free hand go to his forehead in a military salute, and he saw him click his heels together and stand at attention. Another man was coming down the broad marble steps, an erect, slender man in evening clothes. He advanced to Rainsford and held out his hand.

In a cultivated voice marked by a slight accent that gave it added precision and deliberateness, he said: "It is a very great pleasure and honor to welcome Mr. Sanger Rainsford, the celebrated hunter, to my home."

Automatically Rainsford shook the man's hand.

"I've read your book about hunting snow leopards in Tibet, you see," explained the man. "I am General Zaroff."

Rainsford's first impression was that the man was singularly handsome; his second was that there was an original, almost bizarre quality about the general's face. He was a tall man past middle age, for his hair was a vivid white; but his thick eyebrows and pointed military mustache were as black as the night from which Rainsford had come. His eyes, too, were black and very bright. He had high cheekbones, a sharp-cut nose, a spare, dark face, the face of a man used to giving orders, the face of an aristocrat. Turning to the giant in uniform, the general made a sign. The giant put away his pistol, saluted, withdrew.

"Ivan is an incredibly strong fellow," remarked the general, "but he has the misfortune to be deaf and dumb. A simple fellow, but, I'm afraid, like all his race, a bit of a savage."

"Is he Russian?"

"He is a Cossack,"[5] said the general, and his smile showed red lips and pointed teeth. "So am I."

"Come," he said, "we shouldn't be chatting here. We can talk later. Now you want clothes, food, rest. You shall have them. This is a most restful spot."

Ivan had reappeared, and the general spoke to him with lips that moved but gave forth no sound.

"Follow Ivan, if you please, Mr. Rainsford," said the general. "I was about to have my dinner when you came. I'll wait for you. You'll find that my clothes will fit you, I think."

It was to a huge, beam-ceilinged bedroom with a canopied bed big enough for six men that Rainsford followed the silent giant. Ivan laid out an evening suit, and Ransford, as he put it on, noticed that it came from a London tailor who ordinarily cut and sewed for none below the rank of duke.

The dining room to which Ivan conducted him was in many ways remarkable. There was a medieval magnificence about it; it suggested a baronial hall of feudal times with its oaken panels, its high ceiling, its vast refectory table where two-score men could sit down to eat. About the hall were the mounted heads of many animals—lions, tigers, elephants, moose, bears; larger or more perfect specimens Rainsford had never seen. At the great table the general was sitting, alone.

"You'll have a cocktail, Mr. Rainsford," he suggested. The cocktail was surpassingly good; and, Rainsford noted, the table appointments were of the finest—the linen, the crystal, the silver, the china.

They were eating borscht, the rich, red soup with whipped cream so dear to Russian palates. Half apologetically General Zaroff said: "We do our best to preserve the amenities of civilization here. Please forgive any lapses. We are well off the beaten track, you know. Do you think the champagne has suffered from its long ocean trip?"

"Not in the least," declared Rainsford. He was finding the general a most thoughtful and affable host, a true cosmopolite.[6] But there was one small trait of the general's that made Rainsford uncomfortable. Whenever he looked up from his plate he found the general studying him, appraising him narrowly.

"Perhaps," said General Zaroff, "you were

---

4. **astrakhan** (as′trə·kən): curly fur of very young lambs.
5. **Cossack** (käs′ak): Cossacks were elite horsemen and warriors of southern Russia, famous for their fierceness in battle.

6. **cosmopolite** (käz·mäp′ə·līt′): sophisticated citizen of the world.

surprised that I recognized your name. You see, I read all books on hunting published in English, French, and Russian. I have but one passion in my life, Mr. Rainsford, and it is the hunt.''

''You have some wonderful heads here,'' said Rainsford as he ate a particularly well-cooked filet mignon. ''That Cape buffalo is the largest I ever saw.''

''Oh, that fellow. Yes, he was a monster.''

''Did he charge you?''

''Hurled me against a tree,'' said the general. ''Fractured my skull. But I got the brute.''

''I've always thought,'' said Rainsford, ''that the Cape buffalo is the most dangerous of all big game.''

For a moment the general did not reply; he was smiling his curious red-lipped smile. Then he said slowly: ''No. You are wrong, sir. The Cape buffalo is not the most dangerous big game.'' He sipped his wine. ''Here in my preserve on this island,'' he said in the same slow tone, ''I hunt more dangerous game.''

Rainsford expressed his surprise. ''Is there big game on this island?''

The general nodded. ''The biggest.''

''Really?''

''Oh, it isn't here naturally, of course. I have to stock the island.''

''What have you imported, general?'' Rainsford asked. ''Tigers?''

The general smiled. ''No,'' he said. ''Hunting tigers ceased to interest me some years ago. I exhausted their possibilities, you see. No thrill left in tigers, no real danger. I live for danger, Mr. Rainsford.''

The general took from his pocket a gold cigarette case and offered his guest a long black cigarette with a silver tip; it was perfumed and gave off a smell like incense.

''We will have some capital hunting, you and I,'' said the general. ''I shall be most glad to have your society.''

''But what game——'' began Rainsford.

''I'll tell you,'' said the general. ''You will be

amused, I know. I think I may say, in all modesty, that I have done a rare thing. I have invented a new sensation. May I pour you another glass of port, Mr. Rainsford?''

"Thank you, general.''

The general filled both glasses, and said: "God makes some men poets. Some He makes kings, some beggars. Me He made a hunter. My hand was made for the trigger, my father said. He was a very rich man with a quarter of a million acres in the Crimea,[7] and he was an ardent sportsman. When I was only five years old he gave me a little gun, specially made in Moscow for me, to shoot sparrows with. When I shot some of his prize turkeys with it, he did not punish me; he complimented me on my marksmanship. I killed my first bear in the Caucasus[8] when I was ten. My whole life has been one prolonged hunt. I went into the army—it was expected of noblemen's sons—and for a time commanded a division of Cossack cavalry, but my real interest was always the hunt. I have hunted every kind of game in every land. It would be impossible for me to tell you how many animals I have killed.''

The general puffed at his cigarette.

"After the debacle[9] in Russia I left the country, for it was imprudent for an officer of the Czar to stay there. Many noble Russians lost everything. I, luckily, had invested heavily in American securities, so I shall never have to open a tearoom in Monte Carlo[10] or drive a taxi in Paris. Naturally, I continued to hunt—grizzlies in your Rockies, crocodiles in the Ganges, rhinoceroses in East Africa. It was in Africa that the Cape buffalo hit me and laid me up for six months. As soon as I recovered I started for the Amazon to hunt jaguars, for I had heard they were unusually cunning. They weren't.'' The Cossack sighed. "They were

---

7. **Crimea** (krī·mē′ə): an area in the Soviet Union bordering the Black Sea.
8. **Caucasus** (kô′kə·səs): mountainous region in the Soviet Union between the Black and Caspian seas.
9. **debacle** (di·bäk′l): stunning, ruinous collapse. Zaroff refers to the overthrow of the Czar in the Russian Revolution of 1917.
10. **Monte Carlo** (män′ti kär′lō): resort city and gambling center in Monaco on the Mediterranean Sea, associated with the very rich.

no match at all for a hunter with his wits about him and a high-powered rifle. I was bitterly disappointed. I was lying in my tent with a splitting headache one night when a terrible thought pushed its way into my mind. Hunting was beginning to bore me! And hunting, remember, had been my life. I have heard that in America businessmen often go to pieces when they give up the business that has been their life.''

"Yes, that's so,'' said Rainsford.

The general smiled. "I had no wish to go to pieces,'' he said. "I must do something. Now, mine is an analytical mind, Mr. Rainsford. Doubtless that is why I enjoy the problems of the chase.''

"No doubt, General Zaroff.''

"So,'' continued the general, "I asked myself why the hunt no longer fascinated me. You are much younger than I am, Mr. Rainsford, and have not hunted as much, but you perhaps can guess the answer.''

"What was it?''

"Simply this: hunting had ceased to be what you call 'a sporting proposition.' It had become too easy. I always got my quarry. Always. There is no greater bore than perfection.''

The general lit a fresh cigarette.

"No animal had a chance with me anymore. That is no boast; it is a mathematical certainty. The animal had nothing but his legs and his instinct. Instinct is no match for reason. When I thought of this it was a tragic moment for me, I can tell you.''

Rainsford leaned across the table, absorbed in what his host was saying.

"It came to me as an inspiration what I must do,'' the general went on.

"And that was?''

The general smiled the quiet smile of one who has faced an obstacle and surmounted it with success. "I had to invent a new animal to hunt,'' he said.

"A new animal? You're joking.''

"Not at all,'' said the general. "I never joke about hunting. I needed a new animal. I found one. So I bought this island, built this house, and here I do my hunting. The island is perfect for my

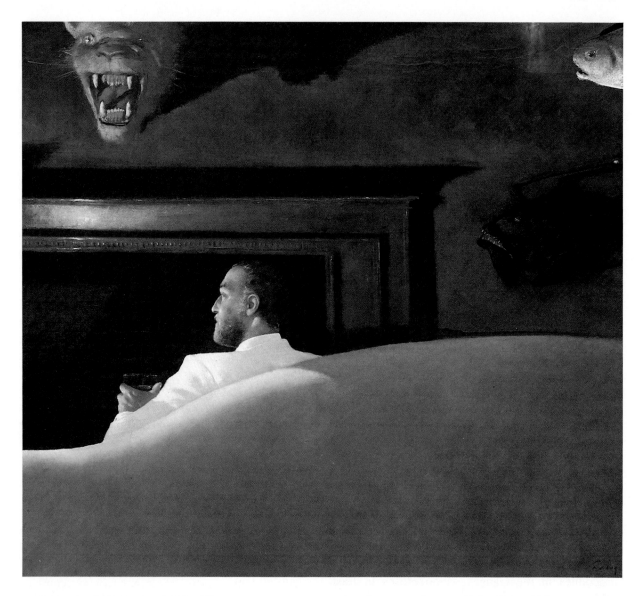

Casanova by Julio Larraz (1987). Oil.

© Julio Larraz. Courtesy Nohra Haime Gallery, New York.

purposes—there are jungles with a maze of trails in them, hills, swamps——''

''But the animal, General Zaroff?''

''Oh,'' said the general, ''it supplies me with the most exciting hunting in the world. No other hunting compares with it for an instant. Every day I hunt, and I never grow bored now, for I have a quarry with which I can match my wits.''

Rainsford's bewilderment showed in his face.

''I wanted the ideal animal to hunt,'' explained the general. ''So I said: 'What are the attributes of an ideal quarry?' And the answer was, of course: 'it must have courage, cunning, and, above all, it must be able to reason.' ''

''But no animal can reason,'' objected Rainsford.

''My dear fellow,'' said the general, ''there is one that can.''

''But you can't mean——'' gasped Rainsford.

''And why not?''

''I can't believe you are serious, General Zaroff. This is a grisly joke.''

''Why should I not be serious? I am speaking of hunting.''

"Hunting? Good God, General Zaroff, what you speak of is murder."

The general laughed with entire good nature. He regarded Rainsford quizzically. "I refuse to believe that so modern and civilized a young man as you seem to be harbors romantic ideas about the value of human life. Surely your experiences in the war——"

"Did not make me condone cold-blooded murder," finished Rainsford stiffly.

Laughter shook the general. "How extraordinarily droll you are!" he said. "One does not expect nowadays to find a young man of the educated class, even in America, with such a naive, and, if I may say so, mid-Victorian point of view. It's like finding a snuffbox in a limousine. Ah, well, doubtless you had Puritan ancestors. So many Americans appear to have had. I'll wager you'll forget your notions when you go hunting with me. You've a genuine new thrill in store for you, Mr. Rainsford."

"Thank you, I'm a hunter, not a murderer."

"Dear me," said the general, quite unruffled, "again that unpleasant word. But I think I can show you that your scruples are quite ill-founded."

"Yes?"

"Life is for the strong, to be lived by the strong, and, if need be, taken by the strong. The weak of the world were put here to give the strong pleasure. I am strong. Why should I not use my gift? If I wish to hunt, why should I not? I hunt the scum of the earth—sailors from tramp ships—lascars,[11] blacks, Chinese, whites, mongrels—a thoroughbred horse or hound is worth more than a score of them."

"But they are men," said Rainsford hotly.

"Precisely," said the general. "That is why I use them. It gives me pleasure. They can reason, after a fashion. So they are dangerous."

"But where do you get them?"

The general's left eyelid fluttered down in a wink. "This island is called Ship-Trap," he answered. "Sometimes an angry god of the high seas sends them to me. Sometimes, when Providence

is not so kind, I help Providence a bit. Come to the window with me."

Rainsford went to the window and looked out toward the sea.

"Watch! Out there!" exclaimed the general, pointing into the night. Rainsford's eyes saw only blackness, and then, as the general pressed a button, far out to sea Rainsford saw the flash of lights.

The general chuckled. "They indicate a channel," he said, "where there's none: giant rocks with razor edges crouch like a sea monster with wide-open jaws. They can crush a ship as easily as I crush this nut." He dropped a walnut on the hardwood floor and brought his heel grinding down on it. "Oh, yes," he said, casually, as if in answer to a question, "I have electricity. We try to be civilized here."

"Civilized? And you shoot down men?"

A trace of anger was in the general's black eyes, but it was there for but a second, and he said, in his most pleasant manner: "Dear me, what a righteous young man you are! I assure you I do not do the thing you suggest. That would be barbarous. I treat these visitors with every consideration. They get plenty of good food and exercise. They get into splendid physical condition. You shall see for yourself tomorrow."

"What do you mean?"

"We'll visit my training school," smiled the general. "It's in the cellar. I have about a dozen pupils down there now. They're from the Spanish bark *San Lucar* that had the bad luck to go on the rocks out there. A very inferior lot, I regret to say. Poor specimens and more accustomed to the deck than to the jungle."

He raised his hand, and Ivan, who served as waiter, brought thick Turkish coffee. Rainsford, with an effort, held his tongue in check.

"It's a game, you see," pursued the general blandly. "I suggest to one of them that we go hunting. I give him a supply of food and an excellent hunting knife. I give him three hours' start. I am to follow, armed only with a pistol of the smallest caliber and range. If my quarry eludes me for three whole days, he wins the game. If I find him"—the general smiled—"he loses."

"Suppose he refuses to be hunted?"

"Oh," said the general, "I give him his option,

---

11. **lascars** (las′kərz): Asian sailors, especially from India.

Animals by Rufino Tamayo (1941).
Oil on canvas, 30⅛″ × 40″.

of course. He need not play that game if he doesn't wish to. If he does not wish to hunt, I turn him over to Ivan. Ivan once had the honor of serving as official knouter[12] to the Great White Czar, and he has his own ideas of sport. Invariably, Mr. Rainsford, invariably they choose the hunt.''

''And if they win?''

The smile on the general's face widened. ''To date I have not lost,'' he said.

Then he added, hastily: ''I don't wish you to think me a braggart, Mr. Rainsford. Many of them afford only the most elementary sort of problem. Occasionally I strike a tartar.[13] One almost did win. I eventually had to use the dogs.''

''The dogs?''

''This way, please. I'll show you.''

The general steered Rainsford to a window. The lights from the windows sent a flickering illumination that made grotesque patterns on the courtyard below, and Rainsford could see moving about there a dozen or so huge black shapes; as they turned toward him, their eyes glittered greenly.

''A rather good lot, I think,'' observed the general. ''They are let out at seven every night. If anyone should try to get into my house—or out of it—something extremely regrettable would occur to him.'' He hummed a snatch of song from the Folies Bergère.[14]

---

12. **knouter** (nout′ər): person who beats criminals with a knout, a kind of leather whip.
13. **strike a tartar:** that is, get more than one bargained for.

14. **Folies Bergère** (fô′lē ber·zher′): famous musical nightclub in Paris.

"And now," said the general, "I want to show you my new collection of heads. Will you come with me to the library?"

"I hope," said Rainsford, "that you will excuse me tonight, General Zaroff. I'm really not feeling at all well."

"Ah, indeed?" the general inquired solicitously. "Well, I suppose that's only natural, after your long swim. You need a good, restful night's sleep. Tomorrow you'll feel like a new man, I'll wager. Then we'll hunt, eh? I've one rather promising prospect—"

Rainsford was hurrying from the room.

"Sorry you can't go with me tonight," called the general. "I expect rather fair sport—a big, strong black. He looks resourceful—Well, good night, Mr. Rainsford; I hope you have a good night's rest."

The bed was good and the pajamas of the softest silk, and he was tired in every fiber of his being, but nevertheless Rainsford could not quiet his brain with the opiate of sleep. He lay, eyes wide open. Once he thought he heard stealthy steps in the corridor outside his room. He sought to throw open the door; it would not open. He went to the window and looked out. His room was high up in one of the towers. The lights of the château were out now, and it was dark and silent, but there was a fragment of sallow moon, and by its wan light he could see, dimly, the courtyard; there, weaving in and out in the pattern of shadow, were black, noiseless forms; the hounds heard him at the window and looked up, expectantly, with their green eyes. Rainsford went back to the bed and lay down. By many methods he tried to put himself to sleep. He had achieved a doze when, just as morning began to come, he heard, far off in the jungle, the faint report of a pistol.

General Zaroff did not appear until luncheon. He was dressed faultlessly in the tweeds of a country squire. He was solicitous about the state of Rainsford's health.

"As for me," sighed the general, "I do not feel so well. I am worried, Mr. Rainsford. Last night I detected traces of my old complaint."

To Rainsford's questioning glance the general said: "Ennui. Boredom."

Then, taking a second helping of crêpes suzette,[15] the general explained: "The hunting was not good last night. The fellow lost his head. He made a straight trail that offered no problems at all. That's the trouble with these sailors; they have dull brains to begin with, and they do not know how to get about in the woods. They do excessively stupid and obvious things. It's most annoying. Will you have another glass of Chablis, Mr. Rainsford?"

"General," said Rainsford firmly, "I wish to leave this island at once."

The general raised his thickets of eyebrows; he seemed hurt. "But, my dear fellow," the general protested, "you've only just come. You've had no hunting——"

"I wish to go today," said Rainsford. He saw the dead black eyes of the general on him, studying him. General Zaroff's face suddenly brightened.

He filled Rainsford's glass with venerable Chablis from a dusty bottle.

"Tonight," said the general, "we will hunt—you and I."

Rainsford shook his head. "No, general," he said. "I will not hunt."

The general shrugged his shoulders and delicately ate a hothouse grape. "As you wish, my friend," he said. "The choice rests entirely with you. But may I not venture to suggest that you will find my idea of sport more diverting than Ivan's?"

He nodded toward the corner to where the giant stood, scowling, his thick arms crossed on his hogshead of chest.

"You don't mean——" cried Rainsford.

"My dear fellow," said the general, "have I not told you I always mean what I say about hunting? This is really an inspiration. I drink to a foeman worthy of my steel—at last."

The general raised his glass, but Rainsford sat staring at him.

"You'll find this game worth playing," the general said enthusiastically. "Your brain against

---

15. **crêpes suzette** (krep' soo·zet'): thin pancakes folded with hot orange sauce and served in flaming brandy.

mine. Your woodcraft against mine. Your strength and stamina against mine. Outdoor chess! And the stake is not without value, eh?"

"And if I win——" began Rainsford huskily.

"I'll cheerfully acknowledge myself defeated if I do not find you by midnight of the third day," said General Zaroff. "My sloop will place you on the mainland near a town."

The general read what Rainsford was thinking.

"Oh, you can trust me," said the Cossack. "I will give you my word as a gentleman and a sportsman. Of course you, in turn, must agree to say nothing of your visit here."

"I'll agree to nothing of the kind," said Rainsford.

"Oh," said the general, "in that case—But why discuss that now? Three days hence we can discuss it over a bottle of Veuve Cliquot,[16] unless——"

The general sipped his wine.

Then a businesslike air animated him. "Ivan," he said to Rainsford, "will supply you with hunting clothes, food, a knife. I suggest you wear moccasins; they leave a poorer trail. I suggest too that you avoid the big swamp in the southeast corner of the island. We call it Death Swamp. There's quicksand there. One foolish fellow tried it. The deplorable part of it was that Lazarus followed him. You can imagine my feelings, Mr. Rainsford. I loved Lazarus; he was the finest hound in my pack. Well, I must beg you to excuse me now. I always take a siesta after lunch. You'll hardly have time for a nap, I fear. You'll want to start, no doubt. I shall not follow till dusk. Hunting at night is so much more exciting than by day, don't you think? Au revoir, Mr. Rainsford, au revoir."

General Zaroff, with a deep, courtly bow, strolled from the room.

From another door came Ivan. Under one arm he carried khaki hunting clothes, a haversack of food, a leather sheath containing a long-bladed hunting knife; his right hand rested on a cocked revolver thrust in the crimson sash about his waist. . . .

---

16. **Veuve Cliquot** (vüv kli·kō'): a brand of fine champagne.

Rainsford had fought his way through the bush for two hours. "I must keep my nerve. I must keep my nerve," he said through tight teeth.

He had not been entirely clearheaded when the château gates snapped shut behind him. His whole idea at first was to put distance between himself and General Zaroff, and, to this end, he had plunged along, spurred on by the sharp rowels of something very like panic. Now he had got a grip on himself, had stopped, and was taking stock of himself and the situation.

He saw that straight flight was futile; inevitably it would bring him face to face with the sea. He was in a picture with a frame of water, and his operations, clearly, must take place within that frame.

"I'll give him a trail to follow," muttered Rainsford, and he struck off from the rude paths he had been following into the trackless wilderness. He executed a series of intricate loops; he doubled on his trail again and again, recalling all the lore of the fox hunt and all the dodges of the fox. Night found him leg-weary, with hands and face lashed by the branches, on a thickly wooded ridge. He knew it would be insane to blunder on through the dark, even if he had the strength. His need for rest was imperative and he thought: "I have played the fox, now I must play the cat of the fable." A big tree with a thick trunk and outspread branches was nearby, and, taking care to leave not the slightest mark, he climbed up into the crotch and stretching out on one of the broad limbs, after a fashion, rested. Rest brought him new confidence and almost a feeling of security. Even so zealous a hunter as General Zaroff could not trace him there, he told himself; only the devil himself could follow that complicated trail through the jungle after dark. But, perhaps, the general was a devil——

An apprehensive night crawled slowly by like a wounded snake, and sleep did not visit Rainsford, although the silence of a dead world was on the jungle. Toward morning when a dingy gray was varnishing the sky, the cry of some startled bird focused Rainsford's attention in that direction. Something was coming through the bush, coming slowly, carefully, coming by the same winding way Rainsford had come. He flattened himself down on the limb, and through a screen of leaves almost as thick as tapestry, he watched. The thing that was approaching was a man.

It was General Zaroff. He made his way along with his eyes fixed in utmost concentration on the ground before him. He paused, almost beneath the tree, dropped to his knees and studied the ground. Rainsford's impulse was to hurl himself down like a panther, but he saw the general's right hand held something metallic—a small automatic pistol.

The hunter shook his head several times, as if he were puzzled. Then he straightened up and took from his case one of his black cigarettes; its pungent incense-like smoke floated up to Rainsford's nostrils.

Rainsford held his breath. The general's eyes had left the ground and were traveling inch by inch up the tree. Rainsford froze there, every muscle tensed for a spring. But the sharp eyes of the hunter stopped before they reached the limb where Rainsford lay; a smile spread over his brown face. Very deliberately he blew a smoke ring into the air; then he turned his back on the tree and walked carelessly away, back along the trail he had come. The swish of the underbrush against his hunting boots grew fainter and fainter.

Then pent-up air burst hotly from Rainsford's lungs. His first thought made him feel sick and numb. The general could follow a trail through the woods at night; he could follow an extremely difficult trail; he must have uncanny powers; only by the merest chance had the Cossack failed to see his quarry.

Rainsford's second thought was even more terrible. It sent a shudder of cold horror through his whole being. Why had the general smiled? Why had he turned back?

Rainsford did not want to believe what his reason told him was true, but the truth was as evident as the sun that had by now pushed through the morning mists. The general was playing with him! The general was saving him for another day's sport! The Cossack was the cat; he was the mouse. Then it was that Rainsford knew the full meaning of terror.

"I will not lose my nerve. I will not."

He slid down from the tree, and struck off again into the woods. His face was set and he forced the machinery of his mind to function. Three hundred yards from his hiding place he stopped where a huge dead tree leaned precariously on a smaller, living one. Throwing off his sack of food, Rainsford took his knife from its sheath and began to work with all his energy.

The job was finished at last, and he threw himself down behind a fallen log a hundred feet away. He did not have to wait long. The cat was coming again to play with the mouse.

Following the trail with the sureness of a bloodhound came General Zaroff. Nothing escaped those searching black eyes, no crushed blade of grass, no bent twig, no mark, no matter how faint, in the moss. So intent was the Cossack on his stalking that he was upon the thing Rainsford had made before he saw it. His foot touched the protruding bough that was the trigger. Even as he touched it, the general sensed his danger and leaped back with the agility of an ape. But he was not quite quick enough; the dead tree, delicately adjusted to rest on the cut living one, crashed down and struck the general a glancing blow on the shoulder as it fell; but for his alertness, he must have been smashed beneath it. He staggered, but he did not fall; nor did he drop his revolver. He stood there, rubbing his injured shoulder, and Rainsford, with fear again gripping his heart, heard the general's mocking laugh ring through the jungle.

"Rainsford," called the general, "if you are within the sound of my voice, as I suppose you are, let me congratulate you. Not many men know how to make a Malay man-catcher. Luckily, for me, I too have hunted in Malacca.[17] You are proving interesting, Mr. Rainsford. I am going now to have my wound dressed; it's only a slight one. But I shall be back. I shall be back."

When the general, nursing his bruised shoulder, had gone, Rainsford took up his flight again. It was flight now, a desperate, hopeless flight, that carried him on for some hours. Dusk came, then darkness, and still he pressed on. The ground grew

---

17. **Malacca** (mə·lak′ə): a state in the southeast Asian nation of Malaysia.

softer under his moccasins; the vegetation grew ranker, denser; insects bit him savagely. Then, as he stepped forward, his foot sank into the ooze. He tried to wrench it back, but the muck sucked viciously at his foot as if it were a giant leech. With a violent effort, he tore loose. He knew where he was now. Death Swamp and its quicksand.

His hands were tight closed as if his nerve were something tangible that someone in the darkness was trying to tear from his grip. The softness of the earth had given him an idea. He stepped back from the quicksand a dozen feet or so, and, like some huge prehistoric beaver, he began to dig.

Rainsford had dug himself in in France[18] when a second's delay meant death. That had been a placid pastime compared to his digging now. The pit grew deeper; when it was above his shoulders, he climbed out and from some hard saplings cut stakes and sharpened them to a fine point. These stakes he planted in the bottom of the pit with the points sticking up. With flying fingers he wove a rough carpet of weeds and branches and with it he covered the mouth of the pit. Then, wet with sweat and aching with tiredness, he crouched behind the stump of a lightning-charred tree.

He knew his pursuer was coming; he heard the padding sound of feet on the soft earth, and the night breeze brought him the perfume of the general's cigarette. It seemed to Rainsford that the general was coming with unusual swiftness; he was not feeling his way along, foot by foot. Rainsford, crouching there, could not see the general, nor could he see the pit. He lived a year in a minute. Then he felt an impulse to cry aloud with joy, for he heard the sharp crackle of the breaking branches as the cover of the pit gave way; he heard the sharp scream of pain as the pointed stakes found their mark. He leaped up from his place of concealment. Then he cowered back. Three feet from the pit a man was standing, with an electric torch in his hand.

"You've done well, Rainsford," the voice of the general called. "Your Burmese tiger pit has claimed one of my best dogs. Again you score. I

think, Mr. Rainsford, I'll see what you can do against my whole pack. I'm going home for a rest now. Thank you for a most amusing evening."

At daybreak Rainsford, lying near the swamp, was awakened by the sound that made him know that he had new things to learn about fear. It was a distant sound, faint and wavering, but he knew it. It was the baying of a pack of hounds.

Rainsford knew he could do one of two things. He could stay where he was and wait. That was suicide. He could flee. That was postponing the inevitable. For a moment he stood there, thinking. An idea that held a wild chance came to him, and, tightening his belt, he headed away from the swamp.

The baying of the hounds drew nearer, then still nearer, nearer, ever nearer. On a ridge Rainsford climbed a tree. Down a watercourse, not a quarter of a mile away, he could see the bush moving. Straining his eyes, he saw the lean figure of General Zaroff; just ahead of him Rainsford made out another figure whose wide shoulders surged through the tall jungle weeds; it was the giant Ivan, and he seemed pulled forward by some unseen force; Rainsford knew that Ivan must be holding the pack in leash.

They would be on him any minute now. His mind worked frantically. He thought of a native trick he had learned in Uganda. He slid down the tree. He caught hold of a springy young sapling and to it he fastened his hunting knife, with the blade pointing down the trail; with a bit of wild grapevine he tied back the sapling. Then he ran for his life. The hounds raised their voices as they hit the fresh scent. Rainsford knew now how an animal at bay feels.

He had to stop to get his breath. The baying of the hounds stopped abruptly, and Rainsford's heart stopped too. They must have reached the knife.

He shinnied excitedly up a tree and looked back. His pursuers had stopped. But the hope that was in Rainsford's brain when he climbed died, for he saw in the shallow valley that General Zaroff was still on his feet. But Ivan was not. The knife, driven by the recoil of the springing tree, had not wholly failed.

18. **dug himself in in France:** dug a foxhole for protection in World War I (1914–1918).

"Nerve, nerve, nerve!" he panted, as he dashed along. A blue gap showed between the trees dead ahead. Ever nearer drew the hounds. Rainsford forced himself on toward that gap. He reached it. It was the shore of the sea. Across a cove he could see the gloomy gray stone of the château. Twenty feet below him the sea rumbled and hissed. Rainsford hesitated. He heard the hounds. Then he leaped far out into the sea. . . .

When the general and his pack reached the place by the sea, the Cossack stopped. For some minutes he stood regarding the blue-green expanse of water. He shrugged his shoulders. Then he sat down, took a drink of brandy from a silver flask, lit a perfumed cigarette, and hummed a bit from *Madame Butterfly.*

General Zaroff had an exceedingly good dinner in his great paneled dining hall that evening. With it he had a bottle of Pol Roger and half a bottle of Chambertin.[19] Two slight annoyances kept him from perfect enjoyment. One was the thought that it would be difficult to replace Ivan; the other was that his quarry had escaped him; of course the American hadn't played the game—so thought the general as he tasted his after-dinner liqueur. In his library he read, to soothe himself, from the works of Marcus Aurelius.[20] At ten he went up to his bedroom. He was deliciously tired, he said to himself, as he locked himself in. There was a little moonlight, so, before turning on his light, he went to the window and looked down at the courtyard. He could see the great hounds, and he called: "Better luck another time," to them. Then he switched on the light.

---

19. **Pol Roger** (pôl′rō·zhā′) . . . **Chambertin** (shan′ber·tan′): respectively, a brand of fine champagne and a kind of red burgundy.
20. **Marcus Aurelius** (ô·rē′lē·əs): Roman emperor and Stoic philosopher (A.D. 121–180).

The Voice of the Casuarina by Julio Larraz (1986). Oil.

© Julio Larraz. Courtesy Nohra Haime Gallery, New York.

A man, who had been hiding in the curtains of the bed, was standing there.

"Rainsford!" screamed the general. "How in God's name did you get here?"

"Swam," said Rainsford. "I found it quicker than walking through the jungle."

The general sucked in his breath and smiled. "I congratulate you," he said. "You have won the game."

Rainsford did not smile. "I am still a beast at bay," he said, in a low, hoarse voice. "Get ready, General Zaroff."

The general made one of his deepest bows. "I see," he said. "Splendid! One of us is to furnish a repast for the hounds. The other will sleep in this very excellent bed. On guard, Rainsford. . . ."

He had never slept in a better bed, Rainsford decided.

An Escape Story?

I think that this very popular story, "The Most Dangerous Game," is a fine illustration of an "escape story." It's fun to read; it helps us pass an hour or two (it helps us "escape" from real life for a time), but does it reveal very much about human life and the real, complex world we live in?

"The Most Dangerous Game" is an adventure story, and it has all the appeal of a Hollywood scare-o-rama, complete with an elegant evil villain, his huge brute of a manservant, a castle, a dark jungle, bloodthirsty animals, and hideous man traps.

Besides these attention-getting elements, there is a "hunting" theme. Rainsford is a world-class hunter, and he lets us know early on that he's pursued wild animals all over the world and is a major authority on the subject. It has not occurred to him that *he* might be prey before the story ends, and boy, is he mistaken.

But here's where I think the problems come in. For such a know-it-all, isn't Rainsford short on good sense when he leaps onto the rail of a ship plowing through the sea? And how does Zaroff run this elegant castle? Does he use some of his victims as servants? Rainsford divides the world into the hunted and the hunters. Where would he put his doctor? his mail carrier? his mother? Rainsford doesn't seem real to me; he seems to be lifted from countless adventure stories told in comic books and on TV and movies.

General Zaroff, his opponent, is the same. He is as steeped in villainy as they come. Do you believe there could be a man rich enough and crazy enough to buy an island and build a castle on it so he can live there and hunt human beings? Or is it more likely that the writer has dreamt up such a character just to scare the pants off us?

And what about that missing part of the plot? Rainsford is cornered, hounds after him, no place to be but the terrible razor-rock rimmed sea. Cut. Next thing we know he's in the general's bedroom. Next thing we know he's in the general's bed. But what happened? How did he get there and how did he dispatch the superman Zaroff? Did the author lose some pages? Or did he decide he didn't like them and think we'd never notice that they're gone?

That's what *I* think about "The Most Dangerous Game"—that it's "escape" fiction. And that is why it's fun to read. But nothing's believable in it—not the characters, not the plot, not even the violence. I wasn't afraid for a minute that Rainsford would really be chewed up by one of those hounds.

Still, people never forget this story. What do you think of it?

—John Leggett

Responding to the Story

Analyzing the Story

Identifying Facts

1. To hook our interest at once, most adventure stories plunge a hero into a dangerous situation. How does Rainsford end up on Ship-Trap Island, which is hardly a place one wants to be?
2. What are Rainsford's first impressions of the repellent General Zaroff? What shocking discoveries does he make about his host's passion for hunting?
3. According to Zaroff, what is the most dangerous game, and why does he think so?
4. During the three days that he is hunted, what strategies does Rainsford use to elude the crafty Zaroff? What happens to each of Rainsford's attempts to win his **conflict** with Zaroff?

Interpreting Meanings

5. What happens to Zaroff at the end of the story?
6. What details right at the start of the story **foreshadow** danger? What details describing Zaroff's unusual dental features and lips aroused your curiosity? (Why do they make Zaroff seem particularly sinister?)
7. Reread Rainsford's discussion with Whitney at the start of the story, about the feelings of hunted animals. How does this conversation **foreshadow** later developments in the plot? Do you think Rainsford finally changes his feelings about hunting?
8. Some **plots** are so fantastic or contrived that readers have to suspend their disbelief. This means that if we do not believe something in a story is possible, the writer hopes we'll just ignore it. Did any details in this story demand that you suspend your disbelief? Compare your responses in class.
9. If you were directing a movie of this story, what actors would you cast as Rainsford? Zaroff? Ivan? If you wanted to add a woman to your movie, what role would you create for her?

Writing About the Story

A Creative Response

1. **Writing a Sequel.** It is morning. Sangar Rainsford has just awakened in General Zaroff's very good bed. What happens next? Write the next episode in Rainsford's adventure. (Does he stay on Ship-Trap Island and turn it into a beach club, or does he go home and work on behalf of endangered species?)
2. **Filling in the Missing Details.** Imagine that you are Rainsford as an old man writing about your life's adventures. How did you get from the sea up to Zaroff's bedroom? What happened when you fought your host? Write your account of this unusual incident in your life.

A Critical Response

3. **Comparing Adventure Stories.** Stories like "The Most Dangerous Game" have always been popular, in books and in movies or on TV. Think of some current adventure movies, and in a brief essay compare one of them to Rainsford's story. Here are some elements you should consider. Before you write, you might complete a chart like this:

	Rainsford's tale	A movie
1. Hero and his values		
2. Villain		
3. Setting		
4 What is at stake		
5. Hero's exploits: Are they believable?		
6. Level of violence		

Reading About the Writer

Richard Connell (1893–1949) today is known for one story, "The Most Dangerous Game." He began his writing career at the age of ten when he covered baseball games in his native Poughkeepsie, New York, for the newspaper that his father edited. Later, at Harvard, Connell wrote for the humorous magazine called *The Lampoon* and for *The Daily Crimson*. Connell frequently wrote humorous stories. In fact, some readers of "The Most Dangerous Game" think that the character of Zaroff, who hunts human beings and yet hums tunes from romantic operas and reads philosophy, makes fun of the typical evil villain.

After serving in World War I, Connell began to write fiction and screenplays for Hollywood movies. Though he published novels and over 300 short stories, "The Most Dangerous Game" is his only work still in print. The story has been filmed under several titles: *The Most Dangerous Game* (1932); *A Game of Death* (1945); and *Run for the Sun* (1956), a loose adaptation in which a writer and a woman crash in the jungle where a German war criminal chases them with guns and hounds.

THE BIRDS

Daphne du Maurier

On December the third, the wind changed overnight, and it was winter. Until then the autumn had been mellow, soft. The leaves had lingered on the trees, golden-red, and the hedgerows were still green. The earth was rich where the plow had turned it.

Nat Hocken, because of a wartime disability, had a pension and did not work full time at the farm. He worked three days a week, and they gave him the lighter jobs: hedging, thatching, repairs to the farm buildings.

Although he was married, with children, his was a solitary disposition; he liked best to work alone. It pleased him when he was given a bank to build up or a gate to mend at the far end of the peninsula, where the sea surrounded the farmland on either side. Then, at midday, he would pause and eat the pasty that his wife had baked for him and, sitting on the cliff's edge, would watch the birds. Autumn was best for this, better than spring. In spring the birds flew inland, purposeful, intent; they knew where they were bound; the rhythm and ritual of their life brooked no delay. In autumn those that had not migrated overseas but remained to pass the winter were caught up in the same driving urge, but because migration was denied them, followed a pattern of their own. Great flocks of them came to the peninsula, restless, uneasy, spending themselves in motion; now wheeling, circling in the sky, now settling to feed on the rich, new-turned soil; but even when they fed, it was as though they did so without hunger, without desire. Restlessness drove them to the skies again.

Black and white, jackdaw and gull, mingled in strange partnership, seeking some sort of liberation, never satisfied, never still. Flocks of starlings, rustling like silk, flew to fresh pasture, driven by the same necessity of movement, and the smaller birds, the finches and the larks, scattered from tree to hedge as if compelled.

Nat watched them, and he watched the sea birds too. Down in the bay they waited for the tide. They had more patience. Oyster catchers, redshank, sanderling, and curlew watched by the water's edge; as the slow sea sucked at the shore and then withdrew, leaving the strip of seaweed bare and the shingle[1] churned, the sea birds raced and ran upon the beaches. Then that same impulse to flight seized upon them too. Crying, whistling, calling, they skimmed the placid sea and left the shore. Make haste, make speed, hurry and begone; yet where, and to what purpose? The restless urge of autumn, unsatisfying, sad, had put a spell upon them, and they must flock, and wheel, and cry; they must spill themselves of motion before winter came.

"Perhaps," thought Nat, munching his pasty by the cliff's edge, "a message comes to the birds in autumn, like a warning. Winter is coming. Many of them perish. And like people who, apprehensive of death before their time, drive themselves to work or folly, the birds do likewise."

The birds had been more restless than ever this fall of the year, the agitation more marked because the days were still. As the tractor traced its path up and down the western hills, the figure of the farmer silhouetted on the driving seat, the whole machine and the man upon it, would be lost momentarily in the great cloud of wheeling, crying birds. There were many more than usual; Nat was sure of this. Always, in autumn, they followed the plow, but not in great flocks like these, nor with such clamor.

Nat remarked upon it when hedging was finished for the day. "Yes," said the farmer, "there are more birds about than usual; I've noticed it too. And daring, some of them, taking no notice of the tractor. One or two gulls came so close to my head this afternoon I thought they'd knock my cap off! As it was, I could scarcely see what I was doing when they were overhead and I had the sun

---

1. **shingle:** pebbly beach.

in my eyes. I have a notion the weather will change. It will be a hard winter. That's why the birds are restless.''

Nat, tramping home across the fields and down the lane to his cottage, saw the birds still flocking over the western hills, in the last glow of the sun. No wind, and the gray sea calm and full. Campion in bloom yet in the hedges, and the air mild. The farmer was right, though, and it was that night the weather turned. Nat's bedroom faced east. He woke just after two and heard the wind in the chimney. Not the storm and bluster of a sou'westerly gale, bringing the rain, but east wind, cold and dry. It sounded hollow in the chimney, and a loose slate rattled on the roof. Nat listened, and he could hear the sea roaring in the bay. Even the air in the small bedroom had turned chill: a draft came under the skirting of the door, blowing upon the bed. Nat drew the blanket round him, leaned closer to the back of his sleeping wife, and stayed wakeful, watchful, aware of misgiving without cause.

Then he heard the tapping on the window. There was no creeper on the cottage walls to break loose and scratch upon the pane. He listened, and the tapping continued until, irritated by the sound, Nat got out of bed and went to the window. He opened it, and as he did so something brushed his hand, jabbing at his knuckles, grazing the skin. Then he saw the flutter of the wings and it was gone, over the roof, behind the cottage.

It was a bird; what kind of bird he could not tell. The wind must have driven it to shelter on the sill.

He shut the window and went back to bed but, feeling his knuckles wet, put his mouth to the scratch. The bird had drawn blood. Frightened, he supposed, and bewildered, the bird, seeking shelter, had stabbed at him in the darkness. Once more he settled himself to sleep.

Presently the tapping came again, this time more forceful, more insistent, and now his wife woke at the sound and, turning in the bed, said to him, "See to the window, Nat, it's rattling.''

"I've already seen to it," he told her; "there's some bird there trying to get in. Can't you hear the wind? It's blowing from the east, driving the birds to shelter.''

"Send them away," she said, "I can't sleep with that noise.''

He went to the window for the second time, and now when he opened it, there was not one bird upon the sill but half a dozen; they flew straight into his face, attacking him.

He shouted, striking out at them with his arms, scattering them; like the first one, they flew over the roof and disappeared. Quickly he let the window fall and latched it.

"Did you hear that?" he said. "They went for me. Tried to peck my eyes." He stood by the window, peering into the darkness, and could see nothing. His wife, heavy with sleep, murmured from the bed.

"I'm not making it up," he said, angry at her suggestion. "I tell you the birds were on the sill, trying to get into the room.''

Suddenly a frightened cry came from the room across the passage where the children slept.

"It's Jill," said his wife, roused at the sound, sitting up in bed. "Go to her, see what's the matter.''

Nat lit the candle, but when he opened the bedroom door to cross the passage the draft blew out the flame.

There came a second cry of terror, this time from both children, and stumbling into their room, he felt the beating of wings about him in the darkness. The window was wide open. Through it came the birds, hitting first the ceiling and the walls, then swerving in midflight, turning to the children in their beds.

"It's all right, I'm here," shouted Nat, and the children flung themselves, screaming, upon him, while in the darkness the birds rose and dived and came for him again.

"What is it, Nat, what's happened?" his wife called from the further bedroom, and swiftly he pushed the children through the door to the passage and shut it upon them, so that he was alone now in their bedroom with the birds.

He seized a blanket from the nearest bed and, using it as a weapon, flung it to right and left about him in the air. He felt the thud of bodies, heard the fluttering of wings, but they were not yet defeated, for again and again they returned to the assault, jabbing his hands, his head, the little stabbing beaks sharp as pointed forks. The blanket became a weapon of defense; he wound it about his head, and then in greater darkness beat at the birds with his bare hands. He dared not stumble to the door and open it, lest in doing so the birds should follow him.

How long he fought with them in the darkness he could not tell, but at last the beating of the wings about him lessened and then withdrew, and through the density of the blanket he was aware of light. He waited, listened; there was no sound except the fretful crying of one of the children from the bedroom beyond. The fluttering, the whirring of the wings had ceased.

He took the blanket from his head and stared about him. The cold gray morning light exposed the room. Dawn and the open window had called the living birds; the dead lay on the floor. Nat gazed at the little corpses, shocked and horrified. They were all small birds, none of any size; there must have been fifty of them lying there upon the floor. There were robins, finches, sparrows, blue tits, larks, and bramblings, birds that by nature's law kept to their own flock and their own territory, and now, joining one with another in their urge for battle, had destroyed themselves against the bedroom walls or in the strife had been destroyed by him. Some had lost feathers in the fight; others had blood, his blood, upon their beaks.

Sickened, Nat went to the window and stared out across his patch of garden to the fields.

It was bitter cold, and the ground had all the hard, black look of frost. Not white frost, to shine in the morning sun, but the black frost that the east wind brings. The sea, fiercer now with the turning tide, white-capped and steep, broke harshly in the bay. Of the birds there was no sign. Not a sparrow chattered in the hedge beyond the garden gate, no early missel thrush or blackbird pecked on the grass for worms. There was no sound at all but the east wind and the sea.

Nat shut the window and the door of the small bedroom and went back across the passage to his own. His wife sat up in bed, one child asleep beside her, the smaller in her arms, his face bandaged. The curtains were tightly drawn across the window, the candles lit. Her face looked garish in the yellow light. She shook her head for silence.

"He's sleeping now," she whispered, "but only just. Something must have cut him, there was blood at the corner of his eyes. Jill said it was the birds. She said she woke up, and the birds were in the room."

His wife looked up at Nat, searching his face for confirmation. She looked terrified, bewildered, and he did not want her to know that he was also shaken, dazed almost, by the events of the past few hours.

"There are birds in there," he said, "dead birds, nearly fifty of them. Robins, wrens, all the little birds from hereabouts. It's as though a madness seized them, with the east wind." He sat down on the bed beside his wife and held her hand. "It's the weather," he said; "it must be that, it's the hard weather. They aren't the birds, maybe, from here around. They've been driven down from upcountry."

"But, Nat," whispered his wife, "it's only this night that the weather turned. There's been no snow to drive them. And they can't be hungry yet. There's food for them out there in the fields."

"It's the weather," repeated Nat. "I tell you, it's the weather."

His face, too, was drawn and tired, like hers. They stared at one another for a while without speaking.

"I'll go downstairs and make a cup of tea," he said.

The sight of the kitchen reassured him. The cups and saucers, neatly stacked upon the dresser, the table and chairs, his wife's roll of knitting on her basket chair, the children's toys in a corner cupboard.

He knelt down, raked out the old embers, and relit the fire. The glowing sticks brought normality; the steaming kettle and the brown teapot, comfort and security. He drank his tea, carried a cup up to his wife. Then he washed in the scullery[2] and, putting on his boots, opened the back door.

The sky was hard and leaden, and the brown hills that had gleamed in the sun the day before looked dark and bare. The east wind, like a razor, stripped the trees, and the leaves, crackling and

---

2. **scullery:** a room next to the kitchen where the dishes are washed.

dry, shivered and scattered with the wind's blast. Nat stubbed the earth with his boot. It was frozen hard. He had never known a change so swift and sudden. Black winter had descended in a single night.

The children were awake now. Jill was chattering upstairs and young Johnny crying once again. Nat heard his wife's voice, soothing, comforting. Presently they came down. He had breakfast ready for them, and the routine of the day began.

"Did you drive away the birds?" asked Jill, restored to calm because of the kitchen fire, because of day, because of breakfast.

"Yes, they've all gone now," said Nat. "It was the east wind brought them in. They were frightened and lost; they wanted shelter."

"They tried to peck us," said Jill. "They went for Johnny's eyes."

"Fright made them do that," said Nat. "They didn't know where they were in the dark bedroom."

"I hope they won't come again," said Jill. "Perhaps if we put bread for them outside the window they will eat that and fly away."

She finished her breakfast and then went for her coat and hood, her schoolbooks, and her satchel. Nat said nothing, but his wife looked at him across the table. A silent message passed between them.

"I'll walk with her to the bus," he said. "I don't go to the farm today."

And while the child was washing in the scullery he said to his wife, "Keep all the windows closed, and the doors too. Just to be on the safe side. I'll go to the farm. Find out if they heard anything in the night." Then he walked with his small daughter up the lane. She seemed to have forgotten her experience of the night before. She danced ahead of him, chasing the leaves, her face whipped with the cold and rosy under the pixie hood.

"Is it going to snow, Dad?" she said. "It's cold enough."

He glanced up at the bleak sky, felt the wind tear at his shoulders.

"No," he said, "it's not going to snow. This is a black winter, not a white one."

All the while he searched the hedgerows for the birds, glanced over the top of them to the fields beyond, looked to the small wood above the farm where the rooks and jackdaws gathered. He saw none.

The other children waited by the bus stop, muffled, hooded like Jill, the faces white and pinched with cold.

Jill ran to them, waving. "My dad says it won't snow," she called, "it's going to be a black winter."

She said nothing of the birds. She began to push and struggle with another little girl. The bus came ambling up the hill. Nat saw her onto it, then turned and walked back toward the farm. It was not his day for work, but he wanted to satisfy himself that all was well. Jim, the cowman, was clattering in the yard.

"Boss around?" asked Nat.

"Gone to market," said Jim. "It's Tuesday, isn't it?"

He clumped off round the corner of a shed. He had no time for Nat. Nat was said to be superior. Read books and the like. Nat had forgotten it was Tuesday. This showed how the events of the preceding night had shaken him. He went to the back door of the farmhouse and heard Mrs. Trigg singing in the kitchen, the wireless[3] making a background to her song.

"Are you there, missus?" called out Nat.

She came to the door, beaming, broad, a good-tempered woman.

"Hullo, Mr. Hocken," she said. "Can you tell me where this cold is coming from? Is it Russia? I've never seen such a change. And it's going on, the wireless says. Something to do with the Arctic Circle."

"We didn't turn on the wireless this morning," said Nat. "Fact is, we had trouble in the night."

"Kiddies poorly?"

"No . . ." He hardly knew how to explain it. Now, in daylight, the battle of the birds would sound absurd.

He tried to tell Mrs. Trigg what had happened, but he could see from her eyes that she thought his story was the result of a nightmare.

"Sure they were real birds," she said, smiling, "with proper feathers and all? Not the funny-

---

3. **wireless:** radio.

shaped kind that the men see after closing hours on a Saturday night?"

"Mrs. Trigg," he said, "there are fifty dead birds, robins, wrens, and such, lying low on the floor of the children's bedroom. They went for me; they tried to go for young Johnny's eyes."

Mrs. Trigg stared at him doubtfully.

"Well there, now," she answered, "I suppose the weather brought them. Once in the bedroom, they wouldn't know where they were to. Foreign birds maybe, from that Arctic Circle."

"No," said Nat, "they were the birds you see about here every day."

"Funny thing," said Mrs. Trigg, "no explaining it, really. You ought to write up and ask the *Guardian*. They'd have some answer for it. Well, I must be getting on."

She nodded, smiled, and went back into the kitchen.

Nat, dissatisfied, turned to the farm gate. Had it not been for those corpses on the bedroom floor, which he must now collect and bury somewhere, he would have considered the tale exaggeration too.

Jim was standing by the gate.

"Had any trouble with the birds?" asked Nat.

"Birds? What birds?"

"We got them up our place last night. Scores of them, came in the children's bedroom. Quite savage they were."

"Oh?" It took time for anything to penetrate Jim's head. "Never heard of birds acting savage," he said at length. "They get tame, like, sometimes. I've seen them come to the windows for crumbs."

"These birds last night weren't tame."

"No? Cold, maybe. Hungry. You put out some crumbs."

Jim was no more interested than Mrs. Trigg had been. It was, Nat thought, like air raids in the war. No one down this end of the country knew what the Plymouth folk had seen and suffered. You had to endure something yourself before it touched you. He walked back along the lane and crossed the stile[4] to his cottage. He found his wife in the kitchen with young Johnny.

"See anyone?" she asked.

"Mrs. Trigg and Jim," he answered. "I don't think they believed me. Anyway, nothing wrong up there."

"You might take the birds away," she said. "I daren't go into the room to make the beds until you do. I'm scared."

"Nothing to scare you now," said Nat. "They're dead, aren't they?"

He went up with a sack and dropped the stiff bodies into it, one by one. Yes, there were fifty of them, all told. Just the ordinary, common birds of the hedgerow, nothing as large even as a thrush. It must have been fright that made them act the way they did. Blue tits, wrens—it was incredible to think of the power of their small beaks jabbing at his face and hands the night before. He took the sack out into the garden and was faced now with a fresh problem. The ground was too hard to dig. It was frozen solid, yet no snow had fallen, nothing had happened in the past hours but the coming of the east wind. It was unnatural, queer. The weather prophets must be right. The change was something connected with the Arctic Circle.

The wind seemed to cut him to the bone as he stood there uncertainly, holding the sack. He could see the white-capped seas breaking down under in the bay. He decided to take the birds to the shore and bury them.

When he reached the beach below the headland he could scarcely stand, the force of the east wind was so strong. It hurt to draw breath, and his bare hands were blue. Never had he known such cold, not in all the bad winters he could remember. It was low tide. He crunched his way over the shingle to the softer sand and then, his back to the wind, ground a pit in the sand with his heel. He meant to drop the birds into it, but as he opened up the sack the force of the wind carried them, lifted them, as though in flight again, and they were blown away from him along the beach, tossed like feathers, spread and scattered, the bodies of the fifty frozen birds. There was something ugly in the sight. He did not like it. The dead birds were swept away from him by the wind.

"The tide will take them when it turns," he said to himself.

He looked out to sea and watched the crested

---

4. **stile:** steps that help people climb over a low wall.

breakers, combing green. They rose stiffly, curled, and broke again, and because it was ebb tide the roar was distant, more remote, lacking the sound and thunder of the flood.

Then he saw them. The gulls. Out there, riding the seas.

What he had thought at first to be the white caps of the waves were gulls. Hundreds, thousands, tens of thousands . . . They rose and fell in the trough of the seas, heads to the wind, like a mighty fleet at anchor, waiting on the tide. To eastward and to the west, the gulls were there. They stretched as far as his eye could reach, in close formation, line upon line. Had the sea been still, they would have covered the bay like a white cloud, head to head, body packed to body. Only the east wind, whipping the sea to breakers, hid them from the shore.

Nat turned and, leaving the beach, climbed the steep path home. Someone should know of this. Someone should be told. Something was happening, because of the east wind and the weather, that he did not understand. He wondered if he should go to the call box by the bus stop and ring up the police. Yet what could they do? What could anyone do? Tens of thousands of gulls riding the sea there in the bay because of storm, because of hunger. The police would think him mad, or drunk, or take the statement from him with great calm. "Thank you. Yes, the matter has already been reported. The hard weather is driving the birds inland in great numbers." Nat looked about him. Still no sign of any other bird. Perhaps the cold had sent them all from upcountry? As he drew near to the cottage his wife came to meet him at the door. She called to him, excited. "Nat," she said, "it's on the wireless. They've just read out a special news bulletin. I've written it down."

"What's on the wireless?" he said.

"About the birds," she said. "It's not only here; it's everywhere. In London, all over the country. Something has happened to the birds."

Together they went into the kitchen. He read the piece of paper lying on the table.

"Statement from the Home Office at 11 A.M. today. Reports from all over the country are coming in hourly about the vast quantity of birds flocking above towns, villages, and outlying districts, causing obstruction and damage and even attacking individuals. It is thought that the Arctic air stream, at present covering the British Isles, is causing birds to migrate south in immense numbers and that intense hunger may drive these birds to attack human beings. Householders are warned to see to their windows, doors, and chimneys, and to take reasonable precautions for the safety of their children. A further statement will be issued later."

A kind of excitement seized Nat; he looked at his wife in triumph.

"There you are," he said. "Let's hope they'll hear that at the farm. Mrs. Trigg will know it wasn't any story. It's true. All over the country. I've been telling myself all morning there's something wrong. And just now, down on the beach, I looked out to sea and there are gulls, thousands of them, tens of thousands—you couldn't put a pin between their heads—and they're all out there, riding on the sea, waiting."

"What are they waiting for, Nat?" she asked.

He stared at her, then looked down again at the piece of paper.

"I don't know," he said slowly. "It says here the birds are hungry."

He went over to the drawer where he kept his hammer and tools.

"What are you going to do, Nat?"

"See to the windows and the chimneys too, like they tell you."

"You think they would break in, with the windows shut? Those sparrows and robins and such? Why, how could they?"

He did not answer. He was not thinking of the robins and the sparrows. He was thinking of the gulls. . . .

He went upstairs and worked there the rest of the morning, boarding the windows of the bedrooms, filling up the chimney bases. Good that it was his free day and he was not working at the farm. It reminded him of the old days, at the beginning of the war. He was not married then, and he had made all the blackout boards for his mother's house in Plymouth. Made the shelter too. Not that it had been of any use when the moment came. He wondered if they would take these precautions up at the farm. He doubted it.

Too easygoing, Harry Trigg and his missus. Maybe they'd laugh at the whole thing. Go off to a dance or a whist drive.[5]

"Dinner's ready." She called him, from the kitchen.

"All right. Coming down."

He was pleased with his handiwork. The frames fitted nicely over the little panes and at the bases of the chimneys.

When dinner was over and his wife was washing up, Nat switched on the one o'clock news. The same announcement was repeated, the one which she had taken down during the morning, but the news bulletin enlarged upon it. "The flocks of birds have caused dislocation in all areas," read the announcer, "and in London the sky was so dense at ten o'clock this morning that it seemed as if the city was covered by a vast black cloud.

"The birds settled on rooftops, on window ledges, and on chimneys. The species included blackbird, thrush, the common house sparrow, and, as might be expected in the metropolis, a vast quantity of pigeons and starlings and that frequenter of the London river, the black-headed gull. The sight has been so unusual that traffic came to a standstill in many thoroughfares, work was abandoned in shops and offices, and the streets and pavements were crowded with people standing about to watch the birds."

Various incidents were recounted, the suspected reason of cold and hunger stated again, and warnings to householders repeated. The announcer's voice was smooth and suave. Nat had the impression that this man, in particular, treated the whole business as he would an elaborate joke. There would be others like him, hundreds of them, who did not know what it was to struggle in darkness with a flock of birds. There would be parties tonight in London, like the ones they gave on election nights. People standing about, shouting and laughing, getting drunk. "Come and watch the birds!"

Nat switched off the wireless. He got up and started work on the kitchen windows. His wife watched him, young Johnny at her heels.

"What, boards for down here too?" she said. "Why, I'll have to light up before three o'clock. I see no call for boards down here."

"Better be sure than sorry," answered Nat. "I'm not going to take any chances."

"What they ought to do," she said, "is to call the Army out and shoot the birds. That would soon scare them off."

"Let them try," said Nat. "How'd they set about it?"

"They have the Army to the docks," she answered, "when the dockers strike. The soldiers go down and unload the ships."

"Yes," said Nat, "and the population of London is eight million or more. Think of all the buildings, all the flats and houses. Do you think they've enough soldiers to go around shooting birds from every roof?"

"I don't know. But something should be done. They ought to do something."

Nat thought to himself that "they" were no doubt considering the problem at that very moment, but whatever "they" decided to do in London and the big cities would not help the people here, three hundred miles away. Each householder must look after his own.

"How are we off for food?" he said.

"Now, Nat, whatever next?"

"Never mind. What have you got in the larder?"

"It's shopping day tomorrow, you know that. I don't keep uncooked food hanging about; it goes off. Butcher doesn't call till the day after. But I can bring back something when I go in tomorrow."

Nat did not want to scare her. He thought it possible that she might not go to town tomorrow. He looked in the larder for himself and in the cupboard where she kept her tins. They would do for a couple of days. Bread was low.

"What about the baker?"

"He comes tomorrow too."

He saw she had flour. If the baker did not call she had enough to bake one loaf.

"We'd be better off in the old days," he said, "when the women baked twice a week, and had pilchards[6] salted, and there was food for a

---

5. **whist drive:** a marathon card game.

6. **pilchards:** a kind of fish.

family to last a siege, if need be."

"I've tried the children with tinned fish; they don't like it," she said.

Nat went on hammering the boards across the kitchen windows. Candles. They were low in candles too. That must be another thing she meant to buy tomorrow. Well, it could not be helped. They must go early to bed tonight. That was, if . . .

He got up and went out of the back door and stood in the garden, looking down toward the sea. There had been no sun all day, and now, at barely three o'clock, a kind of darkness had already come, the sky sullen, heavy, colorless like salt. He could hear the vicious sea drumming on the rocks. He walked down the path, halfway to the beach. And then he stopped. He could see the tide had turned. The rock that had shown in midmorning was now covered, but it was not the sea that held his eyes. The gulls had risen. They were circling, hundreds of them, thousands of them, lifting their wings against the wind. It was the gulls that made the darkening of the sky. And they were silent. They made not a sound. They just went on soaring and circling, rising, falling, trying their strength against the wind.

Nat turned. He ran up the path, back to the cottage.

"I'm going for Jill," he said. "I'll wait for her at the bus stop."

"What's the matter?" asked his wife. "You've gone quite white."

"Keep Johnny inside," he said. "Keep the door shut. Light up now, and draw the curtains."

"It's only just gone three," she said.

"Never mind. Do what I tell you."

He looked inside the toolshed outside the back door. Nothing there of much use. A spade was too heavy, and a fork no good. He took the hoe. It was the only possible tool, and light enough to carry.

He started walking up the lane to the bus stop and now and again glanced back over his shoulder.

The gulls had risen higher now; their circles were broader, wider; they were spreading out in huge formation across the sky.

He hurried on; although he knew the bus would not come to the top of the hill before four o'clock, he had to hurry. He passed no one on the way.

He was glad of this. No time to stop and chatter.

At the top of the hill he waited. He was much too soon. There was half an hour still to go. The east wind came whipping across the fields from the higher ground. He stamped his feet and blew upon his hands. In the distance he could see the clay hills, white and clean, against the heavy pallor of the sky. Something black rose from behind them, like a smudge at first, then widening, becoming deeper, and the smudge became a cloud, and the cloud divided again into five other clouds, spreading north, east, south, and west, and they were not clouds at all; they were birds. He watched them travel across the sky, and as one section passed overhead, within two or three hundred feet of him, he knew, from their speed, they were bound inland, upcountry; they had no business with the people here on the peninsula. They were rooks, crows, jackdaws, magpies, jays, all birds that usually preyed upon the smaller species; but this afternoon they were bound on some other mission.

"They've been given the towns," thought Nat; "they know what they have to do. We don't matter so much here. The gulls will serve for us. The others go to the towns."

He went to the call box, stepped inside, and lifted the receiver. The exchange would do. They would pass the message on.

"I'm speaking from the highway," he said, "by the bus stop. I want to report large formations of birds traveling upcountry. The gulls are also forming in the bay."

"All right," answered the voice, laconic,[7] weary.

"You'll be sure and pass this message on to the proper quarter?"

"Yes . . . yes . . ." Impatient now, fed up. The buzzing note resumed.

"She's another," thought Nat, "she doesn't care. Maybe she's had to answer calls all day. She hopes to go to the pictures tonight. She'll squeeze some fellow's hand and point up at the sky and say 'Look at all them birds!' She doesn't care."

The bus came lumbering up the hill. Jill climbed

---

7. **laconic** (lə·kän′ ik): terse, or wanting to use as few words as possible.

out, and three or four other children. The bus went on toward the town.

"What's the hoe for, Dad?"

They crowded around him, laughing, pointing.

"I just brought it along," he said. "Come on now, let's get home. It's cold, no hanging about. Here, you. I'll watch you across the fields, see how fast you can run."

He was speaking to Jill's companions, who came from different families, living in the council houses.[8] A shortcut would take them to the cottages.

"We want to play a bit in the lane," said one of them.

"No, you don't. You go off home or I'll tell your mammy."

They whispered to one another, round-eyed, then scuttled off across the fields. Jill stared at her father, her mouth sullen.

"We always play in the lane," she said.

"Not tonight, you don't," he said. "Come on now, no dawdling."

He could see the gulls now, circling the fields, coming in toward the land. Still silent. Still no sound.

"Look, Dad, look over there, look at all the gulls."

"Yes. Hurry, now."

"Where are they flying to? Where are they going?"

"Upcountry, I dare say. Where it's warmer."

He seized her hand and dragged her after him along the lane.

"Don't go so fast. I can't keep up."

The gulls were copying the rooks and crows. They were spreading out in formation across the sky. They headed, in bands of thousands, to the four compass points.

"Dad, what is it? What are the gulls doing?"

They were not intent upon their flight, as the crows, as the jackdaws had been. They still circled overhead. Nor did they fly so high. It was as though they waited upon some signal. As though some decision had yet to be given. The order was not clear.

"Do you want me to carry you, Jill? Here, come pick-a-back."

This way he might put on speed; but he was wrong. Jill was heavy. She kept slipping. And she was crying too. His sense of urgency, of fear, had communicated itself to the child.

"I wish the gulls would go away. I don't like them. They're coming closer to the lane."

He put her down again. He started running, swinging Jill after him. As they went past the farm turning, he saw the farmer backing his car out of the garage. Nat called to him.

"Can you give us a lift?" he said.

"What's that?"

Mr. Trigg turned in the driving seat and stared at them. Then a smile came to his cheerful, rubicund[9] face.

"It looks as though we're in for some fun," he said. "Have you seen the gulls? Jim and I are going to take a crack at them. Everyone's gone bird crazy, talking of nothing else. I hear you were troubled in the night. Want a gun?"

Nat shook his head.

The small car was packed. There was just room for Jill, if she crouched on top of petrol tins on the back seat.

"I don't want a gun," said Nat, "but I'd be obliged if you'd run Jill home. She's scared of the birds."

He spoke briefly. He did not want to talk in front of Jill.

"OK," said the farmer, "I'll take her home. Why don't you stop behind and join the shooting match? We'll make the feathers fly."

Jill climbed in, and, turning the car, the driver sped up the lane. Nat followed after. Trigg must be crazy. What use was a gun against a sky of birds?

Now Nat was not responsible for Jill, he had time to look about him. The birds were circling still above the fields. Mostly herring gull, but the black-backed gull amongst them. Usually they kept apart. Now they were united. Some bond had brought them together. It was the black-backed gull that attacked the smaller birds, and

---

8. **council houses:** public housing, built for lower-income families after the war.

9. **rubicund** (roō′ bi·kund′): reddish, rosy.

even newborn lambs, so he'd heard. He'd never seen it done. He remembered this now, though, looking above him in the sky. They were coming in toward the farm. They were circling lower in the sky, and the black-backed gulls were to the front, the black-backed gulls were leading. The farm, then, was their target. They were making for the farm.

Nat increased his pace toward his own cottage. He saw the farmer's car turn and come back along the lane. It drew up beside him with a jerk.

"The kid has run inside," said the farmer. "Your wife was watching for her. Well, what do you make of it? They're saying in town the Russians have done it. The Russians have poisoned the birds."

"How could they do that?" asked Nat.

"Don't ask me. You know how stories get around. Will you join my shooting match?"

"No, I'll get along home. The wife will be worried else."

"My missus says if you could eat gull there'd be some sense in it," said Trigg. "We'd have roast gull, baked gull, and pickle 'em into the bargain. You wait until I let off a few barrels into the brutes. That'll scare 'em."

"Have you boarded your windows?" asked Nat.

"No. Lot of nonsense. They like to scare you on the wireless. I've had more to do today than to go round boarding up my windows."

"I'd board them now, if I were you."

"Garn. You're windy. Like to come to our place to sleep?"

"No, thanks all the same."

"All right. See you in the morning. Give you a gull breakfast."

The farmer grinned and turned his car to the farm entrance.

Nat hurried on. Past the little wood, past the old barn, and then across the stile to the remaining field.

As he jumped the stile he heard the whir of wings. A black-backed gull dived down at him from the sky, missed, swerved in flight, and rose to dive again. In a moment it was joined by others, six, seven, a dozen, black-backed and herring mixed. Nat dropped his hoe. The hoe was useless.

Covering his head with his arms, he ran toward the cottage. They kept coming at him from the air, silent save for the beating wings. The terrible, fluttering wings. He could feel the blood on his hands, his wrists, his neck. Each stab of a swooping beak tore his flesh. If only he could keep them from his eyes. Nothing else mattered. He must keep them from his eyes. They had not learned yet how to cling to a shoulder, how to rip clothing, how to dive in mass upon the head, upon the body. But with each dive, with each attack, they became bolder. And they had no thought for themselves. When they dived low and missed, they crashed, bruised and broken, on the ground. As Nat ran he stumbled, kicking their spent bodies in front of him.

He found the door; he hammered upon it with his bleeding hands. Because of the boarded windows no light shone. Everything was dark.

"Let me in," he shouted, "it's Nat. Let me in."

He shouted loud to make himself heard above the whir of the gulls' wings.

Then he saw the gannet, poised for the dive, above him in the sky. The gulls circled, retired, soared, one after another, against the wind. Only the gannet remained. One single gannet above him in the sky. The wings folded suddenly to its body. It dropped like a stone. Nat screamed, and the door opened. He stumbled across the threshold, and his wife threw her weight against the door.

They heard the thud of the gannet as it fell.

His wife dressed his wounds. They were not deep. The backs of his hands had suffered most, and his wrists. Had he not worn a cap they would have reached his head. As to the gannet . . . the gannet could have split his skull.

The children were crying, of course. They had seen the blood on their father's hands.

"It's all right now," he told them. "I'm not hurt. Just a few scratches. You play with Johnny, Jill. Mammy will wash these cuts."

He half shut the door to the scullery so that they could not see. His wife was ashen. She began running water from the sink.

"I saw them overhead," she whispered. "They began collecting just as Jill ran in with Mr. Trigg.

I shut the door fast, and it jammed. That's why I couldn't open it at once when you came."

"Thank God they waited for me," he said. "Jill would have fallen at once. One bird alone would have done it."

Furtively, so as not to alarm the children, they whispered together as she bandaged his hands and the back of his neck.

"They're flying inland," he said, "thousands of them. Rooks, crows, all the bigger birds. I saw them from the bus stop. They're making for the towns."

"But what can they do, Nat?"

"They'll attack. Go for everyone out in the streets. Then they'll try the windows, the chimneys."

"Why don't the authorities do something? Why don't they get the Army, get machine guns, anything?"

"There's been no time. Nobody's prepared. We'll hear what they have to say on the six o'clock news."

Nat went back into the kitchen, followed by his wife. Johnny was playing quietly on the floor. Only Jill looked anxious.

"I can hear the birds," she said. "Listen, Dad."

Nat listened. Muffled sounds came from the windows, from the door. Wings brushing the surface, sliding, scraping, seeking a way of entry. The sound of many bodies, pressed together, shuffling on the sills. Now and again came a thud, a crash, as some bird dived and fell. "Some of them will kill themselves that way," he thought, "but not enough. Never enough."

"All right," he said aloud. "I've got boards over the windows, Jill. The birds can't get in."

He went and examined all the windows. His work had been thorough. Every gap was closed. He would make extra certain, however. He found wedges, pieces of old tin, strips of wood and metal, and fastened them at the sides to reinforce the boards. His hammering helped to deafen the sound of the birds, the shuffling, the tapping, and more ominous—he did not want his wife or the children to hear it—the splinter of cracked glass.

"Turn on the wireless," he said. "Let's have the wireless."

This would drown the sound also. He went upstairs to the bedrooms and reinforced the windows there. Now he could hear the birds on the roof, the scraping of claws, a sliding, jostling sound.

He decided they must sleep in the kitchen, keep up the fire, bring down the mattresses, and lay them out on the floor. He was afraid of the bedroom chimneys. The boards he had placed at the chimney bases might give way. In the kitchen they would be safe because of the fire. He would have to make a joke of it. Pretend to the children they were playing at camp. If the worst happened, and the birds forced an entry down the bedroom chimneys, it would be hours, days perhaps, before they could break down the doors. The birds would be imprisoned in the bedrooms. They could do no harm there. Crowded together, they would stifle and die.

He began to bring the mattresses downstairs. At the sight of them his wife's eyes widened in apprehension. She thought the birds had already broken in upstairs.

"All right," he said cheerfully, "we'll all sleep together in the kitchen tonight. More cozy here by the fire. Then we shan't be worried by those silly old birds tapping at the windows."

He made the children help him rearrange the furniture, and he took the precaution of moving the dresser, with his wife's help, across the window. It fitted well. It was an added safeguard. The mattresses could now be lain, one beside the other, against the wall where the dresser had stood.

"We're safe enough now," he thought. "We're snug and tight, like an air-raid shelter. We can hold out. It's just the food that worries me. Food, and coal for the fire. We've enough for two or three days, not more. By that time . . ."

No use thinking ahead as far as that. And they'd be giving directions on the wireless. People would be told what to do. And now, in the midst of many problems, he realized that it was dance music only, coming over the air. Not Children's Hour, as it should have been. He glanced at the dial. Yes, they were on the Home Service all right. Dance records. He switched to the Light program. He knew the reason. The usual programs had been abandoned. This only happened at exceptional times. Elections and such. He tried to remember if it had happened in the war, during the heavy raids on London. But of course. The BBC[10] was not stationed in London during the war. The programs were broadcast from other, temporary quarters. "We're better off here," he thought; "we're better off here in the kitchen, with the windows and the doors boarded, than they are up in the towns. Thank God we're not in the towns."

At six o'clock the records ceased. The time signal was given. No matter if it scared the children, he must hear the news. There was a pause after the pips.[11] Then the announcer spoke. His voice was solemn, grave. Quite different from midday.

"This is London," he said. "A national emergency was proclaimed at four o'clock this afternoon. Measures are being taken to safeguard the lives and property of the population, but it must be understood that these are not easy to effect immediately, owing to the unforeseen and unparalleled nature of the present crisis. Every householder must take precautions to his own building, and where several people live together, as in flats and apartments, they must unite to do the utmost they can to prevent entry. It is absolutely imperative that every individual stay indoors tonight and that no one at all remain on the streets or roads or anywhere outdoors. The birds, in vast numbers, are attacking anyone on sight and have already begun an assault upon buildings; but these, with due care, should be impenetrable. The population is asked to remain calm and not to panic. Owing to the exceptional nature of the emergency, there will be no further transmission from any broadcasting station until 7 A.M. tomorrow."

They played the national anthem. Nothing more happened. Nat switched off the set. He looked at his wife. She stared back at him.

"What's it mean?" said Jill. "What did the news say?"

"There won't be any more programs tonight," said Nat. "There's been a breakdown at the BBC."

"Is it the birds?" asked Jill. "Have the birds done it?"

"No," said Nat, "it's just that everyone's very busy, and then of course they have to get rid of the birds, messing everything up, in the towns. Well, we can manage without the wireless for one evening."

"I wish we had a gramophone,"[12] said Jill; "that would be better than nothing."

She had her face turned to the dresser backed against the windows. Try as they did to ignore it, they were all aware of the shuffling, the stabbing, the persistent beating and sweeping of wings.

"We'll have supper early," suggested Nat, "something for a treat. Ask Mammy. Toasted cheese, eh? Something we all like?"

He winked and nodded at his wife. He wanted the look of dread, of apprehension, to go from Jill's face.

He helped with the supper, whistling, singing, making as much clatter as he could, and it seemed to him that the shuffling and the tapping were not so intense as they had been at first. Presently he went up to the bedrooms and listened, and he no longer heard the jostling for place upon the roof.

"They've got reasoning powers," he thought; "they know it's hard to break in here. They'll try elsewhere. They won't waste their time with us."

Supper passed without incident, and then, when they were clearing away, they heard a new sound, droning, familiar, a sound they all knew and understood.

His wife looked up at him, her face alight. "It's planes," she said; "they're sending out planes after the birds. That's what I said they ought to do all along. That will get them. Isn't that gunfire? Can't you hear guns?"

It might be gunfire out at sea. Nat could not tell. Big naval guns might have an effect upon the gulls out at sea, but the gulls were inland now. The guns couldn't shell the shore because of the population.

"It's good, isn't it," said his wife, "to hear the planes?" And Jill, catching her enthusiasm, jumped up and down with Johnny. "The planes

---

10. **BBC:** British Broadcasting Corporation.
11. **pips:** signals indicating the exact time.

12. **gramophone:** phonograph.

will get the birds. The planes will shoot them.''

Just then they heard a crash about two miles distant, followed by a second, then a third. The droning became more distant, passed away out to sea.

"What was that?'' asked his wife. "Were they dropping bombs on the birds?''

"I don't know,'' answered Nat. "I don't think so.''

He did not want to tell her that the sound they had heard was the crashing of aircraft. It was, he had no doubt, a venture on the part of the authorities to send out reconnaissance forces, but they might have known the venture was suicidal. What could aircraft do against birds that flung themselves to death against propeller and fuselage but hurtle to the ground themselves? This was being tried now, he supposed, over the whole country. And at a cost. Someone high up had lost his head.

"Where have the planes gone, Dad?'' asked Jill.

"Back to base,'' he said. "Come on, now, time to tuck down for bed.''

It kept his wife occupied, undressing the children before the fire, seeing to the bedding, one thing and another, while he went round the cottage again, making sure that nothing had worked loose. There was no further drone of aircraft, and the naval guns had ceased. "Waste of life and effort,'' Nat said to himself. "We can't destroy enough of them that way. Cost too heavy. There's always gas. Maybe they'll try spraying with gas, mustard gas. We'll be warned first, of course, if they do. There's one thing, the best brains of the country will be onto it tonight.''

Somehow the thought reassured him. He had a picture of scientists, naturalists, technicians, and all those chaps they called the back-room boys, summoned to a council; they'd be working on the problem now. This was not a job for the government, for the chiefs of staff—they would merely carry out the orders of the scientists.

"They'll have to be ruthless,'' he thought. "Where the trouble's worst they'll have to risk more lives if they use gas. All the livestock, too, and the soil—all contaminated. As long as every-

one doesn't panic. That's the trouble. People panicking, losing their heads. The BBC was right to warn us of that.''

Upstairs in the bedrooms all was quiet. No further scraping and stabbing at the windows. A lull in battle. Forces regrouping. Wasn't that what they called it in the old wartime bulletins? The wind hadn't dropped, though. He could still hear it roaring in the chimneys. And the sea breaking down on the shore. Then he remembered the tide. The tide would be on the turn. Maybe the lull in battle was because of the tide. There was some law the birds obeyed, and it was all to do with the east wind and the tide.

He glanced at his watch. Nearly eight o'clock. It must have gone high water an hour ago. That explained the lull: the birds attacked with the flood tide. It might not work that way inland, upcountry, but it seemed as if it was so this way on the coast. He reckoned the time limit in his head. They had six hours to go without attack. When the tide turned again, around one-twenty in the morning, the birds would come back. . . .

There were two things he could do. The first to rest, with his wife and the children, and all of them snatch what sleep they could, until the small hours. The second to go out, see how they were faring at the farm, see if the telephone was still working there, so that they might get news from the exchange.

He called softly to his wife, who had just settled the children. She came halfway up the stairs and he whispered to her.

"You're not to go,'' she said at once, "you're not to go and leave me alone with the children. I can't stand it.''

Her voice rose hysterically. He hushed her, calmed her.

"All right,'' he said, "all right. I'll wait till morning. And we'll get the wireless bulletin then too, at seven. But in the morning, when the tide ebbs again, I'll try for the farm, and they may let us have bread and potatoes, and milk too.''

His mind was busy again, planning against emergency. They would not have milked, of course, this evening. The cows would be standing by the gate, waiting in the yard, with the household inside, battened behind boards, as they were here at the cottage. That is, if they had time to take precautions. He thought of the farmer, Trigg, smiling at him from the car. There would have been no shooting party, not tonight.

The children were asleep. His wife, still clothed, was sitting on her mattress. She watched him, her eyes nervous.

"What are you going to do?" she whispered.

He shook his head for silence. Softly, stealthily, he opened the back door and looked outside.

It was pitch dark. The wind was blowing harder than ever, coming in steady gusts, icy, from the sea. He kicked at the step outside the door. It was heaped with birds. There were dead birds everywhere. Under the windows, against the walls. These were the suicides, the divers, the ones with broken necks. Wherever he looked he saw dead birds. No trace of the living. The living had flown seaward with the turn of the tide. The gulls would be riding the seas now, as they had done in the forenoon.

In the far distance, on the hill where the tractor had been two days before, something was burning. One of the aircraft that had crashed; the fire, fanned by the wind, had set light to a stack.

He looked at the bodies of the birds, and he had a notion that if he heaped them, one upon the other, on the windowsills they would make added protection for the next attack. Not much, perhaps, but something. The bodies would have to be clawed at, pecked, and dragged aside before the living birds could gain purchase on the sills and attack the panes. He set to work in the darkness. It was queer; he hated touching them. The bodies were still warm and bloody. The blood matted their feathers. He felt his stomach turn, but he went on with his work. He noticed grimly that every windowpane was shattered. Only the boards had kept the birds from breaking in. He stuffed the cracked panes with the bleeding bodies of the birds.

When he had finished he went back into the cottage. He barricaded the kitchen door, made it doubly secure. He took off his bandages, sticky with the birds' blood, not with his own cuts, and put on fresh plaster.

His wife had made him cocoa and he drank it thirstily. He was very tired.

"All right," he said, smiling, "don't worry. We'll get through."

He lay down on his mattress and closed his eyes. He slept at once. He dreamt uneasily, because through his dreams there ran a thread of something forgotten. Some piece of work, neglected, that he should have done. Some precaution that he had known well but had not taken, and he could not put a name to it in his dreams. It was connected in some way with the burning aircraft and the stack upon the hill. He went on sleeping, though; he did not awake. It was his wife shaking his shoulder that awoke him finally.

"They've begun," she sobbed. "They've started this last hour. I can't listen to it any longer alone. There's something smelling bad too, something burning."

Then he remembered. He had forgotten to make up the fire. It was smoldering, nearly out. He got up swiftly and lit the lamp. The hammering had started at the windows and the doors, but it was not that he minded now. It was the smell of singed feathers. The smell filled the kitchen. He knew at once what it was. The birds were coming down the chimney, squeezing their way down to the kitchen range.

He got sticks and paper and put them on the embers, then reached for the can of paraffin.

"Stand back," he shouted to his wife. "We've got to risk this."

He threw the paraffin onto the fire. The flame roared up the pipe, and down upon the fire fell the scorched, blackened bodies of the birds.

The children woke, crying. "What is it?" said Jill. "What's happened?"

Nat had no time to answer. He was raking the bodies from the chimney, clawing them out onto the floor. The flames still roared, and the danger of the chimney catching fire was one he had to take. The flames would send away the living birds from the chimney top. The lower joint was the difficulty, though. This was choked with the smoldering, helpless bodies of the birds caught by fire. He scarcely heeded the attack on the windows and the door: let them beat their wings, break their beaks, lose their lives in the attempt to force an entry into his home. They would not break in. He thanked God he had one of the old cottages, with small windows, stout walls. Not like the new council houses. Heaven help them up the lane in the new council houses.

"Stop crying," he called to the children. "There's nothing to be afraid of, stop crying."

He went on raking at the burning, smoldering bodies as they fell into the fire.

"This'll fetch them," he said to himself, "the draft and the flames together. We're all right, as long as the chimney doesn't catch. I ought to be shot for this. It's all my fault. Last thing, I should have made up the fire. I knew there was something."

Amid the scratching and tearing at the window boards came the sudden homely striking of the kitchen clock. Three A.M. A little more than four hours yet to go. He could not be sure of the exact time of high water. He reckoned it would not turn much before half past seven, twenty to eight.

"Light up the Primus,"[13] he said to his wife. "Make us some tea, and the kids some cocoa. No use sitting around doing nothing."

That was the line. Keep her busy, and the children too. Move about, eat, drink; always best to be on the go.

He waited by the range. The flames were dying. But no more blackened bodies fell from the chimney. He thrust his poker up as far as it could go and found nothing. It was clear. The chimney was clear. He wiped the sweat from his forehead.

"Come on now, Jill," he said, "bring me some more sticks. We'll have a good fire going directly." She wouldn't come near him, though. She was staring at the heaped singed bodies of the birds.

"Never mind them," he said. "We'll put those in the passage when I've got the fire steady."

The danger of the chimney was over. It could not happen again, not if the fire was kept burning day and night.

"I'll have to get more fuel from the farm tomorrow," he thought. "This will never last. I'll manage, though. I can do all that with the ebb tide. It can be worked, fetching what we need,

when the tide's turned. We've just got to adapt ourselves, that's all."

They drank tea and cocoa and ate slices of bread and Bovril.[14] Only half a loaf left, Nat noticed. Never mind, though, they'd get by.

"Stop it," said young Johnny, pointing to the windows with his spoon, "stop it, you old birds."

"That's right," said Nat, smiling, "we don't want the old beggars, do we? Had enough of 'em."

They began to cheer when they heard the thud of the suicide birds.

"There's another, Dad," cried Jill. "He's done for."

"He's had it," said Nat. "There he goes, the blighter."

This was the way to face up to it. This was the spirit. If they could keep this up, hang on like this until seven, when the first news bulletin came through, they would not have done too badly.

"Give us a cigarette," he said to his wife. "A bit of a smoke will clear away the smell of the scorched feathers."

"There's only two left in the packet," she said. "I was going to buy you some from the co-op."

"I'll have one," he said, "t'other will keep for a rainy day."

No sense trying to make the children rest. There was no rest to be got while the tapping and the scratching went on at the windows. He sat with one arm round his wife and the other round Jill, with Johnny on his mother's lap and the blankets heaped about them on the mattress.

"You can't help admiring the beggars," he said; "they've got persistence. You'd think they'd tire of the game, but not a bit of it."

Admiration was hard to sustain. The tapping went on and on and a new rasping note struck Nat's ear, as though a sharper beak than any hitherto had come to take over from its fellows. He tried to remember the names of birds; he tried to think which species would go for this particular job. It was not the tap of the woodpecker. That would be light and frequent. This was more serious because if it continued long the wood would splinter, as the glass had done. Then he remembered the hawks. Could the hawks have taken

---

13. **Primus:** small portable stove.

14. **Bovril:** a kind of instant beef broth.

over from the gulls? Were there buzzards now upon the sills, using talons as well as beaks? Hawks, buzzards, kestrels, falcons—he had forgotten the birds of prey. He had forgotten the gripping power of the birds of prey. Three hours to go, and while they waited, the sound of the splintering wood, the talons tearing at the wood.

Nat looked about him, seeing what furniture he could destroy to fortify the door. The windows were safe because of the dresser. He was not certain of the door. He went upstairs, but when he reached the landing he paused and listened. There was a soft patter on the floor of the children's bedroom. The birds had broken through. . . . He put his ear to the door. No mistake. He could hear the rustle of wings and the light patter as they searched the floor. The other bedroom was still clear. He went into it and began bringing out the furniture, to pile at the head of the stairs should the door of the children's bedroom go. It was a preparation. It might never be needed. He could not stack the furniture against the door, because it opened inward. The only possible thing was to have it at the top of the stairs.

"Come down, Nat, what are you doing?" called his wife.

"I won't be long," he shouted. "Just making everything shipshape up here."

He did not want her to come; he did not want her to hear the pattering of the feet in the children's bedroom, the brushing of those wings against the door.

At five-thirty he suggested breakfast, bacon and fried bread, if only to stop the growing look of panic in his wife's eyes and to calm the fretful children. She did not know about the birds upstairs. The bedroom, luckily, was not over the kitchen. Had it been so, she could not have failed to hear the sound of them up there, tapping the boards. And the silly, senseless thud of the suicide birds, the death and glory boys, who flew into the bedroom, smashing their heads against the walls. He knew them of old, the herring gulls. They had no brains. The black-backs were different; they knew what they were doing. So did the buzzards, the hawks . . .

He found himself watching the clock, gazing at the hands that went so slowly round the dial. If his theory was not correct, if the attack did not cease with the turn of the tide, he knew they were beaten. They could not continue through the long day without air, without rest, without more fuel, without . . . His mind raced. He knew there were so many things they needed to withstand siege. They were not fully prepared. They were not ready. It might be that it would be safer in the towns, after all. If he could get a message through on the farm telephone to his cousin, only a short journey by train upcountry, they might be able to hire a car. That would be quicker—hire a car between tides . . .

His wife's voice, calling his name, drove away the sudden, desperate desire for sleep.

"What is it? What now?" he said sharply.

"The wireless," said his wife. "I've been watching the clock. It's nearly seven."

"Don't twist the knob," he said, impatient for the first time. "It's on the Home where it is. They'll speak from the Home."

They waited. The kitchen clock struck seven. There was no sound. No chimes, no music. They waited until a quarter past, switching to the Light. The result was the same. No news bulletin came through.

"We've heard wrong," he said. "They won't be broadcasting until eight o'clock."

They left it switched on, and Nat thought of the battery, wondered how much power was left in it. It was generally recharged when his wife went shopping in the town. If the battery failed, they would not hear the instructions.

"It's getting light," whispered his wife. "I can't see it, but I can feel it. And the birds aren't hammering so loud."

She was right. The rasping, tearing sound grew fainter every moment. So did the shuffling, the jostling for place upon the step, upon the sills. The tide was on the turn. By eight there was no sound at all. Only the wind. The children, lulled at last by the stillness, fell asleep. At half past eight Nat switched the wireless off.

"What are you doing? We'll miss the news," said his wife.

"There isn't going to be any news," said Nat. "We've got to depend upon ourselves."

He went to the door and slowly pulled away

the barricades. He drew the bolts and, kicking the bodies from the step outside the door, breathed the cold air. He had six working hours before him, and he knew he must reserve his strength for the right things, not waste it in any way. Food and light and fuel; these were the necessary things. If he could get them in sufficiency, they could endure another night.

He stepped into the garden, and as he did so he saw the living birds. The gulls had gone to ride the sea, as they had done before; they sought sea food and the buoyancy of the tide, before they returned to the attack. Not so the land birds. They waited and watched. Nat saw them, on the hedge-rows, on the soil, crowded in the trees, outside in the field, line upon line of birds, all still, doing nothing.

He went to the end of his small garden. The birds did not move. They went on watching him.

"I've got to get food," said Nat to himself. "I've got to go to the farm to find food."

He went back to the cottage. He saw to the windows and the doors. He went upstairs and opened the children's bedroom. It was empty, except for the dead birds on the floor. The living were out there, in the garden, in the fields. He went downstairs.

"I'm going to the farm," he said.

His wife clung to him. She had seen the living birds from the open door.

"Take us with you," she begged. "We can't stay here alone. I'd rather die than stay here alone."

He considered the matter. He nodded.

"Come on, then," he said. "Bring baskets, and Johnny's pram. We can load up the pram."

They dressed against the biting wind, wore gloves and scarves. His wife put Johnny in the pram. Nat took Jill's hand.

"The birds," she whimpered, "they're all out there in the fields."

"They won't hurt us," he said, "not in the light."

They started walking across the field toward the stile, and the birds did not move. They waited, their heads turned to the wind.

When they reached the turning to the farm, Nat stopped and told his wife to wait in the shelter of the hedge with the two children.

"But I want to see Mrs. Trigg," she protested. "There are lots of things we can borrow if they went to market yesterday; not only bread, and . . ."

"Wait here," Nat interrupted. "I'll be back in a moment."

The cows were lowing, moving restlessly in the yard, and he could see a gap in the fence where the sheep had knocked their way through, to roam unchecked in the front garden before the farmhouse. No smoke came from the chimneys. He was filled with misgiving. He did not want his wife or the children to go down to the farm.

"Don't gib[15] now," said Nat, harshly. "Do what I say."

She withdrew with the pram into the hedge, screening herself and the children from the wind.

He went down alone to the farm. He pushed his way through the herd of bellowing cows, which turned this way and that, distressed, their udders full. He saw the car standing by the gate, not put away in the garage. The windows of the farmhouse were smashed. There were many dead gulls lying in the yard and around the house. The living birds perched on the group of trees behind the farm and on the roof of the house. They were quite still. They watched him.

Jim's body lay in the yard . . . what was left of it. When the birds had finished, the cows had trampled him. His gun was beside him. The door of the house was shut and bolted, but, as the windows were smashed, it was easy to lift them and climb through. Trigg's body was close to the telephone. He must have been trying to get through to the exchange when the birds came for

15. **gib:** balk.

him. The receiver was hanging loose, the instrument torn from the wall. No sign of Mrs. Trigg. She would be upstairs. Was it any use going up? Sickened, Nat knew what he would find.

"Thank God," he said to himself, "there were no children."

He forced himself to climb the stairs, but halfway he turned and descended again. He could see her legs protruding from the open bedroom door. Beside her were the bodies of the black-backed gulls and an umbrella, broken.

"It's no use," thought Nat, "doing anything. I've only got five hours, less than that. The Triggs would understand. I must load up with what I can find."

He tramped back to his wife and children.

"I'm going to fill up the car with stuff," he said. "I'll put coal in it, and paraffin for the Primus. We'll take it home and return for a fresh load."

"What about the Triggs?" asked his wife.

"They must have gone to friends," he said.

"Shall I come and help you, then?"

"No; there's a mess down there. Cows and sheep all over the place. Wait, I'll get the car. You can sit in it."

Clumsily he backed the car out of the yard and into the lane. His wife and the children could not see Jim's body from there.

"Stay here," he said, "never mind the pram. The pram can be fetched later. I'm going to load the car."

Her eyes watched his all the time. He believed she understood; otherwise she would have suggested helping him to find the bread and groceries.

They made three journeys altogether, backward and forward between their cottage and the farm, before he was satisfied they had everything they needed. It was surprising, once he started thinking, how many things were necessary. Almost the most important of all was planking for the windows. He had to go round searching for timber. He wanted to renew the boards on all the windows at the cottage. Candles, paraffin, nails, tinned stuff; the list was endless. Besides all that, he milked three of the cows. The rest, poor brutes, would have to go on bellowing.

On the final journey he drove the car to the bus stop, got out, and went to the telephone box. He waited a few minutes, jangling the receiver. No good though. The line was dead. He climbed onto a bank and looked over the countryside, but there was no sign of life at all, nothing in the fields but the waiting, watching birds. Some of them slept— he could see the beaks tucked into the feathers.

"You'd think they'd be feeding," he said to himself, "not just standing in that way."

Then he remembered. They were gorged with food. They had eaten their fill during the night. That was why they did not move this morning. . . .

No smoke came from the chimneys of the council houses. He thought of the children who had run across the fields the night before.

"I should have known," he thought; "I ought to have taken them home with me."

He lifted his face to the sky. It was colorless and gray. The bare trees on the landscape looked bent and blackened by the east wind. The cold did not affect the living birds waiting out there in the fields.

"This is the time they ought to get them," said Nat; "they're a sitting target now. They must be doing this all over the country. Why don't our aircraft take off now and spray them with mustard gas? What are all our chaps doing? They must know; they must see for themselves."

He went back to the car and got into the driver's seat.

"Go quickly past that second gate," whispered his wife. "The postman's lying there. I don't want Jill to see."

He accelerated. The little Morris bumped and rattled along the lane. The children shrieked with laughter.

"Up-a-down, up-a-down," shouted young Johnny.

It was a quarter to one by the time they reached the cottage. Only an hour to go.

"Better have cold dinner," said Nat. "Hot up something for yourself and the children, some of that soup. I've no time to eat now. I've got to unload all this stuff."

He got everything inside the cottage. It could be sorted later. Give them all something to do during the long hours ahead. First he must see to the windows and the doors.

He went round the cottage methodically, testing every window, every door. He climbed onto the roof also, and fixed boards across every chimney except the kitchen. The cold was so intense he could hardly bear it, but the job had to be done. Now and again he would look up, searching the sky for aircraft. None came. As he worked he cursed the inefficiency of the authorities.

"It's always the same," he muttered. "They always let us down. Muddle, muddle, from the start. No plan, no real organization. And we don't matter down here. That's what it is. The people upcountry have priority. They're using gas up there, no doubt, and all the aircraft. We've got to wait and take what comes."

He paused, his work on the bedroom chimney finished, and looked out to sea. Something was moving out there. Something gray and white amongst the breakers.

"Good old Navy," he said, "they never let us down. They're coming down-channel; they're turning in the bay."

He waited, straining his eyes, watering in the wind, toward the sea. He was wrong, though. It was not ships. The Navy was not there. The gulls were rising from the sea. The massed flocks in the fields, with ruffled feathers, rose in formation from the ground and, wing to wing, soared upward to the sky.

The tide had turned again.

Nat climbed down the ladder and went inside the kitchen. The family were at dinner. It was a little after two. He bolted the door, put up the barricade, and lit the lamp.

"It's nighttime," said young Johnny.

His wife had switched on the wireless once again, but no sound came from it.

"I've been all round the dial," she said, "foreign stations, and that lot. I can't get anything."

"Maybe they have the same trouble," he said, "maybe it's the same right through Europe."

She poured out a plateful of the Triggs' soup, cut him a large slice of the Triggs' bread, and spread their dripping upon it.

They ate in silence. A piece of the dripping ran down young Johnny's chin and fell onto the table.

"Manners, Johnny," said Jill, "you should learn to wipe your mouth."

The tapping began at the windows, at the door. The rustling, the jostling, the pushing for position on the sills. The first thud of the suicide gulls upon the step.

"Won't America do something?" said his wife. "They've always been our allies, haven't they? Surely America will do something?"

Nat did not answer. The boards were strong against the windows and on the chimneys too. The cottage was filled with stores, with fuel, with all they needed for the next few days. When he had finished dinner he would put the stuff away, stack it neatly, get everything shipshape, handy like. His wife could help him, and the children too. They'd tire themselves out, between now and a quarter to nine, when the tide would ebb; then he'd tuck them down on their mattresses, see that they slept good and sound until three in the morning.

He had a new scheme for the windows, which was to fix barbed wire in front of the boards. He had brought a great roll of it from the farm. The nuisance was, he'd have to work at this in the dark, when the lull came between nine and three. Pity he had not thought of it before. Still, as long as the wife slept, and the kids, that was the main thing.

The smaller birds were at the window now. He recognized the light tap-tapping of their beaks and the soft brush of their wings. The hawks ignored the windows. They concentrated their attack upon the door. Nat listened to the tearing sound of splintering wood and wondered how many million years of memory were stored in those little brains, behind the stabbing beaks, the piercing eyes, now giving them this instinct to destroy mankind with all the deft precision of machines.

"I'll smoke that last cigarette," he said to his wife. "Stupid of me—it was the one thing I forgot to bring back from the farm."

He reached for it, switched on the silent wireless. He threw the empty packet on the fire and watched it burn.

Responding to the Story

Analyzing the Story

Identifying Facts

1. On December the third, two apparently minor incidents occur. One involves the farmer and one involves Nat. What are these incidents, and how do they **foreshadow,** or hint at, what the story's **conflict** will be? What fact in the incident involving Nat seems most ominous or threatening to you?

2. List at least five ominous details describing the weather in the paragraph beginning "The sky was hard," page 35. As the story goes on, how does the weather get worse as the birds become more aggressive?

3. Nat keeps trying to find a rational explanation for the birds' behavior. What explanations does he propose? How do other people react to the birds? How do they try to explain the birds' actions?

4. How does the information we get from time to time about the BBC create **suspense**? What details about the planes add to our anxiety?

Interpreting Meanings

5. Is there a **climax** to this story, or do you think the climax is yet to come? Explain.

6. What **resolution** to the conflict might be suggested in the final scene—by the silent wireless and the burning cigarette package?

7. Do you think the scene at the Triggs's **foreshadows** what will happen to Nat and his family? Or do you think they will survive? In other words, do you read this as a doomsday story (about the end of human life on earth)? Or do you read it as a story of humans versus nature, in which humans will triumph because of their superior reasoning powers? Cite details from the story to support your interpretation.

8. Explain why you think the writer chose birds to be the attackers in this story. Would other creatures have done as well?

9. Find at least five details that suggest that an evil force is directing the birds to turn on people. What do you imagine this force might be?

10. Du Maurier at times includes details that seem critical of people and of the way they respond to disaster. Find at least three of these details. Do you think the various people in the story respond to this emergency in believable ways? Explain.

Writing About the Story

A Creative Response

1. **Resolving the Conflict.** What happens next? Write your own resolution to the conflict.

2. **Filling in Details.** "They've been given the towns," thinks Nat on page 40. Who is "giving" certain birds certain assignments? What is their purpose? Where are they operating from? Write a paragraph in which you fill in these missing details from the story.

A Critical Response

3. **Explaining an Opinion.** A story like "The Birds" works when the writer is able to persuade us to believe in events that have never actually happened in real life. Has Daphne du Maurier persuaded you to believe that this conflict with the birds might really have happened as she describes it? Do you find any flaws in the plot? Are any details unbelievable? Are there any coincidences that strain your belief? Write a paragraph telling whether you found the story believable. Cite at least three reasons to explain your opinion.

Analyzing Language and Vocabulary

Clues to Meaning

In the first paragraph, this British writer mentions "hedgerows," a term not used in the United States. In the British Isles, hedgerows are thick rows of bushes that form hedges along country lanes. You could have made a pretty good guess at the meaning of the term by thinking about the meanings of the familiar words *hedge* and *row*.

The following passages contain other British terms you might not be familiar with. By using

context clues (see page 13) and by thinking about familiar words that these words resemble, make educated guesses about their meanings. Test your guesses within the context of each passage, and check all your guesses in the dictionary.

1. ". . . he would pause and eat the *pasty* that his wife had baked for him. . . ."
2. "There was no *creeper* on the cottage walls to break loose and scratch upon the pane."
3. "He wondered if he should go to the *call box* by the bus stop and ring up the police."
4. "He looked . . . in the cupboard where she kept her *tins*."
5. " 'She's another,' thought Nat, 'she doesn't care. . . . She hopes to go to the *pictures* tonight.' "

Reading About the Writer

Daphne du Maurier (1907–   ) was born in London, the daughter of a famous actor and theater manager and the granddaughter of George du Maurier, an author of popular novels.

Although she was an attractive child and grew up in a stimulating, well-to-do family, Daphne shunned the social life her sisters so enjoyed. She preferred solitude and reading.

In 1939, while in her early twenties, she decided to write a novel and secluded herself in an empty house in Cornwall, on the coast of England. The novel turned out to be a romantic family chronicle which grew to 200,000 words in just ten weeks.

As she wrote, she discovered something about writing: "Sometimes my book comes so strongly on me that it's like a restless urge within saying 'Get on! Get on!' "

Remarkably, that book revealed an astonishing gift for storytelling, one that readers have since found irresistible. Du Maurier gave the book the title *The Loving Spirit.* It not only found a publisher at once, but it also became a best seller—and a forerunner of a shelf-full of others, including the three famous romantic novels: *Jamaica Inn, Frenchman's Creek,* and *Rebecca.*

Literature & Language

Using Verb Tenses Correctly

Literary Model

In the following passage from a famous adventure story, a stubborn plantation owner in Brazil finds out what will happen if he does not leave his property before an army of killer ants arrives.

"Unless they alter their course, and there's no reason why they should, they'll reach your plantation in two days at the latest."

Leiningen sucked placidly at a cigar about the size of a corn cob and for a few seconds gazed without answering at the agitated District Commissioner. Then he took the cigar from his lips and leaned slightly forward. With his bristling gray hair, bulky nose, and lucid eyes, he had the look of an aging and shabby eagle.

"Decent of you," he murmured, "paddling all this way just to give me the tip. But you're pulling my leg of course when you say I must do a bunk.[1] Why even a herd of saurians[2] couldn't drive me from this plantation of mine."

The Brazilian official threw up lean and lanky arms and clawed the air with wildly distended fingers. "Leiningen!" he shouted. "You're insane! They're not creatures you can fight—they're an elemental—an 'act of God!' Ten miles long, two miles wide—ants, nothing but ants! And every single one of them a fiend from hell; before you can spit three times they'll eat a full grown buffalo to the bones. I tell you if you don't clear out at once there'll be nothing left of you but a skeleton picked as clean as your own plantation."

—from "Leiningen Versus the Ants,"
Carl Stephenson

---

1. **do a bunk:** make a quick escape.
2. **saurians:** a group of reptiles, including lizards. Leiningen probably refers to the dinosaurs.

Grammar Note

A **verb** is a word that expresses action, a condition, or a state of being. Verbs include action words, such as *spit* and *eat*, and linking verbs, such as *is* and *seem*. One of the most important characteristics of verbs is their ability to express time, or **tense**. Different forms of a verb can indicate whether an action or condition is taking place in the present, the past, or the future.

"You*'re* insane! They*'re* not creatures you can fight—" [present]

Then he *took* the cigar from his lips, and *leaned* slightly forward. [past]

". . . they*'ll eat* a full-grown buffalo to the bones." [future]

Note that Stephenson uses contractions (*you're, they're, they'll*) to suggest everyday speech. A **contraction** is a word formed by combining two words and omitting one or more letters, which are replaced with an apostrophe. *You're* is a contraction for *you are, they're* is a contraction for *they are*, and *they'll* is a contraction for *they will*.

To indicate the precise time of an action or condition, helping verbs are often used with the main verb to form a **verb phrase**. For example, in the last sentence above, the helping verb *will* is used with the main verb *eat* to indicate that the condition described will take place in the future. Other helping verbs include *have, has,* and *had; am, is, are,* and *were;* and *can, could, may, might, must, should,* and *would*. The italicized words in the following sentences are examples of verb phrases.

Two years *have passed* since then.

Black winter *had descended* in a single night.

It *must have been* fright that made them act the way they did.

Examining the Writer's Style

1. List all the events that take place in the present, in the passage by Stephenson. List the events in

chronological order. Compare lists with a partner to see if you agree about the sequence of present events.

2. Now list all the events that might take place in the future.

3. Stephenson's passage contains dialogue in quotation marks, representing the exact words of Leiningen and his visitor. The passage also contains the words of the narrator, the person who is telling the story. What tense is most often used in the passages of dialogue? What tense is used most often in the passages of narration?

Using Correct Verb Tenses in Your Writing

1. **Narrating an Action-Packed Experience.** Imagine that you have witnessed some action-packed event, such as a natural disaster, a sudden accident, an attempted crime. The editor of the school newspaper has asked you to write a news report about the incident.

   a. Before you begin, jot down all the events you want to include in your report. Then make a list of the persons involved in this incident. Decide which eyewitnesses you'll pretend to interview. Remember that newspaper readers want to know **what** happened, **whom** it happened to, **when** it happened, **where** it happened, **why** it happened,

and **how** it happened. (You could extend this story of Leiningen, and report on what takes place next. Does Leiningen face the ants and risk becoming a skeleton, or does he run away?)

   b. After you have gathered the information you need, begin writing your report. Put the comments of the people you have interviewed in quotation marks. What tenses will these people speak in?

   c. Ask a partner to read your report. Then ask your partner to underline all your verbs and verb phrases and to indicate whether they are in the present, past, or future tense. Your partner should also note whether you have stayed mainly in one tense or shifted from one tense to another. Finally, ask your partner if the sequence of events is clear from your report. Revise passages that confuse your partner or in which you shift tenses unnecessarily.

2. **Writing a Diary Entry.** Take the same imaginary events that you wrote a news report on, and rewrite them in the form of a personal diary entry. Imagine that the event occurred to you on the same day that you are writing the entry. Use the present tense as much as possible: "I am running down the street at 6 a.m. when . . ."

SUMMARIZING A PLOT

Writing Assignment

In at least one paragraph, summarize the plot of "Poison" (page 6).

Background

Before you get started on this assignment, you should know what it means "to summarize" something. **To summarize** means simply "to state the main points in brief form." A good plot summary should include these features:

1. The summary should include all the story's important events.
2. The summary should state the events in the order in which they occur.
3. The summary should explain how one event in the story causes or leads to the next one.

Your summary should also tell how the story uses the key elements of a plot. The plots of most stories follow a sequence, which is often diagramed (more or less) like this:

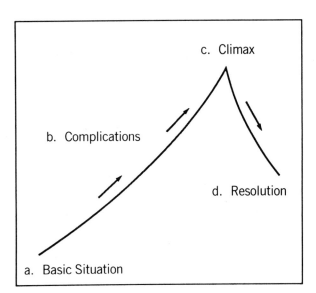

a. Basic Situation
b. Complications
c. Climax
d. Resolution

1. The **basic situation** is the opening of the story, where the **characters** and their **conflict** are introduced. Often, this part of the story includes details that make us feel **suspense**—we are anxious to know "What happens next?"
2. The **complications** are all the problems that arise as the main character takes action to resolve the conflict.
3. The **climax** is the story's high point—the peak of our chart. It is that emotional moment when our suspense and tension are greatest, when we finally realize how the conflict is going to end.
4. The **resolution** is the last part of the story, where the writer ties up the loose ends of the plot and gives the story a sense of completion. In modern stories, the resolution is very, very brief—some stories don't even have one. (This bothers some readers, who prefer a strong sense of "closure" to a story.)

Some versions of this famous diagram are drawn as a pyramid, like this:

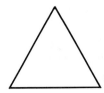

The three points of the pyramid would be the basic situation (or exposition), the climax, and the resolution. According to this pyramid, where would the climax come in the story?

Prewriting

1. Go back and skim "Poison" to review the story's main events. (When you write a summary, never rely on your memory.)
2. As you skim, write down on a piece of paper all the **questions** that you ask yourself as you read the story. (We all automatically ask ourselves questions as we read. The better the reader is, the more questions are asked.) Write the questions in the order that they come to you, and leave enough room for your answers. For example, you might begin with these questions:

It must have been around midnight when I drove home, and as I approached the gates of the bungalow I switched off the headlamps of the car so the beam wouldn't swing in through the window of the side bedroom and wake Harry Pope. But I needn't have bothered. Coming up the drive I noticed his light was still on, so he was awake anyway—unless perhaps he'd dropped off while reading.

I parked the car and went up the five steps to the balcony, counting each step carefully in the dark so I wouldn't take an extra one which wasn't there when I got to the top. I crossed the balcony, pushed through the screen doors into the house itself, and switched on the light in the hall. I went across to the door of Harry's room, opened it quietly, and looked in.

He was lying on the bed and I could see he was awake. But he didn't move. He didn't even turn his head toward me, but I heard him say, "Timber, Timber, come here."

The person who is talking is very thoughtful. I wonder if Harry is hard to get along with.

I wonder why the light is on. It must be important.

Why doesn't Harry move? What is wrong with him?

3. Answer your questions in complete sentences.
4. Organize the details you've cited in your answers by grouping them according to the bare bones of a plot. (You might discard some details as unimportant: that is all right.) Put the details in this order:
   a. The details that work together to make the story's **basic situation.**
   b. The events that **complicate** the story, as the characters take steps to resolve their conflict.
   c. The "big event" that marks the story's **climax.**
   d. The details that **resolve,** or close, the story.
5. Be sure you have summarized the events in their right order. For example, here are some questions about the order of events in "Poison":
   a. Did Timber and Ganderbai pull back the sheet **before or after** they poured the chloroform down the tube?
   b. Did Harry jump up **before or after** he realized the sheet was empty?
   c. Did Harry insult the doctor **before or after** he knew he was safe?
6. Review your list. Have you explained how one event causes or leads to another? If you were summarizing a fairy tale, for example, you wouldn't say: "The king died and then the queen died." Instead, you would show how one event leads to another: "The king died, and so the

queen died of a broken heart." In the case of "Poison," be sure to try to explain the cause of Harry's outburst.

Writing

Here is how a plot summary of "Poison" might begin.

In the beginning of his story "Poison," Roald Dahl makes us suspect at once that something is wrong because we are told that Harry's light is on and because Harry doesn't move. We soon learn from Harry that the basic situation is this: a krait has crawled onto his stomach and is lying there asleep—or so he says.

Checklist for Revision
1. Have you stated the title and author?
2. Have you included all the story's most important events?
3. Have you summarized the events in the order in which they occurred?
4. Have you explained how one event causes or leads to another?

Characters in the plot connect us with the vastness of our secret life, which is endlessly explorable.

—Eudora Welty

Character: Revealing Human Nature

Creating characters—telling us what human beings are like—is the whole point of writing stories. A story is really only interesting to us as readers because of what it tells us about people and how it makes us feel about them. Thus, character, the revelation of human nature, is what a good story is all about.

A magazine editor once told me that all you need to tell a story is a character, an adjective, and a series of choices that the character must make. Let's call our main character George, give him the adjective "stingy," have him invite Donna out for her birthday, and see what happens.

If we are told that he has fifty dollars, yet walks Donna the sixteen blocks to the theater, pretending not to notice the approaching bus, we know our George. We are even delighted when George chooses the balcony seats, which are cheaper than the seats in the orchestra. Later, at the restaurant, we know he'll be looking anxiously at the right-hand side of the menu (where the prices are listed).

What we are curious about is how Donna will respond to this stingy character. But suppose that at the restaurant George recommends, instead of the four-dollar hamburger, the ten-dollar steak? A surprise, a **change** in character! Love, that powerful tonic, has done what no amount of reasoning could do . . . and we recognize with satisfaction a truth, a revelation of how we and our fellow human beings behave.

Of course, people are much more complex than a single adjective can describe, and that is the joy, and the difficulty, of storytelling. How does a writer build a character out of words, someone who will seem to become flesh and blood and rise off the page, a fully realized Scarlett O'Hara or Ebenezer Scrooge or Huck Finn?

Creating Characters—Five Methods

1. Since the writer is painting a portrait in words, the most obvious method of characterization is the character's own **speech.** Think of how you can recognize your friends from what they say— not just from their tone of voice, but also from the kinds of words they use (big inflated words, or little punchy ones; formal words or slangy ones). Think of how people reveal their values by using words that always allude to what things cost, rather than to how pleasurable or beautiful they are. Reading the characters' dialogue in a story is like listening in on a conversation. Just as in real life, dialogue helps reveal human nature—especially if the writer has an ear for the way real people talk.

Character: Revealing Human Nature

> "**All you need to tell a story is a character, an adjective, and a series of choices that the character must make.**"

2. Appearance is another method of creating character. We can tell so much simply from the words a writer uses to describe a person's face. Charles Dickens lets us see Scrooge at once:

> The cold within him froze his old features, nipped his pointed nose, shriveled his cheek, stiffened his gait; made his eyes red, his thin lips blue; and spoke out shrewdly in his grating voice . . .

Clearly, Dickens wants us to think of Scrooge as a character whose cold heart is reflected in his whole appearance.

The kinds of clothes a character wears can give us hints too. As readers, we will respond one way to a character wearing a pin-striped suit and waving an ivory cigarette holder, and another way to a character wearing faded jeans and carrying a copy of *Of Mice and Men*.

3. In fiction, a writer can even take us into the characters' minds to reveal their private **thoughts.** In this sense, fiction has an advantage over real life. We might learn that one character detests her brother's drinking, or that another one sympathizes with his father for his troubles at the office. We might learn how one character secretly feels when he sees the bully picking on the smallest kid in the schoolyard or how another feels as she watches her grandmother's coffin being lowered into the ground.

4. We can learn about characters by watching **how other characters in the story feel about them.** We might learn, for instance, that a salesman is a hearty, good fellow in the eyes of his customers and a generous tipper in the eyes of the local waitress; but he is impatient, cranky, and selfish in the eyes of his family. Dickens tells us what effect Scrooge had on other people:

> Nobody ever stopped him in the street to say, with gladsome looks, "My dear Scrooge, how are you? When will you come to see me?" No beggars implored him to bestow a trifle, no children asked him what it was o'clock, no man or woman ever once in all his life inquired the way to such and such a place, of Scrooge. Even the blind men's dogs appeared to know him; and, when they saw him coming on, would tug their owners into doorways . . .

5. Most of all, we understand characters in fiction from their **actions,** from what we see them doing. How would you react to a girl of sixteen who, when you first meet her in a story, is dyeing her hair green? How would you react to another who, at five-thirty in the morning, is out delivering her newspapers? Scrooge, when we first meet him on Christmas Eve, is working on his accounts— an action that instantly reveals his overriding concern with money.

In fact, characters in a story (and in life) tend to reveal themselves most fully when they are under stress, when they are placed in some situation that demands that they *do* something about it. As we watch the characters in a story take action in response to a conflict, we begin to discover the kinds of people they really are.

> "**H**ow
> would you react
> to a girl of sixteen who,
> when you first meet her
> in a story,
> is dyeing her hair green?
> How would you react
> to another who,
> at five-thirty
> in the morning,
> is out delivering
> her newspapers?"

"The cold within him froze his old features."

Artist John Freas's depiction of Scrooge.

Direct and Indirect Characterization

When a writer shows us a character by describing his or her speech, appearance, thoughts, or actions, we say that the characterization is **indirect.** This means that we ourselves, as readers, have to take all the information we are given about the character and interpret for ourselves the kind of person we are meeting. Indirect characterization is something like meeting people in real life. In real life, people do not wear T-shirts with slogans explaining what kind of people they are. In real life, we observe people, we listen to what they say, and we watch how they act. Then we draw our own conclusions about them.

A writer can use **direct** characterization too. This means that a writer can tell us directly what a character is like or what a person's motives are. A writer might tell us directly that a character is sneaky, honest, evil, innocent, and so on. A writer might tell us directly that a heroine suffers from shyness and hates to go to parties or that another character is self-centered and cares only about adding necklaces to her collection. In a famous listing of adjectives, Dickens even tells us directly what kind of person Scrooge is:

> Oh, but he was a tightfisted hand at the grindstone, Scrooge! a squeezing, wrenching, grasping, scraping, clutching, covetous old sinner!

Modern writers do not often tell us too much directly about their characters. In fiction, as in life itself, it is much more satisfying for us to discover what characters are truly like for ourselves.

> " **I**n real life, people do not wear T-shirts with slogans explaining what kind of people they are."

A CHRISTMAS MEMORY

Truman Capote

Now let's look at a story called ''A Christmas Memory,'' by an accomplished writer named Truman Capote. While you enjoy the story, keep an eye on how the writer reveals to us the character of a woman he never names, but calls simply ''my friend.''

Imagine a morning in late November. A coming of winter morning more than twenty years ago. Consider the kitchen of a spreading old house in a country town. A great black stove is its main feature; but there is also a big round table and a fireplace with two rocking chairs placed in front of it. Just today the fireplace commenced its seasonal roar.

A woman with shorn white hair is standing at the kitchen window. She is wearing tennis shoes and a shapeless gray sweater over a summery calico dress. She is small and sprightly, like a bantam hen; but, due to a long youthful illness, her shoulders are pitifully hunched. Her face is remarkable—not unlike Lincoln's, craggy like that, and tinted by sun and wind; but it is delicate too, finely boned, and her eyes are sherry-colored and timid. ''Oh my,'' she exclaims, her breath smoking the windowpane, ''it's fruitcake weather!''

The person to whom she is speaking is myself. I am seven; she is sixty-something. We are cousins, very distant ones, and we have lived together—well, as long as I can remember. Other people inhabit the house, relatives; and though they have power over us, and frequently make us cry, we are not, on the whole, too much aware of them. We are each other's best friend. She calls me Buddy, in memory of a boy who was formerly her best friend. The other Buddy died in the 1880's, when she was still a child. She is still a child.

''I knew it before I got out of bed,'' she says, turning away from the window with a purposeful excitement in her eyes. ''The courthouse bell sounded so cold and clear. And there were no birds singing; they've gone to warmer country, yes indeed. Oh, Buddy, stop stuffing biscuit and fetch our buggy. Help me find my hat. We've thirty cakes to bake.''

It's always the same: a morning arrives in November, and my friend, as though officially inaugurating the Christmas time of year that exhilarates her imagination and fuels the blaze of her heart, announces: ''It's fruitcake weather! Fetch our buggy. Help me find my hat.''

The hat is found, a straw cartwheel corsaged with velvet roses out-of-doors has faded: it once belonged to a more fashionable relative. Together, we guide our buggy, a dilapidated baby carriage, out to the garden and into a grove of pecan trees. The buggy is mine; that is, it was bought for me when I was born. It is made of wicker, rather unraveled, and the wheels wobble like a drunkard's legs. But it is a faithful object; springtimes, we take it to the woods and fill it with flowers, herbs, wild fern for our porch pots; in the summer, we pile it with picnic paraphernalia and sugar-cane fishing poles and roll it down to the edge of the creek; it has its winter uses, too: as a truck for hauling firewood from the yard to the kitchen, as a warm bed for Queenie, our tough little orange and white rat terrier who has survived distemper and two rattlesnake bites. Queenie is trotting beside it now.

Three hours later we are back in the kitchen hulling a heaping buggyload of windfall pecans. Our backs hurt from gathering them: how hard they were to find (the main crop having been shaken off the trees and sold by the orchard's owners, who are not us) among the concealing leaves, the frosted, deceiving grass. Caarackle! A cheery crunch, scraps of miniature thunder sound as the shells collapse and the golden mound of sweet, oily, ivory meat mounts in the milk-glass bowl. Queenie begs to taste, and now and again my friend sneaks her a mite, though insisting we deprive ourselves. "We mustn't, Buddy. If we start, we won't stop. And there's scarcely enough as there is. For thirty cakes." The kitchen is growing dark. Dusk turns the window into a mirror: our reflections mingle with the rising moon as we work by the fireside in the firelight. At last, when the moon is quite high, we toss the final hull into the fire and, with joined sighs, watch it catch flame. The buggy is empty; the bowl is brimful.

We eat our supper (cold biscuits, bacon, blackberry jam) and discuss tomorrow. Tomorrow the kind of work I like best begins: buying. Cherries and citron, ginger and vanilla and canned Hawaiian pineapple, rinds and raisins and walnuts and whiskey and oh, so much flour, butter, so many eggs, spices, flavorings: why, we'll need a pony to pull the buggy home.

But before these purchases can be made, there is the question of money. Neither of us has any. Except for skinflint sums persons in the house occasionally provide (a dime is considered very big money); or what we earn ourselves from various activities: holding rummage sales, selling buckets of handpicked blackberries, jars of homemade jam and apple jelly and peach preserves, rounding up flowers for funerals and weddings. Once we won seventy-ninth prize, five dollars, in a national football contest. Not that we know a fool thing about football. It's just that we enter any contest we hear about: at the moment our hopes are centered on the fifty-thousand-dollar Grand Prize being offered to name a new brand of coffee (we suggested "A.M."; and, after some hesitation, for my friend thought it perhaps sacrilegious, the slogan "A.M.! Amen!"). To tell the truth, our only *really* profitable enterprise was the Fun and Freak Museum we conducted in a backyard woodshed two summers ago. The Fun was a stereopticon[1] with slide views of Washington and New York lent us by a relative who had been to those places (she was furious when she discovered

why we'd borrowed it); the Freak was a three-legged biddy chicken hatched by one of our own hens. Everybody hereabouts wanted to see that biddy: we charged grownups a nickel, kids two cents. And took in a good twenty dollars before the museum shut down due to the decease of the main attraction.

But one way and another we do each year accumulate Christmas savings, a Fruitcake Fund. These moneys we keep hidden in an ancient bead purse under a loose board under the floor under a chamber pot under my friend's bed. The purse is seldom removed from this safe location except to make a deposit, or, as happens every Saturday, a withdrawal; for on Saturdays I am allowed ten cents to go to the picture show. My friend has never been to a picture show, nor does she intend to: "I'd rather hear you tell the story, Buddy. That way I can imagine it more. Besides, a person my age shouldn't squander their eyes. When the Lord comes, let me see Him clear." In addition to never having seen a movie, she has never: eaten in a restaurant, traveled more than five miles from home, received or sent a telegram, read anything except funny papers and the Bible, worn cosmetics, cursed, wished someone harm, told a lie on purpose, let a hungry dog go hungry. Here are a few things she has done, does do: killed with a hoe the biggest rattlesnake ever seen in this county (sixteen rattles), dip snuff (secretly), tame hummingbirds (just try it) till they balance on her finger, tell ghost stories (we both believe in ghosts) so tingling they chill you in July, talk to herself, take walks in the rain, grow the prettiest japonicas in town, know the recipe for every sort of old-time Indian cure, including a magical wart-remover.

Now, with supper finished, we retire to the room in a faraway part of the house where my friend sleeps in a scrap-quilt-covered iron bed painted rose pink, her favorite color. Silently, wallowing in the pleasures of conspiracy, we take the bead purse from its secret place and spill its contents on the scrap quilt. Dollar bills, tightly rolled and green as May buds. Somber fifty-cent pieces, heavy enough to weight a dead man's eyes. Lovely dimes, the liveliest coin, the one that really jingles. Nickels and quarters, worn smooth as

---

1. **stereopticon:** a kind of slide projector.

creek pebbles. But mostly a hateful heap of bitter-odored pennies. Last summer others in the house contracted to pay us a penny for every twenty-five flies we killed. Oh, the carnage of August: the flies that flew to heaven! Yet it was not work in which we took pride. And, as we sit counting pennies, it is as though we were back tabulating dead flies. Neither of us has a head for figures; we count slowly, lose track, start again. According to her calculations, we have $12.73. According to mine, exactly $13. "I do hope you're wrong, Buddy. We can't mess around with thirteen. The cakes will fall. Or put somebody in the cemetery. Why, I wouldn't dream of getting out of bed on the thirteenth." This is true: she always spends thirteenths in bed. So, to be on the safe side, we subtract a penny and toss it out the window.

Of the ingredients that go into our fruitcakes, whiskey is the most expensive, as well as the hardest to obtain: state laws forbid its sale. But everybody knows you can buy a bottle from Mr. Haha Jones. And the next day, having completed our more prosaic shopping, we set out for Mr. Haha's business address, a "sinful" (to quote public opinion) fish-fry and dancing café down by the river. We've been there before, and on the same errand; but in previous years our dealings have been with Haha's wife, an iodine-dark Indian woman with brassy peroxided hair and a dead-tired disposition. Actually, we've never laid eyes on her husband, though we've heard that he's an Indian too. A giant with razor scars across his cheeks. They call him Haha because he's so gloomy, a man who never laughs. As we approach his café (a large log cabin festooned inside and out with chains of garish-gay naked light bulbs and standing by the river's muddy edge under the shade of river trees where moss drifts through the branches like gray mist) our steps slow down. Even Queenie stops prancing and sticks close by. People have been murdered in Haha's café. Cut to pieces. Hit on the head. There's a case coming up in court next month. Naturally these goings-on happen at night when the colored lights cast crazy patterns and the victrola[2] wails. In the daytime

---

2. **victrola:** an old term for a record player.

Haha's is shabby and deserted. I knock at the door, Queenie barks, my friend calls: "Mrs. Haha, ma'am? Anyone to home?"

Footsteps. The door opens. Our hearts overturn. It's Mr. Haha Jones himself! And he *is* a giant; he *does* have scars; he *doesn't* smile. No, he glowers at us through Satan-tilted eyes and demands to know: "What you want with Haha?"

For a moment we are too paralyzed to tell. Presently my friend half-finds her voice, a whispery voice at best: "If you please, Mr. Haha, we'd like a quart of your finest whiskey."

His eyes tilt more. Would you believe it? Haha is smiling! Laughing, too. "Which one of you is a drinkin' man?"

"It's for making fruitcakes, Mr. Haha. Cooking."

This sobers him. He frowns. "That's no way to waste good whiskey." Nevertheless, he retreats into the shadowed café and seconds later appears carrying a bottle of daisy yellow unlabeled liquor. He demonstrates its sparkle in the sunlight and says: "Two dollars."

We pay him with nickels and dimes and pennies. Suddenly, jangling the coins in his hand like a fistful of dice, his face softens. "Tell you what," he proposes, pouring the money back into our bead purse, "just send me one of them fruitcakes instead."

"Well," my friend remarks on our way home, "there's a lovely man. We'll put an extra cup of rasins in *his* cake."

The black stove, stoked with coal and firewood, glows like a lighted pumpkin. Eggbeaters whirl, spoons spin round in bowls of butter and sugar, vanilla sweetens the air, ginger spices it; melting, nose-tingling odors saturate the kitchen, suffuse the house, drift out to the world on puffs of chimney smoke. In four days our work is done. Thirty-one cakes, dampened with whiskey, bask on window sills and shelves.

Who are they for?

Friends. Not necessarily neighbor friends: indeed, the larger share are intended for persons we've met maybe once, perhaps not at all. People who've struck our fancy. Like President Roosevelt. Like the Reverend and Mrs. J. C. Lucey, Baptist missionaries to Borneo who lectured here

In four days our work is done. A scene from the television adaptation of "A Christmas Memory."

last winter. Or the little knife grinder who comes through town twice a year. Or Abner Packer, the driver of the six o'clock bus from Mobile, who exchanges waves with us every day as he passes in a dust-cloud whoosh. Or the young Wistons, a California couple whose car one afternoon broke down outside the house and who spent a pleasant hour chatting with us on the porch (young Mr. Wiston snapped our picture, the only one we've ever had taken). Is it because my friend is shy with everyone *except* strangers that these strangers, and merest acquaintances, seem to us our truest friends? I think yes. Also, the scrapbooks we keep of thank-you's on White House stationery, time-to-time communications from California and Borneo, the knife grinder's penny post cards, make us feel connected to eventful worlds beyond the kitchen with its views of a sky that stops.

Now a nude December fig branch grates against the window. The kitchen is empty, the cakes are gone; yesterday we carted the last of them to the post office, where the cost of stamps turned our purse inside out. We're broke. That rather depresses me, but my friend insists on celebrating—with two inches of whiskey left in Haha's bottle. Queenie has a spoonful in a bowl of coffee (she likes her coffee chicory-flavored and strong). The rest we divide between a pair of jelly glasses. We're both quite awed at the prospect of drinking straight whiskey; the taste of it brings screwed-up expressions and sour shudders. But by and by we begin to sing, the two of us singing different songs simultaneously. I don't know the words to mine, just: *Come on along, come on along, to the darktown strutters' ball.* But I can dance: that's what I mean to be, a tap-dancer in the movies. My dancing shadow rollicks on the walls; our voices rock the chinaware; we giggle as if unseen hands were tickling us. Queenie rolls on her back, her paws plow the air, something like a grin stretches her black lips. Inside myself, I feel warm and sparky as those crumbling logs, carefree as the wind in the chimney. My friend waltzes round the stove, the hem of her poor calico skirt pinched between her fingers as though it were a party dress: *Show me the way to go home,* she sings, her tennis shoes squeaking on the floor. *Show me the way to go home.*

Enter: two relatives. Very angry. Potent with eyes that scold, tongues that scald. Listen to what they have to say, the words tumbling together into a wrathful tune: "A child of seven! whiskey on his breath! are you out of your mind? feeding a child of seven! must be loony! road to ruination! remember Cousin Kate? Uncle Charlie? Uncle Charlie's brother-in-law? shame! scandal! humiliation! kneel, pray, beg the Lord!"

Queenie sneaks under the stove. My friend gazes at her shoes, her chin quivers, she lifts her skirt and blows her nose and runs to her room. Long after the town has gone to sleep and the house is silent except for the chimings of clocks and the sputter of fading fires, she is weeping into a pillow already as wet as a widow's handkerchief.

"Don't cry," I say, sitting at the bottom of her bed and shivering despite my flannel nightgown that smells of last winter's cough syrup, "don't cry," I beg, teasing her toes, tickling her feet, "you're too old for that."

"It's because," she hiccups, "I *am* too old. Old and funny."

"Not funny. Fun. More fun than anybody. Listen. If you don't stop crying you'll be so tired tomorrow we can't go cut a tree."

She straightens up. Queenie jumps on the bed (where Queenie is not allowed) to lick her cheeks. "I know where we'll find real pretty trees, Buddy. And holly, too. With berries big as your eyes. It's way off in the woods. Farther than we've ever been. Papa used to bring us Christmas trees from there: carry them on his shoulder. That's fifty years ago. Well, now: I can't wait for morning."

Morning. Frozen rime[3] lusters the grass; the sun, round as an orange and orange as hot-weather moons, balances on the horizon, burnishes the silvered winter woods. A wild turkey calls. A renegade hog grunts in the undergrowth. Soon, by the edge of knee-deep, rapid-running water, we have to abandon the buggy. Queenie wades the stream first, paddles across, barking complaints at the swiftness of the current, the pneumonia-making coldness of it. We follow, holding our shoes and equipment (a hatchet, a burlap sack) above our heads. A mile more: of chastising thorns, burs

---

3. **rime:** frost.

and briers that catch at our clothes; of rusty pine needles brilliant with gaudy fungus and molted feathers. Here, there, a flash, a flutter, an ecstasy of shrillings remind us that not all the birds have flown south. Always, the path unwinds through lemony sun pools and pitch vine tunnels. Another creek to cross: a disturbed armada of speckled trout froths the water round us, and frogs the size of plates practice belly flops; beaver workmen are building a dam. On the farther shore, Queenie shakes herself and trembles. My friend shivers, too: not with cold but enthusiasm. One of her hat's ragged roses sheds a petal as she lifts her head and inhales the pine-heavy air. "We're almost there; can you smell it, Buddy?" she says, as though we were approaching an ocean.

And, indeed, it is a kind of ocean. Scented acres of holiday trees, prickly-leafed holly. Red berries shiny as Chinese bells: black crows swoop upon them screaming. Having stuffed our burlap sacks with enough greenery and crimson to garland a dozen windows, we set about choosing a tree. "It should be," muses my friend, "twice as tall as a boy. So a boy can't steal the star." The one we pick is twice as tall as me. A brave, handsome brute that survives thirty hatchet strokes before it keels with a creaking, rending cry. Lugging it like a kill, we commence the long trek out. Every few yards we abandon the struggle, sit down, and pant. But we have the strength of triumphant huntsmen; that and the tree's virile, icy perfume revive us, goad us on. Many compliments accompany our sunset return along the red clay road to town; but my friend is sly and noncommittal when passers-by praise the treasure perched in our buggy: what a fine tree and where did it come from? "Yonderways," she murmurs vaguely. Once a car stops and the rich mill owner's lazy wife leans out and whines: "Giveya twobits cash for that ol tree." Ordinarily my friend is afraid of saying no; but on this occasion she promptly shakes her head: "We wouldn't take a dollar." The mill owner's wife persists. "A dollar, my foot! Fifty cents. That's my last offer. Goodness, woman, you can get another one." In answer, my friend gently reflects: "I doubt it. There's never two of anything."

Home: Queenie slumps by the fire and sleeps till tomorrow, snoring loud as a human.

A trunk in the attic contains: a shoebox of ermine tails (off the opera cape of a curious lady who once rented a room in the house), coils of frazzled tinsel gone gold with age, one silver star, a brief rope of dilapidated, undoubtedly dangerous candylike light bulbs. Excellent decorations, as far as they go, which isn't far enough: my friend wants our tree to blaze "like a Baptist window," droop with weighty snows of ornament. But we can't afford the made-in-Japan splendors at the five-and-dime. So we do what we've always done: sit for days at the kitchen table with scissors and crayons and stacks of colored paper. I make sketches and my friend cuts them out: lots of cats, fish too (because they're easy to draw), some apples, some watermelons, a few winged angels devised from saved-up sheets of Hershey-bar tin foil. We use safety pins to attach these creations to the tree; as a final touch, we sprinkle the branches with shredded cotton (picked in August for this purpose). My friend, surveying the effect, clasps her hands together. "Now honest, Buddy. Doesn't it look good enough to eat?" Queenie tries to eat an angel.

After weaving and ribboning holly wreaths for all the front windows, our next project is the fashioning of family gifts. Tie-dye scarves for the ladies, for the men a home-brewed lemon and licorice and aspirin syrup to be taken "at the first Symptoms of a Cold and after Hunting." But when it comes time for making each other's gift, my friend and I separate to work secretly. I would like to buy her a pearl-handled knife, a radio, a whole pound of chocolate-covered cherries (we tasted some once and she always swears: "I could live on them, Buddy, Lord yes I could—and that's not taking His name in vain"). Instead, I am building her a kite. She would like to give me a bicycle (she's said so on several million occasions: "If only I could, Buddy. It's bad enough in life to do without something *you* want; but confound it, what gets my goat is not being able to give somebody something you want *them* to have. Only one of these days, I will, Buddy. Locate you a bike. Don't ask how. Steal it, maybe"). Instead, I'm fairly certain that she is building me a kite—the same as last year, and the year before: the year before that we exchanged slingshots. All of which is fine by me. For we are champion kite-fliers who study the wind like sailors; my friend, more accomplished than I, can get a kite aloft when there isn't enough breeze to carry clouds.

Christmas Eve afternoon we scrape together a nickel and go to the butcher's to buy Queenie's traditional gift, a good gnawable beef bone. The bone, wrapped in funny paper, is placed high in the tree near the silver star. Queenie knows it's there. She squats at the foot of the tree, staring up in a trance of greed: when bedtime arrives she refuses to budge. Her excitement is equaled by my own. I kick the covers and turn my pillow as though it were a scorching summer's night. Somewhere a rooster crows: falsely, for the sun is still on the other side of the world.

"Buddy, are you awake?" It is my friend, calling from her room, which is next to mine; and an instant later she is sitting on my bed holding a candle. "Well, I can't sleep a hoot," she declares. "My mind's jumping like a jack rabbit. Buddy, do you think Mrs. Roosevelt will serve our cake at dinner?" We huddle in the bed, and she squeezes my hand I-love-you. "Seems like your hand used to be so much smaller. I guess I hate to see you grow up. When you're grown up, will we still be friends?" I say always. "But I feel so bad, Buddy. I wanted so bad to give you a bike. I tried to sell my cameo Papa gave me. Buddy—" she hesitates, as though embarrassed. "I made you another kite." Then I confess that I made her one, too; and we laugh. The candle burns too short to hold. Out it goes, exposing the starlight, the stars spinning at the window like a visible caroling that slowly, slowly daybreak silences. Possibly we doze; but the beginnings of dawn splash us like cold water: we're up, wide-eyed and wandering while we wait for others to waken. Quite deliberately my friend drops a kettle on the kitchen floor. I tap-dance in front of closed doors. One by one the household emerges, looking as though they'd like to kill us both; but it's Christmas, so they can't. First, a gorgeous breakfast: just everything you can imagine—from flapjacks and fried squirrel to hominy grits and honey-in-the-comb. Which puts everyone in a good humor except my

friend and I. Frankly, we're so impatient to get at the presents we can't eat a mouthful.

Well, I'm disappointed. Who wouldn't be? With socks, a Sunday school shirt, some handkerchiefs, a hand-me-down sweater, and a year's subscription to a religious magazine for children, *The Little Shepherd*. It makes me boil. It really does.

My friend has a better haul. A sack of Satsumas,[4] that's her best present. She is proudest, however, of a white wool shawl knitted by her married sister. But she *says* her favorite gift is the kite I built her. And it *is* very beautiful; though not as beautiful as the one she made me, which is blue and scattered with gold and green Good Conduct stars; moreover, my name is painted on it, "Buddy."

"Buddy, the wind is blowing."

The wind is blowing, and nothing will do till we've run to a pasture below the house where Queenie has scooted to bury her bone (and where, a winter hence, Queenie will be buried, too). There, plunging through the healthy, waist-high grass, we unreel our kites, feel them twitching at the string like sky fish as they swim into the wind. Satisfied, sun-warmed, we sprawl in the grass and peel Satsumas and watch our kites cavort. Soon I forget the socks and hand-me-down sweater. I'm as happy as if we'd already won the fifty-thousand-dollar Grand Prize in that coffee-naming contest.

"My, how foolish I am!" my friend cries, suddenly alert, like a woman remembering too late she has biscuits in the oven. "You know what I've always thought?" she asks in a tone of discovery, and not smiling at me but a point beyond. "I've always thought a body would have to be sick and dying before they saw the Lord. And I imagined that when He came it would be like looking at the Baptist window: pretty as colored glass with the sun pouring through, such a shine you don't know it's getting dark. And it's been a comfort: to think of that shine taking away all the spooky feeling. But I'll wager it never happens. I'll wager at the very end a body realizes the Lord has already shown Himself. That things as they are"—her hand circles in a gesture that gathers clouds and

---

4. **Satsumas:** oranges.

kites and grass and Queenie pawing earth over her bone—"just what they've always seen, was seeing Him. As for me, I could leave the world with today in my eyes."

This is our last Christmas together.

Life separates us. Those who Know Best decide that I belong in a military school. And so follows a miserable succession of bugle-blowing prisons, grim reveille-ridden summer camps. I have a new home too. But it doesn't count. Home is where my friend is, and there I never go.

And there she remains, puttering around the kitchen. Alone with Queenie. Then alone. ("Buddy dear," she writes in her wild hard-to-read script, "yesterday Jim Macy's horse kicked Queenie bad. Be thankful she didn't feel much. I wrapped her in a Fine Linen sheet and rode her in the buggy down to Simpson's pasture where she can be with all her Bones . . .") For a few Novembers she continues to bake her fruitcakes single-handed; not as many, but some: and, of course, she always sends me "the best of the batch." Also, in every letter she encloses a dime wadded in toilet paper: "See a picture show and write me the story." But gradually in her letters she tends to confuse me with her other friend, the Buddy who died in the 1880's; more and more thirteenths are not the only days she stays in bed: a morning arrives in November, a leafless birdless coming of winter morning, when she cannot rouse herself to exclaim: "Oh my, it's fruitcake weather!"

And when that happens, I know it. A message saying so merely confirms a piece of news some secret vein had already received, severing from me an irreplaceable part of myself, letting it loose like a kite on a broken string. That is why, walking across a school campus on this particular December morning, I keep searching the sky. As if I expected to see, rather like hearts, a lost pair of kites hurrying toward heaven.

Woodstove by Andrew Wyeth (1962). Watercolor.

Collection of The William A. Farnsworth Library and Art Museum, Rockland, Maine.

Responding to the Story

Analyzing the Story

Identifying Facts

1. Who is narrating this story, and how old is he when these events take place? What is his relationship to the old woman he calls "my friend"?
2. Give examples of how other members of the family treat Buddy and his friend.
3. While it isn't a dominant element, there is a **plot** in "A Christmas Memory." On the surface, at least, it has to do with making fruitcakes and giving them away—indeed, with most of the rituals of Christmas generosity. Exactly what obstacles do Buddy and his friend have to overcome in order to make their gifts of fruitcakes?
4. What does Buddy's friend discover while flying her kite on their last Christmas day together?

Interpreting Meanings

5. The second paragraph offers a head-to-toe portrait of Buddy's friend. Which details about her **physical appearance** do you think are most important in revealing the kind of person she is?
6. In the third paragraph, Buddy tells us that his friend is "still a child." We usually think of a child as loving, joyful, believing, trusting, and innocent of the evil or meanness we might find in the adult world. Find at least two of her **actions** that reveal that Buddy's friend is a child in any of these ways.
7. On page 63 Buddy lists the **actions** his friend has never done and the actions she has done. Which facts in these lists do you think are most important in revealing the old woman's character and values?
8. What does Buddy's friend say "gets her goat"? What does this **speech** reveal about her character?
9. Some people feel that this is a story about two people who are in search of love. Do you agree? (Consider the reasons why they work so hard to send fruitcakes to total strangers.) Explain whether you think Buddy and his friend get what they want.

10. The ending of "A Christmas Memory" has an emotional impact for most of us—we share in Buddy's sense of loss to a point where we might even feel tears rising. But other readers might find the story too sentimental for their taste. How do you feel about this story and the way it ends?

Writing About the Story

A Creative Response

1. **Describing a Person.** Think of a person you know well, perhaps a parent, a relative, a friend, or a neighbor. Describe this person, showing us something about his or her personality. First, give us some **physical details** about the person's face, hands, or clothing. Second, let us hear the character **speak.** Give him or her a line to say and tell us how it sounds—harsh, musical, critical, loving, bored, whining, amused, angry, or pleading. Third, show your character in **action**—walking down the street, parking a car, or cooking breakfast—something that is typical of what that character does. Although you can change the person's name if you like, choose a real person to describe, and don't make up anything. Write a paragraph.

A Critical Response

2. **Responding to a Character.** Is Buddy's friend a realistic character? Or is she so eccentric, or odd, that she seems unbelievable to you? In a paragraph, give your response to these questions. Cite at least two of the old woman's actions or speeches that support your responses to her.
3. **Analyzing Character.** For an exercise on analyzing the character of Buddy's friend, see page 91.

Analyzing Language and Vocabulary

Figures of Speech

Truman Capote's descriptive details help us use our own imaginations to bring his setting and characters to life. Many of the descriptive details in his story are **figures of speech**—that is, they are statements that compare one thing to something else, something very different from it. In the second paragraph, for example, the narrator compares his friend to a bantam hen. A bantam hen is very different from a human being, but if we use our imaginations, we can picture a person who is small, vigorous, and jumpy, the way a bantam hen is.

Here are some other figures of speech from the story. Answer the questions to show that you understand the comparisons they are based on.

1. "... the Christmas time of year ... fuels the blaze of her heart." (Page 62)
   a. What is the old woman's heart compared to?
   b. If Christmas fuels the blaze of her heart, does it make her loving or indifferent?
2. "Enter: two relatives. Very angry. Potent with eyes that scold, tongues that scald." (Page 66)
   a. What are the relatives' tongues compared to?
   b. If their tongues scald, are their words kind or hurtful?
3. " ... the stars spinning at the window like a visible caroling that slowly, slowly daybreak silences." (Page 68)
   a. What are the stars compared to?
   b. In what way does daybreak "silence" them?
4. " ... the beginnings of dawn splash us like cold water." (Page 68)
   a. What is dawn compared to?
   b. Why is this an appropriate way to describe waking up early?
5. " ... we unreel our kites, feel them twitching at the string like sky fish as they swim into the wind." (Page 68)
   a. What are the kites compared to?
   b. What is the kite string compared to?
   c. What is the wind compared to?

Reading About the Writer

Truman Capote (1924–1984) says he was "sort of dragged up" by assorted elderly relatives who lived in "dirt-road Alabama." He was born in New Orleans, but his father deserted the family, and the boy was shunted about while his mother lived in New York with a new husband. For several years, he attended military academies, which he hated. When he was seventeen, he abandoned formal schooling for good and moved to New York City to learn to write.

Capote came to national prominence with the publication of his first novel, *Other Voices, Other Rooms.* His most famous novel is probably *Breakfast at Tiffany's.* It was made into a movie starring Audrey Hepburn as Holly Golightly, the story's unpredictable and "lost" heroine, who comes to New York from the South to make her fortune.

Capote's most talked-about book is not fiction at all, but an account of a mass murder that took place in Kansas. Called *In Cold Blood*, the book took Capote seven years of research and writing and involved him in much controversy. Capote called the book a "nonfiction novel"—that is, it is a narrative that reads like a novel but whose events are all true.

"A Christmas Memory" was made into a television movie and shown during the Christmas season of 1966. Geraldine Page played Buddy's friend and won an Emmy award for her performance. The photograph in this story is from that production.

THE NO-GUITAR BLUES

Gary Soto

The Mexican-American boy who is the hero of this story is called Fausto. Perhaps you know the old legend of Faust, about the man who sells his soul to the devil in exchange for knowledge and worldly power. You may decide that Soto had something like that legend in mind when he wrote this story about a boy who lives in Fresno, California.

In any case, Fausto's problem is *wanting* something in the worst way. This situation is familiar to all of us, powerfully so when we are young.

Before you read, write a few sentences in your journal explaining what you would do if someone gave you money that you wanted badly but that you did not earn fairly.

The moment Fausto saw the group Los Lobos on "American Bandstand," he knew exactly what he wanted to do with his life—play guitar. His eyes grew large with excitement as Los Lobos ground out a song while teenagers bounced off each other on the crowded dance floor.

He had watched "American Bandstand" for years and had heard Ray Camacho and the Teardrops at Romain Playground, but it had never occurred to him that he too might become a musician. That afternoon Fausto knew his mission in life: to play guitar in his own band; to sweat out his songs and prance around the stage; to make money and dress weird.

Fausto turned off the television set and walked outside, wondering how he could get enough money to buy a guitar. He couldn't ask his parents because they would just say, "Money doesn't grow on trees" or "What do you think we are, bankers?" And besides, they hated rock music. They were into the *conjunto* music of Lydia Mendoza, Flaco Jimenez, and Little Joe and La Familia. And, as Fausto recalled, the last album they bought was *The Chipmunks Sing Christmas Favorites*.

But what the heck, he'd give it a try. He returned inside and watched his mother make tortillas. He leaned against the kitchen counter, trying to work up the nerve to ask her for a guitar. Finally, he couldn't hold back any longer.

"Mom," he said, "I want a guitar for Christmas."

She looked up from rolling tortillas. "Honey, a guitar costs a lot of money."

"How 'bout for my birthday next year," he tried again.

"I can't promise," she said, turning back to her tortillas, "but we'll see."

Fausto walked back outside with a buttered tortilla. He knew his mother was right. His father was a warehouseman at Berven Rugs, where he made good money but not enough to buy everything his children wanted. Fausto decided to mow lawns to earn money, and was pushing the mower down the street before he realized it was winter and no one would hire him. He returned the mower and picked up a rake. He hopped onto his sister's bike (his had two flat tires) and rode north to the nicer section of Fresno in search of work. He went door-to-door, but after three hours he managed to get only one job, and not to rake leaves. He was asked to hurry down to the store to buy a loaf of bread, for which he received a grimy, dirt-caked quarter.

He also got an orange, which he ate sitting at the curb. While he was eating, a dog walked up and sniffed his leg. Fausto pushed him away and threw an orange peel skyward. The dog caught it and ate it in one gulp. The dog looked at Fausto and wagged his tail for more. Fausto tossed him a slice of orange, and the dog snapped it up and licked his lips.

"How come you like oranges, dog?"

The dog blinked a pair of sad eyes and whined.

"What's the matter? Cat got your tongue?" Fausto laughed at his joke and offered the dog another slice.

At that moment a dim light came on inside Fausto's head. He saw that it was sort of a fancy dog, a terrier or something, with dog tags and a shiny collar. And it looked well fed and healthy. In his neighborhood, the dogs were never licensed, and if they got sick they were placed near the water heater until they got well.

This dog looked like he belonged to rich people. Fausto cleaned his juice-sticky hands on his pants and got to his feet. The light in his head grew brighter. It just might work. He called the dog, patted its muscular back, and bent down to check the license.

"Great," he said. "There's an address."

The dog's name was Roger, which struck Fausto as weird because he'd never heard of a dog with a human name. Dogs should have names like Bomber, Freckles, Queenie, Killer, and Zero.

Fausto planned to take the dog home and collect a reward. He would say he had found Roger near the freeway. That would scare the daylights out of the owners, who would be so happy that they would probably give him a reward. He felt bad about lying, but the dog *was* loose. And it might even really be lost, because the address was six blocks away.

Fausto stashed the rake and his sister's bike behind a bush, and, tossing an orange peel every time Roger became distracted, walked the dog to his house. He hesitated on the porch until Roger began to scratch the door with a muddy paw. Fausto had come this far, so he figured he might as well go through with it. He knocked softly. When no one answered, he rang the doorbell. A man in a silky bathrobe and slippers opened the door and seemed confused by the sight of his dog and the boy.

"Sir," Fausto said, gripping Roger by the collar. "I found your dog by the freeway. His dog license says he lives here." Fausto looked down at the dog, then up to the man. "He does, doesn't he?"

The man stared at Fausto a long time before saying in a pleasant voice, "That's right." He pulled his robe tighter around him because of the cold and asked Fausto to come in. "So he was by the freeway?"

"Uh—huh."

"You bad, snoopy dog," said the man, wagging his finger. "You probably knocked over some trash cans, too, didn't you?"

Fausto didn't say anything. He looked around, amazed by this house with its shiny furniture and a television as large as the front window at home. Warm bread smells filled the air and music full of soft tinkling floated in from another room.

"Helen," the man called to the kitchen. "We have a visitor." His wife came into the living room wiping her hands on a dish towel and smiling. "And who have we here?" she asked in one of the softest voices Fausto had ever heard.

"This young man said he found Roger near the freeway."

Fausto repeated his story to her while staring at a perpetual clock with a bell-shaped glass, the kind his aunt got when she celebrated her twenty-fifth anniversary. The lady frowned and said, wagging a finger at Roger, "Oh, you're a bad boy."

"It was very nice of you to bring Roger home," the man said. "Where do you live?"

"By that vacant lot on Olive," he said. "You know, by Brownie's Flower Place."

The wife looked at her husband, then Fausto. Her eyes twinkled triangles of light as she said, "Well, young man, you're probably hungry. How about a turnover?"

"What do I have to turn over?" Fausto asked, thinking she was talking about yard work or something like turning trays of dried raisins.

"No, no, dear, it's a pastry." She took him by the elbow and guided him to a kitchen that sparkled with copper pans and bright yellow wallpaper. She guided him to the kitchen table and gave him a tall glass of milk and something that looked

like an *empanada*. Steamy waves of heat escaped when he tore it in two. He ate with both eyes on the man and woman who stood arm-in-arm smiling at him. They were strange, he thought. But nice.

"That was good," he said after he finished the turnover. "Did you make it, ma'am?"

"Yes, I did. Would you like another?"

"No, thank you. I have to go home now."

As Fausto walked to the door, the man opened his wallet and took out a bill. "This is for you," he said. "Roger is special to us, almost like a son."

Fausto looked at the bill and knew he was in trouble. Not with these nice folks or with his parents but with himself. How could he have been so deceitful? The dog wasn't lost. It was just having a fun Saturday walking around.

"I can't take that."

"You have to. You deserve it, believe me," the man said.

"No, I don't."

"Now don't be silly," said the lady. She took the bill from her husband and stuffed it into Fausto's shirt pocket. "You're a lovely child. Your parents are lucky to have you. Be good. And come see us again, please."

Fausto went out, and the lady closed the door. Fausto clutched the bill through his shirt pocket.

He felt like ringing the doorbell and begging them to please take the money back, but he knew they would refuse. He hurried away, and at the end of the block, pulled the bill from his shirt pocket: it was a crisp twenty-dollar bill.

"Oh, man, I shouldn't have lied," he said under his breath as he started up the street like a zombie. He wanted to run to church for Saturday confession,[1] but it was past four-thirty, when confession stopped.

He returned to the bush where he had hidden the rake and his sister's bike and rode home slowly, not daring to touch the money in his pocket. At home, in the privacy of his room, he examined the twenty-dollar bill. He had never had so much money. It was probably enough to buy a secondhand guitar. But he felt bad, like the time he stole a dollar from the secret fold inside his older brother's wallet.

Fausto went outside and sat on the fence. "Yeah," he said. "I can probably get a guitar for twenty. Maybe at a yard sale—things are cheaper."

---

1. **confession:** in the Roman Catholic Church, a sacrament in which a person seeks forgiveness by telling a priest his or her sins.

His mother called him to dinner.

The next day he dressed for church without anyone telling him. He was going to go to eight o'clock mass.

"I'm going to church, Mom," he said. His mother was in the kitchen cooking *papas* and *chorizo con huevos*. A pile of tortillas lay warm under a dishtowel.

"Oh, I'm so proud of you, Son." She beamed, turning over the crackling *papas*.

His older brother, Lawrence, who was at the table reading the funnies, mimicked, "Oh, I'm so proud of you, my son," under his breath.

At Saint Theresa's he sat near the front. When Father Jerry began by saying that we are all sinners, Fausto thought he looked right at him. Could he know? Fausto fidgeted with guilt. No, he thought. I only did it yesterday.

Fausto knelt, prayed, and sang. But he couldn't forget the man and the lady, whose names he didn't even know, and the *empanada* they had given him. It had a strange name but tasted really good. He wondered how they got rich. And how that dome clock worked. He had asked his mother once how his aunt's clock worked. She said it just worked, the way the refrigerator works. It just did.

Fausto caught his mind wandering and tried to concentrate on his sins. He said a Hail Mary and sang, and when the wicker basket came his way, he stuck a hand reluctantly in his pocket and pulled out the twenty-dollar bill. He ironed it between his palms, and dropped it into the basket. The grown-ups stared. Here was a kid dropping twenty dollars in the basket while they gave just three or four dollars.

There would be a second collection for Saint Vincent de Paul,[2] the lector announced. The wicker baskets again floated in the pews, and this time the adults around him, given a second chance to show their charity, dug deep into their wallets and purses and dropped in fives and tens. This time Fausto tossed in the grimy quarter.

---

2. **Saint Vincent de Paul** (1581–1660): founder of religious orders that care for the sick and poor. St. Vincent de Paul societies today minister to the needy.

Fausto felt better after church. He went home and played football in the front yard with his brother and some neighbor kids. He felt cleared of wrongdoing and was so happy that he played one of his best games of football ever. On one play, he tore his good pants, which he knew he shouldn't have been wearing. For a second, while he examined the hole, he wished he hadn't given the twenty dollars away.

Man, I coulda bought me some Levi's, he thought. He pictured his twenty dollars being spent to buy church candles. He pictured a priest buying an armful of flowers with *his* money.

Fausto had to forget about getting a guitar. He spent the next day playing soccer in his good pants, which were now his old pants. But that night during dinner, his mother said she remembered seeing an old bass guitarron the last time she cleaned out her father's garage.

"It's a little dusty," his mom said, serving his favorite enchiladas, "But I think it works. Grandpa says it works."

Fausto's ears perked up. That was the same kind the guy in Los Lobos played. Instead of asking for the guitar, he waited for his mother to offer it to him. And she did, while gathering the dishes from the table.

"No, Mom, I'll do it," he said, hugging her. "I'll do the dishes forever if you want."

It was the happiest day of his life. No, it was the second-happiest day of his life. The happiest was when his grandfather Lupe placed the guitarron, which was nearly as huge as a washtub, in his arms. Fausto ran a thumb down the strings, which vibrated in his throat and chest. It sounded beautiful, deep and eerie. A pumpkin smile widened on his face.

"OK, *hijo*, now you put your fingers like this," said his grandfather, smelling of tobacco and aftershave. He took Fausto's fingers and placed them on the strings. Fausto strummed a chord on the guitarron, and the bass resounded in their chests.

The guitarron was more complicated than Fausto imagined. But he was confident that after a few more lessons he could start a band that would someday play on "American Bandstand" for the dancing crowds.

Responding to the Story

Analyzing the Story

Identifying Facts

1. Stories are often driven by characters who **want** something very badly and who take steps to get it. What does Fausto want so desperately? Why does he want it?
2. Describe the steps Fausto takes to get what he wants.
3. What **complications** arise, to cause a **conflict** in Fausto's heart?
4. How does Fausto **resolve** his conflict? How is he rewarded at the story's end?

Interpreting Meanings

5. Guilt is what Fausto feels at the story's **climax.** What is he guilty *about*? Would you have felt the same way? Why?
6. That Fausto ends up with a guitarron provides the story with a happy **resolution**. Would you have liked the story as well if he had not been rewarded at the end? Why?

Writing About the Story

A Critical Response

Analyzing a Character. To show us the true character of Fausto, Gary Soto puts the boy in a tight situation and lets us watch as he gets out of it. In a brief essay, analyze Fausto's character—in other words, "take Fausto apart" and explain why he decides to resolve his conflict the way he does. Before you write, review the story to gather information about Fausto's actions and feelings. Then fill out a chart like the following:

Fausto's actions/ feelings	What they reveal
1. Goes to work to earn money for a guitar.	1. He's not lazy. He has ambition.

Reading About the Writer

Gary Soto (1952–   ), like Fausto in this story, grew up as part of a Mexican-American family in Fresno, California. Much of his award-winning fiction and poetry draws on his Mexican-American heritage and childhood memories. In his collection of poems for young adults, called *A Fire in My Hands*, Soto says, "I tried to remain faithful to the common things of my childhood—dogs, alleys, my baseball mitt, curbs, and the fruit of the valley. . . . I wanted to give these things life." Soto currently teaches Chicano Studies and English at the University of California at Berkeley.

Focusing on Background
"Stories sometimes begin with memories"

"I was sucking on a popsicle, playing checkers with my sister, doing nothing on a hot summer day, when a lawn-sniffing beagle wandered onto our block. Immediately, I got it into my head to rescue that dog because I thought it was lost. I hopped off the porch with my sister in tow, and called, 'Here, boy,' snapping my fingers, patting my thigh. Foolishly, the dog stopped. I pulled on his collar, the jingle of dog tags rattling under his chin. Sure enough, he was lost: the dog tag was etched with the name of a faraway street. I hauled the poor pooch into our backyard and telephoned the owner to inform her that her dog was found. The owner arrived at our house after a few hours. She was glad to see the dog, and I was glad when she opened her purse and gave me and my sister each a two-dollar bill. So stories sometimes begin with memory, and a memory is what initiated "No-Guitar Blues," way back in the mid-sixties when there were no leash laws and plenty of roaming dogs."

—Gary Soto

THANK YOU, M'AM

Langston Hughes

She was a large woman with a large purse that had everything in it but hammer and nails. It had a long strap and she carried it slung across her shoulder. It was about eleven o'clock at night, and she was walking alone, when a boy ran up behind her and tried to snatch her purse. The strap broke with the single tug the boy gave it from behind. But the boy's weight and the weight of the purse combined caused him to lose his balance so, instead of taking off full blast as he had hoped, the boy fell on his back on the sidewalk and his legs flew up. The large woman simply turned around and kicked him right square in his blue jeaned sitter. Then she reached down, picked the boy up by his shirt front, and shook him until his teeth rattled.

After that the woman said, "Pick up my pocketbook, boy, and give it here."

She still held him. But she bent down enough to permit him to stoop and pick up her purse. Then she said, "Now ain't you ashamed of yourself?"

Firmly gripped by his shirt front, the boy said, "Yes'm."

The woman said, "What did you want to do it for?"

The boy said, "I didn't aim to."

She said, "You a lie!"

By that time two or three people passed, stopped, turned to look, and some stood watching.

"If I turn you loose, will you run?" asked the woman.

"Yes'm," said the boy.

"Then I won't turn you loose," said the woman. She did not release him.

"I'm very sorry lady, I'm sorry," whispered the boy.

"Um-hum! And your face is dirty. I got a great mind to wash your face for you. Ain't you got nobody home to tell you to wash your face?"

"No'm," said the boy.

"Then it will get washed this evening," said the large woman starting up the street, dragging the frightened boy behind her.

He looked as if he were fourteen or fifteen, frail and willow-wild, in tennis shoes and blue jeans.

The woman said, "You ought to be my son. I would teach you right from wrong. Least I can do right now is to wash your face. Are you hungry?"

"No'm," said the being-dragged boy. "I just want you to turn me loose."

"Was I bothering *you* when I turned that corner?" asked the woman.

"No'm."

"But you put yourself in contact with *me*," said the woman. "If you think that that contact is not going to last awhile, you got another thought coming. When I get through with you, sir, you are going to remember Mrs. Luella Bates Washington Jones."

Sweat popped out on the boy's face and he began to struggle. Mrs. Jones stopped, jerked him around in front of her, put a half-nelson about his neck, and continued to drag him up the street. When she got to her door, she dragged the boy inside, down a hall, and into a large kitchenette-furnished room at the rear of the house. She switched on the light and left the door open. The boy could hear other roomers laughing and talking in the large house. Some of their doors were open, too, so he knew he and the woman were not alone. The woman still had him by the neck in the middle of her room.

She said, "What is your name?"

"Roger," answered the boy.

"Then, Roger, you go to that sink and wash your face," said the woman, whereupon she turned him loose—at last. Roger looked at the door—looked at the woman—looked at the door—*and went to the sink.*

"Let the water run until it gets warm," she said. "Here's a clean towel."

"You gonna take me to jail?" asked the boy, bending over the sink.

"Not with that face, I would not take you no-where," said the woman. "Here I am trying to get home to cook me a bite to eat and you snatch my pocketbook! Maybe you ain't been to your supper either, late as it be. Have you?"

"There's nobody home at my house," said the boy.

"Then we'll eat," said the woman. "I believe you're hungry—or been hungry—to try to snatch my pocketbook."

"I wanted a pair of blue suede shoes," said the boy.

"Well, you didn't have to snatch *my* pocketbook to get some suede shoes," said Mrs. Luella Bates Washington Jones. "You could of asked me."

"M'am?"

The water dripping from his face, the boy looked at her. There was a long pause. A very long pause. After he had dried his face and, not knowing what else to do, dried it again, the boy turned around, wondering what next. The door was open. He could make a dash for it down the hall. He could run, run, run, run, *run!*

The woman was sitting on the daybed. After awhile she said, "I were young once and I wanted things I could not get."

There was another long pause. The boy's mouth opened. Then he frowned, but not knowing he frowned.

The woman said, "Um-hum! You thought I was going to say *but,* didn't you? You thought I was going to say, *but I didn't snatch people's pocket-books.* Well, I wasn't going to say that." Pause. Silence. "I have done things, too, which I would not tell you, son—neither tell God, if He didn't already know. So you set down while I fix us something to eat. You might run that comb through your hair so you will look presentable."

In another corner of the room behind a screen was a gas plate and an icebox. Mrs. Jones got up and went behind the screen. The woman did not watch the boy to see if he was going to run now, nor did she watch her purse which she left behind her on the daybed. But the boy took care to sit on the far side of the room where he thought she could easily see him out of the corner of her eye, if she wanted to. He did not trust the woman *not* to trust him. And he did not want to be mistrusted now.

"Do you need somebody to go the store," asked the boy, "maybe to get some milk or some-thing?"

"Don't believe I do," said the woman, "unless you just want sweet milk yourself. I was going to make cocoa out of this canned milk I got here."

"That will be fine," said the boy.

She heated some lima beans and ham she had in the icebox, made the cocoa, and set the table. The woman did not ask the boy anything about where he lived, or his folks, or anything else that would embarrass him. Instead, as they ate, she told him about her job in a hotel beauty shop that stayed open late, what the work was like, and how all kinds of women came in and out, blondes, redheads, and Spanish. Then she cut him a half of her ten-cent cake.

"Eat some more, son," she said.

When they were finished eating she got up and said, "Now, here, take this ten dollars and buy yourself some blue suede shoes. And next time, do not make the mistake of latching onto *my* pock-etbook *nor nobody else's*—because shoes come by devilish like that will burn your feet. I got to get my rest now. But I wish you would behave yourself, son, from here on in."

She led him down the hall to the front door and opened it. "Goodnight! Behave yourself, boy!" she said, looking out into the street.

The boy wanted to say something else other than, "Thank you, m'am," to Mrs. Luella Bates Washington Jones, but he couldn't do so as he turned at the barren stoop and looked back at the large woman in the door. He barely managed to say "Thank you," before she shut the door. And he never saw her again.

Responding to the Story

Analyzing the Story

Identifying Facts

1. Identify the main **characters** and describe their **conflict.**
2. Describe the unusual steps Mrs. Jones takes to resolve the conflict.
3. Describe the **internal conflict** the boy experiences as he sits in Mrs. Jones's room.

Interpreting Meanings

4. Do you think Mrs. Jones's strategy worked? Did Roger **change** in any way? Find details from the story to support your interpretation.
5. Which of these **characteristics** would you attribute to Mrs. Jones?

   a. Fearless   **d.** Suspicious
   b. Kind   **e.** Generous
   c. Angry   **f.** Trustful

   Find details from the story to support your answers.
6. From what you know about Roger, would you infer that he is a hardened criminal? Does the writer suggest a reason why Roger is snatching purses? Explain.
7. Why do you think Mrs. Jones told Roger that she too had done things she was not proud of?
8. What do you think the boy wanted to say, other than "Thank you, m'am"?

Writing About the Story

A Creative Response

1. **Extending the Story.** Write a letter that Roger sends to Mrs. Jones ten years later. In a separate paragraph, describe Mrs. Jones's circumstances as she is reading the letter.

A Critical Response

2. **Responding to Characters.** Did you find these characters believable? What did you think of Mrs. Jones's solution to her purse-snatching problem? Write your response in a paragraph. Open with a statement explaining in general how the story affected you.

Reading About the Writer

Langston Hughes (1902–1967) is famous chiefly as a poet (see page 253), but he also wrote stories, an autobiography, and novels. Hughes was born in Joplin, Missouri. During his life he traveled—or wandered—to many parts of the world, but he is chiefly associated with Harlem, in New York City, which is the setting of many of his poems and of the story "Thank You, M'am."

BLUES AIN'T NO MOCKIN BIRD

Toni Cade Bambara

Before you start this story, think about what "the blues" are in music. The title of the story comes from an old Mississippi song, in which black people sing the blues as a response to trouble. The song tells us that the blues are not self-pitying, nor are they songs about death (as the legendary song of the mockingbird is said to be). The blues are really fighting songs. As you read the story, decide which character understands what the blues really are.

The puddle had frozen over, and me and Cathy went stompin in it. The twins from next door, Tyrone and Terry, were swingin so high out of sight we forgot we were waitin our turn on the tire. Cathy jumped up and came down hard on her heels and started tap-dancin. And the frozen patch splinterin every which way underneath kinda spooky. "Looks like a plastic spider web," she said. "A sort of weird spider, I guess, with many mental problems." But really it looked like the crystal paperweight Granny kept in the parlor. She was on the back porch, Granny was, making the cakes drunk. The old ladle dripping rum into the Christmas tins, like it used to drip maple syrup into the pails when we lived in the Judsons' woods, like it poured cider into the vats when we were on the Cooper place, like it used to scoop buttermilk and soft cheese when we lived at the dairy.

"Go tell that man we ain't a bunch of trees."

"Ma'am?"

"I said to tell that man to get away from here with that camera." Me and Cathy look over toward the meadow where the men with the station wagon'd been roamin around all mornin. The tall man with a huge camera lassoed to his shoulder was buzzin our way.

"They're makin movie pictures," yelled Tyrone, stiffenin his legs and twistin so the tire'd come down slow so they could see.

"They're makin movie pictures," sang out Terry.

"That boy don't never have anything original to say," say Cathy grown-up.

By the time the man with the camera had cut across our neighbor's yard, the twins were out of the trees swingin low and Granny was onto the steps, the screen door bammin soft and scratchy against her palms. "We thought we'd get a shot or two of the house and everything and then——"

"Good mornin," Granny cut him off. And smiled that smile.

"Good mornin," he said, head all down the way Bingo does when you yell at him about the bones on the kitchen floor. "Nice place you got here, aunty. We thought we'd take a——"

"Did you?" said Granny with her eyebrows. Cathy pulled up her socks and giggled.

"Nice things here," said the man, buzzin his camera over the yard. The pecan barrels, the sled, me and Cathy, the flowers, the printed stones along the driveway, the trees, the twins, the toolshed.

"I don't know about the thing, the it, and the stuff," said Granny, still talkin with her eyebrows. "Just people here is what I tend to consider."

Camera man stopped buzzin. Cathy giggled into her collar.

"Mornin, ladies," a new man said. He had come up behind us when we weren't lookin. "And

Her World by Philip Evergood
(1945). Watercolor.

The Metropolitan Museum of Art,
Arthur H. Hearn Fund, 1950.
(50.29)

gents," discoverin the twins givin him a nasty look. "We're filmin for the county," he said with a smile. "Mind if we shoot a bit around here?"

"I do indeed," said Granny with no smile. Smilin man was smiling up a storm. So was Cathy. But he didn't seem to have another word to say, so he and the camera man backed on out the yard, but you could hear the camera buzzin still. "Suppose you just shut that machine off," said Granny real low through her teeth and took a step down off the porch and then another.

"Now, aunty," Camera said, pointin the thing straight at her.

"Your mama and I are not related."

Smilin man got his notebook out and a chewed-up pencil. "Listen," he said moving back into our yard, "we'd like to have a statement from you . . . for the film. We're filmin for the county, see. Part of the food stamp campaign. You know about the food stamps?"

Granny said nuthin.

"Maybe there's somethin you want to say for the film. I see you grow your own vegetables," he smiled real nice. "If more folks did that, see, there'd be no need——"

Granny wasn't sayin nuthin. So they backed on out, buzzin at our clothesline and the twins' bicycles, then back on down to the meadow. The twins were danglin in the tire, lookin at Granny. Me and Cathy were waitin, too, cause Granny always got somethin to say. She teaches steady with no let-up. "I was on this bridge one time," she started off. "Was a crowd cause this man was goin to jump, you understand. And a minister was there and the police and some other folks. His woman was there, too."

"What was they doin?" asked Tyrone.

"Tryin to talk him out of it was what they was doin. The minister talkin about how it was a mortal sin, suicide. His woman takin bites out of her own hand and not even knowin it, so nervous and cryin and talkin fast."

"So what happened?" asked Tyrone.

"So here comes . . . this person . . . with a camera, takin pictures of the man and the minister and the woman. Takin pictures of the man in his misery about to jump, cause life so bad and people

been messin with him so bad. This person takin up the whole roll of film practically. But savin a few, of course."

"Of course," said Cathy, hatin the person. Me standin there wonderin how Cathy knew it was "of course" when I didn't and it was *my* grandmother.

After a while Tyrone say, "Did he jump?"

"Yeh, did he jump?" say Terry all eager.

And Granny just stared at the twins till their faces swallow up the eager and they don't even care any more about the man jumpin. Then she goes back onto the porch and lets the screen door go for itself. I'm lookin to Cathy to finish the story cause she knows Granny's whole story before me even. Like she knew how come we move so much and Cathy ain't but a third cousin we picked up on the way last Thanksgivin visitin. But she knew it was on account of people drivin Granny crazy till she'd get up in the night and start packin. Mumblin and packin and wakin everybody up sayin, "Let's get on away from here before I kill me somebody." Like people wouldn't pay her for things like they said they would. Or Mr. Judson bringin us boxes of old clothes and raggedy magazines. Or Mrs. Cooper comin in our kitchen and touchin everything and sayin how clean it all was. Granny goin crazy, and Granddaddy Cain pullin her off the people, sayin, "Now, now, Cora." But next day loadin up the truck, with rocks all in his jaw, madder than Granny in the first place.

"I read a story once," said Cathy soundin like Granny teacher. "About this lady Goldilocks who barged into a house that wasn't even hers. And not invited, you understand. Messed over the people's groceries and broke up the people's furniture. Had the nerve to sleep in the folks' bed."

"Then what happened?" asked Tyrone. "What they do, the folks, when they come in to all this mess?"

"Did they make her pay for it?" asked Terry, makin a fist. "I'd've made her pay me."

I didn't even ask. I could see Cathy actress was very likely to just walk away and leave us in mystery about this story which I heard was about some bears.

"Did they throw her out?" asked Tyrone, like

his father sounds when he's bein extra nasty-plus to the washin-machine man.

"Woulda," said Terry. "I woulda gone upside her head with my fist and——"

"You woulda done whatcha always do—go cry to Mama, you big baby," said Tyrone. So naturally Terry starts hittin on Tyrone, and next thing you know they tumblin out the tire and rollin on the ground. But Granny didn't say a thing or send the twins home or step out on the steps to tell us about how we can't afford to be fightin amongst ourselves. She didn't say nuthin. So I get into the tire to take my turn. And I could see her leanin up against the pantry table, starin at the cakes she was puttin up for the Christmas sale, mumblin real low and grumpy and holdin her forehead like it wanted to fall off and mess up the rum cakes.

Behind me I hear before I can see Granddaddy Cain comin through the woods in his field boots. Then I twist around to see the shiny black oilskin cuttin through what little left there was of yellows, reds, and oranges. His great white head not quite round cause of this bloody thing high on his shoulder, like he was wearin a cap on sideways. He takes the shortcut through the pecan grove, and the sound of twigs snapping overhead and underfoot travels clear and cold all the way up to us. And here comes Smilin and Camera up behind him like they was goin to do somethin. Folks like to go for him sometimes. Cathy say it's because he's so tall and quiet and like a king. And people just can't stand it. But Smilin and Camera don't hit him in the head or nuthin. They just buzz on him as he stalks by with the chicken hawk slung over his shoulder, squawkin, drippin red down the back of the oilskin. He passes the porch and stops a second for Granny to see he's caught the hawk at last, but she's just starin and mumblin, and not at the hawk. So he nails the bird to the toolshed door, the hammerin crackin through the eardrums. And the bird flappin himself to death and droolin down the door to paint the gravel in the driveway red, then brown, then black. And the two men movin up on tiptoe like they was invisible or we were blind, one.

"Get them persons out of my flower bed, Mister Cain," say Granny moanin real low like at a funeral.

"How come your grandmother calls her husband 'Mister Cain' all the time?" Tyrone whispers all loud and noisy and from the city and don't know no better. Like his mama, Miss Myrtle, tell us never mind the formality as if we had no better breeding than to call her Myrtle, plain. And then this awful thing—a giant hawk—come wailin up over the meadow, flyin low and tilted and screamin, zigzaggin through the pecan grove, breakin branches and hollerin, snappin past the clothesline, flyin every which way, flyin into things reckless with crazy.

"He's come to claim his mate," say Cathy fast, and ducks down. We all fall quick and flat into the gravel driveway, stones scrapin my face. I squinch my eyes open again at the hawk on the door, tryin to fly up out of her death like it was just a sack flown into by mistake. Her body holdin her there on that nail, though. The mate beatin the air overhead and clutchin for hair, for heads, for landin space.

The camera man duckin and bendin and runnin and fallin, jigglin the camera and scared. And Smilin jumpin up and down swipin at the huge bird, tryin to bring the hawk down with just his raggedy ole cap. Granddaddy Cain straight up and silent, watchin the circles of the hawk, then aimin the hammer off his wrist. The giant bird fallin, silent and slow. Then here comes Camera and Smilin all big and bad now that the awful screechin thing is on its back and broken, here they come. And Granddaddy Cain looks up at them like it was the first time noticin, but not payin them too much mind cause he's listenin, we all listenin, to that low groanin music comin from the porch. And we figure any minute, somethin in my back tells me any minute now, Granny gonna bust through that screen with somethin in her hand and murder on her mind. So Granddaddy say above the buzzin, but quiet, "Good day, gentlemen." Just like that. Like he'd invited them in to play cards and they'd stayed too long and all the sandwiches were gone and Reverend Webb was droppin by and it was time to go.

They didn't know what to do. But like Cathy say, folks can't stand Granddaddy tall and silent and like a king. They can't neither. The smile the men smilin is pullin the mouth back and showin the teeth. Lookin like the wolf man, both of them. Then Granddaddy holds his hand out—this huge hand I used to sit in when I was a baby and he'd carry me through the house to my mother like I was a gift on a tray. Like he used to on the trains. They called the other men just waiters. But they spoke of Granddaddy separate and said, The Waiter. And said he had engines in his feet and motors in his hands and couldn't no train throw him off and couldn't nobody turn him round. They were big enough for motors, his hands were. He held that one hand out all still and it gettin to be not at all a hand but a person in itself.

"He wants you to hand him the camera," Smilin whispers to Camera, tiltin his head to talk secret like they was in the jungle or somethin and come upon a native that don't speak the language. The men start untyin the straps, and they put the camera into that great hand speckled with the hawk's blood all black and crackly now. And the hand don't even drop with the weight, just the fingers move, curl up around the machine. But Granddaddy lookin straight at the men. They lookin at each other and everywhere but at Granddaddy's face.

"We filmin for the county, see," say Smilin. "We puttin together a movie for the food stamp program . . . filmin all around these parts. Uhh, filmin for the county."

"Can I have my camera back?" say the tall man with no machine on his shoulder, but still keepin it high like the camera was still there or needed to be. "Please, sir."

Then Granddaddy's other hand flies up like a sudden and gentle bird, slaps down fast on top of the camera and lifts off half like it was a calabash[1] cut for sharing.

"Hey," Camera jumps forward. He gathers up the parts into his chest and everything unrollin and fallin all over. "Whatcha tryin to do? You'll ruin the film." He looks down into his chest of metal reels and things like he's protectin a kitten from the cold.

"You standin in the missus' flower bed," say Granddaddy. "This is our own place."

The two men look at him, then at each other, then back at the mess in the camera man's chest, and they just back off. One sayin over and over all the way down to the meadow, "Watch it, Bruno. Keep ya fingers off the film." Then Granddaddy picks up the hammer and jams it into the oilskin pocket, scrapes his boots, and goes into the house. And you can hear the squish of his boots headin through the house. And you can see the funny shadow he throws from the parlor window onto the ground by the string-bean patch. The hammer draggin the pocket of the oilskin out so Granddaddy looked even wider. Granny was hummin now—high, not low and grumbly. And she was doin the cakes again, you could smell the molasses from the rum.

"There's this story I'm goin to write one day," say Cathy dreamer. "About the proper use of the hammer."

"Can I be in it?" Tyrone say with his hand up like it was a matter of first come, first served.

"Perhaps," say Cathy, climbin onto the tire to pump us up. "If you there and ready."

---

1. **calabash:** a kind of fruit.

Responding to the Story

Analyzing the Story

Identifying Facts

1. Which **characters** play a part in this story's **conflict**? Which characters are only onlookers?
2. What details in the first paragraph tell us that the family has lived in many different places?

What details later on in the story explain why Granny has moved so often?
3. Why do the two men want to film the family? Why does Granny resent the film crew?
4. What **action** does Granddaddy Cain finally take to **resolve** Granny's conflict with the camera crew?

Interpreting Meanings

5. This strong story is rich in **character**. The central character—the one our attention is focused on—is obviously Granny. Is Granny proud, sensitive, independent? Find at least three of Granny's **speeches** or **actions** that reveal the kind of person she is.

6. Explain why Granny tells the children the story about the man on the bridge. What does that particular story reveal about her values?

7. That shrewd observer Cathy seems to want to imitate Granny. Why does Cathy bring up the story about Goldilocks? How does "Cathy teacher" interpret the story?

8. How are the suffering hawks in the story like Granny and her husband? Explain whether or not you think Granddaddy Cain treats the birds the way the film crew treats his family.

9. Think back now to the story's title, and what it says about "the blues." Toni Bambara says that though many outside experts have tried to interpret the blues, only the people who sing them can understand what they are about. In this story, how are the cameramen like those outside experts? What have they failed to understand about Granny and her family?

10. What does Granddaddy Cain's response to the cameramen reveal about his **character**? Suppose you were in the places of Granny and Granddaddy Cain in this story. Describe how you would have responded to the film crew.

Writing About the Story

A Creative Response

1. **Narrating a Related Incident.** Think of an incident in which you resented someone's invasion of your privacy or sense of self-respect. If you have never experienced such an invasion personally, perhaps you've watched it happen to someone else—perhaps on television, where human misery often makes up the bulk of the evening news. Tell about this incident in a paragraph, and explain how it made you feel.

A Critical Response

2. **Analyzing Character.** Think of three adjectives that you would use to describe the character of Granny. Then find at least three incidents from the story that illustrate her character. Look for examples of Granny's **words,** her **actions,** and her **effect on others.** Write a topic sentence using the three adjectives, and develop the topic with the examples you've chosen from the story. Write a paragraph. (For help, see the exercise on page 91.)

3. **Describing the Story's Effect.** In her comment that follows (see "Focusing on Background"), Toni Bambara says that she prefers "upbeat" fiction and that she likes "energetic fun" and "optimism." In a paragraph, explain whether or not you believe this story's effect is upbeat and optimistic. Refer to the story to support your opinion.

4. **Comparing the Character in a Story to the Speaker of a Poem.** In a paragraph, compare the speaker of the following poem with Granny. The chart should help you outline exactly their similarities. Fill this out before you write.

> **Silent, but . . .**
> I may be silent, but
> I'm thinking.
> I may not talk, but
> Don't mistake me for a wall.
> —Tsuboi Shigeji

	Bambara	Shigeji
Line from beginning of story that sounds like poem.		
How Granny and speaker of poem do *not* want to be treated.		
How they *do* want to be treated.		

Analyzing Language and Vocabulary

Dialects

As language is spoken, it changes. All of us, in fact, alter language slightly. We take the sounds we first learn from our parents, brothers, and sisters, and then we add what we hear at school, at work, on the radio, on TV, and in the movies.

Thus, our own particular speech soon becomes as distinctive as the features on our face. We sometimes can even recognize a person simply by overhearing a single spoken word. When we meet new people for the first time, their speech can tell us about the region they come from and about their social, economic, and educational backgrounds.

For this reason, a writer tries to breathe life into a fictional character by letting us hear *how* the person speaks, as well as *what* the person says.

Suppose a writer is setting a story in a particular region—for instance, the deep South or a barrio in Los Angeles or the Flatbush section of Brooklyn. The way the people in the story speak must persuade us (even if we've never been to these places) that they are using the region's special grammar and expressions and pronunciations—in other words, that they are speaking its **dialect.**

Having an "ear" for dialect—being able to hear the peculiarities of speech, its rhythm and flow, the words that are emphasized, the contractions, the slang, the pronunciations—is critical for a writer. The writer with a sensitive ear will record the Bostonians' broad *a*'s, the way they pronounce *r*'s for *h*'s and *h*'s for *r*'s, so that "idea" becomes "idear" and "dear" becomes "deah." In a story set in a rural black neighborhood in Arkansas, the writer will hear "ask" become "aks" and "my" become "mah," and will notice how final consonants are dropped so that "don't" becomes "don."

You saw how deftly Toni Cade Bambara reproduces a regional black dialect in "Blues Ain't No Mockin Bird." Flannery O'Connor's stories take us into another area of Southern upcountry with true regional inflection. Here is a conversation from "A View of the Woods":

> "Let's go get us an ice-cream cone," he suggested, looking at her with concern.
>
> "I don't want no ice-cream cone," she said.
>
> . . . "How'd you like to visit the ten-cent store while I tend to a little bidnis of mine?" he asked. "You can buy yourself something with a quarter I brought along."
>
> "I ain't got nothing to do in no ten-cent store," she said. "I don't want no quarter of yours."

That "bidnis" in the man's mouth is so exactly right that, when we hear it, the scene opens before us convincingly, and we know we're in the presence of an artist.

Ernest Hemingway became a master of writing English speech with the flavor of Spanish. By inverting sentence structure, he was able to give his dialogue a formality that makes us think we are listening to Spanish. Thus, Montoya speaks to Jake Barnes in *The Sun Also Rises:*

> "Tonight at seven o'clock they bring in the Villar bulls, and tomorrow come the Miuras. Do you all go down?"

Here is Mark Twain depicting one of his backwoods dialects in *Huckleberry Finn:*

> "I'll learn people to bring up a boy to put on airs over his own father and let on to be better'n what *he* is. You lemme catch you fooling around that school again, you hear? Your mother couldn't read, and she couldn't write, nurther, before she died. None of the family couldn't before *they* died. *I* can't; and here you're a-swelling yourself up like this."

1. Dialects have several features. Among these features are the use of nonstandard grammar and the pronunciation of certain words in nonstandard ways. In Bambara's story, for example, Cathy says: "That boy don't never have anything original to say." (If this speech were written in standard English, it would say: "That boy doesn't ever have anything original to say.") In another common example of dialect, the narrator says that they were "stompin" on the ice. (In standard English, the speaker would say "stomping.") Look through the story and find at least ten other examples of dialect. Arrange your examples under two headings:

Changes in grammar	Changes in pronunciation

2. Take one of Granny's speeches or conversations in "Blues Ain't No Mockin Bird," and rewrite it in standard, formal English, without Granny's unusual pronunciations and grammar. How much of Granny's character is lost when her dialect is taken away from her?

3. Listen to an actual conversation—in the bus, at the dinner table, in a restaurant, at a ball game. Reproduce in writing the exact speech of the people talking. Try to help your readers hear the particular ways the speakers pronounce words, construct sentences, and create special rhythms in their speech. If good live dialogue doesn't come your way, you may find material on TV.

Reading About the Writer

Toni Cade Bambara (1939–   ) says she writes upbeat fiction because she was raised on stories of champions: Harriet Tubman, Ida B. Wells, Paul Robeson, and her Grandmother Annie. She grew up in Harlem, Brooklyn, and Jersey City. She attended schools in New York City and the South, and she graduated from Queens College in New York.

In the sixties, Bambara studied theater in Italy and mime in France. When she returned to New York, she became interested in dance, but she also did social work in local hospitals and community centers. Eventually she turned to teaching, and over the years she has taught at various colleges and universities, including Rutgers University in New Brunswick, New Jersey, and Spelman College in Atlanta, Georgia.

"Blues Ain't No Mockin Bird" comes from Bambara's first collection of stories, called *Gorilla, My Love.* Many of these stories are told in the voice of a sassy young girl who is tough, compassionate, and brave. Bambara has also published another short-story collection called *The Sea Birds Are Still Alive* and a novel, *The Salt Eaters.*

The name Bambara is the name of a tribe in northwest Africa. Toni Cade found the name in a sketchbook packed away in her great-grandmother's trunk, and she took it for her own.

Focusing on Background
A Comment from the Writer

"Folks come up to me 'lowing as how since I am a writer I would certainly want to hear blah, blah, blah, blah. They . . . tell me about every ugly overheard and lived-through nightmare imaginable. They've got the wrong writer. The kid can't use it. I straightaway refer them to the neighborhood healer, certain that anyone so intoxicated would surely welcome a cleansing. But they persist—'Hey, this is for real, square business. The truth.' I don't doubt that the horror tales are factual. I don't even doubt that ugly is a truth for somebody . . . somehow. But I'm not convinced that ugly is *the* truth that can save us, redeem us. The old folks teach that. Be triflin' and ugly and they say, 'Deep down, gal, you know that ain't right,' appealing to a truth about our deep-down nature. Good enough for me. Besides, I can't get happy writing ugly weird. If I'm not laughing while I work, I conclude that I am not communicating nourishment, since laughter is the most sure-fire healant I know. I don't know all my readers, but I know well for whom I write. And I want for them no less than I want for myself— wholesomeness.

"It all sounds so la-di-da and tra-la-la. I can afford to be sunny. I'm but one voice in the chorus. The literature(s) of our time are a collective effort, dependent on so many views, on so many people's productions. There's a lot of work to do, a lot of records to get straight, a lot of living to share, a lot to plumb. This reader wants it all—the oddball, the satiric, the grim, the ludicrous, what have you. As for my own writing, I prefer the upbeat. It pleases me to blow three or four choruses of just sheer energetic fun and optimism. . . ."

—Toni Cade Bambara

Using Adjectives to Create Character

Literary Model

In this passage from his novel *David Copperfield*, Charles Dickens uses adjectives to bring the awesome Miss Murdstone to life.

> It was Miss Murdstone who was arrived, and a gloomy-looking lady she was: dark, like her brother, whom she greatly resembled in face and voice, and with very heavy eyebrows, nearly meeting over her large nose, as if, being disabled by the wrongs of her sex from wearing whiskers, she had carried them to that account. She brought with her two uncompromising hard black boxes, with her initials on the lids in hard brass nails. When she paid the coachman she took her money out of a hard steel purse, and she kept the purse in a very jail of a bag which hung upon her arm by a heavy chain, and shut up like a bite. I had never, at that time, seen such a metallic lady altogether as Miss Murdstone was.
>
> —from *David Copperfield,*
> Charles Dickens

Grammar Note

Adjectives are words that modify nouns or pronouns—that is, they describe persons, places, or things. Adjectives make something more definite. Truman Capote on page 62 uses two adjectives to describe Buddy's cousin:

"A woman with *shorn, white* hair . . ."

Later on, on the same page, he uses other adjectives to describe her eyes:

". . . her eyes are *sherry-colored* and *timid* . . ."

As you can see, adjectives can be single words or compound words. Whole phrases can also function as adjectives. Capote, still describing Buddy's unusual cousin, says:

"She is *small* and *sprightly, like a Bantam hen.*"

Examining the Writer's Style

Working with a partner, use the following suggestions and questions to fill out the "adjective chart" below.

1. Make a list of all the adjectives Dickens uses to describe Miss Murdstone herself.
2. What adjective is used most often to describe Miss Murdstone's possessions?
3. How does this adjective relate to the word *metallic*?
4. List at least five other details in this description that relate in some way to *metallic*.
5. Look at your list of adjectives and choose the one that makes Miss Murdstone most vivid to you. Explain your choice. Are there any adjectives you would change, or add to this list?

Adjectives	Adjectives used most often	Five details relating to "metallic"

Using Adjectives in Your Writing

1. **Describing a Real Person.** Suppose you are a reporter for an entertainment magazine. Write a description of an actual musician, movie star, or some other entertainer, as the first paragraph of a biographical profile.

   a. Before you write, put a picture of the person in your mind. Begin with the face. Think about how the face reveals the person's personality. Then think about the person's special characteristics. Use adjectives to paint a picture of the person with words. Do not use the person's name in your description.

   b. Trade descriptions with a partner. Identify the adjectives in your partner's description. You might mark the most vivid descriptive passages in some color (perhaps yellow). Then mark in another color (perhaps blue) any passages that should be revised, using more effective adjectives. Be careful not to overuse adjectives.

   c. Rewrite your own description based on your partner's response to it. Then read your description to your classmates to see if they can determine the identity of the entertainer.

2. **Reworking Miss Murdstone.** Suppose you are Charles Dickens and you have changed your mind about the character of Miss Murdstone. Now you would like to suggest that she is not "metallic," but something else—perhaps she is "soft," or "sunny," or "sugary." You probably will want to give your character a new name also, since *Murdstone* has a bleak quality about it. Before you begin rewriting Dickens's description, fill out a chart with adjectives that fit your new character. Remember that adjectives can be single words, compound words, or phrases.

A Box of Adjectives

If you sometimes find it hard to think of adjectives, here are some that can be used to describe a character directly. You might make a second list of adjectives that describe character traits that are opposite to each of these:

sly	shallow
creative	clever
emotional	childlike
loving	brave
loyal	generous
possessive	dishonest
insecure	witty

ANALYZING CHARACTER

Writing Assignment

Write a four- or five-paragraph essay analyzing the character of Buddy's friend in "A Christmas Memory" (page 62).

Background

When you analyze a character, you take a person apart to see what makes him or her "tick." Remember that in stories, as in life, character can be revealed in five ways: by **speech,** by **appearance,** by **thoughts,** by **what other people in the story say or think about the character,** by **actions.** In fiction, character can also be directly revealed by the author: Jane is selfish. Buster is frequently silly.

Prewriting

1. To gather ideas for your character analysis, you might try a technique called **clustering.** Here is how it works: Form a small group with one or two classmates. Then use the following steps to make a cluster of the characteristics of Buddy's friend:

    a. Write the character's name on a sheet of paper. Circle it.

    b. For three minutes, exchange ideas aloud. Think of as many words as possible that describe the personality of Buddy's friend— write down anything that occurs to you when you think about her.

    c. Circle these character traits, and connect them to the name with a line.

    A partially completed cluster about Buddy's friend might look like this:

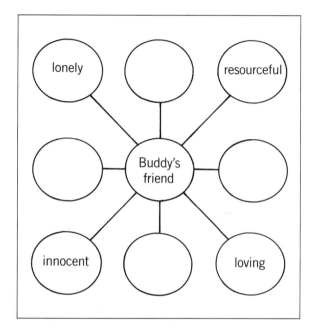

2. Continue clustering by yourself; include any ideas or associations that occur to you.

3. Review your diagram to be sure you've included all the traits that you learned from Buddy's friend's **speech,** from her **appearance,** from her **thoughts,** from **what other characters think** of her, and from her **actions.**

4. Now you are ready to focus your ideas and find details from the story to support them. Another "diagram" might help. Write down three character traits you'd like to focus on and draw a box around each one. Underneath each box, "hang" three more boxes. In each of these boxes, give an example of an action or a conversation (etc.) from the story which illustrates that characteristic of Buddy's friend. Be sure to write in sentences. As an example, one part of the following diagram has been completed.

1. She is resourceful.	2.	3.
She gets whiskey for free.		
She saves money for ingredients.		
She enters contests to win money.		

5. Look over your boxed ''outline'' of character traits. Then write a general statment that summarizes the character of Buddy's friend as you see it. This general statement will be the **thesis statement** of your essay—it will state your main topic.

Writing

Now you are ready to write. You have thought a great deal about Buddy's friend and have enough material to describe her character in four or five paragraphs. In the first paragraph, sum up the topic of your essay with a thesis statement. Then, in the next three paragraphs, discuss three personality traits. Use three specific examples from the story to illustrate each trait. End your essay with a good concluding sentence in the fourth paragraph, or write a fifth paragraph that summarizes your character analysis.

Here is how you might begin a character analysis of Buddy's friend. Notice that the first sentence contains the essay's thesis statement.

In "A Christmas Memory," Truman Capote draws a portrait of an odd but loving old woman who is a lonely young boy's best friend. Buddy's friend has childlike innocence in spite of her age, and in spite of the cruel way she is treated by her relatives. Although this old woman has almost no money, she is resourceful enough to find a way to make Christmas fruitcakes. And her great love is revealed when we discover that she sends the cakes to strangers. Through Buddy's eyes, we see how a lonely little boy was blessed by this woman's love and friendship.	**States the thesis.** **Cites one character trait.** **Cites a second character trait.** **Cites a third character trait.**

Checklist for Revision
1. Have you cited the story's author and title?
2. Have you included a thesis statement?
3. Have you discussed three personality traits?
4. Have you used at least three details from the story to illustrate each character trait?
5. Do you have a good conclusion?

Every story would be another story . . . if it took up its characters and plot and happened somewhere else.

—Eudora Welty

Setting: A Sense of Place

A storyteller, like a travel agent, can help gather you up from wherever you are and put you down in another setting on earth or, for that matter, on a distant planet. That other setting may be a spot you've always wanted to visit, such as a deluxe hotel in Hawaii, or a place where you don't want to be, such as a sinking ship.

Escape—getting away from the same old sights, smells, and obligations—is certainly one of the easy pleasures of reading. But if that is all that happens, our reading experience is just a diversion. In fact, the term "escape reading" suggests that this kind of reading does not have much to do with our lives in the real world.

Setting as a Background

Setting tells us where and when the story takes place. Setting can include the locale of the story, the weather, the time of day, and the time period. One purpose of setting is to provide **background**— a place for the characters to live and act in. A good setting helps to make the story real and believable.

Truman Capote opens his story "A Christmas Memory" (page 62) by ordering us to imagine a setting: a morning in late November "more than twenty years ago" (longer ago today), a kitchen in a "spreading" old house in a country town, a black stove, a round table, a fireplace with two rocking chairs—and in the fireplace, the season's first roaring fire. This setting provides the backdrop for the story's characters. Because it is so vividly described, we feel that we are there.

Setting and Conflict

In some stories, setting even provides the **conflict.** One of the oldest story plots in the world is the one in which a person fights against something in the physical world—a drought, a horde of ants, the heat of the desert, the leeches in the jungle.

Setting and Character

Places where people live and make their homes can reveal a great deal about their **characters.** Setting is often used in stories to tell us something about the people who live in it. In "A Christmas Memory," for example, we learn that Buddy's friend sleeps in a "scrap-quilt-covered iron bed, painted rose pink" and that she grows the "prettiest japonicas in town." This setting suggests her simplicity and her yearning for beauty. (Imagine how differently we would feel about her if she slept in a pile of rags that smelled sour, or if her yard was muddy with no flowers.) In contrast to Buddy's friend, Mr. Haha Jones lives in a different setting. His café is "festooned inside and out with chains of garish-gay naked light bulbs." It stands by the river's "muddy edge." The moss on the trees is like "gray mist." His café is, in daylight, "shabby and deserted." There is something sinister about Haha's setting, as there is about Haha's character (even though he is also kind).

Setting and Atmosphere

Setting can also provide **atmosphere** or **mood**—it can affect the way we feel. Some settings naturally make us feel fear or uneasiness (midnight, a lonely house, the scraping of a branch on the window). Other settings naturally make us feel happy (morning, a garden, the song of a bird). The setting of the Sherlock Holmes stories creates, for us today, the mysterious atmosphere of old London: the gas-lit streets, the fog that shrouds the city, the horse-drawn carriages, the lonely houses in the nearby countryside where deeds of wickedness are committed.

The Houses of Parliament, London by Claude Monet (1904). Oil.

Musée D'Orsay, Paris

How Is Setting Created?

Language is what takes us to Holmes's London or to Capote's rural Alabama. One of the wonders of language is that it can summon up a place for us so immediately. Language can reach us through our five senses and put us right in the middle of the action, along with the characters themselves.

Suppose we read about Rudyard Kipling's India or Jack London's Alaska or Ernest Hemingway's Spain, and then go to check out the actual place itself. We often find that the real place is not quite equal to the picture we had already formed in our minds. This is a tribute not only to the skill of the writer, but also to our own fertile imaginations.

Like the other elements of storytelling, painting a setting is a skill. To create a believable setting, or one that can make us feel pleasure, mystery, or fear, the writer must select the right detail, or image. **Images** are words that call forth the use of one of our senses—sight, smell, touch, hearing, and at times, even taste.

Suppose a writer wants us to imagine a setting as ordinary as the drugstore where Ellen is telling Harold she never wants to see him again. We would get tired of a list of all the objects the couple sees on the shelves. Similarly, we would get tired of a list of all the trees, rocks, and puddles in the mountain pass where the outlaws are waiting for the stagecoach. However, you will be amazed at what your own imagination will supply if the writer prompts it with the right image. In the drugstore scene, the right image might be a row of bottles, each bearing the label *Poison.* In the mountain pass the right image might be a circling vulture or the water that seeps into the outlaws' cracked boots.

If we are told that we are landing near a canal on Mars and that the light outside is very white, we'll supply not only the glare in the window of the spaceship, but also the intense heat, the dryness of the air, possibly even the sweat trickling down the pilot's back.

When a writer supplies a few right images, we will provide the rest of the scenery. We might draw from our own experience, or we might go beyond our memory into our instincts and into the pool of our subconscious. There we will find all kinds of unaccountable knowledge—of desert islands, palaces, and planets—where, so far as we know, we have never been.

This exercise of our imaginations is what makes fiction a more personal and mind-enhancing experience than, for all their lazy pleasures, the ready-made images of movies and television.

Thinking About Setting

Thus, when we read, we can leave our actual bodies at home while our imaginations wing us off to places like Istanbul or Tierra del Fuego or Venus. (There's another advantage to fictional travel: we won't encounter drinking water that makes us sick.) But setting in fiction can also be crucial to a story. When you read, ask yourself these questions about the story's setting:

1. What kind of a place does the story take place in? What do I know about its season, climate, and time of day?

2. Are the characters in any kind of conflict with their setting?

3. Does their setting (their homes, yards, towns, and traditions) help me to understand the nature of the characters?

4. What kind of atmosphere does the setting create? Is it a place I'd like to live in, or one I'd probably avoid?

"**T**here's another advantage to fictional travel: we won't encounter drinking water that makes us sick."

TOP MAN

James Ramsey Ullman

The setting of "Top Man" is essential to the story. This, in fact, is the very purest form of story—in which a person is in conflict with the environment. As you read, notice how the mountain is even given human characteristics, so that it seems to become a character in the story.

The gorge bent. The walls fell suddenly away and we came out on the edge of a bleak, boulder-strewn valley. And there it was.

Osborn saw it first. He had been leading the column, threading his way slowly among the huge rock masses of the gorge's mouth. Then he came to the first flat, bare place and stopped. He neither pointed nor cried out, but every man behind him knew instantly what it was. The long file sprang taut, like a jerked rope. As swiftly as we could, but in complete silence, we came out into the open ground where Osborn stood, and raised our eyes with his. In the records of the Indian Topographical Survey it says:

Kalpurtha: a mountain in the Himalayas, altitude 28,900 ft. The highest peak in British India and fourth highest in the world. Also known as K3. A Tertiary formation of sedimentary limestone——

There were men among us who had spent months of their lives—in some cases, years—reading, thinking, planning about what now lay before us, but at that moment statistics and geology, knowledge, thought and plans, were as remote and forgotten as the faraway Western cities from which we had come. We were men bereft of everything but eyes, everything but the single, electric perception: There it was!

Before us the valley stretched away into miles of rocky desolation. To right and left it was bounded by low ridges which, as the eye followed them, slowly mounted and drew closer together until the valley was no longer a valley at all, but a narrowing, rising corridor between the cliffs. What happened then I can describe only as a single, stupendous crash of music. At the end of the corridor and above it—so far above it that it shut out half the sky—hung the blinding white mass of K3.

It was like the many pictures I had seen, and at the same time utterly unlike them. The shape was there, and the familiar distinguishing features—the sweeping skirt of glaciers; the monstrous vertical precipices of the face and the jagged ice line of the east ridge; finally the symmetrical summit pyramid that transfixed the sky. But whereas in the pictures the mountain had always seemed unreal—a dream image of cloud, snow, and crystal—it was now no longer an image at all. It was a mass, solid, imminent, appalling. We were still too far away to see the windy whipping of its snow plumes or to hear the cannonading of its avalanches, but in that sudden silent moment every man of us was for the first time aware of it, not as a picture in his mind but as a thing, an antagonist. For all its twenty-eight thousand feet of lofty grandeur, it seemed, somehow, less to tower than to crouch—a white-hooded giant, secret and remote, but living. Living and on guard.

I turned my eyes from the dazzling glare and looked at my companions. Osborn still stood a little in front of the others. He was absolutely motionless, his young face tense and shining, his eyes devouring the mountain as a lover's might devour the face of his beloved. One could feel in the very set of his body the overwhelming desire that swelled in him to act, to come to grips, to conquer. A little behind him were ranged the other men of the expedition: Randolph, our leader, Wittmer and Johns, Doctor Schlapp and Bixler. All were still, their eyes cast upward. Off to one side a little stood Nace, the Englishman, the only one among us who was not staring at K3 for the first time. He had been the last to come up out of the gorge and stood now with arms folded on his chest, squinting at the great peak he had known so long and fought so tirelessly and fiercely. His lean British face, under its mask of stubble and windburn, was expressionless. His lips were a colorless line, and his eyes seemed almost shut. Behind the sahibs[1] ranged the porters, bent over their staffs, their brown, seamed faces straining upward from beneath their loads.

For a long while no one spoke or moved. The

---

1. **sahibs:** "sirs," a term formerly used in colonial India, referring to Europeans.

only sounds between earth and sky were the soft hiss of our breathing and the pounding of our hearts.

Through the long afternoon we wound slowly between the great boulders of the valley and at sundown pitched camp in the bed of a dried-up stream. The porters ate their rations in silence, wrapped themselves in their blankets, and fell asleep under the stars. The rest of us, as was our custom, sat close about the fire that blazed in the circle of tents, discussing the events of the day and the plans for the next. It was a flawlessly clear Himalayan night and K3 tiered up into the blackness like a monstrous sentinel lighted from within. There was no wind, but a great tide of cold air crept down the valley from the ice fields above, penetrating our clothing, pressing gently against the canvas of the tents.

"Another night or two and we'll be needing the sleeping bags," commented Randolph.

Osborn nodded. "We could use them tonight, would be my guess."

Randolph turned to Nace. "What do you say, Martin?"

The Englishman puffed at his pipe a moment. "Rather think it might be better to wait," he said at last.

"Wait? Why?" Osborn jerked his head up.

"Well, it gets pretty nippy high up, you know. I've seen it thirty below at twenty-five thousand on the east ridge. Longer we wait for the bags, better acclimated we'll get."

Osborn snorted. "A lot of good being acclimated will do if we have frozen feet."

"Easy, Paul, easy," cautioned Randolph. "It seems to me Martin's right."

Osborn bit his lip, but said nothing. The other men entered the conversation, and soon it had veered to other matters: the weather, the porters and pack animals, routes, camps and strategy— the inevitable, inexhaustible topics of the climber's world.

There were all kinds of men among the eight of us, men with a great diversity of background and interest. Sayre Randolph, whom the Alpine Club had named leader of our expedition, had for years been a well-known explorer and lecturer. Now in his middle fifties, he was no longer equal to the grueling physical demands of high climbing, but served as planner and organizer of the enterprise. Wittmer was a Seattle lawyer, who had recently made a name for himself by a series of difficult ascents in the Coast Range of British Columbia. Johns was an Alaskan, a fantastically strong, able sourdough,[2] who had been a ranger in the U.S. Forest Service and had accompanied many famous Alaskan expeditions. Schlapp was a practicing physician from Milwaukee; Bixler, a government meteorologist[3] with a talent for photography. I, at the time, was an assistant professor of geology at an eastern university.

Finally, and preeminently, there were Osborn and Nace. I say "preeminently," because even at this time, when we had been together as a party for little more than a month, I believe all of us realized that these were the two key men of our venture. None, to my knowledge, ever expressed it in words, but the conviction was there, nevertheless, that if any of us were eventually to stand on the hitherto unconquered summit of K3, it would be one of them, or both. They were utterly dissimilar men. Osborn was twenty-three and a year out of college, a compact, buoyant mass of energy and high spirits. He seemed to be wholly unaffected by either the physical or mental hazards-of mountaineering and had already, by virtue of many spectacular ascents in the Alps and Rockies, won a reputation as the most skilled and audacious of younger American climbers. Nace was in his forties—lean, taciturn, introspective. An official in the Indian Civil Service, he had explored and climbed in the Himalayas for twenty years. He had been a member of all five of the unsuccessful British expeditions to K3, and in his last attempt had attained to within five hundred feet of the summit, the highest point which any man had reached on the unconquered giant. This had been the famous tragic attempt in which his fellow climber and lifelong friend, Captain Furness, had slipped and fallen ten thousand feet to his death. Nace rarely mentioned his name, but on the steel head of his ice ax were engraved the words: TO MARTIN FROM JOHN. If fate were to grant that the

---

2. **sourdough:** strictly speaking, a prospector or settler in the American West.
3. **meteorologist:** weather expert.

ax of any one of us should be planted upon the summit of K3, I hoped it would be his.

Such were the men who huddled about the fire in the deep, still cold of that Himalayan night. There were many differences among us, in temperament as well as in background. In one or two cases, notably that of Osborn and Nace, there had already been a certain amount of friction, and as the venture continued and the struggles and hardships of the actual ascent began, it would, I knew, increase. But differences were unimportant. What mattered—all that mattered—was that our purpose was one—to conquer the monster of rock and ice that now loomed above us in the night; to stand for a moment where no man, no living thing, had ever stood before. To that end we had come from half a world away, across oceans and continents to the fastnesses[4] of inner Asia. To that end we were prepared to endure cold, exhaustion, and danger, even to the very last extremity of human endurance. Why? There is no answer, and at the same time every man among us knew the answer; every man who has ever looked upon a great mountain and felt the fever in his blood to climb and conquer knows the answer. George Leigh Mallory, greatest of mountaineers, expressed it once and for all when he was asked why he wanted to climb unconquered Everest. "I want to climb it," said Mallory, "because it's there."

Day after day we crept on and upward. The naked desolation of the valley was unrelieved by any motion, color, or sound, and, as we progressed, it was like being trapped at the bottom of a deep well or in a sealed court between great skyscrapers. Soon we were thinking of the ascent of the shining mountain not only as an end in itself but as an escape.

In our nightly discussions around the fire, our conversation narrowed more and more to the immediate problems confronting us, and during them I began to realize that the tension between Osborn and Nace went deeper than I had at first surmised. There was rarely any outright argument between them—they were both far too able mountain men to disagree on fundamentals—but I saw that at almost every turn they were rubbing each other the wrong way. It was a matter of personalities chiefly. Osborn was talkative, enthusiastic, optimistic, always chafing to be up and at it, always wanting to take the short, straight line to the given point. Nace, on the other hand, was matter-of-fact, cautious, slow. He was the apostle of trial and error and watchful waiting. Because of his far greater experience and intimate knowledge of K3, Randolph almost invariably followed his advice, rather than Osborn's, when a difference of opinion arose. The younger man usually capitulated with good grace, but I could tell that he was irked.

During the days in the valley I had few occasions to talk privately with either of them, and only once did either mention the other in any but the most casual manner. Even then, the remarks they made seemed unimportant, and I remember them only in view of what happened later.

My conversation with Osborn occurred first. It was while we were on the march, and Osborn, who was directly behind me, came up suddenly to my side.

"You're a geologist, Frank," he began without preamble. "What do you think of Nace's theory about the ridge?"

"What theory?" I asked.

"He believes we should traverse[5] under it from the glacier up. Says the ridge itself is too exposed."

"It looks pretty mean through the telescope."

"But it's been done before. He's done it himself. All right, it's tough—I'll admit that. But a decent climber could make it in half the time the traverse will take."

"Nace knows the traverse is longer," I said, "but he seems certain it will be much easier for us."

"Easier for him is what he means." Osborn paused, looking moodily at the ground. "He was a great climber in his day. It's a shame a man can't be honest enough with himself to know when he's through." He fell silent and a moment later dropped back into his place in line.

It was that same night, I think, that I awoke to

---

4. **fastnesses:** places protected by high walls (here, by the mountains).

5. **traverse:** cross in a zigzag movement.

find Nace sitting up in his blanket and staring at the mountain.

"How clear it is," I whispered.

The Englishman pointed. "See the ridge?"

I nodded, my eyes fixed on the great, twisting spine of ice that climbed into the sky. I could see now, more clearly than in the blinding sunlight, its huge indentations and jagged, wind-swept pitches.

"It looks impossible," I said.

"No, it can be done. Trouble is, when you've made it, you're too done in for the summit."

"Osborn seems to think its shortness would make up for its difficulty."

Nace was silent a long moment before answering. Then for the first and only time I heard him speak the name of his dead companion. "That's what Furness thought," he said quietly. Then he lay down and wrapped himself in his blanket.

For the next two weeks the uppermost point of the valley was our home and workshop. We established our base camp as close to the mountain as we could, less than half a mile from the tongue of its lowest glacier, and plunged into the arduous tasks of preparation for the ascent. Our food and equipment were unpacked, inspected and sorted, and finally repacked in lighter loads for transportation to more advanced camps. Hours on end were spent poring over maps and charts and studying the monstrous heights above us through telescope and binoculars. Under Nace's supervision, a thorough reconnaissance of the glacier was made and the route across it laid out; then began the backbreaking labor of moving up supplies and establishing the advance stations.

Camps I and II were set up on the glacier itself, in the most sheltered sites we could find. Camp III we built at its upper end, as near as possible to the point where the great rock spine of K3 thrust itself free of ice and began its precipitous ascent. According to our plans, this would be the advance base of operations during the climb; the camps to be established higher up, on the mountain proper, would be too small and too exposed to serve as anything more than one or two nights' shelter. The total distance between the base camp and Camp III was only fifteen miles, but the utmost daily progress of our porters was five miles,

and it was essential that we should never be more than twelve hours' march from food and shelter. Hour after hour, day after day, the long file of men wound up and down among the hummocks[6] and crevasses of the glacier, and finally the time arrived when we were ready to advance.

Leaving Doctor Schlapp in command of eight porters at the base camp, we proceeded easily and on schedule, reaching Camp I the first night, Camp II the second, and the advance base the third. No men were left at Camps I and II, inasmuch as they were designed simply as caches for food and equipment; and, furthermore, we knew we would need all the manpower available for the establishment of the higher camps on the mountain proper.

For more than three weeks now the weather had held perfectly, but on our first night at the advance base, as if by malignant prearrangement of Nature, we had our first taste of the supernatural fury of a high Himalayan storm. It began with great streamers of lightning that flashed about the mountain like a halo; then heavily through the weird glare snow began to fall. The wind howled about the tents with hurricane frenzy, and the wild flapping of the canvas dinned in our ears like machine-gun fire.

There was no sleep for us that night or the next. For thirty-six hours the storm raged without lull, while we huddled in the icy gloom of the tents. At last, on the third morning, it was over, and we came out into a world transformed by a twelve-foot cloak of snow. No single landmark remained as it had been before, and our supplies and equipment were in the wildest confusion. Fortunately, there had not been a single serious injury, but it was another three days before we had regained our strength and put the camp in order.

Then we waited. The storm did not return, and the sky beyond the ridges gleamed flawlessly clear, but night and day we could hear the roaring thunder of avalanches on the mountain above us. To have ventured so much as one step into that savage, vertical wilderness before the new-fallen snow froze tight would have been suicidal. We chafed or waited patiently, according to our indi-

---

6. **hummocks:** ridges or rises in the ice.

vidual temperaments, while the days dragged by.

It was late one afternoon that Osborn returned from a short reconnaissance up the ridge. His eyes were shining and his voice jubilant.

"It's tight!" he cried. "Tight as a drum! We can go!" All of us stopped whatever we were doing. His excitement leaped like an electric spark from one to another. "I went about a thousand feet, and it's sound all the way. What do you say, Sayre? Tomorrow?"

Randolph hesitated a moment, then looked at Nace.

"Better give it another day or two," said the Englishman.

Osborn glared at him. "Why?" he challenged.

"It's generally safer to wait until——"

"Wait! Wait!" Osborn exploded. "Don't you ever think of anything but waiting? The snow's firm, I tell you!"

"It's firm down here," Nace replied quietly, "because the sun hits it only two hours a day. Up above it gets the sun twelve hours. It may not have frozen yet."

"The avalanches have stopped."

"That doesn't necessarily mean it will hold a man's weight."

"It seems to me, Martin's point——" Randolph began.

Osborn wheeled on him. "Sure," he snapped. "I know. Martin's right. The cautious bloody English are always right. Let him have his way, and we'll be sitting here twiddling our thumbs until the mountain falls down on us." His eyes flashed to Nace. "Maybe with a little less of that bloody cautiousness, you English wouldn't have made such a mess of Everest. Maybe your pals Mallory and Furness wouldn't be dead."

"Osborn!" commanded Randolph sharply.

The youngster stared at Nace for another moment, breathing heavily. Then, abruptly, he turned away.

The next two days were clear and windless, but we still waited, following Nace's advice. There were no further brushes between him and Osborn, but an unpleasant air of restlessness and tension hung over the camp. I found myself chafing, almost as impatiently as Osborn himself, for the moment when we would break out of that mad-dening inactivity and begin the assault.

At last the day came. With the first paling of the sky, a roped file of men, bent almost double beneath heavy loads, began slowly to climb the ice slope just beneath the jagged line of the great east ridge. In accordance with a prearranged plan, we proceeded in relays; this first group consisting of Nace, Johns, myself, and eight porters. It was our job to ascend approximately two thousand feet in a day's climbing and establish Camp IV at the most level and sheltered site we could find. We would spend the night there and return to the advance base next day, while the second relay, consisting of Osborn, Wittmer, and eight more porters, went up with their loads. This process was to continue until all necessary supplies were at Camp IV, and then the whole thing would be repeated between Camps IV and V, and V and VI. From VI, at an altitude of about 26,000 feet, the ablest and fittest men—presumably Nace and Osborn—would make the direct assault on the summit. Randolph and Bixler were to remain at the advance base throughout the operations, acting as directors and coordinators. We were under the strictest orders that any man, sahib or porter, who suffered illness or injury should be brought down immediately.

How shall I describe those next two weeks beneath the great ice ridge of K3? In a sense, there was no occurrence of importance, and at the same time everything happened that could possibly happen, short of actual disaster. We established Camp IV, came down again, went up again, came down again. Then we crept laboriously higher. The wind increased, and the air grew steadily colder and more difficult to breathe. One morning two of the porters awoke with their feet frozen black; they had to be sent down. A short while later Johns developed an uncontrollable nosebleed and was forced to descend to a lower camp. Wittmer was suffering from splitting headaches, and I, from a continually dry throat. But providentially, the one enemy we feared the most in that icy, gale-lashed hell did not again attack us—no snow fell. And day by day, foot by foot, we ascended.

It is during ordeals like this that the surface trappings of a man are shed and his secret mettle laid bare. There were no shirkers or quitters

among us—I had known that from the beginning—
but now, with each passing day, it became more
manifest which were the strongest and ablest
among us. Beyond all argument, these were Osborn and Nace.

Osborn was magnificent. All the boyish impatience and moodiness which he had exhibited earlier were gone, and, now that he was at last at
work in his natural element, he emerged as the
peerless mountaineer he was. His energy was inexhaustible, and his speed, both on rock and ice,
almost twice that of any other man in the party.
He was always discovering new routes and short-
cuts; and there was such vigor, buoyancy, and
youth in everything he did that it gave heart to all
the rest of us.

In contrast, Nace was slow, methodical, un-
spectacular. Since he and I worked in the same
relay, I was with him almost constantly, and to
this day I carry in my mind the clear image of the
man—his tall body bent almost double against
endless, shimmering slopes of ice; his lean brown
face bent in utter concentration on the problem in
hand, then raised searchingly to the next; the
bright prong of his ax rising, falling, rising, falling
with tireless rhythm, until the steps in the glassy
incline were so wide and deep that the most
clumsy of the porters could not have slipped from
them had he tried. Osborn attacked the mountain,
head on. Nace studied it, sparred with it, wore it
down. His spirit did not flap from his sleeve like
a pennon;[7] it was deep inside him, patient, indomitable.

The day came soon when I learned from him
what it is to be a great mountaineer. We were
making the ascent from Camp IV to V, and an
almost perpendicular ice wall had made it necessary for us to come out for a few yards on the
exposed crest of the ridge. There were six of us
in the party, roped together, with Nace leading,
myself second, and four porters bringing up the
rear. The ridge at this particular point was free of
snow, but razor-thin, and the rocks were covered
with a smooth glaze of ice. On either side the
mountain dropped away in sheer precipices of five
thousand feet.

7. **pennon:** flag or pennant.

Suddenly the last porter slipped. In what seemed to be the same instant I heard the ominous scraping of boot nails and, turning, saw a wildly gesticulating figure plunge sideways into the abyss. There was a scream as the next porter followed him. I remember trying frantically to dig into the ridge with my ax, realizing at the same time it would no more hold against the weight of the falling men than a pin stuck in a wall. Then I heard Nace shout, "Jump!" As he said it, the rope went tight about my waist, and I went hurtling after him into space on the opposite side of the ridge. After me came the nearest porter.

What happened then must have happened in five yards and a fifth of a second. I heard myself cry out, and the glacier, a mile below, rushed up at me, spinning. Then both were blotted out in a violent spasm, as the rope jerked taut. I hung for a moment, an inert mass, feeling that my body had been cut in two; then I swung in slowly to the side of the mountain. Above me the rope lay tight and motionless across the crest of the ridge, our weight exactly counterbalancing that of the men who had fallen on the far slope.

Nace's voice came up from below. "You chaps on the other side!" he shouted. "Start climbing slowly! We're climbing too!"

In five minutes we had all regained the ridge. The porters and I crouched panting on the jagged rocks, our eyes closed, the sweat beading our faces in frozen drops. Nace carefully examined the rope that again hung loosely between us.

"All right, men," he said presently. "Let's get on to camp for a cup of tea."

Above Camp V the whole aspect of the ascent changed. The angle of the ridge eased off, and the ice, which lower down had covered the mountain like a sheath, lay only in scattered patches between the rocks. Fresh enemies, however, instantly appeared to take the place of the old. We were now laboring at an altitude of more than 25,000 feet—well above the summits of the highest surrounding peaks—and day and night, without protection or respite, we were buffeted by the savage fury of the wind. Worse than this was that the atmosphere had become so rarefied it could scarcely support life. Breathing itself was a major physical effort, and our progress upward consisted of two or three painful steps, followed by a long period of rest in which our hearts pounded wildly and our burning lungs gasped for air. Each of us carried a small cylinder of oxygen in our pack, but we used it only in emergencies, and found that, though its immediate effect was salutary, it left us later even worse off than before.

But the great struggle was now mental rather than physical. The lack of air induced a lethargy of mind and spirit; confidence and the powers of thought and decision waned. The mountain, to all of us, was no longer a mere giant of rock and ice; it had become a living thing, an enemy, watching us, waiting for us, hostile, relentless.

On the fifteenth day after we had first left the advance base, we pitched Camp VI at an altitude of 26,500 feet. It was located near the uppermost extremity of the great east ridge, directly beneath the so-called shoulder of the mountain. On the far side of the shoulder the stupendous north face of K3 fell sheer to the glaciers, two miles below. Above it and to the left rose the symmetrical bulk of the summit pyramid. The topmost rocks of its highest pinnacle were clearly visible from the shoulder, and the intervening fifteen hundred feet seemed to offer no insuperable obstacles.

Camp VI, which was in reality no camp at all but a single tent, was large enough to accommodate only three men. Osborn established it with the aid of Wittmer and one porter; then, the following morning, Wittmer and the porter descended to Camp V, and Nace and I went up. It was our plan that Osborn and Nace should launch the final assault—the next day, if the weather held—with myself in support, following their progress through binoculars and going to their aid or summoning help from below if anything went wrong. As the three of us lay in the tent that night, the summit seemed already within arm's reach, victory securely in our grasp.

And then the blow fell. With fiendishly malignant timing, which no power on earth could have made us believe was a simple accident of nature, the mountain hurled at us its last line of defense. It snowed.

For a day and a night the great flakes drove down upon us, swirling and swooping in the wind, blotting out the summit, the shoulder, everything beyond the tiny white-walled radius of our tent. At last, during the morning of the following day, it cleared. The sun came out in a thin blue sky, and the summit pyramid again appeared above us, now whitely robed in fresh snow. But still we waited. Until the snow either froze or was blown away by the wind, it would have been the rashest courting of destruction for us to have ascended a foot beyond the camp. Another day passed. And another.

By the third nightfall our nerves were at the breaking point. For hours on end we had scarcely moved or spoken, and the only sounds in all the world were the endless moaning of the wind outside and the harsh, sucking noise of our breathing. I knew that, one way or another, the end had come. Our meager food supply was running out; even with careful rationing, there was enough left for only two more days.

Presently Nace stirred in his sleeping bag and sat up. "We'll have to go down tomorrow," he said quietly.

For a moment there was silence in the tent. Then Osborn struggled to a sitting position and faced him.

"No," he said.

"There's still too much loose snow above. We can't make it."

"But it's clear. As long as we can see——"

Nace shook his head. "Too dangerous. We'll go down tomorrow and lay in a fresh supply. Then we'll try again."

"Once we go down we're licked. You know it."

Nace shrugged. "Better to be licked than——" The strain of speech was suddenly too much for him and he fell into a violent paroxysm of coughing. When it had passed, there was a long silence.

Then, suddenly, Osborn spoke again. "Look, Nace," he said, "I'm going up tomorrow."

The Englishman shook his head.

"I'm going—understand?"

For the first time since I had known him, I saw Nace's eyes flash in anger. "I'm the senior member of this group," he said. "I forbid you to go!"

With a tremendous effort, Osborn jerked himself to his feet. "You forbid me? This may be your sixth time on this mountain, and all that, but you don't own it! I know what you're up to. You

haven't got it in you to make the top yourself, so you don't want anyone else to get the glory. That's it, isn't it? Isn't it?" He sat down again suddenly, gasping for breath.

Nace looked at him with level eyes. "This mountain has licked me five times," he said softly. "It killed my best friend. It means more to me to lick it than anything else in the world. Maybe I'll make it and maybe I won't. But if I do, it will be as a rational, intelligent human being, not as a fool throwing my life away——"

He collapsed into another fit of coughing and fell back in his sleeping bag. Osborn, too, was still. They lay there inert, panting, too exhausted for speech.

It was hours later that I awoke from dull, uneasy sleep. In the faint light I saw Nace fumbling with the flap of the tent.

"What is it?" I asked.

"Osborn. He's gone."

The words cut like a blade through my lethargy. I struggled to my feet and followed Nace from the tent.

Outside, the dawn was seeping up the eastern sky. It was very cold, but the wind had fallen, and the mountain seemed to hang suspended in a vast stillness. Above us the summit pyramid climbed bleakly into space, like the last outpost of a spent, lifeless planet. Raising my binoculars, I swept them over the gray waste. At first I saw nothing but rock and ice; then, suddenly, something moved.

"I've got him," I whispered.

As I spoke, the figure of Osborn sprang into clear focus against a patch of ice. He took three or four slow upward steps, stopped, went on again. I handed the glasses to Nace.

The Englishman squinted through them a moment, returned them to me, and re-entered the tent. When I followed, he had already laced his boots and was pulling on his outer gloves.

"He's not far," he said. "Can't have been gone more than half an hour." He seized his ice ax and started out again.

"Wait," I said. "I'm going with you."

Nace shook his head. "Better stay here."

"I'm going with you," I said.

He said nothing further, but waited while I

made ready. In a few moments we left the tent, roped up, and started off.

Almost immediately we were on the shoulder and confronted with the paralyzing two-mile drop of the north face, but we negotiated the short exposed stretch without mishap and in ten minutes were working up the base of the summit pyramid. Our progress was creepingly slow. There seemed to be literally no air at all to breathe, and after almost every step we were forced to rest.

The minutes crawled into hours, and still we climbed. Presently the sun came up. Its level rays streamed across the clouds far below and glinted from the summits of distant peaks. But, although the pinnacle of K3 soared a full five thousand feet above anything in the surrounding world, we had scarcely any sense of height. The stupendous wilderness of mountains and glaciers that spread beneath us to the horizon was flattened and remote, an unreal, insubstantial landscape seen in a dream. We had no connection with it or it with us. All living, all awareness, purpose, and will, was concentrated in the last step and the next—to put one foot before the other; to breathe; to ascend. We struggled on in silence.

I do not know how long it was since we had left the camp—it might have been two hours, it might have been six—when we suddenly sighted Osborn. We had not been able to find him again since our first glimpse through the binoculars, but now, unexpectedly and abruptly, as we came up over a jagged outcropping of rock, there he was. He was at a point, only a few yards above us, where the mountain steepened into an almost vertical wall. The smooth surface directly in front of him was obviously unclimbable, but two alternate routes were presented. To the left, a chimney cut obliquely across the wall, forbiddingly steep, but seeming to offer adequate holds. To the right was a gentle slope of snow that curved upward and out of sight behind the rocks. As we watched, Osborn ascended to the edge of the snow, stopped, and tested it with his foot; then, apparently satisfied that it would bear his weight, he stepped out on the slope.

I felt Nace's body tense. "Paul!" he cried out.

His voice was too weak and hoarse to carry. Osborn continued his ascent.

Nace cupped his hands and called his name again, and this time Osborn turned. "Wait!" cried the Englishman.

Osborn stood still, watching us, as we struggled up the few yards to the edge of the snow slope. Nace's breath came in shuddering gasps, but he climbed faster than I had ever seen him climb before.

"Come back!" he called. "Come off the snow!"

"It's all right! The crust is firm!" Osborn called back.

"But it's melting! There's"—Nace paused, fighting for air—"there's nothing underneath!"

In a sudden, horrifying flash I saw what he meant. Looked at from directly below, at the point where Osborn had come to it, the slope on which he stood appeared as a harmless covering of snow over the rocks. From where we were now, however, a little to one side, it could be seen that it was in reality no covering at all, but merely a cornice or unsupported platform clinging to the side of the mountain. Below it was not rock, but ten thousand feet of blue air.

"Come back!" I cried. "Come back!"

Osborn hesitated, then took a downward step. But he never took the next. For in that same instant the snow directly in front of him disappeared. It did not seem to fall or to break away. It was just soundlessly and magically no longer there. In the spot where Osborn had been about to set his foot there was now revealed the abysmal drop of the north face of K3.

I shut my eyes, but only for a second, and when I reopened them Osborn was still, miraculously, there.

Nace was shouting, "Don't move! Don't move an inch!"

"The rope," I heard myself saying.

The Englishman shook his head. "We'd have to throw it, and the impact would be too much. Brace yourself and play it out." As we spoke, his eyes were traveling over the rocks that bordered the snow bridge. Then he moved forward.

I wedged myself into a cleft in the wall and let out the rope which extended between us. A few yards away, Osborn stood in the snow, transfixed, one foot a little in front of the other. But my eyes now were on Nace. Cautiously, but with astonishing rapidity, he edged along the rocks beside the cornice. There was a moment when his only support was an inch-wide ledge beneath his feet, another where there was nothing under his feet at all and he supported himself wholly by his elbows and hands. But he advanced steadily, and at last reached a shelf wide enough for him to turn around on. At this point he was perhaps six feet away from Osborn.

"It's wide enough here to hold both of us," he said in a quiet voice. "I'm going to reach out my ax. Don't move until you're sure you have a grip on it. When I pull, jump."

He searched the wall behind him and found a hold for his left hand. Then he slowly extended his ice ax, head foremost, until it was within two feet of Osborn's shoulder.

"Grip it!" he cried suddenly. Osborn's hands shot out and seized the ax. "Jump!"

There was a flash of steel in the sunlight, and a hunched figure hurtled inward from the snow to the ledge. Simultaneously another figure hurtled out. The haft of the ax jerked suddenly from Nace's hand, and he lurched forward and downward. A violent, sickening spasm convulsed my body as the rope went taut. Then it was gone. Nace did not seem to hit the snow; he simply disappeared through it, soundlessly. In the same instant the snow itself was gone. The frayed, yellow end of broken rope spun lazily in space.

Somehow my eyes went to Osborn. He was crouched on the ledge where Nace had been a moment before, staring dully at the ax he held in his hands. Beyond his head, not two hundred feet above, the white, untrodden pinnacle of K3 stabbed the sky.

Perhaps ten minutes passed, perhaps a half hour. I closed my eyes and leaned forward motionless against the rock, my face against my arm. I neither thought nor felt; my body and mind alike were enveloped in a suffocating numbness. Through it at last came the sound of Osborn moving. Looking up, I saw he was standing beside me.

"I'm going to try to make the top," he said tonelessly.

I merely stared at him.

"Will you come?"

I shook my head slowly. Osborn hesitated a moment, then turned, and began slowly climbing the steep chimney above us. Halfway up he paused, struggling for breath. Then he resumed his laborious upward progress and presently disappeared beyond the crest.

I stayed where I was, and the hours passed. The sun reached its zenith above the peak and sloped away behind it. And at last I heard above me the sound of Osborn returning. As I looked up, his figure appeared at the top of the chimney and began the descent. His clothing was in tatters, and I could tell from his movements that only the thin flame of his will stood between him and collapse. In another few minutes he was standing beside me.

"Did you get there?" I asked.

He shook his head slowly. "I couldn't make it," he answered. "I didn't have what it takes."

We roped together silently and began the descent to the camp. There is nothing more to be told of the sixth assault on K3—at least not from the experiences of the men who made it. Osborn and I reached Camp V in safety, and three days later the entire expedition gathered at the advance base. It was decided, in view of the appalling tragedy that had occurred, to make no further attempt on the summit, and we began the evacuation of the mountain.

It remained for another year and other men to reveal the epilogue.

The summer following our attempt a combined English-Swiss expedition stormed the peak successfully. After weeks of hardship and struggle, they attained the topmost pinnacle of the giant, only to find that what should have been their great moment of triumph was, instead, a moment of the bitterest disappointment. For when they came out at last upon the summit, they saw that they were not the first. An ax stood there. Its haft was embedded in rock and ice, and on its steel head were the engraved words: To Martin From John.

They were sporting men. On their return to civilization they told their story, and the name of the conqueror of K3 was made known to the world.

Responding to the Story

Analyzing the Story

Identifying Facts

1. How would you describe the exact **conflict** in "Top Man"? Find the passage on page 100 that tells exactly what these men want.
2. Find at least three **images** in the description of this mountain **setting** that help us feel as if we are there.
3. At several points in the story, K3 is given human characteristics, so that it seems to become a **character** in the story. Find at least three details in the story that make K3 seem like a human enemy.
4. Describe the **conflict** that takes place on the human level, between Osborn and Nace.
5. On page 103 the narrator says of Nace: "The day came soon when I learned from him what it is to be a great mountaineer." How does Nace show he is a great mountaineer?

Interpreting Meanings

6. Who is the winner in the **conflict** between the men and K3?
7. Who would you say is the real "top man" in this story, and why?
8. Ullman uses a significant object in his story that might be described by writers as a **gimmick.** What is the gimmick, or significant object, used in this story? Why does Osborn place this object on the mountain? What ideas or values do you think the object might stand for?
9. As the characters of Osborn and Nace were revealed, did you find yourself taking sides, favoring one over the other? Did your feelings change as the story went on? Explain.
10. What reasons does this story offer for why people face danger they do not have to face? Can you think of other reasons people want to conquer settings like K3?

Writing About the Story

A Creative Response

1. **Describing a Setting.** List five cold words for a mountain snowstorm; list five more for a winter morning in the suburbs. List five wet words for a fast stream; list another five for an ocean seen from a ship's deck. List five hot, dry words for a desert; list another five for an attic in August. Then take any one of these lists and write a paragraph that uses those words to place the reader "there."

A Critical Response

2. **Contrasting Fiction with a Journal Entry.** Read Ullman's true account of the disappearance of Mallory and Irvine in the 1924 British expedition to Mount Everest (page 109). Then make a list of the details in the fictional story that are like the details in the true account. Make another list of details in the fictional story that are different from details in the true account. Present your findings in at least two paragraphs. In a third paragraph, tell which account was more interesting to you, and why.
3. **Contrasting Characters.** The characters of Nace and Osborn are in sharp, plainly drawn contrast. In a paragraph, explain how the men are "utterly dissimilar in character." Before you write, fill out a chart like the following, in which you list their specific differences:

Nace	Osborn
1.	1.
2.	2.
etc.	etc.

4. **Extending a Statement.** When Mallory was asked why he kept trying to conquer Everest, he replied: "Because it's there." Here another speaker responds to people who tell her something is impossible (a fen is a swamp):

> **I May, I Might, I Must**
>
> If you will tell me why the fen
> appears impassable, I then
> will tell you why I think that I
> can get across it if I try.
> —Marianne Moore

In a paragraph, explain how Mallory's statement and the poet's statement could apply to many challenges in life—not only to actual mountains and actual fens.

Analyzing Language and Vocabulary

Context Clues

Use context clues to make educated guesses at the meanings of the italicized words in the sentences that follow. Write out your own definitions, and then check your guesses against the dictionary's entries.

1. "We were men *bereft* of everything but eyes, everything but the single, electric perception: There it was!"
2. "No men were left at Camps I and II, inasmuch as they were designed simply as *caches* for food and equipment . . ."
3. "We *chafed* or waited patiently, according to our individual temperaments, while the days dragged by."
4. "Each of us carried a small cylinder of oxygen in our pack, but we used it only in emergencies, and found that, though its immediate effect was *salutary,* it left us later even worse off than before."
5. "He collapsed into another fit of coughing and fell back in his sleeping bag. Osborn, too, was still. They lay there *inert,* panting, too exhausted for speech."

Reading About the Writer

James Ramsey Ullman (1907–1971) once said that he led a double life, as a writer and as a mountain climber. Born and raised in New York City, he also said that such "roots" as he had were firmly anchored in Central Park. His first book, *The Other Side of the Mountain,* is about a journey he made across the Andes and down the Amazon River. He followed this with articles, short stories, and novels, many of them about mountaineering.

Ullman also wrote two popular histories of mountaineering, *High Conquest* and *The Age of Mountaineering.* They are accounts of real mountain expeditions, but their exciting, fast pace makes them read like adventure fiction.

In 1963, Ullman realized a lifelong dream when he became a member of the first American expedition to the summit of the world, Mount Everest.

Ullman believed that climbing earth's heights means little in itself. That people *want* to climb them means everything. "It is not the summit that matters," he said, "but the fight for the summit. Not the victory, but the game itself."

Focusing on Background
"Where did the story come from?"

"Top Man" is fiction, and K3 in the story is a fictional mountain, but Ullman might have based some details of his story on actual events. The following report, from Ullman's book *The Age of Mountaineering,* is about a 1924 English expedition to Mount Everest.

As the report opens, the English team has made several unsuccessful attempts to reach the summit. Norton and Somervell are two of the expedition members. Mallory is George Leigh Mallory, thirty-eight years old. At this time, he was a master at Cambridge University and one of the most respected mountaineers in the world.

"Norton and Somervell's assault was the next-to-last in the adventure of 1924. One more was to come—and, with it, mystery and tragedy.

"Bitterly chagrined at the failure of his first effort, Mallory was determined to have one last fling before the monsoon struck. . . .

"Mallory moved with characteristic speed. With young Andrew Irvine as partner he started upward from the col the day after Norton and Somervell descended. They spent the first night at Camp V and the second at Camp VI, at 26,800. Unlike Norton and Somervell, they planned to use oxygen on the final dash and to follow the crest of the northeast ridge instead of traversing the north face to the couloir. The ridge appeared to present more formidable climbing difficulties than the lower route, particularly near the base of the summit pyramid where it buckled upward in two great rock-towers which the Everesters called the First and Second Steps. Mallory, however, was all for the frontal attack and had frequently expressed the belief that the steps could be surmounted. The last Tigers descending that night from the highest camp to the col brought word that both climbers were in good condition and full of hope for success.

"One man only was to have another glimpse of Mallory and Irvine.

"On the morning of June eighth—the day set for the assault on the summit—Odell, the geologist, who had spent the night alone at Camp V, set out for VI with a rucksack of food. The day was as mild and windless as any the expedition had experienced, but a thin gray mist clung to the upper reaches of the mountain, and Odell could see little of what lay above him. Presently, however, he scaled the top of a small crag at about twenty-six thousand feet, and, standing there, he stopped and stared. For a moment the mist cleared. The whole summit ridge and final pyramid of Everest was unveiled, and high above him, on the very crest of the ridge, he saw two tiny figures outlined against the sky. They appeared to be at the base of one of the great steps, not more than seven or eight hundred feet below the final pinnacle. As Odell watched, the figures moved slowly upward. Then, as suddenly as it had parted, the mist closed in again, and they were gone.

"The feats of endurance that Odell performed during the next forty-eight hours are unsurpassed by those of any mountaineer. That same day he went to Camp VI with his load of provisions, and then even higher, watching and waiting. But the mountaintop remained veiled in mist, and there was no sign of the climbers returning. As night came on, he descended all the way to the col, only to start off again the following dawn. Camp V was empty. He spent a solitary night there in sub-zero cold and the next morning ascended again to Camp VI. It was empty too. With sinking heart he struggled upward for another thousand feet, searching and shouting, to the very limit of human endurance. The only answering sound was the deep moaning of the wind. The great peak above him loomed bleakly in the sky, wrapped in the loneliness and desolation of the ages. All hope was gone. Odell descended to the highest camp and signaled the tidings of tragedy to the watchers far below.

"So ended the second attempt on Everest—and, with it, the lives of two brave men. The bodies of George Mallory and Andrew Irvine lie somewhere in the vast wilderness of rock and ice that guards the summit of the world. Where and how death overtook them no one knows. And whether victory came before the end no one knows either. Our last glimpse of them is through Odell's eyes—two tiny specks against the sky, fighting upward.

"For nine years after the 1924 assault no climbers approached Everest. Tibet again closed its gates to Westerners, and it was not until 1933 that permission was once more granted for an expedition to try its luck. By this time most of the veterans of the previous attempts were too old for another ordeal on the mountain, but a capable team of younger men was assembled by the Mount Everest Committee. . . .

"A dramatic discovery was made . . . an hour's climb above Camp VI. On the tilted slabs just below the summit ridge [the climbers] came suddenly upon a solitary, rusted ice ax. The name of the Swiss maker, still plainly stamped on its head, left no possibility of doubt as to how it had come there: it was either Mallory's or Irvine's. Some mountaineers have claimed this to be an indication that Mallory and Irvine reached the top. Odell, they argue, saw them at a point much farther along the ridge; neither climber, presumably, would have attempted to go on without his ax, and the logical supposition, therefore, is that it was dropped in an accident on the way down. Others merely shrug their shoulders. Whatever one chooses to believe, there is no proof. The ax is no more than a tantalizing hint at the fate of the lost climbers."

—James Ramsey Ullman

ANTAEUS

Borden Deal

In Greek mythology, Antaeus was a giant whose strength came from his mother, the Earth. As long as his feet were on the ground, Antaeus had superhuman strength. Then Hercules came along. Learning the giant's secret, Hercules merely lifted Antaeus off the ground so that his strength ebbed away. Then he easily strangled Antaeus to death. Be alert for the passage in the story that explains the connection between Antaeus and a modern boy named T. J.

This was during the wartime, when lots of people were coming North for jobs in factories and war industries, when people moved around a lot more than they do now, and sometimes kids were thrown into new groups and new lives that were completely different from anything they had ever known before. I remember this one kid, T. J. his name was, from somewhere down South, whose family moved into our building during that time. They'd come North with everything they owned piled into the back seat of an old-model sedan that you wouldn't expect could make the trip, with T. J. and his three younger sisters riding shakily on top of the load of junk.

Our building was just like all the others there, with families crowded into a few rooms, and I guess there were twenty-five or thirty kids about my age in that one building. Of course, there were a few of us who formed a gang and ran together all the time after school, and I was the one who brought T. J. in and started the whole thing.

The building right next door to us was a factory where they made walking dolls. It was a low building with a flat, tarred roof that had a parapet all around it about head-high, and we'd found out a long time before that no one, not even the watchman, paid any attention to the roof because it was higher than any of the other buildings around. So my gang used the roof as a headquarters. We could get up there by crossing over to the fire escape from our own roof on a plank and then going on up. It was a secret place for us, where nobody

else could go without our permission.

I remember the day I first took T. J. up there to meet the gang. He was a stocky, robust kid with a shock of white hair, nothing sissy about him except his voice; he talked in this slow, gentle voice like you never heard before. He talked different from any of us and you noticed it right away. But I liked him anyway, so I told him to come on up.

We climbed up over the parapet and dropped down on the roof. The rest of the gang were already there.

"Hi," I said. I jerked my thumb at T. J. "He just moved into the building yesterday."

He just stood there, not scared or anything, just looking, like the first time you see somebody you're not sure you're going to like.

"Hi," Blackie said. "Where are you from?"

"Marion County," T. J. said.

We laughed. "Marion County?" I said. "Where's that?"

He looked at me for a moment like I was a stranger, too. "It's in Alabama," he said, like I ought to know where it was.

"What's your name?" Charley said.

"T. J.," he said, looking back at him. He had pale blue eyes that looked washed-out, but he looked directly at Charley, waiting for his reaction. He'll be all right, I thought. No sissy in him, except that voice. Who ever talked like that?

"T. J.," Blackie said. "That's just initials. What's your real name? Nobody in the world has just initials."

"I do," he said. "And they're T. J. That's all the name I got."

His voice was resolute with the knowledge of his rightness, and for a moment no one had anything to say. T. J. looked around at the rooftop and down at the black tar under his feet. "Down yonder where I come from," he said, "we played out in the woods. Don't you-all have no woods around here?"

"Naw," Blackie said. "There's the park a few blocks over, but it's full of kids and cops and old women. You can't do a thing."

T. J. kept looking at the tar under his feet. "You mean you ain't got no fields to raise nothing in?—no watermelons or nothing?"

"Naw," I said scornfully. "What do you want to grow something for? The folks can buy everything they need at the store."

He looked at me again with that strange, unknowing look. "In Marion County," he said, "I had my own acre of cotton and my own acre of corn. It was mine to plant and make ever' year."

He sounded like it was something to be proud of, and in some obscure way it made the rest of us angry. Blackie said, "Who'd want to have their own acre of cotton and corn? That's just work. What can you do with an acre of cotton and corn?"

T. J. looked at him. "Well, you get part of the bale offen your acre," he said seriously. "And I fed my acre of corn to my calf."

We didn't really know what he was talking about, so we were more puzzled than angry; otherwise, I guess, we'd have chased him off the roof and wouldn't let him be part of our gang. But he was strange and different, and we were all attracted by his stolid sense of rightness and belonging, maybe by the strange softness of his voice contrasting our own tones of speech into harshness.

He moved his foot against the black tar. "We could make our own field right here," he said softly, thoughtfully. "Come spring we could raise us what we want to—watermelons and garden truck and no telling what all."

"You'd have to be a good farmer to make these tar roofs grow any watermelons," I said. We all laughed.

But T. J. looked serious. "We could haul us some dirt up here," he said. "And spread it out even and water it, and before you know it, we'd have us a crop in here." He looked at us intently. "Wouldn't that be fun?"

"They wouldn't let us," Blackie said quickly.

"I thought you said this was you-all's roof," T. J. said to me. "That you-all could do anything you wanted to up here."

"They've never bothered us," I said. I felt the idea beginning to catch fire in me. It was a big idea, and it took a while for it to sink in; but the more I thought about it, the better I liked it. "Say," I said to the gang. "He might have something there. Just make us a regular roof garden, with flowers and grass and trees and everything. And all ours, too," I said. "We wouldn't let anybody up here except the ones we wanted to."

"It'd take a while to grow trees," T. J. said quickly, but we weren't paying any attention to him. They were all talking about it suddenly, all excited with the idea after I'd put it in a way they would catch hold of it. Only rich people had roof gardens, we knew, and the idea of our own private domain excited them.

"We could bring it up in sacks and boxes," Blackie said. "We'd have to do it while the folks weren't paying any attention to us, for we'd have to come up to the roof of our building and then cross over with it."

"Where could we get the dirt?" somebody said worriedly.

"Out of those vacant lots over close to school," Blackie said. "Nobody'd notice if we scraped it up."

I slapped T. J. on the shoulder. "Man, you had a wonderful idea," I said, and everybody grinned at him, remembering that he had started it. "Our own private roof garden."

He grinned back. "It'll be ourn," he said. "All ourn." Then he looked thoughtful again. "Maybe I can lay my hands on some cotton seed, too. You think we could raise us some cotton?"

We'd started big projects before at one time or another, like any gang of kids, but they'd always petered out for lack of organization and direction. But this one didn't; somehow or other T. J. kept it going all through the winter months. He kept talking about the watermelons and the cotton we'd raise, come spring, and when even that wouldn't work, he'd switch around to my idea of flowers and grass and trees, though he was always honest enough to add that it'd take a while to get any trees started. He always had it on his mind, and he'd mention it in school, getting them lined up to carry dirt that afternoon, saying in a casual way that he reckoned a few more weeks ought to see the job through.

Our little area of private earth grew slowly. T. J. was smart enough to start in one corner of the building, heaping up the carried earth two or three feet thick so that we had an immediate result to look at, to contemplate with awe. Some of the evenings T. J. alone was carrying earth up to the building, the rest of the gang distracted by other enterprises or interests, but T. J. kept plugging along on his own, and eventually we'd all come back to him again, and then our own little acre would grow more rapidly.

He was careful about the kind of dirt he'd let us carry up there, and more than once he dumped a sandy load over the parapet into the areaway below because it wasn't good enough. He found out the kinds of earth in all the vacant lots for blocks around. He'd pick it up and feel it and smell it, frozen though it was sometimes, and then he'd say it was good growing soil or it wasn't worth anything, and we'd have to go on somewhere else.

Thinking about it now, I don't see how he kept us at it. It was hard work, lugging paper sacks and boxes of dirt all the way up the stairs of our own building, keeping out of the way of the grownups so they wouldn't catch on to what we were doing. They probably wouldn't have cared, for they didn't pay much attention to us, but we wanted to keep it secret anyway. Then we had to go through the trap door to our roof, teeter over a plank to the fire escape, then climb two or three stories to the parapet, and drop them down onto the roof. All that for a small pile of earth that sometimes didn't seem worth the effort. But T. J. kept the vision bright within us, his words shrewd and calculated toward the fulfillment of his dream; and he worked harder than any of us. He seemed

driven toward a goal that we couldn't see, a particular point in time that would be definitely marked by signs and wonders that only he could see.

The laborious earth just lay there during the cold months, inert and lifeless, the clods lumpy and cold under our feet when we walked over it. But one day it rained, and afterward there was a softness in the air, and the earth was live and giving again with moisture and warmth.

That evening T. J. smelled the air, his nostrils dilating with the odor of the earth under his feet. "It's spring," he said, and there was a gladness rising in his voice that filled us all with the same feeling. "It's mighty late for it, but it's spring. I'd just about decided it wasn't never gonna get here at all."

We were all sniffing at the air, too, trying to smell it the way that T. J. did, and I can still remember the sweet odor of the earth under our feet. It was the first time in my life that spring and spring earth had meant anything to me. I looked at T. J. then, knowing in a faint way the hunger within him through the toilsome winter months, knowing the dream that lay behind his plan. He was a new Antaeus, preparing his own bed of strength.

"Planting time," he said. "We'll have to find us some seed."

"What do we do?" Blackie said. "How do we do it?"

"First we'll have to break up the clods," T. J. said. "That won't be hard to do. Then we plant the seeds, and after a while they come up. Then you got you a crop." He frowned. "But you ain't got it raised yet. You got to tend it and hoe it and take care of it, and all the time it's growing and growing, while you're awake and while you're asleep. Then you lay it by when it's growed and let it ripen, and then you got you a crop."

"There's those wholesale seed houses over on Sixth," I said. "We could probably swipe some grass seed over there."

T. J. looked at the earth. "You-all seem mighty set on raising some grass," he said. "I ain't never put no effort into that. I spent all my life trying not to raise grass."

"But it's pretty," Blackie said. "We could play

on it and take sunbaths on it. Like having our own lawn. Lots of people got lawns."

"Well," T. J. said. He looked at the rest of us, hesitant for the first time. He kept on looking at us for a moment. "I did have it in mind to raise some corn and vegetables. But we'll plant grass."

He was smart. He knew where to give in. And I don't suppose it made any difference to him, really. He just wanted to grow something, even if it was grass.

"Of course," he said, "I do think we ought to plant a row of watermelons. They'd be mighty nice to eat while we was a-laying on that grass."

We all laughed. "All right," I said. "We'll plant us a row of watermelons."

Things went very quickly then. Perhaps half the roof was covered with the earth, the half that wasn't broken by ventilators, and we swiped pocketfuls of grass seed from the open bins in the wholesale seed house, mingling among the buyers on Saturdays and during the school lunch hour. T. J. showed us how to prepare the earth, breaking up the clods and smoothing it and sowing the grass seed. It looked rich and black now with moisture, receiving of the seed, and it seemed that the grass sprang up overnight, pale green in the early spring.

We couldn't keep from looking at it, unable to believe that we had created this delicate growth. We looked at T. J. with understanding now, knowing the fulfillment of the plan he had carried along within his mind. We had worked without full understanding of the task, but he had known all the time.

We found that we couldn't walk or play on the delicate blades, as we had expected to, but we didn't mind. It was enough just to look at it, to realize that it was the work of our own hands, and each evening, the whole gang was there, trying to measure the growth that had been achieved that day.

One time a foot was placed on the plot of ground, one time only, Blackie stepping onto it with sudden bravado. Then he looked at the crushed blades and there was shame in his face. He did not do it again. This was his grass, too, and not to be desecrated. No one said anything, for it was not necessary.

T. J. had reserved a small section for watermelons, and he was still trying to find some seed for it. The wholesale house didn't have any watermelon seeds, and we didn't know where we could lay our hands on them. T. J. shaped the earth into mounds, ready to receive them, three mounds lying in a straight line along the edge of the grass plot.

We had just about decided that we'd have to buy the seeds if we were to get them. It was a violation of our principles, but we were anxious to get the watermelons started. Somewhere or other, T. J. got his hands on a seed catalog and brought it one evening to our roof garden.

"We can order them now," he said, showing us the catalog. "Look!"

We all crowded around, looking at the fat, green watermelons pictured in full color on the pages. Some of them were split open, showing the red, tempting meat, making our mouths water.

"Now we got to scrape up some seed money," T. J. said, looking at us. "I got a quarter. How much you-all got?"

We made up a couple of dollars among us and T. J. nodded his head. "That'll be more than enough. Now we got to decide what kind to get. I think them Kleckley Sweets. What do you-all think?"

He was going into esoteric matters beyond our reach. We hadn't even known there were different kinds of melons. So we just nodded our heads and agreed that yes, we thought the Kleckley Sweets too.

"I'll order them tonight," T. J. said. "We ought to have them in a few days."

"What are you boys doing up here?" an adult voice said behind us.

It startled us, for no one had ever come up here before in all the time we had been using the roof of the factory. We jerked around and saw three men standing near the trap door at the other end of the roof. They weren't policemen or night watchmen, but three men in plump business suits, looking at us. They walked toward us.

"What are you boys doing up here?" the one in the middle said again.

We stood still, guilt heavy among us, levied by the tone of voice, and looked at the three strangers.

The men stared at the grass flourishing behind us. "What's this?" the man said. "How did this get up here?"

"Sure is growing good, ain't it?" T. J. said conversationally. "We planted it."

The men kept looking at the grass as if they didn't believe it. It was a thick carpet over the earth now, a patch of deep greenness startling in the sterile industrial surroundings.

"Yes, sir," T. J. said proudly. "We toted that earth up here and planted that grass." He fluttered the seed catalog. "And we're just fixing to plant us some watermelon."

The man looked at him then, his eyes strange and faraway. "What do you mean, putting this on the roof of my building?" he said. "Do you want to go to jail?"

T. J. looked shaken. The rest of us were silent, frightened by the authority of his voice. We had grown up aware of adult authority, of policemen and night watchmen and teachers, and this man sounded like all the others. But it was a new thing to T. J.

"Well, you wasn't using the roof," T. J. said. He paused a moment and added shrewdly, "So we just thought to pretty it up a little bit."

"And sag it so I'd have to rebuild it," the man said sharply. He started turning away, saying to another man beside him, "See that all that junk is shoveled off by tomorrow."

"Yes, sir," the man said.

T. J. started forward. "You can't do that," he said. "We toted it up here, and it's our earth. We planted it and raised it and toted it up here."

The man stared at him coldly. "But it's my building," he said. "It's to be shoveled off tomorrow."

"It's our earth," T. J. said desperately. "You ain't got no right!"

The men walked on without listening and descended clumsily through the trapdoor. T. J. stood looking after them, his body tense with anger, until they had disappeared. They wouldn't even argue with him, wouldn't let him defend his earth-rights.

He turned to us. "We won't let 'em do it," he said fiercely. "We'll stay up here all day tomorrow and the day after that, and we won't let 'em do it."

We just looked at him. We knew there was no stopping it.

He saw it in our faces, and his face wavered for a moment before he gripped it into determination. "They ain't got no right," he said. "It's our earth. It's our land. Can't nobody touch a man's own land."

We kept looking at him, listening to the words but knowing that it was no use. The adult world had descended on us even in our richest dream, and we knew there was no calculating the adult world, no fighting it, no winning against it.

We started moving slowly toward the parapet and the fire escape, avoiding a last look at the green beauty of the earth that T. J. had planted for us, had planted deeply in our minds as well as in our experience. We filed slowly over the edge and down the steps to the plank, T. J. coming last, and all of us could feel the weight of his grief behind us.

"Wait a minute," he said suddenly, his voice harsh with the effort of calling.

We stopped and turned, held by the tone of his voice, and looked up at him standing above us on the fire escape.

"We can't stop them?" he said, looking down at us, his face strange in the dusky light. "There ain't no way to stop 'em?"

"No," Blackie said with finality. "They own the building."

We stood still for a moment, looking up at T. J., caught into inaction by the decision working in his face. He stared back at us, and his face was pale and mean in the poor light, with a bald nakedness in his skin like cripples have sometimes.

"They ain't gonna touch my earth," he said fiercely. "They ain't gonna lay a hand on it! Come on."

He turned around and started up the fire escape again, almost running against the effort of climbing. We followed more slowly, not knowing what he intended to do. By the time we reached him, he had seized a board and thrust it into the soil, scooping it up and flinging it over the parapet into the areaway below. He straightened and looked at us.

"They can't touch it," he said. "I won't let 'em lay a dirty hand on it!"

We saw it then. He stooped to his labor again, and we followed, the gusts of his anger moving in frenzied labor among us as we scattered along the edge of earth, scooping it and throwing it over the parapet, destroying with anger the growth we had nurtured with such tender care. The soil carried so laboriously upward to the light and the sun cascaded swiftly into the dark areaway, the green blades of grass crumpled and twisted in the falling.

It took less time than you would think; the task of destruction is infinitely easier than that of creation. We stopped at the end, leaving only a scattering of loose soil, and when it was finally over, a stillness stood among the group and over the factory building. We looked down at the bare sterility of black tar, felt the harsh texture of it under the soles of our shoes, and the anger had gone out of us, leaving only a sore aching in our minds like overstretched muscles.

T. J. stood for a moment, his breathing slowing from anger and effort, caught into the same contemplation of destruction as all of us. He stooped slowly, finally, and picked up a lonely blade of grass left trampled under our feet and put it between his teeth, tasting it, sucking the greenness out of it into his mouth. Then he started walking toward the fire escape, moving before any of us were ready to move, and disappeared over the edge.

We followed him, but he was already halfway down to the ground, going on past the board where we crossed over, climbing down into the areaway. We saw the last section swing down with his weight, and then he stood on the concrete below us, looking at the small pile of anonymous earth scattered by our throwing. Then he walked across the place where we could see him and disappeared toward the street without glancing back, without looking up to see us watching him.

They did not find him for two weeks.

Then the Nashville police caught him just outside the Nashville freight yards. He was walking along the railroad track, still heading South, still heading home.

As for us, who had no remembered home to call us, none of us ever again climbed the escapeway to the roof.

Responding to the Story

Analyzing the Story

Identifying Facts

1. This is a story in which two contrasting **settings** have a strong effect on the characters, particularly on a boy named T. J. Describe the setting T. J. remembers. Describe the setting he is now in.
2. What does T. J. want? What **obstacles** does he have to overcome to get what he wants?
3. What does the narrator realize for the first time when he smells the "sweet odor of the earth" under his feet (page 114)?

Interpreting Meanings

4. In your own words, summarize what the other boys learn from T. J. Why do you think they never returned to the rooftop setting?

5. Locate the passage that mentions Antaeus in the story. Explain the connection between what happens to Antaeus in the old myth and what happens to T. J. in this modern story.
6. Think about the word *escapeway* in the last sentence. In what ways was that passage to the roof an "escape" for the boys?
7. At the end of the story, the narrator says that he and the other boys had "no remembered home" to call them. What could the word *home* mean here? Why do you think the city setting couldn't be considered a "home"?

Writing About the Story

A Creative Response

1. **Describing a Setting.** Imagine you have moved to a new community that is very different from the

one where you now live, as T. J. has in this story. Suppose you make new friends who want to know what kind of setting you have come from. In one paragraph tell them about one place where you used to spend a lot of your time. Use **images** that will make your new friends experience this place with each of their five senses. You might tell about your family kitchen, a barn, a garage, a local shop or restaurant—any place you enjoyed and are familiar with. Before you write, make a list of all the specific features of the setting you plan to describe.

A Critical Response

2. **Explaining a Topic Statement.** After the boys destroy the green world they had worked so hard to create, the narrator says: "It took less time than you would think; the task of destruction is infinitely easier than that of creation." In one paragraph explain how this statement applies to the story and how it applies to actual life as well. Use the second part of this quotation as your topic sentence.

Analyzing Language and Vocabulary

Significant Words

On page 115, the writer says this about the grassy setting of T. J.'s rooftop garden:

"This was his grass, too, and not to be *desecrated*."

In another passage, the writer says this about the tarred rooftop:

"We looked down at the bare *sterility* of black tar . . .'"

Look up the words *desecrated* and *sterility* in a dictionary, and answer the following questions:

1. What word means the opposite of *desecrate*?
2. If a church is *desecrated,* what has happened?
3. By using this specific word, what does the writer suggest about T. J.'s feelings for his grass?
4. What word means the opposite of *sterility*?
5. Could T. J.'s grass and garden be described as *sterile*? Why?
6. By using the word *sterility,* what does the writer suggest about the way the boys feel about the city setting?

Reading About the Writer

Like many American writers, **Borden Deal** (1922–1985) was a Southerner. Like his hero T. J., he came from a family of cotton farmers who knew firsthand the hardships of farm life during the 1930's. Deal was born in Mississippi, but as a youth he "beat around" the country for several years looking for work. He was a student at the University of Alabama, on the G.I. bill, when his first story was accepted for publication. A big, friendly man, Deal went on to publish hundreds of short stories and several popular novels.

Focusing on Background
A Comment from the Writer

"My short story 'Antaeus' has a strange history. Though it has been reprinted far more often than any other of my nearly one hundred short stories, it took me *ten years* to get it published the first time! True. It was turned down by every quality and popular magazine in the country, not once but two or three times. Then, on re-reading the story after a year or so, I'd like it all over again, and I'd send it around once more. After a long ten years, the story was finally published by one of the country's finest literary magazines, and the next year it was reprinted in the annual collection called *The Best American Short Stories.* Since then, the story has appeared in hundreds of textbooks and anthologies on every level, from grammar school to college. So you see, when you believe in something, it pays to keep the faith and be persistent—just as, in the story, T. J. is persistent in his faith and feeling for the earth."

—Borden Deal

A MAN CALLED HORSE

Dorothy M. Johnson

Before 1845, most of the West was not part of the United States at all. This unusual story begins in 1845 and is set in Indian territory. The tribe it brings to vivid life is the Crow tribe, which at this time moved frequently over the northern Plains to follow the buffalo herds. The story's conflict involves a clash between two cultures—the white man must adapt to the Crow culture or he will perish. As you read, see if you want "Horse" to escape—or do you find yourself hoping he stays with the Crows?

He was a young man of good family, as the phrase went in the New England of a hundred-odd years ago, and the reasons for his bitter discontent were unclear, even to himself. He grew up in the gracious old Boston home under his grandmother's care, for his mother had died in giving him birth; and all his life he had known every comfort and privilege his father's wealth could provide.

But still there was the discontent, which puzzled him because he could not even define it. He wanted to live among his equals—people who were no better than he and no worse either. That was as close as he could come to describing the source of his unhappiness in Boston and his restless desire to go somewhere else.

In the year 1845, he left home and went out West, far beyond the country's creeping frontier, where he hoped to find his equals. He had the idea that in Indian country, where there was danger, all white men were kings, and he wanted to be one of them. But he found, in the West as in Boston, that the men he respected were still his superiors, even if they could not read, and those he did not respect weren't worth talking to.

He did have money, however, and he could hire the men he respected. He hired four of them, to cook and hunt and guide and be his companions, but he found them not friendly.

They were apart from him and he was still alone. He still brooded about his status in the world, longing for his equals.

On a day in June, he learned what it was to have no status at all. He became a captive of a small raiding party of Crow Indians.

He heard gunfire and the brief shouts of his companions around the bend of the creek just before they died, but he never saw their bodies. He had no chance to fight, because he was naked and unarmed, bathing in the creek, when a Crow warrior seized and held him.

His captor let him go at last, let him run. Then the lot of them rode him down for sport, striking him with their coup sticks. They carried the dripping scalps of his companions, and one had skinned off Baptiste's black beard as well, for a trophy.

They took him along in a matter-of-fact way, as they took the captured horses. He was unshod and naked as the horses were, and like them he had a rawhide thong around his neck. So long as he didn't fall down, the Crows ignored him.

On the second day they gave him his breeches. His feet were too swollen for his boots, but one of the Indians threw him a pair of moccasins that had belonged to the halfbreed, Henri, who was dead back at the creek. The captive wore the moccasins gratefully. The third day they let him ride one of the spare horses so the party could move faster, and on that day they came in sight of their camp.

He thought of trying to escape, hoping he might be killed in flight rather than by slow torture in the camp, but he never had a chance to try. They were more familiar with escape than he was, and knowing what to expect, they forestalled it. The

Camp of the Piegan Indians by Karl Bodmer (1833).

Haesaler/Art Resource, Inc.

only other time he had tried to escape from anyone, he had succeeded. When he had left his home
in Boston, his father had raged and his grandmother had cried, but they could not talk him out
of his intention.

The men of the Crow raiding party didn't bother
with talk.

Before riding into camp they stopped and
dressed in their regalia and in parts of their victims' clothing; they painted their faces black.
Then, leading the white man by the rawhide
around his neck as though he were a horse, they
rode down toward the tepee circle, shouting and
singing, brandishing their weapons. He was unconscious when they got there; he fell and was
dragged.

He lay dazed and battered near a tepee while
the noisy, busy life of the camp swarmed around
him and Indians came to stare. Thirst consumed
him, and when it rained he lapped rain water from
the ground like a dog. A scrawny, shrieking, eter-
nally busy old woman with ragged graying hair
threw a chunk of meat on the grass, and he fought
the dogs for it.

When his head cleared, he was angry, although
anger was an emotion he knew he could not afford.

It was better when I was a horse, he thought—
when they led me by the rawhide around my neck.
I won't be a dog, no matter what!

The hag gave him stinking, rancid grease and
let him figure out what it was for. He applied it
gingerly to his bruised and sun-seared body.

Now, he thought, I smell like the rest of them.

While he was healing, he considered coldly the
advantages of being a horse. A man would be
humiliated, and sooner or later he would strike
back and that would be the end of him. But a
horse had only to be docile. Very well, he would
learn to do without pride.

He understood that he was the property of the
screaming old woman, a fine gift from her son,
one that she liked to show off. She did more yelling at him than at anyone else, probably to impress
the neighbors so they would not forget what a
great and generous man her son was. She was
bossy and proud, a dreadful sag of skin and bones,
and she was a devilish hard worker.

The white man, who now thought of himself as a horse, forgot sometimes to worry about his danger. He kept making mental notes of things to tell his own people in Boston about this hideous adventure. He would go back a hero, and he would say, "Grandmother, let me fetch your shawl. I've been accustomed to doing little errands for another lady about your age."

Two girls lived in the tepee with the old hag and her warrior son. One of them, the white man concluded, was his captor's wife and the other was his little sister. The daughter-in-law was smug and spoiled. Being beloved, she did not have to be useful. The younger sister had bright, wandering eyes. Often enough they wandered to the white man who was pretending to be a horse.

The two girls worked when the old woman put them at it, but they were always running off to do something they enjoyed more. There were games and noisy contests, and there was much laughter. But not for the white man. He was finding out what loneliness could be.

That was a rich summer on the plains, with plenty of buffalo for meat and clothing and the making of tepees. The Crows were wealthy in horses, prosperous, and contented. If their men had not been so avid for glory, the white man thought, there would have been a lot more of them. But they went out of their way to court death, and when one of them met it, the whole camp mourned extravagantly and cried to their God for vengeance.

The captive was a horse all summer, a docile bearer of burdens, careful and patient. He kept reminding himself that he had to be better-natured than other horses, because he could not lash out with hoofs or teeth. Helping the old woman load up the horses for travel, he yanked at a pack and said, "Whoa, brother. It goes easier when you don't fight."

The horse gave him a big-eyed stare as if it understood his language—a comforting thought, because nobody else did. But even among the horses he felt unequal. They were able to look out for themselves if they escaped. He would simply starve. He was envious still, even among the horses.

Humbly he fetched and carried. Sometimes he even offered to help, but he had not the skill for the endless work of the women, and he was not trusted to hunt with the men, the providers.

When the camp moved, he carried a pack trudging with the women. Even the dogs worked then, pulling small burdens on travois[1] of sticks.

The Indian who had captured him lived like a lord, as he had a right to do. He hunted with his peers, attended long ceremonial meetings with much chanting and dancing, and lounged in the shade with his smug bride. He had only two responsibilities: to kill buffalo and to gain glory. The white man was so far beneath him in status that the Indian did not even think of envy.

One day several things happened that made the captive think he might sometime become a man again. That was the day when he began to understand their language. For four months he had heard it, day and night, the joy and the mourning, the ritual chanting and sung prayers, the squabbles and the deliberations. None of it meant anything to him at all.

But on that important day in early fall the two young women set out for the river, and one of them called over her shoulder to the old woman. The white man was startled. She had said she was going to bathe. His understanding was so sudden that he felt as if his ears had come unstopped. Listening to the racket of the camp, he heard fragments of meaning instead of gabble.

On that same important day the old woman brought a pair of new moccasins out of the tepee and tossed them on the ground before him. He could not believe she would do anything for him because of kindness, but giving him moccasins was one way of looking after her property.

In thanking her, he dared greatly. He picked a little handful of fading fall flowers and took them to her as she squatted in front of her tepee, scraping a buffalo hide with a tool made from a piece of iron tied to a bone. Her hands were hideous—most of the fingers had the first joint missing. He bowed solemnly and offered the flowers.

She glared at him from beneath the short, rag-

---

1. **travois** (trə·voi'): a sled, consisting of a net or platform dragged along the ground by two poles.

ged tangle of her hair. She stared at the flowers, knocked them out of his hand, and went running to the next tepee, squalling the story. He heard her and the other women screaming with laughter.

The white man squared his shoulders and walked boldly over to watch three small boys shooting arrows at a target. He said in English, "Show me how to do that, will you?"

They frowned, but he held out his hand as if there could be no doubt. One of them gave him a bow and one arrow, and they snickered when he missed.

The people were easily amused, except when they were angry. They were amused at him, playing with the little boys. A few days later he asked the hag, with gestures, for a bow that her son had just discarded, a man-sized bow of horn. He scavenged for old arrows. The old woman cackled at his marksmanship and called her neighbors to enjoy the fun.

When he could understand words, he could identify his people by their names. The old woman was Greasy Hand, and her daughter was Pretty Calf. The other young woman's name was not clear to him, for the words were not in his vocabulary. The man who had captured him was Yellow Robe.

Once he could understand, he could begin to talk a little, and then he was less lonely. Nobody had been able to see any reason for talking to him, since he would not understand anyway. He asked the old woman. "What is my name?" Until he knew it, he was incomplete. She shrugged to let him know he had none.

He told her in the Crow language, "My name is Horse." He repeated it, and she nodded. After that they called him Horse when they called him anything. Nobody cared except the white man himself.

They trusted him enough to let him stray out of camp, so that he might have got away and, by unimaginable good luck, might have reached a trading post or a fort, but winter was too close. He did not dare leave without a horse; he needed clothing and a better hunting weapon than he had and more certain skill in using it. He did not dare steal, for then they would surely have pursued him, and just as certainly they would have caught

him. Remembering the warmth of the home that was waiting in Boston, he settled down for the winter.

On a cold night he crept into the tepee after the others had gone to bed. Even a horse might try to find shelter from the wind. The old woman grumbled, but without conviction. She did not put him out.

They tolerated him, back in the shadows, so long as he did not get in the way.

He began to understand how the family that owned him differed from the others. Fate had been cruel to them. In a short, sharp argument among the old women, one of them derided Greasy Hand by sneering, "You have no relatives!" and Greasy Hand raved for minutes of the deeds of her father and uncles and brothers. And she had had four sons, she reminded her detractor—who answered with scorn, "Where are they?"

Later the white man found her moaning and whimpering to herself, rocking back and forth on her haunches, staring at her mutilated hands. By that time he understood. A mourner often chopped off a finger joint. Old Greasy Hand had mourned often. For the first time he felt a twinge of pity, but he put it aside as another emotion, like anger, that he could not afford. He thought: What tales I will tell when I get home!

He wrinkled his nose in disdain. The camp stank of animals and meat and rancid grease. He looked down at his naked, shivering legs and was startled, remembering that he was still only a horse.

He could not trust the old woman. She fed him only because a starved slave would die and not be worth boasting about. Just how fitful her temper was he saw on the day when she got tired of stumbling over one of the hundred dogs that infested the camp. This was one of her own dogs, a large, strong one that pulled a baggage travois when the tribe moved camp.

Countless times he had seen her kick at the beast as it lay sleeping in front of the tepee, in her way. The dog always moved, with a yelp, but it always got in the way again. One day she gave the dog its usual kick and then stood scolding at it while the animal rolled its eyes sleepily. The old woman suddenly picked up her axe and cut the dog's head off with one blow. Looking well satisfied with herself, she beckoned her slave to remove the body.

It could have been me, he thought, if I were a dog. But I'm a horse.

His hope of life lay with the girl, Pretty Calf. He set about courting her, realizing how desperately poor he was both in property and honor. He owned no horse, no weapon but the old bow and the battered arrows. He had nothing to give away, and he needed gifts, because he did not dare seduce the girl.

One of the customs of courtship involved sending a gift of horses to a girl's older brother and bestowing much buffalo meat upon her mother. The white man could not wait for some far-off time when he might have either horses or meat to give away. And his courtship had to be secret. It was not for him to stroll past the groups of watchful girls, blowing a flute made of an eagle's wing bone, as the flirtatious young men did.

He could not ride past Pretty Calf's tepee, painted and bedizened;[2] he had no horse, no finery.

Back home, he remembered, I could marry just about any girl I'd want to. But he wasted little time thinking about that. A future was something to be earned.

The most he dared do was wink at Pretty Calf now and then, or state his admiration while she giggled and hid her face. The least he dared do to win his bride was to elope with her, but he had to give her a horse to put the seal of tribal approval on that. And he had no horse until he killed a man to get one. . . .

His opportunity came in early spring. He was casually accepted by that time. He did not belong, but he was amusing to the Crows, like a strange pet, or they would not have fed him through the winter.

His chance came when he was hunting small game with three young boys who were his guards as well as his scornful companions. Rabbits and birds were of no account in a camp well fed on buffalo meat, but they made good targets.

His party walked far that day. All of them at once saw the two horses in a sheltered coulee.[3] The boys and the man crawled forward on their bellies, and then they saw an Indian who lay on the ground, moaning, a lone traveler. From the way the boys inched eagerly forward, Horse knew the man was fair prey—a member of some enemy tribe.

This is the way the captive white man acquired wealth and honor to win a bride and save his life: He shot an arrow into the sick man, a split second ahead of one of his small companions, and dashed forward to strike the still-groaning man with his bow, to count first coup. Then he seized the hobbled horses.

By the time he had the horses secure, and with them his hope for freedom, the boys had followed, counting coup with gestures and shrieks they had practiced since boyhood, and one of them had the scalp. The white man was grimly amused to see the boy double up with sudden nausea when he had the thing in his hand. . . .

There was a hubbub in the camp when they rode in that evening, two of them on each horse. The captive was noticed. Indians who had ignored him as a slave stared at the brave man who had struck first coup and had stolen horses.

The hubbub lasted all night, as fathers boasted loudly of their young sons' exploits. The white man was called upon to settle an argument between two fierce boys as to which of them had struck second coup and which must be satisfied with third. After much talk that went over his head, he solemnly pointed at the nearest boy. He didn't know which boy it was and didn't care, but the boy did.

The white man had watched warriors in their triumph. He knew what to do. Modesty about achievements had no place among the Crow people. When a man did something big, he told about it.

The white man smeared his face with grease and charcoal. He walked inside the tepee circle, chanting and singing. He used his own language.

"You heathens, you savages," he shouted. "I'm going to get out of here someday! I am going to get away!" The Crow people listened respect-

---

2. **bedizened:** dressed in a showy way.

3. **coulee:** a ravine.

Chan-Chä-Viá-Teüin, Teton Sioux, by Karl Bodmer (c. 1840). Watercolor and pencil.

Joslyn Art Museum, Omaha, Nebraska.

fully. In the Crow tongue he shouted, "Horse! I am Horse!" and they nodded.

He had a right to boast, and he had two horses. Before dawn, the white man and his bride were sheltered beyond a far hill, and he was telling her, "I love you, little lady. I love you."

She looked at him with her great dark eyes, and he thought she understood his English words—or as much as she needed to understand.

"You are my treasure," he said, "more precious than jewels, better than fine gold. I am going to call you Freedom."

When they returned to camp two days later, he was bold but worried. His ace, he suspected, might not be high enough in the game he was playing without being sure of the rules. But it served.

Old Greasy Hand raged—but not at him. She complained loudly that her daughter had let herself go too cheap. But the marriage was as good as any Crow marriage. He had paid a horse.

He learned the language faster after that, from Pretty Calf, whom he sometimes called Freedom. He learned that his attentive, adoring bride was fourteen years old.

One thing he had not guessed was the difference

that being Pretty Calf's husband would make in his relationship to her mother and brother. He had hoped only to make his position a little safer, but he had not expected to be treated with dignity. Greasy Hand no longer spoke to him at all. When the white man spoke to her, his bride murmured in dismay, explaining at great length that he must never do that. There could be no conversation between a man and his mother-in-law. He could not even mention a word that was part of her name.

Having improved his status so magnificently, he felt no need for hurry in getting away. Now that he had a woman, he had as good a chance to be rich as any man. Pretty Calf waited on him; she seldom ran off to play games with other young girls, but took pride in learning from her mother the many women's skills of tanning hides and making clothing and preparing food.

He was no more a horse but a kind of man, a half-Indian, still poor and unskilled but laden with honors, clinging to the buckskin fringes of Crow society.

Escape could wait until he could manage it in comfort, with fit clothing and a good horse, with hunting weapons. Escape could wait until the camp moved near some trading post. He did not plan how he would get home. He dreamed of being there all at once and of telling stories nobody would believe. There was no hurry.

Pretty Calf delighted in educating him. He began to understand tribal arrangements, customs, and why things were as they were. They were that way because they had always been so. His young wife giggled when she told him, in his ignorance, things she had always known. But she did not laugh when her brother's wife was taken by another warrior. She explained that solemnly with words and signs.

Yellow Robe belonged to a society called the Big Dogs. The wife stealer, Cut Neck, belonged to the Foxes. They were fellow tribesmen; they hunted together and fought side by side, but men of one society could take away wives from the other society if they wished, subject to certain limitations.

When Cut Neck rode up to the tepee, laughing and singing, and called to Yellow Robe's wife,

"Come out! Come out!" she did as ordered, looking smug as usual, meek and entirely willing. Thereafter she rode beside him in ceremonial processions and carried his coup stick, while his other wife pretended not to care.

"But why?" the white man demanded of his wife, his Freedom. "Why did our brother let his woman go? He sits and smokes and does not speak."

Pretty Calf was shocked at the suggestion. Her brother could not possibly reclaim his woman, she explained. He could not even let her come back if she wanted to—and she probably would want to when Cut Neck tired of her. Yellow Robe could not even admit that his heart was sick. That was the way things were. Deviation meant dishonor.

The woman could have hidden from Cut Neck, she said. She could even have refused to go with him if she had been *ba-wurokee*—a really virtuous woman. But she had been his woman before, for a little while on a berrying expedition, and he had a right to claim her.

There was no sense in it, the white man insisted. He glared at his young wife. "If you go, I will bring you back!" he promised.

She laughed and buried her head against his shoulder. "I will not have to go," she said. "Horse is my first man. There is no hole in my moccasin."

He stroked her hair and said, *"Ba-wurokee."*

With great daring, she murmured, *"Hayha,"* and when he did not answer, because he did not know what she meant, she drew away, hurt.

"A woman calls her man that if she thinks he will not leave her. Am I wrong?"

The white man held her closer and lied, "Pretty Calf is not wrong. Horse will not leave her. Horse will not take another woman, either." No, he certainly would not. Parting from this one was going to be harder than getting her had been. *"Hayha,"* he murmured. "Freedom."

His conscience irked him, but not very much. Pretty Calf could get another man easily enough when he was gone, and a better provider. His hunting skill was improving, but he was still awkward.

There was no hurry about leaving. He was used to most of the Crow ways and could stand the rest. He was becoming prosperous. He owned five horses. His place in the life of the tribe was secure, such as it was. Three or four young women, including the one who had belonged to Yellow Robe, made advances to him. Pretty Calf took pride in the fact that her man was so attractive.

By the time he had what he needed for a secret journey, the grass grew yellow on the plains and the long cold was close. He was enslaved by the girl he called Freedom and, before the winter ended, by the knowledge that she was carrying his child. . . .

The Big Dog society held a long ceremony in the spring. The white man strolled with his woman along the creek bank, thinking: When I get home I will tell them about the chants and the drumming. Sometime. Sometime.

Pretty Calf would not go to bed when they went back to the tepee.

"Wait and find out about my brother," she urged. "Something may happen."

So far as Horse could figure out, the Big Dogs were having some kind of election. He pampered his wife by staying up with her by the fire. Even the old woman, who was a great one for getting sleep when she was not working, prowled around restlessly.

The white man was yawning by the time the noise of the ceremony died down. When Yellow Robe strode in, garish and heathen in his paint and feathers and furs, the women cried out. There was conversation, too fast for Horse to follow, and the old woman wailed once, but her son silenced her with a gruff command.

When the white man went to sleep, he thought his wife was weeping beside him.

The next morning she explained.

"He wears the bearskin belt. Now he can never retreat in battle. He will always be in danger. He will die."

Maybe he wouldn't, the white man tried to convince her. Pretty Calf recalled that some few men had been honored by the bearskin belt, vowed to the highest daring, and had not died. If they lived through the summer, then they were free of it.

"My brother wants to die," she mourned. "His heart is bitter."

Yellow Robe lived through half a dozen clashes with small parties of raiders from hostile tribes.

His honors were many. He captured horses in an enemy camp, led two successful raids, counted first coup and snatched a gun from the hand of an enemy tribesman. He wore wolf tails on his moccasins and ermine skins on his shirt, and he fringed his leggings with scalps in token of his glory.

When his mother ventured to suggest, as she did many times, "My son should take a new wife, I need another woman to help me," he ignored her. He spent much time in prayer, alone in the hills or in conference with a medicine man. He fasted and made vows and kept them. And before he could be free of the heavy honor of the bearskin belt, he went on his last raid.

The warriors were returning from the north just as the white man and two other hunters approached from the south, with buffalo and elk meat dripping from the bloody hides tied on their restive ponies. One of the hunters grunted, and they stopped to watch a rider on the hill north of the tepee circle.

The rider dismounted, held up a blanket and dropped it. He repeated the gesture.

The hunters murmured dismay. "Two! Two men dead!" They rode fast into the camp, where there was already wailing.

A messenger came down from the war party on the hill. The rest of the party delayed to paint their faces for mourning and for victory. One of the two dead men was Yellow Robe. They had put his body in a cave and walled it in with rocks. The other man died later, and his body was in a tree.

There was blood on the ground before the tepee to which Yellow Robe would return no more. His mother, with her hair chopped short, sat in the doorway, rocking back and forth on her haunches, wailing her heartbreak. She cradled one mutilated hand in the other. She had cut off another finger joint.

Pretty Calf had cut off chunks of her long hair and was crying as she gashed her arms with a knife. The white man tried to take the knife away, but she protested so piteously that he let her do as she wished. He was sickened with the lot of them.

Savages! he thought. Now I will go back! I'll go hunting alone, and I'll keep on going.

But he did not go just yet, because he was the

only hunter in the lodge of the two grieving women, one of them old and the other pregnant with his child.

In their mourning, they made him a pauper again. Everything that meant comfort, wealth, and safety they sacrificed to the spirits because of the death of Yellow Robe. The tepee, made of seventeen fine buffalo hides, the furs that should have kept them warm, the white deerskin dress, trimmed with elk teeth, that Pretty Calf loved so well, even their tools and Yellow Robe's weapons—everything but his sacred medicine objects—they left there on the prairie, and the whole camp moved away. Two of his best horses were killed as a sacrifice, and the women gave away the rest.

They had no shelter. They would have no tepee of their own for two months at least of mourning, and then the women would have to tan hides to make it. Meanwhile they could live in temporary huts made of willows, covered with skins given them in pity by their friends. They could have lived with relatives, but Yellow Robe's women had no relatives.

The white man had not realized until then how terrible a thing it was for a Crow to have no kinfolk. No wonder old Greasy Hand had only stumps for fingers. She had mourned, from one year to the next, for everyone she had ever loved. She had no one left but her daughter, Pretty Calf.

Horse was furious at their foolishness. It had been bad enough for him, a captive, to be naked as a horse and poor as a slave, but that was because his captors had stripped him. These women had voluntarily given up everything they needed.

He was too angry at them to sleep in the willow hut. He lay under a sheltering tree. And on the third night of the mourning he made his plans. He had a knife and a bow. He would go after meat, taking two horses. And he would not come back. There were, he realized, many things he was not going to tell when he got back home.

In the willow hut, Pretty Calf cried out. He heard rustling there, and the old woman's querulous voice.

Some twenty hours later his son was born, two months early, in the tepee of a skilled medicine woman. The child was born without breath, and the mother died before the sun went down.

The white man was too shocked to think whether he should mourn, or how he should mourn. The old woman screamed until she was voiceless. Piteously she approached him, bent and trembling, blind with grief. She held out her knife and he took it.

She spread out her hands and shook her head. If she cut off any more finger joints, she could do no more work. She could not afford any more lasting signs of grief.

The white man said, "All right! All right!" between his teeth. He hacked his arms with the knife and stood watching the blood run down. It was little enough to do for Pretty Calf, for little Freedom.

Now there is nothing to keep me, he realized. When I get home, I must not let them see the scars.

He looked at Greasy Hand, hideous in her grief-burdened age, and thought: I really am free now! When a wife dies, her husband has no more duty toward her family. Pretty Calf had told him so, long ago, when he wondered why a certain man moved out of one tepee and into another.

The old woman, of course, would be a scavenger. There was one other with the tribe, an ancient crone who had no relatives, toward whom no one felt any responsibility. She lived on food thrown away by the more fortunate. She slept in shelters that she built with her own knotted hands. She plodded wearily at the end of the procession when the camp moved. When she stumbled, nobody cared. When she died, nobody would miss her.

Tomorrow morning, the white man decided, I will go.

His mother-in-law's sunken mouth quivered. She said one word, questioningly. She said, *"Eero-oshay?"* She said, "Son?"

Blinking, he remembered. When a wife died, her husband was free. But her mother, who had ignored him with dignity, might if she wished ask him to stay. She invited him by calling him Son, and he accepted by answering Mother.

Greasy Hand stood before him, bowed with years, withered with unceasing labor, loveless and childless, scarred with grief. But with all her burdens, she still loved life enough to beg it from him, the only person she had any right to ask. She was stripping herself of all she had left, her pride.

He looked eastward across the prairie. Two thousand miles away was home. The old woman would not live forever. He could afford to wait, for he was young. He could afford to be magnanimous, for he knew he was a man. He gave her the answer. *"Eegya,"* he said. "Mother."

He went home three years later. He explained no more than to say, "I lived with Crows for a while. It was some time before I could leave. They called me Horse."

He did not find it necessary either to apologize or to boast, because he was the equal of any man on earth.

Responding to the Story

Analyzing the Story

Identifying Facts

1. List the details we are given about the Boston **setting.** Why is the man unhappy there?
2. In contrast to her brief summary of the hero's own culture, the writer shows us an enormous amount about Crow customs. Explain what you learned from the story about at least five Crow customs.
3. How does the man become a "horse"?
4. Name the two things that happen one day to make Horse think that he might become a man again.
5. Explain why Horse marries Pretty Calf. Describe what happens to his status in the Crow community after his marriage.

Interpreting Meanings

6. By the end of the story, how has Horse changed? In your own words, explain what he discovers about himself—and other people—in his years with the Crows. How did becoming a "horse" help him become a man?
7. Did you make a judgment about Crow society when you learned about "counting coup" or about how a grieving mother would chop off one joint of her finger for each dead child? Explain how the writer wants you to feel about the Crows. Name at least two incidents in the story that remind us that all people share common human feelings.
8. Did you want Horse to get home to Boston, or did you want him to stay with the Crows? In light of your answer, explain whether you found the

story's **resolution** satisfactory. If not, tell how you would have resolved Horse's **conflict.**
9. It has been said that there are only two reasons why people read. One is for information, the other for entertainment. Did you enjoy this story because of the information it gives about an unusual setting? Or, did you enjoy it because it was entertaining and suspenseful? Explain how you responded to the story.

Writing About the Story

A Creative Response

1. **Writing a Journal Entry.** Imagine that the man called Horse is home in Boston and that he writes an entry in his journal describing his first days back in his "own world." What would he think of his own culture now? Would he be critical of any customs? Does he miss anything about the Crows? Write a paragraph that Horse might enter in his journal. Have Horse use the first-person pronoun "I."
2. **Describing an Alien Culture.** Suppose you are transported to a strange setting and culture, either in this world or in another one. In a paragraph describe three unusual sights and one unusual custom (regarding eating, caring for children, or settling disputes). Tell how you feel as a stranger in this strange land.

A Critical Response

3. **Analyzing a Movie's Plot.** Many movies and TV shows involve a **conflict of cultures.** In some of these stories, an alien from another world is set down on earth and must survive in a bewildering

new society. If you have seen such a movie or show recently, write about it in a paragraph. Name at least two ways in which the alien's ways clash with the ways of the new world. Is the alien presented as innocent or as evil? Tell how the conflict is finally resolved.

4. **Describing Setting.** Look back at pages 121–122 when the man first enters the Crow camp. Note the **images** that help you see, smell, taste, and hear the setting as the man experienced it. Then write a paragraph naming at least four images that helped you feel as if you were there. Before you write, list the images on a chart like this one:

Sight	Smell	Taste	Hearing
1.	1.	1.	1.
2.	2.	2.	2.
etc.	etc.	etc.	etc.

5. **Supporting a Topic Statement.** Write a paragraph in which you provide details from the story to support the last sentence in Jack Schaefer's paragraph (see "Focusing on Background," which follows). If you do not agree with Jack Schaefer, rephrase his statement to make it state your own opinion.

Analyzing Language and Vocabulary

Words from the American Indians

The Crows in this story spoke a form of Siouan, one of the six great "superfamilies" of languages spoken by the American Indians. Thousands of place names on this continent are derived from American Indian languages like Siouan. The early settlers also borrowed many Indian words to name new things they found in the new world. The following questions ask about words derived from some of the American Indian languages. Use a dictionary to find the answers.

1. What Indian language is the word *moccasin* derived from?
2. What Indian language does *tepee* come from?
3. According to your dictionary, what language does the word *caucus* come from, and what did it originally mean?
4. How are these three words used in American English today?
5. What do these place names mean, and what Indian languages are they derived from?

Iowa	Chicago
Texas	Milwaukee
Minnesota	Miami

Reading About the Writer

Dorothy M. Johnson (1905–   ) grew up in Montana. When she was an adult she moved East and tried hard to be an Easterner, but she finally returned home to Montana in the 1950's. At this point, according to Jack Schaefer (another famous Western writer), she began to write "the stories that only Dorothy Johnson could write." Three of her stories—"The Hanging Tree," "The Man Who Shot Liberty Valance," and "A Man Called Horse"—were made into movies. Johnson was welcomed into the Blackfoot tribe in Montana as an honorary member. Her tribal name is "Kills-Both-Places."

Focusing on Background
A Critic Talks About Dorothy Johnson

"No one has written with more understanding of the mountain men who first penetrated the Indian wilderness and of the white settlers who met hardship in hostile Indian territory. And no one has written with keener perception of the Indians themselves, the displaced persons who saw their lands being taken and their way of life crumbling before the inevitable white advance. Here is no glamoriz-ing, no romantic gilding, of settlers or of Indians. Here is something finer and more gripping, the honest portrayal of good and bad, of strength and frailty, of the admirable and the contemptible, in both white settlements and Indian villages. . . ."

—Jack Schaefer
(author of *Shane*)

Literature & Language

Using Connotation to Create Mood

Literary Model

In this passage from a famous short story, a man approaches the gloomy house owned by his friends the Ushers, where he plans a visit.

> During the whole of a dull, dark, and soundless day in the autumn of the year, when the clouds hung oppressively low in the heavens, I had been passing alone, on horseback, through a singularly dreary tract of country, and at length found myself, as the shades of the evening drew on, within view of the melancholy House of Usher. I know not how it was—but, with the first glimpse of the building, a sense of insufferable gloom pervaded my spirit. . . . I looked upon the scene before me—upon the mere[1] house, and the simple landscape features of the domain—upon the bleak walls—upon the vacant eye-like windows—upon a few rank sedges—and upon a few white trunks of decayed trees—with an utter depression of soul. . . . There was an iciness, a sinking, a sickening of the heart—an unredeemed dreariness of thought. . . . What was it—I paused to think—what was it that so unnerved me in the contemplation of the House of Usher? . . . I reined my horse to the precipitous brink of a black and lurid tarn[2] that lay in unruffled luster by the dwelling, and gazed down—but with a shudder even more thrilling than before—upon the remodeled and inverted images of the gray sedge and the ghastly tree stems and the vacant and eye-like windows.
>
> —from "The Fall of the House of Usher,"
> Edgar Allan Poe

---

1. **mere:** a marshy lake. (The house is beside the lake.)
2. **tarn:** a small mountain pool or lake.

A Note on Connotation

All words have literal, or denotative, meanings—these are meanings that appear in the dictionary. Some words also have connotative meanings. **Connotations** are the emotions and associations that have become associated with a word through usage. Writers pay particular attention to the connotations of words when they want to create mood or atmosphere. For example, notice the words Poe chooses in describing the House of Usher:

> I looked upon the scene before me—upon the mere house, and the simple landscape features of the domain—upon the *bleak* walls—upon the *vacant eye-like* windows—upon a few *rank* sedges—and upon a few white trunks of *decayed* trees—with an utter *depression of soul*.

The narrator is describing a deteriorating old house, but the adjectives *bleak*, *vacant*, *eye-like*, *rank*, *decayed*, and *depression of soul* suggest that the house suffers from something more horrifying than ordinary aging. The italicized words create the story's main mood or atmosphere. Over and over again, Poe chooses words that are associated with gloom, dread, death, and emptiness or sterility.

Examining the Writer's Style

Working with a small group of classmates, study the rest of this passage and examine the meanings of key words and their emotional effects.

First, list words from the passage that have strong emotional associations. Then see if all members of your group agree with the feelings associated with these words. Or do the words suggest different feelings to different people? Use a cluster chart like the one on the next page to group words together that seem to convey similar feelings or emotional effects.

After you create cluster maps for Poe's key words, think of other groups of words that suggest other strong connotations. For example, you might create cluster maps containing words that you associate with peace, or joy, or springtime.

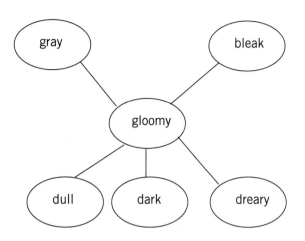

Using Connotations in Your Writing

1. **Describing a Setting.** Imagine that a family emergency has made it necessary for you to spend the summer with a relative you hardly know. This person lives in an unusual house in a distant state, or even in a foreign country. Write a letter to your best friend at home describing the place where you are living. Use words that not only describe your new surroundings but also suggest how you feel about them.

   a. Begin by imagining a detailed picture of your setting. (If you like to draw, you may want to make a drawing of the house or of a particular room.) Jot down adjectives and nouns that describe specific features of the setting (sights, colors, weather, sounds, temperatures). Then think about the overall feeling that you wish to get across to your friend. Does the setting frighten, disgust, relax, or enchant you, for example? Use the words you have chosen to write a letter that will leave your friend in no doubt about how you feel about your summer home.

   b. Exchange letters with a classmate. Circle all the words in your classmate's letter that stir your emotions. Then tell your friend what overall feeling or mood you got from reading the letter. Ask your classmate to do the same for your letter.

   c. If your reader experienced the feeling you intended to get across, you have achieved your purpose. If you did not communicate your intended feeling, rewrite your letter. When revising, look at the words your classmate marked in your letter. Have you used enough connotative words to make a single strong impression?

2. **Re-creating the House of Usher.** Try to change the entire mood of this description of the Ushers' house. You can do this by using words with very different connotations. You might want to go back to the clusters you created in the preceding exercise and substitute words with entirely different connotations for Poe's words. Try to keep the general outline of the original passage, in which a narrator on horseback comes upon a house. Here are some details you'll have to change: season, weather, landscape, time of day, and feelings and mood of the person on horseback.

EXPLAINING THE FUNCTION OF SETTING

Writing Assignment

Describe the setting of "Top Man" (page 96) and explain how the setting functions in the story. Write two paragraphs.

Background

You've seen that setting can work three ways in fiction: (1) Setting can be the source of the story's **conflict:** the characters might struggle with the weather, with a creature, or with a feature of the landscape. (2) Setting can reveal **character:** it can show us how people respond to their environment, or it can show us where a character makes a home or what a character's culture is. (3) Setting can create a story's **mood or atmosphere:** it can act as background music for the story's actions.

Prewriting

Filling out the following charts will give you raw material for your essay on setting. Be sure to cite details from the story where they apply. For some sections of the charts, nothing in the story will apply; leave those sections blank.

```
1. What is the setting?
   Historical period?_____
   Country or locale?_____
   Season of the year?_____
   Weather?_____
   Time of day?_____
   Sights?_____
   Sounds?_____
   Tastes?_____
   Smells?_____
   Other details that establish a sense of place?__
   _____
```

```
2. Are the characters in conflict with their setting?
   What do the characters want, and does the set-
   ting keep them from getting it?_____
   _____
```

```
3. What does the setting tell us about the characters?
   What feelings or attitudes do the main charac-
   ters reveal toward their setting?
   Fear?_____
   Pleasure?_____
   Challenge?_____
   Dislike?_____
   Respect?_____
   Other?_____
```

```
4. Do the details of the setting create an atmosphere?
   Which of the following words describe the at-
   mosphere or mood created by the setting?
   Which details from the story support this judg-
   ment?
   Gloomy?_____
   Cheerful?_____
   Mysterious?_____
   Threatening?_____
   Other?_____
```

Writing

Your answers to the items on Chart 1 will give you material to complete the first part of the assignment (to describe the **setting**). Your answers to Charts 2, 3, and 4 will give you material to complete the second part of the assignment (to explain the setting's function).

In your first paragraph, describe the setting, using the details you've cited on the chart. In the second paragraph, state how the setting functions in the story. Cite at least one detail from the story to support your statement. You might think that the setting has more than one function in the story.

Here is how a famous mystery writer analyzes the setting of Sherlock Holmes's rooms. Perhaps you have read one of Arthur Conan Doyle's stories about the famous detective, who lived at 221B Baker Street, London, many years ago. Mrs. Hudson was Holmes's housekeeper.

There is probably no room in crime fiction that we enter with a keener sense of instant recognition than that claustrophobic upstairs sitting room at 221B Baker Street. Baker Street is now one of the dullest of London's main thoroughfares, and it is difficult, walking these wide pavements, to picture those foggy Victorian evenings with the inevitable veiled lady alighting from her hansom cab outside the door of the celebrated Sherlock Holmes.

But we can see every detail of the room into which Mrs. Hudson will usher her: the sofa on which Holmes reclines during his periods of meditation; the violin case propped against the wall; the shelves of scrapbooks; the bullet marks in the wall; the two broad windows overlooking the street; the twin armchairs on each side of the fireplace; the desk with the locked drawer containing Holmes's confidential records; the central table with "its white cloth and glimmer of china and metal" waiting for Mrs. Hudson to clear away.

The mental scene has, of course, been reinforced countless times in films and on television, but what is remarkable is that so vivid a picture should be produced by so few actual facts. Paradoxically, I can find no passage in the books that describes the room at length and in detail. Instead, Sir Arthur Conan Doyle builds up the scene through a series of stories object by object, and the complete picture is one that the reader himself creates and furnishes in his own imagination from this accumulation of small details.

Few things reveal the essential self more surely than the rooms in which we live, the objects with which we choose to surround ourselves, the books we place on our shelves, all those small household gods that help reaffirm identity and provide comfort and a sense of security. But the description in crime fiction of domestic interiors, furnishings, and possessions does more than denote character; it creates mood and atmosphere, enhances suspense, and is often crucial to the plot.

—P. D. James
(author of *The Black Tower*)

Checklist for Revision

1. Have you cited the title of the story and its author?
2. Have you described where and when the story takes place?
3. Have you explained how the setting functions in the story?
4. Have you supported your statements with specific details from the story?

When we speak of point of view, we simply mean the person the writer has chosen to see the story and to tell it as well. In broad terms, there are three points of view: **omniscient, third-person limited,** and **first person.**

Let's look from an upper window into a sunny street. A young man pauses, puts down the case he is carrying, takes from it a trumpet, and begins to play "Stardust."

Presently, a young woman appears in the window above him. Smiling, she sways her head in time with his tune. A large brown dog saunters up, sits in front of the musician, and howls along with the horn. A second window opens to reveal a man in pajamas. He complains that the noise has awakened him, and if it doesn't stop he will call the police.

The trumpeter hesitates. The young woman applauds and tosses a shower of coins into the trumpet case. The musician bows and plays the theme song from *Cats.* The dog resumes howling, and the man in the pajamas slams his window.

A policeman appears, orders the trumpeter to move on, examines the dog's collar to find him unlicensed, and leads him off. Soon the girl appears in the doorway and, after a moment's hesitation, hurries off in the direction taken by the trumpeter.

Suppose we're interested enough in these events to want to make a story out of them. We'd have three choices:

The Omniscient Point of View

We could tell our story from the **third-person omniscient** point of view. *Omniscient* means "all knowing." *Third-person* simply means that this narrator refers to all the characters in the story as "he" or "she"—in other words, this narrator is not a character in the story and never uses the first-person pronoun "I" to refer to himself or herself. This point of view is often just called "omniscient."

The omniscient narrator knows everything, as would a god who is looking down on earthly characters. This omniscient narrator is able to tell us everything about every character (including how each one thinks and feels). The omniscient narrator can tell us about the past, present, and future. The omniscient narrator is also able to comment directly on the events and the characters. If an omniscient narrator were to tell our story, we might learn that the girl will be married to the musician in a year's time, that the musician is adored by dogs and small children, and that the man in pajamas is lazy and prefers cats. This omniscient point of view is the one many people are most familiar with. We first hear it in fairy tales and children's stories.

Point of View: Who Is Telling the Story?

"We can't imagine what a spider thinks, Louisa, because it's a whole different life style."

© Drawing by Ziegler.

© 1991 The New Yorker Magazine, Inc.

Third-Person Limited

We could tell our story from a **third-person limited** point of view. This means that the narrator will focus in on the thoughts and feelings of just one character. With this point of view, we feel we are experiencing the events of the story chiefly through the memory and senses of only one character. This point of view permits us to share intensely in one character's reactions to everything that happens in the story.

If a third-person limited narrator were to tell our story, we would learn a great deal about the private history and the thoughts and feelings and reactions of one character in the story, but we would not learn as much about the others.

The First Person ("I")

We could let one of the characters tell our story, using the **first-person** point of view. Now one of the characters in the story will be talking to us, using "I," the first-person pronoun, from which this point of view gets its name. When a character in the story is the narrator, we can know only what this person observes and hears about the other characters. All of our information comes from what this one character chooses—or is able—to tell us.

Point of View Makes a Difference

Imagine how the events in our story would be colored if we let the trumpeter tell his own story: we might hear how he needs to earn money, how proud he is of his technique, how he loves the flattery of the girl's response, how he even enjoys the accompaniment of the large brown dog, and how he is shocked by the response of the man in pajamas and angry at the policeman.

Suppose we let the girl tell the story; she will now be the narrator. Perhaps she looks forward to further acquaintance with the trumpeter. She might describe the sidewalk episode as a romantic one, glowing with expectations of a new love to replace the old one who said goodbye last week. If she tells the story, the reader might not even meet the man in the pajamas, the large brown dog, or the policeman. Suppose we let the man in the pajamas tell the story. He would most likely explain why he is in pajamas, sleeping till noon. Now the story might become tragic—that very night, he might tell us, he had fallen asleep at the warehouse and had lost his job because he had been kept awake the day before by a barking dog.

Even the dog could tell the story. His view of events might be equally tragic. He might describe the episode to the other dogs in the pound, while waiting (without much hope) to be rescued by someone in need of a large brown dog. The dog, of course, would not be interested in the impulses that sent the girl out after the trumpeter.

I remember well my sensation as we first entered the house. I knew instantly that something was very wrong. I realized that my father's chair had been sat in, as well as my mother's and my own. The porridge we had left on the table to cool had been partially eaten. None of this, however, prepared me for what we were about to discover upstairs. . . .

Drawing by Whitney Darrow.

The more you think about it, the more you realize what a huge difference point of view makes to a story. You realize how one character's feelings, memories, and prejudices can give the same events entirely different meanings.

While readers are rarely even aware of the point-of-view problem, writers and student writers talk about it constantly, and the best of them are always experimenting with it. In telling the trumpeter's story, they would probably be tempted to let the large brown dog tell it, just to see the difference.

The Narrator Is Not the Writer

Remember that the narrator of the story is not necessarily the story's author. In "Blues Ain't No Mockin Bird" (page 8), the voice we hear is the voice of one of Granny's young grandchildren—this is not the writer, who is Toni Cade Bambara. In "The Cask of Amontillado" (page 210), the voice we hear is the voice of a murderer—this is not the author, who is Edgar Allan Poe, who certainly never walled up a man alive.

Is the Narrator Telling the Truth?

The writer expects us to question any storytelling voice. In particular, any story told in the first person (that is, by someone who calls himself or herself "I") should be watched carefully for reliability. One interesting illustration of this is the famous Japanese tale "Rashomon." This is a four-way story of a murder. The events of the violent crime are retold four times, by the three principal characters and by a witness. Each time, only the narrator is changed, yet each time the story becomes dramatically different, in impact and in meaning. By the time the fourth person has told the tale, we are not sure of what really happened. We do not know which narrator has told us the truth—perhaps none of them did.

How to Identify Point of View

To identify a story's point of view, ask yourself these questions:

1. Is the story told by someone who is not in the story, who never uses "I," but who speaks of all the characters as "he" or "she"? (If so, you have a third-person narrator.)

2. Does this third-person narrator tell you the private thoughts or motivations or life histories of many characters? (If so, you have an **omniscient** narrator.)

3. Or does this third-person narrator zoom in on the thoughts and feelings of only one character in the story? (If so, you have a **third-person limited** narrator.)

4. Is the narrator a character in the story, who speaks of himself or herself as "I"? (If so, you have a **first-person** narrator.)

> " **W**hile readers are rarely even aware of the point-of-view problem, writers and student writers talk about it constantly, and the best of them are always experimenting with it. "

SNOW

Julia Alvarez

If you have stayed in the tropics all your life, you do not know what it's like to see a winter sky fill with snow. If you have never left the northern part of the United States, you do not know what it's like, deep in December, to feel the warm sun on your bare arms.

The first short-short story that follows is narrated by a young girl who has just moved to New York City from the Dominican Republic, a small country that is 575 miles southeast of Miami, Florida. As you might predict from the title, Alvarez's story will have something to do with snow.

Before you read her story, review what you know about the Cuban Missile Crisis, which took place in 1962. John F. Kennedy was then President of the United States, and Fidel Castro was Premier of Cuba. Cuba is an ally of the Soviet Union; in 1962, both countries were Communist and considered threats to the United States.

Our first year in New York we rented a small apartment with a Catholic school nearby, taught by the Sisters of Charity, hefty women in long black gowns and bonnets that made them look peculiar, like dolls in mourning. I liked them a lot, especially my grandmotherly fourth-grade teacher, Sister Zoe. I had a lovely name, she said, and she had me teach the whole class how to pronounce it. *Yo-lan-da.* As the only immigrant in my class, I was put in a special seat in the first row by the window, apart from the other children so that Sister Zoe could tutor me without disturbing them. Slowly, she enunciated the new words I was to repeat: *laundromat, corn flakes, subway, snow.*

Soon I picked up enough English to understand holocaust was in the air. Sister Zoe explained to a wide-eyed classroom what was happening in Cuba. Russian missiles were being assembled, trained supposedly on New York City. President Kennedy, looking worried too, was on the television at home, explaining we might have to go to war against the Communists. At school, we had air-raid drills: An ominous bell would go off and we'd file into the hall, fall to the floor, cover our heads with our coats, and imagine our hair falling out, the bones in our arms going soft. At home, Mami and my sisters and I said a rosary for world peace. I heard new vocabulary: *nuclear bomb, radioactive fallout, bomb shelter.* Sister Zoe explained how it would happen. She drew a picture of a mushroom on the blackboard and dotted a flurry of chalkmarks for the dusty fallout that would kill us all.

The months grew cold, November, December. It was dark when I got up in the morning, frosty when I followed my breath to school. One morning as I sat at my desk daydreaming out the window, I saw dots in the air like the ones Sister Zoe had drawn—random at first, then lots and lots. I shrieked, "Bomb! Bomb!" Sister Zoe jerked around, her full black skirt ballooning as she hurried to my side. A few girls began to cry.

But then Sister Zoe's shocked look faded. "Why, Yolanda dear, that's snow!" She laughed. "Snow."

"Snow," I repeated. I looked out the window warily. All my life I had heard about the white crystals that fell out of American skies in the winter. From my desk I watched the fine powder dust the sidewalk and parked cars below. Each flake was different, Sister Zoe had said, like a person, irreplaceable and beautiful.

MY LUCY FRIEND WHO SMELLS LIKE CORN

Sandra Cisneros

You must read this next short-short story aloud, to hear the feelings expressed by a very young Mexican American girl who yearns to have a friend. This story is a "monologue"—that is, it is a speech delivered by a single character.

If you don't know Spanish, perhaps a Spanish-speaking classmate can help you with some of the names. In Spanish, the vowels (a, e, i, o, u) are pronounced ä (ah), ā, ēe, ō (oh), ōo. Most words are accented on their next-to-last syllable. Lucy's last name is pronounced än·gwē·än'ō.

Before you read, write in your journal a few of your thoughts about children's need for friends. When you were younger, what did you like to do with your best friend? What did you like about this friend?

Lucy Anguiano, Texas girl who smells like corn, like Frito Bandito chips, like tortillas, something like that warm smell of nixtamal or bread the way her head smells when she's leaning close to you over a paper cut-out doll or on the porch when we are squatting over marbles trading this pretty crystal that leaves a blue star on your hand for that giant cat-eye with a grasshopper green spiral in the center like the juice of bugs on the windshield when you drive to the border, like the yellow blood of butterflies. *Have you ever eated dog food? I have.* After crunching like ice, she opens her big mouth to prove it, only a pink tongue rolling around in there like a blind worm, and Janey looking in because she said show me. But me I like that Lucy, corn smell hair and aqua flip flops just like mine which we bought at the K-mart for only 79¢ same time. I'm going to sit in the sun, don't care if it's a million trillion degrees outside, so my skin can get so dark it's blue where it bends like Lucy's. Her whole family like that. Eyes like knife slits. Lucy and her sisters. Norma, Margarita, Ofelia, Herminia, Nancy, Olivia, Cheli, y la Amber Sue.

Screen door with no screen. BANG! Little black dog biting his fur. Fat couch on the porch. Some of the windows painted blue, some pink because her Daddy got tired that day or forgot. Mama in the kitchen feeding clothes into the wringer washer and clothes rolling out all stiff and twisted and flat like paper. Lucy got her arm stuck once and had to yell Maaa! and her Mama had to put the machine in reverse and then her hand rolled back, the finger black and later, the nail fell off. *But did your arm get flat like the clothes? What happened to your arm? Did they have to pump it with air?* No, only the finger, and she didn't cry neither.

Lean across the porch rail and pin the pink sock of the baby Amber Sue on top of Cheli's flowered t-shirt, and the blue jeans of la Ofelia over the inside seam of Olivia's blouse, over the flannel nightgown of Margarita so it don't stretch out, and then you take the workshirts of their Daddy and hang them upside down like this, and this way all the clothes don't get so wrinkled and take up less space and you don't waste pins. The girls all wear each other's clothes, except Olivia who is stingy, because there ain't no boys here. Only girls and one father who is never home hardly and one mother who says *Ay! I'm real tired* and so many sisters there's no time to count them.

Cumpleaños de Lala y Tudi (Birthday Party) by Carmen Lomas Garza (1989). Oil on canvas. 36″ × 48″.

© 1989 Carmen Lomas Garza.

I'm sitting in the sun even though it's the hottest part of the day, the part that makes the streets dizzy, when the heat makes a little hat on the top of your head and bakes the dust and weed grass and sweat up good, all steamy and smelling like sweet corn.

I want to rub heads and sleep in a bed with little sisters, some at the top and some at the feets. I think it would be fun to sleep with sisters you could yell at one at a time or all together, instead of alone on the fold-out chair in the living room.

When I get home Abuelita[1] will say *Didn't I tell you?* and I'll get it because I was supposed to wear this dress again tomorrow. But first I'm going to jump off an old pissy mattress in the Anguiano yard. I'm going to scratch your mosquito bites, Lucy, so they'll itch you, then put mercurochrome smiley faces on them. We're going to trade shoes and wear them on our hands. We're going to walk over to Janey Ortiz's house and say *We're never ever going to be your friend again forever!* We're going to run home backwards and we're going to run home frontwards, look twice under the house where the rats hide and I'll stick one foot in there because you dared me, sky so blue and heaven inside those white clouds. I'm going to peel a scab from my knee and eat it, sneeze on the cat, give you three M&M's I've been saving for you since yesterday, comb your hair with my fingers and braid it into teeny-tiny braids real pretty. We're going to wave to a lady we don't know on the bus. Hello! I'm going to somersault on the rail of the front porch even though my chones[2] show. And cut paper dolls we draw ourselves, and color in their clothes with crayons, my arm around your neck. And when we look at each other, our arms gummy from an orange popsicle we split, we could be sisters, right? We could be, you and me waiting for our teeths to fall and money. You laughing something into my ear that tickles, and me going Ha Ha Ha Ha. Her and me, my Lucy friend who smells like corn.

---

1. **Abuelita** (ä·bwä·lē′tä): "little grandmother" (in English, she might say Granny).

2. **chones** (chō′näs): pants.

Responding to the Stories

Analyzing the Stories

Snow

Identifying Facts

1. What frightening events are happening in Cuba during this story?
2. What mistake does Yolanda make when she first sees snow?

Interpreting Meanings

3. How can you tell that this story is told from the **first-person point of view?** Suppose Sister Zoe were telling the story. What might you know that Yolanda can't tell you?
4. Yolanda tells us about two new sets of English words that she learns from Sister Zoe. How do the "war words" differ from the "peacetime words"? How would the second list of words make a child feel?
5. As much as anything, this story reveals the **character** of Sister Zoe. What does Sister Zoe's last remark tell you about the way she treats her students?
6. How do you think people today would respond to a crisis like this one? How do you think such situations affect young children?

My Lucy Friend Who Smells Like Corn

Identifying Facts

1. The narrator is talking about Lucy, but she does include a few clues about herself and her family. List all the facts you can discover about this young narrator.

Interpreting Meanings

2. How old do you think these girls are? What details make you think so?
3. Where does this narrator indicate that she wants to be like Lucy? Why do you think she likes Lucy so much?
4. The narrator might not be aware of it, but some details in her monologue suggest that Lucy's family might not have much money. What details are they?

5. Do you find any hints that the narrator is really lonely at home? What are they?
6. In a monologue like this, we learn a great deal about the **character** of the speaker. What adjectives would you use to describe this young girl?
7. This story succeeds or fails depending on how you feel about the narrator's voice. How do you respond to this story? Do you think this voice sounds like that of a real girl?

Writing About the Stories

A Creative Response

1. **Writing from Another Point of View.** To see how important point of view is, let another character tell her or his version of each story. Here are some ideas:
   a. Let another classmate tell about Yolanda, the only immigrant in the class.
   b. Let Sister Zoe tell about the Cuban Missile Crisis and how she feels as she prepares her students for an emergency.
   c. Let Lucy tell us something about her friend.
   d. There is a third girl mentioned twice in the "Lucy" story. Who is she? Let her speak to us.

   In your retelling, use the **first-person point of view,** that is, let your new narrator tell the story using the first-person pronoun "I."

2. **Writing a Monologue.** Write a short monologue in the voice of a real person. You will have to use the first-person point of view. Try to find words and construct sentences that imitate the way your character talks and thinks. Before you write, gather your ideas in a chart like this:

	Story
Narrator	
Age of narrator	
Event or person described	
Feelings I want to express	

You may want your narrator to be yourself.

Analyzing Language and Vocabulary

Sentence Fragments and Grammar
(An Oral Activity)

The "Lucy" story is told in the voice you'd hear if this young narrator were talking to you, person to person. In fact, when we read the story, we feel we are overhearing a little girl's private thoughts—her wishes, her fears, her joys.

Prepare this story about Lucy for oral presentation, before an audience. Notice how the long rambling statements, the short punchy fragments, and the slang all work to recreate the special rhythms of the narrator's personal voice. As part of your preparation, do the following:

1. Reread the first long "sentence" aloud. Is this a complete sentence—that is, does it have a subject and a verb and express a complete thought? What words in this "sentence" would you emphasize? Where would you pause?
2. Go through the story and find at least six very brief sentence fragments—that is, statements that express only partial thoughts. (You should find some that are only one word.) How would you read these fragments?
3. Where does this young narrator make grammatical mistakes or use slang words—language which would not be appropriate if she were addressing a parent-teacher meeting?
4. What emotional changes can you chart in this monologue? That is, where does this young narrator reveal different feelings—jealousy, happiness, love, awe, sadness, determination?

Reading About the Writers

At the age of ten, **Julia Alvarez** (1950–   ) left her home in the Dominican Republic and emigrated with her family to New York City. The Alvarez children went to Catholic schools and learned English, sometimes painstakingly, as the story "Snow" shows. "Snow" is from Alvarez's first book of fiction, *How the Garcia Girls Lost Their Accents.* The other Garcia girls—besides Yolanda—are Carla, Sandra, and Sofia. Alvarez has also published a book of poetry called *Homecoming.* She now teaches at her alma mater, Middlebury College, in Vermont.

Sandra Cisneros (1954–   ) was born in Chicago to a Mexican father and a Mexican-American mother. It is no wonder, given her six boisterous brothers, that Cisneros identified with the lone sister in the fairy tale "Six Swans" (her last name means "swan keeper"). Cisneros's first novel, based loosely on her childhood, is called *The House on Mango Street.* She also has published two collections of poems, *Bad Boys* and *My Wicked Wicked Ways.* The "My Lucy Friend" story is part of a new collection called *Woman Hollering Creek.* Cisneros often gives readings of her work. To hear her read is to watch an actress at work. Standing alone at the podium, reading a story aloud, Cisneros can fill the stage with people.

Focusing on Background
A Great English Teacher

"In sixth grade, I had one of the first of a lucky line of great English teachers who began to nurture a love of the language, a love that had been there since a childhood of listening closely to words. Sister Bernadette did not make our class interminably diagram sentences from a workbook or learn a catechism of grammar rules. Instead, she asked us to write little stories imagining we were snowflakes, birds, pianos, a stone in the pavement, a star in the sky. What would it feel like to be a flower with roots in the ground? If the clouds could talk, what would they say? She had an expressive, dreamy look that was accentuated by her face being framed in a wimple. Supposing, just supposing . . . My mind would take off, soaring into possibilities, a flower with roots, a star in the sky, a cloud full of sad sad tears, a piano crying out each time its back was tapped, music only to our ears."

—Julia Alvarez

THE HAT

Jessamyn West

The plot of this story has to do with a teen-age girl's yearning for a hat, our discovery of why she wants the hat, and what happens when she gets it. But these incidents of the plot are interesting only insofar as they reveal Cress's experience with love. As you read, notice how the narrator helps you to see how all the main characters in the story are, in fact, moved by love.

It was a hot August morning, Saturday, six-thirty o'clock, and Mr. and Mrs. Delahanty still lingered at the breakfast table. Six-thirty is midmorning for a rancher in summer; but Mrs. Delahanty hadn't finished talking about the hat.

"It's perfectly clear why she wants it," she said.

It wasn't perfectly clear to Mr. Delahanty. Besides, he thought it would be interesting to know what one woman thinks of another's reasons for buying a hat, even though the second is only thirteen and her daughter.

"Why?" he asked.

"Edwin," said Mrs. Delahanty.

Mr. Delahanty put down his coffee which was too hot, anyway, for a hot morning.

"Edwin!" he exclaimed.

"Oh yes," Mrs. Delahanty assured him.

Mr. Delahanty decided to drink his coffee. After drinking, he asked, "How does the hat figure in it?"

"I think Cress thinks this hat would make Edwin see her in a new light. Frail and feminine."

"Better let her have it, hadn't you?" asked Mr. Delahanty. "Not that I like the idea of encouraging Edwin in any way."

"This hat," Mrs. Delahanty said, "wouldn't encourage anyone. This hat . . . Oh, Cress," she cried, "don't slip around that way. You gave me a start. What are you doing up this hour of the day anyway?"

During summer vacation Cress, unless she had projects of her own afoot, had to be routed from bed.

"I couldn't sleep," she said. She could tell from their faces that they had been talking about her. "And I wanted to ask Father something before he went out to work." She sat down at the table and turned toward her father as if they were two together, though seated unfortunately at a table with a stranger. "Can I call the store and tell them that if they'll hold the hat, you'll come in and look at it with me when we go to town tonight?"

"I've looked at it, Cress," said her mother.

"Mother," said Cress very sweetly, "I was speaking to Father. May I?"

"You don't have to ask permission of me, Cress, to speak to your father."

"Thank you, Mother," said Cress. "May I, Father?"

"Well," said Mr. Delahanty, "I don't suppose there'd be any harm in taking a look. Would there, Gertrude? Though you mustn't count on me for any expert advice about a hat, Cress."

Cress leaned toward her father. "Daddy," she said—she hadn't called her father Daddy for years but somehow the word seemed right and natural to her this morning—"Daddy, if you thought a hat was beautiful and becoming, I'd know it was beautiful and becoming. Or if you thought it was ugly and unsuitable, I'd know it was ugly and unsuitable. Do you know what, Daddy?" Cress said and leaned toward her father, admiring the philosophic lines which ran, not from his nose to his mouth and which she thought made people look sour, but from his cheekbone to his jawbone. "Do you know what?"

"No, Cress," said Mr. Delahanty, "I don't. But I'm waiting to be told."

"I think you probably have instinctive taste."

Mrs. Delahanty laughed, quite loud and long for so early in the morning.

Cress looked at her mother with a mingling of shock and disapproval on her face.

"Were you laughing at me or Daddy, Mother?" she asked politely.

"The two of you," said Mrs. Delahanty. "You and your daddy. Your daddy, Cress, can't tell a bonnet from a bushel basket. Not if the basket has a flower on it, anyway."

"Well, Gertrude," said Mr. Delahanty, "I may not be an expert on hats. I grant you that. But I think I know a pretty hat when I see one."

"That's why I want you to see this hat, Daddy," cried Cress. "It's so downright beautiful."

"That hat, Cress," said her mother, "is the most unsuitable object for a girl of thirteen years to put on her head I ever laid my eyes on."

"Just what do you mean by unsuitable, Gertrude?" asked Mr. Delahanty.

"I mean that hat was never intended for a thirteen-year-old girl. It's for an older—woman," concluded Mrs. Delahanty, wasting irony.

Mr. Delahanty poured himself a glass of milk. "You mean it ties under the chin?" he asked. "Or has . . ." He took a drink of milk, visibly running out of what suggested to him the hat of an older woman.

"Or has a black veil?" Cress helped him.

"No," said Mrs. Delahanty, "it hasn't got a black veil, and it doesn't tie under the chin. But every single other thing on this earth that hat has got."

"Now, Gertrude," said Mr. Delahanty, "maybe you'd just better tell me what this hat is really like."

Mrs. Delahanty had a musing look in her eyes. "John, do you remember the chamber of commerce dinner last fall? In Santa Ana?"

"I remember we were there."

"Do you remember the table decorations?"

"No," said Mr. Delahanty, "I can't say I remember the table decorations."

"Well, it's a pity you can't, because then you would know what this hat looks like."

Cress did not like the way her mother had of being funny about serious matters. It was objec-

tionable in anyone, in any mature person that is, and particularly so in a mother. When I have a child, Cress thought, I'll be serious and understanding the rest of my days.

"The table decorations," said Mrs. Delahanty reminiscently, "were horns of plenty, made out of straw mats. And out of them came spilling every fruit, grain, and flower ever grown in Orange County. Cress's hat would look right at home on that table."

"Oh Mother!" cried Cress.

"Except," said Mrs. Delahanty, "that those horns of plenty were of natural-colored straw, while this hat . . ." She paused, searching the room for some object with which to compare it. "While this hat," she concluded, "is an indescribable color."

"Oh Mother," cried Cress again. "It isn't. It's flamingo red."

"I've always considered red a nice warm color," said Mr. Delahanty.

"This is the warmest red, if it *is* red," agreed Mrs. Delahanty, "you ever laid eyes on. And its size!" Once again Mrs. Delahanty's eyes searched the kitchen without finding a comparable object. "It's just unbelievable," she said, shaking her head.

"Which all adds up to saying, I gather," said Mr. Delahanty, "that this hat Cress wants is large and flowered. Is that right, Cress? Is that the way it strikes you?"

The way the hat struck Cress was so overwhelming that she felt she might search the whole world over and still not find any word, any comparison which would explain it or the way she felt about it. The hat was summertime. It was deep and broad like summer. It caused soft scallops of shadow, like summer shadows under the densest trees, to fall across her face. It was like a poem; it was as much, "The rose is in full bloom, the riches of Flora are lavishly strown," as though Keats when he wrote had been thinking of it. The person wearing it would be languorous, gentle, and delicate. Looking at herself in the store mirror with that hat on, she had heard herself saying to Edwin, "If you'll be kind enough to give me your arm I think I'd like to stroll a little before the dew comes out." And she had seen how she would look, saying that, glancing appealingly upward at Edwin from under the brim of the shadow-casting, summery, flower-laden hat.

"Well, Cress?" asked her father.

"Oh, yes!" said Cress. "That's how it strikes me. May I call the store and say you'll come in tonight to look at it?"

"There's no rush, is there?" asked Mr. Delahanty. "Could look Monday as well as tonight, couldn't we?"

"The rush," said Cress, "is because I want it to wear to the beach tomorrow. That is, if you approve of it, Daddy."

"What's the idea, Cress?" asked her father. "A hat to the beach? You usually put on your bathing cap before we leave the house."

"Tomorrow," said Cress, "I'm not going to go thrashing about in the water. I'm going to walk about and observe."

"You're not going to be able to observe much, Cress," said her mother, "with that hat hanging down over your eyes."

Cress ignored this. "Father, may or may not I call the S.Q.R.? You don't have to promise to buy it or like it. Only to look at it."

"I guess looking never did any harm," said Mr. Delahanty.

"Now you've gone and done it," said Mrs. Delahanty, when Cress had gone.

"Done what?" asked Mr. Delahanty, innocently.

"Promised her that monstrosity. And all in the world she wants it for is to parade around Balboa in it tomorrow hoping Edwin will catch sight of her."

"Is Edwin in Balboa?"

"His family is. And as far as I know they haven't abandoned him."

"I didn't promise to buy the hat," protested Mr. Delahanty. "All I said I'd do was look at it."

Wearing the hat, Cress felt just as she had known she would: gentle and fragile and drooping. Beautiful, too. Running, with it on, would be utterly out of the question. Even sitting with it on had its difficulties, for the hat with its burden of fruits and flowers had to be balanced just so.

"Father," she called from the back seat, "will

you please roll up your window? It's blowing my hat."

"Cress," said Mr. Delahanty, "it's at least ninety in here now and I'm not going to roll this window up another inch. We're barely getting enough fresh air to keep us alive as it is."

"It's blowing the flowers off my hat," cried Cress.

"A few will never be missed," said Mr. Delahanty.

Mrs. Delahanty leaned across her husband and rolled up his window.

"How I could signal, if the need suddenly arose, I don't know," Mr. Delahanty told her, "apart from the fact that I'm suffocating right now."

"Nonsense," said Mrs. Delahanty. "Besides we'll be there in a few minutes."

"Steer for me for a minute, will you, Gertrude?" asked Mr. Delahanty. "I want to get out of this coat before I have a heat stroke."

How ridiculous! Cress felt just right. Warm, summery warm, of course, but though the car windows were tightly closed she could feel the freshness of the sea breeze which was bending the brown grass by the roadside, shaking the palm fronds, ruffling the white leghorns' tails up over their backs like untidy skirts. She could smell the strange salt freshness of the sea, the far, nonland scent of its never-quiet water; and suddenly, in a little gap between two brown hills, she saw the sea itself, blue in the hot air, rippling and glinting under the sun like the scales of big silver-blue fish. Cress sighed so deeply with pleasure that her hat rocked unsteadily and she righted it, holding it for a minute with both hands at just the angle which she hoped it would have when Edwin saw her.

Because Edwin would see her, of course. It was impossible to believe that she, having become the owner of the most beautiful hat, should be in the same town with Edwin without his seeing it and her.

After her father parked the car, he got out his own and her mother's bathing suits; then the two of them stood for a time looking at her.

"Well, times change," said Mr. Delahanty. "Times change. I never thought I'd live to see the day, Cress, when you'd elect to tramp up and down the boardwalk on a hot day instead of going swimming with us."

"I'm going to walk and observe," said Cress, holding onto her hat which was hard to control in the stiff sea breeze which was blowing. "I'm getting a little old for just sporting around in the water."

"Observe," said Mr. Delahanty, seriously regarding her. "I can only hope, Cress, the shoe won't be too decidedly on the other foot."

"Now, John," said Mrs. Delahanty, and though she wasn't ordinarily a mother much given to kissing, she managed to get sufficiently under the brim of Cress's hat to give her a loving kiss.

"You're all right, Crescent," she said. "That hat's a little unusual, but I don't know that I'd want a daughter of mine trigged out like everyone else. Have a good time. And I hope you see Edwin."

"Oh Mother," said Cress earnestly, for the knowledge of her mother's understanding was as comforting to her as confession after sin.

"Run on now," said Mrs. Delahanty.

"We'll meet you at Tiny's at four," said her father, "and have some ice cream before we go home."

At first, Cress was so certain of seeing Edwin that she walked along the boardwalk, really observing and truly, except for the difficulties she had keeping her hat righted, enjoying the sights and smells of the town and the sea. Now and then in front of a plate glass window which served her as mirror she stopped to admire her hat, to get it on straight again, and to poke up the stray hairs which kept dangling down from her not very solid kid-curler curls. Her mother had tried to persuade her not to wear a middy[1] and skirt, saying they didn't go well with her hat. She was glad she hadn't listened to her. A middy was a nautical costume, and what, unless you actually went to sea, was more nautical than the shore? And her hat was the heart of summer, and where was the heart of summer to be found if not in August at the beach? No, looking at herself in the plate glass

windows she passed, she was very content with what she saw: under the large hat her neck looked slender and reedlike, a blossom's stem; her eyes were shadowed, her entire aspect gentle, and even, she thought, mysterious. She was glad she had worn her high-heeled patent leather pumps, too. They made her teeter a little, but a swaying gait, she thought, suited the day, the hat, and her own personality, besides denying in the sharpest way possible the tomboy she was afraid Edwin thought her, and who would, no doubt, have worn sneakers.

What with observing, keeping her hat on straight, and practicing on occasional strangers the look of melting surprise with which she planned to greet Edwin, the first hour went by quickly. After the quietness of the ranch, where a whole day often passed with no other sounds than her own and her father's and mother's voices, and where the chief diversions, perhaps, were those of digging up a trap-door spider, or freeing a butcher-bird's victim, the sights and sounds of a beach town on a Sunday afternoon were almost too exciting to be borne.

First, there was the strange light touch of the penetrating wind off the sea on her warm inland body. Then there was the constant, half-heard beat of the surf, hissing as it ran smoothly up the sand, thundering as it crashed against the rocks of the breakwater. There were all the smells of salt and seaweed, of fish and water and wind. There were all the human smells too of the hundreds of people who filled the boardwalk: ladies in print dresses smelling like passing gardens; swimmers with their scents of suntan oils and skin lotions; there were the smells of the eating places: of mustard and onions, of hamburgers frying; and the sudden sharp smell of stacks of dill pickles, as brisk in the nose as a sudden unintended inhalation of sea water. There was the smell of frying fish from the many fish grottos.[2] And outside these places, in the middle of the boardwalk like miniature, land-locked seas, the glass tanks, where passers-by might admire the grace and color of their dinners before eating them. It was hard to say who did

---

1. **middy:** a blouse with a sailor collar.

2. **fish grottos:** little cavelike places that sell fish on this boardwalk.

the most looking; fish outward from these side-walk aquariums, at the strange pale gill-less pedestrians, or pedestrians inward at the finny swimmers.

Cress liked them both. Solemn fish and passers-by, some also solemn, with problems sun and water had not made them forget. For the first hour this was enough for Cress: being a part of this abundance and knowing that at any minute she would see Edwin. For in a town of one street how could she miss him?

Then suddenly the first hour was gone by; it was past three, and already the wind seemed a little sharper, the sun less bright, the boardwalk less crowded. More of her hair had come un-curled; her hat took more righting to keep it straight; her neck ached from holding her head high enough to see out from under the hat's brim;

occasional stabs of pain shot up the calves of legs unaccustomed to the pull of high heels. A thought, with the swiftness of a stone dropping through water, settled in her mind: he isn't coming. It was a possibility she had not even thought about before. She had thought he would *have* to come. The hat was *for* him. The day was *for* him. How could she possibly, without seeing him, meet her father and mother, say yes, say no, eat ice cream, get in the car, go home, take off her hat, go to bed, sleep?

It was fifteen after three. At first she had been willing that Edwin see her first. Now, she searched every figure, every slight, short man or boy's figure, for as great a distance as she could make them out, saying, "Be Edwin." So strongly did she will it that she thought she might, by determination alone, transform a stranger into Edwin.

It was three-thirty. It was fifteen of four. Her hat was on one side, her mouth weary from practicing her smile on strangers, the pleat out of her freshly starched skirt, her feet mere stumps of pain. Still, she would not give up. "Edwin, appear, Edwin appear," she willed.

Edwin did appear, crossing the street a block away, small and neat and thin in white duck pants and a white shirt. He crossed and turned toward Cress, walking steadily toward her. In two minutes or three he would see her, and see the hat and notice her new gentleness. All tiredness and pain left Cress. She could very easily have flown, or played a piece she had never seen before on the piano, or kissed a mad dog and not been bitten. She had just time to arrange herself, resettle her hat, give her now completely uncurled hair a quick comb upward. To do this she took her hat off, stood on tiptoe, and with fingers which trembled with excitement managed to get it up onto the top of one of the rectangular glass aquariums which by chance stood conveniently before her in the middle of the sidewalk.

Before she, herself, understood what had happened someone was jovially yelling, "Hey, sis, bread crumbs is what you feed them," and there was her hat, slowly, gracefully settling among the startled fish of the aquarium.

The man who had yelled was a short fat man, wearing pants, but no shirt or undershirt. He had sand in the hair on his chest; like dandruff, Cress thought wildly, unable for shame to raise her eyes to his face. "What's the idea, sis?" he asked.

Forcing her eyes away from the sandy dandruff, Cress saw that her hat, still gradually, gracefully floundering, was bleeding flamingo red into the aquarium, so that the amazed fish now swam in sunset waters.

"I thought it had a top," she whispered to no one in particular.

"The hat, sis?" asked the shirtless man.

"The glass place for the fish," Cress whispered. "I thought it had a top."

"It didn't, sis."

"I was resting my hat on it," Cress whispered, "while I fixed my hair."

"You was resting your hat on air, sis."

"It dropped," said Cress. "It fell right out of my hands."

"Gravity, sis," said the fat man. "It was gravity."

"Will it make the fish sick?" asked Cress.

"Make 'em die, sis, in my opinion. Make 'em all puke and throw up their shoestrings I should think."

"What'll I do?" asked Cress.

"Watch 'em die," said the fat man comfortably. "That big one's a goner already."

Cress wanted to die herself. She willed it very hard, but she couldn't. She couldn't even faint, though she held her breath and willed her heart to stop beating. But a sort of numbness did come over her, making all the voices blurred and indistinct, making all the people, and there were dozens, hundreds it seemed to Cress, now pressed about the aquarium, distant and hazy.

It was a field day for fish and humans. It was a great occasion for fish, who had had nothing more exciting to look forward to than death in the frying pan: a big blunt-nosed fish swam at the hat as if to ram it; smaller fish circled it curiously; nervous fish parted the darkening waters in a fishy frenzy. It was a glorious moment for humans, too, a sight they had never expected to see. Someone, a worthy man dedicated to service, brought out the fish grotto proprietor. He came in his white apron and tall chef's hat, brandishing a long-handled ladle and happy at first to see his fish arousing so much interest. He shouldered his way through the crowd, his bloodshot eyes bright with pleasure, until he caught sight of vermilion waters, frantic fish, and the heart of summer, still partially afloat among them. He had had a long hard day frying fish. This was the last straw, fish dying without frying.

"In Heaven's name," he cried, sadly, "who is murdering my fish?"

Cress was too frightened to reply.

"She is," said the fat man, pointing. "Sis, here, done it."

"What does she mean?" the fish grotto proprietor cried. Cress opened her mouth, but not a sound came out. She was as speechless as the fish.

"Sis here was resting her hat on the top of the aquarium," explained the fat man.

"There ain't no top," said the fish grotto owner. "Is she blind?"

"More or less, I reckon," said the fat man. "You kind of blind, sis?" he asked kindly.

Cress was able only to moan a little. With a long shudder, like a capsized ship coming to rest, her hat settled to the bottom of the aquarium. It lay there at a crazy angle, one side held up by a small castle with which the fish grotto proprietor had attempted to give his aquarium a romantic, gothic air. Out of a castle window one frightened fish eye peered, trying to penetrate the murky waters, make out if this was the end of the world for fish. It looked to be. Flowers and fruits were now adding their colors to that of the flamingo red straw. Streaks of purple from pansies and violets, puffs of sulphurous yellow from the daisies, veins of green from stems and flowers richly marbled the general red of the water. And the hat, in form as well as color, was suffering a sea-change. It was softening up, flattening out. Each minute it looked less and less like a hat.

Cress finally found her voice. "Save my hat," she whispered.

"It's too late," the fish grotto proprietor said, "to speak of saving anything. Hat or fishes. They are all goners. Let 'em die together."

"Die?" asked Cress.

"Poisoned," said the fish proprietor, pointing

to his frantic fish, the vari-colored water. "What've you got agin fish, kid?"

"I like fish," Cress whispered.

"She likes fish," said the fat man. "Hate to consider what she might do if she didn't." Those who had gathered about the aquarium laughed. Somewhere among them must be Edwin, Cress thought: seeing her, seeing her face trembling with the effort not to cry, seeing her beautiful hat, its colors fading out among an aquarium full of fish. The laughter was not malicious; it was lazy Sunday afternoon laughter; lazy Sunday afternoon laughers, watching, as if at play, to see what the fish proprietor would do, if he were villain or hero, straight man or clown. But it might as well have been malicious; it shamed Cress to the bone. It was unthinkable that anyone after such public humiliation could live. She would do nothing wild nor dramatic, simply refuse food, fade quietly away, die.

"Poisoned," declared the fish proprietor again, gloomily, "deliberately poisoned."

"I think you're mistaken about their being poisoned."

It was impossible, Cress thought, that anyone should be defending her: let alone Edwin—Edwin, who was always a victim himself.

"I think that color is probably from pure vegetable dyes," said Edwin. Edwin's face was as white as his shirt, and Cress could see that his upper lip trembled. But he was defending her, defying the fish grotto proprietor, not ashamed to be on the side of a person who had been publicly laughed at.

"It might even be good for the fish," suggested Edwin, "that pure vegetable dye."

"Good for them!" cried the fish proprietor. "Them fish have been scared to death at the very least, poison or no poison. Hats descending on them! I wouldn't feed them fish to a cat now. Their nervous systems have been shook up. You related to this girl?"

"No," said Edwin.

"Well, someone," said the fish proprietor, coming to the crux of the matter, "has got to pay for my ruined fish."

"That'll be me, I reckon," said Mr. Delahanty who, without enthusiasm, was pushing his way through the crowd. He took the ladle from the fish owner's hand, and being a tall man was able, by stretching a little, to fetch up the hat, heavy and dripping, from the bottom of the aquarium. He held the hat toward Cress, who without a word took it. Then Mr. Delahanty handed the ladle back to its owner.

"I'll pay ten dollars," he said.

"Twenty-five," said the fish grotto proprietor. "Not a cent less. Those were fancy fish and not to be picked up every day in the week."

"Eleven," said Mr. Delahanty.

"I was fond of those fish," said their owner. "They were pets, so to speak."

"Eleven fifty," said Mr. Delahanty.

"It was cruelty to animals putting that hat in with them. I could turn you in to the S.P.C.A."

"Twelve," said Mr. Delahanty.

They settled for fifteen, Mr. Delahanty getting the fish.

Cress, the hat, and the fish, in an oversized kettle loaned by the fish man, occupied the back of the car on the trip home. It was a slow trip because speed tended to slosh the water in the kettle, together with a fish or two, out on the floor. It was a silent trip because Cress was thinking, and because up in the front seat, while Mr. and Mrs. Delahanty had plenty to say, they didn't want to be overheard by Cress.

They were nearly home before Mrs. Delahanty said, very low, "What a terrible thing to happen! It might mark her emotionally for life."

Mr. Delahanty agreed. "It wouldn't have been so bad though if that Edwin hadn't had to turn up in time to see it all."

"I know. She wanted to be such a lady—for him. That hat . . . and the curls . . . and then the hat in with the fish, the curls gone, and all those people laughing. I'm a grown person, John, but I just don't think I could live down such a thing. I think I might just stick my head in that bucket of fish and end everything."

As if her own words had put an idea into her mind, Mrs. Delahanty looked quickly around.

"Cress," she cried, "what have you got that hat on your head for?"

"It'll shrink if I don't," said Cress very calmly.

"Well, let it. Let it shrink. And you've got all those colors dribbling down your face and neck."

"I'm trying to keep them mopped up," said Cress, mopping some more.

"Throw that hat away," ordered Mrs. Delahanty. "Toss it out the window, Cress. You don't ever have to wear it again. We'll get you a new one."

"Oh no," cried Cress, "I love it. I'm going to keep it all my life."

"Keep it all your life?" Mrs. Delahanty asked, feeling rather dazed. "Cress, that hat didn't look too good in the first place. I can't begin to tell you what it looks like now. Throw it away!"

"No," said Cress stubbornly. "I want to keep it to remember today by."

"Remember today," repeated Mrs. Delahanty, who was beginning to feel increasingly that she and her daughter were not speaking of the same day at all. "Why in the world do you want to remember today?"

"Because of the brave way Edwin defended me," said Cress.

"Oh," said Mrs. Delahanty faintly.

"He was really wonderful, Mother. He defied that man."

"I'm afraid we missed that, Cress."

"And I was stricken, Mother, really stricken. It was the first time Edwin ever saw me stricken. He didn't even know I could be. He's always been the stricken one so far. The most I'd dared hope for was to be gentle. Then," said Cress with great satisfaction, "stricken."

There was complete silence in the car for some time.

"Don't you think I was, Mother?" Cress asked anxiously.

"Yes," said Mrs. Delahanty with conviction, "I think that's about the word for it."

"And whenever I wear this hat, he'll remember."

Mrs. Delahanty took her husband's handkerchief from his pocket and handed it back to her daughter. "Tuck this around your neck, Cress. It'll keep those colors from staining your middy."

With one hand Cress tucked the handkerchief about her neck, with the other she kept her hat in place.

Responding to the Story

Analyzing the Story

Identifying Facts

1. What is the **problem** that Cress thinks the hat will solve—in other words, what does she want, and how does she hope the hat will help her get it?
2. What **complications** develop as Cress sets out, wearing the hat, to resolve her problem?
3. The **climax** of the story is a "rescue scene" involving the ill-starred hat. Why is Cress so surprised to find *Edwin* coming to her rescue?
4. There is a surprise for the reader at the **resolution** of the story. Like her parents, we probably feel that Cress has just suffered a humiliating experience that she wants to forget. However, Cress feels quite the opposite. Why is she so happy? Why does she want to keep the hat all her life?

Interpreting Meanings

5. Find at least three passages that indicate that this narrator is **omniscient**. (Look for passages that reveal the thoughts and feelings of three characters.) Did this point of view help you understand the **motives** of the characters? Explain.
6. What do Cress's thoughts and actions and her choice of clothing tell you about her **character**—is she a realist or a romantic? Is she confident in herself, or insecure? Cite details from the story to support your opinion.
7. Is Cress lucky to have the parents she has? Explain how you responded to the **characters** of Mr. and Mrs. Delahanty.
8. Edwin's brave defense of Cress might have been based on something other than traditional male chivalry. Did he rescue Cress only because of her helplessness? What other possible explanation can you suggest for his behavior?
9. Clearly, this is a story about a young girl's early experience with love. Do you think love also affects the actions of all the main characters in the story? Explain.
10. Did the writer persuade you that Cress's experience is typical of what might happen to a girl her age? Cite details from the story that struck you as either believable, or unbelievable.

Writing About the Story

A Creative Response

1. **Using Another Point of View.** Suppose that Edwin were to narrate his part in this story. Begin with the moment he sees Cress at the tank and let Edwin tell his side of the story, using the first-person pronoun, "I." Be sure to have Edwin describe his feelings for Cress, his response to her hat, and his reasons for rescuing her. Have him tell us if he feels happy at the end of the story, or embarrassed, or disappointed, and why.
2. **Describing an Object.** Write a paragraph describing something that you once desired because you thought it would make you more attractive—perhaps a piece of clothing, jewelry, a bicycle. Be sure to describe how this "possession" made you feel about yourself and your effect on others.

A Critical Response

3. **Responding to a Different Ending.** Jessamyn West says that this story is based on a real incident from her own life, but that she changed the outcome of the conflict. Read what she says here about the incident that inspired this story (see "Focusing on Background," which follows). Explain how the story would have created a different effect if it had ended as it did in real life. Which ending do you prefer? Why? Write a paragraph.

Analyzing Language and Vocabulary

Allusions

One of the complications in this story occurs when Cress's lavishly decorated hat falls into a fish tank. As it sinks to the bottom, its purple, yellow, green, and red colors all run together and stain the fish water:

> And the hat, in form as well as color, was suffering a sea-change. It was softening up, flattening out. Each minute it looked less and less like a hat.

The phrase "suffering a sea-change" is an **allusion,** or reference, to Shakespeare's play *The Tempest.* In the passage alluded to, a sailor is telling a young man that his father has drowned:

> Full fathom five thy father lies:
>   Of his bones are coral made;
> Those are pearls that were his eyes;
>   Nothing of him that doth fade,
> But doth suffer a sea-change
> Into something rich and strange.

In one or more sentences explain Jessamyn West's allusion to a "sea-change." In light of what is actually happening to the hat, is the allusion to Shakespeare's "sea-change" meant to be serious or humorous?

Here is another allusion to Shakespeare's "sea-change," this time in a news story. What has undergone a "sea-change" here?

> WASHINGTON, Sept. 24—President Reagan, delivering a spirited defense of his economic policies, accused the Democrats today of mistaking compassion for practical solutions and insisted that voters still endorsed "the sea-change in American politics" that he said his program had wrought.

Reading About the Writer

Jessamyn West (1902–1984) was born of Irish Quaker parents in Indiana, but she moved to California as a child and she lived there the rest of her long life. When she was twenty-nine, she was stricken with tuberculosis so severely that her doctors thought she would die. Her stubborn mother refused to let Jessamyn give up. With infinite patience, she nursed Jessamyn—telling stories about her own life was part of her long therapy—and eventually she helped restore her daughter to health.

As a result of her mother's storytelling, Jessamyn began to write stories of her own. "The Hat" is an excerpt from *Cress Delahanty,* her collection of stories about a lively California girl. In the first story, Cress is twelve; in the last, she is sixteen.

While Jessamyn West has written more than a dozen books, she is best known for her novel *The Friendly Persuasion,* which was later made into a movie starring Gary Cooper. This best-selling book is a touching portrait of a Quaker family modeled on her own ancestors, who lived in Indiana around the time of the Civil War.

In her autobiography *Hide and Seek,* Jessamyn recalls a girlhood that resembles Cress's girlhood. Like Cress, she was forever in love and in silent agony over it. "My heart pounded, my lips trembled, my eyelids fluttered," she says of her symptoms. "By a process unclear to me then and now, I would gradually fall out of love with one boy and into love with another. Suddenly, characteristics in someone thereto unnoticed would strike me with overpowering charm."

Focusing on Background
A Comment from the Writer

"I've written a number of stories. Some I have forgotten completely. Others, like 'The Hat,' because it is so largely autobiographical, I remember clearly. I was the unfortunate girl who put her hat on top of the topless fish aquarium and so lost it. There *is* some fiction in the story. There was no long-armed, speedy young man to save my hat for me. The fishhouse owner did the job himself. And like the hero in the earlier story (not mine), who 'threw the glove, but not with love, right into the lady's face,'[1] my hat came back to me."

—Jessamyn West

---

1. If you are curious about this reference, you'll find the explanation in a poem called "The Glove and the Lions" by Leigh Hunt.

THE OLD DEMON

Pearl S. Buck

This story takes place in China during the Chinese-Japanese War (1937–1945). Like many stories set during wartime, this one is not about battles and politics. It is about particular individuals in a particular setting. Notice how the point of view helps us understand how one woman is affected by a conflict she did not cause and knows very little about.

Old Mrs. Wang knew of course that there was a war. Everybody had known for a long time that there was a war going on and that Japanese were killing Chinese. But still it was not real and no more than hearsay since none of the Wangs had been killed. The Village of Three Mile Wangs on the flat banks of the Yellow River, which was old Mrs. Wang's clan village, had never even seen a Japanese. This was how they came to be talking about Japanese at all.

It was evening and early summer, and after her supper Mrs. Wang had climbed the dike steps, as she did every day, to see how high the river had risen. She was much more afraid of the river than of the Japanese. She knew what the river would do. And one by one the villagers had followed her up the dike, and now they stood staring down at the malicious yellow water, curling along like a lot of snakes, and biting at the high dike banks.

"I never saw it as high as this so early," Mrs. Wang said. She sat down on a bamboo stool that her grandson, Little Pig, had brought for her, and spat into the water.

"It's worse than the Japanese, this old devil of a river," Little Pig said recklessly.

"Fool!" Mrs. Wang said quickly. "The river god will hear you. Talk about something else."

So they had gone on talking about the Japanese. . . . How, for instance, asked Wang, the baker, who was old Mrs. Wang's nephew twice removed, would they know the Japanese when they saw them?

Mrs. Wang at this point said positively, "You'll know them. I once saw a foreigner. He was taller than the eaves of my house, and he had mud-colored hair and eyes the color of a fish's eyes. Anyone who does not look like us—that is a Japanese."

Everybody listened to her since she was the oldest woman in the village and whatever she said settled something.

Then Little Pig spoke up in his disconcerting way. "You can't see them, Grandmother. They hide up in the sky in airplanes."

Mrs. Wang did not answer immediately. Once she would have said positively, "I shall not believe in an airplane until I see it." But so many things had been true which she had not believed—the Empress, for instance, whom she had not believed dead, was dead. The Republic,[1] again, she had not believed in because she did not know what it was. She still did not know, but they had said for a long time there had been one. So now she merely stared quietly about the dike where they all sat around her. It was very pleasant and cool, and she felt nothing mattered if the river did not rise to flood.

"I don't believe in the Japanese," she said flatly.

They laughed at her a little, but no one spoke. Someone lit her pipe—it was Little Pig's wife, who was her favorite, and she smoked it.

"Sing, Little Pig!" someone called.

So Little Pig began to sing an old song in a high, quavering voice, and old Mrs. Wang listened

---

1. **Republic:** The Revolution of 1911, led by Sun Yat-sen, overthrew the dynasty that had ruled China since 1644. The republic established by the revolution lasted until 1949.

and forgot the Japanese. The evening was beautiful, the sky so clear and still that the willows overhanging the dike were reflected even in the muddy water. Everything was at peace. The thirty-odd houses which made up the village straggled along beneath them. Nothing could break this peace. After all, the Japanese were only human beings.

"I doubt those airplanes," she said mildly to Little Pig when he stopped singing.

But without answering her, he went on to another song.

Year in and year out she had spent the summer evenings like this on the dike. The first time she was seventeen and a bride, and her husband had shouted to her to come out of the house and up the dike, and she had come, blushing and twisting her hands together, to hide among the women while the men roared at her and made jokes about her. All the same, they had liked her. "A pretty piece of meat in your bowl," they had said to her husband. "Feet a trifle big,"[2] he had answered deprecatingly. But she could see he was pleased, and so gradually her shyness went away.

He, poor man, had been drowned in a flood when he was still young. And it had taken her years to get him prayed out of Buddhist purgatory.[3] Finally she had grown tired of it, what with the child and the land all on her back, and so when the priest said coaxingly, "Another ten pieces of silver and he'll be out entirely," she asked, "What's he got in there yet?"

"Only his right hand," the priest said, encouraging her.

Well, then, her patience broke. Ten dollars! It would feed them for the winter. Besides, she had had to hire labor for her share of repairing the dike, too, so there would be no more floods.

"If it's only one hand, he can pull himself out," she said firmly.

She often wondered if he had, poor silly fellow. As like as not, she had often thought gloomily in

Beneficent Rain (detail) by Chang Yü-ts'ai. Ink on silk.

the night, he was still lying there, waiting for her to do something about it. That was the sort of man he was. Well, some day, perhaps, when Little Pig's wife had had the first baby safely and she had a little extra, she might go back to finish him out of purgatory. There was no real hurry, though.

"Grandmother, you must go in," Little Pig's wife's soft voice said. "There is a mist rising from the river now that the sun is gone."

"Yes, I suppose I must," old Mrs. Wang agreed. She gazed at the river a moment. That river—it was full of good and evil together. It

---

2. **feet a trifle big:** Chinese women of certain upper classes used to have their feet bound from an early age in order to make them smaller. Small feet were considered attractive, and they indicated that the woman did not have to work.
3. **Buddhist purgatory:** a state in which the dead are purified before they can achieve nirvana, a state of perfect freedom and bliss.

would water the fields when it was curbed and checked, but then if an inch were allowed it, it crashed through like a roaring dragon. That was how her husband had been swept away—careless, he was, about his bit of the dike. He was always going to mend it, always going to pile more earth on top of it, and then in a night the river rose and broke through. He had run out of the house, and she had climbed on the roof with the child and had saved herself and it while he was drowned. Well, they had pushed the river back again behind its dikes, and it had stayed there this time. Every day she herself walked up and down the length of the dike for which the village was responsible and examined it. The men laughed and said, ''If anything is wrong with the dikes, Granny will tell us.''

It had never occurred to any of them to move the village away from the river. The Wangs had lived there for generations, and some had always escaped the floods and had fought the river more fiercely than ever afterward.

Little Pig suddenly stopped singing.

''The moon is coming up!'' he cried. ''That's not good. Airplanes come out on moonlight nights.''

''Where do you learn all this about airplanes?''

old Mrs. Wang exclaimed. "It is tiresome to me," she added, so severely that no one spoke. In this silence, leaning upon the arm of Little Pig's wife, she descended slowly the earthen steps which led down into the village, using her long pipe in the other hand as a walking stick. Behind her the villagers came down, one by one, to bed. No one moved before she did, but none stayed long after her.

And in her own bed at last, behind the blue cotton mosquito curtains which Little Pig's wife fastened securely, she fell peacefully asleep. She had lain awake a little while thinking about the Japanese and wondering why they wanted to fight. Only very coarse persons wanted wars. In her mind she saw large coarse persons. If they came, one must wheedle them, she thought, invite them to drink tea, and explain to them, reasonably—only why should they come to a peaceful farming village . . . ?

So she was not in the least prepared for Little Pig's wife screaming at her that the Japanese had come. She sat up in bed muttering, "The tea bowls—the tea——"

"Grandmother, there's no time!" Little Pig's wife screamed. "They're here—they're here!"

"Where?" old Mrs. Wang cried, now awake.

"In the sky!" Little Pig's wife wailed.

They had all run out at that, into the clear early dawn, and gazed up. There, like wild geese flying in autumn, were great birdlike shapes.

"But what are they?" old Mrs. Wang cried.

And then, like a silver egg dropping, something drifted straight down and fell at the far end of the village in a field. A fountain of earth flew up, and they all ran to see it. There was a hole thirty feet across, as big as a pond. They were so astonished they could not speak, and then, before anyone could say anything, another and another egg began to fall and everybody was running, running. . . .

Everybody, that is, but Mrs. Wang. When Little Pig's wife seized her hand to drag her along, old Mrs. Wang pulled away and sat down against the bank of the dike.

"I can't run," she remarked. "I haven't run in seventy years, since before my feet were bound. You go on. Where's Little Pig?" She looked around. Little Pig was already gone. "Like his

grandfather," she remarked, "always the first to run."

But Little Pig's wife would not leave her, not, that is, until old Mrs. Wang reminded her that it was her duty.

"If Little Pig is dead," she said, "then it is necessary that his son be born alive." And when the girl still hesitated, she struck at her gently with her pipe. "Go on—go on," she exclaimed.

So unwillingly, because now they could scarcely hear each other speak for the roar of the dipping planes, Little Pig's wife went on with the others.

By now, although only a few minutes had passed, the village was in ruins, and the straw roofs and wooden beams were blazing. Everybody was gone. As they passed they had shrieked at old Mrs. Wang to come on, and she had called back pleasantly:

"I'm coming—I'm coming!"

But she did not go. She sat quite alone watching now what was an extraordinary spectacle. For soon other planes came, from where she did not know, but they attacked the first ones. The sun came up over the fields of ripening wheat, and in the clear summery air the planes wheeled and darted and spat at each other. When this was over, she thought, she would go back into the village and see if anything was left. Here and there a wall stood, supporting a roof. She could not see her own house from here. But she was not unused to war. Once bandits had looted their village, and houses had been burned then, too. Well, now it had happened again. Burning houses one could see often, but not this darting silvery shining battle in the air. She understood none of it—not what those things were, nor how they stayed up in the sky. She simply sat, growing hungry, and watching.

"I'd like to see one close," she said aloud. And at that moment, as though in answer, one of them pointed suddenly downward, and, wheeling and twisting as though it were wounded, it fell head down in a field which Little Pig had plowed only yesterday for soybeans. And in an instant the sky was empty again, and there was only this wounded thing on the ground and herself.

She hoisted herself carefully from the earth. At

her age she need be afraid of nothing. She could, she decided, go and see what it was. So, leaning on her bamboo pipe, she made her way slowly across the fields. Behind her in the sudden stillness two or three village dogs appeared and followed, creeping close to her in their terror. When they drew near to the fallen plane, they barked furiously. Then she hit them with her pipe.

"Be quiet," she scolded, "there's already been noise enough to split my ears!"

She tapped the airplane.

"Metal," she told the dogs. "Silver, doubtless," she added. Melted up, it would make them all rich.

She walked around it, examining it closely. What made it fly? It seemed dead. Nothing moved or made a sound within it. Then, coming to the side to which it tipped, she saw a young man in it, slumped into a heap in a little seat. The dogs growled, but she struck at them again and they fell back.

"Are you dead?" she inquired politely.

The young man moved a little at her voice, but did not speak. She drew nearer and peered into the hole in which he sat. His side was bleeding.

"Wounded!" she exclaimed. She took his wrist. It was warm, but inert, and when she let it go, it dropped against the side of the hole. She stared at him. He had black hair and a dark skin like a Chinese, and still he did not look like a Chinese.

"He must be a Southerner," she thought. Well, the chief thing was, he was alive.

"You had better come out," she remarked. "I'll put some herb plaster on your side."

The young man muttered something dully.

"What did you say?" she asked. But he did not say it again.

"I am still quite strong," she decided after a moment. So she reached in and seized him about the waist and pulled him out slowly, panting a good deal. Fortunately he was rather a little fellow and very light. When she had him on the ground, he seemed to find his feet; and he stood shakily and clung to her, and she held him up.

"Now if you can walk to my house," she said, "I'll see if it is there."

Then he said something quite clearly. She listened and could not understand a word of it. She pulled away from him and stared.

"What's that?" she asked.

He pointed at the dogs. They were standing growling, their ruffs up. Then he spoke again, and as he spoke he crumpled to the ground. The dogs fell on him, so that she had to beat them off with her hands.

"Get away!" she shouted. "Who told *you* to kill him?"

And then, when they had slunk back, she heaved him somehow onto her back; and, trembling, half carrying, half pulling, she dragged him to the ruined village and laid him in the street while she went to find her house, taking the dogs with her.

Her house was quite gone. She found the place easily enough. This was where it should be, opposite the water gate into the dike. She had always watched that gate herself. Miraculously it was not injured now, nor was the dike broken. It would be easy enough to rebuild the house. Only, for the present, it was gone.

So she went back to the young man. He was lying as she had left him, propped against the dike, panting and very pale. He had opened his coat, and he had a little bag from which he was taking out strips of cloth and a bottle of something. And again he spoke, and again she understood nothing. Then he made signs, and she saw it was water he wanted, so she took up a broken pot from one of many blown about the street, and, going up the dike, she filled it with river water and brought it down again and washed his wound, and she tore off the strips he made from the rolls of bandaging. He knew how to put the cloth over the gaping wound and he made signs to her and she followed these signs. All the time he was trying to tell her something, but she could understand nothing.

"You must be from the South, sir," she said. It was easy to see he had education. He looked very clever. "I have heard your language is different from ours." She laughed a little to put him at his ease, but he only stared at her somberly with dull eyes. So she said brightly, "Now if I could find something for us to eat, it would be nice."

He did not answer. Indeed he lay back, panting

still more heavily, and stared into space as though she had not spoken.

"You would be better with food," she went on. "And so would I," she added. She was beginning to feel unbearably hungry.

It occurred to her that in Wang the baker's shop there might be some bread. Even if it were dusty with fallen mortar, it would still be bread. She would go and see. But before she went she moved the soldier a little so that he lay in the edge of shadow cast by a willow tree that grew in the bank of the dike. Then she went to the baker's shop. The dogs were gone.

The baker's shop was, like everything else, in ruins. No one was there. At first she saw nothing but the mass of crumpled earthen walls. But then she remembered that the oven was just inside the door, and the door frame still stood erect, supporting one end of the roof. She stood in this frame, and, running her hand in underneath the fallen roof inside, she felt the wooden cover of the iron caldron. Under this there might be steamed bread. She worked her arm delicately and carefully in. It took quite a long time, but, even so, clouds of lime and dust almost choked her. Nevertheless she was right. She squeezed her hand under the cover and felt the firm smooth skin of the big steamed bread rolls, and one by one she drew out four.

"It's hard to kill an old thing like me," she remarked cheerfully to no one, and she began to eat one of the rolls as she walked back. If she had a bit of garlic and a bowl of tea—but one couldn't have everything in these times.

It was at this moment that she heard voices. When she came in sight of the soldier, she saw surrounding him a crowd of other soldiers, who had apparently come from nowhere. They were staring down at the wounded soldier, whose eyes were now closed.

"Where did you get this Japanese, Old Mother?" they shouted at her.

"What Japanese?" she asked, coming to them.

"This one!" they shouted.

"Is he a Japanese?" she cried in the greatest astonishment. "But he looks like us—his eyes are black, his skin——"

"Japanese!" one of them shouted at her.

"Well," she said quietly, "he dropped out of the sky."

"Give me that bread!" another shouted.

"Take it," she said, "all except this one for him."

"A Japanese monkey eat good bread?" the soldier shouted.

"I suppose he is hungry also," old Mrs. Wang replied. She began to dislike these men. But then, she had always disliked soldiers.

"I wish you would go away," she said. "What are you doing here? Our village has always been peaceful."

"It certainly looks very peaceful now," one of the men said, grinning, "as peaceful as a grave. Do you know who did that, Old Mother? The Japanese!"

"I suppose so," she agreed. Then she asked, "Why? That's what I don't understand."

"Why? Because they want our land, that's why!"

"Our land!" she repeated. "Why, they can't have our land!"

"Never!" they shouted.

But all this time while they were talking and chewing the bread they had divided among themselves, they were watching the eastern horizon.

"Why do you keep looking east?" old Mrs. Wang now asked.

"The Japanese are coming from there," the man replied who had taken the bread.

"Are you running away from them?" she asked, surprised.

"There are only a handful of us," he said apologetically.

"We were left to guard a village—Pao An, in the county of——"

"I know that village," old Mrs. Wang interrupted. "You needn't tell me. I was a girl there. How is the old Pao who keeps the teashop in the main street? He's my brother."

"Everybody is dead there," the man replied. "The Japanese have taken it—a great army of men came with their foreign guns and tanks, so what could we do?"

"Of course, only run," she agreed. Nevertheless she felt dazed and sick. So he was dead, that one brother she had left! She was now the last of her father's family.

But the soldiers were straggling away again, leaving her alone.

"They'll be coming, those little black dwarfs," they were saying. "We'd best go on."

Nevertheless, one lingered a moment, the one who had taken the bread, to stare down at the young wounded man, who lay with his eyes shut, not having moved at all.

"Is he dead?" he inquired. Then, before Mrs. Wang could answer, he pulled a short knife out of his belt. "Dead or not, I'll give him a punch or two with this——"

But old Mrs. Wang pushed his arm away.

"No, you won't," she said with authority. "If he is dead, then there is no use in sending him into purgatory all in pieces. I am a good Buddhist myself."

The man laughed. "Oh well, he is dead," he answered; and then, seeing his comrades already at a distance, he ran after them.

A Japanese, was he? Old Mrs. Wang, left alone with this inert figure, looked at him tentatively. He was very young, she could see, now that his eyes were closed. His hand, limp in unconsciousness, looked like a boy's hand, unformed and still growing. She felt his wrist but could discern no pulse. She leaned over him and held to his lips the half of her roll which she had not eaten.

"Eat," she said very loudly and distinctly. "Bread!"

But there was no answer. Evidently he was dead. He must have died while she was getting the bread out of the oven.

There was nothing to do then but to finish the bread herself. And when that was done, she wondered if she ought not to follow after Little Pig and his wife and all the villagers. The sun was mounting and it was growing hot. If she were going, she had better go. But first she would climb the dike and see what the direction was. They had gone straight west, and as far as eye could look westward was a great plain. She might even see a good-sized crowd miles away. Anyway, she could see the next village, and they might all be there.

So she climbed the dike slowly, getting very hot. There was a slight breeze on top of the dike and it felt good. She was shocked to see the river very near the top of the dike. Why, it had risen in the last hour!

"You old demon!" she said severely. Let the river god hear it if he liked. He was evil, that he was—so to threaten flood when there had been all this other trouble.

She stooped and bathed her cheeks and her wrists. The water was quite cold, as though with fresh rains somewhere. Then she stood up and gazed around her. To the west there was nothing except in the far distance the soldiers still half-running, and beyond them the blur of the next village, which stood on a long rise of ground. She had better set out for that village. Doubtless Little Pig and his wife were there waiting for her.

Just as she was about to climb down and start out, she saw something on the eastern horizon. It was at first only an immense cloud of dust. But, as she stared at it, very quickly it became a lot of black dots and shining spots. Then she saw what it was. It was a lot of men—an army. Instantly she knew what army.

"That's the Japanese," she thought. Yes, above them were the buzzing silver planes. They circled about, seeming to search for someone.

"I don't know who you're looking for," she muttered, "unless it's me and Little Pig and his wife. We're the only ones left. You've already killed my brother Pao."

She had almost forgotten that Pao was dead. Now she remembered it acutely. He had such a nice shop—always clean, and the tea good and the best meat dumplings to be had and the price always the same. Pao was a good man. Besides, what about his wife and his seven children? Doubtless they were all killed, too. Now these Japanese were looking for her. It occurred to her that on the dike she could easily be seen. So she clambered hastily down.

It was when she was about halfway down that she thought of the water gate. This old river—it had been a curse to them since time began. Why should it not make up a little now for all the wickedness it had done? It was plotting wickedness again, trying to steal over its banks. Well, why not? She wavered a moment. It was a pity, of course, that the young dead Japanese would be swept into the flood. He was a nice-looking boy, and she had saved him from being stabbed. It was not quite the same as saving his life, of course, but still it was a little the same. If he had been alive, he would have been saved. She went over to him and tugged at him until he lay well near the top of the bank. Then she went down again.

She knew perfectly how to open the water gate. Any child knew how to open the sluice[4] for crops. But she knew also how to swing open the whole gate. The question was, could she open it quickly enough to get out of the way?

"I'm only one old woman," she muttered. She hesitated a second more. Well, it would be a pity not to see what sort of a baby Little Pig's wife would have, but one could not see everything. She had seen a great deal in this life. There was an end to what one could see, anyway.

She glanced again to the east. There were the Japanese coming across the plain. They were a long clear line of black, dotted with thousands of glittering points. If she opened this gate, the impetuous water would roar toward them, rushing into the plains, rolling into a wide lake, drowning them, maybe. Certainly they could not keep

marching nearer and nearer to her and to Little Pig and his wife who were waiting for her. Well, Little Pig and his wife—they would wonder about her—but they would never dream of this. It would make a good story—she would have enjoyed telling it.

She turned resolutely to the gate. Well, some people fought with airplanes and some with guns, but you could fight with a river, too, if it were a wicked one like this one. She wrenched out a huge wooden pin. It was slippery with silvery green moss. The rill[5] of water burst into a strong jet. When she wrenched one more pin, the rest would give way themselves. She began pulling at it, and felt it slip a little from its hole.

"I might be able to get myself out of purgatory with this," she thought, "and maybe they'll let me have that old man of mine, too. What's a hand of his to all this? Then we'll——"

The pin slipped away suddenly, and the gate burst flat against her and knocked her breath away. She had only time to gasp, to the river:

"Come on, you old demon!"

Then she felt it seize her and lift her up to the sky. It was beneath her and around her. It rolled her joyfully hither and thither, and then, holding her close and enfolded, it went rushing against the enemy.

---

4. **sluice** (sloos): an artificial channel or passage for water, with a gate or valve at one end to regulate the flow.

5. **rill:** a little brook or stream.

Responding to the Story

Analyzing the Story

Identifying Facts

1. At the beginning of the story, what two forces present possible **conflicts** to the villagers? Which of these forces are they more afraid of? Why?
2. Find the passages that reveal how Mrs. Wang thinks about the Japanese. Why does she find it so difficult to "believe in" them or to understand why they want to fight?
3. In the **flashback** beginning on page 154, what

do we learn about Mrs. Wang's background that explains her feelings toward the river?
4. When the Japanese start bombing the village, why does Mrs. Wang refuse to leave? What weapon does she use to fight the enemy army?

Interpreting Meanings

5. Why does Mrs. Wang continue to help the pilot even after she learns that he is Japanese? What does this **action** tell us about her **character**?
6. After trying to save the Japanese pilot, why does she then decide to fight his army?

7. At the **resolution** of the story, Mrs. Wang is killed by "the old demon." Why is she willing to die? How do you think the writer wants us to feel about her death—is it tragic or triumphant? Cite details from the story to support your interpretation.

8. What **point of view** does the writer use in telling this story? Whose thoughts does this point of view allow us to share? Why do you think Pearl Buck chose to tell the story from this character's point of view, rather than from the point of view of another character, such as Little Pig?

9. In your own words, summarize what the events of this story reveal about war and what it can do to individuals who might otherwise care for one another.

10. Pearl Buck is an old China hand, and her stories usually teach a great deal about Chinese life and culture. What can you guess from details in this story about how the Chinese regard those who have attained great age? What do you think of these attitudes?

Writing About the Story

A Creative Response

1. **Using Another Point of View.** Tell about Mrs. Wang's encounter with the Japanese pilot from the point of view of the pilot. What does he think of this enemy who helps him? What are his ideas about war? How does he feel about the Chinese? How does he feel about death? Write a paragraph, letting the dying Japanese pilot speak, using the first-person pronoun, "I."

A Critical Response

2. **Analyzing Character.** *Mrs. Wang is a practical person, who takes things at face value, does whatever she thinks must be done, and accepts her fate.* Write a paragraph using details from the story to support this analysis of Mrs. Wang's character. Or, identify some other aspect of her character and write your paragraph about it.

Analyzing Language and Vocabulary

Context Clues

Use context clues to select the correct meaning of each italicized word below. Do any passages, in your opinion, offer no context clues at all?

1. ". . . the villagers had followed her up the *dike,* and now they stood staring down at the malicious yellow water, curling along like a lot of snakes, and biting at the high *dike* banks." (a) a wall of earth made to prevent flooding (b) a bridge made to span a river (c) a platform overlooking a river (d) a tower

2. ". . . now they stood staring down at the *malicious* yellow water, curling along like a lot of snakes, and biting at the high dike banks." (a) spiteful (b) peaceful (c) helpful (d) dirty

3. "Then Little Pig spoke up in his *disconcerting* way. 'You can't see them, Grandmother. They hide up in the sky in airplanes.' " (a) calm (b) predictable (c) upsetting (d) angry

4. ". . . the men roared at her and made jokes about her. . . . 'A pretty piece of meat in your bowl,' they had said to her husband. 'Feet a trifle big,' he had answered *deprecatingly.* But she could see he was pleased. . . . " (a) in a belittling way (b) in an angry tone (c) in a proud voice (d) in a whisper

Reading About the Writer

Although **Pearl Buck** (1892–1973) was born in West Virginia, she was as familiar with China as she was with her native country. When she was only five months old, her missionary parents left America, and their young daughter spent her early life in the turbulent setting of China during the first part of this century.

When she was sixteen, Pearl was sent back to Virginia to attend Randolph-Macon Women's College, but shortly after graduating she returned to China and married an American agricultural missionary there. The couple settled in Nanking, and they were there in 1927 when the city was invaded. Ten minutes after they fled their home, it was burned to the ground, and the manuscript of Pearl Buck's first novel was destroyed in the flames.

But she threw herself back into writing when she learned that her only child, Carol, was hopelessly retarded and would need costly special care. By 1931 she had published her moving account of Chinese peasant life, *The Good Earth.* This novel was on the best-seller list for twenty-one months, received the Pulitzer Prize, became both a play and a hit movie, and has been translated into more than thirty languages.

Pearl Buck's enormous literary output earned her the Nobel Prize for literature in 1938.

Literature & Language

Using Pronouns Correctly

Literary Model

In the following passage, Gwendolyn Brooks describes Maud Martha's and her family's feelings as they wait for the father's return from a trip to the loan office.

> Papa was to have gone that noon, during his lunch hour, to the office of the Home Owners' Loan. If he had not succeeded in getting another extension, they would be leaving this house in which they had lived for more than fourteen years. There was little hope. The Home Owners' Loan was hard. They sat, making their plans.
>
> "We'll be moving into a nice flat[1] somewhere," said Mama. "Somewhere on South Park, or Michigan, or in Washington Park Court." Those flats, as the girls and Mama knew well, were burdens on wages twice the size of Papa's. This was not mentioned now.
>
> "They're much prettier than this old house," said Helen. "I have friends I'd just as soon not bring here. And I have other friends that wouldn't come down this far for anything, unless they were in a taxi."
>
> Yesterday, Maud Martha would have attacked her. Tomorrow she might. Today she said nothing. She merely gazed at a little hopping robin in the tree, her tree, and tried to keep the fronts of her eyes dry.
>
> —from *Maud Martha*,
> Gwendolyn Brooks

---

1. **flat:** apartment.

Grammar Note

Although Gwendolyn Brooks refers to at least five different people in this excerpt, she does not keep repeating their given names. She uses pronouns instead. A **pronoun** is a word that takes the place of one or more nouns. Pronouns can replace the names of persons, places, and things and make it possible for writers to avoid endless repetition of the same nouns.

The following chart lists the personal pronouns and their possessive forms.

Personal Pronouns			
Singular	I, me	you	he, him, she, her, it
Plural	we, us	you	they, them
Possessive Forms			
Singular	my, mine	your, yours	his, her, hers, its
Plural	our, ours	your, yours	their, theirs

Note how the italicized personal pronouns replace the names of persons and things in the following sentences from the passage by Brooks:

> Papa was to have gone that noon, during *his* lunch hour, to the office of the Home Owners' Loan. If *he* had not succeeded in getting another extension, *they* would be leaving this house in which *they* had lived for more than fourteen years.

The word to which a pronoun refers (and which it replaces) is the **antecedent** of the pronoun. The antecedents of the italicized personal pronouns in these sentences are in bold type:

> Those **flats** . . . were burdens on wages twice the size of Papa's. . . . "*They're* much prettier than this old house," said **Helen**. . . .
>
> Yesterday, **Maud Martha** would have attacked *her.* Tomorrow *she* might. Today *she* said nothing.

Good writers take care that all the pronouns they use have clear antecedents. In other words, they make sure that the context, or the text surrounding each pronoun, makes it clear to whom or to what each pronoun refers. In the following example, note that there are two possible antecedents to which the pronoun might refer:

Mary liked **Jane** and knew *she* couldn't tell a lie.

Other commonly used pronouns include the demonstrative pronouns: *this*, *that*, *these*, and *those*. Demonstrative pronouns may refer back to a noun, pronoun, or clause. Here, for example, the entire statement in bold type is the antecedent of the pronoun *this*, which is in italics.

Those flats, as the girls and Mama knew well, **were burdens on wages twice the size of Papa's.** *This* was not mentioned now.

Examining the Writer's Use of Pronouns

With a partner, examine the way Gwendolyn Brooks uses pronouns.

1. On a chart like the one below, make a list of each pronoun and its antecedent used in the passage from *Maud Martha*. Are all the antecedents immediately clear? If not, remember that this is an excerpt from a longer work, so the complete context is not here.

Pronoun	Antecedent
his	Papa

2. To see how the use of pronouns avoids needless repetition, rewrite the passage from *Maud Martha*, replacing each pronoun with the noun that it refers to. Note how awkward the English language would be if it didn't have pronouns.

Pronouns are useful in determining the point of view of a story or novel. In a first-person narrative, the person telling the story will refer to himself or herself as "I." The reader will see all the other characters and events through the mind of the "I" telling the story. If a story is written in the third person, the narrator, or person telling the story, is outside the action. This "third-person narrator" tells the reader what "he," "she," or "they" are doing or thinking or feeling.

1. Is the passage from *Maud Martha* written in the first or third person? What sentences in the excerpt make the point of view clear to you?

2. Suppose you decide to change the point of view of the *Maud Martha* excerpt. What pronouns would you have to change? Rewrite the passage from the other point of view. Does the rewritten passage have a different effect on you? Why or why not?

Using Pronouns in Your Writing

1. **Writing a Third-Person Narrative.** The family in *Maud Martha* faces the loss of a home. Imagine another situation in which a family faces a problem. Write a third-person narrative in which you present the problem. Tell how each family member feels about it and how each wants to solve it. Remember, as the third-person narrator, you are *not* a character in the story.

2. **Writing a First-Person Narrative.** Write a narrative about a family problem from the first-person point of view of one member of the family. You may want to use the same characters you invented for the preceding exercise. Remember that in a story written from the first-person point of view, the "I" is the narrator and a character in the story at the same time. Such a story might begin like this:

Late last night when I came back to our house, its door was open and the lights on, but no one was home—not even my grandmother, and she never goes out.

ANALYZING POINT OF VIEW

Writing Assignment

Write an essay discussing the effect of the point of view in the story "My Lucy Friend Who Smells Like Corn" (page 139). Include in your essay a description of how a change in point of view might affect your response to the story. Write three paragraphs.

Background

As you learned from pages 135–137, there are basically three kinds of point of view:

1. **Omniscient point of view:** The story is told by an all-knowing narrator who is not a character in the story at all. This narrator speaks in the third person (not "I") and can tell us everything about every event and every character—past, present, and future.
2. **Limited third-person point of view:** The story is also told by an all-knowing narrator who speaks in the third person, but now this narrator focuses on the thoughts and feelings of just one character.
3. **First-person point of view:** The story is told by a character who is in the story and who uses the first-person pronoun, "I."

Point of view is one of the most important elements of storytelling. Point of view controls what we as readers know about the characters and events of a story, what we do not know about them, and how we feel about them. Remember that some points of view are deliberately unreliable. In some stories, we are supposed to wonder, "Is this narrator telling me the truth?"

Prewriting

This writing assignment calls for three tasks: (1) to

find out what the story's point of view is; (2) to describe how the point of view affects the story; and (3) to imagine how a different point of view would change the story.

Filling out the following chart might help you with the three parts of the assignment:

"My Lucy Friend . . ."	The story's point of view:	Different point of view:
1. Who is the narrator?		
2. Which of the three points of view is the story told from?		
3. What does the narrator know that no one else could know?		
4. What does the narrator *not* know?		
5. What are the narrator's biases, if any?		
6. How does the point of view affect the way you feel about the characters? (Does it help you identify with a character? Does it make you sympathize more with one character than with another?)		

Writing

In your first paragraph, name the story and the story's author, and identify the story's point of view. If the story has an identifiable narrator, name her.

In your second paragraph, discuss at least one way the point of view affects the story. (Refer to the details on the left side of your chart.)

In your third paragraph, name at least one way in which the story would be changed if a new point of view were substituted for the one actually used by Cisneros. Be specific in identifying the new point of view. (Refer to the right side of your chart.)

Following is a paragraph which begins an essay on the point of view in "My Lucy Friend . . ." You could use this paragraph to begin your essay, but it would be better if you write your own beginning.

Sandra Cisneros's story with the crazy title "My Lucy Friend Who Smells Like Corn" is told from the first-person point of view. The person talking in the story is a really young girl. I guess she might be around six years old because she says that she is waiting for her teeth to fall out. This little kid never tells us her name, but we don't have to know her name because what she says in this story tells a lot about her character. One thing you have to know right away is that the story uses a lot of incorrect grammar, which put me off at first but then I could see that this is exactly how a little kid would talk. I got used to this unusual point of view.

Cites author and title.
Names the point of view.
Identifies the narrator.

Checklist for Revision

1. Have you cited the story's title and author?
2. Have you identified the story's point of view in the first paragraph?
3. Have you discussed one way this point of view affects the story in your second paragraph?
4. Have you clearly identified a new point of view in the third paragraph?
5. Have you discussed one way this point of view would change the story?
6. Have you supported your ideas with specific details from the story?

Theme:
What Does
the Story Mean?

> *Theme . . . is not imposed on the story but evoked from within it.*
>
> —John Gardner

A story can excel in any number of ways—in the strength of its plot, in the reality of its characters, in the gracefulness of its language. But what often gives a story importance, what makes us remember a story long after we've read it, is the idea on which it is built.

This central idea of a story is called its **theme.** The theme of the story is not the same as its subject. The **subject** is simply the topic of the story. A topic can be stated in one or two words: love, war, growing up. The theme makes some revelation about the subject. A theme is always a statement; it must always be expressed in at least one sentence.

Usually, the theme reveals a truth about human behavior. That truth is usually one that the author has discovered out of experience: for example, that in certain circumstances it is a mistake to marry only for love; or that as one grows old, death becomes less terrifying. In order to communicate this idea, the writer builds a whole fictional house.

The theme is usually not stated directly in the story at all. An essayist would state a theme directly as a way of getting the main idea across clearly, but the fiction writer has a different purpose. The fiction writer lets the story's characters act the idea out for us. The fiction writer hopes that we will feel the characters' experiences so strongly that the truth revealed to them will be revealed to us as well.

If the theme of a story seems fresh and true, if we say, "Yes, I see what you mean, yet I hadn't quite thought of it that way before," or "I hadn't felt quite so strongly about it before," then the story takes on a greater depth. We have penetrated the surface of human behavior, into what the author wants us to recognize about it. Although a theme is usually invisible and unstated, it can be the story's most forceful element. A powerful theme can be why a story gets to our hearts and lingers in our minds.

In previous eras, fiction was widely regarded as a way to teach morality—the right and wrong ways to behave. One could usually be sure in those days that a wicked character in a story would be punished and a virtuous one would be rewarded. Fiction is not usually regarded as a way to teach morality today. Yet, that conflict between what we know *ought* to be in a perfect world and what *is* in a disorderly, imperfect world is still the central business of literature. The theme in a story should be seen as a reflection of this basic conflict in human experience.

Thinking Critically About a Theme

Sometimes it is wise to question the writer's presentation of a theme. We will want to discover whether the writer is presenting a

> " **The** fiction writer hopes that we will feel the characters' experiences so strongly that the truth revealed to them will be revealed to us as well."

truth about life, or whether the writer is trying to force us into accepting a view of life that we reject because we think it is false.

It's the wise reader who makes a judgment about a writer's view of the world, who doesn't accept a story as true just because it's in print. The wise reader asks: Is this story's view of life too romantic? Is it too cynical? Is it too simple? Is it too narrow-minded? Is this writer an overzealous salesperson who is trying to get me to buy an idea that is false or shoddy?

Much of the fiction in popular magazines is weak in this way. We often speak of it as "slick" fiction, not only because it is often found in magazines printed on slick paper, but because such stories themselves have a smooth, shiny surface but little depth.

"Formula" fiction is another way of putting it—such stories are written to a plan that satisfies the general preference for "sweet" stories over truthful ones. Think of the usual romance novel in which a happy outcome is assured, and you'll have one commercially successful formula.

As wise readers, we should make our own critical judgments not only about fiction; we should also make them about what we see on television and what we read in advertisements and in the newspapers.

How to Find a Story's Theme

Here are some questions to ask yourself when you are searching for a story's theme.

1. Does the title signify something special about the story, and does it point to the truth it reveals about life? When you have finished the story, think about the title, to see if it might add new meaning to the story. (Not all titles do this.)

2. Does the main character change in the course of the story? Does the main character realize something he or she hadn't known before?

3. Are any important statements about life or people made in the story—either by the narrator or by characters in the story?

4. Test your statement of theme on the story—does it apply to the whole story, not just to parts of it?

> "Is this writer an overzealous salesperson who is trying to get me to buy an idea that is false or shoddy?"

THE SCARLET IBIS

James Hurst

The story told here is set in the American South. Its climax takes place in 1918, the year World War I was to end in Europe. You will find references in the story to battles being fought in remote parts of the world, but the story is not about the wider war. It is a story about a smaller but equally tragic battle that took place between two young brothers. Read to the end of the paragraph on this page that starts "It was bad enough." Then stop, and write down at least three questions that the storyteller has made you wonder about. When you finish the story, see if your questions have been answered.

It was in the clove of seasons, summer was dead but autumn had not yet been born, that the ibis lit in the bleeding tree. The flower garden was stained with rotting brown magnolia petals, and ironweeds grew rank amid the purple phlox.[1] The five o'clocks by the chimney still marked time, but the oriole nest in the elm was untenanted and rocked back and forth like an empty cradle. The last graveyard flowers were blooming, and their smell drifted across the cotton field and through every room of our house, speaking softly the names of our dead.

It's strange that all this is still so clear to me, now that that summer has long since fled and time has had its way. A grindstone stands where the bleeding tree stood, just outside the kitchen door, and now if an oriole sings in the elm, its song seems to die up in the leaves, a silvery dust. The flower garden is prim, the house a gleaming white, and the pale fence across the yard stands straight and spruce. But sometimes (like right now), as I sit in the cool, green-draped parlor, the grindstone begins to turn, and time with all its changes is ground away—and I remember Doodle.

Doodle was just about the craziest brother a boy ever had. Of course, he wasn't a crazy crazy like old Miss Leedie, who was in love with Pres-

ident Wilson and wrote him a letter every day, but was a nice crazy, like someone you meet in your dreams. He was born when I was six and was, from the outset, a disappointment. He seemed all head, with a tiny body which was red and shriveled like an old man's. Everybody thought he was going to die—everybody except Aunt Nicey, who had delivered him. She said he would live because he was born in a caul[2] and cauls were made from Jesus' nightgown. Daddy had Mr. Heath, the carpenter, build a little mahogany coffin for him. But he didn't die, and when he was three months old Mama and Daddy decided they might as well name him. They named him William Armstrong, which was like tying a big tail on a small kite. Such a name sounds good only on a tombstone.

I thought myself pretty smart at many things, like holding my breath, running, jumping, or climbing the vines in Old Woman Swamp, and I wanted more than anything else someone to race to Horsehead Landing, someone to box with, and someone to perch with in the top fork of the great pine behind the barn, where across the fields and swamps you could see the sea. I wanted a brother. But Mama, crying, told me that even if William Armstrong lived, he would never do these things with me. He might not, she sobbed, even be "all there." He might, as long as he lived, lie on the rubber sheet in the center of the bed in the front bedroom where the white marquisette[3] curtains billowed out in the afternoon sea breeze, rustling like palmetto fronds.

It was bad enough having an invalid brother, but having one who possibly was not all there was unbearable, so I began to make plans to kill him by smothering him with a pillow. However, one afternoon as I watched him, my head poked between the iron posts of the foot of the bed, he looked straight at me and grinned. I skipped through the rooms, down the echoing halls, shouting, "Mama, he smiled. He's all there! He's all there!" and he was.

When he was two, if you laid him on his stom-

---

1. **bleeding tree . . . ironweeds . . . phlox:** types of flowering plants. A bleeding tree is a bleeding-heart plant.

2. **caul** (kôl): a membrane that sometimes encloses the head of a newborn baby like a cap. Some people think a caul brings good luck.

3. **marquisette** (mär′ki·zet′): a thin, meshlike fabric.

ach, he began to try to move himself, straining terribly. The doctor said that with his weak heart this strain would probably kill him, but it didn't. Trembling, he'd push himself up, turning first red, then a soft purple, and finally collapse back onto the bed like an old worn-out doll. I can still see Mama watching him, her hand pressed tight across her mouth, her eyes wide and unblinking. But he learned to crawl (it was his third winter), and we brought him out of the front bedroom, putting him on the rug before the fireplace. For the first time he became one of us.

As long as he lay all the time in bed, we called him William Armstrong, even though it was formal and sounded as if we were referring to one of our ancestors, but with his creeping around on the deerskin rug and beginning to talk, something had to be done about his name. It was I who renamed him. When he crawled, he crawled backward, as if he were in reverse and couldn't change gears. If you called him, he'd turn around as if he were going in the other direction, then he'd back right up to you to be picked up. Crawling backward made him look like a doodlebug[4] so I began to call him Doodle, and in time even Mama and Daddy thought it was a better name than William Armstrong. Only Aunt Nicey disagreed. She said caul babies should be treated with special respect since they might turn out to be saints. Renaming my brother was perhaps the kindest thing I ever did for him, because nobody expects much from someone called Doodle.

Although Doodle learned to crawl, he showed no signs of walking, but he wasn't idle. He talked so much that we all quit listening to what he said. It was about this time that Daddy built him a go-cart, and I had to pull him around. At first I just paraded him up and down the piazza, but then he started crying to be taken out into the yard and it ended up by my having to lug him wherever I went. If I so much as picked up my cap, he'd start crying to go with me, and Mama would call from wherever she was, "Take Doodle with you."

He was a burden in many ways. The doctor

had said that he mustn't get too excited, too hot, too cold, or too tired and that he must always be treated gently. A long list of don'ts went with him, all of which I ignored once we got out of the house. To discourage his coming with me, I'd run with him across the ends of the cotton rows and careen him around corners on two wheels. Sometimes I accidentally turned him over, but he never told Mama. His skin was very sensitive, and he had to wear a big straw hat whenever he went out. When the going got rough and he had to cling to the sides of the go-cart, the hat slipped all the way down over his ears. He was a sight. Finally, I could see I was licked. Doodle was my brother, and he was going to cling to me forever, no matter what I did, so I dragged him across the burning cotton field to share with him the only beauty I knew, Old Woman Swamp. I pulled the go-cart through the saw-tooth fern, down into the green dimness where the palmetto fronds whispered by the stream. I lifted him out and set him down in the soft rubber grass beside a tall pine. His eyes were round with wonder as he gazed about him, and his little hands began to stroke the rubber grass. Then he began to cry.

"For heaven's sake, what's the matter?" I asked, annoyed.

"It's so pretty," he said. "So pretty, pretty, pretty."

After that day Doodle and I often went down into Old Woman Swamp. I would gather wildflowers, wild violets, honeysuckle, yellow jasmine, snakeflowers, and water lilies, and with wire grass we'd weave them into necklaces and crowns. We'd bedeck ourselves with our handiwork and loll about thus beautified, beyond the touch of the everyday world. Then when the slanted rays of the sun burned orange in the tops of the pines, we'd drop our jewels into the stream and watch them float away toward the sea.

There is within me (and with sadness I have watched it in others) a knot of cruelty borne by the stream of love, much as our blood sometimes bears the seed of our destruction, and at times I was mean to Doodle. One day I took him up to the barn loft and showed him his casket, telling him how we all had believed he would die. It was

---

4. **doodlebug:** a type of insect; also, a shuttle train that goes back and forth between stations.

covered with a film of Paris green[5] sprinkled to kill the rats, and screech owls had built a nest inside it.

Doodle studied the mahogany box for a long time, then said, "It's not mine."

"It is," I said. "And before I'll help you down from the loft, you're going to have to touch it."

"I won't touch it," he said sullenly.

"Then I'll leave you here by yourself," I threatened, and made as if I were going down.

Doodle was frightened of being left. "Don't go leave me, Brother," he cried, and he leaned toward the coffin. His hand, trembling, reached out, and when he touched the casket he screamed. A screech owl flapped out of the box into our faces, scaring us and covering us with Paris green. Doodle was paralyzed, so I put him on my shoulder and carried him down the ladder, and even when we were outside in the bright sunshine, he clung to me, crying, "Don't leave me. Don't leave me."

When Doodle was five years old, I was embarrassed at having a brother of that age who couldn't walk, so I set out to teach him. We were down in Old Woman Swamp and it was spring and the sick-sweet smell of bay flowers hung everywhere like a mournful song. "I'm going to teach you to walk, Doodle," I said.

He was sitting comfortably on the soft grass, leaning back against the pine. "Why?" he asked.

I hadn't expected such an answer. "So I won't have to haul you around all the time."

"I can't walk, Brother," he said.

"Who says so?" I demanded.

"Mama, the doctor—everybody."

"Oh, you can walk," I said, and I took him by the arms and stood him up. He collapsed onto the grass like a half-empty flour sack. It was as if he had no bones in his little legs.

"Don't hurt me, Brother," he warned.

"Shut up. I'm not going to hurt you. I'm going to teach you to walk." I heaved him up again, and again he collapsed.

This time he did not lift his face up out of the rubber grass. "I just can't do it. Let's make honeysuckle wreaths."

"Oh yes you can, Doodle," I said. "All you got to do is try. Now come on," and I hauled him up once more.

It seemed so hopeless from the beginning that it's a miracle I didn't give up. But all of us must have something or someone to be proud of, and Doodle had become mine. I did not know then that pride is a wonderful, terrible thing, a seed that bears two vines, life and death. Every day that summer we went to the pine beside the stream of Old Woman Swamp, and I put him on his feet at least a hundred times each afternoon. Occasionally I too became discouraged because it didn't seem as if he was trying, and I would say, "Doodle, don't you *want* to learn to walk?"

He'd nod his head, and I'd say, "Well, if you don't keep trying, you'll never learn." Then I'd paint for him a picture of us as old men, white-haired, him with a long white beard and me still pulling him around in the go-cart. This never failed to make him try again.

Finally one day, after many weeks of practicing, he stood alone for a few seconds. When he fell, I grabbed him in my arms and hugged him, our laughter pealing through the swamp like a ringing bell. Now we knew it could be done. Hope no longer hid in the dark palmetto thicket but perched like a cardinal in the lacy toothbrush tree, brilliantly visible. "Yes, yes," I cried, and he cried it too, and the grass beneath us was soft and the smell of the swamp was sweet.

With success so imminent, we decided not to tell anyone until he could actually walk. Each day, barring rain, we sneaked into Old Woman Swamp, and by cotton-picking time Doodle was ready to show what he could do. He still wasn't able to walk far, but we could wait no longer. Keeping a nice secret is very hard to do, like holding your breath. We chose to reveal all on October eighth, Doodle's sixth birthday, and for weeks ahead we mooned around the house, promising everybody a most spectacular surprise. Aunt Nicey said that, after so much talk, if we produced anything less tremendous than the Resurrection, she was going to be disappointed.

At breakfast on our chosen day, when Mama, Daddy, and Aunt Nicey were in the dining room, I brought Doodle to the door in the go-cart just as

---

5. **Paris green:** a poisonous green insecticide powder.

usual and had them turn their backs, making them cross their hearts and hope to die if they peeked. I helped Doodle up, and when he was standing alone I let them look. There wasn't a sound as Doodle walked slowly across the room and sat down at his place at the table. Then Mama began to cry and ran over to him, hugging him and kissing him. Daddy hugged him too, so I went to Aunt Nicey, who was thanks praying in the doorway, and began to waltz her around. We danced together quite well until she came down on my big toe with her brogans,[6] hurting me so badly I thought I was crippled for life.

Doodle told them it was I who had taught him to walk, so everyone wanted to hug me, and I began to cry.

"What are you crying for?" asked Daddy, but I couldn't answer. They did not know that I did it for myself; that pride, whose slave I was, spoke to me louder than all their voices, and that Doodle walked only because I was ashamed of having a crippled brother.

Within a few months Doodle had learned to walk well and his go-cart was put up in the barn loft (it's still there) beside his little mahogany coffin. Now, when we roamed off together, resting often, we never turned back until our destination had been reached, and to help pass the time, we took up lying. From the beginning Doodle was a terrible liar, and he got me in the habit. Had anyone stopped to listen to us, we would have been sent off to Dix Hill.

My lies were scary, involved, and usually pointless, but Doodle's were twice as crazy. People in his stories all had wings and flew wherever they wanted to go. His favorite lie was about a boy named Peter who had a pet peacock with a ten-foot tail. Peter wore a golden robe that glittered so brightly that when he walked through the sunflowers they turned away from the sun to face him. When Peter was ready to go to sleep, the peacock spread his magnificent tail, enfolding the boy gently like a closing go-to-sleep flower, burying him in the gloriously iridescent, rustling vortex. Yes, I must admit it. Doodle could beat me lying.

Doodle and I spent lots of time thinking about our future. We decided that when we were grown we'd live in Old Woman Swamp and pick dog-tongue for a living. Beside the stream, he planned, we'd build us a house of whispering leaves and the swamp birds would be our chickens. All day long (when we weren't gathering dog-tongue) we'd swing through the cypresses on the rope vines, and if it rained we'd huddle beneath an umbrella tree and play stickfrog. Mama and Daddy could come and live with us if they wanted to. He even came up with the idea that he could marry Mama and I could marry Daddy. Of course, I was old enough to know this wouldn't work out, but the picture he painted was so beautiful and serene that all I could do was whisper Yes, yes.

Once I had succeeded in teaching Doodle to walk, I began to believe in my own infallibility and I prepared a terrific development program for him, unknown to Mama and Daddy, of course. I would teach him to run, to swim, to climb trees, and to fight. He, too, now believed in my infallibility, so we set the deadline for these accomplishments less than a year away, when, it had been decided, Doodle could start to school.

That winter we didn't make much progress, for I was in school and Doodle suffered from one bad cold after another. But when spring came, rich and warm, we raised our sights again. Success lay at the end of summer like a pot of gold, and our campaign got off to a good start. On hot days, Doodle and I went down to Horsehead Landing, and I gave him swimming lessons or showed him how to row a boat. Sometimes we descended into the cool greenness of Old Woman Swamp and climbed the rope vines or boxed scientifically beneath the pine where he had learned to walk. Promise hung about us like leaves, and wherever we looked, ferns unfurled and birds broke into song.

That summer, the summer of 1918, was blighted. In May and June there was no rain and the crops withered, curled up, then died under the thirsty sun. One morning in July a hurricane came out of the east, tipping over the oaks in the yard and splitting the limbs of the elm trees. That afternoon it roared back out of the west, blew the

---

6. **brogans:** heavy, ankle-high shoes.

fallen oaks around, snapping their roots and tearing them out of the earth like a hawk at the entrails of a chicken. Cotton bolls were wrenched from the stalks and lay like green walnuts in the valleys between the rows, while the cornfield leaned over uniformly so that the tassels touched the ground. Doodle and I followed Daddy out into the cotton field, where he stood, shoulders sagging, surveying the ruin. When his chin sank down onto his chest, we were frightened, and Doodle slipped his hand into mine. Suddenly Daddy straightened his shoulders, raised a giant knuckly fist, and with a voice that seemed to rumble out of the earth itself began cursing heaven, hell, the weather, and the Republican Party.[7] Doodle and I, prodding each other and giggling, went back to the house, knowing that everything would be all right.

And during that summer, strange names were heard through the house: Château-Thierry,[8] Amiens, Soissons, and in her blessing at the supper table, Mama once said, "And bless the Pearsons, whose boy Joe was lost in Belleau Wood."

So we came to that clove of seasons. School was only a few weeks away, and Doodle was far behind schedule. He could barely clear the ground when climbing up the rope vines, and his swimming was certainly not passable. We decided to double our efforts, to make that last drive and reach our pot of gold. I made him swim until he turned blue and row until he couldn't lift an oar. Wherever we went, I purposely walked fast, and although he kept up, his face turned red and his eyes became glazed. Once, he could go no further, so he collapsed on the ground and began to cry.

"Aw, come on, Doodle," I urged. "You can do it. Do you want to be different from everybody else when you start school?"

"Does it make any difference?"

"It certainly does," I said. "Now, come on," and I helped him up.

As we slipped through the dog days, Doodle began to look feverish, and Mama felt his forehead, asking him if he felt ill. At night he didn't sleep well, and sometimes he had nightmares, crying out until I touched him and said, "Wake up, Doodle. Wake up."

It was Saturday noon, just a few days before school was to start. I should have already admitted defeat, but my pride wouldn't let me. The excitement of our program had now been gone for weeks, but still we kept on with a tired doggedness. It was too late to turn back, for we had both wandered too far into a net of expectations and had left no crumbs behind.

Daddy, Mama, Doodle, and I were seated at the dining-room table having lunch. It was a hot day, with all the windows and doors open in case a breeze should come. In the kitchen Aunt Nicey was humming softly. After a long silence, Daddy spoke. "It's so calm, I wouldn't be surprised if we had a storm this afternoon."

"I haven't heard a rain frog," said Mama, who believed in signs, as she served the bread around the table.

"I did," declared Doodle. "Down in the swamp."

"He didn't," I said contrarily.

"You did, eh?" said Daddy, ignoring my denial.

"I certainly did," Doodle reiterated, scowling at me over the top of his iced-tea glass, and we were quiet again.

Suddenly, from out in the yard, came a strange croaking noise. Doodle stopped eating, with a piece of bread poised ready for his mouth, his eyes popped round like two blue buttons. "What's that?" he whispered.

I jumped up, knocking over my chair, and had reached the door when Mama called, "Pick up the chair, sit down again, and say excuse me."

By the time I had done this, Doodle had excused himself and had slipped out into the yard. He was looking up into the bleeding tree. "It's a great big red bird!" he called.

The bird croaked loudly again, and Mama and Daddy came out into the yard. We shaded our eyes with our hands against the hazy glare of the sun and peered up through the still leaves. On the topmost branch a bird the size of a chicken, with scarlet feathers and long legs, was perched precariously. Its wings hung down loosely, and as we watched, a feather dropped away and floated

7. **Republican Party:** at this time most Southern farmers were staunch Democrats.
8. **Château-Thierry** (sha·tō′ tye·rē′), **Amiens** (à·myan′), **Soissons** (swả·sôn′), **Belleau** (be·lō′) **Wood:** World War I battle sites in France.

slowly down through the green leaves.

"It's not even frightened of us," Mama said.

"It looks tired," Daddy added. "Or maybe sick."

Doodle's hands were clasped at his throat, and I had never seen him stand still so long. "What is it?" he asked.

Daddy shook his head. "I don't know, maybe it's——"

At that moment the bird began to flutter, but the wings were uncoordinated, and amid much flapping and a spray of flying feathers, it tumbled down, bumping through the limbs of the bleeding tree and landing at our feet with a thud. Its long, graceful neck jerked twice into an S, then straightened out, and the bird was still. A white veil came over the eyes, and the long white beak unhinged. Its legs were crossed and its clawlike feet were delicately curved at rest. Even death did not mar its grace, for it lay on the earth like a broken vase of red flowers, and we stood around it, awed by its exotic beauty.

"It's dead," Mama said.

"What is it?" Doodle repeated.

"Go bring me the bird book," said Daddy.

I ran into the house and brought back the bird book. As we watched, Daddy thumbed through its pages. "It's a scarlet ibis," he said, pointing to a picture. "It lives in the tropics—South America to Florida. A storm must have brought it here."

Sadly, we all looked back at the bird. A scarlet ibis! How many miles it had traveled to die like this, in *our* yard, beneath the bleeding tree.

"Let's finish lunch," Mama said, nudging us back toward the dining room.

"I'm not hungry," said Doodle, and he knelt down beside the ibis.

"We've got peach cobbler for dessert," Mama tempted from the doorway.

Doodle remained kneeling. "I'm going to bury him."

"Don't you dare touch him," Mama warned. "There's no telling what disease he might have had."

"All right," said Doodle. "I won't."

Daddy, Mama, and I went back to the dining-room table, but we watched Doodle through the open door. He took out a piece of string from his pocket and, without touching the ibis, looped one end around its neck. Slowly, while singing softly "Shall We Gather at the River," he carried the bird around to the front yard and dug a hole in the flower garden, next to the petunia bed. Now we were watching him through the front window, but he didn't know it. His awkwardness at digging the hole with a shovel whose handle was twice as long as he was made us laugh, and we covered our mouths with our hands so he wouldn't hear.

When Doodle came into the dining room, he found us seriously eating our cobbler. He was pale and lingered just inside the screen door. "Did you get the scarlet ibis buried?" asked Daddy.

Doodle didn't speak but nodded his head.

"Go wash your hands, and then you can have some peach cobbler," said Mama.

"I'm not hungry," he said.

"Dead birds is bad luck," said Aunt Nicey, poking her head from the kitchen door. "Specially *red* dead birds!"

As soon as I had finished eating, Doodle and I hurried off to Horsehead Landing. Time was short, and Doodle still had a long way to go if he was going to keep up with the other boys when he started school. The sun, gilded with the yellow cast of autumn, still burned fiercely, but the dark green woods through which we passed were shady and cool. When we reached the landing, Doodle said he was too tired to swim, so we got into a skiff and floated down the creek with the tide. Far off in the marsh a rail was scolding, and over on the beach locusts were singing in the myrtle trees. Doodle did not speak and kept his head turned away, letting one hand trail limply in the water.

After we had drifted a long way, I put the oars in place and made Doodle row back against the tide. Black clouds began to gather in the southwest, and he kept watching them, trying to pull the oars a little faster. When we reached Horsehead Landing, lightning was playing across half the sky and thunder roared out, hiding even the sound of the sea. The sun disappeared and darkness descended, almost like night. Flocks of marsh crows flew by, heading inland to their roosting trees, and two egrets, squawking, arose from the oyster-rock shallows and careened away.

Doodle was both tired and frightened, and when

he stepped from the skiff he collapsed onto the mud, sending an armada of fiddler crabs rustling off into the marsh grass. I helped him up, and as he wiped the mud off his trousers, he smiled at me ashamedly. He had failed and we both knew it, so we started back home, racing the storm. We never spoke (What are the words that can solder cracked pride?), but I knew he was watching me, watching for a sign of mercy. The lightning was near now, and from fear he walked so close behind me he kept stepping on my heels. The faster I walked, the faster he walked, so I began to run. The rain was coming, roaring through the pines, and then, like a bursting Roman candle, a gum tree ahead of us was shattered by a bolt of lightning. When the deafening peal of thunder had died, and in the moment before the rain arrived, I heard Doodle, who had fallen behind, cry out, "Brother, Brother, don't leave me! Don't leave me!"

The knowledge that Doodle's and my plans had come to naught was bitter, and that streak of cruelty within me awakened. I ran as fast as I could, leaving him far behind with a wall of rain dividing us. The drops stung my face like nettles,[9] and the wind flared the wet glistening leaves of the bordering trees. Soon I could hear his voice no more.

---

9. **nettles:** plants with leaves that sting.

I hadn't run too far before I became tired, and the flood of childish spite evanesced as well. I stopped and waited for Doodle. The sound of rain was everywhere, but the wind had died and it fell straight down in parallel paths like ropes hanging from the sky. As I waited, I peered through the downpour, but no one came. Finally I went back and found him huddled beneath a red nightshade bush beside the road. He was sitting on the ground, his face buried in his arms, which were resting on his drawn-up knees. "Let's go, Doodle," I said.

He didn't answer, so I placed my hand on his forehead and lifted his head. Limply, he fell backward onto the earth. He had been bleeding from the mouth, and his neck and the front of his shirt were stained a brilliant red.

"Doodle! Doodle!" I cried, shaking him, but there was no answer but the ropy rain. He lay very awkwardly, with his head thrown far back, making his vermilion neck appear unusually long and slim. His little legs, bent sharply at the knees, had never before seemed so fragile, so thin.

I began to weep, and the tear-blurred vision in red before me looked very familiar. "Doodle!" I screamed above the pounding storm and threw my body to the earth above his. For a long, long time, it seemed forever, I lay there crying, sheltering my fallen scarlet ibis from the heresy of rain.

Responding to the Story

Analyzing the Story

Identifying Facts

1. What do we know about the **narrator** of the story? What details at the start of the story tell us that the events he is about to relate took place many years ago?
2. Why does the narrator teach Doodle to walk? Why does he cry when his family congratulates him for his effort?
3. After Doodle has learned to walk, what does his brother try to teach him, to prepare him for school?

4. How does Doodle respond to the scarlet ibis and to its death?

Interpreting Meanings

5. Why does Doodle die? To what extent do you think his brother is responsible for his death? By the end of the story, whom do you pity more—the narrator or Doodle?
6. On one level the **conflict** that powers this story involves the narrator's actual struggle to make his brother like everyone else. On another level, the narrator experiences an **internal conflict.** Describe the narrator's internal conflict. Is it

ever **resolved**? How do you know?

7. What do the narrator's **actions** and **thoughts** reveal about his **character**: Is he jealous? Loving? Cruel? Generous? Cite passages from the story to support your answer.

8. In the last sentence, the narrator calls his brother his "fallen scarlet ibis." In what ways does the scarlet ibis resemble Doodle? How are their deaths similar—both in appearances and in cause?

9. The **theme** of this story reveals a truth about the effects of love and pride. In one sentence or more, state what you think is the theme of the story. In spite of what's been said about theme rarely being stated in a story, there are several passages of the story where the narrator or Doodle puts his finger on the essence of the theme. Find at least two of these passages.

10. What incidents from life as you know it could illustrate the good and bad effects of human pride?

Writing About the Story

A Creative Response

1. **Using Another Point of View.** "The Scarlet Ibis" would be a different story if it had been told from the point of view of Doodle. Pick a key scene from the story and tell it from the **third-person limited** point of view, through Doodle's senses and feelings. Write a paragraph or two.

A Critical Response

2. **Explaining a Response to a Theme.** Do you think this story reveals a genuine truth about people? Are we often cruel to those we love? Can pride cause us to be destructive and to hurt even those we love? Write a paragraph or more explaining your opinion of one of these ideas. Give at least two reasons for your response.

3. **Analyzing a Character.** Look back at the passage on page 173 describing Doodle's "lies." Write a paragraph in which you analyze Doodle's tales. What do his characters want? What kind of world do they live in? Why would Doodle tell this kind of story? What do his stories reveal about his own wants?

4. **Analyzing Setting.** There is a distinct feeling of nature in "The Scarlet Ibis"—the seasons, the drought, the vegetation identified by name, the details of the Old Woman Swamp. In one para-

graph, cite at least five **images** describing the setting that helped give you a vivid sense of being there. In a second paragraph, cite three images describing the vegetation that create an atmosphere of sorrow and loss.

Analyzing Language and Vocabulary

Symbols

We communicate by means of symbols. We use sounds to stand for things in the outer physical world and for ideas in our own inner worlds. The sounds themselves are not the things or ideas; the sounds only symbolize, or stand for, these things and ideas.

In literature, a symbol is somewhat different. In literature, a **symbol** is a specific object, person, or event that stands for something more or for something other than itself.

In "The Scarlet Ibis" the ibis is obviously used as a symbol for Doodle. How do we know this? The story must give us some clues.

1. Find the sentence at the end of "The Scarlet Ibis" that clearly links Doodle and the red bird.

2. In question 8, you noted the similarities between Doodle and the red bird. Go back and reread closely all the passages in the story where the ibis is mentioned. Where does Doodle show that he himself identifies with the bird?

3. Explain how both Doodle and the bird are placed in worlds in which they cannot survive. (Where is the scarlet ibis's natural habitat?)

4. In a sentence, state the broader meaning that you think the ibis has in the story.

5. What examples can you give in which the color red is used as a symbol of love or of courage or of a heroic death?

Reading About the Writer

James Hurst (1922–   ) was born on a farm by the sea in North Carolina. He worked for thirty-four years for a bank in New York City before he retired to New Bern, North Carolina, a town very near his birthplace. He reminds readers of "The Scarlet Ibis" to think of how the war raging among "brothers" in Europe is related to the conflict between Doodle and his brother. In both cases, people suffer because others try to make them over "in their own image."

THE BRIDGE

Nicolai Chukovski

This story's action is set in modern Russia, but it deals with a situation that could happen anywhere in the world. If you have ever felt unsure of yourself or of your future, you'll see that the conflict in "The Bridge" is universal. As you read, think of how the story's title points directly to its theme.

I just can't see him going," Gramma said, turning over the potato cake in the pan with a knife. "He's scared of everything."

"He'll go," Aunt Nadya replied from the depth of the kitchen. "He has to go. He'll be better off there."

Gramma sighed loudly. She wasn't at all convinced Kostya would be better off there.

Kostya had heard every word. He stood not far from the open window amid the currant shrubs, quickly picking the berries and shoving them into his mouth. Since it had been decided he would have to go away, Kostya was spending hours at a time in these shrubs, their luxurious, end-of-July growth serving as an excellent hiding place. He liked to be alone and not have to talk to anyone. Through the branches creeping over the windowsill into the shade-filled kitchen, he could see Gramma's hands moving over the kerosene burner and hear the sizzling of the frying pancakes.

"He's scared of everything . . . everything," Gramma repeated. "He's afraid to buy a stamp in the post office. How'll he go?"

Kostya's mouth was getting sour from the berries. He worked his way out of the shrubbery, found his bicycle on the dark porch, and he opened the kitchen door. Aunt Nadya was peeling potatoes—since it was Sunday she hadn't gone to work in the factory but was helping Gramma. The peels coiled like spirals over Aunt Nadya's thick, manlike fingers. Gramma, a squat, little woman, had just turned over another sizzling pancake. She looked up at the boy. Kostya knew that the mountain of potato cakes piled up in a plate at the burner was being baked for him—one more sign that his going-away was final.

"I'm going for a little ride," he said glumly, hoisting the small bicycle over his shoulder.

Gramma sighed, stepping heavily from foot to foot. "Go on, have your last ride," Aunt Nadya told him without lifting her face from the potatoes. "You won't be doing it there."

Kostya walked the bicycle through the open wicket[1] and threw his long leg over the frame. The bike, a juvenile size bought a long time ago, had become too small for him. This year he had shot up to almost twice his previous height, though otherwise he remained the same: narrow shoulders, a thin neck with a protruding Adam's apple, and slightly protuberant,[2] translucent ears. Mechanically Kostya rode out into the alley, hedged by dusty elder thickets. His sharp knees almost touched his chin but he didn't mind—he was much too used to it. Mechanically he swerved to his left to cut into the open fields; he didn't want to meet anybody and didn't want anybody to disturb his thoughts.

Last spring after he was graduated from high school, barely getting promoted, Kostya had decided that going to the institute was out of the question. There had been a time his marks were no worse than anybody else's, but after his mother had died, a year and a half ago, he hadn't attended school for several months, and he had fallen too far behind to catch up. Everybody in class had

---

1. **wicket:** small gate.
2. **protuberant** (prō·tōō′ bər·ənt): sticking out.

known that Kostya never learned his lessons. He had become shy and unsure of himself, and the shyness had compounded his confusion whenever he'd been called to the blackboard.

And then his awkwardness. In company he'd either keep quiet or blurt out anything that came to his mind, then feel ashamed of himself. He had begun to avoid people, go swimming by himself, had even given up the soccer team. Once he had been shortchanged in the bakery shop, and instead of reminding the saleswoman that she had made a mistake, he had told his grandmother that he had lost the money. Gramma was the only one with whom he felt at ease, unafraid. But now he'd have to leave her. . . .

This was the third year Gramma hadn't worked in the factory but had lived on her pension. Aunt Nadya had four little children; her husband had gone into construction work somewhere on the Volga;[3] and there were rumors he had himself another woman—for the last year he hadn't sent home a kopeck.[4] The whole settlement where Kostya had been born and lived all his starless seventeen years was made up of people working in the factory. It was a women's factory where a true man wouldn't be caught working. Lads would leave the settlement as soon as they were graduated, and Kostya, too, would have to leave and stop living at Gramma's and Aunt Nadya's expense. But where? Uncle Vassily Petrovitch, Gramma's brother, had asked him to come, promising Gramma to take good care of him and find him a job. Everybody had thought that this was good and right, that a bright future was ahead of him . . . everybody but Kostya. Deep inside he was afraid nothing would come out of it, yet he didn't dare tell anybody.

He didn't dare confess to anybody how frightening was the thought of leaving Gramma. Uncle Vassily Petrovitch loomed in Kostya's mind like a cold, strict old man of whom even Gramma was afraid. Quite often she had warned him "not to do anything to spite your uncle." Uncle Vasya had left for Siberia many years ago, before Kostya was even born, when his mother was still a little

girl. He had been a tugboat captain on that great Siberian river that flows into the Arctic Ocean, but now he was more than that—he was a chief over a whole fleet of boats. Kostya often saw this river on a large map hanging in the classroom; with all its winding tributaries it reminded him of some strange plant with many weird roots stretching and stretching. . . . Uncle Vasya often asked that Kostya come. "I'll enter him in the River Technicum[5] together with my son Kolya," he wrote. "They will drill them there so that in three years both of them will become fine navigators." When Gramma had read that letter she flinched and cast Kostya a frightened look at the word "drill." And yet tonight they would go to the railroad station and wait for the Moscow train arriving at five in the morning. He would leave all by himself for Moscow, the unfamiliar big city he had never seen before, and in Moscow he'd have to find his way to another railroad station, board another train leaving for Siberia, and he'd be all by himself with nothing to remind him of Gramma's comfort apart from the potato pancakes in the basket. . . .

It was a warm but sunless, overcast day. Kostya rode out of the settlement and turned onto the highway running amid wavy fields. To the right, about three kilometers away, stretched the river— wide at times, hiding at times behind soft hills. The cloud-covered sky seemed to be hanging low over the usually busy highway, now deserted because it was Sunday. A warm, hay-scented breeze caressed the boy's face, as though careful not to disturb his thinking.

Deep in his thoughts, Kostya pushed the pedals, unaware of a little bird that kept perching on a telegraph post ahead of him, swinging its long tail, and seeming to wait until he caught up with it, then flying up again, perching on another post, farther away, and waiting again. The boy did not notice it nor the old, thick-leaved linden trees— the remnants of an old road on which this highway was constructed—shooting up here and there like petrified explosions. Kostya pedaled onward

---

3. **Volga:** one of the most important rivers in Russia. It flows through Stalingrad and into the Caspian Sea.
4. **kopeck:** a coin. There are 100 kopecks to the ruble.

5. **River Technicum:** a technical school that specializes in naval training.

where the gray ribbon of the macadam[6] ran into the sunless twilight, rising softly or sloping gently.

Each time Kostya reached a crest of the wavy road, he had an excellent view to the next crest. Each time he was on the top of a hill he could see a green depression through which the road made a straight cut, first running down then up toward the crest where it butted against the sky and disappeared.

Hurdling one of these crests, Kostya sighted in the distance a minute, colored dot moving in the same direction. It occurred to him he might have noticed it before but had paid it no attention. There might have been a two-kilometer span between them—he only had a glimpse of it, looming blue and yellow, before it reached the next crest and vanished.

Kostya began to pedal faster. He dashed downhill, bouncing over a little bridge that spanned the two banks of a gully, then climbed the uphill stretch, using the impetus gained from the downdrive. He hurdled the crest and saw again the yellow-blue dot—bigger now, just beginning to move up the next rise. The distance between them had been shortened considerably; he could see it was somebody on a bicycle. How odd, he thought, so gaily dressed, yellow on top, blue below. Quite intrigued, Kostya leaned forward, pumping harder and harder, trying for greater speed.

As soon as he came over the next crest, he realized that the cyclist ahead of him was a girl wearing a blue skirt and yellow blouse, her fair hair falling down her back. She had been pedaling unhurriedly until she heard him coming from behind. As she turned her face to him, the glimpse Kostya caught was brief: a round, babyish face. There were still about two hundred meters separating them, and when she turned away again, her plump, little calves in the white socks began to push harder—the girl didn't want to be outdistanced.

She spurted ahead. Kostya leaned forward on the bars, pumping with all his might. Yet he was unable to cut the distance by much—she seemed to be quite good. On the next rise he appeared to

gain a little, but when they came down the slope and the bikes rolled on their own, he stayed back somewhat. Her bike's better than mine, he thought. Yet the excitement of the chase added will to his strength—on the next rise he gained considerably and covered the next downhill stretch, long as it was, without giving in a meter. Now he could see her well; no more than thirteen or fourteen. At times the girl turned her head slightly, seeming to try to catch a glimpse of him from the corner of her eye. Then he saw her chubby cheek, and a moment later he'd see her trying desperately to keep him from catching up with her. But he was drawing inexorably closer.

The girl's hair fluttered in the wind, exposing the back of her neck. They sped out of the fields, plunging into a forest of aspen, spruce, and birch trees that seemed to rise into a solid wall. As the distance between the bicycles stubbornly decreased, Kostya was overcome by a sense of triumph. The girl's glances were more frequent; every time she tried to have a look at him her bike made a little zigzag, and he gained a few meters. He was sure now to catch up with her, probably on the next rise.

A recently laid asphalt road turned off the highway into the forest, right at the start of the rise. Kostya knew where it led: toward the river where a new bridge was being built to connect the state farms on both sides. But what he did not suspect was that the pursued bicycle would turn off to that road.

The girl made the turn abruptly. It was so sudden that he almost flashed by. She might have thought he would follow the highway and stop pursuing her. But Kostya had become so intensely elated that all he could think of now was catching up with her. He, too, swerved from the highway and spurted after her.

The road was downhill all the way. Both bicycles were tearing down at their maximum speeds, the girl steadily about ten meters ahead of Kostya. But he didn't care anymore—the road only led to the bridge now under construction, and she'd have no choice but to stop there.

The road approached the bridge at an angle; through the tree trunks at the right, the mirror of the river flashed far below under its steep bank.

---

6. **macadam** (mə·kad′əm): a road surfaced with crushed stones and tar or asphalt.

Cement barrels, sifters, and wooden scaffolding loomed before their eyes, together with piles upon piles of scrap concrete—the unfinished structure was right in front of them.

The bridgework had no top layer yet but it spanned both banks. It looked like a net scaled by a formless hodgepodge of wood in which the future metallic slickness could only be vaguely surmised. Now because it was Sunday, instead of the unceasing hum of work, a deep silence stood over the river.

Everything happened so fast that Kostya had no time to consider the danger. Suddenly he saw that the asphalt was coming to an end, and a four-plank trestle, laid over a sand embankment, led to the bridge. The girl pedaled ahead at top speed. Kostya was so shocked that before he had time to recover his wits he found himself, too, bouncing along those planks. He gripped the bar firmly to avoid veering off onto the sand. But the sand wasn't what bothered him. What frightened him was the realization that the trestle ran from the embankment onto the truss, across the unfenced iron girders which served as a narrow path for the bridge workers—high above the water. Was she insane? She was coming to the end of the embankment without slowing down!

"Brake! Brake!" he managed to shout out. But then he choked on his own words.

The girl half turned at the sound of his voice. Again she glanced at him from the corner of one eye. Her bicycle, making a slight zigzag, almost pulled her off the planks. But she managed to straighten out the wheel and spurt straight ahead, onto the truss, over the narrow path suspended high above the water.

Something is terribly wrong here, flashed through Kostya's mind. He should have braked short of the bridge but for some uncanny reason he hadn't done so. His bike carried him onto the truss, onto those same planks, high above the water. . . .

There was no more time to stop, turn, or look back. The only way was straight ahead—with no letup of speed. His hand must not jerk. He knew he couldn't stand the suspense; he'd weaken from fear. But he must go on . . . because of her . . . because her bike was straight ahead. . . .

Kostya couldn't tear his eyes away from the girl. She rode evenly, unswervingly, yet he sensed a desperate tension in that straightness. How can she stand it! Oh, if she only doesn't get it into her head to look back! How far is it to the end of the bridge? If she can only keep her hand from jerking! If only she'll not try to look back! She's over more than half—one more minute, and it'll be all over. Just that she doesn't look back!

The girl did look back.

She turned her head just slightly, just to make sure from the corner of her eye that he was behind. As she turned, her front wheel gave a slight jerk. A second, a long eternity, she struggled with it, trying to make it straight. But she couldn't. Her bike veered into the air, into emptiness. . . .

He didn't see her fall. She simply disappeared from the bridge—she and her bike. Abruptly he did something he had thought was impossible—he put on the brakes and jumped off onto the planks. He looked down. The water was way, way down, glistening with a dull, firm shine like a metal—streaming away, somewhere beyond the bridge. He saw her bike, caught by its frame at the end of a beam, sticking out from behind the rough scaffolding, still swinging slightly. But the girl was nowhere in sight.

Stunned, Kostya put down his bike and dived.

He pierced the surface of the water with his hands and felt it close above him as he was dragged down by the current. Although stung by the fall, he had the presence of mind to open his eyes and look for her. All he could see were hazy outlines of some huge blocks and posts. After touching the bottom, he felt himself pulled up. He turned over under the water and surfaced.

The current pulled him to the bridge span. He came close to a concrete abutment not cleared yet of some wooden casing and piles of lumber. Above, fragments of the cloudy sky seemed to be peeking through the many-storied net of girders, crossbeams, and timbering. The current was strong, too strong for any resistance. Kostya drifted with it, turning, whirling, not even trying to fight it until . . . he saw her, just around the bend.

The top of her head appeared behind a pile of timber sticking out of the water at the bridge span.

Up to her mouth in water, the girl clutched the pile with both hands, right in front of a foaming whirl. Kostya couldn't see her whole face but her cheek and one eye, and from the look of that eye—large, frightened—he knew that she was holding with her last strength. One more moment and the current would carry her away.

"Hold on!" he shouted, choking on a mouthful of water. Now there was only one thing to be afraid of, that the current would carry him by her. He'd never be able to get back to her against it. Kostya tried desperately to gain control of his movements. His wet trousers and canvas slippers hampered his effort. Nonetheless, he managed to throw out his left arm and grab that same pile. As the current whirled him around and around he hung on, his shoulder touching hers.

The girl's pale, wet face was close to his, her wide-open eyes bright with tension. He hoped she would believe that he would be able to save her. But how? He didn't have the slightest idea himself what to do next.

High up, the concrete abutment towered like a tremendous giant. Its surface was too smooth to offer a hold. Kostya looked back—behind them the river grew wide.

"You know how to swim?" he asked.

She shook her head.

Kostya knew that the girl couldn't hold on much longer. He looked back again; the left bank was not too far away. By himself he'd probably make it. To the right, in the direction of the current, the river made a bend. To the left, oblong stones jutted out of the water. There, he should try to get over there. . . .

He looked at the girl again. He'd have to act fast, as long as she still had some strength left. "Let go," he ordered.

"No, no."

"You must listen to me," he said gravely. He pulled her hand away from the pile and tried to put it on his shoulder. Immediately her other hand slipped off the pile and now the girl clung to him with both hands. Under the burden Kostya let go, and both of them began to sink. The whirl pulled them under. In desperation he forcibly pried open her hands and pushed her away. Thrashing wildly, the girl rose to the surface by herself. He, too, came up, snorted, and looked around. The girl kept thrashing right beside him. Her round face rose for a moment out of the water; her mouth gasped for air before she began to sink again. The bridge with all its mass of iron and wood seemed to be rapidly backing away.

Kostya wound her short, chubby arm around his neck. Her other arm which was about to clutch him he pushed aside. "Don't you dare," he said sternly. "You must obey me."

She obeyed and stopped clinging to him. As they began to float more steadily, Kostya struggled stubbornly, stroking with one arm and cutting across the current toward the stones. The girl's soft arm rested confidently, though heavily, against his neck, pressing his face into the water. But Kostya knew how to handle himself. As long as her face remained above water, he'd be able to lift his head for a breath of air, then let it be submerged.

The girl stopped struggling. She calmed down and obviously had more confidence in him than he had in himself. "I'll do whatever you say," she whispered into his ear. But he felt he was weakening, and he was afraid the current would not let them reach the stones. He tried to drift to the shore but the whirls carried him to the right, around the stones, toward the rapids. Two times he tried to reach bottom with his feet; on the third try he touched it.

Although the water reached above his ears, he managed to keep afloat. The shallow from which the stones protruded had apparently extended quite far. Seeing him stand, the girl tried to stand up too. After she swallowed some water and choked, Kostya picked her up and, stepping carefully, he carried her to the shore.

Fifteen minutes later they were sitting on the sloping bank amid elm trees, watching the water through the branches. Their clothes were hung on the trees to dry—he had only his trunks on, she had on panties and a white undershirt. Her seminakedness embarrassed him; he tried not to sit too close to her nor glance at her too often. She, however, seemed not to mind. Her innocent, bright eyes were full of confidence as they admired him through strands of wet hair that kept falling onto her face.

Their bicycles lay side by side on the grass. Kostya had removed them from the bridge by himself. The zeal of achievement had made him feel light and fearless. It hadn't been too difficult to get his bicycle, although when he had stepped onto those planks once again he had asked himself how he was able to ride on that narrow, unfenced path. An hour ago he'd probably not have had the courage to walk on it; but now he ambled without fear, without having to look at his feet. To recover the girl's bike wasn't that easy; he had to clamber down the timbering and hoist the thing with his feet while hanging on the girder with his hands. He had enjoyed his work, however, knowing that she stood there on the shore, watching him, admiring him. He hadn't been afraid to fall into the water because that would have only been a repeat jump. But he had been concerned he might drop the bicycle. He hadn't. He rolled them both up onto the shore, toward the elm tree where their clothes were hung to dry.

"You can do everything." The girl looked at Kostya with admiring eyes.

"I can," he confirmed. "Had I dropped your bike I'd have given you mine." He felt like being extremely generous; as a matter of fact, he was sorry he couldn't give her his bike.

"I'd not have taken it for anything," she said. "You are leaving?"

"Yes, tonight."

"For long?"

"Forever."

"And when will you come back?" she asked.

"Probably never."

The impression his words made on her affected him too.

"Never," the girl repeated slowly. "How far are you going?"

"Very far," he replied. "I'm taking the Moscow train tonight."

She asked if he was going to the district capital. She had apparently thought the district capital was very far.

"Uh uh," Kostya said. "The day after tomorrow I'll be in Moscow."

"In Moscow?" she asked respectfully.

"But only for a day," he explained. "Got to do some sightseeing."

"You're going even farther?" she asked incredulously.

He nodded. "To Siberia."

She became quiet. He sensed how impressive that name sounded to her.

"Who's going with you?" she asked again.

"I'm going by myself."

While he answered her questions, Kostya began to see his trip in a new light. He had suddenly made a discovery—he found out something about himself he had never known: he could accomplish tasks. The future, which up to now had appeared fearful, suddenly became a grandiose adventure within reach.

"I'll guide big ships," Kostya said, getting up from excitement. "Diesel motor ships."

"Where to?"

"To the Arctic Ocean. Beyond the Arctic Circle and back. Through the taiga, tundra,[7] all kinds of animals," Kostya recalled what he knew about Siberia. He was waiting for her to ask if he really knew how to guide diesel motor ships, but she didn't. Perhaps she had some doubts if he really could do everything. He, too, had some doubts.

---

7. **taiga** (tī′ gə), **tundra** (tun′ drə): The taiga is a moist, subarctic evergreen forest region. North of it lies the tundra, a treeless plain whose subsoil level is permanently frozen.

"I'll learn," he said, thinking of Uncle Vasya. "What one man can do another man can, too."

There was silence for a while. Narrow-shouldered, long-legged, upright, Kostya stared into the water glistening through the trees. Absorbed in his new ideas, he seemed to have forgotten about the girl who sat with her arms around her round knees, glancing at him timidly from time to time.

"Is somebody coming to see you off?" she asked softly.

"They are." He nodded.

"Who?"

Kostya knew that Gramma and Aunt Nadya would come with him to the station, but somehow he didn't feel like telling it to the girl. He made no reply.

"I'll come too, may I?" she asked in a pattering whisper, brushing off her wet hair from her forehead. "We live next to the station. I'll just jump out of the window and run up. May I?" The girl talked fast, as if she were afraid he might stop her. "I won't be in anybody's way, they won't even see me. I'll just watch. May I, may I?"

Kostya didn't answer. He looked at her with a joyous wonderment in his heart—it was a hitherto unknown tenderness which he realized was also a new discovery.

Responding to the Story

Analyzing the Story

Identifying Facts

1. At the beginning of the story, what are we told about Kostya's **appearance** and his **character**? (Look at what the author tells you directly and at what you learn from other characters.)

2. Why does Kostya have to leave home, and why is he so afraid of leaving?

3. Explain how Kostya's leisurely, absent-minded bicycle ride turns into an athletic contest. Find the details that tell how he feels as he is chasing the girl on the bicycle.

4. Describe the **physical conflict** Kostya faces as he tries to rescue the girl.

Interpreting Meanings

5. One way to identify a story's **theme** is to think about what the main character learns during the course of the story. Find the passage that tells you what Kostya discovers about himself as a result of his climactic scene on the bridge. Why couldn't he have learned this at home, outside the kitchen window, where we first see him?

6. How does this new revelation **change** him as a

person? How does it change his feelings about his own future?

7. In a sentence or more, state what you think is the **theme** of this story—what does it reveal about how young people learn to have confidence in themselves? In crossing this real bridge, how did Kostya "bridge," or cross over, from childhood to maturity?

8. The last line of the story suggests that Kostya has made not one, but two discoveries. What do you think is the second one?

9. Explain whether you think the change in Kostya is believable. Will it last? Why?

10. The **setting** of this story is Russia. What details in the **plot** and **characterization** would have to change if it were to take place in the United States, at the present time?

Writing About the Story

A Creative Response

1. **Writing an Ending.** What happens at the train station that night? Does the girl show up to see Kostya off? Does she stay in the background, or does Kostya introduce her to his grandmother and aunt? Write a paragraph or more to end the story.

A Critical Response

2. **Analyzing Stories.** "The Bridge" is a **rite-of-passage story** (see page 186), as are several other stories in this book. Select one of the stories you have read so far in which the main character goes through some sort of growing-up experience. You could choose "Antaeus" (page 111) or "The Hat" (page 143). Write at least one paragraph explaining how this story and "The Bridge" can be seen as rite-of-passage stories. Before you write, fill out a chart like the one that follows:

	"The Bridge"	Other story
What does the main character learn?		
How does he or she learn it?		
Does the character change? How?		
Does the story end happily or unhappily?		

Analyzing Language and Vocabulary

Sentences, Style, and Oral Reading

Style refers to a writer's characteristic way of using language. Many writers develop styles that their readers recognize at once. Style is created by many elements: by word choice (plain words or fancy words); by sentence structure (long sentences or short ones); by the use of description (or its absence); by the use of dialogue (or its absence).

"The Bridge" and "The Scarlet Ibis" (page 168) are examples of two different storytelling styles.

1. Read aloud the opening passages of each story. Which story tells you directly, through dialogue, what the problem is going to be?

2. Which story opens with a descriptive passage that creates an atmosphere or mood?

3. Which story's opening sounds more poetic? Which opening seems more dramatic?

4. Read aloud the passage in "The Bridge" beginning "There was no more time to stop" and ending "The girl did look back" (pages 181–182). Practice reading the passage until you are satisfied that your voice conveys suspense and drama. Is suspense in the passage created by a series of long, leisurely poetic sentences? Or is it created by short sentences that clip along quickly?

Reading About the Writer

The dates marking the life of the Russian writer **Nicolai Chukovski** (1904–1965) show that he survived the Russian Revolution of 1917 and the enormous devastation caused by World War II. Chukovski was the son of a popular children's writer. He himself concentrated on historical fiction, accounts of voyages of exploration, and short stories. Very few of his writings have been translated into English.

Focusing on Background
Rite-of-Passage Stories

The word *rite* specifically refers to any kind of ceremony that is always practiced on a particular occasion. Bringing a tree into the house and decorating it every Christmas can be a rite. Lighting the Sabbath candles is a rite, and so are exchanging marriage vows and folding the flag at a military funeral.

A "rite of passage" refers to a ceremony marking the time when a person passes from one stage of life to another. Birth and death are, of course, natural rites of passage that take place at the beginning and the end of life. But there are other rites of passage that occur in between.

A universal rite of passage is the passage from childhood to adulthood. Religions usually mark this passage by a ceremony. The *bar* or *bat mitzvah* marks a Jewish boy's or girl's entry into the adult community of the synagogue. In some Christian religions, confirmation marks a boy's or girl's acceptance as an adult of the responsibilities of his or her faith.

There are other, unofficial, rites of passage that also mark this entry into adult life. Often these involve tests, even pain. For example, a boy's first shave is a kind of a rite of passage that marks his entry into manhood. "The Bridge" presents the experience of first love as a rite of passage into the adult world. "The Hat" (page 143) is another story based on this idea of first love as a preparation for adult life.

This passage from childhood to maturity has turned out to be a rich mine for American writers. Some American writers, in fact, have discovered in this particular rite of passage a theme and a structure for their finest work. Perhaps this passage from childhood to adulthood is a central concern of American fiction because we are a relatively young nation, and because youth is so much admired among us.

More than a hundred years ago, a writer from Massachusetts named Louisa May Alcott published a novel about the coming of age of four sisters—Meg, Jo, Beth, and Amy March. Their story is called *Little Women.* This novel might strike some people as sentimental today (some would call it a "tear-jerker"), but it remains a classic coming-of-age story, one that can still move even the hardest late-model heart.

No writer of any nationality ever made a better choice of subject matter than Mark Twain did when he chose to write about growing up in a frontier town along the Mississippi River. Huckleberry Finn and Tom Sawyer are probably literature's most widely known and beloved boys. Readers of Twain's two masterpieces do more than simply "read" about Huck's raft ride down the Mississippi or about Tom persuading a gullible boy to whitewash a fence for him—they make Huck's and Tom's experiences a part of their own lives.

You can name many books published today that are especially popular because they deal with that rite of passage known as adolescence. In fact, many of today's YA (Young Adult) novels are centered around this rite of passage.

For some reason, many stories about growing up have a humorous side. It is difficult for those who are enduring adolescence to see any humor in it—they know only the agony of a first defeat, a first heartbreak, a first rejection. They may even find humor condescending.

Perhaps adults laugh or smile at teen-age experiences only because they are recalling an agony that they know now is well behind them and that they also now realize was not quite as bad as it seemed to be at the time. Our laughter at the ordeals of adolescence might have another explanation as well—when people laugh, they are also very close to crying.

RED DRESS

Alice Munro

"Red Dress" is set in rural Ontario, in Canada. Like "The Bridge" (page 178), this is a coming-of-age story. The incident that takes the narrator into a new stage of life, however, is not a physical conflict that tests her strength. The setting of this girl's "trial" is merely a dance. But, like a physical conflict, the dance tests her courage and confidence. You will have to decide how well she responds to the test.

My mother was making me a dress. All through the month of November I would come from school and find her in the kitchen, surrounded by cut-up velvet and scraps of tissue-paper pattern. She worked at an old treadle machine[1] pushed up against the window to get the light and also to let her look out, past the stubble fields and bare vegetable garden, to see who went by on the road. There was seldom anybody to see.

The red velvet material was hard to work with; it pulled, and the style my mother had chosen was not easy either. She was not really a good sewer. She liked to make things; that is different. Whenever she could, she tried to skip basting and pressing, and she took no pride in the fine points of tailoring, the finishing of buttonholes and the overcasting[2] of seams as, for instance, my aunt and my grandmother did. Unlike them she started off with an inspiration, a brave and dazzling idea; from that moment on, her pleasure ran downhill. In the first place she could never find a pattern to suit her. It was no wonder; there were no patterns made to match the ideas that blossomed in her head. She had made me, at various times when I was younger, a flowered organdy dress with a high Victorian neckline edged in scratchy lace, with a poke bonnet[3] to match; a Scottish plaid outfit with a velvet jacket and tam; an embroidered peasant

blouse worn with a full red skirt and black laced bodice. I had worn these clothes with docility, even pleasure, in the days when I was unaware of the world's opinion. Now, grown wiser, I wished for dresses like those my friend Lonnie had, bought at Beale's store.

I had to try it on. Sometimes Lonnie came home from school with me and she would sit on the couch watching. I was embarrassed by the way my mother crept around me, her knees creaking, her breath coming heavily. She muttered to herself. Around the house she wore no corset or stockings; she wore wedge-heeled shoes and ankle socks; her legs were marked with lumps of blue-green veins. I thought her squatting position shameless, even obscene; I tried to keep talking to Lonnie so that her attention would be taken away from my mother as much as possible. Lonnie wore the composed, polite, appreciative expression that was her disguise in the presence of grownups. She laughed at them and was a ferocious mimic, and they never knew.

My mother pulled me about and pricked me with pins. She made me turn around, she made me walk away, she made me stand still. "What do you think of it, Lonnie?" she said around the pins in her mouth.

"It's beautiful," said Lonnie, in her mild, sincere way. Lonnie's own mother was dead. She lived with her father who never noticed her, and this, in my eyes, made her seem both vulnerable and privileged.

"It *will* be, if I can ever manage the fit," my mother said. "Ah, well," she said theatrically, get-

---

1. **treadle** (tred′ ′l) **machine:** an old-fashioned sewing machine operated by pumping a foot pedal.
2. **overcasting:** sewing over the edge of the fabric to prevent unraveling.
3. **poke bonnet:** a bonnet with a wide front brim.

Girl at a Sewing Machine by Edward Hopper (1921). Oil.   Thyssen-Bornemisza Collection, Lugano, Switzerland.

ting to her feet with a woeful creaking and sighing, "I doubt if she appreciates it." She enraged me, talking like this to Lonnie, as if Lonnie were grown up and I were still a child. "Stand still," she said, hauling the pinned and basted dress over my head. My head was muffled in velvet, my body exposed, in an old cotton school slip. I felt like a great raw lump, clumsy and goose-pimpled. I wished I was like Lonnie, light-boned, pale, and thin; she had been a Blue Baby.

"Well nobody ever made me a dress when I was going to high school," my mother said. "I made my own, or I did without." I was afraid she was going to start again on the story of her walking seven miles to town and finding a job waiting on tables in a boarding-house, so that she could go to high school. All the stories of my mother's life which had once interested me had begun to seem melodramatic, irrelevant, and tiresome.

"One time I had a dress given to me," she said. "It was a cream-colored cashmere wool with royal blue piping down the front and lovely mother-of-pearl buttons. I wonder what ever became of it?"

When we got free, Lonnie and I went upstairs

to my room. It was cold, but we stayed there. We talked about the boys in our class, going up and down the rows and saying, "Do you like him? Well, do you half-like him? Do you *hate* him? Would you go out with him if he asked you?" Nobody had asked us. We were thirteen, and we had been going to high school for two months. We did questionnaires in magazines, to find out whether we had personality and whether we would be popular. We read articles on how to make up our faces to accentuate our good points and how to carry on a conversation on the first date. . . . We had made a pact to tell each other everything. But one thing I did not tell was about this dance, the high-school Christmas Dance for which my mother was making me a dress. It was that I did not want to go.

At high school I was never comfortable for a minute. I did not know about Lonnie. Before an exam, she got icy hands and palpitations, but I was close to despair at all times. When I was asked a question in class, any simple little question at all, my voice was apt to come out squeaky or else hoarse and trembling. . . . My hands became slippery with sweat when they were required to work the blackboard compass. I could not hit the ball in volleyball; being called upon to perform an action in front of others made all my reflexes come undone. I hated Business Practice because you had to rule pages for an account book, using a straight pen, and when the teacher looked over my shoulder, all the delicate lines wobbled and ran together. I hated Science; we perched on stools under harsh lights behind tables of unfamiliar, fragile equipment and were taught by the principal of the school, a man with a cold, self-relishing voice—he read the Scriptures every morning—and a great talent for inflicting humiliation. I hated English because the boys played bingo at the back of the room while the teacher, a stout, gentle girl, slightly cross-eyed, read Wordsworth at the front. She threatened them, she begged them, her face red and her voice as unreliable as mine. They offered burlesqued apologies, and when she started to read again, they took up rapt postures, made swooning faces, crossed their eyes, flung their hands over their

hearts. Sometimes she would burst into tears; there was no help for it; she had to run out into the hall. Then the boys made loud mooing noises; our hungry laughter—oh, mine too—pursued her. There was a carnival atmosphere of brutality in the room at such times, scaring weak and suspect people like me.

But what was really going on in the school was not Business Practice and Science and English. There was something else that gave life its urgency and brightness. That old building, with its rock-walled clammy basements and black cloakrooms and pictures of dead royalties and lost explorers, was full of the tension and excitement of sexual competition, and in this, in spite of daydreams of vast successes, I had premonitions of total defeat. Something had to happen, to keep me from that dance.

With December came snow, and I had an idea. Formerly I had considered falling off my bicycle and spraining my ankle, and I had tried to manage this, as I rode home along the hard-frozen, deeply rutted country roads. But it was too difficult. However, my throat and bronchial tubes were supposed to be weak; why not expose them? I started getting out of bed at night and opening my window a little. I knelt down and let the wind, sometimes stinging with snow, rush in around my bared throat. I took off my pajama top. I said to myself the words "blue with cold," and as I knelt there, my eyes shut, I pictured my chest and throat turning blue, the cold, grayed blue of veins under the skin. I stayed until I could not stand it any more, and then I took a handful of snow from the windowsill and smeared it all over my chest, before I buttoned my pajamas. It would melt against the flannelette, and I would be sleeping in wet clothes, which was supposed to be the worst thing of all. In the morning, the moment I woke up, I cleared my throat, testing for soreness, coughed experimentally, hopefully, touched my forehead to see if I had fever. It was no good. Every morning, including the day of the dance, I rose defeated, and in perfect health.

The day of the dance I did my hair up in steel curlers. I had never done this before, because my hair was naturally curly, but today I wanted the protection of all possible female rituals. I lay on the couch in the kitchen, reading *The Last Days of Pompeii*,[4] and wishing I was there. My mother, never satisfied, was sewing a white lace collar on the dress; she had decided it was too grown-up looking. I watched the hours. It was one of the shortest days of the year. Above the couch, on the wallpaper, were old games of X's and O's,[5] old drawings and scribblings my brother and I had done when we were sick with bronchitis. I looked at them and longed to be back safe behind the boundaries of childhood.

When I took out the curlers my hair, both naturally and artificially stimulated, sprang out in an exuberant glossy bush. I wet it; I combed it, beat it with the brush, and tugged it down along my cheeks. I applied face powder, which stood out chalkily on my hot face. My mother got out her Ashes of Roses Cologne, which she never used, and let me splash it over my arms. Then she zipped up the dress and turned me around to the mirror. The dress was princess style, very tight in the midriff. . . .

"Well, I wish I could take a picture," my mother said. "I am really, genuinely proud of that fit. And you might say thank you for it."

"Thank you," I said.

The first thing Lonnie said when I opened the door to her was, "What did you do to your hair?"

"I did it up."

"You look like a Zulu. Oh, don't worry. Get me a comb and I'll do the front in a roll. It'll look all right. It'll even make you look older."

I sat in front of the mirror and Lonnie stood behind me, fixing my hair. My mother seemed unable to leave us. I wished she would. She watched the roll take shape and said, "You're a wonder, Lonnie. You should take up hairdressing."

"That's a thought," Lonnie said. She had on a pale blue crepe dress, with a peplum[6] and bow; it was much more grown-up than mine, even without

the collar. Her hair had come out as sleek as the girl's on the bobby-pin card. I had always thought secretly that Lonnie could not be pretty because she had crooked teeth, but now I saw that crooked teeth or not, her stylish dress and smooth hair made me look a little like a golliwog, stuffed into red velvet, wide-eyed, wild-haired, with a suggestion of delirium.

My mother followed us to the door and called out into the dark, "Au reservoir!" This was a traditional farewell of Lonnie's and mine; it sounded foolish and desolate coming from her, and I was so angry with her for using it that I did not reply. It was only Lonnie who called back cheerfully, encouragingly, "Good night!"

The gymnasium smelled of pine and cedar. Red and green bells of fluted paper hung from the basketball hoops; the high, barred windows were hidden by green boughs. Everybody in the upper grades seemed to have come in couples. Some of the Grade Twelve and Thirteen[7] girls had brought boyfriends who had already graduated, who were young businessmen around the town. These young men smoked in the gymnasium; nobody could stop them; they were free. The girls stood beside them, resting their hands casually on male sleeves, their faces bored, aloof, and beautiful. I longed to be like that. They behaved as if only they—the older ones—were really at the dance, as if the rest of us, whom they moved among and peered around, were, if not invisible, inanimate; when the first dance was announced—a Paul Jones[8]—they moved out languidly, smiling at each other as if they had been asked to take part in some half-forgotten childish game. Holding hands and shivering, crowding up together, Lonnie and I and the other Grade Nine girls followed.

I didn't dare look at the outer circle as it passed me, for fear I should see some unmannerly hurrying-up. When the music stopped I stayed where

---

4. *The Last Days of Pompeii:* a historical novel by Bulwer-Lytton, published in 1834, about a tragic romance taking place just before the city of Pompeii is destroyed by the eruption of Mount Vesuvius.
5. **X's and O's:** tick-tack-toe.
6. **peplum:** a short flounce or ruffle extending from the waist of a dress or blouse.

7. In Ontario at this time, high school went through Grade Thirteen.
8. **Paul Jones:** a dance in which the participants weave in and out of a circle. When the music stops, the two people holding hands are dance partners.

I was, and half-raising my eyes I saw a boy named Mason Williams coming reluctantly toward me. Barely touching my waist and my fingers, he began to dance with me. My legs were hollow; my arm trembled from the shoulder; I could not have spoken. This Mason Williams was one of the heroes of the school; he played basketball and hockey and walked the halls with an air of royal sullenness and barbaric contempt. To have to dance with a nonentity like me was as offensive to him as having to memorize Shakespeare. I felt this as keenly as he did and imagined that he was exchanging looks of dismay with his friends. He steered me, stumbling, to the edge of the floor. He took his hand from my waist and dropped my arm.

"See you," he said. He walked away.

It took me a minute or two to realize what had happened and that he was not coming back. I went and stood by the wall alone. The Physical Education teacher, dancing past energetically in the arms of a Grade Ten boy, gave me an inquisitive look. She was the only teacher in the school who made use of the words social adjustment, and I was afraid that if she had seen or if she found out, she might make some horribly public attempt to make Mason finish out the dance with me. I myself was not angry or surprised at Mason; I accepted his position, and mine, in the world of school, and I saw that what he had done was the realistic thing to do. He was a Natural Hero, not a Student Council type of hero bound for success beyond the school; one of those would have danced with me courteously and patronizingly and left me feeling no better off. Still, I hoped not many people had seen. I hated people seeing. I began to bite the skin on my thumb.

When the music stopped I joined the surge of girls to the end of the gymnasium. Pretend it didn't happen, I said to myself. Pretend this is the beginning, now.

The band began to play again. There was movement in the dense crowd at our end of the floor; it thinned rapidly. Boys came over; girls went out to dance. Lonnie went. The girl on the other side of me went. Nobody asked me. I remembered a magazine article Lonnie and I had read which said *Be gay! Let the boys see your eyes sparkle, let them hear laughter in your voice! Simple, obvious,*

but how many girls forget! It was true; I had forgotten. My eyebrows were drawn together with tension; I must look scared and ugly. I took a deep breath and tried to loosen my face. I smiled. But I felt absurd, smiling at no one. And I observed that girls on the dance floor, popular girls, were not smiling; many of them had sleepy, sulky faces and never smiled at all.

Girls were still going out to the floor. Some, despairing, went with each other. But most went with boys. Fat girls, girls with pimples, a poor girl who didn't own a good dress and had to wear a skirt and sweater to the dance; they were claimed, they danced away. Why take them and not me? Why everybody else and not me? I have a red velvet dress; I did my hair in curlers; I used a deodorant and put on cologne. *Pray*, I thought. I couldn't close my eyes, but I said over and over again in my mind, *Please, me, please*, and I locked my fingers behind my back in a sign more potent than crossing, the same secret sign Lonnie and I used not to be sent to the blackboard in Math.

It did not work. What I had been afraid of was true. I was going to be left. There was something mysterious the matter with me, something that could not be put right like bad breath or overlooked like pimples, and everybody knew it, and I knew it; I had known it all along. But I had not known it for sure; I had hoped to be mistaken. Certainty rose inside me like sickness. I hurried past one or two girls who were also left and went into the girls' washroom. I hid myself in a cubicle.

That was where I stayed. Between dances girls came in and went out quickly. There were plenty of cubicles; nobody noticed that I was not a temporary occupant. During the dances, I listened to the music which I liked but had no part of any more. For I was not going to try any more. I only wanted to hide in here, get out without seeing anybody, get home.

One time after the music started somebody stayed behind. She was taking a long time running the water, washing her hands, combing her hair. She was going to think it funny that I stayed in so long. I had better go out and wash my hands, and maybe while I was washing them she would leave.

It was Mary Fortune. I knew her by name, because she was an officer of the Girls' Athletic

Society and she was on the Honor Roll and she was always organizing things. She had something to do with organizing this dance; she had been around to all the classrooms asking for volunteers to do the decorations. She was in Grade Eleven or Twelve.

"Nice and cool in here," she said. "I came in to get cooled off. I get so hot."

She was still combing her hair when I finished my hands. "Do you like the band?" she said.

"It's all right." I didn't really know what to say. I was surprised at her, an older girl, taking this time to talk to me.

"I don't. I can't stand it. I hate dancing when I don't like the band. Listen. They're so choppy. I'd just as soon not dance as dance to that."

I combed my hair. She leaned against a basin, watching me.

"I don't want to dance and don't particularly want to stay in here. Let's go and have a cigarette."

"Where?"

"Come on, I'll show you."

At the end of the washroom there was a door. It was unlocked and led into a dark closet full of mops and pails. She had me hold the door open, to get the washroom light, until she found the knob of another door. This door opened into darkness.

"I can't turn on the light or somebody might see," she said. "It's the janitor's room." I reflected that athletes always seemed to know more than the rest of us about the school as a building; they knew where things were kept and they were always coming out of unauthorized doors with a bold, preoccupied air. "Watch out where you're going," she said. "Over at the far end there's some stairs. They go up to a closet on the second floor. The door's locked at the top, but there's like a partition between the stairs and the room. So if we sit on the steps, even if by chance someone did come in here, they wouldn't see us."

"Wouldn't they smell smoke?" I said.

"Oh, well. Live dangerously."

There was a high window over the stairs which gave us a little light. Mary Fortune had cigarettes and matches in her purse. I had not smoked before except the cigarettes Lonnie and I made ourselves, using papers and tobacco stolen from her

father; they came apart in the middle. These were much better.

"The only reason I even came tonight," Mary Fortune said, "is because I am responsible for the decorations, and I wanted to see, you know, how it looked once people got in there and everything. Otherwise why bother? I'm not boy-crazy."

In the light from the high window I could see her narrow, scornful face, her dark skin pitted with acne, her teeth pushed together at the front, making her look adult and commanding.

"Most girls are. Haven't you noticed that? The greatest collection of boy-crazy girls you could imagine is right here in this school."

I was grateful for her attention, her company, and her cigarette. I said I thought so too.

"Like this afternoon. This afternoon I was trying to get them to hang the bells and junk. They just get up on the ladders and fool around with boys. They don't care if it ever gets decorated. It's just an excuse. That's the only aim they have in life, fooling around with boys. As far as I'm concerned, they're idiots."

We talked about teachers and things at school. She said she wanted to be a physical education teacher, and she would have to go to college for that, but her parents did not have enough money. She said she planned to work her own way through; she wanted to be independent anyway; she would work in the cafeteria and in the summer she would do farm work, like picking tobacco. Listening to her, I felt the acute phase of my unhappiness passing. Here was someone who had suffered the same defeat as I had—I saw that—but she was full of energy and self-respect. She had thought of other things to do. She would pick tobacco.

We stayed there talking and smoking during the long pause in the music, when, outside, they were having doughnuts and coffee. When the music started again Mary said, "Look, do we have to hang around here any longer? Let's get our coats and go. We can go down to Lee's and have a hot chocolate and talk in comfort, why not?"

We felt our way across the janitor's room, carrying ashes and cigarette butts in our hands. In the closet, we stopped and listened to make sure there was nobody in the washroom. We came back into the light and threw the ashes into the toilet. We had to go out and cut across the dance floor to the cloakroom, which was beside the outside door.

A dance was just beginning. "Go round the edge of the floor," Mary said. "Nobody'll notice us."

I followed her. I didn't look at anybody. I didn't look for Lonnie. Lonnie was probably not going to be my friend any more, not as much as before anyway. She was what Mary would call boy-crazy.

I found that I was not so frightened, now that I had made up my mind to leave the dance behind. I was not waiting for anybody to choose me. I had my own plans. I did not have to smile or make signs for luck. It did not matter to me. I was on my way to have a hot chocolate, with my friend.

A boy said something to me. He was in my way. I thought he must be telling me that I had dropped something or that I couldn't go that way or that the cloakroom was locked. I didn't understand that he was asking me to dance until he said it over again. It was Raymond Bolting from our class, whom I had never talked to in my life. He thought I meant yes. He put his hand on my waist and almost without meaning to, I began to dance.

We moved to the middle of the floor. I was dancing. My legs had forgotten to tremble and my hands to sweat. I was dancing with a boy who had asked me. Nobody told him to; he didn't have to; he just asked me. Was it possible; could I believe it; was there nothing the matter with me after all?

I thought that I ought to tell him there was a mistake, that I was just leaving, I was going to have a hot chocolate with my girlfriend. But I did not say anything. My face was making certain delicate adjustments, achieving with no effort at all the grave absent-minded look of those who were chosen, those who danced. This was the face that Mary Fortune saw, when she looked out of the cloakroom door, her scarf already around her head. I made a weak waving motion with the hand that lay on the boy's shoulder, indicating that I apologized, that I didn't know what had happened and also that it was no use waiting for me. Then I turned my head away, and when I looked again she was gone.

Raymond Bolting took me home and Harold Simons took Lonnie home. We all walked together as far as Lonnie's corner. The boys were having an argument about a hockey game, which Lonnie and I could not follow. Then we separated into couples and Raymond continued with me the conversation he had been having with Harold. He did not seem to notice that he was now talking to me instead. Once or twice I said, "Well I don't know, I didn't see that game," but after a while I decided just to say, "H'm hmm," and that seemed to be all that was necessary.

One other thing he said was, "I didn't realize you lived such a long ways out." And he sniffled. The cold was making my nose run a little too, and I worked my fingers through the candy wrappers in my coat pocket until I found a shabby Kleenex. I didn't know whether I ought to offer it to him or not, but he sniffled so loudly that I finally said, "I just have this one Kleenex, it probably isn't even clean, it probably has ink on it. But if I was to tear it in half we'd each have something."

"Thanks," he said. "I sure could use it."

It was a good thing, I thought, that I had done that, for at my gate, when I said, "Well, goodnight," and after he said, "Oh, yeah. Goodnight," he leaned toward me and kissed me, briefly, with the air of one who knew his job when he saw it, on the corner of my mouth. Then he turned back to town, never knowing he had been my rescuer, that he had brought me from Mary Fortune's territory into the ordinary world.

I went around the house to the back door, thinking, I have been to a dance and a boy has walked me home and kissed me. It was all true. My life was possible. I went past the kitchen window and I saw my mother. She was sitting with her feet on the open oven door, drinking tea out of a cup without a saucer. She was just sitting and waiting for me to come home and tell her everything that had happened. And I would not do it; I never would. But when I saw the waiting kitchen and my mother in her faded, fuzzy paisley kimono, with her sleepy but doggedly expectant face, I understood what a mysterious and oppressive obligation I had, to be happy, and how I had almost failed it, and would be likely to fail it, every time, and she would not know.

Responding to the Story

Analyzing the Story

Identifying Facts

1. Find the passage that explains why the narrator doesn't want to go to the Christmas dance. What does she do to try to get out of going?
2. At the dance, why does the narrator hide in the washroom and then decide to leave with Mary Fortune?
3. Why does the narrator end up staying at the dance? How is her self-esteem saved?

Interpreting Meanings

4. Which of these words would you use to **characterize** the narrator?

   a. Self-confident   d. Angry
   b. Mean   e. Unreliable
   c. Unsure of herself f. Ungrateful

   Consider what she reveals by her **appearance**; by her **actions**; and by her **feelings** about herself, school, and other characters. How did you feel about this girl—did you sympathize with her? Identify with her? Dislike her?

5. What about the **character** of Mary Fortune, who rescues the girl in mid-story and then is abandoned for her pains? Explain why you think Mary Fortune is so scornful about the dance and about "boy-crazy" girls. (Do you think Mary is covering up her real feelings, or do you think she is superior to her classmates?)

6. What does the narrator mean when she says that Raymond had rescued her from "Mary Fortune's territory into the ordinary world" (page 193)? Explain whether you found the girl's response to Raymond's kiss believable.

7. The narrator's feelings about her mother are an important element in "Red Dress." Explain whether you found the girl's embarrassment and irritation natural and understandable, or do you think she is being unfair to her mother?

8. When the narrator comes home from the dance, her mother is waiting for her to "tell her everything that had happened" (page 193). Why do you think the narrator decides that she won't tell her mother about her near-failure that night or about future failures?

9. In a sentence or more, state the **theme** of this story as you interpret it—what ideas about the needs and fears of young people does the story reveal? Do you agree with the story's theme—in other words, do you find it to be a true revelation about life as you know it?

10. Explain whether you think the girl's feelings in this story could also be felt by boys.

Writing About the Story

A Creative Response

1. **Describing an Experience.** Like the narrator in "Red Dress," most of us have suffered humiliating experiences. The truth of the matter, however, is that most humiliating experiences take place only in our own minds—onlookers are often unaware of our suffering. (For instance, how many people at the Christmas dance knew that the narrator was suffering one of life's major defeats when no one asked her to dance?) In one paragraph or more, have a narrator describe a humiliating experience: perhaps at a dance, during a game, on the job, on the stage. Let the narrator tell his or her own story, using the first-person pronoun, "I."

2. **Writing from Another Point of View.** What are the risks a boy is likely to take when he asks a girl to dance? For instance, in "Red Dress," what was Raymond Bolting thinking before he asked the girl to dance? Did another boy want to ask her to dance but then lost his nerve? Write a paragraph in which Raymond or another boy is anxiously considering these risks as he crosses the floor toward the girl. Be sure to describe what *her* response seems like from *his* point of view. Let your narrator be either the boy (using the first-person pronoun, "I") or a third-person limited narrator who focuses on the boy's senses and feelings.

3. **Writing from Another Point of View.** Let us hear what the mother is thinking as she waits for her daughter to return from the dance. Write a paragraph in which the mother tells what she thinks as she waits in the kitchen. Use the first-person pronoun, "I."

A Critical Response

4. **Comparing the Story to a Fairy Tale.** Some people might see a resemblance between this modern story and the Cinderella story, in which a maiden is rescued by Prince Charming, saved from a life of drudgery, and restored to her rightful place in the world. If you can see the resemblances, write a paragraph citing two ways in which this story is like "Cinderella." In a second paragraph, tell how the stories are different in at least one important way. You might consider these elements of Cinderella's story:

> The Cinderella character
> The fairy godmother figure
> The dress for the ball
> The prince charming character
> The happy-ever-after resolution

Analyzing Language and Vocabulary

Connotations

When two people see a red flag, they may both see the same color, but each of them may respond differently to *red*. One may associate the color *red* with blood; the other, with danger. A romantic might think of hearts on Valentine cards and associate *red* with love.

We respond to many words in different ways. Each of us can have a different emotional response to the same word, depending on our individual instincts and experiences.

These associations and emotional responses that a word calls up are its **connotations.** A word also has one or more strict dictionary meanings, which are its **denotations.** The denotation of *New York,* or its dictionary meaning, is "a seaport at the mouth of the Hudson River in the southeast part of New York State." But the word *New York* also has a whole range of connotations, ranging from negative associations with crowds, criminals, or slums to positive associations with glittering skyscrapers, glamor, theater, and Wall Street.

Some words, of course, have more connotative power than others, and some have no connotative power at all. We're not likely to draw many strong associations from the words *lettuce* or *stamp,* but we probably draw strong responses from the words *puppy* and *graveyard.* Words such as *and* and *when* have no feelings associated with them at all.

1. What do you associate with the following words? List the associations that come to you at once. Write down things or events, as well as feelings.

   a. home   g. spring
   b. pig   h. winter
   c. rat   i. California
   d. Democrat   j. gold
   e. Republican k. baby
   f. Midwest   l. politician

2. Here are six moods. Write down two words that you think connote each mood.

   a. peace   d. joy
   b. tension   e. security
   c. sadness   f. terror

3. Sometimes a word has such powerfully unfavorable connotations that we try to avoid using it on certain occasions. As an old saying goes: I am careful; you are thrifty; he is stingy. Here are five words that usually carry negative connotations. For each word, think of at least one other word that means generally the same thing, but which has more favorable connotations.

   a. scrawny   d. smelly
   b. fat   e. cheap
   c. old

4. Words and their connotations are powerful tools in the hands of skillful writers. By the deft choice of a particular word, a writer can call forth a whole range of emotions and associations. Look back at the passage from "Red Dress" on page 187 beginning "I had to try it on." Find at least five words in this description that carry unfavorable judgments against the mother and the way the girl thinks she looks.

5. Rewrite this passage so that the reader is not aware of any judgment being passed on the mother at all. To "neutralize" the emotional effect of the passage, you will have to find substitutes for the unfavorable words in your list.

Reading About the Writer

Alice Munro (1931–   ) is a Canadian writer whose stories and novels are widely read and praised in the United States. She grew up in rural Ontario, the setting of "Red Dress." Two of her story collections are called *Dance of the Happy Shades* and *Something I've Been Meaning to Tell You.*

Using a Variety of Sentences

Literary Model

This short story describes the independent spirit of an old Mexican farmer.

Gentleman of Río en Medio

It took months of negotiation to come to an understanding with the old man. He was in no hurry. What he had the most of was time. He lived up in Río en Medio, where his people had been for hundreds of years. He tilled the same land they had tilled. His house was small and wretched, but quaint. The little creek ran through his land. His orchard was gnarled and beautiful.

The day of the sale he came into the office. His coat was old, green, and faded. I thought of Senator Catron,[1] who had been such a power with these people up there in the mountains. Perhaps it was one of his old Prince Alberts.[2] He also wore gloves. They were old and torn, and his fingertips showed through them. He carried a cane, but it was only the skeleton of a worn-out umbrella. Behind him walked one of his innumerable kin—a dark young man with eyes like a gazelle.

The old man bowed to all of us in the room. Then he removed his hat and gloves, slowly and carefully. Chaplin[3] once did that in a picture, in a bank—he was the janitor. Then he handed his things to the boy, who stood obediently behind the old man's chair.

There was a great deal of conversation about rain and about his family. He was very proud of his large family. Finally we got down to business. Yes, he would sell, as he had agreed, for twelve hundred dollars, in cash. We would buy, and the money was ready. "Don Anselmo," I said to him in Spanish, "we have made a

discovery. You remember that we sent that surveyor, that engineer, up there to survey your land so as to make the deed. Well, he finds that you own more than eight acres. He tells us that your land extends across the river and that you own almost twice as much as you thought." He didn't know that. "And now, Don Anselmo," I added, "these Americans are *buena gente*, they are good people, and they are willing to pay you for the additional land as well, at the same rate per acre, so that instead of twelve hundred dollars you will get almost twice as much, and the money is here for you."

The old man hung his head for a moment in thought. Then he stood up and stared at me. "Friend," he said, "I do not like to have you speak to me in that manner." I kept still and let him have his say. "I know these Americans are good people, and that is why I have agreed to sell to them. But I do not care to be insulted. I have agreed to sell my house and land for twelve hundred dollars and that is the price."

I argued with him, but it was useless. Finally he signed the deed and took the money but refused to take more than the amount agreed upon. Then he shook hands all around, put on his ragged gloves, took his stick, and walked out with the boy behind him.

A month later my friends had moved into Río en Medio. They had replastered the old adobe house, pruned the trees, patched the fence, and moved in for the summer. One day they came back to the office to complain. The children of the village were overrunning their property. They came every day and played under the trees, built little play fences around them, and took blossoms. When they were spoken to, they only laughed and talked back good-naturedly in Spanish.

I sent a messenger up to the mountains for Don Anselmo. It took a week to arrange another meeting. When he arrived, he repeated his previous preliminary performance. He wore the

---

1. **Senator Catron:** Thomas Benton Catron, a senator from New Mexico (1912-1917).
2. **Prince Alberts:** long, double-breasted coats named after Prince Albert of Great Britain.
3. **Chaplin:** Charlie Chaplin, a comic star of silent movies.

Literature & Language/*cont.*

same faded cutaway,[4] carried the same stick, and was accompanied by the boy again. He shook hands all around, sat down with the boy behind his chair, and talked about the weather. Finally I broached the subject. "Don Anselmo, about the ranch you sold to these people. They are good people and want to be your friends and neighbors always. When you sold to them, you signed a document, a deed, and in that deed you agreed to several things. One thing was that they were to have the complete possession of the property. Now, Don Anselmo, it seems that every day the children of the village overrun the orchard and spend most of their time there. We would like to know if you, as the most respected man in the village, could not stop them from doing so in order that these people may enjoy their new home more in peace."

Don Anselmo stood up. "We have all learned to love these Americans," he said, "because they are good people and good neighbors. I sold them my property because I knew they were good people, but I did not sell them the trees in the orchard."

This was bad. "Don Anselmo," I pleaded, "when one signs a deed and sells real property one sells also everything that grows on the land, and those trees, every one of them, are on the land and inside the boundaries of what you sold."

"Yes, I admit that," he said. "You know," he added, "I am the oldest man in the village. Almost everyone there is my relative and all the children of Río en Medio are my *sobrinos* and *nietos*,[5] my descendants. Every time a child has been born in Río en Medio since I took possession of that house from my mother, I have planted a tree for that child. The trees in that orchard are not mine, *señor,* they belong to the children of the village. Every person in Río en Medio born since the railroad came to Santa Fe owns a tree in that orchard. I did not sell the trees because I could not. They are not mine."

There was nothing we could do. Legally we owned the trees, but the old man had been so generous, refusing what amounted to a fortune for him. It took most of the following winter to buy the trees, individually, from the descendants of Don Anselmo in the valley of Río en Medio.

—Juan A. A. Sedillo

Grammar Note

Writers can use different kinds of sentences to vary their style and to express precise relationships between their ideas.

1. A **simple sentence** is a sentence with one independent clause and no subordinate clauses. A **clause** is a group of words that contains a subject and a verb. An **independent clause** expresses a complete thought and can stand by itself. (*He was in no hurry.*) A **subordinate clause** cannot stand alone as a sentence. It presents an incomplete idea. (*When they were spoken to*) The following is an example of a simple sentence from Sedillo's story:

His orchard was gnarled and beautiful.

2. A **complex sentence** consists of at least one subordinate clause and an independent clause. In the next sentence, the word *when* begins the subordinate clause.

When they were spoken to, they only laughed and talked back good-naturedly in Spanish.

The subordinate clauses in complex sentences are used as adjectives, adverbs, and nouns, just as if they were single words. In the following complex

4. **cutaway:** the long coat described as a Prince Albert.
5. *sobrinos* and *nietos:* Spanish for "grandchildren" and "nephews and nieces."

sentences, the subordinate clauses used as adjectives, adverbs, or nouns are italicized.

> Then he handed his things to the boy, *who stood obediently behind the old man's chair.* [adjective clause]

> *When he arrived,* he repeated his previous preliminary performance. [adverb clause]

> *What he had the most of* was time. [noun clause]

3. A **compound sentence** is composed of two or more independent clauses but no subordinate clauses. The independent clauses in compound sentences are often combined with one of the coordinating conjunctions: *and, but, or, nor, for, so, yet.*

> They were old and torn, *and* his fingertips showed through them.

> I argued with him, *but* it was useless.

4. A **compound-complex sentence** is composed of two or more independent clauses and at least one subordinate clause. The subordinate clause is italicized in the following compound-complex sentence.

> "*When you sold to them,* you signed a document, a deed, and in that deed you agreed to several things."

Examining the Writer's Style

The individual way a writer chooses words and shapes sentences is called **style**. Examine the way Sedillo structures his sentences. Does he use a variety of simple, compound, complex, and compound-complex sentences, or does he favor just one or two of these structures? Work with another student to find the answer to this question.

1. Analyze the structure of the sentences in the first three paragraphs of "Gentleman of Río en Medio." Use the following abbreviations: **S** = Simple; **Cd** = Compound; **Cx** = Complex; and **Cd-Cx** =

Compound-Complex. Here is how you would analyze the first paragraph:

> It took months of negotiation to come to an understanding with the old man. [**S**] He was in no hurry. [**S**] What he had the most of was time. [**Cx**] He lived up in Río en Medio, where his people had been for hundreds of years. [**Cx**] He tilled the same land they had tilled. [**Cx**] His house was small and wretched, but quaint. [**S**] The little creek ran through his land. [**S**] His orchard was gnarled and beautiful. [**S**]

As you can see, the majority of the sentences in the first paragraph are simple sentences. Go on to see if this pattern holds true in the next two paragraphs of the story.

2. Another aspect of a writer's style is sentence length. Does Sedillo use mostly long or short sentences, or a mixture of both? Analyze the first and last three paragraphs of "Gentleman of Río en Medio" for sentence length. (Notice that most of the sentences in the first paragraph are short.)

3. After you have analyzed the sentences in the story as a whole, think about the effect of Sedillo's style. Does the story read like a folk tale, a story told to teach a moral lesson, perhaps even a story told for children?

Using Sentence Variety in Your Writing

Changing the Style of a Story. The very same story can be told in a variety of ways. Working in a group, rewrite the story of "Gentleman of Río en Medio," using different sentence structures and making occasional changes in word choice, if you wish. Be sure not to change the events or the personalities of the characters. Read your group's revised version aloud to your classmates, and discuss how your changes in style affect their reactions to the story. The first sentence of a rewritten version might go:

> It took months of negotiation to come to an understanding with the old man, because he was in no hurry and what he had the most of was time.

RESPONDING TO A STORY

Writing Assignment

In at least one paragraph, explain your response to one of the stories you have read in this unit.

Background

There is no such thing as a right or wrong response to a story, any more than there is a right or a wrong response to a painting or to a piece of music. Each of us is an individual, and our response to a story is affected by our reading background, our experiences, and our preferences. Once we read a story, however, it is important to know *what* our response is, to know *why* we respond to it as we do, and to be able to put that response into *words*.

A response should include our reaction to a story—what we thought of the plot, characters, and theme, and WHY. Explaining why is most important. You can't just say, "I liked this story because I thought it was funny." You must tell *what* elements of the story struck you as comical.

You can't just say, "I didn't like the story because it was boring." You must tell why it bored you: was the plot too predictable? Were the characters unbelievable? Was the story told in language that you found difficult?

When you are asked to respond to a story, you are acting as a critic. A critic doesn't necessarily find fault with a story. One critic might point out what he or she thinks are a story's flaws (an unbelievable character, an unsatisfactory ending). But another critic might point out only a story's strong points because, according to that critic, the story has no flaws.

Prewriting

1. To gather material for your response, answer the following questions about your story:

   a. **Is the story chiefly entertainment, or does the writer want to reveal a theme, that is, some important truth about life?** If the story is told chiefly for entertainment, did it succeed in making you feel suspense or amusement or surprise? If the story is intended to reveal some truth about life, consider what that truth is and why it is—or is not—acceptable to you.

   b. **Who is the story's central character, and does that character seem believable to you?** Does the main character seem like a real person, behaving the way human beings behave according to your experience of them?

   c. **Did you identify with the character in any way?** How did this affect your response?

   d. **Is the plot told in a way that keeps you interested?** Is the ending of the story believable? Given the nature of the characters, is the ending logical?

   e. **What kind of language is used in the story?** Are the story's images fresh and imaginative? Do the characters sound natural when they speak, and does their conversation reveal the kind of people they are?

   f. **Is the point of view helpful in revealing the nature of the characters? Does the point of view help to create suspense? Is the narrator of the story reliable?**

   g. **Is the setting important to the story?** If so, has the writer made it vivid and realistic, so that you feel you are there?

2. Find at least one example from the story that supports your statements for each question.
3. Choose one of the above questions to focus on in your written response.

Writing

Open your paragraph with a sentence that states your honest response to the story. Follow this up with details from the story which explain and support your response.

On reading the fairy tale "Cinderella," for example, someone wrote the following response:

I really don't accept the basic theme behind the story "Cinderella." It's just not been my experience that a girl who puts up with her grungy work and cruel treatment will be rewarded by a kindly godmother who turns her rags into a ball gown and furnishes a handsome prince to whisk her out of the kitchen and into the palace. It seems to me to be a romantic view of life. I think stories like this have confused generations of young women who keep expecting a Prince Charming to rescue them from life's problems.

Cites response.
Cites details to support response.

On reading the story "Red Dress," someone wrote this critical response:

I am not sure that I really "liked" Alice Munro's story "Red Dress," but I thought that the main character was believable and that her worries about having a good time at the dance were true to life. I have known many girls who are very unsure of themselves and who think that they are not attractive. I also know many girls who feel that their mothers are going to be unhappy if they are not successful with boys. It seemed to me that the girl's treatment of Mary Fortune at the dance was not very nice, but I am glad the writer put that in. To the main character, success with boys was more important than friendship with the outsider. That was a little sad and it was not admirable, but I think it is a true picture of life. In some ways, this was a painful story to read.

Cites response.

Cites details to support response.

Checklist for Revision
1. Have you cited the story's author and title?
2. Have you stated your response in your first sentence?
3. Have you explained why you feel the way you do?
4. Have you referred to some specific elements or details in the story to explain your response?

Irony: Twists and Surprises in Stories

Surprise is an important ingredient in a good story, just as it is in life itself. In our own lives, we are forever expecting events to develop in a certain way, only to see them turn out otherwise. The election is won by an underdog. A dreaded interview turns into an opportunity we had not dared hope for. The firehouse goes up in flames.

This kind of surprise—this difference between what we expect and what actually happens—is the essence of **irony**.

Verbal Irony: Saying One Thing But Meaning Something Else

The simplest kind of irony is verbal irony, and you use it yourself every day. When you say one thing but mean something else, you are using **verbal irony**. (When your tone is bitter, you might call it sarcasm.) If Marcia looks at a muddy stream, we'd expect her to call it a muddy stream. But if instead she says, "Nice clean water you have here," she is using verbal irony.

Situational Irony: Reversing Our Expectations

In fiction, irony is most apparent in plot. We call this **situational irony**. It occurs when a situation that is expected to happen, or that is intended to happen, is the opposite of what actually does happen.

We feel this kind of irony when the parson's son turns out to be a crook or when the general reveals his cowardice. One of the most famous examples of situational irony is found in the old tale called "Appointment in Samarra," which is retold here by W. Somerset Maugham.

> **DEATH SPEAKS:** There was a merchant in Baghdad who sent his servant to market to buy provisions, and in a little while the servant came back, white and trembling, and said, "Master, just now when I was in the marketplace I was jostled by a woman in the crowd, and when I turned I saw it was Death that jostled me. She looked at me and made a threatening gesture; now, lend me your horse, and I will ride away from this city and avoid my fate. I will go to Samarra, and there Death will not find me." The merchant lent him his horse, and the servant mounted it, and he dug his spurs in its flanks,

> " We are forever expecting events to develop in a certain way, only to see them turn out otherwise. The election is won by an underdog. A dreaded interview turns into an opportunity we had not dared hope for. The firehouse goes up in flames."

and as fast as the horse could gallop he went. Then the merchant went down to the marketplace and he saw me standing in the crowd and he came to me and said, "Why did you make a threatening gesture to my servant when you saw him this morning?" "That was not a threatening gesture," I said, "it was only a start of surprise. I was astonished to see him in Baghdad, for I had an appointment with him tonight in Samarra."

—W. Somerset Maugham

There is a childish, or perhaps cowardly, logic in the belief that we can avoid the consequences of bad news simply by running away from it. This is what the servant believes when he tries to outwit fate by being out of town when Death calls. But a surprise awaits the servant when he reaches Samarra: he thinks that when he gets there he will have escaped Death. Ironically, just the opposite happens. By running to Samarra, he has actually run to meet Death.

Situational irony cuts deeply into our feelings. Even though we believe we can control our own lives, we know that chance or the unexpected often has the last word. When irony is put to work in fiction, it is often what touches us the most. Irony can move us toward tears or laughter, because we sense we are close to the truth of life.

> " When irony is put to work in fiction, it is often what touches us the most. Irony can move us toward tears or laughter, because we sense we are close to the truth of life."

Dramatic Irony: Withholding Knowledge

Irony comes from the Greek word *eirōneia,* which means "a withholding of knowledge." This is the kind of irony we associate with a play or movie; we call it **dramatic irony**. We sense this kind of irony, when we, in the audience, know something that the characters on stage or on the screen do not know. In a movie murder mystery, for example, we know, but the character does not know, that the murderer is waiting in the elevator. In a stage comedy, we know, but the hero does not know, that the "girl" he is flirting with is really his pal Joe fooling him with a disguise. Dramatic irony can take place in novels and stories, too. When Little Red Riding Hood calls on Grandma, she does not know, but we do, that Grandma's bonnet conceals a wolf.

What Is the Purpose of Irony?

When you sense the use of irony in a story, ask yourself: What is the purpose of this irony?

1. Does the use of irony create comedy? Is it there for laughs?

2. Does the irony create a sense of tragedy? Is it there to make me feel sadness or puzzlement at the unexpected nature of life?

3. Is the irony there to make me think about people in a new and unexpected way?

Little Red Riding Hood by J. Hetzel, after an engraving by Gustave Doré.　　　The Bettmann Archive

THE LITTLE GIRL AND THE WOLF

James Thurber

James Thurber, one of our most celebrated humorists (see also page 383), shows us in the next two stories just how short a story can be. See how **these short-shorts use irony to spoof, or make fun of, the old fairy tales we read as children.**

One afternoon a big wolf waited in a dark forest for a little girl to come along carrying a basket of food to her grandmother. Finally a little girl did come along and she was carrying a basket of food. "Are you carrying that basket to your grandmother?" asked the wolf. The little girl said yes, she was. So the wolf asked her where her grandmother lived and the little girl told him and he disappeared into the wood.

When the little girl opened the door of her grandmother's house she saw that there was somebody in bed with a nightcap and nightgown on. She had approached no nearer than twenty-five feet from the bed when she saw that it was not her grandmother but the wolf, for even in a nightcap a wolf does not look any more like your grandmother than the Metro-Goldwyn lion looks like Calvin Coolidge.[1] So the little girl took an automatic out of her basket and shot the wolf dead.

Moral: It is not so easy to fool little girls nowadays as it used to be.

---

1. **Metro-Goldwyn lion . . . Calvin Coolidge:** the lion was used in the opening credits of Metro-Goldwyn movies. Calvin Coolidge was the thirtieth President of the United States, who did not look at all like a roaring lion.

THE PRINCESS AND THE TIN BOX

James Thurber

Once upon a time, in a far country, there lived a King whose daughter was the prettiest princess in the world. Her eyes were like the cornflower, her hair was sweeter than the hyacinth, and her throat made the swan look dusty.

From the time she was a year old, the Princess had been showered with presents. Her nursery looked like Cartier's[1] window. Her toys were all made of gold or platinum or diamonds or emeralds. She was not permitted to have wooden blocks or china dolls or rubber dogs or linen books, because such materials were considered cheap for the daughter of a King.

When she was seven, she was allowed to attend the wedding of her brother and throw real pearls at the bride instead of rice. Only the nightingale, with his lyre of gold, was permitted to sing for the Princess. The common blackbird, with his boxwood flute, was kept out of the palace grounds. She walked in silver-and-samite slippers to a sapphire-and-topaz bathroom and slept in an ivory bed inlaid with rubies.

On the day the Princess was eighteen, the King sent a royal ambassador to the courts of five neighboring kingdoms to announce that he would give his daughter's hand in marriage to the prince who brought her the gift she liked the most.

The first prince to arrive at the palace rode a swift white stallion and laid at the feet of the Princess an enormous apple made of solid gold which he had taken from a dragon who had guarded it for a thousand years. It was placed on a long ebony table set up to hold the gifts of the Princess's suitors. The second prince, who came on a gray charger, brought her a nightingale made of a thousand diamonds, and it was placed beside the golden apple. The third prince, riding on a black horse, carried a great jewel box made of platinum and sapphires, and it was placed next to the diamond nightingale. The fourth prince, astride a fiery yellow horse, gave the Princess a gigantic heart made of rubies and pierced by an emerald arrow. It was placed next to the platinum-and-sapphire jewel box.

Now the fifth prince was the strongest and handsomest of all the five suitors, but he was the son of a poor king whose realm had been overrun by mice and locusts and wizards and mining engineers so that there was nothing much of value left in it. He came plodding up to the palace of the Princess on a plow horse, and he brought her a small tin box filled with mica and feldspar and hornblende[2] which he had picked up on the way.

The other princes roared with disdainful laughter when they saw the tawdry gift the fifth prince had brought to the Princess. But she examined it with great interest and squealed with delight, for all her life she had been glutted with precious stones and priceless metals, but she had never seen tin before or mica or feldspar or hornblende. The tin box was placed next to the ruby heart pierced with an emerald arrow.

"Now," the King said to his daughter, "you must select the gift you like best and marry the prince that brought it."

The Princess smiled and walked up to the table and picked up the present she liked the most. It

---

1. **Cartier's** (kär′tē·āz): an expensive jewelry store in New York City.

2. **mica . . . hornblende:** types of ordinary rocks.

was the platinum-and-sapphire jewel box, the gift of the third prince.

"The way I figure it," she said, "is this. It is a very large and expensive box, and when I am married, I will meet many admirers who will give me precious gems with which to fill it to the top. Therefore, it is the most valuable of all the gifts my suitors have brought me, and I like it the best."

The Princess married the third prince that very day in the midst of great merriment and high revelry. More than a hundred thousand pearls were thrown at her and she loved it.

Moral: All those who thought that the princess was going to select the tin box filled with worthless stones instead of one of the other gifts will kindly stay after class and write one hundred times on the blackboard, "I would rather have a hunk of aluminum silicate than a diamond necklace."

Responding to the Stories

Analyzing the Stories

Identifying Facts

1. Why didn't the wolf's disguise fool the little girl?
2. Why does the Princess like the jewel box best?

Interpreting Meanings

3. Explain how these stories are **ironic**—tell what you *expected* each heroine to do, and how the stories reversed your expectations.
4. How do you think Thurber wants you to feel about the original fairy tales and their heroines? Explain whether you think he wants you to admire *his* heroines.
5. What "moral" do you think the original story of Red Riding Hood teaches children?
6. Suppose the Princess had chosen the tin box and married the poor prince. What "moral" would that story teach?
7. Do Thurber's morals strike you as true to life as you know it today? Explain your opinion.

Writing About the Stories

A Creative Response

1. **Reversing a Familiar Plot.** Think of another familiar fairy tale or fable (such as the stories of Cinderella, the Three Bears, the Princess and the Pea, Hansel and Gretel, the Tortoise and the Hare, or the Fox and the Grapes). In a paragraph, change the original plot so that the ending reverses our expectations in a surprising and comical way.
2. **Extending the Stories.** Write a paragraph that explains what the little girl does after she shoots

© 1940 James Thurber, © 1968 Helen Thurber.
From *Fables for Our Time*, Harper & Row, Inc.

the wolf. Write another paragraph describing the Princess's first year of married life.

3. **Putting a Character in a Different Setting.** Choose a traditional fairy-tale heroine, and imagine that she wakes up one day in the modern world. Write a paragraph describing how she behaves during a high-school dance, a football game, a rock concert, or any other social situation you can think of. (You may want to use a hero instead.)

THE SNIPER

Liam O'Flaherty

This story is set in Dublin, Ireland, in the 1920's. During that time a civil war was taking place in Ireland. On one side were the Republicans; they wanted Ireland to become a republic, totally free from British rule. On the other side were the Free Staters; they had compromised with Britain and obtained only a limited amount of independence. Like all civil wars, this one tore families apart. It pitted children against parents, sister against sister, brother against brother. As you read, notice how the writer helps you feel as if you are right there on a Dublin rooftop.

The long June twilight faded into night. Dublin lay enveloped in darkness but for the dim light of the moon that shone through fleecy clouds, casting a pale light as of approaching dawn over the streets and the dark waters of the Liffey.[1] Around the beleaguered Four Courts[2] the heavy guns roared. Here and there through the city, machine guns and rifles broke the silence of the night, spasmodically, like dogs barking on lone farms. Republicans and Free Staters were waging civil war.

On a rooftop near O'Connell Bridge, a Republican sniper lay watching. Beside him lay his rifle and over his shoulders were slung a pair of field glasses. His face was the face of a student, thin and ascetic, but his eyes had the cold gleam of the fanatic. They were deep and thoughtful, the eyes of a man who is used to looking at death.

He was eating a sandwich hungrily. He had eaten nothing since morning. He had been too excited to eat. He finished the sandwich, and, taking a flask of whisky from his pocket, he took a short draught. Then he returned the flask to his pocket. He paused for a moment, considering whether he should risk a smoke. It was dangerous. The flash might be seen in the darkness, and there were enemies watching. He decided to take the risk.

Placing a cigarette between his lips, he struck a match, inhaled the smoke hurriedly and put out the light. Almost immediately, a bullet flattened itself against the parapet of the roof. The sniper took another whiff and put out the cigarette. Then he swore softly and crawled away to the left.

Cautiously he raised himself and peered over the parapet. There was a flash and a bullet whizzed over his head. He dropped immediately. He had seen the flash. It came from the opposite side of the street.

He rolled over the roof to a chimney stack in the rear, and slowly drew himself up behind it, until his eyes were level with the top of the parapet. There was nothing to be seen—just the dim outline of the opposite housetop against the blue sky. His enemy was under cover.

Just then an armored car came across the bridge and advanced slowly up the street. It stopped on the opposite side of the street, fifty yards ahead. The sniper could hear the dull panting of the motor. His heart beat faster. It was an enemy car. He wanted to fire, but he knew it was useless. His bullets would never pierce the steel that covered the gray monster.

Then round the corner of a side street came an old woman, her head covered by a tattered shawl. She began to talk to the man in the turret of the car. She was pointing to the roof where the sniper lay. An informer.

The turret opened. A man's head and shoulders appeared, looking toward the sniper. The sniper raised his rifle and fired. The head fell heavily on the turret wall. The woman darted toward the side street. The sniper fired again. The woman whirled

---

1. **the Liffey:** the great river that runs through Dublin.
2. **Four Courts:** government buildings in Dublin.

round and fell with a shriek into the gutter.

Suddenly from the opposite roof a shot rang out and the sniper dropped his rifle with a curse. The rifle clattered to the roof. The sniper thought the noise would wake the dead. He stooped to pick the rifle up. He couldn't lift it. His forearm was dead. "I'm hit," he muttered.

Dropping flat onto the roof, he crawled back to the parapet. With his left hand he felt the injured right forearm. The blood was oozing through the sleeve of his coat. There was no pain—just a deadened sensation, as if the arm had been cut off.

Quickly he drew his knife from his pocket, opened it on the breastwork of the parapet, and ripped open the sleeve. There was a small hole where the bullet had entered. On the other side there was no hole. The bullet had lodged in the bone. It must have fractured it. He bent the arm below the wound. The arm bent back easily. He ground his teeth to overcome the pain.

Then taking out his field dressing, he ripped open the packet with his knife. He broke the neck of the iodine bottle and let the bitter fluid drip into the wound. A paroxysm of pain swept through him. He placed the cotton wadding over the wound and wrapped the dressing over it. He tied the ends with his teeth.

Then he lay still against the parapet, and, closing his eyes, he made an effort of will to overcome the pain.

In the street beneath all was still. The armored car had retired speedily over the bridge, with the machine gunner's head hanging lifeless over the turret. The woman's corpse lay still in the gutter.

The sniper lay still for a long time nursing his wounded arm and planning escape. Morning must not find him wounded on the roof. The enemy on the opposite roof covered his escape. He must kill that enemy and he could not use his rifle. He had only a revolver to do it. Then he thought of a plan.

Taking off his cap, he placed it over the muzzle of his rifle. Then he pushed the rifle slowly upward over the parapet, until the cap was visible from the opposite side of the street. Almost immediately there was a report, and a bullet pierced the center of the cap. The sniper slanted the rifle forward. The cap slipped down into the street. Then catching the rifle in the middle, the sniper dropped his left hand over the roof and let it hang, lifelessly. After a few moments he let the rifle drop to the street. Then he sank to the roof, dragging his hand with him.

Crawling quickly to the left, he peered up at the corner of the roof. His ruse had succeeded. The other sniper, seeing the cap and rifle fall, thought that he had killed his man. He was now standing before a row of chimney pots, looking across, with his head clearly silhouetted against the western sky.

The Republican sniper smiled and lifted his revolver above the edge of the parapet. The distance was about fifty yards—a hard shot in the dim light, and his right arm was paining him like a thousand devils. He took a steady aim. His hand trembled with eagerness. Pressing his lips together, he took a deep breath through his nostrils and fired. He was almost deafened with the report and his arm shook with the recoil.

Then when the smoke cleared he peered across and uttered a cry of joy. His enemy had been hit. He was reeling over the parapet in his death agony. He struggled to keep his feet, but he was slowly falling forward, as if in a dream. The rifle fell from his grasp, hit the parapet, fell over, bounded off the pole of a barber's shop beneath, and then clattered on the pavement.

Then the dying man on the roof crumpled up and fell forward. The body turned over and over in space and hit the ground with a dull thud. Then it lay still.

The sniper looked at his enemy falling and he shuddered. The lust of battle died in him. He became bitten by remorse. The sweat stood out in beads on his forehead. Weakened by his wound and the long summer day of fasting and watching on the roof, he revolted from the sight of the shattered mass of his dead enemy. His teeth chattered, he began to gibber to himself, cursing the war, cursing himself, cursing everybody.

He looked at the smoking revolver in his hand, and with an oath he hurled it to the roof at his feet. The revolver went off with the concussion and the bullet whizzed past the sniper's head. He was frightened back to his senses by the shock. His nerves steadied. The cloud of fear scattered from his mind and he laughed.

Taking the whisky flask from his pocket, he emptied it at a draught. He felt reckless under the influence of the spirit. He decided to leave the roof now and look for his company commander, to report. Everywhere around was quiet. There was not much danger in going through the streets. He picked up his revolver and put it in his pocket. Then he crawled down through the skylight to the house underneath.

When the sniper reached the laneway on the street level, he felt a sudden curiosity as to the identity of the enemy sniper whom he had killed. He decided that he was a good shot, whoever he was. He wondered did he know him. Perhaps he had been in his own company before the split in the army. He decided to risk going over to have a look at him. He peered around the corner into O'Connell Street. In the upper part of the street there was heavy firing, but around here all was quiet.

The sniper darted across the street. A machine gun tore up the ground around him with a hail of bullets, but he escaped. He threw himself face downward beside the corpse. The machine gun stopped.

Then the sniper turned over the dead body and looked into his brother's face.

Responding to the Story

Analyzing the Story

Identifying Facts

1. This brief dramatic story has the strong impact of simplicity. What facts are we told directly about the sniper as he lies in wait? What does any sniper want to do?
2. Why does the sniper kill the old woman? What happens to him after he fires his weapon?
3. What trick does the sniper use to force his enemy from cover? How does the sniper feel as he takes aim at his enemy and fires?

Interpreting Meanings

4. How does the sniper feel after he has killed his enemy and watched him fall to the ground? Why do you think his feelings now change?
5. Explain the **irony** in the story's last sentence.
6. What do you think the sniper feels when he discovers the identity of the man he has killed? How does the discovery make you feel?
7. How does the writer want us to feel about the sniper? Which of his actions contribute to our feelings about him?
8. How would you state the **theme** of this story—how does the writer want us to feel about war and what it can do to human beings?
9. This story is set in Ireland during the 1920's. In what other **setting** could you imagine similar events taking place?

Writing About the Story

A Creative Response

1. **Completing the Story.** Two important parts of this story are missing. One is the opening, which tells us why the two brothers ended up on opposite sides in the civil war. The other is the closing, which tells what happens to the sniper after he discovers he has killed his brother. Write a paragraph summarizing what you imagine one of these missing parts would be.

A Critical Response

2. **Comparing the Story with a Poem.** This famous poem by a British writer has many resemblances to the story "The Sniper." A soldier is speaking.

The Man He Killed

"Had he and I but met
By some old ancient inn,
We should have sat us down to wet
Right many a nipperkin!°

"But ranged as infantry,
And staring face to face,
I shot at him as he at me,
And killed him in his place.

"I shot him dead because—
Because he was my foe,
Just so: my foe of course he was;
That's clear enough; although

"He thought he'd 'list,° perhaps,
Offhand like—just as I—
Was out of work—had sold his traps°—
No other reason why.

"Yes, quaint and curious war is!
You shoot a fellow down
You'd treat if met where any bar is,
Or help to half-a-crown."°
          —Thomas Hardy

In a paragraph, compare the poem with the story. Consider these questions:

a. What incident occurs in each selection?
b. How is each incident **ironic**?
c. What do both selections say about war?

Reading About the Writer

Liam O'Flaherty (1897–1984) was born on one of the Aran Islands off the west coast of Ireland. He fought in France during World War I and later became involved in the civil war at home. O'Flaherty's best-known novel is *The Informer,* which, like "The Sniper," is set during the Irish "troubles." *The Informer* was made into one of Hollywood's great movies, directed by John Ford.

---

4. **nipperkin:** beer glass.
13. **'list:** enlist.
15. **traps:** possessions.
20. **half-a-crown:** a coin.

THE CASK OF AMONTILLADO

Edgar Allan Poe

Centuries ago in Europe, people often buried their dead in long, winding, underground tunnels, called catacombs. Some wealthy families even had their own private underground burial vaults. In addition to bodies, people sometimes kept wine in these vaults, which were dark and cool. (Amontillado in this story is a kind of wine.) Poe's famous story is set in the catacombs of an Italian city, several centuries ago. It is carnival time. During carnival, in February or March, many Christians used to celebrate wildly before the start of Lent, when they gave up meat and pleasure to atone for their sins.

After you finish the first paragraph, stop and ask yourself: According to this narrator, what makes a perfect crime?

The thousand injuries of Fortunato I had borne as best I could; but when he ventured upon insult, I vowed revenge. You, who so well know the nature of my soul, will not suppose, however, that I gave utterance to a threat. *At length* I would be avenged; this was a point definitively settled—but the very definitiveness with which it was resolved precluded the idea of risk. I must not only punish, but punish with impunity.[1] A wrong is unredressed when retribution overtakes its redresser. It is equally unredressed when the avenger fails to make himself felt as such to him who has done the wrong.

It must be understood that neither by word nor deed had I given Fortunato cause to doubt my good will. I continued, as was my wont, to smile in his face, and he did not perceive that my smile *now* was at the thought of his immolation.[2]

He had a weak point—this Fortunato—although in other regards he was a man to be respected and even feared. He prided himself on his connoisseurship, in wine. Few Italians have the true virtuoso spirit. For the most part their enthusiasm is adopted to suit the time and opportunity—to practice imposture upon the British and Austrian millionaires. In painting and gemmary, Fortunato, like his countrymen, was a quack—but in the matter of old wines he was sincere. In this respect I did not differ from him materially: I was skillful in the Italian vintages myself and bought largely whenever I could.

It was about dusk, one evening during the supreme madness of the carnival season, that I encountered my friend. He accosted me with excessive warmth, for he had been drinking much. The man wore motley.[3] He had on a tight-fitting parti-striped dress, and his head was surmounted by the conical cap and bells. I was so pleased to see him that I thought I should never have done wringing his hand.

I said to him, "My dear Fortunato, you are luckily met. How remarkably well you are looking today! But I have received a pipe[4] of what passes for amontillado, and I have my doubts."

"How?" said he. "Amontillado? A pipe? Impossible! And in the middle of the carnival!"

"I have my doubts," I replied; "and I was silly enough to pay the full amontillado price without consulting you in the matter. You were not to be found, and I was fearful of losing a bargain."

---

1. **with impunity** (im·pyoo′ nə·tē): without fear of being punished in return.
2. **immolation:** destruction, sacrifice.
3. **motley:** a costume of many colors, worn by a clown or jester.
4. **pipe:** large cask.

"Amontillado!"

"I have my doubts."

"Amontillado!"

"And I must satisfy them."

"Amontillado!"

"As you are engaged, I am on my way to Luchesi. If anyone has a critical turn, it is he. He will tell me——"

"Luchesi cannot tell amontillado from sherry."

"And yet some fools will have it that his taste is a match for your own."

"Come, let us go."

"Whither?"

"To your vaults."

"My friend, no; I will not impose upon your good nature. I perceive you have an engagement. Luchesi——"

"I have no engagement; come."

"My friend, no. It is not the engagement, but the severe cold with which I perceive you are afflicted. The vaults are insufferably damp. They are encrusted with niter."[5]

"Let us go, nevertheless. The cold is merely nothing. Amontillado! You have been imposed upon. And as for Luchesi, he cannot distinguish sherry from amontillado."

Thus speaking, Fortunato possessed himself of my arm. Putting on a mask of black silk and drawing a roquelaire[6] closely about my person, I suffered him to hurry me to my palazzo.

There were no attendants at home; they had absconded to make merry in honor of the time. I had told them that I should not return until the morning, and had given them explicit orders not to stir from the house. These orders were sufficient, I well knew, to insure their immediate disappearance, one and all, as soon as my back was turned.

I took from their sconces two flambeaus,[7] and giving one to Fortunato, bowed him through several suites of rooms to the archway that led into the vaults. I passed down a long and winding staircase, requesting him to be cautious as he followed. We came at length to the foot of the descent, and stood together on the damp ground of the catacombs of the Montresors.

The gait of my friend was unsteady, and the bells upon his cap jingled as he strode.

"The pipe," said he.

"It is farther on," said I; "but observe the white web-work which gleams from these cavern walls."

He turned toward me, and looked into my eyes with two filmy orbs that distilled the rheum[8] of intoxication.

"Niter?" he asked, at length.

"Niter," I replied. "How long have you had that cough?"

"Ugh! ugh! ugh!—ugh! ugh! ugh!—ugh! ugh! ugh!—ugh! ugh! ugh!—ugh! ugh! ugh!"

My poor friend found it impossible to reply for many minutes.

"It is nothing," he said, at last.

"Come," I said, with decision, "we will go back; your health is precious. You are rich, respected, admired, beloved; you are happy, as once I was. You are a man to be missed. For me it is no matter. We will go back; you will be ill, and I cannot be responsible. Besides, there is Luchesi——"

"Enough," he said; "the cough is a mere nothing; it will not kill me. I shall not die of a cough."

"True—true," I replied; "and, indeed, I had no intention of alarming you unnecessarily—but you should use all proper caution. A draft of this Médoc[9] will defend us from the damps."

Here I knocked off the neck of a bottle which I drew from a long row of its fellows that lay upon the mold.

"Drink," I said, presenting him the wine.

He raised it to his lips with a leer. He paused and nodded to me familiarly, while his bells jingled.

"I drink," he said, "to the buried that repose around us."

"And I to your long life."

He again took my arm, and we proceeded.

"These vaults," he said, "are extensive."

---

5. **niter** (nī′ tər): a white or gray salt deposit.
6. **roquelaire** (räk′ ə·lôr): a heavy knee-length cloak.
7. **sconces** (skän′ səz): brackets attached to the wall for holding **flambeaus** (flam′ bōz), which are torches or candles.

8. **rheum** (ro͞om): a watery discharge.
9. **Médoc** (mā′ dôk): a type of wine.

"The Montresors," I replied, "were a great and numerous family."

"I forget your arms."[10]

"A huge human foot d'or, in a field azure; the foot crushes a serpent rampant whose fangs are imbedded in the heel."[11]

"And the motto?"

"*Nemo me impune lacessit.*"[12]

---

10. **arms:** coat of arms, the insignia of a family.
11. **foot d'or . . . heel:** the Montresor coat of arms shows a huge golden foot against a blue background, with the foot crushing a serpent that is rearing up and biting the heel.
12. *Nemo . . . lacessit:* Latin for "No one attacks me with impunity."

"Good!" he said.

The wine sparkled in his eyes and the bells jingled. My own fancy grew warm with the Médoc. We had passed through walls of piled bones, with casks and puncheons[13] intermingling, into the inmost recesses of the catacombs. I paused again, and this time I made bold to seize Fortunato by an arm above the elbow.

---

13. **puncheons** (pun' chǝnz): large casks for beer or wine.

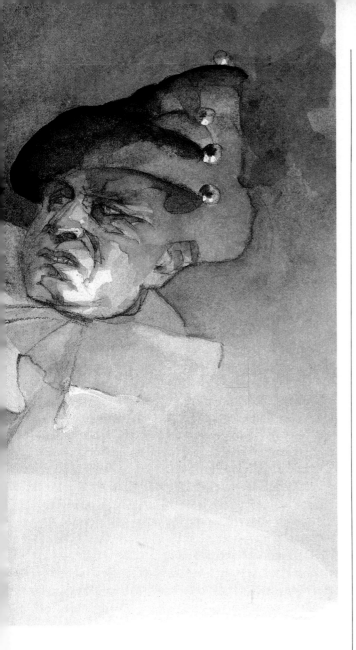

"The niter!" I said. "See, it increases. It hangs like moss upon the vaults. We are below the river's bed. The drops of moisture trickle among the bones. Come, we will go back ere it is too late. Your cough——"

"It is nothing," he said; "let us go on. But first, another draft of the Médoc."

I broke and reached him a flagon of de Grâve. He emptied it at a breath. His eyes flashed with a fierce light. He laughed and threw the bottle upward with a gesticulation I did not understand.

I looked at him in surprise. He repeated the movement—a grotesque one.

"You do not comprehend?" he said.

"Not I," I replied.

"Then you are not of the brotherhood."

"How?"

"You are not of the masons."[14]

"Yes, yes," I said, "yes, yes."

"You? Impossible! A mason?"

"A mason," I replied.

"A sign," he said.

"It is this," I answered, producing a trowel from beneath the folds of my roquelaire.

"You jest," he exclaimed, recoiling a few paces. "But let us proceed to the amontillado."

"Be it so," I said, replacing the tool beneath the cloak and again offering him my arm. He leaned upon it heavily. We continued our route in search of the amontillado. We passed through a range of low arches, descended, passed on, and, descending again, arrived at a deep crypt, in which the foulness of the air caused our flambeaus rather to glow than flame.

At the most remote end of the crypt there appeared another less spacious. Its walls had been lined with human remains, piled to the vault overhead, in the fashion of the great catacombs of Paris. Three sides of this interior crypt were still ornamented in this manner. From the fourth the bones had been thrown down, and lay promiscuously[15] upon the earth, forming at one point a mound of some size. Within the wall thus exposed by the displacing of the bones, we perceived a still interior recess, in depth about four feet, in width three, in height six or seven. It seemed to have been constructed for no especial use within itself, but formed merely the interval between two of the colossal supports of the roof of the catacombs and was backed by one of their circumscribing walls of solid granite.

It was in vain that Fortunato, uplifting his dull torch, endeavored to pry into the depth of the recess. Its termination the feeble light did not enable us to see.

---

14. **masons:** Freemasons or masons are members of a secret society whose principles are brotherhood, charity, and mutual aid. Bricklayers are also called masons. Like most secret organizations, the Masons had secret signs and gestures that only fellow Masons understood.

15. **promiscuously:** casually.

"Proceed," I said; "herein is the amontillado. As for Luchesi——"

"He is an ignoramus," interrupted my friend, as he stepped unsteadily forward, while I followed immediately at his heels. In an instant he had reached the extremity of the niche, and finding his progress arrested by the rock, stood stupidly bewildered. A moment more and I had fettered[16] him to the granite. In its surface were two iron staples, distant from each other about two feet horizontally. From one of these depended a short chain, from the other a padlock. Throwing the links about his waist, it was but the work of a few seconds to secure it. He was too much astounded to resist. Withdrawing the key, I stepped back from the recess.

"Pass your hand," I said, "over the wall; you cannot help feeling the niter. Indeed it is *very* damp. Once more let me *implore* you to return. No? Then I must positively leave you. But I must first render you all the little attentions in my power."

"The amontillado!" ejaculated my friend, not yet recovered from his astonishment.

"True," I replied; "the amontillado."

As I said these words I busied myself among the pile of bones of which I have before spoken. Throwing them aside, I soon uncovered a quantity of building stone and mortar. With these materials and with the aid of my trowel, I began vigorously to wall up the entrance of the niche.

I had scarcely laid the first tier of the masonry when I discovered that the intoxication of Fortunato had in a great measure worn off. The earliest indication I had of this was a low moaning cry from the depth of the recess. It was *not* the cry of a drunken man. There was then a long and obstinate silence. I laid the second tier, and the third, and the fourth; and then I heard the furious vibrations of the chain. The noise lasted for several minutes, during which, that I might harken to it with the more satisfaction, I ceased my labors and sat down upon the bones. When at last the clanking subsided, I resumed the trowel and finished without interruption the fifth, the sixth, and the seventh tier. The wall was now nearly upon a level with my breast. I again paused and, holding the flambeaus over the mason-work, threw a few feeble rays upon the figure within.

A succession of loud and shrill screams, bursting suddenly from the throat of the chained form, seemed to thrust me violently back. For a brief moment I hesitated—I trembled. Unsheathing my rapier,[17] I began to grope with it about the recess; but the thought of an instant reassured me. I placed my hand upon the solid fabric of the catacombs and felt satisfied. I reapproached the wall; I replied to the yells of him who clamored. I re-echoed—I aided—I surpassed them in volume and in strength. I did this, and the clamorer grew still.

It was now midnight, and my task was drawing to a close. I had completed the eighth, the ninth, and the tenth tier. I had finished a portion of the last and the eleventh; there remained but a single stone to be fitted and plastered in. I struggled with its weight; I placed it partially in its destined position. But now there came from out the niche a low laugh that erected the hairs upon my head. It was succeeded by a sad voice, which I had difficulty in recognizing as that of the noble Fortunato. The voice said—

"Ha! ha! ha!—he! he! he!—a very good joke indeed—an excellent jest. We will have many a rich laugh about it at the palazzo—he! he! he!—over our wine—he! he! he!"

"The amontillado!" I said.

"He! he! he!—he! he! he!—yes, the amontillado. But is it not getting late? Will not they be awaiting us at the palazzo—the Lady Fortunato and the rest? Let us be gone."

"Yes," I said, "let us be gone."

"For the love of God, Montresor!"

"Yes," I said, "for the love of God!"

But to these words I harkened in vain for a reply. I grew impatient. I called aloud—

"Fortunato!"

No answer. I called again—

"Fortunato!"

No answer still. I thrust a torch through the remaining aperture and let it fall within. There came forth in return only a jingling of the bells. My heart grew sick—on account of the dampness

---

16. **fettered:** chained.

17. **rapier** (rā′ pē·ər): a slender, double-edged sword.

of the catacombs. I hastened to make an end of my labor. I forced the last stone into its position; I plastered it up. Against the new masonry I re-erected the old rampart of bones. For the half of a century no mortal has disturbed them. *In pace requiescat.*[18]

---

18. *In pace requiescat:* Latin for "May he rest in peace."

Responding to the Story

Analyzing the Story

Identifying Facts

1. This well-known Poe story is remembered for its grisly masonry job, but it is also a splendid illustration of the power of **point of view.** Briefly identify the narrator of this story. What detail in the first paragraph tells us that he is talking to someone directly?
2. What does this narrator tell us is the **motive** for his crime? Name the two features he looks for in perfect revenge—that is, how must a wrong be truly redressed, or corrected?
3. According to Montresor, what kind of **character** is his enemy, Fortunato? What weaknesses of Fortunato allow him to be lured to his death?
4. Exactly how does Montresor get his revenge?
5. At the **resolution** of the story, what do we learn about *when* these events took place? Explain whether Montresor has succeeded in punishing "with impunity"—that is, without being punished himself.

Interpreting Meanings

6. Poe uses all the elements of storytelling to create his eerie effects. Name at least five **images** describing this underground **setting** that contribute to your sense of horror and dread.
7. Part of the story's horrifying effect also comes from our sense of irony. How does Poe use **dramatic irony**—that is, what do *we* know that Fortunato does *not* know about why he has been invited down into the vaults?
8. Which of Montresor's comments to the unsuspecting Fortunato are examples of **verbal irony**—that is, which comments mean something different from what Fortunato *thinks* they mean?
9. Why is it **ironic** that Fortunato is dressed as a jester? Why is it **ironic** that all this time a carnival is taking place over the heads of the two wine lovers? What **irony** can you find in the victim's name, *Fortunato*? (You can make an educated guess about what it means.)
10. What sign does Montresor give Fortunato to prove he is a mason? How does Montresor's proof **foreshadow** to us the crime that is about to occur?
11. Poe deliberately raises questions about Montresor's reliability as a narrator. What details in his story suggest that Montresor is insane and has imagined "the thousand injuries" and the insult? On the other hand, what evidence in the story supports Montresor's claim that Fortunato did in fact injure and insult him?
12. Poe never identifies Montresor's listener. Some readers think the murderer is talking to a priest who is hearing his death-bed confession. This would suggest that Montresor seeks forgiveness for his crime. What are your feelings about this theory? Do you find any evidence in the story that Montresor regrets his crime?

Writing About the Story

A Creative Response

1. **Using Another Point of View.** Suppose this story had not been told by Montresor. Let's say we had heard the gullible Fortunato's side of the story. Write out the beginning of this story as if it is being told by Fortunato. Begin when the two men meet at dusk, and end when they start their journey underground. Let Fortunato tell what *he* thinks of Montresor. Was he guilty of the thousand injuries and the insult? Have Fortunato use the first-person pronoun, "I."
2. **Extending the Story.** What happens to Fortunato after Montresor leaves him alive, manacled behind a wall of stone? Write an ending to Fortunato's story.

3. Writing a Resolution. What response does the mysterious listener make to Montresor's story? Pretend you are the person to whom Montresor is finally confessing. Write out what you say to the murderer after he utters the words "*In pace requiescat.*" Use the first-person pronoun, "I."

A Critical Response

4. Explaining a Response to the Story. Poe once said: "Villains do not always, nor even generally, meet with punishment and shame in reality." Perhaps this explains why he ended this story the way he did. In a paragraph, explain your response to the story's ending. Do you think Poe should have punished Montresor for his crime? Or do you think the ending is more effective and horrifying as it is? Explain your response.

Analyzing Language and Vocabulary

Clues to Word Meanings

Many words in Poe's story are footnoted, but probably other words in the story were unfamiliar to you. You could make an educated guess about the meanings of many of these words by thinking about their relationship to other words that you probably are familiar with.

For example, in the first paragraph, Poe's narrator says: "At length I would be avenged." If you were uncertain about the meaning of the word *avenged,* a clue could be found in the word's similarity to the more familiar word *revenge.*

The italicized words in the following passages might be unfamiliar to you. But each word is similar to another word you might be more familiar with. Make an educated guess about the meaning of each italicized word. Check all your guesses in a dictionary.

1. "For the most part their enthusiasm is adopted to suit the time and opportunity—to practice *imposture* upon the British and Austrian millionaires."
   a. What is an *impostor?*
   b. Could *imposture* have a related meaning and fit in this context?
2. "In painting and *gemmary*, Fortunato, like his countrymen, was a quack . . ."
   a. What familiar word is found within the word *gemmary?*
   b. What does the related word *gemology* mean?
3. "He had on a tight-fitting *parti*-striped dress, and his head was surmounted by the *conical* cap and bells."
   a. What word that sounds like *parti* fits the context?
   b. What word is *conical* built on?
4. "I suffered him to hurry me to my *palazzo.*"
   a. *Palazzo* is an Italian word. What English word does it sound like?
   b. What does the related word *palatial* mean?
5. "He laughed and threw the bottle upward with a *gesticulation* I did not understand."
   a. What word does *gesticulation* resemble?
   b. What does the verb *gesticulate* mean?
6. ". . . Fortunato . . . endeavored to pry into the depth of the recess. Its *termination* the feeble light did not enable us to see."
   a. What word is *termination* built on?
   b. What familiar word does it resemble?

Reading About the Writer

The brief life of **Edgar Allan Poe** (1809–1849) was as haunted as his extraordinary poems and short stories. Poe was born in Boston, the son of traveling actors. His father deserted the family, and his mother died in a theatrical rooming house in Richmond, Virginia, before Poe was three years old. The little boy was taken in as a foster child by the wealthy and childless Allan family of Richmond. As a schoolboy, Poe delighted his foster parents with his brilliant scholarship and athletic ability. But he dismayed them with his moodiness and irresponsibility. The friction that arose between Poe and his foster father was never resolved.

Poe entered the University of Virginia and was an outstanding student, but he received very little money from John Allan. To make money, he gambled, and he ran up debts that Allan refused to pay. Poe left the university after only a year.

He enlisted in the army and did well, and in a desperate attempt to regain his foster father's approval, he entered West Point. But again he was in need of money, and again he ran up gambling debts that Allan refused to pay. Poe soon gave up all hopes of receiving support from his foster father. Unable to resign from West Point without Allan's approval, he deliberately provoked a court-martial and was expelled.

Poe had been writing poetry since childhood. During these troubled years, he published several books of poetry, but they went largely ignored. A friend found him a job as editor of a literary magazine, but he lost the position because of his drinking.

Poe's emotional life became chaotic and unstable. He badly needed the security of a family, and he seemed to find it in the family of his aunt, Maria Clem, of Baltimore. In 1836 Poe married his thirteen-year-old cousin, Virginia Clem, and the threesome moved to New York City, where they set up house together.

In spite of bad health and the terrible lack of money, Poe wrote regularly and he had increasing success. But his one refuge in life was threatened when Virginia showed signs of tuberculosis. When she died at the age of twenty-five, Poe broke down completely. Two years later, at the age of forty, he died after a drinking bout in Baltimore.

Poe's most famous stories include "The Fall of the House of Usher," "The Tell-Tale Heart," "The Pit and the Pendulum," "The Masque of the Red Death," and the world's first detective story, "The Murders in the Rue Morgue." Several of his stories have been made into movies. Among his most famous poems are "The Raven" and "Annabel Lee." Today, Poe is recognized as one of the most important of all American writers. He was among the first of our writers to explore the dark side of the human mind.

Focusing on Background
"Where did the story come from?"

Many people have searched for the sources of Poe's famous story "The Cask of Amontillado." It is possible, of course, that Poe just made the whole idea up. But it is also possible that Poe based his tale on a true story.

In the following passage, a "literary detective" suggests that Poe found the germ of his story in a letter written by the Reverend Joel Tyler Headley, a popular writer of Poe's day. Headley wrote this letter about his travels in Italy, and he published it in the *New York Evening Mirror* on July 12, 1845. The letter was called: "A Sketch: A Man Built in a Wall." Here is part of the literary detective's report:

"The letter by Headley may be summed up briefly. He and his companion enter the little town of San Giovanni, in Italy. They are shown through the church of San Lorenzo. In the wall of the church is a niche covered with 'a sort of trapdoor,' containing an upright human skeleton. This ghastly spectacle had been discovered by workmen some years previous to Headley's visit, but it had not been disturbed. Headley describes the skeleton in detail and concludes that the victim had died of suffocation after having been walled up alive. The history of the immurement is not known, but Headley gives an account of his retrospective view of the event:

The victim was walled up by his enemies in a spirit of revenge. He had been bound securely, and the niche prepared for him. When the opening was large enough, he was placed in it. The walling-up process began. Gradually, it neared completion; the last stone was fitted in and revenge was satisfied.

"We find more than an echo of this account in Poe's 'The Cask of Amontillado.' It will be recalled that here, too, the scene is laid in Italy, and the action is motivated by a spirit of revenge. Further, the characters involved in the plot are of the nobility. Headley writes, 'Men of rank were engaged in it [the torturing of their enemies], for none other could have got the control of a church, and none but a distinguished victim would have caused such great precaution in the murderers.' Poe makes use of a similar tradition of nobility, for he speaks of the Montresors as a 'great and numerous family' and describes their armorial bearings. . . .

"The similarities in the accounts of Poe and Headley may be summed up briefly: The scenes are laid in Italy; the characters involved are of the nobility; the deeds of murder are incited by revenge; the same method of immurement is resorted to; and there are similar descriptive details."

—Joseph S. Schick

THE NECKLACE

Guy de Maupassant

This famous story takes place in Paris in the late 1880's. At that time and in that place, social classes were all-important; people were born into a certain class and that was usually where they remained. This story is about a woman who was born into a middle-class family—clerks would be something like minor office workers today. The problem with this young woman is, first, that she is very beautiful, and, second, that she is very dissatisfied with her class, or station in life. Remember that at this time in France (and in most of the world), women could not go out and get jobs the way they can today. Women for the most part were totally dependent on their husbands for support and for their status in society. Women managed their homes, but the world beyond the home was dominated by men.

The story's theme has to do with human vanity and its rewards. Notice how this theme is revealed by the irony contained in the very last line.

She was one of those pretty and charming girls, born, as if by an accident of fate, into a family of clerks. With no dowry, no prospects, no way of any kind of being met, understood, loved, and married by a man both prosperous and famous, she was finally married to a minor clerk in the Ministry of Education.

She dressed plainly because she could not afford fine clothes, but she was as unhappy as a woman who has come down in the world; for women have no family rank or social class. With them, beauty, grace, and charm take the place of birth and breeding. Their natural poise, their instinctive good taste, and their mental cleverness are the sole guiding principles which make daughters of the common people the equals of ladies in high society.

She grieved incessantly, feeling that she had been born for all the little niceties and luxuries of living. She grieved over the shabbiness of her apartment, the dinginess of the walls, the worn-out appearance of the chairs, the ugliness of the draperies. All these things, which another woman of her class would not even have noticed, gnawed at her and made her furious. The sight of the little Breton girl[1] who did her humble housework roused in her disconsolate regrets and wild daydreams. She would dream of silent chambers, draped with Oriental tapestries and lighted by tall bronze floor lamps, and of two handsome butlers in knee breeches, who, drowsy from the heavy warmth cast by the central stove, dozed in large overstuffed armchairs.

She would dream of great reception halls hung with old silks, of fine furniture filled with priceless curios, and of small, stylish, scented sitting rooms just right for the four o'clock chat with intimate friends, with distinguished and sought-after men whose attention every woman envies and longs to attract.

When dining at the round table, covered for the third day with the same cloth, opposite her husband, who would raise the cover of the soup tureen, declaring delightedly, "Ah! a good stew! There's nothing I like better . . . ," she would dream of fashionable dinner parties, of gleaming silverware, of tapestries making the walls alive with characters out of history and strange birds in a fairyland forest; she would dream of delicious dishes served on wonderful china, of gallant compliments whispered and listened to with a sphinxlike[2] smile as one eats the rosy flesh of a

---

1. **Breton** (bret' 'n) **girl:** a girl from Brittany, a province in northwestern France.

2. **sphinxlike:** mysterious. (The sphinx was a mythological creature who asked riddles.)

trout or nibbles at the wings of a grouse.

She had no evening clothes, no jewels, nothing. But those were the things she wanted; she felt that was the kind of life for her. She so much longed to please, be envied, be fascinating and sought after.

She had a well-to-do friend, a classmate of convent-school days whom she would no longer go to see, simply because she would feel so distressed on returning home. And she would weep for days on end from vexation, regret, despair, and anguish.

Then one evening, her husband came home proudly holding out a large envelope.

"Look," he said, "I've got something for you."

She excitedly tore open the envelope and pulled out a printed card bearing these words:

"The Minister of Education and Mme. Georges Ramponneau beg M. and Mme. Loisel to do them the honor of attending an evening reception at the Ministerial Mansion on Friday, January 18."

Instead of being delighted, as her husband had hoped, she scornfully tossed the invitation on the table, murmuring, "What good is that to me?"

"But, my dear, I thought you'd be thrilled to death. You never get a chance to go out, and this is a real affair, a wonderful one! I had an awful time getting a card. Everybody wants one; it's much sought after, and not many clerks have a chance at one. You'll see all the most important people there."

She gave him an irritated glance and burst out impatiently, "What do you think I have to go in?"

He hadn't given that a thought. He stammered, "Why, the dress you wear when we go to the theater. That looks quite nice, I think."

He stopped talking, dazed and distracted to see his wife burst out weeping. Two large tears slowly rolled from the corners of her eyes to the corners of her mouth; he gasped, "Why, what's the matter? What's the trouble?"

By sheer willpower she overcame her outburst and answered in a calm voice while wiping the tears from her wet cheeks:

"Oh, nothing. Only I don't have an evening dress and therefore I can't go to that affair. Give the card to some friend at the office whose wife can dress better than I can."

He was stunned. He resumed, "Let's see, Mathilde. How much would a suitable outfit cost—one you could wear for other affairs too—something very simple?"

She thought it over for several seconds, going over her allowance and thinking also of the amount she could ask for without bringing an immediate refusal and an exclamation of dismay from the thrifty clerk.

Finally, she answered hesitatingly, "I'm not sure exactly, but I think with four hundred francs I could manage it."

He turned a bit pale, for he had set aside just that amount to buy a rifle so that, the following summer, he could join some friends who were getting up a group to shoot larks on the plain near Nanterre.[3]

However, he said, "All right. I'll give you four hundred francs. But try to get a nice dress."

As the day of the party approached, Mme. Loisel seemed sad, moody, ill at ease. Her outfit was ready, however. Her husband said to her one evening, "What's the matter? You've been all out of sorts for three days."

And she answered, "It's embarrassing not to have a jewel or a gem—nothing to wear on my dress. I'll look like a pauper: I'd almost rather not go to the party."

He answered, "Why not wear some flowers? They're very fashionable this season. For ten francs you can get two or three gorgeous roses."

She wasn't at all convinced. "No. . . . There's nothing more humiliating than to look poor among a lot of rich women."

But her husband exclaimed, "My, but you're silly! Go see your friend Mme. Forestier, and ask her to lend you some jewelry. You and she know each other well enough for you to do that."

She gave a cry of joy. "Why, that's so! I hadn't thought of it."

The next day she paid her friend a visit and told her of her predicament.

Mme. Forestier went toward a large closet with mirrored doors, took out a large jewel box, brought it over, opened it, and said to Mme. Lo-

---

3. **Nanterre** (nän·ter′): a town near Paris.

isel: "Pick something out, my dear."

At first her eyes noted some bracelets, then a pearl necklace, then a Venetian cross, gold and gems, of marvelous workmanship. She tried on these adornments in front of the mirror, but hesitated, unable to decide which to part with and put back. She kept on asking, "Haven't you something else?"

"Oh, yes, keep on looking. I don't know just what you'd like."

All at once she found, in a black satin box, a superb diamond necklace; and her pulse beat faster with longing. Her hands trembled as she took it up. Clasping it around her throat, outside her high-necked dress, she stood in ecstasy looking at her reflection.

Then she asked, hesitatingly, pleading, "Could I borrow that, just that and nothing else?"

"Why, of course."

She threw her arms around her friend, kissed her warmly, and fled with her treasure.

The day of the party arrived. Mme. Loisel was a sensation. She was the prettiest one there, fashionable, gracious, smiling, and wild with joy. All the men turned to look at her, asked who she was, begged to be introduced. All the Cabinet officials wanted to waltz with her. The minister took notice of her.

She danced madly, wildly, drunk with pleasure, giving no thought to anything in the triumph of her beauty, the pride of her success, in a kind of happy cloud composed of all the adulation, of all the admiring glances, of all the awakened longings, of a sense of complete victory that is so sweet to a woman's heart.

She left around four o'clock in the morning. Her husband, since midnight, had been dozing in a small empty sitting room with three other gentlemen whose wives were having too good a time.

He threw over her shoulders the wraps he had brought for going home, modest garments of everyday life whose shabbiness clashed with the stylishness of her evening clothes. She felt this and longed to escape, unseen by the other women who were draped in expensive furs.

Loisel held her back.

"Hold on! You'll catch cold outside. I'll call a cab."

But she wouldn't listen to him and went rapidly down the stairs. When they were on the street, they didn't find a carriage; and they set out to hunt for one, hailing drivers whom they saw going by at a distance.

They walked toward the Seine,[4] disconsolate and shivering. Finally on the docks they found one of those carriages that one sees in Paris only after nightfall, as if they were ashamed to show their drabness during daylight hours.

It dropped them at their door in the Rue des Martyrs,[5] and they climbed wearily up to their apartment. For her, it was all over. For him, there was the thought that he would have to be at the Ministry at ten o'clock.

Before the mirror, she let the wraps fall from her shoulders to see herself once again in all her glory. Suddenly she gave a cry. The necklace was gone.

Her husband, already half undressed, said, "What's the trouble?"

She turned toward him despairingly, "I . . . I . . . I don't have Mme. Forestier's necklace."

"What! You can't mean it! It's impossible!"

They hunted everywhere, through the folds of the dress, through the folds of the coat, in the pockets. They found nothing.

He asked, "Are you sure you had it when leaving the dance?"

"Yes, I felt it when I was in the hall of the Ministry."

"But if you had lost it on the street we'd have heard it drop. It must be in the cab."

"Yes, quite likely. Did you get its number?"

"No. Didn't you notice it either?"

"No."

They looked at each other aghast. Finally Loisel got dressed again.

"I'll retrace our steps on foot," he said, "to see if I can find it."

And he went out. She remained in her evening clothes, without the strength to go to bed, slumped in a chair in the unheated room, her mind a blank.

Her husband came in around seven o'clock.

---

4. **the Seine** (sen): the river that runs through Paris.
5. **Rue des Martyrs** (roo dā mär·tēr'): a street in Paris, meaning "the street of the martyrs."

Interrupted Reading by
Jean-Baptiste Camille Corot (1865). Oil.

Mr. and Mrs. Potter Palmer Collection (bequest of
Berthe Honoré Palmer). (1922.410) The Art Institute of Chicago.

He had had no luck.

He went to the police station, to the newspapers to post a reward, to the cab companies, everywhere the slightest hope drove him.

That evening Loisel returned, pale, his face lined; still he had learned nothing.

"We'll have to write your friend," he said, "to tell her you have broken the catch and are having it repaired. That will give us a little time to turn around."

She wrote to his dictation.

At the end of a week, they had given up all hope.

And Loisel, looking five years older, declared, "We must take steps to replace that piece of jewelry."

The next day they took the case to the jeweler whose name they found inside. He consulted his records. "I didn't sell that necklace, madame," he said. "I only supplied the case."

Then they went from one jeweler to another hunting for a similar necklace, going over their recollections, both sick with despair and anxiety.

They found, in a shop in Palais Royal,[6] a string of diamonds which seemed exactly like the one they were seeking. It was priced at forty thousand francs. They could get it for thirty-six.

They asked the jeweler to hold it for them for three days. And they reached an agreement that he would take it back for thirty-four thousand if the lost one was found before the end of February.

Loisel had eighteen thousand francs he had inherited from his father. He would borrow the rest.

He went about raising the money, asking a thousand francs from one, four hundred from another, a hundred here, sixty there. He signed notes, made ruinous deals, did business with loan sharks, ran the whole gamut of moneylenders. He compromised the rest of his life, risked his signature without knowing if he'd be able to honor it, and then, terrified by the outlook of the future, by the blackness of despair about to close around him, by the prospect of all the privations of the body and tortures of the spirit, he went to claim the new necklace with the thirty-six thousand francs which he placed on the counter of the shopkeeper.

When Mme. Loisel took the necklace back, Mme. Forestier said to her frostily, "You should have brought it back sooner; I might have needed it."

She didn't open the case, an action her friend was afraid of. If she had noticed the substitution, what would she have thought? What would she have said? Would she have thought her a thief?

Mme. Loisel experienced the horrible life the needy live. She played her part, however, with sudden heroism. That frightful debt had to be paid. She would pay it. She dismissed her maid; they rented a garret under the eaves.

She learned to do the heavy housework, to perform the hateful duties of cooking. She washed dishes, wearing down her shell-pink nails scouring the grease from pots and pans; she scrubbed dirty linen, shirts, and cleaning rags which she hung on a line to dry; she took the garbage down to the street each morning and brought up water, stopping on each landing to get her breath. And, clad like a peasant woman, basket on arm, guarding sou[7] by sou her scanty allowance, she bargained with the fruit dealers, the grocer, the butcher, and was insulted by them.

Each month notes had to be paid, and others renewed to give more time.

Her husband labored evenings to balance a tradesman's accounts, and at night, often, he copied documents at five sous a page.

And this went on for ten years.

Finally, all was paid back, everything including the exorbitant rates of the loan sharks and accumulated compound interest.

Mme. Loisel appeared an old woman now. She became heavy, rough, harsh, like one of the poor. Her hair untended, her skirts askew, her hands red, her voice shrill, she even slopped water on her floors and scrubbed them herself. But, sometimes, while her husband was at work, she would sit near the window and think of that long-ago evening when, at the dance, she had been so beautiful and admired.

---

6. **Palais Royal** (pä·le rō·yäl′): a fashionable shopping district in Paris.

7. **sou** (sōō): an old French coin, worth about a cent.

What would have happened if she had not lost that necklace? Who knows? Who can say? How strange and unpredictable life is! How little there is between happiness and misery!

Then one Sunday when she had gone for a walk on the Champs Élysées[8] to relax a bit from the week's labors, she suddenly noticed a woman strolling with a child. It was Mme. Forestier, still young-looking, still beautiful, still charming.

Mme. Loisel felt a rush of emotion. Should she speak to her? Of course. And now that everything was paid off, she would tell her the whole story. Why not?

She went toward her. "Hello, Jeanne."

The other, not recognizing her, showed astonishment at being spoken to so familiarly by this common person. She stammered, "But . . . madame . . . I don't recognize . . . You must be mistaken."

"No, I'm Mathilde Loisel."

Her friend gave a cry, "Oh, my poor Mathilde,

how you've changed!"

"Yes, I've had a hard time since last seeing you. And plenty of misfortunes—and all on account of you!"

"Of me . . . How do you mean?"

"Do you remember that diamond necklace you loaned me to wear to the dance at the Ministry?"

"Yes, but what about it?"

"Well, I lost it."

"You lost it! But you returned it."

"I brought you another just like it. And we've been paying for it for ten years now. You can imagine that wasn't easy for us who had nothing. Well, it's over now, and I am glad of it."

Mme. Forestier stopped short. "You mean to say you bought a diamond necklace to replace mine?"

"Yes. You never noticed, then? They were quite alike."

And she smiled with proud and simple joy.

Mme. Forestier, quite overcome, clasped her by the hands. "Oh, my poor Mathilde. But mine was fake. Why, at most it was worth only five hundred francs!"

---

8. **Champs Élysées** (shän·zā·lē·zā′): a famous and fashionable avenue in Paris.

Responding to the Story

Analyzing the Story

Identifying Facts

1. The working of the **irony** in this classic story depends on the **character** of its central figure, Mathilde Loisel. Name three important facts that you learn about the character of Mathilde from the first two paragraphs.
2. According to paragraphs 3 and 4, what kind of life does Mathilde want? How do her dreams contrast with the life she really leads?
3. What **actions** do the Loisels take to resolve the problem posed by the missing necklace?
4. As a result of losing the necklace, what kind of life do the Loisels begin to lead? Find the details that describe how Mathilde **changes**, both in **character** and **physical appearance**, as a result of her struggle.

Interpreting Meanings

5. When Mme. Forestier reveals the necklace was only a fake, the force of the **irony** is felt. Explain why her revelation is ironic.
6. Describe how you felt about Mathilde at the story's beginning, and how you felt about her by the time it ended. Did you suffer with her in the moment she discovers her loss and during her ten years of penance?
7. What did you think about Mathilde's husband? Did you admire him for his steadfastness, his loyalty, and his undertaking responsibility to replace the lost necklace? Or did you feel he was too indulgent with his vain Mathilde? Explain your feelings.
8. Do you think this story is critical of Mathilde only? Or do you think the writer is saying that

something is wrong with the values of a whole society? Tell why you feel as you do.

9. In one sentence or more, state what you think is the **theme** of this story. Explain whether or not you believe this theme still applies to life today.

Writing About the Story

A Creative Response

1. **Extending the Story.** Write a paragraph telling what might happen after Mme. Forestier reveals that the necklace was a fake. Does she return the difference in value between the original necklace and the one she received as a replacement? Do the Loisels now begin to live a different kind of life? Is it too late for Mathilde to recapture the past—her beauty and social triumph? Or has she learned something during those ten years that makes her unwilling to try?

2. **Writing a New Ending.** Suppose the story had another kind of ending. Suppose the Loisels had *not* lost the necklace. What kind of life do you think they would have led after the party? Would Mathilde have been happy? Would her husband have been happy? Would they have been happy with each other? Write a paragraph.

A Critical Response

3. **Responding to the Story.** In at least one paragraph, explain your response to this story's **plot** and **characters**. Tell whether or not you found the plot believable and the motives of the characters convincing. Use specific incidents from the story to support your opinion.

4. **Applying the Story to Life Today.** Could the events of this story happen today? In a paragraph, give your answer to this question. Consider these points:

   a. Could a young woman today be unhappy with her "class" as Mathilde was?

   b. How could a modern woman change her life if she felt this way?

   c. What if a couple today lost a valuable necklace—what could they do to pay the owner for it?

   d. Would a woman today be able to find a job—as Mathilde could not?

   e. Do you think a husband today would act as M. Loisel did?

Reading About the Writer

One of the world's greatest short-story writers, **Guy de Maupassant** (1850–1893) was born in Normandy, the French province that is the setting for much of his fiction. After his parents separated, de Maupassant was raised by his mother, who was a close friend of the great novelist Gustave Flaubert.

Flaubert set out to instruct the young de Maupassant in the art of fiction. He explained that good writing depends upon seeing things anew, rather than recording what people before us have thought. Flaubert also said: "Whatever you want to say, there is only one word to express it, only one verb to give it movement, only one adjective to qualify it."

For years de Maupassant sent Flaubert his writing exercises every week and then met to discuss his work over lunch. With the success of his story "Ball of Fat," de Maupassant, now aged thirty, quit his job as a minor clerk with the Naval Ministry and began to put his great energy into writing. He quickly achieved enormous popularity. In the space of eleven years, he wrote at a hectic pace and produced nearly three hundred stories and six novels. De Maupassant is best known for his stories about ordinary people caught up in unpleasant events. Many of his stories, like "The Necklace," contain surprise "whiplash" endings.

His novel *The Horla* has been called one of the most terrifying stories of madness ever written. It foretold de Maupassant's own tragic fate of illness, insanity, and early death. He died in a Paris asylum when he was only forty-two years old.

Literature & Language

Choosing Words to Create Tone

Literary Model

The following passage is from Mary Shelley's famous horror novel called *Frankenstein*. The narrator is a scientist named Dr. Frankenstein who has just accidentally created a monster in his laboratory.

It was on a dreary night of November that I beheld the accomplishment of my toils. With an anxiety that almost amounted to agony, I collected the instruments of life around me, that I might infuse a spark of being into the lifeless thing that lay at my feet. It was already one in the morning; the rain pattered dismally against the panes, and my candle was nearly burnt out, when, by the glimmer of the half-extinguished light, I saw the dull yellow eye of the creature open. It breathed hard, and a convulsive motion agitated its limbs.

How can I describe my emotions at this catastrophe, or how delineate the wretch whom with such infinite pains and care I had endeavored to form? His limbs were in proportion, and I had selected his features as beautiful. Beautiful!—Great God! His yellow skin scarcely covered the work of muscles and arteries beneath. His hair was of a lustrous black, and flowing; his teeth of a pearly whiteness. But these luxuriances only formed a more horrid contrast with his watery eyes, that seemed almost of the same color as the dun white sockets in which they were set, his shriveled complexion and straight black lips.

—from *Frankenstein*,
Mary Shelley

A Note on Diction

Diction refers to a writer's or speaker's choice of words. Writers choose words carefully in order to express their precise meanings. Writers also choose words to communicate their feelings. The writer's feeling about a subject is called **tone**. Tone can usually be summed up by one or two adjectives, such as *humorous, critical, nostalgic, sarcastic, satirical,* or *loving*.

Look at the italicized words used to describe an armored car in this passage from "The Sniper" by Liam O'Flaherty. How does the writer feel about this car?

The sniper could feel the *dull panting* of the motor. His heart beat faster. It was an *enemy* car. He wanted to fire, but he knew it was useless. His bullets would never pierce the *steel* that covered the *gray monster*.

The combined effect of the italicized words is to create a fearful, ominous tone. The car seems like a living enemy. Violence and death seem close at hand. If you changed the words, you'd create a different tone (try changing the italicized words in the last sentence to *brilliant steel* and *dove-colored little box*).

Examining the Writer's Style

Work with a partner to study the effects of Mary Shelley's word choice.

1. How do the words and phrases listed below make you feel about the setting of the passage from *Frankenstein*?

   dreary night   rain pattered dismally
   one in the morning   candle nearly burnt out

   What one word would you use to sum up the narrator's feelings about this setting?

2. Make a list of all the words and phrases in the passage that refer to Frankenstein's monstrous creation. Look for nouns as well as adjectives. What word would you use to indicate the narrator's attitude toward his creation?

Literature & Language/*cont.*

Literary Model

Here is a passage from the novel *My Ántonia* by Willa Cather. As you read, look for words that suggest how the narrator feels about the snake.

I whirled around, and there, on one of those dry gravel beds, was the biggest snake I had ever seen. He was sunning himself, after the cold night, and he must have been asleep when Ántonia screamed. When I turned, he was lying in long loose waves, like a letter "W." He twitched and began to coil slowly. He was not merely a big snake, I thought—he was a circus monstrosity. His abominable muscularity, his loathsome, fluid motion, somehow made me sick. He was as thick as my leg and looked as if millstones couldn't crush the disgusting vitality out of him. He lifted his hideous little head, and rattled. I didn't run because I didn't think of it—if my back had been against a stone wall I couldn't have felt more cornered. I saw his coils tighten—now he would spring, spring his length, I remembered. I ran up and drove at his head with my spade, struck him fairly across the neck, and in a minute he was all about my feet in wavy loops.

—from *My Ántonia*,
Willa Cather

Examining the Writer's Style

1. Make a list of all the words that describe what the snake looks like and how it moves. Then in a word or two describe the narrator's attitude toward the snake.
2. Where does the narrator tell you directly how he feels about the snake?

Creating Tone in Your Writing

1. **Writing About an Animal.** Write a description of an animal. You may write about a new pet, a wild animal, or even about an imaginary beast in a fantasy setting. Be sure that you use words to reveal the way you feel about the animal. Will you express fear, affection, horror, disgust, amusement?
   a. Using a chart like the following, begin by listing words that describe the physical features, movement, and behavior (including sounds) of your animal. Be sure the words you choose work together to communicate your general feeling about the animal.

ANIMAL: Parrot		
TONE: Amused		
Appearance	**Movement**	**Behavior**
red/white/ blue fixed gaze face forward steely eyes	jerky head flappy wings tongue darts in and out	nervous watchful croaks "Te adoro."

   b. Using the words from your list, begin writing about the animal. Make sure you describe actions as well as appearance.
   c. Share your description with a classmate. Ask this reader to describe the feeling or tone of your description. If your partner does not get the tone you intended, search for words that will express your feelings more vividly.
2. **Changing the Tone.** Because word choice determines tone, changing key words in a piece of writing should alter its tone. Try changing the tone of the passage from *Frankenstein*. You might, for example, make the tone triumphant or loving. Then change the tone of the passage from *My Ántonia* to one of admiration or awe or affection. Go back to the lists you made earlier of key words in each passage to find the words you will need to change.

COMPARING AND CONTRASTING STORIES

Writing Assignment

Write a three-paragraph essay in which you compare and contrast one of the following pairs of stories:
1. "The Sniper" (page 206) and "The Scarlet Ibis" (page 168)
2. "Red Dress" (page 187) and "The Hat" (page 143)
3. "The No-Guitar Blues" (page 72) and "Thank You, M'am" (page 77)

Background

Strictly speaking, **to compare** means "to point out similarities"; **to contrast** means "to point out differences."

When you have an assignment like this one, your first job is to decide on the stories you want to use in your essay. Select stories you have strong feelings about—nothing is worse than working with material that does not interest you. Your second job is to find the characteristics that the stories have in common. Your third job is to find the ways in which the stories are different.

As you think about the stories, concentrate on the storytelling elements. Look for similarities and differences in **plot, character, theme, point of view, and setting.**

In addition to the way they use the basic elements of fiction, stories can also be compared and contrasted in terms of their tone. **Tone** refers to the writer's attitude toward the characters and events in the story. Tone is never directly stated in a story. It is a quality you have to "pick up" from the writer's language, or "read between the lines" to discover.

Let's say you've chosen to compare and contrast "The Sniper" with "The Scarlet Ibis."

Prewriting

1. Review the two stories and take notes. Put your notes on a chart that looks like this:

	Title of story #1	Title of story #2
Plot (What happens? What is the conflict?)		
Characters (What do the characters learn? Do they change?)		
Theme (What does the story tell me about life and people?)		
Setting (Where and when do the events take place?)		
Point of view (Who tells the story?)		
Tone (How does the writer feel about the characters?)		

2. Make two lists of items from the chart. In one list, cite all the stories' similarities. In the other list, cite all their differences. Your lists might start off like this:

Similarities
a. In both stories, a brother kills his brother.
b. etc.

Differences
a. In "The Sniper" the brother is killed directly by the other brother's bullet. But in "The Scarlet Ibis" Doodle's death is only indirectly caused by his older brother.
b. etc.

3. Once you finish these lists, you will have gathered enough information for your essay. Then look over your lists and decide what your thesis statement will be. For starters, you might write something like this:

a. "The Sniper" by Liam O'Flaherty and "The

Scarlet Ibis'' by James Hurst are both about conflicts between brothers, but the stories are very different in tone. One story has a tone of horror and anger at the senselessness of war. The other story has a tone of sadness, because Doodle's brother didn't really want to cause his death.

b. "The Sniper" by Liam O'Flaherty and "The Scarlet Ibis" by James Hurst are very different in setting. The characters are also different. But the stories are alike in theme. I think both stories reveal how pressure to conform can cause death and destruction. Both stories also reveal what happens when we do not show mercy to other people.

Writing

Write your essay, organizing it like this:

1. **Paragraph 1:** Cite the titles and the authors of the stories, and state the thesis of your essay.
2. **Paragraph 2:** Discuss at least one difference between the stories.
3. **Paragraph 3:** Discuss at least one similarity between the stories, and summarize your findings in a concluding sentence.

Checklist for Revision

1. Have you cited the titles and authors of the two stories?
2. Have you opened your essay with a thesis statement?
3. Have you discussed at least one similarity and one difference between the stories?

THE ELEMENTS OF POETRY

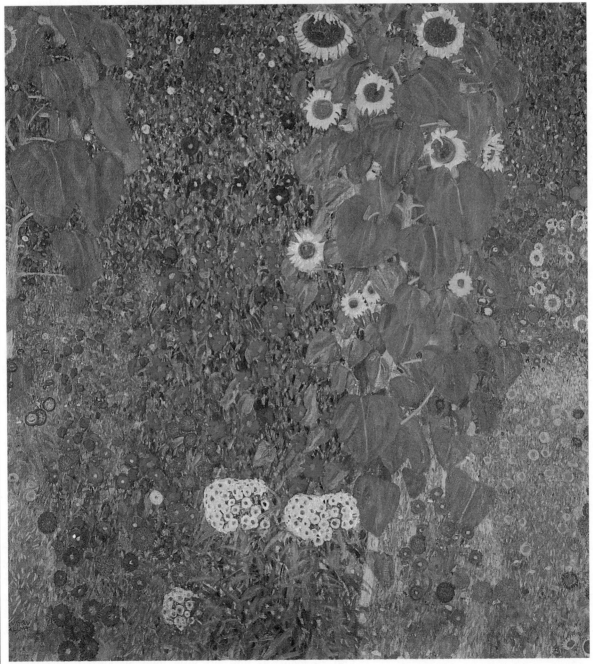

Rural Garden with Sunflowers
by Gustav Klimt (1950). Oil.

Österreichische Galerie,
Vienna/Fotostudio Otto

UNIT TWO

John Malcolm Brinnin

WHAT IS POETRY?

An introduction by **John Malcolm Brinnin**

Poetry can do a hundred and one things, delight, sadden, disturb, amuse, instruct—it may express every possible shade of emotion, and describe every conceivable kind of event, but there is only one thing that all poetry must do: it must praise all it can for being and for happening.

—W. H. Auden

The Imagination at Play

Many important books have been written to explain what poetry is, how it came to be, and how it works. But no matter how seriously we take these discussions of poetry, we must remember that poetry is also a form of playing. Just as we all play at games for the pleasure and challenge we find in them, so do poets play with words, rhymes, and rhythms. This does not mean that poets are not serious about their ideas and feelings. It means rather that poets "play" by using their imaginations.

The sounds of language provide for one kind of play. Tongue twisters are universal favorites: "A bit of better butter will make my bitter batter better" or "Sister Susie's sewing socks for soldiers." The sense of language provides for another kind of play— the play of meanings:

Motto for a Dog House
I love this little house because
It offers, after dark,
A pause for rest, a rest for paws,
A place to moor my bark.

—Arthur Guiterman

The simplest kind of play with meanings is **punning.** One kind of punning involves playing with a word that can have two different meanings at once. You'll get half the fun of Guiterman's little poem if you know two meanings for the word *bark.* Another kind of punning involves playing with words that sound the same but are spelled differently. If you spotted the word that sounds like *paws,* you caught the other pun in this poem.

Play in poetry is like any other kind of play: it lets us use our imaginations; it gives us pleasure and satisfaction. The difference between poetry and other forms of play is that in poetry, the

> "**S**enators, traffic cops, firefighters, and tax collectors have to write in language that is plain and serviceable and literally true. Otherwise, the messages they want us to get will not be clear."

Singing Birds, painted by Elisa Blackgoat when she was a student at the Montezuma Creek Elementary School, Arizona.

playing is done with words, and words, of course, always involve meaning.

Play, then, is what separates poets from other users of the language. Those who write the rules we have to obey cannot play with the language. Senators, traffic cops, firefighters, and tax collectors have to write in language that is plain and serviceable and literally true. Otherwise, the messages they want us to get will not be clear. Imagine the confusion of passengers at a lifeboat drill aboard ship if the commanding officer's voice over the loudspeaker were to tell them: "When you hear seven toot-a-toots, slip into your Mae West, and be ready to hit the drink."

A Record of Our Spiritual History

When we want to know the values, the character, and the particular genius of any country—ancient or modern—we turn first to its poets. From them we learn what statistics and charts and economic surveys cannot tell us. We learn what common experiences unite their people. We learn what they cherish from the past and what they aspire to in the future.

The English poet Percy Bysshe Shelley said that poets were "the unacknowledged legislators of the world." This means he believed that poets were law-makers, who gave expression to the values we live by. And while it would be difficult to put this conviction to any practical test, history provides much evidence to show that the minds of poets have functioned like antennae. Poets express the beliefs, hopes, and ambitions that are eventually recognized by everyone. Ultimately, these values become part of a nation's sense of identity.

Americans who want to know their own history may turn to the huge volumes of the *Congressional Record*. Americans who want to understand their history can do no better than to turn to their poets. Poets have registered every development in our national life, from the time of the Pilgrim landings to the threatening turmoil and breathtaking achievements of the days we live in. The practical language of the elected legislator supplies the record; the imaginative language of the "unacknowledged legislators" gives that record both its meaning and its spiritual dimensions.

Reading a Poem

The first thing we notice about any poem is that it looks different from a story or play. Poems are written in lines that break at certain points. When you read a poem, it is important that you know how to "read" its lines.

1. Look for punctuation in the poem indicating where sentences begin and end. Most poems are written in full sentences.

2. Do not stop at the end of a line if there is no period, comma, colon, semicolon, or dash there. If a line of poetry has no punctuation at its end, the poet intends you to read right on to the next line to complete the sense of the sentence.

3. If you have trouble with a passage of a poem, look for the subject, verb, and complement of each sentence. Try to decide what words the clauses and phrases modify.

4. Look up words you do not understand. Poetry uses few words, so every one counts.

5. Be alert for comparisons.

> "Americans who want to know their own history may turn to the huge volumes of the *Congressional Record*. Americans who want to understand their history can do no better than to turn to their poets."

6. Read the poem aloud. Poets are not likely to work in silence. You should try to **hear** the poem with your ears, as well as **understand** it with your mind, and **feel** it in your heart.

7. After you have read the poem, and answered questions on it, read it again. This time, the poem will mean much more to you.

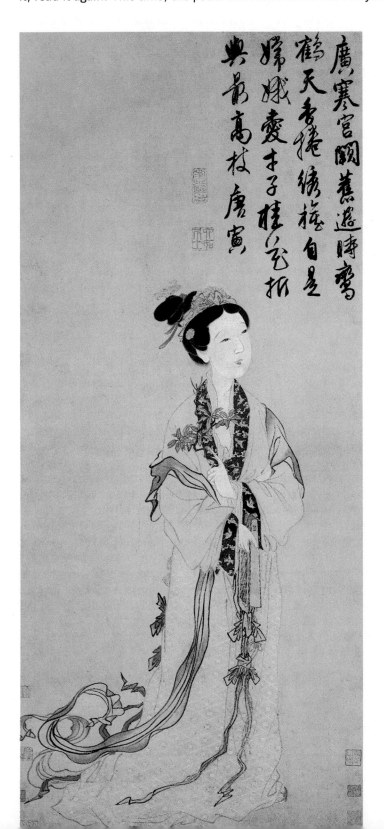

The poem in the painting was written by the artist. This poet-painter was once a famous scholar, until he was disgraced. His poem on the scroll is addressed to a woman he calls the Moon Goddess, Ch'ang O:

**She was long ago a resident of the Moon Palace,
Where phoenixes and cranes gathered, and embroidered banners fluttered in heavenly fragrance.
Ch'ang O, in love with the gifted scholar,
Presents him with the topmost branch of the cassia tree.**
—T'ang Yin

Moon Goddess Ch'ang O
by T'ang Yin (15th century).
Ink and colors on paper.

The Metropolitan Museum of Art, Gift of Douglas Dillon, 1981. (1981.4.2)

What Is Poetry?   233

Imagery: Seeing Things Freshly

Imagery is one of the elements that gives poetry its forcefulness. Images are basically copies of things you can see. Photographers usually attempt to make exact copies of what they see. Poets work with language, so they can't make exact copies of the world. But poets do try to capture in a few exact words those particular aspects of things that will help us see them freshly.

Images in poetry can do even more than help us see things. An **image** is a single word or a phrase that appeals to one of our senses. An image can help us see color or motion. Sometimes it can also help us hear a sound, smell an odor, feel texture or temperature, or even taste a sweet, sour, or salty flavor.

Suppose you come across an old house that has been empty for years. If you were going to photograph the house, you'd probably give us the kind of image we call realistic—the house caught by the camera's eye, just as it might be recorded by the human eye. "The camera never lies," we say, and though this isn't always true, we usually accept a photograph in the same way we accept a document—as a register of fact.

But suppose you were an artist and wanted to paint a portrait of the house. You would now emphasize certain aspects of the house—certain features would be deliberately distorted, and certain features might even be omitted. As an artist, you might emphasize the age of the house by making its siding look as worn and wrinkled and cracked as an old shoe. Or you might emphasize the emptiness of the house by painting clouds reflected in windows without curtains and doors opening onto deserted hallways. In each case, as an artist, you would give the actual visual thing (the house) a certain twist, a particular shading.

So it is with poets. Edwin Arlington Robinson saw an empty house and emphasized its loneliness:

Through broken walls and gray
The winds blow bleak and shrill;
They are all gone away.

—from "The House on the Hill,"
Edwin Arlington Robinson

Robert Frost saw an empty house and emphasized the new life that had moved in:

> "There are bees in this wall." He struck the clapboards,
> Fierce heads looked out; small bodies pivoted.
> We rose to go. Sunset blazed on the windows.
>
> —from "The Black Cottage,"
> Robert Frost

Imagery is part of a poet's style. It is the product of the poet's own way of seeing the world. Just as we learn to recognize certain painters at once by noticing the colors and shapes that mark their works, so we learn to identify poets by paying attention to their imagery. Of course, the time and place in which poets live determine the kind of imagery they use. Poets who live in cities will usually draw upon the street scenes and industrial landscapes they know so well. Poets who live far from cities will usually draw their images from what they see of country life.

Imagery and Feelings

An image can be so fresh, so powerful, that it can speak to our deepest feelings. An image can be so phrased that it makes us feel joy or grief, wonder or horror, love or disgust.

Here is a poem that uses images to help us see a scene on the Great Lakes, and to hear the sounds made by a boat lost in the mist. But what readers remember most about this little poem is the way the images make them feel:

> **Lost**
> Desolate and lone
> All night long on the lake
> Where fog trails and mist creeps,
> The whistle of a boat
> Calls and cries unendingly,
> Like some lost child
> In tears and trouble
> Hunting the harbor's breast
> And the harbor's eyes.
>
> —Carl Sandburg

Certain images here help us see the scene at once: night, a lake, fog trailing, mist creeping, a desolate and lonely boat. Other images help us hear the boat's whistle and cries. The long, sad "o" sounds in the first two lines even echo the sound of the foghorn. But the most powerful image in the poem is the last one, which makes us see the lost boat as a child hunting for its mother. It would be hard to read this poem without sensing the loneliness of all lost things, searching for the docks and the lights of their own harbors.

> "An image can be so fresh, so powerful, that it can speak to our deepest feelings."

The title of this poem has to be read as its first
line. When you get to line 4, stop and decide who
"I"—the speaker—is.

If the Owl Calls Again

John Haines

At dusk
from the island in the river
and it's not too cold,

I'll wait for the moon
5   to rise,

then take wing and glide
to meet him.

We will not speak,
but hooded against the frost
10   soar above
the alder flats, searching
with tawny eyes.

And then we'll sit
in the shadowy spruce and
15   pick the bones
of careless mice,
while the long moon drifts
toward Asia
and the river mutters
20   in its icy bed.

And when morning climbs
the limbs
we'll part without a sound,

fulfilled, floating
25   homeward as
the cold world awakens.

Responding to the Poem

Analyzing the Poem

Identifying Details

1. Look at the first three stanzas, and describe what this speaker imagines he will do if the owl calls again.
2. When will the imagined flight begin, and when will it end? What fact about owls does this remind you of?
3. What **images** help you visualize this scene? What **image** tells you how the river sounds?

Interpreting Meanings

4. What would the owl and his companion be "searching" for? (line 11) Why are the mice "careless"?
5. Does the speaker think he'll enjoy his flight, or will it be painful or sad? Which word in the last stanza tells you how he'd feel?
6. These questions have assumed that the speaker of the poem is the poet. Who or what else could this speaker be?
7. Have you ever wondered what an animal's life was like? What do you think you might discover if you could share an animal's perceptions and experiences for a day?

Writing About the Poem

A Creative Response

1. **Creating Images.** Write a paragraph entitled "When the ——— Calls Again." Imitate Haines's fantasy, but have the call come from another creature: grizzly bear, tiger, hawk, cobra, earthworm, robin, mole, seagull, cat. Use at least three images to help your reader see, smell, or taste what you would experience if you accompanied this creature on its daily rounds.

A Critical Response

2. **Explaining an Opinion.** Read the comment by John Haines that follows. What details in this comment relate to the poem you have just read? Quote from the poem to support your opinion. Write one paragraph.

Reading About the Writer

John Haines (1924–   ) homesteaded for years in the Alaskan wilderness. Drawing upon that experience, he writes of a cold, white landscape in which humans are only incidental. Their thinking minds become but a small factor in a world that is governed by instinct. For readers whose idea of Alaska has been formed by "The Cremation of Sam McGee" and other rousing ballads by Robert W. Service, the work of John Haines is a revelation. Another of his poems appears on page 272 of this book.

Focusing on Background
A Comment from the Poet

"When you live a long time alone in the woods, with mostly animals for companions, some strange things happen inside your head. It is as if an older consciousness of nature, overgrown by education, slowly begins to reassert itself—the barriers come down, and the lines between human and animal, between yourself and the forest world, become indistinct. Something like the ancient religious dread comes back to claim its territory. I feel that this was the case with me at the time. And the evidence is there in the poems, if it is anywhere."

—John Haines

Bats are mammals. Like those other mammals, porpoises, bats have long fascinated humans because they behave in ways that most mammals do not. Unlike nearly all other mammals, bats fly and porpoises live under water. It is easy to forget that, like all other mammals, they nourish their young with milk. No matter how much we learn about their habits, bats remain mysterious. Some people once regarded bats as taboo. They shunned them as food because they thought they were a "crossed species"—part bird and part furry animal. Before you read, name all the things you think of when you look at this picture of a bat.

The Bat

Theodore Roethke

By day the bat is cousin to the mouse.
He likes the attic of an aging house.

His fingers make a hat about his head.
His pulse beat is so slow we think him dead.

5   He loops in crazy figures half the night
Among the trees that face the corner light.

But when he brushes up against a screen,
We are afraid of what our eyes have seen:

For something is amiss or out of place
10   When mice with wings can wear a human face.

Responding to the Poem

Analyzing the Poem

Identifying Details

1. This poet presents **images** of a daytime bat and of a nighttime bat. How does he describe a bat during the day?
2. In contrast, what does the bat do at night?
3. What three creatures does the poet see combined in the bat, according to the last line?

Interpreting Meanings

4. What are the "fingers" of the bat? How could they seem to make a hat about his head?

5. If we call someone "batty," what do we mean? What **image** of the bat's behavior at night explains how this comparison came to be used?
6. Everything in this poem builds up to one strong final **image**. This is the picture of the bat the poet wants his readers to keep. Why do you think this image makes the speaker feel afraid?

Writing About the Poem

A Creative Response

1. **Extending the Poem.** What other creatures with humanlike faces or humanlike ways might make

some people—not everyone—feel that something is amiss or out of place? Write a brief paragraph in which you name three of these creatures. Explain what feature or action makes these creatures seem almost human.

A Critical Response

2. **Writing About Images.** Write a paragraph naming three images used in this poem that help you imagine the bat the poet is describing. Name two images that help you see the bat and one image that helps you hear it. At the end of your paragraph, tell whether the poem succeeded in making you feel something about bats.

Reading About the Writer

Theodore Roethke (1908–1963) was a big, bearish man who wrote with great delicacy about small creatures and with great tenderness about the formative experiences of his own life. Roethke's great poetic theme was the secret life of nature and the mysterious ways in which nature is reflected in human life. Born in Michigan to a family of German immigrants, he achieved an outstanding reputation as a teacher at Penn State, at Bennington College in Vermont, and at the University of Washington in Seattle. He died at the height of a much-honored and still-expanding poetic career. Another of his poems appears on page 340 of this book.

The speaker of this poem is a mother, who is combing her daughter's hair. As you read, let her words create pictures in your mind. You will see several generations of mothers and daughters, as the speaker takes you back into time. Before you read, you should know that *plaiting* (plāt′ing) means "braiding."

Combing

Gladys Cardiff

Bending, I bow my head
And lay my hand upon
Her hair, combing, and think
How women do this for
5   Each other. My daughter's hair
Curls against the comb,
Wet and fragrant—orange
Parings. Her face, downcast,
Is quiet for one so young.

10   I take her place. Beneath
My mother's hands I feel
The braids drawn up tight
As a piano wire and singing,
Vinegar-rinsed. Sitting
15   Before the oven I hear
The orange coils tick
The early hour before school.

She combed her grandmother
Mathilda's hair using
20   A comb made out of bone.
Mathilda rocked her oak wood
Chair, her face downcast,
Intent on tearing rags
In strips to braid a cotton
25   Rug from bits of orange
And brown. A simple act,

Preparing hair. Something
Women do for each other,
Plaiting the generations.

Responding to the Poem

Analyzing the Poem

Identifying Details
1. In the first stanza, what does this mother think as she lays her hand on her daughter's hair?
2. In the second stanza, who is sitting and who is doing the combing? Who is combing and who is in the chair in the third stanza?
3. What lines help you **smell** a fragrance, **feel** the tightness of braids, and **hear** a clock?

Interpreting Meanings
4. What does the poet mean when she says that "preparing hair" is "plaiting the generations"?
5. What single color do you see in all three stanzas? Describe what you **see** each time this color is mentioned.
6. What do you think the speaker means by "singing" in line 13?
7. What other things do family members do for each other that tie or braid generations together?

Writing About the Poem

A Creative Response
Using Verb Forms in a Poem. This poem consists of many *-ing* words. (Before you start to write your own poem, make a list of all the *-ing* words you can find in "Combing," beginning with the title.) Then write at least three lines of a poem in which you use *-ing* words to describe a scene from your own childhood.

Before you write, picture in your mind the scene you want to describe, and jot down various verbs that describe what you see happening. Open each line of your poem with one of your *-ing* words, like this:

> Waking . . .
> Hopping . . .
> Looking . . .

Illustrating the Poem

Make a collage (kə·läzh) illustrating the scenes you see in this poem. A **collage** is a picture that consists of bits of many different materials, all arranged together to make a picture that satisfies the artist. Collages might consist of images from magazines, newsprint, words, scraps of material, flowers, seeds, stones, etc. Before you start to collect your images, decide what color you'd like to dominate your collage. Do you want to suggest a happy or a sad mood?

Reading About the Writer
Gladys Cardiff (1942–   ) had a Cherokee father and an Irish/Welsh mother. She was born in Montana, where her parents taught on the Blackfoot Reservation, and she grew up in Seattle. Cardiff says that writing for her is an art of celebration. She especially connects her poetry with an old Cherokee blessing and prayer: "Let the paths from every direction recognize each other."

The most famous form of Japanese poetry is *haiku*. (English speakers say hī′ kōō. In Japanese, the word has three syllables and, since Japanese is unaccented, all syllables are given the same emphasis: ha·i·ku.) Using only three lines and—in the original Japanese—only seventeen syllables, haiku work by means of suggestion. They use a few precise images to capture the feeling of a single moment. As you read these haiku, see if you can visualize the scene so briefly sketched in each poem. Then let this scene serve as the starting-off place for a train of your own thoughts and feelings.

Haiku

Get out of my road
and allow me to plant these
bamboos, Mr. Toad.

        —Miura Chora

A morning glory
Twined round the bucket:
I will ask my neighbor
    for water.

        —Chiyo

The old pond;
A frog jumps in:
Sound of water.

        —Matsuo Bashō

A dragonfly!
The distant hills
Reflected in his eyes.

        —Kobayashi Issa

Morning Glories by Suzuki Kiitsu (detail from a six-fold screen) (19th century). Color and gold leaf on paper.

The Metropolitan Museum of Art, New York, Seymour Fund, 1954. (54.69.1)

Responding to the Poems

Here are some of the many characteristics of haiku. Can you find each of these features in the haiku here? Are there variations?

1. A haiku has only seventeen syllables—five syllables in lines 1 and 3 and seven syllables in line 2.
2. A haiku usually presents images from daily life.
3. A haiku often brings together two images for comparison.
4. A haiku usually contains a seasonal word or suggestion or symbol (*kigo*).
5. A haiku presents a sudden moment of discovery—a moment of enlightenment (*satori*).

Try writing haiku of your own. Before you write, jot down the images you will want to present, to describe each single fleeting moment. For each haiku, try to use a seasonal word or clue.

Analyzing Language and Vocabulary

A Problem for Translators

Haiku are written as if they were telegrams and each word cost money. The Japanese language has no articles (*a, an, the*), practically no pronouns, and in general does not indicate whether a noun is singular or plural. Moreover, it is expected that the recipients of the haiku "telegram"—the readers—will add their own associations to the poet's.

Obviously, translating such condensed poetry into English is a great challenge, especially since English usually needs more than seventeen syllables to express the original haiku's ideas completely. Translations of haiku usually differ greatly.

Perhaps the most famous haiku (at least to English speakers) is the one here by Bashō, about the pond and the frog. Compare that translation with these versions:

An old silent pond . . .
  Into the pond a frog jumps
Splash! Silence again.

—Translated by Peter Beilenson
    and Harry Behn

Tired old pool, asleep
  When suddenly a frog leaps
Then water-ripple!

—Translated by Richard Foerster

Here is Bashō's haiku in the original Japanese, with the English translation provided. You might want to try your own translation. (*Ya* is a word frequently used in haiku to mean something like "Lo!" Translators often indicate it with a colon, since it suggests a kind of equation.)

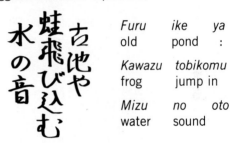

Furu	*ike*	*ya*
old	pond	:
Kawazu	*tobikomu*	
frog	jump in	
Mizu	*no*	*oto*
water		sound

Reading About the Writers

Miura Chora (1729–1780) wrote in the middle of a long period of peace, called the Tokugawa Period. Like the other poets here, he draws his images from very ordinary things, such as this toad.

Chiyo (1703–1775) was the greatest of the women haiku writers. Some people claim her poems are not true haiku because they are too explicit. These critics say her poems are not suggestive enough. But Chiyo's admirers remind us that some people mistake "haziness" in haiku for profound thought. (There are many bad haiku out there!)

Matsuo Bashō (1644–1694) is considered the developer of the haiku form as well as its greatest master. Bashō was a deeply spiritual man who became a Zen monk in his later years. His haiku show a zest for life, a sense that nothing is unimportant, and an awareness that all things in life are related.

Kobayashi Issa's life (1763–1828) was very sad, but his poetry is very human, full of tender simplicity and wry humor. Many of his haiku, like the one here, deal affectionately with insects.

Southbound on the Freeway

May Swenson

A tourist came in from Orbitville,
parked in the air, and said:

The creatures of this star
are made of metal and glass.

5   Through the transparent parts
you can see their guts.

Their feet are round and roll
on diagrams—or long

measuring tapes—dark
10   with white lines.

They have four eyes.
The two in the back are red.

Sometimes you can see a 5-eyed
one, with a red eye turning

15   on the top of his head.
He must be special—

the others respect him,
and go slow,

when he passes, winding
20   among them from behind.

They all hiss as they glide,
like inches, down the marked

tapes. Those soft shapes,
shadowy inside

25   the hard bodies—are they
their guts or their brains?

Responding to the Poem

Analyzing the Poem

Identifying Details

1. What **images** help you to see the creatures that the tourist sees?
2. What **images** help you hear the sounds the creatures make?
3. Which important detail about these creatures does the tourist mention twice? What *are* the "soft shapes"? What does the tourist think they might be?

Interpreting Meanings

4. Part of our enjoyment of this riddle comes from trying to figure out exactly what the visitor is looking at. What *are* their "feet," the "measuring tapes," and their "eyes"?
5. Why do "the others" have respect for the "5-eyed one"?
6. It could be that for all of her humor, this poet may be making a serious comment about life on Earth. If so, what do you suspect she might be saying about us and our dependence on machines?

Writing About the Poem

A Creative Response

1. **Describing a Sight.** Suppose this visitor landed at the Super Bowl during the football game. In a brief paragraph or poem, describe this sight from the point of view of the visitor. Use the first two lines of this poem as your opening.

A Critical Response

2. **Expressing a Response to a Poem.** Read May Swenson's comment on her poem, which follows. Then write your response to what she says about her own poem and about poetry in general. In your response, include an explanation of how the poem affected you.

Reading About the Writer

May Swenson (1919–   ), born in Utah, has lived most of her adult life in or near New York City. Her poems are often characterized by their unusual forms—some of them make unique typographical patterns up and down a page or across it. Swenson has a gift for close observation of animal life and of the curiosities of human existence.

Focusing on Background
A Comment from the Poet

" 'Southbound on the Freeway' makes you see, feel, and experience something *before* you know its name. That's why neither the title nor the text specifically states what is being described. *You* discover the answer, solve the poem like a riddle, by reading it. Just as a visitor from a planet different from Earth could mistake our speeding cars for the inhabitants and might suppose the people in them to be guts or brains—so we, closely examining something for the first time, might reach imaginative conclusions—ones that contain kernels of symbolic truth. Once you discover what each poem is *about,* and name the subject for yourself, next you might notice what is hinted at beyond that: Haven't cars in our world really become more conspicuous, more important than people? Remember, however, that poems don't *have to* carry messages or have purposes, other than to arouse and surprise you and wake up all your senses. Let them give you a new and unexpected view of things, especially things already familiar and quite ordinary."

—May Swenson

Literature & Language

Using Imagery

1. To see how images can be drawn from all sorts of things we observe in life, create two images for each of the following categories. Have one image suggest something pleasant and the other suggest something unpleasant. Try to include images that suggest how a thing looks, smells, tastes, sounds, or feels to touch.

	Pleasant	Unpleasant
Animal images		
Flower (or plant) images		
Water images		
Sky images		
Earth images		
City images		
Country images		

2. In each of the following quotations, tell what sensation the image or images evoke (sight, sound, taste, touch, smell). Explain whether each sensation is unpleasant or pleasant, and cite the words that evoke those feelings.

   a. The sun that brief December day
      Rose cheerless over hills of gray

      —from "Snowbound,"
      John Greenleaf Whittier

   b. . . . a mile of warm sea-scented beach
      —from "Meeting at Night,"
      Robert Browning

   c. The tossing, blooming, perfumed grass
      —from "The Flower-Fed Buffaloes,"
      Vachel Lindsay

   d. The doors are twisted on broken hinges.
      Sheets of rain swish through on the wind.
      —from "Four Preludes on Playthings
      of the Wind," Carl Sandburg

   e. He stirred his velvet head
      Like one in danger . . .
      —from "A Bird Came Down the Walk,"
      Emily Dickinson

3. Suppose we were to describe that bird's head with a different adjective:

   He stirred his flea-bitten head.
   He stirred his snakelike head.
   He stirred his bony head.

   Would you feel differently about the bird or about touching his head? Rewrite the other images in item 2, using descriptive words that evoke different emotions.

4. The following poem was written when the poet was a forest-fire lookout on Sourdough Mountain, in the state of Washington. His poem consists of little more than a series of very precise images. (You'll get the sense of this poem if you pause slightly at the end of each line—whether or not a mark of punctuation is used.)

   Mid-August at Sourdough Mountain Lookout
   Down valley a smoke haze
   Three days heat, after five days rain
   Pitch glows on the fir-cones
   Across rocks and meadows
   Swarms of new flies.

   I cannot remember things I once read
   A few friends, but they are in cities.
   Drinking cold snow-water from a tin cup
   Looking down for miles
   Through high still air.

   —Gary Snyder

   a. List the images in Snyder's poem that appeal to four of your senses: to sight, touch (sensations of heat and cold), hearing, and taste.
   b. Considering all these images, tell how you think the speaker feels about where he is and what he is doing.

5. The next poem was written by a poet who was a member of a group of writers who thought that imagery was the most important element of poetry. She and her friends tried to find hard and

precise images that would carry the emotion and message of a poem almost instantly.

Music

The neighbor sits in his window and plays
    the flute.
From my bed I can hear him,
And the round notes flutter and tap about
    the room,
And hit against each other,
Blurring to unexpected chords.
It is very beautiful,
With the little flute-notes all about me,
In the darkness.

In the daytime,
The neighbor eats bread and onions with
    one hand
And copies music with the other.
He is fat and has a bald head,
So I do not look at him,
But run quickly past his window.
There is always the sky to look at,
Or the water in the well!

But when night comes and he plays his
    flute,
I think of him as a young man,
With gold seals hanging from his watch,
And a blue coat with silver buttons.
As I lie in my bed
The flute-notes push against my ears and
    lips,
And I go to sleep, dreaming.

—Amy Lowell

a. What images in the first stanza help you hear what the speaker hears in the darkness?

b. What sights does the speaker see in the daytime? What do you think she smells?

c. The speaker calls the sounds in the first stanza "beautiful." How would you describe the way she feels about the sights in the second stanza?

d. How do night and the sounds transform what she sees in daytime (in the last stanza)?

e. How do you think the speaker feels about the musician of her imagination? Why?

Writing

Using Images in a Poem. Here are four groups of nouns. Take one of these groups and create images for a poem of your own. (You can replace any of these nouns if you wish to.) Before you write, decide what emotion you would like to express.

1. window, door, mirror, frame, mist, moonlight
2. shadow, streetlamp, puddle, gutter, paper
3. field, sun, soccer ball, sneaker, blade of grass
4. shop, saw, wood, dust, ray of light, thumb

IDENTIFYING IMPLIED IDEAS

Writing Assignment

In a paragraph, state the main idea implied in the poem "The Gift" by Louise Glück. If you do not understand any part of the poem, say so. In a second paragraph, tell how you responded to the poem and give reasons for your response.

Background

Poetry uses the language of suggestion, rather than the language of direct statement. This means that every time we read poetry we must identify implied ideas. For us readers, this is part of the pleasure of reading poetry: we must use our own minds and imaginations to reach for the meaning that the poet only hints at.

Any **implied idea** is an idea that is suggested, rather than one that is directly stated. The reader or observer must make an **inference,** or educated guess, about what the implied idea is. The interesting thing about the poem "Southbound on the Freeway" is that the tourist from Orbitville makes the wrong inference as he looks down at the highway. He sees all the visual clues, but his educated guess is wrong.

You have had to make inferences about meaning in all the poems you've read so far. For examples:

1. In Sandburg's poem on page 235, you have to make an **inference** about whom or what the title "Lost" refers to. What guess did you make? What evidence did you base your guess on?

2. In Haines's poem on page 236, what **inference** did you make to explain why the mice would be called "careless" in line 16? (Another way of posing the same question is to ask: What does the poet imply happened to the mice?) Did clues in the poem help you infer the meaning of the line? Or do you know this answer from your own experience?

3. In Roethke's poem on page 238, you have to make an **inference** as to what Roethke is referring to in the last line. What is he referring to when he talks of "mice"? What evidence in the poem helps you make this inference?

4. In Cardiff's poem "Combing" on page 240, you have to **infer** whom the pronoun *she* refers to in line 18.

5. In Cardiff's poem you also have to make more complex **inferences.** You have to infer what the "orange parings" are in lines 7–8 (there is no orange in the poem). You also have to infer what the poet means by "plaiting the generations" in the final line.

6. In Chiyo's haiku on page 242, you have to **infer** why the speaker does not use the well, but instead asks his neighbor for water. Unless you make this inference, you will miss the whole point of the poem.

7. In Snyder's poem on page 246, you have to make an **inference** to decide how the poet feels about his setting: does he like it, or is he unhappy? What is your guess? What details in the poem allow you to make this inference? Do you think your inference is fully justified, or could someone else disagree with it?

Prewriting

1. To do the writing assignment above, you first have to read "The Gift" carefully. When you have an assignment like this, it is a good idea to ask yourself questions as you read. Write your questions down, and try to answer them as you go along. Here is a sample of the questions one reader asked as the poem was read:

The Gift

Lord, You may not recognize me
speaking for someone else.
I have a son. He is
so little, so ignorant.
He likes to stand
at the screen door calling
oggie, oggie, entering
language, and sometimes
a dog will stop and come up
the walk, perhaps
accidentally. May he believe
this is not an accident?
At the screen
welcoming each beast in
love's name, Your emissary.

—Louise Glück

What could the title mean? (I don't know yet.)

Whom is the speaker addressing? (The Lord; this sounds like a prayer.)

Whom is she speaking for? (Her son)

Does she mean that her son is dumb, or that he is not aware of the harsh realities of life?

What does *oggie* refer to? (A dog; I see in the next lines.)

"Entering language": probably the little boy is just learning to talk?

What happens when he calls a dog? (It comes, sometimes.)

What does she ask the Lord? (That her son will believe the dogs come to him *because* he calls them, not by accident.)

Who is welcoming each beast? (Her son)

Whom does *Your* refer to? (It must be the Lord because the *Y* is capitalized.)

What is an emissary? (A person sent on a specific mission; this must mean that the little son is sent by the Lord to show how much God loves all creatures.)

2. You might have questions that are very different from these. If so, write them down and provide the answers. If you don't know the answers, you might ask to discuss your questions in class.

3. Now decide what you think the title means. Based on your close reading of the poem, make inferences to answer these questions: **Who or what is the gift? Who has received the gift? Who has sent it?**

4. **What is the meaning of the poem, as you see it?** Write a statement explaining the meaning or "message" the poet is sharing with you.

5. As you formulate your statement of what the poem means, think also about this question: **In your opinion, what is the most important word in the poem?**

Writing

Now you should be ready to write your paragraph. You could organize your material in one of two ways.

1. You could state the main idea of the poem in your opening sentence. Then you could provide details from the poem to support your inference.

2. Or, you could first sum up what the poem "says," line by line. Then, in the final statement of the paragraph, you could state the general meaning of the poem, as you infer it.

3. Perhaps you do not fully understand the meaning of the poem. If this happens, say so in your paragraph, and cite the particular lines or words that puzzle you.

4. If you wish, in another paragraph, tell how you responded to the poem. Did it remind you of any experiences of your own? Be specific.

Checklist for Revision

1. Have you cited the title and author?
2. Have you stated clearly the meaning of the poem, as you see it, in either your first sentence or your last one?
3. Have you cited details from the poem to support your interpretation?
4. If any parts of the poem continue to puzzle you, have you explained clearly which parts these were, citing lines or words?

Similes and Metaphors: Seeing Connections

> Poetry is simply made of metaphor. So also is philosophy—and science, too, for that matter. . . . Every poem is a new metaphor inside or it is nothing. And there is a sense in which all poems are the same old metaphor always.
>
> —Robert Frost

One of the ways that poets play with language is by using figurative language—expressions which put aside literal meanings in favor of imaginative connections. A **figure of speech** is always based on a comparison, and it is not literally true. If someone says to you, "Listen, I'm going to give you a piece of my mind," you don't say, "OK, I'll bring a plate to put it on." You understand that the speaker is using a figure of speech. You might even respond with another figure of speech: "Keep your shirt on" or "Spill it" or "Cool it!"

Figurative language can be a kind of shorthand. An idea that, on a literal level, would have to be spelled out is, on an imaginative level, instantly communicated. Think of all the words you'd have to use to explain, literally, what these common expressions say at once: "Judy's uptight." "The check bounced." "Gilford's laid back." "Let's wrap it up." "Keep it on the back burner."

Connections between two very different things are what give figurative language its meaning. One thing is always seen in terms of something else. When we say, "Put it on the back burner," we're talking about some project or idea as if it were a pot of stew that doesn't need the cook's immediate attention and therefore can be put on the back burner of a stove.

Figures of Speech in Everyday Language

Many figures of speech that were once fresh and original have been completely absorbed into our everyday language. We use them without realizing that they are not literally true. When we think about our language, in fact, we realize that figures of speech are the foundation of thousands and thousands of expressions.

When we refer to the "roof of the mouth" or the "arm of the chair" or the "foot of the bed," we are using figurative language. In each case, we are imaginatively relating a part of the body to things that have nothing to do with the body.

Try this experiment: Pretend you are a person from another country who knows the English language only on a literal level. You have no idea of the figures of speech that are commonplace to Americans. Then, imagine how you'd feel if one morning a new American friend of yours (say a newspaper reporter) were to tell you that he was "off to the salt mines," where he was really "in the doghouse." It seems that yesterday he'd been "barking up the wrong tree" on an important story and had ended up with "egg all over his face." When his boss threatened to "give him the ax" if he didn't "get on the ball," he "saw red" and "blew his top," telling the boss to "take a hike." For a while, "the fur was flying," but then he realized that he'd better "simmer down," "get off his high horse," "eat crow," and "pass the peace pipe," even though the guy "drove him up the wall." Otherwise, the "fat would really be in the fire," because he had to "bring home the bacon."

Even the languages of science and business are based on figures of speech. Dentists talk about "building bridges." Biologists talk about "the bloodstream." Stockbrokers talk about "the market crash." Even our newest technology, computer science, has already coined its own figures of speech in terms such as "menus," "bugs," "windows," "software," and "hardware."

Similes

A simile is the very simplest form of figurative language. In a **simile,** two dissimilar things are clearly compared by words such as *like, as, than,* or *resembles.* "The moon shines *like* a fifty-cent piece." "Eva's eyes are *as* green *as* emeralds." "Lucy feels lighter *than* a grasshopper." Like all figures of speech, similes make new connections between familiar objects or feelings. Good similes reveal hidden connections between things we never thought had anything in common.

Here is a poem that uses an unusual simile to describe an ordinary fork:

Fork

This strange thing must have crept
Right out of hell.
It resembles a bird's foot
Worn around the cannibal's neck.

As you hold it in your hand,
As you stab with it into a piece of meat,
It is possible to imagine the rest of the bird:
Its head which like your fist
Is large, bald, beakless, and blind.

—Charles Simic

Metaphors

Similes are easily recognized because of the connectives they contain (*like, as, than,* or *resembles*): "My head is *like* a disorganized file cabinet," or "The sky is *as* green *as* pea soup." When the connective is omitted, we have a metaphor: "My head *is* a disorganized file cabinet," or "The sky *is* a bowl of pea soup." A **metaphor,** then, is a comparison between two unlike things, in which one thing becomes another thing without the use of the word *like, as, than,* or *resembles.* The difference between a met-

> "**E**ven the languages of science and business are based on figures of speech. Dentists talk about 'building bridges.' Stockbrokers talk about 'the market crash.'"

Simile using the word *resembles* compares the fork to a bird's foot.

Simile using the word *like* compares the person's fist to the bird's head.

aphor and a simile is a matter of emphasis. In a simile, the two things remain separate ("My head is *like* a disorganized file cabinet"), but in a metaphor they are united ("My head *is* a disorganized file cabinet," or "The file cabinet in my head is disorganized").

A metaphor can be direct or implied. A **direct metaphor** directly compares the two things by the use of a verb such as *is*. An **implied metaphor** implies or suggests the comparison between the two things, without using *is*. If we say "The city is a sleeping woman," we are using a direct metaphor. If we say "The city sleeps peacefully," we use an implied metaphor. Both metaphors identify a city that has its lights out with a person who has quietly fallen into the darkness of sleep.

Here is a poem that uses the two kinds of metaphor: direct and implied.

First Snow

The old black dog comes in one evening
with the first few snowflakes on his back
and falls asleep, throwing his bad leg out
at our excitement. This is the night
when one of us gets to say, as if it were news,
that no two snowflakes are ever alike;
the night when each of us remembers something
snowier. The kitchen is a kindergarten
steamy with stories. The dog gets stiffly up
and limps away, seeking a quiet spot
at the heart of the house. Outside,
in silence, with diamonds in his fur,
the winter night curls round the legs of the trees,
sleepily blinking snowflakes from his lashes.

—Ted Kooser

If you look closely, you'll see two other implied metaphors in the poem: the "heart of the house" and the "legs of the trees." We know that a house does not literally have a heart and that trees do not have legs. But if we use our imagination, we can "see" how the life-center of a home can be like the heart that gives life to the body, just as the long trunks of a tree are like the legs that support a body.

Metaphor is the most flexible and suggestive element of figurative language. It is a means by which all experience can be imaginatively connected. According to an old Hebrew saying, "The world is a wedding"—and in that, we have a single metaphor that defines all metaphors.

Metaphor directly identifies the kitchen with a kindergarten where stories are told.

Metaphor implies that the snowflakes are diamonds.
Metaphor implies that the winter night is a sleeping animal.

"According to an old Hebrew saying, 'The world is a wedding'—and in that, we have a single metaphor that defines all metaphors."

When the playwright Lorraine Hansberry wrote a play about the hopes and courage and defeats of a black family in America, it was quite natural that she would find her title in one of the lines from this poem: *A Raisin in the Sun*.

Harlem

Langston Hughes

What happens to a dream deferred?

Does it dry up
like a raisin in the sun?
Or fester like a sore—
5   And then run?
Does it stink like rotten meat?
Or crust and sugar over—
like a syrupy sweet?

Maybe it just sags
10   like a heavy load.

Or does it explode?

Responding to the Poem

Analyzing the Poem

Identifying Details

1. What do you think the "dream" is?
2. How would you define "a dream deferred"?
3. What five **similes** does the poet use to restate the first question—that is, to what does he compare a "dream deferred"?

Interpreting Meanings

4. What final **metaphor** is implied when the poet uses the word "explode"—what are we to understand that the dream has become? Why might a "dream deferred" one day "explode"?
5. What is the significance of the poem's title? Would the title "Iowa City" or "Palm Beach" do just as well? Why?
6. Do you think this poem still has a message for people today? Explain.

Writing About the Poem

A Critical Response

Analyzing Figures of Speech. To be effective, metaphors and similes have to make some kind of sense. In six sentences, tell how a "dream deferred" could "dry up," "fester," "stink," "crust and sugar over," "sag," and "explode."

Reading About the Writer

Langston Hughes (1902–1967) was the most widely read and influential black poet of his time. That enormous area of New York City known as Harlem was the source of much of his writing—particularly in the 1920's and 1930's, when Harlem was the flourishing center of black culture in music, dance, and fashion. A great part of Hughes's inspiration came from the rhythms and diction of jazz.

This poem is a riddle; it describes its subject, but does not name it. As you read the poem, monitor your reading. Note the questions that come to your mind. Note words or passages that puzzle you. Note where you had to stop and re-read. Then discuss your responses in class. (You might find help under "Analyzing Language and Vocabulary" on the next page.)

A Narrow Fellow in the Grass

Emily Dickinson

A narrow fellow in the grass
Occasionally rides;
You may have met him—did you not?
His notice sudden is.

5   The grass divides as with a comb,
A spotted shaft is seen;
And then it closes at your feet
And opens further on.

He likes a boggy acre,
10 A floor too cool for corn.
Yet when a boy, and barefoot,
I more than once, at noon,

Have passed, I thought, a whip-lash
Unbraiding in the sun—
15 When, stooping to secure it,
It wrinkled, and was gone.

Several of nature's people
I know, and they know me;
I feel for them a transport
20 Of cordiality;°

But never met this fellow,
Attended or alone,
Without a tighter breathing,
And zero at the bone.

20. **cordiality:** friendly feelings.

Responding to the Poem

Analyzing the Poem

Identifying Details

1. Who or what is the "narrow fellow"?
2. Many clues to the "narrow fellow's" identity are presented as **similes** or **metaphors.** In stanza 2, what simile describes his movement in the grass? What metaphor describes his appearance?
3. In stanza 4, what **metaphor** suggests what the "fellow" once reminded the speaker of?
4. How does the speaker feel about this "fellow"? How does he feel about other creatures?

Interpreting Meanings

5. The most important **metaphor** in the poem occurs in the last line. What kind of feeling could be imagined as a "zero at the bone"? What do you think "zero" refers to here? What do you think "a tighter breathing" is?
6. In stanza 3, why do you think the speaker mentions that he was barefoot?
7. Do you think the speaker's feelings are common? If so, why do you think so few people feel "a transport of cordiality" for this "narrow fellow"?

Writing About the Poem

A Critical Response

Analyzing the Speaker. In reading poetry, it is usually a mistake to assume that the speaker is the poet. Often a poet will speak from someone else's point of view. In "A Narrow Fellow in the Grass," the speaker is clearly not Emily Dickinson. How do we know? Why do you think the poet chose a speaker different from herself? (Keep in mind that this poem was written around 1865. One early reader of this poem, in fact, couldn't believe it was written by a woman. He asked how in the world a *girl* could know that a boggy field wasn't good for growing corn.) Write a brief paragraph in which you give your answers to these two questions about the speaker in this poem.

Analyzing Language and Vocabulary

Inversions and "Understood" Words

To make their rhythms and rhymes "fit," poets of-

ten **invert,** or reverse, the normal English word order of a sentence. Normally, the positions of the main parts of a sentence are subject-verb-complement. (I studied math.) Normally, a prepositional phrase follows the verb it modifies. (Calvin went across the border.) When these normal positions are not followed, we have inversion. (Math I studied. Across the border went Calvin.) Usually, a writer will reverse normal word order in order to give a particular word emphasis. In our examples, stress would be placed on "math" and "across the border."

Poets also often omit words and phrases. When this is done, the poem often seems like a riddle, demanding that you figure out the missing part. The words that are missing are said to be "understood."

1. What would the normal English word order be for lines 1 and 2?
2. What would the normal English word order be for line 4: "His notice sudden is"?
3. What would be the more informal way of saying "Did you not"?
4. Diagram the sentence making up lines 11–16. What changes would you have to make in line 15 to make the diagram come out right?
5. How would you put lines 17 and 18 in normal English word order?
6. What word is understood in line 21—that is, what is the subject of the sentence that makes up the last stanza?

Reading About the Writer

Emily Dickinson (1830–1886) lived a life of such determined privacy that it bordered on the kind of seclusion we associate with hermits. For most of her life, her day-to-day experience was limited to what she could glimpse of village life through her window in Amherst, Massachusetts. But her mind was informed by wide reading in English literature and in the Bible. Her imagination was always ready to turn the simplest of observations into poetry. Almost completely unknown in her lifetime, Dickinson died without the slightest notion that she would soon be regarded as one of the greatest of American poets. Other poems by Dickinson are on pages 269, 285, 312, and 366 of this book.

Alice Walker is a black poet, and she is speaking here specifically of black women of her mother's generation. But could these metaphors apply to all mothers who fight for better lives for their children? Do you think the metaphors in the poem make this tribute especially strong?

Women

Alice Walker

They were women then
My mama's generation
Husky of voice—stout of
Step
5   With fists as well as
Hands
How they battered down
Doors
And ironed
10 Starched white
Shirts
How they led
Armies
Headragged generals
15 Across mined
Fields
Booby-trapped
Ditches
To discover books
20 Desks
A place for us
How they knew what we
Must know
Without knowing a page
25 Of it
Themselves.

Responding to the Poem

Analyzing the Poem

Identifying Details

1. List three things that these women tried to obtain for their children.

Interpreting Meanings

2. "Women" is based on a **metaphor.** To recognize it, you have to remember that a metaphor can be a comparison never openly stated. Here the comparison is between two kinds of actions or struggles. What are these two actions?
3. What "doors" did these women actually batter down? How could ironing "starched white / shirts" be regarded as part of their struggle?
4. When the poet speaks of "headragged generals," what **image** does she want you to see in your mind's eye? What armies are these "generals" actually leading?
5. What might the "mined / fields" and "booby-trapped / ditches" stand for?
6. What do you think these women knew their children had to know?

Writing About the Poem

A Creative Response

1. **Describing People.** How would you describe the women or men of the present generation? Do they engage in any struggles? Do they make any sacrifices? What do they want for their children—and how do they go about getting it? Write a paragraph or poem describing these women or men.

A Critical Response

2. **Describing an Attitude.** How would you say this poet feels about the women of her mother's generation? Does she admire them? Resent them? Sneer at them for being ignorant? What does she mean by the line "They were women then"? Write a paragraph answering these questions.

Reading About the Writer

Alice Walker (1944–   ) was born in Eatonton, Georgia, the eighth child of parents who were share-croppers. She has written poetry and fiction, and a biography of the poet Langston Hughes for children. In 1983 her novel *The Color Purple* won the Pulitzer Prize.

Focusing on Background
A Comment from the Poet

Alice Walker has said that this poem is for her mother. In an interview, she once talked about her mother and other important people in her life. "I also had terrific teachers. When I was four and my mother had to go work in the fields, my first-grade teacher let me start in her class. Right on through grammar school and high school and college, there was one—sometimes even two—teachers who saved me from feeling alone; from worrying that the world I was stretching to find might not even exist.

"Of course, the schools were all-black and that gave us a feeling that they really belonged to us. If they needed desks or a stage, the men in the community built them. My parents gave what they called get-togethers to raise money for the grammar school when I was there. There was a lot of self-help and community.

"My teachers lent me books: *Jane Eyre* was my friend for a long time. Books became my world, because the world I was in was very hard. My mother was working as a maid, so she was away from six-thirty in the morning until after dark. . . . I was supposed to take care of the house and do the cooking. I was twelve, coming home to an empty house and cleaning and fixing dinner—for people who didn't really appreciate the struggle it was to fix it. I missed my mother very much."

—Alice Walker

Before you read this poem, think about the epigraph, the quotation at the beginning. Borges (bôr'hāz) is a great poet from Argentina. Are you startled by the claim he makes? How does it make you feel? What could it mean?

The mention of Tampico (tam·pē'kō), in line 1, shows that the poem is set in Mexico. Tampico is a port on the Gulf of Mexico.

Making a Fist

Naomi Shihab Nye

"We forget that we are all dead men conversing with dead men."
JORGE LUIS BORGES

For the first time, on the road north of Tampico,
I felt the life sliding out of me,
a drum in the desert, harder and harder to hear.
I was seven, I lay in the car
5 watching palm trees swirl a sickening pattern past the glass.
My stomach was a melon split wide inside my skin.

"How do you know if you are going to die?"
I begged my mother.
We had been traveling for days.
10 With strange confidence she answered,
"When you can no longer make a fist."

Years later I smile to think of that journey,
the borders we must cross separately,
stamped with our unanswerable woes.
15 I who did not die, who am still living,
still lying in the backseat behind all my questions,
clenching and opening one small hand.

(Opposite) *Sons of My Compadre* by Diego Rivera (1930). Oil.

Banco Nacional de Mexico.

Responding to the Poem

Analyzing the Poem

Identifying Facts

1. Find the two **metaphors** in the first stanza that describe the way the speaker felt in the car.
2. What was the little girl's question? What was her mother's answer?

Interpreting Meanings

3. Obviously, the girl was not dying in the car. What do you think was actually happening to her?
4. The first part of the poem describes a car journey that took the family across the Mexican-U.S. border. What larger meanings might the words *journey* and *borders* have in lines 12–13?
5. What does the speaker mean when she says she is "still lying in the backseat," clenching and opening one small hand? (What does she fear now? Think back on the Borges quote.)
6. Do you think the girl was comforted by her mother's response to her question? Why or why not? Why do you suppose the mother said what she did?
7. Making a fist is often a gesture of defiance. Do you think Nye is thinking of that idea here?

Writing About the Poem

A Creative Response

Creating Metaphors. When Nye writes "My stomach was a melon split wide inside my skin," she not only makes an imaginative connection but also conveys a distinct feeling of bloated queasiness. Write three other metaphors beginning "My stomach was . . ." to convey other sensations, such as nervousness, fullness, hunger, fear, or anger. (Or, you might describe a headache or a toothache.)

Reading About the Writer

Naomi Shihab Nye (1952–   ) makes her home in San Antonio, Texas. Nye has written three collections of poetry, *Different Ways to Pray, Hugging the Jukebox*, and *Yellow Glove*, and has been awarded the Lavan Younger Poets Award by the Academy of American Poets. Many of her poems are inspired by childhood memories and her Palestinian heritage. Nye is also a songwriter, with two albums to her credit, *Rutabaga-Roo* and *Lullaby Raft*. Like the bards of old, she has traveled to many places reading her poetry. A recent teaching assignment has taken her across the Pacific to the University of Hawaii. "Being alive is a common road," observes Nye. "It's what we notice makes us different."

Focusing on Background
"I am certain I did not make this up"

"A few people have asked why I selected such an ominous quotation from the great Argentinian writer Borges to lead off this simple scene from childhood. To me, it wasn't negative at all. It felt liberating— as in, why worry? Anything bad that happens will be long gone someday soon.

"Of course I wasn't thinking that when I was seven years old, and sick in the back seat of my parents' car. I was just worried about staying alive.

"Writing about it long later, I thought how scenes can become talismans, something we grip onto for reassurance in difficult times. What do you remember vividly whenever you're in trouble?

"The irony is my mother doesn't remember this scene at all. She can't believe she would have given me such a strange answer. Whatever the stretches of my imagination may be, I am certain I did not make this up."

—Naomi Shihab Nye

William Wordsworth wrote six poems about a young girl named Lucy. The mystery of the girl's identity has never been solved. The mention of the River Dove in England reveals that Lucy lived in the countryside—but little else is known about her. Was she a real person? Was she imaginary? Perhaps we will never know. . . .

She Dwelt Among the Untrodden Ways

William Wordsworth

She dwelt among the untrodden ways
   Beside the springs of Dove,
A maid° whom there were none to praise
   And very few to love.

5   A violet by the mossy stone
   Half hidden from the eye!
Fair as a star, when only one
   Is shining in the sky.

She lived unknown, and few could know
10   When Lucy ceased to be;
But she is in her grave, and oh,
   The difference to me!

3. **maid:** a young unmarried woman.

Responding to the Poem

Analyzing the Poem

Identifying Details

1. What two details do we know about the place where Lucy lived? Define *springs* and *untrodden.*
2. How did most people feel about Lucy during her lifetime? How did they react to her death?
3. How were the speaker's feelings about Lucy different from everyone else's?
4. In stanza 2, the speaker uses figurative language to describe Lucy. What **metaphor** does he use? What **simile**?

Interpreting Meanings

5. What do the two very different things she is compared to tell us about Lucy?
6. The poet indicates that Lucy lived and died in obscurity. How has this poem, written in 1799, made her immortal?
7. What do you think the speaker means when he says of Lucy's death, "Oh, the difference to me!"

Writing About the Poem

A Creative Response

1. **Creating Figures of Speech.** Imitate Wordsworth's second verse and create a metaphor and a simile to describe someone's character and appearance. Your metaphor should use an ordinary plant or flower; your simile should use some feature of the universe. Use your subject's name as your title.

A Critical Response

2. **Proposing an Answer to a Question.** Who do you think Lucy was? Was she a country girl whom the poet knew, who died young? Was she the poet's sister Dorothy, who lived with her brother all her life? The poem was written when William and Dorothy lived alone together; a few years later William married. Though Dorothy Wordsworth lived a long life, some people believe that William wrote the Lucy poems thinking of how sad he would be if his sister died. In a paragraph, tell who you think Lucy was and why the poet loved her, even though the rest of the world saw nothing special in her.

Analyzing Language and Vocabulary

Word Histories

When Wordsworth refers to Lucy as a "maid," he does not mean that she is a household servant. Years ago it was common to refer to a young unmarried girl as a "maid." The word comes from an old Indo-European word meaning "youngster," or "unmarried." The word *Mac* that precedes some surnames is derived from the same word: *MacDonald* means "son of Donald," or "youngster of Donald." Over the years, the word *maid* and its related form, *maiden,* have taken on other meanings.

1. What is a ship's maiden voyage?
2. What is a woman's maiden name?
3. What is a "maid of honor" in a wedding?
4. Why do you think the word *maid* came to refer to a household servant?
5. If Wordsworth had called Lucy a "matron," how would your image of her change?

Reading About the Writer

William Wordsworth (1770–1850) was the most influential voice among a group of early nineteenth-century poets who would come to be known as the Romantics. In his brief lyrics, Wordsworth celebrated the simple virtues of people who lived close to the soil. In his long poems, he explored the relationship of nature to the human world. Like many Romantics, Wordsworth was drawn to a philosophy known as *pantheism*—the belief that God is revealed in the laws and forces of nature. Wordsworth's other Lucy poems are called "Lucy Gray, or Solitude," "Strange Fits of Passion Have I Known," "Three Years She Grew in Sun and Shower," "A Slumber Did My Spirit Steal," and "I Traveled Among Unknown Men." The Lucy poems and almost all his other work are associated with the incredibly beautiful Lake District in England, where the poet lived nearly all his life.

Cities figure importantly in both these poems. Sandburg got his impression by observing fog over Chicago's waterfront on Lake Michigan. Eliot's city is London—at a time when "the soot that falls from chimneys" was produced by soft coal burned in furnaces and fireplaces. Are these foggy city scenes quiet or noisy?

Fog

Carl Sandburg

The fog comes
on little cat feet.

It sits looking
over harbor and city
on silent haunches
and then moves on.

"The yellow fog . . ."

T. S. Eliot

The yellow fog that rubs its back upon the windowpanes,
The yellow smoke that rubs its muzzle on the windowpanes
Licked its tongue into the corners of the evening,
Lingered upon the pools that stand in drains,
Let fall upon its back the soot that falls from chimneys,
Slipped by the terrace, made a sudden leap,
And seeing that it was a soft October night,
Curled once about the house, and fell asleep.

from "The Love Song of J. Alfred Prufrock"

Responding to the Poems

Analyzing the Poems

Both of these poems compare the movement of fog to the behavior of a cat. Notice that neither poet comes right out and says "The fog is like a cat" or "The fog moves like a cat" or even "The fog *is* a cat." Both poets use **implied metaphors.** (Notice, in fact, that Eliot never even uses the word *cat* at all.)

Identifying Details

1. What parts of a cat's body are mentioned in Sandburg's poem?
2. What parts of a cat's body are mentioned in Eliot's poem? What catlike actions does Eliot describe?
3. Where does the fog end up in Sandburg's poem? In Eliot's?

Interpreting Meanings

4. Why do you think these two poets chose to describe fog in terms of a cat's actions? Could fog just as well be compared to an elephant or a canary or a snake? Explain.
5. A recent CBS morning weather report began with this **metaphor:** "It's little cat feet out there for large swatches of the country. . . ." What was the weather like? (Notice that there is a second **metaphor** here as well—what is the newscaster comparing the country to by using the word *swatches*?)

Writing About the Poems

A Creative Response

1. **Extending a Metaphor.** Extend either of the metaphors in these two poems even further—that is, think of other catlike qualities and actions that might be applied to fog. Write three sentences.

A Critical Response

2. **Comparing Poems.** Write at least a paragraph in which you compare these two poems. Name at least three ways in which they are similar. Filling out a chart like the one that follows will help you identify the elements the poems have in common. At the end of your composition, tell which "fog" poem you liked better, and why. (For help in writing a comparison, see page 285.)

	Sandburg	Eliot
Setting		
Metaphors		
Mood		

Reading About the Writers

Carl Sandburg (1878–1967) was born to Swedish immigrants in Galesburg, Illinois. As a poet, he is associated with the democratic mass of people, particularly with laborers in cities and on farms, and with the drifting population of hobos and itinerant workers. He is also remembered as the poet of Chicago, in the days when that city was the expanding center of stockyards and steel mills and railroads. As a writer of prose, he is best known for his four-volume biography of Abraham Lincoln. Sandburg was one of those who changed the nature of poetry by insisting that the rhythms of American speech could best be caught in free verse (see page 289). He also believed that poetry should not only be read but performed. Sandburg gave recitals with guitar accompaniment many years before that kind of presentation of music and words became part of American pop culture.

T. S. Eliot (1888–1965) was born in St. Louis, Missouri, where his father was Chancellor of Washington University. True to the custom of his old and aristocratic New England family, Eliot was sent to a prep school, Milton Academy, near Boston. He continued his education at Harvard and at the Sorbonne in Paris. Eventually, he moved to London. Eliot's most famous poem, *The Waste Land,* was a landmark in modern literature.

The following lines are spoken by a character called "the melancholy Jaques" (pronounced jā′ kwēz) in Shakespeare's comedy *As You Like It*. Here the lines are presented as a separate poem, under the title they have come to be known by. Jaques is called "melancholy" because he has a very gloomy view of life, as you'll see by what he says here.

The Seven Ages of Man

William Shakespeare

All the world's a stage,
And all the men and women merely players;
They have their exits and their entrances,
And one man in his time plays many parts,
His acts being seven ages. At first the infant,
Mewling and puking in the nurse's arms;
And then the whining schoolboy, with his satchel
And shining morning face, creeping like snail
Unwillingly to school. And then the lover,
Sighing like furnace, with a woeful ballad
Made to his mistress' eyebrow. Then a soldier,
Full of strange oaths, and bearded like the pard,°
Jealous in honor, sudden and quick in quarrel,
Seeking the bubble reputation
Even in the cannon's mouth. And then the justice,°
In fair round belly with good capon° lined,
With eyes severe and beard of formal cut,
Full of wise saws° and modern instances;
And so he plays his part. The sixth age shifts
Into the lean and slippered pantaloon,°
With spectacles on nose and pouch on side;
His youthful hose,° well saved, a world too wide
For his shrunk shank; and his big manly voice,
Turning again toward childish treble, pipes
And whistles in his sound. Last scene of all,
That ends this strange eventful history,
Is second childishness and mere oblivion,
Sans° teeth, sans eyes, sans taste, sans everything.

5 · 10 · 15 · 20 · 25 (line numbers)

12. **pard:** leopard.

15. **justice:** judge.
16. **capon:** fat chicken.

18. **saws:** sayings.

20. **pantaloon:** silly, flirtatious old man.

22. **hose:** stockings.

28. **sans:** without (French).

Responding to the Poem

Analyzing the Poem

Identifying Details

1. As a playwright, Shakespeare quite naturally thought in terms of the theater. These lines open with a famous **metaphor** that compares the world to a stage. What does Jaques compare men and women with?
2. Jaques extends his **metaphor** by describing one person's life as though it were a play made up of seven acts. In each act, the person gets older. Name the seven acts of a person's life.

Interpreting Meanings

3. In the first two acts, what **images** help you picture childhood as Jaques sees it? What **simile** describes the schoolboy's attitude toward school? Do these pictures of childhood seem mocking, or are they appealing in any way?
4. In Shakespeare's day, it was fashionable to compose serious love poems celebrating the perfection of a lady's eyes, lips, or complexion. Find the lines where Jaques makes fun of this type of poetry. What **simile** describes the sighs of the person who writes it?
5. In lines 13 and 14, what does Jaques compare "reputation" to? What point about the permanence of a reputation is he making by using this **metaphor**? What kind of person would seek reputation "even in the cannon's mouth"?
6. If the justice's belly is "lined with good capon," what do we know about him? What details make the justice seem like a ridiculous character?

7. According to Jaques, what physical and mental changes take place as a man reaches the sixth and seventh ages? Does he make old age seem dignified or worth striving for? Explain.

8. These famous lines were written nearly four hundred years ago. Of all the seven ages of man that Shakespeare characterizes, which have remained true to life in the twentieth century? Have any changed?

9. If Shakespeare were writing the same speech today, what new "parts" might he write? (Think of new social and economic conditions that he might take into account in presenting the seven ages of modern man or woman.)

Writing About the Poem

A Creative Response

1. **Extending the Poem.** Can these "seven ages" be applied to women as well as to men? Write a poem or a paragraph called "The Seven Ages of Woman." Start with the infant. What will you end with? What attitude will you take toward your stages of life?

2. **Extending the Poem.** Suppose each of these seven actors had a chance to deliver one speech as he, or she, climbed up to occupy the spotlight on the stage of life. Write out seven one-line comments each player might deliver upon making an entrance.

A Critical Response

3. **Paraphrasing a Poem.** To *paraphrase* a passage means to restate it in your own words. Because a paraphrase restates complex or difficult ideas in plainer words, it is often longer than the original passage (and never as interesting). Write a paraphrase of Jaques's speech. Be sure to explain in your own words each figure of speech. Pretend you are writing the paraphrase for a reader who has had trouble understanding Jaques's language. Here is how a paraphrase might go for lines 1–2:

> The whole world can be compared to a stage, and all the men and women in the world can be compared to actors and actresses on this stage.

Analyzing Language and Vocabulary

Multiple Meanings

In this speech, Jaques uses at least four words that mean several things, but for the purposes of this speech, only one precise meaning is intended.

1. In Shakespeare's time, soldiers usually traveled to parts of the world that most ordinary people never got to. When Shakespeare says in line 12 that the soldier is "full of *strange* oaths," does he mean that the oaths (or curses) are "foreign and alien" or that they are "peculiar and odd"? (There is a distinction, if you think carefully about the words.)

2. When Shakespeare calls these seven ages a "*strange* eventful history" in line 26, does *strange* mean "foreign and alien" or "peculiar and odd"?

3. The word *fair* can mean: (a) "a festival or carnival," (b) "attractive," (c) "light in complexion," (d) "free from storms, as in *a fair day*," (e) "just and honest, as in *a fair trial*," (f) "neither very good nor very bad, as in *a fair condition*." Which meaning does Shakespeare intend when he calls the justice's belly "fair" in line 16?

4. How does the context tell you that the word *saws* in line 18 refers to a saying, not to a cutting tool?

5. The word *hose* comes from an old word meaning "to conceal or to hide." What does the word mean in line 22 in Jaques's speech?

Like a movie thriller, a good poem can keep us on the edge of our seats by exciting our imaginations and saying the unexpected. This poem begins with a warning. What could a poem possibly do to you that you should avoid it the way you'd avoid a barking dog? Be sure to read this warning poem aloud.

Beware: Do Not Read This Poem

Ishmael Reed

tonite, *thriller* was
abt an ol woman, so vain she
surrounded herself w/
    many mirrors

5 It got so bad that finally she
locked herself indoors & her
whole life became the
    mirrors

one day the villagers broke
10 into her house, but she was too
swift for them, she disappeared
    into a mirror
each tenant who bought the house
after that, lost a loved one to
15   the ol woman in the mirror:
    first a little girl
    then a young woman
    then the young woman/s husband

the hunger of this poem is legendary
20 it has taken in many victims
back off from this poem
it has drawn in yr feet
back off from this poem
it has drawn in yr legs
25 back off from this poem
it is a greedy mirror
you are into this poem, from
    the waist down
nobody can hear you can they?

30 this poem has had you up to here
    belch
this poem aint got no manners
you cant call out frm this poem
relax now & go w/ this poem
35 move & roll on to this poem

do not resist this poem
this poem has yr eyes
this poem has his head
this poem has his arms
40 this poem has his fingers
this poem has his fingertips

this poem is the reader & the
    reader this poem

statistic: the us bureau of missing persons reports
45   that in 1968 over 100,000 people disappeared
    leaving no solid clues
        nor trace   only
a space   in the lives of their friends

(Opposite) *Untitled* by Romare Bearden (1965–1966). Collage.

Courtesy of ACA Galleries, New York, and the Estate of Romare Bearden.

Responding to the Poem

Analyzing the Poem

Identifying Facts

1. What happens in the movie thriller described in the first three stanzas?
2. What **metaphor** describes the old woman's "whole life" in the second stanza?
3. In the fourth stanza, what **metaphor** is used in warning readers to "back off from this poem"?
4. What is happening to the reader in the fifth stanza? What advice does the speaker give "you"?

Interpreting Meanings

5. According to the last stanza, what has become of all those missing persons?
6. Think of what the poet might mean by saying "this poem" is a "greedy mirror." What does he want you to see when you gaze into it?
7. In what way is the reader of this poem like the "ol woman in the mirror"? Where is the poem also compared to a ravenous creature?
8. Readers know they are enjoying a story, poem, or play when they are so caught up in its imaginary realm that they feel removed from the here and now. Do you think this is what this poem is all about? Can a poem be dangerous? Discuss your interpretations.

Writing About the Poem

A Creative Response

Extending the Poem. Write another stanza for the poem that describes what happens next. Write as "I," the reader who has "become" the poem. If you wish, imitate Reed's unusual typography, grammar, and spellings.

Reading About the Writer

Ishmael Reed (1938–   ), as a fellow poet noted, "alters our notion of what is possible." Known for his bold, brash, and blunt style, Reed has written several satiric novels that blend African American vernacular with standard English and hip jargon. As the title of one of his books indicates, Reed believes "writin' is fightin' " and ought to stir up controversy. His books of poetry include *Conjure* and *New and Collected Poems*. His own imprint as a publisher is I Reed Books. A native of Tennessee (his daughter is named for her father's home state), Reed makes his home in Oakland, California. You shouldn't be surprised to hear Reed saying: "My novels and poems are meant to be read aloud. That's why jazz musicians have been able to adapt my stuff."

Literature & Language

Using Similes and Metaphors

1. Tell what two things are being compared in each of the following quotations. What do you imagine the two parts of each simile have in common?

   a. I saw Eternity the other night
   Like a great ring of pure and endless light,
   All calm, as it was bright

   —from "The World," Henry Vaughan

   b. and there's the moon, thinner than a watchspring

   —from "what time is it . . . ,"
   E. E. Cummings

   c. The Roman Road runs straight and bare
   As the pale parting-line in hair

   —from "The Roman Road,"
   Thomas Hardy

   d. . . . some dreams
   hang in the air like smoke
   touching everything.

   —Lucille Clifton

2. In each of the following quotations, name the two different things the poet is bringing together in a metaphor. Then tell what you imagine these two things have in common. Some quotations contain more than one metaphor.

   a. The Lord is my shepherd; I shall not want.
   He maketh me to lie down in green pastures:
   He leadeth me beside the still waters.

   —Psalm 23

   b. The wind was a torrent of darkness among the gusty trees,
   The moon was a ghostly galleon tossed among cloudy seas

   —from "The Highwayman,"
   Alfred Noyes

   c. But Flynn preceded Casey, as did also Jimmy Blake,

And the former was pudding, and the latter was a fake.

   —from "Casey at the Bat,"
   Ernest Lawrence Thayer

   d. The lightning is a yellow fork
   From tables in the sky

   —from "The lightning is . . . ,"
   Emily Dickinson

   e. The lightning showed a yellow beak
   And then a livid claw.

   —from "The Wind begun to rock the grass,"
   Emily Dickinson

3. The following poem uses half of a simile as its title. When you read the poem, you'll see what the poet imagines as the other half.

Harder than Granite

It is a pity the shock-waves
Of the present population-explosion must push in here too.
They will certainly within a century
Eat up the old woods I planted and throw down my stonework: Only the little tower,
Four-foot-thick-walled and useless may stand for a time.
That and some verses. It is curious that flower-soft verse
Is sometimes harder than granite, tougher than a steel cable, more alive than life.

—Robinson Jeffers

   a. What does "here" refer to in line 2?
   b. What does the poet know is going to disappear someday?
   c. What is "harder than granite"? What other similes does the poet use to describe the toughness and durability of his subject?

d. There are also implied metaphors in this little verse. When the poet talks of the "shock-waves / of the present population-explosion," what two distinct things is he comparing?

e. What metaphor describes poetry in line 6?

f. How can poetry be both "soft" and "hard" at the same time?

4. Metaphors are used not only by poets. Each of the following newspaper headlines contains an *implied metaphor.* Answer the question after each headline to show that you recognize the two dissimilar things being compared.

a. Islanders Lick Wounds; Series Resumes Tonight
(What are the Islanders compared to?)

b. New Crisis Knocks Lisbon Off Course
(What is Lisbon compared to?)

c. Congress Predicts Anemic Recovery
(What is the recovery compared to?)

d. Taxpayers Are Drained
(What are the taxpayers compared to?)

e. Senate Committee Grills President
(What is the committee's action compared to?)

f. NBC Shelving "Taxi"; To Go to New Time
(What is NBC's action compared to?)

g. President Believes America on the Mend
(What is America compared to?)

h. President Puts Lid on News Leaks
(What is the President's action compared to? What comparison is the term "news leak" based on?)

i. GOP Unveils Budget Alternative
(What is the GOP's action compared to?)

j. Storm of Complaints Hits Capitol Hill
(What does the storm stand for?)

Writing

1. Creating Similes to Describe Emotions or Ideas. Here are some common emotions and ideas: love, hate, anger, mischief, honesty, grief, stinginess, generosity, ambition, laziness, hunger, despair, joy, innocence, carelessness, neatness, sloppiness, thirstiness, restlessness, dreaminess, pain, lightheartedness, giddiness, drowsiness, selfishness, jealousy, cowardice, moodiness. Choose any five of these as the starting points of your imaginative comparisons, and then make up five similes in which you compare these emotions or ideas to some object or person.

2. Creating Metaphors to Describe Emotions or Ideas. Take five other ideas or emotions from this list, and make up metaphors that compare the idea or emotion to an object or a person. Write direct metaphors, using the verb *is*: "Love is . . . ," "Hate is . . ."

3. Extending a Simile or Metaphor. Select one of your similes or metaphors and extend it for three or four lines—or for as long as you can and still make sense. As a model, use this poem by Emily Dickinson. In what ways can you sensibly imagine fame as having a "song," a "sting," and a "wing"?

> Fame is a bee.
> It has song—
> It has a sting—
> Ah, too, it has a wing.
>
> —Emily Dickinson

RESPONDING TO FIGURES OF SPEECH

Writing Assignment

In a paragraph, identify the main metaphor in the poem "Harlem" and tell whether or not you think it is effective. Include a description of how the metaphor and the poem made you feel.

Background

To be effective, metaphors and similes must meet the "reality" test—that is, the terms of the comparison have to have something in common, even though in all other ways they may be totally different. Here are five figures of speech. First, identify each figure of speech and tell what qualities are being compared. Then discuss in class whether each one meets the reality test. You probably will not all agree on your evaluations.

1. The fog clunked in on elephant feet.
2. Fear is a slow melting of the bones.
3. She was as delicate as a twelve-speed bicycle.
4. Miranda has ruby eyes.
5. Howard is as handsome as a hard-boiled egg.

Prewriting

1. Be sure you can identify the main metaphor in Hughes's poem. Remember that a metaphor has to have two parts: the actual thing being discussed, and the other, different thing it is being likened to.
2. Put the metaphor to the reality test and decide if you think it passes.
3. Think of how the metaphor makes you feel about the poem and its subject. To discover how you feel, you might ask yourself: **How would a different metaphor affect the way I feel about the poem?** For example, how would I feel if the dream de-

ferred were compared to a soda that had lost its fizz? Or to a car that had run out of gas?

Writing

1. First, in your opening sentence, explain what the major metaphor in the poem is.
2. Next, explain whether or not the metaphor meets the reality test.
3. Finally, describe how the metaphor affects the way you feel about the poem and its subject.

Here is how one reader responded to the metaphor in Carl Sandburg's poem "Fog" on page 263:

> The chief and only metaphor in "Fog" by Carl Sandburg is the comparison of fog to a cat. The metaphor passes the reality test, although at first you wouldn't think that fog and a cat could have anything in common. In fact, this metaphor comes close to flunking the reality test. But the poet does make me see how fog could be seen as a cat: both are silent and soft and both are even mysterious—at least that's how I feel about cats. (They are kind of sneaky, the way fog can be when it creeps up on you, silently, without any warning, and suddenly you are surrounded.) I like the poem. First, it was pretty easy to read (to be honest!); second, it did help me imagine the silence of a foggy city; and third, well, I just like cats.

Checklist for Revision

1. Have you cited the poem's author and title?
2. Have you explained in your opening sentence what the major metaphor in the poem is?
3. Have you explained the terms of the comparison, to show how the metaphor "works"?
4. Have you described your response to the poem and the metaphor?

Personification: Making the World Human

Personification is a special kind of metaphor in which we give human qualities to something that is not human—to an animal, an object, or even an idea. "The sun smiled on us," we might say, or "The ocean scribbles long sentences on the shore." Actually, the sun simply goes on being the sun, without the human ability to smile. The ocean goes on being an ocean, without the human ability to write sentences. Yet there is something in our minds that continually leads us to project our own human actions and feelings onto natural phenomena. In the following lines, see what Shakespeare imagines the wind to be:

> Blow, blow thou winter wind.
> Thou art not so unkind
>   As man's ingratitude.
> Thy tooth is not so keen,
> Because thou art not seen,
>   Although thy breath be rude.
>
> —from *As You Like It,*
>   William Shakespeare

The wind can be kind or unkind.

The wind has a tooth.

The wind has rough breath.

Here, the wind—a nonhuman force—has not only a "tooth" and "breath," but also the ability to be kind or unkind. Breath is something that only living creatures have. Kindness and unkindness are traits that we ascribe *only* to humans: the wind has been personified. Through the poet's imagination, it has become a kind of person.

Just as metaphor is common in everyday speech, so is personification. A recent headline personified computers when it announced:

Every Computer "Whispers" Its Secrets

Another headline personified the country of China:

China Depicted as Struggling Giant

Another one personified the White House:

White House Digs in Its Heels on Budget Issue

Sometimes personification simply involves giving life and feelings to things that are inanimate, or lifeless. When we say that a tooth is angry or a cough is stubborn or a computer is friendly or love is blind, we are using a kind of personification. Personification in all its forms is yet another example of how we continually use our imaginations to give life and meaning to all aspects of the nonhuman world.

> "**W**hen we say that a tooth is angry or a cough is stubborn or a computer is friendly or love is blind, we are using a kind of personification."

As you read this poem, be sure you know just what the poet is personifying. Suppose the poem had no title: would you know what "they" are? What clues would tell you?

The Legend of the Paper Plates

John Haines

They trace their ancestry
back to the forest.
There all the family stood,
proud, bushy, and strong.

5   Until hard times,
when from fire and drought
the patriarchs° crashed.

The land was taken for taxes,
the young people cut down
10   and sold to the mills.

Their manhood and womanhood
was crushed, bleached
with bitter acids,
their fibers dispersed
15   as sawdust
among ten million offspring.

You see them at any picnic,
at ball games, at home,
and at state occasions.

20   They are thin and pliable,
porous and identical.
They are made to be thrown away.

7. **patriarchs:** the aged and respected male heads of families. (The female equivalents would be matriarchs.)

Responding to the Poem

Analyzing the Poem

Identifying Details

1. Whom does "they" refer to in stanza 1? Who or what is the "family"?
2. Whom or what does "them" refer to in line 17?
3. A legend is an old story that is usually handed down from generation to generation. In brief, what *is* the legend of the paper plates?

Interpreting Meanings

4. What is **personified** as the "patriarchs"? Why would the patriarchs be the first to fall?
5. What is **personified** as the "young people"? On a literal level, what happens to them?
6. What are the "offspring," or children, of these young people?
7. How do the descendants of the family as described in the last stanza contrast with the family in stanza 1?
8. What is the effect of the **personification** in this poem? In other words, how does it make you feel about the trees and their fate?
9. What is the poet's attitude toward the "consumer culture," where things are made to be thrown away? Do you agree with him, or do you have other opinions? Explain.

Writing About the Poem

A Creative Response

1. **Extending the Poem.** Take some other disposable product that is made from a natural resource and write a brief poem or paragraph entitled "The Legend of _____." Complete the title with the name of your product. Then tell what the product's natural "ancestry" is and what we do to that natural resource to manufacture today's disposable product.

A Critical Response

2. **Explaining the Poet's Purpose.** In a paragraph, explain what you think the poet's purpose was in writing this poem. Do you think he accomplished his purpose? (In deciding on the poet's purpose, you might think about this question:

What does John Haines want me to think about each time I see a paper plate?)

Analyzing Language and Vocabulary

Synonyms and Antonyms

A **synonym** is a word that has the same or almost the same meaning as another word. The word *deduct* is a synonym for the word *subtract.* An **antonym** is a word that is opposite or nearly opposite in meaning to another word. The word *add* is an antonym for the word *subtract.*

Column A below contains words from Haines's poem. For each word in Column A, find a synonym and an antonym from Column B. On a separate sheet of paper, write each word from Column A and indicate its synonym and antonym from Column B.

A	B
proud	flood
strong	gathered
drought	weak
dispersed	humble
thin	thick
pliable	rigid
porous	impermeable
identical	permeable
	distinct
	haughty
	slender
	flexible
	robust
	dryness
	scattered
	same

Synonyms are not always interchangeable; often synonyms will have subtle but distinct shades of meaning that distinguish one word from another. Try substituting the synonyms given in Column B for the words John Haines has used in his poem. Which ones do you think could be substituted for the words in the poem without losing the precise meaning Haines had in mind? Which synonyms could *not* be substituted because they suggest slightly different meanings? A dictionary will help.

How would you personify the seasons of the year,
or the months? Watch for the comical way this
poet personifies February and winter.

March 1st

Kathleen Spivack

Coming out of the house on a fresh March morning,
I saw February still meandering around
like laundry caught in a Bendix.° Stray shreds
of cloud, like pillow slips, were rent° from
5   her large endlessness. Outdated,
her decrepit body garlanded itself disgracefully
with powder. She luxuriated in old age.
Even her graying sheets were still there,
tattered, heaped carelessly on the street,
10   bearing the indentation of someone's huge body
and furred with a fine fringe of soot.
She had been plump, she had been heavy, sitting
on top of us since January. Winter, you
old clothes hamper, what mildew
15   still molders inside you before March
dribbles a bit, dries up, and is done for?

3. **Bendix:** brand name of a washing machine.
4. **rent:** torn.

February Thaw by Charles Burchfield (1920).
Watercolor over pencil.

The Brooklyn Museum.
John B. Woodward Memorial Fund. (21.104)

Responding to the Poem

Analyzing the Poem

Identifying Details

1. What does the speaker see when she leaves her house on March 1?
2. What **simile** immediately reveals what February reminds her of? What **simile** does she use to describe the clouds?
3. What details **personify** February in lines 5–13? What comic image do you get of February in lines 12 and 13?
4. What **metaphor** does the poet use when she addresses winter at the end of the poem?

Interpreting Meanings

5. The word *snow* is never mentioned, and yet we see snow all through the poem. Find two places where you know that the speaker is talking about snow, even though she doesn't actually use the word.
6. What does the speaker mean when she says that March will "dribble" a bit?
7. How does the poet want you to feel about this winter scene—lighthearted, solemn, frightened? Explain.

Writing About the Poem

A Creative Response

1. **Addressing a Season.** The speaker, in a humorous mood, addresses winter as "you old clothes hamper." Write four more lines like this in which you address a season (or month) of the year and compare it to something else: "Spring, you _____," "July, you _____," and so on.
2. **Writing a Poem.** Look at today's weather report in the paper. Write a poem about it, in which you compare the weather to a person. For the title of your poem, use today's date.
3. **Writing a Report Based on a Poem.** Write a straightforward weather report for the local newspaper, telling what the weather is like on this March 1. Include in your report a prediction of the weather for March 2 and 3. Get your weather details from the poem.

Reading About the Writer

The poetry of **Kathleen Spivack** (1938–   ) has appeared in many magazines and anthologies. Spivack lives in Boston and teaches poetry to children. Of her collection of poetry called *Flying Inland,* one critic said: her "poems are studded with images that have the look and feel of fresh paint. She has an ear attuned to speech as we hear it, an eye that flinches at nothing."

You'll have to be able to imagine a streetcar as you read this poem. Streetcars ran on steel rails, were powered by electricity from charged wires overhead, and had bells that clanged. When for some reason the connection between the streetcar and the overhead wires was broken, the motorman had to get out and reconnect it, often to the sound of cracklings and spittings and other strange noises, and to flashes of electricity as swift as lightning.

My Mother Remembers Spanish Influenza

John Ratti

I was the first person in our town
to catch the Spanish influenza.
I heard it come over on the streetcar,
hissing and snapping to itself
5   as it crossed the river.
And when the car stopped at the foot of our hill,
the bell rang twice, the flu got off
and burst inside my head
like sparklers on the Fourth of July.
10   Soon it was smooth and hot as rails in the sun,
running inside my head, metal on metal, ice on ice.
When it began to go away,
the neighborhood children took it, piece by piece,
on the thick, round wheels of their roller skates.
15   Mother brought me a white paper bag
of coconut macaroons.
I ate three and was sick
into the gray metal basin
filled with disinfectant and water
20   that was kept near my bed.
Mother doubted that the flu came on the streetcar.
It seemed more likely to her
that my two young uncles
had brought it back from France with them,
25   hidden in the silk webbing
that stretched between the carved ivory fingers
of the painted fan they had given me.
But I knew better.
I could still hear it, when Mother left the room at night,
30   whispering to itself about itself
as it came across the river on the last car.
It stopped at the foot of our hill for a second,
and then rode on down the valley to the carbarn,
where it waited out the night.

A photograph taken during the flu epidemic mentioned in the poem. Note the masks on the faces of the men.

Responding to the Poem

Analyzing the Poem

Identifying Details

1. Who is the speaker in this poem?
2. How does the speaker think she caught the Spanish influenza? How does her mother think she caught it?
3. Find at least two passages in the poem where the speaker **personifies** the Spanish influenza.

Interpreting Meanings

4. What adjectives would you use to describe the kind of person the speaker imagines the Spanish influenza to be? Point out specific words or lines that give you this impression.
5. What specific symptoms of her illness do you think the speaker is describing in lines 8–11?
6. Why does the speaker think that the neighborhood children "took it" away with them on the wheels of their roller skates?
7. What elements of this speaker's memories seem nightmarish to you?

Writing About the Poem

A Creative Response

1. **Writing a Poem.** Write a poem of your own, or a paragraph if you prefer, about how you felt during an illness. In your own writing, try to **personify** the illness. Use **figures of speech** to tell your reader what kind of a person the fever or chills or other unpleasant feelings reminded you of. In this poem, the child associates her illness with the sounds of the streetcar. Did you associate any sounds or events with your own childhood sickness?

A Critical Response

2. **Explaining an Opinion.** In his comment that follows, the poet says he wanted his poem to say something of what it felt like to be a child. In a paragraph, tell whether he succeeded in reminding you of what a part of childhood was like. Give at least one reason to support your opinion.

Focusing on Background
A Comment from the Poet

"All through my childhood, my mother would periodically recall how ill she had been as an eight- or nine-year-old when 'the flu,' the dread Spanish influenza that hit war-weary Europe and the United States at the end of World War I in 1918–1919, finally caught up with her. She had run a very high temperature—there were no antibiotics in those days—and was delirious at times. But she remembered certain incidents from that dreamlike time of sickness and confusion quite vividly—so vividly that she made her memories very nearly become my memories. Many years later, when I set out to write a group of poems about my mother's childhood, I remembered still her story of the Spanish influenza. Poetry was the most natural way to try and capture this kind of atmosphere, in this case the atmosphere of being a child and sick, at a distant point in time. Poetry can or should make one *feel* what was—and childhood is about feeling. When I sat down to write the poem, I blended things my mother's recounting of the story always included—the vaguely sinister sound of the trolley car, the painful sound of roller-skate wheels on concrete when your head aches terribly, the bag of coconut macaroons that her mother brought her, and the present, the beautiful ivory fan one of her young soldier uncles brought her from France—with my own experience of sickness. Put together, her raw material and my own sense perceptions and memories of the town in which she and I both were born made a poem which I hope says something of what it *feels* like, sometimes, to be a child. If, through a poem's special magic and movement, we can tie the past to things we know and feel now, then we can truly understand what the past, any past, was like, and we can feel it come alive again—vividly, painfully, and sometimes with laughter."

—John Ratti

Have you ever dreamed of one day stumbling over the very thing you have always dreamed of own-ing? Name one thing you dream of, and tell how you'd feel upon finding it.

Fifteen

William Stafford

South of the Bridge on Seventeenth
I found back of the willows one summer
day a motorcycle with engine running
as it lay on its side, ticking over
5   slowly in the high grass. I was fifteen.

I admired all that pulsing gleam, the
shiny flanks, the demure headlights
fringed where it lay; I led it gently
to the road and stood with that
10   companion, ready and friendly. I was fifteen.

We could find the end of a road, meet
the sky out on Seventeenth. I thought about
hills, and patting the handle got back a
confident opinion. On the bridge we indulged
15   a forward feeling, a tremble. I was fifteen.

Thinking, back farther in the grass I found
the owner, just coming to, where he has flipped
over the rail. He had blood on his hand, was pale—
I helped him walk to his machine. He ran his hand
20   over it, called me a good man, roared away.

I stood there, fifteen.

Responding to the Poem

Analyzing the Poem

Identifying Details

1. Find the lines of the poem that tell you what the speaker dreams of doing with the motorcycle.
2. What word in stanza 4 tells us why he went looking for the owner of the motorcycle? What does he discover in the grass that brings him back to reality?

Interpreting Meanings

3. Find at least five words or phrases that **personify** the motorcycle as something alive and capable of human feelings. What words reveal how the boy feels about this machine?
4. Why do you think the motorcycle means so much to the boy?
5. What do you think the speaker means by saying "We could . . . meet / the sky out on Seventeenth"? In what other way could a motorcycle rider "meet the sky"?
6. How many times does the speaker remind us of his age? Does the mention of his age affect you differently each time you hear it? Why?
7. At the end of the poem, the owner of the cycle calls the speaker a "good man." How do you think the speaker feels about these words?

Writing About the Poem

A Creative Response

1. **Personifying a Machine.** Describe a machine in terms that make the machine seem human. Before you write, list the parts of the machine and think of how they could seem human. The engine of a car, for example, could be its "lungs." The bottom of a boat could be its "fat belly." The vacuum cleaner's suction could be its "breath." Write three sentences.

A Critical Response

2. **Explaining a Poem's Message.** In a paragraph, tell what you think the message of this poem is. You might find the message by asking yourself this question: What did the boy in the poem learn when he was fifteen?

Analyzing Language and Vocabulary

Words and Distinct Meanings

The first word of each item in the list that follows is used in "Fifteen." Find the line where it is used, and, using a dictionary, tell exactly what the word means in the poem. Then define the second word to show that you understand its distinction from the first word.

1. pulsing; panting
2. flanks; shanks
3. demure; demur
4. fringed; ringed
5. companion; compatriot
6. confident; confidential
7. indulged; divulged
8. tremble; treble

Reading About the Writer

William Stafford (1914–   ) has spent most of his life in Oregon, where he teaches at Lewis and Clark College. He was born in Kansas and educated at the University of Kansas and the University of Iowa. He has said that writing is "one of the great, free human activities. . . . For the person who follows with trust and forgiveness what occurs to him, the world remains always ready and deep, an inexhaustible environment. . . ."

List three things that immediately come to your mind when you read the title of this poem.

Slumnight

Colette Inez

TV gunning down
the hours
serves as sheriff
in a room
5   where one yawn
triggers off another,

                sends time scuffling
                into night.
                Wars slugged out
10   on vacant lots
                sign an armistice
                with sleep.

                                Turned to a wall,
                                the children dream
                      15   and the moon pulls up
                                in a squadcar.

Responding to the Poem

Analyzing the Poem

Identifying Details

1. What are the people in the poem doing?

Interpreting Meanings

2. At once, the TV set is **personified** as a sheriff. How is this TV set like a person who keeps law and order? How would TV "gun down" the hours?

3. What word **personifies** time? What do you picture time doing?

4. The wars slugged out on vacant lots are also **personified**. What does it mean to say that they sign an "armistice" with sleep?

5. Finally, the most fantastic **personification** of all: who or what does the moon become?

6. What specific words and **images** in this poem suggest that life in this setting is violent? How would you describe the poet's attitude toward the role of television in these people's lives?

Writing About the Poem

A Creative Response

Creating Personifications. Write a poem in imitation of this one, in which you personify **TV, time, the outside activities,** and **the moon.**

Reading About the Writer

Colette Inez (1931–   ) was educated at Hunter College and has lived most of her life in New York City. She has been a high-school teacher in the city and a teacher in antipoverty and English-as-a-second-language programs. This poem is from a collection called *The Woman Who Loved Worms,* which won the National Book Award in 1972.

Literature & Language

Using Personification

1. Name the figure who would personify each of the following ideas:

   a. a person who goes from rags to riches
   b. love
   c. Christmas
   d. hatred of Christmas
   e. the New Year
   f. science that has gone out of control
   g. death
   h. time

2. Here are some examples of personification in poetry. For each quotation, tell what is being personified, and tell which words create the personification.

   a. And what is so rare as a day in June?
      Then, if ever, come perfect days;
      Then Heaven tries earth if it be in tune,
      And over it softly her warm ear lays

      —from "The Vision of Sir Launfal,"
      James Russell Lowell

   b. Time, you old gypsy man,
      Will you not stay?
      Put up your caravan
      Just for one day?

      —from "Time, You Old Gypsy Man,"
      Ralph Hodgson

   c. The shattered water made a misty din.
      Great waves looked over others coming in,
      And thought of doing something to the shore
      That water never did to land before.

      —from "Once by the Pacific,"
      Robert Frost

   d. In the morning the buildings stand
      smooth and shaven and straight

      —from "The Skyscrapers of the
      Financial District Dance with
      Gasman," Marge Piercy

3. In this poem, the speaker complains about the way winter has been personified over the years.

   Winter Portrait

   A wrinkled, crabbed man they picture thee,
   Old Winter, with a rugged beard as gray
   As the long moss upon the apple tree;
   Blue lipped, an ice drop at thy sharp blue nose,
   Close muffled up, and on thy dreary way
   Plodding alone through sleet and drifting snows.
   They should have drawn thee by the high-leaped hearth,
   Old Winter! seated in thy great armed chair,
   Watching the children at their Christmas mirth.

   —Robert Southey

   a. According to this speaker, how is winter usually personified? Why would this picture of winter be a common one?
   b. How does this typical personification make you feel about winter—what kind of person is the season?
   c. How would the speaker prefer to personify winter?
   d. What does the speaker's suggestion reveal about the way *he* feels about winter?

Writing

Personifying the Seasons. Take the four seasons of the year and write three sentences in which you personify each of them. Be sure to describe what each one should look like, what each should wear, and what each should be doing that would characterize that season as you know it. Will the season be a man, a woman, or a child? What will your own mood be?

COMPARING AND CONTRASTING POEMS

Writing Assignment

Write a four-paragraph essay comparing and contrasting the two "wind" poems by James Stephens and Emily Dickinson which follow.

Background

When two poems have something specific in common, such as a subject or an image or a figure of speech, they can be **compared** (their likenesses can be pointed out), or they can be **contrasted** (their differences can be pointed out). As you read these two poems about the wind, you'll find that each poem personifies the wind as a man. But there the likenesses end.

The Wind

The wind stood up, and gave a shout;
He whistled on his fingers, and

Kicked the withered leaves about,
And thumped the branches with his hand,

And said he'd kill, and kill, and kill;
And so he will! And so he will!

—James Stephens

The Wind Tapped Like a Tired Man

The wind tapped like a tired man,
And like a host, "Come in,"
I boldly answered; entered then
My residence within

A rapid, footless guest,
To offer whom a chair
Were as impossible as hand
A sofa to the air.

No bone had he to bind him,
His speech was like the push
Of numerous hummingbirds at once
From a superior bush.

His countenance a billow,
His fingers, if he pass,
Let go a music, as of tunes
Blown tremulous in glass.

He visited, still flitting;
Then, like a timid man,
Again he tapped—'twas flurriedly—
And I became alone.

—Emily Dickinson

Prewriting

Part 1: Paraphrasing. Paraphrasing—restating the text of the poem in your own words—is a good way to test your comprehension of what the poem says, line by line. Some poems are confusing because they use **inverted word order.** This means that a sentence does not follow the usual English order of subject-verb-object (or complement):

. . . entered then
My residence within
A rapid, footless guest

This sounds strange at first, but you can puzzle it out. Paraphrased, with the words in normal order, the lines might read:

A rapidly moving but footless guest then entered my home.

How would you paraphrase these lines?

   a. And like a host, "Come in,"
   I boldly answered . . .
   b. No bone had he to bind him

Sometimes poets omit words. Paraphrase these lines to show which words are missing:

To offer whom a chair
Were as impossible as hand
A sofa to the air.

Be sure you know the meanings of all the words in the poem:

a. What is a **superior** bush? (Of better quality than other bushes? Or higher than the other bushes?)
b. What is a **billow**?
c. What would a **tremulous** sound be like?
d. **Flurriedly** is a word the poet seems to have made up. What two words has she combined to make the new word?

Part 2: Finding the Similarities and Differences. Now "take each poem apart" and compare their elements. Use the following chart:

	Stephens	Dickinson
Subject (What is the poem about?)		
Speaker (Is the speaker in the poem identified? If so, what do you know about the speaker?)		
Imagery (What sensory details does the poet use to describe the wind and help us see or hear it?)		
Figurative language (How does the poet use simile, metaphor, or personification?)		
Meaning (What kind of wind do you think the poet is talking about?)		
Response (How do you feel about the poem? Why?)		

Make two lists: in one, list all the ways in which the poems are similar; in the other, list all the ways in which they are different. Your lists might begin like this:

Similarities
a. Both poems personify the wind as a man.
b. Both poems give the wind fingers.

Differences
a. Stephens's wind shouts, kicks, thumps on branches, and wants to kill.
b. Dickinson's wind is tired and timid.

Finally, study your lists, then ask yourself: What ideas about the wind occur to me as I think about these lists? Your answer to this question could be your **thesis statement.**

Writing

Write your essay according to the following plan:
1. **Paragraph 1:** Cite the title and author of each poem, and include a thesis statement.
2. **Paragraph 2:** Present details showing how the two poems are similar.
3. **Paragraph 3:** Present details showing how the two poems are different.
4. **Paragraph 4:** Explain your response to the poems, discussing your feelings (which may be similar or different) for each one.

If you want, you might begin your essay like this:

James Stephens's poem "The Wind" and Emily Dickinson's poem "The Wind Tapped Like A Tired Man" make me imagine two very different kinds of wind. I know both of these winds.

Checklist for Revision
1. Have you cited the titles and authors?
2. Have you put your thesis statement in the first paragraph?
3. Have you compared the poems in the second paragraph and contrasted them in the third paragraph?
4. Have you described your response to the poems in the fourth paragraph?
5. Have you correctly cited quotations from the poems to support your statements?

The Sounds of Poetry: Rhythm

So far we've been concerned with the sense of poetry and with how poets use figurative language. Now we will look at the ways poets play with sound and at how poetic speech shares, even duplicates, some of the qualities of music. One of these musical qualities is **rhythm,** and rhythm is based on repetition. Without repetition of some sort, there can be no composition in music and no pattern in poetry. In music, composition takes many forms. In poetry, sound patterns can be organized (1) as meter or (2) as free verse.

Meter: A Pattern of Stressed Syllables

Perhaps the best way to think of meter in poetry is to think of the metronome in music. A metronome is an instrument that measures time and usually sits on top of the piano. A metronome moves with regularity, back and forth, at whatever speed the musician has chosen. It never varies but, like a clock, makes its tick and tock over and over again.

What the metronome does for the musician is to provide a basic beat that must be kept—but not too well, not exactly. Music that followed the beat of the metronome exactly would be so dull and monotonous that it would put an audience to sleep. What musicians must learn is both to keep the beat and to make variations on it. Every musician knows you must be *off*beat—without ever forgetting that you can't be "off" until you have a sense of what's "on."

The same is true for poets. When a poet chooses to write in a meter, that meter, like the metronome's beat, is "given." The meter sets the basic mechanical beat, around which, and over which, and even against which, the poet's own voice must play.

Poetry that is written in **meter** has a regular pattern of stressed and unstressed syllables in each line.

The following poem is written in perfect meter. The poet always alternates an unstressed syllable with a stressed syllable (da DAH). He does this four times in the first and third lines of each verse, and he does it three times in the other lines. The stressed syllables in the first verse are marked ′ ; the unstressed syllables are marked ◡ .

If you read the poem aloud, you will see that it is easy to detect its metrical beat. All you have to do is listen, and the beat will come through to you as clearly as the tune of a hymn or the beat of a rock song.

> "All you have to do is listen, and the beat will come through to you as clearly as the tune of a hymn or the beat of a rock song."

The poet imagines here that Simon the Cyrenian is speaking. Simon was a man from Cyrene, a province in Africa, and was the passer-by who was ordered by the Roman soldiers to help Christ bear the cross.

Simon the Cyrenian Speaks

He never spoke a word to me,
　　And yet He called my name;
He never gave a sign to me,
　　And yet I knew and came.

At first I said, "I will not bear
　　His cross upon my back;
He only seeks to place it there
　　Because my skin is black."

But He was dying for a dream,
　　And He was very meek,
And in His eyes there shone a gleam
　　Men journey far to seek.

It was Himself my pity bought;
　　I did for Christ alone
What all of Rome could not have wrought
　　With bruise of lash or stone.

　　　　　　　　　　—Countee Cullen

Scanning a Poem

When poets write in meter as Cullen has done, they are playing a game with language. The challenge is to express feelings in language that has a regular pattern of stressed and unstressed syllables. Cullen chose to work in **iambs.** This means he has written his poem so that a stressed syllable always follows an unstressed syllable (da DAH). (You may think meter is artificial, but if you listen to our spoken English language, you will find that very often we speak in iambs.)

An iamb is an example of a poetic foot—a foot being the basic building block of meter. A **foot** usually consists of one stressed syllable and one or more unstressed syllables. The first and third lines of each stanza in Cullen's poem contain four feet (or four iambs). The second and fourth lines contain three feet (or three iambs).

English poetry has several other kinds of feet. Here is a trochee from Edgar Allan Poe's famous poem "The Raven." A **trochee** is a foot made up of a stressed syllable followed by an unstressed syllable (DAH da); it is the opposite of an iamb:

Once upon a midnight dreary, while I pondered weak and weary

Here is an anapest from Lord Byron's poem "The Destruction of Sennacherib." An **anapest** is a foot made up of three syllables in which two unstressed syllables are followed by a stressed syllable (da da DAH):

˘ ˘ ´ ˘ ˘ ´ ˘ ˘ ´ ˘ ˘ ´
The Assyrian came down like the wolf on the fold

Here is a nursery rhyme's use of a **dactyl** (line 1), where one stressed syllable is followed by two unstressed syllables. (What foot is used in line 2?)

´ ˘ ˘ ´ ˘ ˘ ´
Hickory, dickory, dock
The mouse ran up the clock

A **spondee** is a foot that is made up of two stressed syllables:

´ ´ ˘ ´
We real cool. We
´ ˘ ´
Left school. We

´ ˘ ´
Lurk late. . . .
—From "We Real Cool,"
Gwendolyn Brooks

When you analyze a poem to show its meter, you are **scanning** the poem. Scanning a poem is like analyzing the construction of a song. You are trying to take the poem apart to see how the poet has used words to create verbal music.

Remember that poets rarely use absolutely regular meter for an entire poem. They will almost always deliberately add slight variations, just as a songwriter will add interesting variations in beat or register. In fact, sharps and flats in music, pauses, and unexpected changes in beat—all of these are devices similar to those used by the poet, who is, after all, also a singer of songs.

Free Verse

Up until the last century, all poetry in English was written with a strict concern for meter. But eventually, some poets began to rebel against the old poetic "rules." They insisted that new rhythms were necessary to create new moods. Many poets abandoned meter and began writing what is called "free verse."

Free verse is poetry that is "free" of regular meter—that is, free of a strict pattern of stressed syllables and unstressed syllables. This new kind of poetry sounds very close to prose and to everyday spoken language. But free verse is free only in the sense that it is liberated from the formal rules governing meter. Poets writing in free verse pay very close attention to the rhythmic rise and fall of the voice, to pauses, and to the balances between long and short phrases.

The following poem is written in free verse. When you read it aloud, you'll notice how close to ordinary spoken language it sounds at first. But then you'll notice how it soars into the kind of language used by preachers and orators, especially in its use of repeated words and phrases.

> "**S**harps and flats
> in music,
> pauses, and unexpected
> changes in beat
> —all of these
> are devices similar to
> those used by the poet,
> who is, after all,
> also a singer of songs."

I Hear America Singing

I hear America singing, the varied carols I hear,
Those of mechanics, each one singing his as it should be
    blithe and strong,
The carpenter singing his as he measures his plank or beam,
The mason singing his as he makes ready for work, or leaves
    off work,
The boatman singing what belongs to him in his boat, the
    deckhand singing on the steamboat deck,
The shoemaker singing as he sits on his bench, the hatter
    singing as he stands,
The woodcutter's song, the plowboy's on his way in the morn-
    ing, or at noon intermission or at sundown,
The delicious singing of the mother, or of the young wife at
    work, or of the girl sewing or washing,
Each singing what belongs to him or her and to none else,
The day what belongs to the day—at night the party of young
    fellows, robust, friendly,
Singing with open mouths their strong melodious songs.

—Walt Whitman

Builders #1 by Jacob Lawrence (1972).
Watercolor and gouache.

The Saint Louis Art Museum.
Purchase: Eliza McMillan Fund.

"Flannan Isle" is a mystery story—and a true one. If we are to come close to solving the mystery of what has happened to the keepers of the light, we have to examine the clues. Look for clues in the actual evidence seen by the rescue party and in the psychological evidence provided by the speaker in the poem.

Flannan Isle

Wilfrid Wilson Gibson

"Though three men dwell on Flannan Isle
To keep the lamp alight,
As we steered under the lee,° we caught
No glimmer through the night!"

5   A passing ship at dawn had brought
The news; and quickly we set sail,
To find out what strange thing might ail
The keepers of the deep-sea light.
The winter day broke blue and bright,
10 With glancing sun and glancing spray,
While o'er the swell our boat made way,
As gallant as a gull in flight.

But as we neared the lonely Isle,
And looked up at the naked height,
15 And saw the lighthouse towering white,
With blinded lantern that all night
Had never shot a spark
Of comfort through the dark,
So ghostly in the cold sunlight
20 It seemed that we were struck the while
With wonder all too dread for words.

And as into the tiny creek
We stole beneath the hanging crag,
We saw three queer, black, ugly birds—
25 Too big by far in my belief
For guillemot or shag°—
Like seamen sitting bolt upright
Upon a half-tide reef;
But as we neared, they plunged from sight
30 Without a sound or spurt of white.
And still too mazed° to speak,

We landed, and made fast the boat,
And climbed the track in single file—

3. **lee:** sheltered side of the island.

26. **guillemot or shag:** species of sea bird.

31. **mazed:** dazed or bewildered.

Each wishing he were safe afloat
35 On any sea, however far,
So be it far from Flannan Isle:
And still we seemed to climb and climb,
As though we'd lost all count of time,
And so must climb forevermore.
40 Yet all too soon we reached the door—
The black, sun-blistered lighthouse door,
That gaped for us ajar.

As on the threshold for a spell
We paused, we seemed to breathe the smell
45 Of limewash and of tar,
Familiar as our daily breath,
As though 'twere some strange scent of death:
And so, yet wondering, side by side
We stood a moment, still tongue-tied:
50 And each with black foreboding eyed
The door, ere we should fling it wide
To leave the sunlight for the gloom:
Till, plucking courage up, at last
Hard on each other's heels we passed
55 Into the living room.

Yet as we crowded through the door,
We only saw a table, spread
For dinner, meat and cheese and bread;
But all untouched; and no one there;
60 As though when they sat down to eat,
Ere they could even taste,
Alarm had come; and they in haste
Had risen and left the bread and meat:
For at the table-head a chair
65 Lay tumbled on the floor.
We listened; but we only heard
The feeble chirping of a bird
That starved upon its perch:
And, listening still, without a word
70 We set about our hopeless search.

We hunted high, we hunted low;
And soon ransacked the empty house;
Then o'er the island, to and fro,
We ranged, to listen and to look
75 In every cranny, cleft, or nook
That might have hid a bird or mouse.
But though we searched from shore to shore,
We found no sign in any place:

West Point, Prout's Neck by Winslow Homer
(1900). Oil on canvas.

Sterling and Francine Clark Art Institute,
Williamstown, Massachusetts.

And soon again stood face to face
80 Before the gaping door:
And stole into the room once more
As frightened children steal.

Ay: though we hunted high and low,
And hunted everywhere,
85 Of the three men's fate we found no trace
Of any kind in any place,
But a door ajar, and an untouched meal,
And an overtoppled chair.

And so we listened in the gloom
90 Of that forsaken living room—
A chill clutch on our breath—
We thought how ill-chance came to all
Who kept the Flannan Light;
And how the rock had been the death
95 Of many a likely lad;
How six had come to a sudden end,
And three had gone stark mad:

And one whom we'd all known as friend
Had leapt from the lantern one still night,
100 And fallen dead by the lighthouse wall:
And long we thought
On the three we sought,
And of what might yet befall.

Like curs a glance has brought to heel,
105 We listened, flinching there:
And looked, and looked, on the untouched meal
And the overtoppled chair.

We seemed to stand for an endless while,
Though still no word was said,
110 Three men alive on Flannan Isle,
Who thought on three men dead.

Responding to the Poem

Analyzing the Poem

Identifying Details

1. Who speaks the poem's first four lines? Who speaks the poem's remaining lines?
2. What is the mission of the search party?
3. A good part of the poem is taken up with **images** and expressions of **foreboding**—that is, signs or omens building up our suspense by warning us of disaster to come. The first hint of disaster occurs in line 7: What is it? What is the first image of foreboding seen by the searchers as they near the island?
4. In stanza 4, what do they see that is a sign of something wrong? In stanza 6, what happens to the familiar smell of lime and tar?
5. What do the men see in stanza 7 that alarms them even further?
6. What is the final result of the search for the missing keepers of the light? What do the searchers realize had happened to the previous lighthouse keepers?
7. The number three figures importantly in the poem, as if it is some omen of ill luck. How many threes or multiples of three can you find? How many men all together had been victims of "ill-chance" on Flannan Isle?

Interpreting Meanings

8. At the very end of the poem, the men are speechless. What do you think their fears are?
9. The "three queer, black, ugly birds" the rescue party sees in stanza 4 are significant. What do you think these black birds might be, or what might they stand for?
10. What bad news is suggested by the fact that the bird in stanza 7 is starved on its perch? How does its "feeble chirping" affect the scene's mood?
11. The poet avoids a singsong effect by forcing you not to stop at the ends of certain lines. To get the sense of these lines, you must read right on over into the next line. Such lines are called **run-on lines.** Run-on lines are simple to spot in this poem because they do not end with a punctuation mark. Lines 1 and 3, for example, are run on. A line whose sense naturally is completed at the end of a line is called an **end-stopped line.** End-stopped lines usually end with a punctuation mark, signaling you to pause. Lines 2 and 4, for example, are end stopped. Read the poem aloud. Which lines force you to run on to the next line to get their sense and to avoid a singsong beat?
12. Which lines do you think are so paced that they build up our suspense? How should these lines be read aloud?

Writing About the Poem

A Creative Response

Concluding the Story. Write your own solution to the mystery of Flannan Isle. Do you feel that human or natural forces caused the men to disappear? Or do you feel that the mystery has to do with the intrusion of unearthly or supernatural forces? In your account, use all the evidence you can find in the poem.

Before you write your own solution to the mystery, read the comment that follows ("Focusing on Background"), which summarizes an operatic version of the story.

Analyzing Language and Vocabulary

Connotations

You know that many words in the English language carry **connotations**—strong feelings and associations that are not necessarily part of their dictionary definitions. In this poem, for example, Flannan Isle is described as "lonely" (line 13). The word *lonely* strictly speaking means "standing apart from others." The word *alone* means the same thing, and so does the word *solitary.* But neither *alone* nor *solitary* suggests the feeling of sadness or longing for company that we have come to associate with the word *lonely.* Try substituting *alone* or *solitary* for *lonely* in the poem, and see if you sense the difference in feeling.

1. The *height* is called "naked" (line 14). Would your visual image of the height be the same if it were just described as "having no trees on it"? Does the image of a "naked height" seem pleasant or unpleasant?

2. When you read of "cold sunlight" (line 19), do you feel a sense of comfort provided by the sun? Or do you feel a chilliness and harshness? Would the phrase "weak sunlight" have the same emotional effect?
3. What do you visualize when you read that the door "gaped" (line 42)? How is a "gaping" door different from a door that is merely "opened"?
4. Make a list of words in the poem that connote these feelings and associations: darkness, death, mystery, emptiness, coldness.

Reading About the Writer

Wilfrid Wilson Gibson (1878–1962) was an Englishman whose poems often present compelling stories told with a sharp edge of irony. Gibson was a friend of Robert Frost, who lived near the Gibsons for a time in England. Frost, however, was often critical of Gibson's poems—this might have had to do with the fact that Gibson at the time was a much more popular poet than Frost was.

Focusing on Background
Another Version of the Story

This poem is based on a real-life incident so bizarre that Gibson is not the only person who has been inspired by the mystery.

On December 26, 1900, a supply ship visiting the Flannan Isles lighthouse, in the Outer Hebrides off the coast of Scotland, found the lighthouse deserted and the lighthouse beam extinguished. Everything was in order, but there was not a single trace of the three keepers, and nothing to indicate what might have happened to them. They had simply disappeared.

In 1980, Peter Maxwell Davies wrote a chamber opera called *The Lighthouse,* based on the mystery of Flannan Isle. Here is his version of what happened.

The prologue of the opera is set in an Edinburgh courtroom. Three officers, facing a court of inquiry investigating the disappearance of the keepers, tell conflicting stories of their visit to the empty lighthouse. The next scene flashes back to the lighthouse. We see the three keepers eating supper, playing cards, and singing songs. One keeper, named Blazes, tells of his brutal Glasgow childhood, when he bashed an old woman to death and let his father hang for the murder. Another keeper, Sandy, sings a sentimental song about a young friend. The third keeper, Arthur, sings a hymn. As the fog rolls in and the tide rises, Arthur starts the foghorn. Aloft in the lightroom, he sings to himself a song about a Beast whose cry is heard across the sleeping world. "One night," he sings, "that cry will be answered from the deep." Now we see that confinement and boredom have driven the three men mad. Their songs now express old guilts. Blazes sees the old woman and his dead parents. Sandy sees his friend, long since dead, whom he betrayed. Arthur returns from the lightroom crying that he has seen the Beast coming out from his grave deep below the tide. Hysteria seizes the three men and they sing a defiant song about the Beast as the lights of the approaching ship grow brighter and brighter. Suddenly the three officers are on stage again, in the courtroom. They say they had to defend themselves—the keepers had gone crazy; they had become beasts. At the end of the opera, we see the lighthouse again, but its functioning has been made automatic. Three ghostly keepers sit at supper, their conversation lost as the orchestra repeats the motif "The lighthouse is now automatic."

On the day of the opera's first performance, the real Flannan Isle's light stopped working, and a helicopter had to take a crew out to restart it.

Kidnap Poem

Nikki Giovanni

ever been kidnapped
by a poet
if i were a poet
i'd kidnap you

5   put you in my phrases
and meter you to jones beach
or maybe coney island
or maybe just to my house

lyric you in lilacs
10 dash you in the rain

alliterate the beach
to complement my see

play the lyre for you
ode you with my love song
15 anything to win you
wrap you in the red Black green
show you off to mama

yeah if i were
a poet i'd kid
20 nap you

The Lovers (Somali Friends) by Lois Mailou Jones (1950). Casein.

Courtesy the Evans-Tibbs Collection, Washington, D.C.

297

Responding to the Poem

Analyzing the Poem

Identifying Facts

1. Name three places the poet/kidnapper says she might take "you."
2. List all the unusual things in lines 9–17 that the poet would do to win "you."
3. Read the poem aloud to hear the rhythm of the **free verse**. Where does **alliteration** help create rhythm? Notice that Giovanni uses no punctuation at all. Where would you pause or make a full stop? What words would you emphasize?

Interpreting Meanings

4. Part of the fun of this poem comes from the way it uses the terminology of poetry. How many nouns connected with poetry are used as verbs? What do you imagine each one means here?
5. Poets love **puns**, which are plays on words to suggest two or more meanings. What puns do you spot in lines 13 and 19–20?
6. Use an almanac or encyclopedia to find pictures of the flags of Kenya, Malawi, and Zambia. How does knowing the colors of these African flags add to your understanding of line 16 and the significance of "Black"—the only capitalized word in the entire poem?
7. Maybe this poet is using kidnapping as a **metaphor** to describe the relationship between a poet and a reader. If so, what "weapons" does a poet use to "capture" or kidnap a reader? Do you think this is what the poem is about? Or is it merely a love poem?

Writing About the Poem

A Creative Response

Writing a Poem. Imitate the structure of Giovanni's poem and write a free-verse poem addressed to someone you like a lot. Your first lines should state the metaphor your poem will be based on. For examples:

> ever been "kidnapped" by a musician
>
> ever been "kidnapped" by a painter
>
> ever been "kidnapped" by a computer hack

You must use as verbs at least three nouns relating to the profession of the speaker:

> I'd treble you with trills
> put you in my chorus

Reading About the Writer

Nikki Giovanni (1943–   ) was born in Knoxville, Tennessee, and grew up in Cincinnati, Ohio. She is affectionately called the Princess of Black Poetry because of the large and enthusiastic crowds she attracts whenever she gives public readings of her work. Behind all Giovanni's poetry, according to one critic, are "the creation of racial pride and the communication of individual love." "I write out of my own experiences—" Giovanni says, "which also happen to be the experiences of my people." She has published collections of essays and several books of poetry, including *Re: Creation* and *Ego-Tripping and Other Poems for Children,* in which "Kidnap Poem" appeared. She says she is not flattered when students who take her classes try to write poems that sound like hers. "*I* already sound like me," she says. "I want my students to hear their own voices."

To catch the full emotional content of this poem, read it aloud. Note how it uses the simple, direct diction of folk poetry. Does the poet convince you that this is how a real woman might speak?

Woman Work

Maya Angelou

I've got the children to tend
The clothes to mend
The floor to mop
The food to shop
5   Then the chicken to fry
The baby to dry
I got company to feed
The garden to weed
I've got the shirts to press
10   The tots to dress
The cane to be cut
I gotta clean up this hut
Then see about the sick
And the cotton to pick

15   Shine on me, sunshine
Rain on me, rain

Fall softly, dewdrops
And cool my brow again.

Storm, blow me from here
20   With your fiercest wind
Let me float across the sky
'Til I can rest again.

Fall gently, snowflakes
Cover me with white
25   Cold icy kisses and
Let me rest tonight.

Sun, rain, curving sky
Mountain, oceans, leaf and stone
Star shine, moon glow
30   You're all that I can call my own.

Responding to the Poem

Analyzing the Poem

Identifying Details

1. Stanzas 2–5 are based on **apostrophe**—that is, a direct address to someone or something that cannot understand or respond. What are the things this speaker addresses? What does she ask of each of them?

Interpreting Meanings

2. In your own words, explain what this woman wants from life.
3. Sometimes people think "woman's work" is not as difficult or as important as "man's work." Do you think this poet wants you to see "woman's work" in another light? Explain.
4. Read this poem aloud and listen to its rhythm. Is it written in **free verse** or does it have a **regular metrical beat** or is it a mixture of both? What sentence patterns does the poet repeat?
5. How do you think this woman would respond to the message in Whitman's poem (page 290)?

Writing About the Poem

A Creative Response

Imitating the Poem. Write a poem from your own point of view, telling about your typical day. Imitate the structure of this poem: open with the words "I've got . . ." and list the things you have to do. Then give a list of the things you feel you can really call your own. If you prefer, use an invented character as your speaker.

This poem starts out in a voice that sounds like an adult's. Read the poem aloud, so that you hear how, in line 32, the voice becomes a child's. Before you read, decide what you think the title means.

The Fury of Overshoes

Anne Sexton

They sit in a row
outside the kindergarten,
black, red, brown, all
with those brass buckles.
5 Remember when you couldn't
buckle your own
overshoe
or tie your own
shoe
10 or cut your own meat,
and the tears
running down like mud
because you fell off your
tricycle?
15 Remember, big fish,
when you couldn't swim
and simply slipped under
like a stone frog?
The world wasn't
20 yours,
It belonged to
the big people.
Under your bed

sat the wolf
25 and he made a shadow
when cars passed by
at night.
They made you give up
your night light
30 and your Teddy
and your thumb.
Oh, overshoes,
don't you
remember me,
35 pushing you up and down
in the winter snow?
Oh, thumb,
I want a drink,
it is dark,
40 where are the big people,
when will I get there,
taking giant steps
all day
each day
45 and thinking
nothing of it?

Responding to the Poem

Analyzing the Poem

Identifying Details

1. You wouldn't think that anyone could write a poem about overshoes. But although overshoes are what start this poet thinking, we soon realize they are just an excuse to talk about something else. Name at least seven childhood feelings and experiences the overshoes remind her of.

2. What questions does the poet ask at the end of the poem?

Interpreting Meanings

3. Whom do you think the speaker is talking to in lines 5–31? Who could "they" be in line 28?
4. "Giant steps" can mean, of course, just "long steps." "Giant steps" is also the name of a game

children play. What larger idea could "giant steps" stand for in line 42?

5. What could the speaker mean by "get there" in line 41?

6. What evidence in the poem suggests that the speaker still has some of the feelings she experienced as a child? How would you describe these feelings?

7. Anne Sexton wrote this poem in **free verse.** No rules or meter told her when to end one line and begin another. She had to rely completely on her own sense of timing and spacing, on her own feeling of the "rightness" of how the poem sounds. Read the poem aloud, paying careful attention to when you should pause. Do you think these very short lines are appropriate to the subject and "voices" in this poem?

8. Suppose you were the "big fish" being spoken to in lines 5-31. How would you answer the poet?

Writing About the Poem

A Creative Response

Imitating the Poem. Anne Sexton looks at a row of overshoes sitting outside a kindergarten classroom and remembers her own childhood. The overshoes do not remind her of pleasant things; they call forth memories of being small and awkward and fearful. Write a poem or a paragraph in which you tell what some childhood objects remind you of. But choose something that calls forth pleasant, secure memories. Be sure to choose a title for your list of memories. (Objects you might use include crayons, dolls, cars, comic books, and so on.)

Reading About the Writer

Anne Sexton (1928–1974) was born in Newton, Massachusetts. She was a central figure in a group of poets who tended to write frankly about the most private aspects of their lives. Sexton's poems are often about her childhood, her marriage, her children, and her parents. She once said that poetry should be a "shock to the senses. It should almost hurt." In 1967 she won the Pulitzer Prize for poetry.

Creating Rhythm

1. Rhythm is a constant and universal fact of life. Rhythms are part of human life, and they are part of the natural life of the planet we live on. **Rhythm** is any more or less regular pattern of recurrence. If we were to make a list of common, ordinary rhythms, we might start with the following three. Can you add at least three more to this list? Consider mechanical rhythms as well as natural ones.

   > heartbeat
   > seasons
   > day and night

2. English is an accented language, so every word in English with more than one syllable has a pattern of stressed and unstressed syllables. To practice **scanning**—that is, indicating which syllables are stressed and which are unstressed—mark the stressed and unstressed syllables of these ordinary English words. Use this mark ⌣ to indicate an unstressed syllable; use this mark ´ to indicate a stressed one.

incessantly	hesitate	farewell
eradicate	slippery	undress
terrestrial	difference	forgive
afternoon	garnet	headstart
comprehend	morning	jetset
unaware	omen	hemidemi-semiquaver

3. Even your own name, and everyone else's name, has a regular metric beat:

   > John Fitzgerald Kennedy
   > Leonard Bernstein
   > Mario Cuomo
   > Ernesto Galarza
   > Eleanor Roosevelt
   > Ralph Bunche
   > Natalia Makarova
   > Chita Rivera

   Write down your own name and the names of three other people; how do the names "scan"?

4. Try the same thing with your town, your state, and the name of your school.

4. Nursery rhymes have strong, usually singsong meters, which help children remember them. For the same reason, wise old sayings also have more or less regular patterns of stressed and unstressed syllables. What is the pattern of stressed and unstressed syllables in these examples?

   a. Jack Sprat could eat no fat,
      His wife could eat no lean.
      And so between the two of them
      They licked the platter clean.
   b. Waste not, want not.
   c. Haste makes waste.
   d. Ask me no questions, I'll tell you no lies.

5. Write down the words to a song that you know well. Scan the first verse of the song—that is, indicate the stressed and unstressed syllables—to show whether or not the songwriter has followed a meter. If you choose "The Star-Spangled Banner," for example, the first line would be scanned like this:

   Oh, say can you see, by the dawn's early light

6. There is a kind of rhythm in everyday speech as well as in song. To catch this rhythm, you have to be sure your ear is attuned to the stressed and unstressed syllables in what you read and hear. How many strong stresses are found in these famous statements?

   a. We hold these truths to be self-evident, that all men are created equal. . . .

      —from The Declaration of Independence

   b. . . . government of the people, by the people, for the people, shall not perish from the earth.

      —from "The Gettysburg Address," Abraham Lincoln

c. Hitch your wagon to a star.

—Ralph Waldo Emerson

d. Hear me, my chiefs, my heart is sick and sad. From where the sun now stands, I will fight no more forever.

—Chief Joseph

e. I only regret that I have but one life to lose for my country.

—Nathan Hale

7. The following little poem is written in meter, though the poet doesn't follow the same meter in every line. Copy the poem on a separate piece of paper and scan it, indicating which syllables should be stressed and which should be unstressed. Compare your scanning with what your classmates do. Are there variations in the way you could read this poem? No punctuation appears at the ends of the lines. Should you read each line so that your voice runs on to the next? Or should you pause briefly at the ends of several lines?

Blackberry Sweet

Black girl black girl
lips as curved as cherries
full as grape bunches
sweet as blackberries

Black girl black girl
when you walk you are
magic as a rising bird
or a falling star

Black girl black girl
what's your spell to make
the heart in my breast
jump stop shake

—Dudley Randall

8. Copy this next poem out on a separate piece of paper and scan it, indicating which syllables are stressed and which are unstressed. Are there any variations in the pattern? Which line in this poem is *not* a run-on line? That is, which line ends with a punctuation mark?

The Hardship of Accounting

Never ask of money spent
Where the spender thinks it went.
Nobody was ever meant
To remember or invent
What he did with every cent.

—Robert Frost

9. Poetry written in free verse is written without strict meter. Free verse tends to imitate the natural rhythms of everyday speech, and the writer is usually very careful to balance long phrases and short phrases. One way rhythm is created in free verse is by the repetition of words and phrases. Here is a famous verse from the Bible. Read it aloud to feel the natural rhythm of the lines. How does repetition create the rhythm?

To every thing there is a season,
And a time to every purpose under the heaven:
A time to be born, and a time to die;
A time to plant, and a time to pluck up that
    which is planted;
A time to kill, and a time to heal;
A time to break down, and a time to build up;
A time to weep, and a time to laugh;
A time to mourn, and a time to dance;
A time to cast away stones, and a time to
    gather stones together;
A time to embrace, and a time to refrain from
    embracing;
A time to get, and a time to lose;
A time to keep, and a time to cast away;
A time to rend, and a time to sew;
A time to keep silence, and a time to speak;
A time to love, and a time to hate;
A time of war, and a time of peace.

—Ecclesiastes 3:1–8

The Sounds of Poetry: Rhyme and Other Sound Effects

Among the forms of repetition that contribute to a poem's rhythm, rhyme is the easiest one to recognize. **Rhyme** is the repetition of the sound of a stressed syllable and any syllables that follow: "nails" and "whales"; "material" and "cereal"; "icicle" and "bicycle."

Until very recently, poets considered rhyme essential, and readers expected it. Today, rhyme is a matter of choice—except for those professional versifiers who, like sausage-makers, grind out the little singsong messages found on greeting cards.

Some of our greatest poets continue to explore the endless possibilities of rhyme. Others have turned away from it; they believe that deep feeling is best expressed in language close to familiar speech.

Modern poets who use rhyme feel that it not only helps to make a poem sing, but that it also defines the shape of a poem and holds it together. Rhyme enhances the music of a poem with chiming sounds. It sets up in the reader a pleasing sense of expectation. We expect that the pattern of sounds introduced in the opening lines of a poem will be skillfully sustained until the poem is concluded. Readers also know that poems with a regular pattern of rhyme, or a **rhyme scheme,** are especially easy to memorize.

In spite of the advantage of rhyme, many poets have turned away from it because they feel that just about all of the words in the English language that can be rhymed have long ago been used up. The contemporary poet who would like to continue the practice of using rhyme is faced with having to repeat rhymes that have echoed down the centuries. Or the poet faces the challenge of making new rhymes that might turn out to be strained.

Approximate Rhyme

Some poets have solved this problem by using **approximate rhyme**—that is, words that do not have exact chiming sounds, but that repeat only some sounds. These approximate rhymes are also called "half rhymes," "off rhymes," or "slant rhymes." Readers who dislike them call them "imperfect rhymes." In any case, all of them are substitutes for familiar "head-on" rhymes like "June" and "moon" or "hollow" and "follow." Instead of being an exact echo, approximate rhyme is a partial echo: "hollow" and "mellow" or "look" and "back."

E. E. Cummings was an American poet who found endless possibilities in the language for **exact rhymes** (*may/day, stone/alone, me/sea*) and approximate rhymes (*milly/molly, star/were*). Read this lively poem aloud to enjoy the sounds.

maggie and milly and molly and may
went down to the beach(to play one day)

and maggie discovered a shell that sang
so sweetly she couldn't remember her troubles,and

milly befriended a stranded star
whose rays five languid fingers were;

and molly was chased by a horrible thing
which raced sideways while blowing bubbles:and

may came home with a smooth round stone
as small as a world and as large as alone.

For whatever we lose(like a you or a me)
it's always ourselves we find in the sea

—E. E. Cummings

Internal Rhyme

Rhymes usually occur at the ends of lines. They are seldom spaced more than four lines apart, for the simple reason that an interval longer than that is too long for the chiming sound to be clearly heard. But rhyme can also occur inside the lines. Rhyme inside a line of poetry is called **internal rhyme.** Cummings uses an internal rhyme in line 2 (*play/day*). Here are lines from a famous poem which uses two internal rhymes ("remember" and "ember") to chime with "December":

Ah, distinctly I remember it was in the bleak December;
And each separate dying ember wrought its ghost upon the floor.

—from "The Raven," Edgar Allan Poe

Onomatopoeia: Fitting Sound to Sense

Beyond rhythm and the forms it may take, the most important aspect of sound in poetry is one with a forbidding name: **onomatopoeia** (än′ə·mat′ə·pē′ə). *Onomatopoeia* means fitting the sound of the words to the sense of the words.

Literally, *onomatopoeia* means "the making of words." Long ago, it came into the English language from the Greek. It has eventually come to mean not merely word-making, but word-making by imitating sounds. We use onomatopoeia when we say a gun "bangs" or a cannon "booms." We use onomatopoeia when we say that bacon cooking in the frying pan "sizzles." A child uses onomatopoeia when he or she describes the sound of a rooster crowing in the morning as "cock-a-doodle-do."

In its simplest form, then, onomatopoeia is no more than a single word that echoes a natural sound (hiss, slap, rumble, snarl, moan, drip) or a mechanical sound (click, zing, whack, clickety-clack, putt-putt, toot).

Alliteration

Alliteration means the repetition of the same consonant sound in several words: **m**oney **m**ad, **h**ot and **h**eavy, **d**og **d**ays, **d**rip **d**ry, **w**ash and **w**ear, **r**eady and **r**a**r**ing to go. Alliteration can also be the repetition of similar sounds: a series of *p*'s and *b*'s, of *s*'s and *z*'s, of *d*'s and *t*'s, of *m*'s and *n*'s. Alliteration can also be used to echo sounds. Here is a famous example:

> The silken sad uncertain rustling of each purple curtain
>
> —from "The Raven,"
> Edgar Allan Poe

Alliteration (the repetition of rustling *s* sounds in *silken sad uncertain*) and onomatopoeia (the word *rustling*) together imitate the sound wind makes when it blows past heavy silk draperies.

If you look back at the poem by E. E. Cummings on page 305, about the girls who went to the sea, and if you read it aloud, you'll hear a great deal of alliteration. In the first line, we hear four girls' names that begin with "m." (Can you think of others he might have used?) Notice also the "s" sound in "shell that sang/so sweetly" and "stranded star." And of course there are the "b's" that sound like someone blowing bubbles.

Onomatopoeia is natural to us. Suppose we want to describe the movement of a snake through the grass. We would not say it goes "bumping along like a buggy on a cobblestone street," because that is not at all what a snake in the grass sounds like. But if we say the snake "slithered swiftly across the smooth floor of the grass," we might be satisfied: we have imitated in words the sound we might actually hear.

"Griping, greedy, grasping, grotesque, gruesome, grisly—do you know any other good 'grr' words?"

Drawing by Ed Fisher.
© 1984 The New Yorker Magazine, Inc.

Since this poem supplies the lyrics for one of the most famous American folk songs, you've almost certainly heard it sung at one time or another.

Carried along by the music, you may have thought it was a sentimental love song. If so, read these verses carefully—you'll be surprised.

Clementine

Percy Montross

In a cavern, in a canyon, excavating for a mine,
Dwelt a miner, forty-niner,° and his daughter, Clementine.

2. **forty-niner:** one of the people who went west looking for gold during the California gold rush of 1849.

REFRAIN:
Oh, my darling, oh, my darling, oh, my darling Clementine,
You are lost and gone forever, dreadful sorry, Clementine.

5   Light she was and like a fairy, and her shoes were number nine,
Herring boxes without topses, sandals were for Clementine.

Drove her ducklings to the water, every morning just at nine,
Hit her foot against a splinter, fell into the foaming brine.

Ruby lips above the water, blowing bubbles soft and fine,
10 Alas, for me! I was no swimmer, so I lost my Clementine.

In a churchyard, near the canyon, where the myrtle doth entwine,
There grow roses and other posies fertilized by Clementine.

Then the miner, forty-niner, soon began to droop and pine,
Thought he ought to join his daughter, now he's with his Clementine.

15 In my dreams she still doth haunt me, robed in garments soaked in brine
Though in life I used to kiss her, now she's dead, I draw the line.

Responding to the Poem

Analyzing the Poem

Identifying Details

1. What details tell you where Clementine lived? Who is speaking?
2. What happened to "darling Clementine"?
3. This song is a good example of the kind of joke, based on surprise and exaggeration, known as "frontier humor." What examples of surprise and exaggeration can you find?
4. **Rhymes, alliteration,** and a bouncy **rhythm** lend humor and liveliness to this love song. Look at the **end rhymes**—those at the end of each line. What name do they all rhyme with?
5. The first use of **internal rhyme** comes in line 2: "miner" and "forty-niner." The first use of **alliteration** occurs in line 1: "In a **c**avern, in a **c**anyon, ex**c**avating for a mine." Find ten other lines that contain sound effects created by alliteration and internal rhymes. How do you have to pronounce the phrase "ought to" in line 14 to produce a funny internal rhyme?

Interpreting Meanings

6. A **parody** is a comical, exaggerated imitation of something serious. This song is a parody of a sentimental love song about a delicate young woman. How would we expect a romantic speaker to react when Clementine falls into the duck pond? How does this speaker actually react? What other unromantic sentiments does the poem express?
7. Why do you think some versions of "Clementine" omit the final stanza?

Writing About the Poem

A Creative Response

Writing a Poem in Meter. Make up your own words to the tune of "Clementine." Try to make the end of every line rhyme with the same sound. If you need inspiration, you might find it by thinking of love songs set on some contemporary frontier: the moon, outer space, a computer lab.

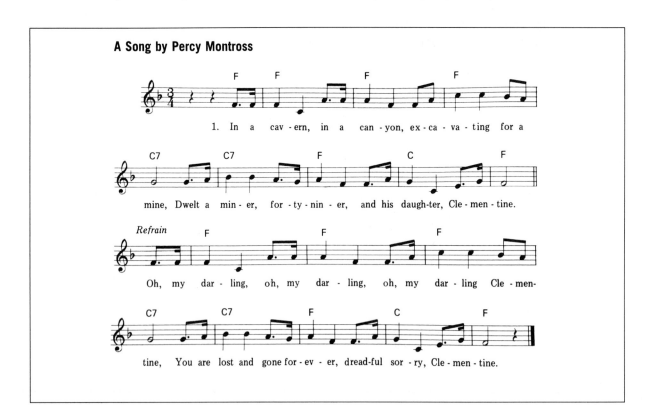

A Song by Percy Montross

1. In a cav-ern, in a can-yon, ex-ca-va-ting for a mine, Dwelt a min-er, for-ty-nin-er, and his daugh-ter, Cle-men-tine.

Refrain

Oh, my dar-ling, oh, my dar-ling, oh, my dar-ling Cle-men-tine, You are lost and gone for-ev-er, dread-ful sor-ry, Cle-men-tine.

When stories become as famous as Daniel Defoe's novel *Robinson Crusoe* (1720), they are always open to new interpretations and new twists. In Defoe's novel, Crusoe was a shipwrecked sailor who washed up on a desert island. Crusoe took in several pets—a parrot, a goat, a dog, and a cat. His one human companion was another man, whom Crusoe discovered on the island and named Friday. Read the first two stanzas of this poem aloud. Do the rhythms and rhymes suggest something serious to come, or do they suggest a comic Crusoe story?

Robinson Crusoe's Story

Charles Edward Carryl

    The night was thick and hazy
    When the "Piccadilly Daisy"
Carried down the crew and captain in the sea;
    And I think the water drowned 'em
5   For they never, never found 'em.
And I know they didn't come ashore with me.

    Oh 'twas very sad and lonely
    When I found myself the only
Population on this cultivated shore;
10   But I've made a little tavern
    In a rocky little cavern
And I sit and watch for people at the door.

    I spent no time in looking
    For a girl to do my cooking,
15 As I'm quite a clever hand at making stews;
    But I had the fellow Friday,
    Just to keep the tavern tidy,
And to put a Sunday polish on my shoes.

    I have a little garden
20   That I'm cultivating lard in,
As the things I eat are rather tough and dry;
    For I live on toasted lizards,
    Prickly pears, and parrot gizzards,
And I'm really very fond of beetle-pie.

25   The clothes I had were furry,
    And it made me fret and worry
When I found the moths were eating off the hair;
    And I had to scrape and sand 'em,
    And I boiled 'em and I tanned 'em,
30 Till I got the fine morocco suit I wear.

I sometimes seek diversion
In a family excursion
With the few domestic animals you see;
And we take along a carrot
35   As refreshment for the parrot,
And a little can of jungleberry tea.

Then we gather as we travel,
Bits of moss and dirty gravel,
And we chip off little specimens of stone;
40   And we carry home as prizes
Funny bugs, of handy sizes,
Just to give the day a scientific tone.

If the roads are wet and muddy,
We remain at home and study—
45   For the goat is very clever at a sum—
And the dog, instead of fighting,
Studies ornamental writing,
While the cat is taking lessons on the drum.

We retire at eleven,
50   And we rise again at seven;
And I wish to call attention, as I close,
To the fact that all the scholars
Are correct about their collars,
And particular in turning out their toes.

Illustration by N. C. Wyeth for the
novel *Robinson Crusoe* by Daniel
Defoe.

The Granger Collection, New York.

Responding to the Poem

Analyzing the Poem

The humor in this poem is in the service of **satire,** the kind of writing that, while it makes you laugh, also makes you see how wrong or silly some aspect of human nature is. This poem comments on the way the British in the nineteenth century tried to make all the countries they colonized into "new Englands." This Robinson Crusoe turns even a bleak desert island into a model of a cozy British establishment.

Identifying Details

1. How does Robinson Crusoe show that he is from a nation of shopkeepers?
2. The British have a reputation for occupying their time productively. What practical or educational activities do Crusoe and his "family" engage in?
3. British schoolmasters were very strict about their students' posture and dress codes. What fact does Crusoe want to point out about his scholars?
4. When, right off the bat, a poem begins to bounce along as this one does, you can be pretty sure that it's going to be lighthearted. Rhyme and rhythm so obvious are meant to please you. They might even make you a little nervous, as the poet sets up an elaborate scheme of rhythm and rhyme that threatens to collapse at any moment, yet never does. Read aloud the **end rhymes.** Which lines in each stanza always rhyme with one another? What clever rhyme has the poet thought of to go with "garden"?

Interpreting Meanings

5. This poem satirizes not only the British tendency to re-create "little Englands" wherever they went; it also makes fun of the general human desire to cling to the familiar, even in the most exotic surroundings. Which details about Crusoe's life do you think specifically make fun of this human tendency?
6. Much of the humor in this poem comes from its fantastic or improbable quality—we don't believe for a minute that a man cast off on a desert island could do some of these things. Which specific features and facts about Crusoe's life are absurd?

7. What do you think of the illustration for the poem (see the opposite page)? Do you think it is appropriate? Why or why not?

Writing About the Poem

A Creative Response

Adapting a Poem for TV. This poem might remind you of certain TV programs in which shipwrecked persons make cozy homes for themselves on deserted islands. Suppose this Robinson Crusoe were to be the basis of a TV series or a daytime cartoon series, and suppose you were the producer. Write a paragraph in which you describe the series. What will the general tone of the series be—light comedy, satire, serious drama? Who will the main character be? Who will the other characters be? Will you have a villain? What, in general, will be the main conflict, or problem, that the characters must face?

Reading About the Writer

Charles Edward Carryl (1841–1920) was a New York stockbroker who began writing stories for his two children. He was so enormously successful as a fantasy writer that he became known as "America's Lewis Carroll." This businessman (whose writings also included memos of stock transactions) was especially praised for his use of wordplay and nonsense.

To understand this poem, you have to know what a moor is, what heather is, and what a billow is.

Think also for a moment of things you can imagine but have never seen.

I Never Saw a Moor

Emily Dickinson

I never saw a moor—
I never saw the sea—
Yet know I how the heather looks
And what a billow be.

5   I never spoke with God
Nor visited in Heaven—
Yet certain am I of the spot
As if the checks° were given.

8. **checks:** colored railway checks that conductors gave to passengers when they collected their tickets. The ticket's color assured the conductor that the passenger had paid a fare to a specific destination.

Responding to the Poem

Analyzing the Poem

Identifying Details

1. In stanza 1, what does the poet say she knows? In stanza 2, what does she say she is certain of?

Interpreting Meanings

2. In what way does stanza 1 appear to be stating a contradiction? How does this "contradiction" reveal the power of imagination?
3. How does stanza 2 demonstrate the power of faith?
4. Describe the **rhyme scheme** in this poem by using a letter of the alphabet to indicate each new rhyme. What examples of **slant rhyme** does the poem contain? What do you think of this kind of "off rhyme"?
5. What do you think of the poem's message?

Writing About the Poem

A Creative Response

Extending the Poem. In a paragraph, name at least three things that you can picture in your mind, even though you have never seen them. Then name three things you have faith in, even though you have never seen or touched them. (If you prefer, you can list these things in the form of a poem.)

Analyzing Language and Vocabulary

Precise Diction

Emily Dickinson published only seven poems while she was alive. After her death, her sister discovered hundreds of poems carefully put away. Friends of the poet's family then set to work to copy the poems (Dickinson's handwriting was often hard to make out) and to try to get them published. In this process, the friends made changes in the poems.

1. The word *billow* in line 4 was changed to the word *wave*. What sound effect would be lost if *billow* became *wave*?
2. The word *checks* in the last line was changed to *chart*, meaning "a map." By using the word *checks*, what comparison did Dickinson want to suggest?
3. Would you be more certain of getting to Heaven (or any destination) if you were on a train with a ticket, or if you were using a map and trying to find your own way?

This poem was written with great care for rhyme and meter, yet it has the ''feel'' of free verse. Read it aloud to hear its music. Where do variations in meter keep it from sounding singsong?

Boy at the Window

Richard Wilbur

Seeing the snowman standing all alone
In dusk and cold is more than he can bear.
The small boy weeps to hear the wind prepare
A night of gnashings and enormous moan.

5   His tearful sight can hardly reach to where
The pale-faced figure with bitumen° eyes
Returns him such a god-forsaken stare
As outcast Adam gave to Paradise.

The man of snow is, nonetheless, content,

10   Having no wish to go inside and die.
Still, he is moved to see the youngster cry.
Though frozen water is his element,
He melts enough to drop from one soft eye
A trickle of the purest rain, a tear

15   For the child at the bright pane surrounded by
Such warmth, such light, such love, and so much fear.

6. **bitumen:** coal.

Responding to the Poem

Analyzing the Poem

Identifying Details

1. The first stanza is written from the point of view of the boy. Where is he? Why is he weeping?
2. The second stanza is told from the point of view of the snowman. Why is the "man of snow" content?
3. The boy himself appears fortunate, surrounded by "such warmth, such light, such love. . . ." What word in the last line reveals why the snowman sheds a tear for him?

Interpreting Meanings

4. Describe what the weather conditions would be like during a "night of gnashings and enormous moan." Which words in this description (line 4) are **onomatopoeic**? What words would a TV weather report use to describe the same weather?
5. In stanza 1, the poet **alludes,** or refers, to the story of Adam and Eve's expulsion from Paradise. Why does the poet think of the boy as the creator and the snowman as Adam? What does the expression "god-forsaken" mean?
6. If you were asked what the poem is about, you might say that it is about a boy and a snowman. But what is the poem also saying about pity and sympathy? Name at least two fears any child might have to face in life.
7. Both the snowman and the boy cry for one another. In the poem, who actually has more reason to feel sorry for the other? In what ways is this **ironic**—or just the opposite of what we think it should be?
8. Find at least three examples of **internal rhyme**—rhymes that occur inside lines that are close together in the poem. One **rhyming sound** connects the boy's stanza with the snowman's stanza. What sound do you hear chiming in both stanzas? How does this sound add to the poem's emotional effect?

Writing About the Poem

A Creative Response

Writing from Another Point of View. The snowman eventually has to "die." Write a paragraph or a poem telling how the snowman feels as the sun becomes warm enough to melt him. Is he content because this is the way things are? Did he expect to live forever? Is he now afraid? Does he think of the boy who made him? Have the snowman speak in the first person, using "I."

Reading About the Writer

Richard Wilbur (1921–   ), born in New Jersey, has lived most of his adult life in New England, with several important periods of residence in France, Italy, and New Mexico. Critics have pointed out that Wilbur shares some of the characteristics of another New England poet, Robert Frost. Like Frost, Wilbur is at ease with nature and its lessons, though he writes about his experiences with the sophistication of a man of wit and learning. In a time when raw and slapdash poetry has been widely accepted, Wilbur continues to write with the elegance and gravity that has always set him apart.

The Sea of Ice by Caspar David Friedrich (1823). Oil.

Hamburger Kunsthalle, Hamburg
Ralph Kleinhempel

**This poem is one of the shortest Frost ever wrote.
How could the very shortness of the poem reflect
its sense?**

Fire and Ice

Robert Frost

Some say the world will end in fire,
Some say in ice.
From what I've tasted of desire
I hold with those who favor fire.
5   But if it had to perish twice,
I think I know enough of hate
To say that for destruction ice
Is also great
And would suffice.

Responding to the Poem

Analyzing the Poem

Identifying Details

1. What emotion does the speaker compare to fire? What emotion does he compare to ice?

Interpreting Meanings

2. How could the world end in fire? How could it end in ice? (Think of what you know about war, the Bible, physics, geology, and even astronomy, and you'll find clues that will suggest some answers.)
3. How would you define "desire"? How is it like fire?
4. Explain why the speaker would feel that "hate" and "ice" have something in common.
5. Explain how "desire" could cause the world to end. Explain how "hate" could also do the job.
6. Here is a serious poem that uses sound effects to drive home its point. What words in the poem **rhyme**? In what way do the rhymes help emphasize the subject of the poem?

Writing About the Poem

A Critical Response

1. **Explaining an Opinion.** Fire and ice are two extremes of nature. Either of them could, by itself, put an end to all living things. Desire and hate are two human emotions; we can be "consumed with desire," or "hardened by hate." Which emotion, desire or hate, do you feel is more destructive? Write a paragraph explaining your opinion.
2. **Developing a Topic Statement.** "This poem talks about the end of the world, but desire or hatred could also put an end to an individual life or happiness." Write a paragraph in which you give at least two examples to develop this topic statement.

Reading About the Writer

Robert Frost (1874–1963) was the last American poet to achieve the status of a national figure on the order of certain sports or movie stars. His poems reflect the same cranky independence and homespun wisdom that brought about the American Revolution. Many are set in New England, but all reach beyond their settings to speak to everyone. Frost was widely read and much honored from the moment his first book appeared. As an old man, he played a prominent part in the ceremonies in which his friend John F. Kennedy was inaugurated President of the United States in 1961.

Here a speaker holds a shell up to his ear and hears its strange sounds. Read the poem aloud to hear how it echoes the sounds of the place the shell is supposed to have come from.

The Shell

James Stephens

And then I pressed the shell
Close to my ear,
And listened well.

And straightway, like a bell,
5   Came low and clear
The slow, sad murmur of far distant seas

Whipped by an icy breeze
Upon a shore
Wind-swept and desolate.

10   It was a sunless strand that never bore
The footprint of a man,
Nor felt the weight

Since time began
Of any human quality or stir,
15   Save what the dreary winds and waves incur.

And in the hush of waters was the sound
Of pebbles, rolling round;
Forever rolling, with a hollow sound:

And bubbling seaweeds, as the waters go,
20   Swish to and fro
Their long cold tentacles of slimy grey;

There was no day;
Nor ever came a night
Setting the stars alight

25   To wonder at the moon:
Was twilight only, and the frightened croon,
Smitten to whimpers, of the dreary wind

And waves that journeyed blind . . .
And then I loosed my ear. —Oh, it was sweet
30   To hear a cart go jolting down the street!

Responding to the Poem

Analyzing the Poem

Identifying Details

1. Find the **image** that describes what the speaker first hears when he puts the shell to his ear.
2. Find at least ten **images** that describe the sights and sounds of the place these sounds come from.
3. The poet uses **onomatopoeia** to echo the strange sounds he hears in the shell. What specific words in lines 6 and 16 echo the sound of the sea?
4. List at least four other examples of **onomatopoeia** in stanzas 6, 7, and 9—words that echo the sounds of waters, pebbles, seaweeds, and wind.
5. What hard consonant sounds in the last line echo the sounds made by the cart?

Interpreting Meanings

6. Why do you think the speaker feels that it is "sweet" to hear the sounds of the cart?
7. What other ordinary sounds could make you feel relieved or comforted?
8. Do you think the "sounds in a shell" would suggest these images to everyone? Might they remind someone else of a happy place? Why or why not?

Writing About the Poem

A Creative Response

1. **Using Onomatopoeia.** As an exercise in describing sounds, close your eyes and listen for a few minutes to the sounds you hear around you. Write three sentences describing the sounds; use words with sounds that echo what you hear. Here are some commonly used onomatopoeic words:

murmur	rumble	gush
ticktock	drum	roar
honk	buzz	whistle
snap	hum	clatter
hush	chatter	sob
patter	groan	moan
drip	sputter	crack
rustle	splash	whisper
tap		

A Critical Response

2. **Developing a Topic Statement.** "The mood of this poem is mournful and gloomy, except for the ending, where the mood is broken by a cart's jolting sound." In a paragraph, develop this topic sentence. You should list at least four specific **onomatopoeic** words with sounds that create the mournful, gloomy mood. You should also list three visual **images** that reinforce this mood. At the end of your paragraph, write one sentence, telling how you responded to the poem.

Reading About the Writer

Poet and novelist **James Stephens** (1882–1950) was born in Dublin, Ireland, to working-class parents. Because of a childish theft, he was sent to the Meath Protestant Industrial School for Boys. There he received not only punishment for his "crime," but a good education as well. A few years after the Irish Free State was established in 1922, Stephens moved to London. But he was always homesick and used to haunt one of the train stations in London, hoping to find an old friend arriving from home. Stephens had a gift for fantasy and humor. He is well-known for his collections of Irish fairy tales and for his fantasy novel *The Crock of Gold*. He has another poem on page 285 of this book.

Literature & Language

Creating Sounds

1. Rhyme is not limited to poems. Just as figurative language is used in everyday speech and in newspapers, so is rhyme used in ordinary speech. Here are three common word combinations that rhyme. Can you add at least four more to this list?

   hi-fi
   boob tube
   fair and square

2. Here are three ordinary compound words that use alliteration. Can you add at least four more to this list?

   crisscross
   spick-and-span
   wishy-washy

3. Advertisers know how powerful rhyme is: they use it to fix in our memories the names of their products and to make us remember what their products supposedly will do for us. Look through magazines and newspapers, and closely observe commercials on TV. Can you find slogans that use rhyme, alliteration, or onomatopoeia?

4. Think of a song that's popular now, or any song that you particularly like or know well. Does it use rhyme, alliteration, or onomatopoeia?

5. Here are some political slogans of the past. Where do they use alliteration and rhyme to fix the name of the candidate in your mind?

   Van, Van, is a used-up man! (1840)
   Tippecanoe and Tyler too! (1840)
   I like Ike! (1952)
   All the way with LBJ! (1964)

6. English spellings and pronunciation are often used as a source of humor. The following poem bases its whole message on a peculiarity in English: there are words in English that are spelled the same but pronounced differently, and there are words in English that are pronounced the same but spelled differently. Make a list of the words in this tongue twister that rhyme. Make another list of words that look as if they should rhyme, but don't. (Such words are called "eye rhymes.")

Hints on Pronunciation for Foreigners

I take it you already know
Of tough and bough and cough and dough?
Others may stumble but not you,
On hiccough, thorough, lough, and through?
Well done! And now you wish, perhaps,
To learn of less familiar traps?

Beware of heard, a dreadful word
That looks like beard and sounds like bird,
And dead: it's said like bed, not bead—
For goodness sake don't call it "deed"!
Watch out for meat and great and threat.
(They rhyme with suite and straight and debt.)
A moth is not a moth in mother
Nor both in bother, broth in brother,
And here is not a match for there
Nor dear and fear for bear and pear,
And then there's dose and rose and lose—
Just look them up—and goose and choose,
And cork and work and card and ward,
And font and front and word and sword,
And do and go and thwart and cart—
Come, come, I've hardly made a start!
A dreadful language? Man alive!
I'd mastered it when I was five!

—T.S.W.

7. Think of four exact rhymes to go with each of these words:

stone	horn	moon
soup	song	time
snow	clothes	shore

8. Think of two exact rhymes and two approximate rhymes for each of these words:

ocean	warm	beard
wash	bush	power

9. Read the following poem carefully, and then answer the questions that follow.

One A.M.

The storm came home too blind to stand:
He thwacked down oaks like chairs
And missing foothold in the dark
Rolled ominous downstairs,

And fumbling with a giant hand
Made nine white tries to scratch
Against a shuddering wall of air
The strict head of his match.

—X. J. Kennedy

a. How is the storm personified?
b. What is literally happening outside in lines 2–4?
c. What are the "nine white tries" the storm makes?
d. What is the "shuddering wall of air"? Does the word *shuddering* suggest any sound to you?
e. What metaphor does the poet use to describe the fire the storm might cause?
f. What is the rhyme scheme of stanza 1?
g. Which rhyming sounds from stanza 1 are repeated in stanza 2, as a way of linking the stanzas together musically?
h. Which word in stanza 1 is onomatopoeic—that is, which word echoes its sense?
i. What rolling long vowel sound is repeated in line 4?
j. What word in line 6 echoes its sense?

Writing

Using Onomatopoeia. This comic description of a pig eating is by a famous British humorist:

A sort of gulpy, gurgly, plobby, squishy, wooflesome sound, like a thousand eager men drinking soup. . . .

—P. G. Wodehouse

Write a sentence describing the sounds made by the following things. Try to use onomatopoeia and alliteration to echo the sounds you hear.

a rainy, windy night
a cat eating dry pet food
a drummer practicing
a city street
a person eating a carrot

RESPONDING TO A POEM

Writing Assignment

Write a three-paragraph essay in which you explain your response to any poem you have read in this unit.

Background

Everyone has some kind of response to a particular poem. But except for limited responses such as "It's nice" or "I don't like it" or "It's all right, I guess" or "It's boring," no one finds it easy to say exactly what that response is. Talking or writing about your response to a poem is difficult because it's like having to pin down a reaction to taste. (It is also difficult to explain why you might like peanut butter or why you might hate carrot juice.)

One thing to remember is that poems don't just happen. Poems are made. Like anything else put together by the human hand and mind, a poem is open to human judgment. We are entitled to ask three questions about any poem:

> How *well* is the poem made?
> What's the point of it?
> Is it worthy of my attention?

Most "made" things are designed to make life simpler, more comfortable, or more efficient. We judge these things in terms of how well they work. Poems have no practical purpose whatsoever, yet we also judge them as if they did—we analyze them in terms of how well they "work." Certain practical things—the butter churn, the hitching post, the shoe button—have become obsolete and have disappeared simply because they are no longer useful. Poems do not become obsolete. But, like things that served the practical needs of only a limited period of history, poems can disappear, simply because they no longer excite the response which first greeted them.

Some of the poems in this book have been read for centuries, some for only a few years. Like all poems, these are on trial, pleading their cases before a new generation, a new audience. Since you are a member of one of these new generations, you come to a poem with experiences different from anything that people have brought to the poem before. Yet your expectations of poetry are just about the same as those held by readers a century ago.

In each step of the process of defining your response, it's important to remain independent. Say what you actually think and feel, and do not be impressed by some notion of what you *ought* to think and feel. Once you've given a poem several readings, once you're sure that you've paid close attention to every image and figure of speech, nothing will help you find the words you need more quickly than faith in your own opinion.

Prewriting

1. The first step is to choose a poem you responded to strongly—one that has delighted you or irritated you, or one that has some special connection with your own experience. Write one sentence stating in general how this poem made you feel.
2. To gather reasons for your response, answer the following questions about the poem's **content** and **construction**. Remember that everything included in the poem is probably there for a good reason.

CONTENT: What does the poem say to you, as the reader?
   a. What experiences or feelings does the poem remind you of or make you think about?
   b. Does anything in the poem make you feel surprise? Irritation? Delight? Suspense? Sadness? Awe?
   c. Does the poem say anything about its subject that you would have liked to say yourself?
   d. What is the poem's message, or main idea, and is it one you'll remember? Or is it one you reject?

e. Does the poem confirm an idea about life that you always believed was true but never knew you knew it before?

CONSTRUCTION: What makes this piece of writing a poem and not a newspaper item? How is the poem put together?

a. Does the poem use **rhyme** and **meter**? Or is it written in **free verse**?

b. What **sound effects** does the poet use, and are they used for a purpose?

c. If you were to write a letter to the poet saying how the poem affected you, what lines or phrases would you mention?

d. Is the **title** of the poem important?

3. Select three answers from each group of questions that best explain your response.

4. Look for details and quotations from the poem that support your response.

Writing

You could follow this plan in writing your essay:

1. Paragraph 1: Briefly tell what the subject of the poem is. State your response to the poem.

2. Paragraph 2: Name at least three ways in which your response is related to the poem's construction (its rhyme, rhythm, and sound effects).

3. Paragraph 3: Name at least three ways in which your response is related to the poem's content.

Here is a response that one reader wrote about the following poem, "Running":

Running
1933
(North Caldwell, New Jersey)

What were we playing? Was it prisoner's base?
I ran with whacking keds
Down the cart-road past Rickard's place,
And where it dropped beside the tractor-sheds

Leapt out into the air above a blurred
Terrain, through jolted light,
Took two hard lopes, and at the third
Spanked off a hummock-side exactly right,

And made the turn, and with delighted strain
Sprinted across the flat
By the bull-pen, and up the lane.
Thinking of happiness, I think of that.

—Richard Wilbur

Though I wasn't even alive in 1933 and have never even seen North Caldwell, New Jersey, I like the way Richard Wilbur begins "Running" by telling where and when the poem takes place. This helps to make the subject of the poem—a boy's run—real for me. It also makes me think that some of the things I do today may become important memories sometime in the future.

When I first read the poem, it was over so quickly that I hardly noticed that the end of every line rhymed with another line. Then I saw that every stanza had the same construction. The underlying meter is iambic. The first line of each stanza has five strong stresses, the second has three, the third has four, and the last line of each stanza is like the first. I happen to be interested in the way poems are put together, so for me the question was:

> Cites title and author.
>
> Names the subject.
>
> Describes his or her response to the poem.
> Begins to discuss the poem's construction.
> Mentions rhyme.
>
> Mentions meter.

How could a poem so formal in design seem so free in effect? That's the poet's secret, I guess, but I suddenly understood that using free verse isn't the only way to make a poem sound like the kind of talk I hear every day. Then I looked for alliteration or onomatopoeia. Sure enough, they are there. Seventeen words have *p* or *b* in them—in a poem only twelve lines long! I saw that the poet used these sounds because they imitate the sounds someone running in tennis shoes would make (he calls them keds).

Mentions sound effects.

Most of all, I like the poet's main idea—that happiness comes from something as simple, yet perfect, as a run. I like to jog, and sometimes I feel a rush of happiness when I pass the corner of Atlantic Avenue and Second Street and see the sun shining on the windows of the house there. I think his phrase "jolted light" is just right to describe what light looks like when you are running. I know that Richard Wilbur is a grown man now, with children and even a grandson of his own, but I like to think there are still some experiences that unite old people with young people. It makes me feel that when I am an adult, I won't think that the things I like to do now are unimportant. If I wrote to Richard Wilbur, I'd ask if we could run a mile or two together—not to see who's faster, but just for the fun of it. I wonder if running would still mean happiness for him.

Discusses the poem's main idea and how it makes him or her feel.

Ends with a clincher statement.

Checklist for Revision

1. Have you cited the poem's title and author and subject?
2. Have you described your general response to the poem?
3. Have you discussed at least three details about the poem's construction?
4. Have you discussed at least three details about the poem's content?
5. If you quoted from the poem, did you quote correctly?
6. Did you use quotation marks to indicate direct quotations?
7. Have you ended your essay with a good clincher statement?

Tone: Revealing an Attitude

Tone is not easy to define, because it is a quality of language that tends to be *suggested* rather than *stated*. **Tone** is a speaker's attitude—toward a subject or toward an audience. Tone can be sarcastic, teasing, critical, serious, playful, angry, admiring, ironic, and so on. (Painters can also reveal tones. The artist below, for example, has taken a mocking tone toward the poor poet, who counts out verses in a leaky attic.)

When we speak out loud, we reveal tone by using our voice and even body gestures. We use our voice to indicate emphasis—that is, we give weight to particular words. We can also vary our pitch and volume and use pauses.

The Poor Poet
by Karl Spitzweg (1839). Oil.

Nationalgalerie Staatliche Museen
Preussischer Kulturbesitz, West Berlin

Take a simple sentence such as "School starts next week." By emphasizing different words and by varying your pitch, volume, and pauses, you can change your tone:

School starts next week. (Sincere)
School starts next week? (Disbelieving)
School starts next week! (Excited)
School starts next week. (Disgusted)

When a poem is printed on a page, we can't hear its tone in the way we can hear a tone of voice. But a poem does convey a tone, and until you've heard its tone, you haven't grasped the poet's complete message.

Diction and Tone

One way to reveal tone is through word choice, or **diction.** If a poet sees a red face and describes it as "beefy," the tone is critical, maybe even sarcastic—no one wants to look like a side of beef. But if the poet describes the face as "rosy" or "robust," the tone is positive and approving.

If a poet compares the world to a rose, the tone is approving—the world seems beautiful. But if a poet compares the world to a prickly cactus, the world does not seem so beautiful, and we sense a cynical tone.

If the poet describes a gaping wound as a minor scratch, we sense an ironic tone—we know the poet is saying one thing but really means something else.

William Wordsworth's tone was solemn when he said, "A slumber did my spirit steal." If we said, "I conked out," we'd be saying more or less the same thing, but our tone would be completely different.

William Shakespeare was adoring when he asked his lover, "Shall I compare thee to a summer's day?" But when he stated in another poem, "My mistress' eyes are nothing like the sun," he was mocking poets who use such exaggerated comparisons.

Sounds and Tone

Rhythms and **rhymes** can also convey tone. If we hear a lively, bouncy rhythm and jingly rhymes, the poet is probably not taking a solemn tone. If a poem is slow-moving and stately, the poet is probably not taking a light, humorous tone.

When Ogden Nash tells us: "Any hound a porcupine nudges / Can't be blamed for harboring grudges," we laugh. Those bouncy rhythms and jingly rhymes reveal to us at once that Nash, as usual, was being playful and funny.

When we read a poem, we must try to hear the poet's tone of voice, his or her emphasis. We must look at the words the poet has chosen and listen to the way the poem sounds. Once we catch the poet's tone of voice, we will become aware of a particular attitude, and the meaning of the poem will be complete.

> " Until you've heard its tone, you haven't grasped the poet's complete message."

Think of at least two different tones you might find in a letter to a sixth-grade teacher. Then read aloud to hear this letter's tone. Which passage in the poem best expresses its tone?

Dear Mrs. McKinney of the Sixth Grade:

David Kherdian

Hands down, you were my favorite
teacher at Garfield elementary,
or at any school since:
your stern, austere face, that
5   held an objective judgment of
everything in charge;
the patient way you taught,
out of a deep belief and respect
for learning,
10   and the good books you chose
to read aloud—
in particular, Mark Twain;
and the punishment you handed
out (a twin cheek twist, just
15   once, with forefingers and thumbs)
embarrassed us only because
we had failed ourselves,
for we had wisely learned from you
the need for discipline and regard.

20   Long after I left that place
I saw you once waiting for a bus,
and though I returned your warm
smile, I hurried on.
Why didn't I stop, as I could
25   see you wanted me to? I deeply
regretted it for weeks, and there
are moments when I remember it still.
And nothing, not poem, not time,
not anything for which I might
30   stand proud, can erase that seeming
failure of feeling and regard on
my part.
I loved you, I really did, and I
wish now that in stopping and chatting
35   with you for a moment I could have
shown it to you then,
instead of now, in this poem,
in which only time and loss, not
you and I, are the subject to be held.

Responding to the Poem

Analyzing the Poem

Identifying Details

1. Written in the form of a letter, this poem, like any good personal letter, is both casual and direct. It is a communication between two people who have shared an experience. What four reasons does the poet give for Mrs. McKinney's being his favorite teacher? What did he learn from her?
2. What incident prompted the poet to write this "letter"?

Interpreting Meanings

3. Why do you think the poet wants to share this "letter" with strangers, as well as with Mrs. McKinney, if she is still alive?
4. Taking into account what he reveals about himself and about Mrs. McKinney, how would you answer the poet's question in lines 24–25?
5. How does the speaker feel now about his experience at the bus stop? Is his **tone** one of amusement? Regret? Indifference? Bitterness?
6. What feelings expressed in this poem do you think most people would identify with?

Writing About the Poem

A Creative Response

Answering the Poet. What must Mrs. McKinney have thought of the boy she knew who smiled at her but did not stop to speak? To supply some of the missing answers, pretend that you are Mrs. McKinney, that you got on the bus, went home, and wrote a letter or poem beginning "Dear David Kherdian: . . ."

Reading About the Writer

David Kherdian (1931–) was born into an Armenian-American family in Racine, Wisconsin. He now lives in Oregon. This poem is from a book of poetry called *I Remember Root River.*

Focusing on Background
A Comment from the Poet

"It might be said that *everything* a poet writes is an open letter to the world—but, in truth, the poet is really writing to the interior witness *in himself.* Nevertheless, on occasion, the addressee is someone real, someone on the outside who did exist, and in the case of Mrs. McKinney (a teacher I loved and respected), the subject acts as a catalytic agent for the poet's conscience. Perhaps what this poem is really saying is that we need the exterior world to experience the inner world. Unless we can establish a correspondence between the two—is this the poet's job?—we are limited by our senses only, by the exterior world only. Then, little by little, the business of living will take us and we will become gradually lost to what is ours to treasure, protect, and develop—ourselves."

—David Kherdian

Before you read, write down what you think this title might mean. Then read the poem aloud, and listen to the speaker's tone of voice. The material on the next page explains the source of the title. How would the poem's tone differ if it had been called "A Heroic Death"?

"Out, Out—"

Robert Frost

The buzz saw snarled and rattled in the yard
And made dust and dropped stove-length sticks of wood,
Sweet-scented stuff when the breeze drew across it.
And from there those that lifted eyes could count
5   Five mountain ranges one behind the other
Under the sunset far into Vermont.
And the saw snarled and rattled, snarled and rattled,
As it ran light, or had to bear a load.
And nothing happened: day was all but done.
10   Call it a day, I wish they might have said
To please the boy by giving him the half hour
That a boy counts so much when saved from work.
His sister stood beside them in her apron
To tell them "Supper." At the word, the saw,
15   As if to prove saws knew what supper meant,
Leaped out at the boy's hand, or seemed to leap—
He must have given the hand. However it was,
Neither refused the meeting. But the hand!
The boy's first outcry was a rueful laugh,
20   As he swung toward them holding up the hand,
Half in appeal, but half as if to keep
The life from spilling. Then the boy saw all—
Since he was old enough to know, big boy
Doing a man's work, though a child at heart—
25   He saw all spoiled. "Don't let him cut my hand off—
The doctor, when he comes. Don't let him, sister!"
So. But the hand was gone already.
The doctor put him in the dark of ether.
He lay and puffed his lips out with his breath.
30   And then—the watcher at his pulse took fright.
No one believed. They listened at his heart.
Little—less—nothing!—and that ended it.
No more to build on there. And they, since they
Were not the one dead, turned to their affairs.

Responding to the Poem

Analyzing the Poem

The title of this poem is an **allusion**—a reference to a famous speech by Macbeth in Shakespeare's play of that name. Macbeth has just heard of his wife's death, and he speaks bitterly of the brevity of life:

"Out, out, brief candle!
Life's but a walking shadow, a poor player
That struts and frets his hour upon the stage,
And then is heard no more. It is a tale
Told by an idiot, full of sound and fury,
Signifying nothing."

Identifying Details

1. The poem opens with **onomatopoeia**—words whose sounds imitate their sense. What sinister noises do you hear as the poem opens?
2. Exactly what happens when the sister comes to announce supper?
3. Describe the boy's reaction to the accident.
4. What happens to the boy? What do the others do?

Interpreting Meanings

5. Why do you think the boy died? When the poet says that the boy saw all "spoiled," what does he mean?
6. What is the significance of the comment at the end of the poem: "No more to build on there"?
7. Does Frost suggest that someone is to blame for the tragedy? If so, who? What do you think?
8. What particular words **personify** the saw as an almost human character?
9. The poem ends on a surprising matter-of-fact tone. Why is this tone **ironic**—that is, given what has happened, why is this tone inappropriate? Why do you think no one shows any sign of grief or horror? What message might Frost be giving us, in ending the poem on this tone? What do you think of his message?
10. What connections can you make between Macbeth's words and the particular situation in the poem? What do you think of Macbeth's view of life?

Writing About the Poem

A Creative Response

1. **Writing from Another Point of View.** What were "they" (line 31) really thinking as the boy's heart stopped? Let one of these adults tell the story of the accident, using the first-person pronoun "I." Have your speaker identify his or her relationship to the boy.

A Critical Response

2. **Contrasting the Poem with a News Story.** Frost based his poem on an actual accident recorded in a local newspaper, on March 31, 1901:

SAD TRAGEDY AT BETHLEHEM

Raymond Fitzgerald a Victim of Fatal Accident

Raymond Tracy Fitzgerald, one of the twin sons of Michael G. and Margaret Fitzgerald of Bethlehem, died at his home Thursday afternoon, March 24, as the result of an accident by which one of his hands was badly hurt in a sawing machine. The young man was assisting in sawing up some wood in his own dooryard with a sawing machine and accidentally hit the loose pulley, causing the saw to descend upon his hand, cutting and lacerating it badly. Raymond was taken into the house and a physician was immediately summoned, but he died very suddenly from the effects of the shock, which produced heart failure. . . .

—*The Littleton Courier*

In a brief essay, contrast Frost's poem with the newspaper story.

3. **Responding to a Poem.** Robert Frost often read his poems aloud before audiences. He would not read this poem in public because he felt it was "too cruel." What is your response to the poem—do you think Frost made the situation too cruel? Write a paragraph explaining your response.

Don Marquis (1878–1937) was a newspaper columnist who commented humorously on the society and politics of the early twentieth century. He was also the creator of an unlikely philosopher—"archy," a cockroach. According to his creator, archy learned to produce poems by jumping on typewriter keys. Reading this poem, we are supposed to believe that it was composed by archy during the night and left on the desk where the newspaperman he called "boss" would be sure to see it the next morning. archy often left poems for the "boss."

Since archy is too small to use the shift key, he provides no capitalization for his poem, and he does not bother with punctuation. Read the poem aloud. Let your own sense of speech rhythms and inflections tell you when to pause, where to begin and end sentences, and how to distinguish between the voice of the moth and the voice of archy.

The Lesson of the Moth

Don Marquis

i was talking to a moth
the other evening
he was trying to break into
an electric light bulb
5   and fry himself on the wires

why do you fellows
pull this stunt i asked him
because it is the conventional
thing for moths or why
10   if that had been an uncovered
candle instead of an electric
light bulb you would
now be a small unsightly cinder
have you no sense
15   plenty of it he answered
but at times we get tired
of using it
we get bored with the routine
and crave beauty
20   and excitement
fire is beautiful
and we know that if we get
too close it will kill us
but what does that matter
25   it is better to be happy
for a moment
and be burned up with beauty
than to live a long time

and be bored all the while
30   so we wad all our life up
into one little roll
and then we shoot the roll
that is what life is for
it is better to be a part of beauty
35   for one instant and then cease to
exist than to exist forever
and never be a part of beauty
our attitude toward life
is come easy go easy
40   we are like human beings
used to be before they became
too civilized to enjoy themselves

and before i could argue him
out of his philosophy
45   he went and immolated himself
on a patent cigar lighter
i do not agree with him
myself i would rather have
half the happiness and twice
50   the longevity

but at the same time i wish
there was something i wanted
as badly as he wanted to fry himself
           archy

Responding to the Poem

Analyzing the Poem

Identifying Details

1. At the beginning of the poem, what is the moth trying to do? What does archy think of this behavior?
2. What is the moth's explanation for his behavior? In other words, what is his philosophy of life?
3. In lines 40–42, what does the moth say is wrong with human beings nowadays? According to the moth, what made people become this way?

4. What happens to the moth?
5. After the moth dies, how does archy explain his own philosophy of life? Clearly, archy disagrees with the moth and disapproves of his actions; what does archy envy about him?

Interpreting Meanings

6. What *is* the "lesson of the moth"?
7. What is archy's **tone** in telling his boss about the moth?

   a. awed and envious
   b. angry and resentful
   c. critical and sarcastic

8. If you were telling the story of the moth, what **tone** would you take?

Writing About the Poem

A Creative Response

1. **Imitating the Poem.** Here, a newspaper editorialist pretends to be archy's grandson as he types a letter responding to an article stating that NASA is accepting applications to travel in space with the astronauts:

> **dear nasa**
>
> your administrator james beggs says there s room for civilian passengers on next year s shuttle flights and asks for applications
> please take me
> he says he wants artists and writers who can describe the beauties of the firmament better than those laconic astronauts well my great great grandfather was the famous poet who typed reams of verse by divebombing the keys of don marquis s typewriter archy was only a roach but roaches are survivors everywhere man has been roaches have gone too why not space
> i am a good traveler i won t get seasick or starstruck mr beggs says the passengers will be assigned from time to time to tend the galley or do things like that i know my way round galleys well enough he says he wants them to translate the experience of what they see in space

into real terms for the public   i am a fine translator   i translate that as meaning he would like
the public to get so high on space it will support
his wish to build a manned space station even
though it will cost 20 billion dollars and nasa
isn t sure what on earth to do with it

we certainly know what to do with it   a roach s
reach must exceed its grasp or what s a heaven
for   once we have colonized the galley on mr
beggs s fine new space station we will aim for
the home of our ancestors on the star betelgeuse
which human children can call beetlejuice

why   because we have conquered every habitat on earth and need new frontiers to conquer
new enterprises to stir the imagination   new
spiritual challenges to justify our raison d etre[1]
also those benighted termites may do it first.

nasa   i am the ideal passenger please accept
my application   if you don t well you can expect
me anyway

Write another composition by archy, in which
you give a cockroach's point of view on some
other topic: roach poison, cats, cities, garbage.
Be sure to imitate archy's unique style, whether
you do it on a typewriter or not.

A Critical Response

2. **Expressing an Opinion.** What do you think of the
two philosophies of life offered in this poem? In
a brief paragraph, summarize in your own words
what the two philosophies are and explain how
you feel about each one. Perhaps you don't
agree with either archy or the moth. If that is
the case, say so and tell why.

---

1. **raison d etre** (raison d'être) (rā ′zon det′): French for "reason
for being." (Notice that archy can't type in the apostrophe or
the word's French accent.)

Analyzing Language and Vocabulary

Extended Meanings

The word *immolate* in this poem specifically refers
to a custom from the ancient world, where a sacrificial victim was killed and offered to the gods.
Thus, *to immolate,* strictly speaking, means "to
offer someone or something up to the gods as a
sacrifice."

When the moth "immolates" himself in this
poem, it means something less specific. Here, *immolate* means that the moth offers his life for a
higher cause (at least as he sees it). Thus the meaning of the old word *immolate* has become somewhat
extended, though it still has to do with the idea of
sacrifice or destruction.

Use a dictionary to answer the following questions about this word. Notice that the **etymology** of
the word, given in parentheses either before or after
the definition, will tell you about its history.

1. What does the word *grits* (or *meal*) have to do
with the meaning of *immolate*?
2. How is the word *mill* related to the word *immolate*?
3. When we say that millions of young men were
"immolated" in a war, what do we mean?

Perhaps you might recognize the kind of love this poem is about. Do you think such love is rare in our world today?

"She loved him all her life"

Lynne Alvarez

She loved him all her life
and when she thought he might die
she tied her wrist to his at night
so that his pulse would not flutter
away from her suddenly
and leave her stranded

Responding to the Poem

Analyzing the Poem

Identifying Details

1. This brief poem is over almost as soon as it starts. See if you can **paraphrase** the poem— that is, state what it says in your own words. Be sure you define the word *stranded*.

Interpreting Meanings

2. A **metaphor** is implied in the last three lines. What creature do you think of when you hear the verb *flutter*? What comparison might be implied?
3. Think of at least two other phrases that might have been used in place of "leave her stranded." What image and feeling does the word *stranded* add to the poem that the other phrases do not?
4. Poems about love can reveal all kinds of **tones,** from angry sarcasm to saccharin-sweet sentimentality. How would you describe the way this speaker feels about the old couple's love?

Writing About the Poem

A Creative Response

1. **Extending the Poem.** Write a second stanza, telling what happens one night when the string flutters.

A Critical Response

2. **Analyzing Free Verse.** This poem has no end punctuation, not even at the end of the final line. In a paragraph explain why, in your opinion, Alvarez decided not to conclude her poem with end marks. (Does it have something to do with the poem's subject?) How would you read the final line if you were reading the poem aloud? At the end of your paragraph, tell what you think of poetry like this—as compared with poetry that uses rhyme and meter.

Reading About the Writer

Lynne Alvarez (1947–   ), a poet and playwright, lived for many years in Mexico and now lives in New York City. Poet David Ignatow says that her poetry is unlike any poetry written today: "It has its roots in the poetry of Latin America, yet is violently and vividly the work of a poet in the United States."

Imagine this speaker standing at the bottom of a steep canyon in the Southwestern United States. Hundreds of years ago, high up on the ledges of these canyon walls, a Pueblo people had built their "cliff cities." Eventually, these remarkable builders and artists abandoned their homes and mysteriously disappeared. But the remains of their cliff dwellings, wall paintings, and pottery attest to a rich cultural legacy, which still survives in Pueblo tribes today.

Notice how this speaker, who is looking up at the ruins of the ancient cliff dwellings, feels she is a part of the community that disappeared so many years ago. What does she know will never change in human life?

Slim Man Canyon

For John, May 1972

Leslie Marmon Silko

700 years ago
    people were living here
    water was running gently
    and the sun was warm on pumpkin flowers.
5 It was 700 years ago
      I remember
they were here
     deep in this canyon
     with sandstone walls rising high above them.
10 The rock, the silence, tall sky and flowing water
     sunshine through cottonwood leaves
     the willow smell in the wind
        700 years ago.

The rhythm,
15   the horses' feet, moving strong through
        white deep sand.
Where I come from is like this
     the warmth, the fragrance, the silence.
Blue sky and rainclouds in the distance
20   we ride together
past the cliffs with the stories
      the songs painted on rocks . . . .
    There was a man who loved a woman
    seven hundred years ago.

Responding to the Poem

Analyzing the Poem

Identifying Facts

1. List five **images** that help you imagine life 700 years ago in Slim Man Canyon.

Interpreting Meanings

2. What does this poet think will never change?
3. What words and ideas are repeated in the poem? What point might the poet be trying to make by using this **repetition?**
4. The poet describes moving through the canyon. In what **figurative sense** does the canyon move through the poet?
5. This poem asks the reader to make mental leaps through the canyon's history—from the past to the present and even into the future. Think about the poem's dedication: "for John, May 1972." Then think of how the poet associates the cliffs and rocks with stories and songs. How might the last two lines actually refer to the poet and her companion?

6. What is the speaker's **attitude** toward this place? Is she bitter? Sad? Contented? Critical?
7. Do you think most people today are so in touch with a place that they feel they are a part of its history? Talk about your responses.

Writing About the Poem

A Creative Response

1. **Describing a Place.** One of the meanings of *genius* is "guardian spirit of a place." In "Slim Man Canyon," Silko evokes the Pueblo people whose spirits give the canyon its special character. The poet even suggests that she, too, is a part of the canyon's history. Write a paragraph describing a place so special that you would want to be its genius and to have your spirit associated with it always. Describe the place as it looks now and as it might have looked centuries ago. You might open with the words "700 years ago."

A Critical Response

2. **Researching the Background.** In an encyclopedia or American history book, read about Pueblo history, architecture, and culture. In a short report, explain what you learned about the background of the poem and tell how it adds to your understanding of the poet's attitude toward Slim Man Canyon. You might look under these topics: Pueblo, Hopi, Canyon de Chelly, Chaco Canyon, Cliff Dwellings, Anasazi, Zuni.

Reading About the Writer

Leslie Marmon Silko (1948–   ) grew up in the Pueblo community of Laguna in New Mexico and currently teaches at the University of Arizona in Tucson. A novelist and short-story writer, as well as a poet, Silko draws her inspiration from Pueblo culture, ritual, and oral tradition. Her unusual book called *Storyteller* includes poems, short stories, and photographs of the place and the family that gave Silko her roots.

Conquerors

Henry Treece

By sundown we came to a hidden village
Where all the air was still
And no sound met our tired ears, save
For the sorry drip of rain from blackened trees
5   And the melancholy song of swinging gates.
Then through a broken pane some of us saw
A dead bird in a rusting cage, still
Pressing his thin tattered breast against the bars,
His beak wide open. And
10   As we hurried through the weed-grown street,
A gaunt dog started up from some dark place
And shambled off on legs as thin as sticks
Into the wood, to die at last in peace.
No one had told us victory was like this;
15   Not one amongst us would have eaten bread
Before he'd filled the mouth of the gray child
That sprawled, stiff as a stone, before the
      shattered door.
There was not one who did not think of home.

Responding to the Poem

Analyzing the Poem

Identifying Details

1. Who is **speaking** in the poem?
2. Find the two sound **images** that describe what the conquerors hear as they enter the village.
3. What specific **images** of death and destruction do they see?

Interpreting Meanings

4. What do you think happened to the "gray child"?
5. What does the speaker mean when he says: "No one had told us victory was like this"? What do you think the conquerors expected victory to be like? Do you infer from this that they are young, or old and experienced?
6. In what way is the title of this poem **ironic**?
7. What feelings about war is this speaker expressing? Do you share them? Explain.
8. Do you think this poem could apply to events that are happening today? Or does it apply only to World War II? Explain.

Writing About the Poem

A Creative Response

Describing a Scene from a Specific Point of View. This poem might accompany any one of hundreds of tragic newspaper photographs of young soldiers face-to-face with the horrors of war. On the opposite page is a photograph of another kind of reaction to another war experience. Write a paragraph from this child's point of view, and tell what the child has seen and is thinking.

Analyzing Language and Vocabulary

Connotations

Certain words suggest, or **connote**, sadness and decay; certain other words suggest, or connote, happiness and fertility.

1. Make a list of ten words and phrases in this poem that, for you, suggest sadness and decay.
2. When you finish your list, compare it with your classmates' lists. Do all of you agree? Are there any words that have different connotations for different people?
3. Now take the first 12 lines of the poem and eliminate all the sad images you have found, replacing them with happy ones.
4. Compare your rewritten versions. Have any of you used the same new words? Have you now created an entirely new tone for the poem? Have you suggested that the conquerors' feelings are different?

Reading About the Writer

Henry Treece (1911–1966) was an Englishman who served in the Royal Air Force during World War II. In addition to poetry, Treece wrote historical fiction, including many juvenile novels.

A satire makes fun of people or institutions by making them appear ridiculous. In "Needs," the things made to seem foolish are advertising and the gadgets it makes us feel we need. Before you read, be sure you know the difference between a "need" and a "want."

Needs

A. R. Ammons

I want something suited to my special needs
I want chrome hubcaps, pin-on attachments and year round use
    year after year
I want a workhorse with smooth uniform cut, dozer blade and
    snow blade & deluxe steering wheel
I want something to mow, throw snow, tow and sow with
5   I want precision reel blades
I want a console styled dashboard
I want an easy spintype recoil starter
I want combination bevel and spur gears, 14 gauge stamped steel
    housing and washable foam element air cleaner
I want a pivoting front axle and extrawide turf tires
10   I want an inch of foam rubber inside a vinyl covering
and especially if it's not too much, if I can deserve it, even if I
    can't pay for it I want to mow while riding.

Responding to the Poem

Analyzing the Poem

Identifying Details

1. Look at the poet's first line. What has the advertisement probably said to persuade the speaker to buy this particular product?
2. From the details in the poem, tell what kind of machine is being advertised.

Interpreting Meanings

3. Throughout the poem, the speaker says that he wants various features of this product—and yet the poem is entitled "Needs." What point do you think the poem is making about the differences between "wants" and "needs"? What do we really "need" in life?
4. What would you say this poem is about—who or what is its subject? How does the poet **feel** about the subject?
5. Do you agree with the poet that advertisements or commercials on television can make us want things we don't need, perhaps don't deserve, and probably can't always afford? Explain.

Writing About the Poem

A Creative Response

Imitating the Poem. This poem is structured around the features of a particular kind of machine that the poet saw advertised, probably in a magazine. Imitating this poem, write one of your own, based on an advertisement that strikes you as particularly silly or false. Open your sentences with the words "I want" and complete them with the features of the product as itemized in the ad. What kind of a tone will you use, and what point will your poem make?

Analyzing Language and Vocabulary

Coining Words

Americans have been particularly clever in inventing new names for new inventions. Often, the words coined for new inventions or new products are taken from other things already in use. The word *conductor,* for example, had been in use on the stagecoach when it was adapted for use on the railroad. Sometimes new words are given the name of their inventor (the diesel engine was named for Rudolph Diesel).

1. What kind of vehicle first used the term *dashboard* (line 6)? What does the word refer to today? A good dictionary will give you the answers.
2. What does *foam* mean in line 8? How do you think the word came to be applied to a kind of rubber product widely used today (see line 10)?
3. The term *vinyl plastic* is an Americanism (which means it originated in America). What is the "vinyl covering" mentioned in line 10?
4. This speaker wants an "extrawide" turf tire. Americans often combine adjectives like this to suggest size or quality. Give at least three examples of how the adjectives "extra" and "super" are used by advertisers and others to indicate size or superiority.

Reading About the Writer

A. R. Ammons (1928–   ) is a poet of what might be termed "a native stripe." This means that he is thoroughly American, both in his experience as a country boy growing up in South Carolina and in his tendency toward poetic experiment and invention. (One of his longest poems was typewritten on the kind of tape a shopper receives at a check-out counter.) Ammons is a professor of English at Cornell University, but he is anything but academic in his approach to language or thought. In his poems, philosophy and wit work together to show humans in relation to their environment.

Highway: Michigan

Theodore Roethke

Here from the field's edge we survey
The progress of the jaded. Mile
On mile of traffic from the town
Rides by, for at the end of day
5 The time of workers is their own.

They jockey for position on
The strip reserved for passing only.
The drivers from production lines
Hold to advantage dearly won.
10 They toy with death and traffic fines.

Acceleration is their need:
A mania keeps them on the move
Until the toughest nerves are frayed.
They are the prisoners of speed
15 Who flee in what their hands have made.

The pavement smokes when two cars meet
And steel rips through conflicting steel.
We shiver at the siren's blast.
One driver, pinned beneath the seat,
20 Escapes from the machine at last.

Responding to the Poem

Analyzing the Poem

Identifying Details

1. Where is the speaker and what is he looking at?
2. What details in the poem (including the title) tell you that these are auto workers from the assembly lines in Detroit, who are driving home from work in the plants?
3. What happens in the last stanza to two of these cars?

Interpreting Meanings

4. What double meaning can you find in the comment that one driver "escapes from the machine at last"?
5. As you know, **irony** suggests a difference between appearances and reality. What is ironic about the speaker's comment that, on this jammed highway, "the time of workers is their own"?
6. In what ways are these drivers "prisoners of speed"? What do you think they are fleeing from?
7. The poem is concerned with workers involved in a particular kind of job. How do you think the poet **feels** about this work and the effect machines can have on human lives? Do you agree with him? Why?
8. Suppose you had to illustrate this poem. What scene or images would you concentrate on?

Writing About the Poem

A Critical Response

1. **Applying the Poem.** In three sentences, tell how this poem might apply to any worker whose days are spent on a production line or in an office where individuals sometimes feel like cogs in a machine.
2. **Comparing Poems.** In a brief essay, compare this poem to "Southbound on the Freeway" by May Swenson (page 244). Before you write, fill out a chart like the following one, to help you determine the ways the poems are alike and unlike.

	Roethke	Swenson
Who is speaking in the poem?		
What is the speaker looking at?		
What is the poet's attitude toward automobiles in life today?		

Analyzing Language and Vocabulary

Connotations

The fact that the poet chose the word *jaded* in line 2 is important. *Jaded* is a word that carries strong **connotations,** or feelings and associations. The word comes from a Finnish word meaning "a mare," specifically, an old, worn-out horse.

1. What does *jaded* mean in line 2?
2. Use the word *jaded* in two other sentences. Does *jaded* suggest negative feelings toward a subject or positive ones? Explain.
3. Does the word *jaded* in this poem reveal something necessarily true about the drivers, or does it only reveal how the speaker feels about them? Explain.
4. Suppose another observer saw these same drivers and had a different attitude. How would the tone of line 2 change if the drivers were described as "tired," "lonely," or "oppressed"?
5. If someone "toys" with death and traffic fines, what is their attitude toward death and fines? Does the poet know for certain that this is how the drivers feel? Or does the use of this verb reveal the poet's attitude, and not what is actually true about the drivers? Explain.
6. In using the word *mania,* what does the poet suggest about the drivers' frame of mind? Do we know for sure that "a mania keeps them on the move," or is this the poet's way of looking at them? What other needs or feelings might keep the drivers moving on this highway?

This poem comes from a collection of poems called *Spoon River Anthology*. Each poem in this collection is spoken by a person who lies buried in a cemetery in a town in Illinois called Spoon River. The speaker of this poem is a woman who is buried at the back of the cemetery, and she has heard many a gloomy story of woe and bitterness from her companions. Here she stands up and addresses them all. This woman is based on the character of the poet's grandmother, Lucinda Masters. Read the poem aloud. Would you change your tone in line 18?

Lucinda Matlock

Edgar Lee Masters

I went to the dances at Chandlerville,
And played snap-out at Winchester.
One time we changed partners,
Driving home in the moonlight of middle June,
5   And then I found Davis.
We were married and lived together for seventy years,
Enjoying, working, raising the twelve children,
Eight of whom we lost
Ere I had reached the age of sixty.
10   I spun, I wove, I kept the house, I nursed the sick,
I made the garden, and for holiday
Rambled over the fields where sang the larks,
And by Spoon River gathering many a shell
And many a flower and medicinal weed—
15   Shouting to the wooded hills, singing to the green valleys.
At ninety-six I had lived enough, that is all,
And passed to a sweet repose.
What is this I hear of sorrow and weariness,
Anger, discontent, and drooping hopes?
20   Degenerate sons and daughters,
Life is too strong for you—
It takes life to love Life.

Responding to the Poem

Analyzing the Poem

Identifying Details

1. List all the joys Lucinda Matlock knew in life. Then list the tragedies she experienced.
2. What line reveals Lucinda's response to people who are angry, discontented, and hopeless?

Interpreting Meanings

3. Find the words Lucinda Matlock uses to describe death. What do these words reveal about her **attitude** toward death?
4. In line 20, what does the word *degenerate* mean? By calling her neighbors "degenerate," what **feelings** about them does Lucinda reveal?

Woman with Plants by Grant Wood (1929). Oil.

Cedar Rapids Museum of Art

5. The message of the poem is revealed in the last line. How would you define the two meanings of the word *life* here? If you had to put this advice in your own words, what would you say?

6. Which of these words would you use to describe Lucinda Matlock's **tone** as she speaks in this poem?

   a. cynical and disappointed
   b. joyful and proud
   c. complaining and self-pitying

How does Lucinda's tone affect the way you feel about her?

Writing About the Poem

A Critical Response

1. Writing an Answer to the Poem. What do you think of Lucinda Matlock's speech? Suppose someone had not been as fortunate as she was in her marriage and health. Suppose someone had not lived in a town like Spoon River, but instead in a congested city. Would Lucinda's example apply to her? In a brief paragraph, answer Lucinda Matlock as she speaks to you from the Spoon River Cemetery. Tell if you agree or disagree with her message, and why.

2. Comparing Poems. In a brief essay, compare "Lucinda Matlock" with "Women" by Alice Walker (page 256) and "Woman Work" by Maya Angelou (page 299). Before you write, fill out a chart like the following. This will help you see at a glance how the poems are alike and how they are different.

	Masters	Walker	Angelou
Who is the speaker?			
What is the speaker's message?			
What is the speaker's attitude toward life?			

Analyzing Language and Vocabulary

Connotations

We see in this poem how a single word—*degenerate*—can suggest Lucinda Matlock's whole attitude toward her neighbors. *Degenerate* is a word with strong **connotations,** or associations and feelings.

1. Think of two other adjectives that someone else might use to describe the same people that Lucinda Matlock calls "degenerate." One adjective should suggest a feeling of love, and the other adjective should suggest a feeling of pity and sympathy for their hard lives.

2. Let two of Lucinda Matlock's neighbors describe *her.* Have one of them use an adjective that suggests awe and admiration, and have another one use an adjective that suggests dislike.

3. Lucinda Matlock's description of death has strong connotations, and it reveals the way she feels about dying. Think of another way of describing death that reveals a different attitude.

Reading About the Writer

Edgar Lee Masters (1868–1950) was born in Garnett, Kansas, and brought up in Lewiston, Illinois. He followed in his father's footsteps by becoming a lawyer, but he later gave up law for literature. Though he wrote novels and biographies as well as poetry, his literary reputation is based on only one volume, *Spoon River Anthology.* In this collection of poems in free verse, a graveyard of dead people speak their own epitaphs. Masters struck a new note in American literature when he looked behind the scenes in Spoon River and recorded what he saw. Unlike Lucinda Matlock, many of the people who speak from the cemetery tell stories that suggest the failure of the American dream and of our belief in the even hand of justice. Some of the other speakers from Spoon River are "George Gray," "Mrs. George Reece," and " 'Butch' Weldy."

Literature & Language

Expressing a Tone

1. When we speak, we can use our voices to convey tone—that is, our attitude or feeling toward what we're talking about. We can pitch our voices high or low, we can stress certain words for emphasis, we can increase or decrease volume, and we can pause. Say the following sentences aloud: first, express a tone of approval; next, express a tone of disbelief; finally, express a tone of accusation.

   a. Caldwell ate the cabbage.
   b. Caldwell ATE the cabbage.
   c. CALDWELL ate the cabbage.

   How can you use pitch, stress, volume, and pauses to make each of these sentences express two different tones?

   a. That's a bright idea.
   b. Shelley asked Lester to dance.
   c. Albert's going to Paris.

2. In writing, we can use adjectives and adverbs to suggest the way we feel about a subject. For example, we could describe Caldwell's cabbage dinner in at least two ways, to suggest two different attitudes toward it:

   Mushy, smelly cabbage (a tone of disgust)
   Sweet, crisp cabbage (a tone of approval)

   Use adjectives to describe the following nouns so that you suggest two distinct attitudes toward each of them:

   a. eye make-up   d. darkness
   b. dogs   e. liver
   c. rain   f. malls

3. There is no easy formula to follow in detecting the tone of a poem. You must consider all the poem's elements, including its descriptive words, its figures of speech, and its sounds. When you are trying to identify a poem's tone, ask yourself: How does this writer feel about his or her subject? Tone can usually be described by an adjective:

admiring	playful
amused	mocking

angry	nostalgic
affectionate	regretful
compassionate	solemn
ironic	sorrowful

Here are a brief poem and a stanza from another poem. Both of these poets use similes to compare their hearts to other things, things they have found in nature that best fit the way they feel. By examining the similes, you can tell exactly how each speaker feels.

> ### Ebb
> I know what my heart is like
>   Since your love died:
> It is like a hollow ledge
> Holding a little pool
>   Left there by the tide,
>   A little tepid pool,
> Drying inward from the edge.
>
> —Edna St. Vincent Millay

> ### from **A Birthday**
> My heart is like a singing bird
>   Whose nest is in a watered shoot;
> My heart is like an apple tree
>   Whose boughs are bent with thickset fruit;
> My heart is like a rainbow shell
>   That paddles in a halcyon° sea;   6. **halcyon:** very calm.
> My heart is gladder than all these
>   Because my love is come to me.
>
> —Christina Rossetti

a. What similes do the speakers use to describe their hearts?
b. Which similes suggest something full of life?
c. Which simile suggests something empty and dried up?
d. Which poem conveys a happy, expectant tone?
e. Which poem conveys a sad, regretful tone?

4. When we say a poet's tone is **satirical,** we mean that the poet is being critical of some human weakness or foolishness. Satire may use sarcasm, mockery, irony, and exaggeration—anything to make the object of the attack seem ridiculous or hateful. Whatever method is used, the person writing satire always wants to bring about reform or change.

   The next poem was written by a poet who served with the British army in World War I. The "pit" he says he dreams about refers to the trenches. There were twenty-five thousand miles of trenches dug in Europe during that war—enough to circle the entire earth.

Does It Matter?

Does it matter?—losing your leg? . . .
For people will always be kind,
And you need not show that you mind
When the others come in after hunting
To gobble their muffins and eggs.

Does it matter?—losing your sight? . . .
There's such splendid work for the blind;
And people will always be kind,
   As you sit on the terrace remembering
   And turning your face to the light.

   Do they matter?—those dreams from
      the pit? . . .
   You can drink and forget and be glad,
   And people won't say that you're mad;
For they'll know that you've fought for your
   country,
And no one will worry a bit.

—Siegfried Sassoon

   a. The speaker asks three times: "Does it matter?" But he does not answer the question directly. What answers does he give?
   b. Do you think the speaker offers his "answers" sincerely, or is he being ironic? How do you think the speaker feels about people who will "always be kind" and won't "worry a bit"?

   c. What is the poem's *real* answer to the question? *Does* it matter that the soldier has lost his leg, or his sight, or that he has nightmares about the trenches?
   d. How would you describe the tone of this poem?

5. A poet does not always write in the same tone. Here is another poem by Siegfried Sassoon in which he expresses a different tone. This poem was written at the end of the war.

Everyone Sang

Everyone suddenly burst out singing;
And I was filled with such delight
As prisoned birds must find in freedom
Winging wildly across the white
Orchards and dark green fields; on; on; and
   out of sight.

Everyone's voice was suddenly lifted,
And beauty came like the setting sun.
My heart was shaken with tears, and horror
Drifted away. . . . . O, but everyone
Was a bird; and the song was wordless; the
   singing will never be done.

—Siegfried Sassoon

   a. What simile does the poet use to express his feelings of release when he heard that the war was over?
   b. What simile does he use to describe the way "beauty" came to him?
   c. In the last stanza, what metaphor describes the singers?
   d. Which pair of adjectives best describes the poet's tone in this poem: Wistful and sad? Satirical and bitter? Joyful and hopeful?

ANALYZING A POEM

Writing Assignment

Write a five-paragraph essay in which you analyze any one of the following poems: "Flannan Isle" (page 291), "Fire and Ice" (page 315), " 'Out, Out—' " (page 328), or "Lucinda Matlock" (page 342). In your essay, discuss the elements of sound and sense and explain how you responded to the poem.

Background

When you **analyze** a poem, you are taking the poem apart in order to see what's in it and how it works. Your aim is to discover how all the elements of sound and sense in the poem work together to create meaning and feeling. These elements include **images, figures of speech, rhyme, rhythm, sound effects,** and **tone.** Analyzing a poem can help you better understand your own response to it. Sometimes the analysis might even change your initial response.

Prewriting

1. Select one poem to analyze, then read it closely—and more than once. Be sure to read the poem out loud, too: hearing a poem is as important as seeing it on a printed page.
2. **Paraphrase** the poem—that is, restate in your own words what the poem says, stanza by stanza (see page 285). This will help you understand the line-by-line progress of the poem. If you find yourself puzzled by some line or figure of speech, read it again or talk with someone else to try to figure out what puzzles you. Restate the figures of speech in your own words.

3. To gather details about the poem's elements, you might fill out a chart like the following:

	Poem's title
Who is the **speaker**? (Or is the speaker unidentified?)	
What is the speaker talking about? (What is the poem's **subject**?)	
What **images** and **figures of speech** are in the poem? How do they affect the way the poem makes you feel?	
What is the poem's **tone**? (What is the poet's attitude toward the subject?)	
How does the poem use **rhyme, meter, free verse,** or other **sound effects**? Do the sound effects contribute to the sense of the poem?	
How do you **respond** to this poem? How can you explain your response?	

4. Reread the poem once more and find quotations that will support or illustrate your analysis.

Writing

You might use the following plan to organize your essay:

1. **Paragraph 1:** Cite the poem's title and author. State the poem's subject. Identify its speaker.
2. **Paragraph 2:** Paraphrase the poem, stanza by stanza. Point out the poem's important images and explain any figures of speech.
3. **Paragraph 3:** Describe the tone of the poem.
4. **Paragraph 4:** Tell how the poem's sounds contribute to its sense.
5. **Paragraph 5:** Describe and explain your personal response to the poem.

Here is an essay that a reader wrote about the following poem, "Youth's Progress":

Youth's Progress

Dick Schneider of Wisconsin . . . was elected
"Greek God" for an interfraternity ball.

—*Life*

When I was born, my mother taped my ears
So they lay flat. When I had aged ten years,
My teeth were firmly braced and much improved.
Two years went by; my tonsils were removed.

At fourteen, I began to comb my hair
A fancy way. Though nothing much was there,
I shaved my upper lip—next year, my chin.
At seventeen, the freckles left my skin.

Just turned nineteen, a nicely molded lad,
I said goodbye to Sis and Mother; Dad
Drove me to Wisconsin and set me loose.
At twenty-one, I was elected Zeus.

—John Updike

"Youth's Progress" by John Updike is based on a magazine article. The poem is about a boy who was elected "Greek God" for a ball sponsored by his university's fraternity organization. The speaker is that boy himself—not actually, but as the poet *imagines* the boy might speak.

    The boy, a typical American kid, gives an outline of his life up to the time he was chosen to be Zeus. In the first stanza, he tells how his ears were taped so they wouldn't stick out, how his crooked teeth were braced, and how his bad tonsils were taken out. In the second stanza, he says that when he was fourteen, he combed his hair in a fancy way. Though he still didn't have much of a beard, he shaved his upper lip and, a year later, he could shave his chin. When he was seventeen, he lost his freckles. At nineteen, the boy says he was "nicely molded." This is an example of figurative language—because the boy was not literally made of clay or anything else that can be molded or shaped. I think this figure of speech suggests that the boy compares himself to a statue created by a sculptor. Then the boy went to the University of Wisconsin where, at the age of twenty-one, he was elected Zeus for an interfraternity ball.

Marginal annotations:

Cites title and author.
Names the poem's subject.

Names the poem's speaker.

Begins to paraphrase the poem.

Explains a figure of speech.

In this poem, John Updike is poking fun at American college life. The poet's tone is comical and mocking. After all, Zeus was the greatest god of ancient Greece. It's a joke to think that an ordinary American boy who keeps himself in good shape might one day become Zeus. It is also comical to think that someone who once had crooked teeth and protruding ears and freckles could become a Greek god. It's even a joke to imagine that a god could be *elected*.

Describes the poem's tone.

The poem is fun to read because of its rhymes and its regular, bouncy beat, which is bascially iambic pentameter. These elements also contribute to the poem's humorous tone. I think the rhyme of "Zeus" with "loose" is clever because it's unexpected.

Mentions the poem's sounds.

This poem also made me realize that other beauty or popularity contests are just as silly as the fraternity's election of Zeus. After all, how could anyone really be "Miss *Universe*"? How could any ordinary girl or boy be "Homecoming *Queen*" or "Homecoming *King*"? I recommend this poem for school books because it is straightforward, funny, and its message relates to real life.

Explains his or her response.

Checklist for Revision

1. Have you cited the poem's title and author, named the subject, and identified the speaker?
2. Have you paraphrased the poem?
3. Have you explained the figures of speech?
4. Have you described the tone of the poem?
5. Have you discussed the poem's sounds?
6. If you used quotations from the poem, did you cite them correctly and put them in quotation marks?
7. Have you described your personal response to the poem?

Two Kinds of Poetry: Ballads and Lyrics

Some of the oldest poems in the world are concerned with telling stories. These very old story poems survive today from places like ancient Sumeria, Greece, and Britain. Usually they tell about what happened to men (sometimes women) who wanted to achieve some goal out of the ordinary. Some of them had to escape the anger of the gods or face the opposition of their own people. These stories told tales of great heroism. Their characters were larger-than-life figures who fought and schemed their way to victory or who died bravely in the attempt. The oldest of all these story poems, the story of Gilgamesh, King of Sumer, might be over 4000 years old. Many people think the greatest of them is the *Odyssey,* composed by the poet Homer between 900 and 700 B.C. (See page 711.)

During the Middle Ages in Europe, another form of "story song" developed. Ordinary people began to turn up in these stories, and what happened to them could happen to anybody. Whether these later story poems were about heroes or about simple people, they all took the form of *ballads*—a word that comes from a French word meaning "a dancing song."

Ballads: Sung Stories

A **ballad** is a story told with a lilt or a beat that makes it easy to sing or recite from memory. A typical ballad also has a **refrain**—a line, a phrase, or even a whole stanza that is repeated exactly or almost exactly throughout the song.

We do not know the names of the authors of the traditional ballads because the songs were not written down until many years after they were first sung. When people liked a ballad, they would just pass it on from generation to generation by word of mouth. As different singers took over a song, changes were made in it, so that many different forms of the old ballads often exist today.

In our own time, ballads are still widely recited and sung. Many come from people who live in remote areas or from people who are outcasts in some way. We have ballads sung by prisoners, by outlaws, by workers in hazardous jobs such as mining. We have ballads sung by people whose color, race, or religion sometimes causes them to be set apart and deprived of advantages other people take for granted. For centuries, ballads have recounted episodes in the lives of people who found themselves in difficult

> "**M**any ballads come from people who are outcasts in some way."

circumstances: deceived by lovers, betrayed by kings, confronted by injustice. Ballads have expressed people's hopes and fears. They have provided us with folk heroes, like the "steel drivin' man" John Henry, whose individual fates reflect the fate of their whole community.

Today, however, the ballad has undergone a transformation brought about by the music and record business. Instead of growing naturally out of experiences commonly shared, many ballads today are "manufactured" by individual songwriters. Songwriters take the genuine article and imitate it for popular consumption. Most of these imitation ballads come and go without an echo. Others, like "The Ballad of Billy Joe," achieve enormous commercial success.

But whether a ballad is born from the group experience of a people or in the head of a single songwriter, it always has a lilt and it always tells a story—many of them stories as gripping as the sensational front-page stories you read in some newspapers or hear on the evening news.

Lyric Poems: Expressing Feelings

Forms of poetry also developed that did not simply tell a story. One of these poetic forms was the *lyric,* a word which comes from the word *lyre,* a stringed instrument that the ancient Greek poets plucked as they sang their verses. The lyric soon became, and continues to be, the dominant kind of poetry written in the Western world.

Almost all the poems you've read in this unit are lyrics. **Lyrics** are comparatively short poems designed to make one sharp impression on the reader. As you've seen, lyrics can be plain and conversational in language, or they can be highly musical. What distinguishes a lyric poem is its very personal quality. A lyric is a poem that does not tell a story but makes a direct expression of emotion—it is a cry from the heart, a single voice speaking its own feelings. If that voice expresses feelings that are eccentric or cranky or too self-absorbed to be clearly understood, the lyric it produces is apt to remain no more than an expression of personal confusion. But when that voice speaks from a depth of feeling, in words as simple and direct as the feeling itself, the lyric speaks for everyone and to everyone.

Vase painting of musician (detail) (c. 490 B.C.). Terracotta.

The Metropolitan Museum of Art, Fletcher Fund, 1956. (56.171.38)

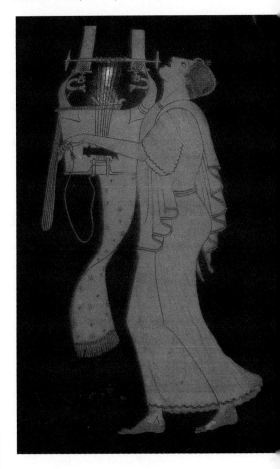

"A lyric poem is a cry from the heart, a single voice speaking its own feeling."

BALLADS

This modern American ballad continues a long tradition by telling a story of sudden tragedy and blood-chilling violence. The ballad is based on an actual event. On Sunday morning, September 15, 1963, in the midst of the struggle for greater civil rights for African Americans, a bomb exploded in the Sixteenth Street Baptist Church in Birmingham, Alabama. Four young girls were killed.

You might try dramatizing this ballad with three speakers. Let one be the young girl who asks the opening question, one the mother, and one the narrator. What kind of music do you think the story should be set to?

Ballad of Birmingham

(On the bombing of a church in Birmingham, Alabama, 1963)

Dudley Randall

"Mother dear, may I go downtown
Instead of out to play,
And march the streets of Birmingham
In a Freedom March today?"

5   "No, baby, no, you may not go,
For the dogs are fierce and wild,
And clubs and hoses, guns and jails
Aren't good for a little child."

"But, mother, I won't be alone.
10   Other children will go with me,
And march the streets of Birmingham
To make our country free."

"No, baby, no, you may not go,
For I fear those guns will fire.
15   But you may go to church instead
And sing in the children's choir."

She has combed and brushed her
    night-dark hair,
And bathed rose petal sweet,
And drawn white gloves on her small
    brown hands,
20   And white shoes on her feet.

The mother smiled to know her child
Was in the sacred place,
But that smile was the last smile
To come upon her face.

25   For when she heard the explosion,
Her eyes grew wet and wild.
She raced through the streets of Birmingham
Calling for her child.

She clawed through bits of glass and brick,
30   Then lifted out a shoe.
"O, here's the shoe my baby wore,
But, baby, where are you?"

Opposite: "One of the main forms of social and recreational activities in which the migrants indulged occurred in the church," No. 54 in the series *The Migration of the Negro* by Jacob Lawrence (1940–1941). Tempera on composition board, 18″ × 12″.

Collection, The Museum of Modern Art, New York. Gift of Mrs. David M. Levy.

Responding to the Poem

Analyzing the Poem

Identifying Facts

1. Why doesn't the mother let her daughter go to the Freedom March?
2. The mother smiles after she sends her daughter to sing in the children's choir. To what kind of place does the mother believe she has sent her child?

Interpreting Meanings

3. The **irony** in this poem intensifies its emotional impact. From the outset, what do *you* know that the mother and daughter do not know? Why is line 22 especially ironic?
4. Of all the emotions that this ballad expresses, anger and bitterness at racial violence seem noticeably absent. What is the overriding emotion created by the ballad? (How did it make you feel?)

An Oral Report

Using newspaper records, books about the Civil Rights Movement of the 1960's, and other historical sources, prepare a factual oral report on the bombing that occurred in Birmingham on September 15, 1963. At the end of your report, explain how knowing the facts either adds to or detracts from the effect of this ballad.

Reading About the Writer

Dudley Randall (1914–) was born in Washington, D.C., and educated at Wayne State University and the University of Michigan. He has lived for many years in Detroit. As publisher of Broadside Press, Randall has been influential in presenting many important works by African American writers, including poets Gwendolyn Brooks and Nikki Giovanni (see page 297).

Focusing on Background
The Story Behind the Ballad

In *Parting the Waters,* a book that won the Pulitzer Prize for History in 1989, Taylor Branch writes about the tragedy that occurred on September 15, 1963, in Birmingham, Alabama:

"That Sunday was the annual Youth Day at the Sixteenth Street Baptist Church. Mamie H. Grier, superintendent of the Sunday school, stopped in at the basement ladies' room to find four young girls who had left Bible classes early and were talking excitedly about the beginning of the school year. All four were dressed in white from head to toe, as this was their day to run the main service for the adults at eleven o'clock. Grier urged them to hurry along and then went upstairs to sit in on her own women's Sunday-school class. They were engaged in a lively debate on the lesson topic, 'The Love That Forgives,' when a loud earthquake shook the entire church and showered the classroom with plaster and debris. Grier's first thought was that it was like a ticker-tape parade. Maxine McNair, a schoolteacher sitting next to her, reflexively went stiff and was the only one to speak. 'Oh, my goodness!' she said. She escaped with Grier, but the stairs down to the basement were blocked and the large stone staircase on the outside literally had vanished. They stumbled through the church to the front door and then made their way around outside through the gathering noise of moans and sirens. A hysterical church member shouted to Grier that her husband had already gone to the hospital in the first ambulance. McNair searched desperately for her only child until finally she came upon a sobbing old man and screamed, 'Daddy, I can't find Denise!' The man helplessly replied, 'She's dead, baby. I've got one of her shoes.' He held a girl's white dress shoe, and the look on his daughter's face made him scream out, 'I'd like to blow the whole town up!' "

—Taylor Branch

Versions of this ballad were popular in England, Scotland, Ireland, and America. It is based on the story of a man come back from the dead to claim his bride. The man had been a mariner, or sailor, in life and engaged to be married. When he did not return home after three years at sea, the young woman married someone else (in most songs, her husband is a carpenter). The version of the ballad printed here was sung in Scotland and Ireland. The meanings of many dialect words should be obvious from their contexts. Other words that might not be so easily figured out are defined in the side notes. Let three speakers present this chilling story of betrayal.

The Demon Lover

Anonymous

"O where have you been, my long, long love,
    This long seven years and mair?"
"O I'm come to seek my former vows
    Ye granted me before."

5   "O hold your tongue of your former vows,
    For they will breed sad strife;
O hold your tongue of your former vows,
    For I am become a wife."

He turned him right and round about,
10   And the tear blinded his ee:
"I wad never hae trodden on Irish ground,
    If it had not been for thee.

"I might hae had a king's daughter,
    Far, far beyond the sea;
15   I might have had a king's daughter,
    Had it not been for love o thee."

"If ye might have had a king's daughter,
    Yer sel ye had to blame;
Ye might have taken the king's daughter,
20   For ye kend° that I was nane.

"If I was to leave my husband dear,
    And my two babes also,
O what have you to take me to,
    If with you I should go?"

25   "I hae seven ships upon the sea—
    The eighth brought me to land—
With four-and-twenty bold mariners,
    And music on every hand."

20. **kend:** knew.

She has taken up her two little babes,
30   Kiss'd them baith cheek and chin:
"O fair ye weel, my ain two babes,
  For I'll never see you again."

She set her foot upon the ship,
  No mariners could she behold;
35 But the sails were o the taffetie,°
  And the masts o the beaten gold.

They had not sailed a league, a league,
  A league but barely three,
When dismal grew his countenance,
40   And drumlie° grew his ee.

They had not sailed a league, a league,
  A league but barely three,
Until she espied his cloven foot,
  And she wept right bitterlie.

35. **taffetie:** taffeta, a fine, shiny fabric.

40. **drumlie:** dark and gloomy.

Island of the Dead by Arnold Böcklin (1880). Oil.   The Metropolitan Museum of Art, Reisinger Fund, 1926. (26.90)

45   "O hold your tongue of your weeping," says he,
          "Of your weeping now let me be;
      I will shew you how lilies grow
          On the banks of Italy."

      "O what hills are yon, yon pleasant hills,
50   That the sun shines sweetly on?"
      "O yon are the hills of heaven," he said,
          "Where you will never win."

      "O whaten mountain is yon," she said,
          "All so dreary wi frost and snow?"
55   "O yon is the mountain of hell," he cried
          "Where you and I will go."

      He strack the tapmast wi his hand,
          The foremast wi his knee,
      And he brake that gallant ship in twain,°
60   And sank her in the sea.

59. **brake . . . in twain:** broke in two.

Responding to the Poem

Analyzing the Poem

Identifying Details

1. This ballad is basically a **dialogue** between two people. Who speaks first, and what does the speaker want to know? How does the other person answer?

Interpreting Meanings

2. Surprisingly enough, the woman agrees to join the man—even though it means abandoning her husband and babies. What can you infer about her motives? What can you infer about why the man went to Ireland in the first place?
3. In line 34 the story changes. What details in the description of the boat hint that the story has shifted into something fantastic? At what point do we know that the man is a demon?
4. "The Demon Lover" belongs in the category of folk poetry in which the natural and the supernatural are intertwined. Such a story was meant to teach its listeners a lesson or to point out a moral they might take to heart. How would you state the ballad's moral? Do you think it still applies to people today?

5. A **typical ballad** always has a strong pattern of stressed and unstressed syllables. This steady rhythm makes the ballad easy to memorize and hypnotic to listen to. Read three stanzas of this ballad aloud in a singsong way and listen to the rhythm. How many stressed syllables does each line of a stanza contain?
6. How do you feel about ballads and poetry written with strong rhythms? Do you like this kind of poetry, or do you prefer poems that sound like everyday speech? Why?

Writing About the Poem

A Creative Response

Extending the Ballad. Write one or two extra stanzas for this poem that give more information about the Demon Lover. Try to use the same pattern of rhythm and rhyme that the ballad uses.

This ballad comes from a very old European folk tale about a murder that might have been based on a true incident. The ballad is told in Scottish dialect. The *brand* that Edward is carrying is his sword, the *bluid* is "blood." You should be able to figure out most of the other dialect words by saying them aloud. Let the mother and her son recite their dramatic story aloud.

Edward

Anonymous

"Why does your brand so drip with bluid,
    Edward, Edward?
Why does your brand so drip with bluid,
And why so sad gang° ye, O?"

  5 "O I have killed my hawk so guid,
    Mither, mither,
O I have killed my hawk so guid,
And I had nae mair° but he, O."

"Your hawkes bluid was never so red,
10   Edward, Edward.
Your hawkes bluid was never so red,
My dear son I tell thee, O."
"O I have killed my red-roan steed,
    Mither, mither,
15 O I have killed my red-roan steed,
That erst° was so fair and free, O."

"Your steed was auld and ye have got mair,
    Edward, Edward.
Your steed was auld and ye have got mair:
20 Some other dule ye dree,° O."
"O I have killed my fader dear,
    Mither, mither,
O I have killed my fader dear,
Alas and woe is me, O!"

25 "And whatten° penance will ye dree for that,
    Edward, Edward?
And whatten penance will ye dree for that,
My dear son, now tell me, O?"
"I'll set my feet in yonder boat,
30   Mither, mither,
I'll set my feet in yonder boat,
And I'll fare over the sea, O."

4. **gang:** go.

8. **nae mair:** no more.

16. **erst:** before.

20. **dule ye dree:** grief you suffer.

25. **whatten:** what sort of.

"And what will ye do with your towers and your hall,
    Edward, Edward?
35   And what will ye do with your towers and your hall,
That were so fair to see, O?"
"I'll let them stand till they down fall,
    Mither, mither,
I'll let them stand till they down fall,
40   For here never mair maun° I be, O."

"And what will ye leave to your bairns° and your wife,
    Edward, Edward,
And what will ye leave to your bairns and your wife,
Whan ye gang over the sea, O?"
45   "The warldes room let them beg thrae life,°
    Mither, mither,
The warldes room let them beg thrae life,
For them never mair will I see, O."

"And what will ye leave to your own mither dear,
50   Edward, Edward?
And what will ye leave to your own mither dear,
My dear son, now tell me, O?"
"The curse of hell from me shall ye bear,
    Mither, mither,
55   The curse of hell from me shall ye bear,
Such counsels ye gave to me, O."

A Lady with a Falcon (15th century). Flemish tapestry (detail).

40. **maun:** must.

41. **bairns:** children.

45. **warldes . . . life:** world's space let them beg through life.

Responding to the Poem

Analyzing the Poem

Identifying Facts

1. Immediately, this ballad plunges us into a dramatic situation. What scene do you visualize as the story opens?
2. This ballad, like the others in this unit, tells its story in **dialogue.** Who asks the questions? Who answers them?
3. What lies does Edward tell to account for his bloody sword? How does his mother catch him in the lies?
4. At what point in the song do you find out exactly what Edward has done?
5. We might think that this **climactic moment** is the end of the song, but the questions go on. What four questions does the mother then ask Edward? How does he answer each of them?

Interpreting Meanings

6. The real meaning of this ballad is not stated; we have to infer the meaning from the details provided. What shocking fact do you infer from Edward's last answer to his mother?
7. Ballads never tell us the whole story, and part of the pleasure is reading between the lines. What motives do you think the mother might have had for giving Edward these "counsels"? What do you think her "counsels" were?
8. Why do you think Edward lied to his mother at first?
9. Who do you think is the real villain in this story? Why?
10. This ballad draws out the **suspense** by having both speakers repeat themselves, so that it takes them a while to get to their points. In what lines do you find this use of repetition?
11. Do incidents like this one exist only in these old stories? Or do you find them in newspapers and the TV news today as well? Explain.

Writing About the Poem

A Creative Response

1. **Retelling the Ballad as a News Story.** The stories told in old ballads are not much different from the stories we find on the front pages of some newspapers today. Suppose you were a reporter assigned to cover the story that takes place in "Edward." Write your front-page account of the crime. Be sure to tell **what** happened, **whom** it happened to, **when** it happened, **where** it happened, **why** it happened, and **how** it happened. What will your headline be?
2. **Extending the Story.** What happens to Edward's mother? In a paragraph tell whether Edward's curse comes true.
3. **Extending the Story.** What happens to Edward in his travels over the sea? Write a paragraph reporting on where Edward is ten years after the murder.

Analyzing Language and Vocabulary

Word Histories

In the days when this ballad was sung, Scottish speakers of English used the word *gang* instead of the word *go.* Today, we use the word *gang* to mean other things: we use it as a noun meaning "a group of people" (a street gang) or as a verb meaning "to attack as a group" (to gang up on him). Our word *gang* is related to that old Scottish word *gang.* Checking in a dictionary, you'd see that both words come from an old Gothic word meaning "to go." Long ago, *gang* was also used as a noun meaning "a journey," or "a going."

To answer the following questions, you have to use a dictionary. Look for the information in the dictionary that gives you the word's history, or **etymology.** Usually this information is given in parentheses at the beginning or end of the entry.

1. What archaic (or old) meaning does the word *brand* have in the ballad? Name at least three modern meanings of the word *brand.*
2. What word is the Scottish word *bairn* derived from? What word related to *bairn* do we use today?
3. What does the dictionary tell you about the history of our word *old*? How does this explain why in Scottish dialect the word is still pronounced *auld*?
4. What is the history of our word *father*? How does this explain why in Scottish dialect the word is pronounced *fader*?

Many years ago, gifts were not exchanged on the Nativity—the day that commemorates the birth of Christ. Instead, gifts were exchanged on the twelfth day after the Nativity, the day when the Wise Men brought their gifts to the Infant. Some parts of the United States still honor this day and call it "Old Christmas." The setting of this ballad is Kentucky, on Old Christmas morning. The story is told in dialogue, with one speaker's words in italics. Both speakers are women. Try to imitate the dialect as you read this dialogue aloud.

Old Christmas

Roy Helton

"Where you coming from, Lomey Carter,
    So airly° over the snow?
And what's them pretties° you got in your hand,
    And where you aiming to go?

5   "Step in, honey! Old Christmas morning
    I ain't got nothing much;
Maybe a bite of sweetness and corn bread,
    A little ham meat and such.

"But come in, honey! Sally Anne Barton's
10   Hungering after your face.
Wait till I light my candle up:
    Set down! There's your old place.

"Now where you been so airly this morning?"
    "Graveyard, Sally Anne.
15 *Up by the trace° in the salt-lick meadows*
    Where Taulbe kilt my man."

"Taulbe ain't to home this morning. . . .
    I can't scratch up a light:
Dampness gets on the heads of the matches;
20   But I'll blow up the embers bright."

"Needn't trouble. I won't be stopping:
    Going a long ways still."
"You didn't see nothing, Lomey Carter,
    Up on the graveyard hill?"

25 *"What should I see there, Sally Anne Barton?"*
    "Well, sperits do walk last night."
"There were an elder bush a-blooming
    While the moon still give some light."

2. **airly:** early.

3. **pretties:** probably branches of elder bushes, which are supposed to bloom to honor Christ's birth in December.

15. **trace:** path.

"Yes, elder bushes, they bloom, Old Christmas,
30   And critters kneel down in their straw.
Anything else up in the graveyard?"

"One thing more I saw:
I saw my man with his head all bleeding
Where Taulbe's shot went through."

35   "What did he say?"
                    "He stooped and kissed me."
"What did he say to you?"

"Said, Lord Jesus forguv your Taulbe;
But he told me another word;
40   *He said it soft when he stooped and kissed me.*
That were the last I heard."

"Taulbe ain't to home this morning."
    "I know that, Sally Anne,
For I kilt him coming down through the meadow
45   *Where Taulbe kilt my man.*

"I met him upon the meadow trace
When the moon were fainting fast,
And I had my dead man's rifle gun
And kilt him as he came past."

50   "But I heard two shots."
                    " 'Twas his was second:
    He shot me 'fore he died:
You'll find us at daybreak, Sally Anne Barton:
    I'm laying there dead at his side."

Responding to the Poem

Analyzing the Poem

Identifying Details

1. Where are the speakers as the poem opens, and what are they doing?
2. What question does Sally Anne Barton ask her old friend Lomey Carter in line 13? How does Lomey answer?
3. Taulbe is a relative of Sally Anne's—probably her husband. What did Taulbe do?
4. What did Lomey see on the graveyard hill?
5. What happened as Lomey came back down through the meadow?

Interpreting Meanings

6. What evidence can you find in the poem that suggests that Sally Anne knew all along what had happened on the graveyard hill?
7. Once we know what happened on the hill, what do we learn about just whom (or what) Sally Anne is talking to? What new significance do Lomey's words in lines 21–22 now take on?
8. Lines 38–41 introduce matters we can only guess about. What might have been the word her man spoke to Lomey as he bent to kiss her?
9. Why do you think the storyteller has these events take place on "Old Christmas"? For the purposes of the story, could they have just as well taken place on the Fourth of July or Halloween? Explain.

Writing About the Poem

A Creative Response

1. **Recasting the Ballad into a News Report.** Suppose this incident was being reported on the evening news. Write out what the announcer would say. Include details explaining **who, what, where, when, why,** and **how.** Will the announcer suggest that anything supernatural or ghostly happened on this Old Christmas morning? (Be sure to report on how the crime was discovered.)

A Critical Response

2. **Comparing Poems.** In a paragraph, compare this modern ballad from the Appalachian Mountains with the old Scottish ballad "Edward." Before you write, fill out a chart like the one following to show how the stories are alike or different:

	Old Christmas	Edward
Subject matter		
Supernatural events		
Surprises		
Use of dialogue		
Rhymes		
Rhythms		

Reading About the Writer

Roy Helton was born in Washington, D.C., in 1886 and graduated from the University of Pennsylvania. He taught school and wrote poetry, much of it based on folklore. This ballad is included in his collection called *Lonesome Water.*

LYRIC POEMS

Linda Pastan wrote this lyric in response to a questionnaire. She says, "It started as a kind of joke and surprised me by ending as a poem." Her poem deals here with a matter of great concern to anyone who, in solitude, writes a poem or a story or a novel. Whom am I writing for besides myself? Whom would I most like to communicate with? Does anyone care?

whom do you visualize as your reader?

Linda Pastan

the humanities 5 section man
who has been sharpening
his red pencil
these twenty years

5   my mother
who suspected me
of such thoughts
all along

the running back
10   who after the last touchdown
reads my poems by his locker
instead of the sports page

Responding to the Poem

Analyzing the Poem

Interpreting Meanings

1. "Humanities 5" could be any college course. A "section man" is an assistant to a professor, whose job is to lead discussion sections and correct term papers and exams. What would this man use his red pencil for? Why would the poet be writing for him?
2. In stanza 2, what kinds of thoughts do you think the poet's mother suspected her of "all along"?
3. Which stanza do you think contains the most serious answer to the title question? Explain.

Writing About the Poem

A Creative Response

Imitating the Poem. Suppose you are a writer and you receive the questionnaire asking "Whom do you visualize as your reader?" Name three people you hope will read what you write. Write a poem like Linda Pastan's.

The subject of this lyric is success and victory. But Emily Dickinson chooses to dramatize and define those ideas by talking about their opposites—failure and defeat. If you have ever lost an important game or failed to get something that you wanted so badly you could taste it, you know what the poet is talking about here.

Success Is Counted Sweetest

Emily Dickinson

> Success is counted sweetest
> By those who ne'er succeed.
> To comprehend a nectar
> Requires sorest need.
>
> 5   Not one of all the purple host
> Who took the flag today
> Can tell the definition,
> So clear, of victory,
>
> As he defeated—dying—
> 10   On whose forbidden ear
> The distant strains of triumph
> Burst agonized and clear!

Responding to the Poem

Analyzing the Poem

Identifying Details

1. According to lines 1 and 2, *who* knows how sweet success really is?
2. *Sorest* as used in line 4 means "most intense." What is "a nectar"? How would you **paraphrase** lines 3 and 4—that is, put them into your own words?
3. The "purple host" in line 5 would be a victorious army. Purple is a color often associated with victory or with the spilling of blood in battle. Of all the people who fought in this battle, who knows best what victory is, according to stanzas 2 and 3?

Interpreting Meanings

4. What sounds do you think the defeated soldier hears in the last stanza? Why would the soldier's ear be called "forbidden"? Why do the distant strains of triumph seem "agonized"?
5. What feelings or emotions do you think this famous lyric poem conveys?
6. Do you think these feelings are universal—that is, does everyone experience them from time to time? Explain.

Writing About the Poem

A Creative Response

Applying the Poem to Life. In a paragraph, tell about an incident involving you or someone else that illustrates the truth of this lyric: "Success is counted sweetest / By those who ne'er succeed." Tell what the person in your story wanted, what happened, and how that person could imagine and taste the victory that he or she never won—even more clearly than the victor could.

Those Winter Sundays

Robert Hayden

Sundays too my father got up early
and put his clothes on in the blueblack cold,
then with cracked hands that ached
from labor in the weekday weather made
5   banked fires blaze. No one ever thanked him.

I'd wake and hear the cold splintering, breaking.
When the rooms were warm, he'd call,
and slowly I would rise and dress,
fearing the chronic angers of that house,

10   Speaking indifferently to him,
who had driven out the cold
and polished my good shoes as well.
What did I know, what did I know
of love's austere and lonely offices?°

14. **offices:** services or offerings.

That Gentleman by Andrew Wyeth (1960). Tempera.   Dallas Museum of Art, Dallas Art Association Purchase.

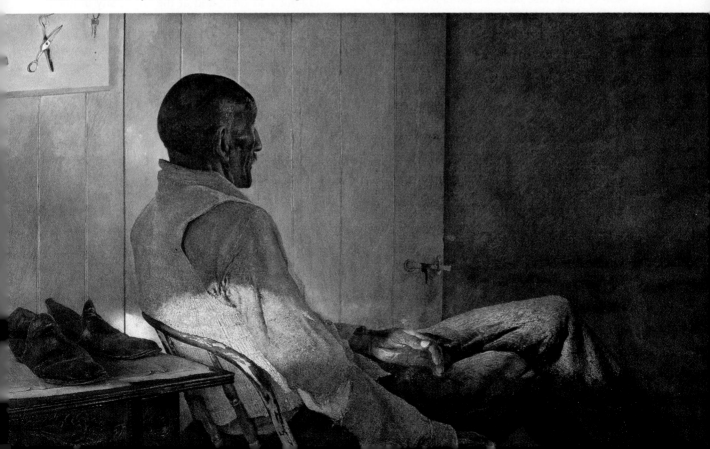

Responding to the Poem

Analyzing the Poem

Identifying Details

1. Name four **images** that help us imagine how cold it was on those winter Sunday mornings.
2. How did the boy respond to his father? How does he explain his response in the last line?
3. To get the full flavor of this poem, note how internal rhymes and other sound echoes make little chiming sounds throughout. Find two examples of **internal rhyme** in stanza 1. Find at least five examples of **alliteration.**
4. Read the first stanza aloud, and **scan** the lines to show which syllables are strongly stressed and which are not. Pay particular attention to the last line of this stanza. Should this line receive strong emphasis? Why?

Interpreting Meanings

5. *Why* do you think no one ever thanked this father?
6. In your own words, explain the "chronic angers" referred to in line 9.
7. The poet says his father "drove out the cold." How can love also be responsible for driving out another kind of cold?
8. This lyric is both a confession and a tribute. What is the poet confessing? What tribute does he pay to his father?

Writing About the Poem

A Creative Response

1. **Telling the Story from Another Point of View.** What are the father's thoughts as he performs his "offices" of love? Write them out in a paragraph, or in a poem. Use the first-person pronoun, "I," and let the father speak.

A Critical Response

2. **Comparing Poems.** In a paragraph, compare "Fire and Ice" by Robert Frost (page 315) with Hayden's poem. Consider these elements:

   a. The use of images of cold
   b. The suggestion that hatred is destructive
   c. The suggestion that love can drive out hatred

Analyzing Language and Vocabulary

One Word, Several Meanings

A key word in this poem is the word *offices* in the last line. The word as it is used in the poem refers to the jobs the father voluntarily performed for his family each Sunday morning. But the word *office* also can refer to daily religious rites, such as those carried out by monks or priests or nuns. Usually, these "offices" consist of saying prayers at certain times of the day and night.

1. In a dictionary, find the meanings of the word *austere.* Which exact meaning does the poet intend here in line 14?
2. Make up a sentence in which you use the word *austere* to mean something different from what it means in the poem.
3. Make up a sentence in which you use the word *offices* to mean something different from what it means in the poem.

Reading About the Writer

Robert Hayden (1913–1980) was born in Detroit and educated there and at the University of Michigan. In his years as professor of English at Fisk University in Tennessee, Hayden was mentor and guide to many black students who were aiming for careers in literature. His own poetry became one of the finest achievements of black literature in recent decades. In fact, Hayden's career might be regarded as an example of poetic justice. A poor freshman who could barely afford a bed in a racially segregated rooming house near the campus of the University of Michigan, Hayden lived to see the day when that same university would invite him to occupy one of its most distinguished professorships.

HOW TO WRITE A POEM

Where poems come from is a mystery. All we know is that a poem is a kind of wedding between something in the outside world that can be observed and pointed at, and some feeling inside the poet that lives like an untold secret in the mind and heart. In a sense, all poems are revelations—they help us discover connections between our inside feelings and the outside world.

The exercises that follow might help you in writing a poem of your own. You should begin your poem with the confidence that you have feelings of your own. The point about feelings is that you have to find an occasion that will urge them into expression.

Getting Started

Your first step is to find a subject that you have some feeling for. Life itself provides many occasions for expression of feelings. Some of the following occasions, or others like them, may already have been part of your own experience:

1. The moment when you learn that your family is moving to another city and you know you'll have to give up friends and neighborhood and everything familiar
2. The day that your grandmother has died and you realize you'll never see her face again and never again open the birthday and Christmas presents she never failed to send
3. That moment when, secretly smiling at someone you've fallen in love with, you see that person looking back and smiling at *you*
4. That moment when, pulling the ripcord of your parachute, you suddenly know you don't *have* a parachute, and you keep falling, falling, down to the parking lot next to the hospital, and—just as you are about to go crashing into Dr. Robinson's white Cadillac—you wake up in a sweat

5. That day when you went back to your old playground and found that all the kids there looked so young

Add to this list important moments or days in your own life. Any one of these moments may provide that spark, that connection between outside events and inside feelings which may lead you to a poem.

Finding a Subject

If this doesn't work for you, there are other ways of finding subjects for poems:

1. The daily newspaper is full of items that might catch your imagination. (John Updike wrote "Youth's Progress," on page 348, after reading a news story in *Life* magazine.)
2. You could pretend that you are Cinderella, a rock star, the Speaker of the House, the last dinosaur (or any other figure from a story or a movie or real life), and write a poem telling your feelings about what's happening to you. (Charles Carryl wrote as if he were Robinson Crusoe on page 309.)
3. You could begin with a question such as "What kind of house would I have lived in in 1600?" "How would I be remembered if I should disappear this very moment?" or "Twenty years from now, who will I be?"
4. You could choose an object and speak to it as though it were capable of understanding what you say. You might call your poem "An Address to a House" or "To a Pizza Pie" or "Words for a Pair of Sneakers."
5. You could decide to write a poem consisting of a series of images. Its title might be "A Catalog of Sounds" or "A Complete List of Everything" or its first line might be "I see——" (or "I smell," "I taste," "I touch," "I hear").
6. You could write a poem consisting of a series of contrasting metaphors: "A cat seems to be _____, but it really is_____"; "Fog seems to be _____, but it really is_____"; "An onion seems to be_____, but it really is_____."

Finding a Form

Once you have an idea for a poem, you have to find a form to write it in.

1. The simplest form for a beginning poet is **free verse**—poetry written in lines that imitate the natural rhythms of speech (see page 289). If you use free verse, take special care to decide when you want to break your lines and to see that no one line is so long that it almost runs off the page. Begin with a statement to catch the reader's attention. Then keep your reader's interest, not only by what you say, but also by using questions, by using dots (. . .) to continue a thought, by using dashes (—) to add a thought, even by using exclamation marks (!).

2. The next simplest forms are poems in **rhymed couplets** (two rhymed lines) or **quatrains** (four rhyming lines). If you use couplets, the last words in each line should rhyme:

> I wish I could unLOCK
> The secrets of a CLOCK

If you use quatrains, you can rhyme just two of the four lines, or you can rhyme the last words in every line (aaaa or abab or aabb). Here is a quatrain in which only two lines are rhymed:

This morning, late for class, I skipped	a
My cornflakes and, gung-ho, de-parted.	b
Nice timing! I made history	c
Before the Civil War got started.	b

3. Perhaps you'll want to try to write a poem in **meter**—that is, to give each line a regular pattern of stressed and unstressed syllables. Two meters are best to begin with. One is a line with six syllables, which alternates an unstressed syllable with a stressed syllable: da/DAH, da/DAH, da/DAH (The dead began to speak). The other is a line with eight syllables, which also alter-

nates an unstressed syllable with a stressed syllable: da/DAH, da/DAH, da/DAH, da/DAH (I wandered lonely as a cloud). If you write in meter, maintain your beat exactly, but at times add a little variation so your verse doesn't become singsong. For instance, you can reverse the beat of the first two syllables in any line, without doing serious harm to your pattern (from da/DAH/ to DAH/da).

Here is a poem written to someone about to write a poem. This poet uses the kind of imagery that usually occurs in dreams—imagery that has no apparent logic to it—but this poet is using illogical combinations of images in order to make a logical point. Though his imagery could occur only in a poem written in the twentieth century, his message applies to the role of poetry in any century.

> **Your Poem, Man. . .**
> unless there's one thing seen
> suddenly against another—a parsnip
> sprouting for a President, or
> hailstones melting in an ashtray—
> nothing really happens. It takes
> surprise and wild connections,
> doesn't it? A walrus chewing
> on a ballpoint pen. Two blue tail-
> lights on Tyrannosaurus Rex. Green
> cheese teeth. Maybe what we wanted
> least. Or most. Some unexpected
> pleats. Words that never knew
> each other till right now. Plug us
> into the wrong socket and see
> what blows up—or what lights up.
> Try
>   untried
>   circuitry,
> new
>   fuses.
> Tell it like it never really was,
> man,
> and maybe we can see it
> like it is.
>
> —Edward Lueders

THE ELEMENTS OF NONFICTION

The Artist Looks at Nature by Charles Sheeler (1943). Oil.   Gift of the Society for Contemporary American Art.
(1944.32) The Art Institute of Chicago.

UNIT THREE   **Sandra Cisneros** and **Janet Burroway**

THE ELEMENTS OF NONFICTION

Two views, by **Sandra Cisneros** *and* **Janet Burroway**

. . . during a time when we have overdosed on visual images accompanied by meager undernourished texts—the news magazines, the nightly roundup—many of our best American writers have been drawn to the imaginative possibilities of short nonfiction.

—Maureen Howard

Fiction/Nonfiction
by *Sandra Cisneros*

> " **The** stories I make up aren't always 'fake,' and the stories I take from the 'real world' aren't always 'non-fake.' "

When I was little and spent a lot of time in the Chicago Public Library, I always had a hard time remembering the difference between the books marked "Fiction" and the books marked "Nonfiction." I think somebody told me the difference once, but I kept forgetting.

The way I made myself remember was like this. "Fiction" means fake and "Nonfiction" means non-fake. This definition seemed to satisfy me then.

So if I had to do a research report on who invented the umbrella, or draw a map of the country that produces the most pistachios, or give an oral presentation on the life of Cleopatra, I knew I had to look in the section marked "Nonfiction." Non-fake. Real stories from the real world.

But if I wanted to read a Hans Christian Andersen fairy tale about a little mermaid, or memorize Beatrix Potter's *The Tale of Tom Kitten,* or follow Alice's adventures through the looking glass, then I had to look on the shelves marked "Fiction." This is where I could find stories that were made up in some writer's head, as opposed to the stories that were plucked from the living world.

Now that I'm not so little anymore and a writer, I find the difference between "Fiction" and "Nonfiction" blurring. I write stories and novels (these can be shelved under "Fiction"), but I also write magazine articles, speeches, book reviews, and essays like the one you're reading here on this page ("Nonfiction"). I write *both* fiction and nonfiction. But the stories I "make up" aren't always "fake," and the stories I take from the "real" world aren't always "non-fake."

Here is something that happened to me. When I began writing my book *The House on Mango Street,* I thought I was writing a memoir, nonfiction, memories of what it had been like for me to be a girl growing up in the city of Chicago. And, yes, the book did begin with my autobiographical memories of people I had known on my block, friends and relatives and neighbors, and, in particular, one sad red house I did not want to belong to. But as the years went by, and the book grew and grew, I realized I wasn't writing nonfiction anymore. That is, I wasn't simply *remembering* real people from my past. I was taking the memory of one girlfriend from the seventh grade, plus adding something one of my students told me, plus blending in a bit of my mama's story about a girl from her own childhood, and there I would have one character who was one-third memory, one-third hearsay, and one-third my mama's history. I couldn't, in all honesty, call my book autobiography any more, because it wasn't nonfiction anymore. It was bits and pieces from real lives, but cut and pasted together like Frankenstein's monster—a creature with the eyes of one person, the arms of another, the body of somebody else, etc., etc., etc. Put them all together and what have you got? Fiction!

Of course, the question students ask the most is, "Is this story *real*?" In other words, how much of this story is "true" (nonfiction)? Well, all of it is true—kind of. All my fiction stories are based on nonfiction, but I add and cut and paste and change the details to make them "more real"—to make the story more interesting. Does this make sense?

Whenever I read my stories from *The House on Mango Street,* my six brothers and my mother say, "It wasn't like that." Or, "We weren't that poor!" They think I'm writing autobiography (nonfiction) about the real house we once lived in at 1525 N. Campbell Street in Chicago. But I'm doing what every good fiction writer does. I'm taking "real" people and "real" events and rearranging them so as to *create* a better story, because "real" life doesn't have shape. But real stories do. No wonder they call writers "liars."

On the other hand, while writing an article for a magazine the other day, I had to rewrite my essay (nonfiction) and add characters that hadn't really been a part of the true event. It was an essay about my father, but the editor kept asking me, "What about your mother? Where is she? Is she still alive?" Yes, she's very much alive, but she played no part in the story I was telling. However, for the sake of the public that might wonder, "What about your mother?," I had to change the facts a bit and add my mother to the story.

See what I mean? Fiction. Nonfiction. Fake? Non-fake? Such rubbery meanings! What is the difference? Now, *you* tell me.

> " **W**henever I read my stories from *The House on Mango Street,* my six brothers and my mother say, 'It wasn't like that.' Or, 'We weren't that poor!' "

> " **I**'m taking 'real' people and 'real' events and rearranging them so as to create a better story, because 'real' life doesn't have shape. But real stories do. No wonder they call writers 'liars.' "

The Writer's Purpose

by *Janet Burroway*

> "Every good writer of nonfiction has a purpose when he or she sits down to write."

Every good writer of nonfiction has a purpose when he or she sits down to write. The purpose may be to explain or inform; to create a mood or stir an emotion; to tell about a series of events; to persuade the reader to believe something or do something. A writer may want to do several of these things in a single essay or report, but he or she will know what the primary purpose of the piece of writing is and will select and arrange words and details that best accomplish that purpose.

Suppose, for instance, that Jim Greene breaks Terry Lewis's arm in the gym on Friday afternoon during a judo workout. Jim says it was an accident; Terry says it was on purpose. Ms. Jeffords, the judo instructor, wasn't looking. Another student, Stan Jones, *was* looking. The principal wants to know exactly what happened, so he asks each one of these people to write down what he or she knows. Ms. Jeffords's account begins:

> Judo throws require both precise timing and exact balance, and at this level (yellow belt) there is always a slight possibility that the participants have insufficient agility or coordination . . .

Ms. Jeffords is not taking sides (though she may very well want to make clear that it wasn't *her* fault). She simply wants to explain how such an accident could have taken place, if it was an accident. Most of her report will be **exposition,** the method of writing whose purpose is to explain or inform, to define, or to clarify an idea. Dictionary and encyclopedia articles, as well as newspaper reports, use exposition.

But Stan Jones, who is better at English than any of the others, and who feels rather important to have been the only witness, wants to write a more detailed and dramatic piece. He also reports on events but he uses a great deal of description.

> The air conditioner in the gym was broken, and the place was like a giant oven. Jim was sweating heavily after the last throw. The neck of his gi was already damp when he moved in. Terry lunged for him and his fingers grabbed, then slipped on the glistening skin . . .

Description is a method of writing that establishes a mood or stirs an emotion. Description works by using **images**—words that help us experience something with our senses: to see it, hear it, smell it, taste it, or touch it.

Jim Greene, who feels innocent and wants to appear as cool and reasonable as possible, sticks to a straight **narration.** This method of writing tells about a series of events, usually in chronological order:

> As best I can understand it, what happened is this: I had just come out of the last throw and had turned around toward Terry, who was getting up to come at me from the left. I made a quarter-turn and moved my left leg forward when he reached for my neck and his hand slipped . . .

Terry Lewis has stronger feelings about it than any of the rest of them—his arm hurts and he's angry that he'll miss the spring tournament. Terry wants to make sure the principal believes that this was no accident. His purpose is **persuasion,** so he will select all the evidence he can to persuade the principal to believe that Jim is responsible.

> I've known Jim Greene had it in for me ever since my brother's dog tags disappeared from my locker and he just laughed. I got my yellow belt three meets ahead of him, and I'm the only one who's ever thrown him three-out-of-four.

These four accounts of the judo accident use the four major methods of writing that we find in nonfiction: *exposition, description, narration,* and *persuasion.* The judo accounts create four different effects and give four different interpretations. Yet they are all based on the same facts! What differs in each case is the purpose of the writer and the method of writing used to accomplish that purpose.

Generally speaking, **exposition** answers the question, "What is it, and how does it work?" **Description** answers the question, "What does it look, sound, smell, feel, taste like?" **Narration** answers, "What happened?" **Persuasion** answers, "What should I feel or do about it?"

The Range of Nonfiction: From the Personal to the Objective

Just a glance at the stacks of nonfiction books in a bookstore will give you an idea of the range of nonfiction. A bookstore might have shelves marked History, Biography, Autobiography, Travel, Science, Criticism, and Politics—and probably even more.

This unit focuses on three popular forms of nonfiction: **Personal Essays, Reports on People and Events,** and **Biography and Autobiography.** You will see that nonfiction can range from a very personal kind of writing (the kind you find in these essays and autobiographies) to a very objective kind of writing (the kind you find in reports and biographies, where the writer is often not a presence at all). When writers are **personal,** or **subjective,** they reveal their feelings and biases. When writers are **objective,** they screen out their private feelings and focus on facts.

What is true of all of these writings, though, is that they are based on a writer's experience with real events and real people. Whether the writer has chosen to present these experiences in a personal way or in an objective way depends on what may be the most important element of nonfiction: the writer's purpose.

> " **J**ust a glance at the stacks of nonfiction books in a bookstore will give you an idea of the range of nonfiction."

Personal Essays
by Janet Burroway

The Amish Letter Writer by Horace Pippin (1940). Oil.

Courtesy Terry Dintenfass Gallery, New York.

Four hundred years ago, a French lawyer named Michel de Montaigne got tired of his practice, sold it, and retired to his country estate. To amuse himself there, he began to write short prose pieces about various topics that came into his mind—cannibals, smells, names, sleeping, friendship, prayers. Probably he had no intention of publishing these pieces at first, but eventually he published three volumes of what he called his *Essais*. Today only historians are interested in the fact that Montaigne was at the court of King Charles IX or was mayor of Bordeaux, but his *Essais* are translated, read, and studied in every language of the Western world.

Essais means "tries" or "attempts" in French, and the name too has lasted. *Essays* or "tries" is a good way to describe these short pieces of nonfiction prose, since no essay will ever say everything there is to say about any subject. There are as many ways of looking at and writing about cannibals, smells, names, and so forth, as there are people to write about them. Montaigne himself understood that a personal essay presents not only its subject but also its writer's personality. He said about his essays, "I have here only made a small bouquet of flowers and have brought nothing of my own but the thread that ties them together."

The essays in this unit were written many centuries after Montaigne wrote his "Essais." But each one still reflects a writer's "attempt" or "try" to talk about a subject with the reader. One writer here talks about a frog-eating bug, another about a screwball family, another about a heroic old woman. Like all personal essays, these are conversational in style and personal in tone and feeling. In all of them, we hear the voice of one particular writer responding in a personal way to some experience that is part of the real world we live in.

Annie Dillard (1945–   ) had written a few articles for magazines and had produced a small book of poetry when she wrote a series of essays called *Pilgrim at Tinker Creek*. At that time, she was living by Tinker Creek in a valley of Virginia's Blue Ridge Mountains. In 1974, much to her surprise, her book of essays won the Pulitzer Prize for general nonfiction. Notice how this essay is about "seeing." "I walk out," she says, "I see something, some event that would otherwise have been utterly missed and lost; or something sees me, some enormous power brushes me with its clean wing, and I resound like a beaten bell. I am an explorer . . ."

THE GIANT WATER BUG

Annie Dillard

A couple of summers ago I was walking along the edge of the island to see what I could see in the water, and mainly to scare frogs. Frogs have an inelegant way of taking off from invisible positions on the bank just ahead of your feet, in dire panic, emitting a froggy "Yike!" and splashing into the water. Incredibly, this amused me, and, incredibly, it amuses me still. As I walked along the grassy edge of the island, I got better and better at seeing frogs both in and out of the water. I learned to recognize, slowing down, the difference in texture of the light reflected from mudbank, water, grass, or frog. Frogs were flying all around me. At the end of the island I noticed a small green frog. He was exactly half in and half out of the water, looking like a schematic diagram of an amphibian, and he didn't jump.

He didn't jump; I crept closer. At last I knelt

on the island's winter-killed grass, lost, dumb-struck, staring at the frog in the creek just four feet away. He was a very small frog with wide, dull eyes. And just as I looked at him, he slowly crumpled and began to sag. The spirit vanished from his eyes as if snuffed. His skin emptied and drooped; his very skull seemed to collapse and settle like a kicked tent. He was shrinking before my eyes like a deflating football. I watched the taut, glistening skin on his shoulders ruck and rumple and fall. Soon, part of his skin, formless as a pricked balloon, lay in floating folds like bright scum on top of the water: it was a monstrous and terrifying thing. I gaped bewildered, appalled. An oval shadow hung in the water behind the drained frog; then the shadow glided away. The frog skin bag started to sink.

I had read about the giant water bug, but never seen one. "Giant water bug" is really the name of the creature, which is an enormous, heavy-bodied brown beetle. It eats insects, tadpoles, fish, and frogs. Its grasping forelegs are mighty and hooked inward. It seizes a victim with these legs, hugs it tight, and paralyzes it with enzymes injected during a vicious bite. That one bite is the only bite it ever takes. Through the puncture shoot the poisons that dissolve the victim's muscles and bones and organs—all but the skin—and through it the giant water bug sucks out the victim's body, reduced to a juice. This event is quite common in warm fresh water. The frog I saw was being sucked by a giant water bug. I had been kneeling on the island grass; when the unrecognizable flap of frog skin settled on the creek bottom, swaying, I stood up and brushed the knees of my pants. I couldn't catch my breath.

Responding to the Essay

Analyzing the Essay

Identifying Facts

1. At the opening of this excerpt, Annie Dillard describes herself as something like a schoolgirl (or boy) playing with frogs. Why was she scaring the frogs?
2. Dillard soon reveals that she sees more than a schoolgirl would. Find at least four **similes** that describe the "monstrous and terrifying" death of the frog.
3. What does the writer tell you directly about her **personal feelings** as she watched the death occur?

Interpreting Meanings

4. This excerpt begins with an amusing walk by a shore and ends with the narrator unable to catch her breath. What do you think Dillard is telling us about nature by beginning and ending in this way?
5. What other natural events might appall or bewilder us? (Think of what you might see on a walk in your own neighborhood.)

Writing About the Essay

A Creative Response

Describing a Scene. Write a paragraph describing as precisely as you can some natural scene you've looked at very, very closely (an ant crawling, a cat cleaning up, a bird eating). Your purpose is to help a reader to **visualize** the scene and to know how it makes you **feel**.

Analyzing Language and Vocabulary

A Greek Root

Annie Dillard says that the frog was half in and half out of the water, looking like a diagram of an *amphibian*. An amphibian, as you probably know, is a creature that can live on both land and water. The word is based on two Greek words, *amphi-*, "on both sides," and *bio,* meaning "life."

Use a dictionary to explain how the sense of *amphi-* is contained in these words:

1. amphibian tank
2. amphitheater
3. amphora (a Greek vase)

Humorist, satirist, illustrator, writer of essays, fables, and children's books, James Thurber (1894–1961) was born and raised in a city that his readers still associate with him—Columbus, Ohio. He graduated from Ohio State University and began his career as a reporter before taking up his long and famous association with *The New Yorker* magazine. When Thurber was asked by an editor to write his own biography, he came up with the essay that is reprinted in part under "Focusing on Background," on page 383. Since Thurber says his account of the bed makes a better recitation than it does a piece of writing, try reading the following essay aloud.

THE NIGHT THE BED FELL

James Thurber

I suppose that the high-water mark of my youth in Columbus, Ohio, was the night the bed fell on my father. It makes a better recitation (unless, as some friends of mine have said, one has heard it five or six times) than it does a piece of writing, for it is almost necessary to throw furniture around, shake doors, and bark like a dog to lend the proper atmosphere and verisimilitude[1] to what is admittedly a somewhat incredible tale. Still, it did take place.

It happened, then, that my father had decided to sleep in the attic one night, to be away where he could think. My mother opposed the notion strongly because, she said, the old wooden bed up there was unsafe; it was wobbly and the heavy headboard would crash down on father's head in case the bed fell, and kill him. There was no dissuading him, however, and at a quarter past ten he closed the attic door behind him and went up the narrow twisting stairs. We later heard ominous creakings as he crawled into bed. Grandfather, who usually slept in the attic bed when he was with us, had disappeared some days before. (On these occasions he was usually gone six or eight days and returned growling and out of temper, with the news that the federal Union was run by a passel of blockheads and that the Army of the Potomac didn't have a chance.)

We had visiting us at this time a nervous first cousin of mine named Briggs Beall, who believed that he was likely to cease breathing when he was asleep. It was his feeling that if he were not awakened every hour during the night, he might die of suffocation. He had been accustomed to setting an alarm clock to ring at intervals until morning, but I persuaded him to abandon this. He slept in my room and I told him that I was such a light sleeper that if anybody quit breathing in the same room with me, I would wake instantly. He tested me the first night—which I had suspected he would—by holding his breath after my regular breathing had convinced him I was asleep. I was not asleep, however, and called to him. This seemed to allay his fears a little, but he took the precaution of putting a glass of spirits of camphor on a little table at the head of his bed. In case I didn't arouse him until he was almost gone, he said, he would sniff the camphor, a powerful reviver. Briggs was not the only member of his family who had his crotchets.[2] Old Aunt Melissa Beall (who could whistle like a man, with two fingers in her mouth) suffered under the premonition that

---

1. **verisimilitude** (ver′ə·si·mil′ə·tōōd): appearance of realism.

2. **crotchets** (kräch′its): peculiar ways; quirks of character.

she was destined to die on South High Street, because she had been born on South High Street and married on South High Street. Then there was Aunt Sarah Shoaf, who never went to bed at night without the fear that a burglar was going to get in and blow chloroform under her door through a tube. To avert this calamity—for she was in greater dread of anesthetics than of losing her household goods—she always piled her money, silverware, and other valuables in a neat stack just outside her bedroom, with a note reading: "This is all I have. Please take it and do not use your chloroform, as this is all I have." Aunt Gracie Shoaf also had a burglar phobia, but she met it with more fortitude. She was confident that burglars had been getting into her house every night for forty years. The fact that she never missed anything was to her no proof to the contrary. She always claimed that she scared them off before they could take anything, by throwing shoes down the hallway. When she went to bed she piled, where she could get at them handily, all the shoes there were about her house. Five minutes after she had turned off the light, she would sit up in bed and say "Hark!" Her husband, who had learned to ignore the whole situation as long ago as 1903, would either be sound asleep or pretend to be sound asleep. In either case he would not respond to her tugging and pulling, so that presently she would arise, tiptoe to the door, open it slightly, and heave a shoe down the hall in one direction, and its mate down the hall in the other direction. Some nights she threw them all, some nights only a couple of pair.

But I am straying from the remarkable incidents that took place during the night that the bed fell on father. By midnight we were all in bed. The layout of the rooms and the disposition[3] of their occupants is important to an understanding of what later occurred. In the front room upstairs (just under father's attic bedroom) were my mother and my brother Herman, who sometimes sang in his sleep, usually "Marching Through Georgia" or "Onward, Christian Soldiers." Briggs Beall and myself were in a room adjoining this one. My brother Roy was in a room across the

---

3. **disposition** (dis′ pə·zish′ən): placement or location.

hall from ours. Our bull terrier, Rex, slept in the hall.

My bed was an army cot, one of those affairs which are made wide enough to sleep on comfortably only by putting up, flat with the middle section, the two sides which ordinarily hang down like the sideboards of a drop-leaf table. When these sides are up, it is perilous to roll too far toward the edge, for then the cot is likely to tip completely over, bringing the whole bed down on top of one, with a tremendous banging crash. This, in fact, is precisely what happened, about two o'clock in the morning. (It was my mother who, in recalling the scene later, first referred to it as "the night the bed fell on your father.")

Always a deep sleeper, slow to arouse (I had lied to Briggs), I was at first unconscious of what had happened when the iron cot rolled me onto the floor and toppled over on me. It left me still warmly bundled up and unhurt, for the bed rested above me like a canopy. Hence I did not wake up, only reached the edge of consciousness and went back. The racket, however, instantly awakened my mother, in the next room, who came to the immediate conclusion that her worst dread was realized: the big wooden bed upstairs had fallen on father. She therefore screamed, "Let's go to your poor father!" It was this shout, rather than the noise of my cot falling, that awakened Herman, in the same room with her. He thought that mother had become, for no apparent reason, hysterical. "You're all right, Mamma!" he shouted, trying to calm her. They exchanged shout for shout for perhaps ten seconds: "Let's go to your poor father!" and "You're all right!" That woke up Briggs. By this time I was conscious of what was going on, in a vague way, but did not yet realize that I was under my bed instead of on it. Briggs, awakening in the midst of loud shouts of fear and apprehension, came to the quick conclusion that he was suffocating and that we were all trying to "bring him out." With a low moan, he grasped the glass of camphor at the head of his bed and instead of sniffing it poured it over himself. The room reeked of camphor. "Ugf, ahfg," choked Briggs, like a drowning man, for he had almost succeeded in stopping his breath under the deluge of pungent spirits. He leaped out of bed and groped toward the open window, but he came up against one that was closed. With his hand, he beat out the glass, and I could hear it crash and tinkle on the alleyway below. It was at this juncture that I, in trying to get up, had the uncanny sensation of feeling my bed above me! Foggy with sleep, I now suspected, in my turn, that the whole uproar was being made in a frantic endeavor to extricate me from what must be an unheard-of and perilous situation. "Get me out of this!" I bawled. "Get me out!" I think I had the nightmarish belief that I was entombed in a mine. "Gugh," gasped Briggs, floundering in his camphor.

By this time my mother, still shouting, pursued by Herman, still shouting, was trying to open the door to the attic, in order to go up and get my father's body out of the wreckage. The door was stuck, however, and wouldn't yield. Her frantic pulls on it only added to the general banging and confusion. Roy and the dog were now up, the one shouting questions, the other barking.

Father, farthest away and soundest sleeper of all, had by this time been awakened by the battering on the attic door. He decided that the house was on fire. "I'm coming, I'm coming!" he wailed in a slow, sleepy voice—it took him many minutes to regain full consciousness. My mother, still believing he was caught under the bed, detected in his "I'm coming!" the mournful, resigned note of one who is preparing to meet his Maker. "He's dying!" she shouted.

"I'm all right!" Briggs yelled to reassure her. "I'm all right!" He still believed that it was his own closeness to death that was worrying mother. I found at last the light switch in my room, unlocked the door, and Briggs and I joined the others at the attic door. The dog, who never did like Briggs, jumped for him—assuming that he was the culprit in whatever was going on—and Roy had to throw Rex and hold him. We could hear father crawling out of bed upstairs. Roy pulled the attic door open, with a mighty jerk, and father came down the stairs, sleepy and irritable but safe and sound. My mother began to weep when she saw him. Rex began to howl. "What in the name of God is going on here?" asked father.

The situation was finally put together like a gigantic jigsaw puzzle. Father caught a cold from prowling around in his bare feet but there were no other bad results. "I'm glad," said mother, who always looked on the bright side of things, "that your grandfather wasn't here."

Roy had to throw Rex.

© 1933, 1961 by James Thurber. From *My Life and Hard Times,* Harper & Row.

Responding to the Essay

Analyzing the Essay

Identifying Facts

1. In the second to the fourth paragraphs, Thurber introduces ten members of his family and a dog—a great number of characters for so short a space. What specific details describe each character and his or her "crotchets"?
2. At first, Thurber leads us to believe that the bed fell on his father. But it didn't (a bed fell on *him,* sort of). Why does Thurber think of it as the night the bed fell on his father?
3. At the end of the essay, Thurber says that the situation had to be put together "like a gigantic jigsaw puzzle." His essay is a **narrative** that puts that jigsaw puzzle together. List the events that were triggered off after the bed fell. Tell how one event led directly to another.

Interpreting Meanings

4. The purpose of **satire** is to make us laugh at people's foolishness or failings, and Thurber is a master of satire. One of the ways Thurber satirizes his family members is by contrasting what really happens with what they think happens. (Notice that Thurber entitles his illustration "Roy had to throw Rex," but it looks as if Rex is really throwing Roy.) In all of the confusion, what did each family member—Mother, Herman, Briggs, Thurber, Father, and the dog—*think* was happening?
5. What other foolish ideas or actions could Thurber be mocking in this comic essay?
6. Thurber says the night the bed fell was the "high-water mark" of his youth. What is a high-water mark? If this was the high-water mark, what is Thurber suggesting the rest of his youth in Columbus, Ohio, was like—in terms of excitement?

Writing About the Essay

A Creative Response

1. **Narrating a Series of Events.** Write a narrative about some actual "disaster" that happened to a family but which turned out all right. Tell **what** happened, **when** it happened, **where** it happened, and **who** was involved. Your narrative may be serious or funny, but try to use some descriptive details that will help us "see" some of the family members involved. One of your purposes in writing should be to create a sense of what this family is like.

A Critical Response

2. **Expressing an Opinion.** The first paragraph of the essay ends, "Still, it did take place," suggesting a nonfiction writer's anxiety to show that his piece is based on fact—even if the facts here can only be verified by Thurber's memory. Do you find events in the essay that make you agree that it's a "somewhat incredible tale"? Do you think Thurber is exaggerating to make his points? Write at least a paragraph giving your opinion on these questions. Cite at least one detail from the essay to support your answer to each question.

Analyzing Language and Vocabulary

Word Roots

Thurber says that he could add "verisimilitude" to his story by throwing furniture around, shaking doors, and barking like a dog. *Verisimilitude* is built on roots from two Latin words: *verus* meaning "true" and *similis* meaning "similar" or "same." Thus, *verisimilitude* means "similar to reality or close to what is true."

Here are some questions about five other words that are built on the Latin words *verus* or *similis*. A dictionary will help you with the answers.

1. What is an eternal *verity*?
2. If a lawyer asks you to *verify* a statement, are you expected (a) to produce proof to show that it is false or (b) to produce proof to show that it is true?
3. Which of these words means the opposite of *falseness:* (a) vivacity, (b) veracity, or (c) velocity?
4. Which of these words uses the root *similis: stimulated* or *simulated*?
5. Which of these words uses the root *similis: simile* or *smile*?

Focusing on Background
About Thurber by Thurber

"James Thurber was born on a night of wild portent and high wind in the year 1894, at 147 Parsons Avenue, Columbus, Ohio. The house, which is still standing, bears no tablet or plaque of any description and is never pointed out to visitors. Once Thurber's mother, walking past the place with an old lady from Fostoria, Ohio, said to her, 'My son James was born in that house,' to which the old lady, who was extremely deaf, replied, 'Why, on the Tuesday morning train, unless my sister is worse.' Mrs. Thurber let it go at that.

"The infant Thurber was brought into the world by an old practical nurse named Margery Albright, who had delivered the babies of neighbor women before the Civil War. He was, of course, much too young at the time to have been affected by the quaint and homely circumstances of his birth. . . . Not a great deal is known about his earliest years, beyond the fact that he could walk when he was only two years old and was able to speak whole sentences by the time he was four.

"Thurber's boyhood (1900–1913) was pretty well devoid of significance. I see no reason why it should take up much of our time. There is no clearly traceable figure or pattern in this phase of his life. If he knew where he was going, it is not apparent from this distance. He fell down a great deal during this period, because of a trick he had of walking into himself. His gold-rimmed glasses forever needed straightening, which gave him the appearance of a person who hears somebody calling but can't make out where the sound is coming from. Because of his badly focused lenses, he saw, not two of everything, but one and a half. Thus, a four-wheeled wagon would not have eight wheels for him, but six. How he succeeded in preventing these two extra wheels from getting into his work, I have no way of knowing.

"Thurber's life baffles and irritates the biographer because of its lack of design. One has the disturbing feeling that the man contrived to be some place without actually having gone there. His drawings, for example, sometimes seem to have reached completion by some other route than the common one of intent.

"The writing is, I think, different. In his prose pieces he appears always to have started from the beginning and to have reached the end by way of the middle. It is impossible to read any of the stories from the last line to the first without experiencing a definite sensation of going backward. This seems to me to prove that the stories were written and did not, like the drawings, just suddenly materialize.

"Thurber's very first bit of writing was a so-called poem entitled 'My Aunt Mrs. John T. Savage's Garden at 185 South Fifth Street, Columbus, Ohio.' It is of no value or importance except insofar as it demonstrates the man's appalling memory for names and numbers. He can tell you to this day the names of all the children who were in the fourth grade when he was. He remembers the phone numbers of several of his high-school chums. He knows the birthdays of all his friends and can tell you the date on which any child of theirs was christened. He can rattle off the names of all the persons who attended the lawn fete of the First M.E. Church of Columbus in 1907. This ragbag of precise but worthless information may have helped him in his work, but I don't see how. . . ."

—James Thurber

Grandson of two rabbis and the son of another, Isaac Bashevis Singer (1904–1991) was born in Radzymin, near Warsaw, Poland. His family wanted him to continue the rabbinical tradition, and so he studied in a Warsaw seminary. But he soon discovered that his real love was language and that he could best express and practice his religious beliefs through literature.

He began writing in Hebrew but complained that the language seemed artificial. "Nobody spoke it where I lived." So he switched to Yiddish, a language based on Medieval High German and written in the Hebrew alphabet. In 1935 Singer became alarmed at the rise of Nazism in Poland and sailed to America. There he eventually married, became a United States citizen, and settled in New York City.

His first literary success in America came with a translation of *The Family Moskat*, a novel about several generations of a Jewish family living in the Warsaw ghetto. More than two dozen books followed, including *In My Father's Court* and *A Day of Pleasure*, from which the essay "The Washwoman" is taken. Singer was awarded the Nobel Prize for literature in 1978.

Despite his great success as a writer, Singer would rewrite and rewrite. He once told an interviewer that one of his friends as a writer had been the wastebasket.

Singer said that "the Yiddish mentality is not haughty. It does not take victory for granted. It does not demand and command but it muddles through, sneaks by, smuggles itself amidst the powers of destruction, knowing somewhere that God's plan for creation is still at the very beginning."

This essay is about a time and a place that are probably strange to you. Despite this, are Singer's characters like some people you know? How can their behavior be explained?

THE WASHWOMAN

Isaac Bashevis Singer

Our home had little contact with Gentiles.[1] The only Gentile in the building was the janitor. Fridays he would come for a tip, his "Friday money." He remained standing at the door, took off his hat, and my mother gave him six groschen.[2]

Besides the janitor there were also the Gentile washwomen who came to the house to fetch our laundry. My story is about one of these.

She was a small woman, old and wrinkled. When she started washing for us, she was already past seventy. Most Jewish women of her age were sickly, weak, broken in body. All the old women in our street had bent backs and leaned on sticks when they walked. But this washwoman, small and thin as she was, possessed a strength that came from generations of peasant forebears. Mother would count out to her a bundle of laundry that had accumulated over several weeks. She would lift the unwieldy pack, load it on her narrow shoulders, and carry it the long way home. She lived on Krochmalna Street too, but at the other end, near the Wola section. It must have been a walk of an hour and a half.

She would bring the laundry back about two weeks later. My mother had never been so pleased with any washwoman. Every piece of linen sparkled like polished silver. Every piece was neatly ironed. Yet she charged no more than the others. She was a real find. Mother always had her money ready, because it was too far for the old woman to come a second time.

Laundering was not easy in those days. The old

---

1. **Gentiles** (jen' tīlz): persons who are not Jewish.
2. **groschen:** a coin in Polish currency.

Jewish boys studying in Warsaw, before the Nazis invaded Poland.

Photograph by Roman Vishniac

woman had no faucet where she lived but had to bring in the water from a pump. For the linens to come out so clean, they had to be scrubbed thoroughly in a washtub, rinsed with washing soda, soaked, boiled in an enormous pot, starched, then ironed. Every piece was handled ten times or more. And the drying! It could not be done outside because thieves would steal the laundry. The wrung-out wash had to be carried up to the attic and hung on clotheslines. In the winter it would become as brittle as glass and almost break when touched. And there was always a to-do with other housewives and washwomen who wanted the attic clotheslines for their own use. Only God knows all the old woman had to endure each time she did a wash!

She could have begged at the church door or entered a home for the penniless and aged. But there was in her a certain pride and love of labor with which many Gentiles have been blessed. The old woman did not want to become a burden, and so she bore her burden.

My mother spoke a little Polish, and the old woman would talk with her about many things. She was especially fond of me and used to say I looked like Jesus. She repeated this every time she came, and Mother would frown and whisper to herself, her lips barely moving, "May her words be scattered in the wilderness."

The woman had a son who was rich. I no longer remember what sort of business he had. He was ashamed of his mother, the washwoman, and never came to see her. Nor did he ever give her a groschen. The old woman told this without rancor. One day the son was married. It seemed that he had made a good match. The wedding took place in a church. The son had not invited the old mother to his wedding, but she went to the church and waited at the steps to see her son lead the "young lady" to the altar.

The story of the faithless son left a deep impression on my mother. She talked about it for weeks and months. It was an affront not only to the old woman but to the entire institution of motherhood. Mother would argue, "Nu, does it pay to make sacrifices for children? The mother uses up her last strength, and he does not even know the meaning of loyalty."

And she would drop dark hints to the effect that she was not certain of her own children: Who knows what they would do some day? This, however, did not prevent her from dedicating her life to us. If there was any delicacy[3] in the house, she would put it aside for the children and invent all sorts of excuses and reasons why she herself did not want to taste it. She knew charms that went back to ancient times, and she used expressions she had inherited from generations of devoted mothers and grandmothers. If one of the children complained of a pain, she would say, "May I be your ransom and may you outlive my bones!" Or she would say, "May I be the atonement for the least of your fingernails." When we ate she used to say, "Health and marrow in your bones!" The day before the new moon she gave us a kind of candy that was said to prevent parasitic worms.

If one of us had something in his eye, Mother would lick the eye clean with her tongue. She also fed us rock candy against coughs, and from time to time she would take us to be blessed against the evil eye. This did not prevent her from studying *The Duties of the Heart, The Book of the Covenant,* and other serious philosophic works.

But to return to the washwoman. That winter was a harsh one. The streets were in the grip of a bitter cold. No matter how much we heated our stove, the windows were covered with frostwork and decorated with icicles. The newspapers reported that people were dying of the cold. Coal became dear. The winter had become so severe that parents stopped sending children to cheder[4] and even the Polish schools were closed.

On one such day the washwoman, now nearly eighty years old, came to our house. A good deal of laundry had accumulated during the past weeks. Mother gave her a pot of tea to warm herself, as well as some bread. The old woman sat on a kitchen chair trembling and shaking, and warmed her hands against the teapot. Her fingers were gnarled from work, and perhaps from arthritis too. Her fingernails were strangely white. These hands spoke of the stubbornness of mankind, of the will to work not only as one's strength permits but beyond the limits of one's power. Mother counted and wrote down the list: men's undershirts, women's vests, long-legged drawers, bloomers, petticoats, shifts, featherbed covers, pillowcases, sheets, and the men's fringed garments. Yes, the Gentile woman washed these holy garments as well.

The bundle was big, bigger than usual. When the woman placed it on her shoulders, it covered her completely. At first she swayed, as though she were about to fall under the load. But an inner obstinacy seemed to call out: No, you may not fall. A donkey may permit himself to fall under his burden, but not a human being, the crown of creation.

It was fearful to watch the old woman staggering out with the enormous pack, out into the frost, where the snow was dry as salt and the air was filled with dusty white whirlwinds, like goblins

---

3. **delicacy:** a special, often expensive food.

4. **cheder** (khä´dər): Hebrew school for religious instruction.

dancing in the cold. Would the old woman ever reach Wola?

She disappeared, and Mother sighed and prayed for her.

Usually the woman brought back the wash after two or, at the most, three weeks. But three weeks passed, then four and five, and nothing was heard of the old woman. We remained without linens. The cold had become even more intense. The telephone wires were now as thick as ropes. The branches of the trees looked like glass. So much snow had fallen that the streets had become uneven, and sleds were able to glide down many streets as on the slopes of a hill. Kindhearted people lit fires in the streets for vagrants to warm themselves and roast potatoes in, if they had any to roast.

For us the washwoman's absence was a catastrophe. We needed the laundry. We did not even know the woman's address. It seemed certain that she had collapsed, died. Mother declared she had had a premonition, as the old woman left our house that last time, that we would never see our things again. She found some old torn shirts and washed and mended them. We mourned, both for the laundry and for the old, toil-worn woman who had grown close to us through the years she had served us so faithfully.

More than two months passed. The frost had subsided, and then a new frost had come, a new wave of cold. One evening, while Mother was sitting near the kerosene lamp mending a shirt, the door opened and a small puff of steam, followed by a gigantic bundle, entered. Under the bundle tottered the old woman, her face as white as a linen sheet. A few wisps of white hair straggled out from beneath her shawl. Mother uttered a half-choked cry. It was as though a corpse had entered the room. I ran toward the old woman and helped her unload her pack. She was even thinner now, more bent. Her face had become more gaunt, and her head shook from side to side as though she were saying no. She could not utter a clear word, but mumbled something with her sunken mouth and pale lips.

After the old woman had recovered somewhat, she told us that she had been ill, very ill. Just what her illness was, I cannot remember. She had been so sick that someone had called a doctor, and the doctor had sent for a priest. Someone had informed the son, and he had contributed money for a coffin and for the funeral. But the Almighty had not yet wanted to take this pain-racked soul to Himself. She began to feel better, she became well, and as soon as she was able to stand on her feet once more, she resumed her washing. Not just ours, but the wash of several other families too.

"I could not rest easy in my bed because of the wash," the old woman explained. "The wash would not let me die."

"With the help of God you will live to be a hundred and twenty," said my mother, as a benediction.

"God forbid! What good would such a long life be? The work becomes harder and harder . . . my strength is leaving me . . . I do not want to be a burden on anyone!" The old woman muttered and crossed herself, and raised her eyes toward heaven.

Fortunately there was some money in the house, and Mother counted out what she owed. I had a strange feeling: the coins in the old woman's washed-out hands seemed to become as worn and clean and pious as she herself was. She blew on the coins and tied them in a kerchief. Then she left, promising to return in a few weeks for a new load of wash.

But she never came back. The wash she had returned was her last effort on this earth. She had been driven by an indomitable[5] will to return the property to its rightful owners, to fulfill the task she had undertaken.

And now at last her body, which had long been no more than a shard[6] supported only by the force of honesty and duty, had fallen. Her soul passed into those spheres where all holy souls meet, regardless of the roles they played on this earth, in whatever tongue, of whatever creed. I cannot imagine paradise without this Gentile washwoman. I cannot even conceive of a world where there is no recompense for such effort.

---

5. **indomitable** (in·däm′it·ə·b'l): undefeatable.
6. **shard** (shärd): a fragment, as of a clay pot.

Responding to the Essay

Analyzing the Essay

Identifying Facts

1. The first sentence states a fact that is important to the essay. Explain how the washwoman was different from the writer's family.
2. What does Singer tell us directly about the old woman's **character**? Which of her actions reveal the kind of person she is?
3. Describe how the washwoman's son treated her. How did the writer's own mother feel about this "faithless son"?
4. Summarize what happened during the winter, after the washwoman picked up a very large load of laundry. What sentence tells you most clearly how surprised the family was to see her return?
5. Where does the narrator expect to meet this washwoman again, and why?
6. Singer wants his winter setting and his character to come alive for us. Find at least three **similes** in the essay that help you picture the setting and the old washwoman.

Interpreting Meanings

7. What did the washwoman mean when she said, "The wash would not let me die"?
8. Singer had a "strange feeling" about the coins his mother placed into the hands of the washwoman. Why do you think he imagined the coins had become "clean and pious"? What kind of money would not be "clean and pious"? (What about the son's riches?)
9. What do you think is Singer's main **purpose** in writing this essay about the old washwoman?
10. Why do you suppose some people turn out to be courageous and honest like the washwoman, but others turn out to be worthless, like her son? Are the washwoman and her son like some people you know? Explain.

Writing About the Essay

A Creative Response

1. **Describing a Character.** Write a paragraph describing an old person you have known. Before you begin, decide on the central idea you want to get across. (Your idea might be stated: "Mr. D. is an expert on World War II aircraft"; "Aunt L. likes cats better than children"; or "The blind man at the newsstand 'sees' better than most people.") Then list specific details that will convey this idea to your reader. Can you get your point across better by describing the person's looks or actions? Or will you tell about an event in which the old person was involved? You may, like Singer, use both techniques.

A Critical Response

2. **Comparing Characters.** In a paragraph, compare the narrator's mother with the washwoman. How are their beliefs and lives different? Are any of their values alike? What kind of mother is each woman? At the end of your paragraph, tell how the two women help Singer to express his ideas about the differences and likenesses among people.
3. **Inferring the Main Idea.** For this exercise, see page 396.

Born in Salinas, California, John Steinbeck (1902–1968) worked at many jobs—apprentice painter, laboratory assistant, ranch hand, fruit picker, construction worker—before he discovered he wanted to be a writer. When he did turn to writing, he worked as a reporter, a war correspondent, a novelist, a playwright, and an essayist.

In 1938, Steinbeck received the Drama Critics Award for his dramatization of his own novel *Of Mice and Men*. In 1940, he won the Pulitzer Prize for his novel *The Grapes of Wrath*. In 1962, he was awarded the Nobel Prize for literature, which he said he did not deserve, and which made him feel "wrapped and shellacked." Ten of his novels have been made into movies. The most famous is probably *East of Eden*. It starred James Dean and became the central myth of a generation of rootless and rebellious students in the 1950's and 1960's.

In 1960, Steinbeck started out for a ten-thousand-mile tour of the United States. He drove a homemade camper which he called Rocinante, after the broken-down horse that the Spanish knight Don Quixote rode on his quests. An aged, cross-toothed French poodle named Charley was his only companion. Steinbeck wanted to rediscover his native land, not in its cities, but in its ever-diminishing heartland—its mountains, deserts, and villages. This essay is from the book he wrote about that journey, called *Travels with Charley: In Search of America*.

Like most people, Steinbeck has opinions. Stop after you read the first paragraph. Do you agree with his opinions here?

CHARLEY IN YELLOWSTONE

John Steinbeck

I must confess to a laxness in the matter of National Parks. I haven't visited many of them. Perhaps this is because they enclose the unique, the spectacular, the astounding—the greatest waterfall, the deepest canyon, the highest cliff, the most stupendous works of man or nature. And I would rather see a good Brady[1] photograph than Mount Rushmore. For it is my opinion that we enclose and celebrate the freaks of our nation and of our civilization. Yellowstone National Park is no more representative of America than is Disneyland.

This being my natural attitude, I don't know what made me turn sharply south and cross a state line to take a look at Yellowstone. Perhaps it was a fear of my neighbors. I could hear them say, "You mean you were that near to Yellowstone and didn't go? You must be crazy." Again it might have been the American tendency in travel. One goes, not so much to see but to tell afterward. Whatever my purpose in going to Yellowstone, I'm glad I went because I discovered something about Charley I might never have known.

A pleasant-looking National Park man checked me in, and then he said, "How about that dog? They aren't permitted in except on leash."

"Why?" I asked.

"Because of the bears."

"Sir," I said, "this is an unique dog. He does not live by tooth or fang. He respects the right of cats to be cats although he doesn't admire them. He turns his steps rather than disturb an earnest caterpillar. His greatest fear is that someone will point out a rabbit and suggest that he chase it. This is a dog of peace and tranquility. I suggest

---

1. **Brady:** Mathew Brady (1823?–1896), the famous Civil War photographer.

that the greatest danger to your bears will be pique[2] at being ignored by Charley.''

The young man laughed. ''I wasn't so much worried about the bears,'' he said. ''But our bears have developed an intolerance for dogs. One of them might demonstrate his prejudice with a

---

2. **pique** (pēk): mild anger.

clip on the chin, and then—no dog.''

''I'll lock him in the back, sir. I promise you Charley will cause no ripple in the bear world, and as an old bear-looker, neither will I.''

''I just have to warn you,'' he said. ''I have no doubt your dog has the best of intentions. On the other hand, our bears have the worst. Don't leave food about. Not only do they steal but they are critical of anyone who tries to reform them. In a word, don't believe their sweet faces, or you might get clobbered. And don't let the dog wander. Bears don't argue."

We went on our way into the wonderland of nature gone nuts, and you will have to believe what happened. The only way I can prove it would be to get a bear.

Less than a mile from the entrance I saw a bear beside the road, and it ambled out as though to flag me down. Instantly a change came over Charley. He shrieked with rage. His lips flared, showing wicked teeth that have some trouble with a dog biscuit. He screeched insults at the bear, which hearing, the bear reared up and seemed to me to overtop Rocinante. Frantically I rolled the windows shut and, swinging quickly to the left, grazed the animal, then scuttled on while Charley raved and ranted beside me, describing in detail what he would do to that bear if he could get at him. I was never so astonished in my life. To the best of my knowledge Charley had never seen a bear and in his whole history had showed great tolerance for every living thing. Besides all this, Charley is a coward, so deep-seated a coward that he has developed a technique for concealing it. And yet he showed every evidence of wanting to get out and murder a bear that outweighed him a thousand to one. I don't understand it.

A little farther along two bears showed up, and the effect was doubled. Charley became a maniac. He leaped all over me, he cursed and growled, snarled and screamed. I didn't know he had the ability to snarl. Where did he learn it? Bears were in good supply, and the road became a nightmare. For the first time in his life Charley resisted reason, even resisted a cuff on the ear. He became a primitive killer lusting for the blood of his enemy, and up to this moment he had had no enemies. In a bearless stretch, I opened the cab, took Charley by the collar, and locked him in the house. But that did no good. When we passed other bears, he leaped on the table and scratched at the windows trying to get out at them. I could hear canned goods crashing as he struggled in his mania. Bears simply brought out the Hyde in my Jekyll-headed dog. What could have caused it? Was it a pre-breed memory of a time when the wolf was in him? I know him well. Once in a while he tries a

bluff, but it is a palpable lie. I swear that this was no lie. I am certain that if he were released he would have charged every bear we passed and found victory or death.

It was too nerve-wracking, a shocking spectacle, like seeing an old, calm friend go insane. No amount of natural wonders, of rigid cliffs and belching waters, of smoking springs could even engage my attention while that pandemonium went on. After about the fifth encounter I gave up, turned Rocinante about, and retraced my way. If I had stopped the night and bears had gathered to my cooking, I dare not think what would have happened.

At the gate the park guard checked me out. "You didn't stay long. Where's the dog?"

"Locked up back there. And I owe you an apology. That dog has the heart and soul of a bear-killer, and I didn't know it. Heretofore he has been a little tender-hearted toward an underdone steak."

"Yeah!" he said. "That happens sometimes. That's why I warned you. A bear dog would know his chances, but I've seen a Pomeranian go up like a puff of smoke. You know, a well-favored bear can bat a dog like a tennis ball."

I moved fast, back the way I had come, and I was reluctant to camp for fear there might be some unofficial non-government bears about. That night I spent in a pretty auto court near Livingston. I had my dinner in a restaurant, and when I had settled in with a drink and a comfortable chair and my bathed bare feet on a carpet with red roses, I inspected Charley. He was dazed. His eyes held a faraway look and he was totally exhausted, emotionally no doubt. Mostly he reminded me of a man coming out of a long, hard drunk—worn out, depleted, collapsed. He couldn't eat his dinner, he refused the evening walk, and once we were in he collapsed on the floor and went to sleep. In the night I heard him whining and yapping, and when I turned on the light his feet were making running gestures and his body jerked and his eyes were wide open, but it was only a night bear. I awakened him and gave him some water. This time he went to sleep and didn't stir all night. In the morning he was still tired. I wonder why we think the thoughts and emotions of animals are simple.

Responding to the Essay

Analyzing the Essay

Identifying Facts

1. What facts does Steinbeck give about Charley to prove to us that his dog did not "live by tooth or fang"?
2. What discovery about his faithful and peaceable Charley did Steinbeck make?
3. What does Steinbeck think might explain Charley's behavior?

Interpreting Meanings

4. What does Steinbeck mean by the remark that "bears brought out the Hyde in my Jekyll-headed dog"? (Who were Dr. Jekyll and Mr. Hyde?)
5. Writers often describe animals as if they had human motives, emotions, and characteristics (a technique called **anthropomorphism**). Steinbeck uses the technique when he says about Charley: "He respects the rights of cats to be cats although he doesn't admire them." *Respect, rights,* and *admiration* are ideas that relate to human society, but we have no way of knowing whether animals have such ideas at all. Find at least four other passages where Steinbeck writes about animals as if they are human. How do these descriptions affect your response to Charley?
6. What **pun,** or joke involving words that have similar sounds, can you find in Steinbeck's description of Charley's troubled sleep?
7. What does Steinbeck mean when he says that Yellowstone "is no more representative of America than is Disneyland"? The word *enclose* in the opening paragraph gives you a clue. Do you agree with Steinbeck? Why?
8. "The American tendency in travel," Steinbeck says, is that "one goes, not so much to see but to tell afterward." What does he mean? Do you find that this is true?

Writing About the Essay

A Creative Response

1. **Narrating an Experience.** Use Steinbeck's last sentence as the topic sentence of a paragraph of your own. Narrate an experience of your own to support what Steinbeck says about the thoughts and emotions of animals. Tell **what** happened to an animal you know, **where** and **when** it happened, and **whom** it happened to. Tell the name of your animal, if it has one.

A Critical Response

2. **Comparing Experiences.** For a moment, think of Annie Dillard (page 377) and John Steinbeck as real characters in their own essays. How are their experiences with nature similar? How do they both respond to what they see? Are their views of nature similar? Compare the experiences of these characters in a paragraph.

Analyzing Language and Vocabulary

Active Verbs

Throughout the essay, Steinbeck contrasts the tranquil creature Charley has always been with the bloodthirsty maniac he becomes in the presence of bears. In writing of Charley-the-maniac, Steinbeck uses one of the most powerful devices available to a writer—the use of many and varied active verbs. Here are some of the verbs Steinbeck has chosen:

shriek	rant	struggle	graze
curse	screech	scream	rave
flare	growl	swing	leap
scratch	rear	snarl	

Each sentence that follows also describes the movement of an animal, but the verb in each sentence is dull and lifeless. For each of these verbs, list at least five other verbs that could be used to give the reader a more vivid picture of what the animal is doing.

1. The snake moved through the weeds.
2. The cat went after the beetle.
3. The deer went across the street.
4. The mosquito flew around the bed.
5. The bird sang in the rosebush.

Literature & Language

Using the Descriptive and Narrative Modes

Literary Model

In the following excerpt from his autobiography, a writer describes his grandmother and the special relationship he had with her when he was a child.

My grandmother!

She stood among my other relations mocking me when I no longer spoke Spanish. "*Pocho*,"[1] she said. But then it made no difference. (She'd laugh.) Our relationship continued. Language was never its source. She was a woman in her eighties during the first decade of my life. A mysterious woman to me, my only living grandparent. A woman of Mexico. The woman in long black dresses that reached down to her shoes. My one relative who spoke no word of English. She had no interest in *gringo*[2] society. She remained completely aloof from the public. Protected by her daughters. Protected even by me when we went to Safeway together and I acted as her translator. Eccentric woman. Soft. Hard.

When my family visited my aunt's house in San Francisco, my grandmother searched for me among my many cousins. She'd chase them away. Pinching her granddaughters, she'd warn them all away from me. Then she'd take me to her room, where she had prepared for my coming. There would be a chair next to the bed. A dusty jellied candy nearby. And a copy of *Life en Español* for me to examine. "There," she'd say. I'd sit there content. A boy of eight. *Pocho*. Her favorite. I'd sift through the pictures of earthquake-destroyed Latin American cities and blond-wigged Mexican movie stars. And all the while I'd listen to the sound of my grandmother's voice. She'd pace around the room, searching through closets and drawers,

telling me stories of her life. Her past. They were stories so familiar to me that I couldn't remember the first time I'd heard them. I'd look up sometimes to listen. Other times she'd look over at me. But she never seemed to expect a response. Sometimes I'd smile or nod. (I understood exactly what she was saying.) But it never seemed to matter to her one way or another. It was enough I was there. . . .

The last time I saw my grandmother I was nine years old. I can tell you some of the things she said to me as I stood by her bed. I cannot, however, quote the message of intimacy she conveyed with her voice. She laughed, holding my hand. Her voice illumined disjointed memories as it passed them again. She remembered her husband, his green eyes, the magic name of Narciso. His early death. She remembered the farm in Mexico. The eucalyptus nearby. (Its scent, she remembered, like incense.) She remembered the family cow, the bell around its neck heard miles away. A dog. She remembered working as a seamstress. How she'd leave her daughters and son for long hours to go into Guadalajara to work. And how my mother would come running toward her in the sun—her bright yellow dress—to see her return. "Mmmaaammmmááá," the old lady mimicked her daughter (my mother) to her son. She laughed. There was the snap of a cough. An aunt came into the room and told me it was time I should leave. "You can see her tomorrow," she promised. And so I kissed my grandmother's cracked face. And the last thing I saw was her thin, oddly youthful thigh, as my aunt rearranged the sheet on the bed.

At the funeral parlor a few days after, I knelt with my relatives during the rosary. Among their voices but silent, I traced, then lost, the sounds of individual aunts in the surge of the common prayer. And I heard at that moment what I have since heard often again—the sounds the women

---

1. **pocho:** a Mexican-American who, in the process of adapting to America, forgets his Mexican heritage.
2. **gringo:** foreign; American.

Literature & Language/*cont.*

in my family make when they are praying in sadness. When I went up to look at my grandmother, I saw her through the haze of a veil draped over the open lid of the casket. Her face appeared calm—but distant and unyielding to love. It was not the face I remembered seeing most often. It was the face she made in public when the clerk at Safeway asked her some question and I would have to respond. It was her public face the mortician had designed with his dubious art.

—from *Hunger of Memory*,
Richard Rodriguez

A Note on the Descriptive Mode

Description is the mode of writing that uses sensory details to help readers see a subject clearly. The language of descriptive writing is specific and often appeals to one or more of the five senses: sight, hearing, taste, smell, touch. Figures of speech, such as similes and metaphors, are frequently used in description.

Note the specific words that help us to picture people and places in Rodriguez's description:

woman in long black dresses that reached down to her shoes; dusty jellied candy; green eyes; scent like incense; bright yellow dress; snap of a cough; cracked face; thin, oddly youthful thigh

Examining the Writer's Style

Answer the following questions to analyze the techniques Richard Rodriguez uses to help us see his grandmother:

1. What details in the second paragraph give a picture of what the writer's grandmother looked like? What details of behavior reveal her character?
2. What sensory details does the grandmother recall from her youth? Which senses do these memories appeal to?
3. Description usually establishes a mood or evokes an emotion. How would you describe Rodriguez's mood or his feelings as he recollects his grandmother?

Literary Model

Here is a narrative from the autobiography of an actress. At the time these events occurred, the writer was young, unemployed, and alone for the first time on Christmas Eve, in the big, impersonal city of New York.

I waited in the hall downstairs for the last mail delivery of the day—the one that would surely bring word from home—Christmas cards, a letter, and of course the box from Dad and my sister with presents and homemade candy and cookies. But the postman came and went and there was nothing. He explained about the blizzard in the West that had delayed all the mails.

Now it was dark and still snowing great, dry, fluffy flakes. The city was white and sparkling like a mica-covered greeting card. I could no longer keep Christmas at bay. The aloneness engulfed me. I couldn't cry because the ache in my throat was too hard and the knot in my middle too tight. Panic set in. I was going down for the third time. I yanked on overshoes, lunged into coat and hood, ran down the block, streaked up the stairs to the elevated, and headed for Broadway where there were people.

At Times Square the lights glittered on sifting snow in the air and powdery snow underfoot. There were happy people everywhere—people in couples, people in parties, people with other people. I felt shamefully conspicuous. I joined a laughing group, walking as close as I dared, trying to look as though I belonged to them. I followed them to a theater entrance where a big sign blazed out "MITZI HAJOS—IN LADY BILLY." I bought a single seat. The orchestra was tuning up, as I walked in elaborately consulting my watch, looking about, and shaking my head in annoyance, as if the friend I expected was late in arriving. It was warm inside and the air was pervaded with that unique theater smell and sound of an audience looking forward to a performance. The overture played, the lights dimmed, the house quieted, and the curtain rose, and then—the magic gradually happened. Mitzi Hajos, Lady Billy, of course, disguised as a boy, sang and danced and made jokes that surprised me into laughing. The knot in my stomach began to loosen. I was not, after all, going down for the third time. I was safe and sheltered on a little island of light and music and color. And I was not alone. The actors, the audience, and I were somehow companions sharing the particular experience that is theater. At intermission most of the people walked to the lobby and I sat still, but my throat didn't ache any more, and I waited, comforted, for the next act to begin.

When the final curtain had shut me out, once again I edged close to a group and scuffed my way through the soft snow to the elevated. There were few passengers that night. The right-angled seats in the center of the car were empty. I sat close in the corner of one and turned my face to the snowy window, and then I cried. I cried my way back to the 86th Street Station, to the empty apartment, and to sleep. The lump inside me had dissolved and Christmas Eve was over.

—from *Openings and Closings*,
Dorothy Stickney

A Note on the Narrative Mode

Narration is the mode of writing which tells "what happened" over a period of time. Stories, which recount a series of related events, are the most common forms of narrative. Whether true or imagined, stories often relate events in chronological order—that is, in the order in which the events actually occurred in time.

Examining the Writer's Style

1. List five major events that occur in this narrative. Are events presented in the order in which they actually occurred? Look for words that give clues to the time of events.
2. A closer look at this excerpt will reveal that it has descriptive as well as narrative elements. What does the writer tell us about the time, date, and weather? Why are these details important?
3. What specific words and sensory details does the writer use to help us imagine her situation and share her feelings?
4. The writer became a famous actress. What main point does her narrative make about the theater and what it can do for people?

Using Narration and Description in Your Writing

Narrating a Series of Events. Write at least one paragraph in which you relate certain events that happened to you or to someone else.

1. Before you write, think of some event that was important or interesting in some way: a party that worked (or failed); an audition for a play that got you a part (or didn't); a Saturday that was boring (or exciting).
2. Then list all the events you want to include.
3. Put your events in chronological order.
4. List some descriptive details that will help your reader know **where** you were and **how** you were feeling.
5. If it will help your reader follow your narrative, use words that set the time: *at 6 A.M.; at noon; when night fell;* and so on.

INFERRING THE MAIN IDEA

Writing Assignment

In a paragraph, explain what you think the main or controlling idea is in the essay "The Washwoman" by Isaac Singer (page 384). In a second paragraph, tell what you think of this idea.

Background

Often, an essayist, like a short-story writer, does not state directly the main idea of the essay. Instead, the writer gives us the pleasure of discovering the idea on our own. The writer allows us to make an **inference,** or educated guess, about what all the separate details in the essay mean, or add up to.

Remember, when you state the main idea of an essay, the statement is yours; probably no other reader will ever state the main idea in exactly the way you state it. Remember also that an idea has to be stated in a complete sentence. A **topic** can be stated in one word (work); to state an **idea** you need a subject and verb. (Work has taught me to value vacations.)

Prewriting

Answering these questions should help you discover the main idea of the essay.

Finding the Main Idea:

1. **Who or what is the essay about?** (Its title is "The Washwoman": is this the essay's subject, or is it something else?)
2. If the essay is chiefly a narrative, ask: **What happens in the essay?**
3. If the essay is chiefly descriptive, ask: **What mood or feeling is expressed in the essay?**
4. **How does the writer feel about the subject of his essay?** How do you know?

5. **Did the writer discover something about this subject that he is sharing with us?**
6. **Does the writer make any direct statements that give you a clue to the meaning of his essay?**
7. **Write a statement that summarizes the meaning you've found in the essay.** Test your statement against the essay: is it broad enough to cover everything that is important in the essay?

Identifying Your Response:

1. **Did the experience described in the essay remind you of any experience of your own or of anyone close to you?**
2. **Did you identify with any character in the essay—that is, did you feel that any person in the essay was like you in some way?** (Remember that the narrator is also a character in the essay.)
3. **Did the writer make any remarks in this essay that you disagree with?**
4. **Did he make any statements that you particularly liked or found very thoughtful?**
5. **Did he use loaded language in the essay, or manipulate your feelings in any way?** (See page 195 for a discussion of loaded words.)

Writing

Open your first paragraph with a sentence that states the central meaning of the essay, as you see it. Then supply at least three details from the essay to support what you say. Open your second paragraph with a sentence that states your general response to the essay. In the rest of this paragraph, give at least three reasons that explain why you feel this way about the essay (about its characters or its message).

Checklist for Revision

1. Have you cited the author and title in your first paragraph?
2. Have you opened each paragraph with a topic sentence?
3. Have you provided supporting details?
4. If you've quoted directly from the essay, have you used quotation marks?

Report is a term often used by magazine and newspaper people. You might have noticed that a "reporter" will often speak of writing a "story," but almost never of writing an "essay."

"Hooking" Our Interest

In fact, most reports are kinds of expository essays. This means that they take as their subject some object or event that the writer basically wants to inform us about: a book, a place, an achievement or a crime, a new discovery. A good reporter can "hook" our interest whether or not we were interested in the subject before we began to read. To understand *why* we as readers bite the hook and "get interested," we need to focus on the techniques the reporter has used. We need to look at the reporter's language: the **images** used to make people and places seem immediate and real; the **figures of speech** used to describe the unfamiliar in terms of the familiar. We need to look for **human interest**—those stories and details that will help us see the way the event affected ordinary human lives.

Though you may not know it, you are quite an expert judge of reports: you have been reading them for years. Whether the report is a magazine article on the dangers of eating junk food, or a newspaper interview with a police detective, or a book-length account about a mountain expedition—*you* are always able to answer the fundamental question: Does this interest me?

Understanding why something interests you always makes it more interesting still, and understanding why always involves learning the rules and the terms of the game. That is why people take the time to learn the difference between a pop fly and a foul or between a *mousse* and a *moussaka.* Just as learning the rules and the terms of the game will make you a better ballplayer or a better cook, so learning the elements that make an interesting report will help you write so that people will say of your report: "Read this!"

The Facts, Please!

Thus, a good reporter must write an interesting report or we won't finish reading it. A good reporter must also write an accurate and objective report, or we will end up not trusting the writer.

Accuracy means that the reporter has the facts straight and that they are presented clearly. **Objectivity** means that the reporter is fair—that he or she doesn't let personal bias or prejudice get in the way of presenting the truth.

As a reader, you must exercise critical judgment when you read reports. You may have to distinguish between "facts" and "fiction" presented as if it were fact. Sometimes reports are really only **propaganda**—that is, they distort the facts in order to manipulate the way we think. Reports can be distorted or inaccurate for another reason: Sometimes, as we all know, facts just do not sell as well as fiction does.

Reports on People and Events

> "**S**ometimes, as we all know, facts just do not sell as well as fiction does."

FROM
COMING INTO THE COUNTRY

John McPhee

John McPhee (1931–   ) is one of those writers who seems to be able to make any subject interesting. He was born, raised, and still lives in Princeton, New Jersey. He has written for television and for such magazines as *Time, National Geographic,* and *The New Yorker.* He has written on hundreds of subjects—tennis, a prep-school teacher, nuclear safeguards, canoes, and the Swiss army knife will give you five. His 1967 book *Oranges* is, just as the title suggests, a historical, geographical, botanical, and anecdotal study of oranges. But *The Deltoid Pumpkin Seed,* written in 1973, is not about pumpkins at all, but about an experimental aircraft.

One of his reviewers commented, "Sometimes it seems that McPhee deliberately chooses unpromising subjects, just to show what he can do with them. . . . McPhee's powers of description are such that we often feel the shock of recognition even when what is being described is totally outside our experience."

This is an extract from *Coming into the Country.* The "country" is Alaska. After you have read the first paragraph, stop, and look at the photographs that are used to illustrate the story. What do you predict the "death postponed" is going to be?

T he country is full of stories of unusual deaths—old Nimrod Robertson lying down on a creek in overflow and letting it build around him a sarcophagus of ice; the trapper on the Kandik who apparently knocked himself out when he tripped and fell on his own firewood and froze to death before he came to—and of stories also of deaths postponed. There are fewer of the second. I would like to add one back—an account that in essence remains in the country but in detail has largely disappeared.

On a high promontory in the montane ruggedness around the upper Charley River lies the wreckage of an aircraft that is readily identifiable as a B-24. This was the so-called Liberator, a medium-range bomber built for the Second World War. The wreckage is in the dead center of the country, and I happened over it in a Cessna early in the fall of 1975, during a long and extremely digressive flight that began in Eagle and ended many hours later in Circle. The pilot of the Cessna said he understood that the crew of the Liberator had bailed out, in winter, and that only one man had survived. I asked around to learn who might know more than that—querying, among others, the Air Force in Fairbanks, the Gelvins, various old-timers in Circle and Central, some of the river people, and Margaret Nelson, in Eagle, who had packed parachutes at Ladd Field, in Fairbanks, during the war. There had been one survivor— everyone agreed. No one knew his name. He had become a symbol in the country, though, and was not about to be forgotten. It was said that he alone had come out—long after all had been assumed dead—because he alone, of the widely scattered crew, was experienced in wilderness, knew how to live off the land, and was prepared to deal with the hostile cold. Above all, he had found a cabin, during his exodus, without which he would have died for sure.

"And the government tries to stop us from building them now."

"Guy jumped out of an airplane, and he would have died, but he found a cabin."

If the survivor had gone on surviving for what was now approaching thirty-five years, he would in all likelihood be somewhere in the Lower Forty-eight. When I was home, I made a try to find him. Phone calls ricocheted around Washington for some days, yielding only additional phone numbers. The story was just too sketchy. Did I know how many bombers had been lost in that war? At length, I was given the name of Gerard Hasselwander, a historian at the Albert F. Simpson Historical Research Center, Maxwell Air Force Base, Alabama. I called him, and he said that if I did not even know the year of the crash he doubted he could help me. Scarcely two hours later, though, he called back to say that he had had a free moment or two at the end of his lunch hour and had browsed through some microfilm. To his own considerable surprise, he had found the survivor's name, which was Leon Crane. Crane's home when he entered the Army Air Force had been in Philadelphia, but Hasselwander had looked in a Philadelphia directory, and there was no Leon Crane in it now. However, he said, Leon Crane had had two brothers who were also in the service—in the Army Medical Corps—during the Second World War. One of them was named Morris. In the Philadelphia directory, there was a Dr. Morris Crane.

When I called the number, someone answered and said Dr. Crane was not there.

I asked when he would return.

"I don't know," was the reply. "He went to Leon's."

The Liberator, making cold-weather propeller tests above twenty thousand feet, went into a spin, dived toward the earth, and, pulling out, snapped its elevator controls.[1] It then went into another spin, and the pilot gave the order to abandon ship. There were five aboard. Leon Crane was the co-pilot. He was twenty-four, and he had been in Alaska less than two months. Since the plane was falling like a swirling leaf, he had to drag himself against heavy centrifugal force toward the open bomb bay. He had never used a parachute. The outside air temperature was at least thirty degrees below zero. When he jumped, he forgot his mittens. The day was December 21st.

The plane fiercely burned, not far away from where he landed, and he stood watching it, up to his thighs in snow. He was wearing a hooded down jacket, a sweater, winter underwear, two pairs of trousers, two pairs of socks, and felt-lined military mukluks. He scanned the mountainsides but could see nothing of the others. He thought he had been the second one to go out of the plane, and as he fell he thought he saw a parachute open in the air above him. He shouted into the winter silence. Silence answered. Months later, he would learn that there had been two corpses in the aircraft. Of the two other fliers no track or trace was ever found. "Sergeant Pompeo, the crew chief, had a thick set of glasses. He must have lost them as soon as he hit the airstream. Without them, he really couldn't see. What was he going to do when he got down there?"

For that matter, what was Crane going to do? He had no food, no gun, no sleeping bag, no mittens. The plane had been meandering in search of

_____

1. **elevator controls:** wing flaps moved to change altitude.

suitable skies for the tests. Within two or three hundred miles, he had no idea where he was.

Two thousand feet below him, and a couple of miles east, was a river. He made his way down to it. Waiting for rescue, he stayed beside it. He had two books of matches, a Boy Scout knife. He started a fire with a letter from his father, and for the first eight days he did not sleep more than two hours at a time in his vigilance to keep the fire burning. The cold awakened him anyway. Water fountained from a gap in the river ice, and that is what he lived on. His hands, which he to some extent protected with parachute cloth or in the pockets of his jacket, became cut and abraded from tearing at spruce boughs. When he spread his fingers, the skin between them would split. Temperatures were probably ranging between a high of thirty below zero and a low around fifty. The parachute, as much as anything, kept him alive. It was twenty-eight feet in diameter, and he wound it around him so that he was at the center of a great cocoon. Still, he said, his back would grow cold while his face roasted, and sparks kept igniting the chute.

He was telling me some of this on a sidewalk in Philadelphia when I asked him how he had dealt with fear.

He stopped in surprise, and looked contemplatively up the street toward Independence Hall, his graying hair wisping out to the sides. He wore a business suit and a topcoat, and he had bright, penetrating eyes. He leaned forward when he walked. "Fear," he repeated. "I wouldn't have used that word. Think about it: there was not a lot I could do if I were to panic. Besides, I was sure that someone was going to come and get me."

All that the search-and-rescue missions had to go on was that the Liberator had last been heard from above Big Delta, so the search area could not be reduced much below forty thousand square miles. Needless to say, they would not come near finding him. He thought once that he heard the sound of an airplane, but eventually he realized that it was a chorus of wolves. In his hunger, he tried to kill squirrels. He made a spear and threw it awkwardly as they jumped and chattered in the spruce boughs. He made a bow and arrow, using a shroud line from his parachute, but when he released the arrow it shot off at angles ridiculously oblique to the screeching, maddening squirrels. There was some rubber involved in the parachute assembly, and he used that to make a slingshot, which was worse than the bow and arrow. When he fell asleep by the fire, he dreamed of milkshakes, dripping beefsteaks, mashed potatoes, and lamb chops, with lamb fat running down his hands. Awake, he kicked aside the snow and found green moss. He put it in his mouth and chewed and chewed some more, but scarcely swallowed any. Incidentally, he was camped almost exactly where, some twenty-five years later, Ed and Virginia Gelvin would build a cabin from which to trap and hunt.

Crane is a thoroughly urban man. He grew up in the neighborhood of Independence Hall, where he lives now, with an unlisted number. That part of the city has undergone extensive refurbishment in recent years, and Crane's sons, who are residential builders and construction engineers, have had a part in the process. Crane, more or less retired, works for them, and when I visited him I followed him from building to building as he checked on the needs and efforts of carpenters, bricklayers, plumbers. He professed to have no appetite for wild country, least of all for the expanses of the North. As a boy, he had joined a city Scout troop, and had become a First Class Scout, but that was not to suggest a particular knowledge of wilderness. When he flew out of Fairbanks that morning in 1943, his lifetime camping experience consisted of one night on the ground—with his troop, in Valley Forge.

He decided on the ninth day that no help was coming. Gathering up his parachute, he began to slog his way downriver, in snow sometimes up to his waist. It crossed his mind that the situation might be hopeless, but he put down the thought as he moved from bend to bend by telling himself to keep going because "right around that curve is what you're looking for." In fact, he was about sixty miles from the nearest human being, almost a hundred from the nearest group of buildings large enough to be called a settlement. Around the next bend, he saw more mountains, more bare jagged rock, more snow-covered sweeps of alpine tundra, contoured toward another river bend.

"Right around that curve is what you're looking for," he told himself again. Suddenly, something was there. First, he saw a cache,[2] high on legs in the air, and then a small cabin, with a door only three feet high. It was like the lamb chops, with the grease on his fingers, but when he pushed at the door it was wood and real. The room inside was nine by ten: earth floor, low ceiling, a bunk made of spruce. It was Alaskan custom always to leave a cabin open and stocked for anyone in need. Split firewood was there, and matches, and a pile of prepared shavings. On a table were sacks of dried raisins, sugar, cocoa, and powdered milk. There was a barrel stove, frying pans on the wall. He made some cocoa and, after so long a time without food, seemed full after a couple of sips. Then he climbed a ladder and looked in the cache, lifting a tarp to discover hammers, saws, picks, drills, coiled rope, and two tents. No one, he reasoned, would leave such equipment far off in the wilderness. "I figured civilization was right around the corner. I was home free."

So he stayed just a night and went on down the river, anxious to get back to Ladd Field. The moon came up after the brief light of day, and he kept going. He grew weak in the deep cold of the night, and when the moon went below the mountains he began to wander off the stream course, hitting boulders. He had been around many corners, but no civilization was there. Now he was sinking into a dream-hazy sleep-walking numbed-out oblivion; but fear, fortunately, struck through and turned him, upriver. He had not retraced his way very far when he stopped and tried to build a fire. He scraped together some twigs, but his cut and bare hands were shaking so—at roughly fifty below zero—that he failed repeatedly to ignite a match. He abandoned the effort, and moved on through the snow. He kept hitting boulders. He had difficulty following his own tracks. He knew now that he would die if he did not get back to the cabin, and the detached observer within him decided he was finished. Left foot, right foot— there was no point in quitting, even so. About noon, he reached the cabin. With his entire body shaking, he worked at a fire until he had one going.

---

2. **cache** (kash): storage place.

Then he rolled up in his parachute and slept almost continuously for three full days.

In his excitement at being "right around the corner from civilization," he had scarcely looked in the cache, and now he found rice, flour, beans, powdered eggs, dried vegetables, and beef—enough for many weeks, possibly months. He found mittens. He found snowshoes. He found long johns, socks, mukluks. He found candles, tea, tobacco, and a corncob pipe. He found ammunition, a .22. In the cabin, he mixed flour, peas, beans, sugar, and snow, and set it on the stove. That would be his basic gruel—and he became enduringly fond of it. Sometimes he threw in eggs and vegetables. He covered his hands with melted candle wax, and the bandage was amazingly effective. He developed a routine, with meals twice a day, a time for hunting, a fresh well chopped daily through the four-foot river ice. He slept eighteen hours a day, like a wintering bear—not truly hibernating, just lying there in his den. He felt a need to hear a voice, so he talked to himself. The day's high moment was a pipeful of tobacco puffed while he looked through ten-year-old copies of *The Saturday Evening Post*. He ransacked the magazines for insights into the woods lore he did not know. He learned a thing or two. In a wind, it said somewhere in the *Post,* build your fire in a hole. He shot and ate a ptarmigan, and had the presence of mind to look in its stomach. He found some overwintering berries there, went to the sort of bushes they had come from, and shot more ptarmigan. Cardboard boxes, the magazines, and other items in the cabin were addressed to "Phil Berail, Woodchopper, Alaska." Contemplating these labels, Crane decided that Alaska was a fantastic place—where someone's name and occupation were a sufficient address. One day, an old calendar fell off the wall and flipped over on its way to the floor. On the back was a map of Alaska. He stared at it all day. He found Woodchopper, on the Yukon, and smiled at his foolishness. From the terrain around him, the northward flow of the stream, the relative positions of Fairbanks and Big Delta, he decided—just right—that he was far up the Charley River. The smile went back where it came from.

He decided to wait for breakup, build a raft,

and in late May float on down to the Yukon. After five or six weeks, though, he realized that his food was going to give out in March. There was little ammunition with which to get meat, and he had no confidence anyway in his chances with the rifle. If he stayed, he would starve. He felt panic now, but not enough to spill the care with which he was making his plans. He had set off willy-nilly once before and did not want to repeat the mistake. He patched his clothes with parachute cloth, sewing them with shroud lines. He made a sled from some boards and a galvanized tub. He figured closely what the maximum might be that he could drag and carry. On February 12th, he left. The sled would scarcely budge at first, and snow bunched up before it. Wearing a harness he had made, he dragged the sled slowly downriver. Berail's snowshoes had Indian ties. Try as he would, he could not understand how to secure them to his feet. The snowshoes were useless. Up to his knees, and sometimes to his hips, he walked from dawn until an hour before dark each day. He slept beside bonfires that burned all night. Blizzards came up the river some days, and driving williwaws—winds of a force that could literally stop him in his tracks. He leaned against the wind. When he could, he stepped forward. Once, at the end of a day's hard walking, he looked behind him—on the twisting mountain river—and saw where he had started at dawn. The Charley in summer—clear-flowing within its canyon walls, with grizzlies fishing its riffles, Dall sheep on the bluffs, and peregrines above it in the air—is an extremely beautiful Alaskan river (it has been called the loveliest of all), but for Leon Crane it was little more than brutal. He came to a lead one day, a patch of open water, and, trying to use some boulders as stepping stones, he fell in up to his armpits. Coming out, barging through snowdrifts, he was the center of a fast-forming block of ice. His matches were dry. Shaking as before, he managed this time to build a fire. All day, he sat steaming beside it, removing this or that item of clothing, drying it a piece at a time.

After a couple of weeks on the river, he found another cabin, with a modest but welcome food cache—cornmeal, canned vegetables, Vienna sausage. He sewed himself a backpack and aban-

doned his cumbersome sled. Some seven or eight days on down the river, he came around a bend at dusk and found cut spruce tops in parallel rows stuck in the river snow. His aloneness, he sensed, was all but over. It was the second week of March, and he was eighty days out of the sky. The arrangement of treetops, obviously, marked a place where a plane on skis might land supplies. He looked around in near darkness and found a toboggan trail. He camped, and next day followed the trail to a cabin—under smoke. He shouted toward it. Al Ames, a trapper, and his wife, Neena, and their children appeared in the doorway. "I am Lieutenant Leon Crane, of the United States Army Air Forces," he called out. "I've been in a little trouble." Ames took a picture, which hangs on a wall in Philadelphia.

Crane remembers thinking, Somebody must be saving me for something, but I don't know what it is. His six children, who owe themselves to that trip and to Phil Berail's fully stocked Charley River cabin, are—in addition to his three sons in the construction business—Mimi, who is studying engineering at Barnard; Rebecca, who is in the master's program in architecture at Columbia; and Ruth, a recent graduate of the Harvard Medical School. Crane himself went on to earn an advanced degree in aeronautical engineering at the Massachusetts Institute of Technology and spent his career developing helicopters for Boeing Vertol.

"It's a little surprising to me that people exist who are interested in living on that ground up there," he told me. "Why would anyone want to take someone who wanted to *be* there and throw them out? Who could *care*?"

Al Ames, who had built his cabin only two years before, harnessed his dogs and mushed Crane down the Yukon to Woodchopper, where a plane soon came along and flew him out.

Crane met Phil Berail at Woodchopper and struggled shyly to express to him his inexpressible gratitude. Berail, sixty-five, was a temporary postmaster and worked for the gold miners there. He had trapped from his Charley River cabin. He was pleased that it had been useful, he said. For his part, he had no intention of ever going there again. He had abandoned the cabin four years before.

Responding to the Report

Analyzing the Report

Identifying Facts

1. How did McPhee first learn about and get interested in Leon Crane's story?
2. Trace McPhee's detective work in search of Leon Crane. What dramatic moment in the reporter's search is not directly described?
3. What were some of Leon Crane's first problems after the crash?
4. What thought kept Crane moving along the river? What ultimately saved his life?

Interpreting Meanings

5. We feel a sense of **irony** when we expect one thing to be true and find in reality just the opposite. McPhee reveals an irony when he records the Yukon inhabitants' opinions on Leon Crane. They said that "he alone had come out—long after all had been assumed dead—because he alone, of the widely scattered crew, was experienced in wilderness, knew how to live off the land, and was prepared to deal with the hostile cold" (page 399). What facts in Crane's actual story make this opinion ironic?
6. What does McPhee mean when he says on page 404 that Crane's six children "owe themselves to that trip and to Phil Berail's fully stocked . . . cabin"?
7. One of McPhee's **purposes** in writing his book on Alaska was to show how new government regulations are changing life in the wilderness. For example, new laws call for the destruction of cabins built by homesteaders on what is now Federal land. One of those cabins was the key to Crane's survival. How do you think McPhee wants you to feel about these new laws?
8. Did this report hook your interest? Why, or why not?

Writing About the Report

A Creative Response

1. **Reporting on a Process.** Choose a subject you've always wanted to know about. It may be any-thing—how a computer works or how people feel about last Saturday's game or the wildlife of your area or how to apply eye makeup or the best shoes for dirt-track jogging. Then go and find out about it. Write a paragraph in which you report on what you found out and the process you used to find out about it. You can begin by simply explaining **what** you want to know, and **why.** Then tell **where** you went, **what** you did, **whom** you talked to, or **what** books you read. Let readers discover the information in the same order you did (McPhee provides an example).

A Critical Response

2. **Analyzing the Report.** In a paragraph, explain how Leon Crane's experience, though told as a report, resembles a short story. Build your paragraph around the answers to these questions: Who is the **main character** and what does he want? What **conflicts** does he encounter as he tries to get what he wants? What is the **climax** of the story? What is its **resolution?** What idea about life (or **theme**) does the story express?

Analyzing Language and Vocabulary

Words and Their Contexts

Cite the context clues that help you make educated guesses at the meaning of each italicized word below. Check your answers in a dictionary.

1. " . . . old Nimrod Robertson lying down on a creek in overflow and letting it build around him a *sarcophagus* of ice . . ." (Page 399)
2. "On a high *promontory* in the *montane* ruggedness around the upper Charley River lies the wreckage of an aircraft . . ." (Page 399)
3. "Since the plane was falling like a swirling leaf, he had to drag himself against heavy *centrifugal* force toward the open bomb bay." (Page 400)
4. "He was wearing a hooded down jacket, a sweater, winter underwear, two pairs of trousers, two pairs of socks, and felt-lined military *mukluks*." (Page 400)
5. "His hands . . . became cut and *abraded* from tearing at spruce boughs." (Page 400)

An archaeologist is a "digger," someone who looks for artifacts that have been left in the earth by people who lived long ago. You might not realize that much of what archaeologists discover comes from ancient burial sites and garbage dumps. These are places where the artifacts people use every day are often preserved.

The writer of this report on archaeology is a scholar of the civilizations of ancient Israel, Greece, and Rome. This report is one of twenty-six very readable essays in Dr. Bertman's book called *Doorways Through Time*. The book includes other essays in archaeology with such interesting titles as "Voices from the Tomb" (mummies in Egypt), "The Dark Labyrinth" (ancient Crete), "The Murmuring Ashes" (Pompeii), and "Bodies in the Bog" (Denmark).

The report you are about to read is about the greatest archaeological discovery ever made in Egypt. You have probably studied Egypt, and you know that the Egyptians established their kingdoms in the fertile valley of the Nile River about 3000 B.C. You probably also know that they were ruled by pharaohs; that they wrote in unusual pictographs called hieroglyphics; that they believed that after death a person's soul made a long journey through the underworld to join the god Osiris. You also surely know about the pyramids, built as tombs for the great pharaohs. Today the pyramids look as if they were made only of rough rock, but centuries ago they were capped with fine white limestone, and they shone like stars across the desert sands.

The Egyptians were master goldsmiths. (They brought gold back from their frequent military forays into gold-rich Nubia, to the south.) It was rumors of buried gold treasure that over the centuries lured diggers of all sorts (honest ones and thieves) to search for the hidden tombs of the pharaohs.

Before you read, think of what archaeologists of the distant future might discover about our civilization today. What artifacts do you think will survive? What will they reveal about us and our lives? Could our remains tell these future diggers the kind of people we *really* are?

BEHIND THE GOLDEN MASK: Tutankhamun and His Queen

Stephen Bertman

I am thy first love, I am thy garden,
Scented with spices, fragrant with flowers.
Deep runs my channel, smoothed by thy tillage,
Cooled by the North Wind, filled by the Nile.

If anything can convey the humanness of the past, it is this—an ancient love poem. The sentiments it contains have traveled across three thousand years of history. Yet, despite the distance in time, the poem's content witnesses the feelings we hold in common with those who once lived long ago.

Of all the love poems in the world, the oldest are the love poems of ancient Egypt, composed in the second millennium B.C. These poems speak to us of love, the most fragile of all human emotions. They survive because human beings have always felt the impulse to express their inner life in some external form, to give to an invisible spirit material expression. Thus antique passions live on, inked onto now-crumbling papyrus or traced on the shards of vases once whole. If it is marvelous that material artifacts endure from lost civilizations, how much more marvelous it is that

Presentation of Nubian tribute to Tutankhamun (restored). Detail #1: center section. Copy of a wall painting from the Tomb of Amenhotep Huy (T 40). XVIII Dynasty, c. 1360 B.C.

Egyptian Expedition of The Metropolitan Museum of Art, New York. Rogers Fund, 1930. (30.4.21)

human emotions can be faithfully transmitted after thousands of years.

It is the land of Egypt itself that has enabled us to have these poems: on the wet banks of the Nile grew papyrus reeds that were transmuted into the world's oldest paper; in the dry sands of the desert, the scrolls were kept from decay.

Yet it is one thing to possess an ancient scroll; something else to understand its meaning. For almost two thousand years the meaning of hieroglyphics was forgotten until a chance discovery by Napoleon's troops near a delta village called Rosetta. Found in 1799, the Rosetta Stone, as it came to be called, proved to be the key that unlocked the secrets of Egyptian literature.

The Rosetta Stone contained a bilingual inscription, a single message written out in two different languages. At the top were Egyptian hieroglyphics; at the bottom, the same message in Greek.

Since ancient Greek could be read and understood, scholars were able to deduce the general meaning of the Egyptian text. By 1822 the Rosetta Stone was completely deciphered, thanks to the insights of English scientist Thomas Young and the labors of French linguist Jean François Champollion.

With the decipherment of hieroglyphic writing and the eventual translation of Egyptian literature, the long-silent Sphinx[1] was finally free to speak. From stories of adventure, bits of wisdom and humor, and erotic verse there emerged the essential humanity of the ancient Egyptian, a humanity that had for too long been hidden behind a veil of mysticism and otherworldliness.

*   *   *

---

1. **Sphinx** (sfinks): a colossal statue in Egypt with a lion's body. A *sphinx* is also a creature who speaks in riddles.

In 1922, one hundred years after the Rosetta Stone had been deciphered, an astounding event took place which further altered our perception of ancient Egypt. After searching in vain for five years through the pharaonic graveyard known as the Valley of the Kings, English archaeologist Howard Carter made the most sensational find in the history of archaeology, the discovery of King Tut's tomb.

Carter and his financial backer, Lord Carnarvon, had been searching for the one royal tomb not accounted for in the archaeological record, the tomb of a minor ruler named Tutankhamun.[2] Boyking at the age of eight, Tutankhamun had come to the throne in the aftermath of religious revolution. His brother, the pharaoh Akhenaton,[3] had taken the radical step of instituting monotheism[4] in Egypt, antagonizing the powerful priesthoods of the land by closing their temples and confiscating their rich estates. In place of the many gods of Egypt, Akhenaton venerated only one, the god Aton, symbolized by the life-giving disc and benevolent rays of the sun. Following a philosophy of love, Akhenaton encouraged a new spirit of tender naturalism in Egyptian art, a spirit present in affectionate family portraits of the pharaoh, his beautiful queen, Nefertiti,[5] and their daughters.

But Akhenaton's tenderness, when transferred to foreign policy, only acted to antagonize Egypt's military establishment in what had heretofore been an age of expansive imperialism. When Akhenaton died, the religious and military hierarchy sought out a legitimate heir who could become the instrument by which the old ways might be reestablished. They even convinced him to change his name from Tutankh*aton* to Tutankh*amun* in order to symbolize the restored primacy of Amun, god of the Egyptian state.

Tutankhamun's reign was brief: he died in 1352 B.C. at the age of eighteen or nineteen with no notable accomplishments; but he lived during the most glorious period of Egyptian history, the eigh-

---

2. **Tutankhamun** (to͞ot′an·kä′mən).
3. **Akhenaton** (ä′kə·nä′t′n).
4. **monotheism**: the worship of one god. The Egyptians were **polytheistic**: they worshiped many gods.
5. **Nefertiti** (nef′ər·tē′tē).

teenth dynasty. Surely, thought Carter and Carnarvon, if his tomb could be found, it would reflect the splendor of that age. Yet apart from some remnants of his funeral—floral wreaths and common vases found in a pit—no material trace of his death had ever been uncovered.

On November 4, 1922, while excavating beneath the rough foundations of an ancient work camp, Carter's men came upon a step cut into the bedrock of the valley floor, the first of sixteen buried steps that led down to a sealed doorway bearing Tutankhamun's name. Beyond the sealed doorway was a rubble-filled passageway and beyond that a second sealed door. Carter prepared to enter the tomb.

Slowly, desperately slowly it seemed to us as we watched, the debris that encumbered the lower part of the doorway was removed, until at last we had the whole door clear before us. The decisive moment had arrived. With trembling hands I made a tiny breach in the upper-lefthand corner. Darkness and blank space, as far as an iron testing rod could reach, showed that whatever lay beyond was empty. Candle tests were applied as a precaution against possible foul gases, and then, widening the hole a little, I inserted the candle and peered in, Lord Carnarvon, Lady Evelyn, and [my assistant] Callender standing anxiously beside me to hear the verdict. At first I could see nothing—the hot air escaping from the chamber caused the candle flame to flicker—but presently, as my eyes grew accustomed to the light, details of the room within emerged slowly from the mist: strange animals, statues, and gold—everywhere the glint of gold. For the moment—an eternity it must have seemed to the others—I was struck dumb with amazement, and when Lord Carnarvon, unable to stand the suspense any longer, inquired anxiously, ''Can you see anything?'' it was all I could do to get out the words, ''Yes, wonderful things.'' Widening the hole a little farther so that we could both see, we inserted an electric torch.

—Howard Carter

The tomb Carter was to enter was crammed with almost five thousand objects, mostly personal possessions placed in the tomb so that they might accompany the pharaoh into the spirit world and brighten his days. For Tutankhamun's delight there were perfumes jarred in alabaster (including a pine-scented after-shave lotion) and labeled cannisters of roast duck and veal (the meat all properly embalmed so it would last forever). Packed away for his comfort were ostrich feather fans to cool him, pairs of gold-tooled slippers, and the Egyptian version of the pillow, a curved neck rest of stone. Game boards (for a game like Parcheesi) were provided to help him while away his leisure hours. For more active pursuits, chariots were garaged in the tomb, their parts neatly stacked up, awaiting reassembly in the spirit world. Souvenirs of Tutankhamun's childhood were there too: a child-sized chair of ebony and ivory (just a bit over two feet tall) and the model boats he had fashioned as a boy, boats that would now magically transport his soul across the heavenly ocean to the western horizon where the god Osiris waited to greet him.

Inside a crypt the body of Tutankhamun rested in a brown quartzite sarcophagus carved with the images of protective goddesses, their arms lovingly outstretched. Within the sarcophagus were four interlocking coffins, the first three of gilded wood, the innermost of one-eighth-inch-thick 22-carat gold. Inside, with face and shoulders encased in a golden portrait mask, was Tutankhamun's linen-swathed mummy, encrusted in golden jewelry and amulets. A gold-bladed dagger had been laid by his side for protection. The petals of spring floral wreaths, tenderly placed over his corpse more than three thousand Aprils ago, still lay intact.

Perhaps *she* had placed them there—Ankhesenamun,[6] his queen—for she too lives on in the tomb, through images of graciousness and quiet affection and through hieroglyphs that caption her acts of reverent love. ''Ankhesenamun, the Great Royal Wife, beloved of the Great Enchantress, the Heiress, Great of Favors, Mistress of Upper

---

6. **Ankhesenamun** (ank'hē·sen·ä'mən).

A wall painting (below) showing Tutankhamun as Osiris. The pharaohs hoped to be reborn from the dead, just as the god Osiris was. (Bottom right) Jars for precious ointments, showing King Tutankhamun, found in his tomb. (Top right) A throne depicting Tutankhamun and his queen.

Tutankhamun's
funeral mask.
Gold with lapis
and carnelian.

and Lower Egypt, Lady of Graciousness, Sweet of Love, the Great Wife whom he loves, Lady of the Two Lands.''

Symbols of their marriage contract are contained in an alabaster box: two locks of hair wrapped in linen beside an ivory pomegranate, symbol of fertility. But Tutankhamun was not her first husband. Years earlier, when she was only a little girl, she had been made to marry her own father, Akhenaton. Why had this happened?

In ancient Egypt the royal bloodline was traced through the female. Estranged from his wife Nefertiti, Akhenaton had chosen to marry one of their daughters as a way of protecting the legitimacy of his reign. Thus, for reasons of state, father and daughter were wed.

When Akhenaton died, Ankhesenamun was given in marriage again, this time (at perhaps age eleven or twelve) to Tutankhamun, himself then only an eight- or nine-year-old boy. These two royal children, used by others and old before their time, would come to share a decade of life and young love.

In the tomb, on a wooden chest veneered in ivory, Ankhesenamun stands, a diminutive figure beneath a bower, holding bouquets of poppies and lotus in both hands. She holds the flowers out to her sovereign lord, Tutankhamun, her dark hair flowing down her left shoulder, her diaphanous gown revealing abdomen and thigh.

On the great golden throne chair she applies perfumed ointment to her husband's shoulder as he waits to appear before his courtiers. Rays of the benevolent sun descend and end in human hands holding the *ankh*,[7] hieroglyphic symbol of life, to the nostrils of Tutankhamun, that he might inhale its vitalizing fragrance.

On the sides of a golden shrine, Ankhesenamun sits on a soft hassock as her husband pours perfumed water into her hand, her right breast visible through her bodice. In another setting, a papyrus marsh, Tutankhamun sits on a folding stool among the bulrushes, his pet lion crouching beside him. The king takes aim with bow and arrow as wild ducks, flushed from a papyrus thicket, take wing. Before him sits the young queen, holding another arrow in her hand for the time when her husband might require it, pointing with her other hand to a nest of fledglings and bidding him spare the birds' mother.

Such a papyrus marsh is the setting of yet another love poem from ancient Egypt, verses that could have been uttered by a young prince named Tutankhamun before the flowers of the wreath had been picked, before the final door was sealed.

> Even when the birds rise
> Wave mass on wave mass in great flight
> I see nothing, I am blind
> Caught up as I am and carried away
> Two hearts obedient in their beating
> My life caught up with yours
> Your beauty the binding.

* * *

Far from Egypt near the Turkish village of Boghazköy[8] sprawl the ruins of Hattusas, capital of the ancient Hittite empire. Once the Hittites were among the mightiest nations on earth, a military superpower that vied with Egypt for control of the Near East; today their name is obscure even to the educated—a humbling commentary on the place present-day nation-states may someday have in humankind's cultural memory.

Excavated at the beginning of the twentieth century, the royal palace at Hattusas has yielded over ten thousand inscribed tablets, the archives of the Hittite empire. Among the annals are two texts that bear upon the story of Ankhesenamun.

In one, a Hittite king named Mursilis describes the reign of his father Suppiluliumas,[9] a monarch of the fourteenth century B.C. and a contemporary of Tutankhamun. Tutankhamun's royal title, Nebkheperura,[10] appears here in its Hittite spelling, *Bibhururiyas*[11] (*Nibhururiyas* in a more accurate parallel text).

> Because . . . their lord Bibhururiyas [Tutankhamun] had just died, the Egyptian queen [Ankhesenamun], who had become a widow, sent an envoy to my father and wrote him as follows: "My husband died and I have no son. People say that you have many sons. If you were to send me one of your sons, he might become my husband. I am loathe to take a servant of mine and make him my husband."
>
> When my father heard that, he called the great into council (saying): "Since of old such a thing has never happened before me." He proceeded to dispatch Hattu-zitis, the chamberlain, (saying): "Go! Bring you reliable information back to me. They may try to deceive me: As to whether they have a prince bring reliable information back to me!" . . . The Egyptian queen answered my

---

7. *ankh* (ank): a cross with a loop at top.

8. **Boghazköy** (bō·gäz′koi).
9. **Suppiluliumas** (su′pē·lōō·lē′ōō·məs).
10. **Nebkheperura** (neb′ke·pə·rōō′rä).
11. *Bibhururiyas* (bib′hōō·rōō′rē·əs).

father in a letter as follows: "Why do you say: 'They may try to deceive me'? If I had a son, would I write to a foreign country in a manner which is humiliating to myself and my country? You do not trust me and tell me even such a thing. He who was my husband died and I have no sons. Shall I perhaps take one of my servants and make him my husband? I have not written to any other country; I have only written to you. People say that you have many sons. Give me one of your sons and he is my husband and king in the land of Egypt."

Mursilis concludes:

Because my father was generous, he complied with the lady's wishes and decided for (sending) the son.

For once Ankhesenamun had taken her destiny (and that of her nation) into her own hands, boldly offering kingship to a son of an enemy emperor and proposing a historic wedding of imperialistic rivals. She may well have feared that not to do so would mean being forced to marry someone else, perhaps someone she detested—for what he was or what he stood for. Instead, she decided to act, before the seventy days of mourning were ended and Tutankhamun's body was placed in its tomb.

Yet others, more powerful and even more devious, had learned of the secret message and decided to intervene. As Mursilis records in a later entry: "When my father gave them one of his sons, they killed him as they led him there."

After this, little is heard of Ankhesenamun. An aged courtier named Eye becomes the next pharaoh; Ankhesenamun, his consort. Two years later, the powerful commander-in-chief of the army, Haremhab, takes the throne. Ankhesenamun is no longer mentioned in Egypt's (or anyone's) annals. Her tomb has never been found.

The deceased Neb-Qued followed by her mother and sister. A wall painting.

Responding to the Report

Analyzing the Report

Identifying Facts

1. Explain how the discovery of the Rosetta Stone helped scholars translate Egyptian hieroglyphics for the first time. According to Bertman, what do we learn about people when we can read their writing?
2. Cite at least five **facts** about Egyptian religious and burial practices that you learned from this report.
3. Why did Tutankhaton change his name?
4. Great discoveries in science are often made by accident. How did Carter and his men find Tut's tomb?

Interpreting Meanings

5. Bertman quotes from several other sources in his report. What does each of these other sources contribute to the report: Human interest? Emotional punch? Support for Bertman's ideas? First-hand accounts?
6. Bertman says that no one knows what became of Ankhesenamun. Does he hint at her fate? What do you think became of her?
7. Do you feel Bertman's report is **objective**? Or does he insert some **subjective** opinions and feelings? Give examples to support your answer.
8. Think about Bertman's **main idea** in this report: Does he suggest that "behind the golden mask" was a man with feelings just like ours? Why does he open with a love poem? Discuss your responses to these ideas.

Writing About the Report

A Creative Response

Digging in the Future. Bertman speculates on what someone in the distant future might learn about *his* life:

> As I sit before my typewriter, the tokens of my life lie scattered on the desk before me: coins and keys, wallet and pen—for better or worse, the pocket symbols of who I am. What could someone learn, I wonder, from these material things I call my own? What could they learn of me?
>
> Could they learn from the keys the amiable locks I turn each day to find my way through life? Could they tell the thoughts that flow from my pen? Could they measure the love I feel for faces pressed tight between wallet calendars and cards?
>
> —Stephen Bertman

Suppose archaeologists ten thousands years from now dig through many strata of earth till they discover the remains of your neighborhood or town or city. What deductions might they make about the people who once lived there? In an essay, cite at least five things the diggers find and tell what they deduce about each "artifact." Use your imagination. Perhaps your diggers make the wrong deductions. For example, diggers might find the subway tunnels in New York City and deduce (wrongly) that the people who once lived there spent all their time underground.

An Oral Report

Working in small groups, prepare to give oral reports on some aspect of life in ancient Egypt that is referred to in Bertman's account. Before you decide on your group topic, review the report and write down all the topics or questions or problems that interest you. Then plan your group assignments. You should include these assignments:

a. Researchers.
b. At least one speaker. (Or will everyone have a chance to speak?)
c. At least one artist to supply visuals or research them.
d. Writers to put the research together into a report.

If you have trouble finding a topic, here are some fascinating ones:

Rosetta Stone	Akhenaton	Nefertiti
Sphinx	polytheism	mummies

Before you read this report about life in Communist China, it is important that you know something about recent Chinese history and about the life of Bette Bao Lord (1938–   ).

Bette Bao was born in Shanghai during the Japanese invasion of China that preceded World War II. Bette's first memories of that bustling city are of the shriek of air-raid sirens and the mass panic as a result of the relentless Japanese bombings. After the war ended, Bette emigrated with her mother and a sister to New York, where her father had been sent as an official of the Nationalist Chinese government. In 1949, however, the Communists defeated the Nationalists, and Mr. Bao lost his post. The Baos decided to remain in the United States.

Bette Bao graduated from Tufts University in 1959. She married Winston Lord, who became a United States diplomat in China. In the early 1970's, when the Nixon Administration was working to establish diplomatic relations with the People's Republic of China, Bette Bao Lord had the extraordinary chance to return to her homeland. In 1985, President Reagan named her husband Ambassador to China. From then until 1989, Bette Bao Lord—by now a well-known author—lived in the United States embassy in Beijing, where she welcomed Chinese artists and writers who wished to discuss their country's movement toward democracy.

Her husband's ambassadorship eventually ended, but Lord returned to Beijing as a consultant for CBS News during the height of the Chinese demonstrations for democratic reforms in 1989. She left Beijing just days before the Communist leaders ordered tanks and troops into Tiananmen Square to put a bloody end to the peaceful protests.

Meanwhile, in the 1960's, Lord had published a book presenting a report on Communist China from the personal perspective of her own family. When the Bao family had emigrated to the United States, one of Lord's sisters, Sansan, had been left behind in China and was adopted by relatives. It was believed that Sansan, being older, could help out the relatives left behind. Lord wanted to give the West "a look at China from the vantage point

of an ordinary person," so she wrote an account of her sister's life as if Sansan had written it herself. The book appeared in 1964 as *Eighth Moon: The True Story of a Young Girl's Life in Communist China*. In 1981, Lord published a fictionalized version of her family's past called *Spring Moon*, which became a best seller. She also wrote a very appealing and humorous children's book based on her own early years in Brooklyn, called *In the Year of the Boar and Jackie Robinson*. "It shows what it's like as an immigrant in a strange place," says Lord. "You don't understand what people say. English sounds like someone gargling water."

The following excerpt from *Eighth Moon* takes place during the period in Chinese history known as the Great Leap Forward. In 1958, China's Communist government tried to promote economic development by forcing people to work on huge government-owned farms. The program failed miserably and resulted in severe food shortages and government rationing.

Before you read, think about all the food you usually eat and drink each day. Then try to estimate the ounces of food you consume on an average day. How many pounds of food do you think you would need each month? In your journal, try to figure out what you would eat if the government allowed you only sixteen ounces of food per day.

Remember that this report reads as if the teenager Sansan herself is speaking.

CORN-HUSK MUFFINS

Bette Bao Lord

Often in that year of 1960 we had two tomatoes along with the usual corn-husk muffins to share among the three of us for dinner. Muffins could no longer satisfy my hunger, for they were dry and contained no oil; they were only corn husks mixed with water and rolled into a ball that was baked until done. Instead of being filled by its bulk, I was curiously more and more hungry.

I longed for more variety. When I worked in the school kitchen, I salvaged the scraps of rotten or dry vegetables thrown on the floor. When I worked on the farms, I gathered wild plants during rest hour. They were bitter, but I was no longer particular. As the year wore on, however, I couldn't even get these bitter plants. Whenever I and my friends would try to pick them, farmers would drive us away, shouting, "Get away from here! If you pick all the wild plants, what do you expect us to eat? Go away! We have to live too."

At home we were living on two to four ounces of vegetables a day and corn-husk muffins at every meal. We longed for noodles, rice, or meat, but these had disappeared from our ration quotas for several months at a time. Thus corn-husk flour became our main staple. This flour was merely the ground-up skin of corn kernels whose meat had already been extracted for export as soup to countries such as Albania.[1] What was left was not at all pleasing. Every day I mixed the flour with water and patted the dough with my hands into a ball which was cooked in the stove. No matter how I tried, there was little I could do to disguise the dry and bland taste of the unhealthy-looking yellow muffins, for we only had two ounces each of sugar and salt a month. We all got very tired of

this diet, but at school we tried to laugh about the food situation and dubbed these awful muffins "golden towers."

The government in the newspapers and at school also deplored the food crisis. Our teacher had repeatedly told us that the weather in the past three years had been so bad that the farmers could not grow enough cotton or grain for all the Chinese people. He would admit the scarcity of food and clothing, but assured us that tomorrow it would be dawn, a dawn when all our hardships would vanish, a dawn toward which everyone must work. And since we all wanted to see the dawn soon, we must all sustain even more hardships in our daily lives.

One of these additional hardships was the reduction of staples. In the past our Street Council had decided on the amount of staples an individual received each month. Now, under the "reduction of staples" campaign, those people who knew you best—your fellow workers or classmates—would decide on your proper share. They knew your daily routine, unlike the Street Council, and were able to judge your needs adequately.

Our teacher supervised the meeting to determine each student's ration allotment of staples, but it was the students who suggested quotas and voted for a consensus. When my name came up, a girl suggested that I should receive 30.8 pounds a month. Big Nose said that the amount was too low because I was active and had a long walk to school each day. He suggested 35.2 pounds, which the class later approved. However, when the teacher notified the party secretary, who also was the principal of the school, he thought it was too much and suggested 33 pounds instead. As a result my ration for a month was set at 33 pounds. While we students held discussions on each other's quotas, it was the party secretary who in fact ruled on these decisions, as in all major ones.

---

1. **Albania:** formerly, China's closest ally among the Communist countries of Eastern Europe.

In our family I received the largest monthly ration of staples, since Mama and Papa both were allotted only 30.8 pounds under the new system. This discrepancy between the adults and the children in a family was according to Chairman Mao's[2] own dictum that students needed more food because they were still growing. Even though my ration was the largest in our house, I tried not to eat more than one pound per day. Two or three times a month I indulged myself and ate more, generally when I was working on the farms and was very hungry at the end of the long day's work. I was without the coupons to buy food toward the end of those months and had to borrow from friends to tide myself over. Because exercise increased my appetite, I had to cut down on the swimming and ice skating that I loved so much.

Even though my ration was more than Mama's or Papa's, I often dipped into their share at the dinner table. I never seemed to have enough to eat. The actual bulk of food I ate was much larger than past dinners of vegetables, rice, and meat. But when dinner was primarily corn-husk muffins, I could eat several pounds at one sitting and still feel empty.

Because rationing was tight, members of a family often fought over portions at the dinner table. When there was so little to eat, an extra bite for one over another was cause for dissatisfaction. No one could afford to invite friends to dinner. It was an unwritten law that guests at a house would leave before mealtime.

My neighbor next door, whom we all affectionately called Big Father, had a great problem because his son and his son's family did stay for dinners. He was an elderly man, his family was his whole life, and he looked forward each Sunday to their visit. But as the food situation deteriorated, he couldn't squeeze out extra portions from his rations for his son, his son's wife, and his five grandchildren. He often passed me in the hall and spoke of his dilemma.

He would say, "What am I to do? There's just barely enough for the old woman and myself if we budget very carefully. Every time the family comes we can't eat for several days. What am I

---

2. **Chairman Mao's:** Mao Tse-Tung (mou′ dzu′do͞ong′) (1893–1976): founder of the People's Republic of China and Chairman of its Communist Party.

going to do? How can I tell my own children not to come to see their old grandfather anymore?"

I suggested, "Why don't you just explain your situation to them. Everyone realizes the hard times."

Big Father would reply on the verge of tears. "How can I? I am too embarrassed. I can't even spare a meal for my children? Also, you know my wife is their stepmother. I don't want them to think they are not loved by her."

I wanted to help, and one Sunday waited for the son. I explained the situation to him, but learned that he already knew the facts. The son said that he was forced to come over for dinner on Sundays because he could not feed his large family any other way. Now, however, he said he would no longer stay for dinner.

That evening I heard loud voices in the hallway. Big Father was shouting, "No, no, please stay and eat with us." The son, shoving his family out, was insisting, "No, we simply couldn't. Our dinner is ready for us at home." Finally the mock fighting stopped and the guests left. Big Father spotted me and said, "It was ridiculous, my saying stay when I meant go, and he saying go when he meant stay."

I replied, "That's the way we Chinese are, so polite and so proud. Do you remember the old story of the seven wives who came to dine together? A platter of eight meat dumplings was put before them and each ate one. All saw the lone remaining dumpling and loudly protested that another should have it—each one was completely full and couldn't eat another bite. Amidst their feminine protests, the lights went out and all were in darkness. Suddenly one screamed and the lights returned. One lady had grabbed for the extra dumpling with her hand and was speared by six pairs of chopsticks."

My story cheered his spirits and we both laughed. But the food situation was a serious one, and at my home we also had our quarrels. I shall never forget one after-supper conversation we had in the fall of 1960. I was cleaning up the table, and Papa and Mama were reading the newspapers. Papa was reading an article on Chairman Mao which impressed him and he commented, "Chairman Mao certainly loves the people."

Mama retorted, "He loves the people, all right; that's why we have nothing to eat."

Papa ignored such remarks from her and looked to me.

"Well, we would have more to eat if Sansan didn't eat so much. Every night she eats more than anyone else."

"But I am hungry and I just can't help it."

Mama began to yell, as she always did when she was excited or aggravated. "You are selfish. Why don't you think about me, your own mother? Children don't love their parents anymore. Parents always suffer because of their children. Why don't you think before you eat? You know that I always try to save some of my rations for the chickens. I eat the leftover food from patients at the hospital so as to eat less at the dinner table so I can save something for my chickens. How can they lay eggs if I don't feed them? You eat your share and part of mine every night. Where are the eggs going to come from? Can you lay eggs? I need my eggs. I can't even buy them on the black market[3] anymore."

She got herself very upset with her own yelling, but I could reply only by saying that I was hungry.

Papa also raised his voice. "So you are hungry! That's no excuse. When you are at school, you hand in a two-ounce coupon and you eat only two ounces. Just because you are at home and no one asks for you to turn in coupons doesn't mean you are entitled to eat more than your share. If you lived at school you wouldn't eat more than you were supposed to. At school you would not ask anyone to share his meal with you. Why do you expect it at home?"

When I didn't answer, no one spoke. Yet I knew the subject was not closed. I went back to the dishes, they to the papers. Later, Papa casually asked me, "Sansan, is the electricity in your room still out of order?"

"Yes. I wear rubber sneakers so I won't get shocks. When do you think the electricians will come to fix it?"

---

3. **black market:** an illegal system for buying and selling goods. The "black market" often thrives when there is rationing.

"A long time from now. It's a big job to fix something under the concrete floor. Maybe five weeks, maybe five months."

"I have already put in a request but have not heard from the electricians yet. I am scared. What if the electricity gets stronger and sneakers won't help?"

Mama offered, "Why don't you move down to our room?"

"No, I'd rather stay upstairs. There's so little room here, and besides, I need to be alone for studying."

"But you can get hurt——"

"I'll be very careful."

Papa closed the subject. "If you don't want to move into our room, we can't force you."

He was about to continue talking when he hesitated and looked over to Mama, who avoided his eyes nervously and picked up the paper instead. Papa then said, "Sansan, have you ever thought of living at school? Winter is coming and the school is so far away. You have to take an hour's ride on the bus and walk almost another hour. When the snow comes, it will be a real hardship for you every morning."

I was completely dumfounded by his suggestion. Papa continued, "I have always said that community living is a good thing; teaches young people how to get along in society. You can use a lesson or two in getting along with others. Maybe then you won't be so stubborn. Living in the dormitory would broaden your outlook, and it is an experience you should have."

I could only say, "I want to stay home."

"The loose wiring in the floor makes it dangerous to stay in your room. It may be months before it is fixed. You won't move into our room. What other choice do you have but to move to school? Winter's coming and there will be less to eat, and at school you can at least be assured of something every day."

"School food tastes bad. I'd rather eat less at home."

"That's just the point, Sansan; you don't eat less at home. You eat more. You eat more than your mother. You eat more than I do. You can't control yourself, you won't control yourself. At least at school you will learn to eat only what is yours." He took a long breath. "It's better you live at school."

"Mama, what do you want me to do?

In an unusually small voice she said, "It is your father's house; you do what your father wants you to."

Papa's mind was made up and I wasn't going to beg. I put away the dishes and went upstairs. I walked carefully into the darkened room and sat on my bed thinking. I couldn't blame them about the food. I did eat too much. I certainly didn't want to stay in their room, and it was probably dangerous to stay any longer in mine. It was a long way to school and winter in Tientsin[4] was very harsh. But even though I had to agree with Papa's logic, I was crying.

I was frightened about living at school. Teachers always campaigned for students to live in the dormitory, and on some occasions even put pressure on them. But in spite of the official encouragement, only twenty out of our class of eighty volunteered to live in. What scared me and the others was the fact that the school authorities kept the identification papers of those students who remained at school. If I lived there my papers would be transferred from my home to the school. The authorities then could send the papers anywhere in the country and I would have no choice but to follow them. They could make me teach after graduation in a faraway area; and I would never get home again. I would have to teach anywhere they wanted me to because without the papers I would be a "black person." I could not get coupons or buy food; I could not work. And no one would have enough to support me. Thus, living at school meant giving up any choice in my future teaching assignment.

The next morning, I took my papers to school. My teacher was very happy that I finally had decided to live there.

---

4. **Tientsin** (tyen'jin'): seaport in northeastern China.

Responding to the Report

Analyzing the Report

Identifying Facts

1. Describe Sansan's corn-husk muffins. (What do you think they tasted like?)
2. List the various things that Sansan ate to try to satisfy her hunger.
3. Staples are basic foods we use all the time: sugar, salt, flour, potatoes or rice. Describe the procedures that determined the amount of staples Sansan received each month.
4. Lord includes some **human-interest** stories to show us the personal effects of rationing on family life. What dilemma did Sansan's neighbor—Big Father—and his son face?
5. What fact about the Chinese does the anecdote about the seven wives illustrate?
6. How did Sansan's adoptive parents resolve the problems caused by their daughter's appetite and the faulty electric wiring in her room?
7. Why was Sansan frightened about living at school?

Interpreting Meanings

8. How did you respond to this report of life in Communist China in the 1960's? What feelings for Sansan and her family did it arouse in you?
9. "I could not think of tomorrow when my stomach was not full today," says Sansan in *Eighth Moon*. How do you think hunger affects a person, a family, and a society?
10. Hunger exists in highly developed societies too. What are some of the causes of hunger in the United States?

Writing About the Report

A Critical Response

Posing Questions for an Interview. Bette Bao Lord presents a picture of China in 1960 in which people must cope not only with hunger but also with frustration and helplessness. Suppose you were going to interview Lord for a TV program. What questions would you like to ask her? Write down at least five questions you'd ask Lord about her life, about Sansan's life, or about her experiences in China.

Maurice Herzog (1919–   ), a Frenchman, and an engineer by profession, was a brilliant mountain climber. In 1950, when he was thirty-one years old, Herzog led the French expedition that scaled Annapurna, a giant mountain in the Himalaya range of Nepal. Annapurna is the tenth highest peak in the world. It rises to a height of 26,502 feet, and until the scaling of Mount Everest in 1953, it was the highest mountain ever climbed.

When Herzog's expedition arrived in Nepal in April of 1950, Annapurna had never been scouted, let alone challenged. In fact, the mountain was scarcely known to the outside world. The Nepalese call the peak "the Goddess of the Harvests" because it stands majestically over the fertile plateau of Pokhara. But for the French climbers in their triumph, Annapurna also meant a harvest of pain and loss.

The French team was accompanied by a group of Sherpa guides—native Nepalese who are expert climbers and who, unlike the French, are accustomed to the rarefied air of the high altitudes.

On the third day of June, Lachenal and Herzog reached the summit of Annapurna. But disaster hit them almost at once, when Herzog watched helplessly as his gloves rolled down the mountain. The rest of their descent was a nightmare of horror. As this selection opens, Herzog and Lachenal have finally found the rest of their party. With hands and feet severely frostbitten, and blinded by the snow, they start the final descent to Camp II.

This chapter is taken from a book that Herzog dictated from a hospital bed a year after the expedition ended. Entitled *Annapurna*, the book became an international best seller.

As you read the first five paragraphs, look for foreshadowings of danger.

The French Climbers	The Sherpas
Maurice Herzog	Ang-Tharkey
Louis "Biscante" Lachenal	Sarki
Lionel Terray	Aila
Gaston Rébuffat	Pansy
Jean Couzy	Foutharkey
Marcel Schatz	Angawa

ANNAPURNA

Maurice Herzog

The descent began—Ang-Tharkey was magnificent, going first and cutting comfortable steps for Terray. Schatz, coming down last, carefully safeguarded the whole party.

Our first group was advancing slowly. The snow was soft, and we sank in up to our knees. Lachenal grew worse: he frequently stopped and moaned about his feet. Rébuffat was a few yards behind me.

I was concerned at the abnormal heat and feared that bad weather would put an end here and now to the epic of Annapurna. It is said that mountaineers have a sixth sense that warns them of danger—suddenly I became aware of danger through every pore of my body. There was a feeling in the atmosphere that could not be ignored. Yesterday it had snowed heavily, and the heat was now working on these great masses of snow which were on the point of sliding off. Nothing in Europe can give any idea of the force of these avalanches. They roll down over a distance of miles and are preceded by a blast that destroys everything in its path.

The glare was so terrific that without glasses it would have been impossible to keep one's eyes open. By good luck we were fairly well spaced out, so that the risk was diminished. The Sherpas no longer remembered the different pitches and oftentimes, with great difficulty, I had to take the lead and be let down on the end of the rope to find the right way. I had no crampons[1] and I could not grasp an ax. We lost height far too slowly for my liking, and it worried me to see my Sherpas going so slowly and carefully and at the same time so insecurely. In actual fact they went very well, but I was so impatient I could no longer judge their performance fairly.

Lachenal was a long way behind us, and every time I turned around he was sitting down in the track. He, too, was affected by snow blindness, though not so badly as Terray and Rébuffat, and he found difficulty in seeing his way. Rébuffat went ahead by guesswork, with agony in his face, but he kept on. We crossed the couloir[2] without incident, and I congratulated myself that we had passed the danger zone.

The sun was at its height, the weather brilliant and the colors magnificent. Never had the mountains appeared to me so majestic as in this moment of extreme danger.

All at once a crack appeared in the snow under the feet of the Sherpas and grew longer and wider. A mad idea flashed into my head—to climb up the slope at speed and reach solid ground. Then I was lifted up by a superhuman force, and, as the Sherpas disappeared before my eyes, I went head over heels. I could not see what was happening. My head hit the ice. In spite of my efforts I could no longer breathe, and a violent blow on my left thigh caused me acute pain. I turned round and round like a puppet. In a flash I saw the blinding light of the sun through the snow which was pouring past my eyes. The rope joining me to Sarki and Aila curled round my neck—the Sherpas shooting down the slope beneath would shortly strangle me, and the pain was unbearable. Again and again I crashed into solid ice as I went hurtling from one serac[3] to another, and the snow crushed me down. The rope tightened around my neck and brought me to a stop. Before I had recovered my wits, I began to pass water, violently and uncontrollably.

I opened my eyes to find myself hanging head downwards with the rope around my neck and my left leg, in a sort of hatchway of blue ice. I put out my elbows toward the walls in an attempt to stop the unbearable pendulum motion which sent me from one side to the other, and I caught a glimpse of the last slopes of the couloir beneath me. My breathing steadied, and I blessed the rope which had stood the strain of the shock.

I simply *had* to try to get myself out. My feet and hands were numb, but I was able to make use of some little nicks in the wall. There was room for at least the edges of my boots. By frenzied jerky movements I succeeded in freeing my left leg from the rope, and then managed to right myself and to climb up a yard or two. After every

---

1. **crampons:** iron plates attached to boots to grip the ice.
2. **couloir** (kōōl·wär′): deep gorge.

3. **serac:** tower of ice.

move I stopped, convinced that I had come to the end of my physical strength, and that in a second I should have to let go.

One more desperate effort, and I gained a few inches. I pulled on the rope and felt something give at the other end—no doubt the bodies of the Sherpas. I called, but hardly a whisper issued from my lips. There was a deathlike silence. Where was Rébuffat?

Conscious of a shadow, as from a passing cloud, I looked up instinctively, and lo and behold! Two scared black faces were framed against the circle of blue sky. Aila and Sarki! They were safe and sound and at once set to work to rescue me. I was incapable of giving them the slightest advice. Aila disappeared, leaving Sarki alone at the edge of the hole; they began to pull on the rope, slowly, so as not to hurt me, and I was hauled up with a power and steadiness that gave me fresh courage. At last I was out. I collapsed on the snow.

The rope had caught over a ridge of ice and we had been suspended on either side. By good luck the weight of the two Sherpas and my own had balanced. If we had not been checked like this we should have hurtled down for another 1500 feet. There was chaos all around us. Where was Rébuffat? I was mortally anxious, for he was unroped. Looking up I caught sight of him less than a hundred yards away:

"Anything broken?" he called out to me.

I was greatly relieved, but I had no strength to reply. Lying flat, and semiconscious, I gazed at the wreckage about me with unseeing eyes. We had been carried down for about 500 feet. It was not a healthy place to linger in—suppose another avalanche should fall! I instructed the Sherpas:

"Now—Doctor Sahib.[4] Quick, very quick!"

By gestures, I tried to make them understand that they must hold me very firm. In doing this I found that my left arm was practically useless. I could not move it at all, the elbow had seized up—was it broken? We should see later. Now, we must push on to Oudot.

---

4. **Doctor Sahib:** Sahib is a term used by the natives to refer to Europeans. Herzog wants to get down the mountain to Doctor Oudot as soon as possible to try to save his hands and feet.

Rébuffat started down to join us, moving slowly; he had to place his feet by feel alone. Seeing him walk like this made my heart ache; he too had fallen and he must have hit something with his jaw, for blood was oozing from the corners of his mouth. Like me, he had lost his glasses and we were forced to shut our eyes. Aila had an old spare pair which did very well for me, and without a second's hesitation Sarki gave his own to Rébuffat.

We had to get down at once. The Sherpas helping me up, I advanced as best I could, reeling about in the most alarming fashion, but they realized now that they must hold me from behind. I skirted round the avalanche to our old track, which started again a little further on.

We now came to the first wall. How on earth should we get down? Again, I asked the Sherpas to hold me firmly:

"Hold me well because . . ."

And I showed them my hands.

"Yes, sir," they replied together like good pupils. I came to the piton;[5] the fixed rope attached to it hung down the wall, and I had to hold on to it—there was no other way. It was terrible: my wooden feet kept slipping on the ice wall, and I could not grasp the thin line in my hands. Without letting go I endeavored to wind it around my hands, but they were swollen and the skin broke in several places. Great strips of it came away and stuck to the rope and the flesh was laid bare. Yet I had to go on down, I could not give up halfway.

"Aila! Pay attention! . . . Pay attention!"

To save my hands I now let the rope slide over my good forearm and lowered myself like this in jerks. On reaching the bottom I fell about three feet, and the rope wrenched my forearm and my wrists. The jolt was severe and affected my feet. I heard a queer crack and supposed I must have broken something—no doubt it was the frostbite that prevented me from feeling any pain.

Rébuffat and the Sherpas came down and we went on, but it all seemed to take an unconscionably long time, and the plateau of Camp II seemed a long way off. I was just about at the limit of my strength. Every minute I felt like giving up; and why, anyway, should I go on when for me everything was over? My conscience was quite easy: everyone was safe, and the others would all get down. Far away below I could see the tents. Just one more hour—I gave myself one more hour and then, wherever I was, I would lie down in the snow. I would let myself go, peacefully. I would be through with it all and could sleep content.

Setting this limit somehow cheered me on. I kept slipping, and on the steep slope the Sherpas could hardly hold me—it was miraculous that they did. The track stopped above a drop—the second and bigger of the walls we had equipped with a fixed rope. I tried to make up my mind, but I could not begin to see how I was going to get down. I pulled off the glove I had on one hand and the red silk scarf that hid the other, which was covered with blood. This time everything was at stake—and my fingers could just look after themselves. I placed Sarki and Aila on the stance from which I had been accustomed to belay[6] them and where the two of them would be able to take the strain of my rope by standing firmly braced against each other. I tried to take hold of the fixed rope; both my hands were bleeding, but I had no pity to spare for myself, and I took the rope between my thumb and forefinger and started off. At the first move I was faced at once with a painful decision: if I let go, we should all fall to the bottom; if I held on, what would remain of my hands? I decided to hold on.

Every inch was a torture I was resolved to ignore. The sight of my hands made me feel sick; the flesh was laid bare and red, and the rope was covered with blood. I tried not to tear the strips right off: other accidents had taught me that one must preserve these bits to hasten the healing process later on. I tried to save my hands by braking with my stomach, my shoulders, and every other possible point of contact. When would this agony come to an end?

I came down to the nose of ice which I myself had cut away with my ax on the ascent. I felt about with my legs—it was all hard. There was no

---

5. **piton:** a metal spike driven into the rock. A rope runs through its eye.

6. **belay:** hold with a rope.

snow beneath. I was not yet down. In panic I called up to the Sherpas:

"Quick . . . Aila . . . Sarki . . . !"

They let my rope out more quickly, and the friction on the fixed rope increased.

My hands were in a ghastly state. It felt as though all the flesh was being torn off. At last I was aware of something beneath my feet—the ledge. I had made it! I had to go along it now, always held by the rope; only three yards, but they were the trickiest of all. It was over. I collapsed, up to the waist in snow—no longer conscious of time.

When I half opened my eyes Rébuffat and the Sherpas were beside me, and I could distinctly see black dots moving about near the tents of Camp II. Sarki spoke to me, and pointed out two Sher-pas coming up to meet us. They were still a long way off, but all the same it cheered me up.

I had to rouse myself; things were getting worse and worse. The frostbite seemed to be gaining ground—up to my calves and my elbows. Sarki put my glasses on for me again, although the weather had turned gray. He put one glove on as best he could; but my left hand was in such a frightful state that it made him sick to look at it, and he tried to hide it in my red scarf.

The fantastic descent continued, and I was sure that every step would be my last. Through the swirling mist I sometimes caught glimpses of the two Sherpas coming up. They had already reached the base of the avalanche cone, and when, from the little platform I had just reached, I saw them stop there, it sapped all my courage.

Snow began to fall, and we now had to make a long traverse over very unsafe ground where it was difficult to guard anyone; then, fifty yards further, we came to the avalanche cone. I recognized Foutharkey and Angawa mounting rapidly toward us. Evidently they expected bad news, and Angawa must have been thinking of his two brothers, Aila and Pansy. The former was with us all right—he could see him in the flesh—but what about Pansy? Even at this distance they started to ask questions, and by the time we reached them they knew everything. I heaved a deep sigh of relief. I felt now as if I had laid down a burden so heavy that I had nearly given way beneath it. Foutharkey was beside me, smiling affectionately. How can anyone call such people "primitive" or say that the rigors of their existence take away all sense of pity? The Sherpas rushed toward me, put down their sacks, uncorked their flasks. Ah, just to drink a few mouthfuls! Nothing more. It had all been such a long time . . .

Foutharkey lowered his eyes to my hands and lifted them again, almost with embarrassment. With infinite sorrow, he whispered: "Poor Bara Sahib—Ah . . ."

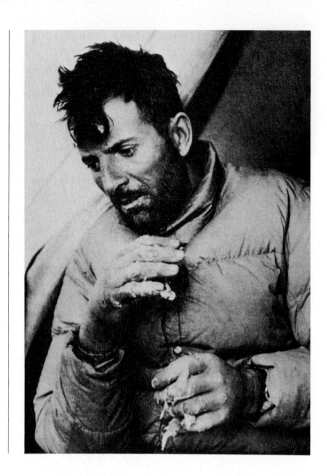

Responding to the Report

Analyzing the Report

Identifying Facts

1. Find at least two details in the third paragraph that create **suspense** by hinting that some disaster is about to happen.
2. Not many people experience a Himalayan avalanche and live to tell about it. What were Herzog's thoughts and sensations as the avalanche struck?
3. The success of reports like this one depends in part on how well the writer can help the reader imagine places and situations that are totally alien. Describe how you picture Herzog's situation as the avalanche cleared. Are all the details clearly described so that you can form a picture of the action he takes to save himself? Explain.
4. What specific **images** does Herzog use to describe how his hands look and feel?

Interpreting Meanings

5. Describe Herzog's attitude toward the Sherpas. Find at least two passages to support your answer.
6. Many people would have given up under the circumstances described here. Where does Herzog talk about this temptation to give up? Why

do you think some people are able to keep going in situations like this, while others cave in?

7. Toward the end of the report, Herzog uses a **point-of-view shift,** in which he shifts from his own point of view and enters the mind of another character. Find where this shift occurs at the end of the chapter. How might Herzog have learned about the thoughts and feelings of the other men?

8. Do you think Herzog portrays any persons as the **heroes** of this part of the story? If so, who are the heroes, and what makes them heroic?

9. Under "Focusing on Background" (page 430), you'll find a report written about Annapurna by a person who was not an eyewitness. Which kind of report do you prefer—a first-person account or a third-person account? Why?

Writing About the Report

A Creative Response

1. **Keeping a Journal and Writing an Autobiographical Report.** Keep a journal for five days, focusing on one single aspect of your life: the care of an animal; your daily encounters with some person; your exercise routine—anything that you do every day. Record your thoughts and feelings. Note details about places and people, including sounds and smells and tastes. Record any changes in your routine. Write freely, for the journal is your property and will be read only by you.

   After five days, look over your journal and prepare to use it as raw material for a brief autobiographical report. First, decide what point you'll make about your routine: is it fascinating, boring, difficult, comical, ordinary? Why do you do it? Then think of a title for your report. In your opening sentences, tell **what** you do and **when** you do it.

2. **Narrating Events.** Chances are that you have not climbed Annapurna or sailed around the world on your own. Nevertheless, you have faced some test of your own personal courage and endurance, have thought that you could not go on, *have* gone on, and have survived. The test may have been something like speaking in front of an audience or facing a person you were afraid of or swimming beyond your depth or simply accomplishing a task when you hated every minute of it. Write a paragraph in which you narrate

the elements of one such experience. Include at least one sentence describing how the test made you feel.

A Critical Response

3. **Analyzing the Report.** Herzog is reporting on true events, but he uses many of the elements of fiction to make his account as exciting as an adventure novel. What is the **conflict** in this report? What questions does Herzog plant in your mind to create **suspense?** Who are the **characters** and what are they like? Write a brief essay explaining three ways in which this report reads like a fictional story.

4. **Explaining a Response.** "What price victory?" asks writer James Ramsey Ullman in the extract that follows. In a paragraph, give your response to this question. Do you think the conquest of mountains, or of space, is worth the human suffering such a victory sometimes entails? Try to give at least two reasons for your response.

Analyzing Language and Vocabulary

Words Frequently Confused

The words in the list that follows are often confused, either in meaning or in pronunciation. Match each word in column A with its correct pronunciation in column B. Then indicate which word correctly fills the blank in each sentence that follows. Use a dictionary.

A	B
1. ascent	1. ə·send′
2. ascend	2. ə·sent′
3. assent	3. ə·sent′
4. descent	4. dē′ s'nt
5. descend	5. di·sent′
6. decent	6. di·send′

1. The ———— began, with the Sherpas leading the way down the mountain.
2. Herzog had his gloves with him on the ———— up the mountain.
3. Herzog had no choice but to ———— to having his fingers and toes amputated.
4. The Sherpas gave the climbers very ———— treatment.
5. The doctor stayed in a base camp and did not ———— to the summit.
6. On the trip down, some of the climbers had to ———— the mountain without proper equipment.

Focusing on Background

The End of the Story

The climbing of Annapurna gained worldwide attention. An old mountaineering hand, James Ramsey Ullman (see his story on page 96), wrote later about the expedition in his book *The Age of Mountaineering.* Here is his epilogue to the Annapurna story:

"Of the four climbers who had spent the night out, Terray was all right, and Rébuffat, though slightly frostbitten and suffering greatly with his eyes, would obviously suffer no permanent effects. But with Herzog and Lachenal it was another matter. The toes of both had turned blue-black, and on Herzog's feet the leaden color extended to the middle of the soles. His hands, from which shreds of rotted skin were hanging, were numb as far as the wrists. In a cramped, dimly lit tent, Oudot worked through the night and all the next day over the two men, administering novocaine to relieve their suffering and injecting them repeatedly with acetylcholine to stimulate the circulation of their blood.

"One day, however, was all that could be spared at Camp II, for the monsoon was now due, and at any moment torrential rains would begin turning the mountainside into a deathtrap of melting snow. Sledges were improvised out of skis and stretched canvas and the crippled men roped onto them for the descent. Inching down the white slopes, their eyes blindfolded, their arms and legs swathed in bandages, they seemed less living men than mummies—except that mummies feel no pain.

"Almost miraculously, the operation was accomplished without mishap, and a few days later they set off from base camp toward civilization—the mountain at last behind them, but a month's nightmare ahead. Herzog and Lachenal had to be carried every step of the way: over glacial moraines, high passes, steep ridges, swollen rivers, and finally through the underbrush of the lowland jungles. Instead of bitter cold there was now cloying, sweltering heat. The two crippled men stank of putrefying flesh, and their pain became so great that Oudot kept them almost constantly under morphine. Herzog, with septicemia, was often delirious, and one day his fever reached 105.6 degrees and it was touch and go whether he would live or die. Massive doses of penicillin pulled him through, however, and the weary caravan struggled on.

"Rain beat down incessantly. The wet earth smoked. And almost every day, amid swarms of flies and crowds of curious villagers, Oudot did the grim work that had to be done on Herzog and Lachenal. For by now it had become obvious that the toes of both men—and Herzog's fingers as well—would have to go; and one by one, the doctor amputated them, before the lethal rot could spread farther into their bodies. By the time the journey was over, Lachenal had lost all his toes and Herzog all his toes and fingers.

"What price victory? . . . It is a question that will be asked and argued as long as men climb mountains, and the only definitive answer is that there is a difference of opinion. . . ."

—from "Bitter Victory,"
James Ramsey Ullman

Literature & Language

Using the Expository and Persuasive Aims

Literary Model

The following paragraphs are from a magazine article about the damage caused to marine animals by plastic waste thrown into the ocean.

The sea is awash in debris. The enormity of this calamity for marine animals of all kinds was masked until recently by the size of the oceans themselves. What harm can a few chunks of plastic cause in a mass of water that spreads over three-quarters of the globe? Such was the response that encouraged indifference among bureaucrats and convenient ignorance among seafarers of all kinds.

But by the early 1980's the need for decisive action had become incontrovertible. During the commercial seal harvest on the Pribilof Islands in the Bering Sea in the years 1981-84, 403 fur seals were found entangled in plastic—chiefly fragments of fishing nets and packing bands, but also rope, monofilament line, six-pack holders, and even lawn-chair material. . . .

In 1987 the United States finally got around to ratifying the section of the International Convention for the Prevention of Pollution from Ships that governs the disposal of trash at sea. (One researcher has estimated that 639,000 plastic containers, including bags, are dumped by the world's merchant ships every day!) All federal agencies now follow the lead taken by the Marine Mammal Commission to stem the tide of plastic trash.

—from "Facing the Tragedy
of Trash in Our Oceans,"
Frank Graham, Jr.

A Note on the Expository Aim

Many writers of newspaper and magazine articles have an **expository aim**; that is, their purpose is to inform or explain. News and magazine writers provide facts, statistics, and examples to support their main ideas. A **fact** is something that can be proven true by concrete information. A **statistic** is a fact that is based on numbers. **Examples** are specific instances, or illustrations, of a general idea.

Examining the Writer's Style

The following questions will help you appreciate the writer's expository techniques:

1. What main idea is the writer trying to get across? Which sentence best summarizes the main idea?
2. What facts, statistics, and examples does the writer use to support the main idea? List these in chart form if you wish.
3. What effect did these details have on you?

Literary Model

In this letter to the editor of a newspaper, a writer wants to persuade readers to share his view of the value of books.

To the Editor:

Sweeping claims are being made that an educational revolution via the computer is on the horizon, and some educators go so far as to see the computer replacing books in classrooms and libraries.

Yet you noted in an Aug. 6 news article, "In the Land of Sony, the Abacus Is Still King," that the survival of the abacus is not merely a matter of tradition. It rests in the belief that it provides a conceptual sense of mathematics that is lacking in electronic calculators.

Predictions of the demise of the book as a result of electronic technology remind me of similar predictions that accompanied other inventions.

The demise of the stenographer was predicted with the invention of the Dictaphone, the demise of the theater with the invention of the talking motion picture, the demise of the concert hall with the invention of the phonograph, the demise of the motion picture with the invention of television, and the demise of handwriting with the invention of the typewriter (albeit the ballpoint pen has led to some very poor scripts).

Aside from being easily portable and readable, in comparison with an electronic screen, and aside from its physical attractiveness, the book (with its pages) conveys a tactile quality and pleasure that no push-button circuitry can provide—even when one is only browsing or skimming through a book, or making marginal notations (preferably only on the pages of one's own books). Moreover, the book can be read while sitting, standing, or lying down. It can even grace the walls of a home library or den when it is not being read.

The physical attributes of a book and its printed pages are far more personal than the computer screen or printout, as indicated by the common practice of writing one's name in a book to designate valued ownership or of writing an inscription when presenting a book as a gift to a friend.

But the book is more than this. Its physical quality is intimately linked to the very evolution of human language and thought. We would do well to heed the advice of Norbert Wiener, a pioneer of the new technology, who wrote in one of his books, "Render unto man the things which are man's and unto the computer the things which are the computer's."

Incidentally, if one should want to learn how to program or use a computer, there are many good books on the subject.

—Daniel Tanner
Professor of Education
Rutgers University

A Note on the Persuasive Aim

Writers with a **persuasive aim** wish to convince you to accept a point of view or to take a particular action. Writers whose aim is persuasion use both logical arguments and appeals to emotion. In evaluating persuasion, you must distinguish between **facts** (which can be proved to be true) and mere **opinions**.

Examining the Writer's Techniques

The following questions will help you analyze Tanner's persuasive techniques:
1. How would you sum up the opinion expressed by the writer of this letter?
2. What facts does the writer use to show that predictions about other inventions have proved untrue?
3. What reasons does he offer to support his opinion? Do his reasons rely on logic, appeals to emotion, or both?
4. What ironic point does he make in the last sentence?
5. Has the writer changed or confirmed your views about computers or books? Why or why not?

Using Expository and Persuasive Aims

1. **Writing an Expository Article.** Write an informative article for the school newspaper or for the newsletter of a club to which you belong. Choose a topic you already know something about. You might write about the food in your school cafeteria; roller blading, or another sport; collecting comic books; or cycling on city streets. Begin by stating your main idea in a topic sentence. Then support this idea with facts, statistics, or examples. Ask a partner to read your article, and revise any confusing or vague details.

2. **Writing a Persuasive Letter to the Editor.** Write a letter to the local newspaper expressing your point of view about one of their recent articles. Or write a letter to the program director of a television station, giving your opinion of a program or a commercial. Your intention is to persuade people to accept your opinion. Identify your issue and state your opinion clearly. Then give good, convincing reasons for your views.

LOOKING FOR EVIDENCE AND APPEALS TO EMOTION

Writing Assignment

In a four-paragraph essay, identify the facts used by reporter Harry Caudill, in the portion of his news article that follows, to support this main idea: **The Pittston Company is responsible for a horrible disaster in Buffalo Creek.** Then, cite passages in which you think Caudill uses language to appeal to your emotions.

Background

Evidence. If a reporter makes a general statement, but fails to support it with some kind of strong factual evidence, we will not be persuaded that his or her central idea is valid. For example, in his third paragraph, Caudill opens with a statement claiming the Pittston Company was guilty of neglect and indifference.

You should be able to find two facts that Caudill provides to persuade us that this general statement is factually true.

Appeals to Emotion. Given the enormity of this disaster, it would not be surprising to find that Caudill has used language and specific details to affect the way we feel about the victims and the mining company. The words that appeal to one reader's emotions are noted in the side notes to the article. Your responses might be very different. As you read, take note of your own responses to Caudill's language, using a separate piece of paper.

BUFFALO CREEK, W. Va.—Last February 26 here in Logan County an enormous mountain of slag and other waste deposited by the Buffalo Mining Company collapsed after several days of heavy rain. Atop the heap hundreds of feet over the Buffalo Creek Valley sat a 14.2 acre lake like a pool of gravy in a mound of mashed potato. Together the 132 million gallons of water from the lake and the waste mixed into a 30-foot high batter of gob that slopped down the steep valley, tearing through a dozen hamlets, smashing and burying hundreds of houses, sweeping away roads and bridges. At least 125 persons died. Over 4,000 of the valley's 5,000 residents, mostly from poor mining families, saw their homes destroyed.

Now, more than six months later, desolation and despair are nearly all that is left in Buffalo Creek Valley. . . . Where thousands of people once lived on cinder-coated streets, many acres now stand vacant and await the future.

Unfortunately, much of that future is dependent on those whose neglect and indifference were responsible for the disaster: the Pittston Company, owner of Buffalo Mining and the

"Batter of gob" is disgusting. "Slopped" is disgusting. My feelings would not be strong at all if the writer had just said "a 30-foot high flood that rushed down the steep valley."

He makes me feel sympathy because the people are poor. They will have a harder time recovering.

"Neglect" and "indifference" make me feel the mining company is to blame.

nation's fourth-largest coal producer. A huge corporation with immense profits and influential connections has simply eradicated a whole string of communities—and done it with astonishing composure.

For years Pittston blithely disregarded state and federal laws prohibiting discharge of industrial wastes into navigable streams and "tributaries thereof" and proceeded to rid itself of slate, shale, coal, and sludge simply by dumping them into a hollow. . . .

—from "Buffalo Creek Aftermath,"
Harry M. Caudill

> The fact that they make a lot of money makes me feel more angry. "Influential connections" suggest something corrupt.
> If they really did this with "composure," I would feel outraged.
> "Blithely" is loaded with judgment against the company. If the word were omitted, the passage would not be as strong. Is it true?

Prewriting

1. Skim the report and list the important evidence that supports the main idea that the slag heap deposited by the Pittston Company caused a disaster.
2. Find the facts that support Caudill's statement that the company was negligent and indifferent.
3. Now look at the ways Caudill describes the disaster and its victims. Examine these passages carefully to see if you can find any descriptive details or words that make you feel horror or sympathy or disgust or rage at the mining company.

Writing

Organize your data now, using this format if you wish:

1. **Paragraph 1:** State the main idea of this part of Caudill's report.
2. **Paragraph 2:** Cite the facts that support the main idea.
3. **Paragraph 3:** Cite any appeals to emotion you have found in the report. Describe the way Caudill wants you to feel about the disaster.
4. **Paragraph 4:** State your own response to the disaster and to the way it is reported by Caudill in this part of his report.

Checklist for Revision

1. Have you cited the title of the report and the writer's name?
2. Have you stated the main idea of the report in your first paragraph?
3. Do you have some strong facts to support the main idea?
4. Have you indicated whether or not you found appeals to your emotions?
5. Have you cited examples of such language?
6. Have you explained your response?

I n Greek, the word *bios* means "life," and *graphia* means "writ-ing." A **biography** is therefore a "written life," or the story of a life. *Auto* in the same language means "self," so an **autobiog-raphy** is the written story of the writer's own life. (These roots are familiar in dozens of English words: an *automobile* is a machine that moves by itself, that is, without a horse to pull it; *biology* is the study of life; *graphite* is the substance in a pencil that makes it write . . . and so on.)

Biography: The Story of a Life

A biographer who sets out to write the story of someone else's life must do a great deal of study and research. We'd expect someone who is going to write a biography of Anne Frank, for example, to read all about the rise of Nazism in Germany in the 1930's. We'd expect the biographer to find out what kinds of schools Anne went to and what kinds of books and newspapers she read. We'd expect the writer to interview people who knew Anne, the people who helped her family hide, and the people who knew her in the camp where she died. We'd expect that the biographer would probably visit the places where Anne lived and the prison where she died. And then we would expect that all this acquired knowledge would be recorded accurately and arranged so as to make all the places, people, atmospheres, and events of Anne's life come alive in the writing.

Autobiography: The Story of the Writer's Own Life

Anne Frank, when she sat down to write her own diary, needed no such research. Her "research" was the daily living of her very own life. She already knew what people, places, and events were at the center of her life. Her purpose as a writer was to record the personal reactions and emotions of her experience, day by day.

A diary like Anne's is one sort of autobiography. Its particular form is that the life is recorded as it is lived, a day or a week at a time. A writer may also sit down to write an autobiography that is a record from memory of his or her entire life up to the time of writing. In either case, what we expect from autobiography is the kind of personal, internal knowledge that cannot be researched, because no one can get into another person's mind.

Objectivity or Subjectivity?

What we look for in biography is factual accuracy and **objectivity.** This means that we want an unbiased account of the person the biography deals with—we do not want the account distorted by the writer's own prejudices.

But in autobiography, we look for **subjectivity**—that is, we want this writer to "get personal." We want to know what the writer thinks about her grandmother or how the writer feels about his home town or why the writer has always been afraid of cats.

The advantage of biography is perspective: an outsider can tell us things about the background, history, influences, and effectiveness of another person—things that that person may not have realized or cared to write about. The advantage of autobiography, on the other hand, is that we can learn about the motives, emotions, fears, hopes, doubts, and joys that only the writer can know.

Joseph P. Lash (1909–1987) was born in New York City and was educated at City College and Columbia University. He is best known as a biographer, particularly of Franklin Delano Roosevelt.

Lash was at work on one of the Roosevelt biographies when the president of Radcliffe College asked if he would write a biography of Radcliffe's famous graduate, the blind and deaf Helen Keller. Lash at first refused, but his wife pointed out to him that it was an unusual honor for a man to be asked by a women's college to write a book about a woman. He read and was enchanted by Helen Keller's autobiography, *The Story of My Life*. He decided that "it would be good for me to get away for a time from those power-oriented men, Roosevelt, Churchill, and Stalin."

Lash's research took him from Massachusetts to New York, Washington, Iowa, Illinois, California, and Tuscumbia, Alabama. He read newspapers and correspondence, studied journals, and interviewed friends and relatives of Helen Keller. He found that it was impossible to write a book about Helen Keller that was not also a book about her teacher, Annie Sullivan. Therefore, his book *Helen and Teacher* starts with Annie.

The Miracle Worker, on page 494 in the drama section of this book, is a dramatization of the relationship between the extraordinary pupil and her extraordinary tutor. The excerpt that follows forms most of the first chapter of *Helen and Teacher*. Read carefully the first two paragraphs: What would you say is Lash's feeling for Annie?

"ANNIE"

Joseph P. Lash

In 1880, when Annie Sullivan, aged fourteen, was permitted to enroll in the Perkins Institution for the Blind in South Boston and begin her schooling, she discovered that history for her schoolmates was the Civil War. For Annie there was only one event in history, the Great Famine in Ireland of 1847 that had subsequently driven her impoverished young parents, like thousands of others, to the United States. "I knew very little about my parents," she said later. "There was no Bible record of births and deaths in my family. A few facts have been dug out of church and municipal records. I know that Limerick, Ireland, was their birthplace. I presume, without knowing the facts, that they were victims of the 'hungry forties.' . . . They left all that was dear to them and came to a strange land, perhaps with Tom Hood's cry upon their lips,

'O God, that bread should be so dear,
And flesh and blood so cheap!' "

Annie was born in April 1866 in Feeding Hills, a village outside of Springfield, Massachusetts, in circumstances of poverty that were not uncommon among Irish immigrants. But the destitution of the Sullivans was starker and more desolate than even that of their compatriots. Annie's father, red-haired Thomas Sullivan, was not only illiterate and unskilled but a drinker and a brawler, and shiftless. Her gentle mother, born Alice Cloesy (spelled Cloahassy on Annie's baptismal certificate), was tubercular, and after a fall when Annie was three or four, was unable to walk again except on crutches. She bore five children. Annie, christened Johanna, was the oldest. The fifth, John, died before he was three months old. A sister, Nellie, had died before that. Her little brother Jimmie was born with a tubercular hip. Only Mary, next to the youngest, did not ail. Annie, although physically robust, contracted trachoma when she was about five. Untreated, this was gradually destroying her vision. One of her earliest memories was a neighbor saying, "She would be so pretty if it were not for her eyes." A woman urged her mother to wash them in geranium water, and Annie remembers thin hands dabbing her "bad" eyes.

Half-blind, hot-tempered like her father, Annie responded to the miseries within and about her by lashing out, childishly, throwing things, going into tantrums. "What a terrible child," the neighbors said. "You little devil," her father often shouted, and tried to control her by beatings so severe that, to save her, Annie's mother would try to hide her little daughter. Horror followed horror. Her mother, "gentle Alice Cloesy," as her neighbors from Limerick called her, died. This was Annie's memory of that dreadful event as she told it fifty years later to Nella Braddy, with a vividness of detail and dramatic sweep that testified to her narrative power:

I am being dragged out of bed. I had a feeling that something very unusual had happened, and I must let them do with me as they liked. I was taken into a room where people were moving about. Soon Jimmie and Mary were there too. They were crying, and other children came and looked at us. Then a blank space. The next thing I remember, I was back in my mother's room. The men were taking the slats out of the trundle-bed and putting them on carpenters' horses. I was intensely interested and watched them quietly. They put three or four slats together. When their work was finished, and they went away, two women laid on the slats the mattress that was on the trundle-bed, then they went over to my mother's bed. I wondered what they were going to do, and I was afraid. I must have made a noise, for I was jerked out of the room. When I went into it again, I saw my mother on the improvised bed. I was astonished to see her in a brown habit which the priests had brought. Her hair was very smooth, and she looked so still! Her hands were crossed. There were white bands around her neck and her sleeves, and there was something on her breast which I knew was a word in white. Many years afterward, when I read "Jesu" in print, I realized in a flash that was the word I had seen on the death robe. There was also a green ribbon round her neck with a little cross which I had never seen and which almost touched her hands. I saw Mary and Jimmie sobbing, and Mary was sitting at my father's knee. I didn't cry or move. Somehow they didn't seem to belong to me or I to them. They seemed more like other people who were sitting around—strangers. I don't remember anyone speaking to me or anything that happened afterward, until my father, Jimmie, Mary, and I were together in a big, black carriage. And I was furious with Jimmie because he wouldn't give me his place by the window so that I could watch the horses. He began to cry, saying I hurt him, and my father struck me sharply on the side of my head. A fire of hatred blazed up in me which burned for many years.

There was no money for the funeral, and the town helped to defray the expenses. She was buried in Potter's Field,[1] a kinswoman told Annie years later. She remembered her father saying after the funeral, "God put a curse on me for leaving Ireland and the old folks." Then he would rage wildly against "the landlords" and weep.

Although the other Sullivans had lost patience with Thomas, an uncle took in Mary and Jimmie, while eight-year-old Annie undertook to keep house for her father in a dilapidated little cabin on her uncle's farm. Her memories of this brief period were not punctuated with hostility and rage. She did not go to school, and no one ever read stories to her, but her imagination and mind were fired by the Irish folklore with which her father regaled her in his heavy brogue.

"My colleen bawn, you can't hear the little people in this new land," my father would say, "but in Ireland the brake[2] is full of voices, lowlike, and many are the times I heard them meself. When it's still-like, and night is coming on like a black rook spreading its wings—it's then you hear them talking of the sheep that

---

1. **Potter's Field:** public land set aside for burial of very poor or unknown persons.
2. **brake** (brāk): thicket.

went astray on the shepherd and how the wheezing soul of old Patrick Munn passed on the wind of last night and how Mrs. Shea's new baby had cut its teeth before ever it was born. As swately as mating doves they whisper. But if any man or woman meddles with them, they'll nurse a grudge till the end of time. There was Michael Doane who kicked a stone in a cairn. 'Let them move it as can,' he says, and turns his back. The next night the stone was moved to his doorstep! Mike never knew a peaceful night until they put him under six feet of Irish soil.''

To her father, the River Shannon that flowed through Limerick was holy water. Once he took her to a Westfield oculist, and when that visit did nothing for her eyes, he sought to comfort her by saying that a drop from the River Shannon would cure them. How, she wanted to know. ''I've told ye more times than ye's got fingers and toes that the Shannon begins in the eyes of the Lord hisself. He looking down from the high place and seeing the beautiful green land of Ireland He had created, not minding what He was doing, tears gushed out of His eyes, like the springs out of the hills, and there in the great plain afore Limerick, the Shannon began. Galway and Killslee have mountains, I hear say; but Limerick has the river Shannon for her glory.''

He also filled his daughter with hate for landlords. In his father's house there had been four windows, he told her, but three of them were boarded up. Why? asked Annie. ''Because openings are taxed in Ireland. You pay the landlord for air and light. Everything belongs to the landlord. He owns the farm you till. He grows fat on the harvest you reap. You handle the spade, follow the plough, plant, sow, and he is always before you or behind you like your own shadow. He orders you about, 'This must be done today, that must be begun tomorrow.' With difficulty you keep from splitting his head wide-open with the spade, but you only curse the devil under your breath.'' Irish hatred of landlords and the British, he told her, ''smoulders on and on like turf-fire.''

Even the run-down shack on her uncle's place was too much for her father to maintain. He gave

it up, and she too went to live in the house of her uncle and aunt who had taken in Jimmie and Mary. Her uncle was doing well as a tobacco farmer; but, unable to get any help from her father toward the children's support, he appealed to the town. Mary was taken in by another aunt. On February 22, 1876, Annie and Jimmie, who was on a crutch because of his diseased hip, were delivered in a Black Maria[3] to the state poorhouse in Tewksbury. It was an isolated, forbidding huddle of grimy structures. The attendant who received them proposed to separate them, sending Annie to the women's ward and Jimmie to the men's; but Annie, whose whole childhood had been one abandonment after another, protested with such passionate sobs that the attendant relented and sent them both to a women's ward. No matter that it was unpainted, overcrowded, peopled with misshapen, diseased, often manic women; they were together.

Somehow it all seemed ''very homelike'' to Annie. The children's cots were next to each other. They had the ''dead house'' where corpses were prepared for burial to play in, and old issues of the *Godey's Lady's Book* and the *Police Gazette* to cut up. It seemed homelike to Annie, too, because most of the women were Irish, the Catholic priest was always about—and she was no stranger to filth and disease.

In the years that Annie was at Tewksbury the poorhouse cared for an average of 940 men, women, and children. The mortality rate was very high, particularly among the children. In the summer there were no screens to keep out the mosquitos and flies, and in the winter the heating often broke down because of rusty pipes. The superintendent repeatedly begged the state for a separate building in which to house the dangerous inmates, especially those with delirium tremens and offensive diseases. Men and women were inadequately separated. . . . Every day at the blast of a whistle the women rushed to the narrow windows crying, ''The Horribles! The Horribles!'' to watch the procession of the men to the dining hall. Deformed, legless, some with

---

3. **Black Maria:** patrol wagon.

"The essence of poverty is shame."
Annie at age 15, the year after she left Tewksbury.

faces distorted by cancer or goiters, they pushed like animals to get to their food, often using canes and crutches as prods if someone slowed down or got in their way. For almost all of six years this constituted Annie's whole world.

Death was a common occurrence, and all her life Annie remembered the clatter of the cots being wheeled over the wooden floor in the dead house. Then the dead house claimed Jimmie. She awoke suddenly in the middle of the night and, sensing the empty space next to her, knew immediately what had happened. She began to tremble. She crept to the dead room and, feeling his cold body under the sheets, began to scream, wakening everyone. As the women dragged her away, she clung to the lifeless body and kicked and screamed. Only when it was light was she permitted to go into the dead room again and sit on a chair beside the bed. Then the sheet was lifted for her and again she flung herself on the little body "and kissed and kissed and kissed his face—the dearest thing in the world—the only thing I had ever loved." Later the matron allowed her to go outside to pick an armful of flowers. These she placed on the little body. She begged to be allowed to follow the coffin to the burial ground. No priest was there as it was lowered into the bare, sandy spot. "When I got back, I saw that they had put Jimmie's bed back in its place. I sat down between my bed and his empty bed, and I hoped desperately to die. I believe very few children have ever been so completely left alone as I was."

Although the Catholic Church was a constant and comforting presence in the almshouse, the priest because of illness had not come to Jimmie's funeral. Fifty years later, in 1927, after she revisited Tewksbury together with Nella, she tried to put Jimmie's death into unrhymed verse:

> The women told each other how they liked
>   to look at him
> Cutting out pictures.
> "His hair was curly, you mind,
> You'd think it was done on curl-papers,
> And his eyes were like the sky at night
> With stars shining in them.
> They shouldn't bury the dead little boy Jim-
> mie

> Before the priest comes,
> Heathens that they are!
> If God heard the prayers of the poor,
> He'd strike them dead for their hard hearts.
> The sister will miss the dead little boy, I say,
> It's crazed with grief she is—anyone can see
>   that.
> She was never hard with him,
> And her having a bad temper
> The pair of them was like two turtle-doves
>   together.
> That'll make her trouble, I'm telling you.
> It's a time they had getting him out,
> And her holding fast to the pine box!
> Holy Mother! It would melt the hardest heart
>   to hear
> How the girl is grieving,
> But they have stones for hearts.
> God's curse be on them that have stones for
>   hearts!
> What's that you said, woman?"
> I said, God pity the little dead boy's sister.
> It's a fair prayer that—
> And God be merciful to the poor wherever
>   they are,
> And God rest the soul of the little dead boy
>   Jimmie.

Not long after Jimmie's death, an estrangement from the Church began. Someone gave her an Agnus Dei[4] to wear around her neck. Curious to see whether it really held the body of the Lord as she had been told, she broke open the silken covers. When the priest learned what she had done, he scolded her. "You have wounded the body of the Lord." That outraged her, and she told him she was through with confession. He imposed penances—fasting and telling her beads—but that only made her more defiant. After a time he was transferred and another priest—Father Barbara, a Jesuit—replaced him, and her attitude toward the Church shifted again. Father Barbara, a big man, was warm and protective. He befriended the young girl, and she responded to his concern. One day he announced, "This is no place for you, little

---

4. **Agnus Dei:** a small cloth-covered disk of wax stamped with the figure of a lamb, blessed by the Pope. The lamb would stand for Christ. *Agnus dei* means "lamb of God" in Latin.

woman; I am going to take you away.'' So in February 1877, almost a year after she arrived, she went to the Hospital of Les Soeurs de la Charité in Lowell, Massachusetts. There she underwent another operation. Two had been performed at Tewksbury, but they had not helped her vision. This one, too, while providing some relief from pain and the shooting lights in her eyes, left her vision so blurred that she continued to be listed on the public records as blind.

Father Barbara now was a frequent companion, in the church next door where he took her around the Stations of the Cross, along the banks of the Merrimac where they strolled hand in hand, and in the hospital ward in the evening when he read her the lives of the saints and told her how Protestants had persecuted the Catholics. He was kind and fatherly. . . . But this idyll came to an end. Father Barbara took her to Boston to some friends for whom she was to do light kitchenwork. But her eyes troubled her, and she was sent to the city infirmary for two more operations. She came out of the hospital to discover that the Boston family did not want her back and that Father Barbara had been sent to another part of the country. So it was back to Tewksbury despite her screams of rage and protest. This time she was placed in a ward of younger women, many of them unwed and pregnant. Although some in the ward were diseased and crippled . . . , it was a relief to her to be with younger women.

"Very much of what I remember about Tewksbury is indecent, cruel, melancholy,'' she told Nella Braddy fifty years later, ''gruesome in the light of grown-up experience; but nothing corresponding with my present understanding of these ideas entered my child mind. Everything interested me. I was not shocked, pained, grieved, or troubled by what happened. Such things happened. People behaved like that—that was all that there was to it. It was all the life I knew. Things impressed themselves upon me because I had a receptive mind. Curiosity kept me alert and keen to know everything.'' . . .

Maggie Hogan, the quiet little woman in charge of her ward, took a special interest in her. She introduced Annie to Tewksbury's small library and persuaded a mildly deranged girl, Tilly, to read to Annie books that she selected, mostly by Irish authors. Later Annie selected the books herself. Those that she remembered and listed for her biographer were: *Caste, The Octoroon, The Lamplighter, Ten Nights in a Barroom, The Breadwinner, Cast up by the Sea, Winiford, Stepping Heavenward, Darkness and Daylight, Tempest and Sunshine,* a life of St. Theresa, and ''the story of some saint who gave Jesus her rosary and He turned it into jewels.''

Annie's overriding ambition was to get out of the almshouse and to go to school. The women in the ward accused her of putting on airs when she spoke of it, which was often. ''She'll be walking out of here some day on the arm of the Emperor of Penzance,'' they scoffed. A sense that she was different, that she wanted something more from life than these women did, was always with her. Even in the first months at Tewksbury she had talked of wanting to go to school when she heard from a blind inmate that there were schools for the blind. One of the women had made light of her ambition, saying that ''education doesn't make any difference, if the Lord wills otherwise; Our life is the Lord's and death's.'' She had retorted hotly, ''I don't see what the Lord has to do with it. And all the same, I'm going to school when I grow up.''

Her chance to escape from Tewksbury came when she heard that an investigating commission headed by Frank B. Sanborn, chairman of the State Board of Charities, had arrived to inspect the institution. Gruesome stories about Tewksbury were rife in the state, even rumors of skins being sold from dead bodies to make shoes. She followed the group from ward to ward, trying to screw up her courage to approach it directly. Finally, as the men stood at the gate, she acted. Without knowing which figure was the exalted Mr. Sanborn, she flung herself into the group, crying, ''Mr. Sanborn, Mr. Sanborn, I want to go to school!'' ''What's the matter with you?'' a voice asked. ''I can't see very well.'' ''How long have you been here?'' She was unable to tell him. The men left, but soon afterward a woman came and told her she was to leave Tewksbury and go to school.

Two calico dresses were found for her. The red

Annie Sullivan and her famous pupil,
Helen Keller (1893).

one she wore; the blue one, along with a coarse-grained chemise and two pairs of black cotton stockings, was tied up in a newspaper bundle. The women in the ward crowded around her shouting advice as she walked to the Black Maria. "Don't tell anyone you came from the poorhouse." "Keep your head up, you're as good as any of them." "Be a good girl and mind your teachers." When Tim, the driver, handed her over to a state charity official, he added his own bit of advice: "Don't ever come back to this place. Do you hear? Forget this and you will be all right."

In Boston, the charity worker handed her over to another official. When he told her Annie came from Tewksbury, she patted the girl on the head. "Poor child," she said pityingly. Annie's face burned. She had thought the calico dress pretty, but the woman's pity suddenly aroused in her a sense of how poorly dressed she must be. "The essence of poverty," she told Nella Braddy, "is shame. Shame to have been overwhelmed by ugliness, shame to be a hole in the perfect pattern of the universe."

That day—October 7, 1880—she entered the Perkins Institution for the Blind.

Responding to the Biography

Analyzing the Biography

Identifying Facts

1. When Annie got to school at the age of fourteen, she discovered "that history for her schoolmates was the Civil War." But for Annie there was "only one event in history, the Great Famine in Ireland of 1847." Annie had never been in Ireland and had not even been born in 1847. Why was the famine, for her, the "only event in history"?

2. Joseph Lash is writing a biography of Annie Sullivan, but he also quotes passages written by Sullivan herself. What key experiences of Annie's life do we hear her tell in her own words?

3. How does Lash describe Annie's father? What influences did her father have on Annie?

4. An important period in Annie's early life was her time at the state poorhouse at Tewksbury, Massachusetts. Years ago, people unable to provide for themselves were put into such places. As you see in Annie's story, children might even go to the poorhouses without their parents. Often the inmates were not only the poor; sometimes, as at Tewksbury, mentally ill people were also sheltered there. How did Annie end up at Tewksbury? Cite at least three details that help you imagine what life was like there for Annie.

Interpreting Meanings

5. Annie Sullivan is a mistreated, unhappy child, whose dearest people in the world—her mother and her brother—die within a few years of each other. Yet we are shown Annie as a spirited, hot-tempered, and independent person. What details does Lash use to reveal these **characteristics** of Annie?

6. What do you think Annie meant when she said (on page 444): "The essence of poverty is shame"? How would you say Annie learned to feel both shame and pride?

7. Biographers can be critical of their subjects or admiring or both. How would you describe Lash's **attitude** toward Annie Sullivan in this part of his biography?

8. Do you find any passages in this biography that Lash might have "reconstructed"? Explain.

9. This story of Annie's early life is not a pleasant one. How do you think Lash wants this part of the story to affect you?

10. Could any of Annie's experiences happen to a child today? Explain.

Writing About the Biography

A Creative Response

1. **Writing a Biographical Account.** Write a paragraph about a significant event or period in the life of

someone you know. Do your research by interviewing your subject: Ask **what** happened, **when** it happened, **how** he or she felt, and **why** the event seems important. You may want to record your interview on tape so that you can play it over and become familiar with it. If you can't do this, take notes. If things seem to be missing or unclear when you examine the interview later, consult the relative or friend to make additions or corrections. After you write your paragraph, show it to your subject to see how accurately you have reported the event and its significance. You yourself should not appear in the report at all.

A Critical Response

2. **Evaluating the Biography.** Write two paragraphs. In the first, tell what you think is Lash's purpose in writing this part of Annie's life story. In the second, tell what you think of the way the story is written. Before you write, fill out a chart like the following, to be sure you have enough material for your evaluation.

Evaluating the Biography	Answers and Details
1. Did the writer accomplish his purpose?	
2. Is the story interesting?	
3. Is it well written?	
4. How do you feel about the specific details describing the poorhouse horrors?	

3. **Distinguishing Facts from Opinion.** For this exercise, based on "Annie," see page 485.

Analyzing Language and Vocabulary

Word Roots

Bio-, graph-, and *auto-* are word roots. A root is simply a core word, with a fairly constant meaning. Many word roots have been taken into English from other languages—many of them from Latin and Greek. When you know word roots, you can figure out the meaning of many unfamiliar words.

Each of the following items cites a word root and gives its meaning in parentheses. The three words that follow are built on the word root. Use a dictionary to define each of these three words. Explain how the word root is part of the word's meaning.

1. *bio-* ("life"): biology, biosphere, bionic.
2. *graph-* ("writing"): graphic, anagram, seismograph.
3. *auto-* ("self"): autocratic, automatic, automation.
4. *am-* ("love or friendliness"): amateur, amity, amiable.
5. *anim-* ("mind, will, or spirit"): animosity, magnanimous, animated.
6. *phil-* ("love"): philosophy, Anglophile, Philadelphia.
7. *dem-* ("people"): democracy, demagogue, epidemic.
8. *man-* ("hand"): manufacture, manacle, manipulate.
9. *scrip-* ("write"): scripture, conscript, inscription.
10. *vis-* ("see or sight"): invisible, visual, vista.

Write a brief answer to each of the following questions about word roots. You will have to use a dictionary.

1. What root that means "tyrant" is found in *tyrannosaurus*? When people coined the word *tyrannosaurus* to name this particular dinosaur, why do you think they built the word on "tyrant"?
2. What root do the words *muscle* and *mouse* have in common?
3. What root do the words *astonish* and *thunder* have in common?
4. What root do the words *pedestrian* and *pedestal* have in common? Does the word *pediatrician* share this root? Explain.
5. Tell how the words *senator, senior,* and *senile* all share a common root. Why is this root appropriate for these words?

Ernesto Galarza (1905–1984) was an immigrant to America. He was born in the village of Jalcocotán, in the west of Mexico, near the point where the Gulf of California joins the Pacific. During his early years, the Mexican Revolution threatened the peace of the rural mountain villages, and Ernesto and his family left Jalcocotán for the city, seeking work and peace. Eventually, they settled in Sacramento, California. They lived in what Galarza calls "a rented corner of the city," the community, or *barrio,* of foreign émigrés. There, like thousands of other refugees, the boy confronted the values and customs of American city life—gradually, and often with difficulty, adjusting to his adopted country.

Eventually, Galarza became an American citizen. He took his Ph.D. from Columbia University in New York, then returned to California to teach. When Galarza's two daughters were small, he began telling them and his wife stories of his childhood. *Barrio Boy* is the book that resulted from these reminiscences.

After you finish this part of Galarza's true story, go back over it and select the incident that you think is most significant or most important. Does everyone agree?

BARRIO BOY

Ernesto Galarza

In Tucson, when I had asked my mother again if the Americans were having a revolution, the answer was: "No, but they have good schools, and you are going to one of them." We were by now settled at 418 L Street and the time had come for me to exchange a revolution for an American education.

The two of us walked south on Fifth Street one morning to the corner of O Street and turned right. Half of the block was occupied by the Lincoln School. It was a three-story wooden building, with two wings that gave it the shape of a double-T connected by a central hall. It was a new building, painted yellow, with a shingled roof that was not like the red tile of the school in Mazatlán. I noticed other differences, none of them very reassuring.

We walked up the wide staircase hand in hand and through the door, which closed by itself. A mechanical contraption screwed to the top shut it behind us quietly.

Up to this point the adventure of enrolling me in the school had been carefully rehearsed. Mrs. Dodson had told us how to find it, and we had circled it several times on our walks. Friends in the *barrio* explained that the director was called a principal and that it was a lady and not a man. They assured us that there was always a person at the school who could speak Spanish.

Exactly as we had been told, there was a sign on the door in both Spanish and English: "Principal." We crossed the hall and entered the office of Miss Nettie Hopley.

Miss Hopley was at a roll-top desk to one side, sitting in a swivel chair that moved on wheels. There was a sofa against the opposite wall, flanked by two windows and a door that opened on a small balcony. Chairs were set around a table, and framed pictures hung on the walls of a man with long white hair and another with a sad face and a black beard.

The principal half turned in the swivel chair to look at us over the pinch glasses crossed on the ridge of her nose. To do this she had to duck her head slightly as if she were about to step through a low doorway.

What Miss Hopley said to us we did not know, but we saw in her eyes a warm welcome, and when she took off her glasses and straightened up

she smiled wholeheartedly, like Mrs. Dodson. We were, of course, saying nothing, only catching the friendliness of her voice and the sparkle in her eyes while she said words we did not understand. She signaled us to the table. Almost tiptoeing across the office, I maneuvered myself to keep my mother between me and the gringo lady. In a matter of seconds I had to decide whether she was a possible friend or a menace. We sat down.

Then Miss Hopley did a formidable[1] thing. She stood up. Had she been standing when we entered she would have seemed tall. But rising from her chair she soared. And what she carried up and up with her was a buxom superstructure, firm shoulders, a straight sharp nose, full cheeks slightly molded by a curved line along the nostrils, thin lips that moved like steel springs, and a high forehead topped by hair gathered in a bun. Miss Hopley was not a giant in body, but when she mobilized it to a standing position she seemed a match for giants. I decided I liked her.

She strode to a door in the far corner of the office, opened it, and called a name. A boy of about ten years appeared in the doorway. He sat down at one end of the table. He was brown like us, a plump kid with shiny black hair combed straight back, neat, cool, and faintly obnoxious.

Miss Hopley joined us with a large book and some papers in her hand. She, too, sat down, and the questions and answers began by way of our interpreter. My name was Ernesto. My mother's name was Henriqueta. My birth certificate was in San Blas. Here was my last report card from the Escuela Municipal Número 3 para Varones de Mazatlán, and so forth. Miss Hopley put things down in the book and my mother signed a card.

As long as the questions continued, Doña Henriqueta could stay and I was secure. Now that they were over, Miss Hopley saw her to the door, dismissed our interpreter, and without further ado took me by the hand and strode down the hall to Miss Ryan's first grade.

Miss Ryan took me to a seat at the front of the room, into which I shrank—the better to survey her. She was, to skinny, somewhat runty me, of a withering height when she patrolled the class. And

when I least expected it, there she was, crouching by my desk, her blond radiant face level with mine, her voice patiently maneuvering me over the awful idiocies of the English language.

During the next few weeks Miss Ryan overcame my fears of tall, energetic teachers as she bent over my desk to help me with a word in the pre-primer. Step by step, she loosened me and my classmates from the safe anchorage of the desks for recitations at the blackboard and consultations at her desk. Frequently she burst into happy announcements to the whole class. "Ito can read a sentence," and small Japanese Ito, squint-eyed and shy, slowly read aloud while the class listened in wonder: "Come, Skipper, come. Come and run." The Korean, Portuguese, Italian, and Polish first-graders had similar moments of glory, no less shining than mine the day I conquered "butterfly," which I had been persistently pronouncing in standard Spanish as boo-ter-flee. "Children," Miss Ryan called for attention. "Ernesto has learned how to pronounce *butterfly*!" And I proved it with a perfect imitation of Miss Ryan. From that celebrated success, I was soon able to match Ito's progress as a sentence reader with "Come, butterfly, come fly with me."

Like Ito and several other first-graders who did not know English, I received private lessons from Miss Ryan in the closet, a narrow hall off the classroom with a door at each end. Next to one of these doors Miss Ryan placed a large chair for herself and a small one for me. Keeping an eye on the class through the open door, she read with me about sheep in the meadow and a frightened chicken going to see the king, coaching me out of my phonetic ruts in words like *pasture, bow-wow-wow, hay,* and *pretty,* which to my Mexican ear and eye had so many unnecessary sounds and letters. She made me watch her lips and then close my eyes as she repeated words I found hard to read. When we came to know each other better, I tried interrupting to tell Miss Ryan how we said it in Spanish. It didn't work. She only said "oh" and went on with *pasture, bow-wow-wow,* and *pretty.* It was as if in that closet we were both discovering together the secrets of the English language and grieving together over the tragedies of Bo-Peep. The main reason I was graduated with

---

1. **formidable** (fôr′mə·də·b'l): displaying power.

honors from the first grade was that I had fallen in love with Miss Ryan. Her radiant, no-nonsense character made us either afraid not to love her or love her so we would not be afraid, I am not sure which. It was not only that we sensed she was with it, but also that she was with us.

Like the first grade, the rest of the Lincoln School was a sampling of the lower part of town where many races made their home. My pals in the second grade were Kazushi, whose parents spoke only Japanese; Matti, a skinny Italian boy; and Manuel, a fat Portuguese who would never get into a fight but wrestled you to the ground and just sat on you. Our assortment of nationalities included Koreans, Yugoslavs, Poles, Irish, and home-grown Americans.

Miss Hopley and her teachers never let us forget why we were at Lincoln: for those who were alien, to become good Americans; for those who were so born, to accept the rest of us. Off the school grounds we traded the same insults we heard from our elders. On the playground we were sure to be marched up to the principal's office for calling someone a wop, a chink, a dago, or a greaser. The school was not so much a melting pot as a griddle where Miss Hopley and her helpers warmed knowledge into us and roasted racial hatreds out of us.

At Lincoln, making us into Americans did not mean scrubbing away what made us originally foreign. The teachers called us as our parents did, or as close as they could pronounce our names in Spanish or Japanese. No one was ever scolded or punished for speaking in his native tongue on the playground. Matti told the class about his mother's down quilt, which she had made in Italy with the fine feathers of a thousand geese. Encarnación acted out how boys learned to fish in the Philippines. I astounded the third grade with the story of my travels on a stagecoach, which nobody else in the class had seen except in the museum at Sutter's Fort. After a visit to the Crocker Art Gallery and its collection of heroic paintings of the golden age of California, someone showed a silk scroll with a Chinese painting. Miss Hopley herself had a way of expressing wonder over these matters before a class, her eyes wide open until they popped slightly. It was easy for me to feel that becoming a proud American, as she said we should, did not mean feeling ashamed of being a Mexican.

The Americanization of Mexican me was no smooth matter. I had to fight one lout who made fun of my travels on the *diligencia*[2] and my barbaric translation of the word into "diligence." He doubled up with laughter over the word until I straightened him out with a kick. In class I made points explaining that in Mexico roosters said "qui-qui-ri-qui" and not "cock-a-doodle-doo," but after school I had to put up with the taunts of a big Yugoslav who said Mexican roosters were crazy.

But it was Homer who gave me the most lasting lesson for a future American.

Homer was a chunky Irishman who dressed as if every day was Sunday. He slicked his hair between a crew cut and a pompadour. And Homer was smart, as he clearly showed when he and I ran for president of the third grade.

Everyone understood that this was to be a demonstration of how the American people vote for president. In an election, the teacher explained, the candidates could be generous and vote for each other. We cast our ballots in a shoe box and Homer won by two votes. I polled my supporters and came to the conclusion that I had voted for Homer and so had he. After class he didn't deny it, reminding me of what the teacher had said— we could vote for each other but didn't have to.

The lower part of town was a collage of nationalities in the middle of which Miss Nettie Hopley kept school with discipline and compassion. She called assemblies in the upper hall to introduce celebrities like the police sergeant or the fire chief, to lay down the law of the school, to present awards to our athletic champions, and to make important announcements. One of these was that I had been proposed by my school and accepted as a member of the newly formed Sacramento Boys Band. "Now, isn't that a wonderful thing?" Miss Hopley asked the assembled school, all eyes on me. And everyone answered in a chorus, including myself, "Yes, Miss Hopley."

---

2. *diligencia* (dē·lē·hän′sē·ə): Spanish for a type of stagecoach.

It was not only the parents who were summoned to her office and boys and girls who served sentences there who knew that Nettie Hopley meant business. The entire school witnessed her sizzling Americanism in its awful majesty one morning at flag salute.

All the grades, as usual, were lined up in the courtyard between the wings of the building, ready to march to classes after the opening bell. Miss Shand was on the balcony of the second floor off Miss Hopley's office, conducting us in our lusty singing of "My Country tiz-a-thee." Our principal, as always, stood there like us, at attention, her right hand over her heart, joining in the song.

Halfway through the second stanza she stepped forward, held up her arm in a sign of command, and called loud and clear: "Stop the singing." Miss Shand looked flabbergasted. We were frozen with shock.

Miss Hopley was now standing at the rail of the balcony, her eyes sparking, her voice low and resonant, the words coming down to us distinctly and loaded with indignation.

"There are two gentlemen walking on the school grounds with their hats on while we are singing," she said, sweeping our ranks with her eyes. "We will remain silent until the gentlemen come to attention and remove their hats." A minute of awful silence ended when Miss Hopley, her gaze fixed on something behind us, signaled Miss Shand and we began once more the familiar hymn. That afternoon, when school was out, the word spread. The two gentlemen were the Superintendent of Schools and an important guest on an inspection.

I came back to the Lincoln School after every summer, moving up through the grades with Miss Campbell, Miss Beakey, Mrs. Wood, Miss Applegate, and Miss Delahunty. I sat in the classroom adjoining the principal's office and had my turn answering her telephone when she was about the building, repeating the message to the teacher, who made a note of it. Miss Campbell read to us during the last period of the week about King Arthur, Columbus, Buffalo Bill, and Daniel Boone, who came to life in the reverie of the class through the magic of her voice. And it was Miss Campbell who introduced me to the public library on Eye Street, where I became a regular customer.

All of Lincoln School mourned together when Eddie, the blond boy everybody liked, was killed by a freight train as he crawled across the tracks going home one day. We assembled to say goodbye to Miss Applegate, who was off to Alaska to be married. Now it was my turn to be excused from class to interpret for a parent enrolling a new student fresh from Mexico. Graduates from Lincoln came back now and then to tell us about high school. A naturalist entertained us in assembly, imitating the calls of the meadow lark, the water ouzel, the oriole, and the killdeer. I decided to become a bird man after I left Lincoln.

In the years we lived in the lower part of town, La Leen-Con, as my family called it, became a benchmark in our lives, like the purple light of the Lyric Theater and the golden dome of the Palacio de Gobierno[3] gleaming above Capitol Park.

---

3. **Palacio de Gobierno** (pä·lä′sē·ō dä go′b'yer′nō): Spanish for "the Govenor's mansion."

Responding to the Autobiography

Analyzing the Autobiography

Identifying Facts

1. This autobiography was written by an adult, but it is told so that we feel we are experiencing everything through a child's eyes. For example, what is the "mechanical contraption" that shuts the door on page 446? Who is the man in the picture with the "long white hair" and who is the one with a "sad face and a black beard" (page 446)?

2. "America is . . . the great melting pot, where all the races of Europe are melting and re-forming!" This famous metaphor originated in a play

by a man named Israel Zangwill. A melting pot makes everyone the same. What different **metaphor** does Galarza use to describe the Lincoln School? Give an example of how this school helped the children to remain proud of their national identities, while they became "Americans."

Interpreting Meanings

3. Galarza says that Homer gave him "the most lasting lesson for a future American." He doesn't explain what the lesson was. What do you infer that he learned from Homer?
4. Miss Hopley's "sizzling Americanism" gave him a different kind of lesson. What does her demand that the two gentlemen remove their hats during the song suggest to you about her idea of "Americanism"?
5. The word *benchmark* is used by surveyors to indicate a permanent landmark, whose position and attitude are fixed. The word has also come to mean any point of reference used in judging quality. Tell in your own words what Galarza implies about the school when he says it was a "benchmark" for his family. Do you think people regard schools this way today? Should they?
6. Writers can reveal any number of **tones** or attitudes when they look back on their school days. They can feel nostalgic, bitter, critical, approving. How would you describe Galarza's tone?
7. How is this story of a childhood different in mood from the story of Annie Sullivan (page 437)?

Writing About the Autobiography

A Creative Response

1. **Narrating an Experience.** The "new-child-in-town-and-school" story is a familiar one, and yet the *experience* of this is something everyone knows firsthand, to some degree. What was your beginning in education like? Did you begin somewhat like Galarza, a person from far away in a new place, or did you begin formal schooling in your home town? In either case, what were those first days like? What elements of strangeness do you think everyone was feeling? Can you remember any names of teachers and classmates? Tell in a paragraph about those days, and let us know if they now appear comic, difficult, frightening, or even significant to you.

A Critical Response

2. **Responding to the Autobiography.** What response did you have to this autobiographical account? Did you find it believable? Did you learn anything from this particular boy's experiences? Do you think anything in Ernesto's experience applies to life and education in America today? Write at least a paragraph explaining your response.

Analyzing Language and Vocabulary

Affixes

Galarza describes his "Americanization." The word is a combination of a noun, *American,* and two affixes: *-ize* and *-ation. Americanization* means "made into an American" (just as *colonization* means "made into a colony").

Affixes are parts of words that are added to a word to form new words. A *prefix* is added to the front of a word (*non*violent, *ex*-senator). A *suffix* is added to the end of a word (digi*tal*, national*ize*).

In the left-hand list below is a list of prefixes and suffixes, and their meanings. Create at least ten new words by adding one of these prefixes or suffixes to each word in the right-hand list. Check your words in a dictionary for meaning or spelling.

Prefixes	Words
dis-, "not, the opposite of"	**a.** alert
anti-, "against"	**b.** Atlantic
sub-, "under or beneath"	**c.** happy
super-, "above or extra"	**d.** guilt
trans-, "across or beyond"	**e.** nation
	f. satisfied
Suffixes	**g.** sonic
-ize, "to make or cause to be"	**h.** standard
-hood, "state, rank, condition"	**i.** terror
-less, "without"	**j.** war
-ness, "quality of, state of"	

Use a dictionary to answer these questions:

1. What is the meaning of the suffix that the words *humanoid* and *asteroid* have in common?
2. Does *inflammable* mean "not flammable" or "very flammable"?
3. Does *intolerable* mean "not tolerable" or "very tolerable"?
4. What is the difference between the prefixes *anti-* and *ante-*? What does *antiwar* mean? What does *antebellum* mean?

A native of the small town of Jackson, Mississippi, Willie Morris (1934–   ) traveled all the way to the University of Texas to take his undergraduate degree.

Morris has contributed articles and stories to many publications. He is also the author of several books: an autobiography, called *North Toward Home,* from which this story is taken; a juvenile novel, *Good Old Boy;* a volume of essays about the town where he spent his childhood, *Yazoo;* a novel, *The Last of the Southern Girls;* and an account of a high-school football star, *The Courting of Marcus Dupree.*

Willie Morris's love of sports began early and has lasted all his life. At Yazoo City High School in Mississippi, he played forward on the "starting five" of the basketball team, led the school's 1951 Indians with a batting average of .300, and played football with the Tribe against Canton in the oldest high-school football rivalry in Mississippi.

In the foreword of his collection of sports stories, *Always Stand in Against the Curve,* Morris recalls himself, "as I was on a summer's afternoon when I was seventeen. . . . Surely there is a wisp of immortality in us then, poised at that juncture before the world seizes hold of us. And for many of us, especially from what was the small-town South, sports was a nexus for much that was meaningful to us: dexterity, fulfillment, radiant well-being—and pain and struggle and disappointment."

Morris's editor adds: "For Willie Morris, sports provide a kind of gentle center in the eye of the storm of experience, a clean world of movement and action to which one can retreat—in the present or in one's memories—to work out the bruises of living. Athletics is also part of the ritual of youth, of learning about winning and losing, of heroes and disillusionment, of finding a way to face the world."

As you read this story, try to imagine the small town that Willie Morris writes about. And watch for the passage that explains the title: What do you *think* the "phantom of Yazoo" refers to?

THE PHANTOM OF YAZOO

Willie Morris

I decided not to try out for the American Legion Junior Baseball team that summer. Legion baseball was an important thing for country boys in those parts, but I was too young and skinny, and I had heard that the coach, a dirt farmer known as Gentleman Joe, made his protégés lie flat in the infield while he walked on their stomachs; he also forced them to take three-mile runs through the streets of town, talked them into going to church, and persuaded them to give up Coca-Colas. A couple of summers later, when I did go out for the team, I found out that Gentleman Joe did in fact insist on these soul-strengthening rituals; because of them, we won the Mississippi State Championship, and the merchants in town took up a collection and sent us all the way to St. Louis to see the Cards play the Phillies. My main concern that earlier summer, however, lay in the more academic aspects of the game. I knew more about baseball, its technology and its ethos,[1] than all the firemen and store experts put together. Having read most of its literature, I could give a sizable lecture on the infield-fly rule alone, which only a thin minority of the

---

1. **ethos** (ē'thäs): the central spirit of a group of people.

townspeople knew existed. Gentleman Joe was held in some esteem for his strategical sense, yet he was the only man I ever knew who could call for a sacrifice bunt with two men out and not have a bad conscience about it. I remember one dismaying moment that came to me while I was watching a country semi-pro game. The home team had runners on first and third with one out, when the batter hit a ground ball to the first baseman, who stepped on first then threw to second. The shortstop, covering second, stepped on the base but made no attempt to tag the runner. The man on third had crossed the plate, of course, but the umpire, who was not very familiar with the subtleties of the rules, signaled a double play. Sitting in the grandstand, I knew that it was not a double play at all and that the run had scored, but when I went down, out of my Christian duty, to tell the manager of the local team that he had just been done out of a run, he told me I was crazy. This was the kind of brainpower I was up against.

That summer the local radio station, the one where we broadcast our Methodist programs, started a baseball quiz program. A razor blade company offered free blades, and the station chipped in a dollar, all of which went to the first listener to telephone with the right answer to the day's baseball question. If there was no winner, the next day's pot would go up a dollar. At the end of the month they had to close down the program because I was winning all the money. It got so easy, in fact, that I stopped phoning in the answers some afternoons so that the pot could build up and make my winnings more spectacular. I netted about $25 and a ten-year supply of double-edged, smooth-contact razor blades before they gave up. One day, when the jackpot was a mere two dollars, the announcer tried to confuse me. ''Babe Ruth,'' he said, ''hit sixty home runs in 1927 to set the major-league record. What man had the next-highest total?'' I telephoned and said, ''George Herman Ruth. He hit fifty-nine in another season.'' My adversary, who had developed an acute dislike of me, said that was not the correct answer. He said it should have been *Babe* Ruth. This incident angered me, and I won for the next four days, just for the devil of it.

On Sunday afternoons, we sometimes drove out of town and along hot, dusty roads to baseball fields that were little more than parched red clearings, the outfield sloping out of the woods and ending in some tortuous gully full of yellowed paper, old socks, and vintage cow dung. One of the backwoods teams had a fastball pitcher named Eckert, who didn't have any teeth, and a fifty-year-old left-handed catcher named Smith. Since there were no catcher's mitts made for left-handers, Smith had to wear a mitt on his throwing hand. In his simian[2] posture he would catch the ball and toss it lightly into the air and then whip his mitt off and catch the ball in his bare left hand before throwing it back. It was a wonderfully lazy way to spend those Sunday afternoons—my father and my friends and I sitting in the grass behind the chicken-wire backstop with eight or ten dozen farmers, watching the wrong-handed catcher go through his contorted gyrations, and listening at the same time to our portable radio, which brought us the rising inflections of a baseball announcer called the Old Scotchman. The sounds of the two games, our own and the one being broadcast from Brooklyn or Chicago, merged and rolled across the bumpy outfield and the gully into the woods; it was a combination that seemed perfectly natural to everyone there.

I can see the town now on some hot, still weekday afternoon in midsummer: ten thousand souls and nothing doing. Even the red water truck was a diversion, coming slowly up Grand Avenue with its sprinklers on full force, the water making sizzling steam-clouds on the pavement while half-naked black children followed the truck up the street and played in the torrent until they got soaking wet. Over on Broadway, where the old men sat drowsily in straw chairs on the pavement near the Bon-Ton Café, whittling to make the time pass, you could laze around on the sidewalks—barefoot, if your feet were tough enough to stand the scalding concrete—watching the big cars with out-of-state plates whip by, the driver hardly knowing and certainly not caring what place this was. Way up that fantastic hill, Broadway seemed to end in a seething mist—little heat mirages that

---

2. **simian** (sim′ē·ən): apelike.

THE SATURDAY EVENING POST

An Illustr...
...led A°...   ...klin

Volume 205, Number 15

10c. in Canada
(INCLUDING TAX)

October 8, 1932

5c. THE COPY

Sheridan

PRESENTING
LILY MARS

By
BOOTH TARKINGTON

shimmered off the asphalt; on the main street itself there would be only a handful of cars parked here and there, and the merchants and the lawyers sat in the shade under their broad awnings, talking slowly, aimlessly, in the cryptic summer way. The one o'clock whistle at the sawmill would send out its loud bellow, reverberating up the streets to the bend in the Yazoo River, hardly making a ripple in the heavy somnolence.

But by two o'clock almost every radio in town was tuned in to the Old Scotchman. His rhetoric dominated the place. It hovered in the branches of the trees, bounced off the hills, and came out of the darkened stores; the merchants and the old men cocked their ears to him, and even from the big cars that sped by, their tires making lapping sounds in the softened highway, you could hear his voice being carried past you out into the delta.

The Old Scotchman's real name was Gordon McLendon, and he described the big-league games for the Liberty Broadcasting System, which had outlets mainly in the South and the Southwest. He had a deep, rich voice, and I think he was the best rhetorician, outside of Bilbo and Nye Bevan, I have ever heard. Under his handling, a baseball game took on a life of its own. As in the prose of the *Commercial Appeal*'s Walter Stewart, his games were rare and remarkable entities; casual pop flies had the flow of history behind them, double plays resembled the stark clashes of old armies, and home runs deserved acknowledgment on earthen urns. Later, when I came across Thomas Wolfe,[3] I felt I had heard him before, from Shibe Park, Crosley Field, or Yankee Stadium.

One afternoon I was sitting around my house listening to the Old Scotchman, admiring the vivacity of a man who said he was a contemporary of Connie Mack. (I learned later that he was twenty-nine.) That day he was doing the Dodgers and the Giants from the Polo Grounds. The game, as I recall, was in the fourth inning, and the Giants were ahead by about 4 to 1. It was a boring game, however, and I began experimenting with my father's shortwave radio, an impressive mechanism a

couple of feet wide, which had an aerial that almost touched the ceiling and the name of every major city in the world on its dial. It was by far the best radio I had ever seen; there was not another one like it in town. I switched the dial to shortwave and began picking up African drum music, French jazz, Australian weather reports, and a lecture from the British Broadcasting Company on the people who wrote poems for Queen Elizabeth. Then a curious thing happened. I came across a baseball game—the Giants and the Dodgers, from the Polo Grounds. After a couple of minutes I discovered that the game was in the eighth inning. I turned back to the local station, but here the Giants and Dodgers were still in the fourth. I turned again to the shortwave broadcast and listened to the last inning, a humdrum affair that ended with Carl Furillo popping out to shortstop, Gil Hodges grounding out second to first, and Roy Campanella lining out to center. Then I went back to the Old Scotchman and listened to the rest of the game. In the top of the ninth, an hour or so later, a ghostly thing occurred; to my astonishment and titillation, the game ended with Furillo popping out to short, Hodges grounding out second to first, and Campanella lining out to center.

I kept this unusual discovery to myself, and the next day, an hour before the Old Scotchman began his play-by-play of the second game of the series, I dialed the shortwave frequency, and, sure enough, they were doing the Giants and the Dodgers again. I learned that I was listening to the Armed Forces Radio Service, which broadcast games played in New York. As the game progressed I began jotting down notes on the action. When the first four innings were over, I turned to the local station just in time to get the Old Scotchman for the first batter. The Old Scotchman's account of the game matched the shortwave's almost perfectly. The Scotchman's, in fact, struck me as being considerably more poetic than the one I had heard first. But I did not doubt him, since I could hear the roar of the crowd, the crack of the bat, and the Scotchman's precise description of foul balls that fell into the crowd, the gestures of the base coaches, and the expression on the face of a small boy who was eating a lemon popsicle in a

3. **Thomas Wolfe** (1900–1938): the novelist from Asheville, North Carolina. He had a very poetic style and wrote books that many people regard as American epics.

box seat behind first base. I decided that the broadcast was being delayed somewhere along the line, maybe because we were so far from New York.

That was my first thought, but after a close comparison of the two broadcasts for the rest of the game, I sensed that something more sinister was taking place. For one thing, the Old Scotchman's description of the count on a batter, though it jibed 90 percent of the time, did not always match. For another, the Scotchman's crowd, compared with the other, kept up an ungodly noise. When Robinson stole second on shortwave, he did it without drawing a throw and without sliding, while for Mississippians the feat was performed in a cloud of angry, petulant dust. A foul ball that went over the grandstand and out of the park for shortwave listeners in Alaska, France, and the Argentine produced for the firemen, bootleggers, farmers, and myself a primitive scramble that ended with a feeble old lady catching the ball on the first bounce to the roar of an assembly that would have outnumbered Grant's at Old Cold Harbor. But the most revealing development came after the Scotchman's game was over. After the usual summaries, he mentioned that the game had been ''recreated.'' I had never taken notice of that particular word before, because I lost interest once a game was over. I went to the dictionary, and under ''recreate'' I found, ''To invest with fresh vigor and strength; to refresh, invigorate (nature, strength, a person or thing).'' The Old Scotchman most assuredly invested a game with fresh vigor and strength, but this told me nothing. My deepest suspicions were confirmed, however, when I found the second definition of the word— ''To create anew.''

So there it was. I was happy to have fathomed the mystery, as perhaps no one else in the whole town had done. The Old Scotchman, for all his wondrous expressions, was not only several innings behind every game he described but was no doubt sitting in some air-conditioned studio in the hinterland, where he got the happenings of the game by news ticker; sound effects accounted for the crack of the bat and the crowd noises. Instead of being disappointed in the Scotchman, I was all the more pleased by his genius, for he made pristine[4] facts more actual than actuality, a valuable lesson when the day finally came that I started reading literature. I must add, however, that this appreciation did not obscure the realization that I had at my disposal a weapon of unimaginable dimensions.

Next day I was at the shortwave again, but I learned with much disappointment that the game being broadcast on shortwave was not the one the Scotchman had chosen to describe. I tried every afternoon after that and discovered that I would have to wait until the Old Scotchman decided to do a game out of New York before I could match his game with the one described live on shortwave. Sometimes, I learned later, these coincidences did not occur for days; during an important Dodger or Yankee series, however, his game and that of the Armed Forces Radio Service often coincided for two or three days running. I was happy, therefore, to find, on an afternoon a few days later, that both the shortwave and the Scotchman were carrying the Yankees and the Indians.

I settled myself at the shortwave with notebook and pencil and took down every pitch. This I did for four full innings, and then I turned back to the town station, where the Old Scotchman was just beginning the first inning. I checked the first batter to make sure the accounts jibed. Then, armed with my notebook, I ran down the street to the corner grocery, a minor outpost of baseball intellection, presided over by my young black friend Bozo, a knowledgeable student of the game, the same one who kept my dog in bologna. I found Bozo behind the meat counter, with the Scotchman's account going full blast. I arrived at the interim between the top and bottom of the first inning.

''Who's pitchin' for the Yankees, Bozo?'' I asked.

''They're pitchin' Allie Reynolds,'' Bozo said. ''Old Scotchman says Reynolds really got the stuff today. He just set 'em down one, two, three.''

The Scotchman, meanwhile, was describing the way the pennants were flapping in the breeze. Phil Rizzuto, he reported, was stepping to the plate.

''Bo,'' I said, trying to sound cut and dried,

---

4. **pristine** (pris·tēn′): spotlessly clean; unpolluted.

"you know what I think? I think Rizzuto's gonna take a couple of fast called strikes, then foul one down the left-field line, and then line out straight to Boudreau at short."

"Yeah?" Bozo said. He scratched his head and leaned lazily across the counter.

I went up front to buy something and then came back. The count worked to nothing and two on Rizzuto—a couple of fast called strikes and a foul down the left side. "This one," I said to Bozo, "he lines straight to Boudreau at short."

The Old Scotchman, pausing dramatically between words as was his custom, said, "Here's the pitch on its way—There's a hard line drive! But Lou Boudreau's there at shortstop, and he's got it. Phil hit that one on the nose, but Boudreau was right there."

Bozo looked over at me, his eyes bigger than they were. "How'd you know that?" he asked.

Ignoring this query, I made my second prediction. "Bozo," I said, "Tommy Henrich's gonna hit the first pitch up against the right-field wall and slide in with a double."

"How come you think so?"

"Because I can predict anything that's gonna happen in baseball in the next ten years," I said. "I can tell you anything."

The Old Scotchman was describing Henrich at the plate. "Here comes the first pitch. Henrich swings, there's a hard smash into right field! . . . This one may be out of here! It's going, going—*No!* It's off the wall in right center. Henrich's rounding first, on his way to second. Here's the relay from Doby . . . Henrich slides in safely with a double!" The Yankee crowd sent up an awesome roar in the background.

"Say, how'd you know that?" Bozo asked. "How'd you know he was gonna wind up at second?"

"I just can tell. I got extra-vision," I said. On the radio, far in the background, the public-address system announced Yogi Berra. "Like Berra right now. You know what? He's gonna hit a one-one pitch down the right-field line—"

"How come you know?" Bozo said. He was getting mad.

"Just a second," I said. "I'm gettin' static." I stood dead still, put my hands up against my tem-

ples and opened my eyes wide. "Now it's comin' through clear. Yeah, Yogi's gonna hit a one-one pitch down the right-field line, and it's gonna be fair by about three or four feet—I can't say exactly—and Henrich's gonna score from second, but the throw is gonna get Yogi at second by a mile."

This time Bozo was silent, listening to the Scotchman, who described the ball and the strike, then said: "Henrich takes the lead off second. Benton looks over, stretches, delivers. Yogi swings." (There was the bat crack.) "There's a line drive down the right side! It's barely inside the foul line. It may go for extra bases! Henrich's rounding third and coming in with a run. Berra's moving toward second. Here comes the throw! . . . And they *get* him! They get Yogi easily on the slide at second!"

Before Bozo could say anything else, I reached in my pocket for my notes. "I've written down here what I think's gonna happen in the first four innings," I said. "Like DiMag. See, he's gonna pop up to Mickey Vernon at first on a one-nothing pitch in just a minute. But don't you worry. He's gonna hit a 380-foot homer in the fourth with nobody on base on a full count. You just follow these notes, and you'll see I can predict anything that's gonna happen in the next ten years." I handed him the paper, turned around, and left the store just as DiMaggio, on a one-nothing pitch, popped up to Vernon at first.

Then I went back home and took more notes from the shortwave. The Yanks clobbered the Indians in the late innings and won easily. On the local station, however, the Old Scotchman was in the top of the fifth inning. At this juncture I went to the telephone and called Firehouse No. 1.

"Hello," a voice answered. It was the fire chief.

"Hello, Chief, can you tell me the score?" I said. Calling the firehouse for baseball information was a common practice.

"The Yanks are ahead, 5–2."

"This is the Phantom you're talkin' with," I said.

"Who?"

"The Phantom. Listen carefully, Chief. Reynolds is gonna open this next inning with a pop-up to Doby. Then Rizzuto will single to left on a one-one count. Henrich's gonna force him at second on a two-and-one pitch but make it to first. Berra's gonna double to right on a nothing-and-one pitch, and Henrich's goin' to third. DiMaggio's gonna foul a couple off and then double down the left-field line, and both Henrich and Yogi are gonna score. Brown's gonna pop out to third to end the inning.''

"Aw, go to the devil,'' the chief said, and hung up.

This was precisely what happened, of course. I phoned No. 1 again after the inning.

"Hello.''

"Hi. This is the Phantom again.''

"Say, how'd you know that?''

"Stick with me,'' I said ominously, "and I'll feed you predictions. I can predict anything that's gonna happen anywhere in the next ten years.'' After a pause I added, "Beware of fire real soon,'' for good measure, and hung up.

I left my house and hurried back to the corner grocery. When I got there, the entire meat counter was surrounded by friends of Bozo's, about a dozen of them. They were gathered around my notes, talking passionately and shouting. Bozo saw me standing by the bread counter. "There he is! That's the one!'' he declared. His colleagues turned and stared at me in undisguised awe. They parted respectfully as I strolled over to the meat counter and ordered a dime's worth of bologna for my dog.

A couple of questions were directed at me from the group, but I replied, "I'm sorry for what happened in the fourth. I predicted DiMag was gonna hit a full-count pitch for that homer. It came out he hit it on two-and-two. There was too much static in the air between here and New York.''

"Too much *static*?'' one of them asked.

"Yeah. Sometimes the static confuses my extra-vision. But I'll be back tomorrow if everything's okay, and I'll try not to make any more big mistakes.''

"Big mistakes!'' one of them shouted, and the crowd laughed admiringly, parting once more as I turned and left the store. I wouldn't have been at all surprised if they had tried to touch the hem of my shirt.

*   *   *

That day was only the beginning of my brief season of triumph. A schoolmate of mine offered me five dollars, for instance, to tell him how I had known that Johnny Mize was going to hit a two-run homer to break up one particularly close game for the Giants. One afternoon, on the basis of a lopsided first four innings, I had an older friend sneak into the store and place a bet, which netted me $14.50. I felt so bad about it I tithed $1.45 in church the following Sunday. At Bozo's grocery store I was a full-scale oracle. To the firemen I remained the Phantom, and firefighting reached a peak of efficiency that month, simply because the firemen knew what was going to happen in the late innings and did not need to tarry when an alarm came.

One afternoon my father was at home listening to the Old Scotchman with a couple of out-of-town salesmen from Greenwood. They were sitting in the front room, and I had already managed to get the first three or four innings of the Cardinals and the Giants on paper before they arrived. The Old Scotchman was in the top of the first when I walked in and said hello. The men were talking business and listening to the game at the same time.

"I'm gonna make a prediction,'' I said. They stopped talking and looked at me. "I predict Musial's gonna take a ball and a strike and then hit a double to right field, scoring Schoendienst from second, but Marty Marion's gonna get tagged out at the plate.''

"You're mighty smart,'' one of the men said. He suddenly sat up straight when the Old Scotchman reported, "Here's the windup and the pitch coming in . . . Musial *swings*!'' (Bat crack, crowd roar.) "He drives one into right field! This one's going up against the boards! . . . Schoendienst rounds third. He's coming on in to score! Marion dashes around third, legs churning. His cap falls off, but here he *comes*! Here's the toss to the plate. He's nabbed at home. He is *out* at the plate! Musial holds at second with a run-producing double.''

Before I could parry the inevitable questions, my father caught me by the elbow and hustled me

into a back room. "How'd you know that?" he asked.

"I was just guessin'," I said. "It was nothin' but luck."

He stopped for a moment, and then a new expression showed on his face. "Have *you* been callin' the firehouse?" he asked.

"Yeah, I guess a few times."

"Now, you tell me how you found out about all that. I mean it."

When I told him about the shortwave, I was afraid he might be mad, but on the contrary he laughed uproariously. "Do you remember these next few innings?" he asked.

"I got it all written down," I said, and reached in my pocket for the notes. He took the notes and told me to go away. From the yard, a few minutes later, I heard him predicting the next inning to the salesmen.

A couple of days later, I phoned No. 1 again. "This is the Phantom," I said. "With two out, Branca's gonna hit Stinky Stanky with a fast ball,

and then Alvin Dark's gonna send him home with a triple."

"Yeah, we know it," the fireman said in a bored voice. "We're listenin' to a shortwave too. You think you're somethin', don't you? You're Ray Morris's boy."

I knew everything was up. The next day, as a sort of final gesture, I took some more notes to the corner grocery in the third or fourth inning. Some of the old crowd was there, but the atmosphere was grim. They looked at me coldly. "Oh, man," Bozo said, "*we* know the Old Scotchman ain't at that game. He's four or five innings behind. He's makin' all that stuff up." The others grumbled and turned away. I slipped quietly out the door.

My period as a seer was over, but I went on listening to the shortwave broadcasts out of New York a few days more. Then, a little to my surprise, I went back to the Old Scotchman, and in time I found that the firemen, the bootleggers, and the few dirt farmers who had shortwave sets all did the same. From then on, accurate, up-to-the-minute baseball news was in disrepute there. I believe we all went back to the Scotchman not merely out of loyalty but because, in our great isolation, he touched our need for a great and unmitigated[5] eloquence.

---

5. **unmitigated** (un·mit′ə·gāt′id): complete and absolute.

Responding to the Autobiography

Analyzing the Autobiography

Identifying Facts

1. Who was "the Old Scotchman"?
2. What three things did the boy realize when he compared the Old Scotchman's broadcasts with the shortwave broadcasts?
3. What did the boy learn about the meaning of the word *recreated*? (What word might a more critical person have used?)
4. How did the boy use his discovery to become the "Phantom of Yazoo"?
5. Once everyone learned about the earlier live broadcasts of the games, why did they go back to listening to the Old Scotchman?

Interpreting Meanings

6. The "Phantom of Yazoo" went on to become a novelist and journalist. In your own words, explain what the Old Scotchman taught him about the power of words and imagination.
7. The writer uses **overstatement,** or exaggeration, to describe the Old Scotchman's broadcasts. For example, he says on page 455 that casual pop flies "had the flow of history behind them." Find two more overstatements in his description of the Old Scotchman's broadcasts. What do they tell you about the way people felt about the broadcasts?
8. The paragraph beginning "I can see the town now" (page 453) describes the town of Yazoo. What **images** describe what the writer sees and hears? How do these descriptive details convince you that, in this town, the radio broadcasts were events of major excitement?

9. What is more important in TV sports broadcasting today—words or electronic images? Do you think TV broadcasting today has the same imaginative power as the Old Scotchman's broadcasts did? Explain.
10. Explain your response to the comments about sports in the introduction to this story on page 452. (Do you feel the same way?)

Writing About the Autobiography

A Creative Response

Writing an Essay. Most essays use a combination of writing methods—primarily they use description and narration, but often they also use exposition and even persuasion. Write a paragraph about a sport or game. Before you write, decide what your purpose is and which is going to be your basic writing method. Follow *one* of these suggestions:

1. Write an **expository** paragraph explaining how a game is played: Who are the players? What equipment do they use? What are the rules?
2. Write a **descriptive** paragraph in which you re-create the most exciting moment you have witnessed in a sport or game. Use images of sight, sound, smell, taste, and touch to convey the excitement of the moment, of the players, of the onlookers. Decide whether you will describe the moment as a player or as an onlooker.
3. Write a **narrative** paragraph in which you tell what happened as you (or someone else) played a sport or game. Narrate the events in the order in which they occurred. Tell how one event led to another.

4. Write a paragraph **persuading** readers that your favorite sport or game is the best, the most exciting, the most important in the world. (You may try writing a comic essay by choosing an unlikely game—tick-tack-toe or a three-legged race—and use overstatement to create humor.)

Analyzing Language and Vocabulary

Jargon

Baseball has a jargon all its own. **Jargon** is a specialized language used by one profession or group. Doctors, computer scientists, athletes, actors, short-order cooks, soldiers—all have jargon of their own. Like other jargon, the baseball jargon in this story would be confusing to anyone not familiar with the game. How would you explain to someone who had never heard of baseball what this passage means?

> . . . Carl Furillo popping out to shortstop, Gil Hodges grounding out second to first . . .

You would have to say something like this:

> . . . Carl Furillo hits a ball that makes a high but short flight, and it is caught by the person playing the position called shortstop, which is between second and third bases. Gil Hodges hits a ball along the ground, but it is picked up by the second baseman and thrown to the first baseman. It arrives there before Hodges does, so he is out, which means he has to leave the base and so cannot score a point . . .

How much longer the explanation is than the jargon! This is one of jargon's purposes: It's a kind of shorthand for the people in the group using it.

How would you explain to someone who knows nothing about baseball what these lines from Morris's story mean?

1. ". . . there's a hard smash into right field . . ."
2. "Henrich's rounding first . . . Henrich slides in safely with a double."
3. "He's gonna hit a 380-foot homer in the fourth with nobody on base on a full count . . ."
4. ". . . Branca's gonna hit Stinky Stanky with a fast ball, and then Alvin Dark's gonna send him home with a triple."

"One would say of my life," says Maya Angelou (1928–   ), "born loser, had to be—but it's not the truth. In the black community, however bad it looks, there's a lot of love and so much humor."

After she left Stamps, Arkansas, Maya won a scholarship to the California Labor School, where she took evening classes in dance and drama. She also persisted until she was hired as the first black female fare collector with the San Francisco Streetcar Company. In 1954 and 1955 she toured Europe and Africa in a State Department-sponsored production of the opera *Porgy and Bess*.

Angelou also has written and produced a ten-part television series on Africanisms in American life; she has written songs that were recorded by B. B. King; and she has published collections of poems. ("Woman Work" is on page 299 of this book.)

I Know Why the Caged Bird Sings, an autobiography of her first sixteen years, was published in 1970 and was an immediate success.

Maya Angelou is an imposing woman, six feet tall, with a gracious, graceful, and formal manner. She declares a continuing interest in exploring the real character of the black woman, with whom she is impressed: "She has nursed a nation of strangers—literally. And has remained compassionate." At the same time, Angelou's purpose in writing is wider. "I speak to the black experience, but I am always talking about the human condition—about what we can endure, dream, fail at, and still survive."

Think for a few minutes about the unusual title of this autobiography. What kind of a life story does it lead you to expect? See if this extract bears out your predictions.

I KNOW WHY THE CAGED BIRD SINGS

Maya Angelou

1

When I was three and Bailey four, we had arrived in the musty little town, wearing tags on our wrists which instructed—"To Whom It May Concern"—that we were Marguerite and Bailey Johnson, Jr., from Long Beach, California, en route to Stamps, Arkansas, c/o Mrs. Annie Henderson.

Our parents had decided to put an end to their calamitous[1] marriage, and Father shipped us home to his mother. A porter had been charged with our welfare—he got off the train the next day in Ari-zona—and our tickets were pinned to my brother's inside coat pocket.

I don't remember much of the trip, but after we reached the segregated southern part of the journey, things must have looked up. Negro passengers, who always traveled with loaded lunch boxes, felt sorry for "the poor little motherless darlings" and plied us with cold fried chicken and potato salad.

Years later I discovered that the United States had been crossed thousands of times by frightened black children traveling alone to their newly affluent parents in Northern cities or back to grandmothers in Southern towns when the urban North reneged on its economic promises.

The town reacted to us as its inhabitants had

---

1. **calamitous** (kə·lam′ə·təs): characterized by great misfortunes, or calamities.

reacted to all things new before our coming. It regarded us a while without curiosity but with caution, and after we were seen to be harmless (and children), it closed in around us, as a real mother embraces a stranger's child. Warmly, but not too familiarly.

We lived with our grandmother and uncle in the rear of the Store (it was always spoken of with a capital *s*), which she had owned some twenty-five years.

Early in the century, Momma (we soon stopped calling her Grandmother) sold lunches to the sawmen in the lumberyard (east Stamps) and the seedmen at the cotton gin (west Stamps). Her crisp meat pies and cool lemonade, when joined to her miraculous ability to be in two places at the same time, assured her business success. From being a mobile lunch counter, she set up a stand between the two points of fiscal[2] interest and supplied the workers' needs for a few years. Then she had the Store built in the heart of the Negro area. Over the years it became the lay[3] center of activities in town. On Saturdays, barbers sat their customers in the shade on the porch of the Store, and troubadours on their ceaseless crawlings through the South leaned across its benches and sang their sad songs of The Brazos while they played juice harps and cigar-box guitars.

The formal name of the Store was the Wm. Johnson General Merchandise Store. Customers could find food staples, a good variety of colored thread, mash for hogs, corn for chickens, coal oil for lamps, light bulbs for the wealthy, shoestrings, hair dressing, balloons, and flower seeds. Anything not visible had only to be ordered.

Until we became familiar enough to belong to the Store and it to us, we were locked up in a Fun House of Things where the attendant had gone home for life.

Each year I watched the field across from the Store turn caterpillar green, then gradually frosty white. I knew exactly how long it would be before the big wagons would pull into the front yard and load on the cotton pickers at daybreak to carry them to the remains of slavery's plantations.

During the picking season my grandmother would get out of bed at four o'clock (she never used an alarm clock) and creak down to her knees and chant in a sleep-filled voice, "Our Father, thank you for letting me see this New Day. Thank you that you didn't allow the bed I lay on last night to be my cooling board, nor my blanket my winding sheet. Guide my feet this day along the straight and narrow, and help me to put a bridle on my tongue. Bless this house, and everybody in it. Thank you, in the name of your Son, Jesus Christ, Amen."

Before she had quite arisen, she called our names and issued orders and pushed her large feet into homemade slippers and across the bare lyewashed wooden floor to light the coal-oil lamp.

The lamplight in the Store gave a soft makebelieve feeling to our world which made me want to whisper and walk about on tiptoe. The odors of onions and oranges and kerosene had been mixing all night and wouldn't be disturbed until the wooded slat was removed from the door and the early morning air forced its way in with the bodies of people who had walked miles to reach the pickup place.

"Sister, I'll have two cans of sardines."

"I'm gonna work so fast today I'm gonna make you look like you standing still."

"Lemme have a hunk uh cheese and some sody crackers."

"Just gimme a coupla them fat peanut paddies." That would be from a picker who was taking his lunch. The greasy brown paper sack was stuck behind the bib of his overalls. He'd use the candy as a snack before the noon sun called the workers to rest.

In those tender mornings the Store was full of laughing, joking, boasting, and bragging. One man was going to pick two hundred pounds of cotton, and another three hundred. Even the children were promising to bring home fo' bits and six bits.[4]

The champion picker of the day before was the hero of the dawn. If he prophesied that the cotton in today's field was going to be sparse and stick

---

2. **fiscal:** pertaining to money; financial.
3. **lay:** not directly involved with the church or the clergy.

4. **fo' bits and six bits:** two bits is slang for 25¢; so four and six bits are 50¢ and 75¢, respectively.

to the bolls like glue, every listener would grunt a hearty agreement.

The sound of the empty cotton sacks dragging over the floor and the murmurs of waking people were sliced by the cash register as we rang up the five-cent sales.

If the morning sounds and smells were touched with the supernatural, the late afternoon had all the features of the normal Arkansas life. In the dying sunlight the people dragged, rather than their empty cotton sacks.

Brought back to the Store, the pickers would step out of the backs of trucks and fold down, dirt-disappointed, to the ground. No matter how much they had picked, it wasn't enough. Their wages wouldn't even get them out of debt to my grandmother, not to mention the staggering bill that waited on them at the white commissary downtown.

The sounds of the new morning had been replaced with grumbles about cheating houses, weighted scales, snakes, skimpy cotton, and dusty rows. In later years I was to confront the stereotyped picture of gay song-singing cotton pickers with such inordinate rage that I was told even by fellow blacks that my paranoia[5] was embarrassing. But I had seen the fingers cut by the mean little cotton bolls, and I had witnessed the backs and shoulders and arms and legs resisting any further demands.

Some of the workers would leave their sacks at the Store to be picked up the following morning, but a few had to take them home for repairs. I winced to picture them sewing the coarse material under a coal-oil lamp with fingers stiffening from the day's work. In too few hours they would have to walk back to Sister Henderson's Store, get vittles and load, again, onto the trucks. Then they would face another day of trying to earn enough for the whole year with the heavy knowledge that they were going to end the season as they started it—without the money or credit necessary to sustain a family for three months. In cotton-picking time the late afternoons revealed the harshness of black Southern life, which in the early morning had been softened by nature's blessing of grogginess, forgetfulness, and the soft lamplight.

2

When Bailey was six and I a year younger, we used to rattle off the times tables with the speed I was later to see Chinese children in San Francisco employ on their abacuses.[6] Our summer-gray pot-bellied stove bloomed rosy red during winter and became a severe disciplinarian threat if we were so foolish as to indulge in making mistakes.

Uncle Willie used to sit, like a giant black Z (he had been crippled as a child), and hear us testify to the Lafayette County Training Schools' abilities. His face pulled down on the left side, as if a pulley had been attached to his lower teeth, and his left hand was only a mite bigger than Bailey's, but on the second mistake or on the third hesitation his big overgrown right hand would catch one of us behind the collar and in the same moment would thrust the culprit toward the dull red heater, which throbbed like a devil's toothache. We were never burned, although once I might have been when I was so terrified I tried to jump onto the stove to remove the possibility of its remaining a threat. Like most children, I thought if I could face the worst danger voluntarily and *triumph,* I would forever have power over it. But in my case of sacrificial effort I was thwarted. Uncle Willie held tight to my dress, and I only got close enough to smell the clean dry scent of hot iron. We learned the times tables without understanding their grand principle, simply because we had the capacity and no alternative.

The tragedy of lameness seems so unfair to children that they are embarrassed in its presence. And they, most recently off nature's mold, sense that they have only narrowly missed being another of her jokes. In relief at the narrow escape, they vent their emotions in impatience and criticism of the unlucky cripple.

Momma related times without end, and without any show of emotion, how Uncle Willie had been

---

5. **paranoia** (par′ə·noi′ə): feelings of being persecuted or victimized.

6. **abacuses** (ab′ə·kəs′əz): devices with strung beads used for counting.

dropped when he was three years old by a woman who was minding him. She seemed to hold no rancor against the baby sitter, nor for her just God who allowed the accident. She felt it necessary to explain over and over again to those who knew the story by heart that he wasn't "born that way."

In our society, where two-legged, two-armed strong black men were able at best to eke out only the necessities of life, Uncle Willie, with his starched shirts, shined shoes, and shelves full of food, was the whipping boy and butt of jokes of the underemployed and underpaid. Fate not only disabled him but laid a double-tiered barrier in his path. He was also proud and sensitive. Therefore he couldn't pretend that he wasn't crippled, nor could he deceive himself that people were not repelled by his defect.

Only once in all the years of trying not to watch him, I saw him pretend to himself and others that he wasn't lame.

Coming home from school one day, I saw a dark car in our front yard. I rushed in to find a strange man and woman (Uncle Willie said later they were schoolteachers from Little Rock) drinking Dr. Pepper in the cool of the Store. I sensed a wrongness around me, like an alarm clock that had gone off without being set.

I knew it couldn't be the strangers. Not frequently, but often enough, travelers pulled off the main road to buy tobacco or soft drinks in the only Negro store in Stamps. When I looked at Uncle Willie, I knew what was pulling my mind's coattails. He was standing erect behind the counter, not leaning forward or resting on the small shelf that had been built for him. Erect. His eyes seemed to hold me with a mixture of threats and appeal.

I dutifully greeted the strangers and roamed my eyes around for his walking stick. It was nowhere to be seen. He said, "Uh . . . this this . . . this . . . uh, my niece. She's . . . uh . . . just come from school." Then to the couple—"You know . . . how, uh, children are . . . th-th-these days . . . they play all d-d-day at school and c-c-can't wait to get home and pl-play some more."

The people smiled, very friendly.

He added, "Go on out and pl-play, Sister."

The lady laughed in a soft Arkansas voice and said, "Well, you know, Mr. Johnson, they say, you're only a child once. Have you children of your own?"

Uncle Willie looked at me with an impatience I hadn't seen in his face even when he took thirty minutes to loop the laces over his high-topped shoes. "I . . . I thought I told you to go . . . go outside and play."

Before I left I saw him lean back on the shelves of Garret Snuff, Prince Albert, and Spark Plug chewing tobacco.

"No, ma'am . . . no ch-children and no wife." He tried a laugh. "I have an old m-m-mother and my brother's t-two children to l-look after."

I didn't mind his using us to make himself look good. In fact, I would have pretended to be his daughter if he wanted me to. Not only did I not feel any loyalty to my own father, I figured that if I had been Uncle Willie's child I would have received much better treatment.

The couple left after a few minutes, and from the back of the house I watched the red car scare chickens, raise dust, and disappear toward Magnolia.

Uncle Willie was making his way down the long shadowed aisle between the shelves and the counter—hand over hand, like a man climbing out of a dream. I stayed quiet and watched him lurch from one side, bumping to the other, until he reached the coal-oil tank. He put his hand behind that dark recess and took his cane in the strong fist and shifted his weight on the wooden support. He thought he had pulled it off.

I'll never know why it was important to him that the couple (he said later that he'd never seen them before) would take a picture of a whole Mr. Johnson back to Little Rock.

He must have tired of being crippled, as prisoners tire of penitentiary bars and the guilty tire of blame. The high-topped shoes and the cane, his uncontrollable muscles and thick tongue, and the looks he suffered of either contempt or pity had simply worn him out, and for one afternoon, one part of an afternoon, he wanted no part of them.

I understood and felt closer to him at that moment than ever before or since.

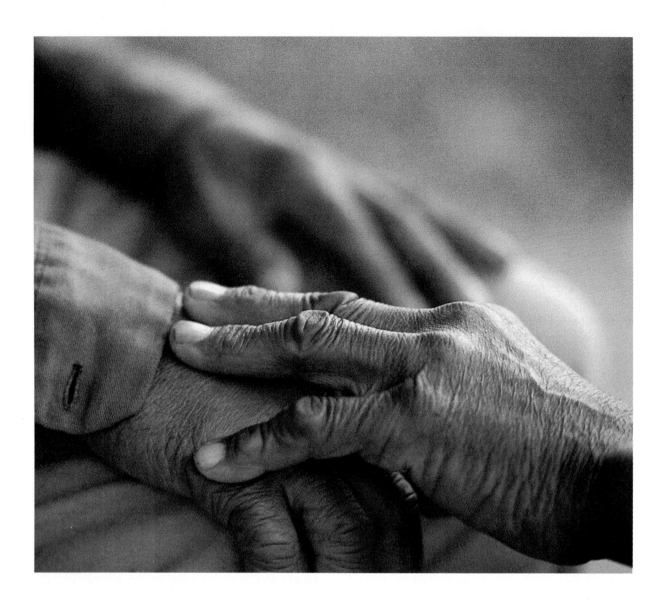

Responding to the Autobiography

Analyzing the Autobiography

Identifying Facts

1. How did the girl and her brother come to live with their grandmother in Stamps, Arkansas?
2. What was the grandmother's role in the life of Stamps?
3. How did the cotton pickers' morning attitudes contrast with the way they felt in the later afternoon? Why did the girl think of the morn-

ing as "supernatural" and of the afternoon as "normal"?

4. The second part of this excerpt concentrates on Uncle Willie. According to the writer, how do children react to lameness, and why? Do you agree?
5. What did Uncle Willie do to make himself "look good" to the schoolteachers from Little Rock? How does the writer explain his unusual behavior?

Interpreting Meanings

6. One **purpose** of this autobiography is to give us a picture of how the black people in Stamps lived. What details does the writer use to support her statement that their life was harsh? Do you think the writer feels that her own life was harsh too? Explain.

7. Another purpose of this autobiography is to give **character** portraits of Momma and Uncle Willie. What does Momma's morning "chant" (page 463) tell about her character?

8. What does it tell about Momma that she "holds no rancor" against God or the baby sitter for Uncle Willie's deformity? Why do you think it was important to Momma that everyone knew that Willie wasn't born that way?

9. What barriers did Uncle Willie have to face and try to conquer? Does the writer feel that Uncle Willie was really cruel?

10. Why did Maya Angelou later feel rage when she confronted the "stereotyped picture" of happy, singing cotton pickers? What other **stereotypes** can you think of? How do you feel about them? (For a definition of stereotype, see page 550.)

Writing About the Autobiography

A Creative Response

1. **Describing a Place.** Review Angelou's descriptions of the Store in the morning and in the evening. Then, think of some place you know very well, and describe in a paragraph the way it looks and sounds and smells in the morning. In another paragraph, describe the same place in the evening, as darkness begins to fall. Decide first what your feelings are about the place in the morning and evening (contentment, joy, peace, sadness, uneasiness, etc.). Then, list the images you will use in each paragraph. If Angelou had made lists, they might have contained the following images.

Morning
soft, make-believe feeling of lamplight
odors of onions, oranges, kerosene
early morning air
tender mornings
laughing, joking, boasting, bragging people
sound of cotton sacks dragging
murmurs of waking people
cash register ringing
morning touched with supernatural

Evening
dying sunlight
people dragging, dirt-disappointed
grumbles
cut fingers
weary limbs
staggering bills
harshness of life
normal

A Critical Response

2. **Explaining a Title.** Here is the final verse of the poem that Angelou drew her title from:

> I know why the caged bird sings, ah me,
> When his wing is bruised and his bosom sore,
> When he beats his bars and would be free;
> It is not a carol of joy or glee,
> But a prayer that he sends from his heart's
>   deep core,
> But a plea, that upward to Heaven he flings—
> I know why the caged bird sings!
>
> —from "Sympathy,"
> Paul Lawrence Dunbar

In a paragraph, explain why, in your opinion, Angelou chose this as the title of her life story. Be sure to explain what you think the caged bird is praying *for*. Is this also what the people in Angelou's story want?

Analyzing Language and Vocabulary

Similes and Metaphors

In each simile and metaphor that follows, name the two things being compared. What feeling does each one suggest to you?

1. *The town of Stamps:* ". . . it closed in around us, as a real mother embraces a stranger's child."

2. *The Store:* ". . . we were locked up in a Fun House of Things where the attendant had gone home for life."

3. *Uncle Willie:* "Uncle Willie used to sit, like a giant black Z . . . his face pulled down on the left side, as if a pulley had been attached to his lower teeth . . ."

4. *The heater:* ". . . the dull red heater, which throbbed like a devil's toothache."

Samuel Langhorne Clemens (1835–1910) was the descendant of slave-holding Virginians, the sixth of seven children of a witty and beautiful mother and a father with grandiose dreams of fortune. Sam was born in Florida, Missouri. When he was four years old, his family moved to Hannibal, Missouri, on the banks of the Mississippi. Sam's childhood was dominated by the river, which he loved, and by the uncertain career of his father. Mr. Clemens managed to be a prominent citizen, even a judge and a justice of the peace, though he was always on the edge of bankruptcy. When Sam was eleven, his father died, and the boy was apprenticed to a printer. This put an end to his formal education.

For the next twenty years, Sam Clemens moved around and shifted from job to job—printer, steamboat pilot, soldier, prospector, reporter, editor, lecturer, publisher. His interests seemed aimless, but he was actually gathering the material and the skills that later helped him produce some of the greatest books in American literature.

Sam Clemens changed life styles as often as he changed jobs: at one time he was Bohemian, then he was respectable; at one time he was an adventurer, then he was exaggeratedly domestic. At various times he was in flight: from the army, from a duel threat, and from a feud with the police. As a humorist, he used a variety of pseudonyms: Thomas Jefferson Snodgrass, W. Epaminandos Adrastus Blab, Sergeant Fathom, and Josh. In 1863 he adopted the pen name by which we know him. "Mark Twain" is from a river phrase ("By the mark, twain!"), meaning the water is "two fathoms deep," which was a safe depth for the Mississippi steamboats.

In 1865 Twain began to be known as a humorist, with the publication of his tall tale "The Celebrated Jumping Frog of Calaveras County." Next he won widespread fame with *The Innocents Abroad*. The "innocents" are a group of naive American tourists. In the same period and using the same talent (he wrote hundreds of love letters), Twain broke through the rebuffs and won the hand of Olivia Langdon of Elmira, New York, a frail and sensitive heiress.

The Clemenses built an enormous house in Hartford, Connecticut—it had twenty rooms, six balconies, and two towers. They had a son, who died in infancy, and three daughters. Twain went about family life with the same intensity that characterized his other undertakings. The daughters were educated at home; the family read together, entertained together, traveled together. Twain's career was thriving. *Roughing It* and *The Adventures of Tom Sawyer* were published. Twain founded his own publishing company, and then he made literary history by writing his great novel, *The Adventures of Huckleberry Finn*.

But troubles soon overtook him in his professional and personal life. He squandered a fortune on the Paige typesetter, an ingenious but impractical machine. His daughter Susy died of spinal meningitis. His beloved wife "Livy" suffered an attack of asthma in 1902 and, never strong, died two years later. A second daughter, Jean, suffered epileptic attacks and died during a seizure in 1909. With the marriage of his last surviving daughter in the same year, Twain was left truly alone, enfeebled by the heart disease that finally claimed his life in April of 1910.

In his lifetime, Twain was famous and popular as a humorist, but his work was taken seriously only by a handful of friends. It is only since his death that Twain has been acknowledged as a giant of American literature, of whom William Faulkner said, "all of us . . . are his heirs."

These excerpts from *Life on the Mississippi* were written when Twain's career was still on the rise. He had already begun writing *Huckleberry Finn*, but he had difficulties with the novel and put it aside for a while. Twain turned instead to writing about his adolescent years as a riverboat pilot—years in which, as he romantically remembered them, he seemed to be "the only unfettered and entirely independent human being that lived upon the earth."

In the chapters that follow, Twain is still an apprentice, or a "cub," on the steamboat. His chief is named Bixby.

Twain's writings are especially lively when they are read aloud. Using at least three readers, read aloud from "I still remember" on page 472 to the end of the chapter on page 476.

LIFE ON THE MISSISSIPPI

Mark Twain

I Take a Few Extra Lessons

The figure that comes before me oftenest, out of the shadows of that vanished time, is that of Brown, of the steamer *Pennsylvania*—the man referred to in a former chapter, whose memory was so good and tiresome. He was a middle-aged, long, slim, bony, smooth-shaven, horse-faced, ignorant, stingy, malicious, snarling, fault-finding, mote-magnifying[1] tyrant. I early got the habit of coming on watch[2] with dread at my heart. No matter how good a time I might have been having with the off watch below, and no matter how high my spirits might be when I started aloft, my soul became lead in my body the moment I approached the pilothouse.

I still remember the first time I ever entered the presence of that man. The boat had backed out from St. Louis and was "straightening down." I ascended to the pilothouse in high feather and very proud to be semiofficially a member of the executive family of so fast and famous a boat. Brown was at the wheel. I paused in the middle of the room, all fixed to make my bow, but Brown did not look around. I thought he took a furtive glance at me out of the corner of his eye, but as not even this notice was repeated, I judged I had been mistaken. By this time he was picking his way among some dangerous "breaks" abreast the woodyards; therefore it would not be proper to interrupt him; so I stepped softly to the high bench and took a seat.

There was silence for ten minutes; then my new boss turned and inspected me deliberately and painstakingly from head to heel for about—as it seemed to me—a quarter of an hour. After which he removed his countenance and I saw it no more for some seconds; then it came around once more, and this question greeted me:

"Are you Horace Bixby's cub?"

"Yes, sir."

After this there was a pause and another inspection. Then:

"What's your name?"

I told him. He repeated it after me. It was probably the only thing he ever forgot; for although I was with him many months he never addressed himself to me in any other way than "Here!" and then his command followed.

"Where was you born?"

"In Florida, Missouri."

A pause. Then:

"Dern sight better stayed there!"

By means of a dozen or so of pretty direct questions, he pumped my family history out of me.

The leads[3] were going now in the first crossing. This interrupted the inquest. When the leads had been laid in, he resumed:

"How long you been on the river?"

I told him. After a pause:

"Where'd you get them shoes?"

I gave him the information.

"Hold up your foot!"

I did so. He stepped back, examined the shoe minutely and contemptuously, scratching his head thoughtfully, tilting his high sugar-loaf hat well forward to facilitate the operation, then ejaculated, "Well, I'll be dod derned!" and returned to his wheel.

What occasion there was to be dod derned about it is a thing which is still as much of a mystery to me now as it was then. It must have been all of fifteen minutes—fifteen minutes of dull, homesick silence—before that long horse-face swung round upon me again—and then what a change! It was as red as fire, and every muscle in it was working. Now came this shriek:

"Here! You going to set there all day?"

I lit in the middle of the floor, shot there by the electric suddenness of the surprise. As soon as I could get my voice I said apologetically: "I have had no orders, sir."

"You've had no *orders*! My, what a fine bird we are! We must have *orders*! Our father was a *gentleman*—owned slaves—and *we've* been to *school*. Yes, we are a gentleman, *too*, and got to have *orders*! ORDERS, is it? ORDERS is what you want! Dod dern my skin, *I'll* learn you to swell yourself up and blow around *here* about your dod

---

1. **mote-magnifying:** in other words, Brown makes even a mote, or speck, seem like something much greater.
2. **watch:** period of duty.

3. **leads** (ledz): weighted lines used to measure the depth of the river.

derned *orders*! G'way from the wheel!'' (I had approached it without knowing it.)

I moved back a step or two and stood as in a dream, all my senses stupefied by this frantic assault.

"What you standing there for? Take that ice pitcher down to the texas-tender![4] Come, move along, and don't you be all day about it!"

The moment I got back to the pilothouse Brown said:

"Here! What was you doing down there all this time?"

"I couldn't find the texas-tender; I had to go all the way to the pantry."

"Derned likely story! Fill up the stove."

I proceeded to do so. He watched me like a cat. Presently he shouted:

"Put down that shovel! Derndest numbskull I ever saw—ain't even got sense enough to load up a stove."

All through the watch this sort of thing went on. Yes, and the subsequent watches were much like it during a stretch of months. As I have said, I soon got the habit of coming on duty with dread. The moment I was in the presence, even in the darkest night, I could feel those yellow eyes upon me and knew their owner was watching for a pretext to spit out some venom on me. Preliminarily he would say:

"Here! Take the wheel."

Two minutes later:

"*Where* in the nation you going to? Pull her down! pull her down!"

After another moment:

"Say! You going to hold her all day? Let her go—meet her! meet her!"

Then he would jump from the bench, snatch the wheel from me, and meet her himself, pouring out wrath upon me all the time.

George Ritchie was the other pilot's cub. He was having good times now; for his boss, George Ealer, was as kindhearted as Brown wasn't. Ritchie had steered for Brown the season before; consequently, he knew exactly how to entertain himself and plague me, all by the one operation.

---

4. **texas-tender:** a person responsible for duties on the "texas," the officers' quarters of a riverboat (so called because it made up the largest area of the boat).

Whenever I took the wheel for a moment on Ealer's watch, Ritchie would sit back on the bench and play Brown, with continual ejaculations of "Snatch her! snatch her! Derndest mudcat I ever saw!" "Here! Where are you going *now*? Going to run over that snag?" "Pull her *down*! Don't you hear me? Pull her *down*!" "There she goes! *Just* as I expected! I *told* you not to cramp that reef. G'way from the wheel!"

So I always had a rough time of it, no matter whose watch it was; and sometimes it seemed to me that Ritchie's good-natured badgering was pretty nearly as aggravating as Brown's dead-earnest nagging.

I often wanted to kill Brown, but this would not answer. A cub had to take everything his boss gave in the way of vigorous comment and criticism; and we all believed that there was a United States law making it a penitentiary offense to strike or threaten a pilot who was on duty. However, I could *imagine* myself killing Brown; there was no law against that; and that was the thing I used always to do the moment I was abed. Instead of going over my river in my mind, as was my duty, I threw business aside for pleasure and killed Brown. I killed Brown every night for months; not in old, stale, commonplace ways, but in new and picturesque ones—ways that were sometimes surprising for freshness of design and ghastliness of situation and environment.

Brown was *always* watching for a pretext to find fault; and if he could find no plausible pretext, he would invent one. He would scold you for shaving a shore and for not shaving it; for hugging a bar and for not hugging it; for "pulling down" when not invited and for *not* pulling down when not invited; for firing up without orders and for waiting *for* orders. In a word, it was his invariable rule to find fault with *everything* you did; and another invariable rule of his was to throw all his remarks (to you) into the form of an insult.

One day we were approaching New Madrid, bound down and heavily laden. Brown was at one side of the wheel, steering; I was at the other, standing by to "pull down" or "shove up." He cast a furtive glance at me every now and then. I had long ago learned what that meant; viz., he was trying to invent a trap for me. I wondered what shape it was going to take. By and by he stepped back from the wheel and said in his usual snarly way:

"Here! See if you've got gumption enough to round her to."

This was simply *bound* to be a success; nothing could prevent it; for he had never allowed me to round the boat to before; consequently, no matter how I might do the thing, he could find free fault with it. He stood back there with his greedy eye on me, and the result was what might have been foreseen: I lost my head in a quarter of a minute and didn't know what I was about; I started too early to bring the boat around, but detected a green gleam of joy in Brown's eye and corrected my mistake. I started around once more while too high up, but corrected myself again in time. I made other false moves and still managed to save myself; but at last I grew so confused and anxious that I tumbled into the very worst blunder of all— I got too far *down* before beginning to fetch the boat around. Brown's chance was come.

His face turned red with passion; he made one bound, hurled me across the house with a sweep of his arm, spun the wheel down, and began to pour out a stream of vituperation[5] upon me which lasted till he was out of breath. In the course of this speech he called me all the different kinds of hard names he could think of, and once or twice I thought he was even going to swear—but he had never done that, and he didn't this time. "Dod dern" was the nearest he ventured to the luxury of swearing, for he had been brought up with a wholesome respect for future fire and brimstone.

That was an uncomfortable hour; for there was a big audience on the hurricane deck. When I went to bed that night, I killed Brown in seventeen different ways—all of them new.

Brown and I
Exchange Compliments

Two trips later I got into serious trouble. Brown was steering; I was "pulling down." My younger brother appeared on the hurricane deck and shouted to Brown to stop at some landing or other, a mile or so below. Brown gave no intimation that he had heard anything. But that was his way: he never condescended to take notice of an underclerk. The wind was blowing; Brown was deaf (although he always pretended he wasn't), and I very much doubted if he had heard the order. If I had had two heads, I would have spoken; but as I had only one, it seemed judicious to take care of it; so I kept still.

Presently, sure enough, we went sailing by that plantation. Captain Klinefelter appeared on the deck and said:

"Let her come around, sir, let her come around. Didn't Henry tell you to land here?"

"*No,* sir!"

"I sent him up to do it."

"He *did* come up; and that's all the good it done, the dod-derned fool. He never said anything."

"Didn't *you* hear him?" asked the captain of me.

Of course I didn't want to be mixed up in this business, but there was no way to avoid it; so I said:

"Yes, sir."

I knew what Brown's next remark would be, before he uttered it. It was:

"Shut your mouth! You never heard anything of the kind."

I closed my mouth, according to instructions. An hour later Henry entered the pilothouse, unaware of what had been going on. He was a thoroughly inoffensive boy, and I was sorry to see him come, for I knew Brown would have no pity on him. Brown began, straightway:

"Here! Why didn't you tell me we'd got to land at that plantation?"

"I did tell you, Mr. Brown."

"It's a lie!"

I said:

"You lie, yourself. He did tell you."

Brown glared at me in unaffected surprise; and for as much as a moment he was entirely speechless; then he shouted to me:

"I'll attend to your case in half a minute!" Then to Henry, "And you leave the pilothouse; out with you!"

It was pilot law and must be obeyed. The boy

---

5. **vituperation** (vi·tōō'pə·rā'shən): abusive language.

started out and even had his foot on the upper step outside the door, when Brown, with a sudden access of fury, picked up a ten-pound lump of coal and sprang after him; but I was between, with a heavy stool, and I hit Brown a good honest blow which stretched him out.

I had committed the crime of crimes—I had lifted my hand against a pilot on duty! I supposed I was booked for the penitentiary sure and couldn't be booked any surer if I went on and squared my long account with this person while I had the chance; consequently I stuck to him and pounded him with my fists a considerable time. I do not know how long, the pleasure of it probably made it seem longer than it really was; but in the end he struggled free and jumped up and sprang to the wheel: a very natural solicitude, for, all this time, here was this steamboat tearing down the river at the rate of fifteen miles an hour and nobody at the helm! However, Eagle Bend was two miles wide at this bank-full stage and correspondingly long and deep: and the boat was steering herself straight down the middle and taking no chances. Still, that was only luck—a body *might* have found her charging into the woods.

Perceiving at a glance that the *Pennsylvania* was in no danger, Brown gathered up the big spyglass, war-club fashion, and ordered me out of the pilothouse with more than Comanche bluster. But I was not afraid of him now; so, instead of going, I tarried and criticized his grammar. I reformed his ferocious speeches for him and put them into good English, calling his attention to the advantage of pure English over the bastard dialect of the Pennsylvania collieries[6] whence he was extracted. He could have done his part to admiration in a cross fire of mere vituperation, of course; but he was not equipped for this species of controversy; so he presently laid aside his glass and took the wheel, muttering and shaking his head; and I retired to the bench. The racket had brought everybody to the hurricane deck, and I trembled when I saw the old captain looking up from amid the crowd. I said to myself, "Now I *am* done for!" for although, as a rule, he was so fatherly and indulgent toward the boat's family, and so

patient of minor shortcomings, he could be stern enough when the fault was worth it.

I tried to imagine what he *would* do to a cub pilot who had been guilty of such a crime as mine, committed on a boat guard-deep with costly freight and alive with passengers. Our watch was nearly ended. I thought I would go and hide somewhere till I got a chance to slide ashore. So I slipped out of the pilothouse and down the steps and around to the texas door and was in the act of gliding within, when the captain confronted me! I dropped my head, and he stood over me in silence a moment or two, then said impressively:

"Follow me."

I dropped into his wake; he led the way to his parlor in the forward end of the texas. We were alone now. He closed the after door; then moved slowly to the forward one and closed that. He sat down; I stood before him. He looked at me some little time, then said:

"So you have been fighting Mr. Brown?"

I answered meekly:

"Yes, sir."

"Do you know that that is a very serious matter?"

"Yes, sir."

"Are you aware that this boat was plowing down the river fully five minutes with no one at the wheel?"

"Yes, sir."

"Did you strike him first?"

"Yes, sir."

"What with?"

"A stool, sir."

"Hard?"

"Middling, sir."

"Did it knock him down?"

"He—he fell, sir."

"Did you follow it up? Did you do anything further?"

"Yes, sir."

"What did you do?"

"Pounded him, sir."

"Pounded him?"

"Yes, sir."

"Did you pound him much? That is, severely?"

"One might call it that, sir, maybe."

"I'm deuced glad of it! Hark ye, never mention

---

6. **collieries** (kăl′yər·ēz): coal mines.

that I said that. You have been guilty of a great crime; and don't you ever be guilty of it again, on this boat. *But*—lay for him ashore! Give him a good sound thrashing, do you hear? I'll pay the expenses. Now go—and mind you, not a word of this to anybody. Clear out with you! You've been guilty of a great crime, you whelp!''

I slid out, happy with the sense of a close shave and a mighty deliverance; and I heard him laughing to himself and slapping his fat thighs after I had closed his door.

When Brown came off watch he went straight to the captain, who was talking with some passengers on the boiler deck, and demanded that I be put ashore in New Orleans—and added:

''I'll never turn a wheel on this boat again while that cub stays.''

The captain said:

''But he needn't come round when you are on watch, Mr. Brown.''

''I won't even stay on the same boat with him. *One* of us has got to go ashore.''

''Very well,'' said the captain, ''let it be yourself,'' and resumed his talk with the passengers.

During the brief remainder of the trip I knew how an emancipated slave feels, for I was an emancipated slave myself. While we lay at landings I listened to George Ealer's flute or to his readings from his two Bibles, that is to say, Goldsmith and Shakespeare, or I played chess with him—and would have beaten him sometimes, only he always took back his last move and ran the game out differently.

A Catastrophe

We lay three days in New Orleans, but the captain did not succeed in finding another pilot, so he proposed that I should stand a daylight watch and leave the night watches to George Ealer. But I was afraid; I had never stood a watch of any sort by myself, and I believed I should be sure to get into trouble in the head of some chute[7] or ground the boat in a near cut through some bar or other. Brown remained in his place, but he would not travel with me. So the captain gave me an order on the captain of the *A.T. Lacey* for a passage to St. Louis, and said he would find a new pilot there and my steersman's berth could then be resumed. The *Lacey* was to leave a couple of days after the *Pennsylvania*.

The night before the *Pennsylvania* left, Henry and I sat chatting on a freight pile on the levee till midnight. The subject of the chat, mainly, was one which I think we had not exploited before—steamboat disasters. One was then on its way to us, little as we suspected it; the water which was to make the steam which should cause it was washing past some point fifteen hundred miles up the river while we talked—but it would arrive at the right time and the right place. We doubted if persons not clothed with authority were of much use in cases of disaster and attendant panic, still they might be of *some* use; so we decided that if a disaster ever fell within our experience we would at least stick to the boat and give such minor service as chance might throw in the way. Henry remembered this, afterward, when the disaster came, and acted accordingly.

The *Lacey* started up the river two days behind the *Pennsylvania*. We touched at Greenville, Mississippi, a couple of days out, and somebody shouted:

''The *Pennsylvania* is blown up at Ship Island, and a hundred and fifty lives lost!''

At Napoleon, Arkansas, the same evening, we got an extra, issued by a Memphis paper, which gave some particulars. It mentioned my brother and said he was not hurt.

Further up the river we got a later extra. My brother was again mentioned, but this time as being hurt beyond help. We did not get full details of the catastrophe until we reached Memphis. This is the sorrowful story:

It was six o'clock on a hot summer morning. The *Pennsylvania* was creeping along, north of Ship Island, about sixty miles below Memphis, on a half head of steam, towing a wood-flat[8] which was fast being emptied. George Ealer was in the pilothouse—alone, I think; the second engineer

---

7. **chute** (shoōt): the swift-running part of a river.

8. **wood-flat:** a large raft for carrying loads of chopped firewood.

and a striker had the watch in the engine room; the second mate had the watch on deck; George Black, Mr. Wood, and my brother, clerks, were asleep, as were also Brown and the head engineer, the carpenter, the chief mate, and one striker; Captain Klinefelter was in the barber's chair, and the barber was preparing to shave him. There were a good many cabin passengers aboard and three or four hundred deck passengers—so it was said at the time—and not very many of them were astir. The wood being nearly all out of the flat now, Ealer rang to "come ahead" full of steam, and the next moment four of the eight boilers exploded with a thunderous crash, and the whole forward third of the boat was hoisted toward the sky! The main part of the mass, with the chimneys, dropped upon the boat again, a mountain of riddled and chaotic rubbish—and then, after a little, fire broke out.

Many people were flung considerable distances and fell in the river; among these were Mr. Wood and my brother and the carpenter. The carpenter was still stretched upon his mattress when he struck the water seventy-five feet from the boat. Brown, the pilot, and George Black, chief clerk, were never seen or heard of after the explosion. The barber's chair, with Captain Klinefelter in it and unhurt, was left with its back overhanging vacancy—everything forward of it, floor and all had disappeared; and the stupefied barber, who was also unhurt, stood with one toe projecting over space, still stirring his lather unconsciously and saying not a word.

When George Ealer saw the chimneys plunging aloft in front of him, he knew what the matter was; so he muffled his face in the lapels of his coat and pressed both hands there tightly to keep this protection in its place so that no steam could get to his nose or mouth. He had ample time to attend to these details while he was going up and returning. He presently landed on top of the unexploded boilers, forty feet below the former pilothouse, accompanied by his wheel and a rain of other stuff, and enveloped in a cloud of scalding steam. All of the many who breathed that steam died; none escaped. But Ealer breathed none of it. He made his way to the free air as quickly as he could; and when the steam cleared away he returned and climbed up on the boilers again and patiently hunted out each and every one of his chessmen and the several joints of his flute.

By this time the fire was beginning to threaten. Shrieks and groans filled the air. A great many persons had been scalded, a great many crippled; the explosion had driven an iron crowbar through one man's body—I think they said he was a priest. He did not die at once, and his sufferings were very dreadful. A young French naval cadet of fifteen, son of a French admiral, was fearfully scalded, but bore his tortures manfully. Both mates were badly scalded, but they stood to their posts, nevertheless. They drew the wood-boat aft, and they and the captain fought back the frantic herd of frightened immigrants till the wounded could be brought there and placed in safety first.

When Mr. Wood and Henry fell in the water they struck out for shore, which was only a few hundred yards away; but Henry presently said he believed he was not hurt (what an unaccountable error!) and therefore would swim back to the boat and help save the wounded. So they parted and Henry returned.

By this time the fire was making fierce headway, and several persons who were imprisoned under the ruins were begging piteously for help. All efforts to conquer the fire proved fruitless, so the buckets were presently thrown aside and the officers fell to with axes and tried to cut the prisoners out. A striker was one of the captives; he said he was not injured, but could not free himself, and when he saw that the fire was likely to drive away the workers he begged that someone would shoot him, and thus save him from the more dreadful death. The fire did drive the axmen away, and they had to listen, helpless, to this poor fellow's supplications till the flames ended his miseries.

The fire drove all into the wood-flat that could be accommodated there; it was cut adrift then, and it and the burning steamer floated down the river toward Ship Island. They moored the flat at the head of the island, and there, unsheltered from the blazing sun, the half-naked occupants had to remain, without food or stimulants, or help for their hurts, during the rest of the day. A steamer came along, finally, and carried the unfortunates

The Mississippi in Time of War (detail).
Lithograph by Currier and Ives (1865).

(57.300.51) The Harry T. Peters Collection.
Museum of the City of New York.

to Memphis, and there the most lavish assistance was at once forthcoming. By this time Henry was insensible. The physicians examined his injuries and saw that they were fatal, and naturally turned their main attention to patients who could be saved.

Forty of the wounded were placed upon pallets on the floor of a great public hall, and among these was Henry. There the ladies of Memphis came every day, with flowers, fruits, and dainties and delicacies of all kinds, and there they remained and nursed the wounded. All the physicians stood watches there, and all the medical students; and the rest of the town furnished money or whatever else was wanted. And Memphis knew how to do all these things well; for many a disaster like the *Pennsylvania*'s had happened near her doors, and she was experienced, above all other cities on the river, in the gracious office of the Good Samaritan.

The sight I saw when I entered that large hall was new and strange to me. Two long rows of prostrate forms—more than forty in all—and every face and head a shapeless wad of loose raw cotton. It was a gruesome spectacle. I watched there six days and nights, and a very melancholy experience it was. There was one daily incident which was peculiarly depressing; this was the removal of the doomed to a chamber apart. It was done in order that the *morale* of the other patients might not be injuriously affected by seeing one of their number in the death agony. The fated one was always carried out with as little stir as possible, and the stretcher was always hidden from sight by a wall of assistants; but no matter: everybody knew what that cluster of bent forms, with its muffled step and its slow movement, meant; and all eyes watched it wistfully, and a shudder went abreast of it like a wave.

I saw many poor fellows removed to the "death room," and saw them no more afterward. But I saw our chief mate carried thither more than once. His hurts were frightful, especially his scalds. He was clothed in linseed oil and raw cotton to his waist, and resembled nothing human. He was often out of his mind; and then his pains would make him rave and shout and sometimes shriek. Then, after a period of dumb exhaustion, his disordered imagination would suddenly transform the great apartment into a forecastle and the hurrying throng of nurses into the crew; and he would come to a sitting posture and shout, "Hump yourselves, *hump* yourselves, you petrifactions, snail-bellies, pallbearers; going to be all *day* getting that hatful of freight out?" and supplement this explosion with a firmament-obliterating eruption of profanity which nothing could stay or stop till his crater was empty. And now and then while these frenzies possessed him, he would tear off handfuls of the cotton and expose his cooked flesh to view. It was horrible. It was bad for the others, of course—this noise and these exhibitions; so the doctors tried to give him morphine to quiet him. But, in his mind or out of it, he would not take it. He said his wife had been killed by that treacherous drug, and he would die before he would take it. He suspected that the doctors were concealing it in his ordinary medicines and in his water—so he ceased from putting either to his lips. Once, when

he had been without water during two sweltering days, he took the dipper in his hand, and the sight of the limpid fluid and the misery of his thirst tempted him almost beyond his strength; but he mastered himself and threw it away, and after that he allowed no more to be brought near him. Three times I saw him carried to the death room, insensible and supposed to be dying; but each time he revived, cursed his attendants, and demanded to be taken back. He lived to be mate of a steamboat again.

But he was the only one who went to the death room and returned alive. Dr. Peyton, a principal physician, and rich in all the attributes that go to constitute high and flawless character, did all that educated judgment and trained skill could do for Henry; but, as the newspapers had said in the beginning, his hurts were past help. On the evening of the sixth day his wandering mind busied itself with matters far away, and his nerveless fingers "picked at his coverlet." His hour had struck; we bore him to the death room, poor boy.

Responding to the Autobiography

Analyzing the Autobiography

Identifying Facts

1. The cubs could not strike or threaten a pilot who was on duty. How did Twain use his imagination to take revenge on Brown?
2. In the chapter called "Brown and I Exchange Compliments," what is it that finally makes the boy act, in fact as well as in his imagination, and hit Brown with the stool?
3. Ironically, according to the opening of "The Catastrophe," how might the argument with Brown have saved Twain's life?
4. In reporting on the explosion of the ship's boilers, Twain relates a few **human-interest stories** to help us understand the horror and freakishness of the disaster in human terms. What happened to the barber and his customer, to George Ealer, to the chief mate, and to Henry?
5. What happened to Brown in the explosion? Does

Twain directly express any feelings about his enemy's fate?

Interpreting Meanings

6. Twain's portrait of Brown on page 472 begins with a long series of adjectives. Which adjectives in this list are simply descriptive? Which ones also pass **judgment** on Brown?
7. Explain the **irony** in the title "Brown and I Exchange Compliments." What would you say Twain and Brown really exchanged?
8. Twain uses **exaggeration** to make a comic story out of his conflict with Brown. But the report of his brother's death is, on the whole, told in a straightforward, **objective** way. What is Twain's **purpose** in each of these two accounts—his experiences with Brown and the steamboat explosion? What response does Twain want you to have to each episode?
9. Twain **alludes** to a parable in the New Testament

when he says on page 478 that the city of Memphis was experienced in the office of "the Good Samaritan." Explain what this allusion means. In your own experience, have any other cities or groups of people also acted as "Good Samaritans" in times of disaster?

Writing About the Autobiography

A Creative Response

1. **Writing a Report with a Human-Interest Story.** Write a report on some momentous event that you know something about. In the style of any good reporter, you will have to tell **what** happened, **when** it happened, **where** it happened, **whom** it happened to, and **why** it happened. Then, to make the event understandable in human terms, include at least one human-interest story to show how the event affected an ordinary person or family.

A Critical Response

2. **Analyzing a Character.** In these first two chapters, Twain brings a character from his Mississippi days to vivid life. Look at how Twain describes Brown, look at what Brown says, and look at how Brown acts. In a paragraph, write a character analysis of Brown. In particular, give your opinion on *why* Brown hated Twain so much. There are clues in Brown's speeches.
3. **Interviewing a Writer.** Suppose you were assigned to interview Twain (first suppose he is still alive). Write out four questions you would ask the great man about his experiences on the Mississippi River. Include one question about truth and fiction.

Analyzing Language and Vocabulary

New Words from Old Ones

When steamboats were invented, a word was needed for the person who steered the ship. The word *pilot* was already in use in sea terminology— it referred to the navigator or the helmsman of sailing vessels. Those ships had taken the word *pilot* from a Greek word meaning "the one who handles the ship's rudder" (the rudder controls direction). When airplanes were invented, the word *pilot* was used again and adapted to a new technology—even though, by this time, the pilot had nothing to do with the sea.

When people need new words for new inventions or experiences, they often turn to the old Latin and Greek roots. For example, *astronauts* did not exist until the twentieth century. To describe these new rocket pilots, the space scientists used two Greek words: *astro,* meaning "stars," and *nautos,* meaning "sailor." These space pilots, then, are "sailors to the stars."

Here are some terms that have been made up or adapted for another new development in contemporary life: computer science. Are all the words defined in a dictionary? What Latin or Greek root is each word built on? What affixes have been added to some of the words to affect their meanings?

1. diskette
2. terminal
3. menu
4. interface
5. microcomputer
6. multifunction
7. digital

Suppose scientists discover a new star or a new galaxy and need a name for it. Or suppose technologists develop a new computer and need a name for it. Here are some Greek and Latin word roots that might be used for such purposes. If you have a knack for word-making, you might try to make up a name of your own. Feel free to combine the following roots with the ones you discovered in the previous exercise.

neo-	"new"
aster-, astro-	"star"
luc-, lum-	"light"
sol-, soli-	"alone, lonely, or singular"
vol-	"turn"
ortho-	"correct"
meter-	"measure"
-onym, onomato-	"word"
nom-	"management or law"
crypt-	"secret"

Punctuating Dialogue

Literary Model

This is an episode from Shirley Jackson's humorous memoir *Life Among the Savages*. The "savages" are her three children. At this point in the story, they are greeting their mother upon her return from the hospital with a new baby.

"There are the children on the porch," I said.

"Beginning to seem like Christmas," my husband said to the taxi driver as I got out, and the taxi driver said, "Snow before morning."

Jannie's hair had obviously not been combed since I left, and as I went up the front walk I was resolving to make her tell immediately where she had hidden the hairbrush. She was wearing her dearest summer sundress, and she was barefoot. Laurie needed a haircut, and he had on his old sneakers, one of which no longer laces, but fastens with a safety pin; I had made a particular point of throwing those sneakers into the garbage can before I left. Sally had chocolate all over her face and *she* was wearing Laurie's fur hat. All three of them were leaning over the porch rail, still and expectant.

I tried to catch hold of all three of them at once, but they evaded me skillfully and ran at their father. "Did you bring it?" Jannie demanded, "did you bring it, did you bring it, did you bring it?"

"Is *that* it you're carrying?" Laurie demanded sternly, "that *little* thing?"

"Did you *bring* it?" Jannie insisted.

"Come indoors and I'll show you," their father said.

They followed him into the living room and stood in a solemn row by the couch. "Now don't touch," their father said, and they nodded all together. They watched while he carefully set the bundle down on the couch and unwrapped it.

Then, into the stunned silence which followed, Sally finally said, "What is it?"

"It's a baby," said their father, with an edge of nervousness to his voice, "it's a baby boy and its name is Barry."

"What's a baby?" Sally asked me.

"It's pretty small," Laurie said doubtfully. "Is that the best you could get?"

"I tried to get another, a bigger one," I said with irritation, "but the doctor said this was the only one left."

"My goodness," said Jannie, "what are we going to do with *that?* Anyway," she said, "you're back."

Suddenly she and Sally were both climbing onto my lap at once, and Laurie came closer and allowed me to kiss him swiftly on the cheek; I discovered that I could reach around all three of them, something I had not been able to do for some time.

"Well," Laurie said, anxious to terminate this sentimental scene, "so now we've got this baby. Do you think it will grow?" he asked his father.

"It's got very small feet," Jannie said. "I really believe they're *too* small."

"Well, if you don't like it we can *always* take it back," said their father.

"Oh, we like it all right, I guess," Laurie said comfortingly. "It's only that I guess we figured on something a little bigger."

"What *is* it?" asked Sally, unconvinced. She put out a tentative finger and touched one toe. "Is this its foot?"

"Please start calling it 'him,'" I said.

"Him?" said Sally. "Him?"

"Hi, Barry," said Laurie, leaning down to look directly into one open blue eye, "hi, Barry, hi, Barry, hi, Barry."

"Hi, Barry," said Jannie.

"Hi, Barry," said Sally. "Is this your foot?"

"I suppose it'll cry a lot?" Laurie asked his father, man to man.

His father shrugged. "Not much else it *can* do," he pointed out.

"I remember Jannie cried all the time," Laurie went on.

"I did not," Jannie said. "You were the one cried all the time."

"Did you get it at the hospital?" Sally asked. She moved Barry's foot up and down and he curled his toes.

"Yes," I said.

"Why didn't you take me?" Sally asked.

"I took you the last time," I said.

"What did you say its name was?" Sally asked.

"Barry," I said.

"Barry?"

"Barry."

"Where did you get it?"

"Well," Laurie said. He sighed and stretched. "Better take a look at those Greek tetradrachms," he said.

"Right," said his father, rising.

"Jannie, you go find that hairbrush," I said.

Laurie, on his way out of the room, stopped next to me and hesitated, obviously trying to think of something congratulatory to say. "I guess it *will* be nice for you, though," he said at last. "Something to keep you busy now we're all grown up."

—from *Life Among the Savages*, Shirley Jackson

A Note on Punctuating Dialogue

Dialogue consists of the exact words of two or more speakers. In short stories, novels, and nonfiction writing, the exact words of speakers always appear in quotation marks.

Dialogue that is not carefully paragraphed, punctuated, and capitalized can be confusing to the reader. For clarity, always follow these rules:

1. A direct quotation begins with a capital letter.
2. When a quoted sentence is divided by an expression like *he said*, the second part of the sentence begins with a small letter. ("Bug off," he said, "or I'll scream.")
3. A direct quotation is set off from the rest of the sentence by a comma, a question mark, or an exclamation point. ("School's out!" Lee shrieked. "I'm OK," Henry said.)
4. Commas and periods are always placed inside closing quotation marks. Question marks and exclamation points are placed inside the quotation marks if the quotation itself is a question or exclamation; otherwise they are placed outside the closing quotes. ("Shall I go home?" Did you say "go home"?)
5. When you write dialogue, begin a new paragraph every time the speaker changes.

Examining the Writer's Techniques

Work with a partner to answer the following questions on Shirley Jackson's use of dialogue:

1. How many different speakers are quoted in this passage? Is it difficult to follow who is speaking? How does the author let you know when the speaker changes?
2. What does Jackson achieve by using expressions such as "Jannie *insisted*" or "Laurie *demanded*," rather than repeating the verb *said?* In what other ways does Jackson give information about her speakers?
3. Suppose you were teaching a younger student how to punctuate dialogue. Go back through Jackson's story and find examples to illustrate each of the five rules of dialogue cited here.

Punctuating Dialogue in Your Writing

Writing a Dialogue. Work with a partner and write a story in which many people speak. Before you write, decide on the issue or topic that will be discussed (a party; what to do with a thousand dollars; what to wear to school). Try to reproduce the way real people speak. Exchange stories. Have you followed all the rules for punctuating dialogue?

Literature & Language

Combining Sentences

Literary Model

This passage is from Antonia Fraser's best-selling biography of Mary Stuart, the ill-fated Queen of Scotland (1542–1587). As this extract opens, Mary has been imprisoned for nineteen years by her cousin, Queen Elizabeth I of England. (Elizabeth saw her Catholic cousin Mary as a threat to her throne and to the Protestant succession in England.) This passage opens on the day Mary is to be beheaded.

The time had come for Jane Kennedy to bind the queen's eyes with the white cloth embroidered in gold which Mary had herself chosen for the purpose the night before. Jane Kennedy first kissed the cloth and then wrapped it gently round her mistress's eyes and over her head so that her hair was covered as by a white turban and only the neck left completely bare. The two women then withdrew from the stage. The queen, without even now the faintest sign of fear, knelt down once more on the cushion in front of the block. She recited aloud in Latin the Psalm *In te Domino confido, non confundar in aeternum*—"In you Lord is my trust, Let me never be confounded"—and then feeling for the block, she laid her head down upon it, placing her chin carefully with both her hands, so that if one of the executioners had not moved them back they too would have lain in the direct line of the ax. The queen stretched out her arms and legs and cried: "*In manus tuas, Domine, confide spiritum meum*"—"Into your hands, O Lord, I commend my spirit"—three or four times. When the queen was lying there quite motionless, Bull's assistant put his hand on her body to steady it for the blow. Even so, the first blow, as it fell, missed the neck and cut into the back of the head. The queen's lips moved, and her servants thought they heard the whispered words: "Sweet Jesus." The second blow severed the neck, all but the smallest sinew, and this was severed by using the ax as a saw. It was about ten o'clock in the morning of Wednesday,

8 February, the queen of Scots being then aged forty-four years old and in the nineteenth year of her English captivity.

In the great hall of Fortheringhay, before the wondering eyes of the crowd, the executioner now held aloft the dead woman's head, crying out as he did so: "God Save the Queen." The lips still moved and continued to do so for a quarter of an hour after the death. But at this moment, weird and moving spectacle, the auburn tresses in his hand came apart from the skull, and the head itself fell to the ground. It was seen that Mary Stuart's own hair had in fact been quite gray and very short at the time of her death: for her execution she had chosen to wear a wig. The spectators were stunned by the unexpected sight and remained silent. It was left to the dean of Peterborough to call out strongly: "So perish all the Queen's enemies," and for Kent, standing over the corpse, to echo: "Such be the end of all the Queen's, and all the Gospel's, enemies." But Shrewsbury could not speak, and his face was wet with tears.

It was now time for the executioners to strip the body of its remaining adornments before handing it over to the embalmers. But at this point a strange and pathetic memorial to that devotion which Mary Stuart had always aroused in those who knew her intimately was discovered: her little lap dog, a Skye terrier, who had managed to accompany her into the hall under her long skirts, where her servants had been turned away, had now crept out from beneath her petticoat and in its distress had stationed itself piteously beneath the severed head and the shoulders of the body. Nor would it be coaxed away, but steadfastly and uncomprehendingly clung to the solitary thing it could find in the hall which still reminded it of its dead mistress. To all others save this poor animal, the sad corpse lying now so still on the floor of the stage, in its red clothes against which the blood stains scarcely showed, with its face now sunken to that of an old woman in the harsh disguise of death, bore little resemblance to her whom they had known only a short while before as Mary Queen of Scots. The spirit had fled the body. The chain was loosed to let the captive go.

—from *Mary Queen of Scots*,
Antonia Fraser

A Note on Sentence Style

To show the relationships among their ideas and to create a pleasing rhythm, good writers will use a variety of sentence structures and lengths. Less competent writers, on the other hand, often use a series of short, choppy, subject-first sentences, such as these:

The queen was lying there. She was quite motionless. Bull's assistant put his hand on her body. He steadied it for the blow. The first blow fell. It missed the neck. It cut into the back of the head.

Compare these sentences with Antonia Fraser's account of the same episode:

When the queen was lying there quite motionless, Bull's assistant put his hand on her body to steady it for the blow. Even so, the first blow, as it fell, missed the neck and cut into the back of the head.

The process by which the first passage above was converted into the second is called sentence combining. **Sentence combining** involves combining words, phrases, clauses, and even whole sentences, to form longer, more complex units. This process can be used to vary the rhythm and the emphasis of a passage. It can also be used to clarify relationships

and time sequences. In Fraser's version of the last sentence, for example, the phrase "the first blow" is set off with commas near the beginning of the sentence for dramatic emphasis. Fraser's first sentence tells *when* the assistant put his hand on the Queen's body and *why* he did so. (It clarifies a time sequence and a cause-and-effect relationship.)

Examining the Writer's Style

Work with a partner to study Antonia Fraser's sentence style.

1. Break down the sentence beginning "She recited aloud," in the first paragraph, into as many short, simple sentences as you can. Then try to combine these simple sentences differently from the way Fraser combined them.
2. Find examples in the passage of simple, subject-first sentences. How many of them are there? Read them aloud. Why do you think Fraser chose to use simple sentences where she did? (Are they dramatic?)
3. Which long sentences clarify relationships between events? Which clarify time sequences?
4. Examine another one of the very long sentences in the passage. Do you think the sentence would have been more effective if it had been broken down into shorter units? Read the long sentence aloud. Where would you pause? What words would you emphasize? Does the sentence sound "good" when it's read aloud?

Combining Sentences in Your Writing

Writing About an Historical Event. Research an event in American history that interests you, such as the death of Dr. Martin Luther King, Jr., the Boston Tea Party, or the first landing of astronauts on the moon. Write a dramatic, detailed account of the event. Use sentence-combining techniques to vary the rhythm of your writing and to clarify relationships and time sequences.

DISTINGUISHING FACTS FROM OPINION

Writing Assignment

In a three-paragraph essay, tell whether Joseph Lash uses only facts, or both facts and opinions, in presenting his account of Annie Sullivan's early life (see page 437). Concentrate on the first eight paragraphs only.

Background

A **fact** is a statement that can be verified somehow—by personal observation, or by reference to an authority (an encyclopedia, a journal, a history book, a newspaper, a letter, etc.). An **opinion** is a statement expressing a personal reaction or a belief about something. An opinion is simply one person's point of view, which another person may or may not agree with.

For example, in her essay on the giant water bug (page 377), Annie Dillard describes the death of the frog. At least two of her sentences do not give actual information at all; instead they reveal her feelings:

"It was a monstrous and terrifying thing. I gaped, bewildered, appalled."

Another observer of this event might feel differently about it. For example, a biologist observing the very same event and writing about it for the magazine *Science* might say this:

The attack was efficient and swift. I watched intently, fascinated.

On the other hand, Dillard's essay is also full of objective facts. Which of these statements from her essay are factual? Which express personal feelings or opinions?

1. "Frogs have an inelegant way of taking off from

invisible positions on the bank just ahead of your feet, in dire panic, emitting a froggy 'Yike!' "
2. "Incredibly, this amused me, and, incredibly, it amuses me still."
3. "It eats insects, tadpoles, fish, and frogs."
4. "Its grasping forelegs are mighty and hooked inward."

As you see from these examples from Dillard's essay, feelings and opinions do not have to be expressed directly. This is because certain words have **connotations**—feelings and associations that become attached to the words, and that can go way beyond their strict dictionary definitions. For example, connotation is at work when one newswriter describes a politician as "rigid" and another newswriter describes the same politician as "firm." The person who says *rigid* has an unfavorable opinion of the politician; the one who says *firm* has a good opinion. Both words mean that the politician is not easily persuaded to change his or her mind, but *firm* has more "favorable connotations" than *rigid* has. We often call words like these **loaded words**—they are loaded with feelings, often with prejudices and biases. Whenever they are used, they reveal the writer's or speaker's feelings; they do not necessarily reveal anything that is factually true.

Select five of these items and write two sentences about each one. In one sentence, use an adjective or figure of speech to reveal your own personal feelings about the item. In the other sentence, describe the item in a way that is factually true.

a. fish
b. spaghetti
c. perfume
d. ankle-strap sandals
e. cutoff jeans
f. cheerleaders
g. smokers
h. a haircut

Prewriting

To gather material for your essay, fill in the following chart. Quote directly from the essay. Under the "Opinions" column, be sure to list any loaded words you might find—words that force you to feel a certain way about a character, a situation, or a setting. (You might feel there are none.)

	Facts	Opinions
1. About Annie's early life.	1. 2. 3. 4. 5.	
2. About Annie herself.	1. 2. 3.	
3. About Annie's father.	1. 2. 3.	
4. About Annie's mother.	1. 2. 3.	
5. About the poorhouse.	1. 2. 3.	

Now look over your chart. Based on your close reading of the first eight paragraphs, would you say that you found mostly facts in Lash's biography or mostly opinions? Write a sentence stating what you found. This will be your thesis statement.

Writing

You can organize your material in this way:

1. **Paragraph 1:** Briefly cite ten important factual details you learned from the first eight paragraphs of the biography. Include details about Annie's early life, about Annie herself, about her father and mother, and about the poorhouse.
2. **Paragraph 2:** Cite any passages of the biography in which you think Lash reveals his personal opinions or feelings, not necessarily facts. Explain what these opinions or feelings are.
3. **Paragraph 3:** Sum up your reading of the biography by stating whether Lash's work consists chiefly of facts or chiefly of opinions. Give at least two reasons for your assessment.

Checklist for Revision
1. Have you cited the author and the title of the selection?
2. Have you included ten of the most important facts from the biography?
3. Have you cited any passages that reveal personal feelings or opinions?
4. If you didn't find any such passages, have you said so?
5. Have you summed up your assessment of the biography and stated it as your thesis statement?

'' 'Rigidity,' according to you. 'Solidity,' according to me.''

Drawing by Donald Reilly
© 1986, The New Yorker Magazine, Inc.

THE ELEMENTS OF DRAMA

The Drama by Honoré Daumier (1860). Oil.

UNIT FOUR

Robert Anderson

THE ELEMENTS OF DRAMA

An introduction by **Robert Anderson**

"All the world's a stage . . ."

—William Shakespeare

Eugene O'Neill, America's first great playwright, said that a play should reveal "the most intense basic human interrelationships." Perhaps this is why, over the years, so many playwrights have written about families. Probably nowhere else do we find such intense feelings as those we find within the family.

Even in the happiest families, we have conflicts, great and small. Parents have dreams for their children. Children have conflicting dreams of their own. Children need to belong to the family and to feel its support; they also need to be independent. There are the inevitable strains from living closely together. There are the problems of aging. The conflicts in a family range from mild, funny blow-ups, to battles royal which break families apart.

Memories of a Saint by René Magritte (1960). Oil.

Menil Foundation, Houston.

A scene from Neil Simon's *Lost in Yonkers* (1991), a dark comedy based on the writer's own childhood.

Conflict: The Basis of Drama

Let's imagine a typical family situation:

> Everything is peaceful in the Norton family's home. They have just finished dinner. Then Sara starts the trouble: she tells her brother that she is going to ask for the family car tonight. Her brother, knowing that Sara disobeyed her parents and kept the car out too late the night before, feels a sense of dread and warns Sara not to ask for it. But Sara is going ahead. It is important to her. She fears she might lose her friends if she can't drive them—she *promised*.

Here we have all the elements for the beginning of a drama. One character, Sara, expresses a "want." ("I want the car.") She is our protagonist. A **protagonist** is generally the person who "drives" the action, who has the "want," who takes the step to achieve a goal. Sara has something at stake (her friends), and there is an obstacle or **antagonist** in her way (her parents and their probable refusal to let her have the car).

In dramatic terms, then, we have the **exposition**—the presentation of the characters and their basic situation; we have the foreshadowing, or suggestions, of a **conflict** (Sara's brother has warned her not to ask for the car); and we have a basic **dramatic question**: "Will Sara get what she wants?"

> Sara then goes to her "ally," her mother, and tells her that she wants to use the car. Her mother tells her she can't: the roads are slick with ice. Then, in irritation, she adds something else: she doesn't care for Sara's friends.

The protagonist has now taken her first step and has met with an obstacle and an unexpected complication: she has discovered that her mother doesn't like her friends.

> "A
> **protagonist**
> is generally the person
> who 'drives' the action,
> who has the 'want,'
> who takes the step
> to achieve a goal."

Sara ignores what her brother and mother say (the protagonist has to, if we're to have a story), and she puts the question to her father.

Now we are moving toward the drama's **climax**—that moment when our tension and emotions are at a peak, when we watch the characters engage in the final struggle that is going to determine the resolution of the problem. (In cowboy movies, this is the moment of the big shootout on Main Street.)

Sara makes her request. The battle begins.

Her father not only says "No" because the roads are bad, but he goes on to reveal other feelings; he says that Sara is showing poor judgment and has become irresponsible. Under the pressure of the situation, Mr. Norton, like Mrs. Norton, reveals what he never would have said under other circumstances.

Now an argument may follow. The mother at first sides with the father; then she starts to defend her daughter. The brother may either run away from the argument, or join in on Sara's side. "You don't understand her. You don't understand either of us." Blow-up. Tears. The pressure-cooker situation has exposed all the characters to themselves and to one another. Sara storms out of the house. The question asked at the beginning of the story is answered: Sara does not get the car. In most homes, the daughter would return and some compromise would be worked out. In a serious drama, Sara might be "gone" forever.

During the working out of the conflict in this family story, something else has taken place. Relationships have changed, and relationships, and what happens to them, are one of the main elements of a play. Sara, who always thought her parents trusted her, finds out what her parents really think. This, in turn, changes her feelings about them (and about herself).

Characters We Care About

Writing about the family can help the playwright with a basic task—to organize the emotions of the audience, to arouse our interest or sympathy for one or more of the characters. (In the old melodramas, where there were real villains, writers organized the emotions of the audience very simply: early in the play they would turn us against the villain by having him kick a dog.)

We are all more or less familiar with the "cast of characters" in families. Though these characters might all be as unique as thumbprints, they are all as similar as thumbs. When my play *I Never Sang for My Father* was produced, I received a number of letters from people asking questions like "How did you know my father?" Of course, I didn't know *their* fathers, but I knew my own. Thus playwrights may write out of feelings for their own particular family, and if they write truly, they sometimes achieve a universality. They may make the audience understand something about *all* families.

> " **W**hen
> my play *I Never Sang for My Father*
> was produced,
> I received a number
> of letters from people
> asking questions like
> 'How did you know
> my father?'
> Of course, I didn't know
> *their* fathers,
> but I knew my own."

This, of course, is one of the aims of art—to reveal the universal in the particular. The characters in plays may seem larger than life, but they are not bizarre, theatrical creatures. The great plays are able to revitalize the familiar. They help us to see our own lives in perspective—our own parents, our own wives or husbands, our own friends. Playwrights strike notes from their own feelings and experiences, and they hope for a responsive chord from the audience.

The "Shock of Recognition"

A play, then, actually exists halfway between the stage and the audience. By choosing the familiar ground of the family, the playwright sometimes finds it easier to "reach" an audience. Spectators in the theater are often doing two things at once: they are watching a play on the stage, and at the same time they are relating it to their own experiences. They are feeling what is known as "the shock of recognition." *"How did you know my father?"*

The four plays in this book dramatize conflicts within the general framework of the family. They examine four easily recognized situations about which hundreds of plays, films, and television dramas have been written. In *The Miracle Worker,* there is a family with a handicapped child. In *Visitor from Forest Hills,* there is a frightened bride. In *The Mother,* there are the problems a family faces with an aging parent. In *Romeo and Juliet,* there are the young, impulsive lovers who will marry despite all obstacles. In the case of Romeo and Juliet, the protagonists' obstacle is a family feud. In more modern plays based on this situation, the obstacles might be race, religion, or social station, as in the musical version of Shakespeare's play—the Bernstein-Sondheim-Laurents *West Side Story.*

"Is It True?"

While playwrights write out of what they know, out of what concerns them, probably very little of their work is strictly autobiographical. The Nobel-Prize-winning novelist William Faulkner said that a writer needs "experience, observation, and imagination." Writers rarely limit themselves to re-creating an actual person as a character in a play. Playwrights may base a character on a person they know, but then they invent and expand to suit the needs of the story. A painter may use a model for a pose or an outline, but after a while, he will become more interested in what is on the canvas. The artist will develop the painting so that it ends up scarcely resembling the original model.

An example of a dramatist who expanded and invented to suit the particular aims of each play was Eugene O'Neill. He used his family as the basis for the comic and sentimental play called *Ah, Wilderness!* as well as for the tragic play called *Long Day's Journey into Night.* The same family—very different plays!

> "The great plays help us to see our own lives in perspective —our own parents, our own wives or husbands, our own friends."

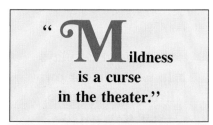
Drama Is a Verb

The dynamic, or drive, of each play in this book is the same: people we care about struggle through crucial situations because they have something important at stake. Note the word *struggle*. *Drama* is, in a sense, a verb. Drama should involve action, and that action can be verbal or physical. In our Norton family story, the action was verbal, as each person in the family tried to achieve his or her ends with words. (The gunfight at high noon would be physical action.)

A Playwright's Concerns: Feeling, Story, and Form

When playwrights sit down to write plays, they have many things to consider. First, they must decide if their feeling about the material is strong enough to hold their interest for the one to three years it might take to write the play. Will they be able to convey this feeling of excitement or humor or emotion to an audience? Mildness is a curse in the theater, and playwrights have to consider whether the feelings they are communicating will have a strong impact.

Next, playwrights must ask whether the story they want to tell is a dramatic one. Does it involve interesting people in a conflict, which moves to a crisis and a climax?

Finally, playwrights must consider the form in which they will write. Probably most of us are more aware of form in painting. We know that a picture may be painted in the more or less realistic style of a Rembrandt or in the impressionistic style of a Monet or in the cubist style of a Picasso.

In somewhat the same way, the story of a play can be told in various forms. It can be told in a conventional straightforward way (often called a linear style), with a beginning, a middle, and an end, presented in chronological order. Or the story can move back and forth in time, with such devices as flashbacks or dream sequences. One recent play, *Betrayal* by Harold Pinter, actually begins at the end of the story and ends at the beginning.

The plays in this book are all more or less conventional in their form. They tell their stories from beginning to end. *The Miracle Worker* uses some memory flashbacks in which we hear the voices that Annie remembers from her childhood. Otherwise, the play moves ahead in a straightforward manner.

Thus, though these plays are varied in style and tone, the pleasure, even the "shock of recognition," awaits you in each one. See if you think that these particular characters and their conflicts reveal universal truths. Do you ask: *"How did you know my family?"*

Rapunzel lets down her hair. A scene from *Into the Woods* (1987), a musical comedy by Stephen Sondheim.

William Gibson's *The Miracle Worker,* a true story, is based on the early life of the blind and deaf Helen Keller and of her teacher, Annie Sullivan. The play was first presented in 1957 on a CBS television program called "Playhouse 90," which fostered excellent work by many of the emerging young playwrights of the period.

William Gibson later expanded his teleplay into the full-length stage play we have here, which opened on Broadway on October 19, 1959. The play retains the fluid quality of its original television form: short, highly dramatic scenes flow into one another, each scene developing conflicts and crises and decisions that move the story into the next scene.

Note particularly the arresting opening scene—evidence of the play's original television form. With no preparation, we are immediately hooked by the family crisis. The play plunges us at once into a desperate situation with "She can't see! . . . She can't hear!" One of the principles of television writing is that you have to capture the attention of the viewers immediately, or they will turn to another channel.

A playwright tells a story by letting us hear what characters say and by letting us watch what they do. This play is an outstanding example of the use of theatrical activity and action. **Activity** is simply any movement on stage: picking up a cup, closing a door. **Action** is dramatically meaningful activity, which helps to move the story forward or which deepens our understanding of characters or of their relationships. A man may close the door just to close the door, or he may close the door to keep someone from leaving the room. The first is activity; the second is action.

Because this play deals with a main character who cannot speak or hear, much of the action must be worked out in physical activity, which is indicated in the long stage directions. Anyone reading what Annie and Helen are expected to do on stage should not be surprised to hear that the actresses who played their roles found the physical exertion exhausting. During the Broadway production, Helen and Annie had to wear padding under their clothing to protect themselves from each other's blows.

Throughout the play, Annie hears "voices" from her past. In the stage production, these voices that haunt Annie were taped and amplified. Speakers placed on the side walls of the theater projected the voices with an echo effect that sounded ghostly and otherworldly. The result was that the people in the theater seemed to hear the voices and their disturbing echo effect in the same way that Annie heard them.

The Miracle Worker was made into an Academy-Award-winning movie and later was again turned back into a television play. This time, on television, Patty Duke, who originally played the child Helen on stage, played the part of Annie. Anne Bancroft originated the part of Annie Sullivan on Broadway.

Before you start the play, you should read the selection from Joseph P. Lash's biography *Helen and Teacher,* on page 437. It tells about Annie Sullivan's early years in the state poorhouse at Tewksbury, Massachusetts.

The Miracle Worker

PLAYBILL
The Playhouse
a weekly magazine for theatregoers

THE MIRACLE WORKER

"**O**ne of the principles of television writing is that you have to capture the attention of the viewers immediately, or they will turn to another channel."

THE MIRACLE WORKER

William Gibson

At another time she asked, "What is a soul?"
"No one knows," I replied; "but we know it is
not the body, and it is that part of us which thinks
and loves and hopes . . . [and] is invisible. . . ."
"But if I write what my soul thinks," she said,
"then it will be visible, and the words will be its
body."

—Annie Sullivan, 1891

The playing space is divided into two areas by a more or less diagonal line, which runs from downstage right to upstage left.

The area behind this diagonal is on platforms and represents the Keller house; inside we see, down right, a family room, and up center, elevated, a bedroom. On stage level near center, outside a porch, there is a water pump.

The other area, in front of the diagonal, is neutral ground; it accommodates various places as designated at various times—the yard before the Keller home, the Perkins Institution for the Blind, the garden house, and so forth.

The less set there is, the better. The stage should be free, airy, unencumbered by walls. Apart from certain practical items—such as the pump, a window to climb out of, doors to be locked—locales should be only skeletal suggestions, and the movement from one to another should be accomplishable by little more than lights.

Characters

A Doctor
Kate, Helen's mother
Keller, Helen's father
Helen
Martha ⎫
Percy ⎭ children of servants
Aunt Ev
James, Captain Keller's son by his first marriage
Anagnos, Director of the Perkins Institution for the Blind, in Boston
Annie Sullivan
Viney, a servant
Blind Girls
A Servant
Offstage Voices

TIME: *The 1880's.*

PLACE: *In and around the Keller homestead in Tuscumbia, Alabama; also, briefly, the Perkins Institution for the Blind, in Boston.*

Act One

Scene 1

It is night over the Keller homestead.

Inside, three adults in the bedroom are grouped around a crib, in lamplight. They have been through a long vigil, and it shows in their tired bearing and disarranged clothing. One is a young gentlewoman with a sweet girlish face, KATE KELLER; *the second is an elderly* DOCTOR, *stethoscope at neck, thermometer in fingers; the third is a hearty gentleman in his forties with chin whiskers,* CAPTAIN ARTHUR KELLER.

Doctor. She'll live.
Kate. Thank God.

[*The* DOCTOR *leaves them together over the crib, packs his bag.*]

Doctor. You're a pair of lucky parents. I can tell you now, I thought she wouldn't.
Keller. Nonsense, the child's a Keller, she has the constitution of a goat. She'll outlive us all.
Doctor (*amiably*). Yes, especially if some of you Kellers don't get a night's sleep. I mean you, Mrs. Keller.
Keller. You hear, Katie?
Kate. I hear.
Keller (*indulgent*). I've brought up two of them, but this is my wife's first, she isn't battle-scarred yet.
Kate. Doctor, don't be merely considerate, will my girl be all right?
Doctor. Oh, by morning she'll be knocking down Captain Keller's fences again.
Kate. And isn't there anything we should do?
Keller (*jovial*). Put up stronger fencing, ha?
Doctor. Just let her get well, she knows how to do it better than we do. (*He is packed, ready to leave.*) Main thing is the fever's gone, these things come and go in infants, never know why. Call it acute congestion of the stomach and brain.
Keller. I'll see you to your buggy, Doctor.
Doctor. I've never seen a baby with more vitality, that's the truth.

[*He beams a good night at the baby and* KATE, *and* KELLER *leads him downstairs with a lamp. They go down the porch steps, and across the* yard, where the DOCTOR goes off left; KELLER stands with the lamp aloft. KATE meanwhile is bent lovingly over the crib, which emits a bleat; her finger is playful with the baby's face.]

Kate. Hush. Don't you cry now, you've been trouble enough. Call it acute congestion, indeed, I don't see what's so cute about a congestion, just because it's yours. We'll have your father run an editorial in his paper, the wonders of modern medicine, they don't know what they're curing even when they cure it. Men, men and their battle scars, we women will have to—(*But she breaks off, puzzled, moves her finger before the baby's eyes.*) Will have to—Helen? (*Now she moves her hand, quickly.*) Helen. (*She snaps her fingers at the baby's eyes twice, and her hand falters; after a moment she calls out, loudly.*) Captain. Captain, will you come—(*But she stares at the baby, and her next call is directly at her ears.*) Captain!

[*And now, still staring, KATE screams. KELLER in the yard hears it, and runs with the lamp back to the house. KATE screams again, her look intent on the baby and terrible. KELLER hurries in and up.*]

Keller. Katie? What's wrong?
Kate. Look. (*She makes a pass with her hand in the crib, at the baby's eyes.*)
Keller. What, Katie? She's well, she needs only time to—
Kate. She can't see. Look at her eyes. (*She takes the lamp from him, moves it before the child's face.*) She can't *see!*
Keller (*hoarsely*). Helen.
Kate. Or hear. When I screamed she didn't blink. Not an eyelash—
Keller. Helen. Helen!
Kate. She can't *hear* you!
Keller. *Helen!*

[*His face has something like fury in it, crying the child's name; KATE, almost fainting, presses her knuckles to her mouth, to stop her own cry. The room dims out quickly.*]

Scene 2

Time, in the form of a slow tune of distant belfry chimes which approaches in a crescendo and then fades, passes; the light comes up again on a day five years later, on three kneeling children and an old dog outside around the pump.*

The dog is a setter named BELLE, *and she is sleeping. Two of the children are black,* MARTHA *and* PERCY. *The third child is* HELEN, *six and a half years old, quite unkempt, in body a vivacious[1] little person with a fine head, attractive, but noticeably blind, one eye larger and protruding; her gestures are abrupt, insistent, lacking in human restraint, and her face never smiles. She is flanked by the other two, in a litter of paper-doll cutouts, and while they speak* HELEN'S *hands thrust at their faces in turn, feeling bafffledly at the movements of their lips.*

Martha (*snipping*). First I'm gonna cut off this doctor's legs, one, two, now then—
Percy. Why you cuttin' off that doctor's legs?
Martha. I'm gonna give him a operation. Now I'm gonna cut off his arms, one, two. Now I'm gonna fix up—(*She pushes* HELEN'S *hand away from her mouth.*) You stop that.
Percy. Cut off his stomach, that's a good operation.
Martha. No, I'm gonna cut off his head first, he got a bad cold.
Percy. Ain't gonna be much of that doctor left to fix up, time you finish all them opera—

[*But* HELEN *is poking her fingers inside his mouth, to feel his tongue; he bites at them, annoyed, and she jerks them away.* HELEN *now fingers her own lips, moving them in imitation, but soundlessly.*]

Martha. What you do, bite her hand?
Percy. That's how I do, she keep pokin' her fingers in my mouth, I just bite 'em off.
Martha. What she tryin' do now?
Percy. She tryin' *talk.* She gonna get mad. Looka her tryin' talk.

[HELEN *is scowling, the lips under her fingertips moving in ghostly silence, growing more and more frantic, until in a bizarre rage she bites at her own fingers. This sends* PERCY *off into laughter, but alarms* MARTHA.]

---

1. **vivacious** (vī·vā′shəs): very lively.

Martha. Hey, you stop now. *(She pulls* HELEN'S *hand down.)* You just sit quiet and—

[But at once HELEN *topples* MARTHA *on her back, knees pinning her shoulders down, and grabs the scissors.* MARTHA *screams.* PERCY *darts to the bell string on the porch, yanks it, and the bell rings.]*

Scene 3

Inside, the lights have been gradually coming up on the main room, where we see the family informally gathered, talking, but in pantomime: KATE *sits darning socks near a cradle, occasionally rocking it;* CAPTAIN KELLER, *in spectacles, is working over newspaper pages at a table; a benign visitor in a hat,* AUNT EV, *is sharing the sewing basket, putting the finishing touches on a big shapeless doll made out of towels; an indolent young man,* JAMES KELLER, *is at the window watching the children.*

With the ring of the bell, KATE *is instantly on her feet and out the door onto the porch, to take in the scene; now we see what these five years have done to her: the girlish playfulness is gone, she is a woman steeled in grief.*

Kate *(for the thousandth time).* Helen. *(She is down the steps at once to them, seizing* HELEN'S *wrists and lifting her off* MARTHA; MARTHA *runs off in tears and screams for momma, with* PERCY *after her.)* Let me have those scissors.

[Meanwhile the family inside is alerted, AUNT EV *joining* JAMES *at the window;* CAPTAIN KELLER *resumes work.]*

James *(blandly).* She only dug Martha's eyes out. Almost dug. It's always almost, no point worrying till it happens, is there?

[They gaze out, while KATE *reaches for the scissors in* HELEN'S *hand. But* HELEN *pulls the scissors back, they struggle for them a moment, then* KATE *gives up, lets* HELEN *keep them. She tries to draw* HELEN *into the house.* HELEN *jerks away.* KATE *next goes down on her knees, takes* HELEN'S *hands gently, and using the scissors like a doll, makes* HELEN *caress and cradle them; she points* HELEN'S *finger houseward.* HELEN'S *whole body*

now becomes eager; she surrenders the scissors. KATE *turns her toward the door and gives her a little push.* HELEN *scrambles up and toward the house, and* KATE, *rising, follows her.]*

Aunt Ev. How does she stand it? Why haven't you seen this Baltimore man? It's not a thing you can let go on and on, like the weather.

James. The weather here doesn't ask permission of me, Aunt Ev. Speak to my father.

Aunt Ev. Arthur. Something ought to be done for that child.

Keller. A refreshing suggestion. What?

[KATE, entering, turns HELEN *to* AUNT EV, *who gives her the towel doll.]*

Aunt Ev. Why, this very famous oculist[2] in Baltimore I wrote you about, what was his name?

Kate. Dr. Chisholm.

Aunt Ev. Yes, I heard lots of cases of blindness people thought couldn't be cured he's cured, he just does wonders. Why don't you write to him?

Keller. I've stopped believing in wonders.

Kate *(rocks the cradle).* I think the Captain will write to him soon. Won't you, Captain?

Keller. No.

James *(lightly).* Good money after bad, or bad after good. Or bad after bad—

Aunt Ev. Well, if it's just a question of money, Arthur, now you're marshal you have this Yankee money. Might as well—

Keller. Not money. The child's been to specialists all over Alabama and Tennessee, if I thought it would do good I'd have her to every fool doctor in the country.

Kate. I think the Captain will write to him soon.

Keller. Katie. How many times can you let them break your heart?

Kate. Any number of times.

[HELEN meanwhile sits on the floor to explore the doll with her fingers, and her hand pauses over the face: this is no face, a blank area of towel, and it troubles her. Her hand searches for features, and taps questioningly for eyes, but no one notices. She then yanks at her AUNT'S *dress, and taps again vigorously for eyes]*

---

2. **oculist** (ŏk′yə·list): eye doctor.

Aunt Ev. What, child?

[*Obviously not hearing,* HELEN *commences to go around, from person to person, tapping for eyes, but no one attends or understands.*]

Kate (*no break*). As long as there's the least chance. For her to see. Or hear, or—

Keller. There isn't. Now I must finish here.

Kate. I think, with your permission, Captain, I'd like to write.

Keller. I said no, Katie.

Aunt Ev. Why, writing does no harm, Arthur, only a little bitty letter. To see if he can help her.

Keller. He can't.

Kate. We won't know that to be a fact, Captain, until after you write.

Keller (*rising, emphatic*). Katie, he can't. (*He collects his papers.*)

James (*facetiously*). Father stands up, that makes it a fact.

Keller. You be quiet! I'm badgered enough here by females without your impudence. (JAMES *shuts up, makes himself scarce.* HELEN *now is groping among things on* KELLER'S *desk, and paws his papers to the floor.* KELLER *is exasperated.*) Katie. (KATE *quickly turns* HELEN *away, and retrieves the papers.*) I might as well try to work in a henyard as in this house—

James (*placating*). You really ought to put her away, Father.

Kate (*staring up*). What?

James. Some asylum. It's the kindest thing.

Aunt Ev. Why, she's your sister, James, not a nobody—

James. Half sister, and half—mentally defective, she can't even keep herself clean. It's not pleasant to see her about all the time.

Kate. Do you dare? Complain of what you *can* see?

Keller (*very annoyed*). This discussion is at an end! I'll thank you not to broach it again, Ev. (*Silence descends at once.* HELEN *gropes her way with the doll, and* KELLER *turns back for a final word, explosive.*) I've done as much as I can bear, I can't give my whole life to it! The house is at sixes and sevens[3] from morning till night over the

child, it's time some attention was paid to Mildred[4] here instead!

Kate (*gently dry*). You'll wake her up, Captain.

Keller. I want some peace in the house, I don't care how, but one way we won't have it is by rushing up and down the country every time someone hears of a new quack. I'm as sensible to this affliction as anyone else, it hurts me to look at the girl.

Kate. It was not our affliction I meant you to write about, Captain.

[HELEN *is back at* AUNT EV, *fingering her dress, and yanks two buttons from it.*]

Aunt Ev. Helen! My buttons.

[HELEN *pushes the buttons into the doll's face.* KATE *now sees, comes swiftly to kneel, lifts* HELEN'S *hand to her own eyes in question.*]

Kate. Eyes? (HELEN *nods energetically.*) She wants the doll to have eyes.

[*Another kind of silence now, while* KATE *takes pins and buttons from the sewing basket and attaches them to the doll as eyes.* KELLER *stands, caught, and watches morosely.* AUNT EV *blinks, and conceals her emotion by inspecting her dress.*]

Aunt Ev. My goodness me, I'm not decent.

Kate. She doesn't know better, Aunt Ev. I'll sew them on again.

James. Never learn with everyone letting her do anything she takes it into her mind to—

Keller. You be quiet!

James. What did I say now?

Keller. You talk too much.

James. I was agreeing with you!

Keller. Whatever it was. Deprived child, the least she can have are the little things she wants.

[JAMES, *very wounded, stalks out of the room onto the porch; he remains here, sulking.*]

Aunt Ev (*indulgently*). It's worth a couple of buttons, Kate, look. (HELEN *now has the doll with eyes, and cannot contain herself for joy; she rocks*

---

3. **at sixes and sevens:** an expression meaning "in neglect and confusion."

4. The Kellers have had a second child.

the doll, pats it vigorously, kisses it.) This child has more sense than all these men Kellers, if there's ever any way to reach that mind of hers.

[*But* HELEN *suddenly has come upon the cradle, and unhesitatingly overturns it; the swaddled baby tumbles out, and* CAPTAIN KELLER *barely manages to dive and catch it in time.*]

Keller. Helen!

[*All are in commotion, the baby screams, but* HELEN, *unperturbed, is laying her doll in its place.* KATE *on her knees pulls her hands off the cradle, wringing them;* HELEN *is bewildered.*]

Kate. Helen, Helen, you're not to do such things, how can I make you understand—

Keller (*hoarsely*). Katie.

Kate. How can I get it into your head, my darling, my poor—

Keller. Katie, some way of teaching her an iota of discipline has to be—

Kate (*flaring*). How can you discipline an afflicted child? Is it her fault?

[HELEN'S *fingers have fluttered to her* MOTHER'S *lips, vainly trying to comprehend their movements.*]

Keller. I didn't say it was her fault.

Kate. Then whose? I don't know what to do! How can I teach her, beat her—until she's black and blue?

Keller. It's not safe to let her run around loose. Now there must be a way of confining her, somehow, so she can't—

Kate. Where, in a cage? She's a growing child, she has to use her limbs!

Keller. Answer me one thing, is it fair to Mildred here?

Kate (*inexorably*). Are you willing to put her away?

[*Now* HELEN'S *face darkens in the same rage as at herself earlier, and her hand strikes at* KATE'S *lips.* KATE *catches her hand again, and* HELEN *begins to kick, struggle, twist.*]

Keller. Now what?

Kate. She wants to talk, like—*be* like you and me. (*She holds* HELEN *struggling until we hear from*

the child her first sound so far, an inarticulate[5] weird noise in her throat such as an animal in a trap might make; and KATE releases her. The second she is free HELEN blunders away, collides violently with a chair, falls, and sits weeping. KATE comes to her, embraces, caresses, soothes her, and buries her own face in her hair, until she can control her voice.) Every day she slips further away. And I don't know how to call her back.

Aunt Ev. Oh, I've a mind to take her up to Baltimore myself. If that doctor can't help her, maybe he'll know who can.

Keller (*presently, heavily*). I'll write the man, Katie. (*He stands with the baby in his clasp, staring at* HELEN'S *head, hanging down on* KATE'S *arm.*)

[*The lights dim out, except the one on* KATE *and* HELEN. *In the twilight,* JAMES, AUNT EV, *and* KELLER *move off slowly, formally, in separate directions;* KATE *with* HELEN *in her arms remains, motionless, in an image which overlaps into the next scene and fades only when it is well under way.*]

Scene 4

Without pause, from the dark down left we hear a man's voice with a Greek accent speaking:

Anagnos. —who could do nothing for the girl, of course. It was Dr. Bell[6] who thought she might somehow be taught. I have written the family only that a suitable governess, Miss Annie Sullivan, has been found here in Boston—

[*The lights begin to come up, down left, on a long table and chair. The table contains equipment for teaching the blind by touch—a small replica of the human skeleton, stuffed animals, models of flowers and plants, piles of books. The chair contains a girl of 20,* ANNIE SULLIVAN, *with a face which in repose is grave and rather obstinate, and when active is impudent, combative, twinkling with all the life that is lacking in* HELEN'S, *and handsome; there is a crude vitality to her. Her suitcase is at*

---

5. **inarticulate** (in'är·tik'yə·lit'): not capable of being understood.
6. **Dr. Bell:** Alexander Graham Bell, the inventor of the telephone, who also worked at methods for teaching the deaf.

her knee. ANAGNOS, *a stocky bearded man, comes into the light only toward the end of his speech.*]

Anagnos. —and will come. It will no doubt be difficult for you there, Annie. But it has been difficult for you at our school too, hm? Gratifying, yes, when you came to us and could not spell your name, to accomplish so much here in a few years, but always an Irish battle. For independence. *(He studies* ANNIE, *humorously; she does not open her eyes.)* This is my last time to counsel you, Annie, and you do lack some—by some I mean *all*—what, tact or talent to bend. To others. And what has saved you on more than one occasion here at Perkins is that there was nowhere to expel you to. Your eyes hurt?

Annie. My ears, Mr. Anagnos. *(And now she has opened her eyes; they are inflamed, vague, slightly crossed, clouded by the granular growth of trachoma,[7] and she often keeps them closed to shut out the pain of light.)*

Anagnos *(severely).* Nowhere but back to Tewksbury, where children learn to be saucy. Annie, I know how dreadful it was there, but that battle is dead and done with, why not let it stay buried?

Annie *(cheerily).* I think God must owe me a resurrection.

Anagnos *(a bit shocked).* What?

Annie *(taps her brow).* Well, He keeps digging up that battle!

Anagnos. That is not a proper thing to say, Annie. It is what I mean.

Annie *(meekly).* Yes. But I know what I'm like, what's this child like?

Anagnos. Like?

Annie. Well—bright or dull, to start off.

Anagnos. No one knows. And if she is dull, you have no patience with this?

Annie. Oh, in grown-ups you have to, Mr. Anagnos. I mean in children it just seems a little—precocious, can I use that word?

Anagnos. Only if you can spell it.

Annie. Premature. So I hope at least she's a bright one.

Anagnos. Deaf, blind, mute—who knows? She is

like a little safe, locked, that no one can open. Perhaps there is a treasure inside.

Annie. Maybe it's empty, too?

Anagnos. Possibly. I should warn you, she is much given to tantrums.

Annie. Means something is inside. Well, so am I, if I believe all I hear. Maybe you should warn *them.*

Anagnos *(frowns).* Annie. I wrote them no word of your history. You will find yourself among strangers now, who know nothing of it.

Annie. Well, we'll keep them in a state of blessed ignorance.

Anagnos. Perhaps *you* should tell it?

Annie *(bristling).* Why? I have enough trouble with people who don't know.

Anagnos. So they will understand. When you have trouble.

Annie. The only time I have trouble is when I'm right. *(But she is amused at herself, as is* ANAGNOS.*)* Is it my fault it's so often? I won't give them trouble, Mr. Anagnos, I'll be so ladylike they won't notice I've come.

Anagnos. Annie, be—humble. It is not as if you have so many offers to pick and choose. You will need their affection, working with this child.

Annie *(humorously).* I hope I won't need their pity.

Anagnos. Oh, we can all use some pity. *(Crisply)* So. You are no longer our pupil, we throw you into the world, a teacher. *If* the child can be taught. No one expects you to work miracles, even for twenty-five dollars a month. Now, in this envelope a loan, for the railroad, which you will repay me when you have a bank account. But in this box, a gift. With our love. *(*ANNIE *opens the small box he extends, and sees a garnet ring. She looks up, blinking, and down.)* I think other friends are ready to say goodbye. *(He moves as though to open doors.)*

Annie. Mr. Anagnos. *(Her voice is trembling.)* Dear Mr. Anagnos, I—*(But she swallows over getting the ring on her finger, and cannot continue until she finds a woebegone joke.)* Well, what should I say, I'm an ignorant, opinionated girl, and everything I am I owe to you?

Anagnos *(smiles).* That is only half true, Annie.

Annie. Which half? I crawled in here like a drowned rat, I thought I died when Jimmie died,

---

7. **trachoma** (trə·kō′mə): a viral inflammation of the eye, which results in ''grainy'' scar tissue.

that I'd never again—come alive. Well, you say with love so easy, and I haven't *loved* a soul since and I never will, I suppose, but this place gave me more than my eyes back. Or taught me how to spell, which I'll never learn anyway, but with all the fights and the trouble I've been here it taught me what help is, and how to live again, and I don't want to say goodbye. Don't open the door, I'm crying.

Anagnos (*gently*). They will not see.

[*He moves again as though opening doors, and in comes a group of girls, 8-year-olds to 17-year-olds; as they walk we see they are blind.* ANAGNOS *shepherds them in with a hand.*]

A Child. Annie?

Annie (*her voice cheerful*). Here, Beatrice.

[*As soon as they locate her voice they throng joyfully to her, speaking all at once;* ANNIE *is down on her knees to the smallest, and the following are the more intelligible fragments in the general hubbub.*]

Children. There's a present. We brought you a going-away present, Annie!

Annie. Oh, now you shouldn't have—

Children. We did, we did, where's the present?

Smallest Child (*mournfully*). Don't go, Annie, away.

Children. Alice has it. Alice! Where's Alice? Here I am! Where? Here!

[*An arm is aloft out of the group, waving a present;* ANNIE *reaches for it.*]

Annie. I have it. I have it, everybody, should I open it?

Children. Open it! Everyone be quiet! Do, Annie! She's opening it. Ssh! (*A settling of silence while* ANNIE *unwraps it. The present is a pair of smoked glasses, and she stands still.*) Is it open, Annie?

Annie. It's open.

Children. It's for your eyes, Annie. Put them on, Annie! 'Cause Mrs. Hopkins said your eyes hurt since the operation. And she said you're going where the sun is *fierce*.

Annie. I'm putting them on now.

Smallest Child (*mournfully*). Don't go, Annie, where the sun is fierce.

Children. Do they fit all right?

Annie. Oh, they fit just fine.

Children. Did you put them on? Are they pretty, Annie?

Annie. Oh, my eyes feel hundreds of per cent better already, and pretty, why, do you know how I look in them? Splendiloquent. Like a race horse!

Children (*delighted*). There's another present! Beatrice! We have a present for Helen, too! Give it to her, Beatrice. Here, Annie! (*This present is an elegant doll, with movable eyelids and a momma sound.*) It's for Helen. And we took up a collection to buy it. And Laura dressed it.

Annie. It's beautiful!

Children. So don't forget, you be sure to give it to Helen from us, Annie!

Annie. I promise it will be the first thing I give her. If I don't keep it for myself, that is, you know I can't be trusted with dolls!

Smallest Child (*mournfully*). Don't go, Annie, to her.

Annie (*her arm around her*). Sarah, dear. I don't *want* to go.

Smallest Child. Then why are you going?

Annie (*gently*). Because I'm a big girl now, and big girls have to earn a living. It's the only way I can. But if you don't smile for me first, what I'll just have to do is—(*She pauses, inviting it.*)

Smallest Child. What?

Annie. Put *you* in my suitcase, instead of this doll. And take *you* to Helen in Alabama!

[*This strikes the children as very funny, and they begin to laugh and tease the smallest child, who after a moment does smile for* ANNIE.]

Anagnos (*then*). Come, children. We must get the trunk into the carriage and Annie into her train, or no one will go to Alabama. Come, come.

[*He shepherds them out and* ANNIE *is left alone on her knees with the doll in her lap. She reaches for her suitcase, and by a subtle change in the color of the light, we go with her thoughts into another time. We hear a boy's voice whispering; perhaps we see shadowy intimations[8] of these speakers in the background.*]

---

8. **intimations** (in·tə·mā′shəns): suggestions, hints.

Boy's Voice. Where we goin', Annie?

Annie (*in dread*). Jimmie.

Boy's Voice. Where we goin'?

Annie. I said—I'm takin' care of you—

Boy's Voice. Forever and ever?

Man's Voice (*impersonal*). Annie Sullivan, aged nine, virtually blind. James Sullivan, aged seven—What's the matter with your leg, Sonny?

Annie. Forever and ever.

Man's Voice. Can't he walk without that crutch? (ANNIE *shakes her head, and does not stop shaking it.*) Girl goes to the women's ward. Boy to the men's.

Boy's Voice (*in terror*). Annie! Annie, don't let them take me—Annie!

Anagnos (*offstage*). Annie! Annie?

[*But this voice is real, in the present, and* ANNIE *comes up out of her horror, clearing her head with a final shake; the lights begin to pick out* KATE *in the* KELLER *house, as* ANNIE *in a bright tone calls back.*]

Annie. Coming!

[*This word catches* KATE, *who stands half turned and attentive to it, almost as though hearing it. Meanwhile* ANNIE *turns and hurries out, lugging the suitcase.*]

Scene 5

The room dims out; the sound of railroad wheels begins from off left, and maintains itself in a constant rhythm underneath the following scene; the remaining lights have come up on the KELLER *homestead.* JAMES *is lounging on the porch, waiting. In the upper bedroom which is to be* ANNIE'S, HELEN *is alone, puzzledly exploring, fingering and smelling things, the curtains, empty drawers in the bureau, water in the pitcher by the washbasin, fresh towels on the bedstead. Downstairs in the family room* KATE *turning to a mirror hastily adjusts her bonnet, watched by a servant in an apron,* VINEY.

Viney. Let Mr. Jimmy go by hisself, you been pokin' that garden all day, you ought to rest your feet.

Kate. I can't wait to see her, Viney.

Viney. Maybe she ain't gone be on this train neither.

Kate. Maybe she is.

Viney. And maybe she ain't.

Kate. And maybe she is. Where's Helen?

Viney. She upstairs, smellin' around. She know somethin' funny's goin' on.

Kate. Let her have her supper as soon as Mildred's in bed, and tell Captain Keller when he comes that we'll be delayed tonight.

Viney. Again.

Kate. I don't think we need say *again*. Simply delayed will do.

[*She runs upstairs to* ANNIE'S *room,* VINEY *speaking after her.*]

Viney. I mean that's what he gone say. "What, again?"

[VINEY *works at setting the table. Upstairs* KATE *stands in the doorway, watching* HELEN'S *groping explorations.*]

Kate. Yes, we're expecting someone. Someone for my Helen. (HELEN *happens upon her skirt, clutches her leg;* KATE *in a tired dismay kneels to tidy her hair and soiled pinafore.*[9]) Oh, dear, this was clean not an hour ago. (HELEN *feels her bonnet, shakes her head darkly, and tugs to get it off.* KATE *retains it with one hand, diverts* HELEN *by opening her other hand under her nose.*) Here. For while I'm gone. (HELEN *sniffs, reaches, and pops something into her mouth, while* KATE *speaks a bit guiltily.*) I don't think one peppermint drop will spoil your supper.

[*She gives* HELEN *a quick kiss, evades her hands, and hurries downstairs again. Meanwhile* CAPTAIN KELLER *has entered the yard from around the rear of the house, newspaper under arm, cleaning off and munching on some radishes; he sees* JAMES *lounging at the porch post.*]

Keller. Jimmie?

James (*unmoving*). Sir?

Keller (*eyes him*). You don't look dressed for anything useful, boy.

---

9. **pinafore** (pin′ə·fôr′): a sleeveless, apronlike garment worn over a dress (usually to keep the dress clean).

James. I'm not. It's for Miss Sullivan.

Keller. Needn't keep holding up that porch, we have wooden posts for that. I asked you to see that those strawberry plants were moved this evening.

James. I'm moving your—Mrs. Keller, instead. To the station.

Keller (heavily). Mrs. Keller. Must you always speak of her as though you haven't met the lady?

[KATE comes out on the porch, and JAMES inclines his head.]

James (ironic). Mother. (He starts off the porch, but sidesteps KELLER'S glare like a blow.) I said mother!

Kate. Captain.

Keller. Evening, my dear.

Kate. We're off to meet the train, Captain. Supper will be a trifle delayed tonight.

Keller. What, again?

Kate (backing out). With your permission, Captain?

[And they are gone. KELLER watches them offstage, morosely. Upstairs HELEN meanwhile has groped for her mother, touched her cheek in a meaningful gesture, waited, touched her cheek, waited, then found the open door, and made her way down. Now she comes into the family room, touches her cheek again; VINEY regards her.]

Viney. What you want, honey, your momma? (HELEN touches her cheek again. VINEY goes to the sideboard, gets a tea-cake, gives it into HELEN'S hand; HELEN pops it into her mouth.) Guess one little tea-cake ain't gone ruin your appetite.

[She turns HELEN toward the door. HELEN wanders out onto the porch, as KELLER comes up the steps. Her hands encounter him, and she touches her cheek again, waits.]

Keller. She's gone. (He is awkward with her; when he puts his hand on her head, she pulls away. KELLER stands regarding her, heavily.) She's gone, my son and I don't get along, you don't know I'm your father, no one likes me, and supper's delayed. (HELEN touches her cheek, waits. KELLER fishes in his pocket.) Here. I brought you

some stick candy, one nibble of sweets can't do any harm.

[He gives her a large stick of candy; HELEN falls to it. VINEY peers out the window.]

Viney (reproachfully). Cap'n Keller, now how'm I gone get her to eat her supper you fill her up with that trash?

Keller (roars). Tend to your work!

[VINEY beats a rapid retreat. KELLER thinks better of it, and tries to get the candy away from HELEN, but HELEN hangs on to it; and when KELLER pulls, she gives his leg a kick. KELLER hops about, HELEN takes refuge with the candy down behind the pump, and KELLER then irately flings his newspaper on the porch floor, stamps into the house past VINEY, and disappears.]

Scene 6

The lights half dim on the homestead, where VINEY and HELEN going about their business soon find their way off. Meanwhile, the railroad sounds off left have mounted in a crescendo to a climax typical of a depot at arrival time, the lights come up on stage left, and we see a suggestion of a station. Here ANNIE in her smoked glasses and disarrayed by travel is waiting with her suitcase, while JAMES walks to meet her; she has a battered paper-bound book, which is a Perkins report,[10] *under her arm.*

James (coolly). Miss Sullivan?

Annie (cheerily). Here! At last. I've been on trains so many days I thought they must be backing up every time I dozed off—

James. I'm James Keller.

Annie. James? (The name stops her.) I had a brother Jimmie. Are you Helen's?

James. I'm only half a brother. You're to be her governess?

Annie (lightly). Well. Try!

James (eying her). You look like half a governess. (KATE enters. ANNIE stands moveless, while

---

10. **Perkins report:** a report on methods of teaching the blind, prepared by the director of the Perkins Institution for the Blind, in Boston.

JAMES *takes her suitcase.* KATE'S *gaze on her is doubtful, troubled.)* Mrs. Keller, Miss Sullivan.

[KATE *takes her hand.*]

Kate *(simply).* We've met every train for two days.

[ANNIE *looks at* KATE'S *face, and her good humor comes back.*]

Annie. I changed trains every time they stopped, the man who sold me that ticket ought to be tied to the tracks—

James. You have a trunk, Miss Sullivan?

Annie. Yes. *(She passes* JAMES *a claim check, and he bears the suitcase out behind them.* ANNIE *holds the battered book.* KATE *is studying her face, and* ANNIE *returns the gaze; this is a mutual appraisal, southern gentlewoman and working-class Irish girl, and* ANNIE *is not quite comfortable under it.)* You didn't bring Helen, I was hoping you would.

Kate. No, she's home.

[*A pause.* ANNIE *tries to make ladylike small talk, though her energy now and then erupts; she catches herself up whenever she hears it.*]

Annie. You—live far from town, Mrs. Keller?

Kate. Only a mile.

Annie. Well. I suppose I can wait one more mile. But don't be surprised if I get out to push the horse!

Kate. Helen's waiting for you, too. There's been such a bustle in the house, she expects something, heaven knows what. *(Now she voices part of her doubt, not as such, but* ANNIE *understands it.)* I expected—a desiccated[11] spinster. You're very young.

Annie *(resolutely).* Oh, you should have seen me when I left Boston. I got much older on this trip.

Kate. I mean, to teach anyone as difficult as Helen.

Annie. *I* mean to try. They can't put you in jail for trying!

Kate. Is it possible, even? To teach a deaf-blind child *half* of what an ordinary child learns—has that ever been done?

Annie. Half?

---

11. **desiccated** (des'i·kāt'əd): dried up.

Kate. A tenth.

Annie *(reluctantly).* No. (KATE'S *face loses its remaining hope; still appraising her youth.)* Dr. Howe did wonders, but—an ordinary child? No, never. But then I thought when I was going over his reports—*(She indicates the one in her hand.)* —he never treated them like ordinary children. More like—eggs everyone was afraid would break.

Kate *(a pause).* May I ask how old you are?

Annie. Well, I'm not in my teens, you know! I'm twenty.

Kate. All of twenty.

[ANNIE *takes the bull by the horns, valiantly.*]

Annie. Mrs. Keller, don't lose heart just because I'm not on my last legs. I have three big advantages over Dr. Howe that money couldn't buy for you. One is his work behind me. I've read every word he wrote about it and he wasn't exactly what you'd call a man of few words. Another is to *be* young, why, I've got energy to do anything. The third is, I've been blind. *(But it costs her something to say this.)*

Kate *(quietly).* Advantages.

Annie *(wry).* Well, some have the luck of the Irish, some do not.

[KATE *smiles; she likes her.*]

Kate. What will you try to teach her first?

Annie. First, last, and—in between—language.

Kate. Language.

Annie. Language is to the mind more than light is to the eye. Dr. Howe said that.

Kate. Language. *(She shakes her head.)* We can't get through to teach her to sit still. You *are* young, despite your years, to have such—confidence. Do you, inside?

[ANNIE *studies her face; she likes her, too.*]

Annie. No, to tell you the truth I'm as shaky inside as a baby's rattle!

[*They smile at each other, and* KATE *pats her hand.*]

Kate. Don't be. (JAMES *returns to usher them off.)* We'll do all we can to help, and to make you feel at home. Don't think of us as strangers, Miss Annie.

Annie (*cheerily*). Oh, strangers aren't so strange to me. I've known them all my life!

[KATE *smiles again,* ANNIE *smiles back, and they precede* JAMES *offstage.*]

Scene 7

The lights dim on them, having simultaneously risen full on the house; VINEY *has already entered the family room, taken a water pitcher, and come out and down to the pump. She pumps real water. As she looks offstage, we hear the clop of hoofs, a carriage stopping, and voices.*

Viney. Cap'n Keller! Cap'n Keller, they comin'! (*She goes back into the house, as* KELLER *comes out on the porch to gaze.*) She sure 'nuff came, Cap'n.

[KELLER *descends, and crosses toward the carriage; this conversation begins offstage and moves on.*]

Keller (*very courtly*). Welcome to Ivy Green, Miss Sullivan. I take it you are Miss Sullivan—

Kate. My husband, Miss Annie, Captain Keller.

Annie (*her best behavior*). Captain, how do you do.

Keller. A pleasure to see you, at last. I trust you had an agreeable journey?

Annie. Oh, I had several! When did this country get so big?

James. Where would you like the trunk, Father?

Keller. Where Miss Sullivan can get at it, I imagine.

"Where would you like the trunk, Father?"

The photographs that illustrate the play are from the movie made in 1962, starring Patty Duke as Helen and Anne Bancroft as Annie.

Annie. Yes, please. Where's Helen?

Keller. In the hall, Jimmie—

Kate. We've put you in the upstairs corner room, Miss Annie, if there's any breeze at all this summer, you'll feel it—

[*In the house the setter* BELLE *flees into the family room, pursued by* HELEN *with groping hands; the dog doubles back out of the same door, and* HELEN *still groping for her makes her way out to the porch; she is messy, her hair tumbled, her pinafore now ripped, her shoelaces untied.* KELLER *acquires the suitcase, and* ANNIE *gets her hands on it too, though still endeavoring to live up to the general air of propertied[12] manners.*]

Keller. *And* the suitcase—

Annie *(pleasantly).* I'll take the suitcase, thanks.

Keller. Not at all, I have it, Miss Sullivan.

Annie. I'd like it.

Keller *(gallantly).* I couldn't think of it, Miss Sullivan. You'll find in the South we—

Annie. Let me.

Keller. —view women as the flowers of civiliza—

Annie *(impatiently).* I've got something in it for Helen! *(She tugs it free;* KELLER *stares.)* Thank you. When do I see her?

Kate. There. There is Helen.

[ANNIE *turns, and sees* HELEN *on the porch. A moment of silence. Then* ANNIE *begins across the yard to her, lugging her suitcase.*]

Keller *(sotto voce[13]).* Katie—

[KATE *silences him with a hand on his arm. When* ANNIE *finally reaches the porch steps she stops, contemplating* HELEN *for a last moment before entering her world. Then she drops the suitcase on the porch with intentional heaviness,* HELEN *starts with the jar, and comes to grope over it.* ANNIE *puts forth her hand, and touches* HELEN'S. HELEN *at once grasps it, and commences to explore it, like reading a face. She moves her hand on to* ANNIE'S *forearm, and dress; and* ANNIE

---

12. **propertied:** rich, well-to-do, befitting someone who owned property.

13. *sotto voce* (sä'tō vō'chā): Italian for "in a low voice."

brings her face within reach of* HELEN'S *fingers, which travel over it, quite without timidity, until they encounter and push aside the smoked glasses.* ANNIE'S *gaze is grave, unpitying, very attentive. She puts her hands on* HELEN'S *arms, but* HELEN *at once pulls away, and they confront each other with a distance between. Then* HELEN *returns to the suitcase, tries to open it, cannot.* ANNIE *points* HELEN'S *hand overhead.* HELEN *pulls away, tries to open the suitcase again;* ANNIE *points her hand overhead again.* HELEN *points overhead, a question, and* ANNIE, *drawing* HELEN'S *hand to her own face, nods.* HELEN *now begins tugging the suitcase toward the door; when* ANNIE *tries to take it from her, she fights her off and backs through the doorway with it.* ANNIE *stands a moment, then follows her in, and together they get the suitcase up the steps into* ANNIE'S *room.*]

Kate. Well?

Keller. She's very rough, Katie.

Kate. I like her, Captain.

Keller. Certainly rear a peculiar kind of young woman in the North. How old is she?

Kate *(vaguely).* Ohh— Well, she's not in her teens, you know.

Keller. She's only a child. What's her family like, shipping her off alone this far?

Kate. I couldn't learn. She's very closemouthed about some things.

Keller. Why does she wear those glasses? I like to see a person's eyes when I talk to—

Kate. For the sun. She was blind.

Keller. Blind.

Kate. She's had nine operations on her eyes. One just before she left.

Keller. Blind, good heavens, do they expect one blind child to teach another? Has she experience at least, how long did she teach there?

Kate. She was a pupil.

Keller *(heavily).* Katie, Katie. This is her first position?

Kate *(bright voice).* She was valedictorian—

Keller. Here's a houseful of grown-ups can't cope with the child, how can an inexperienced half-blind Yankee schoolgirl manage her?

[JAMES *moves in with the trunk on his shoulder.*]

Annie brings her face within reach of Helen's fingers.

James (*easily*). Great improvement. Now we have two of them to look after.

Keller. You look after those strawberry plants!

[JAMES *stops with the trunk.* KELLER *turns from him without another word, and marches off.*]

James. Nothing I say is right.

Kate. Why say anything? (*She calls.*) Don't be long, Captain, we'll have supper right away—

[*She goes into the house, and through the rear door of the family room.* JAMES *trudges in with the trunk, takes it up the steps to* ANNIE'S *room, and sets it down outside the door. The lights elsewhere dim somewhat.*]

Scene 8

Meanwhile, inside, ANNIE *has given* HELEN *a key; while* ANNIE *removes her bonnet,* HELEN *unlocks and opens the suitcase. The first thing she pulls out is a voluminous[14] shawl. She fingers it until she perceives what it is; then she wraps it around her, and acquiring* ANNIE'S *bonnet and smoked glasses as well, dons the lot: the shawl swamps her, and the bonnet settles down upon the glasses, but she stands before a mirror cocking her head to one side, then to the other, in a mockery of adult action.* ANNIE *is amused, and talks to her as one might to a kitten, with no trace of company manners.*

Annie. All the trouble I went to and that's how I look? (HELEN *then comes back to the suitcase, gropes for more, lifts out a pair of female drawers.*) Oh, no. Not the drawers! (*But* HELEN, *discarding them, comes to the elegant doll. Her fingers explore its features, and when she raises it and finds its eyes open and close, she is at first startled, then delighted. She picks it up, taps its head vigorously, taps her own chest, and nods questioningly.* ANNIE *takes her finger, points it to the doll, points it to* HELEN, *and touching it to her own face, also nods.* HELEN *sits back on her heels, clasps the doll to herself, and rocks it. AN-*

NIE *studies her, still in bonnet and smoked glasses like a caricature[15] of herself, and addresses her humorously.*) All right, Miss O'Sullivan. Let's begin with doll. (*She takes* HELEN'S *hand; in her palm* ANNIE'S *forefinger points, thumb holding her other fingers clenched.*) D. (*Her thumb next holds all her fingers clenched, touching* HELEN'S *palm.*) O. (*Her thumb and forefinger extend.*) L. (*Same contact repeated*) L. (*She puts* HELEN'S *hand to the doll.*) Doll.

James. You spell pretty well. (ANNIE *in one hurried move gets the drawers swiftly back into the suitcase, the lid banged shut, and her head turned, to see* JAMES *leaning in the doorway.*) Finding out if she's ticklish? She is.

[ANNIE *regards him stonily, but* HELEN *after a scowling moment tugs at her hand again, imperious.[16]* ANNIE *repeats the letters, and* HELEN *interrupts her fingers in the middle, feeling each of them, puzzled.* ANNIE *touches* HELEN'S *hand to the doll, and begins spelling into it again.*]

James. What is it, a game?

Annie (*curtly*). An alphabet.

James. Alphabet?

Annie. For the deaf. (HELEN *now repeats the finger movements in air, exactly, her head cocked to her own hand, and* ANNIE'S *eyes suddenly gleam.*) Ho. How *bright* she is!

James. You think she knows what she's doing? (*He takes* HELEN'S *hand, to throw a meaningless gesture into it; she repeats this one too.*) She imitates everything, she's a monkey.

Annie (*very pleased*). Yes, she's a bright little monkey, all right.

[*She takes the doll from* HELEN, *and reaches for her hand;* HELEN *instantly grabs the doll back.* ANNIE *takes it again, and* HELEN'S *hand next, but* HELEN *is incensed now; when* ANNIE *draws her hand to her face to shake her head no, then tries to spell to her,* HELEN *slaps at* ANNIE'S *face.* AN-NIE *grasps* HELEN *by both arms, and swings her into a chair, holding her pinned there, kicking,*

---

14. **voluminous** (və·lōō′mə·nəs): large.

15. **caricature** (kar′ə·kə·chər): an exaggerated portrait.
16. **imperious** (im·pir′ē·əs): arrogant, as if used to being obeyed.

while glasses, doll, bonnet fly in various directions. JAMES *laughs.*]

James. She wants her doll back.

Annie. When she spells it.

James. Spell, she doesn't know the thing has a name, even.

Annie. Of course not, who expects her to, now? All I want is her fingers to learn the letters.

James. Won't mean anything to her. (ANNIE *gives him a look. She then tries to form* HELEN'S *fingers into the letters, but* HELEN *swings a haymaker instead, which* ANNIE *barely ducks, at once pinning her down again.*) Doesn't like that alphabet, Miss Sullivan. You invent it yourself?

[HELEN *is now in a rage, fighting tooth and nail to get out of the chair, and* ANNIE *answers while struggling and dodging her kicks.*]

Annie. Spanish monks under a—vow of silence. Which I wish *you'd* take! (*And suddenly releasing* HELEN'S *hands, she comes and shuts the door in* JAMES'S *face.* HELEN *drops to the floor, groping around for the doll.* ANNIE *looks around desperately, sees her purse on the bed, rummages in it, and comes up with a battered piece of cake wrapped in newspaper; with her foot she moves the doll deftly out of the way of* HELEN'S *groping, and going on her knee she lets* HELEN *smell the cake. When* HELEN *grabs for it,* ANNIE *removes the cake and spells quickly into the reaching hand.*) Cake. From Washington up north, it's the best I can do. (HELEN'S *hand waits, baffled.* ANNIE *repeats it.*) C, a, k, e. Do what my fingers do, never mind what it means. (*She touches the cake briefly to* HELEN'S *nose, pats her hand, presents her own hand.* HELEN *spells the letters rapidly back.* ANNIE *pats her hand enthusiastically, and gives her the cake;* HELEN *crams it into her mouth with both hands.* ANNIE *watches her, with humor.*) Get it down fast, maybe I'll steal that back too. Now. (*She takes the doll, touches it to* HELEN'S *nose, and spells again into her hand.*) D, o, l, l. Think it over. (HELEN *thinks it over, while* ANNIE *presents her own hand. Then* HELEN *spells three letters.* ANNIE *waits a second, then completes the word for* HELEN *in her palm.*) L. (*She hands over the doll, and* HELEN *gets a good grip on its leg.*)

Imitate now, understand later. End of the first les— (*She never finishes, because* HELEN *swings the doll with a furious energy, it hits* ANNIE *squarely in the face, and she falls back with a cry of pain, her knuckles up to her mouth.* HELEN *waits, tensed for further combat. When* ANNIE *lowers her knuckles she looks at blood on them; she works her lips, gets to her feet, finds the mirror, and bares her teeth at herself. Now she is furious herself.*) You little wretch, no one's taught you *any* manners? I'll— (*But rounding from the mirror she sees the door slam,* HELEN *and the doll are on the outside, and* HELEN *is turning the key in the lock.* ANNIE *darts over, to pull the knob; the door is locked fast. She yanks it again.*) Helen! Helen, let me out of—

[*She bats her brow at the folly of speaking, but* JAMES, *now downstairs, hears her and turns to see* HELEN *with the key and doll groping her way down the steps;* JAMES *takes in the whole situation, makes a move to intercept* HELEN, *but then changes his mind, lets her pass, and amusedly follows her out onto the porch. Upstairs* ANNIE *meanwhile rattles the knob, kneels, peers through the keyhole, gets up. She goes to the window, looks down, frowns.* JAMES *from the yard sings gaily up to her:*]

James. Buffalo girl, gonna come out tonight,
Come out tonight,
Come out—

[*He drifts back into the house.* ANNIE *takes a handkerchief, nurses her mouth, stands in the middle of the room, staring at door and window in turn, and so catches sight of herself in the mirror, her cheek scratched, her hair disheveled, her handkerchief bloody, her face disgusted with herself. She addresses the mirror, with some irony.*]

Annie. Don't worry. They'll find you, you're not lost. Only out of place. (*But she coughs, spits something into her palm, and stares at it, outraged.*) And toothless. (*She winces.*) Oo! It hurts.

[*She pours some water into the basin, dips the handkerchief, and presses it to her mouth. Standing there, bent over the basin in pain—with the rest of the set dim and unreal, and the lights upon her taking on the subtle color of the past—she hears again, as do we, the faraway voices, and slowly she lifts her head to them; the boy's voice is the same, the others are cracked old crones in a nightmare, and perhaps we see their shadows.*]

Boy's Voice. It hurts. Annie, it hurts.

First Crone's Voice. Keep that brat shut up, can't you, girlie, how's a body to get any sleep in this damn ward?

Boy's Voice. It hurts. It hurts.

Second Crone's Voice. Shut up, you!

Boy's Voice. Annie, when are we goin' home? You promised!

Annie. Jimmie—

Boy's Voice. Forever and ever, you said forever— (ANNIE *drops the handkerchief, averts to the window, and is arrested there by the next cry.*) Annie? Annie, you there? Annie! It *hurts!*

Third Crone's Voice. Grab him, he's fallin'!

Boy's Voice. *Annie!*

Doctor's Voice (*a pause, slowly*). Little girl. Little girl, I must tell you your brother will be going on a—

[*But* ANNIE *claps her hands to her ears, to shut this out; there is instant silence. As the lights bring the other areas in again,* JAMES *goes to the steps to listen for any sound from upstairs.* KELLER *reentering from left crosses toward the house; he passes* HELEN *en route to her retreat under the pump.* KATE *reenters the rear door of the family room, with flowers for the table.*]

Kate. Supper is ready, Jimmie, will you call your father?

James. Certainly. (*But he calls up the stairs, for* ANNIE'S *benefit.*) Father! Supper!

Keller (*at the door*). No need to shout, I've been cooling my heels for an hour. Sit down.

James. Certainly.

Keller. Viney!

[VINEY *backs in with a roast, while they get settled around the table.*]

Viney. Yes, Cap'n, right here.

Kate. Mildred went directly to sleep, Viney?

Viney. Oh yes, that babe's a angel.

Kate. And Helen had a good supper?

Viney (*vaguely*). I dunno, Miss Kate, somehow she didn't have much of a appetite tonight—

Kate (*a bit guilty*). Oh. Dear.

Keller (*hastily*). Well, now. Couldn't say the same for my part, I'm famished. Kate, your plate.

Kate (*looking*). But where is Miss Annie?

[*A silence.*]

James (*pleasantly*). In her room.

Keller. In her room? Doesn't she know hot food must be eaten hot? Go bring her down at once, Jimmie.

James (*rises*). Certainly. I'll get a ladder.

Keller (*stares*). What?

James. I'll need a ladder. Shouldn't take me long.

Kate (*stares*). What shouldn't take you—

Keller. Jimmie, do as I say! Go upstairs at once and tell Miss Sullivan supper is getting cold—

James. She's locked in her room.

Keller. Locked in her—

Kate. What on earth are you—

James. Helen locked her in and made off with the key.

Kate (*rising*). And you sit here and say nothing?

James. Well, everyone's been telling me not to say anything.

[*He goes serenely out and across the yard, whistling.* KELLER *thrusting up from his chair makes for the stairs.*]

Kate. Viney, look out in back for Helen. See if she has that key.

Viney. Yes, Miss Kate. (VINEY *goes out the rear door.*)

Keller (*calling down*). She's out by the pump! (KATE *goes out on the porch after* HELEN, *while* KELLER *knocks on* ANNIE'S *door, then rattles the knob, imperiously.*) Miss Sullivan! Are you in there?

Annie. Oh, I'm in here, all right.

Keller. Is there no key on your side?

Annie (*with some asperity*[17]). Well, if there was a key in here, *I* wouldn't be in here. Helen took it, the only thing on my side is me.

Keller. Miss Sullivan. I—(*He tries, but cannot*

---

17. **asperity** (as·per′ə·tē): sharpness of temper.

510 **The Elements of Drama**

hold it back.) Not in the house ten minutes, I don't see *how* you managed it!

[*He stomps downstairs again, while* ANNIE *mutters to herself.*]

Annie. And even I'm not on my side.
Keller *(roaring).* Viney!
Viney *(reappearing).* Yes, Cap'n?
Keller. Put that meat back in the oven!

[VINEY *bears the roast off again, while* KELLER *strides out onto the porch.* KATE *is with* HELEN *at the pump, opening her hands.*]

Kate. She has no key.
Keller. Nonsense, she must have the key. Have you searched in her pockets?
Kate. Yes. She doesn't have it.
Keller. Katie, she must have the key.
Kate. Would you prefer to search her yourself, Captain?
Keller. No, I would not prefer to search her! She almost took my kneecap off this evening, when I tried merely to—(JAMES *reappears carrying a long ladder, with* PERCY *running after him to be in on things.)* Take that ladder back!
James. Certainly.

[*He turns around with it.* MARTHA *comes skipping around the upstage corner of the house to be in on things, accompanied by the setter* BELLE.]

Kate. She could have hidden the key.
Keller. Where?
Kate. Anywhere. Under a stone. In the flower beds. In the grass—
Keller. Well, I can't plow up the entire grounds to find a missing key! Jimmie!
James. Sir?
Keller. Bring me a ladder!
James. Certainly.

[VINEY *comes around the downstage side of the house to be in on things; she has* MILDRED *over her shoulder, bleating.* KELLER *places the ladder against* ANNIE'S *window and mounts.* ANNIE *meanwhile is running about making herself presentable, washing the blood off her mouth, straightening her clothes, tidying her hair. Another servant enters to gaze in wonder, increasing the gathering ring of spectators.*]

Kate *(sharply).* What is Mildred doing up?
Viney. Cap'n woke her, ma'am, all that hollerin'.
Keller. Miss Sullivan!

[ANNIE *comes to the window, with as much air of gracious normality as she can manage;* KELLER *is at the window.*]

Annie *(brightly).* Yes, Captain Keller?
Keller. Come out!
Annie. I don't see how I can. There isn't room.
Keller. I intend to carry you. Climb onto my shoulder and hold tight.
Annie. Oh, no. It's—very chivalrous of you, but I'd really prefer to—
Keller. Miss Sullivan, follow instructions! I will not have you also tumbling out of our windows. (ANNIE *obeys, with some misgivings.)* I hope this is not a sample of what we may expect from you. In the way of simplifying the work of looking after Helen.
Annie. Captain Keller, I'm perfectly able to go down a ladder under my own—
Keller. I doubt it, Miss Sullivan. Simply hold onto my neck. (*He begins down with her, while the spectators stand in a wide and somewhat awe-stricken circle, watching.* KELLER *half-misses a rung, and* ANNIE *grabs at his whiskers.)* My *neck,* Miss Sullivan!
Annie. I'm sorry to inconvenience you this way—
Keller. No inconvenience, other than having that door taken down and the lock replaced, if we fail to find that key.
Annie. Oh, I'll look everywhere for it.
Keller. Thank you. Do not look in any rooms that can be locked. There.

[*He stands her on the ground.* JAMES *applauds.*]

Annie. Thank you very much.

[*She smooths her skirt, looking as composed and ladylike as possible.* KELLER *stares around at the spectators.*]

Keller. Go, go, back to your work. What are you looking at here? There's nothing here to look at. (*They break up, move off.)* Now would it be possible for us to have supper, like other people? (*He marches into the house.*)

Kate. Viney, serve supper. I'll put Mildred to sleep.

[*They all go in.* JAMES *is the last to leave, murmuring to* ANNIE *with a gesture.*]

James. Might as well leave the l, a, d, d, e, r, hm?

[ANNIE *ignores him, looking at* HELEN; JAMES *goes in too. Imperceptibly the lights commence to narrow down.* ANNIE *and* HELEN *are now alone in the yard,* HELEN *seated at the pump, where she has been oblivious to it all, a battered little savage, playing with the doll in a picture of innocent contentment.* ANNIE *comes near, leans against the house, and taking off her smoked glasses, studies her, not without awe. Presently* HELEN *rises, gropes around to see if anyone is present;* ANNIE *evades her hand, and when* HELEN *is satisfied she is alone, the key suddenly protrudes out of her mouth. She takes it in her fingers, stands thinking, gropes to the pump, lifts a loose board, drops the key into the well, and hugs herself gleefully.* ANNIE *stares. But after a moment she shakes her head to herself; she cannot keep the smile from her lips.*]

Annie. You *devil.* (*Her tone is one of great respect, humor, and acceptance of challenge.*) You think I'm so easily gotten rid of? You have a thing or two to learn, first. I have nothing else to do. (*She goes up the steps to the porch, but turns for a final word, almost of warning.*) And nowhere to go.

[*And presently she moves into the house to the others, as the lights dim down and out, except for the small circle upon* HELEN *solitary at the pump, which ends the act.*]

"Might as well leave the l, a, d, d, e, r, hm?"

Responding to the Play

Analyzing the Play: Act One

Identifying Facts

1. This play plunges us at once into a desperate situation. What do we learn in the first scene?
2. What **actions** is Helen engaged in, in the scene with Percy and Martha? What do these actions indicate about Helen's "wants"?
3. What exactly does each family member (Kate, Captain Keller, James, and Aunt Ev) want to do about Helen in Scene 3? According to her mother, what does Helen want?
4. By the end of this scene, what **decision** has been reached? What **action** has been taken?
5. In Scene 4, with Anagnos and Annie, why is Annie being sent to the Kellers? What do we learn from Anagnos about Annie's background and **character**?
6. Whose voices does Annie hear in Scenes 4 and 8, and what snatches of information do they give us about Annie's early life?
7. New pressures are introduced in Scene 6, where the Kellers meet Annie. How does each member of the family respond to this addition to their already troubled household?
8. You can see the **conflicts** developing between Annie and Helen, and between Annie and the Kellers. What hints of another conflict, between James and his father, have you noticed? What snatch of dialogue in Scene 5 explains what the basis of this conflict might be?

Interpreting Meanings

9. If Annie is the play's **protagonist**, who or what would you say are her **antagonists**—the forces that block her from getting what she wants?
10. Helen's action of putting her fingers to others' mouths is **symbolic**—that is, it signifies or stands for Helen's *desire* for communication. What would you say is symbolic in the fact that the first thing Annie gives Helen is a key?
11. In Scene 5, we see three people giving sweets to Helen. What does this repeated activity suggest about how Helen has always been treated? What might Annie do for Helen that others cannot?
12. Humor is often used to relieve the tone of serious drama. Did you find any lines or scenes in Act One humorous? Explain.
13. By the end of Act One, what questions do you have about what will happen next in *The Miracle Worker*?
14. It has been said that in a play we must have someone to root for. By the end of this act, whom are you rooting for? Is there anyone you do not especially care about? Explain.

Act Two

Scene 1

It is evening.

The only room visible in the KELLER *house is* ANNIE'S, *where by lamplight* ANNIE *in a shawl is at a desk writing a letter; at her bureau* HELEN *in her customary unkempt state is tucking her doll in the bottom drawer as a cradle, the contents of which she has dumped out, creating as usual a fine disorder.*

ANNIE *mutters each word as she writes her letter, slowly, her eyes close to and almost touching the page, to follow with difficulty her penwork.*

Annie. " . . . and, nobody, here, has, attempted, to, control, her. The, greatest, problem, I, have, is, how, to, discipline, her, without, breaking, her, spirit." *(Resolute voice)* "But, I, shall, insist, on, reasonable, obedience, from, the, start—" *(At which point* HELEN, *groping about on the desk, knocks over the inkwell.* ANNIE *jumps up, rescues her letter, rights the inkwell, grabs a towel to stem the spillage, and then wipes at* HELEN'S *hands;* HELEN *as always pulls free, but not until* ANNIE *first gets three letters into her palm.)* Ink. *(*HELEN *is enough interested in and puzzled by this spelling that she proffers her hand again; so* ANNIE *spells and impassively[1] dunks it back in the spillage.)* Ink. It has a name. *(She wipes the hand clean, and leads* HELEN *to her bureau, where she looks for something to engage her. She finds a sewing card, with needle and thread, and going to her knees, shows* HELEN'S *hand how to connect one row of holes.)* Down. Under. Up. And be careful of the needle—*(*HELEN *gets it, and* ANNIE *rises.)* Fine. You keep out of the ink and perhaps I can keep out of—the soup. *(She returns to the desk, tidies it, and resumes writing her letter, bent close to the page.)* "These, blots, are, her, handiwork. I—" *(She is interrupted by a gasp:* HELEN *has stuck her finger, and sits sucking at it, darkly. Then with vengeful resolve she seizes her doll, and is about to dash its brains out on the floor when* ANNIE *diving catches it in one hand, which she at once shakes with hopping pain but otherwise ig-*

nores, patiently.) All right, let's try temperance.[2] *(Taking the doll, she kneels, goes through the motion of knocking its head on the floor, spells into* HELEN'S *hand.)* Bad, girl. *(She lets* HELEN *feel the grieved expression on her face.* HELEN *imitates it. Next she makes* HELEN *caress the doll and kiss the hurt spot and hold it gently in her arms, then spells into her hand.)* Good, girl. *(She lets* HELEN *feel the smile on her face.* HELEN *sits with a scowl, which suddenly clears; she pats the doll, kisses it, wreathes her face in a large artificial smile, and bears the doll to the washstand, where she carefully sits it.* ANNIE *watches, pleased.)* Very good girl—

[*Whereupon* HELEN *elevates the pitcher and dashes it on the floor instead.* ANNIE *leaps to her feet, and stands inarticulate;* HELEN *calmly gropes back to the sewing card and needle.*

ANNIE *manages to achieve self-control. She picks up a fragment or two of the pitcher, sees* HELEN *is puzzling over the card, and resolutely kneels to demonstrate it again. She spells into* HELEN'S *hand.*

KATE *meanwhile coming around the corner with folded sheets on her arm, halts at the doorway and watches them for a moment in silence; she is moved, but level.*]

Kate *(presently).* What are you saying to her?

[ANNIE *glancing up is a bit embarrassed, and rises from the spelling, to find her company manners.*]

Annie. Oh, I was just making conversation. Saying it was a sewing card.
Kate. But does that—*(She imitates with her fingers.)*—mean that to her?
Annie. No. No, she won't know what spelling is till she knows what a word is.
Kate. Yet you keep spelling to her. Why?
Annie *(cheerily).* I like to hear myself talk!
Kate. The Captain says it's like spelling to the fence post.
Annie *(a pause).* Does he, now.
Kate. Is it?
Annie. No, it's how I watch you talk to Mildred.

---

1. **impassively** (im·pas′iv·lē): without emotion, calmly.

2. **temperance** (tem′pər·əns): self-restraint.

She drops her eyes to spell into Helen's hand.

Kate. Mildred.

Annie. Any baby. Gibberish, grown-up gibberish, baby-talk gibberish, do they understand one word of it to start? Somehow they begin to. If they hear it. I'm letting Helen hear it.

Kate. Other children are not—impaired.

Annie. Ho, there's nothing impaired in that head, it works like a mousetrap!

Kate *(smiles)*. But after a child hears how many words, Miss Annie, a million?

Annie. I guess no mother's ever minded enough to count.

[*She drops her eyes to spell into* HELEN'S *hand, again indicating the card;* HELEN *spells back, and* ANNIE *is amused*.]

Kate *(too quickly)*. What did she spell?

Annie. I spelt card. She spelt cake! *(She takes in* KATE'S *quickness, and shakes her head, gently.)* No, it's only a finger-game to her, Mrs. Keller.

What she has to learn first is that things have names.

Kate. And when will she learn?

Annie. Maybe after a million and one words.

[*They hold each other's gaze;* KATE *then speaks quietly.*]

Kate. I should like to learn those letters, Miss Annie.

Annie (*pleased*). I'll teach you tomorrow morning. That makes only half a million each!

Kate (*then*). It's her bedtime. (ANNIE *reaches for the sewing card,* HELEN *objects,* ANNIE *insists, and* HELEN *gets rid of* ANNIE'S *hand by jabbing it with the needle.* ANNIE *gasps, and moves to grip* HELEN'S *wrist; but* KATE *intervenes with a proffered sweet, and* HELEN *drops the card, crams the sweet into her mouth, and scrambles up to search her mother's hands for more.* ANNIE *nurses her wound, staring after the sweet.*) I'm sorry, Miss Annie.

Annie (*indignantly*). Why does she get a reward? For stabbing me?

Kate. Well—(*Then, tiredly*) We catch our flies with honey, I'm afraid. We haven't the heart for much else, and so many times she simply cannot be compelled.

Annie (*ominous*). Yes. I'm the same way myself. (KATE *smiles, and leads* HELEN *off around the corner.* ANNIE *alone in her room picks up things and in the act of removing* HELEN'S *doll gives way to unmannerly temptation: she throttles it. She drops it on her bed, and stands pondering. Then she turns back, sits decisively, and writes again, as the lights dim on her. Grimly:*) "The, more, I, think, the, more, certain, I, am, that, obedience, is, the, gateway, through, which, knowledge, enters, the, mind, of, the, child—"

Scene 2

On the word "obedience" a shaft of sunlight hits the water pump outside, while ANNIE'S *voice ends in the dark, followed by a distant cock crow; daylight comes up over another corner of the sky, with* VINEY'S *voice heard at once.*

Viney. Breakfast ready!

[VINEY *comes down into the sunlight beam, and pumps a pitcherful of water. While the pitcher is brimming we hear conversation from the dark; the light grows to the family room of the house where all are either entering or already seated at breakfast, with* KELLER *and* JAMES *arguing the war.[3]* HELEN *is wandering around the table to explore the contents of the other plates. When* ANNIE *is in her chair, she watches* HELEN. VINEY *reenters, sets the pitcher on the table;* KATE *lifts the almost empty biscuit plate with an inquiring look,* VINEY *nods and bears it off back, neither of them interrupting the men.* ANNIE *meanwhile sits with fork quiet, watching* HELEN, *who at her mother's plate pokes her hand among some scrambled eggs.* KATE *catches* ANNIE'S *eyes on her, smiles with a wry gesture.* HELEN *moves on to* JAMES'S *plate, the male talk continuing,* JAMES *deferential and* KELLER *overriding.*]

James. —no, but shouldn't we give the devil his due, Father? The fact is we lost the South two years earlier when he outthought us behind Vicksburg.[4]

Keller. Outthought is a peculiar word for a butcher.

James. Harness maker, wasn't he?

Keller. I said butcher, his only virtue as a soldier was numbers and he led them to slaughter with no more regard than for so many sheep.

James. But even if in that sense he was a butcher, the fact is he—

Keller. And a drunken one, half the war.

James. Agreed, Father. If his own people said he was I can't argue he—

Keller. Well, what is it you find to admire in such a man, Jimmie, the butchery or the drunkenness?

James. Neither, Father, only the fact that he beat us.

Keller. He didn't.

James. Is it your contention we won the war, sir?

Keller. He didn't beat us at Vicksburg. We lost Vicksburg because Pemberton gave Bragg five thousand of his cavalry and Loring, whom I knew

---

3. **the war:** the Civil War.
4. **Vicksburg:** On July 4, 1863, at Vicksburg, Mississippi, General Ulysses S. Grant's Northern army won a decisive victory in the Civil War.

personally for a nincompoop before you were born, marched away from Champion's Hill with enough men to have held them, we lost Vicksburg by stupidity verging on treason.

James. I would have said we lost Vicksburg because Grant was one thing no Yankee general was before him—

Keller. Drunk? I doubt it.

James. Obstinate.

Keller. Obstinate. Could any of them compare even in that with old Stonewall?[5] If he'd been there we would still have Vicksburg.

James. Well, the butcher simply wouldn't give up, he tried four ways of getting around Vicksburg and on the fifth try he got around. Anyone else would have pulled north and—

Keller. He wouldn't have got around if we'd had a Southerner in command, instead of a half-breed Yankee traitor like Pemberton—(*While this background talk is in progress,* HELEN *is working around the table, ultimately toward* ANNIE'S *plate. She messes with her hands in* JAMES'S *plate, then in* KELLER'S, *both men taking it so for granted they hardly notice. Then* HELEN *comes groping with soiled hands past her own plate, to* ANNIE'S; *her hand goes to it, and* ANNIE, *who has been waiting, deliberately lifts and removes her hand.* HELEN *gropes again,* ANNIE *firmly pins her by the wrist, and removes her hand from the table.* HELEN *thrusts her hands again,* ANNIE *catches them, and* HELEN *begins to flail and make noises; the interruption brings* KELLER'S *gaze upon them.*) What's the matter there?

Kate. Miss Annie. You see, she's accustomed to helping herself from our plates to anything she—

Annie (*evenly*). Yes, but *I'm* not accustomed to it.

Keller. No, of course not. Viney!

Kate. Give her something, Jimmie, to quiet her.

James (*blandly*). But her table manners are the best she has. Well.

[*He pokes across with a chunk of bacon at* HELEN'S *hand, which* ANNIE *releases; but* HELEN *knocks the bacon away and stubbornly thrusts at*

ANNIE'S *plate,* ANNIE *grips her wrists again, the struggle mounts.*]

Keller. Let her this time, Miss Sullivan, it's the only way we get any adult conversation. If my son's half merits that description. (*He rises.*) I'll get you another plate.

Annie (*gripping* HELEN). I have a plate, thank you.

Kate (*calling*). Viney! I'm afraid what Captain Keller says is only too true, she'll persist in this until she gets her own way.

Keller (*at the door*). Viney, bring Miss Sullivan another plate—

Annie (*stonily*). I have a plate, nothing's wrong with the *plate*, I intend to keep it.

[*Silence for a moment, except for* HELEN'S *noises as she struggles to get loose; the* KELLERS *are a bit nonplused,[6] and* ANNIE *is too darkly intent on* HELEN'S *manners to have any thoughts now of her own.*]

James. Ha. You see why they took Vicksburg?

Keller (*uncertainly*). Miss Sullivan. One plate or another is hardly a matter to struggle with a deprived child about.

Annie. Oh, I'd sooner have a more—(HELEN *begins to kick,* ANNIE *moves her ankles to the opposite side of the chair*)—heroic issue myself, I—

Keller. No, I really must insist you—(HELEN *bangs her toe on the chair and sinks to the floor, crying with rage and feigned[7] injury;* ANNIE *keeps hold of her wrists, gazing down, while* KATE *rises.*) Now she's hurt herself.

Annie (*grimly*). No, she hasn't.

Keller. Will you please let her hands go?

Kate. Miss Annie, you don't know the child well enough yet, she'll keep—

Annie. I know an ordinary tantrum well enough, when I see one, and a badly spoiled child—

James. Hear, hear.

Keller (*very annoyed*). Miss Sullivan! You would have more understanding of your pupil if you had some pity in you. Now kindly do as I—

Annie. Pity? (*She releases* HELEN *to turn equally*

---

5. **Stonewall:** General Thomas J. Jackson, nicknamed "Stonewall" by his Southern troops because of his stubborn refusal to give up.

6. **nonplused** (nän·plust'): brought to a halt, perplexed.
7. **feigned** (fānd): pretended or faked.

annoyed on KELLER *across the table; instantly* HELEN *scrambles up and dives at* ANNIE'S *plate. This time* ANNIE *intercepts her by pouncing on her wrists like a hawk, and her temper boils.*) For this *tyrant?* The whole house turns on her whims, is there anything she wants she doesn't get? I'll tell you what I pity, that the sun won't rise and set for her all her life, and every day you're telling her it will, what good will your pity do her when you're under the strawberries, Captain Keller?

Keller (*outraged*). Kate, for the love of heaven will you—

Kate. Miss Annie, please, I don't think it serves to lose our—

Annie. It does you good, that's all. It's less trouble to feel sorry for her than to teach her anything better, isn't it?

Keller. I fail to see where you have taught her anything yet, Miss Sullivan!

Annie. I'll begin this minute, if you'll leave the room, Captain Keller!

Keller (*astonished*). Leave the—

Annie. Everyone, please.

[*She struggles with* HELEN, *while* KELLER *endeavors to control his voice.*]

Keller. Miss Sullivan, you are here only as a paid teacher. Nothing more, and not to lecture—

Annie. I can't *un*teach her six years of pity if you can't stand up to one tantrum! Old Stonewall, indeed. Mrs. Keller, you promised me help.

Kate. Indeed I did, we truly want to—

Annie. Then leave me alone with her. Now!

Keller (*in a wrath*). Katie, will you come outside with me? At once, please.

[*He marches to the front door.* KATE *and* JAMES *follow him. Simultaneously* ANNIE *releases*

"Then leave me alone with her. Now!"

HELEN'S *wrists, and the child again sinks to the floor, kicking and crying her weird noises;* ANNIE *steps over her to meet* VINEY *coming in the rear doorway with biscuits and a clean plate, surprised at the general commotion.*]

Viney. Heaven sakes—
Annie. Out, please.

[*She backs* VINEY *out with one hand, closes the door on her astonished mouth, locks it, and removes the key.* KELLER *meanwhile snatches his hat from a rack, and* KATE *follows him down the porch steps.* JAMES *lingers in the doorway to address* ANNIE *across the room with a bow.*]

James. If it takes all summer, general.

[ANNIE *comes over to his door in turn, removing her glasses grimly; as* KELLER *outside begins speaking,* ANNIE *closes the door on* JAMES, *locks it, removes the key, and turns with her back against the door to stare ominously at* HELEN, *kicking on the floor.* JAMES *takes his hat from the rack, and going down the porch steps joins* KATE *and* KELLER *talking in the yard,* KELLER *in a sputter of ire.*]

Keller. This girl, this—cub of a girl—*presumes*! I tell you, I'm of half a mind to ship her back to Boston before the week is out. You can inform her so from me!
Kate (*eyebrows up*). I, Captain?
Keller. She's a *hireling*![8] Now I want it clear, unless there's an apology and complete change of manner she goes back on the next train! Will you make that quite clear?
Kate. Where will you be, Captain, while I am making it quite—
Keller. At the office!

[*He begins off left, finds his napkin still in his irate hand, is uncertain with it, dabs his lips with dignity, gets rid of it in a toss to* JAMES, *and marches off.* JAMES *turns to eye* KATE.]

James. Will you? (KATE'S *mouth is set, and* JAMES *studies it lightly.*) I thought what she said was exceptionally intelligent. I've been saying it for years.

---

8. *hireling* (hīr′ling): paid servant (used as an insult).

Kate (*not without scorn*). To his face? (*She comes to relieve him of the white napkin, but reverts again with it.*) Or will you take it, Jimmie? As a flag?

Scene 3

JAMES *stalks out, much offended, and* KATE *turning stares across the yard at the house; the lights narrowing down to the following pantomime in the family room leave her motionless in the dark.*

ANNIE *meanwhile has begun by slapping both keys down on a shelf out of* HELEN'S *reach; she returns to the table, upstage.* HELEN'S *kicking has subsided, and when from the floor her hand finds* ANNIE'S *chair empty she pauses.* ANNIE *clears the table of* KATE'S, JAMES'S, *and* KELLER'S *plates; she gets back to her own across the table just in time to slide it deftly away from* HELEN'S *hand. She lifts the hand and moves it to* HELEN'S *plate, and after an instant's exploration,* HELEN *sits again on the floor and drums her heels.* ANNIE *comes around the table and resumes her chair. When* HELEN *feels her skirt again, she ceases kicking, waits for whatever is to come, renews some kicking, waits again.* ANNIE *retrieving her plate takes up a forkful of food, stops it halfway to her mouth, gazes at it devoid of appetite, and half-lowers it; but after a look at* HELEN *she sighs, dips the forkful toward* HELEN *in a for-your-sake toast, and puts it in her own mouth to chew, not without an effort.*

HELEN *now gets hold of the chair leg, and half-succeeds in pulling the chair out from under her.* ANNIE *bangs it down with her rear, heavily, and sits with all her weight.* HELEN'S *next attempt to topple it is unavailing, so her fingers dive in a pinch at* ANNIE'S *flank.* ANNIE *in the middle of her mouthful almost loses it with startle, and she slaps down her fork to round on* HELEN. *The child comes up with curiosity to feel what* ANNIE *is doing, so* ANNIE *resumes eating, letting* HELEN'S *hand follow the movement of her fork to her mouth; whereupon* HELEN *at once reaches into* ANNIE'S *plate.* ANNIE *firmly removes her hand to her own plate.* HELEN *in reply pinches* ANNIE'S *thigh, a good mean pinchful that makes* ANNIE *jump.* ANNIE *sets the fork down, and sits with her*

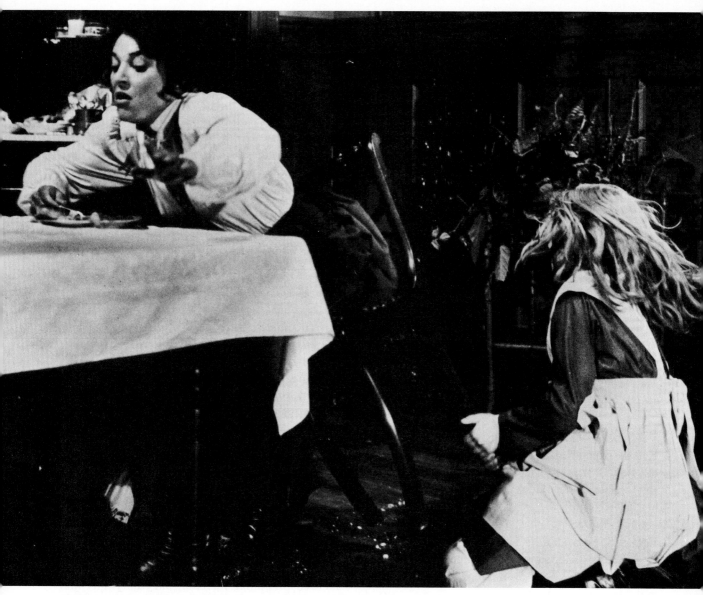

Helen now gets hold of the chair leg.

mouth tight. HELEN *digs another pinch into her thigh, and this time* ANNIE *slaps her hand smartly away;* HELEN *retaliates with a roundhouse fist that catches* ANNIE *on the ear, and* ANNIE'S *hand leaps at once in a forceful slap across* HELEN'S *cheek;* HELEN *is the startled one now.* ANNIE'S *hand in compunction[9] falters to her own face, but when* HELEN *hits at her again,* ANNIE *deliberately slaps her again.* HELEN *lifts her fist irresolute for another roundhouse,* ANNIE *lifts her hand resolute*

for another slap, and they freeze in this posture, while HELEN *mulls it over. She thinks better of it, drops her fist, and giving* ANNIE *a wide berth, gropes around to her* MOTHER'S *chair, to find it empty; she blunders her way along the table upstage, and encountering the empty chairs and missing plates, she looks bewildered; she gropes back to her* MOTHER'S *chair, again touches her cheek and indicates the chair, and waits for the world to answer.*

ANNIE *now reaches over to spell into her hand, but* HELEN *yanks it away; she gropes to the front*

---

9. **compunction** (kəm·punk′shən): regret, or pity for another.

door, tries the knob, and finds the door locked, with no key. She gropes to the rear door, and finds it locked, with no key. She commences to bang on it. ANNIE *rises, crosses, takes her wrists, draws her resisting back to the table, seats her, and releases her hands upon her plate; as* ANNIE *herself begins to sit,* HELEN *writhes out of her chair, runs to the front door, and tugs and kicks at it.* ANNIE *rises again, crosses, draws her by one wrist back to the table, seats her, and sits;* HELEN *escapes back to the door, knocking over her* MOTHER'S *chair en route.* ANNIE *rises again in pursuit, and this time lifts* HELEN *bodily from behind and bears her kicking to her chair. She deposits her, and once more turns to sit.* HELEN *scrambles out, but as she passes* ANNIE *catches her up again from behind and deposits her in the chair;* HELEN *scrambles out on the other side, for the rear door, but* ANNIE *at her heels catches her up and deposits her again in the chair. She stands behind it.* HELEN *scrambles out to her right, and the instant her feet hit the floor* ANNIE *lifts and deposits her back; she scrambles out to her left, and is at once lifted and deposited back. She tries right again and is deposited back, and tries left again and is deposited back, and now feints* ANNIE *to the right but is off to her left, and is promptly deposited back. She sits a moment, and then starts straight over the tabletop, dishware notwithstanding;* ANNIE *hauls her in and deposits her back, with her plate spilling in her lap, and she melts to the floor and crawls under the table, laborious among its legs and chairs; but* ANNIE *is swift around the table and waiting on the other side when she surfaces, immediately bearing her aloft;* HELEN *clutches at* JAMES'S *chair for anchorage, but it comes with her, and halfway back she abandons it to the floor.* ANNIE *deposits her in her chair, and waits.* HELEN *sits tensed, motionless. Then she tentatively puts out her left foot and hand,* ANNIE *interposes her own hand, and at the contact* HELEN *jerks hers in. She tries her right foot,* ANNIE *blocks it with her own, and* HELEN *jerks hers in. Finally, leaning back, she slumps down in her chair, in a sullen biding.*[10]

ANNIE *backs off a step, and watches;* HELEN *offers no move.* ANNIE *takes a deep breath. Both of them and the room are in considerable disorder, two chairs down and the table a mess, but* ANNIE *makes no effort to tidy it; she only sits on her own chair, and lets her energy refill. Then she takes up knife and fork, and resolutely addresses her food.* HELEN'S *hand comes out to explore, and seeing it* ANNIE *sits without moving; the child's hand goes over her hand and fork, pauses—*ANNIE *still does not move—and withdraws. Presently it moves for her own plate, slaps about for it, and stops, thwarted. At this,* ANNIE *again rises, recovers* HELEN'S *plate from the floor and a handful of scattered food from the deranged tablecloth, drops it on the plate, and pushes the plate into contact with* HELEN'S *fist. Neither of them now moves for a pregnant moment—until* HELEN *suddenly takes a grab of food and wolfs it down.* ANNIE *permits herself the humor of a minor bow and warming of her hands together; she wanders off a step or two, watching.* HELEN *cleans up the plate.*

After a glower[11] *of indecision, she holds the empty plate out for more.* ANNIE *accepts it, and crossing to the removed plates, spoons food from them onto it; she stands debating*[12] *the spoon, tapping it a few times on* HELEN'S *plate; and when she returns with the plate she brings the spoon, too. She puts the spoon first into* HELEN'S *hand, then sets the plate down.* HELEN *discarding the spoon reaches with her hand, and* ANNIE *stops it by the wrist; she replaces the spoon in it.* HELEN *impatiently discards it, and again* ANNIE *stops her hand, to replace the spoon in it. This time* HELEN *throws the spoon on the floor.* ANNIE *after considering it lifts* HELEN *bodily out of the chair, and in a wrestling match on the floor closes her fingers upon the spoon, and returns her with it to the chair.* HELEN *again throws the spoon on the floor.* ANNIE *lifts her out of the chair again; but in the struggle over the spoon* HELEN *with* ANNIE *on her back sends her sliding over her head;* HELEN *flees back to her chair and scrambles into it. When* ANNIE *comes after her she clutches it for dear*

---

10. **biding** (bīd′ing): waiting.

11. **glower** (glou′ər): angry look.
12. **debating:** considering.

life; ANNIE *pries one hand loose, then the other, then the first again, then the other again, and then lifts* HELEN *by the waist, chair and all, and shakes the chair loose.* HELEN *wrestles to get free, but* ANNIE *pins her to the floor, closes her fingers upon the spoon, and lifts her kicking under one arm;* with her other hand she gets the chair in place again, and plunks HELEN *back on it. When she releases her hand,* HELEN *throws the spoon at her.*

ANNIE *now removes the plate of food.* HELEN *grabbing finds it missing, and commences to bang*

Annie puts another spoon in her hand.

with her fists on the table. ANNIE *collects a fistful of spoons and descends with them and the plate on* HELEN; *she lets her smell the plate, at which* HELEN *ceases banging, and* ANNIE *puts the plate down and a spoon in* HELEN'S *hand.* HELEN *throws it on the floor.* ANNIE *puts another spoon in her hand.* HELEN *throws it on the floor.* ANNIE *puts another spoon in her hand.* HELEN *throws it on the floor. When* ANNIE *comes to her last spoon she sits next to* HELEN, *and gripping the spoon in* HELEN'S *hand compels her to take food in it up to her mouth.* HELEN *sits with lips shut.* ANNIE *waits a stolid moment, then lowers* HELEN'S *hand. She tries again;* HELEN'S *lips remain shut.* ANNIE *waits, lowers* HELEN'S *hand. She tries again; this time* HELEN *suddenly opens her mouth and accepts the food.* ANNIE *lowers the spoon with a sigh of relief, and* HELEN *spews the mouthful out at her face.* ANNIE *sits a moment with eyes closed, then takes the pitcher and dashes its water into* HELEN'S *face, who gasps astonished.* ANNIE *with* HELEN'S *hand takes up another spoonful, and shoves it into her open mouth.* HELEN *swallows involuntarily, and while she is catching her breath* ANNIE *forces her palm open, throws four swift letters into it, then another four, and bows toward her with devastating pleasantness.*

Annie. Good girl.

[ANNIE *lifts* HELEN'S *hand to feel her face nodding;* HELEN *grabs a fistful of her hair, and yanks. The pain brings* ANNIE *to her knees, and* HELEN *pummels her; they roll under the table, and the lights commence to dim out on them.*]

Scene 4

Simultaneously the light at left has been rising, slowly, so slowly that it seems at first we only imagine what is intimated in the yard: a few ghost-like figures, in silence, motionless, waiting. Now the distant belfry chimes commence to toll the hour, also very slowly, almost—it is twelve—interminably; the sense is that of a long time passing. We can identify the figures before the twelfth stroke, all facing the house in a kind of watch; KATE *is standing exactly as before, but now with the baby* MILDRED *sleeping in her arms, and placed here and there, unmoving, are* AUNT EV *in her hat with a hanky to her nose, and the two children,* PERCY *and* MARTHA, *with necks out-stretched eagerly, and* VINEY *with a knotted kerchief on her head and a feather duster in her hand.*

The chimes cease, and there is silence. For a long moment none of the group moves.

Viney (*presently*). What am I gone do, Miss Kate? It's noontime, dinner's comin', I didn't get them breakfast dishes out of there yet.

[KATE *says nothing, stares at the house.* MARTHA *shifts* HELEN'S *doll in her clutch, and it plaintively says momma.*]

Kate (*presently*). You run along, Martha.

[AUNT EV *blows her nose.*]

Aunt Ev (*wretchedly*). I can't wait out here a minute longer, Kate, why, this could go on all afternoon, too.

Kate. I'll tell the captain you called.

Viney (*to the children*). You hear what Miss Kate say? Never you mind what's going on here. (*Still no one moves.*) You run along tend your own bizness. (*Finally* VINEY *turns on the children with the feather duster.*) Shoo!

[*The two children divide before her. She chases them off.* AUNT EV *comes to* KATE, *on her dignity.*]

Aunt Ev. Say what you like, Kate, but that child is a *Keller.* (*She opens her parasol, preparatory to leaving.*) I needn't remind you that all the Kellers are cousins to General Robert E. Lee. I don't know *who* that girl is. (*She waits; but* KATE *staring at the house is without response.*) The only Sullivan I've heard of—from Boston too, and I'd think twice before locking her up with that kind—is that man John L.[13]

[*And* AUNT EV *departs, with head high. Presently* VINEY *comes to* KATE, *her arms out for the baby.*]

Viney. You give me her, Miss Kate, I'll sneak her in back, to her crib.

---

13. **John L. Sullivan:** a heavyweight boxing champion of the 1880's.

[*But* KATE *is moveless, until* VINEY *starts to take the baby;* KATE *looks down at her before relinquishing her.*]

Kate (*slowly*). This child never gives me a minute's worry.

Viney. Oh yes, this one's the angel of the family, no question 'bout *that*.

[*She begins off rear with the baby, heading around the house; and* KATE *now turns her back on it, her hand to her eyes. At this moment there is the slamming of a door, and when* KATE *wheels,* HELEN *is blundering down the porch steps into the light, like a ruined bat out of hell.* VINEY *halts, and* KATE *runs in;* HELEN *collides with her mother's knees, and reels off and back to clutch them as her savior.* ANNIE *with smoked glasses in hand stands on the porch, also much undone, looking as though she had indeed just taken Vicksburg.* KATE *taking in* HELEN'S *ravaged state becomes steely in her gaze up at* ANNIE.]

Kate. What happened?

[ANNIE *meets* KATE'S *gaze, and gives a factual report, too exhausted for anything but a flat voice.*]

Annie. She ate from her own plate. (*She thinks a moment.*) She ate with a spoon. Herself. (KATE *frowns, uncertain with thought, and glances down at* HELEN.) And she folded her napkin.

[KATE'S *gaze now wavers, from* HELEN *to* ANNIE, *and back.*]

Kate (*softly*). Folded—her napkin?
Annie. The room's a wreck, but her napkin is folded. (*She pauses, then*) I'll be in my room, Mrs. Keller. (*She moves to reenter the house; but she stops at* VINEY'S *voice.*)
Viney (*cheery*). Don't be long, Miss Annie. Dinner be ready right away!

[VINEY *carries* MILDRED *around the back of the house.* ANNIE *stands unmoving, takes a deep breath, stares over her shoulder at* KATE *and* HELEN, *then inclines her head graciously, and goes with a slight stagger into the house. The lights in her room above steal up in readiness for her.*

KATE *remains alone with* HELEN *in the yard, standing protectively over her, in a kind of wonder.*]

Kate (*slowly*). Folded her napkin. (*She contemplates the wild head in her thighs, and moves her fingertips over it, with such a tenderness, and something like a fear of its strangeness, that her own eyes close; she whispers, bending to it.*) My Helen—folded her napkin—

[*And still erect, with only her head in surrender,* KATE *for the first time that we see loses her protracted war with grief; but she will not let a sound escape her, only the grimace of tears comes, and sobs that shake her in a grip of silence. But* HELEN *feels them, and her hand comes up in its own wondering, to interrogate her mother's face, until* KATE *buries her lips in the child's palm.*]

Scene 5

Upstairs, ANNIE *enters her room, closes the door, and stands back against it; the lights, growing on her with their special color, commence to fade on* KATE *and* HELEN. *Then* ANNIE *goes wearily to her suitcase, and lifts it to take it toward the bed. But it knocks an object to the floor, and she turns back to regard it. A new voice comes in a cultured murmur, hesitant as with the effort of remembering a text:*[14]

Man's Voice. This—soul—(ANNIE *puts the suitcase down, and kneels to the object: it is the battered Perkins report, and she stands with it in her hand, letting memory try to speak.*) This—blind, deaf, mute—woman—(ANNIE *sits on her bed, opens the book, and finding the passage, brings it up an inch from her eyes to read, her face and lips following the overheard words, the voice quite factual now.*) Can nothing be done to disinter[15] this human soul? The whole neighborhood would rush to save this woman if she were

---

14. The text is from the writings of Dr. Samuel Gridley Howe, the great director of the Perkins Institution, who had died before Annie arrived there. The words that follow refer to a blind, deaf, and mute woman whom Howe visited in an institution in England.
15. **disinter** (dis·in·tur′): remove from a grave.

buried alive by the caving in of a pit, and labor with zeal until she were dug out. Now if there were one who had as much patience as zeal, he might awaken her to a consciousness of her immortal—(*When the boy's voice comes,* ANNIE *closes her eyes, in pain.*)

Boy's Voice. Annie? Annie, you there?
Annie. Hush.
Boy's Voice. Annie, what's that noise? (ANNIE *tries not to answer; her own voice is drawn out of her, unwilling.*)
Annie. Just a cot, Jimmie.
Boy's Voice. Where they pushin' it?
Annie. To the deadhouse.
Boy's Voice. Annie. Does it hurt, to be dead?

[ANNIE *escapes by opening her eyes, her hand works restlessly over her cheek; she retreats into the book again, but the cracked old crones interrupt, whispering.* ANNIE *slowly lowers the book.*]

First Crone's Voice. There is schools.
Second Crone's Voice. There is schools outside—
Third Crone's Voice. —schools where they teach blind ones, worse'n you—
First Crone's Voice. To read—
Second Crone's Voice. To read and write—
Third Crone's Voice. There is schools outside where they—
First Crone's Voice. There is schools—

[*Silence.* ANNIE *sits with her eyes shining, her hand almost in a caress over the book. Then:*]

Boy's Voice. You ain't goin' to school, are you, Annie?
Annie (*whispering*). When I grow up.
Boy's Voice. You ain't either, Annie. You're goin' to stay here take care of me.
Annie. I'm goin' to school when I grow up.
Boy's Voice. You said we'll be together, forever and ever and ever—
Annie (*fierce*). I'm goin' to school when I grow up!
Doctor's Voice (*slowly*). Little girl. Little girl, I must tell you. Your brother will be going on a journey, soon.

[ANNIE *sits rigid, in silence. Then the boy's voice pierces it, a shriek of terror.*]

Boy's Voice. *Annie!*

[*It goes into* ANNIE *like a sword, she doubles onto it; the book falls to the floor. It takes her a racked moment to find herself and what she was engaged in here; when she sees the suitcase she remembers, and lifts it once again toward the bed. But the voices are with her, as she halts with suitcase in hand.*]

First Crone's Voice. Goodbye, Annie.
Doctor's Voice. Write me when you learn how.
Second Crone's Voice. Don't tell anyone you came from here. Don't tell anyone—
Third Crone's Voice. Yeah, don't tell anyone you came from—
First Crone's Voice. Yeah, don't tell anyone—
Second Crone's Voice. Don't tell any—

[*The echoing voices fade. After a moment* ANNIE *lays the suitcase on the bed; and the last voice comes faintly, from far away.*]

Boy's Voice. Annie. It hurts, to be dead. Forever.

[ANNIE *falls to her knees by the bed, stifling her mouth in it. When at last she rolls blindly away from it, her palm comes down on the open report; she opens her eyes, regards it dully, and then, still on her knees, takes in the print.*]

Man's Voice (*factual*). —might awaken her to a consciousness of her immortal nature. The chance is small indeed; but with a smaller chance they would have dug desperately for her in the pit; and is the life of the soul of less import than that of the body?

[ANNIE *gets to her feet. She drops the book on the bed, and pauses over her suitcase; after a moment she unclasps and opens it. Standing before it, she comes to her decision; she at once turns to the bureau, and taking her things out of its drawers, commences to throw them into the open suitcase.*]

Scene 6

In the darkness down left a hand strikes a match, and lights a hanging oil lamp. It is KELLER'S *hand, and his voice accompanies it, very angry; the lights rising here before they fade on*

ANNIE *show* KELLER *and* KATE *inside a suggestion of a garden house, with a bay-window seat toward center and a door at back.*

Keller. Katie, I will not *have* it! Now you did not see when that girl after supper tonight went to look for Helen in her room—

Kate. No.

Keller. The child practically climbed out of her window to escape from her! What kind of teacher *is* she? I thought I had seen her at her worst this morning, shouting at me, but I come home to find the entire house disorganized by her—Helen won't stay one second in the same room, won't come to the table with her, won't let herself be bathed or undressed or put to bed by her, or even by Viney now, and the end result is that *you* have to do more for the child than before we hired this girl's services! From the moment she stepped off the train she's been nothing but a burden, incompetent, impertinent, ineffectual, immodest—

Kate. She folded her napkin, Captain.

Keller. What?

Kate. Not ineffectual. Helen did fold her napkin.

Keller. What in heaven's name is so extraordinary about folding a napkin?

Kate *(with some humor).* Well. It's more than you did, Captain.

Keller. Katie. I did not bring you all the way out here to the garden house to be frivolous. Now, how does Miss Sullivan propose to teach a deaf-blind pupil who won't let her even touch her?

Kate *(a pause).* I don't know.

Keller. The fact is, today she scuttled any chance she ever had of getting along with the child. If you can see any point or purpose to her staying on here longer, it's more than—

Kate. What do you wish me to do?

Keller. I want you to give her notice.

Kate. I can't.

Keller. Then if you won't, I must. I simply will not—*(He is interrupted by a knock at the back door.* KELLER *after a glance at* KATE *moves to open the door;* ANNIE *in her smoked glasses is standing outside.* KELLER *contemplates her, heavily.)* Miss Sullivan.

Annie. Captain Keller. *(She is nervous, keyed up to seizing the bull by the horns again, and she*

assumes a cheeriness which is not unshaky.) Viney said I'd find you both over here in the garden house. I thought we should—have a talk?

Keller *(reluctantly).* Yes, I— Well, come in. *(*ANNIE *enters, and is interested in this room; she rounds on her heel, anxiously, studying it.* KELLER *turns the matter over to* KATE, *sotto voce.)* Katie.

Kate *(turning it back, courteously).* Captain.

[KELLER *clears his throat, makes ready.*]

Keller. I, ah—wanted first to make my position clear to Mrs. Keller, in private. I have decided I—am not satisfied—in fact, am deeply dissatisfied—with the manner in which—

Annie *(intent).* Excuse me, is this little house ever in use?

Keller *(with patience).* In the hunting season. If you will give me your attention, Miss Sullivan. *(*ANNIE *turns her smoked glasses upon him; they hold his unwilling stare.)* I have tried to make allowances for you because you come from a part of the country where people are—women, I should say—come from who—well, for whom—*(It begins to elude him.)*—allowances must—be made. I have decided, nevertheless, to—that is, decided I—*(vexedly)* Miss Sullivan, I find it difficult to talk through those glasses.

Annie *(eagerly, removing them).* Oh, of course.

Keller *(dourly).* Why do you wear them? The sun has been down for an hour.

Annie *(pleasantly, at the lamp).* Any kind of light hurts my eyes.

[*A silence;* KELLER *ponders her, heavily.*]

Keller. Put them on. Miss Sullivan, I have decided to—give you another chance.

Annie *(cheerfully).* To do what?

Keller. To—remain in our employ. *(*ANNIE'S *eyes widen.)* But on two conditions. I am not accustomed to rudeness in servants or women, and that is the first. If you are to stay, there must be a radical change of manner.

Annie *(a pause).* Whose?

Keller *(exploding).* Yours, young lady, isn't it obvious? And the second is that you persuade me there's the slightest hope of your teaching a child who flees from you now like the plague, to anyone else she can find in this house.

Annie *(a pause)*. There isn't.

[KATE *stops sewing, and fixes her eyes upon* ANNIE.]

Kate. What, Miss Annie?

Annie. It's hopeless here. I can't teach a child who runs away.

Keller *(nonplused)*. Then—do I understand you—propose—

Annie. Well, if we all agree it's hopeless, the next question is what—

Kate. Miss Annie. *(She is leaning toward* ANNIE, *in deadly earnest; it commands both* ANNIE *and* KELLER.*)* I am not agreed. I think perhaps you—underestimate Helen.

Annie. I think everybody else here does.

Kate. She did fold her napkin. She learns, she learns, do you know she began talking when she was six months old? She could say "water." Not really—"wahwah." "Wahwah," but she meant water, she knew what it meant, and only six months old, I never saw a child so—bright, or outgoing—*(Her voice is unsteady, but she gets it level.)* It's still in her, somewhere, isn't it? You should have seen her before her illness, such a good-tempered child—

Annie *(agreeably)*. She's changed.

[*A pause,* KATE *not letting her eyes go; her appeal at last is unconditional, and very quiet.*]

Kate. Miss Annie, put up with it. And with us.

Keller. Us!

Kate. Please? Like the lost lamb in the parable, I love her all the more.

Annie. Mrs. Keller, I don't think Helen's worst handicap is deafness or blindness. I think it's your love. And pity.

Keller. Now what does that mean?

Annie. All of you here are so sorry for her you've kept her—like a pet, why, even a dog you housebreak. No wonder she won't let me come near her. It's useless for me to try to teach her language or anything else here. I might as well—

Kate *(cuts in)*. Miss Annie, before you came we spoke of putting her in an asylum.

[ANNIE *turns back to regard her. A pause.*]

Annie. What kind of asylum?

Keller. For mental defectives.

Kate. I visited there. I can't tell you what I saw, people like—animals, with—*rats,* in the halls, and—*(She shakes her head on her vision.)* What else are we to do, if you give up?

Annie. Give up?

Kate. You said it was hopeless.

Annie. Here. Give up, why, I only today saw what has to be done, to begin! *(She glances from* KATE *to* KELLER, *who stare, waiting; and she makes it as plain and simple as her nervousness permits.)* I—want complete charge of her.

Keller. You already have that. It has resulted in—

Annie. No, I mean day and night. She has to be dependent on me.

Kate. For what?

Annie. Everything. The food she eats, the clothes she wears, fresh—*(She is amused at herself, though very serious.)*—air, yes, the air she breathes, whatever her body needs is a—primer, to teach her out of. It's the only way, the one who lets her have it should be her teacher. *(She considers them in turn; they digest it,* KELLER *frowning,* KATE *perplexed.)* Not anyone who *loves* her, you have so many feelings they fall over each other like feet, you won't use your chances and you won't let me.

Kate. But if she runs from you—*to us*—

Annie. Yes, that's the point. I'll have to live with her somewhere else.

Keller. What!

Annie. Till she learns to depend on and listen to me.

Kate *(not without alarm)*. For how long?

Annie. As long as it takes. *(A pause. She takes a breath.)* I packed half my things already.

Keller. Miss—Sullivan!

[*But when* ANNIE *attends him he is speechless, and she is merely earnest.*]

Annie. Captain Keller, it meets both your conditions. It's the one way I can get back in touch with Helen, and I don't see how I can be rude to you again if you're not around to interfere with me.

Keller *(red-faced)*. And what is your intention if I say no? Pack the other half, for home, and abandon your charge to—to—

Annie. The asylum? (*She waits, appraises* KELLER'S *glare and* KATE'S *uncertainty, and decides to use her weapons.*) I grew up in such an asylum. The state almshouse. (KATE'S *head comes up on this, and* KELLER *stares hard;* ANNIE'S *tone is cheerful enough, albeit level as gunfire.*) Rats— why, my brother Jimmie and I used to play with the rats because we didn't have toys. Maybe you'd like to know what Helen will find there, not on visiting days? One ward was full of the—old women, crippled, blind, most of them dying, but even if what they had was catching there was nowhere else to move them, and that's where they put us. There were younger ones across the hall, prostitutes mostly, with T.B.,[16] and epileptic fits, and a couple of the kind who—keep after other girls, especially young ones, and some insane. Some just had the D.T.'s.[17] The youngest were in another ward to have babies they didn't want, they started at thirteen, fourteen. They'd leave afterward, but the babies stayed and we played with them, too, though a lot of them had—sores all over from diseases you're not supposed to talk about, but not many of them lived. The first year we had eighty, seventy died. The room Jimmie and I played in was the deadhouse, where they kept the bodies till they could dig—

Kate (*closes her eyes*). Oh, my dear—

Annie. —the graves. (*She is immune to* KATE'S *compassion.*) No, it made me strong. But I don't think you need send Helen there. She's strong enough. (*She waits again; but when neither offers her a word, she simply concludes.*) No, I have no conditions, Captain Keller.

Kate (*not looking up*). Miss Annie.

Annie. Yes.

Kate (*a pause*). Where would you—take Helen?

Annie. Ohh—(*Brightly*) Italy?

Keller (*wheeling*). What?

Annie. Can't have everything, how would this garden house do? Furnish it, bring Helen here after a long ride so she won't recognize it, and you can see her every day. If she doesn't know. Well?

Kate (*a sigh of relief*). Is that all?

---

16. **T. B.:** tuberculosis.
17. **D. T.'s:** *delirium tremens*, bodily shaking caused by alcoholism.

Annie. That's all.

Kate. Captain. (KELLER *turns his head; and* KATE'S *request is quiet but firm.*) With your permission?

Keller (*teeth in cigar*). Why must she depend on you for the food she eats?

Annie (*a pause*). I want control of it.

Keller. Why?

Annie. It's a way to reach her.

Keller (*stares*). You intend to *starve* her into letting you touch her?

Annie. She won't starve, she'll learn. All's fair in love and war, Captain Keller. You never cut supplies?

Keller. This is hardly a war!

Annie. Well, it's not love. A siege is a siege.

Keller (*heavily*). Miss Sullivan. Do you *like* the child?

Annie (*straight in his eyes*). Do you?

[*A long pause.*]

Kate. You could have a servant here—

Annie (*amused*). I'll have enough work without looking after a servant! But that boy Percy could sleep here, run errands—

Kate (*also amused*). We can let Percy sleep here, I think, Captain?

Annie (*eagerly*). And some old furniture, all our own—

Kate (*also eager*). Captain? Do you think that walnut bedstead in the barn would be too—

Keller. I have not yet consented to Percy! Or to the house, or to the proposal! Or to Miss Sullivan's—staying on when I—(*But he erupts in an irate surrender.*) Very well, I consent to everything! (*He shakes the cigar at* ANNIE.) For two weeks. I'll give you two weeks in this place, and it will be a miracle if you get the child to tolerate you.

Kate. Two weeks? Miss Annie, can you accomplish anything in two weeks?

Keller. Anything or not, two weeks, then the child comes back to us. Make up your mind, Miss Sullivan, yes or no?

Annie. Two weeks. For only one miracle? (*She nods at him, nervously.*) I'll get her to tolerate me.

[KELLER *marches out, and slams the door.* KATE

on her feet regards ANNIE, *who is facing the door.*]

Kate *(then).* You can't think as little of love as you said. (ANNIE *glances questioning.*) Or you wouldn't stay.

Annie *(a pause).* I didn't come here for love. I came for money!

[KATE *shakes her head to this, with a smile; after a moment she extends her open hand.* ANNIE *looks at it, but when she puts hers out it is not to shake hands, it is to set her fist in* KATE'S *palm.*]

Kate *(puzzled).* Hm?

Annie. A. It's the first of many. Twenty-six!

[KATE *squeezes her fist, squeezes it hard, and hastens out after* KELLER. ANNIE *stands as the door closes behind her, her manner so apprehensive that finally she slaps her brow, holds it, sighs, and, with her eyes closed, crosses herself*[18] *for luck.*]

Scene 7

The lights dim into a cool silhouette scene around her, the lamp paling out, and now, in formal entrances, persons appear around ANNIE *with furniture for the room:* PERCY *crosses the stage with a rocking chair and waits;* MARTHA *from another direction bears in a stool,* VINEY *bears in a small table, and the other servant rolls in a bed partway from left; and* ANNIE, *opening her eyes to put her glasses back on, sees them. She turns around in the room once, and goes into action, pointing out locations for each article; the servants place them and leave, and* ANNIE *then darts around, interchanging them. In the midst of this—while* PERCY *and* MARTHA *reappear with a tray of food and a chair, respectively—* JAMES *comes down from the house with* ANNIE'S *suitcase, and stands viewing the room and her quizzically;* ANNIE *halts abruptly under his eyes, embarrassed, then seizes the suitcase from his hand, explaining herself brightly.*

Annie. I always wanted to live in a doll's house!

[*She sets the suitcase out of the way, and contin-*

ues; VINEY *at left appears to position a rod with drapes for a doorway, and the other servant at center pushes in a wheelbarrow loaded with a couple of boxes of* HELEN'S *toys and clothes.* ANNIE *helps lift them into the room, and the servant pushes the wheelbarrow off. In none of this is any heed taken of the imaginary walls of the garden house; the furniture is moved in from every side and itself defines the walls.*

ANNIE *now drags the box of toys into center, props up the doll conspicuously on top; with the people melted away, except for* JAMES, *all is again still. The lights turn again without pause, rising warmer.*]

James. You don't let go of things easily, do you? How will you—win her hand now, in this place?

Annie *(curtly).* Do I know? I lost my temper, and here we are!

James *(lightly).* No touching, no teaching. Of course, you *are* bigger—

Annie. I'm not counting on force, I'm counting on her. That little imp is dying to know.

James. Know what?

Annie. Anything. Any and every crumb in God's creation. I'll have to use that appetite too. (*She gives the room a final survey, straightens the bed, arranges the curtains.*)

James *(a pause).* Maybe she'll teach you.

Annie. Of course.

James. That she isn't. That there's such a thing as—dullness of heart. Acceptance. And letting go. Sooner or later we all give up, don't we?

Annie. Maybe you all do. It's my idea of the original sin.

James. What is?

Annie *(witheringly).* Giving up.

James *(nettled[19]).* You won't open her. Why can't you let her be? Have some—pity on her, for being what she is—

Annie. If I'd ever once thought like that, I'd be dead!

James *(pleasantly).* You will be. Why trouble? (ANNIE *turns to glare at him; he is mocking.*) Or will you teach me?

---

18. **crosses herself:** makes the sign of the cross, touching her forehead, chest, and both shoulders.

19. **nettled:** irritated.

[*And with a bow, he drifts off.*

Now in the distance there comes the clopping of hoofs, drawing near, and nearer, up to the door; and they halt. ANNIE *wheels to face the door. When it opens this time, the* KELLERS—KATE *in traveling bonnet,* KELLER *also hatted—are standing there with* HELEN *between them; she is in a cloak.* KATE *gently cues her into the room.* HELEN *comes in groping, baffled, but interested in the new surroundings;* ANNIE *evades her exploring hand, her gaze not leaving the child.*]

Annie. Does she know where she is?

Kate (*shakes her head*). We rode her out in the country for two hours.

Keller. For all she knows, she could be in another town—

[HELEN *stumbles over the box on the floor and in it discovers her doll and other battered toys, is pleased, sits to them, then becomes puzzled and suddenly very wary. She scrambles up and back to her mother's thighs, but* ANNIE *steps in, and it is hers that* HELEN *embraces.* HELEN *recoils, gropes, and touches her cheek instantly.*]

Kate. That's her sign for me.

Annie. I know. (HELEN *waits, then recommences her groping, more urgently.* KATE *stands indecisive, and takes an abrupt step toward her, but* ANNIE'S *hand is a barrier.*) In two weeks.

Kate. Miss Annie, I— Please be good to her. These two weeks, try to be very good to her—

Annie. I will. (KATE, *turning then, hurries out. The* KELLERS *cross back of the main house.* ANNIE *closes the door.* HELEN *starts at the door jar, and rushes it.* ANNIE *holds her off.* HELEN *kicks her, breaks free, and careens around the room like an imprisoned bird, colliding with furniture, groping wildly, repeatedly touching her cheek in a growing panic. When she has covered the room, she commences her weird screaming.* ANNIE *moves to comfort her, but her touch sends* HELEN *into a paroxysm[20] of rage: she tears away, falls over her box of toys, flings its contents in handfuls in* ANNIE'S *direction, flings the box too, reels to her feet, rips curtains from the window, bangs and*

kicks at the door, sweeps objects off the mantlepiece and shelf, a little tornado incarnate,[21] all destruction, until she comes upon her doll and, in the act of hurling it, freezes. Then she clutches it to herself, and in exhaustion, sinks sobbing to the floor.* ANNIE *stands contemplating her, in some awe.*) Two weeks. (*She shakes her head, not without a touch of disgusted bewilderment.*) What did I get into now?

[*The lights have been dimming throughout, and the garden house is lit only by moonlight now, with* ANNIE *lost in the patches of dark.*]

Scene 8

KATE, *now hatless and coatless, enters the family room by the rear door, carrying a lamp.* KELLER, *also hatless, wanders simultaneously around the back of the main house to where* JAMES *has been waiting, in the rising moonlight, on the porch.*

Keller. I can't understand it. I had every intention of dismissing that girl, not setting her up like an empress.

James. Yes, what's her secret, sir?

Keller. Secret?

James (*pleasantly*). That enables her to get anything she wants out of you? When I can't.

[JAMES *turns to go into the house, but* KELLER *grasps his wrist, twisting him half to his knees.* KATE *comes from the porch.*]

Keller (*angrily*). She does *not* get anything she—

James (*in pain*). Don't—Don't—

Kate. Captain.

Keller. He's afraid. (*He throws* JAMES *away from him, with contempt.*) What *does* he want out of me?

James (*an outcry*). My God, don't you know? (*He gazes from* KELLER *to* KATE.) Everything you forgot, when you forgot my mother.

Keller. What! (JAMES *wheels into the house.* KELLER *takes a stride to the porch, to roar after him.*) One thing that girl's secret is not, she

---

20. **paroxysm** (par′ək·siz′m): spasm.

21. **tornado incarnate:** a tornado in human form.

doesn't fire one shot and disappear! *(KATE stands rigid, and KELLER comes back to her.)* Katie. Don't mind what he—

Kate. Captain, *I* am proud of you.

Keller. For what?

Kate. For letting this girl have what she needs.

Keller. Why can't my son be? He can't bear me, you'd think I treat him as hard as this girl does Helen— *(He breaks off, as it dawns on him.)*

Kate *(gently)*. Perhaps you do.

Keller. But he has to learn some respect!

Kate *(a pause, wryly)*. Do you like the child? *(She turns again to the porch, but pauses, reluctant.)* How empty the house is tonight.

[After a moment she continues on in. KELLER stands moveless, as the moonlight dies on him.]

Scene 9

The distant belfry chimes toll, two o'clock, and with them, a moment later, comes the boy's voice on the wind, in a whisper:

Boy's voice. Annie. Annie.

[In her patch of dark ANNIE, now in her nightgown, hurls a cup into a corner as though it were her grief, getting rid of its taste through her teeth.]

Annie. No! No pity, I won't have it. *(She comes to HELEN, prone on the floor.)* On either of us. *(She goes to her knees, but when she touches HELEN'S hand the child starts up awake, recoils, and scrambles away from her under the bed. ANNIE stares after her. She strikes her palm on the floor, with passion.)* I *will* touch you! *(She gets to her feet, and paces in a kind of anger around the bed, her hand in her hair, and confronting HELEN at each turn.)* How, How? How do I— *(ANNIE stops. Then she calls out urgently, loudly.)* Percy! Percy! *(She moves swiftly to the drapes, at left.)* Percy, wake up! (PERCY'S *voice comes in a thick sleepy mumble, unintelligible.)* Get out of bed and come in here, I need you. *(ANNIE darts away, finds and strikes a match, and touches it to the hanging lamp; the lights come up dimly in the room, and* PERCY *stands bare to the waist in torn overalls*

between the drapes, with eyes closed, swaying. ANNIE *goes to him, pats his cheeks vigorously.)*

Percy. You awake?

Percy. No'm.

Annie. How would you like to play a nice game?

Percy. Whah?

Annie. With Helen. She's under the bed. Touch her hand.

[She kneels PERCY down at the bed, thrusting his hand under it to contact HELEN'S; HELEN emits an animal sound and crawls to the opposite side, but commences sniffing. ANNIE rounds the bed with PERCY and thrusts his hand again at HELEN; this time HELEN clutches it, sniffs in recognition, and comes scrambling out after PERCY, to hug him with delight. PERCY alarmed struggles, and HELEN'S fingers go to his mouth.]

Percy. Lemme go. Lemme go—(HELEN *fingers her own lips, as before, moving them in dumb imitation.)* She tryin' talk. She gonna hit me—

Annie *(grimly)*. She *can* talk. If she only knew, I'll show you how. She makes letters. *(She opens* PERCY'S *other hand, and spells into it.)* This one is C. C. *(She hits his palm with it a couple of times, her eyes upon HELEN across him;* HELEN *gropes to feel what* PERCY'S *hand is doing, and when she encounters ANNIE'S she falls back from them.)* She's mad at me now, though, she won't play. But she knows lots of letters. Here's another, A. C, a. C, a. *(But she is watching HELEN, who comes groping, consumed with curiosity;* ANNIE *makes the letters in PERCY'S hand, and HELEN pokes to question what they are up to. Then HELEN snatches PERCY'S other hand, and quickly spells four letters into it. ANNIE follows them aloud.)* C, a, k, e! She spells cake, she gets cake. *(She is swiftly over to the tray of food, to fetch cake and a jug of milk.)* She doesn't know yet it means this. Isn't it funny she knows how to spell it and doesn't *know* she knows? *(She breaks the cake in two pieces, and extends one to each;* HELEN *rolls away from her offer.)* Well, if she won't play it with me, I'll play it with you. Would you like to learn one she doesn't know?

Percy. No'm.

[But ANNIE seizes his wrist, and spells to him.]

Annie. M, i, l, k. M is this. I, that's an easy one, just the little finger. L is this— *(And* HELEN *comes back with her hand, to feel the new word.* ANNIE *brushes her away, and continues spelling aloud to* PERCY. HELEN'S *hand comes back again, and tries to get in;* ANNIE *brushes it away again.* HELEN'S *hand insists, and* ANNIE *puts it away rudely.)* No, why should I talk to you? I'm teaching Percy a new word. L. K is this— *(*HELEN *now yanks their hands apart; she butts* PERCY *away, and thrusts her palm out insistently.* ANNIE'S *eyes are bright, with glee.)* Ho, you're *jealous,* are you! *(*HELEN'S *hand waits, intractably²² waits.)* All right. *(*ANNIE *spells into it, milk; and* HELEN *after a moment spells it back to* ANNIE. ANNIE *takes her hand, with her whole face shining. She gives a great sigh.)* Good! So I'm finally back to where I can touch you, hm? Touch and go! No love lost, but here we go. *(She puts the jug of milk into* HELEN'S *hand and squeezes* PERCY'S *shoulder.)* You can go to bed now, you've earned your sleep. Thank you. *(*PERCY *stumbling up weaves his way out through the drapes.* HELEN *finishes drinking, and holds the jug out, for* ANNIE; *when* ANNIE *takes it,* HELEN *crawls onto the bed, and makes for sleep.* ANNIE *stands, looks down at her.)* Now all I have to teach you is—one word. Everything. *(She sets the jug down. On the floor now* ANNIE *spies the doll, stoops to pick it up, and with it dangling in her hand, turns off the lamp. A shaft of moonlight is left on* HELEN *in the bed, and a second shaft on the rocking chair; and* ANNIE, *after putting off her smoked glasses, sits in the rocker with the doll. She is rather happy, and dangles the doll on her knee, and it makes its momma sound.* ANNIE *whispers to it in mock solicitude.)* Hush, little baby. Don't—say a word— *(She lays it against her shoulder, and begins rocking with it, patting its diminutive behind; she talks the lullaby to it humorously at first.)*

Momma's gonna buy you—a mockingbird:
If that—mockingbird don't sing—

[*The rhythm of the rocking takes her into the tune, softly, and more tenderly.*]

Momma's gonna buy you a diamond ring:
If that diamond ring turns to brass—

[*A third shaft of moonlight outside now rises to pick out* JAMES *at the main house, with one foot on the porch step; he turns his body, as if hearing the song.*]

Momma's gonna buy you a looking-glass:
If that looking-glass gets broke—

[*In the family room a fourth shaft picks out* KELLER *seated at the table, in thought; and he, too, lifts his head, as if hearing.*]

Momma's gonna buy you a billy goat:
If that billy goat don't pull—

[*The fifth shaft is upstairs in* ANNIE'S *room, and picks out* KATE, *pacing there; and she halts, turning her head, too, as if hearing.*]

Momma's gonna buy you a cart and bull:
If that cart and bull turns over,
Momma's gonna buy you a dog named Rover:
If that dog named Rover won't bark—

[*With the shafts of moonlight on* HELEN, *and* JAMES, *and* KELLER, *and* KATE, *all moveless, and* ANNIE *rocking the doll, the curtain ends the act.*]

---

22. **intractably** (in·trak′tə·blē): stubbornly.

Responding to the Play

Analyzing the Play: Act Two

Identifying Facts

1. According to Annie's letter and her conversation with Kate Keller in Scene 1, what must be done to help Helen?
2. In contrast, what actions at the breakfast table in Scene 2 reveal the way the Kellers treat Helen?
3. At the breakfast table, the **conflicts** about Helen's treatment turn into an open argument. What point does Annie argue when she loses her temper? How does Annie openly defy the Captain in this scene?
4. What is Annie's goal in that struggle with Helen in Scene 3? What is the outcome of the battle?
5. **Reversals** are an important part of drama. We think something is going well, and then suddenly it is going badly. Or something is going badly, and then suddenly it goes well. When Annie packs her suitcase in Scene 5, what does the audience think she intends to do? What does she really intend? (Did you feel this reversal was exciting?)
6. What makes Annie decide to reveal her past to the shocked Kellers in Scene 6?
7. What bargain has been struck between Annie and the Kellers by the end of Act Two?
8. Why do James and his father argue in Scene 8? The stage direction on page 531 says, "it dawns on him," as Captain Keller breaks off a remark about James. What has dawned on him?

Interpreting Meanings

9. Why does Annie feel that if she teaches Helen only one word, she has taught her "everything"?
10. Annie's voices reveal her **interior conflict**. Why does she seem to feel guilty about her dead brother Jimmie?
11. Why do you think Annie has not given up on this huge task of teaching Helen Keller? What does Annie have at stake? You can find many clues in the voices of Annie's past that speak through her **flashbacks.**
12. After a while, the conflicts in a play wouldn't hold our interest unless the characters involved were also developing and changing. What **changes,** if any, do you see in the main members of the Keller family by the end of Act Two?
13. At this point in the play, what feelings do you have for the major characters: for Annie, Kate, Captain Keller, and James? Tell what you admire about each one, and what you do not admire.
14. Someone once said that the art of playwriting is to get your character up a tree in Act One, throw stones at him (or her) in Act Two, and get him down in Act Three. What new "stones" or more serious problems have been hurled at Annie by the end of this act?

Act Three

Scene 1

The stage is totally dark, until we see ANNIE *and* HELEN *silhouetted on the bed in the garden house.* ANNIE'S *voice is audible, very patient, and worn; it has been saying this for a long time.*

Annie. Water, Helen. This is water. W, a, t, e, r. It has a *name.* (*A silence. Then:*) Egg, e, g, g. It has a *name,* the name stands for the thing. Oh, it's so simple, simple as birth, to explain. (*The lights have commenced to rise, not on the garden house but on the homestead. Then:*) Helen, Helen, the chick *has* to come out of its shell, sometime. You come out, too. (*In the bedroom upstairs, we see* VINEY *unhurriedly washing the window, dusting, turning the mattress, readying the room for use again; then in the family room a diminished group at one end of the table—*KATE, KELLER, JAMES*—finishing up a quiet breakfast; then outside, down right, the other servant on his knees, assisted by* MARTHA, *working with a trowel around a new trellis and wheelbarrow. The scene is one of everyday calm, and all are oblivious to* ANNIE'S *voice.*) There's only one way out, for you, and it's language. To learn that your fingers can talk. And say anything, anything you can name. This is mug. Mug, m, u, g. Helen, it has a *name.* It—has—a—*name.*

[KATE *rises from the table.*]

Keller (*gently*). You haven't eaten, Katie.
Kate (*smiles, shakes her head*). I haven't the appetite. I'm too—restless, I can't sit to it.
Keller. You should eat, my dear. It will be a long day, waiting.
James (*lightly*). But it's been a short two weeks. I never thought life could be so—noiseless, went much too quickly for me.

[KATE *and* KELLER *gaze at him, in silence.* JAMES *becomes uncomfortable.*]

Annie. C, a, r, d. Card. C, a—
James. Well, the house has been practically normal, hasn't it?
Keller (*harshly*). Jimmie.
James. Is it wrong to enjoy a quiet breakfast, after

five years? And you two even seem to enjoy each other—
Keller. It could be even more noiseless, Jimmie, without your tongue running every minute. Haven't you enough feeling to imagine what Katie has been undergoing, ever since—

[KATE *stops him, with her hand on his arm.*]

Kate. Captain. (*To* JAMES) It's true. The two weeks have been normal, quiet, all you say. But not short. Interminable. (*She rises, and wanders out; she pauses on the porch steps, gazing toward the garden house.*)
Annie (*fading*). W, a, t, e, r. But it means *this.* W, a, t, e, r. *This.* W, a, t—
James. I only meant that Miss Sullivan is a boon. Of contention, though, it seems.[1]
Keller (*heavily*). If and when you're a parent, Jimmie, you will understand what separation means. A mother loses a—protector.
James (*baffled*). Hm?
Keller. You'll learn, we don't just keep our children safe. They keep us safe. (*He rises, with his empty coffee cup and saucer.*) There are of course all kinds of separation, Katie has lived with one kind for five years. And another is disappointment. In a child.

[*He goes with the cup out the rear door.* JAMES *sits for a long moment of stillness. In the garden house the lights commence to come up;* ANNIE, *haggard at the table, is writing a letter, her face again almost in contact with the stationery;* HELEN, *apart on the stool, and for the first time as clean and neat as a button, is quietly crocheting an endless chain of wool, which snakes all around the room.*]

Annie. "I, feel, every, day, more, and, more, in—" (*She pauses, and turns the pages of a dictionary open before her; her finger descends the words to a full stop. She elevates her eyebrows, then copies the word.*) "—adequate."

[*In the main house* JAMES *pushes up, and goes to the front doorway, after* KATE.]

---

1. **a boon of contention.** James is making a joke. A "boon" is a blessing. A "bone of contention" is a subject that causes argument or disagreement.

James. Kate? (KATE *turns her glance.* JAMES *is rather wary.*) I'm sorry. Open my mouth, like that fairy tale, frogs jump out.

Kate. No. It has been better. For everyone. *(She starts away, up center.)*

Annie *(writing).* "If, only, there, were, someone, to, help, me, I, need, a, teacher, as, much, as, Helen—"

James. Kate. (KATE *halts, waits.*) What does he want from me?

Kate. That's not the question. Stand up to the world, Jimmie, that comes first.

James *(a pause, wryly).* But the world is him.

Kate. Yes. And no one can do it for you.

James. Kate. *(His voice is humble.)* At least we— Could you—be my friend?

Kate. I am.

[KATE *turns to wander, up back of the garden house.* ANNIE'S *murmur comes at once; the lights begin to die on the main house.*]

Annie. "—my, mind, is, undisiplined, full, of, skips, and, jumps, and—" *(She halts, rereads, frowns.)* Hm. (ANNIE *puts her nose again in the dictionary, flips back to an earlier page, and fingers down the words;* KATE *presently comes down toward the bay window with a trayful of food.)* Disinter—disinterested—disjoin—dis— *(She backtracks, indignant.)* Disinterested, disjoin— Where's disipline? *(She goes a page or two back, searching with her finger, muttering.)* What a dictionary, have to know how to spell it before you can look up how to spell it, disciple, *discipline!* Diskipline. *(She corrects the word in her letter.)* Undisciplined.

[*But her eyes are bothering her, she closes them in exhaustion and gently fingers the eyelids.* KATE *watches her through the window.*]

Kate. What are you doing to your eyes?

[ANNIE *glances around; she puts her smoked glasses on, and gets up to come over, assuming a cheerful energy.*]

Annie. It's worse on my vanity! I'm learning to spell. It's like a surprise party, the most unexpected characters turn up.

Kate. You're not to overwork your eyes, Miss Annie.

Annie. Well. *(She takes the tray, sets it on her chair, and carries chair and tray to* HELEN.*)* Whatever I spell to Helen I'd better spell right.

Kate *(almost wistful).* How—serene she is.

Annie. She learned this stitch yesterday. Now I can't get her to stop! *(She disentangles one foot from the wool chain, and sets the chair before* HELEN. HELEN *at its contact with her knee feels the plate, promptly sets her crocheting down, and tucks the napkin in at her neck, but* ANNIE *withholds the spoon; when* HELEN *finds it missing, she folds her hands in her lap, and quietly waits.* ANNIE *twinkles at* KATE *with mock devoutness.)* Such a little lady, she'd sooner starve than eat with her fingers.

[*She gives* HELEN *the spoon, and* HELEN *begins to eat, neatly.*]

Kate. You've taught her so much, these two weeks. I would never have—

Annie. Not enough. *(She is suddenly gloomy, shakes her head.)* Obedience isn't enough. Well, she learned two nouns this morning, key and water, brings her up to eighteen nouns and three verbs.

Kate *(hesitant).* But—not—

Annie. No. Not that they mean things. It's still a finger-game, no meaning. *(She turns to* KATE, *abruptly.)* Mrs. Keller— *(But she defers it; she comes back, to sit in the bay, and lifts her hand.)* Shall we play our finger-game?

Kate. How will she learn it?

Annie. It will come.

[*She spells a word;* KATE *does not respond.*]

Kate. How?

Annie *(a pause).* How does a bird learn to fly? *(She spells again.)* We're born to use words, like wings, it has to come.

Kate. How?

Annie *(another pause, wearily).* All right. I don't know how. *(She pushes up her glasses, to rub her eyes.)* I've done everything I could think of. Whatever she's learned here—keeping herself clean, knitting, stringing beads, meals, setting-up exercises each morning, we climb trees, hunt eggs, yesterday a chick was born in her hands—all of it I spell, everything we do, we never stop spelling. I go to bed with—writer's cramp from talking so much!

Kate. I worry about you, Miss Annie. You must rest.

Annie. Now? She spells back in her *sleep,* her fingers make letters when she doesn't know! In her bones those five fingers know, that hand aches to—speak out, and something in her mind is asleep, how do I—nudge that awake? That's the one question.

Kate. With no answer.

Annie (*long pause*). Except keep at it. Like this.

[*She again begins spelling—I, need—and* KATE'S *brows gather, following the words.*]

Kate. More—time? (*She glances at* ANNIE, *who looks her in the eyes, silent.*) Here?

Annie. Spell it.

[KATE *spells a word—no—shaking her head;* ANNIE *spells two words—why, not—back, with an impatient question in her eyes; and* KATE *moves her head in pain to answer it.*]

Kate. Because I can't—

Annie. Spell it! If she ever learns, you'll have a lot to tell each other, start now.

[KATE *painstakingly spells in air. In the midst of this the rear door opens, and* KELLER *enters with the setter* BELLE *in tow.*]

Keller. Miss Sullivan? On my way to the office, I brought Helen a playmate—

Annie. Outside please, Captain Keller.

Keller. My dear child, the two weeks are up today, surely you don't object to—

Annie (*rising*). They're not up till six o'clock.

Keller (*indulgent*). Oh, now. What difference can a fraction of one day—

Annie. An agreement is an agreement. Now you've been very good, I'm sure you can keep it up for a few more hours.

[*She escorts* KELLER *by the arm over the threshold; he obeys, leaving* BELLE.]

Keller. Miss Sullivan, you are a tyrant.

Annie. Likewise, I'm sure. You can stand there, and close the door if she comes.

Kate. I don't think you know how eager we are to have her back in our arms—

Annie. I do know, it's my main worry.

Keller. It's like expecting a new child in the house. Well, she *is,* so—composed, so— (*Gently*) attractive. You've done wonders for her, Miss Sullivan.

Annie (*not a question*). Have I.

Keller. If there's anything you want from us in repayment tell us, it will be a privilege to—

Annie. I just told Mrs. Keller. I want more time.

Kate. Miss Annie—

Annie. Another week.

[HELEN *lifts her head, and begins to sniff.*]

Keller. We miss the child. *I* miss her, I'm glad to say, that's a different debt I owe you—

Annie. Pay it to Helen. Give *her* another week.

Kate (*gently*). Doesn't she miss us?

Keller. Of course she does. What a wrench this unexplainable—exile must be to her, can you say it's not?

Annie. No. But I—

[HELEN *is off the stool, to grope about the room; when she encounters* BELLE, *she throws her arms around the dog's neck in delight.*]

Kate. Doesn't she need affection too, Miss Annie?

Annie (*wavering*). She—never shows me she needs it, she won't have any—caressing or—

Kate. But you're not her mother.

Keller. And what would another week accomplish? We are more than satisfied, you've done more than we ever thought possible, taught her constructive—

Annie. I can't promise anything. All I can—

Keller (*no break*). —things to do, to behave like—even look like—a human child, so manageable, contented, cleaner, more—

Annie (*withering*). Cleaner.

Keller. Well. We say cleanliness is next to godliness, Miss—

Annie. Cleanliness is next to nothing, she has to learn that everything has its name! That words can be her *eyes,* to everything in the world outside her, and inside too, what is she without words? With them she can think, have ideas, be reached, there's not a thought or fact in the world that can't be hers. You publish a newspaper, Captain Keller, do I have to tell you what words are? And she has them already—

Keller. Miss Sullivan.

Annie. —eighteen nouns and three verbs, they're in her fingers now, I need only time to push *one* of them into her mind! One, and everything under the sun will follow. Don't you see what she's learned here is only clearing the way for that? I can't risk her unlearning it, give me more time alone with her, another week to—

Keller. Look. *(He points, and* ANNIE *turns.* HELEN *is playing with* BELLE'S *claws; she makes letters with her fingers, shows them to* BELLE, *waits with her palm, then manipulates the dog's claws.)* What is she spelling?

[*A silence.*]

Kate. Water?

[ANNIE *nods.*]

Keller. Teaching a dog to spell. *(A pause)* The dog doesn't know what she means, any more than she knows what you mean, Miss Sullivan. I think you ask too much, of her and yourself. God may not have meant Helen to have the—eyes you speak of.

Annie *(toneless).* I mean her to.

Keller *(curiously).* What is it to you? (ANNIE'S *head comes slowly up.)* You make us see how we indulge her for our sake. Is the opposite true, for you?

Annie *(then).* Half a week?

Keller. An agreement *is* an agreement.

Annie. Mrs. Keller?

Kate *(simply).* I want her back.

[*A wait;* ANNIE *then lets her hands drop in surrender, and nods.*]

Keller. I'll send Viney over to help you pack.

Annie. Not until six o'clock. I have her till six o'clock.

Keller *(consenting).* Six o'clock. Come, Katie.

[KATE *leaving the window joins him around back, while* KELLER *closes the door; they are shut out. Only the garden house is daylit now, and the light on it is narrowing down.* ANNIE *stands watching*

HELEN *work* BELLE'S *claws. Then she settles beside them on her knees, and stops* HELEN'S *hand.*]

Annie *(gently).* No. *(She shakes her head, with* HELEN'S *hand to her face, then spells.)* Dog. D, o, g, Dog. *(She touches* HELEN'S *hand to* BELLE. HELEN *dutifully pats the dog's head, and resumes spelling to its paw.)* Not water. (ANNIE *rolls to her feet, brings a tumbler of water back from the tray, and kneels with it, to seize* HELEN'S *hand and spell.)* Here. Water. *Water. (She thrusts* HELEN'S *hand into the tumbler.* HELEN *lifts her hand out dripping, wipes it daintily on* BELLE'S *hide, and taking the tumbler from* ANNIE, *endeavors to thrust* BELLE'S *paw into it.* ANNIE *sits watching, wearily.)* I don't know how to tell you. Not a soul in the world knows how to tell you. Helen, Helen. *(She bends in compassion to touch her lips to* HELEN'S *temple, and instantly* HELEN *pauses, her hands off the dog, her head slightly averted. The lights are still narrowing, and* BELLE *slinks off. After a moment* ANNIE *sits back.)* Yes, what's it to me? They're satisfied. Give them back their child and dog, both housebroken, everyone's satisfied. But me, and you. (HELEN'S *hand comes out into the light, groping.)* Reach. *Reach!* (ANNIE *extending her own hand grips* HELEN'S; *the two hands are clasped, tense in the light, the rest of the room changing in shadow.)* I wanted to teach you—oh, everything the earth is full of, Helen, everything on it that's ours for a wink and it's gone, and what we are on it, the—light we bring to it and leave behind in—words, why, you can see five thousand years back in a light of words, everything we feel, think, know—and share, in words, so not a soul is in darkness, or done with, even in the grave. And I know, I *know,* one word and I can—put the world in your hand—and whatever it is to me, I won't take less! How, how, how do I tell you that *this*— *(She spells:)* —means a *word,* and the word means this *thing,* wool? *(She thrusts the wool at* HELEN'S *hand;* HELEN *sits, puzzled.* ANNIE *puts the crocheting aside.)* Or this—s, t, o, o, l—means this *thing,* stool? *(She claps* HELEN'S *palm to the stool.* HELEN *waits, uncomprehending.* ANNIE *snatches up her napkin, spells:)* Napkin! *(She forces it on* HELEN'S *hand, waits, discards it, lifts a fold of the child's dress,* *spells:)* Dress! *(She lets it drop, spells:)* F, a, c, e, face! *(She draws* HELEN'S *hand to her cheek, and pressing it there, staring into the child's response-less eyes, hears the distant belfry begin to toll, slowly: one, two, three, four, five, six.)*

Scene 2

On the third stroke the lights stealing in around the garden house show us figures waiting: VINEY, *the other servant,* MARTHA, PERCY *at the drapes, and* JAMES *on the dim porch.* ANNIE *and* HELEN *remain, frozen. The chimes die away. Silently* PERCY *moves the drape rod back out of sight;* VINEY *steps into the room—not using the door—and unmakes the bed; the other servant brings the wheelbarrow over, leaves it handy, rolls the bed off;* VINEY *puts the bed linens on top of a waiting boxful of* HELEN'S *toys, and loads the box on the wheelbarrow;* MARTHA *and* PERCY *take out the chairs, with the trayful, then the table; and* JAMES, *coming down and into the room, lifts* ANNIE'S *suitcase from its corner.* VINEY *and the other servant load the remaining odds and ends on the wheelbarrow, and the servant wheels it off.* VINEY *and the children departing leave only* JAMES *in the room with* ANNIE *and* HELEN. JAMES *studies the two of them, without mockery, and then, quietly going to the door and opening it, bears the suitcase out, and houseward. He leaves the door open.*

KATE *steps into the doorway, and stands.* AN-NIE *lifting her gaze from* HELEN *sees her; she takes* HELEN'S *hand from her cheek, and returns it to the child's own, stroking it there twice, in her mother-sign, before spelling slowly into it.*

Annie. M, o, t, h, e, r. Mother. *(*HELEN *with her hand free strokes her cheek, suddenly forlorn.* ANNIE *takes her hand again.)* M, o, t, h— *(But* KATE *is trembling with such impatience that her voice breaks from her, harsh.)* Let her *come!*

[ANNIE *lifts* HELEN *to her feet, with a turn, and gives her a little push. Now* HELEN *begins groping, sensing something, trembling herself; and* KATE *falling one step in onto her knees clasps her, kissing her.* HELEN *clutches her, tight as she can.*

KATE *is inarticulate, choked, repeating* HELEN'S *name again and again. She wheels with her in her arms, to stumble away out the doorway;* ANNIE *stands unmoving, while* KATE *in a blind walk carries* HELEN *like a baby behind the main house, out of view.*

ANNIE *is now alone on the stage. She turns, gazing around at the stripped room, bidding it silently farewell, impassively, like a defeated general on the deserted battlefield. All that remains is a stand with a basin of water; and here* ANNIE *takes up an eyecup, bathes each of her eyes, empties the eyecup, drops it in her purse, and tiredly locates her smoked glasses on the floor. The lights alter subtly; in the act of putting on her glasses* ANNIE *hears something that stops her, with head lifted. We hear it too, the voices out of the past, including her own now, in a whisper:*]

Boy's Voice. You said we'd be together, forever— You promised, forever and—Annie!
Anagnos' Voice. But that battle is dead and done with, why not let it stay buried?
Annie's Voice *(whispering).* I think God must owe me a resurrection.
Anagnos' Voice. What?

[*A pause, and* ANNIE *answers it herself, heavily.*]

Annie. And I owe God one.
Boy's Voice. Forever and ever— *(*ANNIE *shakes her head.)* —forever, and ever, and— *(*ANNIE *covers her ears.)* —forever, and ever, and ever—

[*It pursues* ANNIE; *she flees to snatch up her purse, wheels to the doorway, and* KELLER *is standing in it. The lights have lost their special color.*]

Keller. Miss—Annie. *(He has an envelope in his fingers.)* I've been waiting to give you this.
Annie *(after a breath).* What?
Keller. Your first month's salary. *(He puts it in her hand.)* With many more to come, I trust. It doesn't express what we feel, it doesn't pay our debt. For what you've done.
Annie. What have I done?
Keller. Taken a wild thing, and given us back a child.

Annie (*presently*). I taught her one thing, no. Don't do this, don't do that—

Keller. It's more than all of us could, in all the years we—

Annie. I wanted to teach her what language is. I wanted to teach her yes.

Keller. You will have time.

Annie. I don't know how. I know without it to do nothing but obey is—no gift, obedience without understanding is a—blindness, too. Is that all I've wished on her?

Keller (*gently*). No, no—

Annie. Maybe. I don't know what else to do. Simply go on, keep doing what I've done, and have—faith that inside she's— That inside it's waiting. Like water, underground. All I can do is keep on.

Keller. It's enough. For us.

Annie. You can help, Captain Keller.

Keller. How?

Annie. Even learning no has been at a cost. Of much trouble and pain. Don't undo it.

Keller. Why should we wish to—

Annie (*abruptly*). The world isn't an easy place for anyone. I don't want her just to obey but to let her have her way in everything is a lie, to *her*, I can't— (*Her eyes fill, it takes her by surprise, and she laughs through it.*) And I don't even love her, she's not my child! Well. You've got to stand between that lie and her.

Keller. We'll try.

Annie. Because *I* will. As long as you let me stay, that's one promise I'll keep.

Keller. Agreed. We've learned something too, I hope. (*A pause*) Won't you come now, to supper?

Annie. Yes. (*She wags the envelope, ruefully.*) Why doesn't God pay His debts each month?

Keller. I beg your pardon?

Annie. Nothing. I used to wonder how I could— (*The lights are fading on them, simultaneously rising on the family room of the main house, where* VINEY *is polishing glassware at the table set for dinner.*) —earn a living.

Keller. Oh, you do.

Annie. I really do. Now the question is, can I survive it!

[KELLER *smiles, offers his arm.*]

Keller. May I?

[ANNIE *takes it, and the lights lose them as he escorts her out.*]

Scene 3

Now in the family room the rear door opens, and HELEN *steps in. She stands a moment, then sniffs in one deep grateful breath, and her hands go out vigorously to familiar things, over the door panels, and to the chairs around the table, and over the silverware on the table, until she meets* VINEY; *she pats her flank approvingly.*

Viney. Oh, we glad to have you back too, prob'ly.

[HELEN *hurries groping to the front door, opens and closes it, removes its key, opens and closes it again to be sure it is unlocked, gropes back to the rear door and repeats the procedure, removing its key and hugging herself gleefully.*

AUNT EV *is next in by the rear door, with a relish tray; she bends to kiss* HELEN'S *cheek.* HELEN *finds* KATE *behind her, and thrusts the keys at her.*]

Kate. What? Oh. (*To* EV) Keys. (*She pockets them, lets* HELEN *feel them.*) Yes, *I'll* keep the keys. I think we've had enough of locked doors, too.

[JAMES, *having earlier put* ANNIE'S *suitcase inside her door upstairs and taken himself out of view around the corner, now reappears and comes down the stairs as* ANNIE *and* KELLER *mount the porch steps. Following them into the family room, he pats* ANNIE'S *hair in passing, rather to her surprise.*]

James. Evening, general.

[*He takes his own chair opposite.*

VINEY *bears the empty water pitcher out to the porch. The remaining suggestion of garden house is gone now, and the water pump is unobstructed;* VINEY *pumps water into the pitcher.*

KATE *surveying the table breaks the silence.*]

Kate. Will you say grace, Jimmie?

[*They bow their heads, except for* HELEN, *who palms her empty plate and then reaches to be sure her mother is there.* JAMES *considers a moment, glances across at* ANNIE, *lowers his head again, and obliges.*]

James (*lightly*). And Jacob was left alone, and wrestled with an angel until the breaking of the day; and the hollow of Jacob's thigh was out of joint, as he wrestled with him; and the angel said, Let me go, for the day breaketh. And Jacob said, I will not let thee go, except thou bless me. Amen. (ANNIE *has lifted her eyes suspiciously at* JAMES, *who winks expressionlessly and inclines his head to* HELEN.) Oh, you angel.

[*The others lift their faces;* VINEY *returns with the pitcher, setting it down near* KATE, *then goes out the rear door; and* ANNIE *puts a napkin around* HELEN.]

Aunt Ev. That's a very strange grace, James.
Keller. Will you start the muffins, Ev?
James. It's from the Good Book, isn't it?
Aunt Ev (*passing a plate*). Well, of course it is. Didn't you know?
James. Yes, I knew.
Keller (*serving*). Ham, Miss Annie?
Annie. Please.
Aunt Ev. Then why ask?
James. I meant it *is* from the Good Book, and therefore a fitting grace.
Aunt Ev. Well. I don't know about *that.*
Kate (*with the pitcher*). Miss Annie?
Annie. Thank you.
Aunt Ev. There's an awful *lot* of things in the Good Book that I wouldn't care to hear just before eating.

[*When* ANNIE *reaches for the pitcher,* HELEN *removes her napkin and drops it to the floor.* ANNIE *is filling* HELEN'S *glass when she notices it; she considers* HELEN'S *bland expression a moment, then bends, retrieves it, and tucks it around* HELEN'S *neck again.*]

James. Well, fitting in the sense that Jacob's thigh was out of joint, and so is this piggie's.
Aunt Ev. I declare, James—
Kate. Pickles, Aunt Ev?

Aunt Ev. Oh, I should say so, you know my opinion of your pickles—
Kate. This is the end of them, I'm afraid. I didn't put up nearly enough last summer, this year I intend to—

[*She interrupts herself, seeing* HELEN *deliberately lift off her napkin and drop it again to the floor. She bends to retrieve it, but* ANNIE *stops her arm.*]

Keller (*not noticing*). Reverend looked in at the office today to complain his hens have stopped laying. Poor fellow, *he* was out of joint, all he could—

[*He stops too, to frown down the table at* KATE, HELEN, *and* ANNIE *in turn, all suspended in mid-motion.*]

James (*not noticing*). I've always suspected those hens.
Aunt Ev. Of what?
James. I think they're Papist.[2] Has he tried—

[*He stops, too, following* KELLER'S *eyes.* ANNIE *now stoops to pick the napkin up.*]

Aunt Ev. James, now you're pulling my—lower extremity, the first thing you know we'll be—

[*She stops, too, hearing herself in the silence.* ANNIE, *with everyone now watching, for the third time puts the napkin on* HELEN. HELEN *yanks it off, and throws it down.* ANNIE *rises, lifts* HELEN'S *plate, and bears it away.* HELEN, *feeling it gone, slides down and commences to kick up under the table; the dishes jump.* ANNIE *contemplates this for a moment, then coming back takes* HELEN'S *wrists firmly and swings her off the chair.* HELEN *struggling gets one hand free, and catches at her mother's skirt; when* KATE *takes her by the shoulders,* HELEN *hangs quiet.*]

Kate. Miss Annie.
Annie. No.
Kate (*a pause*). It's a very special day.
Annie (*grimly*). It will be, when I give in to that.

[*She tries to disengage* HELEN'S *hand;* KATE *lays hers on* ANNIE'S.]

---

2. **Papist:** a derogatory term for Roman Catholics. James jokingly suspects the Papist hens of making trouble for the Protestant reverend.

Kate. Please. I've hardly had a chance to welcome her home—

Annie. Captain Keller.

Keller *(embarrassed).* Oh. Katie, we—had a little talk, Miss Annie feels that if we indulge Helen in these—

Aunt Ev. But what's the child done?

Annie. She's learned not to throw things on the floor and kick. It took us the best part of two weeks and—

Aunt Ev. But only a napkin, it's not as if it were breakable!

Annie. And everything she's learned *is?* Mrs. Keller, I don't think we should—play tug-of-war for her, either give her to me or you keep her from kicking.

Kate. What do you wish to do?

Annie. Let me take her from the table.

Aunt Ev. Oh, let her stay, my goodness, she's only a child, she doesn't have to wear a napkin if she doesn't want to to her first evening—

Annie *(level).* And ask outsiders not to interfere.

Aunt Ev *(astonished).* Out—outsi— I'm the child's *aunt!*

Kate *(distressed).* Will once hurt so much, Miss Annie? I've—made all Helen's favorite foods, tonight.

[*A pause.*]

Keller *(gently).* It's a homecoming party, Miss Annie.

[ANNIE *after a moment releases* HELEN. *But she cannot accept it, at her own chair she shakes her head and turns back, intent on* KATE.]

Annie. She's testing you. You realize?

James *(to* ANNIE*).* She's testing you.

Keller. Jimmie, be quiet. (JAMES *sits, tense.*) Now she's home, naturally she—

Annie. And wants to see what will happen. At your hands. I said it was my main worry, is this what you promised me not half an hour ago?

Keller *(reasonably).* But she's *not* kicking, now—

Annie. And not learning not to. Mrs. Keller, teaching her is bound to be painful, to everyone. I know it hurts to watch, but she'll live up to just what you demand of her, and no more.

James *(palely).* She's testing *you.*

Keller *(testily).* Jimmie.

James. I have an opinion, I think I should—

Keller. No one's interested in hearing your opinion.

Annie. *I'm* interested, of course she's testing me. Let me keep her to what she's learned and she'll go on learning from me. Take her out of my hands and it all comes apart. (KATE *closes her eyes, digesting it;* ANNIE *sits again, with a brief comment for her.*) *Be* bountiful, it's at her expense. *(She turns to* JAMES, *flatly.)* Please pass me more of—her favorite foods.

[*Then* KATE *lifts* HELEN'S *hand, and turning her toward* ANNIE, *surrenders her;* HELEN *makes for her own chair.*]

Kate *(low).* Take her, Miss Annie.

Annie *(then).* Thank you.

[*But the moment* ANNIE *rising reaches for her hand,* HELEN *begins to fight and kick, clutching to the tablecloth, and uttering laments.* ANNIE *again tries to loosen her hand, and* KELLER *rises.*]

Keller *(tolerant).* I'm afraid you're the difficulty, Miss Annie. Now I'll keep her to what she's learned, you're quite right there— (*He takes* HELEN'S *hands from* ANNIE, *pats them;* HELEN *quiets down.*) —but I don't see that we need send her from the table, after all, she's the guest of honor. Bring her plate back.

Annie. If she was a seeing child, none of you would tolerate one—

Keller. Well, she's not, I think some compromise is called for. Bring her plate, please. (ANNIE'S *jaw sets, but she restores the plate, while* KELLER *fastens the napkin around* HELEN'S *neck; she permits it.*) There. It's not unnatural, most of us take some aversion to our teachers, and occasionally another hand can smooth things out. (*He puts a fork in* HELEN'S *hand;* HELEN *takes it. Genially.*) Now. Shall we start all over?

[*He goes back around the table, and sits.* ANNIE *stands watching.* HELEN *is motionless, thinking things through, until with a wicked glee she deliberately flings the fork on the floor. After another moment she plunges her hand into her food, and crams a fistful into her mouth.*]

James (*wearily*). I think we've started all over—

[KELLER *shoots a glare at him, as* HELEN *plunges her other hand into* ANNIE'S *plate.* ANNIE *at once moves in, to grasp her wrist, and* HELEN *flinging out a hand encounters the pitcher; she swings with it at* ANNIE; ANNIE *falling back blocks it with an elbow, but the water flies over her dress.* ANNIE *gets her breath, then snatches the pitcher away in one hand, hoists* HELEN *up bodily under the other arm, and starts to carry her out, kicking.* KELLER *stands.*]

Annie (*savagely polite*). Don't get up!
Keller. Where are you going?
Annie. Don't smooth anything else out for me, don't interfere in any way! I treat her like a seeing child because I *ask* her to see, I *expect* her to see, don't undo what I do!
Keller. Where are you taking her?
Annie. To make her fill this pitcher again!

[*She thrusts out with* HELEN *under her arm, but* HELEN *escapes up the stairs and* ANNIE *runs after her.* KELLER *stands rigid.* AUNT EV *is astounded.*]

Aunt Ev. You let her speak to you like that, Arthur? A creature who *works* for you?
Keller (*angrily*). No. I don't.

[*He is starting after* ANNIE *when* JAMES, *on his feet with shaky resolve, interposes his chair between them in* KELLER'S *path.*]

James. Let her go.
Keller. What!
James (*a swallow*). I said—let her go. She's right. (KELLER *glares at the chair and him.* JAMES *takes a deep breath, then headlong.*) She's right, Kate's right, I'm right, and you're wrong. If you drive her away from here it will be over my dead—chair, has it never occurred to you that on one occasion you might be consummately wrong?

[KELLER'S *stare is unbelieving, even a little fascinated.* KATE *rises in trepidation, to mediate.*]

Kate. Captain.

[KELLER *stops her with his raised hand; his eyes stay on* JAMES'S *pale face, for a long hold. When he finally finds his voice, it is gruff.*]

Keller. Sit down, everyone. (*He sits.* KATE *sits.* JAMES *holds onto his chair.* KELLER *speaks mildly.*) Please sit down, Jimmie.

[JAMES *sits, and a moveless silence prevails;* KELLER'S *eyes do not leave him.* ANNIE *has pulled* HELEN *downstairs again by one hand, the pitcher in her other hand, down the porch steps, and across the yard to the pump. She puts* HELEN'S *hand on the pump handle, grimly.*]

Annie. All right. Pump. (HELEN *touches her cheek, waits uncertainly.*) No, she's not here. Pump! (*She forces* HELEN'S *hand to work the handle, then lets go. And* HELEN *obeys. She pumps till the water comes, then* ANNIE *puts the pitcher in her other hand and guides it under the spout, and the water tumbling half into and half around the pitcher douses* HELEN'S *hand.* ANNIE *takes over the handle to keep water coming, and does automatically what she has done so many times before, spells into* HELEN'S *free palm.*) Water. W, a, t, e, r. Water. It has a—*name*—

[*And now the miracle happens.* HELEN *drops the pitcher on the slab under the spout, it shatters. She stands transfixed.* ANNIE *freezes on the pump handle: there is a change in the sundown light, and with it a change in* HELEN'S *face, some light coming into it we have never seen there, some struggle in the depths behind it; and her lips tremble, trying to remember something the muscles around them once knew, till at last it finds its way out, painfully, a baby sound buried under the debris of years of dumbness.*]

Helen. Wah. Wah. (*And again, with great effort*) Wah. Wah.

[HELEN *plunges her hand into the dwindling water, spells into her own palm. Then she gropes frantically,* ANNIE *reaches for her hand, and* HELEN *spells into* ANNIE'S *hand.*]

Annie (*whispering*). Yes. (HELEN *spells into it again.*) Yes! (HELEN *grabs at the handle, pumps for more water, plunges her hand into its spurt, and grabs* ANNIE'S *to spell it again.*) Yes! Oh, my dear—(*She falls to her knees to clasp* HELEN'S *hand, but* HELEN *pulls it free, stands almost bewildered, then drops to the ground, pats it swiftly,*

And now the miracle happens.

holds up her palm, imperious. ANNIE *spells into*
it.) Ground. (HELEN *spells it back.)* Yes! (HELEN
whirls to the pump, pats it, holds up her palm,
and ANNIE *spells into it.)* Pump. (HELEN *spells it*
back.) Yes! Yes! *(Now* HELEN *is in such an ex-*
citement she is possessed, wild, trembling, cannot
be still, turns, runs, falls on the porch steps, claps
it, reaches out her palm, and ANNIE is at it instantly to spell.) Step. (HELEN has no time to spell
back now, she whirls groping, to touch anything,
encounters the trellis, shakes it, thrusts out her
palm, and ANNIE while spelling to her cries wildly

at the house.) Trellis. Mrs. Keller! *Mrs. Keller!* (*Inside,* KATE *starts to her feet.* HELEN *scrambles back onto the porch, groping, and finds the bell string, tugs it; the bell rings, the distant chimes begin tolling the hour, all the bells in town seem to break into speech while* HELEN *reaches out and* ANNIE *spells feverishly into her hand.* KATE *hurries out, with* KELLER *after her;* AUNT EV *is on her feet, to peer out the window; only* JAMES *remains at the table, and with a napkin wipes his damp brow. From up right and left the servants—* VINEY, *the two children, the other servant—run in, and stand watching from a distance as* HELEN, *ringing the bell, with her other hand encounters her mother's skirt; when she throws a hand out,* ANNIE *spells into it.)* Mother. (KELLER *now seizes* HELEN'S *hand, she touches him, gestures a hand, and* ANNIE *again spells.)* Papa— She *knows!* (KATE *and* KELLER *go to their knees, stammering, clutching* HELEN *to them, and* ANNIE *steps unsteadily back to watch the threesome,* HELEN *spelling wildly into* KATE'S *hand, then into* KELL-ER'S, KATE *spelling back into* HELEN'S; *they cannot keep their hands off her, and rock her in their clasp. Then* HELEN *gropes, feels nothing, turns all around, pulls free, and comes with both hands groping, to find* ANNIE. *She encounters* ANNIE'S *thighs,* ANNIE *kneels to her,* HELEN'S *hand pats* ANNIE'S *cheek impatiently, points a finger, and waits; and* ANNIE *spells into it.)* Teacher. (HELEN *spells it back, slowly;* ANNIE *nods.)* Teacher.

[*She holds* HELEN'S *hand to her cheek. Presently* HELEN *withdraws it, not jerkily, only with reserve, and retreats a step. She stands thinking it over, then turns again and stumbles back to her parents. They try to embrace her, but she has something else in mind, it is to get the keys, and she hits* KATE'S *pocket until* KATE *digs them out for her.*

ANNIE *with her own load of emotion has retreated, her back turned, toward the pump, to sit;* KATE *moves to* HELEN, *touches her hand questioningly, and* HELEN *spells a word to her.* KATE *comprehends it, their first act of verbal communication, and she can hardly utter the word aloud, in wonder, gratitude, and deprivation; it is a moment in which she simultaneously finds and loses a child.*]

Kate. Teacher?

[ANNIE *turns; and* KATE, *facing* HELEN *in her direction by the shoulders, holds her back, holds her back, and then relinquishes her.* HELEN *feels her way across the yard, rather shyly, and when her moving hands touch* ANNIE'S *skirt she stops. Then she holds out the keys and places them in* ANNIE'S *hand. For a moment neither of them moves. Then* HELEN *slides into* ANNIE'S *arms, and lifting away her smoked glasses, kisses her on the cheek.* ANNIE *gathers her in.*

KATE *torn both ways turns from this, gestures the servants off, and makes her way into the house, on* KELLER'S *arm. The servants go, in separate directions.*

The lights are half down now, except over the pump. ANNIE *and* HELEN *are here, alone in the yard.* ANNIE *has found* HELEN'S *hand, almost without knowing it, and she spells slowly into it, her voice unsteady, whispering:*]

Annie. I, love, Helen. (*She clutches the child to her, tight this time, not spelling, whispering into her hair.*) Forever, and— (*She stops. The lights over the pump are taking on the color of the past, and it brings* ANNIE'S *head up, her eyes opening, in fear; and as slowly as though drawn she rises, to listen, with her hand on* HELEN'S *shoulders. She waits, waits, listening with ears and eyes both, slowly here, slowly there: and hears only silence. There are no voices. The color passes on, and when her eyes come back to* HELEN *she can breathe the end of her phrase without fear.*) —ever.

[*In the family room* KATE *has stood over the table, staring at* HELEN'S *plate, with* KELLER *at her shoulder; now* JAMES *takes a step to move her chair in, and* KATE *sits, with head erect, and* KELLER *inclines his head to* JAMES; *so it is* AUNT EV, *hesitant, and rather humble, who moves to the door.*

Outside HELEN *tugs at* ANNIE'S *hand, and* ANNIE *comes with it.* HELEN *pulls her toward the house; and hand in hand, they cross the yard, and ascend the porch steps, in the rising lights, to where* AUNT EV *is holding the door open for them.*

The curtain ends the play.]

"I, love, Helen. Forever, and—ever."

Responding to the Play

Analyzing the Play: Act Three

Identifying Facts

1. The two weeks are now up. (A time limit is always a good way of increasing pressure. We all know this from football and basketball games.) What startling **change** do we see when Helen appears in Scene 1?
2. What has Annie failed to do with Helen? Why won't the Kellers give Annie more time?
3. What does Annie say to Captain Keller about her feelings for Helen in the second scene? What does she say God owes her?
4. In Scene 3, at the dining room table, what surprising **reversal** do we see in Helen's behavior? Why don't the Kellers want to correct Helen?
5. How does James now reveal a major **change** in his character—what does he say and do to help Annie?
6. Why does Annie take Helen to the pump?
7. The **climax** of the play now takes place—in one of the most moving last scenes in the history of the theater. We have been lured into feeling that Helen has gone as far as she can go—that this is good, but still a defeat for Annie *and* Helen. Explain what happens at the pump— what has Helen learned? How do **stage effects** highlight this climactic scene?
8. Where in Act Two did the playwright establish the word *wah wah,* so that its simple utterance can score in this final scene?

Interpreting Meanings

9. What is significant about the fact that Annie no longer hears the voices?
10. Whenever a character announces early in a play that she (or he) will never love again, we sense that she will change her mind before the end, and we wait to see what will change it. Earlier in this play, Annie said she would never love again. Why did she say this? What happens to change her mind? Did you find this change convincing?
11. How is the **climax** of the play the "resurrection," or rebirth, that Annie felt she owed to God and that God owed to her?

12. How has Helen been "born" by the end of the play?
13. The relationship of James to his father has constituted a **subplot,** or sub-story, to the major plot. How is James's **conflict** resolved?
14. What does it mean that Kate has simultaneously found and lost a child?

The Play as a Whole

1. What do you think of the methods Annie used to teach Helen? Do you think she was too cruel?
2. By the end of the play, how do you feel about all the characters? Have your feelings for any of them changed? Explain.
3. Suppose you had to select one scene of this play to present to an audience. Which scene would you select as most important? Why?
4. Is there a message in *The Miracle Worker* that is still important to people today? What do you think this play reveals about children, parents, love, handicaps, and courage?

Writing About the Play

A Creative Response

1. **Writing a Sequel.** Write a scene that could be a sequel to *The Miracle Worker*. Before you write, think of some new **conflict** that will give dramatic tension to the scene. Do Annie and the Kellers now cooperate as Helen's education begins? What about James? Does Annie hear more "voices"? In stage directions, state the **time** and **setting** of your sequel. Gibson called his own sequel *Monday After the Miracle*; what will you call yours?

A Critical Response

2. **Analyzing Theme.** One of the important themes in *The Miracle Worker* is love. Use one of the following statements about love as the topic sentence of an essay. Cite incidents from the play to support your statement.

   a. When Annie was young, she loved Jimmie very much. When Jimmie died, Annie believed she would never love again. The loss of Jimmie haunted Annie until love brought about her resurrection, or rebirth.

b. Until events teach him otherwise, Captain Keller believes that obedience, respect, and proper behavior are sufficient proof of love.

c. Kate Keller loves Helen so much that all she can do is pity and indulge her child. Kate's kind of love is the cause of some of Helen's problems in *The Miracle Worker.* By the end of the play, Kate learns that real love also means losing the one you love.

3. Responding to a Character. In his comment under "Focusing on Background" (see page 548), the playwright says that *The Miracle Worker* is a love letter. In one paragraph, tell which character the "love letter" is directed to. In a second paragraph, explain how you responded to this character: Did you respect her? Fear her? Dislike her? Pity her? Admire her? Try to explain your feelings.

4. Comparing the Play to a Biography. Joseph Lash's story of Annie Sullivan's early life (on page 437 of this book) was published many years after William Gibson wrote his play. In a paragraph, cite at least three ways in which Gibson's account of Annie's early life is different from Lash's account. (Gibson reveals Annie's past through the offstage voices, in Act One, Scenes 4 and 8; and Act Two, Scene 5.) Before you write, you might fill out a chart like this:

Annie's early life	
Lash	Gibson
1.	1.
2.	2.
3.	3.

In a second paragraph, describe your responses to the play and biography. If you had to recommend one of these selections to someone else, which would it be, and why?

5. Comparing the Play to a Letter. Gibson used the letters of Annie Sullivan as one of his sources for the play. Annie wrote the following letter on the climactic day that Helen learned that everything had a name. In one paragraph, cite four details that the playwright altered in writing the scene at the pump. In a second paragraph, tell which you preferred reading, and why: the scene in the play, or the letter.

April 5, 1887

I must write you a line this morning because something very important has happened. Helen has taken the second great step in her education. She has learned that *everything has a name, and that the manual alphabet is the key to everything she wants to know.*

In a previous letter I think I wrote you that "mug" and "milk" had given Helen more trouble than all the rest. She confused the nouns with the verb "drink." She didn't know the word for "drink," but went through the pantomime of drinking whenever she spelled "mug" or "milk." This morning, while she was washing, she wanted to know the name for "water." When she wants to know the name of anything, she points to it and pats my hand. I spelled "w-a-t-e-r" and thought no more about it until after breakfast. Then it occurred to me that with the help of this new word I might succeed in straightening out the "mug-milk" difficulty. We went out to the pump house, and I made Helen hold her mug under the spout while I pumped. As the cold water gushed forth, filling the mug, I spelled "w-a-t-e-r" in Helen's free hand. The word coming so close to the sensation of cold water rushing over her hand seemed to startle her. She dropped the mug and stood as one transfixed. A new light came into her face. She spelled "water" several times. Then she dropped on the ground and asked for its name and pointed to the pump and the trellis, and suddenly turning around she asked for my name. I spelled "Teacher."

Analyzing Language and Vocabulary

Theater Terms

Like all art forms, drama has a special set of terms that describe how it works. The following questions ask you to apply your knowledge of certain dramatic terms, which are in bold type. The questions all apply to *The Miracle Worker.* To answer some questions, you will have to use a dictionary.

1. Give examples of three **stage directions** in the play that reveal character.

2. Give examples of three **stage directions** that indicate action.

3. Where is a **soliloquy** used?

4. List five **properties,** or **props,** that are used in Act One.
5. Find one scene in which **spotlights,** or **spots,** are used for dramatic effect.
6. Where is a **pantomime** called for in Act Two?
7. What is a **subplot**? How do James and his father provide a subplot for this play?
8. What is a **cue**? What is Kate's cue in the second scene of Act One to go out onto the porch?
9. What is **choreography**? Which scene in the play would have to be carefully choreographed?
10. How is Annie's last line the **payoff** of her earlier statement about love (Act One, Scene 4)?

Reading About the Writer

William Gibson (1914–   ) has also written a light, touching comedy called *Two for the Seesaw,* which starred Henry Fonda and Anne Bancroft. He is also the author of a play about the young Shakespeare, *A Cry of Players; Golda,* a play about Golda Meir, who became Prime Minister of Israel; and a book about his family, *A Mass for the Dead.* In 1982, *Monday After the Miracle,* a sequel to *The Miracle Worker,* had a brief run on Broadway.

Focusing on Background
The Playwright Talks About The Miracle Worker

"Tonight at 8 on NBC *The Miracle Worker* will be broadcast in its second television incarnation. Set in 1887, the play recounts the critical events in the first months of Annie Sullivan's struggle to teach the young deaf, mute, and blind Helen Keller how to communicate with the rest of humanity. Its first telecast was live. I wrote that version twenty-three summers ago when *all* television was live, rehearsal time was scant, unwritten pages were improvised, actors went blank over missing props, cameras photographed each other, and everything was sprightlier. So, for example, our first chance to hear the score was in dress rehearsal, violins sobbing away in another studio piped in to us in the control booth; our director, Arthur Penn, groaned, 'This music is killing us!' and an hour later on the air was—unbeknownst to the musicians giving their all—dialing most of it out ad lib. . . .

"No such misadventures will occur in tonight's filmed production. This cast rehearsed in Los Angeles for three weeks, played onstage in Palm Beach for two, and went back to the Coast for another month of filming. But one surprise, for audiences who two decades ago saw Patty Duke as young Helen Keller, may be that she grew up to portray her teacher Annie; her pupil now is played by Melissa Gilbert, at age fifteen, a most familiar figure to viewers of *Little House on the Prairie.*

"I never thought much of the play, till last year. My opinion is hardly objective; after opening night, I can't stand any of my plays and do my best to avoid seeing them. With *The Miracle Worker* I got trapped in venality.[1] I wrote it a second time as a stage play, and a third time as a movie; the present teleplay is my fourth trek through it. My favorite editions now are in those exotic languages I can't tell front from back of. Last year, I saw it in Afrikaans, couldn't comprehend a word, and for the first time thought it looked like a real play—by somebody else. . . .

"What makes for a hit is always an enigma,[2] but one element certainly is common ground between the writer and his audience. The author of *The Miracle Worker* believed in children, was young, energetic, incorrigibly optimistic, no stranger to the 'uplifting' in life; these are not objectionable qualities, and they flowed naturally into the script.

"And it was obviously a love letter. To whom, I would learn later. I like to fall a little in love with my heroines, and the title—from Mark Twain, who said, 'Helen is a miracle, and Miss Sullivan is the miracle worker'—was meant to show where my affections lay. This stubborn girl of twenty, who six years earlier could not write her name, and in one month salvaged Helen's soul, and lived thereafter in its shadow, seemed to me to deserve a star bow."
—William Gibson

1. **venality** (vē·nal′ə·tē): readiness to work for profit.
2. **enigma** (ə·nig′mə): puzzle.

Neil Simon's *Visitor from Forest Hills* is one of three short plays which make up an evening of theater called *Plaza Suite.* Each play takes place in the same suite of rooms at the Plaza Hotel in New York City. *Plaza Suite* opened on Broadway on February 14, 1968.

This play could be called a **comedy,** or it could be called a **farce.** Sometimes it is difficult and often pointless to try to categorize a play as either a comedy or a farce. Theatrical producers occasionally avoid the issue completely by using the term "farce-comedy."

Comedy and Farce

A **farce** is a play in which the playwright concentrates largely on ridiculous situations and comical physical actions (pies in faces; wild chase scenes; screwball dialogues). The characters in a farce tend to be broad, one-dimensional "types." These characters are placed in situations that start out to be reasonable enough, but they soon become ridiculous and absurd. In fact, in a farce, the playwright is under the obligation to be funny almost every minute of the way. That is the sole purpose of a farce: to keep the audience laughing.

Comedy, unlike farce, develops its characters much more fully. Its action grows out of the more complex personalities and more serious attitudes of the characters. Like other serious drama, comedy is concerned with relationships and with changes in relationships. Comedy strives to be funny, but its humor is gentler than the slapstick physical humor in a farce.

Neil Simon, one of the most skillful and successful writers of comedy and farce today, has said that he writes about potentially sad situations from a comic point of view. Walter Kerr, an American theater critic, has said that comedy is tragedy's private diary. In fact, much good comedy has the root of sadness; you laugh only when you also want to cry. For example, in a scene of my comedy *You Know I Can't Hear You When the Water's Running,* an actor is applying for a job. It turns out that the actor is willing to do anything to get the job, even to humiliate himself. The ends to which he will go strike an audience as very funny; but when you think about it, he is also a very sad character.

Both farce and comedy thrive on the contrast between characters with opposite natures. Opposites, of course, usually promise conflicts, and conflict is the basis of drama. You are familiar with the humor that comes from a conflict of opposites in movies and television shows. In *The Odd Couple,* for example, two men are living together; one is a compulsive housekeeper, the other is a mess. Take it from there! This teaming of opposites is good for endless laughs. There have been the cowboy and the lady; the taxi driver and the princess; and the tough guy and the woman missionary. In G. B. Shaw's *Pygmalion* and its musical version, *My Fair Lady,* the highly educated Professor Higgins is teamed with the filthy but charming flower seller, Eliza Doolittle.

Visitor from Forest Hills

PLAYBILL
the national magazine for theatregoers

The Plymouth Theatre

PLAZA SUITE

" **M**uch good comedy has the root of sadness; you laugh only when you also want to cry."

The Battle of the Sexes

Simon's comedy *Visitor from Forest Hills* uses one set of opposites that has served comedy for many years. These characters are a man and a woman—usually husband and wife—and they wage the so-called battle of the sexes.

In such comedies, the man is usually portrayed as a quick-tempered (though loving) husband and father, the domineering head of the household, and the woman is usually portrayed as a slightly addlebrained wife and mother. Of course, it usually develops in these plays that although the wife *seems* flighty and disorganized, she is really more sensible than the husband. Note a similar wife-husband situation in *The Miracle Worker,* where the woman's good sense eventually prevails.

When you read *Romeo and Juliet,* in fact, you will recognize the sixteenth-century squabbling of Lord and Lady Capulet, Juliet's parents, as not much different from the squabbling of Roy and Norma in *Visitor from Forest Hills*. It all is part of the battle of the sexes, and the battle, serious or hilarious, will probably go on forever.

> " When you read *Romeo and Juliet,* you will recognize the sixteenth-century squabbling of Lord and Lady Capulet as not much different from the squabbling of Roy and Norma in *Visitor from Forest Hills*. It is all part of the battle of the sexes."

Types and Stereotypes

At this point we should discuss types and stereotypes. It can be argued that we all fall more or less into **types.** In a way, that is what makes literature possible—we recognize ourselves and others in stories. We all can identify with certain character types: kind people, ambitious people, determined people, easygoing people.

A **stereotype,** however, is another matter. The word comes from a process for making metal plates in printing. A mold is formed, and endless duplicates can be made from the same mold. Over the years, certain religious, racial, sexist, and other stereotypes have developed, which are offensive to us all. Women do not want always to be portrayed as disorganized. Men do not want always to be portrayed as domineering and insensitive.

Though drama and comedy inevitably deal with types, stereotyping comes from lazy thinking. Think again of the image of the thumb and the thumbprint. Thumbs are reasonably the same, but each thumb has a print that makes it unique. A person may belong roughly to a type, but he or she is also an individual. Stereotypes fall back on the same old generalizing—"dumb blonde," "crazy kid," "cruel stepmother"—and we (and blondes and kids and stepmothers) get tired of such thoughtless labels.

At the same time, a sense of humor tells us that we *do* fall into types, that we can be peculiar and funny. At one time recently, when people began attacking stereotypes, there were so many protests from sensitive (and oversensitive) groups that the only creature one could poke fun at was a dog.

VISITOR FROM FOREST HILLS

Neil Simon

Cast of Characters

Norma Hubley
Roy Hubley
Borden Eisler
Mimsey Hubley

Suite 719 at the Plaza. It is three o'clock on a warm Saturday afternoon in spring.

The living room is bedecked with vases and baskets of flowers. In the bedroom one opened valise containing a young woman's street clothes rests on the floor. A very large box, which had held a wedding dress, rests on the luggage rack, and a man's suit lies on the bed. A fur wrap and gloves are thrown over the back of the sofa. Telegrams of congratulation and newspapers are strewn about. The suite today is being used more or less as a dressing room, since a wedding is about to occur downstairs in one of the reception rooms.

As the lights come up, NORMA HUBLEY *is at the phone in the bedroom, impatiently tapping the receiver. She is dressed in a formal cocktail dress and a large hat, looking her very best, as any woman would want to on her daughter's wedding day. But she is extremely nervous and harassed, and with good cause—as we'll soon find out.*

Norma *(on the phone).* Hello? . . . Hello, operator? . . . Can I have the Blue Room, please . . . The Blue Room . . . Is there a Pink Room? . . . I want the Hubley-Eisler wedding . . . The Green Room, that's it. Thank you . . . Could you please hurry, operator, it's an emergency . . . *(She looks over at the bathroom nervously. She paces back and forth.)* Hello? . . . Who's this? . . . Mr. Eisler . . . It's Norma Hubley . . . No, everything's fine . . . Yes, we're coming right down . . . *(She is smiling and trying to act as pleasant and as calm as possible.)* Yes, you're right, it certainly *is* the big day . . . Mr. Eisler, is my husband there? . . . Would you, please? . . . Oh! Well, I'd like to wish you the very best of luck too . . . Borden's a wonderful boy . . . Well, they're *both* wonderful

kids . . . No, no. She's as calm as a cucumber . . . That's the younger generation, I guess . . . Yes, everything seems to be going along beautifully . . . Absolutely beautifully . . . Oh, thank you. *(Her husband has obviously just come on the other end, because the expression on her face changes violently and she screams a rasping whisper filled with doom. Sitting on the bed.)* Roy? You'd better get up here right away, we're in big trouble . . . Don't ask questions, just get up here . . . I hope you're not drunk because I can't handle this alone . . . Don't say anything. Just smile and walk leisurely out the door . . . and then get . . . up here as fast as you can. *(She hangs up, putting the phone back on the night table. She crosses to the bathroom and then puts her head up against the door. Aloud through the bathroom door.)* All right, Mimsey, your father's on his way up. Now, I want you to come out of that bathroom and get married. *(There is no answer.)* Do you hear me? . . . I've had enough of this nonsense . . . Unlock that door! *(That's about the end of her authority. She wilts and almost pleads.)* Mimsey, darling, please come downstairs and get married, you know your father's temper . . . I know what you're going through now, sweetheart, you're just nervous . . . Everyone goes through that on their wedding day . . . It's going to be all right, darling. You love Borden and he loves you. You're both going to have a wonderful future. So please come out of the bathroom! *(She listens; there is no answer.)* Mimsey, if you don't care about your life, think about mine. Your father'll kill me. *(The front doorbell rings.* NORMA *looks off nervously and moves to the other side of the bed.)* Oh . . . he's here! . . . Mimsey! Mimsey, please, spare me this . . . If you want, I'll have it annulled[1] next week, but please come out and get married! *(There is no answer from the bathroom but the front doorbell rings impatiently.)* All right, I'm letting your father in. And heaven help the three of us!

[She crosses through the bedroom into the living room. She crosses to the door and opens it as ROY HUBLEY *bursts into the room.* ROY *is dressed in*

---

1. **annulled** (ə·nuld′): ended.

striped trousers, black tail coat, the works. He looks elegant but he's not too happy in this attire. He is a volatile, explosive man equipped to handle the rigors of the competitive business world, but a nervous, frightened man when it comes to the business of marrying off his only daughter.]

Roy. Why are you standing here? There are sixty-eight people down there drinking my liquor. If there's gonna be a wedding, let's have a wedding. Come on! (*He starts back out the door but sees that* NORMA *is not going anywhere. She sits on the sofa. He comes back in.*) . . . Didn't you hear what I said? There's another couple waiting to use the Green Room. Come on, let's go! (*He makes a start out again.*)

Norma (*very calm*). Roy, could you sit down a minute? I want to talk to you about something.

Roy (*she must be mad*). You want to talk *now*? You had twenty-one years to talk while she was growing up. I'll talk to you when they're in Bermuda. Can we please have a wedding?

Norma. We can't have a wedding until you and I have a talk.

Roy. Are you crazy? While you and I are talking here, there are four musicians playing downstairs for seventy dollars an hour. I'll talk to you later when we're dancing. Come on, get Mimsey and let's go. (*He starts out again.*)

Norma. That's what I want to talk to you about.

Roy (*comes back*). Mimsey?

Norma. Sit down. You're not going to like this.

Roy. Is she sick?

Norma. She's not sick . . . exactly.

Roy. What do you mean, she's not sick exactly? Either she's sick or she's not sick. Is she sick?

Norma. She's not sick.

Roy. Then let's have a wedding! (*He crosses into the bedroom.*) Mimsey, there's two hundred dollars' worth of cocktail frankfurters getting cold downstairs . . . (*He looks around the empty room.*) Mimsey? (*He crosses back to the living room to the side of the sofa. He looks at* NORMA.) . . . Where's Mimsey?

Norma. Promise you're not going to blame me.

Roy. Blame you for what? What did you do?

Norma. I didn't do anything. But I don't want to get blamed for it.

Roy. What's going on here? Are you going to tell me where Mimsey is?

Norma. Are you going to take an oath you're not going to blame me?

Roy. *I take it! I take it!* NOW WHERE . . . IS SHE?

Norma. . . . She's locked herself in the bathroom. She's not coming out and she's not getting married.

[ROY *looks at* NORMA *incredulously. Then, because it must be an insane joke, he smiles at her. There is even the faint glint of a chuckle.*]

Roy (*softly*). . . . No kidding, where is she?

Norma (*turns away*). He doesn't believe me. I'll kill myself.

[ROY *turns and storms into the bedroom. He crosses to the bathroom and knocks on the door. Then he tries it. It's locked. He tries again. He bangs on the door with his fist.*]

Roy. Mimsey? . . . Mimsey? . . . *MIMSEY?* (*There is no reply. Girding himself, he crosses back through the bedroom into the living room to the sofa. He glares at* NORMA.) . . . All right, what did you say to her?

Norma (*jumping up and moving away*). I knew it! I knew you'd blame me. You took an oath. God'll punish you.

Roy. I'm not blaming you. I just want to know what *stupid* thing you said to her that made her do this.

Norma. I didn't say a word. I was putting on my lipstick, she was in the bathroom, I heard the door go click, it was locked, my whole life was over, what do you want from me?

Roy. And you didn't say a word?

Norma. Nothing.

Roy (*ominously moving toward her as* NORMA *backs away*). I see. In other words, you're trying to tell me that a normal, healthy, intelligent twenty-one-year-old college graduate, who has driven me crazy the last eighteen months with wedding lists, floral arrangements, and choices of assorted hors d'oeuvres,[2] has suddenly decided to

---

2. **hors d'oeuvres** (ôr′durvz′): appetizers.

spend this, the most important day of her life, locked in the Plaza Hotel john?

Norma (*making her stand at the mantel*). Yes! Yes! Yes! Yes! Yes!

Roy (*vicious*). YOU MUSTA SAID SOMETHING!

[*He storms into the bedroom.* NORMA *goes after him.*]

Norma. Roy . . . Roy . . . What are you going to do?

Roy (*stopping below the bed*). First I'm getting the college graduate out of the bathroom! Then we're gonna have a wedding and then you and I are gonna have a big talk! (*He crosses to the bathroom door and pounds on it.*) Mimsey! This is your father. I want you and your four-hundred-dollar wedding dress out of there in five seconds!

Norma (*standing at the side of the bed*). Don't threaten her. She'll never come out if you threaten her.

Roy (*to* NORMA). I got sixty-eight guests, nine waiters, four musicians, and a boy with a wedding license waiting downstairs. This is no time to be diplomatic. (*Bangs on the door*) Mimsey! . . . Are you coming out or do we have the wedding in the bathroom?

Norma. Will you lower your voice! Everyone will hear us.

Roy (*to* NORMA). How long you think we can keep this a secret? As soon as that boy says "I do" and there's no one standing next to him, they're going to suspect something. (*He bangs on the door.*) You can't stay in there forever, Mimsey. We only have the room until six o'clock . . . *You hear me?*

[*There is still no reply from the bathroom.*]

Norma. Roy, will you please try to control yourself.

Roy (*with great display of patience, moves to the foot of the bed and sits*). All right, I'll stay here and control myself. You go downstairs and marry the short, skinny kid. (*Exploding*) *What's the matter with you?* Don't you realize what's happening?

Norma (*moving to him*). Yes. I realize what's happening. Our daughter is nervous, frightened, and scared to death.

Roy. Of what? OF WHAT? She's been screaming for two years if he doesn't ask her to marry him, she'll throw herself off the Guggenheim Museum . . . What is she scared of?

Norma. I don't know. Maybe she's had second thoughts about the whole thing.

Roy (*getting up and moving to the bathroom door*). Second thoughts? This is no time to be having *second thoughts*. It's costing me eight thousand dollars for the *first thoughts*. (*He bangs on the door.*) Mimsey, open this door.

Norma. Is that all you care about? What it's costing you? Aren't you concerned about your daughter's happiness?

Roy (*moving back to her below the bed*). Yes! Yes, I'm concerned about my daughter's happiness. I'm also concerned about that boy waiting downstairs. A decent, respectable, intelligent young man . . . who I hope one day is going to teach that daughter of mine to grow up.

Norma. You haven't the faintest idea of what's going through her mind right now.

Roy. Do you?

Norma. It could be anything. I don't know, maybe she thinks she's not good enough for him.

Roy (*looks at her incredulously*). . . . Why? What is he? Some kind of Greek god? He's a plain kid, nothing . . . That's ridiculous. (*Moves back to the door and bangs on it*) Mimsey! Mimsey, open this door. (*He turns to* NORMA.) Maybe she's not in there.

Norma. She's in there. (*Clutches her chest and sits on the side of the bed*) Oh . . . I think I'm having a heart attack.

Roy (*listening at the door*). I don't hear a peep out of her. Is there a window in there? Maybe she tried something crazy.

Norma (*turning to him*). That's right. Tell a woman who's having a heart attack that her daughter jumped out the window.

Roy. Take a look through the keyhole. I want to make sure she's in there.

Norma. She's in there, I tell you. Look at this, my hand keeps bouncing off my chest. (*It does*)

Roy. Are you gonna look in there and see if she's all right or am I gonna call the house detective?

Norma (*getting up and moving below the bed*). Why don't *you* look?

Roy. Maybe she's taking a bath.

Norma. Two minutes before her own wedding?

Roy (crossing to her). What wedding? She just called it off.

Norma. Wouldn't I have heard the water running?

Roy (making a swipe at her hat). With that hat you couldn't hear Niagara Falls! . . . Are you going to look to see what your daughter's doing in the bathroom or do I ask a stranger?

Norma (crossing to the door). I'll look! I'll look! I'll look! (Reluctantly she gets down on one knee and looks through the keyhole with one eye.) Oh . . . !

Roy. What's the matter?

Norma (to him). I ripped my stockings. (Getting up and examining her stocking)

Roy. Is she in there?

Norma. She's in there! She's in there! (Hobbling to the far side of the bed and sitting down on the edge) Where am I going to get another pair of stockings now? How am I going to go to the wedding with torn stockings?

Roy (crossing to the bathroom). If she doesn't show up, who's going to look at you? (He kneels at the door and looks through the keyhole.) There she is. Sitting there and crying.

Norma. I told you she was in there . . . The only one in my family to have a daughter married in the Plaza and I have torn stockings.

Roy (he is on his knees, his eye to the keyhole). Mimsey, I can see you . . . Do you hear me? . . . Don't turn away from me when I'm talking to you.

Norma. Maybe I could run across to Bergdorf's.[3] They have nice stockings. (Crosses to her purse on the bureau in the bedroom and looks through it)

Roy (still through the keyhole). Do you want me to break down the door, Mimsey, is that what you want? Because that's what I'm doing if you're not out of there in five seconds . . . Stop crying on your dress. Use the towel!

Norma (crossing to ROY at the door). I don't have any money. Give me four dollars, I'll be back in ten minutes.

---

3. **Bergdorf's:** Bergdorf Goodman's, an expensive store near the Plaza Hotel.

Roy (gets up and moves below the bed). In ten minutes she'll be a married woman, because I've had enough of this nonsense. (Yells in) All right, Mimsey, stand in the shower because I'm breaking down the door.

Norma (getting in front of the door). Roy, don't get crazy.

Roy (preparing himself for a run at the door). Get out of my way.

Norma. Roy, she'll come out. Just talk nicely to her.

Roy (waving her away). We already had nice talking. Now we're gonna have door breaking. (Through the door) All right, Mimsey, I'm coming in!

Norma. No, Roy, don't! Don't!

[She gets out of the way as ROY hurls his body, led by his shoulder, with full force against the door. It doesn't budge. He stays against the door silently a second; he doesn't react. Then he says calmly and softly.]

Roy. Get a doctor.

Norma (standing below the door). I knew it. I knew it.

Roy (drawing back from the door). Don't tell me I knew it, just get a doctor. (Through the door) I'm not coming in, Mimsey, because my arm is broken.

Norma. Let me see it. Can you move your fingers? (Moves to him and examines his fingers)

Roy (through the door). Are you happy now? Your mother has torn stockings and your father has a broken arm. How much longer is this gonna go on?

Norma (moving ROY's fingers). It's not broken, you can move your fingers. Give me four dollars with your other hand, I have to get stockings.

[She starts to go into his pockets. He slaps her hands away.]

Roy. Are you crazy moving a broken arm?

Norma. Two dollars, I'll get a cheap pair.

Roy (as though she were a lunatic). I'm not carrying any cash today. Rented, everything is rented.

Norma. I can't rent stockings. Don't you even

have a charge plate? *(Starts to go through his pockets again)*

Roy *(slaps her hands away. Then pointing dramatically).* Wait in the Green Room! You're no use to me here, go wait in the Green Room!

Norma. With torn stockings?

Roy. Stand behind the rented potted plant. *(Takes her by the arm and leads her below the bed. Confidentially.)* They're going to call from downstairs any second asking where the bride is. And *I'm* the one who's going to have to speak to them. *Me! Me! Me!* (*The phone rings. Pushing her toward the phone.)* That's them. *You* speak to them!

Norma. What happened to *me me me*?

[*The phone rings again.*]

Roy *(moving to the bathroom door).* Answer it. Answer it.

[*The phone rings again.*]

Norma *(moving to the phone).* What am I going to say to them?

Roy. I don't know. Maybe something'll come to you as you're talking.

Norma *(picks the phone up).* Hello? . . . Oh, Mr. Eisler . . . Yes, it certainly is the big moment. *(She forces a merry laugh.)*

Roy. Stall 'em. Stall 'em. Just keep stalling him. Whatever you do, stall 'em! *(Turns to the door)*

Norma *(on the phone).* Yes, we'll be down in two minutes. *(Hangs up)*

Roy *(turns back to her).* Are you crazy? What did you say that for? I told you to stall him.

Norma. I stalled him. You got two minutes. What do you want from me?

Roy *(shakes his arm at her).* You always panic. The minute there's a little crisis, you always go to pieces and panic.

Norma *(shaking her arm back at him).* Don't wave your broken arm at me. Why don't you use it to get your daughter out of the bathroom?

Roy *(very angry, kneeling to her on the bed).* I could say something to you now.

Norma *(confronting him, kneels in turn on the bed).* Then why don't you say it?

Roy. Because it would lead to a fight. And I don't want to spoil this day for you. *(He gets up and crosses back to the bathroom door.)* Mimsey, this

is your father speaking . . . I think you know I'm not a violent man. I can be stern and strict, but I have never once been violent. Except when I'm angry. And I am really angry now, Mimsey. You can ask your mother.

[*Moves away so* NORMA *can get to the door.*]

Norma *(crossing to the bathroom door).* Mimsey, this is your mother speaking. It's true, darling, your father is very angry.

Roy *(moving back to the door).* This is your father again, Mimsey. If you have a problem you want to discuss, unlock the door and we'll discuss it. I'm not going to ask you this again, Mimsey. I've reached the end of my patience. I'm gonna count to three . . . and . . . I'm warning you, young lady, by the time I've reached three . . . *this door better be open! (Moving away to below the bed)* All right—One! . . . Two! . . . THREE! *(There is no reply or movement from behind the door.* ROY *helplessly sinks down on the foot of the bed.)* . . . Where did we fail her?

Norma *(crosses to the far side of the bed, consoling him as she goes, and sits on the edge).* We didn't fail her.

Roy. They're playing "Here Comes the Bride" downstairs and she's barricaded in a toilet—we must have failed her.

Norma *(sighs).* All right, if it makes you any happier, we failed her.

Roy. You work and you dream and you hope and you save your whole life for this day, and in one click of a door, suddenly everything crumbles. Why? What's the answer?

Norma. It's not your fault, Roy. Stop blaming yourself.

Roy. I'm not blaming myself. I know *I've* done my best.

Norma *(turns and looks at him).* What does that mean?

Roy. It means we're not perfect. We make mistakes, we're only human. I've done my best and we failed her.

Norma. Meaning *I* didn't do my best?

Roy *(turning to her).* I didn't say that. I don't know what your best is. Only *you* know what your best is. Did you do your best?

Norma. Yes, I did my best.

Roy. And I did my best.

Norma. Then we *both* did our best.

Roy. So it's not our fault.

Norma. That's what I said before.

[*They turn away from each other. Then:*]

Roy *(softly)*. Unless one of us didn't do our best.

Norma *(jumping up and moving away)*. I don't want to discuss it any more.

Roy. All right, then what are we going to do?

Norma. I'm having a heart attack, *you* come up with something.

Roy. How? All right, I'll go down and tell them. *(Gets up and moves to the bedroom door)*

Norma *(moving to the door in front of him)*. Tell them? Tell them what?

[*As they move into the living room, she stops him above the sofa.*]

Roy. I don't know. Those people down there deserve some kind of an explanation. They got all dressed up, didn't they?

Norma. What are you going to say? You're going to tell them my daughter is not going to marry their son and that she's locked herself in the bathroom?

Roy. What do you want me to do, start off with two good jokes? They're going to find out *some* time, aren't they?

Norma *(with great determination)*. I'll tell you what you're going to do. If she's not out of there in five minutes, we're going to go out the back door and move to Seattle, Washington! . . . You don't think I'll be able to show my face in this city again, do you? *(ROY ponders this for a moment, then reassures her with a pat on the arm. Slowly he turns and moves into the bedroom. Suddenly, he loses control and lets his anger get the best of him. He grabs up the chair from the dresser, and brandishing it above his head, he dashes for the bedroom door, not even detouring around the bed but rather crossing right over it. NORMA screams and chases after him.)* ROY!

[*At the bathroom door, ROY manages to stop himself in time from smashing the chair against the door, trembling with frustration and anger. Finally, exhausted, he puts the chair down below*

the door and straddles it, sitting leaning on the back. NORMA sinks into the bedroom armchair.]

Roy. . . . Would you believe it, last night I cried. Oh, yes. I turned my head into the pillow and lay there in the dark, crying, because today I was losing my little girl. Some stranger was coming and taking my little Mimsey away from me . . . so I turned my back to you—and cried . . . Wait'll you hear what goes on *tonight!*

Norma *(lost in her own misery)*. I should have invited your cousin Lillie. *(Gestures to the heavens)* She wished this on me, I know it. *(Suddenly ROY begins to chuckle. NORMA looks at him. He chuckles louder, although there is clearly no joy in his laughter.)* Do you find something funny about this?

Roy. Yes, I find something funny about this. I find it funny that I hired a photographer for three hundred dollars. I find it hysterical that the wedding pictures are going to be you and me in front of a locked bathroom! *(Gets up and puts the chair aside)* All right, I'm through sitting around waiting for that door to open. *(He crosses to the bedroom window and tries to open it.)*

Norma *(following after him)*. What are you doing?

Roy. What do you think I'm doing?

[*Finding it impossible to open it, he crosses to the living room and opens a window there. The curtains begin to blow in the breeze.*]

Norma *(crosses after him)*. If you're jumping, I'm going with you. You're not leaving *me* here alone.

Roy *(looking out the window)*. I'm gonna crawl out along that ledge and get in through the bathroom window. *(He starts to climb out the window.)*

Norma. Are you crazy? It's seven stories up. You'll kill yourself. *(She grabs hold of him.)*

Roy. It's four steps, that's all. It's no problem, I'm telling you. Now will you let go of me.

Norma *(struggling to keep him from getting out the window)*. Roy, no! Don't do this. We'll leave her in the bathroom. Let the hotel worry about her. Don't go out on the ledge. *(In desperation, she grabs hold of one of the tails of his coat.)*

Roy *(half out the window, trying to get out as she holds on to his coat)*. You're gonna rip my coat. Let go or you're gonna rip my coat. *(As he tries*

"I can be stern and strict, but I have never once been violent."

The photographs that illustrate the play show the 1969 Broadway cast, starring Maureen Stapleton and Don Porter.

to pull away from her, his coat rips completely up the back, right up to the collar. He stops and slowly comes back into the room. NORMA *has frozen in misery by the bedroom door after letting go of the coat.* ROY *draws himself up with great dignity and control. He slowly turns and moves into the bedroom, stopping by the bed. With great patience, he calls toward the bathroom.*) Hey, you in there . . . Are you happy now? Your mother's got torn stockings and your father's got a rented ripped coat. Some wedding it's gonna be. (*Exploding, he crosses back to the open window in the living room.*) Get out of my way!

Norma (*puts hand to her head*). I'm getting dizzy. I think I'm going to pass out.

Roy (*getting her out of the way*). . . . You can pass out *after* the wedding . . . (*He goes out the window and onto the ledge.*) Call room service. I want a double Scotch the minute I get back.

[*And he disappears from view as he moves across the ledge.* NORMA *runs into the bedroom and catches a glimpse of him as he passes the bedroom window, but then he disappears once more.*]

Norma (*bemoaning her fate*). . . . He'll kill himself. He'll fall and kill himself, that's the way my luck's been going all day. (*She staggers away from the window and leans on the bureau.*) I'm not going to look. I'll just wait until I hear a scream. (*The telephone rings and* NORMA *screams in fright.*) Aggghhh! . . . I thought it was him . . . (*She crosses to the phone by the bed. The telephone rings again.*) Oh . . . what am I going to say? (*She picks it up.*) Hello? . . . Oh, Mr. Eisler. Yes, we're coming . . . My husband's getting Mimsey now . . . We'll be right down. Have some more hors d'oeuvres . . . Oh, thank you. It certainly *is* the happiest day of my life. (*She hangs up.*) No, I'm going to tell him I've got a husband dangling over Fifty-ninth Street. (*As she crosses back to the opened window, a sudden torrent of rain begins to fall. As she gets to the window and sees it*) I knew it! I knew it! It had to happen . . . (*She gets closer to the window and tries to look out.*) Are you all right, Roy? . . . Roy? (*There's no answer.*) He's not all right, he fell. (*She staggers into the bedroom.*) He fell, he fell, he fell, he fell . . . He's dead, I know it. (*She collapses onto*

the armchair.) He's laying there in a puddle in front of Trader Vic's[4] . . . I'm passing out. This time I'm really passing out! (*And she passes out on the chair, legs and arms spread-eagled. The doorbell rings; she jumps right up.*) I'm coming! I'm coming! Help me, whoever you are, help me! (*She rushes through the bedroom into the living room and to the front door.*) Oh, please, somebody, help me, please!

[*She opens the front door and* ROY *stands there dripping wet, fuming, exhausted, and with clothes disheveled[5] and his hair mussed.*]

Roy (*staggering into the room and weakly leaning on the mantelpiece. It takes a moment for him to catch his breath.* NORMA, *concerned, follows him*). She locked the window too. I had to climb in through a strange bedroom. There may be a lawsuit.

[*He weakly charges back into the bedroom, followed by* NORMA, *who grabs his coattails in an effort to stop him. The rain outside stops.*]

Norma (*stopping him below the bed*). Don't yell at her. Don't get her more upset.

Roy (*turning back to her*). Don't get her *upset*? I'm hanging seven stories from a gargoyle in a pouring rain and you want me to worry about her? . . . You know what she's doing in there? She's playing with her false eyelashes. (*Moves to the bathroom door*) I'm out there fighting for my life with pigeons and she's playing with eyelashes . . . (*Crossing back to* NORMA) . . . I already made up my mind. The minute I get my hands on her, I'm gonna kill her. (*Moves back to the door*) Once I show them the wedding bills, no jury on earth would convict me . . . And if by some miracle she survives, let there be no talk of weddings . . . She can go into a convent. (*Slowly moving back to* NORMA *below the bed*) . . . Let her become a librarian with thick glasses and a pencil in her hair, I'm not paying for any more canceled weddings . . . (*Working himself up into a frenzy, he rushes to the table by the armchair*

---

4. **Trader Vic's:** a Polynesian-style restaurant in the Plaza Hotel.
5. **disheveled** (di·shevʹəld): disordered, messy.

and grabs up some newspapers.) Now get her out of there or I start to burn these newspapers and smoke her out.

[NORMA *stops him, soothes him, and manages to get him calmed down. She gently seats him on the foot of the bed.*]

Norma *(really frightened).* I'll get her out! I'll get her out! *(She crosses to the door and knocks.)* Mimsey! Mimsey, please! *(She knocks harder and harder.)* Mimsey, you want to destroy a family? You want a scandal? You want a story in the *Daily News*? . . . Is that what you want? Is it? . . . Open this door! *Open it! (She bangs very hard, then stops and turns to* ROY.) . . . Promise you won't get hysterical.

Roy. What did you do? *(Turns wearily to her)*

Norma. I broke my diamond ring.

Roy *(letting the papers fall from his hand).* Your good diamond ring?

Norma. How many do I have?

Roy *(yells through the door).* Hey, you with the false eyelashes! *(Getting up and moving to the door)* . . . You want to see a broken diamond ring? You want to see eighteen hundred dollars' worth of crushed baguettes?[6] . . . *(He grabs* NORMA'S *hand and holds it to the keyhole.)* Here! Here! *This* is a worthless family heirloom *(Kicks the door)*—and *this* is a diamond bathroom door! *(Controlling himself. To* NORMA) Do you know what I'm going to do now? Do you have any idea? *(*NORMA *puts her hand to her mouth, afraid to hear.* ROY *moves away from the door to the far side of the bed.)* I'm going to wash my hands of the entire Eisler-Hubley wedding. You can take all the Eislers and all the hors d'oeuvres and go to Central Park and have an eight-thousand-dollar picnic . . . *(Stops and turns back to* NORMA) I'm going down to the Oak Room with my broken arm, with my drenched rented ripped suit—and I'm gonna get blind! . . . I don't mean drunk, I mean totally blind . . . *(Erupting with great vehemence)*[7] because I don't want to see you or your crazy daughter again, if I live to be a thousand.

---

6. **baguettes** (ba·gets'): here, diamonds in the shape of long, narrow rectangles.
7. **vehemence** (vē'ə·məns): insistence.

[*He turns and rushes from the bedroom, through the living room to the front door. As he tries to open it,* NORMA *catches up to him, grabs his tail coat, and pulls him back into the room.*]

Norma. That's right. Run out on me. Run out on your daughter. Run out on everybody just when they need you.

Roy. You don't need me. You need a rhinoceros with a blowtorch—because no one else can get into that bathroom.

Norma *(with rising emotion).* I'll tell you who can get into that bathroom. Someone with love and understanding. Someone who cares about that poor kid who's going through some terrible decision now and needs help. Help that only *you* can give her and that *I* can give her. *That's* who can get into that bathroom now.

[ROY *looks at her solemnly . . . Then he crosses past her, hesitates and looks back at her, and then goes into the bedroom and to the bathroom door.* NORMA *follows him back in. He turns and looks at* NORMA *again. Then he knocks gently on the door and speaks softly and with some tenderness.*]

Roy. Mimsey! . . . This is Daddy . . . Is something wrong, dear? . . . *(He looks back at* NORMA, *who nods encouragement, happy about his new turn in character. Then he turns back to the door.)* . . . I want to help you, darling. Mother and I both do. But how can we help you if you won't talk to us? Mimsey, can you hear me? *(There is no answer. He looks back at* NORMA.)

Norma *(at the far side of the bed).* Maybe she's too choked up to talk.

Roy *(through the door).* Mimsey, if you can hear me, knock twice for yes, once for no. *(There are two knocks on the door. They look at each other encouragingly.)* Good. Good . . . Now, Mimsey, we want to ask you a very, very important question. Do you want to marry Borden or don't you?

[*They wait anxiously for the answer. We hear one knock, a pause, then another knock.*]

Norma *(happily).* She said yes.

Roy *(despondently).* She said no. *(Moves away from the door to the foot of the bed)*

Norma. It was two knocks. Two knocks is yes. She wants to marry him.

Roy. It wasn't a double knock "yes." It was two single "no" knocks. She doesn't want to marry him.

Norma. Don't tell me she doesn't want to marry him. I heard her distinctly knock "yes." She went *(Knocks twice on the foot of the bed)* "Yes, I want to marry him."

Roy. It wasn't *(Knocks twice on the foot of the bed)* . . . It was *(Knocks once on the foot of the bed)* . . . and then another *(Knocks once more on the foot of the bed)* . . . That's "no," twice, she's not marrying him. *(Sinks down on the side of the bed)*

Norma *(crossing to the door).* Ask her again. *(Into the door)* Mimsey, what did you say? Yes or no? *(They listen. We hear two distinct loud knocks.* NORMA *turns to* ROY.*)* . . . All right? There it is in plain English . . . You never *could* talk to your own daughter. *(Moves away from the door)*

Roy *(getting up wearily and moving to the door).* Mimsey, this is not a good way to have a conversation. You're gonna hurt your knuckles . . . Won't you come out and talk to us? . . . Mimsey?

Norma *(leads* ROY *gently to the foot of the bed).* Don't you understand, it's probably something she can't discuss with her father. There are times a daughter wants to be alone with her mother. *(Sits* ROY *down on the foot of the bed, and crosses back to the door)* Mimsey, do you want me to come in there and talk to you, just the two of us, sweetheart? Tell me, darling, is that what you want? *(There is no reply. A strip of toilet paper appears from under the door.* ROY *notices it, pushes* NORMA *aside, bends down, picks it up, and reads it.)* What? What does it say? *(*ROY *solemnly hands it to her.* NORMA *reads it aloud.)* "I would rather talk to Daddy."

[NORMA *is crushed. He looks at her sympathetically. We hear the bathroom door unlock.* ROY *doesn't quite know what to say to* NORMA. *He gives her a quick hug.*]

Roy. I—I'll try not to be too long.

[*He opens the door and goes in, closing it behind him, quietly.* NORMA, *still with the strip of paper in her hand, walks slowly and sadly to the foot of the bed and sits. She looks glumly down at the paper.*]

Norma *(aloud).* . . . "I would rather talk to Daddy" . . . Did she have to write it on this kind of paper? *(She wads up the paper.)* . . . Well—maybe I didn't do my best . . . I thought we had such a good relationship . . . Friends. Everyone thought we were friends, not mother and daughter . . . I tried to do everything right . . . I tried to teach her that there could be more than just love between a mother and a daughter . . . There can be trust and respect and friendship and understanding . . . *(Getting angry, she turns and yells toward the closed door.)* Just because *I* don't speak to my mother doesn't mean *we* can't be different!

[*She wipes her eyes with the paper. The bathroom door opens. A solemn* ROY *steps out, and the door closes and locks behind him. He deliberately buttons his coat and crosses to the bedroom phone, wordlessly.* NORMA *has not taken her eyes off him. The pause seems interminable.*]

Roy *(into the phone).* The Green Room, please . . . Mr. Borden Eisler. Thank you. *(He waits.)*

Norma *(getting up from the bed).* . . . I'm gonna have to guess, is that it? . . . It's so bad you can't even tell me . . . Words can't form in your mouth, it's so horrible, right? . . . Come on, I'm a strong person, Roy. Tell me quickly, I'll get over it . . .

Roy *(into the phone).* Borden? Mr. Hubley . . . Can you come up to 719? . . . Yes, now . . . *(He hangs up and gestures for* NORMA *to follow him. He crosses into the living room and down to the ottoman,*[8] *where he sits.* NORMA *follows and stands waiting behind him. Finally)* She wanted to talk to me because she couldn't bear to say it to both of us at the same time . . . The reason she's locked herself in the bathroom . . . is she's afraid.

Norma. Afraid? What is she afraid of? That Borden doesn't love her?

Roy. Not that Borden doesn't love her.

Norma. That she doesn't love Borden?

Roy. Not that she doesn't love Borden.

Norma. Then what is she afraid of?

---

8. **ottoman** (ät′ə·mən): an upholstered footstool.

Roy. . . . She's afraid of what they're going to become.

Norma. I don't understand.

Roy. Think about it.

Norma (*crossing above the sofa*). What's there to think about? What are they going to become? They love each other, they'll get married, they'll have children, they'll grow older, they'll become like us. (*Comes the dawn. Stops by the side of the sofa and turns back to* ROY)—I never thought about that.

Roy. Makes you stop and think, doesn't it?

Norma. I don't think we're so bad, do you? . . . All right, so we yell and scream a little. So we fight and curse and aggravate each other. So you blame me for being a lousy mother and I accuse you of being a rotten husband. It doesn't mean we're not happy . . . does it? . . . (*Her voice rising*) Well? . . . Does it? . . .

Roy (*looks at her*). . . . She wants something better. (*The doorbell rings. He crosses to open the door.* NORMA *follows.*) Hello, Borden.

Borden (*stepping into the room*). Hi.

Norma. Hello, darling.

Roy (*gravely*). Borden, you're an intelligent young man. I'm not going to beat around the bush. We have a serious problem on our hands.

Borden. How so?

Roy. Mimsey—is worried. Worried about your future together. About the whole institution of marriage. We've tried to allay her fears, but obviously we haven't been a very good example. It seems you're the only one who can communicate with her. She's locked herself in the bathroom and is not coming out . . . It's up to you now.

[*Without a word,* BORDEN *crosses below the sofa and up to the bedroom, through the bedroom below the bed and right up to the bathroom door. He knocks.*]

Borden. Mimsey? . . . This is Borden . . . Cool it! (*Then he turns and crosses back to the living room. Crossing above the sofa, he passes the Hubleys, and without looking at them, says*) See you downstairs!

[*He exits without showing any more emotion. The Hubleys stare after him as he closes the door. But then the bathroom door opens and* NORMA *and* ROY *slowly turn to it as* MIMSEY, *a beautiful bride, in a formal wedding gown, with veil, comes out.*]

Mimsey. I'm ready now!

[NORMA *turns and moves into the bedroom toward her.* ROY *follows slowly, shaking his head in amazement.*]

Roy. *Now* you're ready? *Now* you come out?

Norma (*admiring* MIMSEY). Roy, please . . .

Roy (*getting angry, leans toward her over the bed*). I break every bone in my body and you come out for "Cool it"?

Norma (*pushing* MIMSEY *toward* ROY). You're beautiful, darling. Walk with your father, I want to look at both of you.

Roy (*fuming. As she takes his arm, to* NORMA). That's how he communicates? That's the brilliant understanding between two people? "Cool it"?

Norma (*gathering up* MIMSEY'S *train, as they move toward the living room*). Roy, don't start in.

Roy. What kind of a person is that to let your daughter marry?

[*They stop above the sofa.* MIMSEY *takes her bridal bouquet from the table behind the sofa, while* NORMA *puts on her wrap and takes her gloves from the back of the sofa.*]

Norma. Roy, don't aggravate me. I'm warning you, don't spoil this day for me.

Roy. Kids today don't care. Not like they did in my day.

Norma. Walk. Will you walk? In five minutes he'll marry one of the flower girls. Will you walk—

[MIMSEY *takes* ROY *by the arm and they move to the door, as* NORMA *follows.*]

Roy (*turning back to* NORMA). Crazy. I must be out of my mind, a boy like that. (*Opens the door*) She was better off in the bathroom. You hear me? Better off in the bathroom . . . (*They are out the door . . .*)

Curtain

"That's the brilliant understanding between two people?
'Cool it'?"

Responding to the Play

Analyzing the Play

Identifying Facts

1. The play's **exposition** is given in a phone conversation. How does Norma describe the way Mimsey feels? What is the *real* problem?
2. What different approaches does Norma first use to try to make Mimsey come out?
3. Many farces or comedies have a **"Jack-in-the-box" character.** This is a character who establishes one attitude and then repeats and repeats it each time he or she "pops up" in the play. The humor comes from this character's predictability. Roy Hubley is the Jack-in-the-box in this play. What is he always concerned about? Find at least three lines that repeat Roy's chief concern.
4. **Tension** is often created when a play's action runs against the clock. Why is time a crucial element in this play?

5. What farcical (farcelike) actions do Norma and Roy Hubley engage in, to get Mimsey out of the bathroom? Describe how they *look* when the play is over and they start downstairs.
6. What do the Hubleys finally realize that Mimsey is afraid of?
7. Borden's time onstage makes up the **climax** of the play. How does he resolve the problem?

Interpreting Meanings

8. Why do you think Borden's "Cool it!" worked, where Norma and Roy's hysterics did not?
9. On the surface, this play is about a frightened bride and her parents' comic efforts to get her to the wedding ceremony. Who, though, receives most of the playwright's attention? Who or what would you say is the *real* subject of *Visitor from Forest Hills*?
10. Neil Simon's plays are usually **satiric**—that is, they make us laugh because they expose the foolish thoughts and actions of certain characters. What flaws in Roy and Norma is Simon making us laugh at?
11. Do you think most parents would behave like Roy and Norma if their daughter locked herself in the bathroom on her wedding day? Describe how some other parents might respond to the Hubleys' unusual problem.

Writing About the Play

A Creative Response

1. **Writing a New Scene.** Think about what Norma and Roy Hubley have said about their own marriage in *Visitor from Forest Hills*. Then write a scene in which Mimsey comes out of the bathroom earlier to talk about marriage with her parents. Before you write, think about these questions: What are Mimsey's real fears about her future? Will Norma side with Mimsey and make Roy even *more* angry about the money he has spent? Or will something happen between Mr. and Mrs. Hubley to make Mimsey finally decide *yes* or *no*? You might use Borden in some comical way to tip the scales of the action. Or you might invent new characters who will add to the comedy and conflict.
2. **Extending the Play.** Write a scene showing Mimsey and Borden twenty-five years from now. Are they like Roy and Norma? Is Borden still "cool"? You might initiate your action by setting your scene on the day *their* daughter is getting married. Do they remember their own wedding-day crisis? What is their daughter like and what does she want? Where will your scene be set? Invent some point of **conflict,** so that your scene will have movement: a beginning, a middle, and an end.

A Critical Response

3. **Analyzing Character.** Neil Simon has said that it's important, in comedy, "to make your characters likable even when you're exposing their worst faults." Think about the characters' "worst faults" in this play. Despite these faults, do you find each character likable or not? Has the playwright arranged for each character to say or do something likable even as he or she reveals a fault? In an essay, write an analysis of the characters of Norma and Roy. Tell whether or not you think Simon succeeded in making these characters likable, even as he exposed their faults.

Reading About the Writer

Neil Simon (1927–) has had a successful comedy on Broadway almost every season. In fact, he often has two plays running at the same time and a movie showing as well. Simon started as a television writer for sitcoms such as *My Three Sons*. He moved on to the theater with his first play, *Come Blow Your Horn*. Since then, he has written for the theater and the movies such works as *The Odd Couple, California Suite, Chapter Two, The Goodbye Girl*, and *Only When I Laugh*. Two of his comedies, *Barefoot in the Park* and *Plaza Suite*, held record-breaking runs on Broadway. Simon's latest comedies, *Brighton Beach Memoirs* and *Biloxi Blues*, are based on his own boyhood and on his stint in the U.S. Army. Simon, who grew up in New York City, says he is always looking at life as a play—he is always on the alert for new characters and new stories. "There is evidence," he says, "that this phenomenon is prevalent among that strange breed called writers, but it is even more prevalent among that strange breed called comic writers."

Focusing on Background

From an Interview with Neil Simon

On Writing for the Theater

"I hated the idea of working in television and having conferences with network executives and advertising executives who told you what audiences wanted and in what region they wanted it. I despised it. I said, 'There will never be any satisfaction for me unless I can write what I feel I want to say.' And so I wrote that first play [*Come Blow Your Horn*]—it was a matter of life and death for me."

On the Distinction Between Comedy and Drama

"My experience has been that if you write a situation well enough, the tension is so great that the audience will laugh whether you provide it or not. But many times when it's either laugh or cry, a lot of them don't want to cry. And they will pick out a moment—a line, a gesture, whatever it is—to laugh at. It becomes part of the play after a while. I expect it night after night—never having intended it in the beginning. There's just so much that they can handle. You force the audience to deal with a great deal in the theater.

"Mike Nichols and I were doing *Plaza Suite* in Boston many years ago, and the first act was too long—it wasn't that it was too long, we were getting too many laughs in a scene that we thought was basically serious. So Mike and I started to cut out all of the laugh lines, and they started to laugh at other lines that they had never laughed at. They just wanted to laugh!"

On Television and the Live Stage

"Because of television, people might have shorter attention spans, I guess, because it's broken up with commercials. But they actually spend more time watching television programs. They spend a whole year watching *Dynasty*. You see a miniseries, I mean, that's hours a night for five nights a week. You've got to cancel all your plans to see *Roots*. So theater is short in comparison."

On the Future of Playwriting

"I'm naïve and optimistic enough to think that plays will always be here despite the fact that it's been a fairly grim season, and we're losing more and more playwrights to films and to television—places where they're guaranteed to make money. And the price of tickets makes it so difficult to put on certain kinds of plays that don't promise to be big smash hits.

"Whenever I go to speak at a school, it's rarely for the drama class. It's always for a film class. There are so few drama classes that are interested in the theater. There'll be about four kids in the group who are interested in plays, but most of them want to know about films."

—Neil Simon

The Mother

Paddy Chayefsky's *The Mother* is a one-hour television play which was produced for NBC on the Philco Television Playhouse in 1954, during the early days of television. This period is called "the Golden Age of television," when the three networks often broadcast twelve live, original plays a week. It was a time when many young men and women who would eventually become successful playwrights and screenwriters were both earning a living and refining their talents in writing for television.

Though *The Mother* is divided into three acts to accommodate commercials, it is about the length of a one-act play, and it is constructed along the simple lines of a one-act play. But the play also has the scenic fluidity of a motion picture.

The story's basic **dramatic question** is a compelling and familiar one: What will become of an aging widowed mother? The story unfolds very simply. The daughter wants the mother to come live with her. The daughter's husband protests that the mother obviously wants to be independent. And the mother herself wants to get a job and live her own life.

The play is perfectly constructed. The story progresses smoothly from scene to scene, from situation to situation. Each scene grows out of the basic question: What will happen to the mother?

But construction is not everything in a play. It is only the means by which to communicate the vision and feelings of the playwright. A play, or any work of art, can display faultless technique, but without heart and vision the work is empty.

At the same time, heart and vision cannot be communicated without skill or craft. The French painter Auguste Renoir said, "First of all be a good craftsman. This will not keep you from being a genius." This is an important point which all young artists, writers, and composers need to remember. Learning the craft is very difficult. We all want to avoid the hard work and be instant geniuses. Our souls may burn with visions of great plays or novels or symphonies, yet it takes years to learn the skills that will allow us to communicate these visions.

In his early television plays—*Marty, The Bachelor Party, The Catered Affair, The Mother*—Chayefsky used his skill to convey his vision of "the little man." Chayefsky had a great gift for catching the everyday rhythms of speech, the common concerns, the common attitudes. This is one reason why his work was so popular. He spoke to and for a great part of the population, with recognizable characters in familiar situations speaking ordinary speech.

But Chayefsky's **characters** do not simply serve his plots or stories. They also have a human complexity. The boss in *The Mother* is a good example. Though he presents obstacles to the mother's wish to work, he is not a "bad" man. In fact, there are no villains here at all. In one way, the definition of a good play is a play in which everyone is right. In life, each person is "right" to himself or herself. One of the tasks of the playwright is to *justify* each character in whatever he or she does—to provide us with understandable **motives,** or reasons, for what they do. But remember: just because we understand a character does not mean we have to forgive the bad things he or she might do.

> "First of all be a good craftsman. This will not keep you from being a genius."

> "In one way, the definition of a good play is a play in which everyone is right."

THE MOTHER

Paddy Chayefsky

Cast of Characters

Old lady
Daughter
Boss
Son-in-law
Black woman
Sister
Mrs. Geegan
Mrs. Kline
Bookkeeper
Puerto Rican girl

Act One

Fade in: Film—a quick group of shots showing New York in a real thunderstorm—rain whipping through the streets—real miserable weather.

Dissolve to: Close-up of an old woman, aged sixty-six, with a shock of gray-white hair, standing by a window in her apartment, looking out, apparently deeply disturbed by the rain slashing against the pane.

We pull back to see that the old woman is wearing an old kimono, under which there is evidence of an old white batiste[1] nightgown. Her gray-white hair hangs loosely down over her shoulders. It is early morning, and she has apparently just gotten out of bed. This is the bedroom of her two-and-a-half-room apartment in a lower-middle-class neighborhood in the Bronx.[2] The bed is still unmade and looks just slept in. The furniture is old and worn. On the chest of drawers there is a galaxy of photographs and portrait pictures, evidently of her various children and grandchildren. She stands looking out the window, troubled, disturbed.

Suddenly the alarm, perched on the little bed table, rings. Camera moves in for close-up of the alarm clock. It reads half past six. The old lady's hand comes down and shuts the alarm off.

Cut to: Close-up of another alarm clock, ring-ing in another apartment. It also reads half past six; but it is obviously a different clock, on a much more modern bed table. This one buzzes instead of clangs. A young woman's hand reaches over and turns it off.

Camera pulls back to show that we are in the bedroom of a young couple. The young woman who has turned the clock off is a rather plain girl of thirty. She slowly sits up in bed, assembling herself for the day. On the other half of the bed, her husband turns and tries to go back to sleep.

Son-in-law (*from under the blankets*). What time is it?
Daughter (*still seated heavily on the edge of the bed*). It's half past six.
Son-in-law (*from under the blankets*). What did you set it so early for?
Daughter. I wanna call my mother. (*She looks out at the window, the rain driving fiercely against it.*) For heaven's sake, listen to the rain! She's not going down today, I'll tell you that, if I have to go over there and chain her in her bed. . . . (*She stands, crosses to the window, studies the rain.*) Boy, look at it rain.
Son-in-law (*still under the covers*). What?
Daughter. I said, it's raining.

[*She makes her way, still heavy with sleep, out of the bedroom into the foyer[3] of the apartment. She pads in her bare feet and pajamas down the foyer to the telephone table, sits on the little chair, trying to clear her head of sleep. A baby's cry is suddenly heard in an off room. The young woman absently goes "Sshh." The baby's cry stops. The young woman picks up the receiver of the phone and dials. She waits. Then . . .*]

Daughter. Ma? This is Annie. Did I wake you up? . . . I figured you'd be up by now. . . . Ma, you're not going downtown today, and I don't wanna hear no arguments . . . Ma, have you looked out the window? It's raining like . . . Ma, I'm not gonna let you go downtown today, do you hear me? . . . I don't care, Ma . . . Ma, I don't care . . . Ma, I'm coming over. You stay there till . . . Ma, stay

---

1. **batiste** (ba·tēst′): a light fabric of cotton and linen.
2. **Bronx:** one of five boroughs that make up New York City.

3. **foyer** (foi′ər): front hall.

there till I come over. I'm getting dressed right now. I'll drive over in the car. It won't take me ten minutes . . . Ma, you're not going out in this rain. It's not enough that you almost fainted in the subway yesterday . . . Ma, I'm hanging up, and I'm coming over right now. Stay there . . . all right, I'm hanging up . . .

[*She hangs up, sits for a minute, then rises and shuffles quickly back up the foyer and back into her bedroom. She disappears into the bathroom, unbuttoning the blouse of her pajamas. She leaves the bathroom door open, and a shaft of light suddenly shoots out into the dark bedroom.*]

Son-in-law (*awake now, his head visible over the covers*). Did you talk to her?

Daughter (*off in bathroom*). Yeah, she was all practically ready to leave.

Son-in-law. Look, Annie, I don't wanna tell you how to treat your own mother, but why don't you leave her alone? It's obviously very important to her to get a job for herself. She wants to support herself. She doesn't want to be a burden on her children. I respect her for that. An old lady, sixty-six years old, going out and looking for work. I think that shows a lot of guts.

[*The daughter comes out of the bathroom. She has a blouse on now and a half-slip.*]

Daughter (*crossing to the closet*). George, please, you don't know what you're talking about, so do me a favor, and don't argue with me. I'm not in a good mood. (*She opens the closet, studies the crowded rack of clothes.*) I'm turning on the light, so get your eyes ready. (*She turns on the light. The room is suddenly bright. She blinks and pokes in the closet for a skirt, which she finally extracts.*) My mother worked like a dog all her life, and she's not gonna spend the rest of her life bent over a sewing machine. (*She slips into the skirt.*) She had one of her attacks in the subway yesterday. I was never so scared in my life when that cop called yesterday. (*She's standing in front of her mirror now, hastily arranging her hair.*) My mother worked like a dog to raise me and my brother and my sister. She worked in my old man's grocery store till twelve o'clock at night. We owe her a little peace of mind, my brother and my sister and

me. She sacrificed plenty for us in her time. (*She's back at the closet, fishing for her topcoat.*) And I want her to move out of that apartment. I don't want her living alone. I want her to come live here with us, George, and I don't want any more arguments about that either. We can move Tommy in with the baby, and she can have Tommy's room. And that reminds me—the baby cried for a minute there. If she cries again, give her her milk because she went to sleep without her milk last night. (*She has her topcoat on now and is already at the door to the foyer.*) All right, I'll probably be back in time to make you breakfast. Have you got the keys to the car? . . . (*She nervously pats the pocket of her coat.*) No, I got them. All right, I'll see you. Good-by, George . . .

[*She goes out into the foyer.*]

Son-in-law. Good-by, Annie . . .

[*Off in some other room, the baby begins to cry again, a little more insistently. The husband raises his eyebrows and listens for a moment. When it becomes apparent that the baby isn't going to stop, he sighs and begins to get out of bed.*

Dissolve to: The old lady standing by the window again. She is fully dressed now, however, even to the black coat and hat. The coat is unbuttoned. For the first time, we may be aware of a black silk mourning band that the old lady has about the sleeve of her coat. Outside, the rain has abated considerably. It is drizzling lightly now. The old lady turns to her daughter, standing at the other end of the bedroom, brushing the rain from her coat. When the old lady speaks, it is with a mild, but distinct, Irish flavor.]

Old lady. It's letting up a bit.

Daughter (*brushing off her coat*). It isn't letting up at all. It's gonna stop and start all day long.

[*The old lady starts out of her bedroom, past her daughter, into her living room.*]

Old lady. I'm going to make a bit of coffee for myself and some Rice Krispies. Would you like a cup?

[*The daughter turns and starts into the living room ahead of her mother.*]

Daughter. I'll make it for you.

Old lady. You won't make it for me. I'll make it myself. (*She crowds past the daughter and goes to the kitchen. At the kitchen doorway, she turns and surveys her daughter.*)

Old lady. Annie, you know, you can drive somebody crazy, do you know that?

Daughter. *I* can drive somebody crazy?! *You're* the one who can drive somebody crazy.

Old lady. Will you stop hovering over me like I was a cripple in a wheel chair? I can make my own coffee, believe me. Why did you come over here? You've got a husband and two kids to take care of. Go make coffee for them, for heaven's sakes. (*She turns and goes into the kitchen, muttering away. She opens a cupboard and extracts a jar of instant coffee.*) I've taken to making instant coffee, would you like a cup?

[*The daughter is standing on the threshold of the kitchen now, leaning against the doorjamb.*]

Daughter. All right, make me a cup, Ma.

[*The old lady takes two cups and saucers out and begins carefully to level out a teaspoonful of the instant coffee into each. The daughter moves into the kitchen, reaches up for something in the cupboard.*]

Daughter. Where do you keep your saccharin, Ma?

[*The old lady wheels and slaps the daughter's outstretched arms down.*]

Old lady. Annie, I'll get it myself! (*She points a finger into the living room.*) Go in there and sit down, will you?! I'll bring the cup in to you!

[*The daughter leans back against the doorjamb, a little exasperated with the old lady's petulant[4] independence. The old lady now takes an old teapot and sets it on the stove and lights a flame under it.*]

Old lady. You can drive me to the subway if you want to do something for me.

Daughter. Ma, you're not going downtown today.

Old lady. I want to get down there extra early today on the off-chance that they haven't given the job to someone else. What did I do with that card from the New York State Employment Service? . . .

[*She shuffles out of the kitchen, the daughter moving out of the doorway to give her passage. The old lady goes to the table in the living room on which sits her battered black purse. She opens it and takes out a card.*]

Old lady. I don't want to lose that. (*She puts the white card back into her purse.*) I'm pretty sure I could have held onto this job, because the chap at the Employment Service called up the boss, you see, over the phone, and he explained to the man that I hadn't worked in quite a number of years . . .

Daughter (*muttering*). Quite a number of years . . .

Old lady. . . . and that I'd need a day or so to get used to the machines again.

Daughter. Did the chap at the Employment Service explain to the boss that it's forty years that you haven't worked?

Old lady (*crossing back to the kitchen*). . . . and the boss understood this, you see, so he would have been a little lenient[5] with me. But then, of course, I had to go and faint in the subway, because I was in such a hurry to get down there, you know, I didn't even stop to eat my lunch. I had brought along some sandwiches, you see, cheese and tomatoes. Oh, I hope he hasn't given the job to anyone else . . .

[*The old lady reaches into the cupboard again for a bowl of sugar, an opened box of Rice Krispies, and a bowl. The daughter watches her as she turns to the refrigerator to get out a container of milk.*]

Daughter. Ma, when are you gonna give up?

[*The old lady frowns.*]

Old lady. Annie, please . . . (*She pours some Rice Krispies into the bowl.*)

Daughter. Ma, you been trying for three weeks now. If you get a job, you get fired before the day is over. You're too old, Ma, and they don't want to hire old people . . .

---

4. **petulant** (pech′oo·lənt): ill-humored.

5. **lenient** (lē′nē·ənt): patient and forgiving.

Old lady. It's not the age . . .

Daughter. They don't want to hire white-haired old ladies.

Old lady. It's not the age at all! I've seen plenty of old people with white hair and all, sitting at those machines. The shop where I almost had that job and he fired me the other day, there was a woman there, eighty years old if she was a day, an old crone of a woman, sitting there all bent over, her machine humming away. The chap at the Employment Service said there's a lot of elderly people working in the needle trades.[6] The young people nowadays don't want to work for thirty-five, forty dollars a week, and there's a lot of old people working in the needle trades.

Daughter. Well, whatever it is, Ma . . .

Old lady (leaning to her daughter). It's my fingers. I'm not sure of them any more. When you get old, y'know, you lose the sureness in your fingers. My eyes are all right, but my fingers tremble a lot. I get very excited, y'know, when I go in for a tryout, y'know. And I'll go in, y'know, and the boss'll say: "Sit down, let's see what you can do." And I get so excited. And my heart begins thumping so that I can hardly see to thread the needle. And they stand right over you, y'know, while you're working. They give you a packet of sleeves or a skirt or something to put a hem on. Or a seam or something, y'know. It's simple work, really. Single-needle machine. Nothing fancy. And it seems to me I do it all right, but they fire me all the time. They say: "You're too slow." And I'm working as fast as I can. I think, perhaps, I've lost the ability in my fingers. And that's what scares me the most. It's not the age. I've seen plenty of old women working in the shops. (She has begun to pour some milk into her bowl of cereal; but she stops now and just stands, staring bleakly down at the worn oilcloth on her cupboard.)

Daughter (gently). Ma, you worked all your life. Why don't you take it easy?

Old lady. I don't want to take it easy. Now that your father's dead and in the grave I don't know what to do with myself.

---

6. **needle trades:** businesses that hire people to sew together clothing pieces—sleeves, skirts, collars, etc.

Daughter. Why don't you go out, sit in the park, get a little sun like the other old women?

Old lady. I sit around here sometimes, going crazy. We had a lot of fights in our time, your father and I, but I must admit I miss him badly. You can't live with someone forty-one years and not miss him when he's dead. I'm glad that he died for his own sake—it may sound hard of me to say that—but I am glad. He was in nothing but pain the last few months, and he was a man who could never stand pain. But I do miss him.

Daughter (gently). Ma, why don't you come live with George and me?

Old lady. No, no, Annie, you're a good daughter.

Daughter. We'll move Tommy into the baby's room, and you can have Tommy's room. It's the nicest room in the apartment. It gets all the sun.

Old lady. I have wonderful children. I thank God every night for that. I . . .

Daughter. Ma, I don't like you living here alone.

Old lady. Annie, I been living in this house for eight years, and I know all the neighbors and the store people, and if I lived with you, I'd be a stranger.

Daughter. There's plenty of old people in my neighborhood. You'll make friends.

Old lady. Annie, you're a good daughter, but I want to keep my own home. I want to pay my own rent. I don't want to be some old lady living with her children. If I can't take care of myself, I'd just as soon be in the grave with your father. I don't want to be a burden on my children . . .

Daughter. Ma, for heaven's sakes . . .

Old lady. More than anything else, I don't want to be a burden on my children. I pray to God every night to let me keep my health and my strength so that I won't have to be a burden on my children . . . (The teapot suddenly hisses. The old lady looks up.) Annie, the pot is boiling. Would you pour the water in the cups?

[The daughter moves to the stove. The old lady, much of her ginger seemingly sapped out of her, shuffles into the living room. She perches on the edge of one of the wooden chairs.]

Old lady. I been getting some pains in my shoulder the last week or so. I had the electric heating pad on practically the whole night. . . . (She looks up *toward the windows again.)* It's starting to rain a little harder again. Maybe, I won't go downtown today after all. Maybe, if it clears up a bit, I'll go out and sit in the park and get some sun.

[In the kitchen, the daughter pours the boiling water into each cup, stirs.]

Daughter *(to her mother, off in the living room).* Is this all you're eating for breakfast, Ma? Let me make you something else . . .

[Dissolve to: A park bench. The old lady and two other old ladies are seated, all bundled up in their cheap cloth coats with the worn fur collars. The second old lady is also Irish. Her name is Mrs. Geegan. The third old lady is possibly Jewish, certainly a New Yorker by intonation. Her name is Mrs. Kline. The rain has stopped; it is a clear, bright, sunny March morning.]

Old lady. . . . Well, it's nice and clear now, isn't it? It was raining something fierce around seven o'clock this morning.

Mrs. Geegan *(grimacing).* It's too ruddy cold for me. I'd go home except my daughter-in-law is cleaning the house, and I don't want to get in her way.

Mrs. Kline. My daughter-in-law should drop dead tomorrow.

Mrs. Geegan. My daughter-in-law gets into an awful black temper when she's cleaning.

Mrs. Kline. My daughter-in-law should grow rich and own a hotel with a thousand rooms and be found dead in every one of them.

Mrs. Geegan *(to the old lady).* I think I'll go over and visit Missus Halley in a little while, would you like to go? She fell down the stairs and broke her hip, and they're suing the owners of the building. I saw her son yesterday, and he says she's awful weak. When you break a hip at that age, you're as good as in the coffin. I don't like to visit Missus Halley. She's always so gloomy about things. But it's a way of killing off an hour or so to lunch. A little later this afternoon, I thought I'd go to confession. It's so warm and solemn in the church. Do you go to Saint John's? I think it's ever so much prettier than Our Lady of Visitation. Why don't you come to Missus Halley's with me,

Missus Fanning? Her son's a sweet man, and there's always a bit of fruit they offer you.

Old lady. I don't believe I know a Missus Halley.

Mrs. Geegan. Missus Halley, the one that fell down the stairs last week and dislocated her hip. They're suing the owners of the building for forty thousand dollars.

Mrs. Kline. They'll settle for a hundred, believe me.

Mrs. Geegan. Oh, it's chilly this morning. I'd go home, but my daughter-in-law is cleaning the house, and she doesn't like me to be about when she's cleaning. I'd like a bottle of beer, that's what I'd like. Oh, my mouth is fairly watering for it. I'm not allowed to have beer, you know. I'm a diabetic. You don't happen to have a quarter on you, Missus Fanning? We could buy a bottle and split it between us. I'd ask my son for it, but they always want to know what I want the money for.

Old lady *(looking sharply at Mrs. Geegan).* Do you have to ask your children for money?

Mrs. Geegan. Oh, they're generous. They always give me whenever I ask. But I'm not allowed to have beer, you see, and they wouldn't give me the twenty-five cents for that. What do I need money for anyway? Go to the movies? I haven't been to the movies in more than a year, I think. I just like a dollar every now and then for an offering at mass. Do you go to seven o'clock novena,[7] Missus Fanning? It's a good way to spend an hour, I think.

Old lady. Is that what you do with your day, Missus Geegan? Visit dying old ladies and go to confession?

Mrs. Geegan. Well, I like to stay in the house a lot, watching television. There's ever so much fun on television in the afternoons, with the kiddie shows and a lot of dancing and Kate Smith and shows like that. But my daughter-in-law's cleaning up today, and she doesn't like me around the house when she's cleaning, so I came out a bit early to sit in the park.

[The old lady regards Mrs. Geegan for a long moment.]

---

7. **novena:** recitation of prayers for nine days, usually to seek some special favor.

Mrs. Kline. My daughter-in-law, she should invest all her money in General Motors stock, and they should go bankrupt.

[*A pause settles over the three old ladies. They just sit, huddled, their cheeks pressed into the fur of their collars. After a moment, the old lady shivers noticeably.*]

Old lady. It's a bit chilly. I think I'll go home. (*She rises.*) Good-by, Missus Geegan . . . Good-by, Missus . . .

[*The other two old ladies nod their goodbys. The old lady moves off screen. We hold for a moment on the remaining two old ladies, sitting, shoulders hunched against the morning chill, faces pressed under their collars, staring bleakly ahead.*

Dissolve to: Door of the old lady's apartment. It opens, and the old lady comes in. She closes the door behind her, goes up the small foyer to the living room. She unbuttons her coat and walks aimlessly around the room, into the bedroom and out again, across the living room and into the kitchen, and then out of the kitchen. She is frowning as she walks and rubs her hands continually as if she is quite cold. Suddenly she goes to the telephone, picks it up, dials a number, waits.]

Old lady (*snappishly*). Is this Mister McCleod?! This is Missus Fanning in Apartment 3F! The place is a refrigerator up here! It's freezing! I want some steam! I want it right now! That's all there is to it! I want some steam right now!

[*She hangs up sharply, turns—scowling—and sits heavily down on the edge of a soft chair, scowling, nervous, rocking a little back and forth. Then abruptly she rises, crosses the living room to the television set, clicks it on. She stands in front of it, waiting for a picture to show. At last the picture comes on. It is the WPIX station signal, accompanied by the steady high-pitched drone that indicates there are no programs on yet. She turns the set off almost angrily.*

She is beginning to breathe heavily now. She turns nervously and looks at the large ornamental clock on the sideboard. It reads ten minutes after eleven. She goes to the small dining table and sits down on one of the hard-back chairs. Her black

purse is still on the table, as it was during the scene with her daughter. Her eyes rest on it for a moment; then she reaches over, opens the purse, and takes out the white employment card. She looks at it briefly, expressionlessly. Then she returns it to the purse and reclasps the purse. Again she sits for a moment, rigid, expressionless. Then suddenly she stands, grabs the purse, and starts out the living room, down the foyer, to the front door of her apartment—buttoning her coat as she goes. She opens the door, goes out.*

Camera stays on door as it is closed. There is the noise of a key being inserted into the lock. A moment later the bolts on the lock shift into locked position. Hold.]

Fade out.

Act Two

Fade in: Film. Lunchtime in the needle-trade district of New York—a quick montage[1] of shots of the streets, jammed with traffic, trucks, and working people hurrying to the dense little luncheonettes for their lunch.

Dissolve to: Interior of the Tiny Tots Sportswear Co., Inc., 137 West Twenty-seventh Street, on the eighth floor. It is lunchtime. We dissolve in on some of the women operators at their lunch. They are seated at their machines, of which there are twenty—in two rows of ten, facing each other. Not all of the operators eat their lunch in: about half go downstairs to join the teeming noontime crowds in the oily little restaurants of the vicinity. The ten or so women whom we see—munching their sandwiches and sipping their containers of coffee and chattering shrilly to one another—all wear worn house dresses. A good proportion of the operators are Negro and Puerto Rican. Not a few of them are gray-haired, or at least unmistakably middle-aged.

The rest of the shop seems to consist of endless rows of pipe racks on which hang finished chil-

---

1. **montage** (män·täzh′): a set or series of images combined for one effect.

dren's dresses, waiting to be shipped. In the mid-
dle of these racks is a pressing machine and
sorting table at which two of the three men who
work in the shop eat their lunch. At the far end of
the loft—in a corner so dark that a light must
always be on over it—is an old, battered roll-top
desk at which sits the bookkeeper, an angular
woman of thirty-five, differentiated from the hand
workers in that she wears a clean dress.

Nearby is the boss, a man in his thirties. He is
bent over a machine, working on it with a screw
driver. The boss is really a pleasant man; he works
under the illusion, however, that gruffness is a
requisite quality of an executive.

Somehow, a tortured passageway has been
worked out between the racks leading to the ele-
vator doors; it is the only visible exit and entrance
to the loft.

As we look at these doors, there is a growing
whirring and clanging announcing the arrival of
the elevator. The doors slide reluctantly open, and
the old lady enters the shop. The elevator doors
slide closed behind her. She stands surrounded by
pipe racks, a little apprehensive.[2] *The arrival of*
the elevator has caused some of the people to look
up briefly. The old lady goes to the presser, a
Puerto Rican.

Old lady. Excuse me, I'm looking for the boss.

[*The presser indicates with his hand the spot*
where the boss is standing, working on the ma-
chine. The old lady picks her way through the
cluttered pipe racks to the bookkeeper, who looks
up at her approach. The boss also looks up briefly
at her approach, but goes back to his work. The
old lady opens her purse, takes out the white card,
and proffers it to the bookkeeper. She mutters
something.]

Bookkeeper. Excuse me, I can't hear what you said.
Old lady. I said, I was supposed to be here yes-terday, but I was sick in the subway—I fainted, you see, and . . .

---

2. **apprehensive** (ap′rə·hen′siv): worried about what will happen next.

[*The boss now turns to the old lady.*]

Boss. What? . . . What? . . .
Old lady. I was sent down from the . . .
Boss. What?
Old lady (*louder*). I was sent down from the New York State Employment Service. I was supposed to be here yesterday.
Boss. Yes, so what happened?
Old lady. I was sick. I fainted in the subway.
Boss. What?
Old lady (*louder*). I was sick. The subway was so hot there, you see—there was a big crush at a Hundred and forty-ninth Street . . .
Boss. You was supposed to be here yesterday.
Old lady. I had a little trouble. They had my daughter down there and everything. By the time I got down here, it was half past five, and the fellow on the elevator—not the one that was here this morning—another fellow entirely. An old man it was. He said there was nobody up here. So I was going to come down early this morning, but I figured you probably had the job filled anyway. That's why I didn't come down till now.
Boss. What kind of work do you do?
Old lady. Well, I used to do all sections except joining and zippers, but I think the fellow at the Employment Service explained to you that it's been a number of years since I actually worked in a shop.
Boss. What do you mean, a number of years?
Old lady. (*mumbling*). Well, I did a lot of sewing for the Red Cross during the war, y'know, but I haven't actually worked in a shop since 1916.
Boss. (*who didn't quite hear her mumbled words*). What?
Old lady. (*louder*). Nineteen sixteen. October.
Boss. Nineteen sixteen.
Old lady. I'm sure if I could work a little bit, I would be fine. I used to be a very fast worker.
Boss. Can you thread a machine?

[*The old lady nods. He starts off through the maze of pipe racks to the two rows of machines. The old lady follows after him, clutching her purse and the white card, her hat still sitting on her head, her coat still buttoned. As they go up the rows of sewing machines, the other operators look up to catch covert[3] glimpses of the new applicant. The boss indicates one of the open machines.*]

Boss. All right. Siddown. Show me how you thread a machine.

[*The old lady sets her purse down nervously and takes the seat behind the machine. The other operators have all paused in their eating to watch the test. The old lady reaches to her side, where there are several spools of thread.*]

Old lady. What kind of thread, white or black?
Boss. White! White!

[*She fumblingly fetches a spool of white thread and, despite the fact she is obviously trembling, she contrives to thread the machine—a process which takes about half a minute. The boss stands towering over her.*]

Boss. Can you make a sleeve?

[*The old lady nods, desperately trying to get the thread through the eye of the needle and over the proper holes.*]

Boss. It's a simple business. One seam. (*He reaches into the bin belonging to the machine next to the one the old lady is working on and extracts a neatly tied bundle of sleeve material. He drops it on the table beside the old lady.*) All right, make a sleeve. Let's see how you make a sleeve. (*He breaks the string and gives her a piece of sleeve material. She takes it, but is so nervous it falls to the floor. She hurriedly bends to pick it up, inserts the sleeve into the machine, and hunches into her work—her face screwed tight with intense concentration. She has still not unbuttoned her coat, and beads of sweat begin to appear on her brow. With painstaking laboriousness, she slowly moves the sleeve material into the machine. The boss stands, impatient and scowling.*) Mama, what are you weaving there, a carpet? It's a lousy sleeve, for Pete's sake.
Old lady. I'm a little unsure. My fingers are a little unsure . . .
Boss. You gotta be fast, Mama. This is week work. It's not piecework. I'm paying you by the hour. I

got twenny dozen cottons here, gotta be out by six o'clock. The truckman isn't gonna wait, you know . . . Mama, Mama, watch what you're doing there . . . (*He leans quickly forward and reguides the material.*) A straight seam, for heaven's sake! You're making it crooked! . . . Watch it! Watch it! Watch what you're doing there, Mama . . . All right, sew. Don't let me make you nervous. Sew . . . Mama, wadda you sewing there, an appendicitis operation? It's a lousy sleeve. How long you gonna take? I want operators here, not surgeons . . . (*Through all this, the terrified old lady tremblingly pushes the material through the machine. Finally, she's finished. She looks up at the boss, her eyes wide with apprehension, ready to pick up her purse and dash out to the street. The boss picks up the sleeve, studies it, then drops it on the table, mutters:*) All right, we'll try you out for a while . . .

[*He turns abruptly and goes back through the pipe racks to the desk. The old lady sits, trembling, a little slumped, her coat still buttoned to the collar. A middle-aged Negro woman, sitting at the next machine over her lunch, leans over to the old lady.*]

Negro woman (*gently*). Mama, what are you sitting there in your hat and coat for? Hang them up, honey. You go through that door over there. (*She points to a door leading into a built-in room. The old lady looks up slowly at this genuine sympathy.*) Don't let him get you nervous, Mama. He likes to yell a lot, but he's okay.

[*The tension within the old lady suddenly bursts out in the form of a soft, staccato[4] series of sighs. She quickly masters herself.*]

Old lady (*smiling at the Negro woman*). I'm a little unsure of myself. My fingers are a little unsure.

[*Cut to: The boss, standing by the desk. He leans down to mutter to the bookkeeper.*]

Boss (*muttering*). How could I say no, will you tell me? How could I say no? . . .
Bookkeeper. Nobody says you should say no.

---

3. **covert:** hidden, concealed.

4. **staccato** (stə·kät′ō): a rapid series of short sharp sounds.

Boss. She was so nervous, did you see how nervous she was? I bet you she's seventy years old. How could I say no? (*The telephone suddenly rings.*) Answer . . .

[*The bookkeeper picks up the receiver.*]

Bookkeeper (*on the phone*). Tiny Tots Sportswear.
Boss (*in a low voice*). Who is it?
Bookkeeper (*on phone*). He's somewhere on the floor, Mister Raymond. I'll see if I can find him. (*She covers the mouthpiece.*)
Boss (*frowning*). Which Raymond is it, the younger one or the older one?
Bookkeeper. The younger one.
Boss. You can't find me.

[*The bookkeeper starts to relay this message, but the boss changes his mind. He takes the receiver.*]

Boss. Hello, Jerry? This is Sam . . . Jerry, for heaven's sake, the twenty dozen just came at half past nine this morning . . . Jerry, I told you six o'clock; it'll be ready six o'clock . . . (*Suddenly lowers his voice, turns away from the bookkeeper, embarrassed at the pleading he's going to have to go through now*) Jerry, how about that fifty dozen faille[5] sport suits . . . Have a heart, Jerry, I need the work. I haven't got enough work to keep my girls. Two of them left yesterday . . . Jerry, please, what kind of living can I make on these cheap cottons? Give me a fancier garment . . . It's such small lots, Jerry. At least give me big lots . . . (*lowering his voice even more*) Jerry, I hate to appeal to you on this level, but I'm your brother-in-law, you know. . . . Things are pretty rough with me right now, Jerry. Have a heart. Send me over the fifty dozen failles you got in yesterday. I'll make a rush job for you . . . please, Jerry, why do you have to make me crawl? All right, I'll have this one for you five o'clock . . . I'll call up the freight man now. How about the failles? . . . Okay, Jerry, thank you, you're a good fellow. . . . All right, five o'clock. I'll call the freight man right now . . . Okay . . . (*He hangs up, stands a moment, sick at his own loss of dignity. He turns to the bookkeeper, head bowed.*) My own brother-in-law . . . (*He shuffles away,*

looks up. The old lady, who had gone into the dressing room to hang up her coat and hat, comes out of the dressing room now. The boss wheels on her.*) Watsa matter with you? I left you a bundle of sleeves there! You're not even in the shop five minutes, and you walk around like you own the place! (*He wheels to the other operators.*) All right! Come on! Come on! What are you sitting there for?! Rush job! Rush job! Let's go! Five o'clock the freight man's coming! Let's go! Let's go!

[*Cut to: The bedroom of the daughter and son-in-law's apartment. The bed has been made, the room cleaned up. The blinds have been drawn open, and the room is nice and bright. The son-in-law sits on one of the straight-back chairs, slumped a little, surly, scowling. The daughter sits erectly on the bed, her back to her husband, likewise scowling. Apparently, angry words have passed between them. The doorbell buzzes off. Neither of them moves for a moment. Then the daughter rises. At her move, the son-in-law begins to gather himself together.*]

Son-in-law. I'll get it.

[*The daughter moves—in sullen, quick silence—past him and out into the foyer. The son-in-law, who has started to rise, sits down again. In the hallway, the daughter pads down to the front door of the apartment. She is wearing a house dress now and house slippers. She opens the door. Waiting at the door is an attractive young woman in her early thirties, in coat and hat.*]

Daughter. Hello, Marie, what are you doing here?
Sister. Nothing. I just came by for a couple of minutes, that's all. I just brought the kids back to school, I thought I'd drop in for a minute, that's all. How's George?

[*She comes into the apartment. The daughter closes the door after her. The sister starts down the hallway.*]

Daughter. You came in right in the middle of an argument.

[*The son-in-law is now standing in the bedroom doorway.*]

---

5. **faille** (fīl): a fabric of ribbed silk.

Son-in-law (*to the sister*). Your sister drives me crazy.

Sister. Watsa matter now?

Daughter (*following her sister up the foyer*). Nothing's the matter. How's Jack? The kids?

[*The two women go into the bedroom, the son-in-law stepping back to let them in.*]

Sister. They're fine. Jack's got a little cold, nothing important. I just took the kids back to school, and I thought I'd drop in, see if you feel like going up to Fordham Road, do a little shopping for a couple of hours. (*To the son-in-law*) What are you doing home?

Son-in-law. It's my vacation. We were gonna leave the kids with my sister, drive downna Virginia, North Carolina, get some warm climate. But your crazy sister don't wanna go. She don't wanna leave your mother . . . (*Turning to his wife*) Your mother can take care of herself better than we can. She's a tough old woman. . . . How many vacations you think I get a year? I don't wanna sit in New York for two weeks, watching it rain.

Sister. Go ahead, Annie. Me and Frank will see that Mom's all right.

Daughter. Sure, you and Frank. Look, Marie, I was over to see Mom this morning . . .

Son-in-law. Half past six she got up this morning, go over to see your mother . . .

Daughter. After what happened yesterday, I decided to put my foot down. Because Mom got no business at her age riding up and down in the subways. You know how packed they are. Anyway, I called Mom on the phone, and she gave me the usual arguments. You know Mom. So anyway, I went over to see her, and she was very depressed. We talked for about an hour, and she told me she's been feeling very depressed lately. It's no good Mom living there alone, and you know it, Marie. Anyway, I think I finally convinced her to move out of there and come and live over here.

Son-in-law. You didn't convince me.

Daughter. George, please . . .

Son-in-law. Look, Annie, I like your mother. We get along fine. We go over visit her once, twice a week, fine. What I like about her is that she doesn't hang all over you like my mother does.

Daughter. This is the only thing I ever asked you in our whole marriage . . .

Son-in-law. This is just begging for trouble. You know that in the bottom of your heart . . .

Daughter. I don't wanna argue any more about it.

Sister. Look, Annie, I think George is right. I think . . .

[*The daughter suddenly wheels on her sister, a long-repressed fury trembling out of her.*]

Daughter (*literally screaming*). You keep outta this! You hear me?! You never cared about Mom in your whole life! How many times you been over there this week? How many times?! I go over every day! Every day! And I go over in the evenings too sometimes!

[*The sister turns away, not a little shaken by this fierce onslaught. The daughter sits down on the bed again, her back to both her husband and sister, herself confused by the ferocity of her outburst. The son-in-law looks down, embarrassed, at the floor. A moment of sick silence fills the room. Then without turning, but in a much lower voice, the daughter goes on.*]

Daughter. George, I been a good wife to you. Did I ever ask you for mink coats or anything? Anything you want has always been good with me. This is the only thing I ever ask of you. I want my mother to live here with me where I can take care of her.

[*The son-in-law looks up briefly at his wife's unrelenting back and then back to the floor again.*]

Son-in-law. All right, Annie. I won't argue any more with you about it.

Sister. I guess I better go because I want to get back in the house before three o'clock when the kids come home from school.

[*Nobody says anything, so she starts for the door. The son-in-law, from his sitting position, looks up briefly at her as she passes, but she avoids his eyes. He stands, follows her out into the foyer. They proceed silently down the foyer to the doorway. Here they pause a minute. The scene is conducted in low, intense whispers.*]

Son-in-law. She don't mean nothing, Marie. You know that.

Sister. I know, I know . . .

Son-in-law. She's a wonderful person. She'd get up at three o'clock in the morning for you. There's nothing she wouldn't do for her family.

Sister. I know, George. I know Annie better than you know her. When she's sweet, she can be the sweetest person in the world. She's my kid sister but many's the time I came to her to do a little crying. But she's gonna kill my mother with all her sacrifices. She's trying to take away my mother's independence. My mother's been on her own all her life. That's the only way she knows how to live. I went over to see my mother yesterday. She was depressed. It broke my heart because I told Jack; I said: "I think my mother's beginning to give up." My mother used to be so sure of herself all the time, and yesterday she was talking there about how maybe she thinks she is getting a little old to work. It depressed me for the rest of the day . . .

Son-in-law. Marie, you know that I really like your mother. If I thought it would work out at all, I would have no objection to her coming to live here. But the walls in this place are made out of paper. You can hear everything that goes on in the next room, and . . .

Sister. It's a big mistake if she comes here. She'll just dry up into bones inside a year.

Son-in-law. Tell that to Annie. Would you do that for me, please?

Sister. You can't tell Annie nothing. Annie was born at a wrong time. The doctor told my mother she was gonna die if she had Annie, and my mother has been scared of Annie ever since. And if Annie thinks she's gonna get my mother to love her with all these sacrifices, she's crazy. My mother's favorite was always our big brother Frank, and Annie's been jealous of him as long as I know. I remember one time when we were in Saint John's school on Daly Avenue—I think Annie was about ten years old, and . . . oh, well, look, I better go. I'm not mad at Annie. She's been like this as long as I know her. *(She opens the door.)* She's doing the worst thing for my mother, absolutely the worst thing. I'll see you, George.

Son-in-law. I'll see you.

[*The sister goes out, closing the door after her. The son-in-law stands a moment. Then, frowning, he moves back up the foyer to the bedroom. His wife is still seated as we last saw her, her back to the door, her hands in her lap—slumped a little, but with an air of rigid stubbornness about her. The son-in-law regards her for a moment. Then he moves around the bed and sits down beside his wife. He puts his arm around her and pulls her to him. She rests her head on his chest. They sit silently for a moment.*

Dissolve to: Interior, the shop. The full complement[6] of working operators are there, all hunched over their machines, and the place is a picture of industry. The women chatter shrilly with each other as they work. A radio plays in the background. Occasionally, one of the operators lifts her head and bellows out: "Work! Work! Jessica! Gimme some work!" . . . The bookkeeper, Jessica, scurries back and forth from her desk to the sorting table—where she picks up small cartons of materials, bringing them to the operators—and back to her desk.

Dissolve to: The old lady and her immediate neighbor, the Negro woman, both bent over their machines, sewing away. The motors hum. The two women move their materials under the plunging needles. The old lady hunches, intense and painfully concentrated, over her work. They sew in silent industry for a moment. Then . . .]

Old lady (*without daring to look up from her work*). I'm getting the feel back, you know?

Negro woman (*likewise without looking up*). Sure, you're gonna be all right, Mama.

Old lady. I used to be considered a very fast operator. I used to work on the lower East Side in those sweatshops, y'know. Six dollars a week. But I quit in October 1916 because I got married and, in those days, y'know, it was a terrible disgrace for a married woman to work. So I quit. Not that we had the money. My husband was a house painter when we got married, which is seasonal work at best, and he had to borrow the

---

6. **complement:** the required or usual number.

money to go to Atlantic City for three days. That was our honeymoon. *(They lapse into silence. A woman's shrill voice from farther down the row of machines calls out: "Work! Hey, Jessica! Bring me some work!" The two women sew silently. Then . . .)* I got a feeling he's going to keep me on here. The boss, I mean. He seems like a nice enough man.

Negro woman. He's nervous, but he's all right.

Old lady. I've been looking for almost four weeks now, y'know. My husband died a little more than a month ago.

Negro woman. My husband died eighteen years ago.

Old lady. He was a very sick man all his life— lead poisoning, you know, from the paints. He had to quit the trade after a while, went into the retail grocery business. He was sixty-seven when he died, and I wonder he lived this long. In his last years, the circulation of the blood in his legs was so bad he could hardly walk to the corner.

Negro woman. My big trouble is arthritis. I get terrible pains in my arms and in my shoulder sometimes.

Old lady. Oh, I been getting a lot of pains in my back, in between my shoulder blades.

Negro woman. That's gall bladder.

Old lady. Is that what it is?

Negro woman. I had that. When you get to our age, Missus Fanning, you gotta expect the bones to rebel.

Old lady. Well, now, you're not such an old woman.

Negro woman. How old do you think I am?

Old lady. I don't know. Maybe forty, fifty.

Negro woman. I'm sixty-eight years old.

[*For the first time, the old lady looks up. She pauses in her work.*]

Old lady. I wouldn't believe you were sixty-eight.

Negro woman. I'm sixty-eight. I got more white hair than you have. But I dye it. You oughtta dye your hair too. Just go in the five-and-ten, pick up some kind of hair dye. Because most people don't like to hire old people with white hair. My children don't want me to work no more, but I'm gonna work until I die. How old do you think that old Greek woman over there is?

Old lady. How old?

Negro woman. She's sixty-nine. She got a son who's a big doctor. She won't quit working either. I like working here. I come in here in the morning, punch the clock. I'm friends with all these women. You see that little Jewish lady down there? That's the funniest little woman I ever met. You get her to tell you some of her jokes during lunch sometime. She gets me laughing sometimes I can hardly stop. What do I wanna sit around my dirty old room for when I got that little Jewish woman there to tell me jokes all day? That's what I tell my children.

[*The old lady turns back to her sewing.*]

Old lady. Oh, I'd like to hear a couple of jokes.

[*At this moment there is a small burst of high-pitched laughter from farther down the rows of machines. Camera cuts to long shot of the rows of operators, singling out a group of three Puerto Rican girls in their twenties. One of them has apparently just said something that made the other two laugh. A fourth Puerto Rican girl, across the table and up from them, calls to them in Spanish: "What happened? What was so funny?" The Puerto Rican girl who made the others laugh answers in a quick patter of high-pitched Spanish. A sudden gust of laughter sweeps all the Puerto Rican girls at the machines. Another woman calls out: "What she say?" One of the Puerto Rican girls answers in broken English.*]

Puerto Rican girl. She say, t'ree week ago, she make a mistake, sewed the belts onna dress backward. Nobody found out. Yesterday, she went in to buy her little girl a dress inna store. They tried to sell her one-a theese dresses . . . *(A wave of laughter rolls up and down the two rows of operators.)* She say, the label onna dress say: "Made in California."

[*They absolutely roar at this.*

Close-up: The old lady joining in the general laughter. She finishes the sleeve she has been working on. It is apparently the last of the bunch. She gathers together in front of her the two dozen other sleeves she has just finished and begins to

"My mother's been on her own all her life. That's the only way she knows how to live."

tie them up with a black ribbon. She lifts her head up and—with magnificent professionalism—calls out.]

Old lady. Work! Work! . . .

[Camera closes down on the bundle of sleeves she has tied together with the black ribbon.

Dissolve to: The same bundle of sleeves. We pull back and see it is now being held by the boss. He is frowning down at them. At his elbow is standing one of the Puerto Rican girls. She is muttering in broken English.]

Puerto Rican girl. So what I do? The whole bunch, same way . . .

Boss *(scowling).* All right, all right. Cut them open, resew the whole bunch . . .

Puerto Rican girl. Cut! I didn't do! I can't cut, sew, five o'clock the truckman . . . I gotta sew them on the blouse. Take two hours . . .

Boss. All right, all right, cut them open, sew them up again . . . *(The girl takes the bundle of sleeves and shuffles away. The boss turns, suddenly deeply weary. He goes to the desk. To the book-keeper)* The old lady come in today, she sewed all the sleeves for the left hand. She didn't make any rights. All lefts . . .

Bookkeeper. So what are you gonna do? It's half past four.

Boss. Call up Raymond for me.

[*The bookkeeper picks up the phone receiver, dials. The boss looks up and through the pipe racks at the old lady, sitting hunched and intense over her machine, working with concentrated meticulousness.[7] The boss's attention is called back to the phone by the bookkeeper. He takes the phone from her.*]

Boss (*in a low voice*). Jerry? This is Sam. Listen, I can't give you the whole twenty dozen at five o'clock. . . . All right, wait a minute, lemme . . . All right, wait a minute. I got fifteen dozen on the racks now . . . Jerry, please. I just got a new operator in today. She sewed five dozen sleeves all left-handed. We're gonna have to cut the seams open, and resew them . . . Look, Jerry, I'm sorry, what do you want from me? I can get it for you by six . . . Jerry, I'll pay the extra freight fee myself . . . Jerry . . . Listen, Jerry, how about those fifty dozen faille sport suits? This doesn't change your mind, does it? . . . Jerry, it's an accident. It could happen to anyone . . . (*A fury begins to take hold of the boss.*) Look, Jerry, you promised me the fifty dozen fai . . . Look, Jerry, you know what you can do with those fifty dozen failles? You think I'm gonna crawl on my knees to you?! (*He's shouting now. Every head in the shop begins to look up.*) You're a miserable human being, you hear that? I'd rather go bankrupt than ask you for another order! And don't come over my house no more! You hear?! I ain't gonna crawl to you! You hear me?! I ain't gonna crawl to you! . . . (*He slams the receiver down, stands, his chest heaving, his face flushed. He looks down at the bookkeeper, his fury still high.*) Fire her! Fire her! Fire her! (*He stands, the years of accumulated humiliation and resentment flooding out of him.*)

Fade out.

---

7. **meticulousness** (mə·tik′yoo·ləs·nəs): great attention to detail.

Act Three

Fade in: Interior of a subway car heading north to the Bronx during the rush hour—absolutely jam-packed. The camera manages to work its way through the dense crowd to settle on the old lady, seated in her black coat and hat, her hands folded in her lap, her old purse dangling from her wrist. She is staring bleakly straight ahead of herself, as if in another world. The train hurtles on.

Dissolve to: Interior of the old lady's apartment—dark—empty. Night has fallen outside. The sound of a key being inserted into the lock. The bolts unlatch, and the door is pushed open. The old lady enters. She closes the door after herself, bolts it. She stands a moment in the dark foyer, then shuffles up the foyer to the living room. She unbuttons her coat, sits down by the table, places her purse on the table. For a moment she sits. Then she rises, goes into the kitchen, turns on the light.

It takes her a moment to remember what she came into the kitchen for. Then, collecting herself, she opens the refrigerator door, extracts a carton of milk, sets it on the cupboard shelf. She opens the cupboard door, reaches in, extracts the box of Rice Krispies and a bowl. She sets the bowl down, begins to open the box of cereal. It falls out of her hands to the floor, a number of the pebbles of cereal rolling out to the floor. She starts to bend to pick the box up, then suddenly straightens and stands breathing heavily, nervously wetting her lips. She moves out of the kitchen quickly now, goes to the table, sits down again, picks up the phone, and dials. There is an edge of desperation in her movements. She waits. Then . . .

Old lady. Frank? Who's this, Lillian? Lillian, dear, this is your mother-in-law, and I . . . oh, I'm sorry, what? . . . Oh, I'm sorry . . . Who's this, the baby sitter? . . . This is Missus Fanning, dear—Mister Fanning's mother, is he in? . . . Is Missus Fanning in? . . . Well, do you expect them in? I mean, it's half past six. Did they eat their dinner already? . . . Oh, I see. Well, when do you . . . Oh, I see . . . No, dear, this is Mister Fanning's mother. Just tell him I called. It's not important. (*She hangs up, leaving her hand still on the phone. Then* *she lifts the receiver again and dials another number. She places a smile on her face and and waits. Then:)* Oh, Marie, dear, how are you . . . this is mother . . . Oh, I'm glad to hear your voice . . . Oh, I'm fine . . . fine. How's Jack and the kids? . . . Well, I hope it's nothing serious . . . Oh, that's good . . . *(She is mustering up all the good humor she has in her.)* Oh my, what a day I had. Oh, wait'll I tell you. Listen, I haven't taken you away from your dinner or anything . . . Oh, I went down to look for a job again . . . Yes, that's right, Annie was here this morning . . . how did you know? . . . Oh, is that right? Well, it cleared up, you know, and I didn't want to just sit around, so I went down to this job, and I got fired again. . . . The stupidest thing. I sewed all left sleeves . . . Well, you know you have to sew sleeves for the right as well as the left unless your customers are one-armed people . . . *(She is beginning to laugh nervously.)* Yes, it's comical, isn't it? . . . Yes, all left-handed . . . *(She bursts into a short, almost hysterical laugh. Her lip begins to twitch, and she catches her laughter in its middle and breathes deeply to regain control of herself.)* Well, how's Jack and the kids? . . . Well, that's fine. What are you doing with yourself tonight? . . . *(A deep weariness seems to have taken hold of her. She rests her head in the palm of her free hand. Her eyes are closed.)* Oh, do you have a baby sitter? . . . Well, have a nice time, give my regards to your mother-in-law . . . No, no, I'm fine . . . No, I was just asking . . . No, no, listen, dear, I'm absolutely fine. I just come in the house, and I'm going to make myself some Rice Krispies, and I've got some rolls somewhere, and I think I've got a piece of fish in the refrigerator, and I'm going to make myself dinner and take a hot tub, and then I think I'll watch some television. What's tonight, Thursday? . . . Well, Groucho Marx is on tonight . . . No, no, I just called to ask how everything was. How's Jack and the kids? . . . That's fine, have a nice time . . . Good-by, dear . . . *(She hangs up, sits erectly in the chair now. Her face wears an expression of the most profound weariness. She rises now and shuffles with no purpose into the center of the dark room, her coat flapping loosely around her. Then she goes to the television set, turns it on. In a moment a jumble of lines appears, and the sound comes up. The lines clear up into Faye and Skitch Henderson engaging each other in very clever chitchat. The old lady goes back to a television-viewing chair, sits down stiffly—her hands resting on the armrests—and expressionlessly watches the show. Camera comes in for a close-up of the old lady, staring wide-eyed right through the television set, not hearing a word of the chitchat. She is breathing with some difficulty. Suddenly she rises and almost lurches back to the table. She takes the phone, dials with obvious trembling, waits. . . .)* Annie? Annie, I wonder if I could spend the night at your house? I don't want to be alone . . . I'd appreciate that very much . . . All right, I'll wait here . . .

[*Dissolve to: Interior of the old lady's bedroom. The son-in-law, in his hat and jacket, is snapping the clasps of an old valise together. Having closed the valise, he picks it off the bed and goes into the living room. The old lady is there. She is seated in one of the straight-back chairs by the table, still in her coat and hat, and she is talking to the daughter—who can be seen through the kitchen doorway, reaching up into the pantry for some of her mother's personal groceries.*]

Old lady. Well, the truth is, I'm getting old, and there's no point saying it isn't true. *(To her son-in-law as he sets the valise down beside her)* Thank you, dear. I always have so much trouble with the clasp. . . . Did you hear the stupid thing I did today? I sewed all left-handed sleeves. That's the mark of a wandering mind, a sure sign of age. I'm sorry, George, to put you to all this inconvenience . . .

Son-in-law. Don't be silly, Ma. Always glad to have you.

Old lady. Annie, dear, what are you looking for?

Daughter *(in the kitchen)*. Your saccharin.

Old lady. It's on the lower shelf, dear. . . . This isn't going to be permanent, George. I'll just stay with you a little while till I get a room somewheres with some other old woman . . .

Daughter *(in the kitchen doorway)*. Ma, you're gonna stay with us, so, for heaven's sake, let's not have no more arguments.

Old lady. What'll we do with all my furniture? Annie, don't you want the china closet?

Daughter. No, Ma, we haven't got any room for it . . .

Old lady. It's such a good-looking piece. What we have to do is to get Jack and Marie and Frank and Lillian and all of us together, and we'll divide among the three of you whatever you want. I've got that fine set of silver—well, it's not the best, of course, silver plate, y'know—it's older than you are, Annie. *(To her son-in-law)* It was a gift of the girls in my shop when I got married. It's an inexpensive set, but I've shined it every year, and it sparkles. *(To her daughter in the kitchen)* Yes, that's what we'll have to do. We'll have to get all of us together one night and I'll apportion out whatever I've got. And whatever you don't want, well, we'll call a furniture dealer . . . *(to her son-in-law)* . . . although what would he pay me for these old things here? . . . *(To her daughter)* Annie, take the china closet . . . It's such a fine piece.

Daughter. Ma, where would we put it?

Old lady. Well, take that soft chair there. You always liked that chair . . .

Daughter. Ma . . .

Old lady. There's nothing wrong with it. It's not torn or anything. The upholstery's fine. Your father swore by that chair. He said it was the only chair he could sit in.

Daughter. Ma, let's not worry about it now. We'll get together sometime next week with Marie and Lillian . . .

Old lady. I want you to have the chair . . .

Daughter. Ma, we got all modern furniture in our house . . .

Old lady. It's not an old chair. We just bought it about six years ago. No, seven . . .

Daughter. Ma, what do we need the . . .

Old lady. Annie, I don't want to sell it to a dealer! It's my home. I don't want it to go piece by piece into a second-hand shop.

Daughter. Ma . . .

Son-in-law. Annie! We'll take the chair!

Daughter. All right, Ma, the chair is ours.

Old lady. I know that Lillian likes those lace linens I've got in the cedar chest. And the carpets. Now these are good carpets, Annie. There's no sense just throwing them out. They're good broadloom.

The first good money your father was making we bought them. When we almost bought that house in Passaic, New Jersey. You ought to remember that, Annie. You were about seven then. But we bought the grocery store instead. Oh, how we scraped in that store. In the heart of the depression. We used to sell bread for six cents a loaf. I remember my husband said: "Let's buy a grocery store. At least we'll always have food in the house." It seems to me my whole life has been hand-to-mouth. Did we ever not worry about the rent? I remember as a girl in Cork,[1] eating boiled potatoes every day. I don't know what it all means, I really don't . . . *(She stares rather abstractedly at her son-in-law.)* I'm sixty-six years old, and I don't know what the purpose of it all was.

Son-in-law. Missus Fanning . . .

Old lady. An endless, endless struggle. And for what? For what? *(She is beginning to cry now.)* Is this what it all comes to? An old woman parceling out the old furniture in her house . . . ? *(She bows her head and stands, thirty years of repressed tears torturously working their way through her body in racking shudders.)*

Daughter. Ma . . .

[*The old lady stands, her shoulders slumped, her head bowed, crying with a violent agony.*]

Old lady *(the words stumbling out between her sobs).* Oh, I don't care . . . I don't care . . .

[*Hold on the old lady, standing, crying.*

Dissolve to: Film. Rain whipping through the streets of New York at night—same film we opened the show with—a frightening thunderstorm.

Dissolve to: The old lady's valise, now open, lying on a narrow single bed. We pull back to see the old lady—in a dress, but with her coat off—rummaging in the valise for something. The room she is in is obviously a little boy's room. There are a child's paintings and drawings and cutouts Scotch-taped to the wall, and toys and things on the floor. It is dark outside, and the rain whacks against the window panes. The old lady finally

---

1. **Cork:** a county and city in Ireland.

extracts from out of the valise a long woolen nightgown and, holding it in both arms, she shuffles to the one chair in the room and sits down. She sets the nightgown in her lap and bends to remove her shoes. This is something of an effort and costs her a few moments of quick breathing. She sits, expressionless, catching her breath, the white nightgown on her lap, her hands folded on it. Even after she regains her breath, she sits this way, now staring fixedly at the floor at her feet. Hold.

Dissolve to: The window of the child's bedroom. It is daylight now, and the rain has stopped. The cold morning sun shines thinly through the white chintz[2] curtains. The camera pulls slowly back and finally comes to rest on the old lady sitting just as we saw her last, unmoving, wrapped in thought, the white nightgown on her lap, her hands folded. From some room off, the thin voice of a baby

---

2. **chintz** (chints): a kind of printed cotton cloth.

suddenly rises and abruptly falls. The old lady looks up.

Then she bends and puts her shoes on. She rises, sets the nightgown on the chair from which she has just risen, moves with a slight edge of purpose down the room to the closet, opens the door, reaches in, and takes out her coat. She puts it on, stands a moment, looking about the room for something. She finds her hat and purse sitting on the chest of drawers. She picks them up. Then she turns to the door of the room and carefully opens it. She looks out onto the hallway. Across from her, the door to her daughter and son-in-law's bedroom stands slightly ajar. She crosses to the door, looks in. Her daughter and son-in-law make two large bundles under their blankets. For a moment she stands and surveys them. Then the daughter turns in her bed so that she faces her mother. Her eyes are open; she has not been asleep. At the sight of her mother in the doorway, she leans upon one elbow.]

Old lady (*in an intense whisper*). Annie, it just

She sits, expressionless, catching her breath, the white nightgown on her lap, her hands folded on it.

wasn't comfortable, you know? I just can't sleep anywheres but in my own bed, and that's the truth. I'm sorry, Annie, honest. You're a fine daughter, and it warms me to know that I'm welcome here. But what'll I do with myself, Annie, what'll I do? . . .

[*The daughter regards her mother for a moment.*]

Daughter. Where are you going, Ma, with your coat on?

Old lady. I'm going out and look for a job. And, Annie, please don't tell me that everything's against me. I know it. Well, I'll see you, dear. I didn't mean to wake you up. . . .

[*She turns and disappears from the doorway. The daughter starts quickly from the bed.*]

Daughter. Ma . . . (*She moves quickly across the room to the door of the hallway. She is in her pajamas. She looks down the hallway, which is fairly dark. Her mother is already at the front door, at the other end.*) Ma . . .

Old lady. I'm leaving the valise with all my things. I'll pick them up tonight. And please don't start an argument with me, Annie, because I won't listen to you. I'm a woman of respect. I can take care of myself. I always have. And don't tell me it's raining because it stopped about an hour ago. And don't say you'll drive me home because I can

get the bus two blocks away. Work is the meaning of my life. It's all I know what to do. I can't change my ways at this late time.

[*For a long moment the mother and daughter regard each other. Then the daughter pads quietly down to the old lady.*]

Daughter (*quietly*). When I'm your age, Ma, I hope I'm like you. (*For a moment the two women stand in the dark hallway. Then they quickly embrace and release each other. The old lady unbolts the door and disappears outside, closing the door after her. The daughter bolts it shut with a click. She turns and goes back up the dark foyer to her own bedroom. She goes in, shuffles to the bed, gets back under the covers. For a moment she just lies there. Then she nudges her sleeping husband, who grunts.*) George, let's drop the kids at your sister's for a week or ten days and drive down to Virginia. You don't want to spend your one vacation a year sitting in New York, watching it rain.

[*The son-in-law, who hasn't heard a word, grunts once or twice more. The daughter pulls the blankets up over her shoulders, turns on her side, and closes her eyes.*]

Fade out.

The End

Responding to the Play

Analyzing the Play

Identifying Facts

Act One

1. In his first long speech in the opening scene, the son-in-law provides the **exposition**. What is the main **problem** for these characters? What does Annie want to do about the problem?

2. As Annie and her mother have breakfast in the second scene, there is a minor **conflict** about who will serve whom. What, however, is the major conflict here?

3. What does the mother tell Annie she wants? Why doesn't she want to live with Annie and George?

4. In the next scene, the mother has taken Annie's advice and gone to the park. Describe Mrs. Geegan's and Mrs. Kline's relationships with their daughters-in-law. What **action** does the mother take after she leaves her two complaining friends "staring bleakly ahead"?

Act Two

5. In the breakfast scene with Annie, we heard

the mother describe her attempts to get and hold a job. How does the first scene of Act Two, in the shop, dramatize the mother's **problems**? What is the outcome of this scene?

6. According to Marie, why is Annie insisting that her mother come and live with her?

7. What **complication** ends Act Two?

Act Three

8. What **change** has come over the mother by the time we see her at Annie's in Act Three? What "want" of the mother's still hasn't changed?

9. We might expect before the final scene that the play's **climax** is over, that the mother has gone along with Annie's wishes, but what is the actual climax? What belief about herself will not allow the mother to stay with Annie?

10. What is the play's final **resolution**?

Interpreting Meanings

11. Do you think this play has a happy ending? Do you find the ending believable or satisfying? Tell specifically why you feel as you do.

12. We have said that in a good play, the characters are real, complex people, and everyone to some extent is "right." Do you believe this applies to the boss; to the mother; to Annie; to George; and to Marie? Explain. Did the playwright succeed in making you care about these characters? Why?

13. Which characters have **changed** by the end of the play? How have they changed?

14. Name at least two options, or choices, that would be available to a person like the mother today. If this play were taking place in a community you are familiar with, would some of the situations have to change? Explain.

Writing About the Play

A Creative Response

1. **Writing Dialogue.** Chayefsky's dialogue sounds like real speech, but it isn't. Real speech is usually more wandering and shapeless. What the writer of a realistic play aims for is **verisimilitude**—that is, something that seems like real speech but which accomplishes a dramatic purpose. Make notes of the real speech you hear around you—on the bus, in a store, at school, at your dinner table. If you have access to a tape recorder, record an actual conversation. Then

write down the conversation, in dialogue form; transcribe it exactly, with all the pauses, incompleted thoughts, repetitions, and sounds such as "ah" and "um." Comparing what you have with Chayefsky's dialogue will give you a good idea of how focused a dramatic conversation must be. Now rewrite your "real conversation" so that it becomes a dramatic dialogue. Have your speakers express their thoughts on one subject in ways that reveal something about their personalities and about their different "wants."

2. **Extending the Play.** Write a scene for *The Mother* that takes place after the final curtain. Will your final scene be happy? Will another surprising **reversal** occur for these characters? What will be your point of **conflict**?

A Critical Response

3. **Analyzing a Scene.** Choose any scene in this play, and in a paragraph explain how it is, in fact, a small play, with its own **problem, conflict,** and **resolution.**

4. **Supporting a Topic Statement.** Below are two topic statements about *The Mother*. Choose one of these statements, and develop its basic idea in a paragraph or more. If you wish, write instead about why you disagree with the statement. Support what you say with details from the play.

   a. Paddy Chayefsky's *The Mother* dramatizes the idea that many old people wish to lead independent lives.

   b. Paddy Chayefsky's *The Mother* is a good example of a play that presents people we care about who are involved in a conflict in which each one has something at stake.

Analyzing Language and Vocabulary

Television Terms

Television works by means of electronic images, as well as by words. Many of the stage directions in *The Mother* are special television terms that provide shooting directions for the camera, which must provide all the images for the screen.

1. What is meant by **fade in** and **fade out**?

2. When the camera **holds** on some image, what is it doing?

3. When the directions say **cut to,** what is going to happen to the image presently on the screen?

4. When an image **dissolves**, does it fade out grad-

ually or does it suddenly switch to another image?

5. Describe an example of a **montage** from a TV show you are familiar with.

Suppose you were adapting one of the other plays in this unit for television. Rewrite the stage directions for an outdoor scene from *The Miracle Worker* and for any scene from *Visitor from Forest Hills* (all of its scenes take place in the same room). Tell what images would come into view on the screen, and how the camera should shoot them. Use the terms **fade in, fade out, dissolve to, cut to,** and **hold.** Other TV camera directions you might need to use are:

voice-over	moving shot
tight on	stock shot
different angle	slow-motion
wider angle	long shot

Reading About the Writer

Paddy Chayefsky (1923–1981) was born in New York City, a place which provides the setting for many of his plays. In his first stage play, *In the Middle of the Night,* Chayefsky in a sense stayed with his "little man." But in his later plays—*The Tenth Man, Gideon, The Passion of Josef D.*—he became more imaginative and enlarged his frame of reference. After some bad reviews of his later plays, Chayefsky became discouraged and disillusioned with the theater. He went on, for the next sixteen years, to write for the motion pictures, and he won three Academy Awards. *The Hospital* and *Network* were particularly notable for their biting satire; the target of *Network* was a television station which had become obsessed with ratings and indifferent to human beings. Chayefsky was planning to return to the theater and was working on a new play when he died suddenly at the age of 58.

Focusing on Background
A Friend Remembers Paddy Chayefsky

"I would call him periodically during the nontheatrical years, urging him to write again for the stage. 'It takes me two or three years to write a play,' he would say. 'All that time and effort deserve more than a two-week run.'

'But three of your four plays were successful. You're way ahead on percentages,' I once said. 'I'm a writer, not a statistician,' he replied.

"The touching part of this immovable self-imposed exile was that Paddy to the day of his death never stopped being a man of the theater he idolized and dreaded. When we first met in 1954, a gentler year, on the crest of the wave of television triumph, he complained about the ephemeral nature of television—'one one-night stand after another,' he described the medium—and spoke lovingly of how he would like to have a full-length play produced in the theater, 'where live people watch live actors bringing words to life.'

"And in the little office on Seventh Avenue where he wrote to a typical Manhattan discipline, punctuated by telephone calls, pastrami sandwiches, and continual visits from his friends, he would fill dozens of dime-store notebooks with disquisitions[1] in longhand on the scenes and characters he was creating. He rarely wrote dialogue in these preliminary discussions with himself. . . . He would endlessly write himself questions about his individuals and images. 'What am I trying to say in this scene?' he would ask himself. 'Should I try a different setting? If so, where? What's the girl's relationship with her father?' And he would answer his own questions, still in longhand, in page after self-probing page. Months later, he would start the play—on the typewriter. . . .

" 'To be a good playwright,' he said, 'is first of all to be a good carpenter. Get your structure right to begin with.' He told me once that in his youth he decided to learn play structure by copying, word by word, in longhand, the entire script of Lillian Hellman's *The Children's Hour,* which he considered one of the most carefully structured plays ever written."

—Arthur Cantor

---

1. **disquisitions:** discussions.

Using the Expository Aim in Drama

Literary Model

Here is the opening scene of the comedy *Life With Father*, written by Howard Lindsay and Russel Crouse. The play debuted on Broadway on November 8, 1939, and ran for a record-breaking 3,224 performances.

As the curtain rises, ANNIE, *the maid, a young Irish girl, is finishing setting the table for breakfast. After an uncertain look at the result she crosses over to her tray on the console table.* VINNIE *comes down the stairs and into the room.* VINNIE *is a charming, lovable, and spirited woman of forty. She has a lively mind which darts quickly away from any practical matter. She has red hair.*

Annie. Good morning, ma'am.

Vinnie. Good morning, Annie. How are you getting along?

Annie. All right, ma'am, I hope.

Vinnie. Now, don't be worried just because this is your first day. Everything's going to be all right—but I do hope nothing goes wrong. (*Goes to the table*) Now, let's see, is the table all set? (ANNIE *follows her.*) The cream and the sugar go down at this end.

Annie (*placing them where* VINNIE *has indicated*). I thought in the center, ma'am; everyone could reach them easier.

Vinnie. Mr. Day sits here.

Annie (*gets a tray of napkins, neatly rolled and in their rings, from the console table*). I didn't know where to place the napkins, ma'am.

Vinnie. You can tell which go where by the rings. (*Takes them from the tray and puts them down as she goes around the table.* ANNIE *follows her.*) This one belongs to Whitney—it has his initial on it, "W"; that one with the little dog on it is Harlan's, of course. He's the baby. This "J" is for John and the "C" is for Clarence. This narrow plain one is mine. And this is Mr. Day's. It's just like mine—except that it got bent one morning. And that reminds me—always be sure

Mr. Day's coffee is piping hot.

Annie. Ah, your man has coffee instead of tea of a morning?

Vinnie. We all have coffee except the two youngest boys. They have their milk. And, Annie, always speak of my husband as Mr. Day.

Annie. I will that.

Vinnie (*correcting her*). "Yes, ma'am," Annie.

Annie. Yes, ma'am.

Vinnie. And if Mr. Day speaks to you, just say: "Yes, sir." Don't be nervous—you'll get used to him.

[CLARENCE, *the eldest son, about seventeen, comes down the stairs and into the room. He is a manly, serious, good-looking boy. Because he is starting in at Yale next year, he thinks he is grown-up. He is redheaded.*]

Clarence. Good morning, Mother. (*He kisses her.*)

Vinnie. Good morning, Clarence.

Clarence. Did you sleep well, Mother?

Vinnie. Yes, thank you, dear. (CLARENCE *goes to* FATHER'S *chair and picks up the morning paper. To* ANNIE.) We always start with fruit, except the two young boys, who have porridge.

[ANNIE *brings the fruit and porridge to the table.* CLARENCE, *looking at the paper, makes a whistling sound.*]

Clarence. Jiminy! Another wreck on the New Haven. That always disturbs the market. Father won't like that.

Vinnie. I do wish that New Haven would stop having wrecks. If they know how it upset your father—(*Sees that* CLARENCE'S *coat has been torn and mended*) My soul and body, Clarence, what's happened to your coat?

Clarence. I tore it. Margaret mended it for me.

Vinnie. It looks terrible. Why don't you wear your blue suit?

Clarence. That looks worse than this one. You know, I burnt that hole in it.

Vinnie. Oh, yes—well, you can't go around

looking like that. I'll have to speak to your father. Oh, dear!

[JOHN, *who is about fifteen, comes down the stairs and into the room.* JOHN *is gangly and a little overgrown. He is redheaded.*]

John. Good morning, Mother. (*He kisses her.*)

Vinnie. Good morning, John.

John (*to* CLARENCE). Who won?

Clarence. I haven't looked yet.

John. Let me see. (*He tries to take the paper away from* CLARENCE.)

Clarence. Be careful!

Vinnie. Boys, don't wrinkle that paper before your father's looked at it.

Clarence (*to* JOHN). Yes!

[VINNIE *turns to* ANNIE.]

Vinnie. You'd better get things started. We want everything ready when Mr. Day comes down. (ANNIE *exits.*) Clarence, right after breakfast I want you and John to move the small bureau from my room into yours.

Clarence. What for? Is somebody coming to visit us?

John. Who's coming?

Vinnie. I haven't said anyone was coming. And don't you say anything about it. I want it to be a surprise.

Clarence. Oh! Father doesn't know yet?

Vinnie. No. And I'd better speak to him about a new suit for you before he finds out he's being surprised by visitors.

—from *Life With Father*,
Howard Lindsay
and Russel Crouse

A Note on the Expository Aim in Drama

The aim or purpose of the opening scene in a drama is usually **expository**. This means that the scene is intended to explain or set forth what the audience needs to know. A good opening scene answers the questions *who, what, where,* and *when.* It does not tell the audience everything; it tells them just enough to get them interested. The opening scene in a play is like an introduction to a stranger at a party: "This is Jane Doe. She's a painter."

Opening scenes are challenging to write because they must inform and, at the same time, tell enough of a story to catch and hold the audience's interest. The more dramatic scenes of a play, those showing conflict and action, are much easier to write.

Over the centuries, dramatists have tried many different devices to convey the necessary information in their opening scenes. At times they have used very obvious means of exposition. For example, a play would open with two servants cleaning a room and gossiping about the main characters, who are soon to appear. This gossip would "set the stage" by providing important information to the audience.

Other playwrights might use the telephone in exposition. A servant or a member of the family would answer the phone and say something like this: "No, Mr. Keller is not in. He's down at his office at the newspaper. Mrs. Keller is up with the baby, who hasn't been well these days."

However, the best way to present exposition is to provide for some interesting activity on stage, which will convey information without the audience knowing it is being informed.

Years ago, a play started with four men playing poker. They were playing the last hand. One man lost and said, "I don't have any money on me. Is it all right if I give you one of my wife's checks?" Another man remarked, "What other kind of check would you have?" The first man reached over and hit him.

Within two minutes, through action and through what was said, the audience learned that the first man was living on his wife's money, that the other men looked down on him, and that he was very touchy about the situation.

Literature & Language/*cont.*

Examining the Writer's Techniques

Answer these questions to examine how Lindsay and Crouse achieved their expository aim:

1. What information in the opening scene of *Life With Father* answers the questions *who, what, where, when*? Fill in the details in a chart like the one below.

WHO:	
WHAT:	
WHERE:	
WHEN:	

2. In this scene, three members of the Day family are introduced. What physical characteristic do they have in common?

3. The major purpose of this opening scene is to prepare us for the entrance of Father. What do Vinnie's remarks to Annie lead us to expect about Father?

4. How is the sorting of the napkin rings used to give information about the family members? How do you suppose Father's napkin ring got bent?

5. What other words or activities hint at or create interest in Father's personality?

6. At the end of the opening scene, Vinnie introduces two situations that will cause **conflict** later in the play. What are they?

Using the Expository Aim in Your Writing

Writing a Scene of Exposition. Write an opening scene for a stage play in which you introduce at least two characters and suggest a conflict to come.

a. Write about one of the following situations or think of a situation of your own:
Two brothers (or sisters) meet after twenty years
A family gets lost while on vacation
A new baby comes home
A body is found in a wheat field
A stranger comes into town

b. Use words or actions to tell your audience *who, what, where,* and *when*. Before you write, you may want to outline these details on a chart like the one opposite.

c. Work with a small group to refine your scene. Have group members read the speeches of the various characters. Then have others, acting as the audience, make suggestions on how to clarify the characters and their situation.

d. Finally, have your group present the scene to the whole class. Ask the audience if the opening scene makes them want to see the rest of the play.

SUPPORTING AN OPINION

Writing Assignment

Suppose Annie Sullivan in the play *The Miracle Worker* (page 494) had never come to the Kellers' house. Could Helen Keller's family have helped her lead a full life without Annie's teaching? Write a five-paragraph essay in which you state your opinion on this question. Support your opinion with details from *The Miracle Worker.*

Background

Many works of literature raise the question "What if . . .?" What if Romeo and Juliet had simply told their parents they were married secretly? What if Anne Frank and her family had fled to England, instead of hiding in the Secret Annexe: what would Anne have become in life? The essay assignment above poses a "what if" question on *The Miracle Worker.*

When you write an essay expressing your opinion about what would have happened "if" in a story or play, you should be sure of two things:

1. Are your own thoughts clear on what your opinion is?
2. Can you point to incidents and details from the story or play to support your prediction or interpretation?

Prewriting

1. First, be sure you understand the terms in the assignment. For example, what is a "full life" in your opinion? Does it include the need to communicate through language with other human beings? Include your definition of "full life" in your essay.
2. Next, decide how you will answer the question posed in the assignment. Your initial response probably will be a quick "yes" or "no." If you think further, however, you might decide that your answer is partly "yes" and partly "no." You must decide which answer is more strongly supported by details from the play. To gather details about Helen's family and how much they might have helped or harmed her, you might fill out a chart like this one (one detail is filled in as a starter):

	Positive influence(s)	Negative influence(s)
Kate Keller	Loves Helen.	Often too lenient.
Captain Keller		
James Keller		
Aunt Ev		
Annie Sullivan		

3. Now think about the information and ideas you have gathered. What is your opinion on the question in the essay assignment? State your opinion in at least one sentence; this will be your thesis statement.
4. Next, search through the play for details to support your point of view. Look for supporting details in the dialogue, in the characters' actions, and in the author's stage directions.
5. Using your notes and your chart, think of three major reasons which support your opinion. These reasons will make up the body of your essay. Examples of such reasons might be:

Helen's life could have been full and happy without Annie's teaching.
a. She was bright.
b. She had a good home, where she was loved and not neglected.
c. She had determination and a desire to communicate.

Helen's life would have been very limited, or even destroyed, without Annie's teaching.
a. It required particular skills to teach Helen a systematic method of communication.

b. Even though Helen's parents loved her, they also spoiled her.

c. Helen's desire to communicate was often evident only in violent, unsocial behavior; if Annie had not come, Helen might have ended up in an insane asylum. (Refer to the act and scene where this possibility is made clear.)

Writing

To write your essay, follow this format:

1. **Paragraph 1:** Introduce the essay and present your opinion in a thesis statement.

2. **Paragraph 2:** State the first reason explaining your opinion and cite examples from the play to support it.

3. **Paragraph 3:** State your second reason and cite supporting examples from the play.

4. **Paragraph 4:** State your third reason and cite supporting examples from the play.

5. **Paragraph 5:** Clinch your essay by restating your main points or by adding a general comment about your opinion.

Here is an example of an introductory paragraph for an essay that supports the view that Helen could not have led a full life without Annie:

> In William Gibson's play *The Miracle Worker*, we see how a gifted teacher can work miracles. In this case, the child is special: she cannot see or hear. She is locked in a world without sound or light. Except for violent behavior, all methods of communication are closed to her. It is my opinion that, without the help of her teacher, Annie Sullivan, Helen Keller would have been locked in her silent, dark world forever, and would probably have ended up in a madhouse.

Cites playwright and title.

Presents an opinion in a thesis statement.

Checklist for Revision

1. Have you included a thesis statement?
2. Have you defined what you think a "full life" is?
3. Have you included three paragraphs in the body of the essay, each stating a reason for your opinion?
4. Have you supported each reason with details from the play?
5. Do you have a concluding paragraph that clinches your main points?

WILLIAM SHAKESPEARE

"Chandos" Portrait. Oil.　　　National Portrait Gallery, London. Photo: The Granger Collection, New York.

UNIT FIVE　　　**Robert Anderson**

WILLIAM SHAKESPEARE

An introduction by **Robert Anderson**

> *He was not of an age, but for all time.*
>
> —Ben Jonson

William Shakespeare's Life

Little is known about the life of William Shakespeare. What is known is mostly derived from church and legal documents—a baptismal registration, a marriage license, and records of real-estate transactions. We also have a few remarks that others wrote about him during his lifetime.

We know that William was born the third of eight children, around April 23, 1564, in Stratford, a market town about one hundred miles northwest of London. His father, John, was a shopkeeper and a man of considerable standing in Stratford, serving at various times as justice of the peace and high bailiff (mayor).

William attended grammar school, where he studied Latin grammar, Latin literature, and rhetoric (the uses of language). As far as we know, he had no further formal education.

At the age of eighteen, he married Anne Hathaway, who was eight years older than he was. Some time after the birth of their second and third children (twins). Shakespeare moved to London, apparently leaving his family to remain in Stratford.

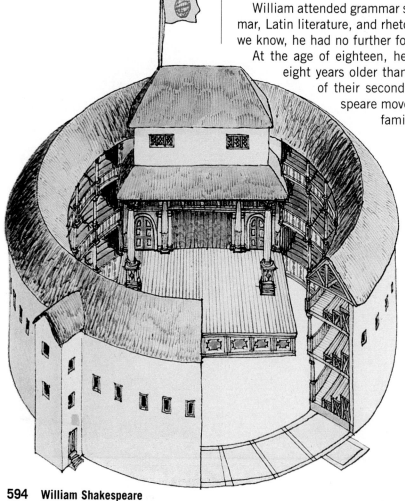

(Left) "The Wooden O," the Globe Theater.

Drawing by David Gentleman.

(Opposite left) Glenn Close as Gertrude, Queen of Denmark, in *Hamlet,* a film directed by Franco Zeffirelli. (Opposite right) A poster showing Denzel Washington as Shakespeare's *Richard III.*

Poster © 1990 by Paul Davis. Courtesy of the artist.

We know that several years later, by 1592, Shakespeare had already become an actor and a playwright. By 1594, he was a charter member of the theatrical company called the Lord Chamberlain's Men, which was later to become the King's Men. (As the names of these acting companies indicate, theatrical groups depended on the support of a wealthy patron—the King's Men were supported by King James himself.) Shakespeare worked with this company for the rest of his writing life. Year after year, he provided it with plays, almost on demand. Shakespeare was the ultimate professional writer. He had a theater that needed plays, actors who needed parts, and a family that needed to be fed.

Romeo and Juliet was probably among the early plays that Shakespeare wrote between 1594 and 1596. By 1612, when he had returned to Stratford to live the life of a prosperous retired gentleman, Shakespeare had written thirty-seven plays, including such masterpieces as *Julius Caesar, Hamlet, Othello, King Lear,* and *Macbeth.*

Shakespeare's plays are still produced all over the world. During a recent Broadway season, one critic estimated that if Shakespeare were alive today, he would be receiving $25,000 a week in royalties for a production of *Othello* alone. The play was attracting larger audiences than any other nonmusical production in town.

Shakespeare died on April 23, 1616, at the age of fifty-two. He is buried under the old stone floor in the chancel of the church in Stratford. Carved over his grave is the following verse:

> Good friend, for Jesus' sake forbear
> To dig the dust enclosed here.
> Blessed be the man that spares these stones
> And cursed be he that moves my bones.

> " **D**uring a recent Broadway season, one critic estimated that if Shakespeare were alive today, he would be receiving $25,000 a week in royalties for a production of *Othello* alone. The play was attracting larger audiences than any other nonmusical production in town."

JOSEPH PAPP PRESENTS

RICHARD III

AUGUST 3–SEPTEMBER 2, 1990
DELACORTE THEATER CENTRAL PARK

©1990 Paul Davis

These are hardly the best of Shakespeare's lines (if indeed they are his at all), but like his other lines, they seem to have worked. His bones lie undisturbed to this day.

Shakespeare's Theater and the Modern Stage

Sometimes playwrights influence the shape and form of a theater, but more often, existing theaters seem to influence the shape and form of plays. It is important that we understand Shakespeare's theater because it influenced the way he wrote his plays.

The "Wooden O"

In 1576, outside the city walls of London, an actor-manager named James Burbage built the first permanent theater in England. He called it The Theater. Up to that time, touring acting companies had played wherever they could rent space. Usually this would be in the courtyards of inns. There the actors would erect a temporary platform stage at one end of the yard and play to an audience which stood around the stage or sat in the tiers of balconies that surrounded the courtyard. (Normally, these balconies were used as passageways to the various rooms of the inn.)

It was natural, then, that the first theater built by Burbage should derive its shape and form from the inns.

In 1599, Burbage's theater was taken down and its timbers were used by Shakespeare and his company to build the Globe Theater. This was the theater for which Shakespeare wrote most of his plays.

In his play *Henry V,* Shakespeare called his theater a "wooden O." It was a large, round (or polygonal) building, three stories high, with a large platform stage that projected from one end into a yard open to the sky. In the back wall of this stage was a curtained-off inner stage. Flanking the inner stage were two doors for entrances and exits. Above this inner stage was a small balcony or upper stage, which could be used to suggest Juliet's balcony or the high walls of a castle or the bridge of a ship. Trap doors were placed in the floor of the main stage for the entrances and exits of ghosts and for descents into hell.

The plays were performed in the afternoon. Since the stage was open to the sky, there was no need for stage illumination. There were very few **sets** (scenery, furniture, etc.). The stage was "set" by the language. A whole forest scene is created in one play when a character announces: "Well, this is the Forest of Arden." But costumes were often elaborate, and the stage might be hung with colorful banners and trappings. (The groundlings, those eight hundred or so people who stood around the stage for the price of a penny, loved a good show. Most people still do.)

We can see that this stage, with its few sets and many acting areas—forestage, inner stage, and upper stage—made for a theater

An afternoon audience flocking to the Globe Theater. Drawn around 1600.

of great fluidity. That is, scene could follow scene with almost cinematic ease.

In one interesting aspect, the theater in Shakespeare's day was very different from the theater we know today. Acting wasn't considered entirely respectable by the English Puritans, so all women's parts were played by boys. Not for many years did women appear on stage in the professional English theater. In Shakespeare's day, Juliet would have been played by a trained boy actor.

The Modern Stage

It has been said that all you need for a theater is "two planks and a passion." Since Shakespeare's time, "the planks" (the stage) have undergone various changes. First, the part of the stage which projected into the yard grew narrower, and the small curtained inner stage grew larger, until there developed what is called the **proscenium stage**. Here, there is no outer stage; there is only the inner stage, and a large curtain separates it from the audience. The effect is like looking inside a window or inside a picture frame. This is the stage most of us know today. It has been standard for well over a hundred years.

But recently, we have seen a reversal of this design. Now, more and more theaters (especially university and regional theaters) are building "thrust" stages, or arena stages. In this kind of theater, the audience once again sits on three or even four sides of the stage.

Like Shakespeare's stage, this kind of "thrust" stage, with its minimal scenery, allows playwrights (if they want) to move their stories rapidly from place to place. They can establish each new scene with a line like "Well, this is the Forest of Arden." Consequently, there has been a temptation to write plays that imitate the style of movies. But this imitation rarely works. Theater and movies are two different media. A theater audience does not necessarily want to be whisked from place to place. People who go to plays often prefer to spend a long, long time watching the subtle development of conflicts among a small group of people, all in one setting. For example, all of the action in Lorraine Hansberry's play *A Raisin in the Sun* takes place inside one small apartment on Chicago's South Side.

Movies are basically a *visual* medium and so must chiefly engage and delight the eye, rather than the ear. (One movie director once referred to a dialogue in a movie as "foreground noise"!) The theater is much more a medium of *words*. When we go to see a play, it is the movement of the *words* rather than the movement of the scenery that delights us.

This difference between the appeal of a movie and the appeal of a play may account for the failure of some successful plays when they are translated to the screen. The movie producer will say: "Open up the story." In "opening up the story," the producer sometimes loses the concentration, the intensity, which was the prime virtue of the play.

A cutaway of the Globe, showing the three stage levels and the dressing and prop rooms.

Drawing by David Gentleman.

"**A**cting wasn't considered entirely respectable by the English Puritans, so all women's parts were played by boys. Juliet would have been played by a trained boy actor.**"**

Shakespeare took the theater of his time, the "wooden O," and used it brilliantly. More recently, American playwrights balked at a theater which was presented to them.

When the great stage designer Jo Mielziner was planning the Vivian Beaumont Theater in the Lincoln Center Complex in New York City, he invited a number of playwrights to come to his studio and view the model for the stage. What we saw was an immense, wide open space. It seemed impossible that such a stage could ever accommodate so many of the American "classics"—*The Glass Menagerie, Long Day's Journey into Night, Life with Father*—which call for confined, intimate, interior settings. But Mielziner said, "We're going to stretch you all."

Unfortunately, we did not stretch. That theater and that stage did not inspire us as Shakespeare's stage had inspired him. After struggling through several seasons, the Beaumont Theater was closed to be redesigned.

Romeo and Juliet

Most of Shakespeare's plays are based on stories that were already well known to his audiences. (He never wrote a play about a contemporary subject.) *Romeo and Juliet* is taken from a long narrative poem by Arthur Brooke, which was published in 1562 as *The Tragicall Historye of Romeus and Juliet.* Brooke's popular poem itself was based on even older Italian stories.

Romeo and Juliet, a very young man and a nearly fourteen-year-old girl, fall in love at first sight. They are caught up in an idealized, almost unreal, passionate love. They are in love with love. In his Prologue, Brooke preaches a moral, which people of his time expected. He says that Romeo and Juliet had to die because they broke laws and married unwisely, against their parents' wishes. But Shakespeare does away with this moralizing. He presents the couple as "star-crossed lovers," doomed to disaster by Fate.

To understand what "star-crossed" means, you have to realize that most people of Shakespeare's time believed in astrology. They believed that the course of their lives was partly determined by the hour, day, month, and year of their birth—hence, "the star" under which they were born. But Shakespeare may not have shared this belief. In a later play, *Julius Caesar,* Shakespeare has a character question this old idea about astrology and the influence of the stars:

> The fault, dear Brutus, is not in our stars,
> But in ourselves that we are underlings.

Although Shakespeare says in the Prologue that Romeo and Juliet are "star-crossed," he does not make them mere victims of Fate. Romeo and Juliet make decisions that lead to their disaster. More important, other characters have a hand in their disaster—they too make decisions that lead to the play's tragic ending.

The Characters

The roster of colorful characters in Shakespeare's plays is extraordinary. In *Romeo and Juliet* we have two of the most notable, Mercutio and the Nurse. Some critics have even suggested that Shakespeare had to kill off Mercutio because he was so attractive he might take over the story. Mercutio is a favorite part with actors, as is the Nurse. She is vividly painted in very few colors, but she is unforgettable.

The lesser characters are not so remarkable, but each is an individual as well as the representative of a type. We can say of many of them, "Oh, yes. I know somebody like that." Tybalt is like all raging bullies. Lord Capulet is like many fussy, loving, but domineering fathers. Benvolio is a typical best friend.

Of the two main characters, Romeo tends to be the less interesting. He is from start to finish an impetuous youth in love. Though it is said that all the world loves a lover, somehow acting a person doing nothing but loving is not very fascinating. Even the greatest actor of our time, Laurence Olivier, did not come off well when he played Romeo. And yet, if Romeo were not this one-note, passionate character, we might not have had a play. Plays tend to be driven by characters who are in some way driven themselves.

Juliet, on the other hand, is a prized part. Actresses find it rewarding to develop the character of Juliet, as she grows from a carefree girl to a mature and deeply committed woman.

The actors at the Globe stood in the middle of thousands of spectators.

Drawing by David Gentleman.

The Poetry

Whatever Shakespeare learned of rhetoric, or language, in grammar school, he parades with relish in *Romeo and Juliet.* He is obviously having a fine time here with puns and wordplay and all the other variations he can ring on the English language.

Romeo and Juliet is written in both prose and poetry. Prose is for the most part spoken by the common people and occasionally by Mercutio when he is joking. Most of the other characters speak in poetry.

Blank Verse. The poetry is largely written in unrhymed iambic pentameter, which is called **blank verse.** The word *blank* just means that there is no rhyme.

A line is written in what is called **iambic meter** when an unstressed syllable is followed by a stressed syllable, as in the word *pre-fer.*

Iambic pentameter simply means that there are five of these iambic units in each line. Here is a perfect example of a line in iambic pentameter, spoken by Romeo:

But soft! What light through yonder window breaks?

Now, obviously, a whole play written in this strict meter would become monotonous and singsong. Shakespeare, therefore, sometimes alters the rhythm to give variety, and sometimes emphasis. In the same speech of Romeo's we find these lines:

Two of the fairest stars in all the heaven
Having some business, do entreat her eyes
To twinkle in their spheres till they return.

We see that here in the first two lines Shakespeare reverses the usual pattern and stresses the first instead of the second syllable. Also, at the end of the first line, he has left an extra unstressed syllable. But notice that still, with all the variations, he has kept *five strong beats* to each line.

Couplets. When Shakespeare uses rhymes, he generally uses **couplets,** two consecutive lines of poetry that rhyme. The couplets often punctuate a character's exit or signal the end of a scene. Here, in the end of Act II, Scene 2, Juliet exits from the balcony with this couplet:

Good night, good night! Parting is such sweet sorrow
That I shall say good night till it be morrow.

A moment later, Romeo ends the scene with another couplet:

Hence will I to my ghostly friar's close cell,
His help to crave and my dear hap to tell.

Reading the Lines. We have all heard people ruin a poem by mechanically pausing at the end of each line, regardless of whether or not the meaning of the line called for such a pause. (Maxwell Anderson, who wrote verse plays in the 1930's and 1940's, had his plays typed as though they were prose, so that the actors would not be tempted to pause at the end of each line.)

Lines of poetry are either end-stopped lines or run-on lines. An **end-stopped line** has some punctuation at its end. A **run-on line** has no punctuation at its end. In a run-on line, the meaning is completed in the line or lines that follow.

In Act II, Scene 2, Juliet speaks in end-stopped lines—lines that end with punctuation marks which require her to pause:

O, Romeo, Romeo! Wherefore art thou Romeo?
Deny thy father and refuse thy name;
Or, if thou wilt not, be but sworn my love,
And I'll no longer be a Capulet.

But Romeo's speech from the same scene consists entirely of run-on lines. The only pause Romeo makes is in the middle of his second line, after the word "lamp."

The brightness of her cheek would shame those stars
As daylight doth a lamp; her eyes in heaven
Would through the airy region stream so bright
That birds would sing and think it were not night.

In the end, the glory of *Romeo and Juliet* is the beauty of the poetry, its imagery, its music, its theatricality. The whole play is brisk and fast moving, and the poetry suits the story of young people dealing with a matter very important to them—passionate, once-in-a-lifetime love.

"In the end, the glory of *Romeo and Juliet* is the beauty of the poetry, its imagery, its music, its theatricality. The poetry suits the story of young people dealing with a matter very important to them —passionate once-in-a-lifetime love."

The Themes

Romeo and Juliet takes place in a universe where (as one critic says) God in His providence is aware of even the fall of a sparrow. In this universe, people believe that what must be, must be, and the heroic people meet their destiny with courage. As you read this play, remember the kind of world it is set in, and think about how it reveals these ideas:

1. How love can confer integrity upon two very young people.
2. How tragedy can be caused when old people's rage is carried over to a younger generation.
3. How humans can often be powerless to bring into being the kind of world we'd like to live in.
4. How innocence, virtue, and beauty can be destroyed.
5. How a disordered and chaotic world can bring disaster down on the humans who live in it.

A Brief Word List

Shakespeare wrote this play almost four hundred years ago. It's not surprising, then, that many words are by now **archaic,** which means that they (or their particular meanings) have disappeared from common use. The sidenotes in the play will help you with these archaic words and with other words and expressions that might be unfamiliar to you. Here are some of the archaic words repeatedly used in the play.

'a: he.
a': on.
an', or **and:** if.
Anon!: Soon! Right away! Coming!
but: if, or only.
Good-den or **go-den** or **God-den:** Good evening. (This would be spoken in the late afternoon. You will still hear people in the British Isles referring to the late afternoon as "evening.")
hap, or **happy:** luck, or lucky.
humor: mood, or moisture.
Jack: a common fellow, an ordinary guy.
maid: a young unmarried girl.
mark: listen.
Marry!: a mild oath, shortened from "By the Virgin Mary!"
nice: trivial, foolish.
owes: owns.
shrift: confession or forgiveness for sins confessed to a priest. To be given absolution after confession was to be **shriven.**
Soft!: Quiet! Hush! Slow up!
Stay!: Wait!
withal: with that, with.
wot: know.

> " **R**omeo *and Juliet* takes place in a universe where (as one critic says) God in His providence is aware of even the fall of a sparrow."

THE TRAGEDY OF ROMEO AND JULIET

William Shakespeare

No one has more poignantly described the beauty of young love . . . and no one has portrayed more honestly . . . the destructiveness of any love which ignores the mortality of those who make it.

—J. A. Bryant, Jr.

Characters

The Montagues

Lord Montague
Lady Montague
Romeo, *son of Montague*
Benvolio, *nephew of Montague and friend of Romeo*
Balthasar, *servant of Romeo*
Abram, *servant of Montague*

The Capulets

Lord Capulet
Lady Capulet
Juliet, *daughter of Capulet*
Tybalt, *nephew of Lady Capulet*
Nurse to Juliet
Peter, *servant to the Nurse*
Sampson ⎱
Gregory ⎰ *servants of Capulet*
An Old Man of the Capulet family

The Others

Prince Escalus, *ruler of Verona*
Mercutio, *a relative of the Prince and friend of Romeo*
Friar Laurence, *a Franciscan priest*
Friar John, *another Franciscan priest*
Count Paris, *a young nobleman, a relative of the Prince*
An Apothecary, *a druggist*
Page to Paris
Chief Watchman
Three Musicians
An Officer

Citizens of Verona, Relatives of both families, Maskers, Guards, Watchmen, and Attendants

Scene: Verona and Mantua, cities in northern Italy

The Prologue

Enter CHORUS.

Chorus.

Two households, both alike in dignity,°
 In fair Verona, where we lay our scene,
From ancient grudge break to new mutiny,
 Where civil blood makes civil hands unclean.°
5 From forth the fatal loins of these two foes
 A pair of star-crossed lovers take their life;
Whose misadventured piteous overthrows
 Doth with their death bury their parents' strife.
The fearful passage of their death-marked love,
10 And the continuance of their parents' rage,
Which, but° their children's end, naught could remove,
 Is now the two hours' traffic° of our stage;
The which if you with patient ears attend,
What here shall miss, our toil shall strive to mend.

[*Exit.*]

1. dignity: rank.

4. That is, where civilians' passions ("civil blood") make their hands unclean (because they have been used for killing).

11. but: except for.

12. traffic: business.

? 14. *This Prologue is spoken by a single actor called "the chorus." The Prologue welcomes the audience and gives them a taste of the story. What will the "two hours' traffic" of this stage be about? What will happen to the two lovers?*

Act I Scene 1. *Verona. A public place.*

Enter SAMPSON *and* GREGORY, *of the house of Capulet, with swords and bucklers (shields).*

Sampson. Gregory, on my word, we'll not carry coals.°
Gregory. No, for then we should be colliers.°
Sampson. I mean, and° we be in choler,° we'll draw.°
Gregory. Ay, while you live, draw your neck out of collar.°
5 **Sampson.** I strike quickly, being moved.
Gregory. But thou art not quickly moved to strike.
Sampson. A dog of the house of Montague moves me.
Gregory. To move is to stir, and to be valiant is to stand.
  Therefore, if thou art moved, thou run'st away.
10 **Sampson.** A dog of that house shall move me to stand. I
  will take the wall° of any man or maid of Montague's.
Gregory. That shows thee a weak slave; for the weakest
  goes to the wall.°
Sampson. 'Tis true; and therefore women, being the
15 weaker vessels, are ever thrust to the wall. Therefore
  I will push Montague's men from the wall and thrust
  his maids to the wall.
Gregory. The quarrel is between our masters and us their
  men.
20 **Sampson.** 'Tis all one. I will show myself a tyrant. When
  I have fought with the men, I will be civil with the
  maids—I will cut off their heads.
Gregory. The heads of the maids?
Sampson. Ay, the heads of the maids or their maidenheads.
25 Take it in what sense thou wilt.
Gregory. They must take it in sense that feel it.
Sampson. Me they shall feel while I am able to stand; and
  'tis known I am a pretty piece of flesh.
Gregory. 'Tis well thou art not fish; if thou hadst, thou
30 hadst been Poor John.° Draw thy tool!° Here comes two
  of the house of Montagues.

[*Enter two other servingmen,* ABRAM *and* BALTHASAR.]

Sampson. My naked weapon is out. Quarrel! I will back
  thee.
Gregory. How? Turn thy back and run?
35 **Sampson.** Fear me not.°
Gregory. No marry. I fear thee!
Sampson. Let us take the law of our sides;° let them begin.
Gregory. I will frown as I pass by, and let them take it as
  they list.

604 William Shakespeare

Stage direction: *The two servants enter, bragging and teasing each other. What actions do you imagine they are engaged in as they cross the city square?*

1. carry coals: do dirty work (put up with insults). People often made jokes about men who carted coal.
2. colliers: coal dealers (men with dirty jobs). Notice how the servants start making jokes based on words that sound the same (*colliers, choler,* and *collar*).
3. and: if. **choler:** anger. **draw:** draw swords.
4. collar: the hangman's noose.

11. take the wall: take the best place on the walk (which is closest to the wall).

13. goes to the wall: is pushed to the rear.

30. Poor John: a kind of salted fish, a poor person's food. **tool:** sword.

Stage direction: *Sampson's and Gregory's swaggering stops when they spot their enemies. How do their next speeches show that they are really cowards? What is Sampson doing when he says "Quarrel! I will back thee"?*

35. Fear me not: distrust me not.

37. That is, stay on the right side of the law.

40   **Sampson.** Nay, as they dare. I will bite my thumb° at them,
     which is disgrace to them if they bear it.
  Abram. Do you bite your thumb at us, sir?
  Sampson. I do bite my thumb, sir.
  Abram. Do you bite your thumb at us, sir?
45   **Sampson** (*aside to* GREGORY). Is the law of our side if I
     say ay?
  Gregory (*aside to* SAMPSON). No.
  Sampson. No, sir, I do not bite my thumb at you, sir; but
     I bite my thumb, sir.
50   **Gregory.** Do you quarrel, sir?
  Abram. Quarrel, sir? No, sir.
  Sampson. But if you do, sir, I am for you. I serve as good
     a man as you.
  Abram. No better.
55   **Sampson.** Well, sir.

  [*Enter* BENVOLIO.]

  Gregory. Say "better." Here comes one of my master's
     kinsmen.
  Sampson. Yes, better, sir.
  Abram. You lie.
60   **Sampson.** Draw, if you be men. Gregory, remember thy
     swashing° blow.

  [*They fight.*]

  Benvolio.
     Part, fools!
     Put up your swords. You know not what you do.

  [*Enter* TYBALT.]

  Tybalt.
     What, art thou drawn among these heartless hinds?°
65   Turn thee, Benvolio; look upon thy death.
  Benvolio.
     I do but keep the peace. Put up thy sword,
     Or manage it to part these men with me.
  Tybalt.
     What, drawn, and talk of peace? I hate the word
     As I hate hell, all Montagues, and thee.
70   Have at thee, coward!

  [*They fight.*]

  [*Enter an* OFFICER, *and three or four* CITIZENS *with clubs,
     bills, and partisans, or spears.*]

  Officer. Clubs, bills, and partisans! Strike! Beat them
     down! Down with the Capulets! Down with the Mon-
     tagues!

40. bite my thumb: an insulting gesture.

42. *It takes the Montague servants some time to speak. How do their actions show that these four servants are very wary of one another?*

56. *How does Gregory change when he spots Benvolio?*

61. swashing: slashing.

63. *What action is Benvolio involved in here?*

64. heartless hinds: cowardly hicks.

65. *Sometimes Tybalt's second line is spoken after a dramatic silence. Why should this line demand our attention?*

69. *This is a key speech. What is Tybalt's mood? How is he shown to be the opposite in nature to Benvolio?*

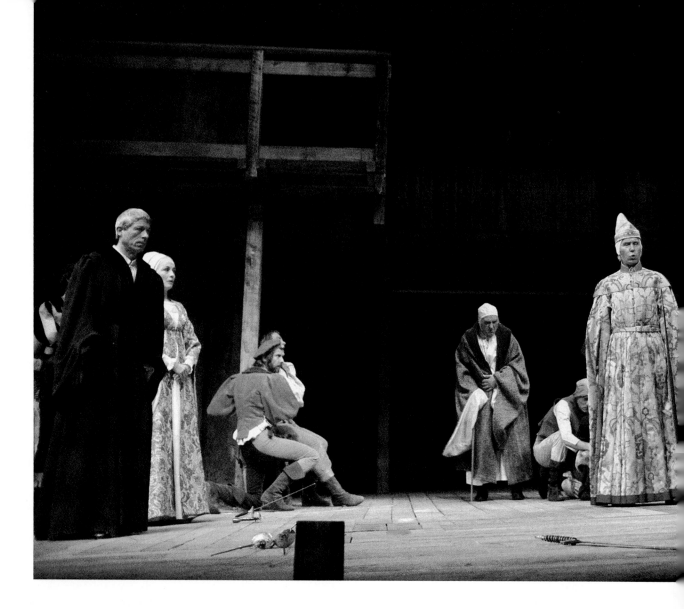

[*Enter old* CAPULET *in his gown, and his wife,* LADY CAP-
ULET.]

Capulet.
 What noise is this? Give me my long sword, ho!
Lady Capulet.
75 A crutch, a crutch! Why call you for a sword?
Capulet.
 My sword, I say! Old Montague is come
 And flourishes his blade in spite° of me.

[*Enter old* MONTAGUE *and his wife,* LADY MONTAGUE.]

Montague.
 Thou villain Capulet!—Hold me not; let me go.
Lady Montague.
 Thou shalt not stir one foot to seek a foe.

75. *In the midst of the tension over Tybalt, we have a comic touch. Why is
Lady Capulet talking about crutches?*

77. in spite of: in defiance of.

78. *Who is holding Montague back?*

"*Throw your mistempered weapons to the ground.*"

The photographs in the play are from the Royal Shakespeare Company, starring Ian McKellan and Francesca Annis.

[*Enter* PRINCE ESCALUS, *with his* TRAIN.]

Prince.

80   Rebellious subjects, enemies to peace,
      Profaners of this neighbor-stainèd steel—
      Will they not hear? What, ho! You men, you beasts,
      That quench the fire of your pernicious rage
      With purple fountains issuing from your veins!
85   On pain of torture, from those bloody hands
      Throw your mistempered° weapons to the ground
      And hear the sentence of your movèd prince.
      Three civil brawls, bred of an airy° word
      By thee, old Capulet, and Montague,
90   Have thrice disturbed the quiet of our streets
      And made Verona's ancient citizens
      Cast by their grave beseeming° ornaments

Stage direction: *The prince and all his attendants enter to the blast of trumpets. Their dignified procession contrasts with the bloody rioting. How do you know from the next speech that the Prince is at first ignored by the brawlers?*

86. **mistempered:** used with bad temper.

87. *Line 88 is spoken after a dramatic pause. What are the brawlers doing now?*
88. **airy:** light or harmless.

92. **grave beseeming:** dignified, as they should be.

To wield old partisans, in hands as old,
Cankered with peace, to part your cankered° hate.
95   If ever you disturb our streets again,
Your lives shall pay the forfeit of the peace.
For this time all the rest depart away.
You, Capulet, shall go along with me;
And, Montague, come you this afternoon,
100   To know our farther pleasure in this case,
To old Freetown, our common judgment place.
Once more, on pain of death, all men depart.

[*Exeunt all but* MONTAGUE, LADY MONTAGUE, *and* BEN-
VOLIO.]

Montague.
Who set this ancient quarrel new abroach?°
Speak, nephew, were you by when it began?

Benvolio.
105   Here were the servants of your adversary
And yours, close fighting ere I did approach.
I drew to part them. In the instant came
The fiery Tybalt, with his sword prepared;
Which, as he breathed defiance to my ears,
110   He swung about his head and cut the winds,
Who, nothing hurt withal, hissed him in scorn.
While we were interchanging thrusts and blows,
Came more and more, and fought on part and part,°
Till the prince came, who parted either part.

Lady Montague.
115   O, where is Romeo? Saw you him today?
Right glad I am he was not at this fray.

Benvolio.
Madam, an hour before the worshiped sun
Peered forth the golden window of the East,
A troubled mind drave me to walk abroad;
120   Where, underneath the grove of sycamore
That westward rooteth from this city side,
So early walking did I see your son.
Towards him I made, but he was ware° of me
And stole into the covert of the wood.
125   I, measuring his affections by my own,
Which then most sought where most might not be
     found,°
Being one too many by my weary self,
Pursued my humor not pursuing his,
And gladly shunned who gladly fled from me.

Montague.
130   Many a morning hath he there been seen,
With tears augmenting the fresh morning's dew,

94. cankered: the first "cankered" means "rusted" (from lack of use in peaceful times); the second means "malignant," like a canker, a running sore.

102. *What has been happening in Verona? What is the Prince's warning?*

103. new abroach: newly opened.

113. on part and part: some on one side, some on the other.

116. *For the first time, Romeo is mentioned, and by his mother, whose human concern is accented by a rhyme. Lady Montague does not say anything else in this scene. What do you imagine she is doing while her husband and Benvolio discuss her son?*

123. ware: aware.

126. He sought for a place where no one could be found. (He wanted to be alone.)

Adding to clouds more clouds with his deep sighs;
But all so soon as the all-cheering sun
Should in the farthest East begin to draw

135   The shady curtains from Aurora's° bed,
Away from light steals home my heavy° son
And private in his chamber pens himself,
Shuts up his windows, locks fair daylight out,
And makes himself an artificial night.

140   Black and portentous must this humor prove
Unless good counsel may the cause remove.

Benvolio.
My noble uncle, do you know the cause?

Montague.
I neither know it nor can learn of him.

Benvolio.
Have you importuned° him by any means?

Montague.
145   Both by myself and many other friends;
But he, his own affections' counselor,
Is to himself—I will not say how true—
But to himself so secret and so close,
So far from sounding° and discovery,

150   As is the bud bit with an envious° worm
Ere he can spread his sweet leaves to the air
Or dedicate his beauty to the sun.
Could we but learn from whence his sorrows grow,
We would as willingly give cure as know.

[*Enter* ROMEO.]

Benvolio.
155   See, where he comes. So please you step aside;
I'll know his grievance, or be much denied.

Montague.
I would thou wert so happy° by the stay
To hear true shrift.° Come, madam, let's away.

[*Exeunt* MONTAGUE *and* LADY MONTAGUE.]

Benvolio.
Good morrow, cousin.

Romeo.   Is the day so young?

Benvolio.
But new struck nine.

160   **Romeo.**   Ay me! Sad hours seem long.
Was that my father that went hence so fast?

Benvolio.
It was. What sadness lengthens Romeo's hours?

Romeo.
Not having that which having makes them short.

---

135. Aurora: goddess of the dawn.
136. heavy: heavy-hearted.

? **141.** *Romeo has been described by his father and his friend. What do we know of him so far?*

144. importuned: questioned.

149. So far from sounding: so far from being sounded out for his mood (as a river is sounded for its depth).
150. envious: evil.

? **Stage direction:** *Romeo at first doesn't see his parents or Benvolio. How do you think he should be acting as he enters?*

157. happy: lucky.
158. shrift: confession.

? **159.** *Benvolio is trying to be casual. What attitude should Romeo convey by his answer to Benvolio's cheery greeting?*

"Ay me! Sad hours seem long."

Benvolio.

I'll pay that doctrine, or else die in debt.°

[*Exeunt.*]

237. **or else die in debt:** or die trying.
? *237. Benvolio can exit here as if he is running after Romeo. The pair will re-enter later, Romeo still being pursued. How are we to feel about Benvolio?*

Scene 2. *A street.*

Enter CAPULET, COUNT PARIS, *and the clown, his* SERVANT.

Capulet.

But Montague is bound° as well as I,
In penalty alike; and 'tis not hard, I think,
For men so old as we to keep the peace.

1. **is bound:** is pledged to keep the peace.

Paris.

Of honorable reckoning° are you both,
5 And pity 'tis you lived at odds so long.
But now, my lord, what say you to my suit?

4. **reckoning:** reputation.

Capulet.

But saying o'er what I have said before:
My child is yet a stranger in the world,
She hath not seen the change of fourteen years;
10 Let two more summers wither in their pride
Ere we may think her ripe to be a bride.

Paris.

Younger than she are happy mothers made.

? *12. Paris is very much at ease with old Capulet and more composed than the lovesick Romeo we just saw. What does Paris want?*

Capulet.

And too soon marred are those so early made.
Earth hath swallowèd all my hopes but she;
15 She is the hopeful lady of my earth.
But woo her, gentle Paris, get her heart;
My will to her consent is but a part.
And she agreed, within her scope of choice°
Lies my consent and fair according° voice.
20 This night I hold an old accustomed° feast,
Whereto I have invited many a guest,
Such as I love; and you among the store,
One more, most welcome, makes my number more.
At my poor house look to behold this night
25 Earth-treading stars° that make dark heaven light.
Such comfort as do lusty young men feel
When well-appareled April on the heel
Of limping winter treads, even such delight
Among fresh fennel° buds shall you this night
30 Inherit° at my house. Hear all, all see,
And like her most whose merit most shall be;
Which, on more view of many, mine, being one,
May stand in number,° though in reck'ning none.°
Come, go with me.

? *15. Why doesn't Capulet want his daughter to marry right away? How is Capulet now different from the man who drew his sword in Scene 1?*

18. **within her scope of choice:** among all she can choose from.
19. **according:** agreeing.
20. **accustomed:** traditional.

25. **Earth-treading stars:** that is, young girls.

29. **fennel:** an herb. Capulet compares the young girls to fennel flowers.
30. **Inherit:** have.

33. **stand in number:** be one of the crowd (of girls). **though in reck'ning none:** though none will be worth more than Juliet is.

[*To* SERVANT, *giving him a paper.*]

Go, sirrah, trudge about

35 Through fair Verona; find those persons out
Whose names are written there, and to them say
My house and welcome on their pleasure stay.°

[*Exit with* PARIS.]

Servant. Find them out whose names are written here? It
is written that the shoemaker should meddle with his
40 yard and the tailor with his last, the fisher with his
pencil and the painter with his nets;° but I am sent to
find those persons whose names are here writ, and can
never find° what names the writing person hath here
writ. I must to the learned. In good time!°

[*Enter* BENVOLIO *and* ROMEO.]

Benvolio.

45 Tut, man, one fire burns out another's burning;
One pain is less'ned by another's anguish;
Turn giddy, and be holp by backward turning;°
One desperate grief cures with another's languish.
Take thou some new infection to thy eye,
50 And the rank poison of the old will die.

Romeo

Your plantain leaf is excellent for that.

Benvolio.

For what, I pray thee?

Romeo.   For your broken° shin.

Benvolio.

Why, Romeo, art thou mad?

Romeo.

Not mad, but bound more than a madman is;
55 Shut up in prison, kept without my food,
Whipped and tormented and—God-den,° good fellow.

Servant. God gi' go-den. I pray, sir, can you read?

Romeo.

Ay, mine own fortune in my misery.

Servant. Perhaps you have learned it without book.
60 But, I pray, can you read anything you see?

Romeo.

Ay, if I know the letters and the language.

Servant. Ye say honestly. Rest you merry.

Romeo. Stay, fellow; I can read.

[*He reads the letter.*]

"Signior Martino and his wife and daughters;
65 County Anselm and his beauteous sisters;

34. *Capulet can be played many ways by actors. Some play him here as a loving, considerate father. Other actors interpret him as a man who chiefly wants a socially advantageous marriage for his daughter. How would you play this scene?*
37. stay: wait.

38. *Like the other servants, this one plays for comedy. He can't read or write. How should he show this bewilderment?*
41. nets: the servant is quoting mixed-up proverbs. He's trying to say that people should attend to what they do best.
43. find: understand.
44. In good time!: Just in time!
44. *The servant looks up from the note to see the young gentlemen enter. He now tries to get them to read the note, while one chases the other across the stage. How do Romeo's comments in the next conversation show that he is trying to change the subject?*

47. be holp by backward turning: be helped by turning in the opposite direction.

52. broken: scratched.

56. God-den: good evening.
56. *Romeo turns to get away and runs into the servant, who has been listening to them in stupefied silence. How should the two gentlemen treat the servant in this little encounter?*

The lady widow of Vitruvio;
Signior Placentio and his lovely nieces;
Mercutio and his brother Valentine;
Mine uncle Capulet, his wife and daughters;
70   My fair niece Rosaline; Livia;
Signior Valentio and his cousin Tybalt;
Lucio and the lively Helena.''
A fair assembly. Whither should they come?

Servant. Up.

75   **Romeo.** Whither? To supper?

Servant. To our house.

Romeo. Whose house?

Servant. My master's.

Romeo.
Indeed I should have asked you that before.

80   **Servant.** Now I'll tell you without asking. My master is
the great rich Capulet; and if you be not of the house
of Montagues, I pray come and crush a cup of wine.
Rest you merry.

[*Exit.*]

Benvolio.
At this same ancient° feast of Capulet's
85   Sups the fair Rosaline whom thou so loves;
With all the admirèd beauties of Verona.
Go thither, and with unattainted° eye
Compare her face with some that I shall show,
And I will make thee think thy swan a crow.

Romeo.
90   When the devout religion of mine eye
Maintains such falsehood, then turn tears to fires;
And these, who, often drowned, could never die,
Transparent heretics,° be burnt for liars!
One fairer than my love? The all-seeing sun
95   Ne'er saw her match since first the world begun.

Benvolio.
Tut! you saw her fair, none else being by,
Herself poised° with herself in either eye;
But in that crystal scales° let there be weighed
Your lady's love against some other maid
100   That I will show you shining at this feast,
And she shall scant° show well that now seems best.

Romeo.
I'll go along, no such sight to be shown,
But to rejoice in splendor of mine own. [*Exeunt.*]

70. *This Rosaline, Capulet's niece, is the girl Romeo is in love with. Some actors read this line to betray to the audience Romeo's secret. How would you have Romeo read this letter? How would he ask his question?*

84. ancient: old, established by an old custom.

87. unattainted: untainted (by prejudice).

89. *What does Benvolio say to lure Romeo to the party?*

93. transparent heretics: his eyes would be easily "seen through"—they would betray the truth.

97. poised: balanced (for comparison).

98. crystal scales: Romeo's eyes.

101. scant: scarcely.

103. *If we know from the letter that Rosaline is to be at the party and that she is the one Romeo loves, we know why he decides to go to Capulet's. Actors usually say these lines to indicate that the decision to go is crucial and fateful. What mood is Romeo in?*

Scene 3. *A room in Capulet's house.*

Enter Capulet's wife, LADY CAPULET, *and* NURSE.

Lady Capulet.
    Nurse, where's my daughter? Call her forth to me.
Nurse.
    Now, by my maidenhead at twelve year old,
    I bade her come. What,° lamb! What, ladybird!
    God forbid, where's this girl? What, Juliet!

[*Enter* JULIET.]

Juliet.
5   How now? Who calls?
Nurse.   Your mother.
Juliet.   Madam, I am here.
    What is your will?
Lady Capulet.
    This is the matter.—Nurse, give leave awhile;
    We must talk in secret. Nurse, come back again.
    I have rememb'red me; thou's° hear our counsel.
10   Thou knowest my daughter's of a pretty age.
Nurse.
    Faith, I can tell her age unto an hour.
Lady Capulet.
    She's not fourteen.
Nurse.   I'll lay fourteen of my teeth—
    And yet, to my teen° be it spoken, I have but four—
    She's not fourteen. How long is it now
15   To Lammastide?°
Lady Capulet.   A fortnight and odd days.
Nurse.
    Even or odd, of all days in the year,
    Come Lammas Eve at night shall she be fourteen.
    Susan and she (God rest all Christian souls!)
    Were of an age.° Well, Susan is with God;
20   She was too good for me. But, as I said,
    On Lammas Eve at night shall she be fourteen;
    That shall she, marry; I remember it well.
    'Tis since the earthquake now eleven years;
    And she was weaned (I shall never forget it),
25   Of all the days of the year, upon that day;
    For I had then laid wormwood to my dug,°
    Sitting in the sun under the dovehouse wall.
    My lord and you were then at Mantua.
    Nay, I do bear a brain. But, as I said,
30   When it did taste the wormwood on the nipple
    Of my dug and felt it bitter, pretty fool,

3. What: an impatient call, like "Hey!" or "Where are you?"

9. thou's: thou shalt.

10. *The Nurse and Lady Capulet are opposites in nature. Lady Capulet sends the Nurse off and then calls her back. Some actresses use this impulsive move to indicate Lady Capulet's reluctance to speak to her daughter about marriage. In contrast, how does the Nurse react in this next scene?*

13. teen: sorrow.

15. Lammastide: a church feast, on August 1.

19. Were of an age: were the same age.

26. wormwood to my dug: applied a bitter substance (wormwood) to her breast to wean the baby.

To see it tetchy° and fall out with the dug!
Shake, quoth the dovehouse!° 'Twas no need, I trow,
To bid me trudge.

35 And since that time it is eleven years,
For then she could stand high-lone;° nay, by th'
   rood,°
She could have run and waddled all about;
For even the day before, she broke her brow;
And then my husband (God be with his soul!

40 'A was a merry man) took up the child.
"Yea," quoth he, "dost thou fall upon thy face?
Thou wilt fall backward when thou hast more wit;°
Wilt thou not, Jule?" and, by my holidam,°
The pretty wretch left crying and said, "Ay."

45 To see now how a jest shall come about!
I warrant, and I should live a thousand years,
I never should forget it. "Wilt thou not, Jule?" quoth he,
And, pretty fool, it stinted° and said, "Ay."

Lady Capulet.
Enough of this. I pray thee hold thy peace.

Nurse.
50 Yes, madam. Yet I cannot choose but laugh
To think it should leave crying and say, "Ay."
And yet, I warrant, it had upon its brow
A bump as big as a young cock'rel's stone;
A perilous knock; and it cried bitterly.

55 "Yea," quoth my husband, "fall'st upon thy face?
Thou wilt fall backward when thou comest to age,
Wilt thou not, Jule?" It stinted and said, "Ay."

Juliet.
And stint thou too, I pray thee, nurse, say I.

Nurse.
Peace, I have done. God mark thee to his grace!
60 Thou wast the prettiest babe that e'er I nursed.
And I might live to see thee married once,
I have my wish.

Lady Capulet.
Marry, that "marry" is the very theme
I came to talk of. Tell me, daughter Juliet,
65 How stands your disposition to be married?

Juliet.
It is an honor that I dream not of.

Nurse.
An honor? Were not I thine only nurse,
I would say thou hadst sucked wisdom from thy teat.

Lady Capulet.
Well, think of marriage now. Younger than you,
70 Here in Verona, ladies of esteem,

32. tetchy: angry.
33. Shake, quoth the dovehouse: the dovehouse shook (from the earthquake).

36. high-lone: alone. **by th'rood:** by the Cross, a mild oath.

42. wit: understanding.
43. by my holidam: by my holy relic.

48. stinted: stopped.
48. *The Nurse must make a strong impression with this speech, which leaves her helpless with laughter. The Nurse directs her chatter to Lady Capulet, but Juliet is listening too. How would Juliet react to her fond Nurse's memories, which refuse to be stifled?*

62. *This short line suggests another dramatic pause. Often, a director will have Juliet rush to the Nurse and kiss her. Her fondness and gaiety with the Nurse must contrast with her reserve toward her mother. How should Juliet react when she speaks in line 66?*

Are made already mothers. By my count,
I was your mother much upon these years
That you are now a maid. Thus then in brief:
The valiant Paris seeks you for his love.

Nurse.

75   A man, young lady! Lady, such a man
As all the world.—Why, he's a man of wax.°

Lady Capulet.

Verona's summer hath not such a flower.

Nurse.

Nay, he's a flower, in faith—a very flower.

Lady Capulet.

What say you? Can you love the gentleman?
80   This night you shall behold him at our feast.
Read o'er the volume of young Paris' face,
And find delight writ there with beauty's pen;
Examine every married lineament,°
And see how one another lends content;°
85   And what obscured in this fair volume lies
Find written in the margent of his eyes.
This precious book of love, this unbound lover,
To beautify him only lacks a cover.
The fish lives in the sea, and 'tis much pride
90   For fair without the fair within to hide.°
That book in many's eyes doth share the glory,
That in gold clasps locks in the golden story;
So shall you share all that he doth possess,
By having him, making yourself no less.

Nurse.

95   No less? Nay, bigger! Women grow by men.

Lady Capulet.

Speak briefly, can you like of Paris' love?

Juliet.

I'll look to like, if looking liking move;
But no more deep will I endart mine eye
Than your consent gives strength to make it fly.

[*Enter* SERVINGMAN.]

100   **Servingman.** Madam, the guests are come, supper served
up, you called, my young lady asked for, the nurse
cursed in the pantry, and everything in extremity. I
must hence to wait. I beseech you follow straight.
                                   [*Exit.*]

Lady Capulet.

We follow thee. Juliet, the county stays.°

Nurse.

105   Go, girl, seek happy nights to happy days. [*Exeunt.*]

76. man of wax: like a wax statue, with a perfect figure.

79. *Notice that Juliet isn't answering. How do you suppose she is feeling during the conversation between the Nurse and her mother about this man they want her to marry?*

83. married lineament: harmonious feature.
84. how one another lends content: how one feature makes the other look good.

90. For fair without the fair within to hide: for handsome men to be embraced by beautiful women.

94. *Lady Capulet has made an elegant appeal to Juliet, to persuade her to consider marrying Paris. Which images in this speech compare Paris to a fine book?*

99. *Juliet says she'll look at Paris to see if she likes him (if liking is brought about by looking). How does she show that she is a dutiful daughter?*

100. *Another comical servant enters, speaking breathlessly, but our attention still must be on Juliet. In some productions, we now hear the sounds of music coming offstage, and Juliet exits excitedly, with little dancing motions. Do we really know much about Juliet yet?*

104. the county stays: the count waits.

Scene 4. *A street.*

Enter ROMEO, MERCUTIO, BENVOLIO, *with five or six other* MASKERS; TORCHBEARERS.

Romeo.
What, shall this speech be spoke for our excuse?°
Or shall we on without apology?

Benvolio.
The date is out of such prolixity.°
We'll have no Cupid hoodwinked° with a scarf,

5   Bearing a Tartar's painted bow of lath,
Scaring the ladies like a crowkeeper;°
Nor no without-book prologue,° faintly spoke
After the prompter, for our entrance;
But, let them measure° us by what they will,

10 We'll measure them a measure° and be gone.

Romeo.
Give me a torch. I am not for this ambling.
Being but heavy, I will bear the light.

Mercutio.
Nay, gentle Romeo, we must have you dance.

Romeo.
Not I, believe me. You have dancing shoes

15 With nimble soles; I have a soul of lead
So stakes me to the ground I cannot move.

Mercutio.
You are a lover. Borrow Cupid's wings
And soar with them above a common bound.

Romeo.
I am too sore enpiercèd with his shaft

20 To soar with his light feathers; and so bound
I cannot bound a pitch° above dull woe.
Under love's heavy burden do I sink.

Mercutio.
And, to sink in it, should you burden love—
Too great oppression for a tender thing.

Romeo.
25 Is love a tender thing? It is too rough,
Too rude, too boist'rous, and it pricks like thorn.

Mercutio.
If love be rough with you, be rough with love;
Prick love for pricking, and you beat love down.
Give me a case to put my visage in.

30 A visor° for a visor! What care I
What curious eye doth quote deformities?°
Here are the beetle brows shall blush° for me.

Benvolio.
Come, knock and enter; and no sooner in

? Stage direction: *It's night. The stage is lit with torches and filled with grotesquely masked young men. The mood is one of excitement—but we are watching Romeo. What does he say in the next speeches to indicate that he is still heavy-hearted?*

1. shall this speech be spoke for our excuse?: shall we introduce ourselves with the usual speeches? (Uninvited maskers were usually announced by a messenger.)
3. The date is out of such prolixity: such speeches are out of fashion now.
4. hoodwinked: blindfolded.

6. crowkeeper: a scarecrow.

7. without-book prologue: memorized.

9. measure: examine.

10. measure them a measure: dance one dance.

? 13. *Mercutio is a key character. Here he comes out of the crowd and speaks to Romeo. They engage in a verbal duel about love. In the following dialogue, how do Mercutio and Romeo differ in their attitudes toward love?*

21. pitch: a measure of height (as in a falcon's flight).

? 29. *Mercutio pauses and asks for a mask. What activity would he be engaged in here?*
30. visor: mask.
31. quote deformities: see imperfections (in the way he looks).
32. Here are the beetle brows shall blush: the mask's heavy eyebrows will blush for him.

Romeo and Juliet **Act I: Scene 4** **619**

But every man betake him to his legs.°

Romeo.

35 A torch for me! Let wantons light of heart
Tickle the senseless rushes° with their heels;
For I am proverbed with a grandsire phrase,°
I'll be a candleholder and look on;
The game was ne'er so fair, and I am done.°

Mercutio.

40 Tut! Dun's the mouse, the constable's own word!
If thou art Dun,° we'll draw thee from the mire
Of this sir-reverence love,° wherein thou stickest
Upon to the ears. Come, we burn daylight, ho!

Romeo.

Nay, that's not so.

Mercutio.   I mean, sir, in delay

45 We waste our lights° in vain, like lights by day.
Take our good meaning, for our judgment sits
Five times in that° ere once in our five wits.

Romeo.

And we mean well in going to this masque,
But 'tis no wit° to go.

Mercutio.   Why, may one ask?

Romeo.

50 I dreamt a dream tonight.

Mercutio.   And so did I.

Romeo.

Well, what was yours?

Mercutio.   That dreamers often lie.

Romeo.

In bed asleep, while they do dream things true.

Mercutio.

O, then I see Queen Mab hath been with you.
She is the fairies' midwife, and she comes

55 In shape no bigger than an agate stone
On the forefinger of an alderman,
Drawn with a team of little atomies°
Over men's noses as they lie asleep;
Her wagon spokes made of long spinners'° legs,

60 The cover, of the wings of grasshoppers;
Her traces,° of the smallest spider web;
Her collars, of the moonshine's wat'ry beams;
Her whip, of cricket's bone; the lash, of film;°
Her wagoner, a small gray-coated gnat,

65 Not half so big as a round little worm
Pricked from the lazy finger of a maid;°
Her chariot is an empty hazelnut,
Made by the joiner squirrel or old grub,
Time out o' mind the fairies' coachmakers.

---

34. **betake him to his legs:** begin dancing.

36. **rushes:** the dance floor is covered with rushes.
37. **grandsire phrase:** old man's saying.

39. **The game . . . I am done:** the game (dancing) was never that good, and I'm exhausted.

? 39. *Despite Mercutio's teasing and Benvolio's urging, what is Romeo determined to do at the dance?*
41. **Dun:** a pun on Romeo's "done"; Dun was the common name used for a horse in an old game called "Dun is in the mire."
42. **sir-reverence love:** "save your reverence," an apologetic expression. Mercutio means, "We'll save you from—pardon me for saying so—love."
45. **lights:** torches.

47. **in that:** in our good meaning.

? 48. *Romeo's mood seems to change abruptly, and he has a foreboding of doom. How would he speak this line about a dream? Would Mercutio's reply be kindly or sharp?*
49. **no wit:** not a good idea.

? 53. *Mercutio is a ringleader and a born entertainer. As he tells this story about Queen Mab, everyone stops and listens in fascinated silence. For the moment, Romeo is in the background. How is Mercutio, in this famous speech, trying to get Romeo's mind off its serious thoughts about dreams and their significance? What gestures will he use to embellish his speech? According to Mercutio, what does Queen Mab have to do with Romeo?*
57. **atomies:** tiny creatures (like atoms).
59. **spinners':** spiders.
61. **traces:** reins and harnesses for a wagon.
63. **film:** a filament of some kind.

66. **lazy finger of a maid:** lazy maids were said to have worms breeding in their fingers.

<table>
<tr><td>70</td><td>And in this state she gallops night by night
Through lovers' brains, and then they dream of love;
On courtiers' knees, that dream on curtsies straight;
O'er lawyers' fingers, who straight dream on fees;
O'er ladies' lips, who straight on kisses dream,</td></tr>
<tr><td>75</td><td>Which oft the angry Mab with blisters plagues,
Because their breath with sweetmeats tainted are.
Sometime she gallops o'er a courtier's nose,
And then dreams he of smelling out a suit;°
And sometime comes she with a tithe pig's° tail</td></tr>
<tr><td>80</td><td>Tickling a parson's nose as 'a lies asleep,
Then he dreams of another benefice.°
Sometime she driveth o'er a soldier's neck,
And then dreams he of cutting foreign throats,
Of breaches, ambuscadoes, Spanish blades,</td></tr>
<tr><td>85</td><td>Of healths° five fathom deep; and then anon
Drums in his ear, at which he starts and wakes,
And being thus frighted, swears a prayer or two
And sleeps again. This is that very Mab
That plaits the manes of horses in the night</td></tr>
<tr><td>90</td><td>And bakes the elflocks° in foul sluttish hairs,
Which once untangled much misfortune bodes.
This is the hag,° when maids lie on their backs,
That presses them and learns them first to bear,
Making them women of good carriage.°</td></tr>
<tr><td>95</td><td>This is she——</td></tr>
</table>

Romeo.   Peace, peace, Mercutio, peace!
     Thou talk'st of nothing.

Mercutio.   True, I talk of dreams;
     Which are the children of an idle brain,
     Begot of nothing but vain fantasy;
     Which is as thin of substance as the air,

100   And more inconstant than the wind, who woos
     Even now the frozen bosom of the North
     And, being angered, puffs away from thence,
     Turning his side to the dewdropping South.

Benvolio.
     This wind you talk of blows us from ourselves.

105   Supper is done, and we shall come too late.

Romeo.
     I fear, too early; for my mind misgives
     Some consequence yet hanging in the stars
     Shall bitterly begin his fearful date
     With this night's revels and expire the term

110   Of a despisèd life, closed in my breast,
     By some vile forfeit of untimely death.
     But he that hath the steerage of my course
     Direct my sail! On, lusty gentlemen!

78. suit: a petitioner who might want to buy his influence at court.
79. tithe pig's: a tithe is a tenth of one's income given to the church. Farmers often gave the parson one pig as a tithe.
81. benefice: means of making a living.

85. healths: toasts to his health.

90. elflocks: elves were thought to tangle hair.

92. hag: nightmare. Nightmares were thought to be spirits who molested women at night.
94. women of good carriage: women who can bear children well.
94. *Mercutio's tone changes here. How are these last details getting into subjects that are more shocking and cynical? Romeo doesn't like this turn of events and cuts Mercutio off.*

103. *Mercutio could be comparing Romeo to the frozen North. If he is, what warning does he give his friend about remaining cold too long?*

106. *Romeo again expresses ominous feelings. Does he give any reasons for his fears? Which words in this speech suggest that he is going to the party because he is in the hands of Fate?*

Benvolio. Strike, drum.

[*They march about the stage, and retire to one side*.]

Scene 5. *A hall in Capulet's house.*

SERVINGMEN *come forth with napkins.*

First Servingman. Where's Potpan, that he helps not to
take away? He shift a trencher!° He scrape a trencher!
Second Servingman. When good manners shall lie all in
one or two men's hands, and they unwashed too, 'tis
5 a foul thing.
First Servingman. Away with the join-stools,° remove the
court cupboard, look to the plate. Good thou, save me
a piece of marchpane,° and as thou loves me, let the
porter let in Susan Grindstone and Nell, Anthony, and
10 Potpan!
Second Servingman. Ay, boy, ready.
First Servingman. You are looked for and called for,
asked for and sought for, in the great chamber.
Third Servingman. We cannot be here and there too.
15 Cheerly, boys! Be brisk awhile, and the longer liver
take all.   [*Exeunt.*]

[*Enter* CAPULET, LADY CAPULET, JULIET, TYBALT,
NURSE, *and all the* GUESTS *and* GENTLEWOMEN, *meeting
the* MASKERS.]

Capulet.
Welcome, gentlemen! Ladies that have their toes
Unplagued with corns will walk a bout° with you.
Ah, my mistresses, which of you all
20 Will now deny to dance? She that makes dainty,°
She I'll swear hath corns. Am I come near ye now?
Welcome, gentlemen! I have seen the day
That I have worn a visor and could tell
A whispering tale in a fair lady's ear,
25 Such as would please. 'Tis gone, 'tis gone, 'tis gone.
You are welcome, gentlemen! Come, musicians, play.

[*Music plays, and they dance.*]

A hall,° a hall! Give room! And foot it, girls.
More light, you knaves, and turn the tables up,
And quench the fire; the room is grown too hot.
30 Ah, sirrah, this unlooked-for sport° comes well.
Nay, sit; nay, sit, good cousin Capulet;
For you and I are past our dancing days.
How long is't now since last yourself and I

Stage direction: *As you read these servants' speeches, note that one speaks in short emphatic sentences and bosses everyone else around. Which one is this? What should be the mood of this short scene?*
2. **trencher:** a wooden plate.

6. **join-stools:** wooden stools made by a carpenter (a joiner).

8. **marchpane:** marzipan.

18. **bout:** dance.

20. **makes dainty:** pretends to be shy.

Stage direction: *The dance, slow and stately, takes place at center stage. Old Capulet and his relative reminisce on the side, but our attention is focused on Romeo (in a mask) and Juliet, who is dancing with someone else. How does the following conversation contrast the two old men with Romeo and Juliet?*
27. **A hall:** clear the floor (for dancing).
30. **unlooked-for sport:** he hadn't expected to find some of the dancers masked.

"A hall, a hall! Give room! And foot it, girls."

Were in a mask?

Second Capulet.   By'r Lady, thirty years.

Capulet.

35 What, man? 'Tis not so much, 'tis not so much;
'Tis since the nuptial of Lucentio,
Come Pentecost as quickly as it will,
Some five-and-twenty years, and then we masked.

Second Capulet.

'Tis more, 'tis more. His son is elder, sir;
40 His son is thirty.

Capulet.   Will you tell me that?
His son was but a ward° two years ago.

Romeo (*to a* SERVINGMAN).

What lady's that which doth enrich the hand
Of yonder knight?

Servingman. I know not, sir.

Romeo.

45 O, she doth teach the torches to burn bright!
It seems she hangs upon the cheek of night
As a rich jewel in an Ethiop's ear—
Beauty too rich for use, for earth too dear!
So shows a snowy dove trooping with crows
50 As yonder lady o'er her fellows shows.
The measure° done, I'll watch her place of stand
And, touching hers, make blessèd my rude° hand.
Did my heart love till now? Forswear it, sight!
For I ne'er saw true beauty till this night.

Tybalt.

55 This, by his voice, should be a Montague.
Fetch me my rapier, boy. What! Dares the slave
Come hither, covered with an antic face,°
To fleer° and scorn at our solemnity?
Now, by the stock and honor of my kin,
60 To strike him dead I hold it not a sin.

Capulet.

Why, how now, kinsman? Wherefore storm you so?

Tybalt.

Uncle, this is a Montague, our foe,
A villain, that is hither come in spite
To scorn at our solemnity this night.

Capulet.

65 Young Romeo is it?

Tybalt.   'Tis he, that villain Romeo.

Capulet.

Content thee, gentle coz, let him alone.
'A bears him like a portly° gentleman,
And, to say truth, Verona brags of him
To be a virtuous and well-governed youth.

---

41. ward: minor.

42. *In some productions, Romeo puts his torch down here, to draw our attention to his urgent question. Where would Juliet be on stage at this point?*

51. measure: dance.

52. rude: rough or simple.

54. *What has happened to Romeo?*

55. *Why would we feel a sense of fear, when we see Tybalt stepping onto center stage again?*

57. antic face: grotesque mask.

58. fleer: jeer.

67. portly: dignified.

70　　I would not for the wealth of all this town
　　　Here in my house do him disparagement.
　　　Therefore be patient; take no note of him.
　　　It is my will, the which if thou respect,
　　　Show a fair presence and put off these frowns,
75　　An ill-beseeming semblance for a feast.
　Tybalt.
　　　It fits when such a villain is a guest.
　　　I'll not endure him.
　Capulet.　　　　　　　He shall be endured.
　　　What, goodman° boy! I say he shall. Go to!°
　　　Am I the master here, or you? Go to!
80　　You'll not endure him, God shall mend my soul!
　　　You'll make a mutiny among my guests!
　　　You will set cock-a-hoop.° You'll be the man!
　Tybalt.
　　　Why, uncle, 'tis a shame.
　Capulet.　　　　　　　Go to, go to!
　　　You are a saucy boy. Is't so, indeed?
85　　This trick may chance to scathe° you. I know what.
　　　You must contrary me! Marry, 'tis time—
　　　Well said, my hearts!—You are a princox°—go!
　　　Be quiet, or—More light, more light!—For shame!
　　　I'll make you quiet. What!—Cheerly, my hearts!
　Tybalt.
90　　Patience perforce° with willful choler° meeting
　　　Makes my flesh tremble in their different greeting.
　　　I will withdraw; but this intrusion shall,
　　　Now seeming sweet, convert to bitt'rest gall.　*[Exit.]*
　Romeo.
　　　If I profane with my unworthiest hand
95　　　This holy shrine, the gentle sin is this:°
　　　My lips, two blushing pilgrims, ready stand
　　　　To smooth that rough touch with a tender kiss.
　Juliet.
　　　Good pilgrim, you do wrong your hand too much,
　　　Which mannerly devotion shows in this;
100　　For saints have hands that pilgrims' hands do touch,
　　　　And palm to palm is holy palmers'° kiss.
　Romeo.
　　　Have not saints lips, and holy palmers too?
　Juliet.
　　　Ay, pilgrim, lips that they must use in prayer.
　Romeo.
　　　O, then, dear saint, let lips do what hands do!
105　　They pray; grant thou, lest faith turn to despair.
　Juliet.
　　　Saints do not move,° though grant for prayers' sake.

77. *What is Capulet's sensible reply to Tybalt's hostility? What feelings is Capulet revealing in his next speeches? Have Capulet's feelings about the Montagues changed since Scene 1?*
78. goodman boy: a scornful phrase. *Goodman* is below the rank of gentleman; *boy* is insulting. **Go to!:** similar to "Go on!" or "Cut it out!"
82. set cock-a-hoop: take the lead in starting trouble.

85. scathe: hurt.

87. princox: rude youngster.

90. patience perforce: enforced patience. **choler:** anger.

94. *In contrast to the raging Tybalt is Romeo, now on center stage with Juliet. Romeo takes Juliet's hand, and in their next 14 lines, the two young speakers' words form a sonnet. Romeo pretends to be a pilgrim going to a saint's shrine. Exactly where do the two young lovers use religious images to talk of their feelings for each other?*
95. the gentle sin is this: this is the sin of a gentleman.
98. *Romeo and Juliet bring the palms of their hands together here. What in their words suggests that this is what they are doing?*
101. palmers': pilgrims going to a holy place. They often carried palms to show they had been to the Holy Land.

106. do not move: do not make the first move.

Romeo.

Then move not while my prayer's effect I take.
Thus from my lips, by thine my sin is purged.

[*Kisses her.*]

Juliet.

Then have my lips the sin that they have took.

Romeo.

110   Sin from my lips? O trespass sweetly urged!
Give me my sin again. [*Kisses her.*]

Juliet.   You kiss by th' book.°

Nurse.

Madam, your mother craves a word with you.

Romeo.

What is her mother?

Nurse.   Marry, bachelor,
Her mother is the lady of the house,

115   And a good lady, and a wise and virtuous.
I nursed her daughter that you talked withal.°
I tell you, he that can lay hold of her
Shall have the chinks.°

Romeo.   Is she a Capulet?
O dear account! My life is my foe's debt.°

Benvolio.

120   Away, be gone; the sport is at the best.

Romeo.

Ay, so I fear; the more is my unrest.

Capulet.

Nay, gentlemen, prepare not to be gone;
We have a trifling foolish banquet towards.°
Is it e'en so? Why then, I thank you all.

125   I thank you, honest gentlemen. Good night.
More torches here! Come on then; let's to bed.
Ah, sirrah, by my fay,° it waxes late;
I'll to my rest.   [*Exeunt all but* JULIET *and* NURSE.]

Juliet.

Come hither, nurse. What is yond gentleman?

Nurse.

130   The son and heir of old Tiberio.

Juliet.

What's he that now is going out of door?

Nurse.

Marry, that, I think, be young Petruchio.

Juliet.

What's he that follows there, that would not dance?

Nurse.

I know not.

108. *In the midst of the swirling dancers, Romeo and Juliet kiss. All of the audience's attention must be on this kiss. What would we fear as we watch, remembering that Tybalt is nearby?*

111. You kiss by th' book: you take my words literally (to get more kisses).

112. *As the Nurse interrupts, the dance ends. Juliet runs off, and Romeo is left alone with the Nurse. What do we know about the Capulets' plans for Juliet that Romeo does not know?*

116. withal: with.

118. chinks: money.

119. My life is my foe's debt: my foe now owns my life.

121. *Romeo stands alone here horrified. What activity goes on around him?*

123. towards: in preparation.

127. fay: faith.

129. *Juliet has moved to the side of the stage. What feelings must she convey in this question? (She is* not *pointing to Romeo.)*

Juliet.

135   Go ask his name.—If he be married,
        My grave is like to be my wedding bed.

Nurse.

        His name is Romeo, and a Montague,
        The only son of your great enemy.

Juliet.

        My only love, sprung from my only hate!
140   Too early seen unknown, and known too late!
        Prodigious° birth of love it is to me
        That I must love a loathèd enemy.

141. **prodigious:** huge and monstrous.

Nurse.

        What's tis? what's tis?

Juliet.   A rhyme I learnt even now
        Of one I danced withal.

144. *What tone of voice would Juliet use here? What has she just realized?*

        [*One calls within, "Juliet."*]

Nurse.   Anon, anon!°
145   Come, let's away; the strangers all are gone.   [*Exeunt.*]

144. **anon:** at once.

Responding to the Play

Analyzing the Play

Act I

Identifying Facts

1. What lines in the Prologue tell you in advance what is going to happen to Romeo and Juliet by the play's end?
2. What does the Prologue say is the only thing that will end their parents' rage?
3. Who is Tybalt, and why is he dangerous?
4. What warning does the Prince give the street brawlers in Scene 1?
5. How does Mercutio in Scene 4 try to snap Romeo out of his depression over Rosaline?
6. Where do Romeo and Juliet meet?

Interpreting Meanings

7. The first scene of *Romeo and Juliet* is a brilliant example of how information can be conveyed through theatrical activity. Look at each segment within the first scene (Gregory-Sampson and the Montague servants; Benvolio-Tybalt; and the Prince's warning). Explain how each episode clarifies the forces at work in this story.
8. In Scene 1 we see that Romeo is a young man who, when he falls in love, falls hopelessly in love, even though in Scene 1 he is in love with the wrong girl. Later, Shakespeare will have Romeo meet Juliet. But before the playwright does this, he must set up obstacles, so that when they do meet and fall in love, we will, in effect, groan at the problems they are going to have to face. What problem or **complication** is presented in Scenes 2 and 3?
9. Scene 4 does not seem to advance the story. The friends could just as well have shown up at the party without this scene. It does have one distinct function, however, and that is to introduce us to Mercutio, who will play an important part in the story later. How would you

characterize Mercutio, based on what he has said and done so far? Is Mercutio a believable character? Have you known people like him?

10. Mercutio is used as a foil to Romeo. The word **foil** in drama means that a character or scene is set up as a contrast to another character or scene. This contrast makes the particular qualities of each character (or scene) stand out vividly. In what specific ways is Mercutio a foil to Romeo?

11. Scene 4 sets up a sense of **foreboding**—a feeling that something bad is about to happen. This feeling will hang over the rest of the story of these "star-crossed lovers." Identify Romeo's specific expressions of foreboding, as he sets off for the party in Scene 4.

12. The story is now under way, and a considerable amount of **suspense** has been generated by this time. If you were watching this play, what questions would you be asking at this point? Write out at least two of them.

13. The action of this play takes place in Italy in the fourteenth century. Which episodes could you imagine taking place today? Would any details have to change?

Analyzing Language and Vocabulary

Shakespeare's Vocabulary

As you see by the word list on page 601, many words in Shakespeare's plays are the same words we use today, but they have different meanings. Sometimes these older meanings are related to the meanings the words have today, but often the meanings are distinct. The word *humor*, for example, comes from a Latin word for "moisture" or "fluid." In Shakespeare's time, people believed there were four basic fluids, or humors, in the body which regulated one's temperament. These four fluids were blood, phlegm, yellow bile, and black bile. The word *humorous* eventually came to refer to another kind of temperament, one that is able to see comedy in situations. Use a dictionary to answer the following questions:

1. What kind of temperament would be *bilious*?
2. What kind of temperament would be *phlegmatic*?
3. If someone showed *choler,* what was he or she displaying?
4. If someone was *melancholy,* what fluid would he or she have too much of?

Here are some other questions on words in the list on page 601. Use a dictionary to find the answers.

1. What did the verb *mark* mean in Shakespeare's day?
2. What is the more common meaning of *mark* as a verb today?
3. What modern expression uses the word *mark* today to mean exactly what it did in Shakespeare's time?
4. Shakespeare's characters frequently wish each other "Good-den." What words are combined in this greeting? What words are combined in our word "goodbye"?
5. In Shakespeare's day, the name *Jack* was used to refer to a common man ("every man jack of them" would mean "every single one of them"). Can you think of three words or expressions used today in which Jack still means, more or less, "a common fellow"?
6. *Hap* in Shakespeare's time meant "luck" or "chance." How does our word *haphazard* still use this old sense of *hap*?

Act II

Enter CHORUS.

Chorus.
Now old desire doth in his deathbed lie,
   And young affection gapes to be his heir;
That fair° for which love groaned for and would die,
   With tender Juliet matched, is now not fair.
5 Now Romeo is beloved and loves again,
   Alike° bewitchèd by the charm of looks;
But to his foe supposed he must complain,°
   And she steal love's sweet bait from fearful hooks.
Being held a foe, he may not have access
10   To breathe such vows as lovers use to° swear,
And she as much in love, her means much less
   To meet her new belovèd anywhere;
But passion lends them power, time means, to meet,
Temp'ring extremities° with extreme sweet.°   [*Exit.*]

3. That fair: Rosaline.

6. Alike: both (both Romeo and Juliet).

7. complain: he must ask Juliet's father, his foe, for her hand in marriage.

10. use to: are used to.

14. extremities: difficulties. **extreme sweet:** very sweet delights.
14. *According to the Prologue, what has happened to Romeo's old love? What is his new problem? What line of the Prologue suggests why these young people fell in love?*

Scene 1. *Near Capulet's orchard.*

Enter ROMEO *alone.*

Romeo.
Can I go forward when my heart is here?
Turn back, dull earth, and find thy center° out.

[*Enter* BENVOLIO *with* MERCUTIO. ROMEO *retires.*]

Benvolio.
Romeo! My cousin Romeo! Romeo!
Mercutio.   He is wise
And, on my life, hath stol'n him home to bed.
Benvolio.
5 He ran this way and leapt this orchard wall.
Call, good Mercutio.
Mercutio.   Nay, I'll conjure too.
Romeo! Humors! Madman! Passion! Lover!
Appear thou in the likeness of a sigh;
Speak but one rhyme, and I am satisfied!
10 Cry but "Ay me!" pronounce but "love" and "dove";
Speak to my gossip° Venus one fair word,
One nickname for her purblind° son and heir,
Young Abraham Cupid,° he that shot so true
When King Cophetua loved the beggar maid!°

2. center: Juliet. The "dull earth" is Romeo, and Juliet is his soul.
Stage direction: *Though the stage direction says that Romeo "retires," Shakespeare did not mean for him to retire quietly, for a few lines later Benvolio says he was running. Romeo has often been played by actors in middle age and leaping over the wall has been a problem for them. Many older Romeos have in fact chosen to "retire" behind the wall. How might this wall be arranged on stage so that we continue to see Romeo hiding in Capulet's orchard and Benvolio and Mercutio in the lane?*

11. gossip: good friend. Venus is the goddess of love.
12. purblind: blind.
13. Young Abraham Cupid: to Mercutio, Romeo seems the very figure of love—old like Abraham in the Bible and young like Cupid.
14. When . . . maid: from a popular ballad.

15 He heareth not, he stirreth not, he moveth not;
    The ape is dead,° and I must conjure him.
    I conjure thee by Rosaline's bright eyes,
    By her high forehead and her scarlet lip,
    By her fine foot, straight leg, and quivering thigh,
20 And the demesnes° that there adjacent lie,
    That in thy likeness thou appear to us!

Benvolio.
    And if he hear thee, thou wilt anger him.

Mercutio.
    This cannot anger him. 'Twould anger him
    To raise a spirit in his mistress' circle°
25 Of some strange nature, letting it there stand
    Till she had laid it and conjured it down.
    That were some spite;° my invocation
    Is fair and honest: in his mistress' name,
    I conjure only but to raise up him.

Benvolio.
30 Come, he hath hid himself among these trees
    To be consorted° with the humorous° night.
    Blind is his love and best befits the dark.

Mercutio.
    If love be blind, love cannot hit the mark.
    And wish his mistress were that kind of fruit
35 As maids call medlars when they laugh alone.
    O, Romeo, that she were, O that she were
    An open et cetera, thou a pop'rin pear!
    Romeo, good night. I'll to my truckle bed;
    This field bed is too cold for me to sleep.
40 Come, shall we go?

Benvolio.   Go then, for 'tis in vain
    To seek him here that means not to be found.

                              [*Exit with others.*]

16. The ape is dead: Romeo is "playing" dead.

20. demesnes: domains.

? 22. *What is Benvolio's tone here? Why would Romeo be angry at Mercutio's remarks?*

24. circle: magical place.

27. spite: cause to be angry.

31. consorted: familiar. **humorous:** damp.

Scene 2. *Capulet's orchard.*

Romeo (*coming forward*).
    He jests at scars that never felt a wound.

[*Enter* JULIET *at a window.*]

    But soft! What light through yonder window breaks?
    It is the East, and Juliet is the sun!
    Arise, fair sun, and kill the envious moon,
5   Who is already sick and pale with grief

? 1. *This begins the balcony scene, one of the most famous scenes in all dramatic literature. In 190 magical lines, the two lovers woo and win each other. (In the wide-open Elizabethan theater, the balcony scene presented no staging problems. In the modern proscenium theaters, however, it is often difficult to have a balcony high enough and yet still visible to people sitting in the last seats of the theater.) Romeo has heard all the joking. Whom is he referring to here, and what kind of "wound" is he talking about?*

That thou her maid° art far more fair than she.
Be not her maid, since she is envious.
Her vestal livery° is but sick and green,°
And none but fools do wear it. Cast it off.
10   It is my lady! O, it is my love!
O, that she knew she were!
She speaks, yet she says nothing. What of that?
Her eye discourses;° I will answer it.
I am too bold; 'tis not to me she speaks.
15   Two of the fairest stars in all the heaven,
Having some business, do entreat her eyes
To twinkle in their spheres till they return.
What if her eyes were there, they in her head?
The brightness of her cheek would shame those stars
20   As daylight doth a lamp; her eyes in heaven
Would through the airy region stream so bright
That birds would sing and think it were not night.
See how she leans her cheek upon her hand!
O, that I were a glove upon that hand,
25   That I might touch that cheek!

Juliet.   Ay me!

Romeo.   She speaks.
O, speak again, bright angel, for thou art
As glorious to this night, being o'er my head,
As is a wingèd messenger of heaven
Unto the white-upturnèd wond'ring eyes
30   Of mortals that fall back to gaze on him
When he bestrides the lazy puffing clouds
And sails upon the bosom of the air.

Juliet.
O Romeo, Romeo! Wherefore art thou Romeo?°
Deny thy father and refuse thy name;
35   Or, if thou wilt not, be but sworn my love,
And I'll no longer be a Capulet.

Romeo (*aside*).
Shall I hear more, or shall I speak at this?

Juliet.
'Tis but thy name that is my enemy.
Thou art thyself though, not° a Montague.
40   What's Montague? It is nor hand, nor foot,
Nor arm, nor face. O, be some other name
Belonging to a man.
What's in a name? That which we call a rose
By any other word would smell as sweet.
45   So Romeo would, were he not Romeo called,
Retain that dear perfection which he owes°
Without that title. Romeo, doff thy name;
And for thy name, which is no part of thee,

6. thou her maid: Juliet, whom Romeo sees as the servant of the virgin goddess Diana.
8. vestal livery: maidenly clothing. **sick and green:** unmarried girls supposedly had "greensickness," or anemia.

13. discourses: speaks.

[?] 25. *Romeo and Juliet rarely talk of each other in straightforward prose. What are some of the metaphors and images that Romeo uses to express his love here?*

33. In other words, "Why is your name Romeo?" (It is the name of her enemy.)

[?] 37. *Juliet does not know Romeo is standing beneath her balcony. What has Romeo now learned at once about her feelings for him?*
39. though, not: even if you were not.

[?] 42. *Short lines like this one usually indicate an interruption or pause. Here, Juliet pauses to think about a question. What does she say in answer to this question about the true significance of a "name"?*

46. owes: owns.

"*O Romeo, Romeo! Wherefore art thou Romeo?*"

Take all myself.

Romeo.   I take thee at thy word.

50   Call me but love, and I'll be new baptized;
Henceforth I never will be Romeo.

Juliet.
What man art thou, that, thus bescreened in night,
So stumblest on my counsel?°

Romeo.   By a name
I know not how to tell thee who I am.

55   My name, dear saint, is hateful to myself
Because it is an enemy to thee.
Had I it written, I would tear the word.

Juliet.
My ears have yet not drunk a hundred words
Of thy tongue's uttering, yet I know the sound.

60   Art thou not Romeo, and a Montague?

Romeo.
Neither, fair maid, if either thee dislike.

Juliet.
How camest thou higher, tell me, and wherefore?
The orchard walls are high and hard to climb,
And the place death, considering who thou art,

65   If any of my kinsmen find thee here.

Romeo.
With love's light wings did I o'erperch° these walls;
For stony limits cannot hold love out,
And what love can do, that dares love attempt.
Therefore thy kinsmen are no stop to me.

Juliet.
70   If they do see thee, they will murder thee.

Romeo.
Alack, there lies more peril in thine eye
Than twenty of their swords! Look thou but sweet,
And I am proof° against their enmity.

Juliet.
I would not for the world they saw thee here.

Romeo.
75   I have night's cloak to hide me from their eyes;
And but° thou love me, let them find me here.
My life were better ended by their hate
Than death proroguèd,° wanting of thy love.

Juliet.
By whose direction found'st thou out this place?

Romeo.
80   By Love, that first did prompt me to inquire.
He lent me counsel, and I lent him eyes.
I am no pilot; yet, wert thou as far
As that vast shore washed with the farthest sea,

53. counsel: private thoughts.

53. *How do you know Romeo has finally spoken aloud to Juliet? What are her feelings in this speech?*

66. o'erperch: fly over.

73. proof: armored.

74. *Juliet is practical. She fears Romeo will be murdered. What is Romeo's tone—is he also fearful and cautious, or is he reckless and elated?*

76. but: if only.

78. prorogued: postponed.

78. *The two lovers will repeatedly remind us that they prefer death to separation. What does this speech tell us of Romeo's intentions? Do you think he is seriously thinking of death here, or is he being impulsive and exaggerating—as many people do when they've fallen head over heels in love?*

I should adventure for such merchandise.

Juliet.

85   Thou knowest the mask of night is on my face;
      Else would a maiden blush bepaint my cheek
      For that which thou hast heard me speak tonight.
      Fain would I dwell on form—fain, fain deny
      What I have spoke; but farewell compliment!°

90   Dost thou love me? I know thou wilt say "Ay";
      And I will take thy word. Yet, if thou swear'st,
      Thou mayst prove false. At lovers' perjuries,
      They say Jove laughs. O gentle Romeo,
      If thou dost love, pronounce it faithfully.

95   Or if thou thinkest I am too quickly won,
      I'll frown and be perverse and say thee nay,
      So thou wilt woo; but else, not for the world.
      In truth, fair Montague, I am too fond,°
      And therefore thou mayst think my havior° light;

100   But trust me, gentleman, I'll prove more true
      Than those that have more cunning to be strange.°
      I should have been more strange, I must confess,
      But that thou overheard'st, ere I was ware,
      My truelove passion. Therefore pardon me,

105   And not impute this yielding to light love,
      Which the dark night hath so discoverèd.°

Romeo.

      Lady, by yonder blessèd moon I vow,
      That tips with silver all these fruit-tree tops—

Juliet.

      O, swear not by the moon, the inconstant moon,

110   That monthly changes in her circle orb,
      Lest that thy love prove likewise variable.

Romeo.

      What shall I swear by?

Juliet.   Do not swear at all;
      Or if thou wilt, swear by thy gracious self,
      Which is the god of my idolatry,

115   And I'll believe thee.

Romeo.   If my heart's dear love—

Juliet.

      Well, do not swear. Although I joy in thee,
      I have no joy of this contract tonight.
      It is too rash, too unadvised, too sudden;
      Too like the lightning, which doth cease to be

120   Ere one can say it lightens. Sweet, good night!
      This bud of love, by summer's ripening breath,
      May prove a beauteous flower when next we meet.
      Good night, good night! As sweet repose and rest
      Come to thy heart as that within my breast!

85. *Juliet's thoughts race now, and she probably speaks rapidly here. Where does she shift from embarrassment to frankness, to pleading, to anxiety, to doubt? Why is she worried that Romeo will think poorly of her?*

89. compliment: good manners.

98. fond: affectionate, tender.
99. havior: behavior.

101. strange: aloof or cold.

106. discovered: revealed.

109. *Why is Juliet afraid of having Romeo swear by the moon? Do you imagine this speech as comic, or would you make Juliet sound genuinely frightened?*

120. *Romeo is quick with vows and promises. Why has Juliet become fearful and cautious?*

Romeo.
125　　O, wilt thou leave me so unsatisfied?
Juliet.
　　　What satisfaction canst thou have tonight?
Romeo.
　　　The exchange of thy love's faithful vow for mine.
Juliet.
　　　I gave thee mine before thou didst request it;
　　　And yet I would it were to give again.
Romeo.
130　　Wouldst thou withdraw it? For what purpose, love?
Juliet.
　　　But to be frank° and give it thee again.
　　　And yet I wish but for the thing I have.
　　　My bounty° is as boundless as the sea,
　　　My love as deep; the more I give to thee,
135　　The more I have, for both are infinite.
　　　I hear some noise within. Dear love, adieu!

[NURSE *calls within.*]

　　　Anon, good nurse! Sweet Montague, be true.
　　　Stay but a little, I will come again.　　　[*Exit.*]
Romeo.
　　　O blessèd, blessèd night! I am afeard,
140　　Being in night, all this is but a dream,
　　　Too flattering-sweet to be substantial.

[*Enter* JULIET *again.*]

Juliet.
　　　Three words, dear Romeo, and good night indeed.
　　　If that thy bent° of love be honorable,
　　　Thy purpose marriage, send me word tomorrow,
145　　By one that I'll procure to come to thee,
　　　Where and what time thou wilt perform the rite;
　　　And all my fortunes at thy foot I'll lay
　　　And follow thee my lord throughout the world.
Nurse (*within*). Madam!
Juliet.
150　　I come anon.—But if thou meanest not well,
　　　I do beseech thee—
Nurse (*within*). Madam!
Juliet.　　　　　　　By and by I come.—
　　　To cease thy strife° and leave me to my grief.
　　　Tomorrow will I send.
Romeo.　　　　　　　So thrive my soul—
Juliet.
155　　A thousand times good night!　　　[*Exit.*]

131. **frank:** generous.

133. **bounty:** capacity for giving.

143. **bent:** intention.

? 148. *What is Juliet making clear to Romeo here? Where does she show that she still fears he may be false with her?*

153. **strife:** efforts (to win her).

? 154. *With this fervent vow, Romeo swears by his immortal soul. What lines that follow indicate that Romeo turns around and heads away from her balcony?*

Romeo.

A thousand times the worse, to want thy light!
Love goes toward love as schoolboys from their books;
But love from love, toward school with heavy looks.

[*Enter* JULIET *again*.]

Juliet.

Hist! Romeo, hist! O for a falc'ner's voice
160 To lure this tassel gentle° back again!
Bondage is hoarse° and may not speak aloud,
Else would I tear the cave where Echo° lies
And make her airy tongue more hoarse than mine
With repetition of "My Romeo!"

Romeo.

165 It is my soul that calls upon my name.
How silver-sweet sound lovers' tongues by night,
Like softest music to attending ears!

Juliet.

Romeo!

Romeo.

      My sweet?

Juliet.

          What o'clock tomorrow
Shall I send to thee?

Romeo.

          By the hour of nine.

Juliet.

170 I will not fail. 'Tis twenty years till then.
I have forgot why I did call thee back.

Romeo.

Let me stand here till thou remember it.

Juliet.

I shall forget, to have thee still stand there,
Rememb'ring how I love thy company.

Romeo.

175 And I'll still stay, to have thee still forget,
Forgetting any other home but this.

Juliet.

'Tis almost morning. I would have thee gone—
And yet no farther than a wanton's° bird,
That lets it hop a little from his hand,
180 Like a poor prisoner in his twisted gyves,°
And with a silken thread plucks it back again,
So loving-jealous of his liberty.

Romeo.

I would I were thy bird.

Juliet.

          Sweet, so would I.
Yet I should kill thee with much cherishing.
185 Good night, good night! Parting is such sweet sorrow
That I shall say good night till it be morrow.   [*Exit*.]

160. tassel gentle: a male falcon.

161. Bondage is hoarse: Juliet is in "bondage" to her parents and must whisper.

162. Echo: a mythical girl who could only repeat others' final words.

178. wanton's: careless child's.

180. gyves: threads holding the bird captive.

184. *What terrible future event does this line foreshadow?*

186. *Why is parting "sweet" to Juliet? (Is she enjoying this prolonged farewell?)*

636 **William Shakespeare**

Romeo.

Sleep dwell upon thine eyes, peace in thy breast!
Would I were sleep and peace, so sweet to rest!
Hence will I to my ghostly friar's° close cell,
His help to crave and my dear hap° to tell.   [*Exit.*]

190

Scene 3. *Friar Laurence's cell.*

Enter FRIAR LAURENCE *alone, with a basket.*

Friar.

The gray-eyed morn smiles on the frowning night,
Check'ring the eastern clouds with streaks of light;
And fleckèd darkness like a drunkard reels
From forth day's path and Titan's burning wheels.°
Now, ere the sun advance his burning eye
The day to cheer and night's dank dew to dry,
I must upfill this osier cage° of ours
With baleful° weeds and precious-juicèd flowers.
The earth that's Nature's mother is her tomb.
What is her burying grave, that is her womb;
And from her womb children of divers kind
We sucking on her natural bosom find,
Many for many virtues excellent,
None but for some, and yet all different.
O, mickle° is the powerful grace that lies
In plants, herbs, stones, and their true qualities;
For naught so vile that on the earth doth live
But to the earth some special good doth give;
Nor aught so good but, strained° from that fair use,
Revolts from true birth,° stumbling on abuse.
Virtue itself turns vice, being misapplied,
And vice sometime by action dignified.

[*Enter* ROMEO.]

Within the infant rind° of this weak flower
Poison hath residence and medicine° power;
For this, being smelt, with that part cheers each part;°
Being tasted, stays all senses with the heart.
Two such opposèd kings encamp them still°
In man as well as herbs—grace and rude will;
And where the worser is predominant,
Full soon the canker° death eats up that plant.

Romeo.

Good morrow, father.

Friar.   Benedicite!°

What early tongue so sweet saluteth me?
Young son, it argues a distemperèd head°

5

10

15

20

25

30

---

189. **ghostly friar's:** spiritual father's.
190. **hap:** luck.

1. *In the absence of lighting, Shakespeare had his characters "set the stage" in their speeches. What "scene" does the Friar set? How are his images of night different from Romeo's images in his "O blessed, blessed night" speech in the last scene?*
4. **Titan's burning wheels:** wheels of the sun-god's chariot.
7. **osier cage:** woven of willow branches.
8. **baleful:** evil or poisonous.

15. **mickle:** great.

19. **strained:** turned aside.
20. **true birth:** true purpose.

22. *What details in the Friar's speech casually suggest that these herbs and flowers have qualities that can heal or kill? Where does the Friar remind us that good can turn to evil, and evil turn to good?*
23. **rind:** skin.
23. *Romeo enters quietly, unseen by the Friar. As the Friar talks of the flower he has picked, how might the audience become uneasy about what might happen to Romeo and Juliet?*
24. **medicine:** medicinal.
25. **For . . . part:** when the flower is smelled each part of the body is stimulated.
27. **still:** always.
30. **canker:** cankerworm, a larva that feeds on leaves.
31. **Benedicite!** (bā′nā·dē′chē·tā): Latin for "Bless you!"

33. **distempered head:** troubled mind.

So soon to bid good morrow to thy bed.
35 Care keeps his watch in every old man's eye,
And where care lodges, sleep will never lie;
But where unbruisèd° youth with unstuffed° brain
Doth couch his limbs, there golden sleep doth reign.
Therefore thy earliness doth me assure
40 Thou art uproused with some distemp'rature;
Or if not so, then here I hit it right—
Our Romeo hath not been in bed tonight.

Romeo.

That last is true. The sweeter rest was mine.

Friar.

God pardon sin! Wast thou with Rosaline?

Romeo.

45 With Rosaline, my ghostly father? No.
I have forgot that name and that name's woe.

Friar.

That's my good son! But where hast thou been then?

Romeo.

I'll tell thee ere thou ask it me again.
I have been feasting with mine enemy,
50 Where on a sudden one hath wounded me
That's by me wounded. Both our remedies
Within thy help and holy physic° lies.
I bear no hatred, blessèd man, for, lo,
My intercession° likewise steads° my foe.

Friar.

55 Be plain, good son, and homely° in thy drift.
Riddling confession finds but riddling shrift.°

Romeo.

Then plainly know my heart's dear love is set
On the fair daughter of rich Capulet;
As mine on hers, so hers is set on mine,
60 And all combined,° save what thou must combine
By holy marriage. When and where and how
We met, we wooed, and made exchange of vow,
I'll tell thee as we pass; but this I pray,
That thou consent to marry us today.

Friar.

65 Holy Saint Francis! What a change is here!
Is Rosaline, that thou didst love so dear,
So soon forsaken? Young men's love then lies
Not truly in their hearts, but in their eyes.
Jesu Maria! What a deal of brine
70 Hath washed thy sallow cheeks for Rosaline!
How much salt water thrown away in waste
To season° love, that of it doth not taste!
The sun not yet thy signs from heaven clears,

37. unbruised: innocent. **unstuffed:** untroubled.

? 44. *Does the Friar approve? How should he speak about this to Romeo?*

52. holy physic: the Friar's power (physic) to make Romeo and Juliet husband and wife.
54. intercession: request. **steads:** helps.

55. homely: plain.

56. shrift: forgiveness (in the confessional).

? 56. *As we have seen, the play is basically written in blank verse, but Shakespeare varies his verse forms from time to time. The Prologues are written in sonnet form. The endings of scenes are marked by rhymed couplets. What is the rhyme scheme of this dialogue?*
60. combined: agreed.

? 65. *In the early part of the play, Shakespeare keeps Romeo's intense love in some kind of perspective by letting us see how others regard him. We have heard Mercutio's sarcastic "The ape is dead." How does Friar Laurence continue with this scolding and ridicule? What actions do you imagine Romeo engaged in as he listens to the priest?*

72. season: preserve (keep fresh, as food was seasoned to keep it from spoiling).

Thy old groans ring yet in mine ancient ears.
75 Lo, here upon thy cheek the stain doth sit
Of an old tear that is not washed off yet.
If e'er thou wast thyself, and these woes thine,
Thou and these woes were all for Rosaline.
And art thou changed? Pronounce this sentence then:
80 Women may fall when there's no strength in men.

Romeo.
Thou chid'st me oft for loving Rosaline.

Friar.
For doting, not for loving, pupil mine.

Romeo.
And bad'st me bury love.

Friar.   Not in a grave
To lay one in, another out to have.

Romeo.
85 I pray thee chide me not. Her I love now
Doth grace° for grace and love for love allow.
The other did not so.

Friar.   O she knew well
Thy love did read by rote, that could not spell.°
But come, young waverer, come go with me.
90 In one respect I'll thy assistant be;
For this alliance may so happy prove
To turn your households' rancor to pure love.

Romeo.
O, let us hence! I stand on° sudden haste.

Friar.
Wisely and slow. They stumble that run fast. [*Exeunt.*]

86. grace: favor.

88. Romeo recited words of love without understanding them.

92. *In these times, it was not at all unusual to form alliances and settle disputes by arranging marriages. How does this explain Friar Laurence's decision to help the young couple?*
93. stand on: I am firm about.
94. *Romeo has gotten what he wants and he dashes off stage. But how do the Friar's last words leave us with a sense that danger lies ahead?*

Scene 4. *A street.*

Enter BENVOLIO *and* MERCUTIO.

Mercutio.
Where the devil should this Romeo be?
Came he not home tonight?

Benvolio.
Not to his father's. I spoke with his man.

Mercutio.
Why, that same pale hardhearted wench, that
    Rosaline,
5 Torments him so that he will sure run mad.

Benvolio.
Tybalt, the kinsman to old Capulet,
Hath sent a letter to his father's house.

7. *Now that the play's love story seems to be heading toward a marriage, Shakespeare turns again to the feuding families. Why is Tybalt looking for Romeo?*

Mercutio. A challenge, on my life.

Benvolio. Romeo will answer it.

10 **Mercutio.** Any man that can write may answer a letter.

Benvolio. Nay, he will answer the letter's master, how he dares, being dared.

Mercutio. Alas, poor Romeo, he is already dead: stabbed with a white wench's black eye; run through the ear
15 with a love song; the very pin° of his heart cleft with the blind bow-boy's butt-shaft; and is he a man to encounter Tybalt?

Benvolio. Why, what is Tybalt?

Mercutio. More than Prince of Cats.° O, he's the coura-
20 geous captain of compliments. He fights as you sing pricksong°—keeps time, distance, and proportion; he rests his minim rests,° one, two and the third in your bosom! The very butcher of a silk button, a duelist, a duelist! A gentleman of the very first house,° of the
25 first and second cause.° Ah, the immortal passado!° The punto reverso!° The hay!°

Benvolio. The what?

Mercutio. The pox of° such antic, lisping, affecting fantasticoes°—these new tuners of accent! "By Jesu,
30 a very good blade! A very tall° man! A very good whore!" Why, is not this a lamentable thing, grandsir, that we should be thus afflicted with these strange flies, these fashionmongers, these pardon-me's, who stand so much on the new form° that they cannot sit
35 at ease on the old bench? O, their bones,° their bones!

[*Enter* ROMEO.]

Benvolio. Here comes Romeo! Here comes Romeo!

Mercutio. Without his roe,° like a dried herring. O flesh, flesh, how art thou fishified! Now is he for the numbers°
that Petrarch flowed in. Laura, to his lady, was a
40 kitchen wench (marry, she had a better love to be-rhyme her), Dido° a dowdy, Cleopatra a gypsy, Helen and Hero hildings° and harlots, Thisbe a gray eye° or so, but not to the purpose. Signior Romeo, bonjour! There's a French salutation to your French slop.° You
45 gave us the counterfeit° fairly last night.

Romeo. Good morrow to you both. What counterfeit did I give you?

Mercutio. The slip, sir, the slip. Can you not conceive?°

Romeo. Pardon, good Mercutio. My business was great,
50 and in such a case as mine a man may strain courtesy.

Mercutio. That's as much as to say, such a case° as yours constrains a man to bow in the hams.

Romeo. Meaning, to curtsy.

---

15. **pin:** center (of a target).

19. **Prince of Cats:** "Tybalt" is the name of a cat in a fable who is known for his slyness.
21. **sing pricksong:** sing with great attention to every note on a printed sheet of music.
22. **minim rests:** shortest rests in a measure.
24. **first house:** first rank.
25. **of . . . cause:** dueling terms ("first" offense is taken; "second" a challenge is given). **passado:** lunge.
26. **punto reverso:** backhand stroke. **hay:** home thrust.
🔲 26. *Mercutio mocks Tybalt's dueling style, but what do we also now know about Tybalt's ability to fight? What do you picture Mercutio doing as he talks of duels? Is he also concerned for Romeo? How do his actions change in the next speech as he mocks the "fashion plates" of his day?*
28. **pox of:** the plague on (a curse on).
29. **fantasticoes:** dandies; men who affect French ways.
30. **tall:** brave.
34. **new form:** new fashions.
35. **bones:** a pun on their use of the French *bon.*
37. **roe:** a pun on roe, a female deer. Roe are also fish eggs, so Mercutio is also suggesting that Romeo has been made "gutless" by love.
38. **numbers:** verses. Petrarch was an Italian poet who wrote verses to a woman named Laura.
41. **Dido:** the famous queen of Carthage in the *Aeneid,* who loved Aeneas. (The women that follow were also great lovers in literature: Cleopatra was the Queen of Egypt loved by Antony; Helen of Troy was loved by Paris; Hero was loved by Leander; Thisbe was loved by Pyramus.)
42. **hildings:** good-for-nothings. **gray eye:** gleam in the eye.
44. **slop:** loose trousers then popular in France.
45. **counterfeit:** slip.
48. **conceive:** understand.
51. **a case:** set of clothes.
🔲 52. *Romeo is being lured by Mercutio to match wits. How can you tell that Romeo soon gets into the spirit of the game and for the moment forgets his romantic problems? In the following verbal duel, the two friends match wits by using puns.*

Mercutio. Thou hast most kindly hit it.

Romeo. A most courteous exposition.

Mercutio. Nay, I am the very pink of courtesy.

Romeo. Pink for flower.

Mercutio. Right.

Romeo. Why, then is my pump° well-flowered.°

Mercutio. Sure wit, follow me this jest now till thou hast worn out thy pump, that, when the single sole of it is worn, the jest may remain, after the wearing, solely singular.

Romeo. O single-soled jest, solely singular for the singleness!°

Mercutio. Come between us, good Benvolio! My wits faint.

Romeo. Swits° and spurs, swits and spurs; or I'll cry a match.

Mercutio. Nay, if our wits run the wild-goose chase, I am done; for thou hast more of the wild goose in one of thy wits than, I am sure, I have in my whole five. Was I with you there for the goose?°

Romeo. Thou wast never with me for anything when thou wast not there for the goose.°

Mercutio. I will bite thee by the ear for that jest.

Romeo. Nay, good goose, bite not!

Mercutio. Thy wit is a very bitter sweeting;° it is a most sharp sauce.

Romeo. And is it not, then, well served in to a sweet goose?°

Mercutio. O, here's a wit of cheveril,° that stretches from an inch narrow to an ell broad!°

Romeo. I stretch it out for that word "broad," which, added to the goose, proves thee far and wide a broad° goose.

Mercutio. Why, is not this better now than groaning for love? Now art thou sociable, now art thou Romeo; now art thou what thou art, by art as well as by nature. For this driveling love is like a great natural° that runs lolling up and down to hide his bauble° in a hole.

Benvolio. Stop there, stop there!

Mercutio. Thou desirest me to stop in my tale against the hair.°

Benvolio. Thou wouldst else have made thy tale large.°

Mercutio. O, thou art deceived! I would have made it short; for I was come to the whole depth of my tale, and meant indeed to occupy the argument no longer.

Romeo. Here's goodly gear!°

[*Enter* NURSE *and her man* PETER.]

59. **pump:** shoe. **well-flowered:** a pun on "well-floored." Men's shoes were "pinked," or cut, with decorations.

65. **singleness:** a pun on "silliness."

? 67. *What exaggerated action do you see Mercutio involved in here?*
68. **Swits:** switches (a pun on "wits").

73. **Was . . . goose?:** Was I right in calling you a goose?

75. **goose:** here, a woman.

78. **bitter sweeting:** a kind of apple.

81. **sweet goose:** sour sauce was considered best for sweet meat.
82. **cheveril:** kid-leather (another reference to fashion).
83. **ell broad:** 45 inches across.

85. **broad:** gross.

90. **natural:** idiot.
91. **bauble:** literally, a trinket or cheap jewel.
? 91. *What does the loyal Mercutio think he has accomplished for Romeo by this game of wits?*
94. **against the hair:** against my inclination.
95. **large:** indecent.

99. **gear:** matter for sport and teasing.

Romeo and Juliet **Act II: Scene 4   641**

100   A sail, a sail!

Mercutio. Two, two! A shirt and a smock.°

Nurse. Peter!

Peter. Anon.

Nurse. My fan, Peter.

105 **Mercutio.** Good Peter, to hide her face; for her fan's the fairer face.

Nurse. God ye good morrow, gentlemen.

Mercutio. God ye good-den,° fair gentlewoman.

Nurse. Is it good-den?

110 **Mercutio.** 'Tis no less, I tell ye; for the bawdy hand of the dial is now upon the prick of noon.

Nurse. Out upon you! What a man are you!

Romeo. One, gentlewoman, that God hath made, himself to mar.

115 **Nurse.** By my troth, it is well said. "For himself to mar," quoth 'a? Gentlemen, can any of you tell me where I may find the young Romeo?

Romeo. I can tell you; but young Romeo will be older when you have found him than he was when you

120 sought him. I am the youngest of that name, for fault of a worse.°

Nurse. You say well.

Mercutio. Yea, is the worst well? Very well took, i' faith! Wisely, wisely.

125 **Nurse.** If you be he, sir, I desire some confidence with you.

Benvolio. She will endite° him to some supper.

Mercutio. A bawd, a bawd, a bawd! So ho!

Romeo. What hast thou found?

130 **Mercutio.** No hare,° sir; unless a hare, sir, in a Lenten pie,° that is something stale and hoar° ere it be spent.

[*He walks by them and sings.*]

An old hare hoar,
And an old hare hoar,
Is very good meat in Lent;
135   But a hare that is hoar
Is too much for a score
When it hoars ere it be spent.

Romeo, will you come to your father's? We'll to dinner thither.

140 **Romeo.** I will follow you.

Mercutio. Farewell, ancient lady. Farewell (*singing*) "Lady, lady, lady." [*Exeunt* MERCUTIO, BENVOLIO.]

Nurse. I pray you, sir, what saucy merchant was this that was so full of his ropery?°

145 **Romeo.** A gentleman, nurse, that loves to hear himself

---

100. *Having established the fact that Tybalt is looking for Romeo, we now return to the love story, with this comic scene involving the Nurse and Peter and the young men. The previous scene might well have seemed to drag if we had not in a sense been promised a confrontation between Romeo and Tybalt. Now the young men laugh openly at the Nurse as she and her servant sail on stage. What does Romeo's comment suggest about her size?*

101. A shirt and a smock: a man (shirt) and a woman (smock).

108. God ye good-den: God grant you a good evening.

121. For fault of a worse: for want of a better.

127. endite: invite. Benvolio mocks the Nurse, for she said "confidence" but meant "conference."

129. *Mercutio, who knows nothing of Romeo's plan to marry Juliet, thinks the Nurse has come to arrange a secret date between Romeo and her mistress. He mocks the Nurse by suggesting that she is a bawd, or "procurer" for Juliet—not a compliment to a woman at all. Mercutio dominates the stage when he's on it. What do you imagine he's doing here?*

130. hare: slang for "a morally loose woman."

131. Lenten pie: a rabbit pie, eaten sparingly during Lent, so that it is around for a long time and gets stale. **hoar:** gray with mould (the old Nurse has gray hair).

142. *Mercutio teases the Nurse about being a flirt by singing the refrain from an old song about a "chaste" lady. The Nurse is outraged and struggles to keep her fine airs. How does Romeo try to calm her down?*

144. ropery: the Nurse means "roguery," or vulgar ways.

---

talk and will speak more in a minute than he will stand to in a month.

Nurse. And 'a speak anything against me, I'll take him down, and 'a were lustier than he is, and twenty such Jacks; and if I cannot, I'll find those that shall. Scurvy knave! I am none of his flirt-gills;° I am none of his skainsmates.° And thou must stand by too, and suffer every knave to use me at his pleasure!

Peter. I saw no man use you at his pleasure. If I had, my weapon should quickly have been out, I warrant you. I dare draw as soon as another man, if I see occasion in a good quarrel, and the law on my side.

Nurse. Now, afore God, I am so vexed that every part about me quivers. Scurvy knave! Pray you, sir, a word; and, as I told you, my young lady bid me inquire you out. What she bid me say, I will keep to myself; but first let me tell ye, if ye should lead her in a fool's paradise, as they say, it were a very gross kind of behavior, as they say; for the gentlewoman is young; and therefore, if you should deal double with her, truly it were an ill thing to be offered to any gentlewoman, and very weak dealing.

Romeo. Nurse, commend me to thy lady and mistress. I protest unto thee—

Nurse. Good heart, and i' faith I will tell her as much. Lord, Lord, she will be a joyful woman.

Romeo. What wilt thou tell her, nurse? Thou dost not mark° me.

Nurse. I will tell her, sir, that you do protest, which, as I take it, is a gentlemanlike offer.

Romeo.
Bid her devise
Some means to come to shrift this afternoon;
And there she shall at Friar Laurence' cell
Be shrived° and married. Here is for thy pains.

Nurse. No, truly, sir; not a penny.

Romeo. Go to! I say you shall.

Nurse. This afternoon, sir? Well, she shall be there.

Romeo.
And stay, good nurse, behind the abbey wall.
Within this hour my man shall be with thee
And bring thee cords made like a tackled stair,°
Which to the high topgallant° of my joy
Must be my convoy° in the secret night.
Farewell. Be trusty, and I'll quit° thy pains.
Farewell. Commend me to thy mistress.

Nurse.
Now God in heaven bless thee! Hark you, sir.

150
155
160
165
170
175
180
185
190

151. flirt-gills: flirty girls.

152. skainsmates: loose women.

153. *Whom is the Nurse talking to here?*

159. *Which part of this speech is delivered to Mercutio? Where does the Nurse turn to Romeo? How might her manner change?*

167. *What warning does the Nurse give Romeo, and why do you think she does this?*

173. mark: listen to.

179. shrived: forgiven of her sins.

180. *The Nurse is all too ready to snatch the coins Romeo offers her. By taking the money, what part has she agreed to play in the elopement?*

185. tackled stair: rope ladder.

186. topgallant: highest platform on the topmast of a ship.
187. convoy: means of conveyance.
188. quit: repay.

Romeo.
What say'st thou, my dear nurse?

Nurse.
Is your man secret? Did you ne'er hear say,
Two may keep counsel, putting one away?

Romeo.
Warrant thee my man's as true as steel.

195 **Nurse.** Well, sir, my mistress is the sweetest lady. Lord,
Lord! When 'twas a little prating thing—O, there is a
nobleman in town, one Paris, that would fain lay knife
aboard;° but she, good soul, had as lieve see a toad, a
very toad, as see him. I anger her sometimes, and tell
200 her that Paris is the properer man; but I'll warrant
you, when I say so, she looks as pale as any clout° in
the versal° world. Doth not rosemary and Romeo begin
both with a letter?

Romeo. Aye, nurse; what of that? Both with an R.

205 **Nurse.** Ah, mocker! That's the dog's name.° R is for the—
no; I know it begins with some other letter; and she
hath the prettiest sententious° of it, of you and rosemary, that it would do you good to hear it.

Romeo. Commend me to thy lady.

210 **Nurse.** Ay, a thousand times. [*Exit* ROMEO.] Peter!

Peter. Anon.

Nurse. Before, and apace.   [*Exit after* PETER.]

198. lay knife aboard: take a slice (lay claim to Juliet).

201. clout: rag (cloth).
202. versal: universal (slang).
202. *The Nurse becomes confiding as she rattles on and on. But what trouble for Romeo and Juliet does she talk about? What is Juliet's feeling for Paris now?*
205. In other words, a dog's growl has an "R" sound (r-r-r-r).

207. sententious: The Nurse means "sentence."

212. *Romeo abruptly rushes offstage, leaving the Nurse with Peter. She bossily pushes Peter onward, to show that she still has authority over someone. How has this scene advanced the love story? What action has been set in motion?*

Scene 5. *Capulet's orchard.*

Enter JULIET.

Juliet.
The clock struck nine when I did send the nurse;
In half an hour she promised to return.
Perchance she cannot meet him. That's not so.
O, she is lame! Love's heralds should be thoughts,
5 Which ten times faster glide than the sun's beams
Driving back shadows over low'ring hills.
Therefore do nimble-pinioned doves° draw Love,
And therefore hath the wind-swift Cupid wings.
Now is the sun upon the highmost hill
10 Of this day's journey, and from nine till twelve
Is three long hours; yet she is not come.
Had she affections and warm youthful blood,

7. nimble-pinioned doves: nimble-winged doves were said to draw the chariot of Venus, the goddess of love.

She would be as swift in motion as a ball;
My words would bandy her° to my sweet love,
15 And his to me.
But old folks, many feign as they were dead—
Unwieldy, slow, heavy, and pale as lead.

[*Enter* NURSE *and* PETER.]

O God, she comes! O honey nurse, what news?
Hast thou met with him? Send thy man away.
Nurse.
20 Peter, stay at the gate.   [*Exit* PETER.]
Juliet.
Now, good sweet nurse—O Lord, why lookest thou sad?
Though news be sad, yet tell them merrily;
If good, thou shamest the music of sweet news
By playing it to me with so sour a face.
Nurse.
25 I am aweary, give me leave awhile.
Fie, how my bones ache! What a jaunce° have I!
Juliet.
I would thou hadst my bones, and I thy news.
Nay, come, I pray thee speak. Good, good nurse, speak.
Nurse.
Jesu, what haste! Can you not stay° awhile?
30 Do you not see that I am out of breath?
Juliet.
How art thou out of breath when thou has breath
To say to me that thou art out of breath?
The excuse that thou dost make in this delay
Is longer than the tale thou dost excuse.
35 Is thy news good or bad? Answer to that.
Say either, and I'll stay the circumstance.°
Let me be satisfied, is't good or bad?
Nurse. Well, you have made a simple° choice; you know
not how to choose a man. Romeo? No, not he. Though
40 his face be better than any man's, yet his leg excels all
men's; and for a hand and a foot, and a body, though
they be not to be talked on, yet they are past compare.
He is not the flower of courtesy, but, I'll warrant him,
as gentle as a lamb. Go thy ways, wench; serve God.
45 What, have you dined at home?
Juliet.
No, no. But all this did I know before.
What says he of our marriage? What of that?
Nurse.
Lord, how my head aches! What a head have I!
It beats as it would fall in twenty pieces.

14. **bandy her:** hit (or send) her back and forth, like a tennis ball.

17. *Juliet has either run on stage or is standing on the balcony. What is her mood as she waits for the Nurse's return?*

26. **jaunce:** weary journey.

29. **stay:** wait.

30. *The actress playing the Nurse can interpret her actions here in several ways. She could be genuinely weary; she could be teasing Juliet; or she could be fearful about the part she has agreed to play in the elopement. How do you imagine the Nurse should play this scene?*

36. **stay the circumstance:** wait for the details.

38. **simple:** foolish.

38. *In comedy, a character is sometimes marked by one peculiarity, one characteristic which can always be counted on for a laugh. You push a button and you always get the same response. Such a character is sometimes called a "Jack-in-the-box" character. What is the Nurse's almost inevitable way of responding when she is asked for information?*

50 My back a'° t' other side—ah, my back, my back!
    Beshrew° your heart for sending me about
    To catch my death with jauncing up and down!
    Juliet.
        I' faith, I am sorry that thou art not well.
        Sweet, sweet, sweet nurse, tell me, what says my love?
55 **Nurse.** Your love says, like an honest gentleman, and a
        courteous, and a kind, and a handsome, and, I warrant,
        a virtuous—where is your mother?
    Juliet.
        Where is my mother? Why, she is within.
        Where should she be? How oddly thou repliest!
60   "Your love says, like an honest gentleman,
        'Where is your mother?' "
    Nurse.   O God's Lady dear!
        Are you so hot?° Marry come up, I trow.°
        Is this the poultice for my aching bones?
        Henceforward do your messages yourself.
    Juliet.
65   Here's such a coil!° Come, what says Romeo?
    Nurse.
        Have you got leave to go to shrift today?
    Juliet.
        I have.
    Nurse.
        Then hie you hence to Friar Laurence' cell;
        There stays a husband to make you a wife.
70   Now comes the wanton blood up in your cheeks:
        They'll be in scarlet straight at any news.
        Hie you to church; I must another way,
        To fetch a ladder, by the which your love
        Must climb a bird's nest soon when it is dark.
75   I am the drudge, and toil in your delight;
        But you shall bear the burden soon at night.
        Go; I'll to dinner; hie you to the cell.
    Juliet.
        Hie to high fortune! Honest nurse, farewell. [*Exeunt.*]

50. a': on.

51. Beshrew: shame on.

52. *What line here indicates that Juliet has tried to humor the Nurse by rubbing her back?*

61. *Juliet can play this scene in several ways. Do you imagine she is angry here? Or is she bewildered? Impatient? Or is she mocking the old Nurse?*
62. hot: angry. **Marry come up, I trow:** something like, "By the Virgin Mary, come off it, I swear."

65. coil: fuss.

69. *At last, the Nurse tells Juliet what she has been waiting for. What do you see Juliet doing as she hears the news?*

78. *Even Juliet puns. What pun does she exit on? What is her mood?*

Scene 6. *Friar Laurence's cell.*

Enter FRIAR LAURENCE *and* ROMEO.

Friar.
    So smile the heavens upon this holy act
    That afterhours with sorrow chide us not!

Romeo.

Amen, amen! But come what sorrow can,
It cannot countervail° the exchange of joy
5   That one short minute gives me in her sight.
Do thou but close our hands with holy words,
Then love-devouring death do what he dare—
It is enough I may but call her mine.

Friar.

These violent delights have violent ends
10 And in their triumph die, like fire and powder,°
Which, as they kiss, consume. The sweetest honey
Is loathsome in his own deliciousness
And in the taste confounds° the appetite.
Therefore love moderately: long love doth so;
15 Too swift arrives as tardy as too slow.

[*Enter* JULIET.]

Here comes the lady. O, so light a foot
Will ne'er wear out the everlasting flint.°
A lover may bestride the gossamers°
That idle in the wanton summer air,
20 And yet not fall; so light is vanity.°

Juliet.

Good even to my ghostly confessor.

Friar.

Romeo shall thank thee, daughter, for us both.

Juliet.

As much to him,° else is his thanks too much.

Romeo.

Ah, Juliet, if the measure of thy joy
25 Be heaped like mine, and that thy skill be more
To blazon° it, then sweeten with thy breath
This neighbor air, and let rich music's tongue
Unfold the imagined happiness that both
Receive in either by this dear encounter.

Juliet.

30 Conceit,° more rich in matter than in words,
Brags of his substance, not of ornament.°
They are but beggars that can count their worth;
But my true love is grown to such excess
I cannot sum up sum of half my wealth.

Friar.

35 Come, come with me, and we will make short work;
For, by your leaves, you shall not stay alone
Till holy church incorporate two in one.   [*Exeunt.*]

4. **countervail:** match or equal.

10. **powder:** gunpowder.

8. *We are continually prepared for the steps Romeo and Juliet might take if they are separated. What does Romeo say here to remind us again of how desperate their love is?*

13. **confounds:** destroys.

15. *What warning does the Friar give about passionate love? What fear does he express for the future?*

17. **flint:** stone.
18. **gossamers:** finest spider threads.

20. **vanity:** fleeting human love.

23. **as much to him:** the same to him.

26. **blazon:** describe.

29. *What is Romeo asking Juliet to do?*

30. **Conceit:** genuine understanding.
31. **ornament:** fancy language.

34. *What is Juliet's response to Romeo's request?*

37. *What do you think the Friar's tone is in this last speech? Is there a slight humorous or teasing note here?*

Responding to the Play

Analyzing the Play

Act II

Identifying Facts

1. What plans do Romeo and Juliet make in Scene 2?
2. What fault does Friar Laurence find in Romeo in Scene 3?
3. Why is Tybalt looking for Romeo in Scene 4?
4. How does Mercutio feel about Tybalt?
5. What part does the Nurse play in Romeo and Juliet's schemes?

Interpreting Meanings

6. The "balcony scene" in Scene 2 is the most famous love scene in the history of the theater. What different feelings and emotions do Romeo and Juliet express in this scene? Which character speaks more cautiously about love, and why?
7. Act II is basically what might be called "a happy act," full of loving and courtship, teasing and humor. But, good dramatist that he is, Shakespeare reminds us in various places of the threatening background. This means he is using **foreshadowing**—providing clues that alert us to what is going to happen later. Point out the lines in this act in which Shakespeare foreshadows the fact that there could be trouble ahead.
8. Mercutio again teases Romeo's romantic love in Scene 4, in much the same way that a group of boys might today tease one of their friends who has fallen head over heels in love. How does Mercutio's sarcastic teasing emphasize Romeo's excessive love? In these scenes with Mercutio, do you find yourself agreeing with Mercutio or sympathizing with Romeo? Explain your answers.
9. Do you think Mercutio is merely teasing Romeo, or is he genuinely worried about his friend? Quote passages to support your answer.
10. In this act, we meet the Nurse, who is one of Shakespeare's great comic characters. The Nurse has only one trick, one source of humor. We laugh at her because she can be counted on to react in a certain way or speak in a certain way. We laugh at the same time that we say, "There she goes again!" But aside from laughing at the Nurse, we are getting an idea of her **character.** Do you think she is a principled person, one who has a strong sense of right and wrong? Or does she seem to be a person who may be easily corrupted—who will do what people want her to do? Find passages to support your answers.
11. The Friar agrees to marry Romeo and Juliet. He wants them to be happy, but he also has another **motive.** Why is the Friar willing to perform this secret marriage? When the audience in a play knows something that a character does *not* know, the writer is using **dramatic irony.** Since the Prologue to this play has told you how it will end, what irony do you feel when you hear the Friar's motives?
12. What other examples of **dramatic irony** can you find in this act—moments when *you* know something that the characters do *not* know?
13. Remember that Shakespeare had to set his stage largely with words. What clues in various speeches help you to visualize the times and the settings of the scenes in Act II?
14. So far, how do you feel about Friar Laurence's schemes? What else might he have done to help Romeo and Juliet?

Analyzing Language and Vocabulary

Shakespeare's Grammar and Vocabulary

Though Shakespeare's English is understandable today, readers often have difficulty with his sentence constructions and with his vocabulary. One of the characteristics of his sentences is the omission of certain words. A characteristic of his vocabulary, of course, is the use of words or expressions that are **archaic** or out of use today or that now have different meanings. For example, in the Prologue the speaker says:

> . . . which if you with patient ears attend,
> What here shall miss, our toil shall strive
>   to mend.

The speaker has omitted words here, and he depends on your instinct and ear to provide them. He has also used the word *attend* in a way not commonly used today. Rewritten, the statement would look like this:

> . . . if you listen with patient ear,
> We'll strive to make clear by our work on
>   stage
> What you have missed from this Prologue.

Here are some passages from Act II that use archaic words or that omit words that are assumed to be understood. Rewrite each passage in the kind of English you would speak today.

1. " 'Tis but my name that is my enemy."
2. "By whose direction found'st thou out this place?"
3. "Dost thou love me?"
4. "I know thou wilt say 'Ay.' "
5. "I'll frown and be perverse and say thee nay."
6. "Where the devil should this Romeo be? Came he not home tonight?"
7. "Out upon you! What a man are you!"
8. "And 'a speak anything against me, I'll take him down, and 'a were lustier than he is, and twenty such Jacks; and if I cannot, I'll find those that shall. Scurvy knave! I am none of his flirt-gills; I am none of his skainsmates. And thou must stand by too, and suffer every knave to use me at his pleasure!"
9. "Is your man secret? Did you ne'er hear say, Two may keep counsel, putting one away?"
10. ". . . but she, good soul, had as lieve see a toad, a very toad, as see him."

Act III Scene 1. *A public place.*

Enter MERCUTIO, BENVOLIO, *and* MEN.

Benvolio.
I pray thee, good Mercutio, let's retire.
The day is hot, the Capels° are abroad,
And, if we meet, we shall not 'scape a brawl,
For now, these hot days, is the mad blood stirring.

5 **Mercutio.** Thou art like one of these fellows that, when
he enters the confines of a tavern, claps me his sword
upon the table and says, "God send me no need of
thee!" and by the operation of the second cup draws
him on the drawer,° when indeed there is no need.

10 **Benvolio.** Am I like such a fellow?

Mercutio. Come, come, thou art as hot a Jack in thy
mood as any in Italy; and as soon moved to be moody,
and as soon moody to be moved.

Benvolio. And what to?

15 **Mercutio.** Nay, and there were two such, we should have
none shortly, for one would kill the other. Thou! Why,
thou wilt quarrel with a man that hath a hair more or
a hair less in his beard than thou hast. Thou wilt
quarrel with a man for cracking nuts, having no other
20 reason but because thou hast hazel eyes. What eye
but such an eye would spy out such a quarrel? Thy
head is as full of quarrels as an egg is full of meat; and
yet thy head hath been beaten as addle° as an egg for
quarreling. Thou hast quarreled with a man for cough-
25 ing in the street, because he hath wakened thy dog
that hath lain asleep in the sun. Didst thou not fall out
with a tailor for wearing his new doublet° before
Easter? With another for tying his new shoes with old
riband? And yet thou wilt tutor me from quarreling!

30 **Benvolio.** And I were so apt to quarrel as thou art, any
man should buy the fee simple of° my life for an hour
and a quarter.

Mercutio. The fee simple? O simple!°

[*Enter* TYBALT *and others.*]

Benvolio. By my head, here come the Capulets.

35 **Mercutio.** By my heel, I care not.

Tybalt.
Follow me close, for I will speak to them.
Gentlemen, good-den. A word with one of you.

Mercutio.
And but one word with one of us?
Couple it with something; make it a word and a blow.

2. **Capels:** Capulets.

? 4. *Romeo's friends enter the stage. Again, Shakespeare "sets the stage" by having the characters tell us what the weather is like. Why does this weather seem to breed trouble?*

9. **draws him on the drawer:** draws his sword on the waiter (who "draws" the drink).

? 18. *Mercutio mocks Benvolio, who is anything but a troublemaker. (Mercutio is the one who can't seem to resist a quarrel.) What do you imagine Benvolio doing, as Mercutio goes on and on? What actions do you imagine Mercutio involved in as his comments become more and more exaggerated?*
23. **addle:** rotten.

27. **doublet:** jacket.

31. **buy the fee simple of:** buy insurance on.

33. **O simple!:** O stupid!

? 34. *How does this talk of quick tempers and short lives foreshadow what will happen next? When did we last see Tybalt onstage, and what did he promise to do against Romeo?*

40 **Tybalt.** You shall find me apt enough to that, sir, and you
will give me occasion.
Mercutio. Could you not take some occasion without
giving?
Tybalt. Mercutio, thou consortest with Romeo.
45 **Mercutio.** Consort?° What, dost thou make us minstrels?
And thou make minstrels of us, look to hear nothing
but discords. Here's my fiddlestick;° here's that shall
make you dance. Zounds,° consort!
Benvolio.
We talk here in the public haunt of men.
50 Either withdraw unto some private place,
Or reason coldly of your grievances,
Or else depart. Here all eyes gaze on us.
Mercutio.
Men's eyes were made to look, and let them gaze.
I will not budge for no man's pleasure, I.

[*Enter* ROMEO.]

Tybalt.
55 Well, peace be with you, sir. Here comes my man.
Mercutio.
But I'll be hanged, sir, if he wear your livery.°
Marry, go before to field,° he'll be your follower!
Your worship in that sense may call him man.
Tybalt.
Romeo, the love I bear thee can afford
60 No better term than this: thou art a villain.°
Romeo.
Tybalt, the reason that I have to love thee
Doth much excuse the appertaining° rage
To such a greeting. Villain am I none.
Therefore farewell. I see thou knowest me not.
Tybalt.
65 Boy, this shall not excuse the injuries
That thou hast done me; therefore turn and draw.
Romeo.
I do protest I never injured thee,
But love thee better than thou canst devise°
Till thou shalt know the reason of my love;
70 And so, good Capulet, which name I tender°
As dearly as mine own, be satisfied.
Mercutio.
O calm, dishonorable, vile submission!
Alla stoccata° carries it away.

[*Draws.*]

Tybalt, you ratcatcher, will you walk?°

---

45. Consort: Mercutio pretends to think that Tybalt means a *consort,* or group of musicians.
47. fiddlestick: violin bow (referring to his sword).
48. Zounds: slang for "By God's wounds."

? **Stage direction:** *Romeo is returning from his secret marriage—he has no thought about hatred and killing. What would he be doing as he enters? How would he react to the tense situation?*

56. livery: servant's uniform. By "man," Tybalt means "target"; but Mercutio uses the word to mean "servant."
57. field: the dueling field.

60. villain: a boor; a clumsy, stupid fellow.

62. appertaining: appropriate.

? **66.** *What insult does Tybalt use to make Romeo want to draw his sword?*

68. devise: imagine.

70. tender: value.
? **71.** *Why does Romeo refuse to duel Tybalt?*

73. Alla stoccata: "at the thrust," a fencing term.

74. walk: make a move.

Tybalt.

75   What wouldst thou have with me?

Mercutio. Good King of Cats, nothing but one of your
        nine lives. That I mean to make bold withal,° and, as
        you shall use me hereafter, dry-beat° the rest of the
        eight. Will you pluck your sword out of his pilcher°

80   by the ears? Make haste, lest mine be about your ears
        ere it be out.

Tybalt. I am for you.

[*Draws.*]

Romeo.

        Gentle Mercutio, put thy rapier up.

Mercutio. Come, sir, your passado!

[*They fight.*]

Romeo.

85   Draw, Benvolio; beat down their weapons.
        Gentlemen, for shame! Forbear this outrage!
        Tybalt, Mercutio, the prince expressly hath
        Forbid this bandying° in Verona streets.
        Hold, Tybalt! Good Mercutio!

75. *Mercutio doesn't know of Romeo's marriage to Juliet (a Capulet). Why is Mercutio so outraged? What feeling should Tybalt express (fear? annoyance?) as he asks Mercutio what he wants?*
77. to make bold withal: to make free with (to take away).
78. dry-beat: thrash.
79. pilcher: scabbard.

Stage direction: *The stage direction above simply says "They fight," but how would you—as director—choreograph the action? Would you have Mercutio challenge Tybalt to protect Romeo? Or would you emphasize Mercutio's dislike of Tybalt? The swordfight can range all over the stage, but where must the three characters be placed when Tybalt stabs Mercutio?*
88. bandying: brawling.

"Come, sir, your passado!"

[TYBALT *under Romeo's arm thrusts* MERCUTIO *in, and flies*.]

Mercutio.   I am hurt.

90   A plague a' both houses! I am sped.°
      Is he gone and hath nothing?

Benvolio.   What, art thou hurt?

Mercutio.
      Ay, ay, a scratch, a scratch. Marry, 'tis enough.
      Where is my page? Go, villain, fetch a surgeon.

                                    [*Exit* PAGE.]

Romeo.
      Courage, man. The hurt cannot be much.

95   **Mercutio.** No, 'tis not so deep as a well, nor so wide as
      a church door; but 'tis enough, 'twill serve. Ask for
      me tomorrow, and you shall find me a grave man. I
      am peppered,° I warrant, for this world. A plague a'
      both your houses! Zounds, a dog, a rat, a mouse, a
100   cat, to scratch a man to death! A braggart, a rogue, a
      villain, that fights by the book of arithmetic!° Why the
      devil came you between us? I was hurt under your arm.

Romeo.
      I thought all for the best.

Mercutio.
      Help me into some house, Benvolio,
105   Or I shall faint. A plague a' both your houses!
      They have made worms' meat of me. I have it,
      And soundly too. Your houses!

                        [*Exeunt* MERCUTIO *and* BENVOLIO.]

Romeo.
      This gentleman, the prince's near ally,°
      My very friend, hath got this mortal hurt
110   In my behalf—my reputation stained
      With Tybalt's slander—Tybalt, that an hour
      Hath been my cousin. O sweet Juliet,
      Thy beauty hath made me effeminate
      And in my temper soft'ned valor's steel!

[*Enter* BENVOLIO.]

Benvolio.
115   O Romeo, Romeo, brave Mercutio is dead!
      That gallant spirit hath aspired° the clouds,
      Which too untimely here did scorn the earth.

Romeo.
      This day's black fate on more days doth depend;°
      This but begins the woe others must end.

[*Enter* TYBALT.]

90. sped: wounded.

98. peppered: given a deadly wound ("peppered" food is ready to eat; Mercutio is "ready" to die).

101. fights by the book of arithmetic: fights according to formal rules for fencing.

? **103.** *How would Romeo say this pathetic line?*

? **107.** *What curse has Mercutio pronounced four times? Some actors playing Mercutio make him seem bitter about his death and hostile to Romeo. Other Mercutios are gallant to the end and extend a hand to Romeo in friendship. How would you play this death speech?*
108. ally: relative. Mercutio was related to Verona's Prince Escalus.

116. aspired: climbed to.
118. depend: hang over.
? **Stage direction:** *Does it seem unlikely that Tybalt would return so soon? He must return, of course, so that Romeo can avenge Mercutio. An alternative would have been to have Romeo attack Tybalt as soon as he stabbed Mercutio, but then Shakespeare would have lost Mercutio's great dying speech. How would you stage Tybalt's return so that it seems believable?*

Benvolio.

120   Here comes the furious Tybalt back again.

Romeo.

        Alive in triumph, and Mercutio slain?

        Away to heaven respective lenity,

        And fire-eyed fury be my conduct now!

        Now, Tybalt, take the "villain" back again

125   That late thou gavest me; for Mercutio's soul

        Is but a little way above our heads,

        Staying for thine to keep him company.

        Either thou or I, or both, must go with him.

Tybalt.

        Thou, wretched boy, that didst consort him here,

130   Shalt with him hence.

Romeo.   This shall determine that.

[They fight. TYBALT falls.]

Benvolio.

        Romeo, away, be gone!

        The citizens are up, and Tybalt slain.

        Stand not amazed. The prince will doom thee death

        If thou art taken. Hence, be gone, away!

Romeo.

135   O, I am fortune's fool!

Benvolio.   Why dost thou stay?

                                        [Exit ROMEO.]

[Enter CITIZENS.]

Citizen.

        Which way ran he that killed Mercutio?

        Tybalt, that murderer, which way ran he?

Benvolio.

        There lies that Tybalt.

Citizen.   Up, sir, go with me.

        I charge thee in the prince's name obey.

[Enter PRINCE, old MONTAGUE, CAPULET, their WIVES, and all.]

Prince.

140   Where are the vile beginners of this fray?

Benvolio.

        O noble prince, I can discover° all

        The unlucky manage° of this fatal brawl.

        There lies the man, slain by young Romeo,

        That slew thy kinsman, brave Mercutio.

Lady Capulet.

145   Tybalt, my cousin! O my brother's child!

        O prince! O cousin! Husband! O, the blood is spilled

134. *What details in Benvolio's speech tell us what Romeo is doing and how he is feeling after this second death?*

135. *What do you think Romeo means by calling himself "fortune's fool"? What does he realize will now happen to him and Juliet?*

Stage direction: *What do you imagine the stage looks like as the Prince and his followers enter?*

141. **discover:** reveal.
142. **manage:** course.

Of my dear kinsman! Prince, as thou art true,
For blood of ours shed blood of Montague.
O cousin, cousin!

Prince.

150   Benvolio, who began this bloody fray?

Benvolio.

     Tybalt, here slain, whom Romeo's hand did slay.
     Romeo, that spoke him fair, bid him bethink
     How nice° the quarrel was, and urged° withal
     Your high displeasure. All this—utterèd

155   With gentle breath, calm look, knees humbly bowed—
     Could not take truce with the unruly spleen°
     Of Tybalt deaf to peace, but that he tilts°
     With piercing steel at bold Mercutio's breast;
     Who, all as hot, turns deadly point to point,

160   And, with a martial scorn, with one hand beats
     Cold death aside and with the other sends
     It back to Tybalt, whose dexterity
     Retorts it. Romeo he cries aloud,
     "Hold, friends! Friends, part!" and swifter than his
        tongue,

165   His agile arm beats down their fatal points,
     And 'twixt them rushes; underneath whose arm
     An envious° thrust from Tybalt hit the life
     Of stout Mercutio, and then Tybalt fled;
     But by and by comes back to Romeo,

170   Who had but newly entertained° revenge,
     And to't they go like lightning; for, ere I
     Could draw to part them, was stout Tybalt slain;
     And, as he fell, did Romeo turn and fly.
     This is the truth, or let Benvolio die.

Lady Capulet.

175   He is a kinsman to the Montague;
     Affection makes him false, he speaks not true.
     Some twenty of them fought in this black strife,
     And all those twenty could but kill one life.
     I beg for justice, which thou, prince, must give.

180   Romeo slew Tybalt; Romeo must not live.

Prince.

     Romeo slew him; he slew Mercutio.
     Who now the price of his dear blood doth owe?

Montague.

     Not Romeo, prince; he was Mercutio's friend;
     His fault concludes but what the law should end,

185   The life of Tybalt.

Prince.   And for that offense
     Immediately we do exile him hence.
     I have an interest in your hate's proceeding,

---

153. nice: trivial. **urged:** mentioned.

156. spleen: anger.
157. tilts: thrusts.

167. envious: full of enmity or hatred.

170. entertained: thought of.

174. *Is Benvolio's testimony about events fully accurate?*

178. *How does Lady Capulet think Tybalt was killed? Why does she think Benvolio is lying?*

My blood° for your rude brawls doth lie a-bleeding;
But I'll amerce° you with so strong a fine
190 That you shall all repent the loss of mine.
I will be deaf to pleading and excuses;
Nor tears nor prayers shall purchase out abuses.
Therefore use none. Let Romeo hence in haste,
Else, when he is found, that hour is his last.
195 Bear hence this body and attend our will.
Mercy but murders, pardoning those that kill.

[*Exit with others.*]

196. *The Prince has heard arguments from both families and has given judgment in the case. What is Romeo's punishment? Why won't the Prince show Romeo mercy?*
The families exit in two separate processions, with their dead. How does this scene contrast with the fighting that has just taken place?

Scene 2. *Capulet's orchard.*

Enter JULIET *alone.*

Juliet.
Gallop apace, you fiery-footed steeds,°
Towards Phoebus' lodging! Such a wagoner
As Phaethon° would whip you to the west
And bring in cloudy night immediately.
5 Spread thy close curtain, love-performing night,
That runaways' eyes may wink,° and Romeo
Leap to these arms untalked of and unseen.
Lovers can see to do their amorous rites,
And by their own beauties; or, if love be blind,
10 It best agrees with night. Come, civil° night,
Thou sober-suited matron all in black,
And learn me how to lose a winning match,
Played for a pair of stainless maidenhoods.
Hood° my unmanned° blood, bating° in my cheeks,
15 With thy black mantle till strange° love grow bold,
Think true love acted simple modesty.
Come, night; come, Romeo; come, thou day in night;
For thou wilt lie upon the wings of night
Whiter than new snow upon a raven's back.
20 Come, gentle night; come, loving, black-browed night;
Give me my Romeo; and, when he shall die,
Take him and cut him out in little stars,
And he will make the face of heaven so fine
That all the world will be in love with night
25 And pay no worship to the garish sun.
O, I have bought the mansion of a love,
But not possessed it; and though I am sold,
Not yet enjoyed. So tedious is this day

Stage direction: *What do we in the audience know that Juliet at this point still does not know?*

1. steeds: horses (that pull the sun god Phoebus' chariot across the sky each day).

3. Phaethon: the reckless son of Phoebus, who couldn't hold the horses.

6. That runaways' eyes may wink: so that the eyes of the sun god's horses may shut.

10. civil: well-behaved.

14. Hood: cover. **unmanned:** unmated. **bating:** fluttering.
15. strange: unfamiliar.

28. *What is the "mansion of a love" Juliet has bought?*

"What hast thou there, the cords
That Romeo bid thee fetch?"

As is the night before some festival
To an impatient child that hath new robes
And may not wear them. O, here comes my nurse,

[*Enter* NURSE, *with a ladder of cords*.]

And she brings news; and every tongue that speaks
But Romeo's name speaks heavenly eloquence.
Now, nurse, what news? What hast thou there, the cords
That Romeo bid thee fetch?

Nurse.   Ay, ay, the cords.
Juliet.
Ay me! What news? Why dost thou wring thy hands?
Nurse.
Ah, weraday!° He's dead, he's dead, he's dead!
We are undone, lady, we are undone!
Alack the day! He's gone, he's killed, he's dead!
Juliet.
Can heaven be so envious?
Nurse.   Romeo can,
Though heaven cannot. O Romeo, Romeo!
Who ever would have thought it? Romeo!

30
35
40

31. *Where does Juliet, in lines of unconscious foreshadowing, make us think of Romeo's death?*

35. *How does the Nurse speak this line?*

37. **weraday!:** well-a-day! (or alas!)

39. *The Nurse rattles on again—but this time, how does she seem to give the wrong news, even as she delays it?*

Juliet.

What devil art thou that dost torment me thus?
This torture should be roared in dismal hell.
45   Hath Romeo slain himself? Say thou but ''Ay,''
And that bare vowel ''I'' shall poison more
Than the death-darting eye of cockatrice.°
I am not I, if there be such an ''Ay,''
Or those eyes' shot that make thee answer ''Ay.''
50   If he be slain, say ''Ay''; or if not, ''No.''
Brief sounds determine of my weal or woe.

Nurse.

I saw the wound, I saw it with mine eyes,
(God save the mark!°) here on his manly breast.
A piteous corse,° a bloody piteous corse;
55   Pale, pale as ashes, all bedaubed in blood,
All in gore-blood. I sounded° at the sight.

Juliet.

O, break, my heart! Poor bankrout,° break at once!
To prison, eyes; ne'er look on liberty!
Vile earth,° to earth resign; end motion here,
60   And thou and Romeo press one heavy bier!

Nurse.

O Tybalt, Tybalt, the best friend I had!
O courteous Tybalt! Honest gentleman!
That ever I should live to see thee dead!

Juliet.

What storm is this that blows so contrary?
65   Is Romeo slaught'red, and is Tybalt dead?
My dearest cousin, and my dearer lord?
Then, dreadful trumpet, sound the general doom!
For who is living, if those two are gone?

Nurse.

Tybalt is gone, and Romeo banishèd;
70   Romeo that killed him, he is banishèd.

Juliet.

O God! Did Romeo's hand shed Tybalt's blood?

Nurse.

It did, it did! Alas the day, it did!

Juliet.

O serpent heart, hid with a flow'ring face!
Did ever dragon keep so fair a cave?
75   Beautiful tyrant! Fiend angelical!
Dove-feathered raven! Wolvish-ravening lamb!
Despisèd substance of divinest show!
Just opposite to what thou justly seem'st—
A damnèd saint, an honorable villain!
80   O nature, what hadst thou to do in hell
When thou didst bower the spirit of a fiend

47. **cockatrice:** a legendary serpent that could kill by a glancing look.

53. **God save the mark!:** God forbid!
54. **corse:** corpse.

56. **sounded:** swooned (fainted).

57. **bankrout:** bankrupt.

59. **Vile earth:** Juliet refers to her own body.
60. *This is one of a series of odd scenes in which we cannot share a character's feelings because we know something that the character does not know. What does Juliet think has happened? How does she foreshadow her own death?*

70. *Why do you think the Nurse waits so long to give Juliet the correct news? Should we feel she is being self-centered here, or is she truly overwhelmed by the news she bears?*

In mortal paradise of such sweet flesh?
Was ever book containing such vile matter
So fairly bound? O, that deceit should dwell
85   In such a gorgeous palace!

Nurse.   There's no trust,
No faith, no honesty in men; all perjured,
All forsworn, all naught, all dissemblers.°
Ah, where's my man? Give me some aqua vitae.°
These griefs, these woes, these sorrows make me old.
90   Shame come to Romeo!

Juliet.   Blistered be thy tongue
For such a wish! He was not born to shame.
Upon his brow shame is ashamed to sit;
For 'tis a throne where honor may be crowned
Sole monarch of the universal earth.
95   O, what a beast was I to chide at him!

Nurse.
Will you speak well of him that killed your cousin?

Juliet.
Shall I speak ill of him that is my husband?
Ah, poor my lord, what tongue shall smooth thy name
When I, thy three-hours wife, have mangled it?
100   But wherefore, villain, didst thou kill my cousin?
That villain cousin would have killed my husband.
Back, foolish tears, back to your native spring!
Your tributary° drops belong to woe,
Which you, mistaking, offer up to joy.
105   My husband lives, that Tybalt would have slain;
And Tybalt's dead, that would have slain my husband.
All this is comfort; wherefore weep I then?
Some word there was, worser than Tybalt's death,
That murd'red me. I would forget it fain;°
110   But O, it presses to my memory
Like damnèd guilty deeds to sinners' minds!
"Tybalt is dead, and Romeo—banishèd."
That "banishèd," that one word "banishèd,"
Hath slain ten thousand Tybalts. Tybalt's death
115   Was woe enough, if it had ended there;
Or, if sour woe delights in fellowship
And needly will be ranked with° other griefs,
Why followed not, when she said "Tybalt's dead,"
Thy father, or thy mother, nay, or both,
120   Which modern° lamentation might have moved°?
But with a rearward° following Tybalt's death,
"Romeo is banishèd"—to speak that word
Is father, mother, Tybalt, Romeo, Juliet,
All slain, all dead. "Romeo is banishèd"—
125   There is no end, no limit, measure, bound,

85. *A moment ago, Juliet thought of Romeo as her very "day in night." Now what does she think of him?*

87. dissemblers: liars.

88. aqua vitae: Latin for "water of life"—here, brandy.

90. *What does the Nurse think about these events? Where does she think the blame lies? Do you see her being selfish here, or is she wholly concerned for Juliet?*

97. *Why does Juliet turn against her Nurse here?*

103. tributary: tears poured out in tribute.

109. fain: willingly.

117. ranked with: accompanied by.

120. modern: ordinary. **moved:** provoked.
121. rearward: rear guard.

124. *Juliet comprehends what has happened. Why does she fix on that one word—banished?*

In that word's death; no words can that woe sound.
Where is my father and my mother, nurse?

Nurse.
Weeping and wailing over Tybalt's corse.
Will you go to them? I will bring you thither.

Juliet.
130   Wash they his wounds with tears? Mine shall be spent,
When theirs are dry, for Romeo's banishment.
Take up those cords. Poor ropes, you are beguiled,
Both you and I, for Romeo is exiled.
He made you for a highway to my bed;
135   But I, a maid, die maiden-widowèd.
Come, cords; come, nurse. I'll to my wedding bed;
And death, not Romeo, take my maidenhead!

Nurse.
Hie to your chamber. I'll find Romeo
To comfort you. I wot° well where he is.
140   Hark ye, your Romeo will be here at night.
I'll to him; he is hid at Laurence' cell.

Juliet.
O, find him! Give this ring to my true knight
And bid him come to take his last farewell.

                                             [*Exit with* NURSE.]

127. *Juliet pauses before she speaks the last line here. How must her tone change as she asks the Nurse about her father and mother?*

137. *Juliet addresses the rope ladder in this speech. What has she decided to do with the ropes?*

139. wot: know.

Scene 3. *Friar Laurence's cell.*

Enter FRIAR LAURENCE.

Friar.
Romeo, come forth; come forth, thou fearful man.
Affliction is enamored of thy parts,
And thou art wedded to calamity.

[*Enter* ROMEO.]

Romeo.
Father, what news? What is the prince's doom?
5   What sorrow craves acquaintance at my hand
That I yet know not?

Friar.   Too familiar
Is my dear son with such sour company.
I bring thee tidings of the prince's doom.

Romeo.
What less than doomsday° is the prince's doom?

Friar.
10   A gentler judgment vanished° from his lips—

3. *When we last saw Romeo he was speaking of himself as "fortune's fool." Now, in the first lines of this scene, how does the Friar remind us again that Romeo seems fated for ill fortune?*

9. doomsday: my death.

10. vanished: escaped.

660   **William Shakespeare**

Not body's death, but body's banishment.

Romeo.

    Ha, banishment? Be merciful, say "death";

    For exile hath more terror in his look,

    Much more than death. Do not say "banishment."

Friar.

15   Here from Verona art thou banishèd.

    Be patient, for the world is broad and wide.

Romeo.

    There is no world without Verona walls,

    But purgatory, torture, hell itself.

    Hence banishèd is banished from the world,

20   And world's exile is death. Then "banishèd"

    Is death mistermed. Calling death "banishèd,"

    Thou cut'st my head off with a golden ax

    And smilest upon the stroke that murders me.

Friar.

    O deadly sin! O rude unthankfulness!

25   Thy fault our law calls death; but the kind prince,

    Taking thy part, hath rushed aside the law,

    And turned that black word "death" to "banishment."

    This is dear mercy, and thou see'st it not.

Romeo.

    'Tis torture, and not mercy. Heaven is here,

30   Where Juliet lives; and every cat and dog

    And little mouse, every unworthy thing,

    Live here in heaven and may look on her;

    But Romeo may not. More validity,°

    More honorable state, more courtship lives

35   In carrion flies than Romeo. They may seize

    On the white wonder of dear Juliet's hand

    And steal immortal blessing from her lips,

    Who, even in pure and vestal modesty,

    Still blush, as thinking their own kisses sin;

40   But Romeo may not, he is banishèd.

    Flies may do this but I from this must fly;

    They are freemen, but I am banishèd.

    And sayest thou yet that exile is not death?

    Hadst thou no poison mixed, no sharp-ground knife,

45   No sudden mean of death, though ne'er so mean,

    But "banishèd" to kill me—"banishèd"?

    O friar, the damnèd use that word in hell;

    Howling attends it! How hast thou the heart,

    Being a divine, a ghostly confessor,

50   A sin-absolver, and my friend professed,

    To mangle me with that word "banishèd"?

Friar.

    Thou fond° mad man, hear me a little speak.

21. *Romeo, like Juliet, fixes on the word* banished. *What does the word mean to him?*

28. *Why is the Friar angry at Romeo?*

33. **validity:** value.

52. **fond:** foolish.

Romeo.

O, thou wilt speak again of banishment.

Friar.

I'll give thee armor to keep off that word;

55 Adversity's sweet milk, philosophy,

To comfort thee, though thou art banishèd.

Romeo.

Yet "banishèd"? Hang up philosophy!

Unless philosophy can make a Juliet,

Displant a town, reverse a prince's doom,

60 It helps not, it prevails not. Talk no more.

Friar.

O, then I see that madmen have no ears.

Romeo.

How should they, when that wise men have no eyes?

Friar.

Let me dispute with thee of thy estate.°

Romeo.

Thou canst not speak of that thou dost not feel.

65 Wert thou as young as I, Juliet thy love,

An hour but married, Tybalt murderèd,

Doting like me, and like me banishèd,

Then mightst thou speak, then mightst thou tear thy hair,

And fall upon the ground, as I do now,

70 Taking the measure of an unmade grave.

[*The* NURSE *knocks.*]

Friar.

Arise, one knocks. Good Romeo, hide thyself.

Romeo.

Not I; unless the breath of heartsick groans

Mistlike infold me from the search of eyes.

[*Knock.*]

Friar.

Hark, how they knock! Who's there? Romeo, arise;

75 Thou wilt be taken.—Stay awhile!—Stand up;

[*Knock.*]

Run to my study.—By and by!—God's will,

What simpleness is this.—I come, I come!

[*Knock.*]

Who knocks so hard? Whence come you? What's your
will?

[*Enter* NURSE.]

60. *For anyone who has never been deeply in love or for anyone who has not lost a love, it may seem that Romeo goes on too much. But it is important that we get the picture of this "fond mad man" in order to understand the action of the play. None of the other characters can understand Romeo's love. They are more level-headed (perhaps less lucky in love?). How is Romeo's response to banishment like Juliet's?*

62. *Whom is Romeo talking about?*

63. estate: situation.

70. *How do you think the Friar responds to these harsh words?*

71. *There is a great deal of action in this scene while the knocks are heard at the door. What action is the Friar engaged in, and what is Romeo doing?*

Nurse.

Let me come in, and you shall know my errand.

80   I come from Lady Juliet.

Friar.   Welcome then.

Nurse.

O holy friar, O, tell me, holy friar,

Where is my lady's lord, where's Romeo?

Friar.

There on the ground, with his own tears made drunk.

Nurse.

O, he is even in my mistress' case,°

84. **case:** condition.

85   Just in her case! O woeful sympathy!

Piteous predicament! Even so lies she,

Blubb'ring and weeping, weeping and blubb'ring.

Stand up, stand up! Stand, and you be a man.

For Juliet's sake, for her sake, rise and stand!

90   Why should you fall into so deep an O?°

90. **an O:** a fit of moaning ("oh, oh, oh").

Romeo (*rises*). Nurse—

? 90. *What action is the Nurse engaged in as she speaks these lines?*

Nurse.

Ah sir, ah sir! Death's the end of all.

Romeo.

Spakest thou of Juliet? How is it with her?

Doth not she think me an old murderer,

95   Now I have stained the childhood of our joy

With blood removed but little from her own?

Where is she? And how doth she! And what says

My concealed lady to our canceled love?

Nurse.

O, she says nothing, sir, but weeps and weeps;

100   And now falls on her bed, and then starts up,

And Tybalt calls; and then on Romeo cries,

And then down falls again.

Romeo.   As if that name,

Shot from the deadly level° of a gun,

103. **level:** aim.

Did murder her; as that name's cursèd hand

105   Murdered her kinsman. O, tell me, friar, tell me,

In what vile part of this anatomy

Doth my name lodge? Tell me, that I may sack°

107. **sack:** plunder and destroy.

The hateful mansion.

[*He offers to stab himself, and* NURSE *snatches the dagger away.*]

Friar.   Hold thy desperate hand.

Art thou a man? Thy form cries out thou art;

110   Thy tears are womanish, thy wild acts denote

The unreasonable fury of a beast.

Unseemly woman in a seeming man!

And ill-beseeming beast in seeming both!

? 108. *Romeo is disarmed without a struggle, and probably stands broken as the Friar, in this long speech, gradually re-establishes control over him. It is important to remember that to the people in this play, suicide was a mortal sin, which damned one to hell forever. Where does the Friar angrily remind Romeo of this?*

Thou hast amazed me. By my holy order,
115   I thought thy disposition better tempered.
Hast thou slain Tybalt? Wilt thou slay thyself?
And slay thy lady that in thy life lives,
By doing damnèd hate upon thyself?
Why railest thou on thy birth, the heaven, and earth?
120   Since birth and heaven and earth,° all three do meet
In thee at once; which thou at once wouldst lose.
Fie, fie, thou shamest thy shape, thy love, thy wit,
Which,° like a usurer, abound'st in all,
And usest none in that true use indeed
125   Which should bedeck° thy shape, thy love, thy wit.
Thy noble shape is but a form of wax,
Digressing from the valor of a man;
Thy dear love sworn but hollow perjury,
Killing that love which thou hast vowed to cherish;
130   Thy wit, that ornament to shape and love,
Misshapen in the conduct° of them both,
Like powder in a skilless soldier's flask,
Is set afire by thine own ignorance,
And thou dismembered with thine own defense.°
135   What, rouse thee, man! Thy Juliet is alive,
For whose dear sake thou wast but lately dead.
There art thou happy.° Tybalt would kill thee,
But thou slewest Tybalt. There art thou happy.
The law, that threatened death, becomes thy friend
140   And turns it to exile. There art thou happy.
A pack of blessings light upon thy back;
Happiness courts thee in her best array;
But, like a misbehaved and sullen wench,
Thou puts up thy fortune and thy love.
145   Take heed, take heed, for such die miserable.
Go get thee to thy love, as was decreed,
Ascend her chamber, hence and comfort her.
But look thou stay not till the watch be set,
For then thou canst not pass to Mantua,
150   Where thou shalt live till we can find a time
To blaze° your marriage, reconcile your friends,
Beg pardon of the prince, and call thee back
With twenty hundred thousand times more joy
Than thou went'st forth in lamentation.
155   Go before, nurse. Commend me to thy lady,
And bid her hasten all the house to bed,
Which heavy sorrow makes them apt unto.
Romeo is coming.

Nurse.
O Lord, I could have stayed here all the night
160   To hear good counsel. O, what learning is!

120. **birth and heaven and earth:** family origin, soul, and body.

123. **Which:** who (speaking of Romeo).

125. **bedeck:** do honor to.

131. **conduct:** management.

134. **And . . . defense:** Romeo's own mind (wit), which should protect him, is destroying him.

137. **happy:** lucky.

151. **blaze:** announce.

154. *What line in this speech suggests that Romeo has been standing listless? Find where the Friar first shames Romeo, then appeals to his common sense, then offers him hope.*
155. *Friar turns to the Nurse. What are his instructions?*

My lord, I'll tell my lady you will come.

Romeo.

Do so, and bid my sweet prepare to chide.

[NURSE *offers to go in and turns again.*]

Nurse.

Here, sir, a ring she bid me give you, sir.

Hie you, make haste, for it grows very late.   [*Exit.*]

Romeo.

165 How well my comfort is revived by this!

Friar.

Go hence; good night; and here stands all your state:°

Either be gone before the watch be set,

Or by the break of day disguised from hence.

Sojourn in Mantua. I'll find out your man,

170 And he shall signify from time to time

Every good hap to you that chances here.

Give me thy hand. 'Tis late. Farewell; good night.

Romeo.

But that a joy past joy calls out on me,

It were a grief so brief to part with thee.

175 Farewell.   [*Exeunt.*]

161. *The Nurse's amazement at what she calls the Friar's "learning" often brings a laugh from the audience and breaks the tension. Romeo thus far has said nothing. How do you imagine he shows that the Friar's speech has brought him back to life?*

166. state: situation.

175. *In spite of Romeo's and Juliet's anguish, the problem at this point seems to be simple. What plans have been made to resolve the young people's difficulties?*

Scene 4. *A room in Capulet's house.*

Enter old CAPULET, *his wife,* LADY CAPULET, *and* PARIS.

Capulet.

Things have fallen out, sir, so unluckily

That we have had no time to move° our daughter.

Look you, she loved her kinsman Tybalt dearly,

And so did I. Well, we were born to die.

5 'Tis very late; she'll not come down tonight.

I promise you, but for your company,

I would have been abed an hour ago.

Paris.

These times of woe afford no times to woo.

Madam, good night. Commend me to your daughter.

Lady Capulet.

10 I will, and know her mind early tomorrow;

Tonight she's mewed up to her heaviness.°

Capulet.

Sir Paris, I will make a desperate tender°

Of my child's love. I think she will be ruled

In all respects by me; nay more, I doubt it not.

15 Wife, go you to her ere you go to bed;

Acquaint her here of my son Paris' love

2. move: persuade (to marry Paris).

7. *Dramatic irony is felt when the audience knows something that the characters on stage do* not *know. What intense dramatic irony does the audience feel as this scene unfolds? What do* we *know that the Capulets and Paris are totally ignorant of?*

11. mewed up to her heaviness: shut away because of her great grief.

12. desperate tender: bold offer.

And bid her (mark you me?) on Wednesday next—
But soft! What day is this?

Paris.   Monday, my lord.

Capulet.

Monday! Ha, ha! Well, Wednesday is too soon.

20 A' Thursday let it be—a' Thursday, tell her,
She shall be married to this noble earl.
Will you be ready? Do you like this haste?
We'll keep no great ado—a friend or two;
For hark you, Tybalt being slain so late,

25 It may be thought we held him carelessly,
Being our kinsman, if we revel much.
Therefore we'll have some half a dozen friends,
And there an end. But what say you to Thursday?

Paris.

My lord, I would that Thursday were tomorrow.

Capulet.

30 Well, get you gone. A' Thursday be it then.
Go you to Juliet ere you go to bed;
Prepare her, wife, against this wedding day.
Farewell, my lord.—Light to my chamber, ho!
Afore me,° it is so very late

35 That we may call it early by and by.
Good night.   [*Exeunt.*]

19. *Capulet is sometimes played as a foolish old man. Why do you think he wants to get Juliet married as soon as possible? What do you think his mood is here?*

32. *Capulet speaks this line to his wife. Lady Capulet sometimes expresses uneasiness about her husband's plans here. Why would she be uneasy?*

34. Afore me: indeed.

36. *Just as we might feel the situation can be rescued, Shakespeare "raises the stakes" with this short scene. How does this scene increase our tension for the scene that follows, the wedding-night scene?*

Scene 5. *Capulet's orchard.*

Enter ROMEO *and* JULIET *aloft.*

Juliet.

Wilt thou be gone? It is not yet near day.
It was the nightingale, and not the lark,
That pierced the fearful hollow of thine ear.
Nightly she sings on yond pomegranate tree.

5 Believe me, love, it was the nightingale.

Romeo.

It was the lark, the herald of the morn;
No nightingale. Look, love, what envious streaks
Do lace the severing clouds in yonder east.
Night's candles are burnt out, and jocund day

10 Stands tiptoe on the misty mountaintops.
I must be gone and live, or stay and die.

Juliet.

Yond light is not daylight; I know it, I.
It is some meteor that the sun exhales°
To be to thee this night a torchbearer

Stage direction: *This scene was probably played on the upper stage in Shakespeare's time. In movies and in some modern stage productions, it is often played with varying degrees of frankness in Juliet's bedroom. Perhaps the fact that in Shakespeare's day Juliet was played by a boy dictated the brevity of the scene and the place where it was played. Would any lines not make sense if the scene were played in the bedroom?*

Juliet's first words here alert us to the time: it must be near morning, when Romeo must be gone to Mantua. We hear the song of a lark, which sings at daybreak. The nightingale, on the other hand, sings at night. Why does Juliet insist she hears the nightingale?

13. exhales: gives off. (It was believed that the sun drew up vapors and ignited them as meteors.)

"Wilt thou be gone? It is not yet near day."

15   And light thee on thy way to Mantua.
      Therefore stay yet; thou need'st not to be gone.

Romeo.
      Let me be taken, let me be put to death.
      I am content, so thou wilt have it so.
      I'll say yon gray is not the morning's eye,
20   'Tis but the pale reflex° of Cynthia's brow;°
      Nor that is not the lark whose notes do beat
      The vaulty heaven so high above our heads.
      I have more care to stay than will to go.
      Come, death, and welcome! Juliet wills it so.
25   How is't, my soul? Let's talk; it is not day.

Juliet.
      It is, it is! Hie hence, be gone, away!
      It is the lark that sings so out of tune,
      Straining harsh discords and unpleasing sharps.
      Some say the lark makes sweet division;°
30   This doth not so, for she divideth us.
      Some say the lark and loathèd toad change eyes;°
      O, now I would they had changed voices too,
      Since arm from arm that voice doth us affray,°
      Hunting thee hence with hunt's-up° to the day.
35   O, now be gone! More light and light it grows.

Romeo.
      More light and light—more dark and dark our woes.

[*Enter* NURSE.]

Nurse. Madam!
Juliet. Nurse?
Nurse.
      Your lady mother is coming to your chamber.
40   The day is broke; be wary, look about.   [*Exit.*]
Juliet.
      Then, window, let day in, and let life out.
Romeo.
      Farewell, farewell! One kiss, and I'll descend.

[*He goes down.*]

Juliet.
      Art thou gone so, love-lord, ay husband-friend?
      I must hear from thee every day in the hour,
45   For in a minute there are many days.
      O, for this count I shall be much in years
      Ere I again behold my Romeo!
Romeo.
      Farewell!
      I will omit no opportunity
50   That may convey my greetings, love, to thee.

20. reflex: reflection. **Cynthia's brow:** Cynthia is the moon.

26. *What has Romeo said that makes Juliet suddenly practical and aware of danger?*

29. division: literally, *division* here refers to a rapid run of notes, but Juliet is punning on the word's other meaning (separation).
31. A fable to explain why the lark, which sings so beautifully, has ugly eyes, and why the toad, which croaks so harshly, has beautiful ones.
33. affray: frighten.
34. hunt's-up: morning song for hunters.

41. *What is Juliet doing as she speaks these lines?*

43. *Where is Romeo now, as Juliet asks him to communicate with her?*

Juliet.

O, think'st thou we shall ever meet again?

Romeo.

I doubt it not; and all these woes shall serve

For sweet discourses in our times to come.

Juliet.

O God, I have an ill-divining soul!

55   Methinks I see thee, now thou art so low,

As one dead in the bottom of a tomb.

Either my eyesight fails, or thou lookest pale.

Romeo.

And trust me, love, in my eye so do you.

Dry° sorrow drinks our blood. Adieu, adieu!   [*Exit.*]

Juliet.

60   O Fortune, Fortune! All men call thee fickle.

If thou art fickle, what dost thou with him

That is renowned for faith? Be fickle, Fortune,

For then I hope thou wilt not keep him long

But send him back.

[*Enter Juliet's mother,* LADY CAPULET.]

Lady Capulet.

65   Ho, daughter! Are you up?

Juliet.

Who is't that calls? It is my lady mother.

Is she not down so late,° or up so early?

What unaccustomed cause procures her hither?

Lady Capulet.

Why, how now, Juliet?

Juliet.   Madam, I am not well.

Lady Capulet.

70   Evermore weeping for your cousin's death?

What, wilt thou wash him from his grave with tears?

And if thou couldst, thou couldst not make him live.

Therefore have done. Some grief shows much of love;

But much of grief shows still some want of wit.

Juliet.

75   Yet let me weep for such a feeling loss.°

Lady Capulet.

So shall you feel the loss, but not the friend

Which you weep for.

Juliet.   Feeling so the loss,

I cannot choose but ever weep the friend.

Lady Capulet.

Well, girl, thou weep'st not so much for his death

80   As that the villain lives which slaughtered him.

Juliet.

What villain, madam?

51. *Remember what the Prologue has told you about what will happen to Romeo and Juliet. How do you feel when you hear Juliet speak this line?*

57. *Friar Laurence might have taken Juliet with Romeo, into exile in Mantua. But we must remember that Juliet is not quite fourteen, and at this point in the story, Friar Laurence thinks the situation can be happily resolved. As the lovers part now, where does Juliet foresee Romeo's doom?*
59. Dry: thirsty (sorrow was thought to drain color from the cheeks).

67. down so late: so late getting to bed.

74. *The actresses playing Lady Capulet have interpreted her character in two ways. Some actresses portray her as loving toward Juliet. Others find in her speeches a signal to play her as distant and strong-willed, to contrast with Juliet's helplessness. What do you think Lady Capulet's tone is here, and how would you play the part?*
75. feeling loss: loss so deeply felt.
78. *All Juliet's lines in this scene have double meanings. Whom is she really grieving for?*

Lady Capulet.   That same villain Romeo.

Juliet (*aside*).

　　Villain and he be many miles asunder—

　　God pardon him! I do, with all my heart;

　　And yet no man like he doth grieve my heart.

Lady Capulet.

85　　That is because the traitor murderer lives.

Juliet.

　　Ay, madam, from the reach of these my hands.

　　Would none but I might venge my cousin's death!

Lady Capulet.

　　We will have vengeance for it, fear thou not.

　　Then weep no more. I'll send to one in Mantua,

90　　Where that same banished runagate° doth live,

　　Shall give him such an unaccustomed dram°

　　That he shall soon keep Tybalt company;

　　And then I hope thou wilt be satisfied.

Juliet.

　　Indeed I never shall be satisfied

95　　With Romeo till I behold him—dead—

　　Is my poor heart so for a kinsman vexed.

　　Madam, if you could find out but a man

　　To bear a poison, I would temper° it;

　　That Romeo should, upon receipt thereof,

100　　Soon sleep in quiet. O, how my heart abhors

　　To hear him named and cannot come to him,

　　To wreak° the love I bore my cousin

　　Upon his body that hath slaughtered him!

Lady Capulet.

　　Find thou the means, and I'll find such a man.

105　　But now I'll tell thee joyful tidings, girl.

Juliet.

　　And joy comes well in such a needy time.

　　What are they, beseech your ladyship?

Lady Capulet.

　　Well, well, thou hast a careful° father, child;

　　One who, to put thee from thy heaviness,

110　　Hath sorted out° a sudden day of joy

　　That thou expects not nor I looked not for.

Juliet.

　　Madam, in happy time!° What day is that?

Lady Capulet.

　　Marry, my child, early next Thursday morn

　　The gallant, young, and noble gentleman,

115　　The County Paris, at Saint Peter's Church,

　　Shall happily make thee there a joyful bride.

Juliet.

　　Now by Saint Peter's Church, and Peter too,

90. runagate: fugitive.

91. unaccustomed dram: unexpected drink (of poison).

❓ **93.** *This is a hard and fearful threat. How does Juliet reply, and with what hidden emotions does she speak her next words? How does she continue to speak with double meanings?*

❓ **95.** *How should lines 95–96 be said to indicate that Juliet intends "dead" to modify "heart"?*

98. temper: mix (she really means "weaken").

102. wreak: avenge (she really means "express").

❓ **105.** *Has Juliet convinced her mother that she wants Romeo dead?*

❓ **107.** *We know what the "tidings" are, but Juliet doesn't. How would she speak these lines?*

108. careful: full of caring (for Juliet).

110. sorted out: selected.

112. in happy time: at a lucky time.

He shall not make me there a joyful bride!
I wonder at this haste, that I must wed

120   Ere he that should be husband comes to woo.
I pray you tell my lord and father, madam,
I will not marry yet; and when I do, I swear
It shall be Romeo, whom you know I hate,
Rather than Paris. These are news indeed!

Lady Capulet.

125   Here comes your father. Tell him so yourself,
And see how he will take it at your hands.

[*Enter* CAPULET *and* NURSE.]

Capulet.

When the sun sets the earth doth drizzle dew,
But for the sunset of my brother's son
It rains downright.

130   How now? A conduit,° girl? What, still in tears?
Evermore showering? In one little body
Thou counterfeits a bark,° a sea, a wind:
For still thy eyes, which I may call the sea,
Do ebb and flow with tears; the bark thy body is,

135   Sailing in this salt flood; the winds, thy sighs,
Who, raging with thy tears and they with them,
Without a sudden calm will overset
Thy tempest-tossèd body. How now, wife?
Have you delivered to her our decree?

Lady Capulet.

140   Ay, sir; but she will none, she gives you thanks.
I would the fool were married to her grave!

Capulet.

Soft! Take me with you,° take me with you, wife.
How? Will she none? Doth she not give us thanks?
Is she not proud? Doth she not count her blest,

145   Unworthy as she is, that we have wrought°
So worthy a gentleman to be her bride?

Juliet.

Not proud you have, but thankful that you have.
Proud can I never be of what I hate,
But thankful even for hate that is meant love.

Capulet.

150   How, how, how, how, chopped-logic?° What is this?
"Proud"—and "I thank you"—and "I thank you not"—
And yet "not proud"? Mistress minion° you,
Thank me no thankings, nor proud me no prouds,
But fettle° your fine joints 'gainst Thursday next

155   To go with Paris to Saint Peter's Church,
Or I will drag thee on a hurdle thither.

120. *Juliet becomes sarcastic as she repeats her mother's words. Despite this shocking news, how does Juliet manage to make a reasonable protest to her mother?*

130. conduit: water pipe (Juliet is weeping).

132. counterfeits a bark: imitates a boat.

139. *Lord Capulet, self-satisfied and certain of his scheme, tries to humor and tease the weeping Juliet. Again, what irony do we feel in this scene?*

142. Soft! Take me with you: Wait! Let me understand you.

145. wrought: arranged.

149. *How does Juliet show that she knows her father loves her, even though she hates what he has done for her?*
150. chopped-logic: hair-splitting.

152. minion: badly behaved girl.

154. fettle: make ready.

Out, you greensickness carrion! Out, you baggage!
You tallow-face!

Lady Capulet. Fie, fie! What, are you mad?

Juliet.
    Good father, I beseech you on my knees,
160   Hear me with patience but to speak a word.

Capulet.
    Hang thee, young baggage! Disobedient wretch!
    I tell thee what—get thee to church a' Thursday
    Or never after look me in the face.
    Speak not, reply not, do not answer me!
165   My fingers itch. Wife, we scarce thought us blest
    That God had lent us but this only child;
    But now I see this one is one too much,
    And that we have a curse in having her.
    Out on her, hilding!

Nurse.   God in heaven bless her!
170   You are to blame, my lord, to rate° her so.

Capulet.
    And why, my Lady Wisdom? Hold your tongue,
    Good Prudence. Smatter with your gossips,° go!

Nurse.
    I speak no treason.

Capulet.   O, God-i-god-en!°

Nurse.
    May not one speak?

Capulet.   Peace, you mumbling fool!
175   Utter your gravity o'er a gossip's bowl,
    For here we need it not.

Lady Capulet.   You are too hot.

Capulet.
    God's bread!° It makes me mad.
    Day, night; hour, tide, time; work, play;
    Alone, in company; still my care hath been
180   To have her matched; and having now provided
    A gentleman of noble parentage,
    Of fair demesnes,° youthful, and nobly trained,
    Stuffed, as they say, with honorable parts,
    Proportioned as one's thought would wish a man—
185   And then to have a wretched puling° fool,
    A whining mammet,° in her fortune's tender,°
    To answer "I'll not wed, I cannot love;
    I am too young, I pray you pardon me"!
    But, and you will not wed, I'll pardon you!°
190   Graze where you will, you shall not house with me.
    Look to't, think on't; I do not use to jest.
    Thursday is near; lay hand on heart, advise:°
    And you be mine, I'll give you to my friend;

158. *What insulting names does Capulet call Juliet? What would Capulet's actions be, as he speaks these vicious words to his only daughter? Whom is Juliet's mother talking to, in her next line?*

160. *In the midst of this drama, we have a recognizable domestic scene, a family argument, which might have been played out in any century. What is Juliet doing as she talks to her father here? What does she do during her father's next speech?*

170. rate: scold (berate).

172. Smatter with your gossips: chatter with your gossipy friends.

173. God-i-god-en!: Get on with you! ("God give you good evening.")

177. God's bread!: an oath on the sacrament of Communion.

182. demesnes (di·māns): domains, or land.

185. puling: whining.
186. mammet: puppet. **fortune's tender:** with all her good fortunes.

188. *Why does Lord Capulet think Juliet won't marry Paris?*
189. I'll pardon you!: I'll give you permission to go!

192. advise: consider.

"I tell thee what—get thee to church a' Thursday
Or never after look me in the face."

And you be not, hang, beg, starve, die in the streets,
195   For, by my soul, I'll ne'er acknowledge thee,
Nor what is mine shall never do thee good.
Trust to't. Bethink you. I'll not be forsworn.°   [*Exit.*]

Juliet.
Is there no pity sitting in the clouds
That sees into the bottom of my grief?
200   O sweet my mother, cast me not away!
Delay this marriage for a month, a week;
Or if you do not, make the bridal bed
In that dim monument where Tybalt lies.

Lady Capulet.
Talk not to me, for I'll not speak a word.
205   Do as thou wilt, for I have done with thee.   [*Exit.*]

Juliet.
O God!—O nurse, how shall this be prevented?

197. forsworn: guilty of breaking his vow.

197. *There is usually a moment of stunned silence onstage after Capulet leaves. What exactly will Lord Capulet do if Juliet refuses to marry Paris? In the next speech, how does Juliet appeal to her mother for help?*

My husband is on earth, my faith in heaven.°
How shall that faith return again to earth
Unless that husband send it me from heaven
210   By leaving earth? Comfort me, counsel me.
Alack, alack, that heaven should practice stratagems
Upon so soft a subject as myself!
What say'st thou? Hast thou not a word of joy?
Some comfort, nurse.

Nurse.   Faith, here it is.
215   Romeo is banished; and all the world to nothing°
That he dares ne'er come back to challenge you;
Or if he do, it needs must be by stealth.
Then, since the case so stands as now it doth,
I think it best you married with the county.
220   O, he's a lovely gentleman!
Romeo's a dishclout° to him. An eagle, madam,
Hath not so green, so quick, so fair an eye
As Paris hath. Beshrew° my very heart,
I think you are happy in this second match,
225   For it excels your first; or if it did not,
Your first is dead—or 'twere as good he were
As living here and you no use of him.

Juliet.
Speak'st thou from thy heart?

Nurse.
And from my soul too; else beshrew them both.
230   **Juliet.** Amen!
Nurse. What?
Juliet.
Well, thou hast comforted me marvelous much.
Go in; and tell my lady I am gone,
Having displeased my father, to Laurence' cell,
235   To make confession and to be absolved.
Nurse.
Marry, I will; and this is wisely done.   [*Exit.*]
Juliet.
Ancient damnation!° O most wicked fiend!
Is it more sin to wish me thus forsworn,
Or to dispraise my lord with that same tongue
240   Which she hath praised him with above compare
So many thousand times? Go, counselor!
Thou and my bosom henceforth shall be twain.°
I'll to the friar to know his remedy.
If all else fail, myself have power to die.   [*Exit.*]

207. **my faith in heaven:** my wedding vow is recorded in heaven.

210. *Romeo and Juliet constantly remind us that they have taken their marriage vows seriously. According to Juliet here, how can these vows be broken?*

215. **all the world to nothing:** it is a safe bet.

223. **Beshrew:** curse.

227. *What is the Nurse's "comfort" and advice for Juliet? Which line in this speech suggests that Juliet has reacted with shock and that the Nurse must pause? Did you expect such advice from the Nurse?*

235. *In most productions, the Nurse has embraced Juliet to comfort her. Now Juliet has made a decision. What do you see Juliet doing as she speaks?*

237. **Ancient damnation!:** Damned old woman!

242. **twain:** separate.

244. *What has Juliet decided about the Nurse? We may wonder why Juliet doesn't just tell her parents why she cannot marry Paris. Why do you think she does not take this easy way out? Is she protecting Romeo, or does she feel abandoned by her parents?*

Responding to the Play

Analyzing the Play

Act III

Identifying Facts

1. What causes the sword fight between Mercutio and Tybalt?
2. How is Mercutio killed?
3. Why does Romeo kill Tybalt?
4. What is Romeo's punishment?
5. What does Juliet threaten in Scene 2, after learning of Romeo's banishment?
6. What is the Friar's plan in Scene 3?
7. What plans have her parents made for Juliet in Scene 4?

Interpreting Meanings

8. This is Mercutio's last act. Some people believe that if Mercutio had remained alive, he might have persuaded Romeo to act more cautiously and realistically. Remember that Mercutio was not a member of either feuding family; he was related to the Prince. Suppose Mercutio had killed Tybalt in this act, as he very nearly did. How would the action have changed? Do you think the old feud would have erupted again as it did? Explain.
9. The **turning point** of a play takes place when something happens that turns the action of the play either upward toward a happy ending or downward toward a tragic ending. Why does Romeo's killing of Tybalt become the turning point of this play—that is, what **actions** does this killing set in motion, actions that will probably lead to tragedy for Romeo and Juliet?
10. We already know that the play ends in the deaths of Romeo and Juliet. Their willingness to die comes as no surprise to us, because we have been forewarned. Point out the instances in this act where each young person mentions this willingness to die if they are separated.
11. The Nurse has been Juliet's friend and counselor throughout the story. If she had remained her friend and supporter, the story might have ended differently. How does the Nurse offend Juliet in this act and cease to be her friend? How does the Nurse's behavior toward Juliet contrast with the Friar's behavior toward Romeo?
12. The last scene in this act, in which Capulet tells Juliet she will marry the man he wants her to marry, might seem familiar to you from movies or TV shows or novels. Are this lord and this lady like fathers and mothers of all centuries? Is Juliet like all their children? Explain.
13. What have the events of this act revealed to you about the **characters** of Romeo and Juliet? Explain how the young lovers are changing. What hard lessons are they learning about life?
14. By the end of Act III, we have reached the highest point of suspense. **Suspense** causes us to ask questions, to wonder anxiously "What will happen next?" Write out the questions you are asking at the end of Act III.

Analyzing Language and Vocabulary

Names in Shakespeare's Plays

In Act II, Scene 2, Juliet, upset to discover that her lover is named Montague, delivers a famous line about the insignificance of names:

> What's in a name? That which we call a
>   rose
> By any other word would smell as sweet.

Names, however, often *are* significant in Shakespeare's plays. A dictionary will help you answer the following questions about three names in *Romeo and Juliet*.

1. What chemical element is Mercutio named for?
2. What characteristics of this element match Mercutio's character?
3. What does it mean to say that someone is *mercurial* in temperament?
4. Benvolio's name is coined from the words *bene* and *volo*. What do these words mean in Latin?
5. How does his name match Benvolio's temperament?
6. How is Tybalt like the cat he is named for?

Act IV Scene 1. *Friar Laurence's cell.*

Enter FRIAR LAURENCE *and* COUNTY PARIS.

Friar.
On Thursday, sir? The time is very short.
Paris.
My father Capulet will have it so,
And I am nothing slow to slack his haste.
Friar.
You say you do not know the lady's mind.
5   Uneven° is the course; I like it not.
Paris.
Immoderately she weeps for Tybalt's death,
And therefore have I little talked of love;
For Venus smiles not in a house of tears.
Now, sir, her father counts it dangerous
10   That she do give her sorrow so much sway,
And in his wisdom hastes our marriage
To stop the inundation of her tears,
Which, too much minded° by herself alone,
May be put from her by society.
15   Now do you know the reason of this haste.
Friar (*aside*).
I would I knew not why it should be slowed,—
Look, sir, here comes the lady toward my cell.

[*Enter* JULIET.]

Paris.
Happily met, my lady and my wife!
Juliet.
That may be, sir, when I may be a wife.
Paris.
20   That "may be" must be, love, on Thursday next.
Juliet.
What must be shall be.
Friar.   That's a certain text.
Paris.
Come you to make confession to this father?
Juliet.
To answer that, I should confess to you.
Paris.
Do not deny to him that you love me.
Juliet.
25   I will confess to you that I love him.
Paris.
So will ye, I am sure, that you love me.

5. Uneven: irregular or unusual.

13. minded: thought about.

15. *According to Paris, why is Capulet pushing his daughter to marry so quickly?*

26. *In this scene, Juliet's action is to keep up appearances and ward off Paris, who presses his attentions on her. She does this by wittily playing with words. We are fascinated by two things here: by what is being done, and by how it is being done. What double meanings does Juliet intend in the exchange with Paris that follows?*

Juliet.
     If I do so, it will be of more price,
     Being spoke behind your back, than to your face.
Paris.
     Poor soul, thy face is much abused with tears.
Juliet.
30   The tears have got small victory by that,
     For it was bad enough before their spite.°
Paris.
     Thou wrong'st it more than tears with that report.
Juliet.
     That is no slander, sir, which is a truth;
     And what I spake, I spake it to my face.
Paris.
35   Thy face is mine, and thou hast slandered it.
Juliet.
     It may be so, for it is not mine own.
     Are you at leisure, holy father, now,
     Or shall I come to you at evening mass?
Friar.
     My leisure serves me, pensive daughter, now.
40   My lord, we must entreat the time alone.
Paris.
     God shield° I should disturb devotion!
     Juliet, on Thursday early will I rouse ye.
     Till then, adieu, and keep this holy kiss.   [*Exit.*]
Juliet.
     O, shut the door, and when thou hast done so,
45   Come weep with me—past hope, past care, past help!
Friar.
     O Juliet, I already know thy grief;
     It strains me past the compass of my wits.
     I hear thou must, and nothing may prorogue° it,
     On Thursday next be married to this county.
Juliet:
50   Tell me not, friar, that thou hearest of this,
     Unless thou tell me how I may prevent it.
     If in thy wisdom thou canst give no help,
     Do thou but call my resolution wise
     And with this knife I'll help it presently.
55   God joined my heart and Romeo's, thou our hands;
     And ere this hand, by thee to Romeo's sealed,
     Shall be the label° to another deed,°
     Or my true heart with treacherous revolt
     Turn to another, this shall slay them both.
60   Therefore, out of thy long-experienced time,
     Give me some present counsel; or, behold,
     'Twixt my extremes and me this bloody knife

31. **spite:** injury or damage (to her face).

? **38.** *Juliet must show here that the tension of keeping up this pretense is unbearable. Where do you think she pauses and changes her tone?*

41. **God shield:** God forbid.

? **45.** *Paris has gone and Juliet has endured his "holy kiss." Whom is she talking to now?*

48. **prorogue:** postpone

? **54.** *What is Juliet holding in her hand? What is she threatening to do?*
57. **label:** seal. **deed:** contract (of marriage).
? **62.** *The Friar has to put up with a good deal of brandishing of knives and daggers from Romeo and Juliet. Now that the Nurse is no longer Juliet's friend, the Friar has to be the confidant of both Juliet and Romeo. He must listen with patience to their threats of suicide if they cannot be together. What line in Juliet's speech indicates that she has paused and that the Friar, for a time, is silent?*

Shall play the umpire, arbitrating that
Which the commission° of thy years and art
65   Could to no issue of true honor bring.
Be not so long to speak. I long to die
If what thou speak'st speak not of remedy.

Friar.
Hold, daughter. I do spy a kind of hope,
Which craves as desperate an execution
70   As that is desperate which we would prevent.
If, rather than to marry County Paris,
Thou hast the strength of will to slay thyself,
Then is it likely thou wilt undertake
A thing like death to chide away this shame,
75   That cop'st° with death himself to scape from it;
And, if thou darest, I'll give thee remedy.

Juliet.
O, bid me leap, rather than marry Paris,
From off the battlements of any tower,
Or walk in thievish ways, or bid me lurk
80   Where serpents are; chain me with roaring bears,
Or hide me nightly in a charnel house,°
O'ercovered quite with dead men's rattling bones,
With reeky° shanks and yellow chapless° skulls;
Or bid me go into a new-made grave
85   And hide me with a dead man in his shroud—
Things that, to hear them told, have made me
     tremble—
And I will do it without fear or doubt,
To live an unstained wife to my sweet love.

Friar.
Hold, then. Go home, be merry, give consent
90   To marry Paris. Wednesday is tomorrow.
Tomorrow night look that thou lie alone;
Let not the nurse lie with thee in thy chamber.
Take thou this vial, being then in bed,
And this distilling° liquor drink thou off;
95   When presently through all thy veins shall run
A cold and drowsy humor;° for no pulse
Shall keep his native° progress, but surcease;°
No warmth, no breath, shall testify thou livest;
The roses in thy lips and cheeks shall fade
100   To wanny° ashes, thy eyes' windows fall
Like death when he shuts up the day of life;
Each part, deprived of supple government,°
Shall, stiff and stark and cold, appear like death;
And in this borrowed likeness of shrunk death
105   Thou shalt continue two-and-forty hours,
And then awake as from a pleasant sleep.

64. **commision:** authority.

75. **cop'st:** negotiates.

77. *What should Juliet's mood be as she delivers this speech? What will she do, rather than marry Paris?*

81. **charnel house:** house where bones from old graves are kept.

83. **reeky:** damp, stinking. **chapless:** jawless.

89. *Juliet must pay strict attention to the Friar's plan, as must the audience. What day does the Friar tell Juliet to take the potion?*

94. **distilling:** penetrating.

96. **humor:** fluid.
97. **native:** natural. **surcease:** stop.

100. **wanny:** pale.

102. **government:** control.
106. *This may be the most implausible part of the play, but we have been prepared for it. Where have we seen the Friar attending his herbs and heard him talk of magical potions before? What will happen to Juliet when she takes the drug?*

Now, when the bridegroom in the morning comes
To rouse thee from thy bed, there art thou dead.
Then, as the manner of our country is,
110   In thy best robes uncovered on the bier
Thou shalt be borne to that same ancient vault
Where all the kindred of the Capulets lie.
In the meantime, against° thou shalt awake,
Shall Romeo by my letters know our drift;°
115   And hither shall he come; and he and I
Will watch thy waking, and that very night
Shall Romeo bear thee hence to Mantua.
And this shall free thee from this present shame,
If no inconstant toy° nor womanish fear
120   Abate thy valor in the acting it.

Juliet.
   Give me, give me! O, tell not me of fear!

Friar.
   Hold! Get you gone, be strong and prosperous
In this resolve. I'll send a friar with speed
To Mantua, with my letters to thy lord.

Juliet.
125   Love give me strength, and strength shall help afford.
Farewell, dear father.   [*Exit with* FRIAR.]

113. against: before.
114. drift: intentions.

? 117. *How is Romeo to be told of this plan, and when is he to watch Juliet wake and take her to Mantua?*
119. toy: whim.

? 122. *What does the Friar give Juliet as she exits? What exactly is his plan?*

? 126. *In some productions, the Friar holds Juliet back for just a moment and silently blesses her. Why would this make us more anxious about the outcome of his plan?*

Scene 2. *A hall in Capulet's house.*

Enter father CAPULET, LADY CAPULET, NURSE, *and* SERVINGMEN, *two or three.*

Capulet.
   So many guests invite as here are writ.
                       [*Exit a* SERVINGMAN.]
Sirrah, go hire me twenty cunning° cooks.

Servingman. You shall have none ill, sir; for I'll try if they can lick their fingers.

Capulet.
5   How canst thou try them so?

Servingman. Marry, sir, 'tis an ill cook that cannot lick his own fingers. Therefore he that cannot lick his fingers goes not with me.

Capulet. Go, be gone.   [*Exit* SERVINGMAN.]
10   We shall be much unfurnished° for this time.
   What, is my daughter gone to Friar Laurence?

Nurse. Ay, forsooth.

? 1. *Capulet is sending his servant off to invite guests to Juliet's wedding. How would this comic and busy domestic scene contrast with the previous one?*
  2. cunning: skillful.

10. unfurnished: unsupplied (without food).

Capulet.
Well, he may chance to do some good on her.
A peevish self-willed harlotry it is.

[*Enter* JULIET.]

Nurse.
15   See where she comes from shrift with merry look.
Capulet.
How now, my headstrong? Where have you been gadding?
Juliet.
Where I have learnt me to repent the sin
Of disobedient opposition
To you and your behests, and am enjoined
20   By holy Laurence to fall prostrate here
To beg your pardon. Pardon, I beseech you!
Henceforward I am ever ruled by you.
Capulet.
Send for the county. Go tell him of this.
I'll have this knot knit up tomorrow morning.
Juliet.
25   I met the youthful lord at Laurence' cell
And gave him what becomèd° love I might,
Not stepping o'er the bounds of modesty.
Capulet.
Why, I am glad on't. This is well. Stand up.
This is as't should be. Let me see the county.
30   Ay, marry, go, I say, and fetch him hither.
Now, afore God, this reverend holy friar,
All our whole city is much bound to him.
Juliet.
Nurse, will you go with me into my closet,°
To help me sort such needful ornaments
35   As you think fit to furnish me tomorrow?
Lady Capulet.
No, not till Thursday. There is time enough.
Capulet.
Go, nurse, go with her. We'll to church tomorrow.
                  [*Exeunt* JULIET *and* NURSE.]
Lady Capulet.
We shall be short in our provision.
'Tis now near night.
Capulet.   Tush, I will stir about,
40   And all things shall be well, I warrant thee, wife.
Go thou to Juliet, help to deck up her.
I'll not to bed tonight; let me alone.
I'll play the housewife for this once. What, ho!
They are all forth; well, I will walk myself

14. *Harlotry means a "good for nothing," a prostitute. Whom is Capulet referring to as "it"?*

15. *Do you think Juliet really has a merry look, or is the Nurse trying to cover up?*

24. *Why do you think Capulet pushes the marriage up to Wednesday?*

26. becomed: proper or becoming.

28. *According to this speech, what has Juliet been doing since she first addressed her father?*

33. closet: private quarters.

37. *The wedding has been changed to take place on Wednesday. Lady Capulet tries to change her husband's mind, perhaps in consideration of Juliet. But she is not successful. How will this affect the timing of the Friar's plans?*

45   To County Paris, to prepare up him
      Against tomorrow. My heart is wondrous light,
      Since this same wayward girl is so reclaimed.

                          [*Exit with* LADY CAPULET.]

47. *Lord Capulet realizes all the servants are gone. What action is he involved in in this speech? What is his new mood?*

Scene 3. *Juliet's chamber.*

Enter JULIET *and* NURSE.

Juliet.
      Ay, those attires are best; but, gentle nurse,
      I pray thee leave me to myself tonight;
      For I have need of many orisons°

3. **orisons:** prayers.

      To move the heavens to smile upon my state,
5   Which, well thou knowest, is cross and full of sin.

[*Enter* LADY CAPULET.]

Lady Capulet.
      What, are you busy, ho? Need you my help?

6. *Lady Capulet is sometimes played here as loving and gentle with Juliet, perhaps suggesting that she is uneasy about her daughter's change of heart. What emotions should her next speech show?*

Juliet.
      No, madam; we have culled such necessaries
      As are behoveful° for our state° tomorrow.

8. **behoveful:** suitable. **state:** ceremonies.

      So please you, let me now be left alone,
10   And let the nurse this night sit up with you;
      For I am sure you have your hands full all
      In this so sudden business.

Lady Capulet.   Good night.
      Get thee to bed, and rest; for thou hast need.

                  [*Exeunt* LADY CAPULET *and* NURSE.]

Juliet.
      Farewell! God knows when we shall meet again.
15   I have a faint cold fear thrills through my veins
      That almost freezes up the heat of life.
      I'll call them back again to comfort me.
      Nurse!—What should she do here?
      My dismal scene I needs must act alone.
20   Come, vial.
      What if this mixture do not work at all?
      Shall I be married then tomorrow morning?
      No, no! This shall forbid it. Lie thou there.

[*Lays down a dagger.*]

      What if it be a poison which the friar
25   Subtly hath ministered to have me dead,

14. *Here is a fine example of the Shakespearean soliloquy, where a character is poised on the edge of action and deliberates its pros and cons. What are the fears and doubts which Juliet must consider before taking the potion?*

Juliet is not standing still as she delivers this speech. What actions is she involved in?

"How if, when I am laid into the tomb,
I wake before the time that Romeo
Come to redeem me?"

Lest in this marriage he should be dishonored
Because he married me before to Romeo?
I fear it is; and yet methinks it should not,
For he hath still been tried° a holy man.
30   How if, when I am laid into the tomb,
I wake before the time that Romeo
Come to redeem me? There's a fearful point!
Shall I not then be stifled in the vault,
To whose foul mouth no healthsome air breathes in,
35   And there die strangled ere my Romeo comes?
Or, if I live, is it not very like
The horrible conceit of death and night,
Together with the terror of the place—
As in a vault, an ancient receptacle
40   Where for this many hundred years the bones
Of all my buried ancestors are packed;
Where bloody Tybalt, yet but green in earth,°
Lies fest'ring in his shroud; where, as they say,
At some hours in the night spirits resort—
45   Alack, alack, is it not like that I,
So early waking—what with loathsome smells,
And shrieks like mandrakes° torn out of the earth,
That living mortals, hearing them, run mad—
I, if I wake, shall I not be distraught,
50   Environèd with all these hideous fears,
And madly play with my forefathers' joints,
And pluck the mangled Tybalt from his shroud,
And, in this rage, with some great kinsman's bone
As with a club dash out my desp'rate brains?
55   O, look! Methinks I see my cousin's ghost
Seeking out Romeo, that did spit his body
Upon a rapier's point. Stay, Tybalt, stay!
Romeo, Romeo, Romeo, I drink to thee.

[*She falls upon her bed within the curtains.*]

29. still been tried: always been proved.

[?] 29. *Audiences always wonder why the Friar has not simply told the families of Romeo's and Juliet's secret wedding, rather than involve them in such a dangerous plan. How does Juliet explain the Friar's actions?*

42. green in earth: newly buried.

47. mandrakes: plants resembling the human body, which were said to grow beneath the gallows and to scream when torn up.

[?] 58. *How is Juliet's vision of night now different from how she saw it in Act III, Scene 2? What "vision" finally makes her seize the potion and drink it down?*

Scene 4. *A hall in Capulet's house.*

Enter LADY CAPULET *and* NURSE.

Lady Capulet.
    Hold, take these keys and fetch more spices, nurse.
Nurse.
    They call for dates and quinces in the pastry.

[*Enter old* CAPULET.]

[?] 1. *How does this peaceful domestic scene contrast with what has just happened? What is everyone preparing for?*

Capulet.

Come, stir, stir, stir! The second cock hath crowed,

The curfew bell hath rung, 'tis three o'clock.

5   Look to the baked meats, good Angelica;

Spare not for cost.

Nurse.   Go, you cotquean,° go,

Get you to bed! Faith, you'll be sick tomorrow

For this night's watching.

Capulet.

No, not a whit. What, I have watched ere now

10   All night for lesser cause, and ne'er been sick.

Lady Capulet.

Ay, you have been a mouse hunt° in your time;

But I will watch you from such watching now.

                    [*Exit* LADY CAPULET *and* NURSE.]

Capulet.

A jealous hood,° a jealous hood!

[*Enter three or four* FELLOWS *with spits and logs and baskets.*]

                              Now, fellow,

What is there?

First Fellow.

15   Things for the cook, sir; but I know not what.

Capulet.

Make haste, make haste.   [*Exit* FIRST FELLOW.]

    Sirrah, fetch drier logs.

Call Peter; he will show thee where they are.

Second Fellow.

I have a head, sir, that will find out logs°

And never trouble Peter for the matter.

Capulet.

20   Mass,° and well said; a merry whoreson, ha!

Thou shalt be loggerhead.°

                    [*Exit* SECOND FELLOW, *with the others.*]

                              Good faith, 'tis day.

The county will be here with music straight,

For so he said he would. (*Play music offstage.*)

                              I hear him near.

Nurse! Wife! What, ho! What, nurse, I say!

[*Enter* NURSE.]

25   Go waken Juliet; go and trim her up.

I'll go and chat with Paris. Hie, make haste,

Make haste! The bridegroom he is come already:

Make haste, I say.   [*Exit.*]

684   William Shakespeare

5. *Angelica is the Nurse's name. How does Lord Capulet treat her now, as opposed to how he treated her in Act III, Scene 5? What humor does the Nurse add to this scene?*

6. cotquean: old woman (a man who acts like an old woman).

11. mouse hunt: woman-chaser or night-prowler.

12. *What is Lady Capulet's tone here?*

13. hood: female.

18. I . . . logs: in other words, "I have a wooden head."

20. Mass: a mild oath, "By the Mass."

21. loggerhead: blockhead.

21. *Capulet fusses around and has his nose in everything. What actions do you imagine the old man involved in, in this scene?*

23. *The music is bridal music, for the wedding. What irony would the audience sense on hearing this music and knowing what has happened to Juliet?*

Scene 5. *Juliet's chamber.*

Nurse.
    Mistress! What, mistress! Juliet! Fast,° I warrant her, she.
    Why, lamb! Why, lady! Fie, you slugabed.
    Why, love, I say! Madam; sweetheart! Why, bride!
    What, not a word? You take your pennyworths° now;
5   Sleep for a week; for the next night, I warrant,
    The County Paris hath set up his rest°
    That you shall rest but little. God forgive me!
    Marry, and amen. How sound is she asleep!
    I needs must wake her. Madam, madam, madam!
10   Ay, let the county take you in your bed;
    He'll fright you up, i' faith. Will it not be?

[Draws aside the curtains.]

    What, dressed, and in your clothes, and down again?
    I must needs wake you. Lady! Lady! Lady!
    Alas, alas! Help, help! My lady's dead!
15   O weraday that ever I was born!
    Some aqua vitae, ho! My lord! My lady!

[Enter LADY CAPULET.]

Lady Capulet.
    What noise is here?
Nurse.   O lamentable day!
Lady Capulet.
    What is the matter?
Nurse.   Look, look! O heavy day!
Lady Capulet.
    O me, O me! My child, my only life!
20   Revive, look up, or I will die with thee!
    Help, help! Call help.

[Enter CAPULET.]

Capulet.
    For shame, bring Juliet forth; her lord is come.
Nurse.
    She's dead, deceased; she's dead, alack the day!
Lady Capulet.
    Alack the day, she's dead, she's dead, she's dead!
Capulet.
25   Ha! Let me see her. Out alas! She's cold,
    Her blood is settled, and her joints are stiff;
    Life and these lips have long been separated.
    Death lies on her like an untimely frost
    Upon the sweetest flower of all the field.

1. Fast: fast asleep.

? 1. *As the Nurse speaks to Juliet and to herself, she is busy arranging clothes, opening windows, and doing things around the room. In what line here does she touch Juliet and discover she is cold?*

4. pennyworths: small naps.

6. set up his rest: become firmly resolved.

? 29. *What actions are taking place on stage as the three actors now find Juliet "dead"?*

Nurse.

30   O lamentable day!

Lady Capulet.   O woeful time!

Capulet.

Death, that hath ta'en her hence to make me wail,
Ties up my tongue and will not let me speak.

[*Enter* FRIAR LAURENCE *and* PARIS, *with* MUSICIANS.]

Friar.

Come, is the bride ready to go to church?

Capulet.

Ready to go, but never to return.

35   O son, the night before thy wedding day
Hath Death lain with thy wife. There she lies,
Flower as she was, deflowerèd by him.
Death is my son-in-law, Death is my heir;
My daughter he hath wedded. I will die

40   And leave him all. Life, living, all is Death's.

Paris.

Have I thought, love, to see this morning's face,
And doth it give me such a sight as this?

Lady Capulet.

Accursed, unhappy, wretched, hateful day!
Most miserable hour that e'er time saw

45   In lasting labor of his pilgrimage!
But one, poor one, one poor and loving child,
But one thing to rejoice and solace in,
And cruel Death hath catched it from my sight.

Nurse.

O woe! O woeful, woeful, woeful day!

50   Most lamentable day, most woeful day
That ever ever I did yet behold!
O day, O day, O day! O hateful day!
Never was seen so black a day as this.
O woeful day! O woeful day!

Paris.

55   Beguiled, divorcèd, wrongèd, spited, slain!
Most detestable Death, by thee beguiled,
By cruel, cruel thee quite overthrown.
O love! O life!—not life, but love in death!

Capulet.

Despised, distressèd, hated, martyred, killed!

60   Uncomfortable time, why cam'st thou now
To murder, murder our solemnity?
O child, O child! My soul, and not my child!
Dead art thou—alack, my child is dead,
And with my child my joys are buried!

49. *Here again, as with Juliet's bemoaning Romeo's supposed death in an earlier scene, we have Lord and Lady Capulet and the Nurse expressing anguish when we, the audience, know that Juliet is not dead. We tend to listen to them, but we are not moved in the way they are. What words of the Capulets here suggest a loving concern for Juliet that seemed to be missing from earlier scenes? Which character enters and plays dumb about the whole situation?*

58. *In your opinion, what might all these people think caused Juliet's death?*

64. *These expressions of grief are by now sounding mechanical and repetitive. Shakespeare might have written them this way to prevent grief at a false death from gaining our sympathy. How could these lines of the parents, of the Nurse, and of Paris also suggest that the speakers' feelings might not be very deep?*

Friar.

65 Peace, ho, for shame! Confusion's cure lives not
In these confusions. Heaven and yourself
Had part in this fair maid—now heaven hath all,
And all the better is it for the maid.
Your part in her you could not keep from death,

70 But heaven keeps his part in eternal life.
The most you sought was her promotion,
For 'twas your heaven she should be advanced;
And weep ye now, seeing she is advanced
Above the clouds, as high as heaven itself?

75 O, in this love, you love your child so ill
That you run mad, seeing that she is well.°
She's not well married that lives married long,
But she's best married that dies married young.
Dry up your tears and stick your rosemary°

80 On this fair corse, and, as the custom is,
And in her best array bear her to church;
For though fond nature° bids us all lament,
Yet nature's tears are reason's merriment.

Capulet.

All things that we ordainèd festival

85 Turn from their office to black funeral—
Our instruments to melancholy bells,
Our wedding cheer to a sad burial feast;
Our solemn hymns to sullen dirges change;
Our bridal flowers serve for a buried corse;

90 And all things change them to the contrary.

Friar.

Sir, go you in; and, madam, go with him;
And go, Sir Paris. Everyone prepare
To follow this fair corse unto her grave.
The heavens do lower° upon you for some ill;

95 Move them no more by crossing their high will.

[*Exeunt, casting rosemary on her and shutting the curtains. The* NURSE *and* MUSICIANS *remain.*]

First Musician.

Faith, we may put up our pipes and be gone.

Nurse.

Honest good fellows, ah, put up, put up!
For well you know this is a pitiful case.   [*Exit.*]

First Musician.

Ay, by my troth, the case may be amended.

[*Enter* PETER.]

100 **Peter.** Musicians, O, musicians, "Heart's ease,"
"Heart's ease"! O, and you will have me live, play

---

65. *The Friar, of course, knows that Juliet is drugged, not dead. His words here suggest that there has been great confusion on stage. What consolation does he offer—and what sharp rebuke does he give the adults?*

76. well: that is, she is in heaven.

79. rosemary: an herb that stands for remembrance.

82. fond nature: foolish human nature.

83. *Why does the Friar say that reason tells us to be "merry" about death?*

90. *Does Capulet express any guilt? Is he still self-centered?*

94. lower: frown.

98. *These are the Nurse's last lines in the play. True to her character, she jokes as she leaves, though she might do this to cover her grief. The musicians are talking about the cases for their instruments. What "case" is the Nurse referring to?*

"Heart's ease."

First Musician. Why "Heart's ease"?

Peter. O, musicians, because my heart itself plays "My
105   heart is full." O, play me some merry dump° to comfort me.

First Musician. Not a dump we! 'Tis no time to play now.

Peter. You will not then?

First Musician. No.

110   **Peter.** I will then give it you soundly.

First Musician. What will you give us?

Peter. No money, on my faith, but the gleek.° I will give
you° the minstrel.

First Musician. Then will I give you the serving-creature.

115   **Peter.** Then will I lay the serving-creature's dagger on
your pate. I will carry° no crotchets. I'll re you, I'll fa
you. Do you note me?

First Musician. And you re us and fa us, you note us.

Second Musician. Pray you put up your dagger, and put
120   out your wit. Then have at you with my wit!

Peter. I will dry-beat° you with an iron wit, and put up
my iron dagger. Answer me like men.

"When griping grief the heart doth wound,
And doleful dumps the mind oppress,
125   Then music with her silver sound"—
Why "silver sound"? Why "music with her silver
sound"? What say you, Simon Catling?°

First Musician. Marry, sir, because silver hath a sweet
sound.

130   **Peter.** Pretty! What say you, Hugh Rebeck?°

Second Musician. I say "silver sound" because musicians
sound for silver.

Peter. Pretty too! What say you, James Soundpost?°

Third Musician. Faith, I know not what to say.

135   **Peter.** O, I cry you mercy,° you are the singer. I will say
for you. It is "music with her silver sound" because
musicians have no gold for sounding.°

"Then music with her silver sound
With speedy help doth lend redress."   [*Exit.*]

140   **First Musician.** What a pestilent knave is this same!

Second Musician. Hang him, Jack! Come, we'll in here,
tarry for the mourners, and stay dinner.

[*Exit with others.*]

---

105. dump: sad tune.

112. gleek: jeer or insult.

113. give you: call you (to be called a min-strel was an insult to a musician).

116. carry: endure.

121. dry-beat: beat soundly.

127. Catling: a lute string.

130. Rebeck: a fiddle.

133. Soundpost: a violin peg.

135. cry you mercy: beg your pardon.

137. no gold for sounding: no money to jingle in their pockets.

142. *Peter, who was always bossed about by the Nurse, here has grabbed at the chance to boss the musicians, who are a step below him socially. Meanwhile, the stage behind them is being cleared of bedroom trappings. What actions do you imagine during this exchange of insults? (Note that they all want to stay for dinner.) How does this scene provide relief for us— and remind us that ordinary life goes on amid tragedy?*

Responding to the Play

Analyzing the Play

Act IV

Identifying Facts

1. What does Juliet threaten to do if the Friar cannot help her, in Scene 1?
2. What is the Friar's plan to get Romeo and Juliet together?
3. What change does Capulet make in the wedding plans, in Scene 2?
4. What is the situation in the Capulet house at the end of Act IV? What religious comfort does the Friar offer the Capulets?

Interpreting Meanings

5. One of the pleasures in watching a play is knowing something that a character on stage does not know. This use of **dramatic irony** gives us the pleasure of **suspense.** We wait anxiously to find out what will happen when the characters discover what we already know. Where is dramatic irony used in Scenes 2, 3, and 4?
6. What trials or tests does Juliet have to face in this act? How does she respond to each challenge? Explain what her responses tell us about the character of this very young girl.
7. Juliet's parents are the **blocking figures** in the play—they want to block the young lovers and prevent them from marrying. Does Shakespeare present the Capulets as ''bad'' characters? Or does he help us see them as complex human beings, not as mere stage villains? Explain your opinion.

Analyzing Language and Vocabulary

Paraphrasing

Read the following passages in their contexts, and then **paraphrase** each one—that is, rephrase each passage in your own words. Try to rephrase each passage so that it sounds as if it is being spoken by a twentieth-century American. If you find a word you do not know, use **context clues** or the side-notes in the play to help you figure out what it means. The first passage is done for you.

a. PARIS.
My father Capulet will have it so,
And I am nothing slow to slack his haste.
Scene 1, Lines 2–3
a. My father-in-law Capulet wants it that way, and I'm not going to slow him down.

1. PARIS.
Immoderately she weeps for Tybalt's death,
And therefore have I little talked of love;
For Venus smiles not in a house of tears.
Scene 1, Lines 6–8

2. JULIET (to the FRIAR).
Be not so long to speak. I long to die
If what thou speak'st speak not of remedy.
Scene 1, Lines 66–67

3. FRIAR LAURENCE (to JULIET).
The roses in thy lips and cheeks shall fade
To wanny ashes, thy eyes' windows fall
Like death when he shuts up the day of life . . .
Scene 1, Lines 99–101

4. LADY CAPULET (to her husband).
We shall be short in our provision.
'Tis now near night.
Scene 2, Lines 38–39

5. JULIET (holding the poison).
Oh, look! Methinks I see my cousin's ghost
Seeking out Romeo, that did spit his body
Upon a rapier's point. Stay, Tybalt, stay!
Scene 3, Lines 55–57

6. FRIAR LAURENCE (to the CAPULETS after they've discovered JULIET's drugged body).
She's not well married that lives married long,
But she's best married that dies married young.
Dry up your tears and stick your rosemary
On this fair corse, and, as the custom is,
And in all her best array bear her to church . . .
Scene 5, Lines 77–81

Act V Scene 1. *Mantua. A street.*

Enter ROMEO.

Romeo.
    If I may trust the flattering truth of sleep,
    My dreams presage° some joyful news at hand.
    My bosom's lord° sits lightly in his throne,
    And all this day an unaccustomed spirit
5   Lifts me above the ground with cheerful thoughts.
    I dreamt my lady came and found me dead
    (Strange dream that gives a dead man leave to think!)
    And breathed such life with kisses in my lips
    That I revived and was an emperor.
10   Ah me! How sweet is love itself possessed,
    When but love's shadows° are so rich in joy!

[Enter Romeo's man BALTHASAR, *booted from riding.]*

    News from Verona! How now, Balthasar?
    Dost thou not bring me letters from the friar?
    How doth my lady? Is my father well?
15   How fares my Juliet? That I ask again,
    For nothing can be ill if she be well.
Balthasar.
    Then she is well, and nothing can be ill.
    Her body sleeps in Capel's monument,
    And her immortal part with angels lives.
20   I saw her laid low in her kindred's vault
    And presently took post° to tell it you.
    O, pardon me for bringing these ill news,
    Since you did leave it for my office,° sir.
Romeo.
    Is it e'en so? Then I defy you, stars!
25   Thou knowest my lodging. Get me ink and paper
    And hire post horses. I will hence tonight.
Balthasar.
    I do beseech you, sir, have patience.
    Your looks are pale and wild and do import
    Some misadventure.
Romeo.   Tush, thou art deceived.
30   Leave me and do the thing I bid thee do.
    Hast thou no letters to me from the friar?
Balthasar.
    No, my good lord.
Romeo.   No matter. Get thee gone.
    And hire those horses. I'll be with thee straight.
                           [Exit BALTHASAR.]
    Well, Juliet, I will lie with thee tonight.

2. **presage:** foretell.
3. **bosom's lord:** heart.

11. **shadows:** dreams.

? 16. *Some actors playing Romeo reveal in this line that they suspect bad news. What, meanwhile, would Balthasar be doing?*

21. **post:** a post horse.

23. **office:** duty.
? 23. *Balthasar must show that he dreads giving his master the tragic news. What do we know that Balthasar does not know?*

? 26. *Some actors move away here, or hide their faces in their hands. Romeo could address the stars or fate defiantly or tonelessly, to suggest defeat. What would you say is Romeo's tone here?*

? 29. *What does Balthasar suggest Romeo looks like, even though he pretends to be calm?*

? 31. *What letter is Romeo waiting for?*

? 34. *This line is spoken in a still, quiet moment. After a pause, what does Romeo immediately set out to do? Does he hesitate at all to consider his course of action, or does he plunge into it?*

35 Let's see for means. O mischief, thou art swift
    To enter in the thoughts of desperate men!
    I do remember an apothecary,
    And hereabouts 'a dwells, which late I noted
    In tattered weeds,° with overwhelming° brows,
40 Culling of simples.° Meager were his looks,
    Sharp misery had worn him to the bones;
    And in his needy shop a tortoise hung,
    An alligator stuffed, and other skins
    Of ill-shaped fishes; and about his shelves
45 A beggarly account° of empty boxes,
    Green earthen pots, bladders, and musty seeds,
    Remnants of packthread, and old cakes of roses
    Were thinly scatterèd, to make up a show.
    Noting this penury,° to myself I said,
50 "And if a man did need a poison now
    Whose sale is present death in Mantua,
    Here lives a caitiff° wretch would sell it him."
    O, this same thought did but forerun my need,
    And this same needy man must sell it me.
55 As I remember, this should be the house.
    Being holiday, the beggar's shop is shut.
    What, ho! Apothecary!

    [*Enter* APOTHECARY.]

Apothecary.   Who calls so loud?
Romeo.
    Come hither, man. I see that thou art poor.
    Hold, there is forty ducats. Let me have
60 A dram of poison, such soon-speeding gear°
    As will disperse itself through all the veins
    That the life-weary taker may fall dead,
    And that the trunk° may be discharged of breath
    As violently as hasty powder fired
65 Doth hurry from the fatal cannon's womb.
Apothecary.
    Such mortal drugs I have; but Mantua's law
    Is death to any he that utters° them.
Romeo.
    Art thou so bare and full of wretchedness
    And fearest to die? Famine is in thy cheeks,
70 Need and oppression starveth in thy eyes,
    Contempt and beggary hangs upon thy back:
    The world is not thy friend, nor the world's law;
    The world affords no law to make thee rich;
    Then be not poor, but break it and take this.
Apothecary.
75 My poverty but not my will consents.

39. **weeds:** clothes. **overwhelming:** overhanging.
40. **simples:** herbs.

45. **account:** number.

49. **penury:** poverty.

52. **caitiff:** miserable.

? 57. *What actions do you imagine Romeo has been engaged in as he delivers this speech about the apothecary?*

60. **gear:** stuff.

63. **trunk:** body.

67. **utters:** sells.

? 74. *What argument does Romeo use to persuade the apothecary to break the law?*

Romeo.
　I pay thy poverty and not thy will.

Apothecary.
　Put this in any liquid thing you will
　And drink it off, and if you had the strength
　Of twenty men, it would dispatch you straight.

Romeo.
80　There is thy gold—worse poison to men's souls,
　Doing more murder in this loathsome world,
　Than these poor compounds that thou mayst not sell.
　I sell thee poison; thou hast sold me none.
　Farewell. Buy food and get thyself in flesh.
85　Come, cordial and not poison, go with me
　To Juliet's grave; for there must I use thee.　[*Exeunt.*]

79. *What actions do you think have taken place before the apothecary gives Romeo instructions for taking the poison?*

83. *What "poison" has Romeo "sold" the apothecary?*

86. *Why does Romeo call the poison a "cordial," which is a kind of medicine that restores the heartbeat?*

Scene 2. *Friar Laurence's cell.*

Enter FRIAR JOHN.

John.
　Holy Franciscan friar, brother, ho!

[*Enter* FRIAR LAURENCE.]

Laurence.
　This same should be the voice of Friar John.
　Welcome from Mantua. What says Romeo?
　Or, if his mind be writ, give me his letter.

John.
5　Going to find a barefoot brother out,
　One of our order, to associate° me
　Here in this city visiting the sick,
　And finding him, the searchers° of the town,
　Suspecting that we both were in a house
10　Where the infectious pestilence did reign,
　Sealed up the doors, and would not let us forth,
　So that my speed to Mantua there was stayed.

Laurence.
　Who bare my letter, then, to Romeo?

John.
　I could not send it—here it is again—
15　Nor get a messenger to bring it thee,
　So fearful were they of infection.

Laurence.
　Unhappy fortune! By my brotherhood,
　The letter was not nice,° but full of charge,°
　Of dear import; and the neglecting it

3. *In the previous scene, we learned that Romeo had received no letters from the Friar. How would the Friar's question immediately put questions in the audience's mind?*

6. associate: accompany.

8. searchers: health officers.

16. *Another accident! By what strange coincidence was the Friar's letter never delivered to Romeo?*

18. nice: trivial. **charge:** importance.

20   May do much danger. Friar John, go hence,
    Get me an iron crow and bring it straight
    Unto my cell.

John.   Brother, I'll go and bring it thee. [*Exit.*]

Laurence.
    Now must I to the monument alone.
    Within this three hours will fair Juliet wake.

25   She will beshrew me much that Romeo
    Hath had no notice of these accidents;°
    But I will write again to Mantua,
    And keep her at my cell till Romeo come—
    Poor living corse, closed in a dead man's tomb! [*Exit.*]

26. accidents: happenings.

? 29. *If we can accept the "accidents of fate," we have here something like a "chase" scene. We know, but the Friar doesn't know, that Romeo is also on his way to the tomb. Why is it essential that the Friar get there first?*

Scene 3. *A churchyard; in it, a monument belonging to the Capulets.*

Enter PARIS *and his* PAGE *with flowers and scented water.*

Paris.
    Give me thy torch, boy. Hence, and stand aloof.
    Yet put it out, for I would not be seen.
    Under yond yew trees lay thee all along,°
    Holding the ear close to the hollow ground.

5   So shall no foot upon the churchyard tread
    (Being loose, unfirm, with digging up of graves)
    But thou shalt hear it. Whistle then to me,
    As signal that thou hearest something approach.
    Give me those flowers. Do as I bid thee, go.

Page (*aside*).
10   I am almost afraid to stand alone
    Here in the churchyard; yet I will adventure.°

                      [*Retires.*]

Paris.
    Sweet flower, with flowers thy bridal bed I strew
      (O woe! thy canopy is dust and stones)
    Which with sweet water nightly I will dew;
15   Or, wanting that, with tears distilled by moans.
    The obsequies° that I for thee will keep
    Nightly shall be to strew thy grave and weep.

[BOY *whistles*.]

    The boy gives warning something doth approach.
    What cursèd foot wanders this way tonight
20   To cross° my obsequies and true love's rite?
    What, with a torch? Muffle° me, night, awhile.

                      [*Retires.*]

3. all along: lie down at full length (on the ground).

? 9. *Paris is the surprise we did not expect. He adds an interesting complication, as well as some action to this scene. He and his servant, probably wearing dark cloaks, enter on the upper stage. Paris makes his way down alone into the tomb or vault. Why is Paris here?*
11. adventure: risk it.

? 13. *In Shakespeare's theater, we would see a tomb at the rear of the stage. Juliet's body, in its burial gown, would be placed in this tomb, on top of a raised structure. Tybalt's body would lie nearby. What atmosphere must be suggested in this scene? How would lighting be used in a modern stage to create such an atmosphere?*
16. obsequies: observances or rituals.

20. cross: interrupt.
21. Muffle: hide.

[*Enter* ROMEO *and* BALTHASAR *with a torch, a mattock, and a crowbar of iron.*]

Romeo.
Give me that mattock and the wrenching iron.
Hold, take this letter. Early in the morning
See thou deliver it to my lord and father.
25   Give me the light. Upon thy life I charge thee,
Whate'er thou hearest or see'st, stand all aloof
And do not interrupt me in my course.
Why I descend into this bed of death
Is partly to behold my lady's face,
30   But chiefly to take thence from her dead finger
A precious ring—a ring that I must use
In dear employment.° Therefore hence, be gone.
But if thou, jealous,° dost return to pry
In what I farther shall intend to do,
35   By heaven, I will tear thee joint by joint
And strew this hungry churchyard with thy limbs.
The time and my intents are savage-wild,
More fierce and more inexorable far
Than empty tigers or the roaring sea.

Balthasar.
40   I will be gone, sir, and not trouble ye.

Romeo.
So shalt thou show me friendship. Take thou that.
Live, and be prosperous; and farewell, good fellow.

Balthasar (*aside*).
For all this same, I'll hide me hereabout.
His looks I fear, and his intents I doubt.   [*Retires.*]

Romeo.
45   Thou detestable maw,° thou womb of death,
Gorged with the dearest morsel of the earth,
Thus I enforce thy rotten jaws to open,
And in despite° I'll cram thee with more food.

[ROMEO *opens the tomb.*]

Paris.
This is that banishèd haughty Montague
50   That murd'red my love's cousin—with which grief
It is supposed the fair creature died—
And here is come to do some villainous shame
To the dead bodies. I will apprehend him.
Stop thy unhallowèd toil, vile Montague!
55   Can vengeance be pursued further than death?
Condemnèd villain, I do apprehend thee.
Obey, and go with me; for thou must die.

22. *Paris enters with flowers and per-fumed water, but Romeo enters with iron tools—a mattock, which is something like a hoe, and a crowbar. Like Paris, Romeo and his servant also enter at the upper level. What strange excuse does Romeo give his servant for wanting to descend into the tomb alone?*

32. dear employment: important business.
33. jealous: curious.

39. *Romeo makes sure his servant will not interrupt him. What do the last three lines tell about his state of mind?*

45. maw: mouth.

48. in despite: to spite you.
48. *Who or what is Romeo talking to here? What is he doing? What "food" is he going to feed this "mouth"?*

51. *What was believed to be the cause of Juliet's sudden "death"?*

54. *What does Paris do as he speaks this line?*

Romeo.

I must indeed; and therefore came I hither.
Good gentle youth, tempt not a desp'rate man.
60 Fly hence and leave me. Think upon these gone;
Let them affright thee. I beseech thee, youth,
Put not another sin upon my head
By urging me to fury. O, be gone!
By heaven, I love thee better than myself,
65 For I come hither armed against myself.
Stay not, be gone. Live, and hereafter say
A madman's mercy bid thee run away.

Paris.

I do defy thy conjurations.°
And apprehend thee for a felon here.

Romeo.

70 Wilt thou provoke me? Then have at thee, boy!

[*They fight.*]

Page.

O Lord, they fight! I will go call the watch.

[*Exit.* PARIS *falls.*]

Paris.

O, I am slain! If thou be merciful,
Open the tomb, lay me with Juliet.   [*Dies.*]

Romeo.

In faith, I will. Let me peruse this face.
75 Mercutio's kinsman, noble County Paris!
What said my man when my betossèd soul
Did not attend° him as we rode? I think
He told me Paris should have married Juliet.
Said he not so, or did I dream it so?
80 Or am I mad, hearing him talk of Juliet,
To think it was so? O, give me thy hand,
One writ with me in sour misfortune's book!
I'll bury thee in a triumphant grave.
A grave? O, no, a lanthorn,° slaught'red youth,
85 For here lies Juliet, and her beauty makes
This vault a feasting presence full of light.
Death, lie thou there, by a dead man interred.

[*Lays him in the tomb.*]

How oft when men are at the point of death
Have they been merry! Which their keepers° call
90 A lightning before death. O, how may I
Call this a lightning? O my love, my wife!
Death, that hath sucked the honey of thy breath,
Hath had no power yet upon thy beauty.
Thou are not conquered. Beauty's ensign° yet

67. *Romeo doesn't attempt even to fight Paris. How do his words here show calmness and maturity?*
68. conjurations: solemn orders.

70. *What has Paris done to provoke Romeo?*

74. *Whatever we thought of Paris before, we understand now that he loved Juliet. What does Romeo do here?*

77. attend: pay attention to.

82. *Romeo has spoken of himself as "fortune's fool." Why does he see Paris as another victim?*
84. lanthorn: a windowed dome.

87. *Romeo, dragging Paris's body across the stage, now sees Juliet. What words indicate that he sees the tomb transformed? Who is the "dead man" in line 87?*

89. keepers: jailers.

94. ensign: flag (signal).

95   Is crimson in thy lips and in thy cheeks,
     And death's pale flag is not advancèd there.
     Tybalt, liest thou there in the bloody sheet?
     O, what more favor can I do to thee
     Than with that hand that cut thy youth in twain
100 To sunder his that was thine enemy?
     Forgive me, cousin! Ah, dear Juliet,
     Why art thou yet so fair? Shall I believe
     That unsubstantial Death is amorous,
     And that the lean abhorrèd monster keeps
105 Thee here in dark to be his paramour?
     For fear of that I still will stay with thee
     And never from this pallet of dim night
     Depart again. Here, here will I remain
     With worms that are thy chambermaids. O, here
110 Will I set up my everlasting rest
     And shake the yoke of inauspicious stars
     From this world-wearied flesh. Eyes, look your last!
     Arms, take your last embrace! And, lips, O you
     The doors of breath, seal with a righteous kiss
115 A dateless° bargain to engrossing° death!
     Come, bitter conduct;° come, unsavory guide!
     Thou desperate pilot,° now at once run on
     The dashing rocks thy seasick weary bark!
     Here's to my love! (*Drinks.*) O true apothecary!
120 Thy drugs are quick. Thus with a kiss I die.

     [*Falls.*]

     [Enter FRIAR LAURENCE, *with lanthorn, crowbar, and*
       spade.]

Friar.
     Saint Francis be my speed! How oft tonight
     Have my old feet stumbled at graves! Who's there?
Balthasar.
     Here's one, a friend, and one that knows you well.
Friar.
     Bliss be upon you! Tell me, good my friend,
125 What torch is yond that vainly lends his light
     To grubs and eyeless skulls? As I discern,
     It burneth in the Capels' monument.
Balthasar.
     It doth so, holy sir; and there's my master,
     One that you love.
Friar.   Who is it?
Balthasar.   Romeo.
Friar.
130 How long hath he been there?

97. *Romeo turns to see Tybalt's body. Is he angry at his enemy, or does he ask forgiveness?*

102. *Where in this speech does Romeo see life in Juliet, reminding us that she is not dead at all?*

108. *Romeo has climbed to Juliet's tomb and lies beside her. What other actions do you see him doing here?*

115. dateless: timeless. **engrossing:** all-encompassing.
116. conduct: guide (the poison).
117. desperate pilot: Romeo himself.

120. *Actors playing Romeo interpret this last speech in different ways: some play him as if he is in a dream; others as if he were mad; others as if he is in full control of himself; others as if he is desperate and out of his mind with grief, desire, and fear. What clues would direct the way you'd interpret Romeo's feelings as he gives his final speech?*

130. *What feelings must the Friar reveal when he hears that Romeo has gotten to the tomb before he has heard of the plan to drug Juliet?*

Balthasar.   Full half an hour.

Friar.

Go with me to the vault.

Balthasar.   I dare not, sir.

My master knows not but I am gone hence,
And fearfully did menace me with death
If I did stay to look on his intents.

Friar.

135   Stay then; I'll go alone. Fear comes upon me.
O, much I fear some ill unthrifty° thing.

Balthasar.

As I did sleep under this yew tree here,
I dreamt my master and another fought,
And that my master slew him.

Friar.   Romeo!

140   Alack, alack, what blood is this which stains
The stony entrance of this sepulcher?
What means these masterless and gory swords
To lie discolored by this place of peace?

[Enters the tomb.]

Romeo! O, pale! Who else? What, Paris too?
145   And steeped in blood? Ah, what an unkind° hour
Is guilty of this lamentable chance!
The lady stirs.

[JULIET rises.]

Juliet.

O comfortable° friar! Where is my lord?
I do remember well where I should be,
150   And there I am. Where is my Romeo?

Friar.

I hear some noise. Lady, come from that nest
Of death, contagion, and unnatural sleep.
A greater power than we can contradict
Hath thwarted our intents. Come, come away.
155   Thy husband in thy bosom there lies dead;
And Paris too. Come, I'll dispose of thee
Among a sisterhood of holy nuns.
Stay not to question, for the watch is coming.
Come, go, good Juliet. I dare no longer stay.

Juliet.

160   Go, get thee hence, for I will not away.

[Exit FRIAR.]

What's here? A cup, closed in my truelove's hand?
Poison, I see, hath been his timeless° end.
O churl!° Drunk all, and left no friendly drop
To help me after? I will kiss thy lips.

136. unthrifty: unlucky.

141. *Where is the Friar as he discovers the bloodstains?*

145. unkind: unnatural.

147. *This short line suggests that the Friar rushes to Juliet and waits for her to speak. What must his feelings be?*

148. comfortable: comforting.

152. *For the Friar, this is a terrible moment. What is his reaction to the noise he hears?*

159. *What does the Friar say will become of Juliet? What is Juliet doing, or refusing to do, as the Friar repeatedly tries to move her?*

160. *It is hard to believe that after all his concern for these two young lovers, the Friar would become a coward at this moment and leave Juliet to harm herself. How must the Friar act here to persuade us that he is frantic and not very sensible?*

162. timeless: untimely.

163. churl: rude fellow (spoken teasingly).

165   Haply some poison yet doth hang on them
         To make me die with a restorative.

[*Kisses him.*]

         Thy lips are warm!
Chief Watchman (*within*). Lead, boy. Which way?
Juliet.
         Yea, noise? Then I'll be brief. O happy° dagger!

[*Snatches Romeo's dagger.*]

170   This is thy sheath; there rust, and let me die.

[*She stabs herself and falls.*]

[*Enter Paris's* BOY *and* WATCH.]

Boy.
         This is the place. There, where the torch doth burn.
Chief Watchman.
         The ground is bloody. Search about the churchyard.

169. happy: lucky (to be here when she needs it).

Stage direction: *Do you see Juliet in her last moments as being half-crazed or calm and purposeful or something else? Do you think this scene can be played either way? Or both ways? How would you do it?*

698   **William Shakespeare**

"Ah, what an unkind hour
Is guilty of this lamentable chance!"

Go, some of you; whoe'er you find attach.
　　　　　　　[*Exeunt some of the* WATCH.]
Pitiful sight! Here lies the county slain;
175　And Juliet bleeding, warm, and newly dead,
Who here hath lain this two days burièd.
Go, tell the prince; run to the Capulets;
Raise up the Montagues; some others search.
　　　　　　　[*Exeunt others of the* WATCH.]
We see the ground whereon these woes do lie,
180　But the true ground° of all these piteous woes
We cannot without circumstance° descry.

180. ground: cause.
181. circumstance: details.

[*Enter some of the* WATCH, *with Romeo's man*
BALTHASAR.]

Second Watchman.
　Here's Romeo's man. We found him in the churchyard.
Chief Watchman.
　Hold him in safety till the prince come hither.

[*Enter* FRIAR LAURENCE *and another* WATCHMAN.]

Third Watchman.

Here is a friar that trembles, sighs, and weeps.

185   We took this mattock and this spade from him

As he was coming from this churchyard's side.

Chief Watchman.

A great suspicion! Stay the friar too.

[*Enter the* PRINCE *and* ATTENDANTS.]

Prince.

What misadventure is so early up,

That calls our person from our morning rest?

[*Enter* CAPULET *and his wife,* LADY CAPULET, *with others.*]

Capulet.

190   What should it be, that is so shrieked abroad?

Lady Capulet.

O, the people in the street cry "Romeo,"

Some "Juliet," and some "Paris"; and all run

With open outcry toward our monument.

Prince.

What fear is this which startles in your ears?

Chief Watchman.

195   Sovereign, here lies the County Paris slain;

And Romeo dead; and Juliet, dead before,

Warm and new killed.

Prince.

Search, seek, and know how this foul murder comes.

Chief Watchman.

Here is a friar, and slaughtered Romeo's man,

200   With instruments upon them fit to open

These dead men's tombs.

Capulet.

O heavens! O wife, look how our daughter bleeds!

This dagger hath mista'en, for, lo, his house°

Is empty on the back of Montague,

205   And it missheathèd in my daughter's bosom!

Lady Capulet.

O me, this sight of death is as a bell

That warns° my old age to a sepulcher.

[*Enter* MONTAGUE *and others.*]

Prince.

Come, Montague; for thou art early up

To see thy son and heir more early down.

Montague.

210   Alas, my liege, my wife is dead tonight!

184. *How do the watchman's words help us picture the state the Friar is in?*

193. *As the tomb begins to fill up with people, noises and cries are heard offstage. What does Lady Capulet suggest is being "shrieked abroad" in Verona?*

203. **house:** sheath.

207. **warns:** summons.

Grief of my son's exile hath stopped her breath.
What further woe conspires against mine age?

Prince.
Look, and thou shalt see.

Montague.
O thou untaught! What manners is in this,
215   To press before thy father to a grave?

Prince.
Seal up the mouth of outrage for a while,
Till we can clear these ambiguities
And know their spring, their head, their true descent;
And then will I be general of your woes°
220   And lead you even to death. Meantime forbear,
And let mischance be slave to patience.
Bring forth the parties of suspicion.

Friar.
I am the greatest, able to do least,
Yet most suspected, as the time and place
225   Doth make against me, of this direful murder;
And here I stand, both to impeach and purge°
Myself condemnèd and myself excused.

Prince.
Then say at once what thou dost know in this.

Friar.
I will be brief, for my short date of breath°
230   Is not so long as is a tedious tale.
Romeo, there dead, was husband to that Juliet;
And she, there dead, that's Romeo's faithful wife.
I married them; and their stolen marriage day
Was Tybalt's doomsday, whose untimely death
235   Banished the new-made bridegroom from this city;
For whom, and not for Tybalt, Juliet pined.
You, to remove that siege of grief from her,
Betrothed and would have married her perforce
To County Paris. Then comes she to me
240   And with wild looks bid me devise some mean
To rid her from this second marriage,
Or in my cell there would she kill herself.
Then gave I her (so tutored by my art)
A sleeping potion; which so took effect
245   As I intended, for it wrought on her
The form of death. Meantime I writ to Romeo
That he should hither come as° this dire night
To help to take her from her borrowed grave,
Being the time the potion's force should cease.
250   But he which bore my letter, Friar John,
Was stayed by accident, and yesternight
Returned my letter back. Then all alone

? **215.** *Whom is Montague talking to here?*

219. general of your woes: leader of your mourning.

226. impeach and purge: charge and punish.

229. date of breath: term of life.

? **230.** *All of what the Friar says here is known by the audience. In some productions, this long speech is cut entirely, but it is important for us to imagine the effect the speech has on the Montagues, the Capulets, and the Prince. This is the moment when they discover what we've known all along. Where do you think the Friar must pause as the families cry out and weep?*

? **237.** *Whom does the Friar mean by "You"?*

247. as: on.

At the prefixèd hour of her waking
Came I to take her from her kindred's vault;
255 Meaning to keep her closely at my cell
Till I conveniently could send to Romeo.
But when I came, some minute ere the time
Of her awakening, here untimely lay
The noble Paris and true Romeo dead.
260 She wakes; and I entreated her come forth
And bear this work of heaven with patience;
But then a noise did scare me from the tomb,
And she, too desperate, would not go with me,
But, as it seems, did violence on herself.
265 All this I know, and to the marriage
Her nurse is privy;° and if aught in this
Miscarried by my fault, let my old life
Be sacrificed some hour before his time
Unto the rigor of severest law.

Prince.
270 We still° have known thee for a holy man.
Where's Romeo's man? What can he say to this?

Balthasar.
I brought my master news of Juliet's death;
And then in post he came from Mantua
To this same place, to this same monument.
275 This letter he early bid me give his father,
And threat'ned me with death, going in the vault,
If I departed not and left him there.

Prince.
Give me the letter. I will look on it.
Where is the county's page that raised the watch?
280 Sirrah, what made your master in this place?

Boy.
He came with flowers to strew his lady's grave;
And bid me stand aloof, and so I did.
Anon comes one with light to ope the tomb;
And by and by my master drew on him;
285 And then I ran away to call the watch.

Prince.
This letter doth make good the friar's words,
Their course of love, the tidings of her death;
And here he writes that he did buy a poison
Of a poor apothecary and therewithal
290 Came to this vault to die and lie with Juliet.
Where be these enemies? Capulet, Montague,
See what a scourge is laid upon your hate,
That heaven finds means to kill your joys with love.
And I, for winking at° your discords too,
295 Have lost a brace° of kinsmen. All are punished.

261. *This line expresses the Friar's view of life. How would the play have been different if both Romeo and Juliet had been able, from the start, to bear their trials "with patience"? How does this also apply to the adults in the play?*

266. privy: an accessory (she knows what has happened).

269. *Does the Friar accept responsibility for his part in the tragedy? What does he say?*
270. still: always.

285. *What would the families be doing as the Prince now pauses to read the letter?*

294. winking at: closing his eyes to.
295. brace: pair (Mercutio and Paris).
295. *We have been repeatedly reminded of the role of fate in this tragedy, but the human characters also admit their responsibility. What does the Prince admit? Do you think that some people have been punished too harshly and some not severely enough?*

"For never was a story of more woe
Than this of Juliet and her Romeo."

Capulet.
O brother Montague, give me thy hand.
This is my daughter's jointure,° for no more
Can I demand.

Montague. But I can give thee more;
For I will raise her statue in pure gold,
300   That whiles Verona by that name is known,
There shall no figure at such rate° be set
As that of true and faithful Juliet.

Capulet.
As rich shall Romeo's by his lady's lie—
Poor sacrifices of our enmity!

Prince.
305   A glooming peace this morning with it brings.
    The sun for sorrow will not show his head.
Go hence, to have more talk of these sad things;
    Some shall be pardoned, and some punishèd;
For never was a story of more woe
310   Than this of Juliet and her Romeo.   [*Exeunt omnes.*]

297. jointure: marriage settlement.

301. rate: value.

? **304.** *The central focus on stage now is not the families, but the bodies of Romeo and Juliet. Over the bodies of their children, the families join hands. What words of Capulet's admit his part in the tragedy?*

? **310.** *As the actors solemnly file out, the Friar is usually the last to exit. Some productions have the fathers leave last. At times, the Nurse reappears and makes the final exit. What different effects would be produced by having different characters be the last to leave the stage?*

Finally, only the bodies are left on stage. Can you describe how lighting would be used as the action closes?

Responding to the Play

Analyzing the Play

Act V

Identifying Facts

1. What news does Romeo's servant bring him in Scene 1?
2. Why does Romeo buy the poison?
3. Why didn't Romeo receive the Friar's letter explaining the change in plans?
4. What does Romeo find when he enters the tomb?
5. What happens to Romeo and then to Juliet?
6. What has become of the feud between the families by the play's end?

Interpreting Meanings

7. The first two scenes of this act include unlucky **coincidences** that may strain our belief. What coincidences conspire to wreck the Friar's plans? Do any of these coincidences seem incredible to you? Explain.
8. **Dramatic irony** has been used throughout this tragedy. In what scene does this sense of irony reach its peak in Act V?
9. The **climax** of a play is its most intensely emotional moment, that moment when we feel overcome with horror or sadness or fear or regret. The climax of Shakespeare's plays always comes in the final act. When in this act would you say the climax takes place—what were your feelings at this moment?
10. In the midst of all the comings and goings, Romeo's mood changes, from the time he says "the time and my intents are savage-wild" in Scene 3, to the lines he speaks before taking the poison, ending with "Thus with a kiss I die." Discuss these changes in Romeo. He is still the same young man, still deeply in love, but there is a difference in his mood by the play's end. How would you describe it?
11. For a final time, the Prince comes in at the end of a fight. What is the difference this time, in what he sees, in what he says, and in what has been accomplished?

The Play as a Whole

1. The Prince turns to the Capulets and Montagues in the last scene and says:

   "See what a scourge is laid upon your hate,
   That heaven finds means to kill your joys
       with love."

   It seems **ironic** that love could kill joy, but how in this play did "love" kill the families' "joys"? In what way is the whole play about the way that "heaven" scourged, or punished, people for *hating*?
2. There have been many references to the workings of Fate in the play. In your opinion, what caused the tragedy of Romeo and Juliet? Do you believe it was due to fate, or to human errors? Explain.
3. Explain how each of the ideas listed on page 601 is revealed in *Romeo and Juliet*. Which of these ideas do you think is the most important one in the play?
4. If you had to select one line or one speech from the play to express its main idea, which line or passage would you select?

Writing About the Play

A Creative Response

1. **Writing a New Ending.** Suppose Romeo and Juliet had survived because the Friar's schemes had worked. Write a scene showing them facing some family problem twenty years later. In their dialogue, make clear what has happened to the Capulets, the Friar, and the Nurse. Use stage directions to tell when and where your scene is set.
2. **Updating a Scene.** Rewrite the balcony scene (Act II, Scene 2) so that it is set today in the backyard of Juliet's suburban home (or on the fire escape of a city apartment). Rewrite Romeo and Juliet's dialogue in contemporary English. Before you write, decide exactly what your setting will be, and describe it in your stage directions.

3. **Writing a Beginning.** Write a paragraph in which you explain what might have caused the feud between the Capulets and the Montagues. Tell *when* the hatred started, and *why* it started.

4. **Updating the Characters.** If Romeo, Juliet, and Mercutio lived today, what would be their preferences in music, clothing, reading, sports, and parties? What future would each one look forward to? Write out a personality profile of each character, as if he or she were living today and attending your school.

A Critical Response

5. **Analyzing a Character.** Write a character analysis, using the following critical comment as your thesis statement. Be sure to use details from the play to support what the critic says about Juliet and how the world treated her.

> Shakespeare's real miracle . . . was Juliet, transformed from an adolescent arrogantly eager to outdo her elders to an appealing child-woman, barely fourteen, who learns to mix courage with her innocence, yet falls victim to a world that only briefly and unintentionally but fatally treats her as a plaything.
>
> —J. A. Bryant, Jr.

6. **Responding to the Characters' Actions.** It would be a mistake to think that this play idealizes the young lovers. Shakespeare is careful to remind us that Romeo and Juliet's love is destructive because it fails to see life as it really is. Romeo and Juliet do not act with caution and patience and wisdom. They act on impulse and in haste. In an essay, tell what you think Romeo and Juliet *should* have done at at least three different points in the play, but failed to do. Do you think they even could have triumphed? Do you think that Mercutio might have helped them had he lived?

7. **Comparing and Contrasting Characters.** The Nurse and Mercutio both have practical, earthy views of life. Both enjoy a joke, and both bring comedy to the play. But they are also totally different. How are Mercutio and the Nurse different in their values and loyalties? Do you admire one character? Were you disappointed in the other one? Write an essay in which you compare and contrast the characters of Mercutio and the Nurse.

8. **Analyzing and Responding to Theme.** On page 601 you'll find some ideas that are revealed in this play. Review these ideas and select one to develop into a statement of theme. Then, in an essay, show how this theme is revealed by certain actions and speeches in the play. At the end of your essay, tell how you feel about this theme of *Romeo and Juliet*.

9. **Applying the Story to Modern Life.** The basic situation of this story arises from a feud between two families. No reason is given for the feud—it seems to be based on mindless hatreds. Think of other stories or movies or TV shows based on hatreds growing out of ignorance of another race, religion, or nationality. Could the story of Romeo and Juliet take place today? Write an essay explaining whether or not you think the basic situation of this play could be set in the 1990's, in a physical setting you are familiar with.

10. **Analyzing Language.** Romeo and Juliet speak of each other and of their feelings in **images** of darkness and light, of day and night. Write an essay in which you trace their use of images, considering particularly these speeches: Romeo's speech in Act II, Scene 2, when he first sees Juliet on the balcony; Juliet's speech in the garden as she waits for Romeo in Act III, Scene 2; Romeo and Juliet's parting speech in Act III, Scene 5; and Romeo's dying speech in Act V, Scene 3. Use the first sentence above as your topic sentence.

Literature & Language

Creating Figures of Speech

The glory of *Romeo and Juliet* is its poetry. Shakespeare's characters invent images and figures of speech so rich and so varied that the play, which has lived now for almost four hundred years, will probably live as long as English continues to be spoken.

Similes

The simplest form of figurative language is the **simile**, a clearly stated comparison between two different things. A simile uses words such as *like* or *as* or *than* in stating its comparison. For example, Romeo, dejected over Rosaline, says of love, "It pricks like thorn." Romeo's simile suggests that love can cause pain, just as a thorn can when it pierces the skin. (And you notice that his figure of speech is about love for *Rosaline*—a name related to *rose,* a beautiful flower with a thorny stem.)

In the following quotations, identify the similes and tell what two different things are brought together in each. In what important way are the two things alike?

1. ROMEO.
O, she doth teach the torches to burn bright!
It seems she hangs upon the cheek of night
As a rich jewel in an Ethiop's ear—
Beauty too rich for use, for earth too dear!
Act I, Scene 5, lines 45–48

2. ROMEO.
O, speak again, bright angel, for thou art
As glorious to this night, being o'er my head,
As is a wingèd messenger of heaven
Unto the white-upturnèd wond'ring eyes
Of mortals that fall back to gaze on him
When he bestrides the lazy puffing clouds
And sails upon the bosom of the air.
Act II, Scene 2, lines 26–32

3. ROMEO.
Love goes toward love as schoolboys from their books;

But love from love, toward school with heavy looks.
Act II, Scene 2, lines 157–158

4. JULIET.
Come, night; come, Romeo; come, thou day in night;
For thou wilt lie upon the wings of night
Whiter than new snow upon a raven's back.
Act III, Scene 2, lines 17–19

5. LORD CAPULET.
Death lies on her like an untimely frost
Upon the sweetest flower of all the field.
Act IV, Scene 5, lines 28–29

Metaphors

Metaphors omit the words *like* or *as* or *than,* and directly identify two different things. When the Nurse says of Paris ". . . he's a flower, a very flower," she immediately identifies Paris's good looks with a beautiful blossom. When Romeo complains that "Love is a smoke raised from the fume of sighs," he identifies love and its fleeting quality with smoke, which disappears as it rises. Metaphors may also be **implied.** The Prince uses implied metaphors when he angrily accuses the citizens: "You men, you beasts,/That quench the fire of your pernicious rage / With purple fountains issuing from your veins." The Prince compares the anger of the citizens with a fire, and the blood issuing from their wounds to purple fountains.

Here are some passages containing metaphors. Tell what each metaphor is, and identify the two things brought together in the comparison. Some passages contain more than one metaphor.

1. ROMEO (to Juliet).
If I profane with my unworthiest hand
  This holy shrine, the gentle sin is this:
My lips, two blushing pilgrims, ready stand
  To smooth that rough touch with a tender kiss.
Act I, Scene 5, lines 94–97

Literature & *Language*/*cont.*

2. ROMEO (under Juliet's balcony).
But soft! What light through yonder window
  breaks?
It is the East, and Juliet is the sun!
> Act II, Scene 2, lines 2–3

3. JULIET (to Romeo).
This bud of love, by summer's ripening breath,
May prove a beauteous flower when next we
  meet.
> Act II, Scene 2, lines 121–122

4. NURSE (to Juliet, about Paris).
. . . I think it best you married with the county.
O, he's a lovely gentleman!
Romeo's a dishclout to him.
> Act III, Scene 5, lines 219–221

5. ROMEO (before Juliet's tomb).
Thou detestable maw, thou womb of death,
Gorged with the dearest morsel of the earth,
Thus I enforce thy rotten jaws to open,
And in despite I'll cram thee with more food.
> Act V, Scene 3, lines 45–48

Personification

Personification is a special kind of metaphor, in which something that is not a person—an object, something in nature, an emotion—is spoken of as if it were human. When Benvolio says that the sun "peered forth the golden windows of the east," he is personifying the sun by saying it "peered," as if it had two eyes and were looking out a window. Here are some quotations from *Romeo and Juliet* that contain personifications. In each, what non-human thing is spoken of as if it were a person? Some passages contain more than one personification.

1. CAPULET.
. . . well-appareled April on the heel
Of limping winter treads . . .
> Act I, Scene 2, lines 27–28

2. PROLOGUE.
Now old desire doth in his deathbed lie,
  And young affection gapes to be his heir.
> Act II, Prologue, lines 1–2

3. JULIET.
. . . Come, civil night,
Thou sober-suited matron all in black,
And learn me how to lose a winning match.
> Act III, Scene 2, lines 10–12

4. ROMEO.
Night's candles are burnt out, and jocund day
Stands tiptoe on the misty mountaintops.
> Act III, Scene 5, lines 9–10

5. ROMEO (to Juliet's "corpse").
. . . Shall I believe
That unsubstantial Death is amorous,
And that the lean abhorrèd monster keeps
Thee here in dark to be his paramour?
> Act V, Scene 3, lines 102–105

Puns

Shakespeare's audience loved puns, which are plays on the multiple meanings of words. (Jokes today are still based on puns. Question: "What has four wheels and flies?" Answer: "A garbage truck." This pun is based on the two meanings of the word *flies*.) Many of the puns in *Romeo and Juliet* go over our heads today because jokes go out of fashion very quickly and some of Shakespeare's word play is done with words we just don't use any more.

Mercutio is the best punster in the play, though Romeo does pretty well in Act III when he matches wits with his friend. When Mercutio spies Romeo coming down the street, he says Romeo comes "without his roe." *Roe* can refer to a female deer, so if Romeo is without his roe, he's without his girl. *Roe* also refers to fish eggs, so "without his roe" can mean that Romeo's been gutted (we'd say he's "gutless"), as a fish is when its eggs are removed. The word *Romeo* without the letters r,o,e is *mo*, and in Shakespeare's day this was a whining sound. Mercutio could be mocking his friend for whining about not being loved by Rosaline.

Here are three more puns from the play. If you can explain the plays on meaning, you'll have caught the jokes.

1. ROMEO (on seeing Mercutio stabbed).
Courage man, the hurt cannot be much.
MERCUTIO.
. . . Ask for me tomorrow, and you shall find me a grave man.
Act III, Scene I, lines 94–97

2. ROMEO.
Give me a torch. I am not for this ambling.
Being but heavy, I will bear the light.
Act I, Scene 4, lines 11–12

3. ROMEO.
. . . You have dancing shoes
With nimble soles; I have a soul of lead
So stakes me to the ground I cannot move.
Act I, Scene 4, lines 14–16

Allusions

One of the books used in the grammar schools of Shakespeare's time was a book of mythology called *Metamorphoses*, by the Roman writer Ovid. Shakespeare knew his mythology very well, and so did most of his audience—they knew much more about it than most people know today. When Shakespeare had Lord Montague say in Act I that the sun is drawing "the shady curtains from Aurora's bed," he could be sure that his audience would know that Aurora was the goddess of dawn. Such references to mythology (or to religion, history, or politics) are called **allusions**. Here are three allusions to mythology from *Romeo and Juliet*. What story or character is Shakespeare alluding to in each?

1. JULIET.
Bondage is hoarse and may not speak aloud,
Else would I tear the cave where Echo lies
And make her airy tongue more hoarse than mine
With repetition of "My Romeo!"
Act II, Scene 2, lines 161–164

2. FRIAR.
The gray-eyed morn smiles on the frowning night,
Check'ring the eastern clouds with streaks of light;
And fleckèd darkness like a drunkard reels
From forth day's path and Titan's burning wheels.
Act II, Scene 3, lines 1–4

3. JULIET.
Gallop apace, you fiery-footed steeds,
Towards Phoebus' lodging! Such a wagoner
As Phaethon would whip you to the west
And bring in cloudy night immediately.
Act III, Scene 2, lines 1–4

TESTING A HYPOTHESIS

Writing Assignment

Write an essay of at least one paragraph in which you give examples to support or refute one of the following statements about the characters in *Romeo and Juliet*:

1. Juliet is more heroic and mature than Romeo.
2. Romeo is a lovelorn character who falls in and out of love very easily.
3. Mercutio is mentally unstable.
4. Mercutio is the most practical and admirable character in the play.
5. Friar Laurence has ulterior motives for helping Romeo and Juliet.

Background

If you were an actor who had gotten a part in a Shakespearean play, you would want to find out as much as you could about your character. When actors get a part, they ask themselves questions such as: "What are my motives? What do I want? Am I greedy, unstable, mature, intelligent, romantic, insensitive? What are my flaws? My strengths?" Some actors go even further: they imagine the house where the character lives, the clothes he or she wears, and what his or her particular mannerisms are.

What an actor does, then, is to form various hypotheses about a character. A **hypothesis** (hī·päth'ə·sis) is a theory or proposition, which must be tested before it can be proven as true. To prove a hypothesis about a character, the actor must look at the script. The character's speeches and actions must support the hypothesis. Finding evidence to support an assumption is called **testing** a hypothesis. (You may be familiar with hypothesis testing as the basis for inquiry in the sciences.)

After your test, you might conclude that there is no evidence to support your assumption, which makes your hypothesis invalid, or not true. Your hypothesis would then have to be revised or thrown out entirely.

Here are some hypotheses. How would you go about testing them?

1. Everything that goes up must come down.
2. All invisible pigs have stripes.
3. All beautiful people are conceited.
4. New cars have too many breakable gadgets.

There are two major ways you can prove or disprove any hypothesis:

1. You can find examples to *support* your idea.
2. You can look for but find no examples that *disagree* with your idea.

Sometimes the only way to prove that a hypothesis is valid is to find no **counterexamples**—examples that disprove the theory. Consider the statement, "All beautiful people are conceited." If you found a beautiful person who was not conceited, you would have a counterexample, or evidence that contradicts your theory. Your hypothesis would be *invalid*. If, on the other hand, you could find no invisible pigs without stripes, this hypothesis (however fantastic) would be valid until proven otherwise.

Prewriting

1. Choose one of the five hypotheses suggested in the writing assignment.
2. Fill out a chart like the following:

Details that support the hypothesis	Details that indicate that the hypothesis is false
1. 2. 3. etc.	1. 2. 3. etc.

On one side, write down everything you can find in *Romeo and Juliet* that supports your hypothesis. Quote what the character says, and cite details telling how he or she acts, or how other people respond to him or her.

3. On the other side, write down all the details that say, "This hypothesis is *not* true." Be careful, and be hard on yourself! Don't start out just looking for points that support your hypothesis. This is not good thinking (your hypothesis just might be wrong).

4. Now look at your notes. Do the points supporting your hypothesis outweigh the counterexamples? If so, your hypothesis is probably correct. However, if your two lists are evenly or closely matched, you probably need to search through the text again. You might also need to reword your hypothesis.

5. Once you have arrived at a valid hypothesis,

select the evidence in your list which most strongly supports your theory. Four or five strong, precise examples will give more powerful support to your hypothesis than ten insignificant details.

Writing

Open your paragraph or essay by stating your hypothesis; this will also be your thesis statement. Next, cite details from the play (what the character says and does) that support your hypothesis. Conclude your essay by summarizing your ideas and examples. Depending on how many details you cite, your essay might be more than one paragraph long.

For example, here is how you might begin an essay based on the hypothesis about Juliet's heroism and maturity:

In Shakespeare's *Romeo and Juliet,* I first thought of Romeo as more heroic and mature, because he is older and takes the lead. Actually, it is Juliet who is more heroic and mature. Juliet knows very well what she risks by loving Romeo. She says, "Although I joy in thee, / I have no joy of this contract tonight. / It is too rash, too unadvised, too sudden; / Too like the lightning, which doth cease to be / Ere one can say it lightens." (See Act II, Scene 2, lines 116–120.)	**Cites the play's title and author.** **States the hypothesis: thesis statement.** **Uses a direct quotation to support the hypothesis.** **Cites the source of the quote.**

Checklist for Revision

1. Have you opened the essay by stating your hypothesis?

2. Have you supported the hypothesis with examples of action and dialogue from the play?

3. Have you checked your direct quotations from the play, to be sure you've quoted accurately?

4. Have you cited the source of each quotation (act, scene, and line numbers)?

5. Have you ended the essay with a summary of the hypothesis and its main supporting points?

THE ELEMENTS OF THE EPIC

Ancient Greek statue. Bronze.

Museo de Magna Graecia, Calabria. Photo: Art Resource

UNIT SIX   **David Adams Leeming**

THE ODYSSEY

An introduction by **David Adams Leeming**

If the world was given to us to explore and master, here is a tale, a play, a song about that endeavor long ago, by no means neglecting self-mastery, which in a sense is the whole point. Electronic brains may help us to use our heads but will not excuse us from that duty, and as to our hearts—cardiograms cannot diagnose what may be most ill about them or confirm what may be best. . . . Nor do I suppose that the pleasure of hearing a story in words has quite gone out. Even movies and TV make use of words. The **Odyssey** *at all events was made for your pleasure, in Homer's words and in mine.*

—Robert Fitzgerald

The Odyssey

> " **T**hese real battles would have taken place as early as 1200 B.C.—a time that was at least as long ago for Homer's audience as the Pilgrims' landing at Plymouth Rock is for us."

The world's most famous epic poems—Homer's *Iliad* and *Odyssey*—were composed between 900 and 700 B.C. The poems describe legendary events that probably can be traced to real historical struggles for control of the waterway leading from the Aegean Sea to the Sea of Marmara and the Black Sea. These real battles would have taken place as early as 1200 B.C.—a time that was at least as long ago for Homer's audience as the Pilgrims' landing at Plymouth Rock is for us.

Homer's first epic was the *Iliad,* which tells of a ten-year war fought on the plains beyond the walls of Troy (a city also known as Ilion). The ruins of Troy can still be seen today in what is now western Turkey. In Homer's story, the Trojan War was fought between the people of Troy and an alliance of early Greek kings (at this time, each island and area of the Greek mainland had its own king). The *Iliad* tells us that the cause of the war was the world's most beautiful woman, Helen. Helen had left her Greek husband, King Menelaus, and had run off with a man called Paris, who was a prince of Troy. The *Odyssey,* Homer's second epic, is the story of the attempt of one Greek soldier, Odysseus, to get home after the Trojan War. All epic poems in the Western world owe something to the basic patterns established by these two stories.

What Is an Epic?

Epics are long narrative poems that tell of the adventures of heroes who embody the values of their particular civilizations. The Greeks for centuries used the *Iliad* and the *Odyssey* in their schools to

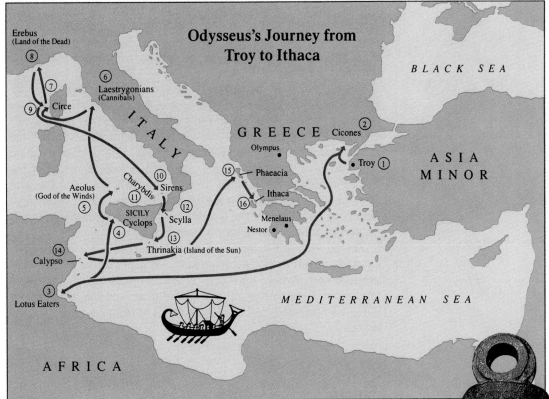

Odysseus's Journey from Troy to Ithaca

Erebus
(Land of the Dead) ⑧

⑦

⑨ Circe

⑥ Laestrygonians
(Cannibals)

ITALY

Aeolus
(God of the Winds)
⑤

Charybdis ⑩ Sirens
⑪

SICILY
Cyclops ④

⑫ Scylla

⑬

Thrinakia (Island of the Sun)

⑭
Calypso

③
Lotus Eaters

AFRICA

GREECE   Cicones ②

Olympus •

⑮ — Phaeacia

Ithaca
⑯

Menelaus •
Nestor •

Troy ① •

BLACK SEA

ASIA
MINOR

MEDITERRANEAN   SEA

teach Greek virtues. And so it is not surprising that later cultures, while admiring the Homeric epics, created their own epics that imitated Homer's style but conveyed their own value systems.

Still, for all the epics that have been written since Homer's time and for all the ones that might have been composed before it, when we think of the word *epic* we think primarily of the *Iliad* and the *Odyssey.* Rome's *Aeneid,* France's *Song of Roland,* Italy's *Divine Comedy,* the very ancient Sumerian tale of Gilgamesh, India's *Mahabharata* and *Ramayana*—all are great poems that happen to be in the epic tradition. But to discover the heart of that tradition, we need to examine Homer's epics.

The *Iliad* is the primary model for the epic of war. The *Odyssey* is the model for the epic of the long journey. The theme of the journey has been the more basic one in Western literature—it is found in Homer, in fairy tales, and in such later stories as *Huckleberry Finn, Moby-Dick,* and *The Hobbit.* Thus, it is the *Odyssey* that has been the more widely read of Homer's two great stories.

The War-Story Background

You will find the background for Odysseus's story in the *Iliad*—the war epic. The action of the *Iliad* is set in the tenth and final year of the Trojan War. According to the *Iliad,* the Greeks had originally attacked Troy to avenge the insult suffered by Menelaus, king of

A mask used in a festival honoring Dionysos. First half of first century A.D.

Greek helmet (6th century B.C.).
Bronze.

The Metropolitan Museum of Art,
Dodge Fund, 1955. (55.11.10)

Sparta, when his wife Helen ran off with Paris, a young prince of Troy. The Greek kings banded together under the leadership of Agamemnon, the brother of Menelaus and the king of Mycenae. In a thousand ships, they sailed across the Aegean Sea and mounted the siege of Troy.

The audience of the *Odyssey* would have known this war story. They would have known that the Greeks were eventually victorious and that they burned Troy to the ground. They would have known all about the greatest of the Greek warriors, Achilles, who was fated to die young in the final year of the war. The audience would probably have heard other epic poems (now lost) that told of the homecomings of the various Greek heroes who survived the war. They would especially have known about the homecoming of Agamemnon, the leader of the Greek forces, who was murdered by his unfaithful wife upon his return from Troy.

Finally, Homer's listeners might well have been particularly fascinated by another homecoming story—this one about a somewhat unusual hero, known as much for his brain as for his brawn. In fact, many legends had already grown up around this hero, whose name was Odysseus. He was the subject of Homer's new epic, the *Odyssey*.

The *Odyssey*'s Hero

In Homer's day, **heroes** were thought of as a special class of aristocrats. Their station in life and their general attitudes placed them somewhere between the gods and ordinary human beings. These heroes might experience pain and death, but they were always sure of themselves, always "on top of the world."

Penelope and Odysseus Reunited
by Romare Bearden (1977). Collage.

Reprinted courtesy of Cordier and Eckstrom Gallery, New York, and the Estate of Romare Bearden.

The *Odyssey* is a portrait of a hero in trouble. We can relate to this hero because we share with him a sense of being somehow lost in a world of difficult choices. Like him, we have to cope with unfair authority figures. Like him, we seem always to have to work very hard to get what we want.

The *Odyssey* is a poem marked by melancholy and a feeling of what might be called "postwar disillusionment." Odysseus is a soldier whose military prowess is scoffed at by the fairy-tale monsters that populate the world of his wanderings. Even the people of his home island, Ithaca, seem to lack respect for him. It is as if society were saying to the returning hero, "You were a great soldier once—or so they say—but times have changed. This is a difficult world, and we have more important things to think about than your heroics."

In the years before the great war, Odysseus had married the beautiful and ever-faithful Penelope, one of several very strong women in the "man's world" of the Greek epic. (One critic, Robert Graves, was so impressed by the unusual importance of women and home and hearth in the *Odyssey* that he believed Homer must have been a woman.)

Penelope and Odysseus had one son, Telemachus (tə·lem′ə·kəs). He was still a toddler when Odysseus was called by Agamemnon and Menelaus to join them in the struggle against Troy. Rather untypically for a Greek hero, Odysseus was a homebody. He preferred not to go to war, and even though he was obligated under a treaty to go, he tried draft-dodging. It was said that when Agamemnon and Menelaus came to fetch him, he pretended to be insane and acted as if he did not recognize his visitors. Instead of entertaining them, he dressed as a peasant and began plowing a field. But the "draft board" was smarter than the wily Odysseus in this case. They threw his baby, Telemachus, in front of his oncoming plow. The hero revealed his sanity by quickly turning the plow aside to avoid running over his son.

The Wooden-Horse Trick

Once in Troy, Odysseus performed extremely well as a soldier and commander. It was he, for example, who thought of the famous wooden-horse trick that would lead to the downfall of Troy. For ten years, the Greeks had been fighting the Trojans, but they were fighting outside Troy's massive walls. They had been unable to break through the walls and enter the city. Odysseus's plan was to build an enormous wooden horse and hide a few Greek soldiers inside its hollow belly. After the horse was built, the Greeks pushed it up to the gates of Troy and withdrew their armies, so that their camp appeared to be abandoned. Thinking that the Greeks had given up the fight and that the horse was a peace offering, the Trojans brought the horse into their city. That night, the Greeks hidden inside the wooden body came out, opened the gates of Troy to the whole Greek army, and began the battle that was to win the war.

Draped warrior (late 6th century B.C.). Bronze.

The Wadsworth Atheneum, Hartford. J. Pierpont Morgan Collection.

" **T**he *Odyssey* is a portrait of a hero in trouble. It is marked by a feeling of what might be called 'postwar disillusionment.' "

The Ancient World and Ours

The world of Odysseus was a harsh place, a world in which violence was all too familiar. In a certain sense, Odysseus and his men act like mere pirates on their journey home. They think nothing of entering a town and carrying off all its worldly goods. The "worldly goods" in an ancient city might well have been such things as pots and pans and cattle and sheep. The "palaces" the Greeks raided might have been little more than elaborate mud and stone farmhouses. Yet, in the struggles of Odysseus, Penelope, and Telemachus in their "primitive" society—a society that has little in common with the high Athenian culture that would develop several centuries later—there is something that has a great deal to do with us.

Odysseus and his family are people searching for the right relationships with each other and with the people around them. They want to find their proper places in life. It is this theme that sets the tone for the *Odyssey* and determines the unusual way in which the poem is structured.

Instead of beginning at the beginning with Odysseus's departure from Troy, the story begins with his son, Telemachus. Telemachus is now twenty years old, threatened in his own home by powerful men who want to rob him of his inheritance, of his mother, and of his self-respect. He is a young man who yearns for the support of a father.

Meanwhile, we hear that Odysseus is stranded on an island, longing to find a way to get back to his wife, child, and home. It is ten years since his sailing from Troy, twenty years since his original departure from Ithaca. If Telemachus is in search of the inner strength represented by the wished-for presence and approval of his father, Odysseus is in search of a way out of what we might today call his "mid-life crisis." He is searching for a way to re-establish a natural balance in his life. The quests of father and son provide a framework for the poem and bring us into it as well, because we all are in search of our real identities, our true selves.

The Gods in the *Odyssey*

This brings us to the mythic and religious questions in the *Odyssey*. **Myths** are stories that use fantasy to express ideas about life that cannot be expressed easily in realistic terms. Most myths are essentially religious because they are concerned with the relationship between human beings and the unknown or spiritual realm.

As you will see, Homer is always concerned with the relationship between humans and gods: Homer is religious. For him, the gods control all things. Athena, the goddess of wisdom, is always at the side of Odysseus in whatever he does. This is appropriate, because Odysseus is known for his mental abilities. In other words, in Homer's stories a god can be an **alter ego,** a spiritual or psychological reflection of a hero's best qualities. A hero's bad tendencies can also be mirrored by the divine beings. The god who works

> "The quests of father and son provide a framework for the poem and bring us into it as well, because we all are in search of our real identities, our true selves."

> "Homer is always concerned with the relationship between humans and gods: Homer is religious."

against Odysseus is Poseidon, the god of the sea, who is known for arrogance and a certain brutishness. It might be said that to find inner peace or "a way home," Odysseus must find a means of reconciling brain and brawn in his own life. Only with Athena's help and with Poseidon's acceptance can he achieve his goal.

Readers have argued that Odysseus and Telemachus are not particularly admirable as heroes because everything they do depends on the help of the gods. But when you think about it, you realize that the religious person of today doesn't think any less of a heroic deed because it is seen as "God's will." We should see the relationship between Odysseus and the gods as a model for what the greatest of the ancient myth-makers saw as religious reality.

Who Was Homer?

Who exactly was this famous myth-maker? No one knows for sure who Homer was. The later Greeks believed he was a blind minstrel who came from the island of Chios. Some scholars feel there must have been two Homers; some think he was just a legend. But scholars have also argued as to whether a man called Shakespeare ever existed. It is almost as if they were saying that Homer and Shakespeare are too good to be true. On the whole, it seems most sensible to take the word of the Greeks themselves and to accept the existence of Homer at least as an ideal model for a class of wandering bards or minstrels later called "rhapsodes."

These **rhapsodes,** or "singers of tales," were the historians and entertainers as well as the myth-makers of their time. There was probably no written history in Homer's day. There were certainly no movies and no television, and there was nothing like a Bible or a book of religious stories. So it was that the minstrels traveled about from community to community singing of recent legendary events or of the doings of heroes, gods, and goddesses. It is as if the composer of the Book of Kings in the Bible, the writer of a book on World War II, and a famous pop singer were combined in one person. For Homer's people, there was no conflict between religion, history, and good fun.

How Were the Epics Told?

Scholars have found that oral epic poets are still composing today in Yugoslavia and other parts of the world. Work done by scholars on these poets suggests that stories like the *Iliad* and *Odyssey* would have been told aloud at first by and for people who could not read and write. The stories would have been composed orally according to a basic set story line. But most of the actual words would have been improvised—made up on the spot—in such a way as to fit a particular rhythm or meter. The singers of these stories would have needed a great deal of talent, and they would have had

> "**S**ome scholars think Homer was just a legend. But scholars have also argued as to whether a man called Shakespeare ever existed. It is almost as if they were saying that Homer and Shakespeare are too good to be true."

Bust of Homer. Marble.

Vatican Museum Pio Clementino.
Photo: Art Resource.

to work very hard. They would also have needed an audience used to listening closely.

We can see from this why there is so much repetition in the Homeric epics. The oral storyteller, in fact, had a store of formulas ready in his memory. He knew formulas for describing the arrival and greeting of guests, for the eating of meals, and for the taking of baths. He knew formulas for describing the sea (it is always "wine-dark") and for describing Athena (she is always "gray-eyed Athena").

Formulas such as these had another advantage: they gave the singer and his audience some breathing time. The audience could relax for a moment and enjoy a familiar and memorable passage, while the singer could think ahead to the next part of his story.

When we think about the audience that listened to these stories, we can also understand the value of the extended comparisons that we call **Homeric** or **heroic similes** today. These similes compare heroic or epic events to simple and easily understandable everyday events—events the audience would recognize instantly. For example, at one point in the *Iliad,* Athena prevents an arrow from striking Menelaus. The singer compares the goddess's actions to an action that every listener would have been familiar with:

> She brushed it away from his skin as lightly as when a mother
> Brushes a fly away from her child who is lying in sweet sleep.

Epic poets such as Homer would come to a city and would go through a part of their repertory while there. A story as long as the *Odyssey* (11,300 lines) could not be told at one sitting. We have to assume, therefore, that if the singer had only a few days in a town, he would summarize some of his story and sing the rest in detail, in as many sittings as he had time for. This is exactly what will happen in the selections from the *Odyssey* that are presented here. We will assume that Homer wants to get his story told to us, but that he has a limited time in which to do it. We will also assume that before retiring at the end of each segment of the performance, Homer's audience, of which we are now a part, will want to think about and talk about that set of stories. Like most audiences, this one will have many questions about the story: Why is Odysseus crying when we first meet him? How do the gods really feel about humans? What does this strange tale have to do with us?

A Live Performance

We can imagine what it would have been like at a live performance of the *Odyssey* because there are many instances in the epic itself in which traveling singers appear and sing their tales. In the court of the Phaeacian king, Alcinous (ăl·sĭn′ō·əs), in Book 8, for instance, there is a particularly wonderful singer who must make us wonder if the blind Homer was painting a self-portrait. Let's picture the setting of a performance before we start the story.

Imagine a large hall full of people who are freshly bathed,

Statuette of a veiled dancer (2nd century B.C.). Bronze.

The Metropolitan Museum of Art. Bequest of Walter C. Baker, 1971. (1972.118.95)

rubbed with fine oils, and draped in clean tunics. Imagine the smell of meat being cooked over charcoal, the sounds of cheerful voices. Imagine wine being freely poured, the flickering reflections of the great cooking fires, and the torches that light the room. A certain anticipation hangs in the air. It is said that the blind minstrel Homer is in the city and that he has new stories about that long war in Troy. Will he appear and entertain tonight?

Characters in the *Odyssey*

The following cast of characters includes only those who take part in the sections of the *Odyssey* included in this book. Note that the Greeks in the *Odyssey* are often referred to as **Achaeans** (ə·kē′ənz) or **Argives** (är′gīvz). *Achaeans* is the most general term, which also includes the people in Ithaca, the island off the west coast of Greece where Odysseus ruled. The word *Achaeans* is taken from the name of an ancient part of northeastern Greece called Achaea. The name *Argives* usually refers to the Greeks who went to fight at Troy.

Bust of Poseidon. Bronze.

The Athens Museum. Photo: Farrell Grehan, Photo Researchers.

The People Home in Ithaca:

Antinous (ăn·tĭn′ō·əs): one of Penelope's leading suitors; an arrogant and mean young noble from Ithaca.

Argos (är′gäs′): Odysseus's old dog.

Eumaeus (yoo·mē′əs): a swineherd, one of Odysseus's loyal servants.

Eurycleia (yoo·ri·klī′yə): Odysseus's old nurse.

Laertes (lā·ûr′tēz): Odysseus's old father, who lives in the country.

Penelope (pə·nĕl′ə·pē): Odysseus's faithful wife.

Philoeteus (fī·loi′tē·əs): a cowherd, one of Odysseus's loyal servants.

The People and Places of Telemachus's Journey:

Helen: known as Helen of Troy, the beautiful wife of King Menelaus. Her elopement with Paris, a prince of Troy, started the Trojan War.

Menelaus (men′ə·lā′əs): brother of Agamemnon, husband of Helen, and king of **Lacedaemon** (las′ə·dē′mən), also known as **Sparta.**

Nestor: the wise king of **Pylos,** and a hero of the Trojan War.

The People and Places of Odysseus's Wanderings:

Aeaea (ē·ē′ə): home of Circe, the witch-goddess.

Alcinous (ăl·sĭn′ō·əs): the king of Phaeacia, father of Nausicaa. Odysseus tells the story of his adventures to Alcinous's court.

" **I**magine the smell of meat being cooked over charcoal, the sounds of cheerful voices. . . . It is said that the blind minstrel Homer is in the city and that he has new stories about that long war in Troy. Will he appear and entertain tonight?"

Hermes Running. Attributed to the Tithonos Painter (475 B.C.). Vase.

The Metropolitan Museum of Art, Fletcher Fund, 1925.

Calypso (kə·lĭp'sō): a beautiful goddess-nymph who lives on Ogygia. She keeps Odysseus for seven years.

Charybdis (kə·rĭb'dĭs): a female monster who sucks in water three times a day to form a deadly whirlpool. (Thought to be a real whirlpool in the Straits of Messina.)

Circe (sŭr'sē): the witch-goddess who turns Odysseus's men into swine.

Cyclops (sī'klŏps): one of the **Cyclopes,** a race of brutish one-eyed giants who live solitary lives as shepherds, supposedly on the island now known as Sicily.

Erebus (er'ə·bəs): the Land of the Dead.

Nausicaa (nô·sik'ā·ə): the beautiful young daughter of King Alcinous and Queen Arete of Phaeacia.

Ogygia (ō·gī'·jə): Calypso's island.

Phaeacia (fē·ā'shə): an island kingdom ruled by King Alcinous. The Phaeacians are shipbuilders and traders.

Polyphemus (pōl'ə·fē'məs): the Cyclops blinded by Odysseus; the son of the sea god Poseidon.

Scylla (sĭl'ə): a female monster with six serpent heads, each head having a triple row of fangs. (Thought to be a dangerous rock in the Straits of Messina.)

Sirens: sea nymphs whose beautiful and mysterious music lures sailors to steer their ships toward the rocks.

Teiresias (tī·rē'sē·əs): a famous blind prophet, from the city of Thebes. Odysseus meets him in the Land of the Dead.

The Gods:

Athena (ə·thē'nə): favorite daughter of Zeus; the great goddess of wisdom and of the arts of war and peace. She favored the Greeks during the Trojan War. She is often called Pallas Athena.

Hermes (hur'mēz): the messenger god.

Olympus (ō·lĭm'pəs): the mountain home of the gods.

Poseidon (pō·sī'dən): brother of Zeus, god of the sea and earth. Called "Earth Shaker" because he is believed to cause earthquakes. Poseidon is an enemy of Odysseus.

Zeus (zoos): the most powerful god, whose home is on Olympus.

FROM
THE ODYSSEY

Homer

Translated by **Robert Fitzgerald**

Part One: A Son Seeks a Father

Book 1: Athena Advises Telemachus

*Homer opens with an **invocation,** or prayer, asking the Muse° to help him sing his tale. Notice how the singer gives his listeners hints about how his story is to end.*

There were nine Muses, daughters of Zeus. They inspired people to produce music, poetry, dance, and all the other arts.

> Sing in me, Muse, and through me tell the story
> of that man skilled in all ways of contending,°
> the wanderer, harried for years on end,
> after he plundered the stronghold
> on the proud height of Troy.

2. **contending:** fighting, arguing.

> 5   He saw the townlands
> and learned the minds of many distant men,
> and weathered many bitter nights and days
> in his deep heart at sea, while he fought only
> to save his life, to bring his shipmates home.
> 10 But not by will nor valor could he save them,
> for their own recklessness destroyed them all—
> children and fools, they killed and feasted on
> the cattle of Lord Helios, the Sun,
> and he who moves all day through heaven
> 15 took from their eyes the dawn of their return.
>
> Of these adventures, Muse, daughter of Zeus,
> tell us in our time, lift the great song again.

We learn that Odysseus is alive, twenty years older than when he had left for the war in Troy. He is being kept prisoner on Ogygia, the island of the nymph Calypso, who wants him for herself.

Meanwhile, the gods on Mount Olympus are discussing Odysseus. His patroness there, the goddess Athena, begs her father, Zeus, to allow Odysseus to return safely to his home in Ithaca. But Odysseus has an enemy among the gods. The sea god, Poseidon, is angry at the hero for having blinded his son, the Cyclops called Polyphemus. Zeus agrees with Athena, and Hermes, the messenger god, is to be sent to Ogygia to command Calypso to free Odysseus.

Athena's next move is to make her way to Ithaca to help Odysseus's young son, Telemachus, cope with another problem. His home—the palace of Odysseus—is overrun by his mother's suitors. Those arrogant men have taken over Odysseus's house. They are partying on the boy's inheritance and are demanding that his mother, Penelope, take one of them as a husband.

Here we now have the main themes of the epic:

1. *A boy must struggle to become a man.*
2. *A soldier must struggle to get home from a war.*
3. *A king must struggle to reclaim a kingdom (Ithaca).*

Now the goddess Athena arrives on the scene in Ithaca. Disguised as Mentor, an old family friend, she mingles with the mob of suitors and waits to talk to Telemachus:

Athena (c. 460 B.C.). Stone.

Acropolis Museum, Athens
Photo: Art Resource

       Long before anyone else, the prince Telemachus
       now caught sight of Athena—for he, too,
20   was sitting there, unhappy among the suitors,
       a boy, daydreaming. What if his great father
       came from the unknown world and drove these men
       like dead leaves through the place, recovering
       honor and lordship in his own domains?
25   Then he who dreamed in the crowd gazed out at Athena.

       Straight to the door he came, irked with himself
       to think a visitor had been kept there waiting,
       and took her right hand, grasping with his left
       her tall bronze-bladed spear. Then he said warmly:

30   "Greetings, stranger! Welcome to our feast.
       There will be time to tell your errand later."

       He led the way, and Pallas Athena followed
       into the lofty hall. The boy reached up
       and thrust her spear high in a polished rack
35   against a pillar, where tough spear on spear
       of the old soldier, his father, stood in order.
       Then, shaking out a splendid coverlet,
       he seated her on a throne with footrest—all
       finely carved—and drew his painted armchair
40   near her, at a distance from the rest.
       To be amid the din, the suitors' riot,
       would ruin his guest's appetite, he thought,
       and he wished privacy to ask for news
       about his father, gone for years.

As Telemachus and the goddess-in-disguise talk, the suitors are partying loudly all around them. Telemachus tells the goddess that the men are eating through all they have, courting his mother, and using his house as if it were theirs to wreck and plunder.

45   Pallas Athena was disturbed, and said:

       "Ah, bitterly you need Odysseus, then!
       High time he came back to engage these upstarts.
       I wish we saw him standing helmeted
       there in the doorway, holding shield and spear,

50 looking the way he did when I first knew him. . . .

                                        If I were you,
I should take steps to make these men disperse.
Listen, now, and attend to what I say:
at daybreak call the islanders to assembly,
55 and speak your will, and call the gods to witness:
the suitors must go scattering to their homes.
Then here's a course for you, if you agree:
get a sound craft afloat with twenty oars
and go abroad for news of your lost father—
60 perhaps a traveler's tale, or rumored fame
issued from Zeus abroad in the world of men.
Talk to that noble sage° at Pylos, Nestor,
then go to Menelaus, the red-haired king
at Sparta, last man home of all the Achaeans.
65 If you should learn your father is alive
and coming home, you could hold out a year.
Or if you learn that he is dead and gone,
then you can come back to your own dear country
and raise a mound for him, and burn his gear,
70 with all the funeral honors due the man,
and give your mother to another husband.

When you have done all this, or seen it done,
it will be time to ponder
concerning these contenders in your house—
75 how you should kill them, outright or by guile.°
You need not bear this insolence° of theirs,
you are a child no longer.''

Book 2: Telemachus Confronts the Suitors

*Frustrated in his attempts to control the suitors, who are older
and more powerful than he is, Telemachus decides to follow
Athena's advice. He tries in public to become his "father's son."*

    When primal Dawn spread on the eastern sky
her fingers of pink light, Odysseus's true son
80 stood up, drew on his tunic and his mantle,
slung on a sword belt and a new-edged sword,
tied his smooth feet into good rawhide sandals,
and left his room, a god's brilliance upon him.
He found the criers with clarion° voices and told them
85 to muster the unshorn° Achaeans in full assembly.
The call sang out, and the men came streaming in;
and when they filled the assembly ground, he entered,
spear in hand, with two quick hounds at heel;
Athena lavished on him a sunlit grace

62. **sage:** wise person.

75. **guile:** slyness, trickery.
76. **insolence:** rudeness, lack of respect.

84. **clarion:** clear and ringing.
85. **unshorn:** unshaven.

90   that held the eye of the multitude. Old men
     made way for him as he took his father's chair.

Telemachus complains of the way his family is treated by the suitors. He especially resents the way they treat his mother. The suitors answer through Antinous, the most arrogant suitor of them all. He demands that Penelope choose one of them in marriage, and he blames her for her trickery.

    "For three years now—and it will soon be four—
    she has been breaking the hearts of the Achaeans,
    holding out hope to all, and sending promises
95   to each man privately—but thinking otherwise.

    Here is an instance of her trickery:
    she had her great loom standing in the hall
    and the fine warp of some vast fabric on it;
    we were attending her, and she said to us:

Scene from the *Odyssey* by Bernardino Pintoricchio (1509). Fresco.

The National Gallery, London. Photo: The Granger Collection, New York.

100 'Young men, my suitors, now my lord is dead,
let me finish my weaving before I marry,
or else my thread will have been spun in vain.
It is a shroud° I weave for Lord Laertes,
when cold death comes to lay him on his bier.°

105 The country wives would hold me in dishonor
if he, with all his fortune, lay unshrouded.'
We have men's hearts; she touched them; we agreed.
So every day she wove on the great loom—
but every night by torchlight she unwove it;

110 and so for three years she deceived the Achaeans.
But when the seasons brought the fourth around,
one of her maids, who knew the secret, told us;
we found her unraveling the splendid shroud.
She had to finish then, although she hated it.

115 Now here is the suitors' answer—
you and all the Achaeans, mark it well:
dismiss your mother from the house, or make her marry
the man her father names and she prefers.
Does she intend to keep us dangling forever?''

*In the face of this stalemate, Telemachus decides to sail away
in search of his father.*

120 The assembly broke up; everyone went home—
the suitors home to Odysseus's house again.
But Telemachus walked down along the shore
and washed his hands in the foam of the gray sea,
then said this prayer:

                  ''O god of yesterday,

125 guest in our house, who told me to take ship
on the hazy sea for news of my lost father,
listen to me, be near me:
the Achaeans only wait, or hope to hinder me,
the damned insolent suitors most of all.''

130 Athena was nearby and came to him,
putting on Mentor's figure and his tone,
the warm voice in a lucid flight of words:

''You'll never be fainthearted or a fool,
Telemachus, if you have your father's spirit;

135 he finished what he cared to say,
and what he took in hand he brought to pass.
The sea routes will yield their distances
to his true son, Penelope's true son—
I doubt another's luck would hold so far.

140 The son is rare who measures with his father,
and one in a thousand is a better man,
but you will have the sap and wit

103. **shroud:** a cloth that is used to wrap up the dead body.
104. **bier** (bir): platform on which a coffin is placed.

and prudence—for you get that from Odysseus—
to give you a fair chance of winning through.
145 So never mind the suitors and their ways,
there is no judgment in them, neither do they
know anything of death and the black terror
close upon them—doom's day on them all. . . ."

*Quietly, Telemachus goes home and again bears the mockery of
the suitors. With the help of his old nurse, Eurycleia, he prepares
for the journey in search of his father. Athena, still disguised as
Mentor, borrows a ship and rounds up a crew, and off they sail
in the night. Telemachus's only concern is a human one: he
worries about his mother and begs the nurse not to tell her he
has gone until some days have passed.*

Book 3: The Visit to Nestor

*At sunrise, Telemachus's ship arrives at Pylos, the land of King
Nestor. Homer's listeners must have felt their interest quickening
at the appearance of this familiar hero of the Trojan War days—
we feel the same pleasure today when a favorite character from
one book or movie suddenly turns up in another. Surrounded by
his faithful sons and subjects, and dutifully offering prayers to
the gods, Nestor stands in perfect contrast to Odysseus's family
and their chaotic situation in Ithaca. Telemachus and Athena
arrive during a religious ritual, in honor of the sea god Poseidon,
the "blue-maned god who makes the islands tremble."*

On the shore
150 black bulls were being offered by the people
to the blue-maned god who makes the islands tremble:
nine congregations, each five hundred strong,
led out nine bulls apiece to sacrifice,
taking the tripes° to eat, while on their altars

154. **tripes:** lining of the stomach.

155 thighbones in fat lay burning for the god.
Here they put in, furled sail, and beached the ship;
but Telemachus hung back in disembarking,
so that Athena turned and said:

"Not the least shyness, now, Telemachus.
160 You came across the open sea for this—
to find out where the great earth hides your father
and what the doom was that he came upon.
Go to old Nestor, master charioteer,°
so we may broach the storehouse of his mind.

163. **charioteer:** Nestor had driven those horse-drawn carts used in ancient times for war.

165 Ask him with courtesy, and in his wisdom
he will tell you history and no lies."

But clear-headed Telemachus replied:

"Mentor, how can I do it, how approach him?
I have no practice in elaborate speeches, and
170 for a young man to interrogate an old man
seems disrespectful—"

                                 But the gray-eyed goddess said:
"Reason and heart will give you words, Telemachus;
and a spirit will counsel others. I should say
the gods were never indifferent to your life."

175 She went on quickly, and he followed her
to where the men of Pylos had their altars.
Nestor appeared enthroned among his sons,
while friends around them skewered the red beef
or held it scorching. When they saw the strangers
180 a hail went up, and all that crowd came forward
calling out invitations to the feast. . . .
Meanwhile the spits were taken off the fire,
portions of crisp meat for all. They feasted,
and when they had eaten and drunk their fill, at last
185 they heard from Nestor, prince of charioteers:

"Now is the time," he said, "for a few questions,
now that our young guests have enjoyed their dinner.
Who are you, strangers? . . ."

*Telemachus says he is Odysseus's son, and he asks for news of
his lost father. Nestor is full of praise for the lost soldier, and he
quickly recognizes the heroic qualities of the son. Notice how
Nestor prepares us for the later entrance of the absent hero
himself.*

                                          "Your father?
190 Well, I must say I marvel at the sight of you:
your manner of speech couldn't be more like his;
one would say No; no boy could speak so well.
And all that time at Ilion, he and I
were never at odds in council or assembly—
195 saw things the same way, had one mind between us
in all the good advice we gave the Argives. . . .
Who knows, your father might come home some day
alone or backed by troops, and have it out with them.
If gray-eyed Athena loved you
200 the way she did Odysseus in the old days,
in Troy country, where we all went through so much—
never have I seen the gods help any man
as openly as Athena did your father—
well, as I say, if she cared for you that way,
205 there would be those to quit this marriage game."

But prudently Telemachus replied:

"I can't think what you say will ever happen, sir.
It is a dazzling hope. But not for me.
It could not be—even if the gods willed it."

210   At this gray-eyed Athena broke in, saying:

"What strange talk you permit yourself, Telemachus.
A god could save the man by simply wishing it—
from the farthest shore in the world."

Book 4: The Visit to Menelaus and Helen

*Nestor sends Telemachus off to continue his search in Sparta.
There, two more favorites of the Trojan War story, King Mene-
laus and his wife, Helen, now live peacefully. Like Homer's
Greek audience, we remember throughout Telemachus's stay in
Sparta that this Helen was the very cause of the Trojan War
itself.*

*Telemachus is awed at Menelaus's palace, luminous with
bronze, gold, amber, silver, and ivory. He does not reveal his
identity to Menelaus or to Helen; Athena is still disguised as
Mentor.*

*The old commander Menelaus begins to tell war stories. As
he reminisces about Odysseus, the absent hero becomes more
and more vivid. Remember that Menelaus does not realize here
that he is talking to Odysseus's own son. Menelaus speaks:*

"No soldier
215   took on so much, went through so much, as Odysseus.
That seems to have been his destiny, and this mine—
to feel each day the emptiness of his absence,
ignorant, even, whether he lived or died.
How his old father and his quiet wife,
220   Penelope, must miss him still!
And Telemachus, whom he left as a newborn child."

Now hearing these things said, the boy's heart rose
in a long pang for his father, and he wept,
holding his purple mantle with both hands
225   before his eyes. Menelaus knew him now,
and so fell silent with uncertainty
whether to let him speak and name his father
in his own time, or to inquire, and prompt him.
And while he pondered, Helen came
230   out of her scented chamber, a moving grace
like Artemis,° straight as a shaft of gold. . . .
Reclining in her light chair with its footrest,
Helen gazed at her husband and demanded:

"Menelaus, my lord, have we yet heard

231. **Artemis** (är′tə·mis): goddess of the hunt.

Helen and Priam, King of Troy.
Krater interior.

Tarquin Museum. Photo: Art Resource

235   our new guests introduce themselves? Shall I
       dissemble° what I feel? No, I must say it.
       Never, anywhere, have I seen so great a likeness
       in man or woman—but it is truly strange!
       This boy must be the son of Odysseus,
240   Telemachus, the child he left at home
       that year the Achaean host made war on Troy—
       daring all for the wanton° that I was.''

236. dissemble: conceal.

242. wanton: immoral woman.

Menelaus and Helen tell Telemachus they have heard that Odysseus is alive, that he is living with the nymph, Calypso, and that he longs for a way of returning home.

    Having increased our suspense, Homer at this point takes us back to Ithaca where we learn that the suitors intend to ambush and kill Telemachus upon his return.

    Now, with the themes of the epic established, we are ready to meet Odysseus in person.

    Here we will imagine that Homer stops for the night. The listeners would now go off to various corners of the local nobleman's house—as Telemachus and his friends would have done after their evening of talk and feasting with Menelaus and Helen. The blind poet might well have taken a glass of wine before turning in. The people who had heard the bard's stories might have asked questions among themselves and looked forward to the next evening's installment.

Responding to the Epic

Analyzing the Epic

Identifying Facts

1. Instead of beginning his epic with the adventures of Odysseus, Homer takes four books to describe the problems and travels of the hero's son, Telemachus. Describe the specific problems that exist in Ithaca with Odysseus gone.
2. What **actions** does Athena advise Telemachus to take? How does Athena use her divine powers to transform Telemachus from time to time?
3. According to Antinous, what trick has Penelope used to deceive the suitors?
4. What does Telemachus learn about his father from Menelaus?
5. How are Telemachus and Athena received by Nestor and his family? How does this contrast with the way the boy is treated in his own home, in Ithaca?

Interpreting Meanings

6. According to the poet's opening prayer to the Muse, why are all of Odysseus's companions going to die before they reach home? What do this and other details tell you about the importance of the gods in Homer's time?
7. We have heard several people talking about the absent hero, including the poet himself in his invocation to the Muse. Describe what we know so far about Odysseus's **character.** What are his main traits?
8. Describe the kind of person Telemachus is. What are his strengths and weaknesses?
9. We all know how hard it is to follow in someone else's footsteps. What are the specific problems that confront Telemachus—or anyone else who feels he must "wear his father's (or mother's) shoes"?
10. What women have you met so far in the epic? Based on what you've seen, describe the roles women seem to take in Homeric society.
11. What elements of the story thus far could be related to life as you know it? Consider the **characters,** their **conflicts,** and the **steps taken** to resolve the conflicts.
12. Suppose you were Telemachus and your father had never returned from a long war, and your mother was pestered by men who wanted to marry her and who were sponging off her. How would you handle your problems?
13. Like all good storytellers, Homer knew he had to make his listeners feel **suspense**—he wanted them to wonder "What will happen next?" List at least three questions a listener would have at this point in the story: include questions about Odysseus, Penelope, and Telemachus.

Analyzing Language and Vocabulary

Figures of Speech

In the following **figures of speech,** the poet compares one thing to something else, something quite different from it in all but a few important ways. Answer the questions after each figure of speech to show that you understand the comparison it is based on.

1. ". . . What if his great father
   came from the unknown world and drove these men
   like dead leaves through the place . . ."
   (Lines 21–23)
   a. What are the dead leaves compared to?
   b. What action do you see when you read this figure of speech?

2. "When primal Dawn spread on the eastern sky
   her fingers of pink light . . ."
   (Lines 78–79)
   a. What aspect of the dawn is being compared to fingers of pink light?
   b. **Personification** is a figure of speech in which something inanimate or not alive is spoken of as if it were a person. What is personified in these lines?

3. ". . . black bulls were being offered by the people
   to the blue-maned god who makes the islands tremble."
   (Lines 150–151)
   a. The blue-maned god is Poseidon. What exactly is his "blue mane"?
   b. What creature usually is spoken of as having a "mane"?

Part Two: The Wanderings of Odysseus

Book 5: Calypso, the Sweet Nymph

*Again the story begins with the gods. Zeus, unable to resist the pleas of his favorite daughter, Athena, sends the messenger-god Hermes to Calypso's island to order Odysseus released. Notice the particularly beautiful **epic simile**—the extended comparison—that gives life to Hermes' swift voyage to Ogygia (lines 251–257), and notice the wonderful description of the nymph's lair. It is important to remember that although Calypso is not described as evil, her seductive charms—even her promises of immortality for Odysseus—threaten to lead the hero away from the straight and narrow path back to Penelope.*

    No words were lost on Hermes the Wayfinder
    who bent to tie his beautiful sandals on,
245 ambrosial,° golden, that carry him over water
    or over endless land in a swish of the wind,
    and took the wand with which he charms asleep—
    or when he wills, awake—the eyes of men.
    So wand in hand he paced into the air,
250 shot from Pieria° down, down to sea level,
    and veered to skim the swell. A gull patrolling
    between the wave crests of the desolate sea
    will dip to catch a fish, and douse his wings;
    no higher above the whitecaps Hermes flew
255 until the distant island lay ahead,
    then rising shoreward from the violet ocean
    he stepped up to the cave. Divine Calypso,
    the mistress of the isle, was now at home.
    Upon her hearthstone a great fire blazing
260 scented the farthest shores with cedar smoke
    and smoke of thyme, and singing high and low
    in her sweet voice, before her loom a-weaving,
    she passed her golden shuttle to and fro.
    A deep wood grew outside, with summer leaves
265 of alder and black poplar, pungent cypress.
    Ornate birds here rested their stretched wings—
    horned owls, falcons, cormorants—long-tongued
    beachcombing birds, and followers of the sea.
    Around the smoothwalled cave a crooking vine
270 held purple clusters under ply of green;
    and four springs, bubbling up near one another
    shallow and clear, took channels here and there
    through beds of violets and tender parsley.
    Even a god who found this place

245. **ambrosial:** fit for the gods.

250. **Pieria:** a place in central Greece, a favorite spot of Hermes. It is not far from Olympus.

275 would gaze, and feel his heart beat with delight:
so Hermes did; but when he had gazed his fill
he entered the wide cave. Now face to face
the magical Calypso recognized him,
as all immortal gods know one another
280 on sight—though seeming strangers, far from home.
But he saw nothing of the great Odysseus,
who sat apart, as a thousand times before,
and racked his own heart groaning, with eyes wet
scanning the bare horizon of the sea. . . .

Hermes tells Calypso that she must give up Odysseus forever.
And now, one quarter of the way through the epic, we are directly
introduced to Odysseus. Notice what this great warrior is doing
when we first meet him.

285 The strong god glittering left her as he spoke,
and now her ladyship, having given heed
to Zeus's mandate, went to find Odysseus

A view of the sea from one of the
Greek islands.

in his stone seat to seaward—tear on tear
brimming his eyes. The sweet days of his lifetime
290   were running out in anguish over his exile,
for long ago the nymph had ceased to please.
Though he fought shy of her and her desire,
he lay with her each night, for she compelled him.
But when day came he sat on the rocky shore
295   and broke his own heart groaning, with eyes wet
scanning the bare horizon of the sea.
Now she stood near him in her beauty, saying:

"O forlorn man, be still.
Here you need grieve no more; you need not feel
300   your life consumed here; I have pondered it,
and I shall help you go. . . ."

Calypso promises Odysseus a raft and provisions, to help him
homeward without harm—provided the gods wish it. Now Odys-
seus and Calypso say goodbye.

Swiftly she turned and led him to her cave,
and they went in, the mortal and immortal.
He took the chair left empty now by Hermes,
305   where the divine Calypso placed before him
victuals and drink of men; then she sat down
facing Odysseus, while her serving maids
brought nectar and ambrosia° to her side.
Then each one's hands went out on each one's feast
310   until they had had their pleasure; and she said:
"Son of Laertes, versatile Odysseus,
after these years with me, you still desire
your old home? Even so, I wish you well.
If you could see it all, before you go—
315   all the adversity you face at sea—
you would stay here, and guard this house, and be
immortal—though you wanted her forever,
that bride for whom you pine each day.
Can I be less desirable than she is?
320   Less interesting? Less beautiful? Can mortals
compare with goddesses in grace and form?"

To this the strategist Odysseus answered:

"My lady goddess, there is no cause for anger.
My quiet Penelope—how well I know—
325   would seem a shade before your majesty,
death and old age being unknown to you,
while she must die. Yet, it is true, each day
I long for home, long for the sight of home.

308. **nectar and ambrosia:** drink and food of the gods.

734   **The Elements of the Epic**

So Odysseus builds the raft and sets sail. But the sea god Poseidon, still angry at Odysseus, is by no means ready to allow an easy passage over his watery domain. He raises a storm and destroys the raft. It is only with the help of Athena and a sea nymph that Odysseus arrives, broken and battered, on the island of Scheria, home of the Phaeacians. There he hides himself in a pile of leaves and falls into a deep sleep.

Farewell to Calypso by Samuel Palmer (1848). Watercolor.

Whitworth Art Gallery, University of Manchester

      A man in a distant field, no hearthfires near,
330   will hide a fresh brand° in his bed of embers
      to keep a spark alive for the next day;
      so in the leaves Odysseus hid himself,
      while over him Athena showered sleep
      that his distress should end, and soon, soon.
335   In quiet sleep she sealed his cherished eyes.

330. **brand:** a burning stick.

Book 6: The Princess Nausicaa

In this important episode, we meet the lovely teen-age princess, Nausicaa, and learn something about domestic life in those days. (Homer is not above telling us about doing laundry or taking baths.) We also learn here something about natural modesty and standards of moral behavior. The world of epic is the world of heroes, but it is also the world of everyday reality.

> Far gone in weariness, in oblivion,
> the noble and enduring man slept on;
> but Athena in the night went down the land
> of the Phaeacians, entering their city. . . .

340 She took her way to a painted bedchamber
  where a young girl lay fast asleep—so fine
  in mould and feature that she seemed a goddess—
  the daughter of Alcínous, Nausicaa.
  On either side, as Graces° might have slept,
345 her maids were sleeping. The bright doors were shut,
  but like a sudden stir of wind, Athena
  moved to the bedside of the girl, and grew
  visible as the shipman Dymas's daughter,
  a girl the princess's age, and her dear friend.
350 In this form gray-eyed Athena said to her:
  "How so remiss, and yet thy mother's daughter?
  leaving thy clothes uncared for, Nausicaa,
  when soon thou must have store of marriage linen,
  and put thy minstrelsy° in wedding dress!
355 Beauty, in these, will make the folk admire,
  and bring thy father and gentle mother joy.
  Let us go washing in the shine of morning!
  Beside thee will I drub,° so wedding chests
  will brim by evening. Maidenhood must end!
360 Have not the noblest born Phaeacians
  paid court to thee, whose birth none can excel?
  Go beg thy sovereign father, even at dawn,
  to have the mule cart and the mules brought round
  to take thy body-linen, gowns, and mantles.
365 Thou shouldst ride, for it becomes thee more,
  the washing pools are found so far from home."

  On this word she departed, gray-eyed Athena,
  to where the gods have their eternal dwelling—
  as men say—in the fastness of Olympus.
370 Never a tremor of wind, or a splash of rain,
  no errant snowflake comes to stain that heaven,
  so calm, so vaporless, the world of light.
  Here, where the gay gods live their days of pleasure,
  the gray-eyed one withdrew, leaving the princess.

344. Graces: three sister goddesses who ruled over pleasure, charm, and beauty in human life.

354. minstrelsy: court singers and entertainers.

358. drub: beat the clothes on rocks, to get the dirt out.

375 And now Dawn took her own fair throne, awaking
the girl in the sweet gown, still charmed by dream.
Down through the rooms she went to tell her parents,
whom she found still at home: her mother seated
near the great hearth among her maids—and twirling
380 out of her distaff yarn dyed like the sea—;
her father at the door, bound for a council
of princes on petition of the gentry.
She went up close to him and softly said:

"My dear Papa, could you not send the mule cart
385 around for me—the gig with pretty wheels?
I must take all our things and get them washed
at the river pools; our linen is all soiled.
And you should wear fresh clothing, going to council
with counselors and first men of the realm.
390 Remember your five sons at home: though two
are married, we have still three bachelor sprigs;
they will have none but laundered clothes each time
they go to the dancing. See what I must think of!"

She had no word to say of her own wedding,
395 though her keen father saw her blush. Said he:

"No mules would I deny you, child, nor anything.
Go along, now; the grooms will bring your gig
with pretty wheels and the cargo box upon it."
He spoke to the stableman, who soon brought round
400 the cart, low-wheeled and nimble;
harnessed the mules, and backed them in the traces.
Meanwhile the girl fetched all her soiled apparel
to bundle in the polished wagon box.
Her mother, for their luncheon, packed a hamper
405 with picnic fare, and filled a skin of wine,
and, when the princess had been handed up,
gave her a golden bottle of olive oil
for softening girls' bodies, after bathing.
Nausicaa took the reins and raised her whip,
410 lashing the mules. What jingling! What a clatter!
But off they went in a ground-covering trot,
with princess, maids, and laundry drawn behind.
By the lower river where the wagon came
were washing pools, with water all year flowing
415 in limpid spillways that no grime withstood.
The girls unhitched the mules, and sent them down
along the eddying stream to crop sweet grass.
Then sliding out the cart's tail board, they took
armloads of clothing to the dusky water,
420 and trod them in the pits, making a race of it.
All being drubbed, all blemish rinsed away,

they spread them, piece by piece, along the beach
whose pebbles had been laundered by the sea;
then took a dip themselves, and, all anointed
425 with golden oil, ate lunch beside the river
while the bright burning sun dried out their linen.
Princess and maids delighted in that feast;
then, putting off their veils,
they ran and passed a ball to a rhythmic beat,
430 Nausicaa flashing first with her white arms. . . .

Soon it was time, she knew, for riding homeward—
mules to be harnessed, linen folded smooth—
but the gray-eyed goddess Athena made her tarry,°
so that Odysseus might behold her beauty
and win her guidance to the town.
435   It happened
when the king's daughter threw her ball off line
and missed, and put it in the whirling stream—
at which they all gave such a shout, Odysseus
awoke and sat up, saying to himself:

440 "Now, by my life, mankind again! But who?
Savages, are they, strangers to courtesy?
Or gentle folk, who know and fear the gods?
That was a lusty cry of tall young girls—
most like the cry of nymphs, who haunt the peaks,
445 and springs of brooks, and inland grassy places.
Or am I amid people of human speech?
Up again, man; and let me see for myself."

He pushed aside the bushes, breaking off
with his great hand a single branch of olive,
450 whose leaves might shield him in his nakedness;
so came out rustling, like a mountain lion,
rain-drenched, wind-buffeted, but in his might at ease,
with burning eyes—who prowls among the herds
or flocks, or after game, his hungry belly
455 taking him near stout homesteads for his prey.
Odysseus had this look, in his rough skin
advancing on the girls with pretty braids;
and he was driven on by hunger, too.
Streaked with brine, and swollen, he terrified them,
460 so that they fled, this way and that. Only
Alcinous's daughter stood her ground, being given
a bold heart by Athena, and steady knees.

She faced him, waiting. And Odysseus came,
debating inwardly what he should do:
465 embrace this beauty's knees in supplication?
or stand apart, and, using honeyed speech,
inquire the way to town, and beg some clothing?

433. **tarry:** linger, be late.

In his swift reckoning, he thought it best
to trust in words to please her—and keep away;
470   he might anger the girl, touching her knees.
So he began, and let the soft words fall:

"Mistress: please: are you divine, or mortal?
If one of those who dwell in the wide heaven,
you are most near to Artemis, I should say—
475   great Zeus's daughter—in your grace and presence.
If you are one of earth's inhabitants,
how blest your father, and your gentle mother,
blest all your kin. I know what happiness
must send the warm tears to their eyes, each time
480   they see their wondrous child go to the dancing!
But one man's destiny is more than blest—
he who prevails, and takes you as his bride.
Never have I laid eyes on equal beauty
in man or woman. I am hushed indeed.
485   So fair, one time, I thought a young palm tree
at Delos near the altar of Apollo—
I had troops under me when I was there
on the sea route that later brought me grief—
but that slim palm tree filled my heart with wonder:
490   never came shoot from earth so beautiful.
So now, my lady, I stand in awe so great
I cannot take your knees.° And yet my case is desperate:
twenty days, yesterday, in the wine-dark sea,
on the ever-lunging swell,° under gale winds,
495   getting away from the Island of Ogygia.
And now the terror of Storm has left me stranded
upon this shore—with more blows yet to suffer,
I must believe, before the gods relent.
Mistress, do me a kindness!
500   After much weary toil, I come to you,
and you are the first soul I have seen—I know
no others here. Direct me to the town,
give me a rag that I can throw around me,
some cloth or wrapping that you brought along.
505   And may the gods accomplish your desire:
a home, a husband, and harmonious
converse with him—the best thing in the world
being a strong house held in serenity
where man and wife agree. Woe to their enemies,
510   joy to their friends! But all this they know best."

Then she of the white arms, Nausicaa, replied:

"Stranger, there is no quirk or evil in you
that I can see. You know Zeus metes out fortune
to good and bad men as it pleases him.

492. The taking of the knees is an act of respect and humility and petition. By kneeling before a person and holding on to his or her knees, a petitioner shows that he or she means no harm but desires mercy or help.
494. **ever-lunging swell:** waves that plunge up and down.

515 Hardship he sent to you, and you must bear it.
But now that you have taken refuge here
you shall not lack for clothing, or any other
comfort due to a poor man in distress.
The town lies this way, and the men are called
520 Phaeacians, who own the land and city.
I am daughter to the Prince Alcinous,
by whom the power of our people stands."

Turning, she called out to her maids-in-waiting:

"Stay with me! Does the sight of a man scare you?
525 Or do you take this one for an enemy?
Why, there's no fool so brash, and never will be,
as to bring war or pillage° to this coast,
for we are dear to the immortal gods,
living here, in the sea that rolls forever,
530 distant from other lands and other men.
No: this man is a castaway, poor fellow;
we must take care of him. Strangers and beggars
come from Zeus: a small gift, then, is friendly.
Give our new guest some food and drink, and take him
535 into the river, out of the wind, to bathe."

They stood up now, and called to one another
to go on back. Quite soon they led Odysseus
under the river bank, as they were bidden;
and there laid out a tunic, and a cloak,
540 and gave him olive oil in the golden flask.
"Here," they said, "go bathe in the flowing water."
But heard now from that kingly man, Odysseus:

"Maids," he said, "keep away a little; let me
wash the brine from my own back, and rub on
545 plenty of oil. It is long since my anointing.
I take no bath, however, where you can see me—
naked before young girls with pretty braids."

They left him, then, and went to tell the princess.
And now Odysseus, dousing in the river,
550 scrubbed the coat of brine from back and shoulders
and rinsed the clot of sea-spume from his hair;
got himself all rubbed down, from head to foot,
then he put on the clothes the princess gave him.
Athena lent a hand, making him seem
555 taller, and massive, too, with crisping hair
in curls like petals of wild hyacinth,
but all red-golden. Think of gold infused
on silver by a craftsman, whose fine art
Hephaestus° taught him, or Athena: one
560 whose work moves to delight: just so she lavished

527. **pillage:** violent looting or stealing.

559. **Hephaestus:** god of crafts.

beauty over Odysseus's head and shoulders.
Then he went down to sit on the sea beach
in his new splendor. There the girl regarded him,
and after a time she said to the maids beside her:

565　"My gentlewomen, I have a thing to tell you.
The Olympian gods cannot be all averse
to this man's coming here among our islanders.
Uncouth he seemed, I thought so, too, before;
but now he looks like one of heaven's people.
570　I wish my husband could be fine as he
and glad to stay forever on Scheria!

Ulysses and Nausicaa by Peter Paul
Rubens (17th century). Oil.

Firenze Gallery. Photo: Art Resource

But have you given refreshment to our guest?"

At this the maids, all gravely listening, hastened
to set out bread and wine before Odysseus,
575 and ah! how ravenously that patient man
took food and drink, his long fast at an end.

The princess Nausicaa now turned aside
to fold her linens; in the pretty cart
she stowed them, put the mule team under harness,
580 mounted the driver's seat, and then looked down
to say with cheerful prompting to Odysseus:

"Up with you now, friend; back to town we go;
and I shall send you in before my father
who is wondrous wise; there in our house with him
585 you'll meet the noblest of the Phaeacians.
You have good sense, I think; here's how to do it:
while we go through the countryside and farmland
stay with my maids, behind the wagon, walking
briskly enough to follow where I lead.
590 But near the town—well, there's a wall with towers
around the Isle, and beautiful ship basins
right and left of the causeway of approach;
seagoing craft are beached beside the road
each on its launching ways. The agora,° | 594. **agora:** marketplace, or town square.
595 with fieldstone benches bedded in the earth,
lies either side Poseidon's shrine—for there
men are at work on pitch-black hulls and rigging,
cables and sails, and tapering of oars.
The archer's craft is not for Phaeacians,
600 but ship designing, modes of oaring cutters
in which they love to cross the foaming sea.
From these fellows I will have no salty talk,
no gossip later. Plenty are insolent.
And some seadog might say, after we passed:
605 'Who is this handsome stranger trailing Nausicaa?
Where did she find him? Will he be her husband?
Or is she being hospitable to some rover
come off his ship from lands across the sea—
there being no lands nearer. A god, maybe?
610 a god from heaven, the answer to her prayer,
descending now—to make her his forever?
Better, if she's roamed and found a husband
somewhere else: none of our own will suit her,
though many come to court her, and those the best.'
615 This is the way they might make light of me.
And I myself should hold it shame
for any girl to flout° her own dear parents, | 617. **flout:** scorn, insult.
taking up with a man, before her marriage."

742   The Elements of the Epic

Book 8: The Song of the Minstrel

Odysseus is received in Book 7 as an unknown guest by Nausicaa's father, King Alcinous, and by the Phaeacian court. To the ancient people of Greece and Asia Minor, all guests were godsent and had to be treated with great care before they could be asked to identify themselves and state their business.

Alcinous orders a banquet for his mystery guest. When everything is prepared, Odysseus is seated in the guest's place of honor. The famous blind minstrel, Demodocus, is called. Odysseus gives the singer a gift of pork crisp with fat and requests a song about the wooden horse of Troy. In effect, he asks for a song about himself.

       The minstrel stirred, murmuring to the god, and soon
620   clear words and notes came one by one, a vision
       of the Achaeans in their graceful ships
       drawing away from shore: the torches flung
       and shelters flaring: Argive soldiers crouched
       in the close dark around Odysseus: and
625   the horse, tall on the assembly ground of Troy. . . .
       For Troy must perish, as ordained, that day
       she harbored the great horse of timber; hidden
       the flower of Achaea lay, and bore
       slaughter and death upon the men of Troy.
630   He sang, then, of the town sacked° by Achaeans
       pouring down from the horse's hollow cave,
       this way and that way raping the steep city . . .

       The splendid minstrel sang it.
                                  And Odysseus
       let the bright molten tears run down his cheeks,
635   weeping the way a wife mourns for her lord
       on the lost field where he has gone down fighting . . .

630. sacked: all its goods taken by force.

Here Alcinous notices Odysseus's tears and demands that his guest reveal his identity.

       ". . . Friend, you must not be
       secretive any longer! Come, in fairness,
       tell me the name you bore in that far country;
640   how were you known to family, and neighbors?
       No man is nameless—no man, good or bad,
       but gets a name in his first infancy,
       none being born, unless a mother bears him!
       Tell me your native land, your coast and city—"

At this moment of suspense, Homer might have put aside his harp until the next night.

Responding to the Epic

Analyzing the Epic

Identifying Facts

1. What **images** does Homer use to help his audience see and smell the fragrant place where the nymph Calypso lives?
2. What does Calypso offer Odysseus to tempt him to stay with her and abandon his quest? What is Odysseus's response?
3. What inspires Nausicaa to organize her washing expedition? What reason does she give her father?
4. In a macho culture like Odysseus's, a hero is by definition a "ladies' man." From the point of view of Homer's audience, Odysseus was not unfaithful to Penelope as long as he kept her in mind as his ultimate goal. Homer never tires of telling us that Odysseus would rather be with Penelope than with Calypso or Circe, who keep him against his will. Thus, to the Greeks, morality does not come into question in Odysseus's relationship with the "witches" in the story. But with Nausicaa it is something else. She is a real human girl ready for marriage. What is Odysseus's condition when Nausicaa sees him first? How does Odysseus use his famed wit to handle this situation and win Nausicaa's confidence?

Interpreting Meanings

5. When we first see Odysseus, he is weeping. Why? We rarely see a twentieth-century hero weeping. What would most people feel today about a hero who cries? What does Odysseus's crying tell us about the values of Homeric society as opposed to modern values?
6. Look back at Odysseus's first speech to Nausicaa, starting at line 472 on page 739. What do we learn about Odysseus's **character** from this speech? What is especially significant about his references to marriage?
7. Based on what she says and does, how would you describe Nausicaa's **character** traits? What does this portrait of Nausicaa reveal about the life and values of a teen-age girl in Homeric society?
8. Look at how Demodocus is treated at Alcinous's banquet. What does this tell us about the role of poets and poetry in Homer's time? Do storytelling and music play a similar role in our society? (How would a contemporary ruler entertain honored guests?)

Analyzing Language and Vocabulary

Homeric Similes

The **Homeric simile** (sometimes called the **epic simile** or the **heroic simile**) is an extended comparison between something that the audience cannot have seen (such as the god Hermes skimming the waves) and something ordinary and domestic which they would have been familiar with (such as a sea gull fishing: see lines 251–257 on page 732).

1. Write out at least three Homeric similes that you find in these episodes. (Include their line numbers.)
2. Explain how each simile brings the audience into the story by comparing a strange or unfamiliar occurrence with something domestic or familiar.
3. Make up three Homeric similes of your own, in which you compare something strange or unfamiliar with something domestic and familiar. You might consider describing something like:

> A space launch
> The surface of Uranus
> A view of a blood sample through a microscope

Writing About the Epic

A Creative Response

Writing a Journal Entry. Suppose you are Nausicaa. Describe your thoughts and feelings as you saw Odysseus come out of hiding and appear before you. Write as if you are writing in a journal. Use the first-person pronoun, "I," as if we were hearing Nausicaa's voice.

Book 9: The Lotus Eaters and the Cyclops

Alcinous's call to Odysseus to reveal his identity is Odysseus's cue to begin telling of the adventures that will literally make his name. Homer's greatest hero is himself a famous storyteller. (Perhaps all successful heroes must contain aspects of their creators.)

The adventures that follow are the ones for which the epic is most remembered. Imagine the excitement of the Phaeacians, having just heard Demodocus sing the story of the Trojan horse, when they discover the identity of their guest. Alcinous has just asked Odysseus to reveal his name:

645   Now this was the reply Odysseus made:

  "I am Laertes' son, Odysseus.

                              Men hold me

  formidable for guile in peace and war:
  this fame has gone abroad to the sky's rim.
  My home is on the peaked sea-mark of Ithaca
650   under Mount Neion's wind-blown robe of leaves,
  in sight of other islands—Doulikhion,
  Same, wooded Zakynthos—Ithaca
  being most lofty in that coastal sea,
  and northwest, while the rest lie east and south.
655   A rocky isle, but good for a boy's training;
  I shall not see on earth a place more dear,
  though I have been detained long by Calypso,
  loveliest among goddesses, who held me
  in her smooth caves, to be her heart's delight,
660   as Circe of Aeaea, the enchantress,
  desired me, and detained me in her hall.
  But in my heart I never gave consent.
  Where shall a man find sweetness to surpass
  his own home and his parents? In far lands
665   he shall not, though he find a house of gold. . . ."

εἴμ' Ὀδυσεὺς Λαερτιάδης, ὃς πᾶσι δόλοισιν
ἀνθρώποισι μέλω, καί μευ κλέος οὐρανὸν ἵκει.
ναιετάω δ' Ἰθάκην εὐδείελον· ἐν δ' ὄρος αὐτῇ,
Νήριτον εἰνοσίφυλλον ἀριπρεπές· ἀμφὶ δὲ νῆσοι
πολλαὶ ναιετάουσι μάλα σχεδὸν ἀλλήλῃσι,
Δουλίχιόν τε Σάμη τε καὶ ὑλήεσσα Ζάκυνθος.

The passage beginning "I am Laertes' son" in the original text.

Odysseus now tells of his voyage from Troy—how many of his men lost their lives during a foolish raid on the Cicones, how Zeus punished the survivors by raising the North Wind against their ships, how they were made to drift aimlessly from place to place, for nine days. Finally, they stopped at the land of the Lotus Eaters. (The people of Southern Europe used to make a drink from the fermented fruit of the lotus plant. The drink was supposed to produce feelings of laziness and dreaminess.) Odysseus is still speaking:

"Upon the tenth
we came to the coastline of the Lotus Eaters,
who live upon that flower. We landed there
to take on water. All ships' companies
670   mustered alongside for the midday meal.
Then I sent out two picked men and a runner
to learn what race of men that land sustained.
They fell in, soon enough, with Lotus Eaters,
who showed no will to do us harm, only
675   offering the sweet Lotus to our friends—
but those who ate this honeyed plant, the Lotus,
never cared to report, nor to return:
they longed to stay forever, browsing on
that native bloom, forgetful of their homeland.
680   I drove them, all three wailing, to the ships,
tied them down under their rowing benches,
and called the rest: 'All hands aboard;
come, clear the beach and no one taste
the Lotus, or you lose your hope of home.'
685   Filing in to their places by the rowlocks
my oarsmen dipped their long oars in the surf,
and we moved out again on our seafaring."

Salvation from the next adventure requires the special intelligence associated with Odysseus's name. Odysseus is the cleverest of the ancient Greek heroes because his divine guardian is the goddess of wisdom, Athena. As a result of this confrontation with the Cyclops named Polyphemus, the one-eyed monster son

The Cyclop (detail) by Odilon Redon (1898). Oil.

State Museum Collection Kroller-Muller, Otterlo, The Netherlands

of the god Poseidon, Odysseus incurs the wrath of the sea god. Polyphemus might be said to represent the brute force and a negative singleness of purpose that any hero must overcome before he can reach home.

It is Odysseus's famed curiosity that leads him to the Cyclops's cave and that makes him insist on waiting for the barbaric giant.

    "We lit a fire, burnt an offering,
and took some cheese to eat; then sat in silence

690 around the embers, waiting. When he came
he had a load of dry boughs on his shoulder
to stoke his fire at suppertime. He dumped it
with a great crash into that hollow cave,
and we all scattered fast to the far wall.

695 Then over the broad cavern floor he ushered
the ewes he meant to milk. He left his rams
and he-goats in the yard outside, and swung
high overhead a slab of solid rock
to close the cave. Two dozen four-wheeled wagons,

700 with heaving wagon teams, could not have stirred
the tonnage of that rock from where he wedged it
over the doorsill. Next he took his seat
and milked his bleating ewes. A practiced job
he made of it, giving each ewe her suckling;

705 thickened his milk, then, into curds and whey,
sieved out the curds to drip in withy baskets,°
and poured the whey to stand in bowls
cooling until he drank it for his supper.
When all these chores were done, he poked the fire,

710 heaping on brushwood. In the glare he saw us.

    'Strangers,' he said, 'who are you? And where from?
What brings you here by sea ways—a fair traffic?
Or are you wandering rogues, who cast your lives
like dice, and ravage other folk by sea?'

715 We felt a pressure on our hearts, in dread
of that deep rumble and that mighty man.
But all the same I spoke up in reply:

    'We are from Troy, Achaeans, blown off course
by shifting gales on the Great South Sea;

720 homeward bound, but taking routes and ways
uncommon; so the will of Zeus would have it.
We served under Agamemnon, son of Atreus—
the whole world knows what city
he laid waste, what armies he destroyed.

725 It was our luck to come here; here we stand,
beholden for your help, or any gifts

706. **withy baskets:** made from willow twigs.

you give—as custom is to honor strangers.
We would entreat you, great Sir, have a care
for the gods' courtesy; Zeus will avenge
the unoffending guest.'

730   He answered this
from his brute chest, unmoved:

                                 'You are a ninny,
or else you come from the other end of nowhere,
telling me, mind the gods! We Cyclopes
care not a whistle for your thundering Zeus

735 or all the gods in bliss; we have more force by far.
I would not let you go for fear of Zeus—
you or your friends—unless I had a whim to.
Tell me, where was it, now, you left your ship—
around the point, or down the shore, I wonder?'

740 He thought he'd find out, but I saw through this,
and answered with a ready lie:

                                 'My ship?
Poseidon Lord, who sets the earth a-tremble,
broke it up on the rocks at your land's end.
A wind from seaward served him, drove us there.

745 We are survivors, these good men and I.'

Neither reply nor pity came from him,
but in one stride he clutched at my companions
and caught two in his hands like squirming puppies
to beat their brains out, spattering the floor.

750 Then he dismembered them and made his meal,
gaping and crunching like a mountain lion—
everything: innards, flesh, and marrow bones.
We cried aloud, lifting our hands to Zeus,
powerless, looking on at this, appalled;

755 but Cyclops went on filling up his belly
with manflesh and great gulps of whey,
then lay down like a mast among his sheep.
My heart beat high now at the chance of action,
and drawing the sharp sword from my hip I went

760 along his flank to stab him where the midriff
holds the liver. I had touched the spot
when sudden fear stayed me: if I killed him
we perished there as well, for we could never
move his ponderous doorway slab aside.

765 So we were left to groan and wait for morning.

When the young Dawn with finger tips of rose
lit up the world, the Cyclops built a fire
and milked his handsome ewes, all in due order,
putting the sucklings to the mothers. Then,

770 his chores being all dispatched, he caught

another brace of men to make his breakfast,
and whisked away his great door slab
to let his sheep go through—but he, behind,
reset the stone as one would cap a quiver.
775 There was a din of whistling as the Cyclops
rounded his flock to higher ground, then stillness.
And now I pondered how to hurt him worst,
if but Athena granted what I prayed for.
Here are the means I thought would serve my turn:

780 a club, or staff, lay there along the fold—
an olive tree, felled green and left to season
for Cyclops's hand. And it was like a mast
a lugger° of twenty oars, broad in the beam—
a deep-seagoing craft—might carry:
785 so long, so big around, it seemed. Now I
chopped out a six-foot section of this pole
and set it down before my men, who scraped it;
and when they had it smooth, I hewed again
to make a stake with pointed end. I held this
790 in the fire's heart and turned it, toughening it,
then hid it, well back in the cavern, under
one of the dung piles in profusion there.
Now came the time to toss for it: who ventured
along with me? Whose hand could bear to thrust
795 and grind that spike in Cyclops's eye, when mild
sleep had mastered him? As luck would have it,
the men I would have chosen won the toss—
four strong men, and I made five as captain.

At evening came the shepherd with his flock,
800 his woolly flock. The rams as well, this time,
entered the cave: by some sheep-herding whim—
or a god's bidding—none were left outside.
He hefted his great boulder into place
and sat him down to milk the bleating ewes
805 in proper order, put the lambs to suck,
and swiftly ran through all his evening chores.
Then he caught two more men and feasted on them.
My moment was at hand, and I went forward
holding an ivy bowl of my dark drink,
looking up, saying:
810   'Cyclops, try some wine.
Here's liquor to wash down your scraps of men.
Taste it, and see the kind of drink we carried
under our planks. I meant it for an offering
if you would help us home. But you are mad,
815 unbearable, a bloody monster! After this,
will any other traveler come to see you?'

783. **lugger:** a type of sailboat.

Ulysses receiving the wine that will later be given to Polyphemus. Krater.

Museo Boliano. Photo: Art Resource

He seized and drained the bowl, and it went down
so fiery and smooth he called for more:

'Give me another, thank you kindly. Tell me,
820 how are you called? I'll make a gift will please you.
Even Cyclopes know the wine grapes grow
out of grassland and loam in heaven's rain,
but here's a bit of nectar and ambrosia!'

Three bowls I brought him, and he poured them down.
825 I saw the fuddle and flush come over him,
then I sang out in cordial tones:

         'Cyclops,

you ask my honorable name? Remember
the gift you promised me, and I shall tell you.
My name is Nohbdy: mother, father, and friends,
everyone calls me Nohbdy.'

830   And he said:

'Nohbdy's my meat, then, after I eat his friends.
Others come first. There's a noble gift, now.'

Even as he spoke, he reeled and tumbled backward,

his great head lolling to one side; and sleep
835 took him like any creature. Drunk, hiccuping,
he dribbled streams of liquor and bits of men.

Now, by the gods, I drove my big hand spike
deep in the embers, charring it again,
and cheered my men along with battle talk
840 to keep their courage up: no quitting now.
The pike of olive, green though it had been,
reddened and glowed as if about to catch.
I drew it from the coals and my four fellows
gave me a hand, lugging it near the Cyclops
845 as more than natural force nerved them; straight
forward they sprinted, lifted it, and rammed it
deep in his crater eye, and I leaned on it
turning it as a shipwright turns a drill
in planking, having men below to swing
850 the two-handled strap that spins it in the groove.
So with our brand we bored that great eye socket
while blood ran out around the red hot bar.
Eyelid and lash were seared; the pierced ball
hissed broiling, and the roots popped.

       In a smithy°
855 one sees a white-hot axhead or an adze°
plunged and wrung in a cold tub, screeching steam—
the way they make soft iron hale and hard—
just so that eyeball hissed around the spike.
The Cyclops bellowed and the rock roared round him,
860 and we fell back in fear. Clawing his face
he tugged the bloody spike out of his eye,
threw it away, and his wild hands went groping;
then he set up a howl for Cyclopes
who lived in caves on windy peaks nearby.
865 Some heard him; and they came by divers° ways
to clump around outside and call:

        'What ails you,
Polyphemus? Why do you cry so sore
in the starry night? You will not let us sleep.
Sure no man's driving off your flock? No man
has tricked you, ruined you?'

       Out of the cave
870 the mammoth Polyphemus roared in answer:

'Nohbdy, Nohbdy's tricked me, Nohbdy's ruined me!'

To this rough shout they made a sage reply:

'Ah well, if nobody has played you foul
875 there in your lonely bed, we are no use in pain

---

854. **smithy:** a blacksmith's shop, where iron work is done.
855. **adze:** a tool like an ax, but with a longer, curved blade.

865. **divers:** diverse, various.

given by great Zeus. Let it be your father,
Poseidon Lord, to whom you pray.'

So saying
they trailed away. And I was filled with laughter
to see how like a charm the name deceived them.
880 Now Cyclops, wheezing as the pain came on him,
fumbled to wrench away the great doorstone
and squatted in the breach with arms thrown wide
for any silly beast or man who bolted—
hoping somehow I might be such a fool.
885 But I kept thinking how to win the game:
death sat there huge; how could we slip away?
I drew on all my wits, and ran through tactics,
reasoning as a man will for dear life,
until a trick came—and it pleased me well.
890 The Cyclops's rams were handsome, fat, with heavy
fleeces, a dark violet.

Three abreast
I tied them silently together, twining
cords of willow from the ogre's bed;
then slung a man under each middle one
895 to ride there safely, shielded left and right.

Ulysses escaping from Polyphemus
(c. 510 B.C.). Krater.

Badisches Landesmuseum, Karlsruhe

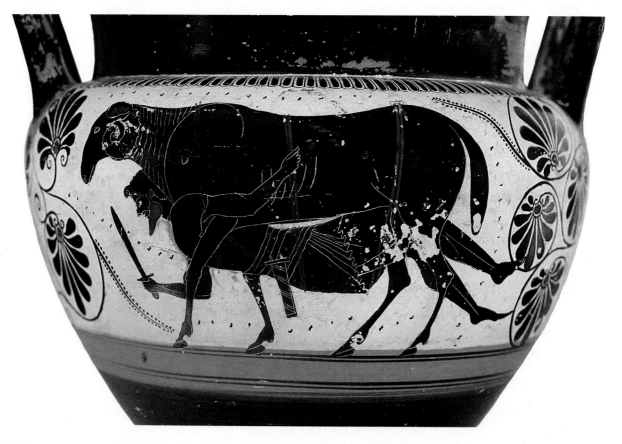

So three sheep could convey each man. I took
the woolliest ram, the choicest of the flock,
and hung myself under his kinky belly,
pulled up tight, with fingers twisted deep
900   in sheepskin ringlets for an iron grip.
So, breathing hard, we waited until morning.

When Dawn spread out her finger tips of rose
the rams began to stir, moving for pasture,
and peals of bleating echoed round the pens
905   where dams with udders full called for a milking.
Blinded, and sick with pain from his head wound,
the master stroked each ram, then let it pass,
but my men riding on the pectoral fleece°
the giant's blind hands blundering never found.

910   Last of them all my ram, the leader, came,
weighted by wool and me with my meditations.
The Cyclops patted him, and then he said:

'Sweet cousin ram, why lag behind the rest
in the night cave? You never linger so,
915   but graze before them all, and go afar
to crop sweet grass, and take your stately way
leading along the streams, until at evening
you run to be the first one in the fold.
Why, now, so far behind? Can you be grieving
920   over your Master's eye? That carrion rogue°
and his accurst companions burnt it out
when he had conquered all my wits with wine.
Nohbdy will not get out alive, I swear.
Oh, had you brain and voice to tell
925   where he may be now, dodging all my fury!
Bashed by this hand and bashed on this rock wall
his brains would strew the floor, and I should have
rest from the outrage Nohbdy worked upon me.'

He sent us into the open, then. Close by,
930   I dropped and rolled clear of the ram's belly,
going this way and that to untie the men.
With many glances back, we rounded up
his fat, stiff-legged sheep to take aboard,
and drove them down to where the good ship lay.
935   We saw, as we came near, our fellows' faces
shining; then we saw them turn to grief
tallying those who had not fled from death.
I hushed them, jerking head and eyebrows up, and in a low
voice told them: 'Load this herd;
940   move fast, and put the ship's head toward the breakers.'
They all pitched in at loading, then embarked
and struck their oars into the sea. Far out,

908. **pectoral fleece:** fleece on the animal's chest area.

920. **carrion rogue:** rotten tramp (carrion is decaying flesh).

as far off shore as shouted words would carry,
I sent a few back to the adversary:

945   'O Cyclops! Would you feast on my companions?
Puny, am I, in a Caveman's hands?
How do you like the beating that we gave you,
you damned cannibal? Eater of guests
under your roof! Zeus and the gods have paid you!'

Ulysses Deriding Polyphemus by
J.M.W. Turner (1829). Oil.

The National Gallery, London.
Photo: The Granger Collection,
New York.

950 The blind thing in his doubled fury broke
a hilltop in his hands and heaved it after us.
Ahead of our black prow it struck and sank
whelmed in a spuming geyser, a giant wave
that washed the ship stern foremost back to shore.

955 I got the longest boathook out and stood
fending us off, with furious nods to all
to put their backs into a racing stroke—

row, row, or perish. So the long oars bent
kicking the foam sternward, making head
960 until we drew away, and twice as far.
Now when I cupped my hands I heard the crew
in low voices protesting:

                                 'Godsake, Captain!
Why bait the beast again? Let him alone!'

'That tidal wave he made on the first throw
all but beached us.'

965   'All but stove us in!'

'Give him our bearing with your trumpeting,
he'll get the range and lob° a boulder.'   967. **lob:** toss.

                                            'Aye
He'll smash our timbers and our heads together!'

I would not heed them in my glorying spirit,
but let my anger flare and yelled:

970   'Cyclops,
if ever mortal man inquire
how you were put to shame and blinded, tell him
Odysseus, raider of cities, took your eye:
Laertes' son, whose home's on Ithaca!'

975 At this he gave a mighty sob and rumbled:

'Now comes the weird° upon me, spoken of old.   976. **weird:** fate.
A wizard, grand and wondrous, lived here—Telemus,
a son of Eurymus; great length of days
he had in wizardry among the Cyclopes,
980 and these things he foretold for time to come:
my great eye lost, and at Odysseus's hands.
Always I had in mind some giant, armed
in giant force, would come against me here.
But this, but you—small, pitiful, and twiggy—
985 you put me down with wine, you blinded me.
Come back, Odysseus, and I'll treat you well,
praying the god of earthquake to befriend you—
his son I am, for he by his avowal
fathered me, and, if he will, he may
990 heal me of this black wound—he and no other
of all the happy gods or mortal men.'

Few words I shouted in reply to him:
'If I could take your life I would and take
your time away, and hurl you down to hell!
995 The god of earthquake could not heal you there!'

At this he stretched his hands out in his darkness
toward the sky of stars, and prayed Poseidon:

'O hear me, lord, blue girdler of the islands,
if I am thine indeed, and thou art father:
1000   grant that Odysseus, raider of cities, never
see his home: Laertes' son, I mean,
who kept his hall on Ithaca. Should destiny
intend that he shall see his roof again
among his family in his fatherland,
1005   far be that day, and dark the years between.
Let him lose all companions, and return
under strange sail to bitter days at home.' "

Book 10: The Bag of Winds and the Witch Circe

*Odysseus and his men land next on the island of Aeolia. There
the wind king, Aeolus, does Odysseus a favor. He puts all the
stormy winds in a bag so that they will not harm the Ithacans.
The bull's hide bag containing the winds is wedged under Odysseus's afterdeck. During the voyage, the suspicious and curious
sailors open the bag (thinking it contains treasure), and the evil
winds roar up into hurricanes to plague the luckless Odysseus
again.*

   *After more of his men are killed and eaten by the gigantic
cannibals called the Laestrygonians, Odysseus's ship lands on
Aeaea, the home of the witch Circe. Here a party of twenty-two
men, led by Eurylochus, goes off to explore the island. Odysseus
is still speaking:*

"In the wild wood they found an open glade,
around a smooth stone house—the hall of Circe—
1010   and wolves and mountain lions lay there, mild
in her soft spell, fed on her drug of evil.
None would attack—oh, it was strange, I tell you—
but switching their long tails they faced our men
like hounds, who look up when their master comes
1015   with tidbits for them—as he will—from table.
Humbly those wolves and lions with mighty paws
fawned on our men—who met their yellow eyes
and feared them.
                 In the entrance way they stayed
to listen there: inside her quiet house
they heard the goddess Circe.
1020   Low she sang
in her beguiling voice, while on her loom
she wove ambrosial fabric sheer and bright,
by that craft known to the goddesses of heaven.

No one would speak, until Polites—most
1025 faithful and likable of my officers, said:
'Dear friends, no need for stealth: here's a young weaver
singing a pretty song to set the air
a-tingle on these lawns and paven courts.
Goddess she is, or lady. Shall we greet her?'

1030 So reassured, they all cried out together,
and she came swiftly to the shining doors
to call them in. All but Eurylochus—
who feared a snare—the innocents went after her.
On thrones she seated them, and lounging chairs,
1035 while she prepared a meal of cheese and barley
and amber honey mixed with Pramnian wine,
adding her own vile pinch, to make them lose
desire or thought of our dear fatherland.
Scarce had they drunk when she flew after them
1040 with her long stick and shut them in a pigsty—
bodies, voices, heads, and bristles, all
swinish now, though minds were still unchanged.
So, squealing, in they went. And Circe tossed them
acorns, mast,° and cornel berries—fodder

1044. **mast:** various kinds of nuts.

1045 for hogs who rut and slumber on the earth.

Down to the ship Eurylochus came running
to cry alarm, foul magic doomed his men!
But working with dry lips to speak a word
he could not, being so shaken; blinding tears
1050 welled in his eyes; foreboding filled his heart.
When we were frantic questioning him, at last
we heard the tale: our friends were gone. . . .''

*Odysseus leaves the ship and rushes to Circe's hall. The god
Hermes stops him to give him a plant that will act as an antidote
to Circe's power. (Homer calls it a* molu; *it might have been a
kind of garlic.) Odysseus uses the* molu *and the witch, overcome
by the plant's magic, frees Odysseus's men. Now, Circe,
"loveliest of all immortals," persuades Odysseus to stay, share
her meat and wine, and restore his heart. After many seasons of
feasting and other pleasures, Odysseus and his men beg Circe
to help them get home:*

"'Son of Laertes and the gods of old,
Odysseus, master mariner and soldier,
1055 you shall not stay here longer against your will;
but home you may not go
unless you take a strange way round and come
to the cold homes of Death and pale Persephone.°
You shall hear prophecy from the rapt° shade

1058. **Persephone** (pər·sef'ə·nē): wife of
Hades and Queen of the Underworld.
1059. **rapt:** completely absorbed in his
thoughts.

1060　of blind Teiresias of Thebes, forever
　　　charged with reason even among the dead;
　　　to him alone, of all the flitting ghosts,
　　　Persephone has given a mind undarkened.'

　　　At this I felt a weight like stone within me,
1065　and, moaning, pressed my length against the bed,
　　　with no desire to see the daylight more."

Book 11: The Land of the Dead

Odysseus is not alone among the ancient heroes who must descend to the Land of the Dead. The Sumerian hero Gilgamesh, the Greek heroes Theseus and Heracles, and many other heroes made similar journeys. It is as if the ancient myth-makers are telling us that the truly significant voyages in life involve journeys to the deepest parts of ourselves, and a confrontation with the darkest reality of all—death.

In the Land of the Dead, Odysseus seeks his destiny. The source of his information is Teiresias, the famous blind prophet from the city of Thebes, whose lack of external sight suggests the presence of true insight. Circe has told Odysseus exactly what rites he must perform to bring Teiresias up from the dead. Odysseus is speaking:

Ulysses descends into Hell. Fresco.

Palazzo Vecchio, Florence. Photo: Art Resource

"Then I addressed the blurred and breathless dead,
vowing to slaughter my best heifer for them
before she calved, at home in Ithaca,
1070 and burn the choice bits on the altar fire;
as for Teiresias, I swore to sacrifice
a black lamb, handsomest of all our flock.
Thus to assuage the nations of the dead
I pledged these rites, then slashed the lamb and ewe,
1075 letting their black blood stream into the wellpit.
Now the souls gathered, stirring out of Erebus,
brides and young men, and men grown old in pain,
and tender girls whose hearts were new to grief;
many were there, too, torn by brazen lanceheads,
1080 battle-slain, bearing still their bloody gear.
From every side they came and sought the pit
with rustling cries; and I grew sick with fear.
But presently I gave command to my officers
to flay° those sheep the bronze cut down, and make

1084. **flay:** strip of skin.

1085 burnt offerings of flesh to the gods below—
to sovereign Death, to pale Persephone.
Meanwhile I crouched with my drawn sword to keep
the surging phantoms from the bloody pit
till I should know the presence of Teiresias. . . .
1090 Soon from the dark that prince of Thebes came forward
bearing a golden staff; and he addressed me:

'Son of Laertes and the gods of old,
Odysseus, master of land ways and sea ways,
why leave the blazing sun, O man of woe,
1095 to see the cold dead and the joyless region?
Stand clear, put up your sword;
let me but taste of blood, I shall speak true.'

At this I stepped aside, and in the scabbard
let my long sword ring home to the pommel silver,
1100 as he bent down to the somber blood. Then spoke
the prince of those with gift of speech:
                                    'Great captain,
a fair wind and the honey lights of home
are all you seek. But anguish lies ahead;
the god who thunders on the land prepares it,
1105 not to be shaken from your track, implacable,°

1105. **implacable:** inflexible, not to be pacified.

in rancor for the son whose eye you blinded.
One narrow strait may take you through his blows:
denial of yourself, restraint of shipmates.
When you make landfall on Thrinakia° first

1109. **Thrinakia** (thri·nā′kē·ə): island where the sun god Helios pastured his sacred cattle.

1110 and quit the violet sea, dark on the land
you'll find the grazing herds of Helios
by whom all things are seen, all speech is known.

Avoid those kine,° hold fast to your intent,
and hard seafaring brings you all to Ithaca.
1115 But if you raid the beeves, I see destruction
for ship and crew. Though you survive alone,
bereft of all companions, lost for years,
under strange sail shall you come home, to find
your own house filled with trouble: insolent men
1120 eating your livestock as they court your lady.
Aye, you shall make those men atone in blood!
But after you have dealt out death—in open
combat or by stealth—to all the suitors,
go overland on foot, and take an oar,
1125 until one day you come where men have lived
with meat unsalted, never known the sea,
nor seen seagoing ships, with crimson bows
and oars that fledge light hulls for dipping flight.
The spot will soon be plain to you, and I
1130 can tell you how: some passerby will say,
'What winnowing fan° is that upon your shoulder?'
Halt, and implant your smooth oar in the turf
and make fair sacrifice to Lord Poseidon:
a ram, a bull, a great buck boar; turn back,
1135 and carry out pure hecatombs° at home
to all wide heaven's lords, the undying gods,
to each in order. Then a seaborne death
soft as this hand of mist will come upon you
when you are wearied out with rich old age,
1140 your country folk in blessed peace around you.
And all this shall be just as I foretell.'

When he had done, I said at once,

                                        'Teiresias,
my life runs on then as the gods have spun it.
But come, now, tell me this; make this thing clear:
1145 I see my mother's ghost among the dead
sitting in silence near the blood. Not once
has she glanced this way toward her son, nor spoken.
Tell me, my lord,
may she in some way come to know my presence?'

To this he answered:

                                        'I shall make it clear
1150 in a few words and simply. Any dead man
whom you allow to enter where the blood is
will speak to you, and speak the truth; but those
deprived will grow remote again and fade.'

1155 When he had prophesied, Teiresias's shade
retired lordly to the halls of Death. . . .''

1113. *Kine* and *beeves* (see line 1115) are old-fashioned plural words for cattle (cows and oxen).

1131. **winnowing fan:** a device used to separate wheat from chaff. (These people would never have seen an oar.)

1135. **hecatombs:** sacrifices of one hundred cattle.

Now Odysseus meets a familiar ghost, his mother Anticleia, who died of a broken heart when her son failed to return from Troy.

                                         "I bit my lip,
          rising perplexed, with longing to embrace her,
          and tried three times, putting my arms around her,
1160   but she went sifting through my hands, impalpable
          as shadows are, and wavering like a dream.
          Now this embittered all the pain I bore,
          and I cried in the darkness:

                                    'O my mother,
          will you not stay, be still, here in my arms,
1165   may we not, in this place of Death, as well,
          hold one another, touch with love, and taste
          salt tears' relief, the twinge of welling tears?
          Or is this all hallucination, sent
          against me by the iron queen, Persephone,
          to make me groan again?'

1170   My noble mother
          answered quickly:

                                'O my child—alas,
          most sorely tried of men—great Zeus's daughter,
          Persephone, knits no illusion for you.
          All mortals meet this judgment when they die.
1175   No flesh and bone are here, none bound by sinew,
          since the bright-hearted pyre° consumed them down—
          the white bones long exanimate°—to ash;
          dreamlike the soul flies, insubstantial.

          You must crave sunlight soon.
                                    Note all things strange
1180   seen here, to tell your lady in after days.'"

1176. **pyre:** a huge fire on which a body is burned in a funeral rite.
1177. **exanimate:** lifeless.

The afterlife envisioned by Homer was not a happy place of rest. This society, which so relished the joys, accomplishments, and passions of the physical life, found little pleasure in an eternal life among mere shadows. After many more encounters in the Land of the Dead, Odysseus returns to Circe's island for further instructions.

Book 12: The Sirens, Scylla and Charybdis

The witch Circe is speaking. She warns Odysseus of the perils that await him—the forces that would prevent him from achieving his destiny.

                      "'Listen with care
to this, now, and a god will arm your mind.
Square in your ship's path are Sirens, crying
beauty to bewitch men coasting by;

1185   woe to the innocent who hears that sound!
He will not see his lady nor his children
in joy, crowding about him, home from sea;
the Sirens will sing his mind away
on their sweet meadow lolling. There are bones

1190   of dead men rotting in a pile beside them
and flayed skins shrivel around the spot.

                      Steer wide;

keep well to seaward; plug your oarsmen's ears
with beeswax kneaded soft; none of the rest
should hear that song.

                      But if you wish to listen,

1195   let the men tie you in the lugger, hand
and foot, back to the mast, lashed to the mast,
so you may hear those harpies'° thrilling voices;
shout as you will, begging to be untied,
your crew must only twist more line around you

1200   and keep their stroke up, till the singers fade. . . .'"

1197. **harpies:** monstrous winged women, greedy for victims.

The next peril lies between two headlands with sheer cliffs. Circe continues:

        "'. . . That is the den of Scylla, where she yaps
abominably, a newborn whelp's° cry,
though she is huge and monstrous. God or man,
no one could look on her in joy. Her legs—

1205   and there are twelve—are like great tentacles,
unjointed, and upon her serpent necks
are borne six heads like nightmares of ferocity,
with triple serried° rows of fangs and deep
gullets of black death. Half her length, she sways

1210   her heads in air, outside her horrid cleft,
hunting the sea around that promontory
for dolphins, dogfish, or what bigger game
thundering Amphitrite° feeds in thousands.
And no ship's company can claim

1215   to have passed her without loss and grief; she takes,
from every ship, one man for every gullet.

The opposite point seems more a tongue of land
you'd touch with a good bowshot, at the narrows.
A great wild fig, a shaggy mass of leaves,

1220   grows on it, and Charybdis lurks below
to swallow down the dark sea tide. Three times

1202. **whelp's:** puppy's.

1208. **serried:** dense, compact.

1213. **Amphitrite** (am·fi·trīt′ē): goddess of the sea, wife of Poseidon.

from dawn to dusk she spews it up
and sucks it down again three times, a whirling
maelstrom;° if you come upon her then

1225 the god who makes earth tremble could not save you.
No, hug the cliff of Scylla, take your ship
through on a racing stroke. Better to mourn
six men than lose them all, and the ship, too. . . .

Then you will coast Thrinakia, the island
1230 where Helios's cattle graze, fine herds, and flocks
of goodly sheep. The herds and flocks are seven,
with fifty beasts in each.

No lambs are dropped,
or calves, and these fat cattle never die. . . .

Now give those kine a wide berth, keep your thoughts
1235 intent upon your course for home,
and hard seafaring brings you all to Ithaca.
But if you raid the beeves, I see destruction
for ship and crew.' "

The Ithacans set off. But Odysseus never reveals to them Circe's
last prophecy—that he will be the only survivor of their long
journey. Odysseus is still speaking to Alcinous's court:

"The crew being now silent before me, I
addressed them, sore at heart:

1240   'Dear friends,
more than one man, or two, should know those things
Circe foresaw for us and shared with me,
so let me tell her forecast: then we die
with our eyes open, if we are going to die,
1245 or know what death we baffle if we can. Sirens
weaving a haunting song over the sea
we are to shun, she said, and their green shore
all sweet with clover; yet she urged that I
alone should listen to their song. Therefore
1250 you are to tie me up, tight as a splint,
erect along the mast, lashed to the mast,
and if I shout and beg to be untied,
take more turns of the rope to muffle me.'

I rather dwelt on this part of the forecast,
1255 while our good ship made time, bound outward down
the wind for the strange island of Sirens.
Then all at once the wind fell, and a calm
came over all the sea, as though some power
lulled the swell.

1224. **maelstrom:** whirlpool.

The crew were on their feet

1260 briskly, to furl the sail, and stow it; then,
each in place, they poised the smooth oar blades
and sent the white foam scudding by. I carved
a massive cake of beeswax into bits
and rolled them in my hands until they softened—

1265 no long task, for a burning heat came down
from Helios, lord of high noon. Going forward
I carried wax along the line, and laid it
thick on their ears. They tied me up, then, plumb°
amidships, back to the mast, lashed to the mast,

1270 and took themselves again to rowing. Soon,
as we came smartly within hailing distance,
the two Sirens, noting our fast ship
off their point, made ready, and they sang. . . .

1268. **plumb:** perfectly vertical.

Ulysses and the Sirens (c. 475 B.C.).
Attic red vase.

The lovely voices in ardor appealing over the water

1275   made me crave to listen, and I tried to say
'Untie me!' to the crew, jerking my brows;
but they bent steady to the oars. Then Perimedes
got to his feet, he and Eurylochus,
and passed more line about, to hold me still.

1280   So all rowed on, until the Sirens
dropped under the sea rim, and their singing
dwindled away.

                          My faithful company
rested on their oars now, peeling off
the wax that I had laid thick on their ears;
then set me free.

1285   But scarcely had that island
faded in blue air than I saw smoke
and white water, with sound of waves in tumult—
a sound the men heard, and it terrified them.
Oars flew from their hands; the blades went knocking

1290   wild alongside till the ship lost way,
with no oarblades to drive her through the water.

Well, I walked up and down from bow to stern,
trying to put heart into them, standing over
every oarsman, saying gently,

                                  'Friends,

1295   have we never been in danger before this?
More fearsome, is it now, than when the Cyclops
penned us in his cave? What power he had!
Did I not keep my nerve, and use my wits
to find a way out for us?

                              Now I say

1300   by hook or crook this peril too shall be
something that we remember.

                        Heads up, lads!
We must obey the orders as I give them.
Get the oarshafts in your hands, and lay back
hard on your benches; hit these breaking seas.

1305   Zeus help us pull away before we founder.

You at the tiller, listen, and take in
all that I say—the rudders are your duty;
keep her out of the combers° and the smoke;
steer for that headland; watch the drift, or we

1310   fetch up in the smother,° and you drown us.'

That was all, and it brought them round to action.
But as I sent them on toward Scylla, I
told them nothing, as they could do nothing.
They would have dropped their oars again, in panic,

1308. **combers:** waves.

1310. **smother:** turmoil.

1315   to roll for cover under the decking. Circe's
        bidding against arms had slipped my mind,
        so I tied on my cuirass° and took up
        two heavy spears, then made my way along
        to the foredeck—thinking to see her first from there,
1320   the monster of the gray rock, harboring
        torment for my friends. I strained my eyes
        upon that cliffside veiled in cloud, but nowhere
        could I catch sight of her.

                                    And all this time,
        in travail,° sobbing, gaining on the current,
1325   we rowed into the strait—Scylla to port
        and on our starboard beam Charybdis, dire
        gorge° of the salt sea tide. By heaven! when she
        vomited, all the sea was like a cauldron
        seething over intense fire, when the mixture
        suddenly heaves and rises.
1330   The shot spume
        soared to the landside heights, and fell like rain.

        But when she swallowed the sea water down
        we saw the funnel of the maelstrom, heard
        the rock bellowing all around, and dark
1335   sand raged on the bottom far below.
        My men all blanched° against the gloom, our eyes
        were fixed upon that yawning mouth in fear
        of being devoured.
                        Then Scylla made her strike,
        whisking six of my best men from the ship.

1340   I happened to glance aft at ship and oarsmen
        and caught sight of their arms and legs, dangling
        high overhead. Voices came down to me
        in anguish, calling my name for the last time.

        A man surf-casting on a point of rock
1345   for bass or mackerel, whipping his long rod
        to drop the sinker and the bait far out,
        will hook a fish and rip it from the surface
        to dangle wriggling through the air:
                            so these
        were borne aloft in spasms toward the cliff.
1350   She ate them as they shrieked there, in her den,
        in the dire grapple,° reaching still for me—
        and deathly pity ran me through
        at that sight—far the worst I ever suffered,
        questing the passes of the strange sea.
                          We rowed on.
1355   The Rocks were now behind; Charybdis, too,
        and Scylla dropped astern.

1317. cuirass (kwĭ·răs′): armor for the breast and back.

1324. travail: agony, pain.

1327. gorge: throat and jaws.

1336. blanched: grew pale.

1351. dire grapple: terrible fight.

Then we were coasting
the noble island of the god, where grazed
those cattle with wide brows, and bounteous flocks
of Helios, lord of noon, who rides high heaven.

1360 From the black ship, far still at sea, I heard
the lowing of the cattle winding home
and sheep bleating; and heard, too, in my heart
the words of blind Teiresias of Thebes
and Circe of Aeaea: both forbade me
1365 the island of the world's delight, the Sun. . . ."

Because they are dying of starvation, Odysseus's men disobey his orders, and shortly after they land, they eat the sacred cattle of the sun god, Helios. When they set sail again, they are punished by death—a thunderbolt from Zeus destroys their boat and all the men drown. Only Odysseus survives. He makes his way to Calypso's island, where we met him originally in Book 5. Odysseus the storyteller has brought us up to date. He can now rest.

Responding to the Epic

Analyzing the Epic
Identifying Facts

1. Describe the **internal conflict** Odysseus and his men encounter in the land of the Lotus Eaters.
2. Describe three strategies that the wily Odysseus uses to outwit the Cyclops Polyphemus. What mistake does the hero make near the end of the Cyclops adventure?
3. What curse concludes the Cyclops adventure—**foreshadowing** trouble ahead for Odysseus?
4. What are Circe's powers? How does Circe first treat Odysseus and his men?
5. Homer's audience would have known who Teiresias was and they would have known that the prophet could not possibly be wrong. Summarize all that Odysseus finds out from Teiresias about his own future.
6. What does Odysseus's mother tell him about death and the soul?
7. Describe the threats posed by the Sirens and by Scylla and Charybdis. How does Odysseus survive these perils?
8. What happens to his men?

Interpreting Meanings

9. What **simile** does Homer use to help his audience see what happens when Scylla whisks six men from Odysseus's ship? What do Odysseus's feelings here tell you about his **character**?
10. It is important to remember, as we listen to Odysseus's adventures, that the *Odyssey* was used as part of Greek children's education for centuries after the poem was written down. How could the adventure with the Lotus Eaters teach them about the temptation to "forget" one's troubles by dropping out? How could the Cyclops adventure be used to teach the dangers of violence and of curiosity?
11. Explain what we can learn about the deceptive nature of beauty from the Circe episode.
12. Odysseus considers the Cyclopes to be barbarians. Describe Polyphemus's home and his way of life, especially his attitude toward the treatment of guests. Explain how the Cyclopes and their society contrast with what we have seen on Ithaca and on Pylos and Sparta.

13. Recall that Books 9–12 of the *Odyssey* are a long narration delivered by Odysseus at the Phaeacian court of King Alcinous. As he tells his adventures, do you ever sense that Odysseus is boastful or arrogant, or do you think he is just being confident? What incidents support your evaluation of his **character**?

14. Books 9–12 of the *Odyssey* tell of Odysseus's most famous adventures; in fact, this is all that many readers know of the *Odyssey*. Why do you think these particular adventures continue to fascinate people? How did you feel about these favorite parts of the *Odyssey*?

you write, fill out a chart like the following, to help you see the ways in which the stories are alike and different:

	Odyssey	Other story
A small person vs. a giant		
Intelligence vs. brute strength		
A surprise upset victory		

Writing About the Epic

A Creative Response

1. **Personifying a Force of Nature.** Homer describes a whirlpool and a dangerous rock as if they were living monsters. In this sense, Scylla and Charybdis are **personified**: they are inanimate (nonliving), but the poet describes them as if they have life. In a paragraph, personify some other violent force of nature. Use details that suggest that the force is a monster with destructive intentions. You might describe one of these forces:

   A volcano
   A tornado
   A tidal wave
   Thunder and lightning
   Snow

   Include details that tell how the monster looks; what it sounds like; what it hunts for; and what happens to people it captures.

2. **Narrating the Fulfillment of a Prophecy.** In lines 1122–1141, the prophet Teiresias tells Odysseus about his future. Several writers after Homer have tried to imagine exactly what this mysterious prophecy means. Write your own story based on this prophecy. Tell **what** Odysseus did, **where** he went, and **when** it happened. In your story be sure to include all the details contained in the prophecy.

A Critical Response

3. **Comparing Stories.** The story of Odysseus versus the Cyclops has parallels in other stories told throughout the ages. In a paragraph, compare this story to another one you have read. Before

Analyzing Language and Vocabulary

The Prefixes *Poly-* and *Mono-*

One of the most useful of the many Greek prefixes adapted into the English language is the prefix *poly-*. We find it used in the *Odyssey* in the name given to the monster Cyclops, Polyphemus. The prefix can mean "many or more than one," "excessive," or "of many kinds or parts." Use a dictionary to answer the following questions:

1. What word uses *poly-* to name a kind of fabric manufactured from several resins?
2. What word uses *poly-* to describe a person who has more than one husband or wife at the same time?
3. Why do you think a growth in the nasal passage or colon is called a *polyp*?
4. What word uses *poly-* to name a belief in many gods?

Use a dictionary to write out the definition of each italicized word in the following sentences:

1. The Lower East Side is a *polyglot* neighborhood.
2. Hawaii is part of *Polynesia*.
3. The geometry teacher drew a *polygon* on the chalkboard.

The prefix *mono-* is opposite in meaning to *poly-*; it means "one," "alone," or "single." Use a dictionary to answer these questions:

1. What word uses *mono-* to name the worship of one God?
2. Why is the infection called *mononucleosis* so named?
3. What word uses *mono-* to describe people who have only one spouse at a time?

Part Three: The Return of the Hero

In Book 13, Odysseus, laden with gifts, is returned in secret to Ithaca in one of the magically swift Phaeacian ships. In Ithaca, Athena herself appears to the hero. She advises him how to proceed and disguises him as a beggar. Notice that this new hero of the postwar age of disillusionment will achieve success not only by physical power but also by guile and wisdom.

In Book 14, Odysseus, in his beggar disguise, finds his way to the house of his old and trusty swineherd, Eumaeus. Eumaeus is the very image of faithfulness in a servant—a quality much prized by Homer's society. The introduction of the so-called servant class as important actors is unusual in epic poetry, and it indicates Homer's originality. Odysseus is simply but politely entertained in the swineherd's hut, but he remains disguised from Eumaeus.

In Book 15, we go back to Telemachus, who is still with Menelaus and Helen. The plots of the father and the son are

Ulysses disguised as a beggar. Attic red figure vase.

Etruscan Museum, Chiusi. Photo: Art Resource

now about to be brought together. Athena appears to the boy and advises him to return home. She warns him that the evil suitors plan to ambush him. Telemachus boards ship for home, lands secretly on Ithaca, and heads toward the cottage of the swineherd. As father and son were moved closer and closer together, the suspense in the audience must have become great. Now Homer is ready for what could be the most dramatic moment in the epic.

Book 16: The Meeting of Father and Son

But there were two men in the mountain hut—
Odysseus and the swineherd. At first light
blowing their fire up, they cooked their breakfast
and sent their lads out, driving herds to root
in the tall timber.

1370   When Telemachus came,
the wolvish troop of watchdogs only fawned on him
as he advanced. Odysseus heard them go
and heard the light crunch of a man's footfall—
at which he turned quickly to say:

                            "Eumaeus,
1375 here is one of your crew come back, or maybe
another friend: the dogs are out there snuffling
belly down; not one has even growled.
I can hear footsteps—"

                    But before he finished
his tall son stood at the door.

                      The swineherd
1380 rose in surprise, letting a bowl and jug
tumble from his fingers. Going forward,
he kissed the young man's head, his shining eyes
and both hands, while his own tears brimmed and fell.
Think of a man whose dear and only son,
1385 born to him in exile, reared with labor,
has lived ten years abroad and now returns:
how would that man embrace his son! Just so
the herdsman clapped his arms around Telemachus
and covered him with kisses—for he knew
1390 the lad had got away from death. He said:

"Light of my days, Telemachus,
you made it back! When you took ship for Pylos
I never thought to see you here again.
Come in, dear child, and let me feast my eyes;
1395 here you are, home from the distant places!
How rarely, anyway, you visit us,

your own men, and your own woods and pastures!
Always in the town, a man would think
you loved the suitors' company, those dogs!''

1400 Telemachus with his clear candor said:

"I am with you, Uncle.° See now, I have come
because I wanted to see you first, to hear from you
if Mother stayed at home—or is she married
off to someone, and Odysseus's bed
1405 left empty for some gloomy spider's weaving?''

1401. **Uncle:** here, an affectionate greeting.

Gently the forester replied to this:

"At home indeed your mother is, poor lady
still in the women's hall. Her nights and days
are wearied out with grieving.''

                                        Stepping back
1410 he took the bronze-shod lance, and the young prince
entered the cabin over the worn door stone.
Odysseus moved aside, yielding his couch,
but from across the room Telemachus checked him:
"Friend, sit down; we'll find another chair
1415 in our own hut. Here is the man to make one!''

The swineherd, when the quiet man sank down,
built a new pile of evergreens and fleeces—
a couch for the dear son of great Odysseus—
then gave them trenchers° of good meat, left over
1420 from the roast pork of yesterday, and heaped up
willow baskets full of bread, and mixed
an ivy bowl of honey-hearted wine.
Then he in turn sat down, facing Odysseus,
their hands went out upon the meat and drink
1425 as they fell to, ridding themselves of hunger . . .

1419. **trenchers:** wooden platters.

*Not realizing that the stranger is his father, Telemachus agrees
to protect him as best he can. But he tells the beggar that he
cannot stay in the palace hall because he will be abused by the
drunken suitors.*

*The swineherd is sent to Penelope with news of her son's
return. And now it seems that even Athena cannot stand the
suspense any longer. She turns to Odysseus, in beggar's rags:*

She tipped her golden wand upon the man,
making his cloak pure white, and the knit tunic
fresh around him. Lithe° and young she made him,
ruddy with sun, his jawline clean, the beard
1430 no longer gray upon his chin. And she
withdrew when she had done.

1428. **Lithe:** limber.

Then Lord Odysseus
reappeared—and his son was thunderstruck.
Fear in his eyes, he looked down and away
as though it were a god, and whispered:

                            "Stranger,
1435   you are no longer what you were just now!
Your cloak is new; even your skin! You are
one of the gods who rule the sweep of heaven!
Be kind to us, we'll make you fair oblation°
and gifts of hammered gold. Have mercy on us!"

1440   The noble and enduring man replied:

"No god. Why take me for a god? No, no.
I am that father whom your boyhood lacked
and suffered pain for lack of. I am he."

Held back too long, the tears ran down his cheeks
as he embraced his son.
1445   Only Telemachus,
uncomprehending, wild
with incredulity,° cried out:

                            "You cannot
be my father Odysseus! Meddling spirits
conceived this trick to twist the knife in me!
1450   No man of woman born could work these wonders
by his own craft, unless a god came into it
with ease to turn him young or old at will.
I swear you were in rags and old,
and here you stand like one of the immortals!"

1455   Odysseus brought his ranging mind to bear
and said:

                "This is not princely, to be swept
away by wonder at your father's presence.
No other Odysseus will ever come,
for he and I are one, the same; his bitter
1460   fortune and his wanderings are mine.
Twenty years gone, and I am back again
on my own island. . . ."
                      Then, throwing
his arms around this marvel of a father,
Telemachus began to weep. Salt tears
1465   rose from the wells of longing in both men,
and cries burst from both as keen and fluttering
as those of the great taloned hawk,
whose nestlings farmers take before they fly.
So helplessly they cried, pouring out tears,
1470   and might have gone on weeping so till sundown. . . .

1438. **oblation:** offering of a sacrifice.

1447. **incredulity:** disbelief.

Responding to the Epic

Analyzing the Epic

Identifying Facts

1. After twenty years, Odysseus finally returns in secret to Ithaca. Once there, whom does he visit and how is he disguised?
2. What **images** in this little episode help us feel as if we were there by appealing to our senses of sight, hearing, and even taste?
3. How does Athena transform Odysseus just before he reveals his identity to Telemachus?

Interpreting Meanings

4. We feel **irony** when a situation seems inappropriate or just the reverse of what we expected. Why is it ironic that Odysseus should return to his kingdom dressed in beggar's rags?
5. **Dramatic irony** in particular refers to a situation in which the readers (or the audience) know more than the characters in the story (or play) know. Where do we get a sense of great dramatic irony in this episode in the swineherd's hut?
6. It is rare in ancient epics for heroic characters to have much to do with ordinary people, but in the *Odyssey,* servants play important roles. How do Odysseus and Telemachus treat Eumaeus? What might Homer be trying to teach us through that treatment?
7. What **simile** describes the feelings of Odysseus and his son as they embrace after twenty years? How would you describe exactly what the father and his son are feeling here?
8. Do you know of any other stories or any movies or TV shows in which the hero (or heroine) appears in a disguise? What do these heroes (or heroines) usually learn while they are in the disguise?
9. Suppose Odysseus were a modern general who finally got home after an absence of twenty years. How do you think he would have approached his old home—if he had had to face the problems that exist in Ithaca?

Book 17: The Beggar and the Faithful Dog

Telemachus returns to the family compound and is greeted tear-fully by his mother and his old nurse, Eurycleia. A soothsayer tells Penelope that Odysseus is alive and is already in Ithaca. The suspense builds, as Odysseus, once again disguised as a beggar, finally returns to his home accompanied only by the swineherd. He has been away for twenty years. Only one creature recognizes him.

An old hound, lying near, pricked up his ears
and lifted up his muzzle. This was Argos,
trained as a puppy by Odysseus,
but never taken on a hunt before
1475 his master sailed for Troy. The young men, afterward,
hunted wild goats with him, and hare, and deer,
but he had grown old in his master's absence.
Treated as rubbish now, he lay at last
upon a mass of dung before the gates—

1480 manure of mules and cows, piled there until
fieldhands could spread it on the king's estate.
Abandoned there, and half destroyed with flies,
old Argos lay.

         But when he knew he heard
Odysseus's voice nearby, he did his best
1485 to wag his tail, nose down, with flattened ears,
having no strength to move nearer his master.
And the man looked away,
wiping a salt tear from his cheek; but he
hid this from Eumaeus. Then he said:

Hound gnawing a bone
(Greek, 2nd century B.C.). Bronze.

The Metropolitan Museum of Art,
Fletcher Fund, 1936. (36.11.12)

1490   "I marvel that they leave this hound to lie
here on the dung pile;
he would have been a fine dog, from the look of him,
though I can't say as to his power and speed
when he was young. You find the same good build
1495   in house dogs, table dogs landowners keep
all for style.''

                And you replied, Eumaeus:
"A hunter owned him—but the man is dead
in some far place. If this old hound could show
the form he had when Lord Odysseus left him,
1500   going to Troy, you'd see him swift and strong.
He never shrank from any savage thing
he'd brought to bay in the deep woods; on the scent
no other dog kept up with him. Now misery
has him in leash. His owner died abroad,
1505   and here the women slaves will take no care of him.
You know how servants are: without a master
they have no will to labor, or excel.
For Zeus who views the wide world takes away
half the manhood of a man, that day
1510   he goes into captivity and slavery.''

Eumaeus crossed the court and went straight forward
into the megaron° among the suitors;
but death and darkness in that instant closed
the eyes of Argos, who had seen his master,
1515   Odysseus, after twenty years.

1512. **megaron:** the great hall, or central room.

In the hall, the beggar is taunted by the suitors, but Penelope supports him. She has heard that the ragged stranger claims to have news of her husband. Unaware of who this beggar is, she invites him to visit her later in the night to talk about Odysseus.

   In Book 18, Penelope appears among the suitors and chastises Telemachus for allowing the stranger to be abused. She certainly must have warmed her husband's heart by doing this and by further singing the praises of her lost Odysseus.

Book 19: Penelope, the Beggar, and the Nurse

After the suitors depart for the night and after Odysseus and Telemachus discuss their strategy, the wily hero goes as appointed to Penelope with the idea of testing her and her maids. (Remember that some of the maids have not been loyal to the household and have worked with the suitors against them.) The faithful wife receives her disguised husband. We can imagine the tension Homer's audience must have felt. Would Odysseus be recognized?

                                                        Willing hands
        brought a smooth bench, and dropped a fleece upon it.
        Here the adventurer and king sat down;
        then carefully, Penelope began:

1520   "Friend, let me ask you first of all:
        who are you, where do you come from, of what nation
        and parents were you born?"

                                        And he replied:
        "My lady, never a man in the wide world
        should have a fault to find with you. Your name
1525   has gone out under heaven like the sweet
        honor of some god-fearing king, who rules
        in equity over the strong: his black lands bear
        both wheat and barley, fruit trees laden bright,
        new lambs at lambing time—and the deep sea
1530   gives great hauls of fish by his good strategy,
        so that his folk fare well.

                                        O my dear lady,
        this being so, let it suffice to ask me
        of other matters—not my blood, my homeland.
        Do not enforce me to recall my pain.
1535   My heart is sore; but I must not be found
        sitting in tears here, in another's house:
        it is not well forever to be grieving.
        One of the maids might say—or you might think—
        I had got maudlin over cups of wine."

        And Penelope replied:

1540   "Stranger, my looks,
        my face, my carriage, were soon lost or faded
        when the Achaeans crossed the sea to Troy,
        Odysseus my lord among the rest.
        If he returned, if he were here to care for me,
1545   I might be happily renowned!
        But grief instead heaven sent me—years of pain.
        Sons of the noblest families on the islands,
        Doulikhion, Same, wooded Zakynthos,
        with native Ithacans, are here to court me,
1550   against my wish; and they consume this house.

Can I give proper heed to guest or suppliant
or herald on the realm's affairs?

                          How could I?

wasted with longing for Odysseus, while here
they press for marriage. . . .

1555   And now, as matters stand at last,
I have no strength left to evade a marriage,
cannot find any further way; my parents
urge it upon me, and my son
will not stand by while they eat up his property.

1560   He comprehends it, being a man full grown,
able to oversee the kind of house
Zeus would endow with honor.

                        But you too

confide in me, tell me your ancestry.
You were not born of mythic oak or stone.''

*Here the beggar spins a yarn about his origins, pretending that
he has met Odysseus on his travels. He cannot resist praising*

Return of Ulysses (5th century B.C.).
Terracotta relief.

The Metropolitan Museum of Art.
Fletcher Fund, 1930. (30.11.9)

1565   Now all these lies he made appear so truthful
         she wept as she sat listening. The skin
         of her pale face grew moist the way pure snow
         softens and glistens on the mountains, thawed
         by Southwind after powdering from the West,
1570   and, as the snow melts, mountain streams run full:
         so her white cheeks were wetted by these tears
         shed for her lord—and he close by her side.
         Imagine how his heart ached for his lady,
         his wife in tears; and yet he never blinked;
1575   his eyes might have been made of horn or iron
         for all that she could see. He had this trick—
         wept, if he willed to, inwardly.

                                              Well, then,
         as soon as her relieving tears were shed
         she spoke once more:

                         "I think that I shall say, friend,
1580   give me some proof, if it is really true
         that you were host in that place to my husband
         with his brave men, as you declare. Come, tell me
         the quality of his clothing, how he looked,
         and some particular of his company."

1585   Odysseus answered, and his mind ranged far:

         "Lady, so long a time now lies between,
         it is hard to speak of it. Here is the twentieth year
         since that man left the island of my father.
         But I shall tell what memory calls to mind.
1590   A purple cloak, and fleecy, he had on—
         a double thick one. Then, he wore a brooch
         made of pure gold with twin tubes for the prongs,
         and on the face a work of art: a hunting dog
         pinning a spotted fawn in agony
1595   between his forepaws—wonderful to see
         how being gold, and nothing more, he bit
         the golden deer convulsed, with wild hooves flying.
         Odysseus's shirt I noticed, too—a fine
         closefitting tunic like dry onion skin,
1600   so soft it was, and shiny. . . ."

         Now hearing these details—minutely true—
         she felt more strangely moved, and tears flowed
         until she had tasted her salt grief again.

The story-telling beggar reveals that he has heard Odysseus is alive and is even now sailing for home. Penelope calls for the old nurse and asks her to wash the guest's feet—a sign of respect and honor. What follows is a scene of great emotional suspense. Eurycleia speaks to the supposed beggar:

                              "My heart within me stirs,
1605   mindful of something. Listen to what I say:
strangers have come here, many through the years,
but no one ever came, I swear, who seemed
so like Odysseus—body, voice, and limbs—
as you do."

                    Ready for this, Odysseus answered:

1610   "Old woman, that is what they say. All who have seen
the two of us remark how like we are,
as you yourself have said, and rightly, too."

Then he kept still, while the old nurse filled up
her basin glittering in firelight; she poured
cold water in, then hot.
1615   But Lord Odysseus
whirled suddenly from the fire to face the dark.
The scar: he had forgotten that. She must not
handle his scarred thigh, or the game was up.
But when she bared her lord's leg, bending near,
she knew the groove at once.
1620   An old wound
a boar's white tusk inflicted, on Parnassus°
years ago. . . .
This was the scar the old nurse recognized;
she traced it under her spread hands, then let go,
1625   and into the basin fell the lower leg
making the bronze clang, sloshing the water out.
Then joy and anguish seized her heart; her eyes
filled up with tears; her throat closed, and she whispered,
with hand held out to touch his chin:

                                  "Oh yes!

1630   *You are Odysseus! Ah, dear child!* I could not
see you until now—not till I knew
my master's very body with my hands!"

Quickly, Odysseus swears Eurycleia to secrecy. Meanwhile, Athena has cast a spell on Penelope so that she has taken no notice of this recognition scene. Penelope adds to the suspense by deciding on a test for the suitors on the next day. Without realizing it, she now has given Odysseus a way to defeat the suitors.

1621. Parnassus: a mountain in central Greece.

Responding to the Epic

Analyzing the Epic

Identifying Facts

1. What is Argos's condition when Odysseus sees him? In telling us how Odysseus's dog is kept, what is Homer also telling us about conditions in Ithaca?
2. Odysseus continues to maintain his disguise by telling "lying tales"—even to his wife. What yarn does the "beggar" tell Penelope? How does he describe Odysseus (and why do you think he adds these details)?
3. Clever as he is, Odysseus slips up when Eurycleia bathes his feet. By what hidden sign does she recognize him?

Interpreting Meanings

4. What do we learn about the **character** of Penelope in her interview with the "beggar"?
5. What do we learn about the **character** of Odysseus in his interview with his wife?
6. Why do you think Odysseus continues to keep his identity hidden from his wife?
7. How is Penelope's interview with the "beggar" **ironic**?
8. The scene between Odysseus and Penelope is one of the most famous scenes in literature. Some readers have suggested that Penelope actually knows the identity of the beggar by now but is not revealing it. What do you think about this interpretation? Support your answer with specific reference to the epic.
9. The *Odyssey* is centuries and centuries old. Are the human feelings revealed by the people in the *Odyssey* still important to people today? Are the needs of people still exactly the same today? Explain.

Analyzing Language and Vocabulary

The Epithet

An **epithet** is an adjective or phrase used to characterize someone. *Good* King Wenceslaus, Katherine *the Great, The Brat Pack, Land of the Free*—these epithets are used to characterize a king, a queen, a group of actors, and a country. The word *epithet* means "put on" or "added."

Homer uses many epithets as formulas to characterize places and people. Penelope, for example, is frequently referred to as "faithful Penelope," and we are instantly reminded of her outstanding character trait.

The following questions focus on some of Homer's famous epithets.

1. Odysseus is called "*versatile* Odysseus," "*wily* Odysseus," "the *strategist*," and "the noble and *enduring* man." What does each italicized word mean?
2. Persephone, the Queen of the Underworld, is called "the iron queen." What does the word *iron* suggest about the realm she rules over and her own character? (Think of how different she would seem if she were called "the golden queen.")
3. Telemachus is called "clear-headed Telemachus." How would you define "clear-headed"?
4. One of Homer's most famous epithets is the formula description "the wine-dark sea." Many scholars and even scientists have argued about this description. Since wine is either red or white or yellowish, and the sea is none of these hues, the description is puzzling. Some say that the ancient Greeks diluted their wine with water and that the alkaline in the water changed the color of the wine from red to blue. Others think the sea was covered with red-colored marine algae. Still others even suggest that the Greeks were color blind. But Robert Fitzgerald, the great translator of the *Odyssey,* thought about the question when he was on a ship sailing into the Aegean Sea:

"The contrast of the bare arid baked land against the sea gave the sea such a richness of hue that I felt as though we were sailing through a bowl of dye. The depth of hue of the water was like the depth of hue of a good red wine."

How would *you* explain Homer's "wine-dark sea"?

Book 21: The Test of the Great Bow

Like many unwilling princesses of myth, fairy tale, and legend,
Penelope proposes an impossible task for those who wish to
marry her. By so doing, she causes the bloody events that lead
to the restoration of her true husband. The test will involve
Odysseus's huge bow, which no one could string except Odysseus
himself. Odysseus had left his bow home in Ithaca twenty years
ago.

Now the queen reached the storeroom door and halted.
Here was an oaken sill, cut long ago
and sanded clean and bedded true. Foursquare
the doorjambs and the shining doors were set
by the careful builder. Penelope untied the strap
around the curving handle, pushed her hook
into the slit, aimed at the bolts inside
and shot them back. Then came a rasping sound
as those bright doors the key had sprung gave way—
a bellow like a bull's vaunt° in a meadow—
followed by her light footfall entering
over the plank floor. Herb-scented robes
lay there in chests, but the lady's milkwhite arms
went up to lift the bow down from a peg
in its own polished bowcase.

                                    Now Penelope
sank down, holding the weapon on her knees,
and drew her husband's great bow out, and sobbed
and bit her lip and let the salt tears flow.
Then back she went to face the crowded hall
tremendous bow in hand, and on her shoulder hung
the quiver spiked with coughing death. Behind her
maids bore a basket full of axheads, bronze
and iron implements for the master's game.
Thus in her beauty she approached the suitors,
and near a pillar of the solid roof
she paused, her shining veil across her cheeks,
her maids on either hand and still,
then spoke to the banqueters:

                                    "My lords, hear me:
suitors indeed, you recommended this house
to feast and drink in, day and night, my husband
being long gone, long out of mind. You found
no justification for yourselves—none
except your lust to marry me. Stand up, then:
we now declare a contest for that prize.
Here is my lord Odysseus's hunting bow.

1635

1640

1645

1650

1655

1660

1665

1642. **vaunt:** boast.

Bend and string it if you can. Who sends an arrow
through iron ax-helve sockets,° twelve in line?
1670   I join my life with his, and leave this place, my home,
my rich and beautiful bridal house, forever
to be remembered, though I dream it only.''

*Many of the suitors boldly try the bow, but not a man can even
bend it enough to string it.*

Two men had meanwhile left the hall:
swineherd and cowherd, in companionship,
1675   one downcast as the other. But Odysseus
followed them outdoors, outside the court,
and coming up said gently:

                              ''You, herdsman,
and you, too, swineherd, I could say a thing to you,
or should I keep it dark?

                                        No, no; speak,
1680   my heart tells me. Would you be men enough
to stand by Odysseus if he came back?
Suppose he dropped out of a clear sky, as I did?
Suppose some god should bring him?
Would you bear arms for him, or for the suitors?''

The cowherd said:

1685   ''Ah, let the master come!
Father Zeus, grant our old wish! Some courier
guide him back! Then judge what stuff is in me
and how I manage arms!''

                              Likewise Eumaeus
fell to praying all heaven for his return,
1690   so that Odysseus, sure at least of these,
told them:

                              ''I am at home, for I am he.
I bore adversities, but in the twentieth year
I am ashore in my own land. I find
the two of you, alone among my people,
1695   longed for my coming. Prayers I never heard
except your own that I might come again.
So now what is in store for you I'll tell you:
If Zeus brings down the suitors by my hand
I promise marriages to both, and cattle,
1700   and houses built near mine. And you shall be
brothers-in-arms of my Telemachus.
Here, let me show you something else, a sign
that I am he, that you can trust me, look:

1669. An ax-helve is the ax handle. The
socket is a hollowed-out place lined with
iron at the end of the handle. The ax slides
into the socket and is secured. Shooting an
arrow through a line of ax-helve sockets
would be an ''impossible task''—something
worthy of a folk hero like Daniel Boone or
the Lone Ranger, or Odysseus.

this old scar from the tusk wound that I got
boar hunting on Parnassus—'' . . .

1705   Shifting his rags
he bared the long gash. Both men looked, and knew
and threw their arms around the old soldier, weeping,
kissing his head and shoulders. He as well
took each man's head and hands to kiss, then said—
1710 to cut it short, else they might weep till dark—

"Break off, no more of this.
Anyone at the door could see and tell them.
Drift back in, but separately at intervals
after me.

                          Now listen to your orders:
1715 when the time comes, those gentlemen, to a man,
will be dead against giving me bow or quiver.
Defy them. Eumaeus, bring the bow
and put it in my hands there at the door.
Tell the women to lock their own door tight.
1720 Tell them if someone hears the shock of arms
or groans of men, in hall or court, not one
must show her face, but keep still at her weaving.
Philoeteus, run to the outer gate and lock it.
Throw the crossbar and lash it.''

Now Odysseus, still in his beggar's clothes, asks to try the bow.
The suitors refuse to allow a mere beggar to try where they have
failed, but Penelope insists that the stranger be given his chance.
The suspense is very great—by this act, Penelope has accepted
her husband as a suitor.

Eumaeus, the swineherd, hands Odysseus the bow and tells
the nurse to retire with Penelope and the maids to the family
chambers (the harem) and to bolt the doors. Odysseus had earlier
told Telemachus to remove the suitors' weapons from the great
hall. Now he takes the bow . . .

1725   And Odysseus took his time,
turning the bow, tapping it, every inch,
for borings that termites might have made
while the master of the weapon was abroad.
The suitors were now watching him, and some
jested among themselves:

1730   "A bow lover!"

"Dealer in old bows!"

                          "Maybe he has one like it
at home!"

"Or has an itch to make one for himself."

"See how he handles it, the sly old buzzard!"

And one disdainful suitor added this:

1735   "May his fortune grow an inch for every inch he bends
          it!"

But the man skilled in all ways of contending,
satisfied by the great bow's look and heft,
like a musician, like a harper, when
with quiet hand upon his instrument
1740   he draws between his thumb and forefinger
a sweet new string upon a peg: so effortlessly
Odysseus in one motion strung the bow.
Then slid his right hand down the cord and plucked it,
so the taut gut vibrating hummed and sang
a swallow's note.
1745   In the hushed hall it smote the suitors
and all their faces changed. Then Zeus thundered
overhead, one loud crack for a sign.
And Odysseus laughed within him that the son
of crooked-minded Cronus° had flung that omen down.
1750   He picked one ready arrow from his table
where it lay bare: the rest were waiting still
in the quiver for the young men's turn to come.
He nocked° it, let it rest across the handgrip,
and drew the string and grooved butt of the arrow,
aiming from where he sat upon the stool.
1755   Now flashed
arrow from twanging bow clean as a whistle
through every socket ring, and grazed not one,
to thud with heavy brazen head beyond.
                                Then quietly
Odysseus said:
                        "Telemachus, the stranger
1760   you welcomed in your hall has not disgraced you.
I did not miss, neither did I take all day
stringing the bow. My hand and eye are sound,
not so contemptible as the young men say.
The hour has come to cook their lordships' mutton—
1765   supper by daylight. Other amusements later,
with song and harping that adorn a feast."
He dropped his eyes and nodded, and the prince
Telemachus, true son of King Odysseus,
belted his sword on, clapped hand to his spear,
1770   and with a clink and glitter of keen bronze
stood by his chair, in the forefront near his father.

1749. **Cronus:** father of Zeus. His epithet is "crooked-minded" because of his schemes to destroy his children.

1753. **nocked:** fit to the bowstring.

Book 22: Death at the Palace

The climax of the story is here. Odysseus is ready to claim his rightful kingdom. But first he must deal with more than a hundred young and hostile suitors. The first one he turns to is Antinous. Antinous has been, all through the story, the meanest of the suitors and their ringleader. He had hit Odysseus with a stool when the hero appeared in the hall as a beggar, and he had ridiculed the disguised king by calling him a bleary vagabond, a pest, and a tramp.

Now shrugging off his rags the wiliest fighter of the islands
leapt and stood on the broad door sill, his own bow in his
    hand.
He poured out at his feet a rain of arrows from the quiver
and spoke to the crowd:

1775   "So much for that. Your clean-cut game is over.
Now watch me hit a target that no man has hit before,
if I can make this shot. Help me, Apollo."°

He drew to his fist the cruel head of an arrow for Antinous
just as the young man leaned to lift his beautiful drinking
    cup,
1780 embossed, two-handled, golden: the cup was in his fingers:
the wine was even at his lips: and did he dream of death?
How could he? In that revelry amid his throng of friends
who would imagine a single foe—though a strong foe in-
    deed—
could dare to bring death's pain on him and darkness on
    his eyes?

1777. Odysseus prays to Apollo because this particular day is one of the god's feast days. Apollo is also the god of archery.

Ulysses slaying Penelope's suitors (c. 440 B.C.). Attic red figure vase.

Staatliche Museen, Berlin.
Photo: The Granger Collection,
New York.

1785 Odysseus's arrow hit him under the chin
and punched up to the feathers through his throat.
Backward and down he went, letting the winecup fall
from his shocked hand. Like pipes his nostrils jetted
crimson runnels,° a river of mortal red,
1790 and one last kick upset his table
knocking the bread and meat to soak in dusty blood.
Now as they craned to see their champion where he lay
the suitors jostled in uproar down the hall,
everyone on his feet. Wildly they turned and scanned
1795 the walls in the long room for arms; but not a shield,
not a good ashen spear was there for a man to take and
   throw.
All they could do was yell in outrage at Odysseus:

"Foul! to shoot at a man! That was your last shot!"
"Your own throat will be slit for this!"

                              "Our finest lad is down!
You killed the best on Ithaca."
1800   "Buzzards will tear your eyes out!"

For they imagined as they wished—that it was a wild shot,
an unintended killing—fools, not to comprehend
they were already in the grip of death.
But glaring under his brows Odysseus answered:

1805 "You yellow dogs, you thought I'd never make it
home from the land of Troy. You took my house to
   plunder,
twisted my maids to serve your beds. You dared
bid for my wife while I was still alive.
Contempt was all you had for the gods who rule wide
   heaven,
1810 contempt for what men say of you hereafter.
Your last hour has come. You die in blood."

As they all took this in, sickly green fear
pulled at their entrails,° and their eyes flickered
looking for some hatch or hideaway from death.
1815 Eurymachus alone could speak. He said:

"If you are Odysseus of Ithaca come back,
all that you say these men have done is true.
Rash actions, many here, more in the countryside.
But here he lies, the man who caused them all.
1820 Antinoüs was the ringleader, he whipped us on
to do these things. He cared less for a marriage
than for the power Cronion° has denied him
as king of Ithaca. For that
he tried to trap your son and would have killed him.

1789. **runnels:** streams.

1813. **entrails:** guts.

1822. **Cronion:** another name for Zeus, meaning "son of Cronus."

1825 He is dead now and has his portion. Spare
your own people. As for ourselves, we'll make
restitution of wine and meat consumed,
and add, each one, a tithe° of twenty oxen
with gifts of bronze and gold to warm your heart.
1830 Meanwhile we cannot blame you for your anger.''

Odysseus glowered under his black brows
and said:

           "Not for the whole treasure of your fathers,
all you enjoy, lands, flocks, or any gold
put up by others, would I hold my hand.
1835 There will be killing till the score is paid.
You forced yourselves upon this house. Fight your way
   out,
or run for it, if you think you'll escape death.
I doubt one man of you skins by." . . .

*Telemachus joins his father in the fight. They are helped by the
swineherd and cowherd. Now the suitors, trapped in the hall
without weapons, are struck right and left by arrows, and many
of them lie dying on the floor.*

At this moment that unmanning thunder cloud,
1840 the aegis, Athena's shield,
took form aloft in the great hall.
           And the suitors mad with fear
at her great sign stampeded like stung cattle by a river
when the dread shimmering gadfly strikes in summer,
in the flowering season, in the long-drawn days.
1845 After them the attackers wheeled, as terrible as eagles
from eyries° in the mountains veering over and diving
   down
with talons wide unsheathed on flights of birds,
who cower down the sky in chutes and bursts along the
   valley—
but the pouncing eagles grip their prey, no frantic wing
   avails,
1850 and farmers love to watch those beakèd hunters.
So these now fell upon the suitors in that hall,
turning, turning to strike and strike again,
while torn men moaned at death, and blood ran smoking
over the whole floor.

*Odysseus now calls forth the maids who have betrayed his house-
hold by associating with the suitors. He orders them to clean up
the house and dispose of the dead. He then "pays" them by
hanging them in the courtyard.*

1828. **tithe:** tax.

1846. **eyries** (er′ēs): nests built in very high
places.

Book 23: Odysseus and Penelope

Eurycleia runs to Penelope to announce the return of Odysseus and the defeat of the suitors. The faithful wife—the perfect mate for the wily Odysseus—suspects a trick from the gods and decides to test her would-be husband. She succeeds in teasing him to distraction.

1855 Crossing the door sill she sat down at once
in firelight, against the nearest wall,
across the room from the lord Odysseus.

                                              There
leaning against a pillar, sat the man
and never lifted up his eyes, but only waited
1860 for what his wife would say when she had seen him.
And she, for a long time, sat deathly still
in wonderment—for sometimes as she gazed
she found him—yes, clearly—like her husband,
but sometimes blood and rags were all she saw.

Telemachus's voice came to her ears:

                                              "Mother,
1865
cruel mother, do you feel nothing,
drawing yourself apart this way from Father?
Will you not sit with him and talk and question him?
What other woman could remain so cold?
1870 Who shuns her lord, and he come back to her
from wars and wandering, after twenty years?
Your heart is hard as flint and never changes!"

Penelope answered:

                                    "I am stunned, child.
I cannot speak to him. I cannot question him.
1875 I cannot keep my eyes upon his face.
If really he is Odysseus, truly home,
beyond all doubt we two shall know each other
better than you or anyone. There are
secret signs we know, we two."

                                              A smile
1880 came now to the lips of the patient hero, Odysseus,
who turned to Telemachus and said:

"Peace: let your mother test me at her leisure.
Before long she will see and know me best.
These tatters, dirt—all that I'm caked with now—
1885 make her look hard at me and doubt me still. . . ."

Odysseus orders Telemachus, the swineherd, and the cowherd to bathe and put on fresh clothing . . .

Greathearted Odysseus, home at last,
was being bathed now by Eurynome
and rubbed with golden oil, and clothed again
in a fresh tunic and a cloak. Athena
1890 lent him beauty, head to foot. She made him
taller, and massive, too, with crisping hair
in curls like petals of wild hyacinth
but all red-golden. Think of gold infused
on silver by a craftsman, whose fine art
1895 Hephaestus taught him, or Athena: one
whose work moves to delight: just so she lavished
beauty over Odysseus's head and shoulders.
He sat then in the same chair by the pillar,
facing his silent wife, and said:

                               "Strange woman,
1900 the immortals of Olympus made you hard,
harder than any. Who else in the world
would keep aloof as you do from her husband
if he returned to her from years of trouble,
cast on his own land in the twentieth year?

1905 Nurse, make up a bed for me to sleep on.
Her heart is iron in her breast."

                                    Penelope
spoke to Odysseus now. She said:

                               "Strange man,
if man you are . . . This is no pride on my part
nor scorn for you—not even wonder, merely.
1910 I know so well how you—how he—appeared
boarding the ship for Troy. But all the same . . .

Make up his bed for him, Eurycleia.
Place it outside the bedchamber my lord
built with his own hands. Pile the big bed
1915 with fleeces, rugs, and sheets of purest linen."

With this she tried him to the breaking point,
and he turned on her in a flash raging:

"Woman, by heaven you've stung me now!
Who dared to move my bed?
1920 No builder had the skill for that—unless
a god came down to turn the trick. No mortal
in his best days could budge it with a crowbar.
There is our pact and pledge, our secret sign,
built into that bed—my handiwork
and no one else's!

Mirror with the head of a woman
(4th century B.C.). Bronze.

The Metropolitan Museum of Art,
Rogers Fund, 1907. (07.256)

1925   An old trunk of olive
grew like a pillar on the building plot,
and I laid out our bedroom round that tree,
lined up the stone walls, built the walls and roof,
gave it a doorway and smooth-fitting doors.
1930 Then I lopped off the silvery leaves and branches,
hewed and shaped the stump from the roots up
into a bedpost, drilled it, let it serve
as model for the rest, I planed them all,
inlaid them all with silver, gold, and ivory,
1935 and stretched a bed between—a pliant web
of oxhide thongs dyed crimson.
                                  There's our sign!
I know no more. Could someone else's hand
have sawn that trunk and dragged the frame away?''
Their secret! as she heard it told, her knees
1940 grew tremulous and weak, her heart failed her.
With eyes brimming tears she ran to him,
throwing her arms around his neck, and kissed him,
murmuring:
                         "Do not rage at me, Odysseus!
No one ever matched your caution! Think
1945 what difficulty the gods gave: they denied us
life together in our prime and flowering years,
kept us from crossing into age together.
Forgive me, don't be angry. I could not
welcome you with love on sight! I armed myself
1950 long ago against the frauds of men,
impostors who might come—and all those many
whose underhanded ways bring evil on! . . .
But here and now, what sign could be so clear
as this of our own bed?
1955 No other man has ever laid eyes on it—
only my own slave, Actoris, that my father
sent with me as a gift—she kept our door.
You make my stiff heart know that I am yours.''
Now from his breast into his eyes the ache
1960 of longing mounted, and he wept at last,
his dear wife, clear and faithful, in his arms,
longed for as the sunwarmed earth is longed for by a
    swimmer
spent in rough water where his ship went down
under Poseidon's blows, gale winds and tons of sea.
1965 Few men can keep alive through a big surf
to crawl, clotted with brine, on kindly beaches
in joy, in joy, knowing the abyss behind:
and so she too rejoiced, her gaze upon her husband,
her white arms round him pressed as though forever.

Book 24: Odysseus and His Father

The ghosts of the suitors drift away through dank places to where the Dead dwell at the world's end.

Odysseus has one more duty. He must go to old Laertes, his grieving father, who lives alone outside of town. A natural story-teller to the end, Odysseus cannot resist teasing his father. He pretends to be a traveler, who had entertained Odysseus five years ago. As Laertes hears his son spoken of, the old man's eyes fill with tears . . .

1970 A cloud of pain had fallen on Laertes.
Scooping up handfuls of the sunburnt dust
he sifted it over his gray head, and groaned,
and the groan went to the son's heart. A twinge
prickling up through his nostrils warned Odysseus
1975 he could not watch this any longer.
He leaped and threw his arms around his father,
kissed him, and said:

                    "Oh, Father, I am he!
Twenty years gone, and here I've come again
to my own land!

               Hold back your tears! No grieving!
1980 I bring good news—though still we cannot rest.
I killed the suitors to the last man!
Outrage and injury have been avenged!"
Laertes turned and found his voice to murmur:

"If you are Odysseus, my son, come back,
1985 give me some proof, a sign to make me sure."

His son replied:

               "The scar then, first of all.
Look, here the wild boar's flashing tusk
wounded me on Parnassus; do you see it? . . .
Again—more proof—let's say the trees you gave me
1990 on this revetted° plot of orchard once.   1990. **revetted:** walled in.
I was a small boy at your heels, wheedling
amid the young trees, while you named each one.
You gave me thirteen pear, ten apple trees,
and forty fig trees. Fifty rows of vines
1995 were promised too, each one to bear in turn.
Bunches of every hue would hang there ripening,
weighed down by the god of summer days."
The old man's knees failed him, his heart grew faint,
recalling all that Odysseus calmly told.

2000 He clutched his son. Odysseus held him swooning
until he got his breath back and his spirit
and spoke again:

                            "Zeus, Father! Gods above!—
you still hold pure Olympus, if the suitors
paid for their crimes indeed, and paid in blood!"

2005 . . . They went home, the two together,
into the stone farmhouse. There Telemachus
and the two herdsmen were already carving
roast young pork, and mixing amber wine.
During these preparations the Sikel woman°
2010 bathed Laertes and anointed him,
and dressed him in a new cloak. Then Athena,
standing by, filled out his limbs again,
gave girth and stature to the old field captain
fresh from the bathing place. His son looked on
2015 in wonder at the godlike bloom upon him,
and called out happily:

                             "Oh, Father,

surely one of the gods who are young forever
has made you magnificent before my eyes!"

*The families of the dead suitors arrive with revenge in their
hearts. A blood feud seems inevitable, and a battle has already
begun, when Pallas Athena, directed by Zeus, ends once and for
all, the power struggle in Ithaca.*

                                "Now hold!"
2020 she cried, "Break off this bitter skirmish;
end your bloodshed, Ithacans, and make peace."

Their faces paled with dread before Athena,
and swords dropped from their hands unnerved, to lie
strewing the ground, at the great voice of the goddess.
2025 Those from the town turned fleeing for their lives.
But with a cry to freeze their hearts
and ruffling like an eagle on the pounce,
the lord Odysseus reared himself to follow—
at which the son of Cronus dropped a thunderbolt
smoking at his daughter's feet.
2030   Athena
cast a gray glance at her friend and said:

"Son of Laertes and the gods of old,
Odysseus, master of land ways and sea ways,
command yourself. Call off this battle now,
2035 or Zeus who views the wide world may be angry."

2009. The Sikel woman is Laertes' servant. *Sikel* might refer to Sicily.

He yielded to her, and his heart was glad.
Both parties later swore to terms of peace
set by their arbiter, Athena, daughter
of Zeus who bears the stormcloud as a shield—
2040   though still she kept the form and voice of Mentor.

Statuette of Zeus (Etruscan, c. 480 B.C.). Bronze.

Collection of the J. Paul Getty Museum, Malibu, California.

Responding to the Epic

Analyzing the Epic

Identifying Facts

1. Just before he steps forward to try the bow, Odysseus reveals his true identity to two other people. Who are they, and why does he reveal himself to them?
2. As the epic reaches its **climax,** two signs are sent from Olympus to indicate the gods' approval of Odysseus. What are they?
3. List at least five **images** and **similes** that help you picture some of the most tense or most horrifying moments in the battle.
4. The tables are turned on the wily Odysseus near the end of the story. How does Penelope test Odysseus after the battle? What characteristic of their marriage bed suggests the strength and endurance of their love?
5. What proofs does Odysseus give his father, Laertes, that it is indeed he, Odysseus, who has returned to Ithaca? How does Athena now transform old Laertes?
6. What is Athena's role at the **resolution** of the epic?

Interpreting Meanings

7. In setting up the test of the bow for the suitors, how is Penelope really saying that she is looking for Odysseus?
8. When Odysseus takes the bow in his hands at line 1736 (page 785), a **simile** compares him to a musician or harper. At what other points in the story has Odysseus been associated with singers of tales? What is significant about this simile and its use at the climactic moment of the *Odyssey*?
9. Is Odysseus's revenge on the suitors and maids excessive? Discuss this question from Odysseus's point of view (remember he was the rightful king) and from your own modern point of view.
10. When Odysseus was held by Calypso on her island, he told the nymph that he wanted to get home to see his wife. Calypso wondered what it was about Penelope that drew Odysseus homeward (see page 734). Now that you have met Penelope, how would you answer Calypso?

11. What important Greek value do you think is expressed in Odysseus's last action—his visit to Laertes? Do we share this value today?

Writing About the Epic

A Creative Response

1. **Setting the Epic in Modern Times.** Write a proposal in which you suggest ways that the *Odyssey* could be made into a movie set in contemporary times. In your proposal, which will be directed to the people who will produce the movie, you will have to explain how you would modernize the *Odyssey*. Use the following chart to organize your ideas. Write two or three paragraphs:

1200 B.C.	Today
a. Trojan War as a background	a.
b. Hero is soldier who fought in war	b.
c. Journeys home around Mediterranean and down to Underworld	c.
d. Uses ships with oars and sails	d.
e. Meets Lotus Eaters, Sirens, Scylla and Charybdis	e.
f. Is tempted by Circe and Calypso	f.
g. Is rescued by a teen-age princess	g.
h. Fortune hunters at home hound his wife	h.
i. Dog lives on garbage heap	i.
j. Son is insulted	j.
k. Gods dominate the action	k.

2. **Casting a Woman as the Voyaging Hero.** Write a brief essay in which you explain how an *Odyssey* could be written with a woman as the voyaging hero. Consider these points in your essay:

   a. Occupation of the heroine
   b. Reason for being away from home
   c. Situation at home
   d. Trials of journey home
   e. How the people blocking the heroine are defeated

A Critical Response

3. **Explaining the Epic's Relevance to the Twentieth Century.** A work of literature cannot be important to us unless it speaks to us and to our lives. In a paragraph, name at least four ways in which the *Odyssey* speaks to you in the twentieth century. You might consider how it says something about these values:

   a. The values of courage, trust, and discipline
   b. The value of home and family
   c. The value of obedience to the divine world
   d. The value of courtesy and respect for all classes of people

4. **Explaining a Theme.** On page 723 the three major themes of the *Odyssey* are very briefly stated. Take one theme, and in an essay explain how it is developed in the epic.

5. **Analyzing the Elements of the Epic.** Write a brief essay in which you cite incidents from the *Odyssey* that show how the epic includes these elements:

   a. It portrays the adventures of a larger-than-life hero.
   b. This hero is on a quest for something of great value.
   c. The epic is huge in scope and portrays domestic life as well as life in the divine world.
   d. It expresses the values of a particular society.

6. **Analyzing Character.** Various epithets describe Odysseus as "wily," "versatile," and a "strategist." In a brief essay, explain how Odysseus shows his cleverness and wit in the episodes with Nausicaa, with the Cyclops, and with Penelope at the end of the story. Consider also the hero's decision not to tell his men the whole of Circe's prophecy (page 764). At the end of your essay, explain how you feel about the character of Odysseus: Is he totally admirable? Is he believable? Is he like a modern hero, or does he seem old-fashioned today? Give at least one reason for your response.

7. **Comparing Stories.** Some of the story elements used in the *Odyssey* are found in legend and folklore. In a four-paragraph essay, explain how at least four situations found in the *Odyssey* are also found in another legend or folktale. Before you write, fill out a chart like the following one:

	Odyssey	Other Story
Magical weapon that works only for one person		
Scars or other signs that reveal true identity		
Divine beings (or fairy godmothers) who assist hero or heroine		
Magical transformations of hero or heroine		

8. **Contrasting Two "Return" Stories.** After any war there are homecoming stories, and the Trojan War was no different. One of the great homecoming stories to come out of that war is Odysseus's. Another homecoming story, which Homer's audience also knew very well, was the horrible story of Agamemnon's return to Mycenae and his wife Clytemnestra. In fact, Odysseus meets Agamemnon in the Land of the Dead and hears the old commander's tragic story. In a good sourcebook on mythology, look up the story of what happened when Agamemnon returned to Mycenae after the war. Then write an essay in which you contrast that homecoming with Odysseus's return to Ithaca and Penelope. (Edith Hamilton's *Mythology* will give you the information you need.) Write three paragraphs. Use the following chart to organize your main points.

	Odysseus	Agamemnon
The faithfulness of the heroes' wives		
The wives' motives for their behavior		
The reception each hero got upon being reunited with his wife		
The children's roles in the stories		

9. **Supporting a Critical Response.** Use one of these quotations as the basis of an essay on the *Odyssey*. Cite specific passages from the epic that you think support the ideas in the statement. If you disagree with the statement, cite specific passages from the epic to support your

own opinion, which you should make clear in your topic sentence. Write at least three paragraphs.

> . . . what has made Homer for three thousand years the greatest poet in the world is his *naturalness*. We love each other as in Homer. We hate each other as in Homer. We are perpetually being interfered with as in Homer by change and fate and necessity, by invisible influences for good, and by invisible influences for evil . . .
> —John Cowper Powys

> . . . the whole problem of the *Odyssey* is for Odysseus to establish his identity.
> —George S. Dimock, Jr.

> There are many women, young and old, enchantresses and queens and serving maids [in the *Odyssey*]. In the "society," as we say, of the *Odyssey*, women can be very distinguished: Athena is powerful in the highest circles, Arete holds equal power with her husband in Phaeacia, Helen has been re-established in the power of her beauty, which if I am not mistaken she makes Telemachus feel. Three of the principal adventures of Odysseus are with exquisite young women of great charm and spirit . . .
> —Robert Fitzgerald

Analyzing Language and Vocabulary

Words from the Epic

Even today, a difficult journey full of adventures and possible hardships is called an *odyssey*. In fact, any kind of wandering, or journey in search of something, is an *odyssey*. We speak of a scientist's "odyssey" in search of the secret of DNA. We speak of Alex Haley's "odyssey" in search of his African roots. John Steinbeck wrote of his "odyssey" in search of America in *Travels with Charley* (his poodle Charley rode with him). (See page 389.)

Here are some questions about some names from the *Odyssey* and some related English words. To answer the questions, you'll need a good dictionary. Look up the words in italics. Right after the word itself in the dictionary, you'll find information in parentheses that gives you the word's history.

1. The Cyclops was a giant with a single enormous eye. What does the word *Cyclops* have in common with our word *cycle*?
2. The Sirens were beautiful women with enchanting voices that lured sailors to steer their ships toward the rocks. Why do you think the warning horn on an ambulance or police car came to be called a *siren*?
3. *Siren* and *sinew* have a common root word, meaning "to tie." How did the Sirens "tie" men who heard their songs? How does the word *sinew* relate to the sense of "tie"?
4. Homer and Demodocus, both great bards, open their epic poems with a prayer to the Muse. There were nine Muses in mythology. They were goddesses who inspired people working in the arts and sciences. How is our word *museum* related to the *Muses*?
5. What does our word *music* have to do with the *Muses*?
6. Athena is often disguised in this epic as *Mentor,* a captain who was a friend of Odysseus's family. As Mentor, she guides the young Telemachus on his own "odyssey" to find his father and reclaim his rightful inheritance. What do we mean today when we say someone is a *mentor*?
7. Olympus was believed to be the home of the gods—it is a real mountain that can be seen today in Greece. Why were the *Olympics* named for this dwelling place of the gods?
8. The gods were believed to remain immortal by eating nectar and ambrosia. You find these divine foods mentioned several times in the *Odyssey*. What does *nectar* have in common with the medical term *necrosis,* which means "the death of tissue"?
9. Why do you think people named a fruit the *nectarine*?
10. The singer Homer and other bards were called *rhapsodes*. What does our word *rhapsody* mean today?

THE ELEMENTS OF AN EPIC

Epics are long narrative poems that tell about the adventures of a hero who represents the values of a particular civilization. As you have seen from reading the *Odyssey,* epic heroes are superhuman—they are braver and stronger than ordinary people are. Usually the epic hero is on a quest for something of great value to him or his people. The villains that try to keep the hero from his quest are usually uglier, more evil, and more cunning than anyone we know in ordinary life. And, in most epics, we find the divine world mixing in with the human world.

The following episode is from the *Aeneid,* the Roman epic written in the first century B.C. by the poet Virgil. It tells of the fall of Troy, but from the point of view of a Trojan prince named Aeneas. In this episode, Aeneas realizes Troy is doomed. He has just seen the Greeks murder the old Trojan king, Priam. All of his men have been killed, and now he worries about his own family (his old father, Anchises; his wife, Creusa; and his little son, Ascanius). All around him, Troy is in flames. Aeneas tells his own story.

The notes on the side will help guide your reading.

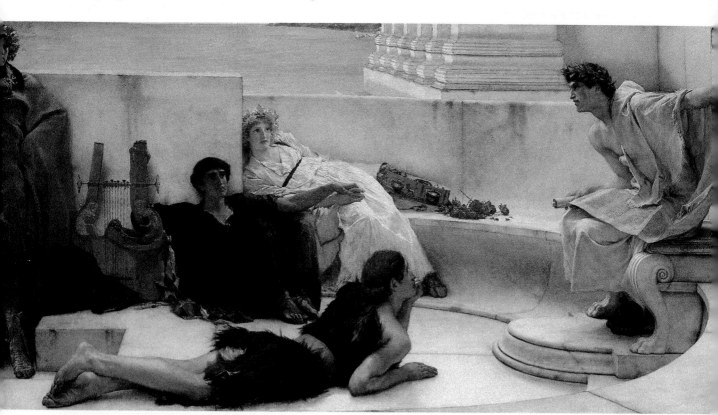

A Reading from Homer
by Sir Lawrence Alma-Tadema (1885). Oil.

Philadelphia Museum of Art,
George W. Elkins Collection

Yes, I was now the one man left of my party. But just
   then,
Hugging close to the threshold of Vesta,° speechlessly hid-
   ing there,
I noticed the daughter of Tyndareus, Helen. The blaze lit
   up
The whole scene as I wandered, peering this way and that.
5 Helen, the scourge of Troy and her own land alike,
In dread anticipation of Trojan wrath at Troy's
Downfall, of Greek revenge, of her cuckolded° husband's
   anger—
Helen, that hateful creature, was crouched by the altar, in
   hiding.
A fire broke out in my heart, a passion of rage to avenge
10 My country's fall and punish her crime by a crime upon her.
Was she going to get away with it? See Sparta again and
   her homeland?
Return as a queen, in triumph? Be once more reunited
With husband, home, parents, and children? Use our Trojan
Ladies for her attendants and Trojan men for slaves?—
15 All this, with Priam put to the sword, and Troy in ashes,
And Troy's shore time and again bathed in a sweat of blood?
Not so, I said. For although to kill a woman earns one
No fame, and victory over a female wins no decorations,
I shall be praised for stamping out an iniquity, punishing
20 One who so richly deserves it; and I shall enjoy fulfilling
My soul with a flame of vengeance, appeasing my people's
   ashes.
Such were my thoughts, the insensate° fury that drove me
   onward,
When to my view—and never before had I seen her so
   clear—
My gentle mother appeared: all glowing with light she came
25 Through the gloom, a goddess manifest, oh, high and hand-
   some as
The heaven dwellers know her. She laid a hand on mine,
Restraining me, then shaped these words with her rosy lips:
   My son, what anguish spurs you to this ungoverned rage?
What madness has driven all thought for love out of your
   heart?
30 Will you not first find out if your aged father, Anchises,
Is where you left him, and whether your wife, Creusa, be
   still

You should at once decide who "I" is.

2. **Vesta:** goddess of the hearth and home.

Do you have a picture of this scene?

7. **cuckolded:** deceived, meaning that his wife was deceiving him with another man.

We hear now the private thoughts of the narrator. Think about what they reveal of his character and values.

These lines foreshadow what is going to happen to the Trojans who are taken prisoners. They help establish motive.

If you don't know what "iniquity" means, the context might help. Make a good guess.

22. **insensate:** unreasonable.

You should notice the words that tell you that this is a ghost. Remember that in the world of the epic, supernatural events often occur.

Remember that Odysseus also met his mother, and that she was also dead. Notice what this woman tells her angry son.

Alive, and little Ascanius? A whole Greek army is surging
Round them on every side, and but for my guardian care
The flames would have got them by now, the fell° sword
    drained their blood.

35 It is not the beauty of hated Helen, it is not Paris,
Though you hold him to blame—the gods, the gods, I tell
    you, are hostile,
It's they who have undermined Troy's power and sent it
    tumbling.

—from the *Aeneid,* Book 2,
translated by C. Day Lewis

34. **fell:** deadly or cruel.

Epics take place in a world where the divinities mingle in human affairs. You should have an idea from this of how the Romans felt about the gods' power.

1. What does Aeneas want to do with Helen? What are his **motives**?
2. Helen eloped with a Trojan prince and willingly lived as his wife for many years in Troy—even though she already had a husband and children in Sparta. What irony can you see in the fact that this woman is now crouched beside the statue of a goddess dedicated to the family and home?
3. What was the Roman attitude toward killing women? Does this suggest that the Romans honored women, or does it suggest something else? Explain.
4. What supernatural event takes place in this part of the epic?
5. What does Aeneas's mother tell him is more important than vengeance?
6. From what the mother says to her son, how would you describe the Roman attitude toward the gods and their relationship to the human world?
7. How do you feel about the ways these people respond to the devastation of their country? Do you think people today would respond in the same ways? Explain.
8. What causes warfare and terrorism today? Are the reasons anything like the cause of the Trojan War? Explain.

Writing

1. **Narrating an Epic Episode.** Narrate one episode of an epic that will be read in the year 3000 by a class of high-school students. Base your epic on a great event of the twentieth century:

   World War I or II
   The atomic blast at Hiroshima
   The Vietnam War

   Choose some incident that will dramatize a code of behavior that your society values. Who will your hero or heroine be? What will his or her quest be? What obstacles will have to be overcome? Will you include any supernatural elements in your story?

2. **Extending an Epic.** You have met the famous Helen of Troy twice now (see also page 729). Add an episode to the *Odyssey* in which you let the readers know how Helen feels now about her role in the war. Start the narration right after Telemachus's visit (page 729) to Sparta. Include a flashback to the war. You could write a monologue in which Helen speaks.

PRESENTING TWO SIDES OF AN ARGUMENT

Writing Assignment

Imagine that Odysseus has been accused of neglecting his responsibility to his kingdom and to his men, resulting in a senseless loss of life and economic chaos in Ithaca. Write an interview in which Odysseus and his accuser (let's call him Demetrius) present their sides of the story.

Background

Besides telling a captivating story, the *Odyssey* also reveals values that were significant in Greek culture. Our culture also has values that make it uniquely American. Our public figures, for example, expect to be held accountable for their actions.

Imagine, then, what would happen if Odysseus were alive today. Would he receive a hero's welcome upon his return? What questions might the returned ruler be asked on the nightly news programs? (Why did he take so long to come home? Why did all of his men die? Could he have done more to save their lives? Was he simply enjoying his adventures too much to make more of an effort to come home? Was he really making a serious effort to surmount circumstances beyond his control?)

Prewriting

1. Prepare for this assignment by listening to a television or radio news interview program. As you listen, note the interviewer's behavior and the kinds of questions he or she asks. Be alert to the following points—which you should also keep in mind as you develop your interview for this assignment:

a. **Does the interviewer act as though there are two sides to the issue?** Remember, there are at least two sides to any complex issue or argument. While you may personally agree with a particular side, you cannot ignore your responsibility to explore *both* sides.

b. **Does the interviewer remain objective?** No matter how you feel about the issue or people involved, your job as an interviewer is to get the facts out and to reveal the character of the person you are interviewing (what is this person like?)—in a way that is fair, honest, and respectful.

c. **Does the interviewer ask specific questions?** With time limits for your interview, you must ask questions directly related to the issue. If the person you're interviewing starts to ramble, you must get him or her to refocus on the subject.

2. List at least five (preferably more) questions that you, as the interviewer on a news program, would ask Odysseus and his accuser, Demetrius.

3. Draw a chart with the answers that both Odysseus and Demetrius would give to your questions. Base their answers on information in the *Odyssey.* Remember that Odysseus and Demetrius should each present one side of the issue. That is, Odysseus should respond to a question with one answer, and Demetrius's answer should present the other side of the issue. For example, your chart could begin like this:

Question	Odysseus	Demetrius
1. Why were you with Circe for so long?	1. I had to stay with her to get her to tell me what I needed to know to get home. I could *not* escape.	1. For at least a time, Odysseus forgot his obligation to his kingdom and instead selfishly enjoyed Circe's attentions.

Writing

After developing your arguments and counterarguments, set up your writing in either an interview format or a dialogue format. If you use the **interview format**, you should follow each speaker's name with a colon (:). Then, write the speaker's comments in sentence form. If you use the **dialogue format**, enclose each speaker's words in quotation marks, and begin a new paragraph when the speaker changes.

Here is how you might use the interview format:

Interviewer: Here on "Faces in the News" today, we will be examining the baffling story of the return of Odysseus, without his crew, after an absence of over twenty years. The government investigation team, led by Demetrius, would like Odysseus to explain his long absence and loss of men. Demetrius, what are your charges?

> Speaker's name is followed by a colon.
> Comments are in sentence form.

Demetrius: We allege that Odysseus, in fact, had no desire to return home quickly. A trip that should have been completed in a matter of days took him ten years to complete.

> One argument is cited.

Odysseus: No, that charge isn't true. Throughout my travels, I made every effort to save the lives of my crew and to extricate us from our troubles. Consider, for example, my ingenious plan for escaping from the horrible Cyclops. And remember that the god Poseidon was dead set against me and tried to kill us all.

> The counterargument is cited.
>
> An example is given from the *Odyssey*.

Checklist for Revision

1. Have you included at least five arguments and counterarguments?
2. Have you included examples from the *Odyssey* to support each speaker's statements?
3. Have you presented arguments on both sides of the issue?
4. Have you correctly used the interview or the dialogue format?

THE ELEMENTS
OF A NOVEL

Watering Time (detail) by Charles Burchfield
(1925). Watercolor.

The Chrysler Museum, Norfolk, Virginia.
Gift of Walter P. Chrysler, Jr.

UNIT SEVEN

John Leggett

THE ELEMENTS OF A NOVEL

An introduction by **John Leggett**

> *In a narrative so plain that a child will enjoy it, yet with double meanings as cruel and comic as any great cartoon, George Orwell presents a parable that may rank as one of the great political satires of our anxious time. . . . the impact goes straight to the forehead of any kind of Goliath, any monstrous totalitarianism. It is a smooth stone indeed, sped by a skillful slinger.*
>
> —Christopher Morley

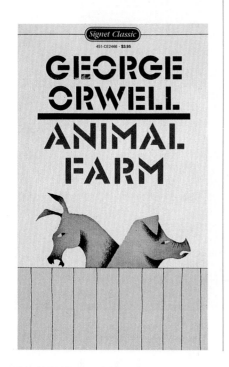

Ask your classmates to define the term **novel,** and see if you all mean the same thing by the word. For example, do you agree on how a novel differs from a short story? Is a novel simply longer than a short story? Surely it is that. Short stories, as a rule, get themselves told within fifteen or twenty book pages, often even less. If a short story is longer than that, some people suspect that the writer hasn't probed deeply enough to tell the story as a full novel, or that the writer hasn't wanted to make the cutting necessary to produce a short story.

Of course, there is a very legitimate mid-sized narrative of about fifty book pages called the **novella** ("little novel"), but for some reason novellas are very rare. Perhaps the length is an awkward one. A fifty-page story is too long for most magazines to use and too brief for a book publisher to bind and sell conveniently in hard cover.

What is a novel? It is a long fictional story, whose length is normally somewhere between a hundred and five hundred book pages, which uses all the elements of storytelling: **plot, character, setting, theme,** and **point of view.** The novel has been the most popular form of storytelling since its appearance in England in the eighteenth century.

Daniel Defoe's *Robinson Crusoe,* a long fictional account of the adventures of a shipwrecked sailor, was published in 1719. It was followed by Samuel Richardson's *Pamela* in 1740, by Henry Fielding's *Tom Jones* in 1749, and by the first true psychological novel, Laurence Sterne's *Tristram Shandy,* in 1760.

The Reach of a Novel

Though novels share all the elements of a short story (see page 3), they differ in their reach or scope. While the short story tends to confine itself to a single important **conflict,** to a few **characters,** to a single **theme,** and to a short span of **time,** the novel can, and usually does, embrace a great many conflicts, multiple themes, and several settings. While James Joyce's huge novel *Ulysses* takes place in a single day, John Galsworthy's novel *The Forsyte Saga* takes thirty-four years to unfold. A novel like Leo Tolstoy's great *War and Peace* introduces us to armies, soldiers, and officers by the barracksful, and to their families at home as well. Charles Dickens stretches another huge canvas for his masterful portrayal of the French Revolution in *A Tale of Two Cities.*

What Does a Novel "Do"?

Why do people read, let alone write, one of these long stories called a novel? People who read a great deal believe that a good novel does two things, and that it does them at the same time. It entertains us, and it tells us something about ourselves or about the world we live in.

If a novel succeeds with us, it so absorbs us in the lives of its characters that they seem like people we actually know, and we must read on to discover what happens to them. If at the same time we are also learning about some huge history-making event like a revolution, then our lives have been stretched with new knowledge and new pleasure. We know a little more than we did about how people behave in good times and in bad. We also know a little more about how to deal with our own lives.

Writing a novel takes an enormous amount of time: several years as a rule, and five or six years is not unusual. Writing a novel has to be done alone, too. As a prisoner in a workroom, the writer draws characters, scenes, and a story out of his or her own mind and heart. "Torture," some writers will tell you. Why do it?

Some say the novelist does it for money; that is how he or she earns a living. But the motive for writing a novel involves more than that. A novel is written out of the writer's belief in a private vision, in a gift of knowledge about what is going on between people here on earth. The writer has some insight into "the purpose of it all" that he or she wants to share. Every once in a while, the insight is worth the sharing, and we have a great novel. But, of course, visions are very personal matters, and we have to make up our own minds about whose vision is worth sharing.

Most novelists start a new book with an idea that interests them or with a character who interests them. From that moment, progress can be like a long journey taken into a wilderness. The writer takes chances and often follows paths that turn out to be the wrong ones.

Writing a novel is generally hard labor. Some writers feel that, day after day, they seem to be dragging a dead weight up a steep

> "As a prisoner in a workroom, the writer draws characters, scenes, and a story out of his or her own mind and heart. 'Torture,' some writers will tell you. Why do it?"

> "A novel is written out of the writer's belief in a private vision, in a gift of knowledge about what is going on between people here on earth."

hill. If they are extremely lucky, one day the weight stirs, it begins to come to life, and it does do some of the work on its own. When this happens, that lucky writer has broken into the lode of inner experience where it is possible to discover the deepest of feelings. From that moment, the writer may feel that the novel is writing itself.

Of course, there are all kinds of novels. They may be good or bad, serious or funny, profound or superficial. They may have to do with **ideas** (as in George Orwell's novel *Animal Farm*) or they may have to do chiefly with **character** (as in Charles Dickens's *Great Expectations*). Most great novels are equally concerned with both character and ideas (as in Harper Lee's *To Kill a Mockingbird*). Novels can also be simply entertainment—as a mystery or spy or science-fiction novel usually is.

For most of us, the worthwhile novels must either inform us of something we're the better for knowing—how it is to work in a coal mine or to be the general of a losing army—or else they must move us in some way, toward tears or laughter. The great novels give us a strong emotional experience—and that is a test of what is worthy in art of every kind.

Where Did the Story Come From?

George Orwell got the idea for *Animal Farm* from seeing a small boy driving a horse and whipping it whenever it tried to turn. "It struck me," said Orwell, "that if only such animals became aware of their strength, we should have no power over them, and that men exploit animals in much the same way as the rich exploit the proletariat [the working class]."

When he began writing *Animal Farm,* Orwell was forty-two years old and a relatively unknown writer. The books he had produced up to then revealed definite political convictions. Orwell disapproved of Britain's privileged class and believed instead in the traditions and virtues of the working class.

These beliefs had been fostered by a visit Orwell made to Spain about ten years earlier. He had gone to Spain in order to write about the Civil War there, and even to fight in it. In fact, he was so badly wounded in battle by a sniper's bullet in his neck that his voice was permanently altered. But the war experience had also given him a horrifying glimpse of political reality. In Spain he saw how liberal, revolutionary causes can be corrupted and evolve into another form of totalitarianism, which he saw as the future's big threat to human freedom. (Totalitarianism is a kind of dictatorship where one political party has total control and all opposition is ruthlessly suppressed.)

Later in Russia, he saw a powerful leader—Joseph Stalin—come up through the revolutionary ranks and end up oppressing the people as badly as they had been oppressed before, under the czars.

To show how a whole nation could be enslaved, Orwell created his fable about the animals of Manor Farm. Orwell said that the

Animal Farm

"**I**ts success surprised even Orwell. The first edition sold out in a month, and by spring it was being translated into nine languages."

Night Pigs by Jamie Wyeth (1979). Oil on board.

© 1979 by James Wyeth. Courtesy of the Brandywine River Museum, Chadds Ford, Pennsylvania.

book was the first "in which I tried, with full consciousness of what I was doing, to fuse political purpose and artistic purpose in one whole."

When *Animal Farm* was published in 1945, its success surprised even Orwell. The first edition sold out in a month, and by spring of 1946 it was being translated into nine languages. It sold over half a million copies and ended Orwell's financial worries.

Along with Orwell's next novel, *Nineteen Eighty-Four, Animal Farm* made its author into the outstanding political satirist of his time. When he died of a neglected lung disease in 1950, at the age of forty-six, he was recognized as the conscience of his generation.

The Life of Orwell (1903–1950)

"George Orwell" is a pen name. He was born Eric Blair in India, into a British family he described as "shabby-genteel." (He took his pen name because he felt "Eric Blair" sounded like a snobbish, upper class name.) Back home in England, Eric was sent to "rich man's schools" where he saw how wealth and privilege prevailed in every situation, and how the strong constantly triumphed over the weak. Instead of going on to the university, he took a post with the police department at Rangoon in Burma.

He did not enjoy this service: "In a job like that you see the dirty work of Empire at close quarters." His health also suffered in the Burmese climate. He had always been an avid reader, and when he returned to England in 1927, in search of another career, he quite naturally chose writing.

He also began to lead a notably Bohemian life. He traveled to Paris, where he lived in filth and poverty, and he spent a year in England, traveling as a tramp. His first book, called *Down and Out in London and Paris,* was about these experiences.

His experience in the Spanish Civil War was critical. What he saw in Barcelona disillusioned him. He returned from Spain bitter toward Communist policy and totalitarianism in general. He then developed the idea for *Animal Farm*—"a nightmare world in which the leader, or some ruling clique, controls not only the future but the past. If the leader says of such and such an event, 'it never happened'—well, it never happened. If he says that two and two are five—well, two and two are five."

By 1948, within two years of his death, Orwell had finished his second masterwork, *Nineteen Eighty-Four.* This novel looks into the future (1984 was then 36 years away) where it finds humankind deprived of a past, of privacy, of freedom, and of individualism. Orwell said that he had not intended this novel as a prophecy but as a warning "that something like *Nineteen Eighty-Four* could happen." "The moral to be drawn from this dangerous, nightmare situation is a simple one," said Orwell: *"Don't let it happen. It depends on you."*

George Orwell as the proprietor of Animal Farm. Drawing by David Levine.

Reprinted with permission from *The New York Review of Books,* © 1966, Nyrev, Inc.

" **D**on't let it happen. It depends on you.''

The Form of *Animal Farm*

Animal Farm combines three different literary forms. First, it is a **fable,** or a beast tale. Fables are usually brief and humorous stories in which animals speak and act like humans. The purpose of a fable is to expose some human failing. The use of animals in a beast fable helps the writer control the reader's feelings: people who are portrayed as pigs, or sheep, or worms do not usually seem very admirable, or dignified. Perhaps Orwell chose this fable form because he had always loved animals and observed them carefully. "Most of my good memories of my childhood, and up to the age of about twenty," he wrote, "are in some way connected with animals."

Animal Farm is also an **allegory,** a story that can be read on two different levels. Each character or event in an allegory stands for something else, and the writer uses these characters and events to convey some moral message. To people who are aware of Orwell's purpose, and of history, the animals' rebellion on Manor Farm is clearly an allegory for the Russian Revolution in 1917, and the pig Napoleon represents the Soviet dictator Joseph Stalin. It is possible to "translate" most of the other events and characters in the novel to some real-life equivalents in Russian history.

Finally, *Animal Farm* is a **satire,** a form of literature that uses ridicule to make specific events and people look foolish or stupid. Satire always has a bite—it seeks out our weaknesses and wrong-doings and forces us to see our behavior with new eyes. Satire usually uses **dramatic irony**—in which we perceive a contrast be-tween what is stated on the page and what is really meant. Satire also uses **situational irony**—in which we realize that there is a discrepancy between what we expect to happen and what actually does happen. *Animal Farm* probably has more irony per page than any other modern novel; watch for it as you read.

Yet, for all the political meanings people have seen in it, *Animal Farm* is not merely a political book. Basically, it is a good story, and that is why people have continued to read it for over forty years. The specific political satire is there for people who want to analyze it, but for most readers the first pleasure is in finding out "what happened" on Manor Farm after the animals took over. The second pleasure lies in recognizing how this barnyard menagerie could be a microcosm of our own society, and of any society—at any time in history, at any place on the planet. What Orwell said about *Nineteen Eighty-Four* could also apply to *Animal Farm:*

"Don't let it happen. It depends on you."

> "Yet, for all the political meanings people have seen in it, *Animal Farm* is not merely a political book. Basically, it is a good story."

> "This barnyard menagerie could be a microcosm of our own society, and of any society —at any time in history, at any place on the planet."

The Themes of the Novel

Though *Animal Farm* is often humorous, it reveals several serious **themes,** or main ideas. Here are some of them:

1. The idea that freedom and individual dignity must be guarded very carefully.

2. The idea that language is a powerful tool; used improperly, it can enslave and confuse us.

3. The idea that weakness can be dominated by strength, fear, and trickery.

4. The idea that hope and vision must be kept alive, or we might live like the animals of Manor Farm.

ANIMAL FARM

George Orwell

I

Mr. Jones, of the Manor Farm, had locked the henhouses for the night, but was too drunk to remember to shut the popholes. With the ring of light from his lantern dancing from side to side, he lurched across the yard, kicked off his boots at the back door, drew himself a last glass of beer from the barrel in the scullery, and made his way up to bed, where Mrs. Jones was already snoring.

As soon as the light in the bedroom went out there was a stirring and a fluttering all through the farm buildings. Word had gone round during the day that old Major, the prize Middle White boar, had had a strange dream on the previous night and wished to communicate it to the other animals. It had been agreed that they should all meet in the big barn as soon as Mr. Jones was safely out of the way. Old Major (so he was always called, though the name under which he had been exhibited was Willingdon Beauty) was so highly regarded on the farm that everyone was quite ready to lose an hour's sleep in order to hear what he had to say.

At one end of the big barn, on a sort of raised platform, Major was already ensconced on his bed of straw, under a lantern which hung from a beam. He was twelve years old and had lately grown rather stout, but he was still a majestic-looking pig, with a wise and benevolent appearance in spite of the fact that his tushes[1] had never been cut. Before long the other animals began to arrive and make themselves comfortable after their different fashions. First came the three dogs, Bluebell, Jessie, and Pincher, and then the pigs, who settled down in the straw immediately in front of the platform. The hens perched themselves on the windowsills, the pigeons fluttered up to the rafters, the sheep and cows lay down behind the pigs and began to chew the cud. The two cart-horses, Boxer and Clover, came in together, walking very slowly and setting down their vast hairy hoofs with great care lest there should be some small animal concealed in the straw. Clover was a stout motherly mare approaching middle life, who had never quite got her figure back after her fourth foal. Boxer was an enormous beast, nearly eighteen hands high, and as strong as any two ordinary horses put together. A white stripe down his nose gave him a somewhat stupid appearance, and in fact he was not of first-rate intelligence, but he was universally respected for his steadiness of character and tremendous powers of work. After the horses came Muriel, the white goat, and Benjamin, the donkey. Benjamin was the oldest animal on the farm, and the worst tempered. He seldom talked, and when he did, it was usually to make some cynical remark—for instance, he would say that God had given him a tail to keep the flies off, but that he would sooner have had no tail and no flies. Alone among the animals on the farm he never laughed. If asked why, he would say that he saw nothing to laugh at. Nevertheless, without openly admitting it, he was devoted to Boxer; the two of them usually spent their Sundays together in the small paddock beyond the orchard, grazing side by side and never speaking.

The two horses had just lain down when a brood of ducklings, which had lost their mother, filed into the barn, cheeping feebly and wandering from side to side to find some place where they would not be trodden on. Clover made a sort of wall round them with her great foreleg, and the ducklings nestled down inside it and promptly fell asleep. At the last moment Mollie, the foolish,

---

1. **tushes:** tusks.

pretty white mare who drew Mr. Jones's trap,[2] came mincing daintily in, chewing at a lump of sugar. She took a place near the front and began flirting her white mane, hoping to draw attention to the red ribbons it was plaited with. Last of all came the cat, who looked round, as usual, for the warmest place and finally squeezed herself in between Boxer and Clover; there she purred contentedly throughout Major's speech without listening to a word of what he was saying.

"Comrades, you have heard already about the strange dream that I had last night. But I will come to the dream later. I have something else to say first. I do not think, comrades, that I shall be with you for many months longer, and before I die, I feel it my duty to pass on to you such wisdom as I have acquired. I have had a long life, I have had much time for thought as I lay alone in my stall, and I think I may say that I understand the nature of life on this earth as well as any animal now living. It is about this that I wish to speak to you.

"Now, comrades, what is the nature of this life of ours? Let us face it: our lives are miserable, laborious, and short. We are born, we are given

just so much food as will keep the breath in our bodies, and those of us who are capable of it are forced to work to the last atom of our strength; and the very instant that our usefulness has come to an end we are slaughtered with hideous cruelty. No animal in England knows the meaning of happiness or leisure after he is a year old. No animal in England is free. The life of an animal is misery and slavery: that is the plain truth.

---

2. **trap:** a light, two-wheeled carriage.

"But is this simply part of the order of nature? Is it because this land of ours is so poor that it cannot afford a decent life to those who dwell upon it? No, comrades, a thousand times no! The soil of England is fertile, its climate is good, it is capable of affording food in abundance to an enormously greater number of animals than now inhabit it. This single farm of ours would support a dozen horses, twenty cows, hundreds of sheep—and all of them living in a comfort and a dignity that are now almost beyond our imagining. Why then do we continue in this miserable condition? Because nearly the whole of the produce of our labor is stolen from us by human beings. There, comrades, is the answer to all our problems. It is summed up in a single word—Man. Man is the only real enemy we have. Remove Man from the scene, and the root cause of hunger and overwork is abolished forever.

"Man is the only creature that consumes without producing. He does not give milk, he does not lay eggs, he is too weak to pull the plow, he cannot run fast enough to catch rabbits. Yet he is lord of all the animals. He sets them to work, he gives back to them the bare minimum that will prevent them from starving, and the rest he keeps for himself. Our labor tills the soil, our dung fertilizes it, and yet there is not one of us that owns more than his bare skin. You cows that I see before me, how many thousands of gallons of milk have you given during this last year? And what has happened to that milk which should have been breeding up sturdy calves? Every drop of it has gone down the throats of our enemies. And you hens, how many eggs have you laid in this last year, and how many of those eggs ever hatched into chickens? The rest have all gone to market to bring in money for Jones and his men. And you, Clover, where are those four foals you bore, who should have been the support and pleasure of your old age? Each was sold at a year old—you will never see one of them again. In return for your four confinements and all your labor in the fields, what have you ever had except your bare rations and a stall?

"And even the miserable lives we lead are not allowed to reach their natural span. For myself I do not grumble, for I am one of the lucky ones. I am twelve years old and have over four hundred children. Such is the natural life of a pig. But no animal escapes the cruel knife in the end. You young porkers who are sitting in front of me, every one of you will scream your lives out at the block within a year. To that horror we all must come—cows, pigs, hens, sheep, everyone. Even the horses and the dogs have no better fate. You,

Boxer, the very day that those great muscles of yours lose their power, Jones will sell you to the knacker,[3] who will cut your throat and boil you down for the foxhounds. As for the dogs, when they grow old and toothless, Jones ties a brick round their necks and drowns them in the nearest pond.

"Is it not crystal clear then, comrades, that all the evils of this life of ours spring from the tyranny of human beings? Only get rid of Man, and the produce of our labor would be our own. Almost overnight we could become rich and free. What then must we do? Why, work night and day, body and soul, for the overthrow of the human race! That is my message to you, comrades: Rebellion! I do not know when that Rebellion will come, it might be in a week or in a hundred years, but I know, as surely as I see this straw beneath my feet, that sooner or later justice will be done. Fix your eyes on that, comrades, throughout the short remainder of your lives! And above all, pass on this message of mine to those who come after you, so that future generations shall carry on the struggle until it is victorious.

"And remember, comrades, your resolution must never falter. No argument must lead you astray. Never listen when they tell you that Man and the animals have a common interest, that the prosperity of the one is the prosperity of the others. It is all lies. Man serves the interests of no creature except himself. And among us animals let there be perfect unity, perfect comradeship in the struggle. All men are enemies. All animals are comrades."

At this moment there was a tremendous uproar. While Major was speaking four large rats had crept out of their holes and were sitting on their hindquarters, listening to him. The dogs had suddenly caught sight of them, and it was only by a swift dash for their holes that the rats saved their lives. Major raised his trotter[4] for silence.

"Comrades," he said, "here is a point that must be settled. The wild creatures, such as rats and rabbits—are they our friends or our enemies? Let us put it to the vote. I propose this question to the meeting: Are rats comrades?"

The vote was taken at once, and it was agreed by an overwhelming majority that rats were comrades. There were only four dissentients,[5] the three dogs and the cat, who was afterward discovered to have voted on both sides. Major continued:

"I have little more to say. I merely repeat, remember always your duty of enmity toward Man and all his ways. Whatever goes upon two legs is an enemy. Whatever goes upon four legs, or has wings, is a friend. And remember also that in fighting against Man, we must not come to resemble him. Even when you have conquered him, do not adopt his vices. No animal must ever live in a house, or sleep in a bed, or wear clothes, or drink alcohol, or smoke tobacco, or touch money, or engage in trade. All the habits of Man are evil. And, above all, no animal must ever tyrannize over his own kind. Weak or strong, clever or simple, we are all brothers. No animal must ever kill any other animal. All animals are equal.

"And now, comrades, I will tell you about my dream of last night. I cannot describe that dream to you. It was a dream of the earth as it will be when Man has vanished. But it reminded me of something that I had long forgotten. Many years ago, when I was a little pig, my mother and the other sows used to sing an old song of which they knew only the tune and the first three words. I had known that tune in my infancy, but it had long since passed out of my mind. Last night, however, it came back to me in my dream. And what is more, the words of the song also came back— words, I am certain, which were sung by the animals of long ago and have been lost to memory for generations. I will sing you that song now, comrades. I am old and my voice is hoarse, but when I have taught you the tune, you can sing it better for yourselves. It is called 'Beasts of England.' "

Old Major cleared his throat and began to sing. As he had said, his voice was hoarse, but he sang well enough, and it was a stirring tune, something between "Clementine" and "La Cucaracha." The words ran:

> *Beasts of England, beasts of Ireland,*
> *Beasts of every land and clime,*
> *Hearken to my joyful tidings*
> *Of the golden future time.*
>
> *Soon or late the day is coming,*
> *Tyrant Man shall be o'erthrown,*
> *And the fruitful fields of England*
> *Shall be trod by beasts alone.*
>
> *Rings shall vanish from our noses,*
> *And the harness from our back,*
> *Bit and spur shall rust forever,*
> *Cruel whips no more shall crack.*

---

3. **knacker:** a person who buys worn-out horses or other domestic animals to slaughter and sell as dog food, fertilizer, etc.
4. **trotter:** foot (of a pig or sheep).
5. **dissentients** (di·sen′shənts): dissenters, those who disagree with the majority opinion (or the opinion being expressed).

Riches more than mind can picture,
Wheat and barley, oats and hay,
Clover, beans, and mangel-wurzels[6]
Shall be ours upon that day.

Bright will shine the fields of England,
Purer shall its waters be,
Sweeter yet shall blow its breezes
On the day that sets us free.

For that day we all must labor,
Though we die before it break;
Cows and horses, geese and turkeys,
All must toil for freedom's sake.

Beasts of England, beasts of Ireland,
Beasts of every land and clime,
Hearken well and spread my tidings
Of the golden future time.

The singing of this song threw the animals into the wildest excitement. Almost before Major had reached the end, they had begun singing it for themselves. Even the stupidest of them had already picked up the tune and a few of the words, and as for the clever ones, such as the pigs and dogs, they had the entire song by heart within a few minutes. And then, after a few preliminary tries, the whole farm burst out into ''Beasts of England'' in tremendous unison. The cows lowed it, the dogs whined it, the sheep bleated it, the horses whinnied it, the ducks quacked it. They were so delighted with the song that they sang it right through five times in succession, and might have continued singing it all night if they had not been interrupted.

Unfortunately, the uproar awoke Mr. Jones,

---

6. **mangel-wurzels:** large beets used as food for cattle.

who sprang out of bed, making sure that there was a fox in the yard. He seized the gun which always stood in a corner of his bedroom, and let fly a charge of number 6 shot into the darkness. The pellets buried themselves in the wall of the barn and the meeting broke up hurriedly. Everyone fled to his own sleeping place. The birds jumped on to their perches, the animals settled down in the straw, and the whole farm was asleep in a moment.

II

Three nights later old Major died peacefully in his sleep. His body was buried at the foot of the orchard.

This was early in March. During the next three months there was much secret activity. Major's speech had given to the more intelligent animals on the farm a completely new outlook on life. They did not know when the Rebellion predicted by Major would take place, they had no reason for thinking that it would be within their own lifetime, but they saw clearly that it was their duty to prepare for it. The work of teaching and organizing the others fell naturally upon the pigs, who were generally recognized as being the cleverest of the animals. Pre-eminent among the pigs were two young boars named Snowball and Napoleon, whom Mr. Jones was breeding up for sale. Napoleon was a large, rather fierce-looking Berkshire boar, the only Berkshire on the farm, not much of a talker, but with a reputation for getting his own way. Snowball was a more vivacious pig than Napoleon, quicker in speech and more inventive, but was not considered to have the same depth of character. All the other male pigs on the farm were porkers.[1] The best known among them was a small fat pig named Squealer, with very round cheeks, twinkling eyes, nimble movements, and a shrill voice. He was a brilliant talker, and when he was arguing some difficult point he had a way of skipping from side to side and whisking his tail which was somehow very persuasive. The others said of Squealer that he could turn black into white.

These three had elaborated old Major's teachings into a complete system of thought, to which they gave the name of Animalism. Several nights a week, after Mr. Jones was asleep, they held secret meetings in the barn and expounded the principles of Animalism to the others. At the beginning they met with much stupidity and apathy. Some of the animals talked of the duty of loyalty to Mr. Jones, whom they referred to as "Master," or made elementary remarks such as "Mr. Jones feeds us. If he were gone, we should starve to death." Others asked such questions as "Why should we care what happens after we are dead?" or "If this Rebellion is to happen anyway, what difference does it make whether we work for it or not?" and the pigs had great difficulty in making them see that this was contrary to the spirit of Animalism. The stupidest questions of all were asked by Mollie, the white mare. The very first question she asked Snowball was: "Will there still be sugar after the Rebellion?"

"No," said Snowball firmly. "We have no means of making sugar on this farm. Besides, you do not need sugar. You will have all the oats and hay you want."

"And shall I still be allowed to wear ribbons in my mane?" asked Mollie.

"Comrade," said Snowball, "those ribbons that you are so devoted to are the badge of slavery. Can you not understand that liberty is worth more than ribbons?"

Mollie agreed, but she did not sound very convinced.

The pigs had an even harder struggle to counteract the lies put about by Moses, the tame raven. Moses, who was Mr. Jones's especial pet, was a spy and a talebearer, but he was also a clever talker. He claimed to know the existence of a mysterious country called Sugarcandy Mountain, to which all animals went when they died. It was situated somewhere up in the sky, a little distance beyond the clouds, Moses said. In Sugarcandy Mountain it was Sunday seven days a week, clover was in season all the year round, and lump sugar and linseed cake grew on the hedges. The animals hated Moses because he told tales and did no work, but some of them believed in Sugarcandy Mountain, and the pigs had to argue very hard to persuade them that there was no such place.

Their most faithful disciples were the two carthorses, Boxer and Clover. These two had great difficulty in thinking anything out for themselves, but having once accepted the pigs as their teachers, they absorbed everything that they were told and passed it on to the other animals by simple arguments. They were unfailing in their attendance at the secret meetings in the barn and led the singing of "Beasts of England," with which the meetings always ended.

Now, as it turned out, the Rebellion was achieved much earlier and more easily than anyone had expected. In past years Mr. Jones, although a hard master, had been a capable farmer, but of late he had fallen on evil days. He had become much disheartened after losing money in a lawsuit, and had taken to drinking more than was good for him. For whole days at a time he would lounge in his Windsor chair in the kitchen, reading the newspapers, drinking, and occasionally feeding Moses on crusts of bread soaked in beer. His men were idle and dishonest, the fields were full of weeds, the buildings wanted roofing, the hedges were neglected, and the animals were underfed.

June came and the hay was almost ready for cutting. On Midsummer's Eve, which was a Saturday, Mr. Jones went into Willingdon and got so drunk at the Red Lion that he did not come back till midday on Sunday. The men had milked the cows in the early morning and then had gone out rabbiting, without bothering to feed the animals. When Mr. Jones got back, he immediately went to sleep on the drawing-room sofa with the *News of the World* over his face, so that when evening came, the animals were still unfed. At last they could stand it no longer. One of the cows broke in the door of the store-shed with her horn, and all the animals began to help themselves from the bins. It was just then that Mr. Jones woke up. The next moment he and his four men were in the store-shed with whips in their hands, lashing out in all directions. This was more than the hungry animals could bear. With one accord, though nothing of the kind had been planned beforehand, they flung themselves upon their tormentors. Jones and his men suddenly found themselves being butted and kicked from all sides. The situation was quite out of their control. They had never seen animals behave like this before, and this sudden uprising of creatures whom they were used to thrashing

---

1. **porkers:** young pigs fattened for use as food (as opposed to boars, which are used for breeding purposes and therefore live long lives).

and maltreating just as they chose frightened them almost out of their wits. After only a moment or two they gave up trying to defend themselves and took to their heels. A minute later all five of them were in full flight down the cart-track that led to the main road, with the animals pursuing them in triumph.

Mrs. Jones looked out of the bedroom window, saw what was happening, hurriedly flung a few possessions into a carpet bag, and slipped out of the farm by another way. Moses sprang off his perch and flapped after her, croaking loudly. Meanwhile the animals had chased Jones and his men out on to the road and slammed the five-barred gate behind them. And so, almost before they knew what was happening, the Rebellion had been successfully carried through: Jones was expelled, and the Manor Farm was theirs.

For the first few minutes the animals could hardly believe in their good fortune. Their first act was to gallop in a body right round the boundaries of the farm, as though to make quite sure that no human being was hiding anywhere upon it; then they raced back to the farm buildings to wipe out the last traces of Jones's hated reign. The harness room at the end of the stables was broken open; the bits, the nose rings, the dog chains, the cruel knives with which Mr. Jones had been used

to castrate the pigs and lambs, were all flung down the well. The reins, the halters, the blinkers, the degrading nosebags, were thrown on to the rubbish fire which was burning in the yard. So were the whips. All the animals capered with joy when they saw the whips going up in flames. Snowball

also threw on to the fire the ribbons with which the horses' manes and tails had usually been decorated on market days.

"Ribbons," he said, "should be considered as clothes, which are the mark of a human being. All animals should go naked."

When Boxer heard this he fetched the small straw hat which he wore in summer to keep the flies out of his ears, and flung it on to the fire with the rest.

In a very little while the animals had destroyed everything that reminded them of Mr. Jones. Napoleon then led them back to the store-shed and served out a double ration of corn[2] to everybody, with two biscuits for each dog. Then they sang "Beasts of England" from end to end seven times running, and after that they settled down for the night and slept as they had never slept before.

But they woke at dawn as usual, and suddenly remembering the glorious thing that had happened, they all raced out into the pasture together. A little way down the pasture there was a knoll that commanded a view of most of the farm. The animals rushed to the top of it and gazed round them in the clear morning light. Yes, it was theirs—everything that they could see was theirs! In the ecstasy of that thought they gamboled round and round, they hurled themselves into the air in great leaps of excitement. They rolled in the dew, they cropped mouthfuls of the sweet summer grass, they kicked up clods of the black earth and snuffed its rich scent. Then they made a tour of inspection of the whole farm and surveyed with speechless admiration the plowland, the hayfield, the orchard, the pool, the spinney.[3] It was as though they had never seen these things before, and even now they could hardly believe that it was all their own.

Then they filed back to the farm buildings and halted in silence outside the door of the farmhouse. That was theirs too, but they were frightened to go inside. After a moment, however, Snowball and Napoleon butted the door open with their shoulders and the animals entered in single file, walking with the utmost care for fear of disturbing anything. They tiptoed from room to room, afraid to speak above a whisper and gazing with a kind of awe at the unbelievable luxury, at the beds with their feather mattresses, the looking glasses, the horsehair sofa, the Brussels carpet, the lithograph of Queen Victoria over the drawing-room mantelpiece. They were just coming down

---

2. **corn:** in British usage, the seeds of any cereal grain, such as wheat or oats.
3. **spinney:** (British) a thicket or grove.

the stairs when Mollie was discovered to be missing. Going back, the others found that she had remained behind in the best bedroom. She had taken a piece of blue ribbon from Mrs. Jones's dressing table and was holding it against her shoulder and admiring herself in the glass in a very foolish manner. The others reproached her sharply, and they went outside. Some hams hanging in the kitchen were taken out for burial, and the barrel of beer in the scullery was stove in[4] with a kick from Boxer's hoof; otherwise nothing in the house was touched. A unanimous resolution was passed on the spot that the farmhouse should be preserved as a museum. All were agreed that no animal must ever live there.

The animals had their breakfast, and then Snowball and Napoleon called them together again.

"Comrades," said Snowball, "it is half-past six and we have a long day before us. Today we begin the hay harvest. But there is another matter that must be attended to first."

The pigs now revealed that during the past three months they had taught themselves to read and write from an old spelling book which had belonged to Mr. Jones's children and which had been thrown on the rubbish heap. Napoleon sent for pots of black and white paint and led the way down to the five-barred gate that gave on to the main road. Then Snowball (for it was Snowball who was best at writing) took a brush between the two knuckles of his trotter, painted out MANOR FARM from the top bar of the gate and in its place painted ANIMAL FARM. This was to be the name of the farm from now onward. After this they went back to the farm buildings, where Snowball and Napoleon sent for a ladder which they caused to be set against the end wall of the big barn. They explained that by their studies of the past three months the pigs had succeeded in reducing the principles of Animalism to Seven Commandments. These Seven Commandments would now be inscribed on the wall; they would form an unalterable law by which all the animals on Animal Farm must live forever after. With some difficulty (for it is not easy for a pig to balance himself on a ladder) Snowball climbed up and set to work, with Squealer a few rungs below him holding the paint pot. The Commandments were written on the tarred wall in great white letters that could be read thirty yards away. They ran thus:

The Seven Commandments

1. *Whatever goes upon two legs is an enemy.*
2. *Whatever goes upon four legs, or has wings, is a freind.*
3. *No animal shall wear clothes.*
4. *No animal shall sleep in a bed.*
5. *No animal shall drink alcohol.*
6. *No animal shall kill any other animal.*
7. *All animals are equal.*

It was very neatly written, and except that "friend" was written "freind" and one of the *s*'s was the wrong way round, the spelling was correct all the way through. Snowball read it aloud for the benefit of the others. All the animals nodded in complete agreement, and the cleverer ones at once began to learn the Commandments by heart.

"Now, comrades," cried Snowball throwing down the paintbrush, "to the hayfield! Let us make it a point of honor to get in the harvest more quickly than Jones and his men could do."

But at this moment the three cows, who had seemed uneasy for some time past, set up a loud lowing. They had not been milked for twenty-four hours, and their udders were almost bursting. After a little thought, the pigs sent for buckets and milked the cows fairly successfully, their trotters being well adapted to this task. Soon there were five buckets of frothing creamy milk at which many of the animals looked with considerable interest.

"What is going to happen to all that milk?" said someone.

---

4. **stove in:** broken or crushed inward.

"Jones used sometimes to mix some of it in our mash," said one of the hens.

"Never mind the milk, comrades!" cried Napoleon, placing himself in front of the buckets. "That will be attended to. The harvest is more important. Comrade Snowball will lead the way. I shall follow in a few minutes. Forward, comrades! The hay is waiting."

So the animals trooped down to the hayfield to begin the harvest, and when they came back in the evening it was noticed that the milk had disappeared.

Responding to the Novel

Analyzing the Novel

Identifying Facts

1. The novel opens with a remarkable scene. A big old pig is waiting for Manor Farm's animals to assemble in the barn. According to old Major, why is Man the enemy of the animals? What does Major urge the animals to do?
2. In Chapter II, what objections do some of the animals raise to the principles of Animalism?
3. Describe the events leading up to the Rebellion at Manor Farm.

Interpreting Meanings

4. Orwell's animals are immediately humanized. How would you describe the **characters** of old Major, Clover, Boxer, Benjamin, and Mollie?
5. How are Snowball, Napoleon, and Squealer characterized? What traits set them apart from the other animals, such as Clover and Boxer? (After reading the description of these three leaders, which of old Major's warnings seems particularly important to keep in mind?)
6. Why is the promise of Sugarcandy Mountain a threat to the Rebellion and to the principles of Animalism? How is Mollie's behavior also a threat?
7. Who do you think is responsible for the disappearance of the milk at the end of Chapter II? What problems in the future of Animal Farm do you think this incident might **foreshadow**?
8. What incidents in the story so far suggest that Commandments 2 and 7 (see page 816) might not be true? Which other commandments do you think might cause trouble in the future?
9. How could the animals represent a human society in miniature? Look especially at Orwell's description of the animals as they assemble in the barn (page 810).
10. Do you think any events in the animals' Rebellion are like events in real rebellions or revolutions you have read about? Explain.
11. Do you identify or sympathize with any characters so far? Do you dislike any of them?

Writing About the Novel

A Creative Response

Writing a Newspaper Story. Write the newspaper story that might have been published the morning after the rebellion at Manor Farm. Tell **what** happened, **where** it happened, **whom** it happened to, and **why** it happened. What will your headline be? What attitude will you take about the Rebellion: do you approve or disapprove? Before you write, decide whether your newspaper readers are people or animals.

III

How they toiled and sweated to get the hay in! But their efforts were rewarded, for the harvest was an even bigger success than they had hoped.

Sometimes the work was hard; the implements had been designed for human beings and not for animals, and it was a great drawback that no animal was able to use any tool that involved standing on his hind legs. But the pigs were so clever that they could think of a way round every difficulty. As for the horses, they knew every inch of the field, and in fact understood the business of mowing and raking far better than Jones and his men had ever done. The pigs did not actually work but directed and supervised the others. With their superior knowledge it was natural that they should assume the leadership. Boxer and Clover would harness themselves to the cutter or the horse rake (no bits or reins were needed in these days, of course) and tramp steadily round and round the field with a pig walking behind and calling out "Gee up, comrade!" or "Whoa back, comrade!" as the case might be. And every animal down to the humblest worked at turning the hay and gathering it. Even the ducks and hens toiled to and fro all day in the sun, carrying tiny wisps of hay in their beaks. In the end they finished the harvest in two days' less time than it had usually taken Jones and his men. Moreover, it was the biggest harvest that the farm had ever seen. There was no wastage whatever; the hens and ducks with their sharp eyes had gathered up the very last stalk. And not an animal on the farm had stolen so much as a mouthful.

All through the summer the work of the farm went like clockwork. The animals were happy as they had never conceived it possible to be. Every mouthful of food was an acute positive pleasure now that it was truly their own food, produced by themselves and for themselves, not doled out to them by a grudging master. With the worthless parasitical human beings gone, there was more for everyone to eat. There was more leisure too, inexperienced though the animals were. They met with many difficulties—for instance, later in the year, when they harvested the corn, they had to tread it out in the ancient style and blow away the chaff[1] with their breath, since the farm possessed no threshing machine—but the pigs with their cleverness and Boxer with his tremendous muscles always pulled them through. Boxer was the admiration of everybody. He had been a hard worker even in Jones's time, but now he seemed more like three horses than one; there were days when the entire work of the farm seemed to rest on his mighty shoulders. From morning to night he was pushing and pulling, always at the spot where the work was hardest. He had made an arrangement with one of the cockerels[2] to call him in the mornings half an hour earlier than anyone else and would put in some volunteer labor at whatever seemed to be most needed, before the regular day's work began. His answer to every problem, every setback, was "I will work harder!"—which he had adopted as his personal motto.

But everyone worked according to his capacity. The hens and ducks, for instance, saved five bushels of corn at the harvest by gathering up the stray grains. Nobody stole, nobody grumbled over his rations, the quarreling and biting and jealousy which had been normal features of life in the old days had almost disappeared. Nobody shirked—or almost nobody. Mollie, it was true, was not good at getting up in the mornings and had a way of leaving work early on the ground that there was a stone in her hoof. And the behavior of the cat was somewhat peculiar. It was soon noticed that when there was work to be done the cat could never be found. She would vanish for hours on end, and then reappear at mealtimes or in the evening after work was over, as though nothing had happened. But she always made such excellent excuses and purred so affectionately that it was impossible not to believe in her good intentions. Old Benjamin, the donkey, seemed quite unchanged since the Rebellion. He did his work in the same slow, obstinate way as he had done it in Jones's time, never shirking and never volunteering for extra work either. About the Rebellion and its results he would express no opinion. When asked whether he was not happier now that Jones was gone, he would say only, "Donkeys live a long time. None of you has ever seen a dead donkey," and the others had to be content with this cryptic answer.

On Sundays there was no work. Breakfast was an hour later than usual, and after breakfast there was a ceremony which was observed every week without fail. First came the hoisting of the flag. Snowball had found in the harness room an old green tablecloth of Mrs. Jones's and had painted on it a hoof and a horn in white. This was run up

---

1. **chaff:** husks that are separated from the grain in threshing.

2. **cockerels** (käk′ər·əlz): young roosters, less than a year old.

the flagstaff in the farmhouse garden every Sunday morning. The flag was green, Snowball explained, to represent the green fields of England, while the hoof and horn signified the future Republic of the Animals which would arise when the human race had been finally overthrown. After the hoisting of the flag all the animals trooped into the big barn for a general assembly which was known as the Meeting. Here the work of the coming week was planned out and resolutions were put forward and debated. It was always the pigs who put forward the resolutions. The other animals understood how to vote, but could never think of any resolutions of their own. Snowball and Napoleon were by far the most active in the debates. But it was noticed that these two were never in agreement: whatever suggestion either of them made, the other could be counted on to oppose it. Even when it was resolved—a thing no one could object to in itself—to set aside the small paddock behind the orchard as a home of rest for animals who were past work, there was a stormy debate over the correct retiring age for each class of animal. The Meeting always ended with the singing of "Beasts of England," and the afternoon was given up to recreation.

The pigs had set aside the harness room as a headquarters for themselves. Here, in the evenings, they studied blacksmithing, carpentering, and other necessary arts from books which they had brought out of the farmhouse. Snowball also busied himself with organizing the other animals into what he called Animal Committees. He was indefatigable[3] at this. He formed the Egg Production Committee for the hens, the Clean Tails League for the cows, the Wild Comrades' Re-education Committee (the object of this was to tame the rats and rabbits), the Whiter Wool Movement for the sheep, and various others, besides instituting classes in reading and writing. On the whole, these projects were a failure. The attempt to tame the wild creatures, for instance, broke down almost immediately. They continued to behave very much as before, and when treated with generosity, simply took advantage of it. The cat joined the Re-education Committee and was very active in it for some days. She was seen one day sitting on a roof and talking to some sparrows who were just out of her reach. She was telling them that all animals were now comrades and that any sparrow who chose could come and perch on her paw; but the sparrows kept their distance.

The reading and writing classes, however, were

---

3. **indefatigable** (in′di·fat′i·gə·b'l): untiring.

a great success. By the autumn almost every animal on the farm was literate in some degree.

As for the pigs, they could already read and write perfectly. The dogs learned to read fairly well, but were not interested in reading anything except the Seven Commandments. Muriel, the goat, could read somewhat better than the dogs, and sometimes used to read to the others in the evenings from scraps of newspaper which she found on the rubbish heap. Benjamin could read as well as any pig but never exercised his faculty. So far as he knew, he said, there was nothing worth reading. Clover learnt the whole alphabet, but could not put words together. Boxer could not get beyond the letter D. He would trace out A, B, C, D, in the dust with his great hoof and then

would stand staring at the letters with his ears back, sometimes shaking his forelock, trying with all his might to remember what came next and never succeeding. On several occasions, indeed, he did learn E, F, G, H, but by the time he knew them, it was always discovered that he had forgotten A, B, C, and D. Finally he decided to be content with the first four letters and used to write them out once or twice every day to refresh his memory. Mollie refused to learn any but the six letters which spelled her own name. She would form these very neatly out of pieces of twig and would then decorate them with a flower or two and walk round them admiring them.

None of the other animals on the farm could get further than the letter A. It was also found that the stupider animals, such as the sheep, hens, and ducks, were unable to learn the Seven Commandments by heart. After much thought Snowball declared that the Seven Commandments could in effect be reduced to a single maxim, namely: "Four legs good, two legs bad." This, he said, contained the essential principle of Animalism. Whoever had thoroughly grasped it would be safe from human influences. The birds at first objected, since it seemed to them that they also had two legs, but Snowball proved to them that this was not so.

"A bird's wing, comrades," he said, "is an organ of propulsion and not of manipulation. It should therefore be regarded as a leg. The distinguishing mark of man is the *hand*, the instrument with which he does all his mischief."

The birds did not understand Snowball's long words, but they accepted his explanation, and all the humbler animals set to work to learn the new maxim by heart. FOUR LEGS GOOD, TWO LEGS BAD was inscribed on the end wall of the barn, above the Seven Commandments and in bigger letters. When they had once got it by heart, the sheep developed a great liking for this maxim, and often as they lay in the field they would all start bleating "Four legs good, two legs bad! Four legs good, two legs bad!" and keep it up for hours on end, never growing tired of it.

Napoleon took no interest in Snowball's committees. He said that the education of the young was more important than anything that could be done for those who were already grown up. It happened that Jessie and Bluebell had both whelped soon after the hay harvest, giving birth between them to nine sturdy puppies. As soon as they were weaned, Napoleon took them away from their mothers, saying that he would make himself responsible for their education. He took them up into a loft which could only be reached by a ladder from the harness room, and there kept them in such seclusion that the rest of the farm soon forgot their existence.

The mystery of where the milk went to was soon cleared up. It was mixed every day into the pigs' mash. The early apples were now ripening, and the grass of the orchard was littered with windfalls.[4] The animals had assumed as a matter of course that these would be shared out equally; one day, however, the order went forth that all the windfalls were to be collected and brought to the harness room for the use of the pigs. At this some of the other animals murmured, but it was no use. All the pigs were in full agreement on this point, even Snowball and Napoleon. Squealer was sent to make the necessary explanations to the others.

"Comrades!" he cried. "You do not imagine, I hope, that we pigs are doing this in a spirit of selfishness and privilege? Many of us actually dislike milk and apples. I dislike them myself. Our sole object in taking these things is to preserve our health. Milk and apples (this has been proved by Science, comrades) contain substances absolutely necessary to the well-being of a pig. We pigs are brainworkers. The whole management and organization of this farm depend on us. Day and night we are watching over your welfare. It is for *your* sake that we drink that milk and eat those apples. Do you know what would happen if we pigs failed in our duty? Jones would come back! Yes, Jones would come back! Surely, comrades," cried Squealer almost pleadingly, skipping from side to side and whisking his tail, "surely there is no one among you who wants to see Jones come back?"

Now if there was one thing that the animals were completely certain of, it was that they did not want Jones back. When it was put to them in this light, they had no more to say. The importance of keeping the pigs in good health was all too obvious. So it was agreed without further argument that the milk and the windfall apples (and also the main crop of apples when they ripened) should be reserved for the pigs alone.

IV

By the late summer the news of what had happened on Animal Farm had spread across half the county. Every day Snowball and Napoleon sent out flights of pigeons whose instructions were to mingle with the animals on neighboring farms, tell them the story of the Rebellion, and teach them the tune of "Beasts of England."

Most of this time Mr. Jones had spent sitting in the taproom of the Red Lion at Willingdon, complaining to anyone who would listen of the mon-

---

4. **windfalls:** fruit blown off a tree by the wind.

strous injustice he had suffered in being turned out of his property by a pack of good-for-nothing animals. The other farmers sympathized in principle, but they did not at first give him much help. At heart, each of them was secretly wondering whether he could not somehow turn Jones's misfortune to his own advantage. It was lucky that the owners of the two farms which adjoined Animal Farm were on permanently bad terms. One of them, which was named Foxwood, was a large, neglected, old-fashioned farm, much overgrown by woodland, with all its pastures worn out and its hedges in a disgraceful condition. Its owner, Mr. Pilkington, was an easygoing gentleman farmer who spent most of his time in fishing or hunting according to the season. The other farm, which was called Pinchfield, was smaller and better kept. Its owner was a Mr. Frederick, a tough, shrewd man, perpetually involved in lawsuits and with a name for driving hard bargains. These two disliked each other so much that it was difficult for them to come to any agreement, even in defense of their own interests.

Nevertheless, they were both thoroughly frightened by the rebellion on Animal Farm and very anxious to prevent their animals from learning too much about it. At first they pretended to laugh, to scorn the idea of animals managing a farm for themselves. The whole thing would be over in a fortnight,[1] they said. They put it about that the animals on the Manor Farm (they insisted on calling it the Manor Farm; they would not tolerate the name "Animal Farm") were perpetually fighting among themselves and were also rapidly starving to death. When time passed and the animals had evidently not starved to death, Frederick and Pilkington changed their tune and began to talk of the terrible wickedness that now flourished on Animal Farm. It was given out that the animals there practiced cannibalism, tortured one another with red-hot horseshoes, and had their females in common. This was what came of rebelling against the laws of Nature, Frederick and Pilkington said.

However, these stories were never fully believed. Rumors of a wonderful farm, where the human beings had been turned out and the animals managed their own affairs, continued to circulate in vague and distorted forms, and throughout that year a wave of rebelliousness ran through the countryside. Bulls which had always been tractable suddenly turned savage, sheep broke down hedges and devoured the clover, cows kicked the pail over, hunters refused their fences and shot their riders on to the other side. Above all, the tune and even the words of "Beasts of England" were known everywhere. It had spread with astonishing speed. The human beings could not contain their rage when they heard this song, though they pretended to think it merely ridiculous. They could not understand, they said, how even animals could bring themselves to sing such contemptible rubbish. Any animal caught singing it was given a flogging on the spot. And yet the song was irrepressible. The blackbirds whistled it in the hedges, the pigeons cooed it in the elms, it got into the din of the smithies and the tune of the church bells. And when the human beings listened to it, they secretly trembled, hearing in it a prophecy of their future doom.

Early in October, when the corn was cut and stacked and some of it was already threshed, a flight of pigeons came whirling through the air and alighted in the yard of Animal Farm in the wildest excitement. Jones and all his men, with half a dozen others from Foxwood and Pinchfield, had entered the five-barred gate and were coming up the cart-track that led to the farm. They were all carrying sticks, except Jones, who was marching ahead with a gun in his hands. Obviously they were going to attempt the recapture of the farm.

This had long been expected, and all preparations had been made. Snowball, who had studied an old book of Julius Caesar's campaigns which he had found in the farmhouse, was in charge of the defensive operations. He gave his orders quickly, and in a couple of minutes every animal was at his post.

As the human beings approached the farm buildings, Snowball launched his first attack. All the pigeons, to the number of thirty-five, flew to and fro over the men's heads and muted[2] upon them from midair; and while the men were dealing with this, the geese, who had been hiding behind the hedge, rushed out and pecked viciously at the calves of their legs. However, this was only a light skirmishing maneuver, intended to create a little disorder, and the men easily drove the geese off with their sticks. Snowball now launched his second line of attack. Muriel, Benjamin, and all the sheep, with Snowball at the head of them, rushed forward and prodded and butted the men from every side, while Benjamin turned around and lashed at them with his small hoofs. But once again the men, with their sticks and their hobnailed boots, were too strong for them; and suddenly, at a squeal from Snowball, which was the

---

1. **fortnight:** two weeks.

2. **muted:** defecated.

signal for retreat, all the animals turned and fled through the gateway into the yard.

The men gave a shout of triumph. They saw, as they imagined, their enemies in flight, and they rushed after them in disorder. This was just what Snowball had intended. As soon as they were well inside the yard, the three horses, the three cows, and the rest of the pigs, who had been lying in ambush in the cowshed, suddenly emerged in their rear, cutting them off. Snowball now gave the signal for the charge. He himself dashed straight for Jones. Jones saw him coming, raised his gun and fired. The pellets scored bloody streaks along Snowball's back, and a sheep dropped dead. Without halting for an instant, Snowball flung his fifteen stone[3] against Jones's legs. Jones was hurled into a pile of dung and his gun flew over his hands. But the most terrifying spectacle of all was Boxer, rearing up on his hind legs and striking out with his great iron-shod hoofs like a stallion. His very first blow took a stablelad from Foxwood on the skull and stretched him lifeless in the mud. At the sight, several men dropped their sticks and tried to run. Panic overtook them, and the next moment all the animals together were chasing them round and round the yard. They were gored, kicked, bitten, trampled on. There was not an animal on the farm that did not take vengeance on them after his own fashion. Even the cat suddenly leapt off a roof onto a cowman's shoulders and sank her claws in his neck, at which he yelled horribly. At a moment when the opening was clear, the men were glad enough to rush out of the yard and make a bolt for the main road. And so within five minutes of their invasion they were in ignominious retreat by the same way as they had come, with a flock of geese hissing after them and pecking at their calves all the way.

All the men were gone except one. Back in the yard Boxer was pawing with his hoof at the stablelad who lay face down in the mud, trying to turn him over. The boy did not stir.

"He is dead," said Boxer sorrowfully. "I had no intention of doing that. I forgot that I was wearing iron shoes. Who will believe that I did not do this on purpose?"

"No sentimentality, comrade!" cried Snowball, from whose wounds the blood was still dripping. "War is war. The only good human being is a dead one."

"I have no wish to take life, not even human life," repeated Boxer, and his eyes were full of tears.

"Where is Mollie?" exclaimed somebody.

Mollie in fact was missing. For a moment there was great alarm; it was feared that the men might have harmed her in some way, or even carried her off with them. In the end, however, she was found hiding in her stall with her head buried among the hay in the manger. She had taken to flight as soon as the gun went off. And when the others came back from looking for her, it was to find that the stablelad, who in fact was only stunned, had already recovered and made off.

The animals had now reassembled in the wildest excitement, each recounting his own exploits in the battle at the top of his voice. An impromptu celebration of the victory was held immediately. The flag was run up and "Beasts of England" was sung a number of times, then the sheep who had been killed was given a solemn funeral, a hawthorn bush being planted on her grave. At the

---

3. **stone:** (British) a unit of weight equal to 14 pounds.

graveside Snowball made a little speech, emphasizing the need for all animals to be ready to die for Animal Farm if need be.

The animals decided unanimously to create a military decoration, "Animal Hero, First Class," which was conferred there and then on Snowball and Boxer. It consisted of a brass medal (they were really some old horse brasses which had been found in the harness room), to be worn on Sundays and holidays. There was also "Animal Hero, Second Class," which was conferred posthumously on the dead sheep.

There was much discussion as to what the battle should be called. In the end, it was named the Battle of the Cowshed, since that was where the ambush had been sprung. Mr. Jones's gun had been found lying in the mud, and it was known that there was a supply of cartridges in the farmhouse. It was decided to set the gun up at the foot of the flagstaff, like a piece of artillery, and to fire it twice a year—once on October the twelfth, the anniversary of the Battle of the Cowshed, and once on Midsummer Day, the anniversary of the Rebellion.

Responding to the Novel

Analyzing the Novel

Identifying Facts

1. During the first summer after the Rebellion, why are the animals so happy? Identify the specific ways in which their lives have improved.
2. Although Commandment 7 states that all animals are equal, certain inequalities quickly become noticeable. Identify at least four of these inequalities.
3. The **characters** of Snowball and Napoleon are sharply contrasted. Describe their different attitudes toward re-educating the animals. What does each pig do to put his beliefs into action?
4. On what point are Snowball and Napoleon in complete agreement?
5. Describe the Battle of the Cowshed. What human ceremonies mark the animals' victory celebration?

Interpreting Meanings

6. Describe the **conflict** over power that is taking place between Snowball and Napoleon. At this point in the novel, which of the pigs are you "rooting for"? Tell why.
7. Compare Snowball's "Four legs good, two legs bad" with the Seven Commandments on page 816. Do you agree that this single maxim contains the "essential principle of Animalism"? Explain why or why not.
8. Besides giving the animals human characteristics, Orwell uses some of our **stereotypes,** or fixed ideas, about animals. Most people, for example, believe that a typical dog is loving, loyal, and highly trainable; and that a typical cat is independent, lazy, and comfort-seeking. Give at least four examples from the novel where animals display what we think of as a typical trait for their species. (Consider the cat, dog, donkey, pig, and sheep.) Do you think Orwell has chosen the right animals for his story?
9. As you read about the Battle of the Cowshed, who did you want to win—the animals or the humans? What do you think Orwell has done—thus far in the novel—to make you feel this way?
10. What do you think might happen next in the story? Think of three possible ways the story might end.

Analyzing Language and Vocabulary

Propaganda Techniques

Propaganda refers to the deliberate attempt to influence a mass audience to act or think a certain way. Usually the term is associated with an intent to deceive. Here are some common propaganda techniques. (Notice that the pigs are experts in propaganda.)

1. **Slogans.** A "catchy" slogan is more easily remembered than a complicated and perhaps more accurate explanation. What slogan do the pigs invent?
2. **Repetition.** When a message is "drummed" into

a listener's consciousness, it tends to be remembered. Which group in the novel is trained to repeat the slogan so loudly and long that all "rational thought" becomes impossible?

3. **Loaded words.** Certain words—like *peace, patriotism, moral*—arouse such strong emotional responses that they are called **loaded words** (they are loaded with feelings). Look back on page 811 at old Major's speech, and find some examples of loaded words. What loaded words can you find in Squealer's explanation of why the pigs take all of the apples and milk? (See page 820.)

4. **Powerful images.** Just as there are loaded words, certain images are loaded with powerful emotional associations. Gardens, rainbows, sunshine, clear streams—these images tend to make us "feel good." Find examples of such "loaded" images in the song "Beasts of England" (see page 812). Can you think of opposite images that would make us feel bad or afraid?

5. **Appeals to our fears.** A powerful propaganda technique is to play on a listener's fears. The message says, in effect, that if you don't do a certain thing (or if you don't think in a certain way), something that you fear very much will happen. How does Squealer use this device in his speech on page 820?

6. **Appeals to our basic desires and needs.** All human beings need food, drink, clothing, and shelter in order to survive. We also have emotional needs: we need to be loved and cared for, to have meaningful work, to have a sense of dignity and self-worth. Look at old Major's speech (pages 811–812) and Squealer's (page 820) to find examples of appeals to some of these desires and needs.

Can you think of how any of these propaganda techniques are used in the world today—either to sell you an idea, a political party, or a product?

V

As winter drew on, Mollie became more and more troublesome. She was late for work every morning and excused herself by saying that she had overslept, and she complained of mysterious pains, although her appetite was excellent. On every kind of pretext she would run away from work and go to the drinking pool, where she would stand foolishly gazing at her own reflection in the water. But there were also rumors of something more serious. One day as Mollie strolled blithely into the yard, flirting her long tail and chewing at a stalk of hay, Clover took her aside.

"Mollie," she said, "I have something very serious to say to you. This morning I saw you looking over the hedge that divides Animal Farm from Foxwood. One of Mr. Pilkington's men was standing on the other side of the hedge. And—I was a long way away, but I am almost certain I saw this—he was talking to you and you were allowing him to stroke your nose. What does that mean, Mollie?"

"He didn't! I wasn't! It isn't true!" cried Mollie, beginning to prance about and paw the ground.

"Mollie! Look me in the face. Do you give me your word of honor that that man was not stroking your nose?"

"It isn't true!" repeated Mollie, but she could not look Clover in the face, and the next moment she took to her heels and galloped away into the field.

A thought struck Clover. Without saying anything to the others, she went to Mollie's stall and turned over the straw with her hoof. Hidden under the straw was a little pile of lump sugar and several bunches of ribbon of different colors.

Three days later Mollie disappeared. For some weeks nothing was known of her whereabouts, then the pigeons reported that they had seen her on the other side of Willingdon. She was between the shafts of a smart dogcart painted red and black, which was standing outside a public house. A fat red-faced man in check breeches and gaiters, who looked like a publican,[1] was stroking her nose and feeding her with sugar. Her coat was newly clipped and she wore a scarlet ribbon around her forelock. She appeared to be enjoying herself, so

the pigeons said. None of the animals ever mentioned Mollie again.

In January there came bitterly hard weather. The earth was like iron, and nothing could be done in the fields. Many meetings were held in the big barn, and the pigs occupied themselves with planning out the work of the coming season. It had come to be accepted that the pigs, who were manifestly cleverer than the other animals, should decide all questions of farm policy, though their decisions had to be ratified by a majority vote. This arrangement would have worked well enough if it had not been for the disputes between Snowball and Napoleon. These two disagreed at every point where disagreement was possible. If one of them suggested sowing a bigger acreage with barley, the other was certain to demand a bigger acreage of oats, and if one of them said that such and such a field was just right for cabbages, the other would declare that it was useless for anything except roots. Each had his own following, and there were some violent debates. At the Meetings Snowball often won over the majority by his brilliant speeches, but Napoleon was better at canvassing support for himself in between times. He was especially successful with the sheep. Of late the sheep had taken to bleating "Four legs good, two legs bad" both in and out of season, and they often interrupted the Meeting with this. It was noticed that they were especially liable to break into "Four legs good, two legs bad" at crucial moments in Snowball's speeches. Snowball had made a close study of some back numbers of the *Farmer and Stockbreeder*, which he had found in the farmhouse, and was full of plans for innovations and improvements. He talked learnedly about field drains, silage,[2] and basic slag,[3] and had worked out a complicated scheme for all the animals to drop their dung directly in the fields, at a different spot every day, to save the labor of cartage. Napoleon produced no schemes of his own, but said quietly that Snowball's would come to nothing and seemed to be biding his time. But of all their controversies, none was so bitter as the one that took place over the windmill.

In the long pasture, not far from the farm buildings, there was a small knoll which was the highest point on the farm. After surveying the ground, Snowball declared that this was just the place for a windmill, which could be made to operate a

---

1. **publican** (pub′li·kən): (British) a saloonkeeper or innkeeper.

2. **silage:** hay, straw, and other cattle feed stored in a **silo,** an airtight pit or tower.
3. **basic slag:** fertilizer that comes from the waste materials of steelmaking.

dynamo[4] and supply the farm with electrical power. This would light the stalls and warm them in winter and would also run a circular saw, a chaff-cutter, a mangel-slicer, and an electric milking machine. The animals had never heard of anything of this kind before (for the farm was an old-fashioned one and had only the most primitive machinery), and they listened in astonishment while Snowball conjured up pictures of fantastic machines which would do their work for them while they grazed at their ease in the fields or improved their minds with reading and conversation.

Within a few weeks Snowball's plans for the windmill were fully worked out. The mechanical details came mostly from three books which had belonged to Mr. Jones—*One Thousand Useful Things to Do About the House, Every Man His Own Bricklayer,* and *Electricity for Beginners.* Snowball used as his study a shed which had once been used for incubators and had a smooth wooden floor, suitable for drawing on. He was closeted there for hours at a time. With his books held open by a stone and with a piece of chalk gripped between the knuckles of his trotter, he would move rapidly to and fro, drawing in line after line and uttering little whimpers of excitement. Gradually the plans grew into a complicated mass of cranks and cogwheels,[5] covering more than half the floor, which the other animals found completely unintelligible but very impressive. All of them came to look at Snowball's drawings at least once a day. Even the hens and ducks came, and were at pains not to tread on the chalk marks. Only Napoleon held aloof. He had declared himself against the windmill from the start. One day, however, he arrived unexpectedly to examine the plans. He walked heavily round the shed, looked closely at every detail of the plans, and snuffed at them once or twice, then stood for a little while contemplating them out of the corner of his eye; then suddenly he lifted his leg, urinated over the plans, and walked out without uttering a word.

The whole farm was deeply divided on the subject of the windmill. Snowball did not deny that to build it would be a difficult business. Stone would have to be carried and built up into walls, then the sails would have to be made, and after that there would be need for dynamos and cables. (How these were to be procured, Snowball did not say.) But he maintained that it could all be done in a year. And thereafter, he declared, so much labor would be saved that the animals would only need to work three days a week. Napoleon, on the other hand, argued that the great need of the moment was to increase food production and that if they wasted time on the windmill they would all starve to death. The animals formed themselves into two factions under the slogan, "Vote for Snowball and the three-day week" and "Vote for Napoleon and the full manger." Benjamin was the only animal who did not side with either faction. He refused to believe either that food would become more plentiful or that the windmill would save work. Windmill or no windmill, he said, life would go on as it had always gone on—that is, badly.

Apart from the disputes over the windmill, there was the question of the defense of the farm. It was fully realized that though the human beings had been defeated in the Battle of the Cowshed they might make another and more determined attempt to recapture the farm and reinstate Mr. Jones. They had all the more reason for doing so because the news of their defeat had spread across the countryside and made the animals on the neighboring farms more restive than ever. As usual, Snowball and Napoleon were in disagreement. According to Napoleon, what the animals must do was to procure firearms and train themselves in the use of them. According to Snowball, they must send out more and more pigeons and stir up rebellion among the animals on the other farms. The one argued that if they could not defend themselves they were bound to be conquered; the other argued that if rebellions happened everywhere they would have no need to defend themselves. The animals listened first to Napoleon, then to Snowball, and could not make up their minds which was right; indeed, they always found themselves in agreement with the one who was speaking at the moment.

At last the day came when Snowball's plans were completed. At the Meeting on the following

4. **dynamo:** an electrical generator.
5. **cogwheels:** notched wheels that mesh with other notched wheels to produce motion.

Sunday the question of whether or not to begin work on the windmill was to be put to the vote. When the animals had assembled in the big barn, Snowball stood up and, though occasionally interrupted by bleating from the sheep, set forth his reasons for advocating the building of the windmill. Then Napoleon stood up to reply. He said very quietly that the windmill was nonsense and that he advised nobody to vote for it, and promptly sat down again; he had spoken for barely thirty seconds and seemed almost indifferent as to the effect he produced. At this Snowball sprang to his feet, and shouting down the sheep, who had begun bleating again, broke into a passionate appeal in favor of the windmill. Until now the animals had been about equally divided in their sympathies, but in a moment Snowball's eloquence had carried them away. In glowing sentences he painted a picture of Animal Farm as it might be when sordid labor was lifted from the animals' backs. His imagination had now run far beyond chaff-cutters and turnip-slicers. Electricity, he said, could operate threshing machines, plows, harrows, rollers, and reapers and binders, besides supplying every stall with its own electric light, hot and cold water, and an electric heater. By the time he had finished speaking, there was no doubt as to which way the vote would go. But just at this moment Napoleon stood up and, casting a peculiar sidelong look at Snowball, uttered a high-pitched whimper of a kind no one had ever heard him utter before.

At this there was a terrible baying sound outside, and nine enormous dogs wearing brass-studded collars came bounding into the barn. They dashed straight for Snowball, who only sprang from his place just in time to escape their snapping jaws. In a moment he was out of the door and they were after him. Too amazed and frightened to speak, all the animals crowded through the door to watch the chase. Snowball was racing across the long pasture that led to the road. He was running as only a pig can run, but the dogs were close on his heels. Suddenly he slipped and it seemed certain that they had him. Then he was up again, running faster than ever; then the dogs were gaining on him again. One of them all but closed his jaws on Snowball's tail, but Snowball whisked it free just in time. Then he put on an extra spurt and, with a few inches to spare, slipped through a hole in the hedge and was seen no more.

Silent and terrified, the animals crept back into the barn. In a moment the dogs came bounding back. At first no one had been able to imagine where these creatures came from, but the problem was soon solved: they were the puppies whom Napoleon had taken away from their mothers and reared privately. Though not yet full-grown, they were huge dogs, and as fierce-looking as wolves. They kept close to Napoleon. It was noticed that they wagged their tails to him in the same way as the other dogs had been used to do to Mr. Jones.

Napoleon, with the dogs following him, now mounted on to the raised portion of the floor where Major had previously stood to deliver his speech. He announced that from now on the Sunday-morning Meetings would come to an end. They were unnecessary, he said, and wasted time.

In future all questions relating to the working of the farm would be settled by a special committee of pigs, presided over by himself. These would meet in private and afterward communicate their decisions to the others. The animals would still assemble on Sunday mornings to salute the flag, sing "Beasts of England," and receive their orders for the week; but there would be no more debates.

In spite of the shock that Snowball's expulsion had given them, the animals were dismayed by this announcement. Several of them would have protested if they could have found the right arguments. Even Boxer was vaguely troubled. He set his ears back, shook his forelock several times, and tried hard to marshal his thoughts; but in the end he could not think of anything to say. Some of the pigs themselves, however, were more articulate. Four young porkers in the front row uttered shrill squeals of disapproval, and all four of them sprang to their feet and began speaking at once. But suddenly the dogs sitting round Napoleon let out deep, menacing growls, and the pigs fell silent and sat down again. Then the sheep broke out into a tremendous bleating of "Four legs good, two legs bad!" which went on for nearly a quarter of an hour and put an end to any chance of discussion.

Afterwards Squealer was sent round the farm to explain the new arrangement to the others.

"Comrades," he said, "I trust that every animal here appreciates the sacrifice that Comrade Napoleon has made in taking this extra labor upon himself. Do not imagine, comrades, that leadership is a pleasure! On the contrary, it is a deep and heavy responsibility. No one believes more firmly than Comrade Napoleon that all animals are equal. He would only be too happy to let you make your decisions for yourselves. But sometimes you might make the wrong decisions, comrades, and then where would we be? Suppose you had decided to follow Snowball, with his moonshine of windmills—Snowball, who, as we now know, was no better than a criminal?"

"He fought bravely at the Battle of the Cowshed," said somebody.

"Bravery is not enough," said Squealer. "Loyalty and obedience are more important. And as to the Battle of the Cowshed, I believe the time will come when we shall find that Snowball's part in it was much exaggerated. Discipline, comrades, iron discipline! That is the watchword for today. One false step, and our enemies would be upon us. Surely, comrades, you do not want Jones back?"

Once again this argument was unanswerable. Certainly the animals did not want Jones back; if the holding of debates on Sunday mornings was liable to bring him back, then the debates must stop. Boxer, who had now had time to think things over, voiced the general feeling by saying: "If Comrade Napoleon says it, it must be right." And from then on he adopted the maxim, "Napoleon is always right," in addition to his private motto of "I will work harder."

By this time the weather had broken and the spring plowing had begun. The shed where Snowball had drawn his plans of the windmill had been shut up, and it was assumed that the plans had been rubbed off the floor. Every Sunday morning at ten o'clock the animals assembled in the big barn to receive their orders for the week. The skull of old Major, now clean of flesh, had been disinterred from the orchard and set up on a stump at the foot of the flagstaff, beside the gun. After the hoisting of the flag, the animals were required to file past the skull in a reverent manner before entering the barn. Nowadays they did not sit all together as they had done in the past. Napoleon, with Squealer and another pig named Minimus, who had a remarkable gift for composing songs and poems, sat on the front of the raised platform, with the nine young dogs forming a semicircle round them, and the other pigs sitting behind. The rest of the animals sat facing them in the main body of the barn. Napoleon read out the orders for the week in a gruff, soldierly style, and after a single singing of "Beasts of England," all the animals dispersed.

On the third Sunday after Snowball's expulsion, the animals were somewhat surprised to hear Napoleon announce that the windmill was to be built after all. He did not give any reason for having changed his mind, but merely warned the animals that this extra task would mean very hard work; it might even be necessary to reduce their rations. The plans, however, had all been prepared, down to the last detail. A special committee of pigs had been at work upon them for the past three weeks. The building of the windmill, with various other improvements, was expected to take two years.

That evening Squealer explained privately to the other animals that Napoleon had never in reality been opposed to the windmill. On the contrary, it was he who had advocated it in the beginning, and the plan which Snowball had drawn on the floor of the incubator shed had actually been stolen from among Napoleon's papers. The windmill was, in fact, Napoleon's own creation. Why, then, asked somebody, had he spoken so strongly against it? Here Squealer looked very sly. That, he said, was Comrade Napoleon's cunning. He had *seemed* to oppose the windmill, simply as a maneuver to get rid of Snowball, who was a dangerous character and a bad influence. Now that Snowball was out of the way, the plan could go forward without his interference. This, said Squealer, was something called tactics. He repeated a number of times, "Tactics, comrades, tactics!" skipping round and whisking his tail with a merry laugh. The animals were not certain what the word meant, but Squealer spoke so persuasively, and the three dogs who happened to be with him growled so threateningly that they accepted his explanation without further questions.

Responding to the Novel

Analyzing the Novel

Identifying Facts

1. Explain why Mollie is never mentioned again on Animal Farm.
2. Snowball and Napoleon are in **conflict** about everything on the farm. Contrast their plans for the farm, their ideas about defending the farm and building the windmill, and their methods of winning support for their ideas.
3. List the specific events that lead to Snowball's expulsion from Animal Farm.
4. List at least four important changes that take place at Animal Farm after Snowball leaves. Even though some of the animals try to protest, why are they unable to stop these changes?

Interpreting Meanings

5. In a totalitarian government, one political party or group maintains complete control and bans all opposition. In what specific ways has Animal Farm now become a totalitarian state?

6. What do you suppose **motivates** Napoleon to change his position on the windmill? What does this suggest about his **character**?
7. After Snowball's expulsion, what happens to democracy and equality on Animal Farm? What new values begin to take their place?
8. What do you think is **foreshadowed** by the dogs' behavior toward Napoleon?
9. Who are the nine dogs that suddenly appear? What group in a human society do you think these dogs would resemble?
10. Squealer and the sheep each fill essential roles in the new society. Explain each one's function. What do you think their human counterparts would be in a totalitarian government?
11. Summarize the propaganda techniques Squealer uses in his arguments on page 828. What pattern do you see emerging in Squealer's method of persuasion?
12. Do Squealer, Napoleon, or Snowball remind you in any way of people you know or have read about? Explain.
13. How *should* the animals respond to Squealer?

VI

All that year the animals worked like slaves. But they were happy in their work; they grudged no effort or sacrifice, well aware that everything that they did was for the benefit of themselves and those of their kind who would come after them, and not for a pack of idle, thieving human beings.

Throughout the spring and summer they worked a sixty-hour week, and in August Napoleon announced that there would be work on Sunday afternoons as well. This work was strictly voluntary, but any animal who absented himself from it would have his rations reduced by half. Even so, it was found necessary to leave certain tasks undone. The harvest was a little less successful than in the previous year, and two fields which should have been sown with roots in the early summer were not sown because plowing had not been completed early enough. It was possible to foresee that the coming winter would be a hard one.

The windmill presented unexpected difficulties. There was a good quarry of limestone on the farm, and plenty of sand and cement had been found in one of the outhouses, so that all the materials for building were at hand. But the problem the animals could not at first solve was how to break up the stone into pieces of suitable size. There seemed no way of doing this except with picks and crowbars, which no animal could use, because no animal could stand on his hind legs. Only after weeks of vain effort did the right idea occur to somebody—namely, to utilize the force of gravity. Huge boulders, far too big to be used as they were, were lying all over the bed of the quarry. The animals lashed ropes round these, and then all together, cows, horses, sheep, any animal that could lay hold of the rope—even the pigs sometimes joined in at critical moments—they dragged them with desperate slowness up the slope to the top of the quarry, where they were toppled over the edge, to shatter to pieces below. Transporting the stone when it was once broken was comparatively simple. The horses carried it off in cartloads, the sheep dragged single blocks, even Muriel and Benjamin yoked themselves into an old governess cart and did their share. By late summer a sufficient store of stone had accumulated, and then the building began, under the superintendence of the pigs.

But it was a slow, laborious process. Frequently, it took a whole day of exhausting effort to drag a single boulder to the top of the quarry, and sometimes when it was pushed over the edge it failed to break. Nothing could have been achieved without Boxer, whose strength seemed equal to that of all the rest of the animals put together. When the boulder began to slip and the animals cried out in despair at finding themselves dragged down the hill, it was always Boxer who strained himself against the rope and brought the boulder to a stop. To see him toiling up the slope inch by inch, his breath coming fast, the tops of his hoofs clawing at the ground, and his great sides matted with sweat, filled everyone with admiration. Clover warned him sometimes to be careful not to overstrain himself, but Boxer would never listen to her. His two slogans, "I will work harder" and "Napoleon is always right," seemed to him a sufficient answer to all problems. He had made arrangements with the cockerel to call him three-quarters of an hour earlier in the mornings instead of half an hour. And in his spare moments, of which there were not many nowadays, he would go alone to the quarry, collect a load of broken stone, and drag it down to the site of the windmill unassisted.

The animals were not badly off throughout the summer, in spite of the hardness of their work. If they had no more food than they had had in Jones's day, at least they did not have less. The advantage of only having to feed themselves and not having to support five extravagant human beings as well was so great that it would have taken a lot of failures to outweigh it. And in many ways the animal method of doing things was more efficient and saved labor. Such jobs as weeding, for instance, could be done with a thoroughness impossible to human beings. And again, since no animal now stole, it was unnecessary to fence off pasture from arable[1] land, which saved a lot of labor on the upkeep of hedges and gates. Nevertheless, as the summer wore on, various unforeseen shortages began to make themselves felt.

---

1. **arable** (ar′ə·b'l): suitable for plowing and producing crops. Farmers keep animals off arable land.

There was need of paraffin oil, nails, string, dog biscuits, and iron for the horses' shoes, none of which could be produced on the farm. Later there would also be need for seeds and artificial manures, besides various tools and, finally, the machinery for the windmill. How these were to be procured, no one was able to imagine.

One Sunday morning, when the animals assembled to receive their orders, Napoleon announced that he had decided upon a new policy. From now onward Animal Farm would engage in trade with the neighboring farms: not, of course, for any commercial purpose, but simply in order to obtain certain materials which were urgently necessary. The needs of the windmill must override everything else, he said. He was therefore making arrangements to sell a stack of hay and part of the current year's wheat crop, and later on, if more money were needed, it would have to be made up by the sale of eggs, for which there was always a market in Willingdon. The hens, said Napoleon, should welcome this sacrifice as their own special contribution towards the building of the windmill.

Once again the animals were conscious of a vague uneasiness. Never to have any dealings with human beings, never to engage in trade, never to make use of money—had not these been among the earliest resolutions passed at that first triumphant Meeting after Jones was expelled? All the animals remembered passing such resolutions: or at least they thought that they remembered it. The four young pigs who had protested when Napoleon abolished the Meetings raised their voices timidly, but they were promptly silenced by a tremendous growling from the dogs. Then, as usual, the sheep broke into "Four legs good, two legs bad!" and the momentary awkwardness was smoothed over. Finally Napoleon raised his trotter for silence and announced that he had already made all the arrangements. There would be no need for any of the animals to come in contact with human beings, which would clearly be most undesirable. He intended to take the whole burden upon his own shoulders. A Mr. Whymper, a solicitor[2] living in Willingdon, had agreed to act as intermediary between Animal Farm and the outside world, and would visit the farm every Monday morning to receive his instructions. Napoleon ended his speech with his usual cry of "Long live Animal Farm!" and after the singing of "Beasts of England" the animals were dismissed.

Afterward Squealer made a round of the farm and set the animals' minds at rest. He assured them that the resolution against engaging in trade and using money had never been passed or even suggested. It was pure imagination, probably traceable in the beginning to lies circulated by Snowball. A few animals still felt faintly doubtful, but Squealer asked them shrewdly, "Are you certain that this is not something that you have dreamed, comrades? Have you any record of such a resolution? Is it written down anywhere?" And since it was certainly true that nothing of the kind existed in writing, the animals were satisfied that they had been mistaken.

Every Monday Mr. Whymper visited the farm as had been arranged. He was a sly-looking little man with side whiskers, a solicitor in a very small way of business, but sharp enough to have realized earlier than anyone else that Animal Farm would need a broker and that the commissions would be worth having. The animals watched his coming and going with a kind of dread, and avoided him as much as possible. Nevertheless, the sight of Napoleon, on all fours, delivering orders to Whymper, who stood on two legs, roused their pride and partly reconciled them to the new arrangement. Their relations with the human race were now not quite the same as they had been before. The human beings did not hate Animal Farm any less now that it was prospering; indeed, they hated it more than ever. Every human being held it as an article of faith that the farm would go bankrupt sooner or later and, above all, that the windmill would be a failure. They would meet in the public houses[3] and prove to one another by means of diagrams that the windmill was bound to fall down or that if it did stand up, then that it would never work. And yet, against their will, they had developed a certain respect for the efficiency with which the animals were managing their own affairs. One symptom of this was that they had begun to call Animal Farm by its proper name and ceased to pretend that it was called the Manor Farm. They had also dropped their championship of Jones, who had given up hope of getting his farm back and gone to live in another part of the county. Except through Whymper, there was as yet no contact between Animal Farm and the outside world, but there were constant rumors that Napoleon was about to enter into a definite business agreement either with Mr. Pilkington of Foxwood or with Mr. Frederick of Pinchfield—but never, it was noticed, with both simultaneously.

---

2. **solicitor** (sə·lis′it·ər): (British) lawyer.

3. **public houses:** (British) bars or saloons.

It was about this time that the pigs suddenly moved into the farmhouse and took up their residence there. Again the animals seemed to remember that a resolution against this had been passed in the early days, and again Squealer was able to convince them that this was not the case. It was absolutely necessary, he said, that the pigs, who were the brains of the farm, should have a quiet place to work in. It was also more suited to the dignity of the Leader (for of late he had taken to speaking of Napoleon under the title of "Leader") to live in a house than in a mere sty. Nevertheless, some of the animals were disturbed when they heard that the pigs not only took their meals in the kitchen and used the drawing room as a recreation room, but also slept in the beds. Boxer passed it off as usual with "Napoleon is always right!" but Clover, who thought she remembered a definite ruling against beds, went to the end of the barn and tried to puzzle out the Seven Commandments which were inscribed there. Finding herself unable to read more than individual letters, she fetched Muriel.

"Muriel," she said, "read me the Fourth Commandment. Does it not say something about never sleeping in a bed?"

With some difficulty Muriel spelled it out.

"It says, 'No animal shall sleep in a bed *with sheets,*'" she announced finally.

Curiously enough, Clover had not remembered that the Fourth Commandment mentioned sheets; but as it was there on the wall, it must have done so. And Squealer, who happened to be passing at this moment, attended by two or three dogs, was able to put the whole matter in its proper perspective.

"You have heard then, comrades," he said, "that we pigs now sleep in the beds of the farmhouse? And why not? You did not suppose, surely, that there was ever a ruling against *beds*? A bed merely means a place to sleep in. A pile of straw in a stall is a bed, properly regarded. The rule was against *sheets,* which are a human invention. We have removed the sheets from the farmhouse beds and sleep between blankets. And very comfortable beds they are too! But not more comfortable than we need, I can tell you, comrades, with all the brainwork we have to do nowadays. You would not rob us of our repose, would you, comrades? You would not have us too tired to carry out our duties? Surely none of you wishes to see Jones back?"

The animals reassured him on this point immediately, and no more was said about the pigs sleeping in the farmhouse beds. And when, some days afterwards, it was announced that from now on the pigs would get up an hour later in the mornings than the other animals, no complaint was made about that either.

By the autumn the animals were tired but happy. They had had a hard year, and after the sale of part of the hay and corn, the stores of food for the winter were none too plentiful, but the windmill compensated for everything. It was almost half built now. After the harvest there was a stretch of clear dry weather, and the animals toiled harder than ever, thinking it well worth while to plod to and fro all day with blocks of stone if by doing so they could raise the walls another foot. Boxer would even come out at nights and work for an hour or two on his own by the light of the harvest moon. In their spare moments the animals would walk round and round the half-finished mill, admiring the strength and perpendicularity of its walls and marveling that they should ever have been able to build anything so imposing. Only old Benjamin refused to grow enthusiastic about the windmill, though, as usual, he would utter nothing beyond the cryptic remark that donkeys live a long time.

November came, with raging southwest winds. Building had to stop because it was now too wet to mix the cement. Finally there came a night when the gale was so violent that the farm buildings rocked on their foundations and several tiles were blown off the roof of the barn. The hens woke up squawking with terror because they had all dreamed simultaneously of hearing a gun off in the distance. In the morning the animals came out of their stalls to find that the flagstaff had been blown down and an elm tree at the foot of the orchard had been plucked up like a radish. They had just noticed this when a cry of despair broke from every animal's throat. A terrible sight had met their eyes. The windmill was in ruins.

With one accord they dashed down to the spot. Napoleon, who seldom moved out of a walk, raced ahead of them all. Yes, there it lay, the fruit of all their struggles, leveled to its foundations, the stones they had broken and carried so laboriously scattered all around. Unable at first to speak, they stood gazing mournfully at the litter of fallen stone. Napoleon paced to and fro in silence, occasionally snuffing at the ground. His tail had grown rigid and twitched sharply from side to side, a sign in him of intense mental activity. Suddenly he halted as though his mind were made up.

"Comrades," he said quietly, "do you know who is responsible for this? Do you know the enemy who has come in the night and overthrown our windmill? SNOWBALL!" he suddenly roared in a voice of thunder. "Snowball has done this thing! In sheer malignity,[4] thinking to set back our plans and avenge himself for his ignominious expulsion, this traitor has crept here under cover of night and destroyed our work of nearly a year. Comrades, here and now I pronounce the death sentence upon Snowball. 'Animal Hero, Second Class' and half a bushel of apples to any animal who brings him to justice. A full bushel to anyone who captures him alive!"

The animals were shocked beyond measure to learn that even Snowball could be guilty of such an action. There was a cry of indignation, and everyone began thinking out ways of catching Snowball if he should ever come back. Almost immediately the footprints of a pig were discovered in the grass at a little distance from the knoll. They could only be traced for a few yards, but appeared to lead to a hole in the hedge. Napoleon snuffed deeply at them and pronounced them to be Snowball's. He gave it as his opinion that Snowball had probably come from the direction of Foxwood Farm.

"No more delays, comrades!" cried Napoleon when the footprints had been examined. "There is work to be done. This very morning we begin

---

4. **malignity** (mə·lig′nə·tē): persistent, intense ill will or desire to harm others.

rebuilding the windmill, and we will build all through the winter, rain or shine. We will teach this miserable traitor that he cannot undo our work so easily. Remember, comrades, there must be no alteration in our plans: they shall be carried out to the day. Forward, comrades! Long live the windmill! Long live Animal Farm!"

VII

It was a bitter winter. The stormy weather was followed by sleet and snow, and then by a hard frost which did not break till well into February. The animals carried on as best they could with the rebuilding of the windmill, well knowing that the outside world was watching them and that the envious human beings would rejoice and triumph if the mill were not finished on time.

Out of spite, the human beings pretended not to believe that it was Snowball who had destroyed the windmill: they said that it had fallen down because the walls were too thin. The animals knew that this was not the case. Still, it had been decided to build the walls three feet thick this time instead of eighteen inches as before, which meant collecting much larger quantities of stone. For a long time the quarry was full of snowdrifts and nothing could be done. Some progress was made in the dry frosty weather that followed, but it was cruel work, and the animals could not feel so hopeful about it as they had felt before. They were always cold, and usually hungry as well. Only Boxer and Clover never lost heart. Squealer made excellent speeches on the joy of service and the dignity of labor, but the other animals found more inspiration in Boxer's strength and his never-failing cry of "I will work harder!"

In January food fell short. The corn ration was drastically reduced, and it was announced that an extra potato ration would be issued to make up for it. Then it was discovered that the greater part of the potato crop had been frosted in the clamps,[1] which had not been covered thickly enough. The potatoes had become soft and discolored, and only a few were edible. For days at a time the animals had nothing to eat but chaff and mangels. Starvation seemed to stare them in the face.

It was vitally necessary to conceal this fact from the outside world. Emboldened by the collapse of the windmill, the human beings were inventing fresh lies about Animal Farm. Once again it was being put about that all the animals were dying of famine and disease, and that they were continually fighting among themselves and had resorted to cannibalism and infanticide. Napoleon was well aware of the bad results that might follow if the real facts of the food situation were known, and he decided to make use of Mr. Whymper to spread a contrary impression. Hitherto the animals had had little or no contact with Whymper on his weekly visits: now, however, a few selected animals, mostly sheep, were instructed to remark casually in his hearing that rations had been increased. In addition, Napoleon ordered the almost empty bins in the storeshed to be filled nearly to the brim with sand, which was then covered up with what remained of the grain and meal. On some suitable pretext Whymper was led through the storeshed and allowed to catch a glimpse of the bins. He was deceived and continued to report to the outside world that there was no food shortage on Animal Farm.

Nevertheless, toward the end of January it became obvious that it would be necessary to procure some more grain from somewhere. In these days Napoleon rarely appeared in public, but spent all his time in the farmhouse, which was guarded at each door by fierce-looking dogs. When he did emerge, it was in a ceremonial manner, with an escort of six dogs who closely surrounded him and growled if anyone came too near. Frequently he did not even appear on Sunday mornings, but issued his orders through one of the other pigs, usually Squealer.

One Sunday morning, Squealer announced that the hens, who had just come in to lay again, must surrender their eggs. Napoleon had accepted, through Whymper, a contract for four hundred eggs a week. The price of these would pay for enough grain and meal to keep the farm going till summer came on and conditions were easier.

When the hens heard this, they raised a terrible outcry. They had been warned earlier that this sacrifice might be necessary but had not believed that it would really happen. They were just getting their clutches ready for the spring sitting, and they protested that to take the eggs away now was murder. For the first time since the expulsion of Jones, there was something resembling a rebellion. Led by three young Black Minorca pullets, the hens made a determined effort to thwart Napoleon's wishes. Their method was to fly up to the rafters and there lay their eggs, which smashed to pieces on the floor. Napoleon acted swiftly and ruthlessly. He ordered the hens' rations to be stopped, and decreed that any animal giving so much as a grain of corn to a hen should be punished by death. The dogs saw to it that these

orders were carried out. For five days the hens held out, then they capitulated and went back to their nesting boxes. Nine hens had died in the meantime. Their bodies were buried in the orchard, and it was given out that they had died of coccidiosis.[2] Whymper heard nothing of this affair, and the eggs were duly delivered, a grocer's van driving up to the farm once a week to take them away.

All this while no more had been seen of Snowball. He was rumored to be hiding on one of the neighboring farms, either Foxwood or Pinchfield. Napoleon was by this time on slightly better terms with the other farmers than before. It happened that there was in the yard a pile of timber which had been stacked there ten years earlier when a beech spinney was cleared. It was well seasoned,

---

1. **clamps:** (British) heaped-up piles of produce covered with straw or earth to prevent freezing.

2. **coccidiosis** (kăk·sĭd′ē·ō′sĭs): an intestinal disease caused by parasites.

and Whymper had advised Napoleon to sell it; both Mr. Pilkington and Mr. Frederick were anxious to buy it. Napoleon was hesitating between the two, unable to make up his mind. It was noticed that whenever he seemed on the point of coming to an agreement with Frederick, Snowball was declared to be in hiding in Foxwood, while, when he inclined toward Pilkington, Snowball was said to be at Pinchfield.

Suddenly, early in the spring, an alarming thing was discovered. Snowball was secretly frequenting the farm by night! The animals were so disturbed that they could hardly sleep in their stalls. Every night, it was said, he came creeping in under cover of darkness and performed all kinds of mischief. He stole the corn, he upset the milk pails, he broke the eggs, he trampled the seedbeds, he gnawed the bark off the fruit trees. Whenever anything went wrong it became usual to attribute it to Snowball. If a window was broken or a drain was blocked up, someone was certain to say that Snowball had come in the night and done it, and when the key of the storeshed was lost, the whole farm was convinced that Snowball had thrown it down the well. Curiously enough, they went on believing this even after the mislaid key was found under a sack of meal. The cows declared unanimously that Snowball crept into their stalls and milked them in their sleep. The rats, which had been troublesome that winter, were also said to be in league with Snowball.

Napoleon decreed that there should be a full investigation into Snowball's activities. With his dogs in attendance he set out and made a careful tour of inspection of the farm buildings, the other animals following at a respectful distance. At every few steps Napoleon stopped and snuffed the ground for traces of Snowball's footsteps, which, he said, he could detect by the smell. He snuffed in every corner, in the barn, in the cowshed, in the henhouses, in the vegetable garden, and found traces of Snowball almost everywhere. He would put his snout to the ground, give several deep sniffs, and exclaim in a terrible voice, "Snowball! He has been here! I can smell him distinctly!" and at the word "Snowball" all the dogs let out bloodcurdling growls and showed their side teeth.

The animals were thoroughly frightened. It seemed to them as though Snowball were some kind of invisible influence, pervading the air about them and menacing them with all kinds of dangers. In the evening Squealer called them together and, with an alarmed expression on his face, told them that he had some serious news to report.

"Comrades!" cried Squealer, making little nervous skips, "a most terrible thing has been discovered. Snowball has sold himself to Frederick of Pinchfield Farm, who is even now plotting to attack us and take our farm away from us! Snowball is to act as his guide when the attack begins. But there is worse than that. We had thought that Snowball's rebellion was caused simply by his vanity and ambition. But we were wrong, comrades. Do you know what the real reason was? Snowball was in league with Jones from the very start! He was Jones's secret agent all the time. It has all been proved by documents which he left behind him and which we have only just discovered. To my mind this explains a great deal, comrades. Did we not see for ourselves how he attempted—fortunately without success—to get us defeated and destroyed at the Battle of the Cowshed?"

The animals were stupefied. This was a wickedness far outdoing Snowball's destruction of the windmill. But it was some minutes before they could fully take it in. They all remembered, or thought they remembered, how they had seen Snowball charging ahead of them at the Battle of the Cowshed, how he had rallied and encouraged them at every turn, and how he had not paused for an instant even when the pellets from Jones's gun had wounded his back. At first it was a little difficult to see how this fitted in with his being on Jones's side. Even Boxer, who seldom asked questions, was puzzled. He lay down, tucked his forehoofs beneath him, shut his eyes, and with a hard effort managed to formulate his thoughts.

"I do not believe that," he said. "Snowball fought bravely at the Battle of the Cowshed. I saw him myself. Did we not give him 'Animal Hero, First Class,' immediately afterward?

"That was our mistake, comrade. For we know now—it is all written down in the secret documents that we have found—that in reality he was trying to lure us to our doom.

"But he was wounded," said Boxer. "We all saw him running with blood."

"That was part of the arrangement!" cried Squealer. "Jones's shot only grazed him. I could show you this in his own writing, if you were able to read it. The plot was for Snowball, at the critical moment, to give the signal for flight and leave the field to the enemy. And he very nearly succeeded—I will even say, comrades, he *would* have succeeded it if had not been for our heroic Leader, Comrade Napoleon. Do you not remember how, just at the moment when Jones and his men had got inside the yard, Snowball suddenly turned and fled, and many animals followed him? And do you not remember, too, that it was just at that moment, when panic was spreading and all seemed lost, that Comrade Napoleon sprang forward with a cry of 'Death to Humanity!' and sank his teeth in Jones's leg? Surely you remember *that*, comrades?'' exclaimed Squealer, frisking from side to side.

Now when Squealer described the scene so graphically, it seemed to the animals that they did remember it. At any rate, they remembered that at the critical moment of the battle Snowball had turned to flee. But Boxer was still a little uneasy.

''I do not believe that Snowball was a traitor at the beginning,'' he said finally. ''What he has done since is different. But I believe that at the Battle of the Cowshed he was a good comrade.''

''Our Leader, Comrade Napoleon,'' announced Squealer, speaking very slowly and firmly, ''has stated categorically[3]—categorically, comrade—that Snowball was Jones's agent from the very beginning—yes, and from long before the Rebellion was ever thought of.''

''Ah, that is different!'' said Boxer. ''If Comrade Napoleon says it, it must be right.''

''That is the true spirit, comrade!'' cried Squealer, but it was noticed he cast a very ugly look at Boxer with his little twinkling eyes. He turned to go, then paused, and added impressively: ''I warn every animal on this farm to keep his eyes very wide open. For we have reason to think that some of Snowball's secret agents are lurking among us at this moment!''

Four days later, in the late afternoon, Napoleon ordered all the animals to assemble in the yard. When they were all gathered together, Napoleon emerged from the farmhouse, wearing both his medals (for he recently awarded himself ''Animal Hero, First Class,'' and ''Animal Hero, Second Class''), with his nine huge dogs frisking round him and uttering growls that sent shivers down all the animals' spines. They all cowered silently in their places, seeming to know in advance that some terrible thing was about to happen.

Napoleon stood sternly surveying his audience; then he uttered a high-pitched whimper. Immediately the dogs bounded forward, seized four of the pigs by the ear and dragged them, squealing with pain and terror, to Napoleon's feet. The pigs' ears were bleeding, the dogs tasted blood, and for a few moments they appeared to go quite mad. To the amazement of everybody, three of them flung themselves upon Boxer. Boxer saw them coming and put out his great hoof, caught a dog in midair, and pinned him to the ground. The dog shrieked for mercy and the other two fled with their tails between their legs. Boxer looked at Napoleon to know whether he should crush the dog to death or let it go. Napoleon appeared to change countenance,[4] and sharply ordered Boxer to let the dog go, whereat Boxer lifted his hoof, and the dog slunk away, bruised and howling.

Presently the tumult died down. The four pigs waited, trembling, with guilt written on every line of their countenances. Napoleon now called upon them to confess their crimes. They were the same four pigs as had protested when Napoleon abolished the Sunday Meetings. Without any further prompting they confessed that they had been secretly in touch with Snowball ever since his expulsion, that they had collaborated with him in destroying the windmill, and that they had entered into an agreement with him to hand over Animal Farm to Mr. Frederick. They added that Snowball had privately admitted to them that he had been Jones's secret agent for years past. When they had finished their confession, the dogs promptly tore their throats out, and in a terrible voice Napoleon demanded whether any other animal had anything to confess.

The three hens who had been the ringleaders in the attempted rebellion over the eggs now came forward and stated that Snowball had appeared to them in a dream and incited them to disobey Napoleon's orders. They, too, were slaughtered. Then a goose came forward and confessed to having secreted six ears of corn during the last year's harvest and eaten them in the night. Then a sheep confessed to having urinated in the drinking

---

3. **categorically:** absolutely; without qualifications or conditions.

4. **countenance** (koun′tə·nəns): facial expression.

pool—urged to do this, so she said, by Snowball—and two other sheep confessed to having murdered an old ram, an especially devoted follower of Napoleon, by chasing him round and round a bonfire when he was suffering from a cough. They were all slain on the spot. And so that tale of confessions and executions went on, until there was a pile of corpses lying before Napoleon's feet and the air was heavy with the smell of blood, which had been unknown there since the expulsion of Jones.

When it was all over, the remaining animals, except for the pigs and dogs, crept away in a body. They were shaken and miserable. They did not know which was more shocking—the treachery of the animals who had leagued themselves with Snowball or the cruel retribution they had just witnessed. In the old days there had often been scenes of bloodshed equally terrible, but it seemed to all of them that it was far worse now that it was happening among themselves. Since Jones had left the farm, until today, no animal had killed another animal. Not even a rat had been killed. They had made their way on to the little knoll where the half-finished windmill stood, and with one accord they all lay down as though huddling together for warmth—Clover, Muriel, Benjamin, the cows, the sheep, and a whole flock of geese and hens—everyone, indeed, except the cat, who had suddenly disappeared just before Napoleon ordered the animals to assemble. For some time nobody spoke. Only Boxer remained on his feet. He fidgeted to and fro, swishing his long black tail against his sides and occasionally uttering a little whinny of surprise. Finally he said:

"I do not understand it. I would not have believed that such things could happen on our farm. It must be due to some fault in ourselves. The solution, as I see it, is to work harder. From now onward I shall get up a full hour earlier in the mornings."

And he moved off at his lumbering trot and made for the quarry. Having got there, he collected two successive loads of stone and dragged them down to the windmill before retiring for the night.

The animals huddled about Clover, not speaking. The knoll where they were lying gave them a wide prospect across the countryside. Most of Animal Farm was within their view—the long pasture stretching down to the main road, the hayfield, the spinney, the drinking pool, the plowed fields where the young wheat was thick and green, and the red roofs of the farm buildings with the smoke curling from the chimneys. It was a clear spring evening. The grass and the bursting hedges were gilded by the level rays of the sun. Never had the farm—and with a kind of surprise they remembered that it was their own farm, every inch of it their own property—appeared to the animals so desirable a place. As Clover looked down the hillside her eyes filled with tears. If she could have spoken her thoughts, it would have been to say that this was not what they had aimed at when they had set themselves years ago to work for the overthrow of the human race. These scenes of terror and slaughter were not what they had looked forward to on that night when old Major first stirred them to rebellion. If she herself had had any picture of the future, it had been of a society of animals set free from hunger and the whip, all equal, each working according to his capacity, the strong protecting the weak, as she had protected the lost brood of ducklings with her foreleg on the night of Major's speech. Instead—she did not know why—they had come to a time when no one dared speak his mind, when fierce, growling dogs roamed everywhere, and when you had to watch your comrades torn to pieces after confessing to shocking crimes. There was no thought of rebellion or disobedience in her mind. She knew that, even as things were, they were far better off than they had been in the days of Jones and that before all else it was needful to prevent the return of the human beings. Whatever happened she would remain faithful, work hard, carry out the orders that were given to her, and accept the leadership of Napoleon. But still, it was not for this that she and all the other animals had hoped and toiled. It was not for this that they had built the windmill and faced the bullets of Jones's gun. Such were her thoughts, though she lacked the words to express them.

At last, feeling this to be in some way a substitute for the words she was unable to find, she began to sing "Beasts of England." The other animals sitting round her took it up, and they sang it three times over—very tunefully, but slowly and mournfully, in a way they had never sung it before.

They had just finished singing it for the third time when Squealer, attended by two dogs, approached them with the air of having something important to say. He announced that, by a special decree of Comrade Napoleon, "Beasts of England" had been abolished. From now onward it was forbidden to sing it.

The animals were taken aback.

"Why?" cried Muriel.

"It's no longer needed, comrade," said Squealer stiffly. "'Beasts of England' was the song of the Rebellion. But the Rebellion is now completed. The execution of the traitors this afternoon was the final act. The enemy both external and internal has been defeated. In 'Beasts of England' we expressed our longing for a better society in days to come. But that society has now been established. Clearly this song has no longer any purpose.''

Frightened though they were, some of the animals might possibly have protested, but at this moment the sheep set up their usual bleating of ''Four legs good, two legs bad,'' which went on for several minutes and put an end to the discussion.

So ''Beasts of England'' was heard no more. In its place Minimus, the poet, had composed another song which began:

Animal Farm, Animal Farm,
Never through me shalt thou come to harm!

and this was sung every Sunday morning after the hoisting of the flag. But somehow neither the words nor the tune ever seemed to the animals to come up to ''Beasts of England.''

Responding to the Novel

Analyzing the Novel

Identifying Facts

1. In Chapters VI and VII, several of the commandments that were established immediately after the Rebellion are broken. Identify at least three of these commandments. What reason do the pigs give for breaking each one?
2. When the Fourth Commandment is changed, why doesn't Clover trust her own memory about its original wording?
3. What frightening new strategy for silencing and manipulating the animals does Squealer use to justify trade with humans?
4. Identify some of the outright lies and distortions of the truth that Squealer uses to prove that Snowball was a traitor from the very beginning.

5. Describe what happens after Napoleon accuses four pigs of being Snowball's secret agents. How does Boxer escape from being attacked by Napoleon's dogs?

Interpreting Meanings

6. What **irony** do you sense in the following passages? (Read them in context first.)
   a. ''All that year the animals worked like slaves.'' (Page 830)
   b. ''This work was strictly voluntary, but any animal who absented himself from it would have his rations reduced by half.'' (Page 830)
   c. ''Then, as usual, the sheep broke into 'Four legs good, two legs bad!' and the momentary awkwardness was smoothed over.'' (Page 831)

d. "Curiously enough, Clover had not remembered that the Fourth Commandment mentioned sheets; but as it was there on the wall, it must have done so." (Page 832)

7. Orwell could have told his story of Animal Farm without including the windmill. What do you think the windmill—and the animals' exhausting work—represents, or **symbolizes**, to the animals? To Orwell?

8. Do you think the animals are really guilty of the crimes they confess to in the barnyard? If not, what horrifying assumption can we make about why they confess anyway? (Is there more than one possible reason?)

9. From Napoleon's perspective, what purpose do the confessions and executions serve?

10. What **irony** do you detect in Boxer's response to them? Clover's response is considered one of the most important passages in the novel (see page 837). Do you see any **irony** in it, or are we meant to agree with what she is thinking?

11. Look back at old Major's speech on page 811. Which of his statements about life on Manor Farm under the rule of Mr. Jones are now true of life on Animal Farm? Explain the **irony** in this situation.

12. What do you suppose is Napoleon's real reason for outlawing the singing of "Beasts of England"? Why is it **ironic** that the animals sing this song at the end of Chapter VII?

13. What do you predict will happen next on Animal Farm? What would have to happen for the animals to be happy again, in the way that they were right after the Rebellion?

VIII

A few days later, when the terror caused by the executions had died down, some of the animals remembered—or thought they remembered—that the Sixth Commandment decreed "No animal shall kill any other animal." And though no one cared to mention it in the hearing of the pigs or the dogs, it was felt that the killings which had taken place did not square with this. Clover asked Benjamin to read her the Sixth Commandment, and when Benjamin, as usual, said that he refused to meddle in such matters, she fetched Muriel. Muriel read the Commandment for her. It ran: "No animal shall kill any other animal *without cause*." Somehow or other, the last two words had slipped out of the animals' memory. But they saw now that the Commandment had not been violated; for clearly there was good reason for killing the traitors who had leagued themselves with Snowball.

Throughout the year the animals worked even harder than they had worked in the previous year. To rebuild the windmill, with walls twice as thick as before, and to finish it by the appointed date, together with the regular work of the farm, was a tremendous labor. There were times when it seemed to the animals that they worked longer hours and fed no better than they had done in Jones's day. On Sunday mornings Squealer, holding down a long strip of paper with his trotter, would read out to them lists of figures proving that the production of every class of foodstuff had increased by two hundred per cent, three hundred per cent, or five hundred per cent, as the case might be. The animals saw no reason to disbelieve him, especially as they could no longer remember very clearly what conditions had been like before the Rebellion. All the same, there were days when they felt that they would sooner have had less figures and more food.

All orders were now issued through Squealer or one of the other pigs. Napoleon himself was not seen in public as often as once in a fortnight. When he did appear, he was attended not only by his retinue of dogs but by a black cockerel who marched in front of him and acted as a kind of trumpeter, letting out a loud "cock-a-doodle-doo" before Napoleon spoke. Even in the farmhouse, it was said, Napoleon inhabited separate apartments from the others. He took his meals alone, with two dogs to wait upon him, and always ate from the Crown Derby dinner service which had been in the glass cupboard in the drawing room. It was also announced that the gun would be fired every year on Napoleon's birthday, as well as on the other two anniversaries.

Napoleon was now never spoken of simply as "Napoleon." He was always referred to in formal style as "our Leader, Comrade Napoleon," and the pigs liked to invent for him such titles as Father of All Animals, Terror of Mankind, Protector of the Sheepfold, Ducklings' Friend, and the like. In his speeches, Squealer would talk with the tears rolling down his cheeks of Napoleon's wisdom, the goodness of his heart, and the deep love he bore to all animals everywhere, even and especially the unhappy animals who still lived in ignorance and slavery on other farms. It had become usual to give Napoleon the credit for every successful achievement and every stroke of good fortune. You would often hear one hen remark to another, "Under the guidance of our Leader, Comrade Napoleon, I have laid five eggs in six days"; or two cows, enjoying a drink at the pool, would exclaim, "Thanks to the leadership of Comrade Napoleon, how excellent his water tastes!" The general feeling on the farm was well expressed in a poem entitled "Comrade Napoleon," which was composed by Minimus and which ran as follows:

Friend of fatherless!
Fountain of happiness!
Lord of the swill[1] bucket! Oh, how my soul is on
Fire when I gaze at thy
Calm and commanding eye,
Like the sun in the sky,
Comrade Napoleon!

Thou are the giver of
All that thy creatures love,
Full belly twice a day, clean straw to roll upon;
Every beast great or small
Sleeps at peace in his stall,
Thou watchest over all,
Comrade Napoleon!

Had I a sucking pig,
Ere he had grown as big
Even as a pint bottle or as a rolling pin,
He should have learned to be
Faithful and true to thee,
Yes, his first squeak should be
"Comrade Napoleon!"

---

1. **swill:** garbage, table scraps, etc., mixed with liquid and used for feeding pigs.

Napoleon approved of this poem and caused it to be inscribed on the wall of the big barn, at the opposite end from the Seven Commandments. It was surmounted by[2] a portrait of Napoleon, in profile, executed by Squealer in white paint.

Meanwhile, through the agency of Whymper, Napoleon was engaged in complicated negotiations with Frederick and Pilkington. The pile of timber was still unsold. Of the two, Frederick was the more anxious to get hold of it, but he would not offer a reasonable price. At the same time there were renewed rumors that Frederick and his men were plotting to attack Animal Farm and to destroy the windmill, the building of which had aroused furious jealousy in him. Snowball was known to be still skulking on Pinchfield Farm. In the middle of the summer the animals were alarmed to hear that three hens had come forward and confessed that, inspired by Snowball, they had entered into a plot to murder Napoleon. They were executed immediately, and fresh precautions for Napoleon's safety were taken. Four dogs guarded his bed at night, one at each corner, and a young pig named Pinkeye was given the task of tasting all his food before he ate it, lest it should be poisoned.

At about the same time it was given out that Napoleon had arranged to sell the pile of timber to Mr. Pilkington; he was also going to enter into a regular agreement for the exchange of certain products between Animal Farm and Foxwood. The relations between Napoleon and Pilkington, though they were only conducted through Whymper, were now almost friendly. The animals distrusted Pilkington, as a human being, but greatly preferred him to Frederick, whom they both feared and hated. As the summer wore on and the windmill neared completion, the rumors of an impending treacherous attack grew stronger and stronger. Frederick, it was said, intended to bring against them twenty men all armed with guns, and he had already bribed the magistrates and police, so that if he could once get hold of the title deeds of Animal Farm they would ask no questions. Moreover, terrible stories were leaking out from Pinchfield about the cruelties that Frederick practiced upon his animals. He had flogged an old horse to death, he starved his cows, he had killed a dog by throwing it into the furnace, he amused himself in the evenings by making cocks fight with splinters of razor blade tied to their spurs. The animals' blood boiled with rage when they heard of these things being done to their comrades, and sometimes they clamored to be allowed to go out in a body and attack Pinchfield Farm, drive out the humans, and set the animals free. But Squealer counseled them to avoid rash actions and trust in Comrade Napoleon's strategy.

Nevertheless, feeling against Frederick continued to run high. One Sunday morning Napoleon appeared in the barn and explained that he had never at any time contemplated selling the pile of timber to Frederick; he considered it beneath his dignity, he said, to have dealings with scoundrels of that description. The pigeons who were still sent out to spread tidings of the Rebellion were forbidden to set foot anywhere on Foxwood and were also ordered to drop their former slogan of "Death to Humanity" in favor of "Death to Frederick." In the late summer yet another of Snowball's machinations[3] was laid bare. The wheat crop was full of weeds, and it was discovered that on one of his nocturnal visits Snowball had mixed weed seeds with the seed corn. A gander who had been privy to the plot had confessed his guilt to Squealer and immediately committed suicide by swallowing deadly nightshade berries. The animals now also learned that Snowball had never—as many of them had believed hitherto—received the order of "Animal Hero, First Class." This was merely a legend which had been spread some time after the Battle of the Cowshed by Snowball himself. So far from being decorated, he had been censured for showing cowardice in the battle. Once again some of the animals heard this with a certain bewilderment, but Squealer was soon able to convince them that their memories had been at fault.

In the autumn, by a tremendous, exhausting effort—for the harvest had to be gathered at almost the same time—the windmill was finished. The machinery had still to be installed, and Whymper was negotiating the purchase of it, but the structure was completed. In the teeth of every difficulty, in spite of inexperience, of primitive implements, of bad luck, and of Snowball's treachery, the work had been finished punctually to the very day! Tired out but proud, the animals walked round and round their masterpiece, which appeared even more beautiful in their eyes than when it had been built the first time. Moreover, the walls were twice as thick as before. Nothing short of explosives would lay them low this time! And when they thought of how they had labored,

---

2. **surmounted by:** underneath; in other words, the portrait was painted above the poem.

3. **machinations** (mak'ə·nā'shənz): evil schemes or plots.

what discouragements they had overcome, and the enormous difference that would be made in their lives when the sails were turning and the dynamos running—when they thought of all this, their tiredness forsook them and they gamboled round and round the windmill, uttering cries of triumph. Napoleon himself, attended by his dogs and his cockerel, came down to inspect the completed work; he personally congratulated the animals on their achievement and announced that the mill would be named Napoleon Mill.

Two days later the animals were called together for a special meeting in the barn. They were struck dumb with surprise when Napoleon announced that he had sold the pile of timber to Frederick. Tomorrow Frederick's wagons would arrive and begin carting it away. Throughout the whole period of his seeming friendship with Pilkington, Napoleon had really been in secret agreement with Frederick.

All relations with Foxwood had been broken off; insulting messages had been sent to Pilkington. The pigeons had been told to avoid Pinchfield Farm and to alter their slogan from "Death to Frederick" to "Death to Pilkington." At the same time Napoleon assured the animals that the stories of an impending attack on Animal Farm were completely untrue and that the tales about Frederick's cruelty to his own animals had been greatly exaggerated. All these rumors had probably originated with Snowball and his agents. It now appeared that Snowball was not, after all, hiding on Pinchfield Farm, and in fact had never been there in his life: he was living—in considerable luxury, so it was said—at Foxwood and had in reality been a pensioner of Pilkington for years past.

The pigs were in ecstasies over Napoleon's cunning. By seeming to be friendly with Pilkington he had forced Frederick to raise his price by twelve pounds. But the superior quality of Napoleon's mind, said Squealer, was shown in the fact that he trusted nobody, not even Frederick. Frederick had wanted to pay for the timber with something called a check, which, it seemed, was a piece of paper with a promise to pay written upon it. But Napoleon was too clever for him. He had demanded payment in real five-pound notes, which were to be handed over before the timber was removed. Already Frederick had paid up; and the sum he had paid was just enough to buy the machinery for the windmill.

Meanwhile the timber was being carted away at high speed. When it was all gone, another special meeting was held in the barn for the animals to inspect Frederick's bank notes. Smiling beatif-ically, and wearing both his decorations, Napoleon reposed on a bed of straw on the platform, with the money at his side, neatly piled on a china dish from the farmhouse kitchen. The animals filed slowly past, and each gazed his fill. And Boxer put out his nose to sniff at the bank notes, and the flimsy white things stirred and rustled in his breath.

Three days later there was a terrible hullabaloo. Whymper, his face deadly pale, came racing up the path on his bicycle, flung it down in the yard and rushed straight into the farmhouse. The next moment a choking roar of rage sounded from Napoleon's apartments. The news of what had happened sped round the farm like wildfire. The bank notes were forgeries! Frederick had got the timber for nothing!

Napoleon called the animals together immediately and in a terrible voice pronounced the death sentence upon Frederick. When captured, he said, Frederick should be boiled alive. At the same time he warned them that after this treacherous deed the worst was to be expected. Frederick and his men might make their long-expected attack at any moment. Sentinels were placed at all the approaches to the farm. In addition, four pigeons were sent to Foxwood with a conciliatory message, which it was hoped might reestablish good relations with Pilkington.

The very next morning the attack came. The animals were at breakfast when the lookouts came racing in with the news that Frederick and his followers had already come through the five-barred gate. Boldly enough the animals sallied forth to meet them, but this time they did not have the easy victory that they had had in the Battle of the Cowshed. There were fifteen men, with half a dozen guns between them, and they opened fire as soon as they got within fifty yards. The animals could not face the terrible explosions and the stinging pellets, and in spite of the efforts of Napoleon and Boxer to rally them, they were soon driven back. A number of them were already wounded. They took refuge in the farm buildings and peeped cautiously out from chinks and knotholes. The whole of the big pasture, including the windmill, was in the hands of the enemy. For the moment even Napoleon seemed at a loss. He paced up and down without a word, his tail rigid and twitching. Wistful glances were sent in the direction of Foxwood. If Pilkington and his men would help them, the day might yet be won. But at this moment the four pigeons, who had been sent out on the day before, returned, one of them bearing a scrap of paper from Pilkington. On it was penciled the words: "Serves you right."

Meanwhile Frederick and his men had halted about the windmill. The animals watched them, and a murmur of dismay went round. Two of the men had produced a crowbar and a sledge hammer. They were going to knock the windmill down.

"Impossible!" cried Napoleon. "We have built the walls far too thick for that. They could not knock it down in a week. Courage, comrades!"

But Benjamin was watching the movements of the men intently. The two with the hammer and the crowbar were drilling a hole near the base of the windmill. Slowly, and with an air almost of amusement, Benjamin nodded his long muzzle.

"I thought so," he said. "Do you not see what they are doing? In another moment they are going to pack blasting powder into that hole."

Terrified, the animals waited. It was impossible now to venture out of the shelter of the buildings. After a few minutes the men were seen to be running in all directions. Then there was a deafening roar. The pigeons swirled into the air, and all the animals, except Napoleon, flung themselves flat on their bellies and hid their faces. When they got up again, a huge cloud of black smoke was hanging where the windmill had been. Slowly the breeze drifted it away. The windmill had ceased to exist!

At this sight the animals' courage returned to them. The fear and despair they had felt a moment earlier were drowned in their rage against this vile, contemptible act. A mighty cry for vengeance went up, and without waiting for further orders they charged forth in a body and made straight for the enemy. This time they did not heed the cruel pellets that swept over them like hail. It was a savage, bitter battle. The men fired again and again, and, when the animals got to close quarters, lashed out with their sticks and their heavy boots. A cow, three sheep, and two geese were killed, and nearly everyone was wounded. Even Napoleon, who was directing operations from the rear, had the tip of his tail chipped by a pellet. But the men did not go unscathed either. Three of them had their heads broken by blows from Boxer's hoofs; another was gored in the belly by a cow's horn; another had his trousers nearly torn off by Jessie and Bluebell. And when the nine dogs of Napoleon's own bodyguard, whom he had instructed to make a detour under cover of the hedge, suddenly appeared on the men's flank, baying ferociously, panic overtook them. They saw that they were in danger of being surrounded. Frederick shouted to his men to get out while the going was good, and the next moment the cowardly enemy was running for dear life. The animals

chased them right down to the bottom of the field and got in some last kicks at them as they forced their way through the thorn hedge.

They had won, but they were weary and bleeding. Slowly they began to limp back towards the farm. The sight of their dead comrades stretched upon the grass moved some of them to tears. And for a little while they halted in sorrowful silence at the place where the windmill had once stood. Yes, it was gone; almost the last trace of their labor was gone! Even the foundations were partially destroyed. And in rebuilding it they could not this time, as before, make use of the fallen stones. This time the stones had vanished too. The force of the explosion had flung them to distances of hundreds of yards. It was as though the windmill had never been.

As they approached the farm Squealer, who had unaccountably been absent during the fighting, came skipping towards them, whisking his tail and beaming with satisfaction. And the animals heard, from the direction of the farm buildings, the solemn booming of a gun.

"What is that gun firing for?" said Boxer.

"To celebrate our victory!" cried Squealer.

"What victory?" said Boxer. His knees were bleeding, he had lost a shoe and split his hoof, and a dozen pellets had lodged themselves in his hind leg.

"What victory, comrade? Have we not driven the enemy off our soil—the sacred soil of Animal Farm?"

"But they have destroyed the windmill. And we had worked on it for two years!"

"What matter? We will build another windmill. We will build six windmills if we feel like it. You do not appreciate, comrade, the mighty thing that we have done. The enemy was in occupation of this very ground that we stand upon. And now—thanks to the leadership of Comrade Napoleon—we have won every inch of it back again!"

"Then we have won back what we had before," said Boxer.

"That is our victory," said Squealer.

They limped into the yard. The pellets under the skin of Boxer's leg smarted painfully. He saw ahead of him the heavy labor of rebuilding the windmill from the foundations, and already in imagination he braced himself for the task. But for the first time it occurred to him that he was eleven years old and that perhaps his great muscles were not quite what they had once been.

But when the animals saw the green flag flying and heard the gun firing again—seven times it was fired in all—and heard the speech that Napoleon made, congratulating them on their conduct, it did seem to them after all that they had won a great victory. The animals slain in the battle were given a solemn funeral. Boxer and Clover pulled the wagon which served as a hearse, and Napoleon himself walked at the head of the procession. Two whole days were given over to celebrations. There were songs, speeches, and more firing of the gun, and a special gift of an apple was bestowed on every animal, with two ounces of corn for each bird and three biscuits for each dog. It was announced that the battle would be called the Battle of the Windmill and that Napoleon had created a new decoration, the Order of the Green Banner, which he had conferred upon himself. In the general rejoicings the unfortunate affair of the bank notes was forgotten.

It was a few days later than this that the pigs came upon a case of whiskey in the cellars of the farmhouse. It had been overlooked at the time when the house was first occupied. That night there came from the farmhouse the sound of loud singing, in which, to everyone's surprise, the strains of "Beasts of England" were mixed up. At about half-past nine Napoleon, wearing an old bowler hat of Mr. Jones's, was distinctly seen to emerge from the back door, gallop rapidly round the yard, and disappear indoors again. But in the morning a deep silence hung over the farmhouse. Not a pig appeared to be stirring. It was nearly nine o'clock when Squealer made his appearance, walking slowly and dejectedly, his eyes dull, his tail hanging limply behind him, and with every appearance of being seriously ill. He called the animals together and told them that he had a terrible piece of news to impart. Comrade Napoleon was dying!

A cry of lamentation went up. Straw was laid down outside the doors of the farmhouse, and the animals walked on tiptoe. With tears in their eyes they asked one another what they should do if their Leader was taken away from them. A rumor went round that Snowball had after all contrived to introduce poison into Napoleon's food. At eleven o'clock Squealer came out to make another announcement. As his last act upon earth, Comrade Napoleon had pronounced a solemn decree: the drinking of alcohol was to be punished by death.

By the evening, however, Napoleon appeared to be somewhat better, and the following morning Squealer was able to tell them that he was well on the way to recovery. By the evening of that day Napoleon was back at work, and on the next day it was learned that he had instructed Whymper to purchase in Willingdon some booklets on brewing and distilling. A week later Napoleon gave orders that the small paddock beyond the orchard, which it had previously been intended to set aside as a grazing ground for animals who were past work, was to be plowed up. It was given out that the pasture was exhausted and needed reseeding; but it soon became known that Napoleon intended to sow it with barley.

About this time there occurred a strange incident which hardly anyone was able to understand. One night at twelve o'clock there was a loud crash in the yard, and the animals rushed out of their stalls. It was a moonlit night. At the foot of the end wall of the big barn, where the Seven Commandments were written, there lay a ladder broken in two pieces. Squealer, temporarily stunned, was sprawling beside it, and near at hand there lay a lantern, a paintbrush, and an overturned pot of white paint. The dogs immediately made a ring round Squealer and escorted him back to the farmhouse as soon as he was able to walk. None of the animals could form any idea as to what this meant, except old Benjamin, who nodded his muzzle with a knowing air and seemed to understand, but would say nothing.

But a few days later Muriel, reading over the Seven Commandments to herself, noticed that there was yet another of them which the animals had remembered wrong. They had thought the Fifth Commandment was "No animal shall drink alcohol," but there were two words that they had forgotten. Actually the Commandment read: "No animal shall drink alcohol *to excess*."

IX

Boxer's split hoof was a long time in healing. They had started the rebuilding of the windmill the day after the victory celebrations were ended. Boxer refused to take even a day off work and made it a point of honor not to let it be seen that he was in pain. In the evenings he would admit privately to Clover that the hoof troubled him a great deal. Clover treated the hoof with poultices[1] of herbs which she prepared by chewing them, and both she and Benjamin urged Boxer to work less hard. "A horse's lungs do not last forever," she said to him. But Boxer would not listen. He had, he said, only one real ambition left—to see the windmill well under way before he reached the age for retirement.

At the beginning, when the laws of Animal Farm were first formulated, the retiring age had been fixed for horses and pigs at twelve, for cows at fourteen, for dogs at nine, for sheep at seven, and for hens and geese at five. Liberal old-age pensions had been agreed upon. As yet no animal had actually retired on pension, but of late the subject had been discussed more and more. Now that the small field beyond the orchard had been set aside for barley, it was rumored that a corner of the large pasture was to be fenced off and turned into a grazing ground for superannuated[2] animals. For a horse, it was said, the pension would be five pounds of corn a day and, in winter, fifteen pounds of hay, with a carrot or possibly an apple on public holidays. Boxer's twelfth birthday was due in the late summer of the following year.

Meanwhile life was hard. The winter was as cold as the last one had been, and food was even shorter. Once again all rations were reduced, except those of the pigs and the dogs. A too rigid equality in rations, Squealer explained, would have been contrary to the principles of Animalism. In any case he had no difficulty in proving to the other animals that they were *not* in reality short of food, whatever the appearances might be. For the time being, certainly, it had been found necessary to make a readjustment of rations (Squealer always spoke of it as a "readjustment," never as a "reduction"), but in comparison with the days of Jones, the improvement was enormous. Reading out the figures in a shrill, rapid voice, he proved to them in detail that they had more oats, more hay, more turnips than they had had in Jones's day, that they worked shorter hours, that their drinking water was of better quality, that they lived longer, that a larger proportion of their young ones survived infancy, and that they had more straw in their stalls and suffered less from fleas. The animals believed every word of it. Truth to tell, Jones and all he stood for had almost faded out of their memories. They knew that life nowadays was harsh and bare, that they were often hungry and often cold, and that they were usually working when they were not asleep. But doubtless it had been worse in the old days. They were glad to believe so. Besides, in those days they had been slaves and now they were free, and that made all the difference, as Squealer did not fail to point out.

There were many more mouths to feed now. In the autumn the four sows had all littered about simultaneously, producing thirty-one young pigs between them. The young pigs were piebald,[3] and as Napoleon was the only boar on the farm, it was possible to guess at their parentage. It was announced that later, when bricks and timber had been purchased, a schoolroom would be built in the farmhouse garden. For the time being, the young pigs were given their instruction by Napoleon himself in the farmhouse kitchen. They took their exercise in the garden and were discouraged from playing with the other young animals. About this time, too, it was laid down as a rule that when

---

1. **poultices** (pōl′tis·əz): hot, soft, moist dressings applied to a sore part of the body.
2. **superannuated** (soo′pər·an′yoo·wāt′id): too old for further work.

3. **piebald:** covered with patches of two different colors, usually black and white.

a pig and any other animal met on the path, the other animal must stand aside: and also that all pigs, of whatever degree, were to have the privilege of wearing green ribbons on their tails on Sundays.

The farm had had a fairly successful year but was still short of money. There were the bricks, sand, and lime for the schoolroom to be purchased, and it would also be necessary to begin saving up again for the machinery for the windmill. Then there were lamp oil and candles for the house, sugar for Napoleon's own table (he forbade this to the other pigs, on the ground that it made them fat), and all the usual replacements such as tools, nails, string, coal, wire, scrap iron, and dog biscuits. A stump of hay and part of the potato crop were sold off, and the contract for eggs was increased to six hundred a week, so that that year the hens barely hatched enough chicks to keep their numbers at the same level. Rations, reduced in December, were reduced again in February, and lanterns in the stalls were forbidden to save oil. But the pigs seemed comfortable enough and, in fact, were putting on weight if anything. One afternoon in late February a warm, rich, appetizing scent, such as the animals had never smelt before, wafted itself across the yard from the little brewhouse, which had been disused in Jones's time, and which stood beyond the kitchen. Someone said it was the smell of cooking barley. The animals sniffed the air hungrily and wondered whether a warm mash was being prepared for their supper. But no warm mash appeared, and on the following Sunday it was announced that from now onward all barley would be reserved for the pigs. The field beyond the orchard had already been sown with barley. And the news soon leaked out

that every pig was now receiving a ration of a pint of beer daily, with half a gallon for Napoleon himself, which was always served to him in the Crown Derby soup tureen.

But if there were hardships to be borne, they were partly offset by the fact that life nowadays had a greater dignity than it had had before. There were more songs, more speeches, more processions. Napoleon had commanded that once a week there should be held something called a Spontaneous Demonstration, the object of which was to celebrate the struggles and triumphs of Animal Farm. At the appointed time the animals would leave their work and march round the precincts of the farm in military formation, with the pigs leading, then the horses, then the cows, then the sheep, and then the poultry. The dogs flanked the procession and at the head of all marched Napoleon's black cockerel. Boxer and Clover always carried between them a green banner marked with the hoof and the horn and the caption, ''Long live Comrade Napoleon!'' Afterward there were recitations of poems composed in Napoleon's honor and a speech by Squealer giving particulars of the latest increases in the production of foodstuffs and on occasion a shot was fired from the gun. The sheep were the greatest devotees of the Spontaneous Demonstration, and if anyone complained (as a few animals sometimes did, when no pigs or dogs were near) that they wasted time and meant a lot of standing about in the cold, the sheep were sure to silence him with a tremendous bleating of ''Four legs good, two legs bad!'' But by and large the animals enjoyed these celebrations. They found it comforting to be reminded that, after all, they were truly their own masters and that the work they did was for their own benefit. So that, what with the songs, the processions, Squealer's lists of figures, the thunder of the gun, the crowing of the cockerel, and the fluttering of the flag, they were able to forget that their bellies were empty, at least part of the time.

In April, Animal Farm was proclaimed a Republic, and it became necessary to elect a President. There was only one candidate, Napoleon, who was elected unanimously. On the same day it was given out that fresh documents had been discovered which revealed further details about Snowball's complicity with Jones. It now appeared that Snowball had not, as the animals had previously imagined, merely attempted to lose the Battle of the Cowshed by means of a stratagem, but had been openly fighting on Jones's side. In fact, it was he who had actually been the leader of the human forces and had charged into battle with the words ''Long live Humanity!'' on his lips.

The wounds on Snowball's back, which a few of the animals still remembered to have seen, had been inflicted by Napoleon's teeth.

In the middle of the summer Moses the raven suddenly reappeared on the farm, after an absence of several years. He was quite unchanged, still did no work, and talked in the same strain as ever about Sugarcandy Mountain. He would perch on a stump, flap his black wings, and talk by the hour to anyone who would listen. "Up there, comrades," he would say solemnly, pointing to the sky with his large beak—"up there, just on the other side of that dark cloud that you can see—there it lies, Sugarcandy Mountain, that happy country where we poor animals shall rest forever from our labors!" He even claimed to have been there on one of his higher flights and to have seen the everlasting fields of clover and the linseed cake and lump sugar growing on the hedges. Many of the animals believed him. Their lives now, they reasoned, were hungry and laborious; was it not right and just that a better world should exist somewhere else? A thing that was difficult to determine was the attitude of the pigs towards

Moses. They all declared contemptuously that his stories about Sugarcandy Mountain were lies, and yet they allowed him to remain on the farm, not working, with an allowance of a gill[4] of beer a day.

After his hoof had healed up, Boxer worked harder than ever. Indeed, all animals worked like slaves that year. Apart from the regular work of the farm and the rebuilding of the windmill, there was the schoolhouse for the young pigs, which

---

4. **gill** (jil): a liquid measure, equal to ¼ pint.

was started in March. Sometimes the long hours on insufficient food were hard to bear, but Boxer never faltered. In nothing that he said or did was there any sign that his strength was not what it had been. It was only his appearance that was a little altered; his hide was less shiny than it had used to be, and his great haunches seemed to have shrunk. The others said, "Boxer will pick up when the spring grass comes on"; but the spring came and Boxer grew no fatter. Sometimes on the slope leading to the top of the quarry, when he braced his muscles against the weight of some vast boulder, it seemed that nothing kept him on his feet except the will to continue. At such times his lips were seen to form the words, "I will work harder"; he had no voice left. Once again Clover and Benjamin warned him to take care of his health, but Boxer paid no attention. His twelfth birthday was approaching. He did not care what happened so long as a good store of stone was accumulated before he went on pension.

Late one evening in the summer, a sudden rumor ran round the farm that something had happened to Boxer. He had gone out alone to drag a load of stone down to the windmill. And sure enough, the rumor was true. A few minutes later two pigeons came racing in with the news: "Boxer has fallen! He is lying on his side and can't get up!"

About half the animals on the farm rushed out to the knoll where the windmill stood. There lay Boxer, between the shafts of the cart, his neck stretched out, unable even to raise his head. His eyes were glazed, his sides matted with sweat. A thin stream of blood had trickled out of his mouth. Clover dropped to her knees at his side.

"Boxer!" she cried, "how are you?"

"It is my lung," said Boxer in a weak voice. "It does not matter. I think you will be able to finish the windmill without me. There is a pretty good store of stone accumulated. I had only another month to go in any case. To tell you the truth, I had been looking forward to my retirement. And perhaps, as Benjamin is growing old too, they will let him retire at the same time and be a companion to me."

"We must get help at once," said Clover. "Run, somebody, and tell Squealer what has happened."

All the other animals immediately raced back to the farmhouse to give Squealer the news. Only Clover remained, and Benjamin, who lay down at Boxer's side, and, without speaking, kept the flies off him with his long tail. After about a quarter of an hour Squealer appeared, full of sympathy and concern. He said that Comrade Napoleon had learned with the very deepest distress of this misfortune to one of the most loyal workers on the farm and was already making arrangements to send Boxer to be treated in the hospital at Willingdon. The animals felt a little uneasy at this. Except for Mollie and Snowball, no other animal had ever left the farm, and they did not like to think of their sick comrade in the hands of human beings. However, Squealer easily convinced them that the veterinary surgeon in Willingdon could treat Boxer's case more satisfactorily than could be done on the farm. And about half an hour later, when Boxer had somewhat recovered, he was with difficulty got on to his feet and managed to limp back to his stall, where Clover and Benjamin had prepared a good bed of straw for him.

For the next two days Boxer remained in his stall. The pigs had sent out a large bottle of pink medicine which they had found in the medicine chest in the bathroom, and Clover administered it to Boxer twice a day after meals. In the evenings she lay in his stall and talked to him, while Benjamin kept the flies off him. Boxer professed not to be sorry for what had happened. If he made a good recovery, he might expect to live another three years, and he looked forward to the peaceful days that he would spend in the corner of the big pasture. It would be the first time that he had had leisure to study and improve his mind. He intended, he said, to devote the rest of his life to learning the remaining twenty-two letters of the alphabet.

However, Benjamin and Clover could only be with Boxer after working hours, and it was in the middle of the day when the van came to take him away. The animals were all at work weeding turnips under the supervision of a pig, when they were astonished to see Benjamin come galloping from the direction of the farm buildings, braying at the top of his voice. It was the first time that they had ever seen Benjamin excited—indeed, it was the first time that anyone had ever seen him gallop. "Quick, quick!" he shouted. "Come at once! They're taking Boxer away!" Without waiting for orders from the pig, the animals broke off work and raced back to the farm buildings. Sure enough, there in the yard was a large closed van, drawn by two horses, with lettering on its side and a sly-looking man in a low-crowned bowler hat sitting on the driver's seat. And Boxer's stall was empty.

The animals crowded round the van. "Goodbye, Boxer!" they chorused, "goodbye!"

"Fools! Fools!" shouted Benjamin, prancing round them and stamping the earth with his small hoofs. "Fools! Do you not see what is written on the side of the van?"

That gave the animals pause, and there was a hush. Muriel began to spell out the words. But Benjamin pushed her aside and in the midst of a deadly silence he read:

"'Alfred Simmonds, Horse Slaughterer and Glue Boiler, Willingdon. Dealer in Hides and Bone Meal. Kennels Supplied.' Do you not understand what that means? They are taking Boxer to the knacker's!"

A cry of horror burst from all the animals. At this moment the man on the box whipped up his horses and the van moved out of the yard at a smart trot. All the animals followed, crying out at the tops of their voices. Clover forced her way to the front. The van began to gather speed. Clover tried to stir her stout limbs to a gallop and achieved a canter. "Boxer!" she cried. "Boxer! Boxer! Boxer!" And just at this moment, as though he had heard the uproar outside, Boxer's face, with the white stripe down his nose, appeared at the small window at the back of the van.

"Boxer!" cried Clover in a terrible voice. "Boxer! Get out! Get out quickly! They're taking you to your death!"

All the animals took up the cry of "Get out, Boxer, get out!" But the van was already gathering speed and drawing away from them. It was uncertain whether Boxer had understood what Clover had said. But a moment later his face disappeared from the window and there was the sound of a tremendous drumming of hoofs inside the van. He was trying to kick his way out. The time had been when a few kicks from Boxer's hoofs would have smashed the van to matchwood. But alas! his strength had left him; and in a few moments the sound of drumming hoofs grew fainter and died away. In desperation the animals began appealing to the two horses which drew the van to stop. "Comrades, comrades!" they shouted. "Don't take your own brother to his death!" But the stupid brutes, too ignorant to realize what was happening, merely set back their ears and quickened their pace. Boxer's face did not reappear at the window. Too late, someone thought of racing ahead and shutting the five-barred gate; but in another moment the van was through it and rapidly disappearing down the road. Boxer was never seen again.

Three days later it was announced that he had died in the hospital at Willingdon, in spite of receiving every attention a horse could have. Squealer came to announce the news to the others. He had, he said, been present during Boxer's last hours.

"It was the most affecting sight I have ever seen!" said Squealer, lifting his trotter and wiping away a tear. "I was at his bedside at the very last. And at the end, almost too weak to speak, he whispered in my ear that his sole sorrow was to have passed on before the windmill was finished. 'Forward, comrades!' he whispered. 'Forward in the name of the Rebellion. Long live Animal Farm! Long live Comrade Napoleon! Napoleon is always right.' Those were his very last words, comrades."

Here Squealer's demeanor suddenly changed. He fell silent for a moment, and his little eyes darted suspicious glances from side to side before he proceeded.

It had come to his knowledge, he said, that a foolish and wicked rumor had been circulated at the time of Boxer's removal. Some of the animals had noticed that the van which took Boxer away was marked "Horse Slaughterer" and had actually jumped to the conclusion that Boxer was being sent to the knacker's. It was almost unbelievable, said Squealer, that any animal could be so stupid. Surely, he cried indignantly, whisking his tail and skipping from side to side, surely they knew their beloved Leader, Comrade Napoleon,

better than that? But the explanation was really very simple. The van had previously been the property of the knacker and had been bought by the veterinary surgeon, who had not yet painted the old name out. That was how the mistake had arisen.

The animals were enormously relieved to hear this. And when Squealer went on to give further graphic details of Boxer's deathbed, the admirable care he had received and the expensive medicines for which Napoleon had paid without a thought as to the cost, their last doubts disappeared and the sorrow that they felt for their comrade's death was tempered by the thought that at least he had died happy.

Napoleon himself appeared at the meeting on the following Sunday morning and pronounced a short oration in Boxer's honor. It had not been possible, he said, to bring back their lamented comrade's remains for interment[5] on the farm, but he had ordered a large wreath to be made from the laurels in the farmhouse garden and sent down to be placed on Boxer's grave. And in a few day's time the pigs intended to hold a memorial banquet in Boxer's honor. Napoleon ended his speech with a reminder of Boxer's two favorite maxims, "I will work harder" and "Comrade Napoleon is always right"—maxims, he said, which every animal would do well to adopt as his own.

On the day appointed for the banquet, a grocer's van drove up from Willingdon and delivered a large wooden crate at the farmhouse. That night there was the sound of uproarious singing, which was followed by what sounded like a violent quarrel and ended at about eleven o'clock with a tremendous crash of glass. No one stirred in the farmhouse before noon on the following day, and the word went round that from somewhere or other the pigs had acquired the money to buy themselves another case of whiskey.

---

5. **interment:** burial.

Responding to the Novel

Analyzing the Novel

Identifying Facts

1. Explain how Squealer manages to convince the animals that each of the following is true:
   a. The Sixth Commandment has not been violated by the slaughter in the barnyard of the animals who confessed to crimes. (Page 840)
   b. The Battle of the Windmill was actually a victory for the animals. (Page 843)
   c. The animals are better off than they were in the days under Farmer Jones before the Rebellion. (Page 845)
2. Name at least four ways in which the pigs' lives are different from those of the other animals on the farm. In what ways has the pigs' behavior come to resemble human behavior?
3. Summarize what happens during the long-negotiated sale of the timber to Mr. Frederick. How does Frederick double-cross Napoleon?
4. Explain how Boxer is betrayed by the pigs. What happens to his body?
5. What is Napoleon's **motive** for betraying Boxer?

Interpreting Meanings

6. When Napoleon thinks he is dying, what is really the matter with him?

7. Why is it **ironic** that the pigs begin to wear green ribbons in their tails?
8. How does the rewriting of history concerning Snowball grow increasingly ridiculous? What change do you detect in the animals' reaction to each new revision of the "facts"?
9. Why do you suppose the pigs encourage Moses the raven to remain on Animal Farm? How might the animals' belief in Sugarcandy Mountain be in the pigs' best interest? Are there parallels to the idea of "Sugarcandy Mountain" in real life?
10. How does Boxer's death **ironically** fulfill old Major's prophecy on page 812?
11. How did you feel as you read about Boxer's illness and death?
12. Reread Squealer's description of Boxer's death (page 849). Why do you suppose the animals go on believing everything that the pigs tell them? At this point in the novel, how do you feel about the animals' gullibility and the pigs' manipulations? Explain your response.
13. Compare and contrast "Beasts of England" with the poem "Comrade Napoleon." Is one a better work of literature, in your opinion?
14. What ending do you predict for the story? What ending would you *like* to find in the next chapter? Does everyone in class agree?

X

Years passed. The seasons came and went, the short animal lives fled by. A time came when there was no one who remembered the old days before the Rebellion, except Clover, Benjamin, Moses the raven, and a number of the pigs.

Muriel was dead; Bluebell, Jessie, and Pincher were dead. Jones too was dead—he had died in an inebriates'[1] home in another part of the country. Snowball was forgotten. Boxer was forgotten, except by the few who had known him. Clover was an old stout mare now, stiff in the joints and with a tendency to rheumy eyes. She was two years past the retiring age, but in fact no animal had ever actually retired. The talk of setting aside a corner of the pasture for superannuated animals had long since been dropped. Napoleon was now a mature boar of twenty-four stone. Squealer was so fat that he could with difficulty see out of his eyes. Only old Benjamin was much the same as ever, except for being a little grayer about the muzzle, and, since Boxer's death, more morose and taciturn[2] than ever.

There were many more creatures on the farm now, though the increase was not so great as had been expected in earlier years. Many animals had been born to whom the Rebellion was only a dim tradition, passed on by word of mouth, and others had been bought who had never heard mention of such a thing before their arrival. The farm possessed three horses now besides Clover. They were fine upstanding beasts, willing workers and good comrades, but very stupid. None of them proved able to learn the alphabet beyond the letter B. They accepted everything that they were told about the Rebellion and the principles of Animalism, especially from Clover, for whom they had an almost filial[3] respect; but it was doubtful whether they understood very much of it.

The farm was more prosperous now and better organized: it had even been enlarged by two fields which had been bought from Mr. Pilkington. The windmill had been successfully completed at last, and the farm possessed a threshing machine and a hay elevator of its own, and various new buildings had been added to it. Whymper had bought himself a dogcart. The windmill, however, had not after all been used for generating electrical power.

It was used for milling corn and brought in a handsome money profit. The animals were hard at work building yet another windmill; when that one was finished, so it was said, the dynamos would be installed. But the luxuries of which Snowball had once taught the animals to dream, the stalls with electric light and hot and cold water, and the three-day week, were no longer talked about. Napoleon had denounced such ideas as contrary to the spirit of Animalism. The truest happiness, he said, lay in working hard and living frugally.

Somehow it seemed as though the farm had grown richer without making the animals themselves any richer—except, of course, for the pigs and the dogs. Perhaps this was partly because there were so many pigs and so many dogs. It was not that these creatures did not work, after their fashion. There was, as Squealer was never tired of explaining, endless work in the supervision and organization of the farm. Much of this work was of a kind that the other animals were too ignorant to understand. For example, Squealer told them that the pigs had to expend enormous labors every day upon mysterious things called "files," "reports," "minutes," and "memoranda." These were large sheets of paper which had to be closely covered with writing, and as soon as they were so covered, they were burnt in the furnace. This was of the highest importance for the welfare of the farm, Squealer said. But still, neither pigs nor dogs produced any food by their own labor; and there were very many of them, and their appetites were always good.

As for the others, their life, so far as they knew, was as it had always been. They were generally hungry, they slept on straw, they drank from the pool, they labored in the fields; in winter they were troubled by the cold, and in summer by the flies. Sometimes the older ones among them racked their dim memories and tried to determine whether in the early days of the Rebellion, when Jones's expulsion was still recent, things had been better or worse than now. They could not remember. There was nothing with which they could compare their present lives: they had nothing to go upon except Squealer's lists of figures, which invariably demonstrated that everything was getting better and better. The animals found the problem insoluble; in any case, they had little time for speculating on such things now. Only old Benjamin professed to remember every detail of his long life and to know that things never had been nor ever could be much better or much worse—hunger, hardship, and disappointment being, so he said, the unalterable law of life.

And yet the animals never gave up hope. More,

---

1. **inebriates** (in·ē′ brē·its): drunkards.
2. **taciturn** (tas′ ə·turn′): silent; uncommunicative.
3. **filial** (fil′ ē·əl): appropriate to a son or daughter.

they never lost, even for an instant, their sense of honor and privilege in being members of Animal Farm. They were still the only farm in the whole county—in all England—owned and operated by animals. Not one of them, not even the youngest, not even the newcomers who had been brought from farms ten or twenty miles away, ever ceased to marvel at that. And when they heard the gun booming and saw the green flag fluttering at the masthead, their hearts swelled with imperishable pride, and the talk turned always toward the old heroic days, the expulsion of Jones, the writing of the Seven Commandments, the great battles in which the human invaders had been defeated. None of the old dreams had been abandoned. The Republic of the Animals which Major had foretold, when the green fields of England should be untrodden by human feet, was still believed in. Some day it was coming: it might not be soon, it might not be within the lifetime of any animal now living, but still it was coming. Even the tune "Beasts of England" was perhaps hummed secretly here and there: at any rate, it was a fact that every animal on the farm knew it, though no one would have dared to sing it aloud. It might be that their lives were hard and that not all of their hopes had been fulfilled; but they were conscious that they were not as other animals. If they went hungry, it was not from feeding tyrannical human beings; if they worked hard, at least they worked for themselves. No creature among them went upon two legs. No creature called any other creature "Master." All animals were equal.

One day in early summer Squealer ordered the sheep to follow him and led them out to a piece of waste ground at the other end of the farm, which had become overgrown with birch saplings. The sheep spent the whole day there browsing at the leaves under Squealer's supervision. In the evening he returned to the farmhouse himself, but as it was warm weather, told the sheep to stay where they were. It ended by their remaining there for a whole week, during which time the other animals saw nothing of them. Squealer was with them for the greater part of every day. He was, he said, teaching them to sing a new song, for which privacy was needed.

It was just after the sheep had returned, on a pleasant evening when the animals had finished work and were making their way back to the farm buildings, that the terrified neighing of a horse sounded from the yard. Startled, the animals stopped in their tracks. It was Clover's voice. She neighed again, and all the animals broke into a gallop and rushed into the yard. Then they saw what Clover had seen.

It was a pig walking on his hind legs.

Yes, it was Squealer. A little awkwardly, as though not quite used to supporting his considerable bulk in that position, but with perfect balance, he was strolling across the yard. And a moment later, out from the door of the farmhouse came a long file of pigs, all walking on their hind legs. Some did it better than others, one or two were even a trifle unsteady and looked as though they would have liked the support of a stick, but every one of them made his way right round the

yard successfully. And finally there was a tremendous baying of dogs and a shrill crowing from the black cockerel, and out came Napoleon himself, majestically upright, casting haughty glances from side to side, and with his dogs gamboling round him.

He carried a whip in his trotter.

There was a deadly silence. Amazed, terrified, huddling together, the animals watched the long line of pigs march slowly round the yard. It was as though the world had turned upside down. Then there came a moment when the first shock had worn off and when, in spite of everything—in spite of their terror of the dogs and of the habit, developed through long years, of never complaining, never criticizing no matter what happened—they might have uttered some word of protest. But just at that moment, as though at a signal, all the sheep burst out into a tremendous bleating of—

"Four legs good, two legs *better!* Four legs good, two legs *better!* Four legs good, two legs *better!*"

It went on for five minutes without stopping. And by the time the sheep had quieted down, the chance to utter any protest had passed, for the pigs had marched back into the farmhouse.

Benjamin felt a nose nuzzling at his shoulder. He looked round. It was Clover. Her old eyes looked dimmer than ever. Without saying anything, she tugged gently at his mane and led him round to the end of the big barn, where the Seven Commandments were written. For a minute or two they stood gazing at the tarred wall with its white lettering.

"My sight is failing," she said finally. "Even when I was young I could not have read what was written there. But it appears to me that that wall looks different. Are the Seven Commandments the same as they used to be, Benjamin?"

For once Benjamin consented to break his rule, and he read out to her what was written on the wall. There was nothing there now except a single Commandment. It ran:

ALL ANIMALS ARE EQUAL
BUT SOME ANIMALS ARE MORE EQUAL THAN OTHERS

After that it did not seem strange when next day the pigs who were supervising the work of the farm all carried whips in their trotters. It did not seem strange to learn that the pigs had bought themselves a wireless set, were arranging to install a telephone, and had taken out subscriptions to *John Bull, Tit-Bits,* and the *Daily Mirror.* It did not seem strange when Napoleon was seen strolling in the farmhouse garden with a pipe in his mouth—no, not even when the pigs took Mr. Jones's clothes out of the wardrobes and put them on, Napoleon himself appearing in a black coat, ratcatcher breeches, and leather leggings, while his favorite sow appeared in the watered silk dress which Mrs. Jones had been used to wear on Sundays.

A week later, in the afternoon, a number of dogcarts drove up to the farm. A deputation of neighboring farmers had been invited to make a tour of inspection. They were shown all over the farm and expressed great admiration for everything they saw, especially the windmill. The animals were weeding the turnip field. They worked diligently, hardly raising their faces from the ground and not knowing whether to be more frightened of the pigs or of the human visitors.

That evening loud laughter and bursts of singing came from the farmhouse. And suddenly, at the sound of the mingled voices, the animals were stricken with curiosity. What could be happening in there, now that for the first time animals and human beings were meeting on terms of equality? With one accord they began to creep as quietly as possible into the farmhouse garden.

At the gate they paused, half frightened to go on, but Clover led the way in. They tiptoed up to the house, and such animals as were tall enough peered in at the dining-room window. There,

round the long table, sat half a dozen farmers and half a dozen of the more eminent pigs, Napoleon himself occupying the seat of honor at the head of the table. The pigs appeared completely at ease in their chairs. The company had been enjoying a game of cards, but had broken off for the moment, evidently in order to drink a toast. A large jug was circulating, and the mugs were being refilled with beer. No one noticed the wondering faces of the animals that gazed in at the window.

Mr. Pilkington, of Foxwood, had stood up, his mug in his hand. In a moment, he said, he would ask the present company to drink a toast. But before doing so, there were a few words that he felt it incumbent upon him to say.

It was a source of great satisfaction to him, he said—and, he was sure, to all others present—to feel that a long period of mistrust and misunderstanding had now come to an end. There had been a time—not that he, or any of the present company, had shared such sentiments—but there had been a time when the respected proprietors of Animal Farm had been regarded, he would not say with hostility, but perhaps with a certain measure of misgiving, by their human neighbors. Unfortunate incidents had occurred, mistaken ideas had been current. It had been felt that the existence of a farm owned and operated by pigs was somehow abnormal and was liable to have an unsettling effect in the neighborhood. Too many farmers had assumed, without due enquiry, that on such a farm a spirit of license and indiscipline would prevail. They had been nervous about the effects upon their own animals, or even upon their human employees. But all such doubts were now dispelled. Today he and his friends had visited Animal Farm and inspected every inch of it with their own eyes, and what did they find? Not only the most up-to-date methods, but a discipline and an orderliness which should be an example to all farmers everywhere. He believed that he was right in saying that the lower animals on Animal Farm did more work and received less food than any animals in the county. Indeed, he and his fellow visitors today had observed many features which they intended to introduce on their own farms immediately.

He would end his remarks, he said, by emphasizing once again the friendly feelings that subsisted, and ought to subsist, between Animal Farm and its neighbors. Between pigs and human beings there was not, and there need not be, any clash of interests whatever. Their struggles and their difficulties were one. Was not the labor problem the same everywhere? Here it became apparent that Mr. Pilkington was about to spring some carefully prepared witticism on the company, but for a moment he was too overcome by amusement to be able to utter it. After much choking, during which his various chins turned purple, he managed to get it out: "If you have your lower animals to contend with," he said, "we have our lower classes!" This *bon mot*[4] set the table in a roar; and Mr. Pilkington once again congratulated the pigs on the low rations, the long working hours, and the general absence of pampering which he had observed on Animal Farm.

And now, he said finally, he would ask the company to rise to their feet and make certain that their glasses were full. "Gentlemen," concluded Mr. Pilkington, "gentlemen, I give you a toast: To the prosperity of Animal Farm!"

There was enthusiastic cheering and stamping of feet. Napoleon was so gratified that he left his place and came round the table to clink his mug against Mr. Pilkington's before emptying it. When the cheering had died down, Napoleon, who had remained on his feet, intimated that he too had a few words to say.

Like all of Napoleon's speeches, it was short and to the point. He too, he said, was happy that the period of misunderstanding was at an end. For a long time there had been rumors—circulated, he had reason to think, by some malignant enemy— that there was something subversive and even revolutionary in the outlook of himself and his colleagues. They had been credited with attempting to stir up rebellion among the animals on neighboring farms. Nothing could be further from the truth! Their sole wish, now and in the past, was to live at peace and in normal business relations with their neighbors. This farm which he had the honor to control, he added, was a cooperative enterprise. The title deeds, which were in his own possession, were owned by the pigs jointly.

He did not believe, he said, that any of the old suspicions still lingered, but certain changes had been made recently in the routine of the farm which should have the effect of promoting confidence still further. Hitherto the animals on the farm had had a rather foolish custom of addressing one another as "Comrade." This was to be suppressed. There had also been a very strange custom, whose origin was unknown, of marching every Sunday morning past a boar's skull which was nailed to a post in the garden. This, too, would be suppressed, and the skull had already been buried. His visitors might have observed, too, the green flag which flew from the masthead. If so, they would perhaps have noted that the white hoof and horn with which it had previously been marked had now been removed. It would be a plain green flag from now onward.

He had only one criticism, he said, to make of Mr. Pilkington's excellent and neighborly speech. Mr. Pilkington had referred throughout to "Animal Farm." He could not of course know—for he, Napoleon, was only now for the first time announcing it—that the name "Animal Farm" had been abolished. Henceforward the farm was to be known as "The Manor Farm"—which, he believed, was its correct and original name.

"Gentlemen," concluded Napoleon, "I will give you the same toast as before, but in a different form. Fill your glasses to the brim. Gentlemen, here is my toast: To the prosperity of The Manor Farm!"

There was the same hearty cheering as before, and the mugs were emptied to the dregs. But as the animals outside gazed at the scene, it seemed to them that some strange thing was happening. What was it that had altered in the faces of the pigs? Clover's old dim eyes flitted from one face to another. Some of them had five chins, some had four, some had three. But what was it that seemed to be melting and changing? Then, the applause having come to an end, the company took up their cards and continued the game that had been interrupted, and the animals crept silently away.

But they had not gone twenty yards when they stopped short. An uproar of voices was coming from the farmhouse. They rushed back and looked through the window again. Yes, a violent quarrel was in progress. There were shoutings, bangings on the table, sharp suspicious glances, furious denials. The source of the trouble appeared to be that Napoleon and Mr. Pilkington had each played an ace of spades simultaneously.

Twelve voices were shouting in anger, and they were all alike. No question, now, what had happened to the faces of the pigs. The creatures outside looked from pig to man, and from man to pig, and from pig to man again; but already it was impossible to say which was which.

---

4. **bon mot** (bōn mō): (French) a witty or clever remark.

Responding to the Novel

Analyzing the Novel

Identifying Facts

1. Even though the animals have finished building the windmill, why don't they have the promised comforts (less work, hot and cold water, light, and heat in every stall) that electricity was supposed to bring them? How does Napoleon explain this change in plans?

2. Contrast the pigs' daily lives with the lives of the other animals on the farm. According to Napoleon, which animals achieve the "truest happiness"?

3. What event turns the animals' world "upside down"? Explain why Squealer had to teach the sheep a new song before this event could take place.

4. Throughout the novel, the pigs change the Seven Commandments to suit their purposes. How do they further modify the commandments in this chapter?

5. At the banquet with the farmers, what does Pilkington admire about Animal Farm? In his toast, what lies does Napoleon tell, and what changes does he announce?

Interpreting Meanings

6. What details in this chapter **satirize,** or ridicule, the work done by bureaucrats?

7. Why does the farm grow richer without making the majority of the animals any richer?

8. Reread the description of the animals' joyous behavior immediately following the Rebellion (page 815). Why is it **ironic** that the pigs begin carrying whips?

9. How do you think the final saying on the barn wall ("All animals are equal, but some animals are more equal than others") relates to the novel's **theme,** or central meaning?

10. Of all the changes that Napoleon announces at the banquet, which would you say is the most significant? Why?

11. In the last scene, what **transformation,** or change, do the animals witness as they peer through the farmhouse windows? How does this transformation express the novel's central **irony**?

12. Reread the passage on page 852 that begins: "None of the old dreams had been abandoned . . . ." Do you think the animals' continuing belief in the coming of the Republic shows that they have not been duped by the pigs after all? Or does it prove instead how truly gullible they are? Explain.

13. Did you find the novel's **resolution** satisfying? Or did you expect or want a different ending? Explain your response.

The Novel as a Whole

1. Briefly summarize the **plot** of Animal Farm. Then tell where you think the plot's **climax** occurs. (Keep in mind that the climax is the moment in the plot, usually toward the end, when our emotional involvement is the greatest.)

2. Identify as many important **conflicts** in the novel as you can. (You should be able to find at least three.) How are each of these conflicts **resolved** by the novel's end? Or are they resolved? Which conflict were you most interested in?

3. Who would you say is the novel's **main character**? (Or does a group function as the main character?) Are any characters **dynamic characters** who undergo some change or development during the course of the novel? Or are they all **static characters** who remain essentially the same throughout the novel? Did you identify or sympathize with any particular characters? Why?

4. Napoleon is clearly an evil villain. Does the novel have a real **hero** or **heroine**? Explain your answer.

5. On every page of Animal Farm, we see outrageous examples of the animals' gullibility. We watch in amazement—and sometimes horror—as the pigs take advantage of this gullibility to betray every ideal of the Rebellion. Although there are occasional faint murmurs of protest, the animals never rise up against the pigs. What point do you think Orwell is making about *human* behavior in the face of tyranny? Do you agree with his point? Do you think it is the **theme** of the novel?

6. Who or what do you think Orwell is **satirizing** in Animal Farm? Satire's intention is to improve society in some way. How do you think Orwell

wants the world to improve? Do you agree with Orwell, or do you have different ideas?

7. In your opinion, why do the pigs betray the ideals of the Rebellion? Could this betrayal have been prevented? (If so, which animal or animals might have stood up to the pigs, and why does each one fail to do so?)

8. Discuss how each of the following quotations relates to *Animal Farm.* Tell whether you think Orwell would agree with each idea. What do you think of each of them?

> **a.** "Those who cannot remember the past are condemned to repeat it."
> —George Santayana
>
> **b.** "Power tends to corrupt and absolute power corrupts absolutely."
> —Lord Acton
>
> **c.** "What experience and history teach is this—that people and governments never have learned anything from history, or acted on principles deduced from it."
> —G. W. F. Hegel
>
> **d.** "In general, the art of government consists in taking as much money as possible from one class of people to give to the other."
> —Voltaire
>
> **e.** "If this is the best of all possible worlds, what then are the others?"
> —Voltaire

9. One publisher who rejected the manuscript of *Animal Farm* wanted Orwell to change the leaders to some animal other than pigs. Why do you think Orwell called this an "imbecile suggestion"? Do you agree with Orwell, or the publisher?

Writing About the Novel

A Creative Response

1. **Writing a New Ending.** Write an eleventh chapter for *Animal Farm.* Tell what happens the day after—or the year after—the final farmhouse scene in Chapter X.

2. **Extending the Story.** What became of Snowball? Write a brief story telling what happened to Snowball after his expulsion from Animal Farm. Did he try to come back? Did he try to organize a Rebellion on another farm? You may invent your story completely, or base your account on facts about the historical figure you think Snowball is based on. (See item 4 below.)

3. **Using Another Point of View.** Select an incident from the novel and let one of the animals tell us about it, using the first-person pronoun, "I."

A Critical Response

4. **Analyzing the Allegory.** One of the novel's first reviewers called it "a brief barnyard history of the Russian Revolution from October [1917] to just beyond the Stalin-Hitler pact." Use a good encyclopedia to find out about Lenin, Stalin, Trotsky, and events in Russia from 1917 to about 1939. Then write a brief essay in which you identify parallels between the characters and plot of *Animal Farm* and actual historical figures and events.

5. **Responding to a Different Ending.** When an animated cartoon was made of *Animal Farm,* it was given a different ending. Here is how one critic responded to the new ending:

> The film version gives *Animal Farm* a happy ending. The animals all the world over, hearing how Napoleon has betrayed the animal cause, rise up against him at the end and in a second revolution expel him. After this second revolution, we are left to believe, a rule of freedom and equality is established and survives. But of course this ending makes nonsense of [Orwell's] whole thesis.
> —Christopher Hollis

In a paragraph or two, tell what you think of the happy ending in the movie version of *Animal Farm.* Do you think this ending could possibly happen; or is it, as Hollis says, nonsensical? Why do you think Orwell decided *not* to end the story happily? Explain your response to this different ending.

6. **Analyzing a Character.** Throughout *Animal Farm* Benjamin expresses a cynical, pessimistic philosophy of life which sets him apart from the other animals. Look back through Chapters II through X (paying particular attention to Chapter X), and write down everything Benjamin says, thinks, or does. Organize this information into two columns, as in the following chart:

Situation or event	Benjamin's response
1. Reading	1. Could read as well as any pig but never did; said there was nothing worth reading (page 819).
2. etc.	2. etc.

Based on this information, summarize Benjamin's philosophy of life, as you interpret it. At the end of your essay, explain whether or not you think Benjamin's philosophy reflects Orwell's own view of life. Or does Orwell see a better approach to life's problems?

7. **Analyzing and Evaluating a Theme.** For help with this assignment, see page 858.

Analyzing Language and Vocabulary

Euphemisms and the Misuse of Language

The word *euphemism* (yo͞o′fə·miz′m) comes from an ancient Greek word meaning "to speak a good sound or good omen." A **euphemism** is an agreeable, inoffensive way of expressing an idea that some people consider unpleasant. For example, you are using a euphemism if you say that someone has "passed away" (instead of "died") or that a person is "between jobs" (instead of "unemployed").

See if you can match the plain, straightforward word or phrase on the left with its euphemism on the right. (These euphemisms have all actually been used.)

1. killing
2. combat
3. lies
4. layoffs
5. an airline crash
6. refugee camps

a. "eliminating redundancies in the human resources area"
b. "a controlled flight into terrain"
c. "disinformation"
d. "violence processing"
e. "new life hamlets"
f. "unlawful or arbitrary deprivation of life"

What euphemism does Squealer use at the beginning of Chapter IX? What "unpleasantness" is it designed to mask?

The dividing line between euphemisms and lies is often fuzzy. Both are misuses of language because they mask or undermine the truth. Why is it a misuse of language to:

1. Describe the Battle of the Windmill as a "victory" for Animal Farm?
2. Say that the animals' way of life had a "greater dignity" than it had had before?
3. Call the animals' weekly march a "Spontaneous Demonstration"?
4. Proclaim Animal Farm a "republic"?

Which of these statements do you think are *not* euphemisms, but are downright lies?

ANALYZING AND EVALUATING A THEME

Writing Assignment

Write a five-paragraph essay in which you analyze the **theme** in *Animal Farm.* At the end of the essay, explain how you responded to Orwell's theme.

Background

Analysis is used whenever you look very closely at the elements (or the smaller parts) that make up a whole work. When you analyze a novel, for example, you look closely at the elements of plot, character, theme, setting, and point of view. You try to understand how all these elements work together to create the story's meaning.

Evaluation involves making a value judgment. In an evaluation, you state whether a work is, in your opinion, well written or poorly written, whether it is believable or not believable, whether it hooked your interest or left you cold. The most important part of an evaluation is giving **reasons** and **evidence** from the novel to back up your opinion.

Prewriting

1. **Asking yourself questions.** First, write out your answers to the questions that follow. Your answers will serve as prewriting notes for your essay.

   a. **Thinking about Theme.** Look at the themes listed on page 809. Which one is most interesting to you?

   b. **Stating a Theme.** In at least one sentence, explain the insight about human nature that you think is revealed by all the events in the novel. Does the novel point to situations that should be changed in a particular society, or does it apply to people everywhere?

   c. **Explaining How Theme Is Revealed.** Summarize the key events in the plot that develop and reveal the theme.

   d. **Direct Statements of Theme.** Is this theme stated directly in any passages in the novel— either by the narrator or by a character? Note these passages that state the theme directly.

   e. **Evaluating the Theme.** Fill out a chart like the following to evaluate Orwell's theme as you have stated it.

Theme evaluation	Answers	Details from novel and page references
1. Do you agree with the theme, or disagree with it or parts of it? Explain.		
2. Is the theme still relevant today? Explain why or why not.		
3. Was the theme easy to spot, or was it too obscure?		

2. **Evaluating your data.** Now look over your prewriting notes, and decide exactly what you are going to cover in your essay. If you have gathered too much information to include in a five-paragraph essay, decide which information is most important. Put an asterisk beside the information in your notes that you'll use in your essay.

3. **Organize your ideas.** The best way to do this is to make an outline. The following outline was written for an essay that analyzes the character of Squealer and his function in the novel.

> I. Introductory paragraph (what Squealer is like; how he uses mind control and deception; brilliant talker; shifty, cowardly, dishonest)

II. Body of essay
   A. Squealer's propaganda techniques
      1. Analysis of one of his "explanations"
         (a) Appeals to authority
         (b) Claims unselfish motives
         (c) Plays on animals' fears
      2. His outright lies—Boxer's death
   B. How Squealer rewrites history
      1. Revises Seven Commandments
      2. Denies that what happened ever happened
         (a) Resolution against trade with people
         (b) Snowball's part in Battle of the Cowshed
      3. How all this emphasizes the importance of written records of the past
   C. Squealer's use of statistics
      1. Statistics as a valid device in logical argument
      2. Use of false statistics

III. Concluding paragraph (my response to Squealer's character and arguments; what I learned about propaganda devices and techniques)

Writing

Begin your essay with an introductory paragraph that contains your **thesis statement,** a general statement that sums up your essay's main idea. The outline you've just read is based on this simple thesis statement:

> Squealer is an unlikeable character who uses mind control and deception to consolidate the pigs' power.

An introductory paragraph and a closing paragraph should discuss this main idea. The three paragraphs in the middle of the essay (the body) should give specific details from the story to support your main idea.

The following essay, developed from the outline, discusses Squealer's role in the novel.

The Character of Squealer

Squealer is an unlikeable character who uses mind control and deception to consolidate the pigs' power. Orwell introduces Squealer as a round-cheeked, twinkling-eyed young porker—a brilliant talker who can turn black into white. When Squealer gets excited in an argument, he skips from side to side, and it is this "shiftiness" in his character that Orwell develops in the novel.

Squealer functions on the farm as Chief Propagandist. It is his job to "explain" unpleasant events to the other animals. Squealer's first job is to explain to the other animals why the pigs take all the milk and apples for themselves. Most pigs, he says, do not even like milk and apples. They eat them for the other animals' well-being (unselfish motives). Squealer claims that Science (appeal to authority) has proved that milk and apples

States the thesis.

Describes character's appearance.

Mentions a major character trait.

Analyzes Squealer's propaganda techniques.

are absolutely essential to the pigs' health and that the animals need the pigs to manage the farm (appeal to self-interest). Lastly, he warns that if the pigs do not get the milk and apples, Jones may come back (plays on animals' fears). Later in the novel, Squealer brilliantly displays his powers of persuasion in explaining why Napoleon chases Snowball off the farm and why Napoleon changes his mind about building the windmill. By the middle of the novel, Squealer abandons propaganda techniques and turns to outright lies, as in his explanation of Boxer's death.

Gives other examples of Squealer's techniques.

One of Squealer's most terrifying techniques is convincing the animals that they remember the past incorrectly. We see this first in his rewording of the Seven Commandments. Later, when Napoleon decides to trade with humans, Squealer convinces the animals that there was never a resolution prohibiting such trade. "Are you certain that this is not something that you have dreamed, comrades? Have you any record of such a resolution? Is it written down anywhere?" (See page 831.) Similarly, Squealer keeps "revising" Snowball's actions at the Battle of the Cowshed until he turns Snowball-the-Great-Hero into Snowball-the-Terrible-Villain. I think Orwell is telling us here that if we don't have written records, we will forget or distort what actually happened in the past.

Shows how Squealer rewrites history.

Example 1.

Example 2.

Example 3.

Finally, Squealer overwhelms the animals with statistics. Though the animals are hungry and miserable, he reads them long lists of figures that prove how well off they are. All of his statistics are lies.

Shows how Squealer uses statistics.

I disliked Squealer for what he does to the other animals, and I despised him as a character, though I think he was very realistic. I really enjoyed analyzing Squealer's arguments because I learned a lot about propaganda devices. The character of Squealer made me aware of how one person can use language to manipulate other people. I think there are Squealers all over the place.

Gives response to character.

WRITING ABOUT LITERATURE

Writing Answers to Essay Questions

The following strategies will help you organize and write your answers to the essay questions that follow each selection in this book. Step-by-step instruction in the writing process may also be found in the Exercises in Critical Thinking and Writing. See the list of these exercises in the index on page 938.

1. Read the essay question carefully. Make sure you understand exactly what the question is asking, and note how much evidence is required. If you are asked to supply three examples, make sure you provide *three*.

2. Identify the key verb in the question. It will tell you what to "do." Look for these key verbs:

- **Analyze (examine or consider).** To *analyze* something is to take it apart to see how it works. Usually, you will be asked to analyze one element of a work and to explain its effect on the work as a whole. For example, you might be asked to analyze the metaphor in Carl Sandburg's poem, "Fog." Restrict your essay to a discussion of metaphor: identify the metaphor and the things compared; tell what the metaphor contributes to the poem as a whole.

- **Compare/Contrast.** When you *compare,* you point out similarities; when you *contrast,* you point out differences. You may be asked, for example, to contrast the characters of Annie and Mrs. Keller in *The Miracle Worker.* You should plan your answer by making a chart or list of differences. Sometimes the word *compare* in an essay question implies both comparison and contrast.

- **Describe.** To *describe* means to paint a picture in words. You might be asked to describe a character or a setting. If you were asked to describe Buddy's friend in "A Christmas Memory," for example, you would write about what you know about her through direct and indirect characterization. You would tell how she looks, acts, speaks, and affects other people.

- **Discuss (examine).** To *discuss* means to comment on or talk about in a general way. For example, you might be asked to discuss the use of suspense in Daphne DuMaurier's "The Birds." You could write about the details that create suspense, the techniques of sustaining suspense, and the effect suspense has on your enjoyment of the story.

- **Evaluate.** An evaluation is a judgment about how good or bad something is. Give force to your evaluation by citing specific details from the work that "prove" your judgment is valid.

- **Illustrate.** To *illustrate* means to provide examples from the work to support an idea or statement. For example, you may be asked to illustrate Penelope's loyalty to Odysseus in the *Odyssey.* Provide at least two examples of Penelope's loyalty; more would be better.

- **Interpret.** To *interpret* something means to explain its meaning or importance. You might be asked to interpret what the ibis symbolizes in James Hurst's story, "The Scarlet Ibis." Tell what you think the symbol means, and then cite specific details from the work to support your interpretation.

- **Explain your response.** This type of question asks you to tell whether you liked or disliked a work, how it made you feel, and what it made you think about. A response question often asks you to explain *why* you responded the way you did. Try to provide one or two reasons for your response.

3. Write a thesis statement stating your essay's main idea. Often, this includes a restatement of a part of the essay question. Include the thesis statement in the introductory paragraph. Suppose a question asked: How would you interpret the symbolism of the ibis in "The Scarlet Ibis"? Your thesis statement might begin: "The ibis in 'The Scarlet Ibis' symbolizes ———.''

4. Gather evidence to support the thesis statement. If you can use your book, look back over the work for examples and illustrations. In a closed-book essay, make notes on all of the supporting details that you remember.

5. Write one paragraph for each main point. Say what you want to say as clearly and simply as possible. A topic sentence for each paragraph will help you stick to the question. Don't pad your answer with unrelated details and ideas.

6. End with a concluding paragraph. Summarize your main points and/or give a personal response to the work.

Writing and Revising an Essay About a Literary Work

You may be asked to choose your own topic for an essay on a specific work.

Prewriting

1. Choose a limited topic that you can cover adequately. If your assignment is an essay of four paragraphs or 500 words, you can't possibly analyze all of the characters in *Romeo and Juliet*. But you do have room to discuss the dominant images of light and darkness in the play. For ideas on the kinds of topics you can choose, review the key verbs on page 861.

2. Write a thesis statement. Ask yourself, "What main idea about my topic do I want to discuss?" Then write one sentence that states your essay's main idea.

3. List two or three main ideas that develop your thesis statement. Jot down the ideas that come to mind when you think about your thesis statement, and choose the strongest two or three.

4. Gather and arrange supporting evidence. Your essay should include quotations, specific details, examples, and incidents from the **primary source**—the literary work you are writing about. You can also include information from **secondary sources**—books, reviews, articles, and interviews about the work or its author.

Before you begin to write, decide which evidence best supports your ideas. Then be hard-hearted: discard weak or unrelated material. Once you've arranged the main ideas and evidence in what seems to you the most logical order, you'll have an informal plan or outline.

Writing

Write a draft of your essay. As you write, follow your outline and notes. Be sure to include enough evidence to "prove" your ideas, and cite the sources correctly. Your essay should have the following form:

I. INTRODUCTORY PARAGRAPH
   Catches audience's interest.
   Tells what the essay will be about.
   Ends or begins with the thesis statement.

II. BODY (Paragraphs 2, 3, etc.)
   Develops the thesis statement.
   Each paragraph includes a topic sentence and supporting evidence.

III. CONCLUSION
   Tells the audience essay is completed.
   Restates or emphasizes thesis statement and main ideas.
   Often includes personal response.

Revising

1. Check to see that you've supported your thesis statement with at least two main ideas and enough evidence.

2. Reread your draft another time for style. Does it "sound" right?

3. Clarify and simplify your writing. Don't hesitate to cut wordy or distracting or repetitive material.

Using Proofreader's Symbols

Use the following proofreader's symbols to correct errors in your paper in spelling and punctuation. Notice that poems and short stories should be put in quotation marks; plays, novels, and longer works of literature should be in italics. In manuscript, italics are indicated by underscoring.

Proofreader's Symbols

≡	Annie sullivan	Capitalize a lower-case letter.
/	*Romeo And Juliet*	Lower-case a capital letter.
∧	"The Cask of Amontillado"	Insert a word.
∧	"Correspondence"	Insert a letter.
⊙	Edna St. Vincent Millay	Add a period.
⋀	Juliet, Romeo, and Tybalt	Add a comma.

⌄⌄	"Fire and Ice ⌄⌄	Insert quotation marks.
—	<u>Romeo and Juliet</u>	Set in italics (for long works of literature).
∿	Odyss~~ue~~s	Change the order of the letters.
⁋	⁋"Poison" begins with a man's desperate plea.	Indent to begin a new paragraph.
ℰ	James Thur~~r~~ber	Leave out (delete) and close up space.

A Model Essay

The following essay shows revisions that the writer made in the first draft.

The Conflict Between Parents and Children in <u>Romeo and Juliet</u>

⁋ *William*
‸Shakespeare wrote <u>Romeo and Juliet</u> almost four hundred years

         still   *people*
ago, yet the play‸speaks strongly to ~~children and to parents~~ today.

       the   *of the play*
One of it~~s~~‸main conflicts ‸is the conflict between parents and their

children. This conflict has two results‸it causes Juliet to change

                             it causes
from a carefree girl to a mature but desperate woman, and‸the play

to
‸ends‸tragically.

     Juliet's
  Because of ~~the~~‸conflict with her parents, her character changes

dramatically. At first, she is ~~young and~~ innocent and obedient‸She

                               ing of
is‸full of life and high spirits‸~~She seems to~~ trust‸everyone. She

first reveals her independence when she marries Romeo in secret

because she knows that her parents will never consent. Shake-

speare's audience would have been shocked by Juliet's behavior.

INTRODUCTION

States thesis.

BODY States topic sentence.

Adds supporting details.

According to one critic, ... in thus boldly asserting her own will,

she violates a sacred canon of Elizabethan life: namely, that chil-

dren, and especially daughters owe obedience to the wishes of their

parents." *(Heilman, 17)* As the play goes on, Juliet must fight her parents on

another issue: ~~their~~ *they are* forcing her to marry Paris, someone she does

not love and of course can't marry anyway. The Capulets become

cruel, and Juliet becomes more pitiable as the play progresses. She

becomes more and more alon*e*, ~~She is~~ cut off from Romeo, her

parents, and the Nurse, *who was* Once her close friend and confid*a*nt*e*. Finally,

Juliet has become so isolated that there is no one she can turn to,

and when she finds Romeo dead she gives in to despair: "My dismal

Uses a quote from the play.

scene I needs must act alone." *(Act IV, Scene 3, line 19)*

States another topic sentence.

The conflict between parents and children cause*s* the play to end

tragically. The Prologue told us in the very beginning that nothing

could end the families' hatred except the deaths of the two young

people. To me, this is very tragic because Romeo and Juliet could

should have been able to ~~not~~ talk honestly with their parents about their love. It is even

Adds supporting details.

worse that, *after they were married,* they could not, ~~once married,~~ just tell their parents

what they had done. Maybe the parents would have been consid- *understanding*

erate, though when Juliet's father says *in Act III, Scene 5, that* she m~~s~~*u*~~u~~t marry or leave

the house, it seems pretty clear, *to me* that she would get no help from

Lord Capulet.

CONCLUSION

In summary, conflict between parents and their children is cen-

Summarizes the main idea.

tral to the play, not only does the conflict change Juliet's character,

but also it reveals the play's tragic theme : about generations of blind prej- *that even true and innocent love cannot overcome*

udice and hatred. At the play's resolution, the feuding families learn

what we all should know: that people must treat one another with

respect and tolerance, even parents and children.

Documenting Sources

Find out which method of documenting sources your teacher prefers that you use.

1. Parenthetical citations give line numbers or page references, or act and scene numbers, or the author's name, or a combination of these items. The following chart illustrates some types of parenthetical citations:

Parenthetical Citations	
Type	Example
Quotation from a prose passage (when the author is cited in the text):	In "The Giant Water Bug," Annie Dillard explains how a frog's "very skull seemed to collapse and settle like a kicked tent" (page 378).
Quotation from a play (act, scene, line):	On first seeing Juliet, Romeo exclaims, "O, she doth teach the torches to burn bright!" (I.5.45) *or* (Act I, Scene 5, line 45).
Quotation from a poem (line number):	Walt Whitman says "I hear America singing" (line 1).
Citation when the author's name is not in text:	According to one critic, *Romeo and Juliet* is "a story of ill luck" (Harrison, 472).

2. Footnotes are usually placed at the bottom of a page. They can be indicated by raised numbers at the end of the quotation. Footnotes are generally numbered consecutively.

[1] Alice Walker, "Beauty: When the Other Dancer Is the Self," *In Search of Our Mother's Gardens* (New York: Harcourt Brace Jovanovich, 1983).

Check a writing handbook, or ask your teacher for the style for footnoting poems, magazine articles, interviews, or books with more than one author.

3. End notes are identical to footnotes except that they appear in a list entitled "Notes" at the end of a paper. End notes are numbered consecutively.

4. A **bibliography** should be included at the end of your essay. This is an alphabetical list of all the sources you used to prepare your essay. Bibliography entries are listed alphabetically by the author's last name.

Harrison, G. B., *Shakespeare: The Complete Works* (New York: Harcourt Brace Jovanovich, 1952).

Check a writing handbook, or ask your teacher for the style for other kinds of bibliography entries.

A HANDBOOK OF LITERARY TERMS

ALLEGORY A story in which the characters and settings and events stand for certain other people or events or concepts. Allegories thus have two meanings: a literal meaning and a symbolic meaning. Long ago, allegories were used for teaching purposes. An old and famous allegory in the English language is *Pilgrim's Progress,* which recounts the adventures of a character called Christian. The hero's journey to the Celestial City brings him up against many trials, all of them standing for pitfalls that face the Christian as he or she travels through this earthly world toward the spiritual world. *Animal Farm* (page 810) is a kind of allegory.

See page 809.

ALLITERATION The repetition of the same consonant sounds in words that are close together in a poem, or the repetition of consonant sounds that are very similar. In this example, the sounds "fl," "t," "n," and "w" are repeated in line 1, and the "s" sound is repeated in line 2:

> Open here I flung the shutter, when, with many a flirt and flutter,
> In there stepped a stately Raven of the saintly days of yore.
>
> —from "The Raven,"
> Edgar Allan Poe

See pages 306, 319, 323.

ALLUSION A reference to a statement, person, place, event, or thing that is known from literature, history, religion, myth, politics, sports, science, or pop culture. Here are two stanzas from a poem that alludes to the Sirens in the *Odyssey* (see page 764):

> This is the one song everyone
> would like to learn: the song
> that is irresistible:
>
> The song that forces men
> to leap overboard in squadrons
> even though they see the beached
> skulls . . .
>
> —from "Siren Song,"
> Margaret Atwood

Odysseus filled his sailors' ears with wax so that they would not hear the Sirens and jump overboard. He himself was able to listen to their beautiful song because he was lashed to the mast and couldn't move. Whenever you hear a reference to a "siren song," you know you are hearing an allusion to the *Odyssey.*

Allusions are used in the daily newspapers too, and often they are used for humor. In an article about President Reagan's indecision about choosing a man named Arthur Burns for a government job, columnist William Safire wrote: "Reagan fiddles while Burns roams." This allusion is a comic turn-around of the famous saying, "Nero fiddled while Rome burned."

See pages 151, 314, 329, 479, 708.

ARGUMENT A special form of persuasion that uses reason to try to convince a reader or listener to think or act in a certain way. Like all persuasive writing, argument is aimed at winning people to the writer's point of view, but argument uses only facts and logical reasoning to achieve its purpose. (Other persuasive writing may use any method of persuasion, including an unashamed appeal to the emotions.) Debate societies use arguments to try to win their points. Good arguments are also sometimes found in editorials and magazine articles.

See also *Persuasion.*

ASIDE Words spoken by a character in a play to the audience or to another character, that are not supposed to be overheard by the others on stage in a scene. Stage directions usually tell when a speech is an "aside." For example, in the opening scene of *Romeo and Juliet* on page 605, there are two asides exchanged between Sampson and Gregory as they pick a fight with the servants of the house of Montague. Sampson and Gregory hear the asides, and so do we in the audience, but Montague's servants do not.

See pages 605, 631.

ASSONANCE The repetition of similar vowel sounds followed by different consonant sounds, especially in words that are close together in a poem. For example, the words "base" and "fade" and the words "young" and "love" are examples of assonance. This line is especially musical because of its assonance:

> Thou foster child of silence and slow time
>
> —from "Ode on a Grecian Urn,"
> John Keats

See also *Alliteration, Onomatopoeia,* and *Rhyme.*

AUTOBIOGRAPHY An account of the writer's own life. Some examples of autobiographies are *Growing Up* by Russell Baker, *I Know Why the Caged Bird Sings* by Maya Angelou (see page 462), and *Barrio Boy* by Ernesto Galarza (see page 446).

See pages 435, 481.

BALLAD A song that tells a story. Folk ballads are composed by unknown singers and are passed on from generation to generation by word of mouth before they are written down. "The Demon Lover" (page 355) is a folk ballad. Literary ballads, on the other hand, are composed by known individuals and are written down in imitation of the old folk ballads. "Old Christmas," by Roy Helton (page 361), is a literary ballad. Ballads usually tell sensational stories of tragedy or adventure, using simple language with a great deal of repetition. They also usually have regular rhythm and rhyme patterns, which make them easy to memorize.

See pages 350, 352.

BIOGRAPHY An account of a person's life, written or told by another person. One of the most famous biographies of all time, written in the eighteenth century, is James Boswell's *Life of Samuel Johnson.* A classic American biography is Carl Sandburg's multi-volumed life of Abraham Lincoln. Today, biographies are written of movie stars, TV personalities, politicians, sports figures, self-made millionaires, even underworld figures. Biographies are among the most popular forms of contemporary literature. "Annie" (page 437) is an excerpt from Joseph Lash's biography of Helen Keller and her teacher Annie Sullivan.

See pages 435, 482.
See also *Autobiography.*

BLANK VERSE Poetry written in unrhymed iambic pentameter. "Blank" means the poetry is not rhymed. "Iambic pentameter" means that each line contains five iambs, or metrical feet, consisting of an unstressed syllable followed by a stressed syllable (˘ ′). Blank verse is the most important poetic form in English epic and dramatic poetry. It is the verse line used in William Shakespeare's plays. Here, for example, are a few lines of blank verse from *Romeo and Juliet*. Juliet is speaking to Romeo on the morning after their marriage:

> ˘ ′ ˘ ˘ ′ ˘ ′ ˘ ′ ˘ ′
> It was the nightingale, and not the lark,
> ˘ ′ ˘ ′ ˘ ′ ˘ ′ ˘ ′
> That pierced the fearful hollow of thine ear . . .
>
> —from *Romeo and Juliet*,
> William Shakespeare

See page 599.
See also *Iambic Pentameter, Meter.*

CHARACTER A person in a story. In some stories, such as Aesop's fables, a character is an animal. In other stories, such as fairy tales, a natural force such as the wind may be a character. In still other stories, a character is a divinity or hero, as are Athena and Odysseus in the *Odyssey* (page 721). But most often a character is an ordinary human being, as is the grandmother in Toni Cade Bambara's "Blues Ain't No Mockin Bird" (page 81).

The process of revealing the personality of a character in a story is called **characterization.** A writer can reveal a character in the following ways:

1. By letting us hear the character speak.
2. By describing how the character looks and dresses.
3. By letting us listen to the character's inner thoughts and feelings.
4. By revealing what other people in the story think or say about the character.
5. By showing us what the character does—how he or she acts.
6. By telling us directly what the character's personality is like: cruel, kind, sneaky, brave, and so on.

The first five ways of revealing a character are known as **indirect characterization.** When a writer uses indirect characterization, we have to use our own judgment to decide what a character is like, based on the evidence the writer gives us. But when a writer uses the sixth method, known as **direct characterization,** we don't have to decide for ourselves; we are told directly what kind of person the character is.

Characters can be classified as static or dynamic. A **static character** is one who does not change much in the course of a story. By contrast, a **dynamic character** changes as a result of the story's events.

Characters can also be classified as flat or round. A **flat character** has only one or two traits, and these can be described in a short phrase. In other words, a flat character is one-dimensional, like a flat piece of cardboard. A **round character,** like a real person, has many different character traits, sometimes contradictory ones. A round character, then, is three-dimensional, solid, and realistic.

See pages 59, 89, 91, 93, 490.

COMEDY In general, a story that ends happily. The hero or heroine of a comedy is usually an ordinary character who overcomes a series of obstacles that block what he or she wants. Comedy is distinct from **tragedy,** in which a great person comes to an unhappy or disastrous end, often through some character flaw or weakness. *Visitor from Forest Hills* by Neil Simon (page 551) is a good example of a dramatic comedy.

See pages 549, 565.
See also *Farce, Tragedy.*

CONFLICT A struggle or clash between opposing characters, or between opposing forces. In an **external conflict,** a character struggles against some outside force. This outside force might be another character, or society as a whole, or some natural force. "The Most Dangerous Game" by Richard Connell (page 14) revolves around the external conflict between the evil General Zaroff and his guest, the hunter Rainsford. By contrast, an **internal conflict** takes place entirely within the character's own mind. An internal conflict is a struggle between opposing needs or desires or emotions within a single person. In Langston Hughes's story "Thank You, M'am" (page 77), the boy goes through an internal conflict as he decides whether or not he will snatch Mrs. Jones's pocketbook, lying within his reach.

See pages 4, 55, 93, 489.

CONNOTATION All the meanings, associations, or emotions that a word suggests. For example, *skinny* and *slender* both have the same literal definition—"thin." But their connotations are completely different. If you say, "That girl is skinny," you are saying something unflattering. If you say, "That girl is slender," you are paying her a compliment. The British philosopher Bertrand Russell once gave a classic example of the different connotations of words: "I am firm. You are obstinate. He is a pigheaded fool."

If you are aware of the connotations of words, you will increase your reading powers. To be unaware of a word's special associations and meanings can be risky, as the following cartoon illustrates:

"Hagar the Horrible" © 1981. Reprinted with special permission of King Features Syndicate.

If only the tailor had thought to say "You'll need a suit of *heroic* proportions," he might have avoided Hagar's wrath.

See pages 195, 295, 337, 341, 344, 485, 824.

COUPLET Two consecutive lines of poetry that rhyme. Alexander Pope wrote this sarcastic couplet for a dog's collar (Kew is a place in England):

> I am his Highness's dog at Kew;
> Pray tell me, Sir, whose dog are you?
> —Alexander Pope

As we see here, couplets work nicely for humor and satire because the punchline comes so quickly. However, they are most often used to express a completed thought. Shakespeare uses a couplet to give a sense of closure to each act of *Romeo and Juliet* (see page 703).

See pages 370, 600.

DENOTATION The literal, dictionary definition of a word.
See page 195.
See also *Connotation*.

DESCRIPTION A kind of writing that is intended to create a mood or emotion, or to re-create a person, a place, a thing, an event, or an experience. Description is one of the four major techniques used in writing. (The others are **narration, exposition,** and **persuasion.**) Description works through images that appeal to the senses of sight, smell, taste, hearing, or touch. Writers use description in all forms of fiction, nonfiction, and poetry. Here is a description of an experience by the Kiowa writer N. Scott Momaday:

My father is at the wheel of a new green pickup, and I am sitting beside him, hugely pleased to be along. The dashboard is gray-brown and to me very beautiful; there are bright knobs in it. My father is wearing gloves, soft leather gloves, and that is unimaginably fine. My dog Blackie is at the rear window, riding high to the wind, looking, laughing in at me. I look out in every direction to see who will notice us, for we are wonderful to behold, speeding along in the new truck, handsome, handsome, our eyes glittering; and otherwise, too, there is so much to see; the wide world is enchanted. The little truck bounces over the dirt roads of the Navajo reservation, raises a great rooster tail of red dust. It is summer and there is a sharp glare on the sand, on the cottonwood leaves. There is a jolt which rattles my bones . . .

—from *The Names*,
N. Scott Momaday

See pages 374, 393.

DIALECT A way of speaking that is characteristic of a particular region or of a particular group of people. Dialects may have a distinct vocabulary, pronunciation system, and grammar. In a sense, we all speak "dialects"; but one dialect usually becomes dominant in a country or culture, and becomes accepted as the standard way of speaking. In this country, for example, the formal written language is known as Standard English. (You usually hear it spoken by TV newscasters on the national channels.) Writers often imitate regional dialects or those that reveal a person's economic or social class, in order to give a story "local color," the sense of being authentic to a place or people. For example, Roy Helton's poem "Old Christmas" (page 361) is written in a dialect from the mountains of Appalachia. Characters in *The Mother* (page 567) use the dialects heard in New York City.

See page 87.

DICTION A writer's or speaker's choice of words. People use different types of words depending on the audience they're addressing, the subject they're discussing, and the effect they're trying to produce. For example, slang words that would be suitable in a casual conversation with a friend ("This song is *far out*") would be unsuitable in a formal essay. Similarly, the language used by a scientist to describe the moon would be different from the language used by a poet.

Diction is an essential element of a writer's **style.** Some writers use simple, down-to-earth, or even slang words (*house, home, digs*); others use ornate, official-sounding, or even flowery language (*domicile, residence, abode*). Notice that the **connotations** of words (rather than their strict, literal meanings, or **denotations**) are an important aspect of diction.

Diction has a tremendous effect on the tone of a piece of writing. In fact, changing the diction of a story or poem can completely transform its effect on us. Here, a humorist makes fun of a certain kind of complicated and pompous diction used by many people today:

> In an effort to make the classics accessible to contemporary readers, I am translating them into the modern American language. Here is the translation of *Little Red Riding Hood:*
>
> Once upon a point in time, a small person named Little Red Riding Hood initiated plans for the preparation, delivery, and transportation of foodstuffs to her grandmother, a senior citizen residing at a place of residence in a wooded area of indeterminate dimensions. . . .
>
> —from "Little Red Riding Hood Revisited," Russell Baker

See pages 276, 312, 325.
See also *Connotation, Style, Tone.*

DRAMA A story that is written to be acted out in front of an audience. The action of a drama is usually driven by a character who wants something very much and who takes steps to get it. The stages of drama are often described as: **exposition, complications, climax,** and **resolution.**

See pages 489–492.

EPIC A long story told in poetry which relates the great deeds of a larger-than-life hero who embodies the values of a particular society. Most epics include elements of myth, legend, folk tale, and history. Their tone is serious and their language is grand. Most epic heroes undertake quests to achieve something of tremendous value to themselves or their people. Often the hero's quest is set in both Heaven and Hell. Homer's *Iliad* and *Odyssey* (see page 721) are the best-known epics in Western civilization. The great epic of ancient Rome is Virgil's *Aeneid*, which, like the *Iliad* and *Odyssey,* is based on events that happened during and after the Trojan War.

The English-speaking people have two major epics. *Beowulf* is about a hero who saves a people from two monsters who are threatening the stability of their kingdom. *Paradise Lost*, written by John Milton in the seventeenth century, is an epic that retells the story of the creation and fall of the human race. The great French national epic is *The Song of Roland*, about a knight of Charlemagne's. The great Spanish national epic is the story of a knight called El Cid.

See pages 713, 798.

EPITHET An adjective or other descriptive phrase that is regularly used to characterize a person, place, or thing. We speak of "Honest Abe," for example, and "America the Beautiful." For a time in the 1980's "The Refrigerator" was an epithet used for a professional football player because of his great size.

Homer created so many descriptive epithets in his *Iliad* and *Odyssey* that his name has been permanently associated with a type of epithet. The *Homeric epithet* in most English translations consists of compound adjectives that are regularly used to modify a particular noun. Three famous examples are "wine-dark sea," "rosy-fingered dawn," "the gray-eyed goddess Athena."

See page 781.

ESSAY A short piece of nonfiction prose that examines a single subject from a limited and usually personal point of view. Most essays can be categorized as either **personal** or **formal.** (Personal essays are also called **informal** or **familiar** essays.)

The **personal essay** is the type of essay included in the nonfiction unit of this book. It generally reveals a great deal about the writer's personality and tastes. Its tone is often conversational, sometimes even humorous, and there may be no attempt to be objective. In fact, in a personal essay we are interested in the writer's feelings and responses to an experience.

The **formal essay** is usually serious, objective, and impersonal in tone. Its purpose is to inform its readers about some topic of interest or to convince them to accept the writer's views. The statements in a formal essay should be supported by facts and logic.

See page 376.

EXPOSITION A kind of writing that explains, gives information, defines, or clarifies an idea. Exposition is one of the four major techniques used in writing. (The others are **narration, description,** and **persuasion.**) We find exposition in news articles, in histories, in biographies (and even in cookbook recipes). In fact, each entry in this *Handbook of Literary Terms* is an example of exposition.

Exposition is also the term for that part of a plot that gives information about the characters and their problems or conflicts.

See pages 5, 374, 489, 588.
See also *Plot.*

FABLE A very brief story in prose or verse that teaches a moral, or a practical lesson about how to get along in life. The characters of most fables are animals that behave and speak like human beings. Some of the oldest fables in the world come from China. If you know any of the Greek fables of Aesop, you'll recognize the clever fox in this fable.

The Tiger Behind the Fox

A tiger caught a fox. The fox said, "You wouldn't dare eat *me!* The gods in Heaven have made me the leader of all animals. It would be a violation of the gods' mandate for you to make a meal of me. If you doubt it, let me walk in front, and you follow to see if any animal dares stand his ground." The tiger consented and went with the fox, nose to heels. Every animal that saw them fled. Amazed, and agreeing that the fox was leader of all the animals, the tiger went on his way.

—Chan Kuo Ts'e

See pages 203, 808.

FARCE A type of comedy in which ridiculous and often stereotyped characters are involved in far-fetched, very silly situations. The humor in farce is based on crude physical action, slapstick, and clowning. Characters may slip on banana peels, get pies thrown in their faces, and knock one another on the head with ladders. Movies starring Abbott and Costello, Laurel and Hardy, and the Marx Brothers are examples of farces.

The word *farce* comes from a Latin word for "stuffing." At one time, farces were used to fill in the waiting time between the acts of a serious play. Even in tragedies, farcical elements are often included to provide comic relief. Shakespeare, for example, frequently lets his "common" characters (such as servants) engage in farcical actions.

See page 549.

FIGURE OF SPEECH A word or phrase that describes one thing in terms of another and is not meant to be understood on a literal level. Figures of speech always involve some sort of imaginative comparison between seemingly unlike things.

Some 250 different types of figures of speech have been identified. The most common are the **simile** ("I wandered lonely as a cloud"), the **metaphor** ("Fame is a bee"), and **personification** ("The wind stood up and gave a shout").

See pages 71, 250, 268, 706.
See also *Metaphor, Personification,* and *Simile.*

FLASHBACK A scene in a movie, play, short story, novel, or narrative poem that interrupts the present action of the plot to "flash backward" and tell what happened at an earlier time. That is, a flashback breaks the normal, chronological movement of the narrative, usually to give the reader or viewer some background information needed to make sense of the story. Much of the *Odyssey* (page 721) is told in the form of a flashback, as Odysseus describes his previous adventures to the Phaeacian court of King Alcinos. A flashback in "The Old Demon" (page 153) tells us about Mrs. Wang's early life. Flashbacks are extremely common storytelling devices in movies. In fact, the word *flashback* comes from film criticism, and it has spread to the rest of literature.

See pages 160, 482, 533.

FOIL A character who is used as a contrast to another character. The daredevil mountain climber Osborn is a foil to the careful, methodical Nace in "Top Man" (page 96). The cynical, sophisticated Mercutio is used as a foil to the romantic, naive Romeo. A writer uses a foil to accentuate and clarify the distinct qualities of two characters. The word *foil* is also used for a thin sheet of shiny metal that is placed beneath a gem to intensify its brilliance. A character who is a foil, like the metal behind the gem, sets off or intensifies the character of another person.

See page 628.

FORESHADOWING The use of clues to hint at events that will occur later in the plot. Foreshadowing is used to build up suspense and sometimes anxiety in the reader or viewer. In a drama, that gun found in a bureau drawer in Act I is likely to foreshadow violence later in the play. In "The Cask of Amontillado" Poe uses foreshadowing skillfully. For example, when Montresor produces a trowel from beneath his cloak, he is foreshadowing the means he will use to murder his enemy. When later he begins to build a wall up around Fortunato, we remember that trowel.

See pages 53, 215, 648.

FREE VERSE Poetry that does not have a regular meter or rhyme scheme. Poets writing in free verse try to capture the natural rhythms of ordinary speech. To create its music, free verse may use **internal rhyme, repetition, alliteration, onomatopoeia,** and other musical devices. Notice all the sound effects that create the music of the following free-verse poem by a Native American writer.

Loneliness

The deafening tic-tic-tic of the clock,
The thunder of my own thoughts rumble 'round
The dark room crowding its silence in upon me.
Where are my friends? What is there to do?
The slow steady pounding of my lonesome heart
The never-ending thump-thump-thump of my pulse
Against a set pillow, the only living sounds to listen to!
Visions drift slowly past my eyes . . .
Visions of scarred, contorted trees standing in barren
    desolate fields . . .
Visions of solitary children standing in deserted alleys
With tears washing clean rivulets down their dirty
    faces . . .
Visions of old men, old women, dying with hopeless-
    ness
And agony twisted into their aged masks of death . . .
Visions of neglected tombstones crumbling by
Abandoned churches . . . Oh God!
Where are my friends?
Someone, please come and talk to me!

—Loyal Shegonee

See pages 289, 299, 301.

IAMBIC PENTAMETER A line of poetry that contains five iambs. An **iamb** is a metrical foot, or unit of measure, consisting of an unstressed syllable followed by a stressed syllable (˘ ′). **Pentameter** comes from the Greek *penta* ("five") and *meter* ("measure"). Here is one iamb: arise. Here is a line measuring five iambs:

But soft! What light through yonder window breaks?

—from *Romeo and Juliet*,
William Shakespeare

Iambic pentameter is by far the most common verse line in English poetry. Other than free verse, iambic pentameter sounds the most like natural speech.

See page 599.
See also *Blank Verse, Meter, Rhythm*.

IMAGERY Language that appeals to the senses. Most images are visual—that is, they create pictures in the reader's mind by appealing to the sense of sight. Images can also appeal to the senses of sound, touch, taste, or smell, or even to several senses at once. While imagery is an element in all types of writing, it is especially important in poetry. The following lines contain images that make us see, hear, and even smell what the speaker experiences as he travels to meet someone he loves.

Then a mile of warm sea-scented beach;
Three fields to cross till a farm appears;
A tap at the pane, the quick sharp scratch
And blue spurt of a lighted match . . .

—from "Meeting at Night,"
Robert Browning

See pages 95, 234, 246, 374, 397, 824.

INVERSION The reversal of the normal word order of a sentence. The elements of a standard English sentence are subject, verb, and complement, and in most sentences this is the order in which they appear. (Ray rowed home.) In most sentences, modifiers precede the words they modify (silky blouse, not blouse silky). Writers use inversion to gain emphasis and variety. They may also use it for more technical reasons—to create a rhyme or to accommodate a given meter. In a statement about Ulysses S. Grant and Robert E. Lee, historian Bruce Catton wrote, "Daring and resourcefulness they had too . . ." Catton inverted the order of the sentence in order to put the important words (*daring* and *resourcefulness*) first.

See page 255.

IRONY A contrast or discrepancy between expectation and reality—between what is said and what is really meant, between what is expected to happen and what really does happen, or between what appears to be true and what is really true.

1. In **verbal irony,** a writer or speaker says one thing but really means something completely different. If you call a bad baseball player "the new Darryl Strawberry," you are using verbal irony. The murderer in Edgar Allan Poe's "The Cask of Amontillado" is using verbal irony when he says to his unsuspecting victim, "Your health is precious" (page 211).

2. **Situational irony** occurs when there is a contrast between what would seem appropriate and what really happens, or when what we expect to happen is in fact the opposite of what really does take place. In the extract from *Coming into the Country* (page 398), John McPhee reports that Leon Crane, who found himself the sole survivor of a plane crash in Alaska, had no wilderness experience except for a one-night camping trip with a Boy Scout troop. Given his inexperience in survival techniques, we'd expect that Crane would have perished, but instead, ironically, he walked out of the wilderness alive.

3. **Dramatic irony** occurs when the audience or the reader knows something important that a character in a play or story does not know. In *Romeo and Juliet,* for example, *we* know, but Romeo does *not*, that when he finds Juliet in the tomb, she is drugged and not really

dead at all. Thus we feel a terrible sense of dramatic irony as we watch Romeo kill himself upon discovering her body.

See pages 201, 648, 809.

LYRIC POETRY Poetry that does not tell a story but aims only at expressing a speaker's emotions or thoughts. Most lyrics are short, and they usually imply, rather than directly state, a single strong emotion. The term *lyric* comes from the Greek. In ancient Greece, lyric poems were recited to the accompaniment of a stringed instrument called the lyre. Today poets still try to make their lyrics "sing," but they rely only on the musical effects they can create with words (such as **rhyme, rhythm,** and **onomatopoeia**).

See pages 351, 365.
See also *Sonnet.*

METAPHOR A figure of speech that makes a comparison between two unlike things, in which one thing becomes another thing without the use of the words *like, as, than,* or *resembles.* The poet Robert Burns's famous comparison, "O my love is like a red, red rose," is a simile. If he had written "O my love *is* a red, red rose" or "O my love blossoms and flowers," he would have been using metaphors.

Notice that the comparison in the second metaphor is implied, or suggested, rather than directly stated (as it is in the first metaphor). An **implied metaphor** does not tell us directly that one thing *is* something else. Instead, it uses words that suggest what the nature of the comparison is. The verbs *blossom* and *flower* imply that the feeling of love is like a blossoming flower.

An **extended metaphor** is a metaphor that is extended, or developed, over several lines of writing or even throughout an entire poem. In the following poem, the soul is identified with an oyster sleeping in its shell. The metaphor is extended for several lines, until we arrive at another metaphor: the poet's art is identified with a precious pearl. (*Hermetic* means "secretive.")

Art

I would like to think
that someday I could open
the hermetic oyster
where my soul sleeps.
Sprinkle on it
the bitter juice of the afternoon.
Eat it
and find a pearl in my mouth.

—Hjalmar Flax

A **dead metaphor** is a metaphor that has become so overused that we no longer even realize that it is a figure of speech—we simply skip over the metaphorical connection it makes. Examples of dead metaphors include *the roof of the mouth, the eye of the storm, the heart of the matter,* and *the arm of a chair.*

A **mixed metaphor** is the inconsistent mixture of two or more metaphors. Mixed metaphors are a common problem in bad writing, and they can often be unintentionally funny. You are using a mixed metaphor if you say "Put it on the back burner and let it germinate" or "That's a very hard blow to swallow" or "Let's set sail and get this show on the road."

See pages 251, 268, 270, 706.
See also *Figure of Speech, Simile.*

METER A generally regular pattern of stressed and unstressed syllables in poetry. When we want to indicate the metrical pattern of a poem, we mark the stressed syllables with the symbol (′) and the unstressed syllables with the symbol (˘). Indicating the metrical pattern of a poem in this way is called **scanning** the poem, or **scansion.** Here is an example of scansion. In these lines, the pattern is very regular.

By day the bat is cousin to the mouse.
He likes the attic of an aging house.

—from "The Bat,"
Theodore Roethke

See pages 287–289.

NARRATION A kind of writing or speaking that tells a story. Narration is one of the four major techniques used in writing. (The others are **description, exposition,** and **persuasion.**) Narration can be any length, from a brief paragraph to an entire book. It is most often found in short stories, novels, plays, epics, and ballads. But narration also occurs in any piece of nonfiction writing that relates a series of events that tell "what happened"—such as a biography, essay, or news story.

See pages 374, 393.
See also *Narrator.*

NONFICTION Prose writing that deals with real people, events, and places. The most popular forms of nonfiction are the **biography,** the **autobiography,** and the **essay.** Other examples of nonfiction include newspaper stories, magazine articles, historical writing, scientific reports, and even personal diaries and letters.

See pages 373–376.
See also *Autobiography, Biography,* and *Essay.*

NOVEL **A long fictional story, whose length is normally somewhere between a hundred and five hundred book pages, which uses all the elements of storytelling: plot, character, setting, theme, and point of view.** Modern writers often do away with one or more of the novel's traditional elements. Some novels today are basically character studies, with only the barest, stripped-down story lines. Other novels tell us little in-depth about their characters and concentrate instead on plot and setting. The novel in this book is a short one, *Animal Farm.*

See page 805.

ONOMATOPOEIA **The use of a word whose sound imitates or suggests its meaning.** Onomatopoeia is so natural to us that we begin using it instinctively as children. *Crackle, pop, fizz, click, zoom,* and *chirp* are all examples of onomatopoeia. Onomatopoeia is an important element in creating the music of poetry. In the poem by Loyal Shegonee, under the entry "Free Verse," onomatopoeia is created by words that imitate the sound of a clock (tic-tic-tic), of thunder (rumble), of the heartbeat (pound), and of the pulse (thump-thump-thump).

See pages 305, 306, 319.
See also *Alliteration, Assonance.*

PERSONIFICATION **A special kind of metaphor in which a nonhuman thing or quality is talked about as if it were human.** Here are a few lines in which poetry itself is personified—that is, it is described as behaving and feeling the way people do:

This poetry gets bored of being alone,
it wants to go outdoors to chew on the winds,
to fill its commas with the keels of rowboats . . .

—from "Living Poetry,"
Hugo Margenat

See pages 271, 284, 707, 731.
See also *Figure of Speech.*

PERSUASION **A kind of writing that aims at convincing the reader or listener to think or act in a certain way.** Examples of persuasive writing are found in newspaper editorials, in speeches, and in many essays and articles. The techniques of persuasion are used in all kinds of advertising. Persuasion can use language that appeals to the emotions, or it can use logic to appeal to reason. When persuasive writing appeals to reason and not to the emotions, it is called **argument.**

Here is part of a famous persuasive speech delivered by Patrick Henry in 1775. In trying to persuade the Virginia colonists to raise arms against the British military

presence in the colonies, Henry appeals first to his listeners' reason, then to their emotions.

I ask gentlemen, sir, what means this martial [warlike] array, if its purpose be not to force us to submission? Can gentlemen assign any other possible motive for it? Has Great Britain any enemy in this quarter of the world, to call for all this accumulation of navies and armies? No, sir, she has none. They are meant for us: they can be meant for no other. They are sent over to bind and rivet upon us those chains which the British ministry have been so long forging.

—from "Speech in the Virginia Convention,"
Patrick Henry

See pages 375, 431.
See also *Argument.*

PLOT **The series of related events that make up a story.** Plot is "what happens" in a story—whether that story is told in the form of a short story, novel, play, or poem. Most plots are built on these "bare bones": A **basic situation,** or **exposition,** tells us who the characters are and, usually, what their conflict is. **Complications** arise, as the characters take steps to resolve the conflict. Eventually, the plot reaches a **climax,** the most exciting moment in the story, when the outcome is decided one way or another. The final part of a story is the **resolution,** or **denouement.** This is when all the story's problems are solved and the story is "closed."

Not all works of fiction or drama have a traditional plot structure. Modern writers often experiment with plot, eliminating at times some or nearly all of the parts of a traditional plot in order to focus on other elements, such as character, point of view, or mood.

See pages 3–5, 57.

POETRY **A kind of rhythmic, compressed language that uses figures of speech and imagery designed to appeal to our emotions and imaginations.** The major forms of poetry are the **lyric,** the **epic,** and the **ballad.** Beyond this, it is difficult to define poetry, though many readers feel it is easy to recognize it. Emily Dickinson once explained how she recognized poetry:

If I read a book and it makes my whole body so cold that no fire can ever warm me, I know that it is poetry. If I feel physically as if the top of my head were taken off, I know that it is poetry.

—Emily Dickinson

See page 231.

POINT OF VIEW The vantage point from which the writer has chosen to tell the story. In broad terms, there are three possible points of view: **omniscient, third-person limited,** and **first person.**

1. In the *omniscient (or "all knowing") point of view,* the person telling the story knows everything there is to know about the characters and their problems. This all-knowing narrator can tell us about the past, the present, and the future of all the characters. This narrator can even tell us what the characters are thinking. The narrator can also tell us what is happening in other places or parts of the world. In the omniscient point of view, the narrator is not in the story at all. In fact, the omniscient narrator is like a god telling the story. This is a very familiar point of view; we hear it in fairy tales from the time we are children: "Once upon a time there lived a small girl whose name was Red Riding Hood."

2. In the *third-person limited point of view,* the narrator focuses on the thoughts and feelings of just one character. With this point of view, we feel we are observing the action through the eyes and with the feelings of one of the characters in the story. If the story of Red Riding Hood were told from this point of view, we'd feel as if we were looking inside her head: "As Little Red Riding Hood hurried toward her grandmother's house, she was not even thinking of wolves with dripping fangs. She was thinking of the chicken sandwiches in her basket, though she was much too good ever to steal one."

3. In the *first-person point of view,* one of the characters is actually telling the story, using the pronoun "I." We get to know the narrator very well, but we can know only what this person knows, observe only what this person observes. All of our information about the story must come from this one person. If Red Riding Hood's story were told from a first-person point of view, we might hear this version: "My granddaughter was late coming along with her basket of food and when she finally arrived I didn't recognize her, her teeth had gotten so big."

See pages 135–137, 162.

PUN A play on the multiple meanings of a word, or on two words that sound alike but have different meanings. Most often puns are used for their humorous effects; they are used in jokes all the time ("What has four wheels and flies?" Answer: "A garbage truck.") Shakespeare was one of the great punsters of all time. The servants in *Romeo and Juliet* make crude puns as they clown around at the start of the play. Later, Romeo and his friend Mercutio trade wits in a series of more sophisticated puns. Since word meanings change so quickly, some of Shakespeare's puns are barely understandable to us today—just as puns popular today will probably be puzzling to people a hundred years from now.

See pages 231, 335, 707.

REFRAIN A repeated word, phrase, line, or group of lines. Though refrains are usually associated with songs and poems, they are also used in speeches and other forms of literature. Refrains are most often used to build rhythms, but they may also provide commentary or build suspense. In the ballad "Edward" (page 358), the names "Edward, Edward," and "Mither, mither" are repeatedly used as refrains.

See page 350.

RHYME The repetition of accented vowel sounds and all sounds following them, in words that are close together in a poem. *Choice* and *voice* are rhymes, as are *tingle* and *jingle.* **End-rhymes** are rhymes at the ends of lines. In this poem, the words *defense/tense, know/go,* and *Spain/Maine* are end-rhymes.

Old Mary

My last defense
Is the present tense.

It little hurts me now to know
I shall not go

Cathedral-hunting in Spain
Nor cherrying in Michigan or Maine.

—Gwendolyn Brooks

Internal rhymes are rhymes in the middle of a line. This line has internal rhymes (*dreary/weary*):

Once upon a midnight dreary, while I pondered, weak and weary

—from "The Raven,"
Edgar Allan Poe

When two words are alike in some sounds, but do not rhyme exactly, they are called **approximate rhymes** (or **near rhymes,** or **slant rhymes**). In the poem above, Brooks uses approximate rhyme with the words *now* and *know.*

The pattern of rhymes in a poem is called a **rhyme scheme.** To indicate the rhyme scheme of a stanza or poem, use a separate letter of the alphabet for each rhyme. For example, the rhyme scheme of Brooks's poem is *aabbcc.*

See pages 304, 319, 325.

RHYTHM A musical quality produced by the repetition of stressed and unstressed syllables, or by the repetition of certain other sound patterns, in poetry and prose. The most obvious kind of rhythm is produced by **meter,** the regular repetition of stressed and unstressed syllables found in some poetry. But writers can also create rhythm by using rhymes, by repeating words and phrases, and even by repeating whole lines or sentences. This stanza by Walt Whitman is written in free verse and so does not follow a metrical pattern. Yet the lines are rhythmical because of Whitman's repeated use of certain sentence structures, words, and sounds:

> Give me the splendid silent sun with all his beams
> full-dazzling,
> Give me juicy autumnal fruit ripe and red from the
> orchard,
> Give me a field where the unmowed grass grows,
> Give me an arbor, give me the trellised grape,
> Give me fresh corn and wheat, give me serene-moving
> animals teaching content,
> Give me nights perfectly quiet as on high plateaus west
> of the Mississippi, and I looking up at the
> stars . . .
>
> —from "Give Me the Splendid Silent Sun,"
> Walt Whitman

See page 325.
See also *Meter.*

SATIRE The kind of writing that ridicules something—a person, a group of people, humanity at large, an attitude or failing, a social institution—in order to reveal a weakness. Most satires try to convince us of a point of view or to persuade us to follow a course of action. They do this by pointing out how the opposite point of view or action is ridiculous or laughable. For example, the TV show *All in the Family* satirized the narrow-minded views of Archie Bunker, making him look so ridiculous that most people would try to avoid being identified with him. Some satires ridicule other works of literature. "The Little Girl and the Wolf" (page 203) and "The Princess and the Tin Box" (page 204), both by James Thurber, satirize fables and fairy tales with great delight. Thurber is not trying to get us to stop reading fables or fairy tales. He just wants to poke fun at some of the standard characters and plots of such stories.

See pages 346, 382, 809, 855.

SETTING The time and place of a story or play. Most often the setting of a narrative is established early in the story. For example, in the fourth paragraph of "The Cask of Amontillado" (page 210), Edgar Allan Poe tells his read-

ers, "It was about dusk, one evening during the supreme madness of the carnival season . . ." Setting often contributes to a story's emotional effect. In "The Cask of Amontillado," the descriptions of the gloomy Montresor palace, with its damp catacombs full of bones, help create the story's mood of horror. Setting can also provide the conflict in a story, as the mountain setting does in "Top Man" (page 96). Setting can also be used to reveal character, as it does in "A Christmas Memory" (page 62).

See pages 93, 131.

SHORT STORY A short fictional prose narrative that usually makes up about ten to twenty book pages. Short stories were first written in the nineteenth century; some say the first short-story writer was Edgar Allan Poe. Short stories are usually built on a plot that consists of these "bare bones": the **basic situation** or **exposition, complications, climax,** and **resolution.** Years ago, most short stories were chiefly notable for their strong plots. Recent writers tend to concentrate more on character development or on the revelation of theme or creation of mood.

See pages 3–5.

SIMILE A figure of speech that makes a comparison between two unlike things, using an explicit word such as *like, as, resembles,* or *than.* Here is a famous simile from an American poem. The poet has been asking someone to read a poem to comfort him:

> And the night shall be filled with music,
> And the cares, that infest the day,
> Shall fold their tents, like the Arabs,
> And as silently steal away.
>
> —from "Day Is Done,"
> Henry Wadsworth Longfellow

Cares and worries would seem to have nothing in common with those nomadic people who set up their tents for a while and then suddenly fold them, pack them up, and slip away into the vastness of the desert. Yet Longfellow helps us to imagine how cares and worries can also just as suddenly disappear, leaving not a trace behind.

See pages 251, 268, 706.
See also *Figures of Speech, Metaphor.*

SOLILOQUY An unusually long speech in which a character on stage alone expresses his or her thoughts aloud. The soliloquy is a very old dramatic convention, in which the audience is supposedly overhearing the private thoughts of the character. Perhaps the most famous soliloquy is the "To be or not to be" speech in Shakespeare's play *Hamlet.* There are also several soliloquies in *Romeo and*

Juliet, including Friar Lawrence's soliloquy at the opening of Act II, Scene 3 (page 637); Juliet's at the end of Act IV, Scene 3 (page 681); and Romeo's in Act V, Scene 3 (page 695).

SONNET A fourteen-line lyric poem, usually written in iambic pentameter, that has one of several rhyme schemes. The oldest kind of sonnet is called the **Italian sonnet,** or the **Petrarchan sonnet,** after the fourteenth-century Italian poet Petrarch. The first eight lines, or octet, of the Italian sonnet pose a question or problem about love or some other subject. The concluding six lines, or **sestet,** respond to the octet. The octet has the rhyme scheme *abba abba;* the sestet has the rhyme scheme *cde cde.*

Another important sonnet form, widely used by William Shakespeare, is called the **Shakespearean sonnet.** It has three four-line units, or **quatrains,** followed by a concluding two-line unit, or **couplet.** The most common rhyme scheme for the Shakespearean sonnet is *abab cdcd efef gg.*

SPEAKER The voice who is talking to us in a poem. Sometimes the speaker is identical to the poet, but often the speaker and the poet are not the same. The poet may be speaking as a child, a woman, a man, a whole people, an animal, or even an object. For example, the speaker in "The Lesson of the Moth" by Don Marquis (page 330) is a cockroach.

See page 255.

STANZA A group of consecutive lines in a poem that form a single unit. A stanza in a poem is something like a paragraph in prose: it often expresses a unit of thought. A stanza may consist of one line, or two, three, four, or any number of lines beyond that. The word *stanza* is an Italian word for "stopping place" or "place to rest." Emily Dickinson's poem "I Never Saw a Moor" (page 312) consists of two four-line stanzas, or **quatrains,** each one expressing a unit of thought.

STEREOTYPE A fixed idea or conception of a character which does not allow for any individuality. Stereotypes are often based on racial, social, religious, sexist, or ethnic prejudices. Some common stereotypes are the ideas that all football players are dumb, that all New Yorkers are rude, that all Texans are rich. Stereotypes are often used in comedies for laughs.

See pages 80, 550.

SUSPENSE The uncertainty or anxiety we feel about what is going to happen next in a story. In "The Most Dangerous Game" (page 14) our curiosity is hooked at once when we hear about Ship-Trap Island and how sailors dread it. When Rainsford lands on that very island and is hunted by the sinister General Zaroff, suspense keeps us on the edge of our seats. We wonder: Will Rainsford be another victim who is hunted down and killed by the evil and weird Zaroff?

See pages 4, 57.
See also *Plot.*

SYMBOL A person, a place, a thing, or an event that stands for itself and for something beyond itself as well. A symbol has a real meaning or existence as itself, while at the same time it represents something else. For example, a scale has a real existence as an instrument for measuring weights but it also is used as a symbol of justice. Other familiar symbols are the cross that symbolizes the Christian religion, the six-pointed star that symbolizes the Jewish religion, and the bald eagle that symbolizes the United States. These are popular symbols that everyone knows, but in literature writers sometimes create new symbols, which must be understood from their context.

See page 177.

THEME The central idea of a work of literature. A theme is not the same as a "subject." The subject of a work can usually be expressed in a word or two: love, childhood, death. The theme is the idea the writer wishes to convey *about* that subject. The theme must be expressed in a statement or sentence. For example, one theme of *Romeo and Juliet* might be stated as: Love is more powerful than family loyalty. A work's theme is not usually stated directly. Most often, the reader has to think about all the elements of the work and use them to make an inference, or educated guess, about what its theme is.

See pages 166, 196.

TONE The attitude a writer takes toward the audience, a subject, or a character. Tone is conveyed through the writer's choice of words and detail. For example, Truman Capote's story "A Christmas Memory" (page 62) is affectionate and nostalgic in tone. Charles Edward Carryl's "Robinson Crusoe's Story" (page 309) is humorous and lightly mocking in tone.

See pages 225, 324, 345.
See also *Diction.*

TRAGEDY A play, novel, or other narrative, depicting serious and important events, in which the main character comes to an unhappy end. In a tragedy, the main character is usually dignified and courageous. This character's downfall may be caused by a character flaw, or it may result from forces beyond his or her control. The tragic hero or heroine usually wins some self-knowledge and wisdom, even though he or she suffers defeat, perhaps even death.

See also *Comedy.*

GRAMMAR, USAGE, AND MECHANICS: A REFERENCE GUIDE

PARTS OF SPEECH

Nouns

1. A *noun* is a word used to name a person, a place, a thing, or an idea.

   EXAMPLES
   woman, doctor, Julia, Dr. Watson [people]
   state, country, Texas, Canada [places]
   car, money, Buick, yen [things]
   bravery, happiness, hate, freedom [ideas]

2. A *common noun* names general persons, places, or things.

   EXAMPLES
   queen, city, novel

3. A *proper noun* names a particular person, place, or thing.

   EXAMPLES
   Elizabeth I, Orlando, *Shane*

4. A *compound noun* is a single noun made up of two or more words. Compound nouns may be common or proper.

   EXAMPLES
   backyard, redwood, evergreen
   red pepper, sister-in-law, Puerto Rico

Pronouns

1. A *pronoun* is a word used in place of a noun or more than one noun. The noun the pronoun stands for is called its *antecedent*.

   EXAMPLES
   Roberta told **her** uncle **she** would arrive early. [The pronouns *her* and *she* refer to the antecedent *Roberta*.]

   John and **I** told Judy that **we** could help.
   John and I told Judy that John and I could help. [In this case, *we* would be the correct pronoun, since it refers to the antecedent *John and I*.]

2. *Personal pronouns* stand for people, places, and things. Here are the personal pronouns:

   EXAMPLES
   I, me, mine, my, myself; you, your, yours, yourself, yourselves; he, him, his, himself; she, her, hers, herself; it, its, itself; we, us, our, ours, ourselves; they, them, their, theirs, themselves

Adjectives

1. An *adjective* is a word used to modify a noun or a pronoun. Adjectives answer questions such as *What kind? Which one? How much?* or *How many?*

   EXAMPLES
   a **tall** tree [What kind?] **this** book [Which one?]
   two pints [How much?] **several** songs [How many?]

2. *A, an,* and *the* are special adjectives called *articles.*

3. A *proper adjective* is an adjective that is formed from a proper noun. Proper adjectives, like proper nouns, are always capitalized.

   EXAMPLES
   Islamic culture, **Chinese** food, **Arthurian** legend

Verbs

1. A *verb* is a word that expresses action or otherwise helps to make a statement.

   EXAMPLES
   Marianne Moore **wrote** great poems. [*Wrote* expresses action.]
   Sylvia Plath **is** a poet. [*Is* does not express action but helps to make a statement.]

2. An *action verb* is a word that expresses a physical or mental action.

EXAMPLES
talk, walk, run, sit [physical actions]
think, imagine, believe [mental actions]

3. A *linking verb* is a word that does not express an action. A linking verb helps to make a statement by joining the subject with a noun or adjective in the predicate.

EXAMPLES
Mel Gibson **is** a terrific actor. [*Is* links the subject *Mel Gibson* with the noun *actor* in the predicate.]
He **looked** handsome in *Hamlet*. [*Looked* links the subject *he* with the adjective *handsome* in the predicate.]

4. A one-word verb is called a *main verb.* Sometimes a main verb is accompanied by other verbs called *helping verbs.* The main verb and the helping verb together make up a *verb phrase.*

EXAMPLE
The baby **had crawled** out of the crib. [The verb phrase is *had crawled*. The main verb is *crawled* and *had* is the helping verb.]

Adverbs

An *adverb* is a word used to modify a verb, an adjective, or another adverb. Adverbs usually answer questions such as: *Where? When? How? To what extent?*

TIPS FOR WRITERS

Use an adverb only after an action verb. Use an adjective after a linking verb to modify a noun or pronoun in the subject of a sentence. If you are uncertain, substitute the verb *is* for the verb. If *is* works, you should use an adjective.

EXAMPLES
The meat tasted good. [*Good* is an adjective that appears after the linking verb *tasted* and modifies the subject noun *meat*. You could also say "The meat *is* good."]
He acted badly. [*Badly* is an adverb that modifies the action verb *acted*. You can't say "He is badly."]

EXAMPLES
He swam **upstream**. [Where?]
We went fishing **yesterday**. [When?]
Please hold this **carefully**. [How?]
The towel is **completely** dry. [To what extent?]

Prepositions

1. A *preposition* is a word used to show the relationship of a noun or a pronoun to some other word in the sentence. Below are common prepositions.

EXAMPLES

about	behind	for	on
above	below	from	over
across	beside	in	since
after	between	into	through
among	beyond	like	to
around	by	near	until
at	during	of	with

2. The noun or pronoun following the preposition is called the *object of the preposition.* Words that modify the object may come between the preposition and the object. Taken together, the preposition, its object, and the modifiers of the object are called a *prepositional phrase.*

EXAMPLE
He took pictures **of the majestic mountains.** [The prepositional phrase is *of the majestic mountains. Of* is the preposition, *mountains* is the object of the preposition, and the words *the majestic* modify *mountains.*]

Conjunctions

1. A *conjunction* is a word that joins words or groups of words.

EXAMPLES
Tamara **and** Raul speak three languages. [The conjunction *and* joins the two words *Tamara* and *Raul.*]
Paula is fluent in Russian **but** not in German. [The conjunction *but* joins the two phrases *in Russian* and *not in German.*]

2. *Coordinating conjunctions* join two or more words, phrases, or sentence parts of equal rank. The words *and, but, or, nor, for, so,* and *yet* are called coordinating conjunctions.

EXAMPLES

Dogs **and** cats are not natural enemies. [The two words *dogs* and *cats* are joined by *and*.]
I will adopt that brown puppy, **or** Johanna will take it. [Two sentences are joined by *or*.]

3. *Correlative conjunctions* are always found in pairs that have other words separating them: *either . . . or, neither . . . nor, both . . . only, not only . . . but also.*

EXAMPLES

Either Dr. Kuhlman **or** Dr. Reidy will take care of your cat.
Neither the veterinarian **nor** his assistant could restrain the cat.

4. *Subordinating conjunctions* are used to introduce subordinate clauses in complex sentences. Common subordinating conjunctions include *after, as soon as, because, if, so that, until, when,* and *while.* (See page 882 for an examination of complex sentences.)

Interjections

An *interjection* is a word that expresses emotion and that is not related grammatically to other words in the sentence.

EXAMPLES

Wow! That suitcase is really heavy to lift.
Well, I wouldn't try to lift it if I were you.

THE SENTENCE

Elements of a Sentence

1. A *sentence* is a group of words expressing a complete thought. A group of words that does not express a complete thought is a *fragment.*

FRAGMENTS

Catches the baseball. [We do not know *who* catches the baseball.]
After he hit the ball. [We do not know *what happened* after he hit the ball.]
The player on third base. [We do not know *what* the player on third base did.]

SENTENCES

Joe Johnson catches the baseball. [The sentence expresses a complete thought.]
After he hit the ball, the player ran to first base.
The player on third base ran to home and scored a run.

2. The *subject* of a sentence is the part about which something is being said. The *simple subject* is the main word in a subject. The *complete subject* is the simple subject and all the words that go with it.

EXAMPLES

The baseball players waited in the dugout. [*The baseball players* is the complete subject. *Players* is the simple subject.]
At home plate stood **several umpires**. [*Several umpires* is the complete subject. *Umpires* is the simple subject.]

3. The *predicate* of a sentence is the part that says something about the subject. The *simple predicate,* or *verb,* is the main word in a predicate. The *complete predicate* is the simple predicate and all the words that go with it.

EXAMPLES

The baseball players **waited in the dugout.** [*Waited in the dugout* is the complete predicate. *Waited* is the simple predicate.]
At home plate stood several umpires. [*At home plate stood* is the complete predicate. *Stood* is the simple predicate.]

4. A *phrase* is a group of related words that is used as a single part of speech and does not contain a verb and its subject. Three common types of phrases include verb phrases, noun phrases, and prepositional phrases.

EXAMPLE

The young children were awakened by the storm. [*The young children* is a noun phrase, *were awakened* is a verb phrase, and *by the storm* is a prepositional phrase.]

TIPS FOR WRITERS

If you want to be certain that your words form a complete sentence, read them aloud. If something sounds wrong, ask questions such as: What happened? What is being said of the subject? Who or what did the action? If you cannot answer one of the questions, then add the necessary information to make your sentence complete.

The rookie pitcher. [What happened? The predicate is missing.]
The rookie pitcher threw the ball. [*Threw the ball* completes the thought.]

---

5. A *clause* is a group of words that contains a verb and its subject and is used as part of a sentence. An *independent clause* expresses a complete thought and can stand by itself as a sentence. A *dependent* (or *subordinate*) clause does not express a complete thought and cannot stand alone.

INDEPENDENT CLAUSE
Since it was their anniversary, **I bought them a gift.** [This clause can stand alone as a sentence.]

DEPENDENT CLAUSE
I was their best man **when they were married.** [This clause cannot stand alone as a sentence.]

Kinds of Sentences

1. A *declarative sentence* makes a statement. It is followed by a period.

2. An *interrogative sentence* asks a question. It is followed by a question mark.

3. An *imperative sentence* gives a command or request. It is followed by a period. Strong commands are followed by exclamation points.

4. An *exclamatory sentence* shows excitement or expresses a strong feeling. It is followed by an exclamation point.

EXAMPLES
The moon is full tonight. [declarative]
Is there a lunar eclipse this year? [interrogative]
Look at the moon through this telescope. [imperative]
Watch out! [imperative]
What a beautiful moon there is tonight! [exclamatory]

Sentence Complements

1. A *complement* is a word or phrase that completes the meaning begun by the subject and verb.

2. The *direct object* receives the action expressed by the verb or names the result of the action. A direct object answers the question *What?* or *Whom?* after the action verb.

EXAMPLES
The publisher signed the young **writer** to an exclusive contract. [*Writer* is the direct object; it receives the action of the verb *signed.*]

The young writer signed the exclusive **contract.** [*Contract* is the direct object; it receives the action of the verb *signed.*]

3. The *indirect object* of the verb precedes the direct object and tells *to whom* (or *what*) or *for whom* (or *what*) the action of the verb is done.

EXAMPLES
My uncle bought **me** a new jacket. [*Me* is the indirect object because it tells *for whom* my uncle bought a new jacket.]
Bob gave the **floor** a second coat of wax. [*Floor* is the indirect object because it tells *to what* Bob gave a second coat of wax.]

4. A *subject complement* is a word which follows a linking verb and refers to (explains or describes) the subject.

5. If the subject complement is a noun or pronoun, it is called a *predicate nominative.*

EXAMPLES
This Friday is a **holiday.** [*Holiday* is a predicate nominative, a noun that renames the subject *Friday.*]
The winner is **you.** [*You* is a predicate nominative. It is a pronoun that renames the subject *winner.*]

6. If the subject complement is an adjective, it is called a *predicate adjective*. A predicate adjective modifies the subject of the sentence.

EXAMPLES
The house is very **large.** [*Large* is a predicate adjective modifying the subject *house.*]
The gardens look **beautiful.** [*Beautiful* is a predicate adjective modifying the subject *gardens.*]

Sentence Structure

1. A *simple sentence* has one independent clause and no dependent (or subordinate) clauses. A simple sentence may have a compound subject, a compound predicate, or both.

EXAMPLES
The kitten played with the string. [simple sentence]
The puppy and its mother slept near each other. [simple sentence with compound subject]
The dog caught the ball and then dropped it. [simple sentence with compound predicate]
The cat and the dog dug holes and buried toys in the backyard. [simple sentence with compound subject and compound predicate.]

2. A *compound sentence* has two or more independent clauses but no dependent (or subordinate) clauses.

EXAMPLES
Robert liked the story by William Faulkner, but his sister Sarah hated it. [This sentence has two independent clauses joined by the conjunction *but*.]
I read a novel by F. Scott Fitzgerald, Abdul read one by Richard Wright, and we both read a great play by Thornton Wilder. [This sentence has three independent clauses, the last two of which are joined by the conjunction *and*.]

3. A *complex sentence* has one independent clause and at least one dependent (subordinate) clause.

EXAMPLE
After I saw the movie, I read the book. [*I read the book* is the independent clause, and *after I saw the movie* is the dependent clause.]

4. A *compound-complex sentence* has two or more independent clauses and at least one dependent (subordinate) clause.

EXAMPLE
Everyone enjoyed the new science fiction movie, and a few of us who really loved it planned to see it again. [*Everyone enjoyed the new science fiction movie* and *a few of us planned to see it again* are both independent clauses. *Who really loved it* is a dependent or subordinate clause.]

TIPS FOR WRITERS

Do not use a comma to separate a compound subject or predicate in which only two elements are joined by a conjunction. Do use commas to separate all the elements in a compound subject or predicate with three or more elements.

EXAMPLES
Julio and Mica have joined the school drama club. [Two elements in a compound subject are not separated by a comma.]
Julio, Sebastian, and Mica have joined the school drama club. [Three elements in a compound subject are separated by commas.]

PROBLEMS OF AGREEMENT

Agreement of Subject and Verb

1. **A verb should agree with its subject in number. Singular subjects take singular verbs. Plural subjects take plural verbs.**

Number is the form of a word that indicates whether the word is singular or plural. When a word refers to one person or thing, it is singular in number. When a word refers to more than one, it is plural in number. *He* and *man* are singular in number. *They* and *men* are plural in number.

EXAMPLES
He cleans the house. [The singular verb *cleans* agrees with the singular subject *he*.]
They clean the house. [The plural verb *clean* agrees with the plural subject *they*.]
Children clean the house. [The plural verb *clean* agrees with the plural subject *children*.]

In the examples above, the main verbs agree in number with their subjects. Like single-word verbs, verb phrases also agree with their subjects. However, in a verb phrase, only the first auxiliary (helping) verb changes its form to agree with a singular or plural subject.

EXAMPLES
A **friend was singing** in the talent show at school.
Two **friends were singing** in the talent show at school.
He has been cleaning the house.
They have been cleaning the house.

2. **The number of the subject is not changed by a phrase following the subject.**

EXAMPLES
This **book** of stories **is** terrible. [*Book* is the subject, not *stories*.]
These **books** about self-help **are** interesting. [*Books* is the subject, not *self-help*.]

Remember that a verb agrees in number with its subject. The subject is never part of a prepositional phrase.

3. **Compound prepositions such as *together with, in addition to, as well as,* and *along with* following the subject do not affect the number of the subject.**

EXAMPLES
Kim, together with her sisters, **is visiting** relatives in China this summer. [The subject of the sentence is singular because it names one person, *Kim*. Therefore, the predicate of the sentence uses the singular verb form *is*.]
Juan and Angelo, along with Pedro, **have been granted** lifeguard licenses. [The subject of the sentence is plural because it names more than one person, *Juan and Angelo*. Therefore, the predicate of the sentence uses the plural verb form *have*.]

TIPS FOR WRITERS

To make certain that you have correctly identified the subject of the sentence, try dropping out the words you think make up the prepositional phrase. If the sentence still makes sense, then you have correctly identified the subject.

That **box** of supplies **is** missing.
That **box is** missing. [When *of supplies* is dropped, the sentence still makes sense. Therefore, *box* is the subject.]
That **supplies is** missing. [When *box of* is dropped, the sentence no longer makes sense. Therefore, *supplies* is not the subject.]

---

4. **The following pronouns are singular: *each, either, neither, one, everyone, everybody, no one, nobody, anyone, anybody, someone, somebody.***

   EXAMPLES
   Each of the dancers **jumps** effortlessly. [*Each one* jumps.]
   Neither of the dancers **is** ready to begin. [*Neither one* is ready.]
   Someone was moving in the wrong direction during rehearsal. [*One* person was moving.]
   Does everyone in your class enjoy dance? [*Everyone* does enjoy.]
   No one is ready to dance. [*Not one* person is ready.]

5. **The following pronouns are plural: *several, few, both, many.***

   EXAMPLES
   Several of the dancers **are** rehearsing.
   Few of the dancers **have** injured themselves.
   Were both of the ballets canceled?
   Many of the dancers **rehearse** daily.

6. **The pronouns *some, all, most, any,* and *none* may be either singular or plural. These pronouns are singular when they refer to a singular word and plural when they refer to a plural word.**

   EXAMPLES
   Some of the ballet **is** sad. [*Some* refers to the singular noun *ballet*.]
   Some of the dancers **are** good. [*Some* refers to the plural noun *dancers*.]

   All of the troupe **has** arrived.
   All of the dancers **have** arrived.

   Most of the music **sounds** familiar.
   Most of the tunes **sound** familiar.

   Was any of the dancing exciting?
   Were any of the dances exciting?

   None of the music **is** dull.
   None of the pieces **are** dull.

TIPS FOR WRITERS

The words *any* and *none* may be singular even when they refer to a plural word if the speaker is thinking of each item individually. The words *any* and *none* are plural only if the speaker is thinking of several items as a group.

Any of these ballets **is** worth seeing. [*Any one ballet* is worth seeing.]
None of the ballets **was** bad. [*Not one ballet* was bad.]
Any of these ballets **are** worth seeing. [*All the ballets* are worth seeing.]
None of the ballets **were** bad. [*No ballets* were bad.]

---

7. **Compound subjects joined by the word *and* are usually plural in form and therefore take a plural verb.**

   A **compound subject** is a subject that contains two or more nouns or pronouns that are the subject of the same verb.

   EXAMPLES
   Anne Sexton and **Adrienne Rich are** poets. [Two persons *are* poets.]
   Melody, rhythm, and **harmony give** form to music. [Three things *give*.]
   He, she, and **I swim** every day in the pool at the school gymnasium. [Three people *swim*.]

8. **Compound subjects that name only one person or thing take a singular verb.**

EXAMPLES
My **coach and trainer is** my uncle. [One person is my coach and trainer.]
Cheddar cheese and grapes makes a good snack. [The one combination makes a snack.]
Ham and eggs is a great breakfast dish.

9. **Singular subjects joined by the words *or* or *nor* take a singular verb.**

EXAMPLE
After lunch, either **Tai** or **Patti washes** the dishes. [*Either* Tai *or* Patti washes the dishes, not both.]

10. **When a singular subject and a plural subject are joined by *or* or *nor*, the verb agrees with the subject nearer the verb.**

ACCEPTABLE
Neither the director nor the **actors were** happy with the performance.
Neither the actors nor the **director was** happy with the performance.

Try to avoid such awkward constructions.

BETTER
The actors were not happy with the performance, and neither was the director.

Other Problems in Subject–Verb Agreement

1. **The contractions *don't* and *doesn't* must agree with their subjects.**

Contractions are two words combined into one, with an apostrophe indicating a letter or letters that are missing. *Don't* is the contraction for *do not*. *Doesn't* is the contraction for *does not*.

With the subjects *I* and *you* and with plural subjects, use the contraction *don't* (*do not*).

EXAMPLES
I **don't** want to.   They **don't** laugh.
You **don't** say.   These **don't** fade.

With singular subjects and with subjects *he, she,* and *it,* use the singular *doesn't* (*does not*). If you are confused about *don't* or *doesn't*, try substituting the full two words for the contraction. *He does not* makes sense, but *He do not* does not.

EXAMPLES
He **doesn't** want to.   One **doesn't** laugh.
She **doesn't** say.   This **doesn't** fade.

2. **Use a plural verb with a collective noun when you are referring to the individual parts or members of the group acting separately. Use a singular verb when you refer to the group acting together as a unit.**

Collective nouns may be either singular or plural in form. Collective nouns are singular in form when they name a *group* of persons or things.

EXAMPLES
army	class	fleet	jury
assembly	committee	flock	public
audience	faculty	group	swarm

EXAMPLES
The class **have** finished their examinations. [*Class* is thought of as several individuals.]
The class **has** voted for its president. [*Class* is thought of as a single unit.]

Be sure that any pronoun referring to the collective noun has the same number as the noun (*their* in the first example, *its* in the second).

3. **A verb agrees with its subject, not with its predicate nominative.**

S   V   PN
The choral **groups are** the main attraction.
S   V   PN
The main **attraction is** the choral groups.

TIPS FOR WRITERS
When the subject follows the verb, find the subject and make sure that the verb agrees with it. The most common uses of the subject-following-verb pattern are in sentences beginning with *here* and *there* and in questions.

Here **is** a **list** of members.
Here **are** two **lists** of members.
There **is** my **book.**
There **are** my **books.**
Where **is Donald**? Where **is Kimi**?
Where **are Donald** and **Kimi**?

---

4. Contractions such as *here's, where's, how's,* and *what's* include the verb *is.* Do not use one of these contractions unless a singular subject follows it.

NONSTANDARD
There's some facts on that topic in a chart at the back of the book.

STANDARD
There **are** some population **numbers** in a table in the first chapter of the book.
In the first chapter of the book, there**'s** a **table** with some population numbers.

5. A word or a phrase stating a weight, a measurement, or an amount of money or time is usually considered one item and takes a singular verb.

EXAMPLES
Two hundred pounds is too heavy for me to lift.
Five miles is a long way to walk.
Ten dollars is too much for a movie ticket.
Two hours is not too long for a feature film.
Two thirds of the movie **was** filmed in Asia.

Sometimes, however, the amount is thought of as individual pieces or parts. If so, a plural verb is used.

EXAMPLES
Three dollars were scattered on the table.
Two vacation days are still coming to me.
Three fourths of the peaches **are** homegrown.

6. The title of a work of art, literature, or music, even when plural in form, takes a singular verb.

EXAMPLES
Three Musicians **is** a well-known painting by Pablo Picasso. [one work of art]
Little Women **is** my favorite novel. [one book]

7. *Every* or *many a* before a subject calls for a singular verb.

EXAMPLES
Every student and parent **was** there.
Many a serious problem **was** avoided through their efforts.

8. A few nouns, although plural in form, take singular verbs.

EXAMPLES
The **news** of her election to the U.S. Senate **is** a relief to everyone.
Measles is becoming a serious health problem in some cities.
Physics is a fascinating subject.

Some nouns that end in *-s* take a plural verb even though they refer to a single item.

EXAMPLES
The **tweezers are** in the cabinet.
Were these **slacks** on sale?
The **pliers are** on the workbench.

Agreement of Pronoun and Antecedent

1. A pronoun should agree with its antecedent in number and gender.

A pronoun refers to a noun or another pronoun that usually comes before it. The word that a pronoun refers to is called its **antecedent.**

A few singular personal pronouns have forms that indicate the **gender** of the antecedent. *He, him,* and *his* are masculine; *she her,* and *hers* are feminine; and *it* and *its* are neuter.

EXAMPLES
Marta plays **her** final match today.
Bo rides **his** bicycle every day.
The **apartment** has **its** own patio.

2. When the antecedent of a personal pronoun is another kind of pronoun, look in a phrase following the antecedent to determine gender.

EXAMPLES
Each of the **women** designs **her** own fabrics.
One of the **boys** brought **his** rabbit to school.

3. When the antecedent may be either masculine or feminine, use both the masculine and the feminine forms.

EXAMPLES
Every one of the students gave a speech about **his or her** hobby.
A **person** should always manage **his or her** finances wisely.

4. **Use a singular pronoun to refer to *each, either, neither, one, everyone, everybody, no one, nobody, anyone, anybody, someone,* or *somebody.***

EXAMPLES
Someone left **his or her** umbrella under that chair.
One of the dogs has a sock in **its** mouth.

Sometimes the meaning of *everyone* and *everybody* is clearly plural. In such cases, the plural pronoun should be used.

CONFUSING
Everyone cheered when **he or she** heard the final score.

CLEAR
Everyone cheered when **they** heard the final score.

5. **Two or more singular antecedents joined by *or* or *nor* should be referred to by a singular pronoun.**

EXAMPLES
Neither **William nor Alexander** hurt **himself** in the game.
Sue or Miko will give **her** speech at the assembly.

6. **Two or more antecedents joined by *and* should be referred to by a plural pronoun.**

EXAMPLES
Myra and Jim walked slowly because **they** wanted to take photographs of the flower exhibit.
Randy and Tom performed **their** duet.

USING VERBS CORRECTLY

The Principal Parts of Verbs

1. **The four principal parts of a verb are the *infinitive,* the *present participle,* the *past,* and the *past participle.***

The principal parts of the verb *sing,* for example, are *sing* (infinitive), *singing* (present participle), *sang* (past), and *sung* (past participle). These principal parts are used to form all of the different verb tenses.

EXAMPLES
The choir **sings** every day.
The choir **is singing** now.
The choir **sang** at two special ceremonies.
The choir **has sung** its final concert.

Notice that the tenses made from the present participle and past participle contain helping verbs, such as *am, is, are, has, have.*

Regular Verbs

2. **A regular verb forms its past and past participle by adding *-d* or *-ed* to the infinitive.**

INFINITIVE	PRESENT PARTICIPLE	PAST	PAST PARTICIPLE
use	using	used	(have) used
risk	risking	risked	(have) risked
help	helping	helped	(have) helped

The present participle of most regular verbs ending in *-e* drops the *-e* before adding *-ing.* One common error in the use of the past and the past participle forms is to leave off the *-d* or *-ed* ending.

NONSTANDARD
She use to play the clarinet.

STANDARD
She **used** to play the clarinet.

NONSTANDARD
We were suppose to meet them in the city for dinner.

STANDARD
We were **supposed** to meet them in the city for dinner.

Another error is doubling the ending.

NONSTANDARD
In the middle of the summer the crops were attackted by locusts.

STANDARD
In the middle of the summer the crops were **attacked** by locusts.

NONSTANDARD
At the swimming pool last summer, he almost drownded.

STANDARD
At the swimming pool last summer, he almost **drowned.**

A few regular verbs have an alternate past form ending in -t: *burned* or *burnt.*

Irregular Verbs

3. **An *irregular verb* forms its past and past participle in some other way than by adding -d or -ed.**

Irregular verbs form their past and past participle in one or more of these ways: changing a vowel, changing consonants, adding -en, making no change at all.

INFINITIVE	PAST	PAST PARTICIPLE
begin	began	(have) begun
bring	brought	(have) brought
choose	chose	(have) chosen
ride	rode	(have) ridden
put	put	(have) put
write	wrote	(have) written

Since most English verbs are regular, people sometimes try to make irregular verbs follow the same pattern. However, such words as *throwed, knowed, shrinked,* or *choosed* are considered nonstandard. If you are not sure about the parts of a verb, look in a dictionary, which lists the principal parts of irregular verbs. In the next column, you will find a list of frequently misused irregular verbs.

Irregular Verbs Frequently Misused

INFINITIVE	PRESENT PARTICIPLE	PAST	PAST PARTICIPLE
arise	arising	arose	(have) arisen
begin	beginning	began	(have) begun
bet	betting	bet	(have) bet
bleed	bleeding	bled	(have) bled
blow	blowing	blew	(have) blown
break	breaking	broke	(have) broken
bring	bringing	brought	(have) brought
burst	bursting	burst	(have) burst
choose	choosing	chose	(have) chosen
come	coming	came	(have) come
dig	digging	dug	(have) dug
do	doing	did	(have) done
drink	drinking	drank	(have) drunk
drive	driving	drove	(have) driven
eat	eating	ate	(have) eaten
fall	falling	fell	(have) fallen
fly	flying	flew	(have) flown
freeze	freezing	froze	(have) frozen
give	giving	gave	(have) given
go	going	went	(have) gone
grow	growing	grew	(have) grown
know	knowing	knew	(have) known
leave	leaving	left	(have) left
lend	lending	lent	(have) lent
put	putting	put	(have) put
ride	riding	rode	(have) ridden
ring	ringing	rang	(have) rung
run	running	ran	(have) run
see	seeing	saw	(have) seen
seek	seeking	sought	(have) sought
shake	shaking	shook	(have) shaken
shrink	shrinking	shrank	(have) shrunk
sink	sinking	sank	(have) sunk
speak	speaking	spoke	(have) spoken
steal	stealing	stole	(have) stolen
sting	stinging	stung	(have) stung
strike	striking	struck	(have) struck
swear	swearing	swore	(have) sworn
swim	swimming	swam	(have) swum
take	taking	took	(have) taken
tear	tearing	tore	(have) torn
throw	throwing	threw	(have) thrown
wear	wearing	wore	(have) worn
win	winning	won	(have) won
write	writing	wrote	(have) written

4. **When the present participle or the past participle is used as a main verb (simple predicate) in a sentence, it always requires a helping verb to form a verb phrase.**

MAIN VERB + HELPING VERB = VERB PHRASE

taking	am	am taking
walking	was	was walking
smiling	were	were smiling
going	have been	have been going
taken	have	have taken
walked	has	has walked
gone	had	had gone
gone	will have	will have gone
stopped	have been	have been stopped

To avoid nonstandard usage, use the helping verb *have*, *has*, or *had* with the past participle.

NONSTANDARD
We already seen that TV program.

STANDARD
We **have** already **seen** that TV program.
or
We already **saw** that TV program.

5. **The time expressed by a verb is called the *tense* of the verb. Every verb in English has six tenses: present, past, future, present perfect, past perfect, future perfect.**

The following list shows six tense forms of *give*. Showing all the forms of a verb in this way is called **conjugating** the verb.

Conjugation of *Give*

Present Tense

Singular	Plural
I give	we give
you give	you give
he, she, *or* it gives	they give

Past Tense

Singular	Plural
I gave	we gave
you gave	you gave
he, she, *or* it gave	they gave

Future Tense

Singular	Plural
I will (shall) give	we will (shall) give
you will give	you will give
he, she, *or* it will give	they will give

Present Perfect Tense

Singular	Plural
I have given	we have given
you have given	you have given
he, she, *or* it has given	they have given

Past Perfect Tense

Singular	Plural
I had given	we had given
you had given	you had given
he, she, *or* it had given	they had given

Future Perfect Tense

Singular	Plural
I will (shall) have given	we will (shall) have given
you will have given	you will have given
he, she, *or* it will have given	they will have given

Each of the six tenses has an additional form called the **progressive form**, which expresses continuing action. It consists of a form of the verb *be* plus the present participle of the verb. The progressive is not a separate tense but an additional form of each of the six tenses in the conjugation.

Progressive Forms
Present Progressive: am, are, is giving
Past Progressive: was, were giving
Future Progressive: will (shall) be giving
Present Perfect Progressive: has, have been giving
Past Perfect Progressive: had been giving
Future Perfect Progressive: will (shall) have been giving

Consistency of Tenses
6. **Do not change needlessly from one tense to another.**

NONSTANDARD
Myron parked the car and locks the doors. [*Parked* is past tense; *locks* is present tense.]
She opened the bottle and pours the champagne. [*Opened* is past tense; *pours* is present tense.]

STANDARD
Myron **parked** the car and **locked** the doors. [*Parked* and *locked* are past tense.]
She **opens** the bottle and **pours** the champagne. [*Opens* and *pours* are present tense.]

The perfect tenses are used to express completed action.

NONSTANDARD
I told her that I studied French for four years. [Since the action of studying was completed before the action of telling, the verb should be *had studied*, not *studied*.]

STANDARD
I told her that I **had studied** French for four years.

Active and Passive Voices

7. A verb in the active voice expresses an action done *by* its subject. A verb in the passive voice expresses an action done *to* its subject.

ACTIVE VOICE
The guide **led** us on a tour through the Baseball Hall of Fame. [The subject, *guide,* performs the action of leading.]

PASSIVE VOICE
We **were led** by the guide on a tour through the Baseball Hall of Fame. [The subject, *we,* receives the action.]

ACTIVE VOICE
The speaker **provided** useful suggestions at the end of the lecture.

PASSIVE VOICE
Useful suggestions **were provided** by the speaker at the end of the lecture.

ACTIVE VOICE
Nathaniel Hawthorne **wrote** *The House of the Seven Gables.*

PASSIVE VOICE
The House of the Seven Gables **was written** by Nathaniel Hawthorne.

ACTIVE VOICE
Someone **has stolen** my wallet.

PASSIVE VOICE
My wallet **has been stolen**.

ACTIVE VOICE
Experts from the museum **repaired** the damaged painting.

PASSIVE VOICE
The damaged painting **was repaired** by experts from the museum.

The active voice is usually more forceful than the passive voice.

WEAK/PASSIVE VOICE
Kim's first boyfriend **will** always **be remembered.**

BETTER/ACTIVE VOICE
Kim **will** always **remember** her first boyfriend.

The following list shows the conjugation of the verb *know* in the passive voice. Compare this conjugation with the one on page 888.

Conjugation of *Know* in the Passive Voice

Present Tense

Singular	Plural
I am known	we are known
you are known	you are known
he, she, *or* it is known	they are known

Past Tense

Singular	Plural
I was known	we were known
you were known	you were known
he, she, *or* it was known	they were known

Future Tense

Singular	Plural
I will be known	we will be known
you will be known	you will be known
he, she, *or* it will be known	they will be known

Present Perfect Tense

Singular	Plural
I have	we have
been known	been known
you have	you have
been known	been known
he, she, *or* it has	they have
been known	been known

Past Perfect Tense

Singular	Plural
I had	we had
been known	been known
you had	you had
been known	been known
he, she, *or* it had	they had
been known	been known

Future Perfect Tense

Singular	Plural
I will have	we will have
been known	been known
you will have	you will have
been known	been known
he, she, *or* it will have	they will have
been known	been known

Special Problems with Verbs

Using *Lie* and *Lay* Correctly

1. The verb *lie* means "to rest or recline," or "to remain lying in a position." *Lie* never takes an object. The verb *lay* means "to put" or "to place" (something). *Lay* usually takes an object. Problems result from the fact that the past tense of *lie* is *lay*. Be sure you know whether you mean "to rest" or "to put."

INFINITIVE	PRESENT PARTICIPLE	PAST	PAST PARTICIPLE
lie	lying	lay	(have) lain
lay	laying	laid	(have) laid

EXAMPLES
I like to **lie** on the grass in the backyard.
The mail is **lying** on the table.
Those books have **lain** there for years.
Yesterday Raul **lay** in bed all day.
How long **has** the mail **lain** there?

Lay those packages down.
I **am laying** the mail on the table.
Raul **laid** the foundation for his house.
Have you **laid** your book aside?

Using *Sit* and *Set* Correctly

2. The verb *sit* means "to rest in an upright, seated position." *Sit* almost never takes an object. The verb *set* means "to put" or "to place" (something). *Set* usually takes an object. Notice that *set* does not change form in the past or past participle.

INFINITIVE	PRESENT PARTICIPLE	PAST	PAST PARTICIPLE
sit	sitting	sat	(have) sat
set	setting	set	(have) set

EXAMPLES
Why don't you **sit** on the rocking chair?
She **is sitting** in the sunshine, dreaming about her vacation.
Grandfather **sat** there for hours, telling us stories of his days as a cadet.
I **have sat** on antique chairs before—but never one this old.

Set your books down over here and your groceries on the kitchen table.
I **am setting** the table for our family reunion dinner.
Marcus **set** the cookies on a plate to cool.
Have you **set** aside some money for the skiing trip to Colorado?
She **has set** the plant on the windowsill.

Using *Rise* and *Raise* Correctly

3. The verb *rise* means "to go in an upward direction." *Rise* never has an object. The verb *raise* means "to move something in an upward direction." *Raise* usually takes an object.

INFINITIVE	PRESENT PARTICIPLE	PAST	PAST PARTICIPLE
rise	rising	rose	(have) risen
raise	raising	raised	(have) raised

EXAMPLES
Look the sun is **rising**!
He **has risen** to the rank of vice president in our corporation.
We left the dough for an hour and it **rose**.
She **rose** in the morning at six o'clock.

They **raised** one hundred dollars for the poor families in their country.
The storekeeper **is raising** his rates for fresh vegetables and fruits.
My mother **has raised** two children.

USING PRONOUNS CORRECTLY

Nominative and Objective Uses

The Case Forms of Personal Pronouns

1. *Case* is the form of a noun or pronoun that shows its use in a sentence. In English, there are three cases: *nominative, objective,* and *possessive.* Nominative means the word is used as a subject. Objective means that the word is used as the object of a verb or a preposition. Possessive means that the word is used to indicate possession.

Choosing the correct case form for a noun is no problem, because the form remains the same in the nominative and objective cases.

EXAMPLE
My **doctor** [nominative] has opened a new office with another **doctor** [objective].

Only in the possessive case does a noun change its form, usually by adding an apostrophe and *s.*

EXAMPLE
My **doctor's** practice is growing.

Personal pronouns, however, have various case forms. In the following example, the pronouns in boldfaced type all refer to the same person. They have three different forms because of their different uses.

EXAMPLE
I [nominative] remembered to bring **my** [possessive] umbrella with **me** [objective].

2. Here are the case forms of personal pronouns. Notice that all personal pronouns, except *you* and *it*, have different nominative and objective forms.

PERSONAL PRONOUNS

Singular

Nominative Case	Objective Case	Possessive Case
I	me	my, mine
you	you	your, yours
he, she, it	him, her, it	his, her, hers, its

Plural

Nominative Case	Objective Case	Possessive Case
we	us	our, ours
you	you	your, yours
they	them	their, theirs

The Nominative Case

1. The *subject* of a verb is in the nominative case.

EXAMPLE
She was pleased that **they** came. [*She* is the subject of *was; they* is the subject of *came.*]

Sometimes you may be unsure about which pronoun to use when both parts of a compound subject are pronouns. To help you choose the correct form, try each pronoun separately with the verb.

EXAMPLE
(She, Her) or (They, Them) will bring salad.

"*She* will bring salad." "*They* will bring salad." "*Her* will bring salad" and "*Them* will bring salad" sound strange. "*She or they will bring salad*" is correct.

TIPS FOR WRITERS

When the pronouns *we* and *they* sound awkward as used in a compound subject, it is a good idea to revise the sentence.

AWKWARD
We and they plan to go together to the concert.

BETTER
We plan to go with **them** to the concert.

2. A *predicate nominative* is in the nominative case.

A **predicate nominative** is a noun or pronoun that follows a linking verb and explains or identifies the subject of the sentence.

A pronoun used as a predicate nominative always follows a form of the verb *be* or a verb phrase ending in *be* or *been.*

EXAMPLES
This is **he**.
It might be **she**.

The Objective Case

3. The *direct object* of a verb is in the objective case.

A *direct object* is a noun or pronoun that receives the action of the verb or shows the result of the action.

EXAMPLES
Rob told **her** about the program last night. [*Rob* is the subject of the verb *told*. Rob told *whom?* The answer is *her.*]

He called **us** soon after receiving the news. [*He* is the subject of the verb *called*. He called *whom?* He called *us.*]

When the object is compound, try each pronoun separately. All parts of the compound must be correct for the sentence to be correct.

NONSTANDARD
Rob's good news delighted her and I. [*Rob's news delighted her* is correct. *Rob's news delighted I* is incorrect. Therefore, *Rob's news delighted her and I* is incorrect. The second pronoun should be *me.*]

STANDARD
Rob's good news delighted her and **me**.

4. The *indirect object* of the verb is in the objective case.

An *indirect object* is a noun or pronoun that tells to whom or for whom something is done. Pronouns used as indirect objects are in the objective case: *me, him, her, us, them.*

EXAMPLE
The clerk gave **her** a receipt.

5. The *object of a preposition* is in the objective case.

A prepositional phrase begins with a preposition and ends with a noun or pronoun, which is the **object of the preposition.** A pronoun used as an object of a preposition must be in the objective case.

EXAMPLES
with **him**   before **me**   next to **us**

Errors often occur when the object of a preposition is compound. You can usually figure out the correct pronouns by trying each one separately in the prepositional phrase.

NONSTANDARD
Marvin sat behind her and I. [*Marvin sat behind her* is correct. *Marvin sat behind I* is incorrect. The correct forms of the pronouns are *her* and *me.*]

STANDARD
Marvin sat behind her and **me.**

Special Pronoun Problems

Using *Who* and *Whom* Correctly

6. *Who* is used as subject or predicate nominative, and *whom* is used as an object.

NOMINATIVE	OBJECTIVE
who	whom
whoever	whomever

In spoken English, the use of *whom* is becoming less common. In fact, when you are speaking, you may correctly begin any question with *who*, regardless of the grammar of the sentence. In written English, however, you should make a distinction between *who* and *whom*.

7. **The use of *who* or *whom* in a subordinate clause depends on how the pronoun functions in the clause.**

When you are choosing between *who* or *whom* in a subordinate clause, follow these steps:

STEP 1: Find the subordinate clause.
STEP 2: Decide how the pronoun is used in the clause—as subject, predicate nominative, object of the verb, or object of a preposition.
STEP 3: Determine the case of the pronoun using the rules of standard English.
STEP 4: Select the correct form of the pronoun.

EXAMPLE
Does he know (*who, whom*) they are?
STEP 1: The subordinate clause is (*who, whom*) *they are.*
STEP 2: In this clause, the subject is *they,* the verb is *are,* and the pronoun is the predicate nominative: *they are* (*who, whom*).
STEP 3: As predicate nominative, the pronoun is in the nominative case.
STEP 4: The nominative form is *who.*
ANSWER: Does he know **who** they are?

Remember that no words outside the clause affect the case of the pronoun. In this example, the entire clause is used as a direct object of the verb *does know,* but the pronoun is used as a predicate nominative (nominative case) within the clause.

EXAMPLE
Thomas A. Edison, (*who, whom*) I read about recently, invented many things.
STEP 1: The subordinate clause is (*who, whom*) *I read about recently.*
STEP 2: In this clause, the subject is *I,* and the verb is *read.* The pronoun is the object of the preposition *about: I read about* (*who, whom*).
STEP 3: The object of a preposition is in the objective case.

STEP 4: The objective form is *whom.*
ANSWER: Thomas A. Edison, **whom** I read about recently, invented many things.

Frequently, in subordinate clauses *whom* is omitted. (This means it is "understood" to be part of the sentence.)

EXAMPLES
The man [whom] I admire is Edison.
The man [whom] I read about was an amazing inventor.

8. **Pronouns used as *appositives* are in the same case as the word to which they refer.**

An **appositive** is a noun or pronoun that follows another noun or pronoun to identify or explain it.

EXAMPLES
The hosts, **he, she,** and **I,** greeted the guests. [Since *hosts* is the subject of the sentence, the pronouns in apposition with it (*he, she, I*) must be in the nominative case.]

Steve introduced the performers, Maryanne, Thomas, and **me.** [Since *performers* is the direct object of *introduced,* the pronoun *me,* which is in apposition to *performers,* must be in the objective case.]

TIPS FOR WRITERS

To figure out the correct form for a pronoun used with an appositive or as an appositive, read the sentence with only the pronoun.

EXAMPLES
Ms. Sato asked two students, Polly and (*he, him*), to help. [Omit the direct object, *students:* Ms. Sato asked Polly and him to help.]
(*We, us*) classmates offered to help. [Omit the appositive, *classmates:* We offered to help.]

The Pronoun in an Incomplete Construction
9. **After *than* and *as* introducing an incomplete construction, use the form of the pronoun that you would use if the construction were completed.**

On the following page are two incomplete constructions. Notice how pronouns change the meaning of the sentence.

EXAMPLES
Tina likes Nan better than **I**.
Tina likes Nan better than **me.**

In the first sentence, the nominative case pronoun *I* is the subject of an understood verb: *Tina likes Nan better than I* [*like Nan*]. In the second sentence, the objective case pronoun *me* is the object of the understood verb: *Tina likes Nan better than* [*Tina likes*] *me.*

EXAMPLES
I call you more often than **he** [calls you].
I call you more often than [I call] **him.**

Did he help Abe as much as **I** [helped Abe]?
Did he help Abe as much as [he helped] **me?**

USING MODIFIERS CORRECTLY

1. **Adjectives and adverbs are modifiers, that is, they state qualities of other parts of speech. Adjectives modify nouns and pronouns. Adverbs modify verbs, adjectives, and other adverbs.**

   EXAMPLES
   tall tree   **leafy** branches   [adjectives]
   walk **quickly**   sing **well**   [adverbs]

2. **Use adjectives to compare one noun with another noun that has the same quality.**

   EXAMPLES
   This tree is **taller** than that one.
   That bush is **prettier** than this one.

3. **Use adverbs to make comparisons between verbs.**

   EXAMPLE
   I mowed the backyard quickly, but Lois mowed the front lawn even **more quickly.**

4. **There are three degrees of comparison:** *positive,* *comparative,* **and** *superlative.*

POSITIVE	COMPARATIVE	SUPERLATIVE
wide	wider	widest
young	younger	youngest
happy	happier	happiest
playful	more playful	most playful
slowly	more slowly	most slowly
good	better	best
bad	worse	worst

5. **A one-syllable modifier regularly forms its comparative and superlative degrees by adding** *-er* **and** *-est.*

POSITIVE	COMPARATIVE	SUPERLATIVE
high	higher	highest
white	whiter	whitest
long	longer	longest

6. **Some two-syllable modifiers form their comparative and superlative degrees by adding** *-er* **and** *-est.* **Other two-syllable modifiers form their comparative and superlative degrees with** *more* **and** *most.*

POSITIVE	COMPARATIVE	SUPERLATIVE
humble	humbler	humblest
lonely	lonelier	loneliest
fearful	more fearful	most fearful
basic	more basic	most basic
swiftly	more swiftly	most swiftly
quickly	more quickly	most quickly

   Some two-syllable modifiers may take either *-er,* *-est* or *more, most: common, commoner, commonest;* or *common, more common, most common.*

   If you are unsure of how a two-syllable modifier is compared, look in an unabridged dictionary.

7. **Modifiers that have more than two syllables form their comparative and superlative degrees with** *more* **and** *most.*

POSITIVE	COMPARATIVE	SUPERLATIVE
dependable	more dependable	most dependable
beautiful	more beautiful	most beautiful
magnificently	more magnificently	most magnificently

8. **Modifiers that indicate less of a quality use the word** *less* **or** *least* **before the modifier.**

POSITIVE	COMPARATIVE	SUPERLATIVE
humid	less humid	least humid
closely	less closely	least closely
damp	less damp	least damp

Irregular Comparison
9. **On the opposite page are some commonly used modifiers that do not follow the regular methods of forming their comparative and superlative degrees.**

POSITIVE	COMPARATIVE	SUPERLATIVE
bad	worse	worst
good	better	best
well	better	best
many	more	most
much	more	most

Do not add the -er, -est or more, most forms to irregularly compared forms: worse, not worser or more worse.

Use of Comparative and Superlative Forms

10. **Use the comparative degree when comparing two things. Use the superlative degree when comparing more than two.**

COMPARATIVE
Writing poetry seems **more demanding** than writing essays.
I think that Emily Dickinson is a **better** poet than Amy Lowell.
A TV program is **less interesting** than a Broadway play.

SUPERLATIVE
The *Iliad* is the **hardest** poem I have ever read.
Writing a sonnet is the **most demanding** assignment I've had so far.
Watching TV is the **least demanding** activity in the world.

In everyday conversation, people sometimes use the superlative degree in comparing two things: *Put your best foot forward.*

11. **Avoid illogical comparisons.**

ILLOGICAL
Ralph is more musical than any member of his family. [Ralph is a member of his own family, and he cannot be more musical than himself. The word *other* should be added.]

LOGICAL
Ralph is more musical than any **other** member of his family.

ILLOGICAL
Carla hits better than everyone. [The word *everyone* includes all people, and Carla is a person. Since she cannot hit better than herself, the word *else* should be added to clarify the meaning.]

LOGICAL
Carla hits better than everyone **else.**

ILLOGICAL
Marianne bakes better cakes and pastries than anyone.

LOGICAL
Marianne bakes better cakes and pastries than anyone **else**.

12. **Avoid double comparisons.**

A **double comparison** is incorrect because it contains both -er and more, or -est and most.

NONSTANDARD
She is more younger than he.

STANDARD
She is **younger** than he.

NONSTANDARD
This is the most warmest coat I've worn since I was in Alaska.

STANDARD
This is the **warmest** coat I've worn since I was in Alaska.

NONSTANDARD
My brother is more taller than I am.

STANDARD
My brother is **taller** than I am.

13. **Be sure your comparisons are clear.**

UNCLEAR
The population of China is greater than the United States. [This sentence incorrectly compares population to a country.]

CLEAR
The population of China is greater than the population of the United States.

UNCLEAR
The running speed of a cheetah is greater than a lion.

CLEAR
The running speed of a cheetah is greater than the running speed of a lion.

UNCLEAR
The surface area of a baseball is less than a basketball.

CLEAR
The surface area of a baseball is less than the surface area of a basketball.

Both parts of an incomplete comparison should be stated if there is any chance of misunderstanding.

UNCLEAR
I helped her more than Frances.

CLEAR
I helped her more than I helped Frances.

CLEAR
I helped her more than Frances helped her.

Dangling Modifiers

14. **A modifying phrase or clause that does not clearly and sensibly modify a word in a sentence is a *dangling modifier*. To correct a dangling modifier, rearrange the words in the sentence or add words to make the meaning logical and clear.**

When a modifying phrase containing a verb comes at the beginning of a sentence, the phrase should be followed by a comma. Immediately after that comma should come the word that the phrase modifies.

DANGLING MODIFIER
Driving along the highway, a deer jumped out from the underbrush. [Was the deer driving along the highway?]

CORRECTED
Driving along the highway, **we** saw a deer jump out from the underbrush.

DANGLING MODIFIER
To interpret the data completely, a computer was used.

CORRECTED
To interpret the data completely, **we** used a computer.

DANGLING MODIFIER
Wrapped in colorful paper, Jim discovered a package lying on the coffee table.

CORRECTED
Wrapped in colorful paper, **a package** lay on the coffee table.
or
Jim discovered a package wrapped in colorful paper lying on the coffee table.

DANGLING MODIFIER
To become a concert pianist, much study and practice are necessary.

CORRECTED
To become a concert pianist, **you** [*or*: a person] must spend years studying and practicing.
or
If you want to become a concert pianist, you must spend years studying and practicing.

DANGLING MODIFIER
While opening the front door, the package slipped out of my hands.

CORRECTED
While I was opening the front door, **the package** slipped out of my hands.

TIPS FOR WRITERS

A sentence may appear to have a dangling modifier when *you* is the understood subject. In such cases, the modifier is not dangling; it is modifying the understood subject.

EXAMPLES
To learn the latest weather prediction, [you] tune in to the Weather channel.
If you want hot food, [you should] try a Thai curry.

Misplaced Modifiers

15. **A *misplaced modifier* is a phrase or clause that sounds awkward because it seems to modify the wrong word(s). Modifying phrases and clauses should be placed as near as possible to the words they modify.**

MISPLACED MODIFIER
I heard about the airplane that crashed on the evening television news.

CORRECTED
I heard on the evening television news about the airplane that crashed.

MISPLACED MODIFIER
My brother told me about the dog that cried in his letter.

CORRECTED
In his letter, my brother told me about the dog that cried.

MISPLACED MODIFIER
I graduated from high school after attending for only three years on Friday.

CORRECTED
On Friday, I graduated from high school after attending for only three years.

MISPLACED MODIFIER
The audience listened to the young cellist with indifference.

CORRECTED
The audience listened with indifference to the young cellist.

MISPLACED MODIFIER
I bought a peach from a grocer that was not ripe.

CORRECTED
I bought a peach that was not ripe from a grocer.

MISPLACED MODIFIER
He is building a cabinet for the kitchen that is made of oak.

CORRECTED
He is building a cabinet that is made of oak for the kitchen.

COMMON USAGE PROBLEMS

a, an
These indefinite articles refer to one of a general group. Use *a* before words beginning with a consonant sound; use *an* before words beginning with a vowel sound.

EXAMPLES
We heard **a** lark and **an** oriole.
Do you want **an** apple, **a** pear, **an** avocado, or **an** egg?
Do you want **an** apple, orange, or apricot?
A herd of cattle has been grazing for **an** hour.

In the last example, *a* is used before *herd* because the *h* in *herd* is pronounced. *An* is used before *hour* because the *h* in *hour* is not pronounced.

accept, except
Accept is a verb that means "to receive." *Except* may be either a verb or a preposition. As a verb, it means "to leave out" or "to omit." As a preposition, *except* means "excluding."

EXAMPLES
I gratefully **accept** the award.
The law **excepts** no one from paying the tax.
All the flowers **except** the roses were destroyed by the winds.
She **accepted** the fact that they weren't coming.

affect, effect
Affect is a verb meaning "to influence." *Effect* used as a verb means "to accomplish." Used as a noun, *effect* means "the result of some action."

EXAMPLES
High temperatures **affect** one's energy.
The hurricane had not **affected** telephone service in the area.
The doctors know that only rest will **effect** a cure for the condition.
The duet music has a soothing **effect** on the patients.

ain't
Avoid the word *ain't* in speaking or writing. Use of this word is always considered to be nonstandard English.

all the farther, all the faster
This should be "as far as" and "as fast as."

DIALECT
This is all the farther we can go.

STANDARD
This is **as far as** we can go.

allusion, illusion
An *allusion is* an intentional reference to something. An *illusion* is a false idea or a misleading appearance.

EXAMPLES
The text has many **allusions** to Greek philosophy.
The image in the lake was an optical **illusion.**

a lot

Do not write the expression *a lot* as one word. It should always be written as two words.

EXAMPLES
I was carrying **a lot** of packages.
She knew **a lot** about India, so we asked her to be in our group.

alumni, alumnae

Alumni is the plural of *alumnus* (a male graduate). *Alumnae* is the plural of *alumna* (a female graduate).

EXAMPLES
Many of the **alumni** of that college have gone on to graduate school.
The **alumnae** voted against coed dormitories.

among

see **between, among.**

amount, number

Use *amount* to refer to a singular word. Use *number* to refer to a plural word.

EXAMPLES
A large **number** of books [plural] are new.
The **amount** of time [singular] needed is too great.

and etc.

Etc. is an abbreviation of the Latin phrase *et cetera*, meaning "*and* other things." Thus, do not use *and* with *etc.*

EXAMPLE
My father collects baseball cards, pennants, team booklets, **etc.** [not *and etc.*]

anywheres, everywheres, nowheres, somewheres

Use these words without the final *s.*

EXAMPLES
That terrier was seen **somewhere** [not *somewheres*] in the neighborhood today.
We looked **everywhere** for her cat.
They stopped the car in the middle of **nowhere**.

as

See **like, as.**

as if

See **like, as if.**

at

Do not use *at* after *where.*

NONSTANDARD
This is where I live at.

STANDARD
This is **where** I live.

bad, badly

Bad is an adjective. *Badly* is an adverb.

EXAMPLES
Her report was organized **badly.**
The chances of going look **bad.**

because

In informal English the expression *The reason is* is often completed with a clause introduced by *because.* In formal English use the conjunction *that* to introduce the clause.

INFORMAL
The reason we went was because we wanted to see her.

FORMAL
The reason we went **was that** we wanted to see her.

being as, being that

Do not use these phrases for *since* or *because.*

NONSTANDARD
Being as it was cold I decided to wear a coat.

STANDARD
Because it was cold I decided to wear a coat.

beside, besides

Beside is a preposition that means "by the side of" someone or something. *Besides* as a preposition means "in addition to." As an adverb, *besides* means "moreover."

EXAMPLES
Sit **beside** me.
Besides poems, the book contained several essays.
Fresh fruit tastes good. **Besides**, it provides fiber for one's diet.

between, among

Use *between* when you are referring to two things at a time, even though they may be part of a group consisting of more than two.

EXAMPLES
There is friction **between** Ann Marie and Nora.
The director could not decide which of the two actors to cast because there was not much difference **between** them.

Use *among* when more than two things or persons are involved.

EXAMPLES
There was friction **among** Ann Marie, Nora, and Nick.
We divided the forty dollars **among** the five of us.
There was total agreement **among** the legislators about the effect of the law.

bring, take
  Bring means "to come carrying something." *Take* means "to go carrying something." Think of *bring* as related to *come, take* as related to *go.*

EXAMPLES
Bring that basket over here.
Now **take** it out to the kitchen.
If you **bring** enough money with you, you can **take** a present home to your mother.

bust, busted
  Avoid using these words as verbs. Use a form of either *burst* or *break.*

EXAMPLES
The pipe **burst** [not *busted*] unexpectedly.
The athlete **broke** [not *busted*] a record.

can't hardly, haven't scarcely
  The words *hardly* and *scarcely* convey a negative meaning. They should never be used with another negative word.

EXAMPLES
I **can** [not *can't*] **hardly** see the stars tonight.
We **have** [not *haven't*] **scarcely** enough vegetables for soup.

can't help but
  Avoid this expression in formal English.

INFORMAL
I can't help but hear how noisy they are.

FORMAL
I can't help **hearing** how noisy they are.

could of
  Do not write *of* with the helping verb *could.* Write *could have.* Also avoid *ought to of, should of, would of, might of,* and *must of.*

EXAMPLES
Luisa **could have** [not *of*] left town by now.
She **ought to have** [not *of*] left by now.
Grandfather **should have** [not *of*] gotten a new sweater.
I **would have** [not *of*] gone had I known.
My sister **might have** [not *of*] been to Paris before.
Jackie **must have** [not *of*] made that sandwich.

discover, invent
  Discover means "to be the first to find, see, or learn about something that already exists." *Invent* means "to be the first to do or make something."

EXAMPLES
Pierre and Marie Curie **discovered** the element radium in 1898.
The sewing machine was **invented** by Elias Howe and revolutionized the garment industry.
Chang **discovered** that the radiator was leaking.

don't, doesn't
  Don't is the contraction of *do not.*
  Doesn't is the contraction of *does not.* Use *doesn't* not *don't,* with *he, she, it, this,* and singular nouns.

EXAMPLES
It **doesn't** [not *don't*] hurt.
Snow **doesn't** [not *don't*] often fall this late in the spring.
This **doesn't** [not *don't*] smell good.

effect
  See **affect, effect.**

emigrate, immigrate
  Emigrate means "to go away from a country."
  Immigrate means "to come into a country."

EXAMPLES
How many people **emigrated** from Europe in the 1920's?
A great number from Europe **immigrated** to the United States.

everywheres

> See **anywheres,** etc.

fewer, less

> *Fewer* is used with numbers. *Less* is used with a quantity. *Fewer* tells "how many"; *less* tells "how much."
>
> EXAMPLES
> There were **fewer** inches of rainfall this year than last.
> The result of the drought is **less** water for the farmers' crops.
> He had **fewer** friends than he thought.
> The teacher had **less** patience with the young children than I had.

good, well

> *Good* is always an adjective. Never use *good* to modify a verb; use *well,* which is an adverb.
>
> NONSTANDARD
> The violinist played good.
>
> STANDARD
> The violinist played **well.**
>
> Although it is usually an adverb, *well* is used as an adjective to mean "healthy."
>
> EXAMPLE
> I feel **well.**
>
> *Feel good* and *feel well* mean different things. *Feel good* means "to feel happy or pleased." *Feel well* simply means "to feel healthy."
>
> EXAMPLES
> The gift made her feel **good.**
> She didn't feel **well,** so she went home early.
> The use of *good* as an adverb is increasing in conversational English, but it should not be used that way in writing.

had of

> See **of.**

had ought, hadn't ought

> Unlike other verbs, *ought* is not used with *had.*
>
> NONSTANDARD
> Myra had ought to be more careful; she hadn't ought to leave her car unlocked.

STANDARD
Myra **ought** to be more careful; she **ought not** to leave her car unlocked.

he, she, they

> Do not use an unnecessary pronoun after a noun. This error is called the **double subject.**
>
> NONSTANDARD
> My brother he bakes his own bread and rolls.
>
> STANDARD
> **My brother** bakes his own bread and rolls.
>
> NONSTANDARD
> Thalia she sews all her own clothes.
>
> STANDARD
> **Thalia** sews all her own clothes.
>
> NONSTANDARD
> The Joneses they fix their own car.
>
> STANDARD
> **The Joneses** fix their own car.

immigrate

> See **emigrate.**

kind, sort, type

> The words *this, that, these,* and *those* should always agree in number with the words *kind, sort, type.*
>
> EXAMPLES
> **This kind** of cereal has more bran than any of **those** other **kinds.**
> **This type** of shirt is made of softer cotton than **those types.**
> **What sort** of dress are you wearing to your sister's birthday party?

learn, teach

> *Learn* means "to acquire knowledge." *Teach* means "to instruct" or "to show how."
>
> EXAMPLE
> A native speaker **teaches** me Russian; I am **learning** to speak the language.

leave, let

> *Leave* means "to go away" or "to depart from."
> *Let* means "to allow" or "to permit."

NONSTANDARD
Leave her sit down and rest because she's dizzy.

STANDARD
Let her sit down and rest.

STANDARD
Let's **leave** early in the morning.

less
See **fewer, less.**

like, as
Like is a preposition. In informal English, *like* is often used as a conjunction meaning "as." In formal English, always use *as* as a conjunction.

EXAMPLES
I don't love anyone **as** I love Pete. [*As* introduces an adverb clause.]
You should take the medicine **as** the doctor recommends. [*The doctor recommends* is a clause and needs the subordinating conjunction *as* to introduce it.]

like, as if
In formal written English, the preposition *like* should not be used for the compound conjunctions *as if* or *as though.*

EXAMPLES
The letter looks **as though** [not *like*] it was written in haste.
She looks **as if** she doesn't feel well.

might of, must of
See **could of.**

no, none, nothing
Do not use these words with another negative.

NONSTANDARD
That question doesn't make no sense.

STANDARD
That question **makes no** sense.
That question **doesn't make any** sense.

NONSTANDARD
The free book won't cost you nothing but postage and handling.

STANDARD
The free book **won't cost you anything** but postage and handling.

The free book **will cost you nothing** but postage and handling.

NONSTANDARD
We looked for fresh rhubarb in the market, but there wasn't none.

STANDARD
We looked for fresh rhubarb in the market, but there **wasn't any.**
We looked for fresh rhubarb in the market, but there **was none.**

nowheres
See **anywheres,** etc.

of
Do not use *of* with prepositions such as *inside, off,* or *outside.*

EXAMPLES
She stepped **off** [not *off of*] the porch **outside** [not *outside of*] the house.
What's **inside** [not *inside of*] that cabinet?
Don't travel **outside** [not *outside of*] the state.

Of is also unnecessary with *had.*

EXAMPLE
If I **had** [not *had of*] run, I would be there.

or, nor
Use *or* with *either*; use *nor* with *neither.*

EXAMPLES
For dinner we have a choice of **either** pasta **or** rice.
Neither Tom **nor** Paul wants potatoes.

ought to of
See **could of.**

rise, raise
See page 890.

shall, will
Some people prefer to use *shall* with first person pronouns and *will* with second and third person pronouns in the future and future perfect tenses. Nowadays, most Americans do not make this distinction. *Will* is acceptable in the first person as well as in the other two.

sit, set
See page 890.

some, somewhat
> In writing, do not use *some* for *somewhat* as an adverb.
>
> NONSTANDARD
> My tennis game has improved some.
>
> STANDARD
> My tennis game has improved **somewhat.**

take, bring
> See **bring, take.**

than, then
> Do not confuse these words. *Than* is a conjunction; it is used to make comparisons. *Then* is an adverb; it tells about time.
>
> EXAMPLES
> This metal is heavier **than** that.
> We opened the book. **Then** we took turns reading aloud.
> This shirt is warmer **than** that one.
> First we'll clean the house and **then** we'll have some fun.

them
> *Them* should not be used as an adjective. Use *those.*
>
> NONSTANDARD
> Do you like them cuff links?
>
> STANDARD
> Do you like **those** cuff links?

this here, that there
> The words *here* and *there* are unnecessary after *this* and *that.*
>
> EXAMPLE
> Are you buying **this** [not *this here*] portable radio instead of **that** [not *that there*] one?

this kind, sort, type
> See **kind,** etc.

type, type of
> Do not use *type* as an adjective before a noun. *Type* is a noun. Do not omit *of* after type.
>
> EXAMPLE
> This **type of** reference is helpful.

way, ways
> Use *way*, not *ways*, in referring to a distance.
>
> EXAMPLE
> We drove a long **way** [not *ways*] on Tuesday.

when, where
> Do not use *when* or *where* incorrectly in writing a definition.
>
> NONSTANDARD
> A "bomb" in show business is when a new play gets bad reviews.
>
> STANDARD
> A "bomb" in show business is a new play that gets bad reviews.

where
> Do not use *where* for *that.*
>
> EXAMPLES
> I heard on a news broadcast **that** [not *where*] Boris Becker had won the tournament.
> I knew **that** [not *where*] you were going to see the championship match.

which, that, who
> The relative pronoun *who* refers to people only; *which* refers to things only; *that* refers to either people or things.
>
> EXAMPLES
> Here is the person **who** will deliver your new rug. [person]
> I chose this pattern, **which** is unusual. [thing]
> This rug is one **that** will wear well. [thing]
> The dealer is a person **that** stands behind her products. [person]

who, whom
> See pages 892–893.

without, unless
> Do not use the preposition *without* in place of the conjunction *unless.*
>
> EXAMPLE
> I cannot go **unless** [not *without*] I do my homework.

would of
> See **could of.**

THE RULES FOR CAPITALIZATION

First Words

1. **Capitalize the first word in every sentence.**

   EXAMPLES
   Many basic terms in theater come from Latin and Greek. **T**he complete list of characters in a play, for example, is Latin: *dramatis personae* ("persons of the drama"). **T**he term for the wall, or plane, separating the stage from the audience is *proscenium*, a Greek word meaning "in front of the tent."

   Traditionally, the first word of each line of poetry is capitalized, but many modern poets do not follow this practice. When you are quoting, use capital letters exactly as they are used in the source of the quotation.

Pronoun *I*

2. **Capitalize the pronoun *I*.**

   EXAMPLES
   Marta and **I** were graduated in June.
   Mom and **I** went shopping.

   The letter *I* came to be capitalized in order to make it distinct on the page. Some modern poets now use the lower-case "i."

Proper Nouns and Proper Adjectives

3. **Capitalize proper nouns and proper adjectives.**
   A **common noun** names general people, places, and things. A **proper noun** names a particular person, place, or thing. Proper adjectives are formed from proper nouns.

   Common nouns are not capitalized unless they begin a sentence or a direct quotation or are included in a title (see pages 906 and 912). Proper nouns are always capitalized.

   COMMON NOUNS
   a **p**laywright, a **n**ation, a **q**ueen, a **p**lanet

   PROPER NOUNS
   Shakespeare, **G**reece, **V**ictoria, **S**aturn

   PROPER ADJECTIVES
   Shakespearean tragedy, **G**reek poetry, **V**ictorian novel, **S**aturnian rings

Some proper names consist of more than one word. In these names, short prepositions (generally, fewer than five letters) and articles are not capitalized.

EXAMPLES
American Museum **o**f Natural History
Frederick **t**he Great
Bank **o**f Boston
Department **o**f Labor
Museum **o**f Science **a**nd History

To find out whether a noun should be capitalized, check in a dictionary. The dictionary will tell you if a word should always be capitalized or if it should be capitalized only in certain uses.

Names of People

4. **Capitalize the names of people.**

   EXAMPLES
   Amanda **B**rissel, **G**abriel **R**odriguez, **F**rank **T**urner, **L**ara **M**ackenzie, **J**effrey **R**osen, **A**llen **B**annon, **V**ictor **B**anerjee

Geographical Names

5. **Capitalize geographical names.**

   TOWNS, CITIES
   Fargo, **C**hicago, **M**oscow, **B**uenos **A**ires, **L**os **A**ngeles, **T**ulsa, **E**asthampton, **M**emphis

   COUNTIES, TOWNSHIPS
   Dade **C**ounty, **E**vanston **T**ownship, **S**oweto **T**ownship, **N**assau **C**ounty

   STATES
   Texas, **H**awaii, **M**ontana, **K**entucky, **S**outh **C**arolina, **A**laska, **O**regon, **N**evada

   REGIONS
   the **E**ast, the **S**outh, the **N**orthwest, the **M**iddle **W**est, **N**ew **E**ngland, **C**ape **C**od, the **S**outheast, the **G**ulf **C**oast

   Words such as *north, west,* and *southeast* are not capitalized when they indicate direction.

   EXAMPLES
   south of town
   traveling **n**orthwest
   canoeing **e**ast
   walking **w**est

However, these words are capitalized when they name a particular place.

EXAMPLES
states in the Northwest
driving in the Southeast
boating in the East
skiing in the West

COUNTRIES
the United States of America, Mexico, the Netherlands, Romania, Italy, Nigeria, Thailand, Mozambique, Gambia

CONTINENTS
South America, Australia, Asia, Europe, Africa, North America, Antarctica

ISLANDS
Block Island, the Greater Antilles, the Isle of Man, the Isle of Wight, Crete

MOUNTAINS
Wasatch Mountains, Mount St. Helens, the Adirondacks, the Great Smoky Mountains, the Urals, the Catskills

BODIES OF WATER
Indian Ocean, Caspian Sea, Columbia River, Chesapeake Bay, Pacific Ocean, Amazon River, Snake River

PARKS
Grand Teton Park, Starved Rock State Park, Sequoia National Park, Yellowstone National Park, Central Park

ROADS, HIGHWAYS, STREETS
Route 66, Interstate 495, Pennsylvania Turnpike, Michigan Avenue, East Ninth Street, Elm Drive, Sunset Boulevard, Santa Monica Freeway

In a hyphenated number, the second word begins with a small letter.

EXAMPLES
Twenty-eighth Street, Thirty-third Avenue, Ninety-sixth Street

Organizations
6. Capitalize names of organizations, businesses, institutions, and government bodies.

ORGANIZATIONS
United Nations, Central Intelligence Agency, National Football League, American Association of Retired Persons, Federal Bureau of Investigation, National Association for the Advancement of Colored People

The word *party* is usually written without a capital letter when it follows a proper adjective.

EXAMPLES
Republican party, Democratic party, Whig party, Communist party

BUSINESSES
General Foods Corporation, Xerox Corporation, General Electric

INSTITUTIONS
United States Coast Guard, University of California at Berkeley, Smith College, New Hyde Park High School, Beth Israel Hospital, Harvard College, Mayo Clinic

Do not capitalize words like *hotel, theater, college, high school,* and *post office* unless they are part of a proper name.

EXAMPLES
Decatur High School	a high school
Waldorf-Astoria Hotel	a hotel in New York
Shubert Theater	a theater in Chicago
Tampa Post Office	a local post office
Boston College	a college in Boston

GOVERNMENT BODIES
Congress, Internal Revenue Service, House of Representatives, Department of Commerce, Department of Agriculture, Department of Housing and Community Renewal

Historical Events
7. Capitalize the names of historical events and periods, special events, and calendar items.

HISTORICAL EVENTS AND PERIODS
Russian Revolution, Shays' Rebellion, World War I, Age of Reason, War Between the States, French Revolution

SPECIAL EVENTS
U.S. Open, World Series, Super Bowl, Macy's Thanksgiving Day Parade, Cannes International Film Festival

CALENDAR ITEMS
Friday, November, Memorial Day, Father's Day, Christmas, Yom Kippur, Easter, April, Mother's Day

---

TIPS FOR WRITERS

Do not capitalize the names of seasons unless they are personified or are part of the names of special events.

EXAMPLES
"I saw old Autumn in the misty morn." [personification]
We will be on the decorating committee for the annual Winter Carnival. [special event]

Nationalities and Races

8. **Capitalize the names of nationalities, races, and peoples.**

EXAMPLES
Brazilian, French, Scandinavian, Slavic, Kikuyu, Seminole, African American, Italian, Polish, Native American

Brand Names

9. **Capitalize the brand names of business products.**

EXAMPLES
Kleenex tissue, Chevrolet, Kodak film, Mitsubishi, Scott towels, Glad trash bags, Cadillac, Stanley tools

Particular Places, Things, Events

10. **Capitalize the names of ships, planets, monuments, awards, and any other particular places, things, or events.**

SHIPS, TRAINS, SPACECRAFT
the *Merrimac*, the *Lusitania*, the *Golden Hind*, the *Orient Express*, Saturn V, Magellan, Soyuz, Apollo 11, the *Metroliner*

PLANETS, STARS
Neptune, Rigel, the Dog Star, Mars, Venus, the North Star, Uranus

Sun, moon, and *earth* are not capitalized unless they are listed with other heavenly bodies.

MONUMENTS, MEMORIALS
Washington Monument, Lincoln Memorial, Vietnam Veterans' Memorial

BUILDINGS
Sears Tower, Empire State Building, Westminster Abbey, Puck Building, Parliament, the New York Stock Exchange

AWARDS
Nobel Prize, Emmy Award, Pulitzer Prize, Purple Heart, Academy Award, Tony Award, People's Choice Award

Specific Courses, Languages

11. **Do *not* capitalize names of school subjects, except for languages or course names followed by a number.**

EXAMPLES
This year I am taking geometry, English, world history, Typing I, a foreign language, and American history.
Jermaine is taking algebra, French II, English literature, world geography, European history, and drama.

Do *not* capitalize the name of a class (*freshman, sophomore, junior, senior*) unless it is used as part of a proper noun.

EXAMPLE
All juniors should meet after school to discuss the Junior-Senior Awards Dinner.

Titles of People

12. **Capitalize the title of a person when it comes before a name.**

EXAMPLES
President Bush   Mr. Valdez
Dr. Schweitzer   Ms. Sato

Do not capitalize a title used alone or following a person's name, especially if the title is preceded by *a* or *the.*

EXAMPLES
We saw the reverend at the park.
Lloyd Bentsen's six-year term as senator from Texas ends in 1995.
A new United States president is elected every four years.
The queen of England is getting old.
My doctor likes to go to the movies.

13. **Capitalize words showing family relationship when used with a person's name but *not* when preceded by a possessive.**

EXAMPLES
Aunt Sally, **C**ousin Fred, **G**randmother, my **m**other, your **b**rother, Harold's **a**unt

Titles of Literary and Other Creative Works

14. **Capitalize the first and last words and all important words in titles of books, periodicals, poems, stories, historical documents, movies, television programs, works of art, and musical compositions.**

Unimportant words in a title are the following:
articles: *a, an, the*
short prepositions (fewer than five letters): *of, to, for, from*
coordinating conjunctions: *and, but, so, nor, or, yet, for*

BOOKS
Island of the Blue Dolphins, Anne of Green Gables, Where the Red Fern Grows, The Summer of the Swans

PERIODICALS
Time, Newsweek, People Magazine

POEM
"The Raven"

STORIES
"The Tell-Tale Heart," "A Christmas Memory," "A Man Called Horse"

HISTORICAL DOCUMENTS
Albany **P**lan of **U**nion, **C**onstitution, **B**ill of **R**ights, **D**eclaration of **I**ndependence, **M**agna **C**arta, **E**dict of **N**antes, **E**mancipation **P**roclamation

TELEVISION PROGRAMS
Wall Street Week, Jeopardy, Cheers, Golden Girls, MacNeil-Lehrer News Hour, The Bill Cosby Show, The Simpsons

WORKS OF ART
Mona Lisa, Waterlilies

MUSICAL COMPOSITIONS
"The Star-Spangled Banner," *Porgy and Bess,* Mozart's *Requiem, The Rite of Spring*

The words *a, an,* and *the* written before a title are capitalized only when they are the first word of a title.

EXAMPLES
A Tale of Two Cities, The Phantom of the Opera, A Bell for Adano

Before the names of magazines and newspapers, *a, an,* and *the* are usually not capitalized.

EXAMPLES
I read the *New York Times.*
Dad reads the *New York Post.*
Jack reads the *Los Angeles Times.*
Moira subscribes to the *Boston Phoenix.*

Religions

15. **Capitalize names of religions and their followers, holy celebrations, holy writings, and specific deities.**

RELIGIONS AND FOLLOWERS
Islam, Hinduism, Catholicism, Judaism, Lutheran, Buddhist, Taoist, Mormon, Quaker, Jehovah's Witness

HOLY DAYS AND SEASONS
Good Friday, Ramadan, Yom Kippur, Easter, Christmas, Hannukah, Lent, Passover, Day of Atonement

HOLY WRITINGS
the Bible, Koran, Veda, Acts of the Apostles, the Talmud

SPECIFIC DEITIES
Allah, God, Jehovah

The word *god* is not capitalized when it refers to one of the several gods of ancient mythology.

EXAMPLE
The Roman emperor paid tribute to the god Jupiter.
The ancient Greeks worshiped the goddess Athena.

PUNCTUATION

End Marks

End marks—*periods, question marks,* and *exclamation points*—are used to indicate the purpose of a sentence.

1. **Use a period to end a statement (*or* declarative sentence).**

EXAMPLES
Our team lost the game.
Janet questioned who they were.
We're not there yet.
She isn't coming.

Notice in the second example that a declarative sentence containing an indirect question is followed by a period.

2. **Use a question mark to end a question (*or* an interrogative sentence).**

EXAMPLES
Can we go together?
Was it on time?
Who knocked on the door?
Where is Sam?

A direct question may have the same word order as a declarative sentence. Since it is a question, however, it is followed by a question mark.

EXAMPLES
We can go together?
It was on time?
He is coming with us?
They know we're here?

TIPS FOR WRITERS
Be sure to distinguish between a declarative sentence that contains an indirect question and an interrogative sentence, which asks a direct question.

INDIRECT QUESTION
Barbara asked **where the program was**. [declarative]

DIRECT QUESTION
Where is the program? [interrogative]

3. **Use an exclamation point to end an exclamation—that is, a statement that shows strong feeling. Use an** exclamation point after an interjection—that is, a word that shows strong feeling.

EXAMPLES
Wow! What a performance!
No way!
Forget it!

4. **Use a period or exclamation point to end an imperative sentence.**

When an imperative sentence makes a request, it is generally followed by a period. Imperative sentences, particularly commands, may also show strong feeling. In such cases, an exclamation point should be used.

EXAMPLES
Please don't run.
Don't run!
Please come over here.
Come over here!

TIPS FOR WRITERS
Some writers overuse the exclamation point. Use this mark of punctuation only after true exclamations or excited commands, usually in dialogue.

5. **Use a period after an abbreviation.**

Personal Names: E. B. White, O. Henry
Titles Used with Names: Mr., Ms., Mrs., Dr.
States: Fla., Miss., Mass., Conn.
Time of Day: A.M., P.M.
Years: B.C., A.D.
Addresses: Ave., St., Rd., Blvd., Pkwy.
Organizations and Companies: Assn., Co.
Units of Measure: lb., oz., in., ft., yd., mi.

Abbreviations for government agencies and international organizations and some other frequently used abbreviations are written without periods. Abbreviations in the metric system are often written without periods, especially in science books.

EXAMPLES
TV, IQ, FM, UFO, ROTC, USAF, UN, rpm, km, cm, ml, kg

The two-letter state abbreviations without periods are used only when the ZIP code number is included.

EXAMPLE
Chicago, IL 60610

If you are unsure about whether to use periods with an abbreviation, look in a dictionary.

TIPS FOR WRITERS

If an abbreviation comes at the end of a statement, do not use an additional period as an end mark. However, use a question mark or an exclamation point if one is needed.

EXAMPLES
Holly was born in Washington, D.C.
When did she leave Washington, D.C.**?**

Commas

1. **Use commas to separate items in a series.**

Notice in the following examples that the number of commas in a series is one less than the number of items in the series.

EXAMPLES
All of the sophomores, juniors, and seniors participated in May Day. [words]
The juniors played Frisbee behind the library, near the lake, and beside the garden. [phrases]
Those who had barbecued the chicken, who had made the salads, and who had baked the pies and cakes were glad that they had helped. [clauses]

When the last two items in a series are joined by *and,* some writers omit the comma before the *and* if the comma is not needed to clarify the meaning.

CLEAR WITH COMMA OMITTED
The sauce had tomatoes, green peppers, onions, garlic and spices.

NOT CLEAR WITH COMMA OMITTED
Our cookbook staff has contributors for appetizers, salads, meats, breads and desserts. [How many contributors are there, four or five? Does one person serve as breads and desserts contributor, or is there a separate contributor for each?]

CLEAR WITH COMMA INCLUDED
Our cookbook staff has contributors for appetizers, salads, meats, breads, and desserts. [five contributors]

Some writers prefer always to use the comma before the *and* in a series. Follow your teacher's instructions on this point.

Some words—such as *bread and butter, rod and reel, table and chairs*—are used in pairs and may be considered one item in a series.

EXAMPLE
My favorite desserts are brownies, cheesecake, and **strawberries and cream.**

2. **If all items in a series are joined by *and* or *or,* do not use commas to separate them.**

EXAMPLE
I bought **scissors and thread and needles.**

3. **Independent clauses in a series are usually separated by semicolons. Short independent clauses, however, may be separated by commas.**

EXAMPLES
As the hurricane wore on, darkness persisted; branches snapped from trees; streets were deserted; streams were teeming with debris.
Tree branches snapped, roofs were blown away, and streams flooded.

4. **Use commas to separate two or more adjectives preceding a noun.**

EXAMPLE
Are you eating that old, stale, dried-out cake?

When the last adjective in a series is thought of as part of the noun, the comma before the adjective is omitted.

EXAMPLES
I vacuumed our **small living room.**
We'll buy **cool, refreshing papaya juice.**

You can use two tests to determine whether an adjective and a noun form a unit.

TEST 1:
Insert the word *and* between the adjectives. If *and* fits sensibly between the adjectives, use a comma. In the first example sentence, *and* cannot be logically inserted: *small and living room.* In the second sentence, *and* sounds logical between the first two adjectives (*cool and refreshing*) but not between the second and third (*refreshing and papaya*).

TEST 2:
Change the order of the adjectives. If the order of the adjectives can be reversed sensibly, use a comma. *Refreshing, cool papaya juice* makes sense, but *papaya refreshing juice* and *living small room* do not.

5. **Use commas before *and, but, or, nor, for, so,* and *yet* when they join independent clauses.**

Do not be misled by compound verbs, which often make a sentence look as though it contains two independent clauses.

COMPOUND SENTENCE
Mother mowed the lawn, and **Father trimmed the hedges.** [two independent clauses]

SIMPLE SENTENCE
Mother **planted** petunias in the garden and **watered** the roses. [one subject with a compound verb]

In the following correctly punctuated compound sentences, notice that independent clauses appear on both sides of the coordinating conjunctions.

Mark turned the switch, and **the screen lit up.**
The family has a car, yet **they always use the city buses.**

TIPS FOR WRITERS
A comma is always used before *for, so,* and *yet* joining two independent clauses. The comma may be omitted, however, before *and, but, or,* or *nor* when the independent clauses are very short and when there is no chance of confusion.

EXAMPLES
He didn't know why, so he asked her to explain.
I saw the play and I enjoyed it.

6. **Use commas to set off nonessential clauses and nonessential participial phrases.**

A *nonessential* (or *nonrestrictive*) clause or participial phrase adds information that is not necessary to the main idea in the sentence. Omitting such a clause or phrase will not change the meaning of the sentence.

NONESSENTIAL CLAUSES
Thomas Clark, **who was senior class president,** plans to attend Howard University.

The Lewises, **who live on South Maple,** often vacation in the Pocono Mountains.

NONESSENTIAL PHRASES
Anna Carroll, **hoping to tour Europe,** studied Spanish diligently.
The Wealth of Nations, **written by Adam Smith,** was first published in 1776.

When a clause or phrase is necessary to the meaning of a sentence—that is, when it tells *which ones*—the clause or phrase is *essential* (or *restrictive),* and commas are *not* used.

Notice how the meaning of each sentence changes when the essential clause or phrase is omitted.

ESSENTIAL CLAUSES
All students **who have studied French** must take the examination.
A book **that I might like** is reviewed in this magazine.

An adjective clause beginning with *that* is usually essential.

ESSENTIAL PHRASES
Problems **that are avoided** lead to bigger problems.
Books **that are missing covers** sometimes sell for bargain prices.

7. **Use a comma after introductory words such as *well, yes, no,* and *why* when they begin a sentence.**

EXAMPLE
No, we're going to stay home.

8. **Use a comma after an introductory participial phrase.**

EXAMPLES
Hoping for rain, the farmers planted their crops in spite of the drought.
Excited by the parade, the children could not sit still.

9. **Use a comma after a series of introductory prepositional phrases.**

EXAMPLES
At the end of the garden on the north side, he planted two trees.
By the end of the hurricane, much property was damaged.

A short introductory prepositional phrase does not require a comma unless the comma is necessary to make the meaning clear.

EXAMPLES
In our library we have many biographies.
In our library, books are classified by the Dewey Decimal System. [The comma is necessary to avoid reading *library books.*]

10. **Use a comma after an introductory adverb clause.**

EXAMPLES
After Martha Graham was given the award, the audience gave her a standing ovation.
When you hear the alarm, you must exit.

11. **Use commas to set off elements that interrupt the sentence.**

EXAMPLES
That song, **in fact,** was never popular.
Tina, **in spite of my warning,** is coming to visit this summer.

If an "interrupter" comes at the beginning or at the end of a sentence, only one comma is needed.

EXAMPLES
Nevertheless, you must buy a gift.
I want the flowers, **of course.**

12. **Use commas to set off appositives and appositive phrases.**

EXAMPLES
My pet, **a cat,** was a birthday present.
My favorite poet, **Wallace Stevens,** was also an insurance executive.
Everyone, **even his great-grandmother,** came to welcome him home.

When an appositive has no modifiers and is closely related to the word preceding it, it should not be set off by commas.

EXAMPLES
The French poet **Verlaine** is my favorite.
We **juniors** sponsored the picnic.

13. **Use commas to set off words used in direct address.**

EXAMPLES
Martha, you must leave now.

I practiced that exercise last week, **Mr. Tai.**
Your homework, **Lee,** needs to be done.

14. **Use commas to set off parenthetical expressions.**

EXAMPLES
Generally speaking, she likes modern art.
She is, **I believe,** from Italy.

A contrasting expression introduced by *not* is parenthetical and must be set off by commas.

EXAMPLE
It was the basil, **not the parsley,** which gave the special flavor.

15. **Use a comma to separate items in dates and addresses.**

EXAMPLE
My brother moved to **Hagerstown, Maryland,** on **Wednesday, August 21, 1991.**

Notice that no comma separates the month and day *(August 21)* because it is considered one item.

16. **Use a comma after the salutation of a friendly letter and after the closing of any letter.**

EXAMPLES
Dear Ms. Wang,
Sincerely yours,
My dear Anna,
Yours very truly,

17. **Use a comma after a name followed by an abbreviation such as** *Jr., Sr.,* **and** *M.D.*

EXAMPLES
David Jefferson, **Jr.**
Ens. Will Austin, **U.S.N.**
Maria Molina, **M.D.**

In a sentence, these abbreviations must be set off by commas:

Martin Luther King, Jr., was an important American civil rights leader.

Semicolons

1. **Use a semicolon between independent clauses in a sentence if they are not joined by** *and, but, or, nor, for, so,* **or** *yet.*

Notice in the following examples that the semicolon replaces the comma and the conjunction joining the independent clauses.

EXAMPLES
First I made the salad**, and** then I began the hamburger.
First I made the salad**;** then I began the hamburger.

Penny will go to Cincinnati**, but** her brother will stay home.
Penny will go to Cincinnati**;** her brother will stay home.

A semicolon can be used between two closely related independent clauses.

EXAMPLE
Paul turned out the lights. Then he went to bed.
Paul turned out the lights**;** then he went to bed.

2. **Use a semicolon between independent clauses joined by conjunctive adverbs or transitional expressions.**

EXAMPLES
George was sick**; however,** the pills helped.
The intersection at the corner of Elm Street and Bates Avenue is dangerous**; for example,** yesterday there were three major car accidents.

When conjunctive adverbs and transitional expressions appear *within* one of the clauses and not *between* clauses, they are usually punctuated as interrupters (set off by commas). The two clauses are still separated by a semicolon.

EXAMPLE
Our youth organization wanted a tournament; our advisor**, however,** discouraged it.

3. **Use a semicolon (rather than a comma) to separate independent clauses joined by a coordinating conjunction when there are commas within the clauses.**

CONFUSING
I went with Jessica, Jill, and Jan, and Mark and Melissa followed.

CLEAR
I went with Jessica, Jill, and Jan; Mark and Melissa followed.

CONFUSING
Opening her journal and turning to a list of topics, Marla looked carefully at the many possibilities, pondering each one, but, in spite of the long list, she still could not decide.

CLEAR
Opening her journal and turning to a list of topics, Marla looked carefully at the many possibilities, pondering each one**;** but, in spite of the long list, she still could not decide.

4. **Use a semicolon between items in a series if the items contain commas.**

EXAMPLES
I have friends in **Athens, Greece; Tokyo, Japan; Zurich, Switzerland; and Warsaw, Poland.**
The band will practice in the morning on **Friday, September 13; Tuesday, September 17; and Thursday, September 19.**

Colons

1. **Use a colon before a list of items, especially after expressions like *the following* and *as follows*.**

EXAMPLES
You will study **the following subjects:** algebra, European history, and geography.
Additional colors are **as follows:** violet, pink, indigo, and turquoise.

If a word is followed by a list of appositives, then the colon is used to make the sentence clear.

EXAMPLES
At the traffic light we saw three signs: To Lawrenceville, To Debron, and To Milford.
You need to add several ingredients: flour, baking soda, and a pinch of salt.

Do not use a colon before a list that follows a verb or a preposition.

INCORRECT
Additional courses are: filmmaking, screenwriting, photography, knitting, and pottery.
You need to go to: the pharmacy, the meat market, and the bakery.

CORRECT
Additional courses are filmmaking, screenwriting, photography, knitting, and pottery.
You need to go to the pharmacy, the meat market, and the bakery.

2. **Use a colon before a long, formal statement or quotation.**

EXAMPLE
Albert Einstein had this to say: "The most beautiful thing we can experience is the mysterious. It is the source of all true art and science."

3. **Use a colon between the hour and the minute.**

EXAMPLES
9:30 P.M.   8:00 A.M.

4. **Use a colon between chapter and verse in referring to passages from the Bible.**

EXAMPLES
Psalms 3:5   Genesis 1:6–14

5. **Use a colon after the salutation of a business letter.**

EXAMPLES
Dear Ms. Davila: Dear Dr. Fenton:
Dear Sir: To Whom It May Concern:

Italics

When writing or typing, indicate italics by underlining. If your composition were to be printed, the underlined words would be set in italics. For example, if you type

Leo Tolstoy wrote <u>War and Peace</u>.

the sentence would be printed like this:

Leo Tolstoy wrote *War and Peace*.

If you use a personal computer, you can probably set words in italics yourself.

1. **Use italics (underlining) for titles of books, plays, films, periodicals, works of art, long musical compositions, television programs, ships, aircraft, and so on.**

BOOKS: *The Adventures of Huckleberry Finn, Animal Farm*
PLAYS: *The Miracle Worker, Death of a Salesman*
FILMS: *Citizen Kane, Dances with Wolves*
PERIODICALS: *Time, Washington Post*
WORKS OF ART: *Mona Lisa, The Last Supper*
TITLES OF LONG MUSICAL COMPOSITIONS: Handel's *Messiah,* the *Jupiter Symphony*

TELEVISION SERIES: *Cheers, The Simpsons*
SHIPS: *Andrea Doria, USS Iowa*
AIRCRAFT, SPACECRAFT: *Enola Gay, Apollo 12*

The words *a, an,* and *the* written before a title are italicized only when they are part of the title. Before the names of newspapers and magazines, however, they are not italicized, even if they are capitalized on the front page of the newspaper or on the cover of the magazine.

EXAMPLES
Do you prefer ***The Adventures of Robin Hood*** or the more recent version with Kevin Costner?
I bought Ernest Hemingway's ***The Sun Also Rises.***
In the museum we saw Rodin's sculpture ***The Kiss.***
I subscribe to the ***New York Times*** and the ***Country Journal.***
Every week I watched ***The Wonder Years.***

Magazine articles, chapter headings, and titles of short poems, short stories, short musical compositions, and individual episodes of TV shows, when referred to in a composition, should be placed in quotation marks, not italicized. See page 914.

2. **Use italics (underlining) for words, letters, and figures referred to as such and for foreign words.**

EXAMPLES
The word ***agape*** comes from Greek.
The word ***Mississippi*** has four ***s***'s and four ***i***'s.
The ***8*** on my application looks like a ***3.***
I gave the woman a bouquet of flowers, and she said, ***"Merci."***

Quotation Marks
1. **Use quotation marks to enclose a direct quotation—a person's exact words.**

EXAMPLES
Joyce said, "It is time to go home."
"Impossible. It is much too early," argued her husband.

2. **Begin a direct quotation with a capital letter.**

EXAMPLES
Before the rehearsal, the soloist said, "**M**y music is not on my stand."
Mr. Horton said, "**T**he rest of the novel, of course." [Although this quotation is not a sentence, it is Mr. Horton's complete remark.]

If the direct quotation is obviously a fragment of the original quotation, it may begin with a small letter.

EXAMPLE
Is the market, as Adam Smith thought, governed by an "invisible hand"? [The quotation is obviously only a phrase from Smith's sentence.]

TIPS FOR WRITERS
Do not use quotation marks for *indirect quotations*.

DIRECT QUOTATIONS
Steven said, "I'm going to mow the lawn."
She exclaimed, "I've never seen such a beautiful horse!"

INDIRECT QUOTATIONS
Steven said that he was going to mow the lawn.
She exclaimed that she had never seen such a beautiful horse.

---

3. **When a quoted sentence is divided into two parts by an interrupting expression, begin the second part with a small letter.**

EXAMPLE
"I know," she said, "that we can complete the project."

If the second part of a quotation is a new sentence, a period (not a comma) follows the interrupting expression; and the second part begins with a capital letter.

EXAMPLE
"I tried to see the penguins," the student said. "The penguin house was closed, though."

An interrupting expression is not a part of a quotation and therefore should never be inside quotation marks.

INCORRECT
"Don't go there, she said, because you might fall."

CORRECT
"Don't go there," she said, "because you might fall."

When two or more sentences by the same speaker are quoted together, use only one set of quotation marks.

INCORRECT
Robert said, "The corridor is long, indeed." "Why aren't there more lights?"

CORRECT
Robert said, "The corridor is long, indeed. Why aren't there more lights?"

4. **Set off a direct quotation from the rest of the sentence by commas or by a question mark or an exclamation point.**

EXAMPLES
The waiter said, "I hope you will enjoy your food," as he placed our appetizers on the table.
Mother said, "Have a wonderful trip!" as she tucked a present into my hand and gave me a hug.

5. **Place commas and periods inside closing quotation marks.**

EXAMPLES
"I haven't seen the exhibition," remarked the professor, "but I understand it has received excellent reviews."
He read aloud "Ode to the End of Summer," a poem by Phyllis McGinley.

6. **Place semicolons and colons outside closing quotation marks.**

EXAMPLES
Socrates once said, "Know thyself"; I wonder what this means?
The following students were cited for "honorable mention": Beth Good, Marty Fisher, and Pat Roads.

7. **If the quotation is a question or an exclamation, place question marks and exclamation points inside the closing quotation marks. Otherwise, place them outside.**

EXAMPLES
"Is it raining?" the nurse asked as I closed my umbrella.
"It's pouring!" I answered.
What is the connotation of "egghead"?

8. **When you write dialogue (a conversation), begin a new paragraph every time the speaker changes.**

EXAMPLE
"It was a feast," Jack murmured, still not daring to glance at his father.
"A feast," Judy agreed.

9. When a quoted passage consists of more than one paragraph, put quotation marks at the beginning of each paragraph and at the end of the entire passage. Do not put quotation marks after any paragraph but the last.

EXAMPLE
   "At nine o'clock last night," read the news story, "someone entered Tom Frank's house, destroyed art pieces on the first floor, and set fire to the house.
   "Local Fire Company Number 5 responded to the alarms, and no injuries were reported."

10. Use single quotation marks to enclose a quotation within a quotation.

EXAMPLES
Perplexed, Tiffany asked, "Which newspaper had as its headline **'Mayor Lowers Taxes'**?"
Mr. Vann said, "In a letter to his wife, the president wrote, **'Debate today was exhausting, but profitable.'** "

11. Use quotation marks to enclose titles of articles, short stories, essays, poems, songs, individual episodes of TV shows, chapters, and other parts of books or periodicals.

EXAMPLES
Please read the section titled **"Nature and Origin of the Mind."**
The article **"Comments on the Fine Arts"** was on the suggested reading list.

Italicize the title of a poem long enough to be published in a separate volume. Such poems are usually divided into titled or numbered sections, such as cantos, parts, or books. Long musical compositions include operas, descriptive titles of symphonies, ballets, oratorios, and concertos.

EXAMPLES
In my report on James Joyce, I plan to quote from **_Ulysses_** and from his story "The Dead."
He sang "Ol' Man River" from **_ShowBoat_**.

Apostrophes

With the Possessive Case
1. Add an apostrophe and an *s* to form the possessive case of a singular noun. The *possessive* of a noun or pronoun shows ownership or relationship.

EXAMPLES
a **school's** reputation   a **family's** tradition
the **president's** vacation   **Charles's** desk
a **dollar's** worth   the **couple's** wedding

2. Add only an apostrophe if the addition of *'s* would make the word awkward to pronounce.

EXAMPLES
for **righteousness'** sake
Hercules' journey

3. Add only an apostrophe to form the possessive case of a plural noun ending in *s*.

EXAMPLES
cities' transportation
students' contributions

Although most plural nouns end in *s*, some are irregular. To form the possessive case of a plural noun that does not end in *s*, add an apostrophe and an *s*.

EXAMPLES
deer's antlers
women's accessories
children's programs

Do not use an apostrophe to form the *plural* of a noun. Remember that the apostrophe shows ownership or relationship.

INCORRECT
Two sisters' left their bookbags and sweaters with the guard.

CORRECT
Two **sisters** left their bookbags and sweaters with the guard.

CORRECT
Two **sisters'** bookbags and sweaters were left with the guard.

INCORRECT
Three dogs' were tied to a tree.

CORRECT
Three **dogs** were tied to a tree.

CORRECT
Three **dogs'** leashes were tied to a tree.

INCORRECT
Ten trucks' had flat tires.

CORRECT
Ten **trucks** had flat tires.

CORRECT
Ten **trucks'** tires were flat.

4. **Do not use an apostrophe with a possessive personal pronoun.**

My, your, her, its, our, and *their* are used before a noun. *Mine, yours, hers, ours,* and *theirs,* on the other hand, are never used before a noun; they are used as subjects, complements, or objects in sentences. *His* may be used in either way.

EXAMPLES
I have **your** pearl necklace. I have a pearl necklace of **yours.**
That is **your** airplane ticket. That airplane ticket is **yours.**
Her painting was beautiful. **Hers** was a beautiful painting.
Renata has **our** cat; Anna has **theirs.**
This is **his** math notebook. This is a math notebook of **his.**

The possessive form of *who* is *whose,* not *who's.* Similarly, do not write *it's* for *its,* or *they're* for *their.*

5. **Add an apostrophe and an *s* to form the possessive case of an indefinite pronoun.**

EXAMPLES
nobody**'s** answer   another**'s** summary
someone**'s** application   neither**'s** preference
everybody**'s** name   anybody**'s** guess

6. **For possessives of compound words, names of organizations and businesses, and words showing joint possession, make only the last word possessive in form.**

COMPOUND WORDS
everyone else's problem
community board's plan
sister-in-law's quilt

ORGANIZATIONS
United Fund's drive
Wildlife Association's campaign
American Cancer Association's research program

BUSINESSES
United Paper Company's employees
American Can Company's production levels
Xerox Corporation's product line

JOINT POSSESSION
Bill and Betty**'s** furniture [The furniture belongs to both Bill and Betty.]
When one of the words showing joint possession is a pronoun, both words should be possessive in form.

EXAMPLES
Patsy's and my stamp collection [not *Patsy and my stamp collection*]
Dad's and my bowling scores have improved a lot since we watched that videotape.

7. **When two or more persons possess something individually, make each of their names possessive in form.**

EXAMPLES
Mrs. Smith's and **Mrs. Linder's** gifts [the gifts of two different women]
Tara's and **Tom's grades** [individual, not joint, possession]

With Contractions

8. **Use an apostrophe to show where letters or numbers have been omitted in a contraction.**

A **contraction** is a shortened form of a word, a figure, or a group of words. The apostrophes in contractions indicate where letters or numerals have been left out.

EXAMPLES
who is . . . who's   I am . . . I'm
is not . . . isn't   were not . . . weren't

EXCEPTION
will not . . . won't

9. **To prevent confusion, use an apostrophe and an *s* to form the plurals of lowercase letters, some uppercase letters, numerals, and some words referred to as words.**

EXAMPLES
Good shoppers mind their *p**'s*** and *q**'s**.*
His *hi**'s*** are hard to hear. [An apostrophe is used because without one the plural spells the word *his.*]

Hyphens

1. **Use a hyphen in some compound nouns.**

EXAMPLES
fire-eater, great-grandfather, sister-in-law

2. **Use a hyphen to divide a word at the end of a line.**

EXAMPLE
The candidate's campaign committee was **di-vided** on the issue of taxes.

Divide an already hyphenated word only at a hyphen.

INCORRECT
The guide this morning is my sis-ter-in-law.

CORRECT
The guide this morning is my **sister-in-law.**

INCORRECT
The grandfather clock was old-fash-ioned.

CORRECT
The grandfather clock was **old-fashioned**.

Do not divide a word so that one letter stands alone.

INCORRECT
The dish with a-pricots is in the pantry.

CORRECT
The dish with **apri-cots** is in the pantry.

INCORRECT
The height of the mountain was a-mazing.

CORRECT
The height of the mountain was **amaz-ing.**

3. **Use a hyphen with compound numbers from *twenty-one* to *ninety-nine* and with fractions used as adjectives.**

EXAMPLES
twenty-five pennies
one-third cup [but *one third* of the pasta]

4. **Use a hyphen with the prefixes *ex-, self-, all-,* and with the suffix *-elect,* and with all prefixes before a proper noun or proper adjective.**

EXAMPLES
ex-wife   **self-**worth
mid-June   **pro-**Western

Dashes

Use a dash to indicate an abrupt break in thought or speech or an unfinished statement or question.

Many words and phrases are used parenthetically; that is, they break into the main thought of a sentence. Most parenthetical elements are set off by commas or parentheses.

EXAMPLES
Joe, **however,** will not go with him.
The question, **he had to admit,** bothered him.

Sometimes, however, these elements demand a stronger emphasis. In such instances, a dash is used.

EXAMPLES
My friend—**if I can call him that**—lied to me.
A hint of saffron—**was it saffron?**—lingered in the kitchen.

Parentheses

Use parentheses to enclose material that is added to a sentence but is not considered of major importance.

EXAMPLES
During the period of the Consulate **(from 1799 to 1804)**, the French republic was governed by three consuls.
Aunt Bea **(no one knows her real age)** has been a fixture in our neighborhood for years.

Punctuation marks are used within parentheses when they belong with the parenthetical matter. However, a punctuation mark is not placed within parentheses if the mark belongs to the sentence as a whole.

EXAMPLES
Fill in the order blank carefully. (Do not use erasable ink.)
This old portrait may soon be worth a fortune (it was painted at the turn of the century**).**

SPELLING

Words with *ie* and *ei*

1. **Write *ie* when the sound is long *e*, except after *c*.**

   EXAMPLES

achieve	shield	ceiling	receipt	conceive
chief	thief	siege	fiend	wield
grief	relief	piece	perceive	yield

2. **Write *ei* when the sound is not long *e*.**

   EXAMPLES

neighbor	weight	forfeit
reign	eight	height
vein	foreign	sleigh

   EXCEPTIONS
   friend, mischief, kerchief, financier

Words with *-cede*, *-ceed*, and *-sede*

3. **Only one English word ends in *-sede: supersede;* only three words end in *-ceed: exceed, proceed,* and *succeed;* all other words with this sound end in *-cede.***

   EXAMPLES

precede	recede	secede
intercede	concede	accede

Adding Prefixes and Suffixes

4. **When a prefix is added to a word, the spelling of the original word itself remains the same.**

   EXAMPLES
   im + mature = **im**mature
   mis + rule = **mis**rule
   dis + regard = **dis**regard
   un + safe = **un**safe
   pre + cook = **pre**cook

5. **When the suffix *-ness* or *-ly* is added to a word, the spelling of the original word remains the same.**

   EXAMPLES
   clear + ly = clear**ly**
   near + ly = near**ly**
   rude + ness = rude**ness**

   EXCEPTIONS
   Words ending in *y* usually change the *y* to *i* before *-ness* and *-ly:*

   *hardy—hard**i**ness; busy—bus**i**ly*

   But most one-syllable adjectives ending in *y* follow rule 5: *shy—shyness; dry—dryly*
   True, due, and *whole* drop the final *e* before *-ly: truly, duly, wholly*

6. **Drop the final silent *e* before adding a suffix that begins with a vowel.**

   EXAMPLES
   muse + ing = musing
   guide + ance = guidance
   grieve + ous = grievous
   graze + ed = grazed

   EXCEPTIONS
   1. Keep the final silent *e* in words ending in *ce* or *ge* before a suffix that begins with *a* or *o: chargeable, noticeable*
   2. To avoid confusion with other words, keep the final silent *e* in some words: *dyeing* and *dying, singeing* and *singing.*

7. **Keep the final silent *e* before adding a suffix that begins with a consonant.**

   EXAMPLES
   nine + ty = nin**e**ty   sure + ly = sur**e**ly
   hate + ful = hat**e**ful   base + less = bas**e**less

   EXCEPTIONS
   nine + th = ninth
   acknowledge + ment = acknowledgment
   judge + ment = judgment

8. **When a word ends in *y* preceded by a consonant, change the *y* to *i* before any suffix except one beginning with *i*.**

   EXAMPLES
   forty + eth = fort**i**eth
   luxury + ous = luxur**i**ous
   rely + ed = rel**i**ed
   cry + ing = cr**y**ing

EXCEPTIONS
1. Some one-syllable words:
   sly + ness = slyness
   sky + ward = skyward
2. *lady* and *baby* with suffixes:
   ladylike   ladyship   babyhood

9. **When a word ends in *y* preceded by a vowel, simply add the suffix.**

   EXAMPLES
   joy + ous = joyous
   boy + hood = boyhood
   display + ed = displayed
   gray + ing = graying

   EXCEPTIONS
   day + ly = daily   pay + ed = paid
   say + ed = said

Doubling Final Consonants
10. **When a word ends in a consonant, double the final consonant before a suffix that begins with a vowel only if the word: (1) has only one syllable or is accented on the last syllable, and (2) ends in a single consonant preceded by a single vowel.**

    EXAMPLES
    stop + ing = stopping
    excel + ence = excellence
    occur + ence = occurrence
    fit + ing = fitting
    repel + ing = repelling

    Otherwise, simply add the suffix.

    EXAMPLES
    pump + ed = pumped
    funnel + ing = funneling
    exist + ence = existence
    borrow + ing = borrowing

Plurals of Nouns
11. **To form the plurals of most English nouns, simply add *s.***

SINGULAR	PLURAL
dog	dogs
coat	coats
pickle	pickles
niece	nieces
tree	trees
bottle	bottles

12. **To form the plurals of other nouns, follow these rules.**

If the noun ends in *s, x, z, ch,* or *sh,* add *es.*

SINGULAR	PLURAL
glass	glasses
fox	foxes
tax	taxes
waltz	waltzes
match	matches
dash	dashes

If the noun ends in *y* preceded by a consonant, change the *y* to *i* and add *es.*

SINGULAR	PLURAL
fly	flies
navy	navies
body	bodies
lady	ladies
candy	candies

EXCEPTION
The plurals of proper nouns: the *Murphys,* the *Barrys.*

If the noun ends in *y* preceded by a vowel add *s.*

SINGULAR	PLURAL
turkey	turkeys
tray	trays
key	keys

For some nouns ending in *f* or *fe,* change the *f* to *v* and add *s* or *es.*

Noticing how the plural is pronounced will help you remember whether to change the *f* to *v.*

SINGULAR	PLURAL
roof	roofs
chief	chiefs
loaf	loaves
knife	knives
self	selves

If the noun ends in *o* preceded by a consonant, add *es.*

SINGULAR	PLURAL
echo	echoes
hero	heroes
torpedo	torpedoes
potato	potatoes

If the noun ends in *o* preceded by a vowel, add *s*.

SINGULAR	PLURAL
patio	patio**s**
stereo	stereo**s**
tattoo	tattoo**s**
video	video**s**
rodeo	rodeo**s**

EXCEPTIONS
SINGULAR	PLURAL
poncho	ponchos
zoo	zoos
tango	tangos

EXCEPTIONS
Nouns for musical terms that end in *o* preceded by a consonant form the plural by adding only *s*.

SINGULAR	PLURAL
soprano	soprano**s**
alto	alto**s**
piano	piano**s**

A number of nouns that end in *o* preceded by a consonant have two plural forms.

SINGULAR	PLURAL
tornado	tornado**s** *or* tornado**es**
flamingo	flamingo**s** *or* flamingo**es**
halo	halo**s** *or* halo**es**
mosquito	mosquito**s** *or* mosquito**es**

The best way to handle plurals of words ending in *o* preceded by a consonant is to check their spelling in a dictionary.

The plurals of some nouns are formed in irregular ways.

SINGULAR	PLURAL
foot	feet
man	men
woman	women
mouse	mice
child	children
tooth	teeth

Some nouns have the same form in both the singular and the plural.

SINGULAR AND PLURAL
deer   moose   Japanese
French   sheep

Plurals of Compound Nouns
13. **If a compound noun is written as one word, form the plural by adding s or es.**

SINGULAR	PLURAL
cupful	cupful**s**
mockup	mockup**s**
backyard	backyard**s**
eyelash	eyelash**es**

If a compound noun is hyphenated or written as two words, make the main noun plural. The *main noun* is the noun that is modified.

SINGULAR	PLURAL
mother-in-law	mother**s**-in-law
brother-in-law	brother**s**-in-law
notary public	notar**ies** public
runner-up	runner**s**-up

EXCEPTIONS
SINGULAR	PLURAL
mock-up	mock-ups
lean-to	lean-tos
drop-off	drop-offs
close-up	close-ups

Plurals of Latin and Greek Loan Words
14. **Some nouns borrowed from Latin and Greek form the plural as in the original language.**

SINGULAR	PLURAL
crisis	cris**es**
diagnosis	diagnos**es**
datum	dat**a**

A few Latin and Greek loan words have two plural forms.

SINGULAR	PLURAL
vertex	verte**xes** *or* verti**ces**
curriculum	curricul**a** *or* curriculum**s**
phenomenon	phenomen**a** or phenomenon**s**

Check a dictionary to find the preferred spelling of such plurals.

Plurals of Numbers, Letters, Symbols, and Words Used as Words
15. **To form the plurals of numerals, most capital letters, symbols, and words used as words, add an s.**

EXAMPLES
Put the **7s** and the **Ls** in the second column.
Change the **&s** to **ands.**

To prevent confusion, use an apostrophe and an *s* to form the plurals of lowercase letters, certain capital letters, and some words used as words.

EXAMPLES
Your *q*'s look like *g*'s.
Ramon got all *A*'s last semester.
His low-pitched *ahem*'s bothered the speaker.

The plurals of decades and centuries may be formed by adding an *s* or an apostrophe and an *s* ('s).

EXAMPLES
My parents were teen-agers during the **'60s.**
Many immigrants came to this country during the **1800's** (*or* **1800s**).

Spelling Numbers

16. **Always spell out a number that begins a sentence.**

    EXAMPLE
    Two thousand seven hundred choral singers attended this year's state Choral Festival.

17. **Within a sentence, spell out numbers that can be written in one word or two words; use numerals for other numbers.**

    EXAMPLES
    I have only **two** weeks in which to write **three** term papers.
    Over the weekend we picked **thirty-two** quarts of strawberries.
    Barb has collected **112** different kinds of rocks.

18. **Spell out numbers used to indicate order.**

    EXAMPLE
    My sister placed **third** [not 3rd] in this year's marathon.

    EXCEPTION
    Use numerals for dates when you include the name of the month. Always use numerals for years.

    EXAMPLE
    Summer school begins on June **12** [not 12th].
    [Writing *the twelfth of June* is also correct.]
    World War I ended in **1918.**

Words Often Confused

You can prevent many spelling errors by learning the difference between the words grouped together in this section. Some of them are confusing because they are *homonyms*—that is, they're pronounced alike. Others are confusing because they're spelled the same or nearly the same.

advice	[noun] *counsel* My grandmother gave me some sound *advice.*
advise	[verb] *to give advice* Everyone *advised* me to get my high school diploma.
affect	[verb] *to influence* The lack of rain will surely *affect* the grain harvest.
effect	[verb] *to accomplish;* [noun] *consequence* or *result* The antibiotic *effected* a rapid cure. Closing down the factory may have a major *effect* on unemployment.
all ready	[pronoun plus adjective] *everyone ready* By dawn, we were *all ready* to take off on our trip.
already	[adverb] *beforehand* I *already* know what you're going to say.
all right	[This is the only acceptable spelling. Although the spelling *alright* appears in some dictionaries, it has not become standard usage.]
altar	*a table or stand at which religious rites are performed* The *altar* is carved from stone.
alter	*to change* I have had to *alter* my plans for the summer.
all together	*everyone in the same place* Dinner is the only time the members of my family are *all together.*
altogether	*entirely* Both your sister and you are *altogether* correct.

born	*given life* Professor Robert Wong was *born* in China in 1952.
borne	*carried; endured* The seeds are *borne* aloft by the wind. She has *borne* more than her share of physical pain.
brake	*a stopping device* The *brakes* on our bus were worn.
break	*to shatter, sever* Did you *break* this bottle?
capital	[noun] *center of government* or *money or property used in business;* [adjective] *punishable by death; of major importance; excellent; uppercase* Austin is the *capital* of Texas. Modernizing the factory will require much *capital.* Killing a police officer is a *capital* offense. One of the *capital* virtues of this city is clean air. It was a *capital* movie. This word should begin with a *capital* letter.
capitol	[noun] *building, statehouse* You can see the *capitol* as you enter the city.
choose	[verb, used for present and future tense, rhymes with *news*] *select* Please *choose* a number.
chose	[verb, past tense, rhymes with *nose*] Yesterday we *chose* our club officers for the year.
clothes	*garments; wearing apparel* I really prefer old *clothes.*
cloths	*pieces of material; fabrics* I use felt *cloths* to polish silver.
coarse	*rough or crude* The texture of this bread is rather *coarse.* I hate to hear *coarse* language.
course	*path of action; progress; unit of study; track or way;* also used with *of* to mean *naturally* or *certainly*

	The pilot almost got off *course.* I'm taking a *course* in Russian. I work at a golf *course.* Of *course,* no one knows but you and me.
complement	[noun] *something that completes or makes perfect;* [verb] *to complete or make perfect* The ship now has its full *complement* of officers. That blue scarf *complements* your red blouse.
compliment	[noun] *a remark that expresses approval, praise, or admiration;* [verb] *to pay a compliment* I welcomed his *compliment.* Let me *compliment* you.
consul	*the representative of a foreign country* The Brazilian *consul* was the first to arrive.
council	*a group called together to accomplish a job* The city *council* has not yet voted.
councilor	*a member of a council* My mother recently met our new district *councilor.*
counsel	[noun] *advice;* [verb] *to give advice* Your *counsel* was most useful. Did you *counsel* him to see a lawyer?
counselor	*one who gives advice* I don't think I'm qualified to act as your college *counselor.*
des´ert	[noun] *a dry region* Death Valley, a *desert* in California and Nevada, contains the lowest point in the Western Hemisphere.
desert´	[verb] *to leave* I hope you won't *desert* me in my time of need.
dessert	[noun] *the final course of a meal* A good *dessert* can be nutritious.
formally	*properly, according to strict rules* She will be *formally* sworn in tomorrow.

formerly	*previously, in the past* The new ambassador *formerly* taught Arabic at our university.
hear	[verb] *to receive sounds through the ears* I can't quite *hear* what you are saying.
here	[adverb] *this place* Be *here* promptly at 5:00 P.M.
ingenious	*clever; resourceful; skillful* What an *ingenious* solution to the problem!
ingenuous	*innocent; trusting; frank* She has an *ingenuous* smile that wins everyone over.
its	[possessive of *it*] Water seeks *its* own level.
it's	[contraction of *it is*] *It's* possible that we shall see snow by nightfall.
later	*after some time; subsequently* I'll meet you *later*.
latter	*the second of two* Almonds or pecans will do, but I prefer the *latter*.
lead	[verb, present tense, pronounced *leed*] *to go first* If you *lead,* I'll follow.
led	[verb, past tense of *lead*, rhymes with bed] Fido *led* us directly to where the keys were.
lead	[noun, pronounced *led*] *a heavy metal;* also *graphite in a pencil* These pipes are made of *lead*.
loose	[adjective, rhymes with *noose*] *free; not close together* The boat came *loose* from its mooring. The nations formed a rather *loose* alliance.
lose	[verb, pronounced *looz*] *to suffer loss* You won't *lose* your way if you follow this map.
moral	[adjective] *having to do with good or right;* [noun] *a lesson in conduct*

	Moral values are important. Each fable has a *moral*.
morale	[noun] *mental condition, spirit* The soldiers' *morale* was high.
passed	[verb, past tense of *pass*] A truck *passed* us swiftly.
past	[noun] *the history of a person;* [adjective] *former;* [preposition] *farther than* I wanted to know more about the general's *past*. Her *past* record shows she has had a lot of experience with computers. It's long *past* the time when we were to leave.
peace	*absence of conflict* During war, *peace* seemed unreachable.
piece	*a part of something* Please take a *piece* of this cake.
personal	*individual; private* Her *personal view* is that we should not buy that gift.
personnel	*a group of people employed in the same work or service; a staff* Most of the *personnel* working in this office work with computers.
plain	[adjective] *not fancy; clear;* [noun] *a flat area of land* I prefer *plain* things to fancy ones. Her meaning seemed *plain*. The central *plains* are the grain belt of the United States.
plane	[noun] *a flat surface or a level;* also *a tool; an airplane* Three points determine a *plane*. They kept the discussion on a high *plane*. First, Chris smoothed the surface with a *plane;* then he sanded the wood. Our *plane* was overbooked.
principal	[noun] *head of a school;* [adjective] *main, most important* The *principal* talked with us. The *principal* issue is one of salary.

[Remember that you have a *pal* in the *principal*.]

principle [noun] *a rule of conduct;* also *a law* or *a main fact*
My friend will not compromise her *principles*.
I am learning the *principles* of chemistry.

quiet *silent, still*
The children are usually *quiet* until just before lunch.

quite *to a great extent or degree; completely*
John is *quite* fluent in German.
He was *quite* happy today.

shone [verb, past tense of *shine*]
The rhinestones *shone* brilliantly under the stage lights.

shown [verb, past participle of *show*] *revealed*
Fiora has just *shown* us how to do the tarantella.

stationary *in a fixed position*
A fixed point is *stationary*.

stationery *writing paper*
Use this new *stationery* for invitations.
[Remember that there is an *e* in *pen* and in *stationery*.]

than [conjunction, used to make comparisons]
Jimmy enjoys country music more *than* rock music.

then [adverb, indicating *at that time* or *next*]
Were you *then* asked to play?
I soaked the beans, and *then* I put them in water to boil.

their [possessive of *they*]
The witnesses gave *their* versions of the incident.

there [adverb] *at a place* [also an expletive used to begin a sentence]
Can you be *there* by noon?
There are too few doctors in this country.

they're [contraction of *they are*]
They're walking up the street.
[If you have trouble, try the words *they are* in the sentence: *They are* walking up the street.]

threw [verb, past tense of *throw*] *hurled*
Marcus *threw* the first ball.

through [preposition] *in one side and out the opposite side*
We drove *through* the tunnel.

to [preposition; also part of the infinitive form of a verb]
I have come *to* a conclusion.
She warned us *to* avoid fat.

too *also* or *more than enough*
I prefer Mozart, and Eve does *too*.
This coffee is *too* sweet.

two *the sum of one + one*
Here are *two* letters that came for you.

waist [noun] *the middle part of the body*
Mamie has a small *waist*.

waste [noun] *discarded material;* [verb] *to squander*
Disposing of *waste* will soon become a major business.
Don't *waste* your time.

weak *feeble; lacking force; opposite of strong*
The colt is *weak* from fever.
The voice was too *weak* to hear.

week *seven days*
Marvin has been away for a *week*.

weather *conditions outdoors*
The *weather* is pleasant today.

whether [conjunction, indicates an alternative or doubt]
I wondered *whether* the event would ever begin.

who's [contraction of *who is, who has*]
I don't know *who's* downstairs.
Who's been eating the salad?

whose [possessive of *who*]
Whose book is this?

GLOSSARY

The glossary below is an alphabetical list of words found in the selections in this book. Use this glossary just as you use a dictionary—to find out the meanings of unfamiliar words. (A few technical, foreign, or more obscure words in this book are not listed here but are defined instead for you in the footnotes that accompany each selection.)

Many words in the English language have more than one meaning. This glossary gives the meanings that apply to the words as they are used in the selections in this book. Words closely related in form and meaning are usually listed together in one entry (*acute* and *acutely*), and the definition is given for the first form.

The following abbreviations are used:

adj., adjective **n.,** noun **v.,** verb
adv., adverb **pl.,** plural form

Unless a word is very simple to pronounce, its pronunciation is given in parentheses. A guide to the pronunciation symbols appears at the bottom of each right-hand glossary page.

For more information about the words in this glossary, or about words not listed here, consult a dictionary.

abate (ə·bāt′) *v.* To make less in amount, degree, or force.

abolish (ə·bäl′ish) *v.* To do away with completely; to put an end to.

abominable (ə·bäm′ə·nə·b'l) *adj.* Nasty and disgusting; vile. —**abominably** *adv.*

abscond (əb·skänd′) *v.* To run away and hide, especially in order to escape the law.

abstracted (ab·strak′tid) *adj.* Withdrawn in mind; preoccupied.

abundance (ə·bun′dəns) *n.* A large quantity; wealth.

abutment (ə·but′mənt) *n.* The point of contact between a support and the thing supported.

accentuate (ak·sen′choo·wāt′) *v.* To emphasize.

accord (ə·kôrd′) *n.* Mutual agreement; harmony.

accost (ə·kôst′) *v.* To approach and speak to, especially in an intrusive way.

accumulate (ə·kyoom′yə·lāt′) *v.* To pile up or gather together, especially over a period of time.

acute *adj.* 1. Having a sharp point. 2. Severe and sharp. 3. Shrill; high in pitch. —**acutely** *adv.*

adulation (aj′ə·lā′shən) *n.* Praise; flattery.

adversary (ad′vər·ser′ē) *n.* An enemy.

adversity (ad·vur′sə·tē) *n.* A state of misfortune; poverty and trouble.

advocate (ad′və·kāt) *v.* To speak or write in support of.

affliction (ə·flik′shən) *n.* A distressing condition; suffering.

affluent (af′loo·wənt) *adj.* Wealthy; rich. —*n.* A stream flowing into a river.

affront (ə·frunt′) *n.* An open, intentional insult; a slight to one's dignity.

aimless *adj.* Having no aim or purpose.

allay (ə·lā′) *v.* To put (fears, etc.) to rest; to calm.

aloof *adj.* Reserved and cool; distant.

amateurish (am′ə·choor′ish) *adj.* Not expert or professional.

amble *v.* To walk at a leisurely pace.

amphibian (am·fib′ē·ən) *n.* Any of a class (Amphibia) of vertebrates that usually begin life in the water, as tadpoles with gills, and later develop lungs: they are coldblooded and scaleless.

angular (aŋ′gyə·lər) *adj.* 1. Having or forming an angle or angles. 2. Having bones that jut out.

apathy (ap′ə·thē) *n.* Lack of emotion or interest.

aperture (ap′ər·cher) *n.* An opening; a hole; a gap.

appease *v.* To pacify or satisfy.

apportion (ə·pôr′shən) *v.* To divide and distribute in shares.

appraisal (ə·prā′z'l) *n.* A judging of quality or worth.

apprentice (ə·pren′tis) *n.* A person who is learning a trade or skill from a master or an expert.

apt *adj.* 1. Inclined or likely. 2. Quick to learn or understand.

arable (ar′ə·b'l) *adj.* Suitable for plowing and producing crops.

arbiter (är′bə·tər) *n.* A person selected to judge a dispute.

ardor (är′dər) *n.* Emotional warmth; passion.

armada (är·mä′də) *n.* A fleet.

articulate (är·tik′yə·lit) *adj.* Expressing oneself easily and clearly.

ashen *adj.* Like ashes, especially in color; pale.

askew (ə·skyoo′) *adj.* To one side; crooked.

asperity (as·per′ə·tē) *n.* Harshness of temper.

asphyxiate (as·fik′sē·āt′) *v.* To suffocate.

assuage (ə·swāj′) *v.* To calm; to pacify.

astray (ə·strā′) *adv.* Off the right path.

atheist (ā′thē·ist) *n.* A person who believes that there is no God.

atone *v.* To make up for a wrongdoing; make amends. —**atonement** *n.*

audacious (ô·dā′shəs) *adj.* Bold; daring.

audible (ô′də·b′l) *adj.* Loud enough to be heard.

avenge (ə·venj′) *v.* To get revenge for.

averse (ə·vʉrs′) *adj.* Not willing; reluctant.

barbaric (bär·ber′ik) *adj.* Crude or uncivilized; wild; unrestrained.

barricade (bar′ə·kād′) *v.* To shut in or keep out with a barrier thrown up hastily for defense. —*n.* Any barrier.

beguile (bi·gīl′) *v.* **1.** To mislead by cheating or tricking. **2.** To charm or delight.

beholden (bi·hōld′ən) *adj.* Obliged to feel grateful; owing thanks.

beleaguer (bi·lē′gər) *v.* **1.** To besiege by encircling, as by an army. **2.** To harass or attack.

bemoan (bi·mōn′) *v.* To moan about; to lament.

benediction (ben′ə·dik′shən) *n.* A blessing.

benevolent (bə·nev′ə·lənt) *adj.* Inclined to do good; kindly.

benign (bi·nīn′) *adj.* Good-natured; kindly.

billow *v.* To surge or swell like a wave.

blight *n.* Anything that destroys or prevents growth.

blithe (blī*th*) *adj.* Showing a cheerful disposition; carefree. —**blithely** *adv.*

bluster *v.* To blow stormily: said of wind.

brace *n.* **1.** A device used as a support; a prop. **2.** A pair.

brandish *v.* To wave, shake, or hold up in a menacing, challenging, or triumphant way.

brash *adj.* Offensively bold; impudent.

brazen *adj.* **1.** Of brass. **2.** Showing no shame; impudent.

breach *n.* An opening; a broken place.

brine *n.* Water full of salt, especially sea water.

broach *v.* **1.** To start a discussion of; to bring up. **2.** To make a hole in so as to let out liquid.

browse *v.* **1.** To nibble or graze. **2.** To glance through a book or other reading material in a casual way, reading passages here and there.

buoyancy (boi′ən·sē) *n.* Lightness of spirit; cheerfulness.

burnish *v.* To make shiny by rubbing; to polish.

cache (kash) *n.* **1.** A place in which stores of food or supplies are hidden. **2.** Any safe place for hiding or storing things.

calamity (kə·lam′ə·tē) *n.* A great misfortune; a disaster.

calibrations (kal′ə·brā′shəns) *n.* The markings on a measuring instrument.

candor (kan′dər) *n.* Honesty; frankness.

caper *v.* To skip or jump about in a gay, playful manner; to frisk.

capitulate (kə·pich′ə·lāt′) *v.* To give up.

careen *v.* To move wildly at full speed.

caricature (kar′ə·kə·chər) *n.* A picture or an imitation of a person, literary style, etc., in which certain features or mannerisms are exaggerated for satirical effect.

carnage (kär′nij) *n.* Bloody and extensive slaughter, especially in battle; bloodshed.

carriage *n.* **1.** A four-wheeled passenger vehicle, usually horse-drawn. **2.** One's manner of carrying the head and body; posture.

censure (sen′shər) *n.* A judgment condemning a person for misconduct.

chloroform (klôr′ə·fôrm′) *n.* An anesthetic.

circumscribe (sʉr′kəm·skrīb′) *v.* To trace a line around; to encircle.

clamor (klam′ər) *n.* A loud outcry; an uproar. —*v.* To cry out, demand, or complain noisily.

close (klōs) *adj.* **1.** Nearby. **2.** Enclosing; tightly surrounding.

commission (kə·mish′ən) *n.* A percentage of the money taken in on sales.

compensate (käm′pən·sāt′) *v.* To make up for.

compliance (kəm·plī′əns) *n.* The act of giving in to a request or demand.

complicity (kəm·plis′ə·tē) *n.* A partnership in wrongdoing.

compound *v.* To increase or intensify by adding elements.

compunction (kəm·puŋk′shən) *n.* A feeling of slight regret for something done.

conciliatory (kən·sil′ē·ə·tôr′ē) *adj.* Tending to win over or make friendly.

confer *v.* **1.** To have a discussion. **2.** To give or grant.

confession (kən·fesh′ən) *n.* **1.** Any act of confessing, or admitting, a fault or a crime. **2.** The confessing of sins to a priest in the sacrament of penance.

confront *v.* To face or oppose boldly and defiantly.

conjure (kän′jər) **up** *v.* **1.** To call to mind. **2.** To cause something to happen as by magic.

connoisseur (kän′ə·sʉr′) *n.* A person who has expert knowledge and keen discrimination in some field.

consecrate (kän′sə·krāt′) *v.* To devote entirely; to dedicate.

conspiracy (kən·spir′ə·sē) *n.* A secret plan.

constitute (kän′stə·to͞ot′) *v.* **1.** To make up; to compose. **2.** To set up; to establish.

consummate (kən·sum′it) *adj.* Complete or perfect in every way; supreme.

---

fat, āpe, cär; ten, ēven; is, bīte; gō, hôrn, to͞ol, look; oil, out; up, fʉr; get; joy; yet; **ch**in; **sh**e; **th**in, **th**en; **zh,** leisure; **ŋ,** ring; ə for *a* in *ago, e* in *agent, i* in *sanity, o* in *comply, u* in *focus;* ′ as in *able* (ā′b′l).

contemplate (kän′təm·plāt′) *v.* **1.** To think about intently; to consider. **2.** To have in mind as a possibility or plan.

contemptible (kən·temp′tə·b′l) *adj.* Deserving of contempt or scorn; worthless.

contemptuous (kən·temp′choo·wəs) *adj.* Full of contempt or scorn; disdainful.

contention (kən·ten′shən) *n.* A statement or point that one argues for as true or valid.

contrary *adj.* **1.** Opposite; differing completely. **2.** Inclined to oppose or disagree.

contrive *v.* **1.** To bring about, as by scheme; to manage. **2.** To think up; to devise; to scheme; to plan.

controversy (kän′trə·vur′sē) *n.* A discussion of a question in which opposing opinions clash; a debate.

conviction *n.* The state or appearance of being convinced, as of the truth of a belief.

counteract (koun′tər·akt′) *v.* To make ineffective through some action.

courier (koor′e·ər) *n.* A messenger.

covert (kuv′ərt) *adj.* Concealed; hidden; disguised; surreptitious.

crest *n.* The top or highest point.

crone *n.* An ugly, withered old woman; a hag.

crop *v.* To cut off or bite off the tops or ends of.

crypt (kript) *n.* An underground chamber, especially under the floor of a church, often serving as a burial place.

cryptic *adj.* Having a hidden or unclear meaning.

cynical (sin′i·k′l) *adj.* Believing that people are motivated in all their actions by selfishness.

deference (def′ər·əns) *n.* A yielding in opinion, judgment, or wishes. —**deferential** *adj.*

defray (di·frā′) *v.* To pay or furnish the money for.

delirium (di·lir′ē·əm) *n.* A state of extreme mental excitement and confusion.

demeanor (di·mēn′ər) *n.* Outward behavior; conduct.

deprecate (dep′rə·kāt′) *v.* To feel and express disapproval of.

depressed *adj.* **1.** Gloomy; dejected; sad. **2.** Pressed down.

depression *n.* **1.** A hollow or low place. **2.** Low spirits; gloominess; dejection.

desecrate (des′ə·krāt′) *v.* To take away the sacredness of; to treat as not sacred.

desiccate (des′i·kāt′) *v.* To dry completely.

desolate (des′ə·lit) *adj.* Left alone; lonely.

desolation (des′ə·lā′shən) *n.* **1.** A deserted or uninhabitable area. **2.** Lonely grief; misery.

despondent (di·spän′dənt) *adj.* Discouraged or hopeless; dejected.

destitution (des′tə·tōō′shən) *n.* Abject poverty.

detain *v.* To keep from leaving; to hold back.

deviation (dē′vē·ā′shən) *n.* A sharp divergence from normal behavior or from a standard.

diaphanous (dī·af′ə·nəs) *adj.* So fine or gauzy in texture as to be transparent or translucent.

differentiate (dif′ə·ren′shē·āt′) *v.* To be or form a difference in or between.

dike *n.* A dam made to prevent flooding from a river.

dilapidated (di·lap′ə·dāt′id) *adj.* Falling into pieces or into disrepair; shabby and neglected.

diligent (dil′ə·jent) *adj.* Hard-working.

diplomatic (dip′lə·mat′ik) *adj.* Politely skillful in dealing with people; tactful.

disciple (di·sī′p′l) *n.* A pupil or follower of any school of religion, learning, art, etc.

disconcert (dis′kən·surt′) *v.* To upset the composure of; to embarrass; to confuse.

disconsolate (dis·kän′sə·lit) *adj.* So unhappy that nothing will comfort.

dispel *v.* To scatter and drive away; to cause to vanish.

disposition (dis′pə·zish′ən) *n.* One's customary frame of mind; one's nature or temperament.

disrepute (dis′ri·pyōōt′) *n.* Bad reputation; disgrace; disfavor.

dissolute (dis′ə·lōōt′) *adj.* Overindulging in disgraceful or immoral activities, such as drinking and gambling.

docile (däs′′l) *adj.* Easy to manage or discipline; obedient. —**docility** *n.*

dogged (dôg′id) *adj.* Not giving in readily; persistent; stubborn.

dole *v.* To give sparingly.

domain (dō·mān′) *n.* Land under one government, ruler, or owner.

douse *v.* To plunge suddenly into liquid.

dowry (dou′rē) *n.* The property that a woman brings to her husband at marriage.

eaves (ēvz) *n. pl.* The lower edges of a roof.

eddy *v.* To move with a circular motion against the main current.

ejaculate (i·jak′yə·lāt′) *v.* To exclaim. —**ejaculation** *n.*

eloquence (el′ə·kwens) *n.* An art or manner of speech or writing that is vivid, forceful, fluent, graceful, and persuasive.

emancipate (i·man′sə·pāt′) *v.* To set free; to release from slavery or restraint.

embankment *n.* A bank of earth, rubble, etc., used to keep back water.

embolden (im·bōl′d′n) *v.* To give courage to; to cause to be bold or bolder.

emboss (im·bôs′) *v.* To decorate with patterns raised above the surface.

eminent (em′ə·nənt) *adj.* Standing high by comparison to others; distinguished.

emphatic (im·fat′ik) *adj.* Using emphasis or force.

endeavor (in·dev'ər) *v.* To try; to attempt.

enduring (in·door'iŋ) *adj.* **1.** Lasting; permanent. **2.** Bearing pain without flinching.

enmity (en'mə·tē) *n.* The bitter feelings of an enemy; hostility.

ensconce (in·skäns') *v.* To place or settle comfortably or snugly.

entrails (en'trālz) *n.* The inner organs; the guts.

entreat *v.* To ask earnestly; to beg.

equity (ek'wət·ē) *n.* Fairness; justice.

errant (er'ənt) *adj.* Roving; wandering.

erroneous (ə·rō'nē·əs) *adj.* Mistaken; wrong.

esoteric (es'ə·ter'ik) *adj.* Only known by a certain group; beyond the understanding of most people.

estrange (ə·strānj') *v.* To turn (a person) from an affectionate, friendly attitude to an indifferent, unfriendly, or hostile one.

evade *v.* To avoid or escape from.

evanesce (ev'ə·nes') *v.* To fade from sight like mist or smoke; to vanish.

exceedingly (ik·sēd'iŋ·lē) *adv.* Extremely; very much.

exodus (ek'sə·dəs) *n.* **1.** The departure of the Israelites from Egypt, in the Bible. **2.** The act of leaving.

exorbitant (ig·zôr'bə·tənt) *adj.* Unreasonably high.

expound (ik·spound') *v.* To state or explain in detail.

extensive (ik·sten'siv) *adj.* Great in amount or area.

exuberant (ig·zoo'bər·ənt) *adj.* **1.** Characterized by good health and high spirits; full of life. **2.** Growing thickly and abundantly.

facetious (fə·sē'shəs) *adj.* Joking or trying to be humorous, especially at an inappropriate time.

facilitate (fə·sil'ə·tāt') *v.* To make easy or easier.

feign (fān) *v.* To make a false show of; to pretend; to simulate.

ferocity (fə·räs'ə·tē) *n.* Wild force or cruelty.

festoon *v.* To hang in, or decorate with, loops or curves.

fetter *v.* To bind with chains.

firmament (fur'mə·mənt) *n.* The sky, viewed poetically as a solid arch or vault.

flabbergast *v.* To make speechless with amazement.

flay *v.* To strip off the skin or hide of.

flinch *v.* To draw back, as from fear or pain; to wince.

formidable (fôr'mə·də·b'l) *adj.* **1.** Causing fear or dread. **2.** Awe-inspiring in size or excellence.

fortitude (fôr'tə·tood') *n.* The strength to bear misfortune or pain calmly and patiently; firm courage.

founder *v.* To fill with water and sink.

frenzy *n.* A wild, frantic outburst of feeling or action.

froth *n.* Whitish bubbles; foam. **—frothing** *adj.*

furl *v.* To roll up tightly and make secure.

furtive *adj.* Slyly secret; sneaky. **—furtively** *adv.*

galaxy (gal'ək·sē) *n.* **1.** A brilliant group of things. **2.** A large grouping of stars.

galvanize (gal'və·nīz') *v.* **1.** To plate (metal) with zinc. **2.** To stimulate as if by electrical shock; to excite.

gambol (gam'b'l) *v.* To jump and skip about in play.

gargoyle (gär'goil) *n.* A waterspout, usually in the form of a grotesquely carved animal or fantastic creature, projecting from the gutter of a building.

garret *n.* An attic.

gaunt (gônt) *adj.* Thin and bony.

gentry *n.* People of high social standing or rank.

gild *v.* To coat with a golden color.

ginger *n.* **1.** An aromatic rootstalk used as a spice. **2.** [Colloquial] vigor; spirit.

gird *v.* To prepare oneself for action.

gore *v.* To pierce with, or as with, a horn or a tusk.

gorge *n.* **1.** A deep narrow pass between steep heights. **2.** A mass that blocks up a passage, as of ice.

grandiose (gran'dē·ōs') *adj.* Having grandeur or magnificence; imposing; impressive.

gullet *n.* The tube leading from the mouth to the stomach; throat.

gyration (jī·rā'shən) *n.* The act of moving in a circular or spiral path; whirling.

haggard (hag'ərd) *adj.* Looking weary and wasted.

hale *adj.* Sound; healthy.

hamper *v.* To keep from moving or acting freely.

harass (hə·ras') *v.* To worry or torment, as with cares, debts, or repeated questions.

harry *v.* To worry or torment; to harass.

herald *n.* A person who makes announcements or delivers state messages.

heresy (her'ə·sē) *n.* The rejection of a belief that is part of church dogma.

hoist *v.* To lift or push up with an effort.

humiliate (hyoo·mil'ē·āt') *v.* To hurt the pride or dignity of by causing to be or seem foolish or contemptible.

hurdle *v.* To jump over.

ignominious (ig'nə·min'ē·əs) *adj.* Shameful; dishonorable.

illiterate (i·lit'ər·it) *adj.* Not knowing how to read or write.

illusion (i·loo'zhən) *n.* A false idea or belief.

imminent (im'ə·nənt) *adj.* Likely or threatening to happen without delay.

---

fat, āpe, cär; ten, ēven; is, bīte; gō, hôrn, tool, look; oil, out; up, fur; get; joy; yet; chin; she; thin, then; zh, leisure; ŋ, ring; ə for *a* in *ago, e* in *agent, i* in *sanity, o* in *comply, u* in *focus;* ' as in *able* (ā'b'l).

immolate (im′ə·lāt′) *v.* To offer or kill as a sacrifice.

immune (i·myo͞on′) *adj.* Exempt from or protected against something disagreeable or harmful.

impalpable (im·pal′pə·b′l) *adj.* Not perceptible to the touch; that cannot be felt.

impassive (im·pas′iv) *adj.* Not feeling or showing emotion.

impending *adj.* About to happen.

imperceptible (im′pər·sep′tə·b′l) *adj.* Barely noticeable; slight; gradual.

imperious (im·pir′ē·əs) *adj.* Overbearing or arrogant. —**imperiously** *adv.*

imperishable (im·per′ish·ə·b′l) *adj.* Indestructible.

impertinent (im·pʉr′t′n·ənt) *adj.* Not showing proper respect or manners.

impetuous (im·pech′o͞o·wəs) *adj.* Moving with great force or violence; rash; impulsive.

impetus (im′pə·təs) *n.* The force of motion.

implement (im′plə·mənt) *n.* A tool; an instrument.

imposture (im·päs′chər) *n.* Pretending to be someone or something one is not.

impound *v.* 1. To lock up or hold by legal authority. 2. To gather and enclose (water) for irrigation.

impoverished (im·päv′ər·ish′d) *adj.* Poor.

impromptu (im·prämp′to͞o) *adj.* Without preparation or advance thought.

imprudence (im·pro͞o′dəns) *n.* An action taken without judgment or caution; rashness; indiscretion.

impudence (im′pyo͞o·dəns) *n.* Shamelessly bold or disrespectful behavior.

inanimate (in·an′ə·mit) *adj.* Not endowed with (animal) life.

incense (in·sens′) *v.* To make very angry; to enrage.

incessant (in·ses′′nt) *adj.* Never ceasing; constant.

incredulous (in·krej′o͞o·ləs) *adj.* Unwilling or unable to believe; doubting.

indices (in′də·sēz′) *n. pl.* Indexes.

indolent (in′də·lənt) *adj.* Lazy; idle.

indomitable (in·däm′it·ə·b′l) *adj.* Not easily discouraged, defeated, or subdued; unconquerable.

indulgence (in·dul′jəns) *n.* 1. A yielding to wishes or desires. 2. Gentleness in punishing or judging; kindness and lenience. —**indulgent** *adj.*

inexorable (in·ek′sər·ə·b′l) *adj.* Not alterable; unrelenting.

infallible (in·fal′ə·b′l) *adj.* Incapable of error; never wrong. —**infallibility** *n.*

inflict *v.* To give or cause (pain, wounds, etc.) by, or as by, striking.

inordinate (in·ôr′d′n·it) *adj.* Lacking restraint or moderation; too great or too many.

insensate (in·sen′sāt) *adj.* 1. Lacking or not able to feel sensation. 2. Without sense; stupid.

insidious (in·sid′ē·əs) *adj.* 1. Treacherous or sly; crafty.

2. Operating in a slow or not easily apparent manner; more dangerous than seems evident.

insoluble (in·säl′yo͞o·b′l) *adj.* Not able to be solved.

instinctive (in·stiŋk′tiv) *adj.* Based on instinct; natural.

interdict (in′tər·dikt′) *n.* An official prohibition or restraint.

intermediary (in′tər·mē′dē·er′ē) *n.* A go-between; a mediator.

interrogate (in·ter′ə·gāt′) *v.* To ask questions of.

intervene (in′tər·vēn′) *v.* 1. To come between as an influencing force in order to modify, settle, or hinder some action or argument. 2. To take place between two events or points in time.

intimation (in′tə·mā′shən) *n.* A hint; an indirect suggestion.

intonation (in′tə·nā′shən) *n.* A particular vocal quality with significant levels and variations of pitch.

intrigue (in·trēg′) *v.* To excite with curiosity; to fascinate.

intuition (in′to͞o·wish′ən) *n.* Immediate understanding or knowing without reasoning.

invariable (in·ver′ē·ə·b′l) *adj.* Never changing.

irate (ī·rāt′) *adj.* Angry; furious.

iridescent (ir′ə·des′′nt) *adj.* Showing shifting changes of color.

irk *v.* To annoy.

irredeemable (ir′i·dēm′ə·b′l) *adj.* Not able to be changed; hopeless.

irrelevant (i·rel′ə·vənt) *adj.* Not to the point; not relating to the subject.

irresolute (i·rez′ə·lo͞ot′) *adj.* Not resolute; indecisive.

irrevocable (i·rev′ə·kə·b′l) *adj.* Not able to be changed or undone; unalterable.

irrupt (i·rupt′) *v.* To burst suddenly or violently.

justification (jus′tə·fi′kā′shən) *n.* A fact that shows something to be just or right; an excuse.

knoll (nōl) *n.* A small hill; a mound.

laborious (lə·bôr′ē·əs) *adj.* Involving or calling for hard work; difficult.

lamentation (lam′ən·tā′shən) *n.* An outward expression of grief; a weeping or wailing.

languid (laŋ′gwid) *adj.* Without vigor or vitality; drooping; weak.

languor (laŋ′gər) *n.* 1. A lack of vigor or vitality; a weakness. 2. Tenderness of mood or feeling.

larder *n.* A place where the food supplies of the household are kept.

lax *adj.* Careless; loose. —**laxness** *n.*

leer *n.* A sidelong look showing evil intent or malicious triumph.

leisurely (lē′zhər·lē) *adv.* In an unhurried manner; slow.

Lilliputian (lil′ə·pyōō′shən) *adj.* **1.** Narrow-minded; petty. **2.** Very small; tiny. (In Jonathan Swift's novel, *Gulliver's Travels,* Lilliput was a society of tiny people.)

limpid *adj.* Perfectly clear; transparent.

linger *v.* To stay because of a reluctance to leave.

lithe (lī*th*) *adj.* Bending easily; supple; limber.

loll *v.* To lean or lounge about in a relaxed or lazy manner.

lucid (lōō′sid) *adj.* Clear to the mind; readily understood.

magnanimous (mag·nan′ə·məs) *adj.* Generous in overlooking insult.

malaria (mə·ler′ē·ə) *n.* An infectious disease characterized by severe chills and fever.

malicious (mə·lish′əs) *adj.* Intentionally mischievous or harmful; spiteful.

maneuver (mə·nōō′vər) *n.* Any movement or procedure intended as a clever step toward a goal; a scheme.

mania *n.* A craze; a wildness.

manifest (man′ə·fest′) *adj.* Evident; obvious.

manipulation (mə·nip′yə·lā′shən) *n.* A skillfull handling or operation; an artful control.

mar *v.* To spoil the perfection of; to damage.

maudlin (môd′lin) *adj.* Foolishly and tearfully sentimental.

maxim *n.* A concisely expressed principle or rule of conduct.

meander (mē·an′dər) *v.* To wander aimlessly; to ramble.

melodramatic (mel′ə·drə·mat′ik) *adj.* Exaggeratedly emotional; sensational.

mete *v.* To distribute; to allot. (Usually used with *out.*)

metropolis (mə·träp′′l·is) *n.* A large city.

mimic *adj.* Inclined to copy; imitative.

misgiving *n.* A disturbed feeling of fear or doubt.

mold *n.* **1.** A pattern or hollow form for giving a certain form to something. **2.** A form or shape.

molten *adj.* Melted or liquefied by heat.

morose (mə·rōs′) *adj.* Ill-tempered and gloomy; sullen.

mortality (môr·tal′ə·tē) *n.* Death on a large scale, as from disease or war.

muster *v.* **1.** To gather together and display; to collect. **2.** To assemble, as for inspection.

negotiate (ni·gō′shē·āt′) *v.* To bargain or discuss with a view to reaching agreement.

nettle *v.* To irritate; to annoy.

noncommittal (nän·kə·mit′′l) *adj.* Not committing one to any point of view or plan; not revealing any definite attitude or purpose.

nonentity (nän·en′tə·tē) *n.* A person or thing of little or no importance.

nonplus (nän·plus′) *v.* To put into a condition of confusion in which one is unable to go, speak, or act further; to bewilder.

notorious (nō·tôr′ē·əs) *adj.* Widely but unfavorably known.

obliterate (ə·blit′ə·rāt′) *v.* To blot out or wear away, leaving no traces; to erase.

oblivion (ə·bliv′ē·ən) *n.* A forgetting or having forgotten; forgetfulness.

obstinacy (äb′stə·nə·sē) *n.* Stubbornness; resistance. — **obstinate** *adj.*

offering *n.* A presentation at worship.

ominous (äm′ə·nəs) *adj.* Serving as a bad omen; threatening.

onslaught (än′slôt′) *n.* A violent, intense attack.

oppressive (ə·pres′iv) *adj.* Weighing heavily on the mind, body, or senses; distressing.

ordain *v.* To decree beforehand; to predetermine.

ornate *adj.* Heavily ornamented.

palpable (pal′pə·b′l) *adj.* **1.** Able to be touched, felt, or handled. **2.** Easily perceived; noticeable.

palpitate (pal′pə·tāt′) *n.* To beat rapidly or flutter: said especially of heart action that one is conscious of. — **palpitation** *n.*

pandemonium (pan′də·mō′nē·əm) *n.* A scene of wild disorder, noise, or confusion.

parapet (par′ə·pit) *n.* A low wall or railing.

paraphernalia (par′ə·fər·nāl′yə) *n.* Any collection of things or equipment.

parasitical (par′ə·sit′ik′l) *adj.* Living at the expense of others.

parry *v.* To turn aside or block (a blow, a question, etc.).

patronize (pa′trə·nīz′) *v.* To treat in a haughty or condescending manner.

pauper (pô′pər) *n.* A person who is extremely poor.

penitentiary (pen′ə·ten′shə·rē) *n.* A prison, especially a state or federal prison for persons convicted of serious crimes.

perpendicular (pur′pən·dik′yə·lər) *adj.* At right angles to a given line or plane; vertical. —**perpendicularity** *n.*

perpetrate (pur′pə·trāt′) *v.* To commit or do.

perpetual (pər·pech′ōō·wəl) *adj.* Continuing without interruption; constant. —**perpetually** *adv.*

petition *n.* **1.** A solemn, earnest request to a deity or superior. **2.** A formal document stating such a request and signed by a number of persons.

---

fat, āpe, cär; ten, ēven; is, bīte; gō, hôrn, tōōl, look; oil, out; up, fur; get; joy; yet; **chin; she; thin,** *th*en; **zh,** leisure; **η,** ring; ə for *a* in *ago, e* in *agent, i* in *sanity, o* in *comply, u* in *focus;* ' as in *able* (ā′b′l).

phonetic (fə·net′ik) *adj.* Of speech sounds or the production of these.

pittance (pit′′ns) *n.* A small amount of money.

plausible (plô′zə·b'l) *adj.* Seemingly true or acceptable.

pliant *adj.* Easily bent.

plunder *v.* To rob or take property by force.

ply *n.* A single thickness, fold, or layer.

pommel *n.* The round knot on the end of the hilt of some swords.

postpone *v.* To put off until later; to delay.

potent (pōt′ ′nt) *adj.* Effective; powerful.

poultice (pol′tis) *n.* A hot, soft, moist mass applied to a sore.

precarious (pri·ker′ē·əs) *adj.* **1.** Dependent upon chance; risky. **2.** Dependent upon circumstances; uncertain; insecure.

preclude *v.* To make impossible, especially in advance; to shut out; to prevent.

predicament (pri·dik′ə·mənt) *n.* A difficult or unpleasant situation.

preeminent (prē·em′ə·nənt) *adj.* Excelling others, especially in a particular quality; surpassing.

preliminary (pri·lim′ə·ner′ē) *adj.* Coming before the main action or business; preparatory.

premonition (pre·mə·nish′ən) *n.* A feeling that something bad will happen.

pretext (prē′tekst) *n.* A false reason; an excuse.

prevail (pri·vāl′) *v.* To gain advantage; to triumph.

priority (prī·ôr′ə·tē) *n.* A condition of being ahead of or before in time, order, or importance.

privation (prī·vā′shən) *n.* A depriving or being deprived.

procure (prō·kyoor′) *v.* To get or bring about by some effort; to obtain.

profess (prə·fes′) *v.* To declare openly; to affirm.

profound (prə·found′) *adj.* Deep; intense.

projectile (prə·jek′t'l) *n.* Anything thrown or designed to be thrown or shot forward, such as a cannon shell or a rocket.

promiscuous (prə·mis′kyoo·wəs) *adj.* **1.** Consisting of different elements mixed together without sorting or discrimination. **2.** Not distinguishing or discriminating.

promontory (präm′ən·tôr′ē) *n.* A peak of high land that juts out into a body of water.

propulsion (prə·pul′shən) *n.* A propelling.

prosperity (prä·sper′ə·tē) *n.* Wealth, success.

prosperous (präs′pər·əs) *adj.* Having continued success; flourishing.

prostrate (präs′trāt) *v.* To throw or put face downward; to lie flat on the ground.

prudent *adj.* Cautious or discreet in conduct. —**prudently** *adv.*

pulverize (pul′və·rīz′) *v.* To break down completely; to demolish.

punctual (puŋk′choo·wəl) *adj.* On time; prompt.

pungent (pun′jənt) *adj.* Producing a sharp sensation of smell or taste.

querulous (kwer′ə·ləs) *adj.* Complaining.

quintessence (kwin·tes′′ns) *n.* The pure, concentrated essence of anything.

quirk (kwʉrk) *n.* An oddness; a peculiarity.

rampart (ram′pärt) *n.* A wall protecting a castle or fort.

rancor (raŋ′kər) *n.* Deep hate or ill will.

rank *adj.* Strong or offensive in smell or taste.

rapt *adj.* Completely absorbed or engrossed.

ratify *v.* To approve; to confirm.

ravage (rav′ij) *v.* To destroy violently; to devastate.

ravenous (rav′ə·nəs) *adj.* Greedily or wildly hungry; famished. —**ravenously** *adv.*

recitation (res′ə·tā′shən) *n.* A reciting, as of facts or events; a recital.

recompense (rek′əm·pens′) *n.* A repayment; a reward.

reconcile (rek′ən·sīl′) *v.* To make friendly again or win over to a friendly attitude.

redress (rē′dres′) *v.* To set right; to remedy.

refurbish (ri·fʉr′bish) *v.* To brighten or fix up; to renovate. —**refurbishment** *n.*

regalia (ri·gāl′yə) *n.* Splendid clothes; finery.

reiterate (rē·it′ə·rāt′) *v.* To repeat.

relent *v.* To become less severe, stern, or stubborn.

reminiscent (rem′ə·nis′′nt) *adj.* Recalling past experiences. —**reminiscently** *adv.*

remnant *n.* What is left over; the remainder.

renegade (ren′ə·gād′) *n.* One who abandons his group to go over to the other side; one who is disloyal.

renowned (ri·nound′) *adj.* Famous.

repress *v.* To keep down or hold back; to restrain.

reproach *v.* To accuse of and blame for a fault.

requisite (rek′wə·zit) *adj.* Required by circumstances; necessary for some purpose.

resolute (rez′ə·loot) *adj.* Having or showing a fixed, firm purpose; determined.

resonant (rez′ə·nənt) *adj.* Having or producing a full, deep, or rich sound.

resplendent (ri·splen′dənt) *adj.* Shining brightly; splendid.

restitution (res′tə·too′shən) *n.* **1.** The return of something to its rightful owner. **2.** A repaying for loss or damage.

resurrection (rez′ə·rek′shən) *n.* A rising from the dead; a coming back to life.

retinue (ret′n·oo′) *n.* A group of assistants, followers, or servants attending a person of importance.

retribution (ret′rə·byoo′shən) *n.* Deserved punishment for evil done.

revelry (rev′l·rē) *n.* Noisy merrymaking.

reverent (rev′ər·ənt) *adj.* Showing respect and awe, as for something sacred.

rhetoric (ret′ər·ik) *n.* **1.** The art of using words effectively in speaking or writing. **2.** Showiness or elaborateness in language or literary style.

rigor (rig′ər) *n.* **1.** A strictness or exactness. **2.** An extreme hardship or difficulty.

rogue (rōg) *n.* A rascal; a scoundrel. **2.** A wandering beggar or tramp; a vagabond.

rouse (rouz) *v.* To stir up; to excite.

rout *v.* To force out.

rover *n.* A person who roves, or wanders.

rubicund (rōō′bi·kund′) *adj.* Reddish, rosy.

ruddy *adj.* Having a healthy red color.

rut *v.* To mate.

ruthless *adj.* Without pity.

sap¹ *n.* Vigor; energy; vitality.

sap² *v.* To weaken; to exhaust.

sarcophagus (sär·käf′ə·gəs) *n.* A stone coffin.

scabbard (skab′ərd) *n.* A sheath or case to hold the blade of a sword or dagger.

scaffolding (skaf′l·diŋ) *n.* A temporary wooden or metal framework for holding workers or materials during a repair or construction job.

scanty *adj.* Barely enough.

schematic (skē·mat′ik) *adj.* Done or organized as a scheme, plan, or diagram.

scourge (skûrj) *n.* Any cause of serious trouble or suffering.

scowl *v.* To contract the eyebrows and lower the corners of the mouth to show displeasure.

scruple (skrōō′p′l) *n.* A feeling of uneasiness about doing something one believes is wrong.

scud *v.* To move or glide along swiftly.

segregated (seg′rə·gāt·id) *adj.* Conforming to a system that separates racial groups.

sentimentality (sen′tə·men·tal′ə·tē) *n.* A display of tender, gentle, or delicate feelings, especially in a superficial way.

serene *adj.* Not disturbed or troubled; calm.

shade *n.* **1.** An area giving protection from the heat and light of the sun. **2.** Anything lacking substance or reality; a phantom or a ghost.

shamble *v.* To walk in a lazy or clumsy manner, barely lifting the feet; to shuffle.

shard *n.* A fragment; a broken piece.

shirk (shûrk) *v.* To neglect or evade doing.

shrewd (shrōōd) *adj.* Clever or sharp in practical affairs.

shuffle *v.* To move by dragging or scraping the feet.

shun *v.* To keep away from; to avoid.

simultaneous (sī′m′l·tā′nē·əs) *adj.* Occurring or done at the same time.

sinister (sin′is·tər) *adj.* Wicked, evil, or dishonest, especially in some dark, mysterious way.

skirmish *n.* A brief fight.

solder (säd′ər) *v.* To join together by melting a metal; to fuse.

solicitude (sə·lis′ə·tōōd′) *n.* Great care or concern.

somber *adj.* Dark; gloomy.

somnolent (säm′nə·lənt) *adj.* Sleepy; drowsy.

sovereign (säv′rən) *adj.* **1.** Of or holding the position of a ruler; reigning. **2.** Excellent; outstanding.

span *v.* To stretch or extend across.

spasm *n.* Any sudden, violent, temporary movement.

spasmodic (spaz·mäd′ik) *adj.* Sudden, violent, and temporary.

spruce *adj.* Neat and trim; dapper.

spume (spyōōm) *n.* Foam; froth; scum. —*v.* To foam or froth.

stealth *n.* Secret or artfully sly action or behavior. —**stealthy** *adj.*

stereotype (ster′ē·ə·tīp′) *n.* An unchanging conception or idea about some group or thing, held by many people and allowing for no individuality.

stolid *adj.* Showing no or little emotion or sensitivity; unexcitable.

stout *adj.* **1.** Strong in body; sturdy. **2.** Fat.

stratagem (strat′ə·jəm) *n.* Any trick or scheme for achieving some purpose.

strategist (strat′ə·jist) *n.* One skilled in strategy, or artful planning, to achieve some purpose.

stricken *adj.* Wounded; greatly affected.

stronghold *n.* A place having strong defenses.

stubble *n.* Short stumps of grain or other crops, left standing after harvesting.

stupendous (stoo·pen′dəs) *adj.* Astonishing; overwhelming.

subsist *v.* To remain alive.

subversive (səb·vûr′siv) *adj.* Tending or trying to overthrow or destroy.

suffice (sə·fīs′) *v.* To be enough.

sullen *adj.* Silent and ill-humored; gloomy; sulky.

summit *n.* The highest point.

suppliant (sup′lē·ənt) *n.* A person who makes a humble request or supplication.

supplicate (sup′lə·kāt′) *v.* To make a humble request of; to petition. —**supplication** *n.*

surly *adj.* Bad-tempered; sullenly rude.

---

fat, āpe, cär; ten, ēven; is, bīte; gō, hôrn, tōōl, look; oil, out; up, fʉr; get; joy; yet; **ch**in; **sh**e; **th**in, **th**en; **zh**, leisure; **ŋ**, ring; ə for *a* in *ago*, *e* in *agent*, *i* in *sanity*, *o* in *comply*, *u* in *focus*; ′ as in *able* (ā′b′l).

surmount *v.* **1.** To place something above or on top of. **2.** To conquer; to overcome.

sustain *v.* To keep up; to maintain.

swell *n.* A large wave that moves without breaking.

swoon *v.* **1.** To faint. **2.** To feel strong emotion.

taciturn (tas′ə·tʉrn′) *adj.* Not liking to talk; quiet.

taut *adj.* Tightly stretched.

teeming *v.* **1.** Full; crowded. **2.** Pouring with rain.

temperance (tem′pər·əns) *n.* Self-restraint in conduct or expression; moderation.

torpor (tôr′pər) *n.* A state of being inactive; a temporary loss of all or part of the power of sensation or of motion.

tourniquet (toor′nə·kit) *n.* A device for compressing a blood vessel, as in preparation for an injection or to stop bleeding.

tractable (trak′tə·b'l) *adj.* Easily managed or controlled.

tranquility (traη·kwil′ə·tē) *n.* Calmness.

translucent (trans·lōō′s'nt) *adj.* Letting light pass through; partially transparent, like frosted glass.

treacherous (trech′ər·əs) *adj.* Not to be trusted; betraying.

tremor (trem′ər) *n.* A trembling; a shivering.

tremulous (trem′yoo·ləs) *adj.* Trembling; quivering.

trepidation (trep′ə·dā′shən) *n.* Fearful uncertainty.

tributary (trib′yoo·ter′ē) *n.* A small stream or river that flows into a larger one.

trough (trôf) *n.* **1.** A long, narrow, open container holding water or food for animals. **2.** A long, narrow hollow, as between waves.

tumult (too′mult) *n.* A noisy commotion; an uproar.

twinge *n.* A sudden, brief, darting pain; a pang.

tyrannize (tir′ə·nīz′) *v.* To govern as a tyrant; to rule cruelly with unlimited power.

unaccountable (un′ə·koun′tə·b'l) *adj.* Unexplainable. — **unaccountably** *adv.*

unanimous (yoo·nan′ə·məs) *adj.* Agreeing completely; united in opinion.

uncanny *adj.* So remarkable or unusual as to seem preternatural.

uncoordinated (un·kō·ôr′d'n·āt′id) *adj.* **1.** Not in harmony or proper order. **2.** Lacking effective action or movement.

uncouth (un·kōōth′) *adj.* Uncultured; crude; boorish.

unforeseen *adj.* Not known beforehand.

unfurl (un·fʉrl′) *v.* To open; to spread out; to unfold.

unhinge *v.* To unlock; to detach.

uniform *adj.* Having the same manner or appearance as others of the same type.

unmitigated (un·mit′ə·gāt′id) *adj.* Not lessened or eased.

unnerve *v.* To cause to lose one's nerve or courage.

unrelenting (un·ri·len′tiη) *adj.* Refusing to yield or relent; inflexible.

unscathed (un·skā*th*d′) *adj.* Not hurt; unharmed.

uproarious (up·rôr′ē·əs) *adj.* Loud; noisy; rowdy.

vain *adj.* **1.** Too proud of one's looks or self. **2.** Without force or effect; unsuccessful.

valor (val′ər) *n.* Great courage; bravery.

vaunt (vônt) *v.* To boast about; to brag of.

veer *v.* To change direction; to turn or swing around.

venture (ven′chər) *v.* To do or go at some risk.

verisimilitude (ver′ə·si·mil′ə·tōōd′) *n.* The appearance of being true or real.

vermilion (vər·mil′yən) *adj.* A bright red color.

versatile (vʉr′sə·t'l) *adj.* Competent in or useful for many things.

vexation (vek·sā′shən) *n.* A state of being disturbed, annoyed, or irritated.

vicinity (və·sin′ə·tē) *n.* The area near or close by.

victuals (vit′'ls) *n. pl.* [Dialect or Colloquial] Items of food, especially when prepared for use.

vigil (vij′əl) *n.* A purposeful watch, usually during the hours of sleep.

vigilance (vij′ə·ləns) *n.* Watchfulness; alertness to danger or trouble.

vigorous (vig′ər·əs) *adj.* Forceful or powerful; energetic.

vile *adj.* **1.** Wicked; sinful. **2.** Highly disagreeable; very bad.

viscous (vis′kəs) *adj.* Having a sticky, fluid consistency.

vituperation (vī·tōō′pə·rā′shən) *n.* Abusive language.

vivacious (vi·vā′shəs) *adj.* Full of life and animation; spirited.

vivacity (vi·vas′ə·tē) *n.* Liveliness; spirit.

volatile (väl′ə·t'l) *adj.* Likely to shift quickly and unpredictably; unstable; explosive.

voluntary (väl′ən·ter′ē) *adj.* Given or done of one's own free will.

vortex (vôr′teks) *n.* A whirling mass.

vulnerable (vul′nər·ə·b'l) *adj.* Able to be wounded or harmed.

waft *v.* To float, as on the wind.

warp *n.* **1.** A distortion, as a twist or bend. **2.** The threads running lengthwise in a loom.

wheedle *v.* To persuade by flattery or coaxing.

wily *adj.* Crafty; sly.

wither *v.* **1.** To dry up, as from great heat; to shrivel. **2.** To cause to quail or feel small, as by a scornful glance.

woeful *adj.* Full of grief; sad.

wrench *v.* To pull or twist suddenly or jerkily.

zest *n.* Keen excitement or enjoyment.

INDEX OF SKILLS

Storytelling 3
Subjectivity 436
Subplot 546
Suspense 4, 57, 360, 877
Symbol 177, 877
Tension in drama 563
Theater terms 547
Theme 166, 177, 185, 601, 877
Third-person point of view 135, 136, 164, 875
Title, meaning of 86
Tone 324, 345, 877
Translation 243
Trochee 288
Turning point of drama 675
Understood words 255
Verbal irony 201, 872

LANGUAGE AND VOCABULARY SKILLS

Affixes 451
Allusions 151, 867
American Indian words 130
Americanisms 339
Antonyms 276
Archaic words 628, 648
British terms 54
Clues to word meanings 54, 216
Coining words 339, 480, 675
Comparisons 71, 469
Connotations 195, 295, 337, 341, 344, 868
Context clues 13, 54, 109, 161, 406, 689
Denotations 195, 869
Dialects 86, 360, 869
Diction 312, 869
Dictionary, using a 13, 54, 109, 118, 130, 216, 282, 360, 368, 378, 382, 406, 429, 445, 451, 480, 547, 628, 675, 769, 797
Epithet 781, 870
Etymologies 130, 262, 332, 339, 360, 378, 382, 445, 628, 675, 769, 797
Euphemisms and the misuse of language 857
Extended word meanings 332
Figures of speech 71, 469, 871
Grammar, Shakespeare's 648
Greek root words 378, 480
Homonyms 282, 429
Inversions 255, 872
Jargon 461, 547, 586
Latin root words 382, 480
Loaded words 824
Metaphors 469, 872

Multiple meanings 267, 335, 368
Names in Shakespeare's plays 675
New words from old ones 480
Paraphrasing 689
Prefixes 451, 769
Propaganda techniques 823
Puns and special meanings 875
Related words 216
Root words 378, 382, 445, 480
Sentences and style 142, 185
Shakespeare's grammar 648
Shakespeare's vocabulary 628, 648
Significant words 118
Similes 469, 876
Style 185
Suffixes 451
Symbols 177, 877
Synonyms 276, 282
Syntax 255, 648
Television terms 586
Theater terms 547
Translation 243
"Understood words" 255, 648
Verbs, active 392
Word histories 130, 262, 332, 339, 360, 378, 382, 445, 628, 675, 769, 797
Word roots 216, 378, 382, 445, 480
Words and distinct meanings 282
Words from the epic 797
Words frequently confused 282, 429

SPEAKING AND LISTENING SKILLS

Becoming aware of dialects 86, 358, 361
Choral speaking 352, 355, 358
Identifying propaganda techniques 823
Identifying rhyme 304, 308, 311, 312, 314, 316, 319, 320, 357, 368, 370, 600
Identifying rhythm and meter 287, 288, 299, 302, 313, 357, 370, 599
Listening for the poet's tone of voice 324–346
Listening to the natural rhythms of speech in free verse 289, 303
Listening to a conversation 87, 586
Oral report 354, 415
Reading a poem aloud 233, 287, 289, 295, 299, 300, 301, 309, 313, 317, 326, 330, 340, 342, 352, 355, 358, 361
Reading aloud end-stopped and run-on lines in poetry 295, 301, 600

Reading prose passages aloud 185, 379, 470
Reproducing a dialogue in writing 87, 586
Rewriting dialect into standard English 87
Scanning a poem 288, 302, 303, 368
Varying voice to suggest different tones 340, 342, 345

COMPOSITION SKILLS

Writing: A Creative Response
Adapting a poem for TV 311
Addressing a season 278
Answering the poet 327
Applying the poem to life 366
Casting a woman as the voyaging hero 795
Completing the story 31, 209, 295
Creating figures of speech 262, 264, 272, 282, 283, 284
Creating images 237
Creating metaphors 260, 272
Creating personifications 282, 283, 284
Creating similes to describe emotions or ideas 272
Describing a person 70, 257, 388
Describing a scene or setting 108, 117, 245, 335, 337, 378, 469
Describing an alien culture 129
Describing an experience 194
Describing an object 151
Digging in the future 415
Extending a metaphor 264, 272
Extending a simile 272
Extending an epic 800
Extending the ballad 357
Extending the play 546, 564, 586, 704
Extending the poem 238, 267, 270, 276, 295, 312, 327, 333
Extending the story 54, 80, 185, 205, 215, 224, 360
Filling in details 31, 54
Imagining a character's thoughts 13
Imitating the poem 299, 301, 331, 339, 365
Keeping a journal 429
Making up a dialogue 12
Narrating a related incident 86
Narrating an epic episode 800

Supporting a topic (or thesis) statement 130, 586, 709, 796, 858
Supporting an opinion 237, 280, 316, 332, 382, 591
Testing a hypothesis 709
Writing about images 239, 705
Writing an answer to the poem 344

CRITICAL THINKING SKILLS

The page numbers in italics refer to critical thinking skills covered in the Critical Thinking and Writing exercises.

Analysis
Analyzing a biography 445
Analyzing a movie's plot 129
Analyzing a poem *248, 347*
Analyzing a report 406, 429, *433*
Analyzing a scene from a play 586
Analyzing a theme 546, 705, *858*
Analyzing an essay *396*
Analyzing character 76, 86, *91,* 161, 177, 480, 564, 705, *709,* 796, 856
Analyzing figures of speech 253
Analyzing free verse 333
Analyzing language 705
Analyzing point of view *164*
Analyzing setting *133,* 177
Analyzing stories 185
Analyzing the allegory 856
Analyzing the elements of the epic 796
Analyzing the speaker in a poem 255
Applying the poem 341
Describing a writer's attitude 257
Distinguishing facts from opinion *485*
Identifying evidence and appeals to emotion *433*
Presenting two sides of an argument *801*
Testing a hypothesis *709*

Comparison and Contrast
Comparing adventure stories 31
Comparing and contrasting characters 108, 388, 705
Comparing and contrasting poems *285,* 341, 344, 364, 368
Comparing and contrasting stories 31, 76, *227,* 769, 796
Comparing experiences 392

Comparing poems 264, 327
Comparing the character in a story to the speaker of a poem 86
Comparing the play to a biography 547
Comparing the play to a letter 547
Comparing the story to a fairy tale 195
Comparing the story to a poem 142, 209
Contrasting characters 108
Contrasting fiction with a journal entry 108
Contrasting the poem with a news story 329
Contrasting two "return" stories 796

Evaluation and Response
Evaluating a poem *321*
Evaluating a short story *199*
Evaluating a theme *858*
Evaluating an essay *396, 433*
Evaluating figures of speech *273*
Responding to a character 70, 80, 547, 705
Responding to a different ending 151, 856
Responding to a play 547, 705
Responding to a poem 245, *248, 273, 321,* 329
Responding to a report 429
Responding to a short story 13, *199,* 216
Responding to a theme 705
Responding to an autobiography 451
Responding to an essay *396*
Responding to figures of speech *273*
Responding to the characters' actions 705

Interpretation
Explaining a poem's message 282
Explaining a theme 796
Explaining the epic's relevance to the twentieth century 796
Explaining the function of setting *133*
Defining an abstract idea *591*
Identifying implied ideas *248*
Identifying loaded words *485*
Identifying point of view *137*
Identifying the main metaphor in a poem *270*
Inferring the main idea of an essay *396*
Making inferences *248, 396*

Oral report 354, 415
Paraphrasing a poem 267, *285*
Stating the main idea of a poem *248*
Summarizing a plot *57*
Summarizing the main idea in an essay *396*

Synthesis
[All of the writing activities listed in the Composition Skills index require synthesis.]

Supporting a topic (or thesis) statement 130, 586, *709,* 796, *858*
Supporting an opinion with reasons and evidence 54, 237, 280, 316, 332, 382, *591, 709*
Writing a poem *369*
Writing an essay *57, 91, 133, 164, 199, 227, 248, 273, 285, 321, 347, 396, 433, 485, 591, 709, 858*
Writing an interview *801*

LITERATURE AND LANGUAGE EXERCISES

For further reinforcement in integrating the study of literature and language, see **Grammar, Usage, and Mechanics: A Reference Guide** on pages 878–923 of the text. This handbook also contains additional tips for writers.

Choosing Words to Create Tone 225
Combining Sentences 483
Creating Figures of Speech 406
Creating Rhythm 302
Creating Sounds 319
Expressing a Tone 345
Punctuating Dialogue 481
Using Adjectives to Create Character 89
Using Connotation to Create Mood 131
Using the Descriptive and Narrative Modes 393
Using the Expository Aim in Drama 588
Using the Expository and Persuasive Aims 431
Using Imagery 246
Using Personification 284
Using Pronouns Correctly 162
Using Similes and Metaphors 271
Using a Variety of Sentences 196
Using Verb Tenses Correctly 55

INDEX OF FEATURES
Focusing on Background

ORGANIZATION OF CONTENTS BY THEMES

The Power of Love

The Search for Identity

Transformations

Defeat and Triumph

War and Peace

Wish and Nightmare

PICTURE CREDITS

Pages: 2 © Jerry Jacka, courtesy Heard Museum, Phoenix, Arizona; 3 © Richard Erdoes; 6–7, 77 illustrations by Floyd Cooper; 17 © Anne Heinemann/The Stock Market; 18 © Jean Miele/The Stock Market; 20 © Anthony Bannister/Animals Animals; 32, 45, 50–51, 181 illustrations by Tom Leamon; 74, left, © Lester Sloan/Woodfin Camp; 74, right © Gary Gershoff/Retna; 96 © Hubert Schriebl/Superstock, Inc.; 99 © Bill O'Connor—Peter Arnold; 103 © Gaston Rebuffat—Photo Researchers; 112 E. Carle/Superstock, Inc.; 140 Photo by Wolfgang Dietze; 147 © Suzanne Szasz—Photo Researchers; 168 © Bruce W. Coleman—Bruce Coleman; 171 © David Meunch—H. Armstrong Roberts; 207 © Milton Heiberg—Photo Researchers; 231 © Bruce Hucko; 236 © H. Armstrong Roberts; 238–239 © Hans Reinhard—Bruce Coleman; 240 © Marcia Keegan; 244 © Michael Tamborino—De Wys; 254 © Jerry White—HBJ Photo; 256 © Day Williams—Photo Researchers; 263 © W. H. Grace—Taurus; 266 © Bruce Roberts—Photo Researchers; 272 © Don Renner; 279 Culver Pictures; 281 © H. Armstrong Roberts; 301 © Hans Gritscher—Peter Arnold; 313 © Peter Arnold; 317 © 1991 Lynn Stone: TSW/Chicago; 326 © Elizabeth Wilcox—Photo Researchers; 330 © D. Lyons—Bruce Coleman; 331 © H. Armstrong Roberts; 334–335 © Guido Alberto Rossi/The Image Bank; 336 Gamma—Liaison; 336, 338 Courtesy, Simplicity Mfg. Co.; 340 © Erich Hartmann; 362–363 © Bruce Roberts—Photo Researchers; 365 © Ron Sherman—Bruce Coleman; 377 © John Mitchell—Photo Researchers; 385 From POLISH JEWS: A Pictorial Record by Roman Vishniac, © 1947 renewed 1975 by Schocken Books, Inc. Reprinted by permission of Pantheon Books, a division of Random House, Inc.; 390 © Margot Conte—Animals, Animals; 398 © DPI; 403 © Barbara Von Hoffmann—Tom Stack Assoc.; 404–405 © Marcello Bertinetti—Photo Researchers; 409 map by Jan Pyk; 411–412 Lee Boltin; 414 Art Resource, New York; 416 Dave Bartruff; 418 © Marc F. Bernheim/Woodfin Camp; 420 © Wally McNamee/Woodfin Camp; 422–427 © Peter Cummings, © Spencer Swanger—Tom Stack Assoc.; 428 Photo by Marcel Ichac. From *Annapurna* by Maurice Herzog. © 1952, renewed 1980 by E. P. Dutton; 435 © Benn Mitchell; 436 © Bob Krist—De Wys; 443 Brown Brothers; 447 © Paul Fusco—Magnum; 454 New York Public Library Picture Collection/Don Renner; 459 Henry Goskinsky, LIFE Magazine, © 1983, Time, Inc.; 465 © Stephen Krasemann—Photo Researchers; 466 © Hanson Carroll—Peter Arnold; 468 © Wasyl Szhodginsky—Photo Researchers; 471 © Cary Wolinsky—Stock, Boston; 487 Photo: Artothek; 489, 992 © 1991 Martha Swope; 493 © PLAYBILL (r), Inc.; 494 The Bettmann Archive; 505–512, 518–522, Museum of Modern Art Film Stills Archives; 515, 543–545, Culver Pictures; 549 © PLAYBILL (r) Inc.; 551–563 © Martha Swope; 567 © Todd Gipstein—Photo Researchers; 580 © Larry Mulvehill—Photo Researchers; 584 © Jan Haleska—Photo Researchers; 593 The Granger Collection; 594, 597–599, from *Shakespeare and His Theatre* by John Russell Brown, illustrated by David Gentleman (Kestrel Books, 1982). © 1982 by David Gentleman, by permission of William Morrow and Company, New York; 595, left, Photofest; 596 The Granger Collection; 602–703 © Reg Wilson; 721 © De Wys; 733 © Farrell Grehan—Photo Researchers; 811–857 illustrations by Joy Batchelor and John Halas from *Animal Farm* by George Orwell (Harcourt Brace Jovanovich), © 1954 Joy Batchelor and John Halas.

INDEX OF FINE ART

INDEX OF AUTHORS AND TITLES